1 MONTH OF
FREE
READING

at

www.ForgottenBooks.com

By purchasing this book you are eligible for one month membership to ForgottenBooks.com, giving you unlimited access to our entire collection of over 1,000,000 titles via our web site and mobile apps.

To claim your free month visit:

www.forgottenbooks.com/free1212867

ISBN 978-0-332-07511-2
PIBN 11212867

FEDERAL DECISIONS.

CASES ARGUED AND DETERMINED

IN THE

SUPREME, CIRCUIT AND DISTRICT COURTS

OF THE

UNITED STATES.

COMPRISING

THE OPINIONS OF THOSE COURTS FROM THE TIME OF THEIR ORGANIZATION TO
THE PRESENT DATE, TOGETHER WITH EXTRACTS FROM THE OPIN-
IONS OF THE COURT OF CLAIMS AND THE ATTORNEYS-
GENERAL, AND THE OPINIONS OF GENERAL
IMPORTANCE OF THE TERRI-
TORIAL COURTS.

ARRANGED BY

WILLIAM G. MYER,

*Author of an Index to the United States Supreme Court Reports;
also Indexes to the Reports of Illinois, Ohio, Iowa, Missouri
and Tennessee, a Digest of the Texas Reports, and
local works on Pleading and Practice.*

VOL. XXIV.

NAME—PURSER OF THE NAVY.

ST. LOUIS, MO.:
THE GILBERT BOOK COMPANY.
1888.

359853

DAVID ATWOOD,
Printer and Stereotyper,
MADISON, WIS,

EXPLANATORY.

1. The cases in this work are arranged by subjects, instead of chronologically. They are assigned to the various general heads of the law, and each subject is divided and subdivided, for convenience of arrangement and reference, with head-notes, or table of contents, at the head of each subject, the same as an ordinary digest.

2. At the head of each division of a subject will be found a digest or summary of the points of law in the cases assigned to such division. This SUMMARY is confined exclusively to the statement of the points of law applicable to the particular division under which the case is published, other points of law in the case, if any, being transferred to other subjects, or to other subdivisions of the same subject. Where points in a case are carried to another division of a subject, they are put into the foot-notes, or notes following the cases, and reference is made to the case by section numbers in parenthesis at the end of the section.

3. The cases in full are arranged, generally, according to the order of the sections of the SUMMARY. Where the court states the facts of the case, it is so indicated by the use of the words STATEMENT OF FACTS at the beginning of the opinion. Where it is necessary to state the facts apart from the opinion, the statement is made as brief as possible, and is confined to the facts necessary to enable the reader to understand the points decided. The cases are also divided into convenient paragraphs, with a brief statement at the beginning of each paragraph of the point of law discussed or decided. Reference is here had to the *italic* sections scattered through the opinion. These take the place of the syllabus usually placed at the head of the opinion, and, besides bringing out every point of law actually decided, in some instances call attention to a review of authorities, as well as various points of law which would ordinarily be classed as *dicta*.

4. At the end of a series of cases is a digest of points applicable to the particular subdivision of the subject. This digest matter is obtained from four sources: 1st. Cases assigned originally to the general head, but digested and thrown out in the final arrangement, not to appear in full in any part of the work. 2d. Points taken from cases which will appear in full under some other division of the same subject. 3d. Points taken from cases which are assigned to some other general head. 4th. A digest of cases from state reports, law periodicals, and the opinions of the Court of Claims and the Attorneys-General.

5. Cases that will not appear in full in any part of the work are denoted by a *star* following the name of the case, thus, DOE *v.* ROE.* The tables of cases will also contain a similar designation of rejected cases, so that in consulting them the reader will readily see whether he is referred to a case in full or only a digest.

6. The *italic* matter at the head of the SUMMARY takes the place of the side-heads, or catchwords, usually prefixed to the sections, and is intended as an index to the contents of the SUMMARY. At the end of each section of the SUMMARY the name of the case of which the section is a digest is given, followed by the numbers of the sections into which the case is divided, so that after the reader has read the section of the SUMMARY, and found that it is what he wants, he can at once turn to the case in full.

CERTIFICATE OF APPROVAL.

[PLEADING.]

The subject of Pleading has been edited by FRANK A. FARNHAM, ESQ., of Boston. I certify that in my opinion he has shown good judgment in printing or digesting cases, and that the points in those digested appear sufficiently in the cases printed in full.

BENJAMIN R. CURTIS.

[PARTNERSHIP.]

I HEREBY CERTIFY, That the cases under the title "Partnership" submitted to me as digested by the general editor of "Federal Decisions," and not appearing important enough to be printed in full under that head. seem to me to have been discarded by him, after being digested, with good discretion.

WILLIAM F. WHARTON. *

---

* Editor of the last edition of STORY ON PARTNERSHIP.

TABLE OF CONTENTS.

TABLE OF CONTENTS.

VOLUMES AND CASES TO BE INCLUDED.

ABBREVIATIONS.

Abbott's Admiralty	Abb. Adm.	Lowell	Low.
Abbott's U. S.	Abb.	McAllister	McAl.
Albany Law Journal	Alb. L. J.	McCahon	McCahon.
American Law Register	Am. L. Reg.	McCrary	McC.
Baldwin	Bald.	McLean	McL.
Bee	Bee.	MacArthur	MacArth.
Benedict	Ben.	Marshall	Marsh.
Bissell	Biss.	Martin	Martin (N. C.).
Black	Black.	Mason	Mason.
Blatchford	Blatch.	Montana Territory	Mont. Ty.
Blatchford's Prize Cases	Bl. Pr. Cas.	Newberry	Newb.
Blatchford & Howland	Bl. & How.	National Bankruptcy Register	N. B. R.
Bond	Bond.	Olcott	Olc.
Brewster	Brewster.	Opinions of Attorneys-General	Opp. Att'y Genl.
Brockenbrough	Marsh.	Oregon	Oreg.
Brown	Brown.	Otto	Otto.
Call	Call (Va.).	Overton	Overton (Tenn.).
Central Law Journal	Cent. L. J.	Paine	Paine.
Chase's Decisions	Chase's Dec.	Peters	Pet.
Chicago Legal News	Ch. Leg. N.	Peters' Admiralty	Pet. Adm.
Clifford	Cliff.	Peters' Circuit Court	Pet. C. C.
Colorado Territory	Colo. Ty.	Philadelphia Reports	Phil.
Connecticut Reports	Conn.	Pittsburgh Reports	Pittsb. R.
Cooke	Cooke (Tenn.).	Sawyer	Saw.
Court of Claims	Ct. Cl.	Smith	Smith (N. H.).
Crabbe	Crabbe.	Sprague	Spr.
Cranch	Cr.	Story	Story.
Cranch's Circuit Court	Cr. C. C.	Sumner	Sumn.
Curtis	Curt.	Taney	Taney.
Dakota Territory	Dak. Ty.	Utah Territory	Utah T'y.
Dallas	Dal.	Vermont Reports	Vt.
Daveis	Dav.	Wallace	Wall.
Day	Day (Conn.).	Wallace's Circuit Court	Wall. C. C.
Deady	Deady.	Wallace, Jr	Wall. Jr.
Dillon	Dill.	Ware	Ware.
Federal Reporter	Fed. R.	Washington	Wash.
Fisher's Patent Cases	Fish. Pat. Cas.	Washington Territory	Wash. Ty.
Flippin	Flip.	Wheaton	Wheat.
Gallison	Gall.	Wheeler's Criminal Cases	Wheeler.
Gilpin	Gilp.	Woods	Woods.
Hempstead	Hemp.	Woodbury & Minot	Woodb. & M.
Hoffman	Hoff.	Woolworth	Woolw.
Holmes	Holmes.	Wyoming Territory	Wyom. Ty.
Howard	How.	Van Ness	Van Ness.
Hughes	Hughes.		
Law and Equity Reporter	Law & Eq. Rep.		
Legal Gazette Reports	Leg. Gaz. R.		

FEDERAL DECISIONS.

NAME.

§ 1. In general.— Where two names have the same original derivation, or where one is an abbreviation or corruption of the other, but both are taken promiscuously, and according to common use, to be the same, though differing in sound, the use of one for the other is not a material misnomer. Gordon *v.* Holiday,[*] 1 Wash., 287.

§ 2. *It seems* that an act of attainder against *Henry* Gordon is void as against one who was baptized and always known and called by the name of *Harry* Gordon. *Ibid.*

§ 8. A name chosen by a person by which he causes himself to be known becomes his name. United States *v.* Winter, 13 Blatch., 276.

§ 4. Material variance.— A letter of credit addressed by mistake to John and Joseph Naylor & Co., but delivered by the bearer to John and Jeremiah Naylor & Co., the firm to which the writer really intended to address the letter, will not support an action of *assumpsit* for funds advanced to the bearer by the latter firm; nor is parol proof admissible to show the intent of the writer, and that the variance was the result of a mistake. Grant *v.* Naylor, 4 Cr., 224.

§ 5. In an action where the declaration stated that E. Brown was attached to answer, and proceeded to allege the drawing of a bill of exchange by Elisha Brown, a bill of exchange signed by E. Brown, such signature being that of Elijah Brown, is not admissible in support of the declaration. Craig *v.* Brown, Pet. C. C., 189.

§ 6. In an action for assault and battery, defendant pleaded that the plaintiff was known and called by the name Jesse Jeffery, and not Jesse Jeffries. A demurrer to this plea was sustained. *Held*, that the court erred; that the names are not *idem sonans.* Marshall *v.* Jeffries,[*] Hemp., 299.

§ 7. Immaterial variance.— Where a commission to take depositions under an order of the court purported to be in a cause between Richard M. Meade, plaintiff, and K., defendant, whereas the name of the plaintiff was Richard W. Meade, the mistake being made by the clerk in making out the commission, *held*, that there was no material variance. Keene *v.* Meade, 8 Pet., 1.

§ 8. If a *dedimus* issue to take depositions in a cause in which Richard M. Meade is plaintiff, whereas the name of the plaintiff was Richard W. Meade, and the commissioners certify that they took the depositions to be read in a cause in which Richard W. Meade was plaintiff, the depositions are admissible, notwithstanding the clerical error in writing an M. for a W. in the commission. Meade *v.* Keane, 3 Cr. C. C., 51.

§ 9. The use of a wrong name by mistake in the body of a deposition is not material if the right name appears in the title of the case. Thus, where the deposition read, "Anderson, the above plaintiff," whereas the plaintiff's name was correctly stated in the title of the case as "Vorce," *held*, immaterial, as the mistake could mislead no one. Voce *v.* Lawrence, 4 McL., 208.

§ 10. Extrinsic evidence.— A patent is not void by reason of an error in the christian name of the patentee if it contains any other matter descriptive of the person for whom it was intended, in which case extrinsic proof is admissible to identify the grantee. Where a patent was issued to Phillipe F. Carlier and A. V. as joint inventors of an improvement in extinguishing fires, there being no such person as Phillipe F. Carlier, *held*, that by reason of this description, Francois Phillipe Carlier being identified as the joint inventor with A. V., and the person intended in the patent, the patent was valid. Northwestern Fire-extinguisher Co. *v.* Philadelphia Fire-extinguisher Co.,[*] 6 Off. Gaz. Pat., 84.

§ 11. Reputation or hearsay is competent proof of the name of a person, place or house. Thus, upon an indictment of one Dodge for selling liquor without a license, the court allowed the prosecution to show that the house where the liquor was sold "was called Dodge's," and that the man who dealt out the liquor "was called Dodge." United States *v.* Dodge, Deady, 186.

§ 12. Use of initials.— A party being indicted by the name of D. K. Olney Winter moved that the indictment be quashed upon the ground that he was not described therein by any christian name. The motion was denied, on the ground that as a person may be known by any of the several names given him at baptism, and may, if he like, place initials before instead of behind such name, it was to be presumed that the name set out in the indictment was the only given name by which the defendant had chosen to be known, and that his manner of writing it was the same as that exhibited in the indictment. United States v. Winter, 13 Blatch., 276.

§ 13. Upon suit by "Terence Nugent, Jr.," to recover the value of cotton seized by the United States during the late rebellion, satisfactory evidence being produced by the claimant to establish his loyalty, *held*, that the appearance of the name of "T. Nugent, Jr.," in the poll list-of those who voted at a presidential election, under the Confederate government, was not sufficient to connect the claimant with that election. Nugent v. United States,* 6 Ct. Cl., 305.

§ 14. In proving a claim against the estate of a bankrupt, founded on a note of the bankrupt given in favor of A. G. Wallace, and signed W. H. Valentine, the full christian names, or at least the first christian name, of each party should appear, either in the documents offered in evidence or in the record of the proceedings; if the creditor's initials merely are stated it is not sufficient. *In re* Valentine, 4 Biss., 317.

§ 15. Presumption as to identity.— Where an alleged offender was described in the mandate, issued by the executive for his arrest, as "George Macdonell," while in the warrant and complaint he was described as "George Macdonell, otherwise Macdonnell," *held*, that the variance was not material, as identity of name raises the presumption of identity of person. *In re* Macdonnell, 11 Blatch., 79.

§ 16. Upon the question of the admissibility of an oath taken by the claimant under an amnesty proclamation, the name, place of residence, and occupation of the claimant being identical with the name, residence, and business of the person described in the amnesty oath, *held*, that the identification of the claimant as the one by whom the oath was taken was sufficient, and that the oath was admissible in evidence. Backer v. United States,* 7 Ct. Cl., 551.

§ 17. Where one set of witnesses describe W. B. as being a respectable man, a deacon in the church, a surveyor, and capable of writing a good hand, and another set describe him as an ignorant, dissipated man, incapable of business, accustomed to hunting, and living the greater part of the time with the Indians, the court may assume that there are two persons of the name of W. B. Coulson v. Walton, 9 Pet., 62.

§ 18. Libelant sued under the name of William *Henry* for a balance of wages due him as cook and steward. In the original articles produced before the commissioner William *Henderson* was entered as cook and steward. The name was signed by a mark, and the handwriting of the witness to the articles was proved. *Held*, that as libelant sued in the capacity of cook and steward, he would be presumed, in the absence of proof, to be the person who signed the shipping articles. Henry v. Curry,* Abb. Adm., 483.

§ 19. Courts of admiralty are too familiar with the habit of sailors to assume a variety of names to lay special stress on an objection of misnomer unaccompanied with evidence that the party was not known by the name ascribed to him. *Ibid.* The administrator of *Lebering* permitted to draw the wages of a mariner who appeared to have been known on board as *Lebrun* or *Lebring*. Ketland v. Lebering,* 2 Wash., 201.

§ 20. Middle name.— The law knows but one christian name, and the omission or insertion of the middle name or of the initial letter of that name is immaterial. Where a deed was offered in evidence in which the grantor described himself as "David Carrick Buchanan, formerly David Buchanan," and the person named in the patent was David Buchanan, *held*, that the deed was admissible as evidence, the jury being left to determine whether David Carrick Buchanan was the same person as David Buchanan named as grantee in the patent. Games v. Stiles, 14 Pet., 322; Dunn v. Games, 1 McL., 321.

§ 21. Where all the papers in the case and the notices published in the newspapers gave the bankrupt's name correctly, but the notices served on the creditors who appeared at the creditors' meeting gave the middle letter of the bankrupt's name as B., instead of D., *held*, that the variance was not material. *In re* Hill,* 6 Int. Rev. Rec., 51.

§ 22. Change of name.— At common law a man may lawfully change his name, and may sue and be sued by his known and recognized name. Hence a plea alleging that the plaintiff's real name, at the commencement of the suit, was and is S. and not L.; that the real name of the husband of the plaintiff at the time of his marriage to her was S. and not L., must be overruled as bad. Linton v. First Nat. Bank of Kittanning, 10 Fed. R., 894; 13 Rep., 487; 28 Int. Rev. Rec., 104.

§ 23. Amendment.— Where the writ was against E. Briddle, and the declaration against E. Biddle, the defendant having given bail by the name of E. Briddle, and pleaded in bar of the action, *held*, that judgment could not be arrested on the ground of misnomer; that the variance being merely matter of form might, by the provisions of the act of congress, be amended at any time. Scull *v.* Briddle, 2 Wash., 200.

§ 24. Misnomer in judgment.— A mere misnomer is not sufficient to exclude the record of a judgment from being given in evidence, if, in point of fact, the party appeared by a wrong name, and, instead of pleading the misnomer, went to issue on other points, and judgment was given against him; and an averment in an action on the judgment that he is the same person, if made out by proof, will fix the liability of the defendant for the judgment. Stevelie *v.* Read, 2 Wash., 274.

§ 25. After judgment rendered, misnomer of the plaintiff cannot be taken advantage of. Breedlove *v.* Nicolet, 7 Pet. 413.

§ 26. In pleadings.— The full christian and surnames of all persons referred to in a bill must be inserted therein; but a bill defective in this respect may be amended. Barth *v.* Makeever, 4 Biss., 206.

§ 27. Demurrer.— At common law a defendant in a criminal case cannot take advantage of a misnomer by demurrer. If he is not proceeded against by his true name, he must so allege in a plea in abatement, and state what his true name is. United States *v.* Howard, 1 Saw., 507.

NATIONAL BANKS.

See BANKS, NATIONAL.

NATIONAL BOUNDARIES.

See COURTS; STATES.

NATURALIZATION.

See CITIZENS AND ALIENS.

NAVIGABLE RIVERS.

See WATER-COURSES.

NAVIGATION LAWS.

See MARITIME LAW.

NAVY.

See WAR.

NEBRASKA.

See STATES.

NEGLIGENCE.

See CARRIERS; TORTS.

NEGOTIABLE PAPER.

See BILLS AND NOTES; BONDS.

NEGROES.

See CITIZENS; CONSTITUTION AND LAWS.

NEUTRALITY.

See WAR.

NEVADA.

See STATES.

NEW HAMPSHIRE.

See STATES.

NEW JERSEY.

See STATES.

NEW MADRID CERTIFICATES.

See LAND.

NEW MEXICO.

See STATES.

NEW TRIAL.

See PRACTICE.

NEW YORK.

See STATES.

NOLLE PROSEQUI.

See CRIMES; PRACTICE.

NON-IMPORTATION LAWS.

See EMBARGO.

NON-INTERCOURSE LAWS.

See WAR.

NON-RESIDENTS.

See COURTS; PRACTICE.

NONSUIT.

See PRACTICE.

NORTH CAROLINA.

See STATES.

NORTHWEST TERRITORY.

See CONSTITUTION AND LAWS; STATES.

NOTARIAL ACT.

See CONVEYANCES; NOTARY PUBLIC.

NOTARY PUBLIC.

[See BILLS AND NOTES]

§ 1. An infant may hold the office of notary public at common law. And a minor is not ineligible because the state statute requires county officers to be twenty-one years old, a notary not being a county officer. So where one was indicted for perjury, and he pleaded that the notary before whom he took the oath was an infant, a demurrer to the plea was sustained. United States v. Bixby,* 9 Fed. R., 78.

§ 2. Use of seal.—Where the copy of a record of the condemnation of property insured was offered in evidence without the seal of the notary who made the copy, there being merely flourishes of the pen on the margin of each page, held, no proof being given that the notary had or had not a seal, that the evidence must be rejected. Talcott v. Delaware Ins. Co., 2 Wash., 449.

§ 3. The notarial seal proves itself in all countries where the law merchant prevails, and it is only necessary that it should conform to the law of the place where the notary acts. An impression upon the paper is as good as upon wax, or any tenaceous substance. Orr v. Lacy, 4 McL., 243.

§ 4. Judicial notice is taken of the seal of a notary public from any part of the world, if impressed upon paper or wax. Such seal authenticates an act of protest, and entitles it to full faith and credit. So held where a certificate was offered in evidence, which had been made in Norway, and which had impressed upon the paper a seal purporting to be that of a notary public in Norway. Pierce v. Indseth, 16 Otto, 546.

§ 5. A notarial seal proves itself. The requisites of such seal are determined by the law of the locality from which the official derives his authority, or if there be no law prescribing what the seal shall be, by the rules of the common law. *In re* Phillips,* 14 N. B. R., 219; 3 Month. West. Jur., 457.

§ 6. In the absence of statutory provision, an official seal is the impression on the paper directly, or on wax, or wafer, attached thereto, made by the official as and for his seal. Hence the seal impression placed upon a document by a notary public signifies authentication of his official character. It is the seal and not its composition or characters of words and devices which raises the presumption of official character, of which courts take judicial notice. Accordingly where a notarial seal affixed to a jurat contained the words "Notarial Seal, Lucas Co., Ohio," the name of the notary being omitted, *held*, sufficient. *Ibid.*

§ 7. Indication of official character.— Under the act of congress of September 16, 1860, providing that certain oaths, affirmations or acknowledgments may be taken before any notary public, and that "when certified under the hand and official seal of such notary they shall have the same force and effect," etc., *held*, that the officer need not state in his certificate that he is a notary public and that such certificate is given under his hand and seal; that if the notary signs his name with the words "Notary Public" thereunder, and his seal contains his name and the words "Notary Public," it is a sufficient indication of his official character. Goodyear v. Hullihen, 3 Hughes, 492; 3 Fish. Pat. Cas., 251.

§ 8. Act of clerk or deputy.— A demand of payment of a foreign bill of exchange and protest for non-payment by the clerk of a notary is of no effect. The notary, who acts under oath, is certainly the only one who can make the protest. Sacrider v. Brown, 3 McL., 481.

§ 9. Taking acknowledgments of deeds.— A notary public is not incompetent to acknowledge and certify a deed of trust, by reason of his interest as one of the beneficiaries in the trust, such acknowledgment being merely a ministerial duty. National Bank of Fredericksburg v. Conway, 1 Hughes, 37.

§ 10. Powers and liabilities as to commercial paper.— In Mississippi, a notary public is a public officer and becomes the agent of the holder of negotiable paper intrusted to him for demand and protest, and is alone liable to the holder for any failure or negligence in the discharge of his official duties, even though the paper is intrusted to him without the knowledge or authority of the holder by a bank to which it has been sent for the purpose of collection. Britton v. Niccolls, 14 Otto, 757. See BILLS AND NOTES.

§ 11. If a notary public, whose duty it is to demand payment of a bill of exchange from the acceptors, goes several times to their office for the purpose of making demand, but finding the doors closed, and no person there to answer his demand, makes out his notarial protest, certifying to these facts, without seeking out the residences of such acceptors, he has made a legal demand and protest, and is not liable to the holder on the ground of negligence by reason of his not having sought the acceptors at their residences. Wiseman v. Chiapella, 23 How.,. 368. If a notary does not remember that he has made demand, he may refer to his book, and then testify that he made demand as therein stated. Thornton v. Caldwell, 1 Cr. C. C.. 524.

§ 12. Power to administer oaths.— A notary public is authorized, under the act of congress of August 15, 1876, to administer the oath required by the laws of the United States to be taken by the directors of national banks. United States v. Neale, 14 Fed. R., 767.

§ 13. Under the act of 1790 a notary public is a proper officer before whom the oaths of persons claiming exemption from military duty under act of March 3, 1863, may be taken. United States v. Sonachall, 4 Biss., 425.

§ 14. Notaries public are proper officers before whom to take verifications to bills and answers, and affidavits in support of, or to oppose, motions for injunction, the notarial acts in such cases being "acts in relation to evidence," within the meaning of the act of congress of July 29, 1854. Blake Crusher Co. v. Ward,* 1 Am. L. T. Rep. (N. S.), 423.

§ 15. Although, under section 2 of chapter 159 of the laws of 1854, notaries public had power to administer oaths in the United States circuit courts, such power is now gone by virtue of section 5596 of the Revised Statutes of 1878. Buerk v. Imhaeuser,* 10 Off. Gaz. Pat., 907.

§ 16. Acts in evidence.— By the laws of Louisiana copies of notarial acts are evidence, the original always remaining in the office of the notary. Thus, where a copy of a bill of sale, executed by a notary in New Orleans, and on record in his office, was offered in evidence in a federal court, *held*, that the court was bound to take judicial notice of the laws of Louisiana and admit the copy as evidence, it being evidence by the state laws. Owings v. Hull, 9 Pet., 607.

§ 17. An entry made by a notary is admissible as evidence after his death, to prove facts contained therein, it being shown that he kept a record of his notarial acts. Nicholls v. Webb, 8 Wheat., 326.

§ 18. Upon trial for engaging in the slave trade, by carrying two blacks from a port in Africa to Brazil, the defendant alleged that the blacks whom he received on board had free papers, as if manumitted. It was adjudged to be evidence of the genuineness of the manumission papers that they were attested and sealed by persons purporting to be Portuguese notaries public on that coast, and who had acted as such in other business; that they were on the kind of paper and under the stamp used there in the public offices; were lodged with the proper authorities in Brazil, and the Portuguese consul there certified to the notaries' being regular officers of his government, and that the American consul in Brazil obtained and sent to this country all these papers with translations. United States v. Libby, 1 Woodb. & M., 221.

§ 19. In bankruptcy.— Proof of debt taken before a notary public under the provisions of the act of June 22, 1874, amending the bankrupt act, is not admissible as proof of the debt unless it be authenticated by the notary's signature and seal, and the impression of the seal must show it to be that of the notary whose acts it purports to authenticate. In re Nebe,* 11 N. B. R., 289.

§ 20. Notaries public are competent to acknowledge letters of attorney to represent creditors. The provision, in general order in bankruptcy No. 84, for their acknowledgment before a register or United States commissioner, is not in exclusion of other methods of proof. In re Butterfield,* 14 N. B. R., 195.

§ 21. Notaries public have authority to take the acknowledgments of creditors to powers of attorney in bankruptcy proceedings. In re McDuffee,* 14 N. B. R., 336.

§ 22. Under the statute of August 15, 1876 (19 Stats., 206, ch. 804), notaries public have authority to swear bankrupts as to their schedules. In re Bailey,* 15 N. B. R., 48.

§ 23. Notaries public have not, under the act of congress of September 16, 1850, or the act of July 29, 1854, the judicial power to take legal proof of a claim, by deposition or otherwise, against the estate of a bankrupt under the bankrupt act. In re Strauss,* 2 N. B. R., 18.

§ 24. A notary public is not authorized to take a creditor's acknowledgment to a power of attorney to vote for assignee, under general order No. 84 in bankruptcy. In re Higgins, 8 Ben., 100.

§ 25. A petition in involuntary bankruptcy was verified before a notary public, proceedings instituted and an adjudication of bankruptcy made by default. Upon petition by a creditor to vacate the adjudication because the petition was verified before a notary, held, that the verification before a notary public was irregular, but as the question of proper verification was one of practice, and not of jurisdiction, and the verification had been recognized as proper and an order of adjudication had been entered, it was too late for the debtor or any creditor to raise the question. In re Gitchell, 8 Ben., 256.

§ 26. The certificate of a notary public in Liverpool of the authority of English assignees in bankruptcy is sufficient to enable them to be admitted as defendants in a suit against the bankrupts in this country. Wilson v. Stewart, 1 Cr. C. C., 129.

NOTES.

See BILLS AND NOTES.

NOTICE.

[See APPEALS; BILLS AND NOTES; BONDS; CONTRACTS; EQUITY. By registration, see CONVEYANCES. Innocent Purchaser, see FRAUD; LAND; SALES. In Bankruptcy, see DEBTOR AND CREDITOR. In Practice, see PRACTICE; WRITS.]

§ 1. Constructive notice is notice imputed by the law to a person not having actual notice; and every person who has actual notice of circumstances sufficient to put a prudent man upon inquiry as to a particular fact, and who omits to make such inquiry with reasonable diligence, is deemed to have constructive notice of the fact itself. Gress v. Evans,* 1 Dak. T'y, 387.

§ 2. To affect a purchaser with constructive notice, it is not enough that he had the means of obtaining, and might by prudent caution have obtained, knowledge of the fact, but whether not obtaining it was an act of gross negligence. Wilson v. Wall, 6 Wall., 83.

§ 3. A mortgage was given in reality to indemnify the mortgagee, but purporting to secure a sum of money payable in one year, and five years afterwards it was assigned, the whole sum appearing from the instrument to be unpaid. *Held*, that the circumstances of the case should have put the assignee upon inquiry, from which he would have learned the true consideration of the mortgage, and that having thus had constructive notice, his rights with reference to the mortgage were no better than those of his assignor, the mortgagee. United States *v.* Sturges, 1 Paine, 525.

§ 4. Party put on inquiry.—Information which makes it the duty of a party to make inquiry, and shows where it may be effectually made, is notice of all facts to which such inquiry might have led. But a party thus put on inquiry is to be allowed a reasonable time to make it before he is affected with notice. Carr *v.* Hilton, 1 Curt., 390.

§ 5. A party put upon inquiry by the known facts is affected with notice of interdependent facts. Oliver *v.* Piatt, 3 How., 333.

§ 6. To be published "once a week."— Where an act of congress required notice to be published once a week for three months, *held*, that a week, within the meaning of the statute, is a definite period of time beginning with Sunday and ending with Saturday, and that a notice published on one day during each week for that time is sufficient, even if more than seven days elapsed between two successive publications. Roukendorff *v.* Taylor, 4 Pet., 349.

§ 7. Where a statute requires a notice to be published "once in each week for four weeks" there should be an interval of seven days between each of the four publications. *In re* King, 7 N. B. R., 279; 5 Ben., 453.

§ 8. Thus, where, under such a statute, notice was published on the 11th, 21st and 27th days of January, and on the 1st and 10th days of February, *held* insufficient. *Ibid.*

§ 9. In writing.—Under the act of congress providing that any person who "shall harbor or conceal" (a fugitive from labor), "after notice that he or she was a fugitive, . . . shall forfeit," etc., *held*, that in order to render a party liable under the law, the notice need not be in writing, or come from the master of the fugitives, or his agent; but that full knowledge, derived from the negroes, or otherwise, that they were fugitives from labor, was sufficient notice to the one harboring them. Jones *v.* Vanzandt, 2 McL., 611.

§ 10. The act of Rhode Island (Digest of 1822, p. 246, sec. 3) provides "that no guardian shall be appointed or removed under this act, unless all persons interested shall have had reasonable notice in writing, signed by the clerk, and served by the town sergeant or constable, that he, she, or they may appear to object to the same." *Held*, that a notice by reading the order of the court is not a "notice in writing," in the sense of the statute, and that the appointment of a guardian, with such notice only, was a nullity. Hart *v.* Gray, 3 Sumn., 339.

§ 11. Service on Sunday.—A notice cannot lawfully be served on Sunday. Chesapeake & Ohio Canal Co. *v.* Bradley, 4 Cr. C. C., 193. Notice of rescission of a contract may be given on Sunday. Pence *v.* Langdon, 9 Otto, 578.

§ 12. A printed tariff of charges at a dry dock, not brought to the notice of the master or owner of the vessel taken into such dock for repairs, is not binding upon such master or owner. Ives *v.* The Steamboat Buckeye State, 1 Newb., 69.

§ 13. Notice by mail.—Where a clause in an insurance policy required notice in writing to be given to the underwriters of any subsequent insurance on the property that the same might be indorsed on the policy, *held*, that evidence of writing and posting a letter notifying the company of subsequent insurance is not evidence of giving the notice required. To constitute such notice the letter must have been received. Carpenter *v.* Providence Washington Ins. Co., 4 How., 185.

§ 14. To be read.—A person chargeable with the duty of giving a notice does not perform that duty by handing the party entitled to notice a paper containing such notice, especially if the person to whom it is handed is directed to use it in a particular way and for a particular purpose, which does not require him to examine or read it. An agent presented, for his principal, United States bonds to the assistant treasurer for payment. The assistant treasurer gave him a receipt for the same and directed him to take the receipt to the cashier in another part of the building. The receipt, which was not examined by the agent, contained the following: "Payment made subject to examination and acceptance of bonds by the department at Washington." Upon examination at Washington, the bonds were found to be forged. Upon suit brought against the agent for the money received on the forged bonds, such money having in the meantime been paid over to his principal, *held*, that the above clause in the receipt was not notice to him of the conditional payment of the bonds. United States *v.* Pinover, 3 Fed. R., 305.

§ 15. Designation of newspaper.— Where a statute requires a notice to be published in a paper where "the place of its publication is nearest the land," the language must be taken as referring to the particular place where the paper is first issued, that is, given to the public for circulation, and not to the place where the papers may be sent for distribution. Leroy *v.* Jamison, 3 Saw., 369.

§ 16. Purchaser.— Where a plaintiff seeks to set up the equitable against the legal title in the defendant, he must aver that the latter purchased with notice, and at the trial conclusively prove such averment. McNeil v. Magee, 5 Mason, 244.

§ 17. Notoriety, at a subsequent time, of an adverse title cannot affect rights of a purchaser antecedently vested. *Ibid.*

§ 18. A purchaser who has notice of such facts as with ordinary diligence would lead him to a full knowledge of an outstanding equity is a purchaser with notice. Hinde v. Vattier, 1 McL., 110.

§ 19. Neither floating rumor nor a notice by one who has no interest in the property is sufficient to affect the conscience of a purchaser. Piatt v. Vattier, 1 McL., 146.

§ 20. Notice to a purchaser, who purchased from one who was a *bona fide* purchaser, without notice, cannot affect the title. *Ibid.*

§ 21. Notice ordinarily sufficient to put a party on inquiry is not necessarily notice of all that might be learned by inquiry where the purchaser had a right to rely upon positive representations of the vendor. Boyce v. Grundy, 3 Pet., 210.

§ 22. A full consideration paid in cash will not protect a purchaser who has notice, actual or constructive, that the vendor is selling to hinder and delay his creditors. A. bought of a merchant, B., at a late hour in the night. his stock of goods. A. knew B.'s general reputation for honesty was bad; that he was not punctual in the payment of his debts; that the value of all the property B. possessed before he purchased the goods did not exceed one-half of the goods purchased; that it was unusual for country merchants to buy exclusively for cash; that he was selling the stock for one-half of its cost, in the height of the business season, and at about the time debts contracted in its purchase would be maturing; that B. had not advertised in any mode his desire to sell the goods; and that he probably had not disclosed his purpose to do so to any other person. A. intended to make money out of the purchase by selling the goods where they were at public auction, and must have known that the same method of disposing of the goods was open to B., and that there was no reason why he should not resort to it if he owed no debts and was honest. *Held*, that A. had constructive notice of the fraudulent character of the sale and could not claim to be a *bona fide* purchaser without notice of the fraud. Singer v. Jacobs, 3 McC., 638.

§ 23. Where a patent to land is issued to William Park Lea instead of William P. Lea, a purchaser of the land from William Park Lea, without notice of the mistake, will be protected in equity; and the actual possession of such purchaser is notice of his title, although his deed be not recorded until long afterwards, so as to bar, under the statute of limitations, any relief sought. Lea v. Polk County Copper Co., 21 How., 493.

§ 24. Where A. mortgaged to B. the whole of his stock in trade, and on the same day made oath to the petition for the benefit of the bankrupt act, and B. subsequently assigned all his right, title and interest in the said stock to a certain bank, *held*, that inasmuch as the bank had notice, at the time when the assignment was made, that A. had failed, and only took it as collateral security for old claims upon B., it was not a *bona fide* purchase for a valuable consideration without notice. Morse v. Godfrey, 3 Story, 364.

§ 25. The pendency of proceedings in bankruptcy is sufficient constructive notice to all grantees of property proceeding from the bankrupt. *Ibid.*

§ 26. A stranded vessel was sold by the master at an inadequate price, and immediately thereafter purchased by himself and the wreck commissioner at the price for which she had just been sold, they taking a special warranty of title. Subsequently A. purchased one-half of the vessel from the wreck commissioner, taking a special warranty relating back to the original sale of the vessel, and later the remaining half from the master, taking a general warranty. While in the hands of B., the new master and quarter owner by purchase from A., the vessel was seized and libeled by the former owners on the ground that the sale made on the beach was unnecessary, illegal and collusive. A. and B. claimed to be *bona fide* purchasers without notice. *Held*, that as A. and B. purchased with a full knowledge of the antecedent history of the vessel, taking special warranty instead of general warranty, contrary to general custom, and as their own title deeds showed who were the original owners, while other papers showed the manner and consideration of the wreck sale and the purchase of the wreck commissioner and the master for a proportionate sum of the original price, they must be considered as having had constructive notice of the fraud practiced upon the owners, and hence were not entitled to hold as *bona fide* purchasers. The Schooner Tilton, 5 Mason, 465.

§ 27. There is no such principle of law as that what is matter of record shall be constructive notice to a purchaser. The true doctrine is, that purchasers are affected with constructive notice of all that is apparent upon the face of the title deeds under which they claim, and of such other facts as those already known necessarily put them upon inquiry for; but of other facts, extrinsic of the title and collateral to it, no constructive notice can be presumed. Dexter v. Harris, 2 Mason, 581.

§ 28. Notice of a lien or incumbrance on property binds the purchaser when received before the actual payment of the purchase money, and arrests all further steps towards the completion of the purchase; and a purchaser, to be protected, must deny notice before the actual payment of the purchase money, and this essential averment cannot be supplied by intendment. Merrill v. Dawson, Hemp., 563; Fowler v. Merrill, 11 How., 375.

§ 29. Notice reaches the conscience of the party, and though he be a purchaser for a valuable consideration, yet, in equity, his rights are the same as were those of the person from whom he purchased. Smith v. Shane, 1 McL., 22.

§ 30. No person is at liberty to remain intentionally ignorant of facts relating to his purchase within his reach, and then claim protection as an innocent purchaser. Jenkins v. Eldredge, 3 Story, 181.

§ 31. A purchase of goods, before seizure, which have become forfeited to the United States, will not purge the forfeiture, when the purchase has been made under a full knowledge of the facts, or of such facts as were sufficient to put the party on inquiry. Where a ship immediately on its return from a voyage, which, under an act of congress, subjected it to forfeiture, was purchased by a party with full knowledge of the facts of the voyage, held, that such purchaser must have had notice of the legal consequences flowing from those acts, and hence was not a bona fide purchaser without notice of the defect of title. The Brig Ploughboy, 1 Gall., 41.

§ 32. Possession by a tenant of an estate at the time of its purchase is constructive notice to the purchaser of the tenant's title, though not of the title of the lessor, or of the party under whom the tenant claims. Flagg v. Mann, 2 Sumn., 486.

§ 33. Where purchasers of real estate, at the time of their purchase, have actual or constructive notice that it is partnership property, it will be chargeable in their hands with the payment of the partnership debts, even though they have no notice of the existence of partnership debts. If they have no notice that it is partnership property, they are exonerated to the extent of the purchase money already paid by them; but so far as the purchase money has not been paid, it is a substituted fund, chargeable in their hands with the same burdens as the real estate. Hoxie v. Carr, 1 Sumn., 173.

§ 34. Confirmation of land titles.— A notice published by the surveyor-general, stating that he had examined and approved of a certain rancho, confirmed to designated parties, and that the plats would be retained in his office, subject to inspection, for four weeks from the date of publication, held, to be insufficient under the act of congress of June 14, 1860, requiring a published notice that a survey and plat of the claim confirmed had been made and approved by the surveyor-general. Leroy v. Jamison, 3 Saw., 369.

§ 35. Title to personal property.— A., a resident of California, directed his agent, B., in New York, to contract for the building of a vessel there, all contracts in relation thereto to be made in the name of B., who was to act as the owner of the vessel and conceal the ownership of A. B. procured the usual builder's certificate in his own name, and had the ship enrolled also in his name. A. having died during the construction of the vessel, his representatives pursued substantially the same line of conduct with reference to the ownership of the ship, except that some of the materials were paid for through another agent. B., being to all appearances owner and possessed of all the indicia of property, sold the vessel. Held, that the purchasers, who were advised by B. that there were parties in California who had advanced money toward building the vessel; that she was originally intended for employment in the waters of that state; that this purpose had been changed; that they now wished the boat sold, and that he, B., was authorized to sell her, did not thereby receive constructive notice of the equitable interest in the heirs or personal representatives of A. Calais Steamboat Co. v. Scudder, 2 Black, 372.

§ 36. Purchase from one executor.— Where property is purchased from one of two joint executors, without the knowledge or consent of the other, and a deed taken from the one executor only, such purchaser takes the property subject to the infirmity of the executor's deed to him, on the principle of caveat emptor, and all subsequent purchasers of him are equally charged with notice. Lipse v. Spears, 4 Hughes, 535.

§ 37. Sale under trust deed.— As the law has prescribed no particular form for the notice of a sale under a trust deed, it is sufficient if, upon the whole matter, it appears calculated reasonably to apprise the public of the property intended to be sold. Where a notice described the property as "lot 99, in P., B., T. and D.'s addition to Georgetown, fronting sixty feet on F. street and one hundred and twenty feet on S. street," held, that the notice was sufficient, although the property was in T.'s addition instead of the one named in the notice. Newman v. Jackson, 12 Wheat., 570.

§ 38. Mortgage.— Where A. promises B. to buy machinery of C., and let B. have it to use at an agreed price per yard for cloth made by it at B.'s factory, A. to furnish the raw cotton and credit B. towards payment for the machinery with what the cloth sells for beyond that price and expenses; and a memorandum at the bottom of the contract calls the machinery collateral security for the money paid for it by A., the contract may be deemed a mortgage of the machinery to A. in equity, and any person buying such machinery of B. knowing the circumstances, or knowing enough to put him on inquiry, cannot hold the machinery without paying A. the balance due. Nor, to constitute notice, is a record of such mortgage necessary. Almy v. Wilber, 2 Woodb. & M., 371.

§ 39. Prior deed or mortgage.— Notice in fact of a prior deed or mortgage may be proved where such prior conveyances have not been recorded, or where by reason of defects in the papers, or the registration thereof. there was no constructive notice. Schultz v. Moore, 1 McL . 520. Actual notice of a deed is sufficient against an attaching creditor of the grantor although the deed was not recorded. Briggs v. French, 2 Sumn., 251.

§ 40. A person having notice of a prior mortgage on a canal boat is not a purchaser in good faith within the meaning of the act of the New York legislature of 1864. And a person who has discovered enough to put him on inquiry is bound to make further inquiry, and whether he does so or not will be charged with notice of everything to which such inquiry would have reasonably led. The Canal Boat Independence, 9 Ben., 895; Pickert v. Canal Boat Independence, 55 How. Pr., 205.

§ 41. Subsequent vendee.— A. conveyed, by unstamped and unrecorded deeds, a portion of his mining claim to certain parties, who in turn conveyed the same to B., by deeds duly stamped and recorded. Later A. conveyed all his interest in the same mining claims to B., by deeds duly stamped and recorded, and afterwards filed a bill to correct a mistake in the latter conveyance to B., but *pendente lite* conveyed to C., who had no notice of the prior conveyances by unstamped and unrecorded deeds, all his interest in the mine. *Held*, that whatever equities A. could have conveyed to any one, as against his prior vendees, had already been conveyed to B., of which conveyance C. had notice, and that therefore all that C. could possibly acquire was the equity, if such existed, on which a reformation of A.'s deed to B. might be obtained. Kinney v. Consolidated Virginia Mining Co., 4 Saw.. 382.

§ 42. Lis pendens.— The general principles by which a third person is charged with notice under the doctrine of *lis pendens* is that the notice attaches only to the thing which is the subject-matter of the suit. *In re* Great Western Telegraph Co.,* 5 Biss., 363.

§ 43. In regard to promissory notes, fair upon their face, an indorsee is not bound to inquire into the consideration of the note or the circumstances out of which it grew. So a *bona fide* indorsee of a note is not charged with notice by a pending suit to declare void a contract made by the litigating parties. *Ibid.*

§ 44. A person purchasing municipal bonds with actual knowledge of a suit pending to avoid the bonds is not an innocent holder. His position is no better than that of his vendor or indorser, although the paper was purchased before maturity, Durant v. Iowa County, 1 Woolw., 69.

§ 45. To make the pendency of a suit notice, so as to affect the conscience of a purchaser, it is essential that the court have jurisdiction over the thing. Carrington v. Brents, 1 McL., 167.

§ 46. The pendency of a suit cannot operate as notice until after the service of process or publication. Dunn v. Games, 1 McL., 321. *Held*, that a purchase of real estate in Virginia pending a suit is void, though the notice of the suit is not filed and recorded pursuant to the provisions of the code. Rutherglen v. Woolf,* 1 Hughes, 78.

§ 47. Where a defendant in ejectment aliens the property in dispute while the proceedings are pending, and the plaintiff ultimately recovers. the vendee cannot set up the statute of limitations as against such plaintiff. although by reason of vexatious delays in the suit he and his vendor have been able to keep the plaintiff out for the period required by statute to give title by possession under color of title. Walden v. Bodley's Heirs, 9 How., 34.

§ 48. Where a vessel, having become subject to a lien for damage by a collision, afterwards comes within the jurisdiction in which to be subject to libel, such presence being known to the libelants and no action being taken. a libel, filed four years after the collision, will not affect the rights of *bona fide* purchasers without notice. And where, pending the collision cause, one of the original purchasers sells his part of the vessel to the other, such part will be subject to no greater liability than that which attached to it in the hands of the seller, as one who has bought in good faith, without notice of an equity, can convey a good title to a purchaser, whether he has or has not notice of the equity. The D. M. French, 1 Low., 48.

§ 49. Where bonds are secured by lien, and an equitable suit is brought to enforce the lien claimed upon property in the hands of the defendants, who are not charged on the bonds in any other sense than that there is a lien upon their property, such suit operates as a *lis pen-*

dens in regard to all defenses set up to the lien, on the principle that the causes of action on the bonds, protected by established rules of law against the consequences of *lis pendens*, are independent of, and entirely collateral to, causes of action arising out of the lien. Stevens *v.* The Railroads, 4 Fed. R., 97.

§ 50. In chancery it is settled that a *lis pendens* is created by filing a bill and actual service of the subpœna. Fowler *v.* Byrd, Hemp., 213.

§ 51. The rule that all persons are bound to take notice of a pending suit does not apply to negotiable securities. Marshall *v.* Town of Elgin, 8 Fed. R., 783; 3 McC., 35.

§ 52. The plea of *lis pendens* in a foreign country is not a good plea in abatement. Lyman *v.* Brown, 2 Curt., 539.

§ 53. A purchaser of bonds for value, before maturity, who had no actual notice of any irregularity in the issuing of such bonds, or as to their invalidity, is unaffected by the pendency, at the time of the purchase, of a suit to declare the bonds invalid. Phelps *v.* Town of Lewiston, 15 Blatch., 131.

§ 54. An order issued by the court requiring a judgment debtor to appear for an examination touching his property, under the Ohio code, does not constitute a *lis pendens* so as to prevent him from mortgaging his property after service of notice upon him, but before his appearance. Gregory *v.* Hewson, 1 Bond, 277.

§ 55. A person who purchases property *pendente lite* does so at his peril, and is as conclusively bound by the results of the litigation, whatever they may be, as if he had been a party to it from the outset. Tilton *v.* Cofield, 3 Otto, 163.

§ 56. The rule that persons dealing with property are bound to take notice of a suit pending with regard to the title thereto, and will, on their peril, purchase the same from any of the parties to the suit, does not apply to negotiable securities purchased before maturity. Such securities are exempt from the rule, whether created before the suit or during its pendency, and whether the suit relates to their origin or transfer. County of Warren *v.* Marcy, 7 Otto, 96.

§ 57. Parties who by themselves or their counsel have had notice of proceedings in a federal court with reference to certain property, cannot claim to be *bona fide* purchasers under proceedings in a state court touching the same matter. Bill *v.* New Albany R. Co., 2 Biss., 390.

§ 58. Where an attachment is properly issued, notice of *lis pendens* may be filed in the clerk's office. United States *v.* Stevenson, 1 Abb., 495.

§ 59. The pendency of a suit is not constructive notice to purchasers of negotiable paper which is the subject of such suit. Preble *v.* Board of Supervisors, 8 Biss., 358.

§ 60. A suit not prosecuted to a decree or judgment is not constructive notice to a person not a *pendente lite* purchaser. Alexander *v.* Pendleton, 8 Cr., 462.

§ 61. Where there are three distinct and independent suits, with an interval of one year between the first and second, and two years between the second and third, the doctrine of *lis pendens* does not apply. Lee County *v.* Rogers, 7 Wall., 181.

§ 62. A purchaser *pendente lite* and those holding under him are chargeable with notice, and must be considered as having purchased subject to the results of the pending suit. Nor is the title of such purchaser fortified by the fact that a decree *pro confesso*, by a default on the publication of notice, was made against a claimant now claiming under the ultimate decree declaring his claim invalid, and that very soon after this and before that default was set aside, the purchase was made and the deed received from one of the parties to the suit. Such purchaser was bound to know the inconclusive character of the decree *pro confesso*, and that by the state law such decree could be set aside by the appearance of the absent defendant, and motion to that effect, especially where such purchaser is the attorney of one of the parties to the suit. Gay *v.* Parpart, 16 Otto, 679.

§ 63. A creditor's bill does not create a *lis pendens*, operating as notice as to real estate, unless it be so definite in the description that any one reading it can learn thereby what property is intended to be made the subject of litigation, and if not thus definite it will be postponed to a junior bill which is properly drawn. Miller *v.* Sherry, 2 Wall., 237.

§ 64. If the person holding the legal title is not made a party to a creditor's bill, the title of a purchaser *pendente lite* will hold good. *Ibid.*

§ 65. In Louisiana *lis pendens* must be pleaded as in *limine litis*. Barras *v.* Bidwell, 3 Woods, 5.

§ 66. Notice to the stockholders of a corporation of the facts which constitute the alleged fraud by means of which a decree was obtained against the corporation is sufficient to conclude the corporation where the stockholders had an opportunity to intervene and defend, but did not do so. Pacific Railroad *v.* Missouri Pacific R'y Co., 12 Fed. R., 641.

§ 67. Where a former shareholder attends a meeting of the board of directors of a corporation, there being but four of the five directors present, and purchases property of the directors, knowing that one of their number was absent, he cannot claim to be a *bona fide* purchaser without notice, where due notice of the meeting had not been given to the absent director as required by the by-laws of the corporation. Farwell *v.* Houghton Copper Works, 8 Fed. R., 66.

§ 68. The knowledge of stockholders in a corporation, the former owners of the property now owned by the corporation, will not affect the corporation with notice of a lien when there are other stockholders who took stock in ignorance of the claim. The Admiral,* 8 Law Rep. (N. S.), 91.

§ 69. A notice to a stockholder, or to a party who afterwards becomes an officer in the company, is not notice to the corporation. The fact that a party receiving notice afterwards becomes an officer in the company will not make it obligatory upon him to give that notice, before received, to the company. *Ibid.*

§ 70. Where the president and cashier of a bank are members of an insolvent firm, and have notice, as members, of the insolvency of their firm, such notice is to be deemed notice to the bank so as to invalidate a transfer of property from the firm to the bank a few days before suspension of business by the former. Nisbit *v.* Macon Bank, 12 Fed. R., 686; 4 Woods, 464.

§ 71. **Transfer of stock.**— Upon transfer of bank stock from A. to B., notice to the board of directors that B. is to hold as trustee only is notice to the bank, and precludes the banking corporation from applying the stock to its own use, for the debt of B., to the prejudice of the rights of the known *cestuis que trust*, unless the power to appropriate in such cases is expressly given by the charter. Mechanics' Bank of Alexandria *v.* Seton, 1 Pet., 299.

§ 72. **Stock.**— Where a corporation paid for certain mineral land in stock which was issued to the directors as paid-up stock, and it ultimately developed that gross fraud had been perpetrated between the parties to the sale and purchase of the mineral land, *held*, that as between the corporation and innocent purchasers of the stock in open market without notice, knowledge, or means of knowledge of the fraud, the shares of stock were paid up as shown by the books of the corporation. Foreman *v.* Bigelow, 4 Cliff., 508.

§ 73. An executor having bank stock devised to him in trust to pay the dividends to certain persons transferred the stock, for his own private purposes, to a third person on the books of the bank, with the assent of the officers of the same, who issued a certificate to such third person, on the faith of which he made advances and incurred liabilities for the individual benefit of the executor. *Held*, 1st, that such third person, having no notice of the misapplication of the money, or of the source of the executor's title, was entitled to hold the stock; 2d, that the bank which issued the certificate, having had notice that the stock belonged originally to the testator, was bound to look to the title of the executor under the will, before it permitted a transfer, and having had notice of the application of the funds to the executor's private use, was liable for the stock to the persons entitled under the will. Lowry *v.* Commercial & Farmers' Bank,* 3 Am. L. J., 111.

§ 74. **To corporation.**— Where the treasurer of a corporation was also the managing agent of the corporation, *held*, that notice to be given to the corporation was properly given to him instead of the board of directors, assembled for the transaction of business. New England Car Spring Co. *v.* Union India Rubber Co., 4 Blatch., 1.

§ 75. **Commercial paper.**— Where bonds of a corporation, negotiable by delivery, were stolen, and sold before maturity to a *bona fide* purchaser without notice, *held*, that the purchaser took a good title to the bonds, and to the coupons which were not due, but not to the overdue coupons. Gilbough *v.* Norfolk & Petersburg R. Co., 1 Hughes, 410.

§ 76. The mere fact that coupons for interest upon bonds of a municipal corporation are overdue and unpaid when such coupons are purchased is not of itself sufficient, without other circumstances to put the purchaser on his guard, to charge such purchaser with notice of defenses to the bonds, especially where the record shows that the sale of the bonds, during all of the time when the coupons were maturing, was restrained by an injunctional order, which was dissolved after the coupons had become due, but before the purchase of the same. Preble *v.* Board of Supervisors, 8 Biss., 358.

§ 77. Notice to bankers of the loss of overdue commercial paper is binding upon them, and if they afterwards purchase such paper in the course of their business, they are liable for the value thereof to the real owners. Vermilye *v.* Adams Express Co., 21 Wall., 188.

§ 78. Bills of exchange drawn on the secretary of war by army officers were accepted by the former and purchased by A. before maturity. Before making the purchase, A. was informed by a public officer that there was an "express law" prohibiting the secretary from making direct advance payment to army contractors, but that it was, and had been, "the custom of the department" to accept such bills. *Held*, that this was sufficient notice to A. of the illegality of the paper, to render the acceptance void in his hands. Peirce *v.* United States,* 1 Ct. Cl., 270.

§ 79. Where the question, whether coupons surrendered by the holder were merely sold, or delivered up for payment and cancellation, depended upon the intention of the holder, *held*, that intention to sell might be inferred from actual or constructive notice that purchase and not payment was being made; and that where the coupons were not paid in the usual manner, by the officers or agents of the company, at the place designated for payment, but, after examination, were sealed up in an envelope, and the holder directed to go elsewhere to get his money, which he did, and the coupons were not delivered up to the company, such constructive notice must be inferred.   Duncan *v.* Mobile & Ohio R. Co., 3 Woods, 567.

§ 80. Fraudulent conveyance.— The rule in equity that a vendee, after notice of the vendor's fraud, is only protected as to payment made before such notice, cannot be applied in a case at law.   Sousteby *v.* Keeley, 2 McC., 103; 11 Fed. R., 578 (FRAUD, §§ 540–42).

§ 81. Appointment of guardian.— Where the law authorizes the appointment of a guardian "after notice given to all persons interested," such notice is necessary to give jurisdiction, and the record must show that notice was given or the appointment will be void. Seavens *v.* Gerke, 3 Saw.. 353.

§ 82. Ownership of telegraph.— Where by contract a telegraph company was allowed to construct its line of telegraph wires along the track of a railroad company, such lines being under the control and operation of the telegraph company, as evidenced by the printed message blanks used, and the fact that all the telegraph business was done in the name of the telegraph company, *held*, that a purchaser of the railroad, at a foreclosure sale, did not acquire any title to the telegraph line as a *bona fide* purchaser thereof for value and without notice.   Western Union Telegraph Co. *v.* Burlington & Southwestern R'y Co., 3 McC., 130.

§ 83. Trustee for creditors.— Where A. gave to B. a deed of trust preferring certain creditors, holders of notes forged by him, in the expectation that if the notes were paid no prosecution would be instituted against him, *held*, that notice to the trustee, B., of A.'s hopes and expectations was not notice to the creditors so as to render the deed of trust void, as a contract, the consideration of which was the compounding of a felony.   Brooks *v.* Marbury, 11 Wheat., 78.

§ 84. Exempt property.—Where goods were set apart by decree of the court as an exemption for the benefit of the family, and such goods were sold by the head of the family, in conjunction with his business partner, *held*, that the purchaser took no title, as he was bound to know that, by the laws of the state, such property could not be sold by the husband without the wife joining in the sale.   *In re* Smith, 2 Hughes, 307.

§ 85. Notice to counsel.— Where A., a trust executor, through his counsel, B., paid to C. a sum of money according to the direction of the will of his testate, C. having been adjudged bankrupt and an assignee appointed more than two years prior to such payment, *held*, that the executor was chargeable with notice of C.'s bankruptcy, by reason of the knowledge of his counsel, B., although the executor himself had no knowledge of the bankruptcy proceedings, and the same had wholly escaped the mind of B., at the time the payment was made. Beecher *v.* Gillespie, 6 Ben., 356.

§ 86. Notice of insolvency.— Where A., being engaged in extensive business operations, pays an extraordinarily large discount for a loan, such fact is not notice, to the parties making the loan, of his insolvency, although commercial paper similar to A.'s was at the same time selling at high rates, if it appear that A.'s pressing need of money, by reason of his desire to hold large quantities of salable products for more favorable prices, was not inconsistent with his pretensions as a man of means.   Golson *v.* Neihoff,* 5 N. B. R., 56.

§ 87. Innocent persons.— When one of two innocent persons must suffer, the one guilty of negligence, or who fails to use the means within his reach to acquire information which would have avoided the injury, must bear the loss.   The Monte Allegre, 9 Wheat., 616.

§ 88. By-laws of a town.— One who owns real estate in a town is bound to take notice of its charter, by-laws and ordinances. Thus, where an ordinance permitted property owners to give their notes for the taxes due, thereby creating an equitable lien upon the property, *held*, that a purchaser of the property was liable for such equitable liens on the property which attached to it while in the hands of its former owner.   Corporation of Georgetown *v.* Smith, 4 Cr. C. C., 91.

§ 89. Notice to a deputy marshal who performs an act is notice to the marshal himself. United States *v.* Bank of Arkansas, Hemp., 460.

NOTICE BY PUBLICATION.

See JUDGMENTS; WRITS.

NOVATION.

See Contracts.

NUISANCE.

See Crimes; Equity; Torts; Water-courses.

NUL TIEL RECORD.

See Pleading.

OATHS.

[See Affidavit; Notary Public.]

§ 1. Who may administer.—A judge of a district court of the United States has power to administer oaths incident to his judicial office, or pertaining to matters arising in his own court, and hence may administer to the clerk of the United States court for his district the oath which is required by law to be made, by such clerk, to his accounts with the government. United States v. Ambrose, 2 Fed. R., 556.

§ 2. A United States consul at Mexico was appointed minister, whereupon he took and subscribed the oath required by the act of July 2, 1862 (12 Stat. at L., p. 502), before the consul-general of Switzerland. *Held*, that he was entitled to no pay as minister under the above act, as the consul-general of Switzerland had no right in the premises, and was not a proper party before whom to take the oath. Otterbourg v. United States,* 5 Ct. Cl., 480.

§ 3. A county judge having power to administer oaths may administer them in any county in the state. Voce v. Lawrence, 4 McL., 203.

§ 4. A state master in chancery is not authorized by any act of congress to administer oaths. Hence affidavits made before such master cannot be read in evidence, when offered in chancery, in a United States circuit court. Haight v. Proprietors of the Morris Aqueduct, 4 Wash., 601.

§ 5. A deputy clerk, being authorized by the court to act during the absence of the clerk, has the right to administer oaths in bankruptcy, and such oaths are presumed to be administered in the presence of the court and by virtue of its authority. United States v. Nihols, 4 McL., 23.

§ 6. Upon the presentation in evidence, in the United States circuit court for the District of Columbia, of a deposition taken in Louisiana before a person who called himself "a commissioner duly appointed by the district court of the United States for the eastern district of Louisiana, under and by virtue of the act of congress entitled 'An act for the more convenient taking of affidavits and bail in civil causes depending in the courts of the United States'" (act of February 20, 1812), it was contended that the commissioners, under the act of 1812, were only authorized to take depositions in causes depending in their own courts, or in the district courts, under the act of 1817. *Held*, that the deposition might be read in evidence. Whitney v. Huntt, 5 Cr. C. C., 120.

§ 7. Where an act of congress requires a person claiming pre-emption rights to make oath of entry, etc., such oath, under the usage of the proper department of the government, may be administered by a state officer having power to administer oaths. United States v. Winchester, 2 McL., 135.

§ 8. Under a rule of the court ordering "that petitioners residing out of the county of W. may verify their petitions before the county clerk of the county in which they reside, and the clerks of the different counties of this district are hereby appointed commissioners to administer oaths to petitioners applying for the benefit of the bankrupt law," *held*, that county clerks outside of the county of W. had no power to administer oaths to persons residing outside of their respective counties. United States v. Deming, 4 McL., 8.

§ 9. A justice of the peace is not incompetent to administer the oath upon the taking of a deposition, by reason of his being deponent's counsel. Atkinson v. Glenn, 4 Cr. C. C., 184.

§ 10. An attachment issued upon affidavit is not insufficient by reason of the affidavit having been taken before a clerk of the circuit court in vacation, the clerk having power to administer oaths in vacation, in such cases. James v. Jenkens, Hemp., 189.

§ 11. Although there is no statute of the United States which expressly authorizes any justice of the peace of a state to administer an oath in support of any claim against the United States under the act of July 5, 1832, the secretary of the treasury, in order to carry into effect the authority given to him to liquidate and pay the claims referred to in such act, having established a regulation authorizing justices of the peace to administer such oaths, *held*, that by virtue of his implied power to make such regulations, oaths thus administered would be within the purview of the act of March 1, 1823. United States v. Bailey, 9 Pet., 238.

§ 12. Presumption.— An officer of the customs, duly commissioned, and acting in the duties of his office, is presumed to have taken the regular oaths. United States v. Bachelder, 2 Gall., 15.

§ 13. Affirmation.— A juror cannot be permitted to make solemn affirmation in lieu of oath, unless it be contrary to his religious principles to take an oath on any occasion. Bryan's Case, 1 Cr. C. C., 151.

§ 14. A juror not a quaker nor attached to any particular religious sect will not be permitted to affirm simply because he prefers affirming to swearing. McIntire's Case, 1 Cr. C. C., 157. ·

OBJECTIONS.

See APPEALS; EVIDENCE; PRACTICE.

OBLIGATION OF CONTRACTS.

See CONSTITUTION AND LAWS.

OBSCENE ARTICLES.

[As to non-mailable matter, see CRIMES.]

An information founded on the act of 1857, chapter 68, was filed against one case of stereoscopic slides, alleging them to be indecent and obscene, and praying for their condemnation and destruction. A part of the slides were admitted to be indecent, but as to the rest the general issue was filed. *Held*, that those only which were found to be indecent could be condemned and destroyed. But it seems that if the information had alleged that those which were not indecent were imported in the same package with those which were indecent, proof of that fact would have authorized their forfeiture. United States v. One Case Stereoscopic Slides,* 1 Spr., 467.

OCCUPYING CLAIMANTS.

See LAND.

OFFICERS.

[See COURTS; GOVERNMENT; WRITS. As to duties in particular cases, see the appropriate general heads of the work.]

I. IN GENERAL. POWERS, DUTIES AND LIABILITIES.

SUMMARY — *Office and officer defined*, § 1.— *How offices to be established; agent of fortifications*, § 2.— *Illegal appointment; liability of appointee*, § 3.— *Acts requiring judgment and discretion*, §§ 4, 5, 7.— *Liability of a sheriff as conservator of the peace*, § 6.

§ 1. An office is "a public charge or employment," and he who performs the duties of the office is an officer. If employed on the part of the United States, he is an officer of the United States. Although an office is "an employment" it does not follow that every employment is an office. A man may be employed under a contract, express or implied, to do an act, or perform a service, without becoming an officer. But if the duty be a continuing one, which is defined by rules prescribed by the government, and not by contract, which an individual is appointed by government to perform, who enters on the duties appertaining to his station without any contract defining them, if those duties continue, though the person be changed, it seems very difficult to distinguish such a charge or employment from an office, or the person performing the duties from an officer. United States *v.* Maurice, §§ 8-17.

§ 2. All offices, except such as are provided for in the constitution, must be established by legislative enactment. The acts of congress from 1794 to 1808, empowering the president to erect fortifications, and appropriating large sums of money to enable him to carry these acts into execution, do not establish the office of agent of fortifications. The army regulations, revised in September, 1816, according to the provisions of the act of April 24, 1816, recognizing such army regulations, and providing for alterations, in connection with the act of March 2, 1821, adopting the revisal of September, 1816, established such office in August, 1818; and the duties of said office were prescribed by such army regulations. *Ibid.*

§ 3. An irregular appointment to an office does not absolve the person appointed from the legal and moral obligation of accounting for public money which has been placed in his hands in consequence of such appointment. *Ibid.*

§ 4. A public officer is not liable to an action, if he falls into error, in a case where the act to be done is not merely a ministerial one, but is one in relation to which it is his duty to exercise judgment and discretion, even though an individual may suffer by his mistake. Kendall *v.* Stokes, §§ 18-21.

§ 5. In the settlement of accounts properly belonging to the postoffice department, upon which it was the duty of the postmaster-general to exercise his judgment, where he committed an error, in supposing that he had a right to set aside allowances for services rendered upon which his predecessor in office had finally decided, but as the case admits he had acted from a sense of public duty and without malice, his mistake in a matter properly belonging to the department over which he presided can give no cause of action against him. (McLEAN, J., dissented.) *Ibid.*

§ 6. Though the powers and duties of a sheriff as conservator of the peace are not strictly judicial, still the preservation of the peace is a public duty, for neglect of which he is amenable to the public, and punishable by indictment only. To render him liable to a civil action for acts not simply ministerial, the plaintiff must allege and prove, 1, that he had a right or privilege; 2, that by the act of the officer he was hindered from the enjoyment of it; and, 3, that the act was done maliciously. So, in an action upon a sheriff's official bond, where the plaintiff alleged that, while engaged in his lawful business, certain evil-disposed persons came about him, hindered and prevented him, threatened his life, with force of arms demanded of him a large sum of money, and imprisoned and detained him for the space of four days, and until he paid them the sum of $2,500 for his enlargement; that the sheriff being present, plaintiff applied to him for protection, and requested him to keep the peace of the state of Maryland; that the sheriff neglected and refused to protect and defend the plaintiff, and to keep the peace, etc., whereby his bond became forfeited, and action accrued to the plaintiff,— *held*, that the sheriff was not liable. South *v.* State of Maryland, §§ 22-24.

§ 7. Report having been made by the warehouse keeper that certain goods were in a perishing condition, the collector directed an examination of them to be made by two United States appraisers, and upon report by them that the goods were in a perishing condition, and that an immediate sale was necessary, the collector ordered them to be sold. They were sold at auction, but only on a day's notice, and at prices considerably less than their value. *Held*, that under the act of congress of August 6, 1846 (Dunlop, U. S. Laws, 1106), providing for the sale forthwith " of goods of a perishable nature, and all gunpowder, firecrackers, and explosive substances " deposited, etc., as to the true condition of the goods, the necessity of a sale, and the degree of promptitude required, the collector was *pro hac vice* a judicial officer, and if he fell into an error, where the act done was not purely ministerial, but one in relation to which his duty was to exercise his judgment and discretion, he was not liable in an action. If a discretion was reposed in him by law, to render him liable it must be proved either that he exercised the power confided in cases not within his jurisdiction, or in a manner not confided to him, as with malice, cruelty or wilful oppression. The briefness of the notice could not be considered *per se* sufficient evidence of fraud or corrupt motive. Gould *v.* Hammond, §§ 25, 26.

[NOTES.— See §§ 27-200.]

UNITED STATES *v.* MAURICE.

(Circuit Court for Virginia: 2 Marshall, 96-118. 1823.)

Opinion by MARSHALL, C. J.

STATEMENT OF FACTS.— This is an action of debt brought upon a bond executed on the 18th day of August, 1818, in the penalty of $20,000, with the following condition: "Whereas the said James Maurice has been appointed agent for fortifications on the part of the United States, now, therefore, if the said James Maurice shall truly and faithfully execute and discharge all the duties appertaining to the said office of agent, as aforesaid, then the above obligation to be void," etc. The breach assigned in the declaration is, that large sums of money came to the hands of the said Maurice, as agent of fortifications, which he was bound by the duties of his office faithfully to disburse and account for, a part of which, namely, $40,000, he has, in violation of his said duty, utterly failed to disburse to the use of the United States, or account for; wherefore, etc.

The defendants, the sureties in the said obligation, prayed oyer of the bond, and of the condition, and then demurred to the declaration. The plaintiff joined in the demurrer. The defendants also pleaded several pleas, on some of which issue has been made up, and on others demurrer has been joined.

§ 8. *What constitutes a public office.*

The first point to be considered is the demurrer to the declaration. The defendants insist that the declaration cannot be sustained, because the bond is void in law, it being taken for the performance of duties of an office, which office has no legal existence, and consequently, no legal duties. No violation of duty, it is said, can take place when no duty exists.

Since the demurrer admits all the facts alleged in the declaration which are properly charged, and denies that those facts create any obligation in law, it must be taken as true that James Maurice was in fact appointed an agent of fortification on the part of the United States; that he received large sums of money in virtue of that appointment, and has failed to apply it to the purpose for which he received it, or to account for it to the United States.

As the securities certainly intended to undertake that Maurice should perform the very acts which he has failed to perform, and as the money of the nation has come into his hands on the faith of this undertaking, it is the duty of the court to hold them responsible, to the extent of this undertaking, unless the law shall plainly interpose its protecting power for their relief, upon the principle that the bond creates no legal obligation. Is this such a bond?

The first step in this inquiry is the character of the bond. Does it, on its face, purport to be a mere official bond, or to be in the nature of a contract? This question is to be answered by a reference to the terms in which its condition is expressed. These leave no shadow of doubt on the mind. The condition refers to no contract, states no undertaking to perform any specific act — refers to nothing — describes nothing which the obligor was bound to do, except to perform the duties of an officer. It recites that he was appointed to an office, and declares that the obligation is to be void if he "shall truly and faithfully execute and discharge all the duties appertaining to the said office." Of the nature of those duties no information whatever is given. Whether the disbursement of public money does or does not constitute a part of them is a subject on which the instrument is entirely silent.

The bond, then, is, on its face, completely an official bond, given, not for the performance of any contract, but for the performance of the duties of an office, which duties were known and had been prescribed by law or by persons authorized to prescribe them.

In his declaration the attorney for the United States has necessarily taken up this idea and proceeded on it. In his assignment of breaches he states that the said James Maurice had been appointed agent of fortifications, and alleges that he had not performed the duties of the said office nor kept the condition of his bond, but that the said condition is broken in this, that while he held and remained in the said office divers large sums of money came to his hands, as agent of fortifications, which he was bound by the duties of his office faithfully to disburse and account for; a part of which, $40,000, he has, in violation of his said duty, utterly failed to disburse or account for. On this breach of his official duty, which is alleged to constitute a breach of the condition of his bond, the action is founded. No allusion is made to any other circumstance whatever as giving cause of action.

The suit, then, is plainly prosecuted for a violation of the duty of office, which is alleged to constitute a breach of an official bond. The court must, on this demurrer, at least, so consider it, and must decide it according to those rules which govern cases of this description. This being a suit upon an official bond, the condition of which binds the obligors only that the officer should perform the duties of his office, it would seem that the obligation could be only co-extensive with these duties. What is their extent? The defendants contend that no such office exists; that James Maurice was never an officer, ,and, of consequence, was never bound by this bond to the performance of any duty whatever.

To estimate the weight of this objection, it becomes necessary to examine the constitution of the United States and the acts of congress in relation to this subject. The constitution, article 2, section 2, declares that the president "shall nominate, and, by and with the advice and consent of the senate, shall appoint ambassadors," etc., "and all other officers of the United States, whose appointments are not herein otherwise provided for, and which shall be established by law."

I feel no diminution of reverence for the framers of this sacred instrument when I say that some ambiguity of expression has found its way into this clause. If the relative "which" refers to the word "appointments," that word is referred to in a sense rather different from that in which it had been used. It is used to signify the act of placing a man in office, and referred to as signifying the office itself. Considering this relative as referring to the word "offices," which word, if not expressed, must be understood, it is not perfectly clear whether the words "which" offices "shall be established by law" are to be construed as ordaining that all offices of the United States shall be established by law, or merely as limiting the previous general words to such offices as shall be established by law. Understood in the first sense, this clause makes a general provision that the president shall nominate, and, by and with the consent of the senate, appoint to all offices of the United States, with such exceptions only as are made in the constitution; and that all offices (with the same exceptions) shall be established by law. Understood in the last sense, this general provision comprehends those offices only which might be established by law, leaving it in the power of the executive, or of those who might be intrusted with the execution of the laws, to create in all laws of legislative omission such offices as might be deemed necessary for their execution, and afterwards to fill those offices.

I do not know whether this question has ever occurred to the legislative or executive of the United States, nor how it may have been decided. In this ignorance of the course which may have been pursued by the government, I shall adopt the first interpretation, because I think it accords best with the general spirit of the constitution, which seems to have arranged the creation of office among legislative powers, and because, too, this construction is, I think, sustained by the subsequent words in the same clause, and by the third clause of the same section.

The sentence which follows, and forms an exception to the general provision which had been made, authorizes congress "by law to vest the appointment of such inferior officers as they think proper in the president alone, in the courts of law, or in the heads of departments." This sentence, I think, indicates an opinion in the framers of the constitution that they had provided for all cases of offices.

The third section empowers the president "to fill up all vacancies that may happen during the recess of the senate, by granting commissions which shall expire at the end of their next session." This power is not confined to vacancies which may happen in offices created by law. If the convention supposed that the president might create an office, and fill it originally without the consent of the senate, that consent would not be required for filling up a vacancy in the same office. The constitution, then, is understood to declare that all offices of the United States, except in cases where the constitution itself may otherwise provide, shall be established by law.

§ 9. *Agent of fortifications.*

Has the office of agent of fortifications been established by law? From the year 1794 to the year 1808, congress passed several acts, empowering the president to erect fortifications, and appropriating large sums of money to enable him to carry these acts into execution. No system for their execution has ever been organized by law. The legislature seems to have left this subject to the discretion of the executive. The president was, consequently, at liberty to employ any means which the constitution and laws of the United States placed under his control. He might, it is presumed, employ detachments from the army, or he might execute the work by contract, in all the various forms which contracts can assume. Might he organize a corps, consisting of laborers, managers, paymasters, providers, etc., with distinct departments of duty, prescribed and defined by the executive, and with such fixed compensation as might be annexed to the various parts of the service? If this mode of executing the law be consistent with the constitution, there is nothing in the law itself to restrain the president from adopting it.   But the general language of the law must be limited by the constitution, and must be construed to empower the president to employ those means only which are constitutional.   According to the construction given in this opinion to the second section of the second article of that instrument, it directs that all offices of the United States shall be established by law; and I do not think that the mere direction that a thing shall be done, without prescribing the mode of doing it, can be fairly construed into the establishment of an office for the purpose, if the object can be effected without one.   It is not necessary, or even a fair inference from such an act, that congress intended it should be executed through the medium of offices, since there are other ample means by which it may be executed, and since the practice of the government has been for the legislature, wherever this mode of executing an act was intended, to organize a system by law, and either to create the several laws expressly or to authorize the president, in terms, to employ such persons as he might think proper, for the performance of particular services.

If, then, the agent of fortifications be an officer of the United States, in the sense in which that term is used in the constitution, his office ought to be established by law, and cannot be considered as having been established by the acts empowering the president, generally, to cause fortifications to be constructed.

Is the agent of fortifications an officer of the United States?   An office is defined to be "a public charge or employment," and he who performs the duties of the office is an officer.   If employed on the part of the United States, he is an officer of the United States.   Although an office is "an employment," it does not follow that every employment is an office.   A man may certainly be employed under a contract, express or implied, to do an act, or perform a service, without becoming an officer.   But if a duty be a continuing one, which is defined by rules prescribed by the government, and not by contract, which an individual is appointed by government to perform, who enters on the duties appertaining to his station, without any contract defining them, if those duties continue, though the person be changed, it seems very difficult to distinguish such a charge or employment from an office, or the person who performs the duties from an officer.

If it may be converted into a contract, it must be a contract to perform the duties of the office of agent of fortifications, and such an office must exist with ascertained duties, or there is no standard by which the extent of the condition can be measured.

The army regulations are referred to in acts of congress, passed previous and subsequent to the execution of the bond under consideration.   A copy of those regulations, purporting to be a revisal made in the war office in September, 1816, conformably to the act of the 24th of April, 1816, has been laid before the court and referred to by both parties.   These regulations provide for the appointment and define the duties of the agents of fortifications.

They are to be governed by the orders of the engineer department in the disbursement of the money placed in their hands.   They are to provide the materials and workmen deemed necessary for the fortifications, and they are to pay the laborers employed.   In the performance of these duties they are directed to make out, first, an "abstract of articles purchased;" secondly, "an abstract of labor performed;" thirdly, "an abstract of pay of mechanics;" and fourthly, "an abstract of contingent expenses."

These duties are those of a purchasing quartermaster, commissary and paymaster. These are important duties. A very superficial examination of the laws will be sufficient to show that duties of this description, if not performed by contract, are performed by persons who are considered as officers of the United States, whose offices are established by law.

If, then, we look at the bond and declaration we find in both every characteristic of an office bond. If we look at the army regulations, the only additional source of information within our reach, we find the duties of an agent of fortifications to be such as would make him an officer of the United States. Is the office established by law? The permanent agents mentioned in the act of March 3, 1809 (ch. 19, sec. 3), are those who are appointed "either for the purpose of making contracts or for the purchase of supplies, or for the disbursement, in any other manner, of moneys for the use of the military establishment of the United States." If this act authorizes the appointment of such agents, and virtually establishes their offices, it cannot, I think, in correct construction, be extended to other persons than those who are employed in some manner in disbursing money "for the use of the military establishment or navy of the United States." "The military establishment" is a term which seems to be well defined in the acts of congress, and to be well understood, and I do not think the act can be construed to comprehend an agent of fortifications.

§ 10. *Object of act of March 3, 1817.*

In the act of March 3, 1817 (ch. 517, sec. 5), it is made the duty of the secretary of war "to prepare general regulations, better defining and prescribing the respective duties and powers in the adjutant-general, inspector-general, quartermaster-general and commissary of ordnance, department of the topographical engineers, of the aids of generals, and generally of the general and regimental staff; which regulations, when approved by the president of the United States, shall be respected and obeyed until altered or revoked by the same authority."

The exclusive object of this section is, I think, the regulation of existing offices. I do not think it can be fairly construed to extend to the establishment of offices. Yet, if under this act subordinate agencies or offices have in fact been introduced, such offices may be established by subsequent acts of congress.

The act of April 24, 1816, "for organizing the general staff, and making farther provision for the army of the United States," section 9, enacts "that the regulations in force before the reduction of the army be recognized, as far as the same shall be found applicable to the service, subject, however, to such alterations as the secretary of war may adopt, with the approbation of the president."

A legislative recognition of the actually existing relations of the army must be understood as giving to those regulations the sanction of the law; and the subsequent words of the sentence authorize the secretary of war to alter those regulations with the approbation of the president. Such alterations have also the sanction of the act of 1816.

This subject appears to have been taken up by the secretary. A pamphlet, entitled "Army Regulations Revised, conformably to the act of 24th of April, 1816," has been laid before the court as authentic, and has been appealed to by both plaintiffs and defendants, as being the same regulations which are approved and adopted by the act of the 2d of March, 1821, section 13.

These regulations direct the appointment of agents of fortifications, and define their duties. They purport to have been revised in the war office, in September, 1816. If the provision they contain respecting agents of fortifications formed a part of the army regulations prior to the act of the 24th of April, 1816, it is recognized by that act. If that provision was first introduced in September, 1816, it may, if approved by the president, be considered as an alteration authorized by that act. The question whether this alteration has been approved by the president is perhaps a question of fact not examinable on this demurrer.

When I consider the act of the 24th of April, 1816, and this revisal in the war office, in connection with the act of the 2d of March, 1821, adopting the revisal of September, 1816, under the name of general regulations of the army, compiled by Major-General Scott (for they are represented as being the same regulations), I feel much difficulty in saying that the office of agent of fortifications was not established by law when this bond was executed. I am more inclined to give this opinion because I am persuaded this cause must be carried before a tribunal which can make that certain which was before uncertain; and because, by overruling the demurrer to the declaration, the other questions of law which occur in the cause, and which would be arrested by sustaining the demurrer to the declaration, will all be brought before the supreme court.

§ 11. *Effect of taking a new official bond to release the sureties on the old bond.*
The defendants pleaded several pleas to the declaration. The second plea is, that the defendant, James Maurice, performed the condition of his bond up to the 26th day of September, 1820, on which day a new bond was executed, in pursuance of the act of the 15th of May, 1820, "providing for the better organization of the treasury department." The plaintiff takes issue on that part of the plea which alleges performance up to the 26th day of September, 1820, and demurs to the residue. The act under which this new bond was executed gives a new and summary remedy against officers of the United States who had received public money for which they had failed to account, and against their sureties, and contains a proviso, "That the summary process herein directed shall not affect any surety of any officer of the United States who became bound to the United States before the passing of this act; but each and every such officer shall, on or before the 30th day of September next, give new and sufficient sureties for the performance of the duties required of such officer." The defendants contend that this new and sufficient bond was a substitute for the old one, and discharged the sureties to the original obligation, so far as respects subsequent transactions.

The plaintiff contends that the bond is cumulative, and that the sureties to the first obligation continue bound for any subsequent as well as any preceding default of the officer. There is certainly no express declaration of the act on this subject; and if the second bond operates a discharge of the first, this effect is produced by implication only; yet the implication is very strong in favor of the construction.

The sole object of the law is to obtain sureties against whom the new and summary remedy it gives might be used. To obtain additional security does not appear to be one of the motives for which it was passed. The direction that the sureties should be " new " and " sufficient " countenances the opinion that they were solely relied on for the subsequent transactions of the officer. If no additional security was intended to be demanded; if the sole object of the law was to coerce the giving of sureties, against whom this new remedy, by distress, might be used, it seems reasonable to think that the legislature supposed the new sureties alone responsible for the subsequent conduct of their officer. It could not escape the consideration of the legislature that the same friends who became bound in the first bond might probably become bound in the second, thinking themselves discharged from the first. But friends may be willing to become bound in a penalty within their resources, or to an amount to which the officer can secure them, and very unwilling to become bound in double that sum. The officer may be able to give security in a penalty of $25,000, and totally unable to give security for $50,000. The government fixes the penalty in which an officer shall give bond and sureties, and is regulated in fixing that penalty by all the considerations which belong to the subject. It ought not to be considered as augmenting that penalty, unless the means used for augmenting it are plain, direct and intelligible. In this case, if the same sureties execute the new bond, they are liable to a double penalty by an act not clearly understood to have that effect. If there are new sureties to the new bond, the attention of the old sureties may be diverted from watching the conduct of the officer, and they may even be induced to relinquish liens on property, in order to enable the officer to find his new sureties.

If the course of legislation on the subject has been such as to furnish to the original sureties reasonable ground for the opinion that they were discharged from all liability for the subsequent conduct of the officer, and reasonable ground for the implication that such was the intention of the legislature, and I think it has, such ought to be the construction of the act. This demurrer, therefore, is overruled.

§ 12. *Appointment to office by the heads of departments. Validity.*

The fifth plea is that James Maurice was never legally appointed, but was, on the 1st day of August, 1818, appointed by the secretary of war, agent of fortifications for Norfolk, Hampton Roads, and the lower part of the Chesapeake Bay, without any provision of law whatever authorizing and empowering him to make such appointment, and directly contrary to an act entitled an act, etc., passed the 3d of March, 1809.

To this plea there is a demurrer. The first question arising on this demurrer respects the validity of this appointment made by the secretary of war. It is too clear, I think, for controversy that appointments to office can be made by heads of departments in those cases only which congress has authorized by law; and I know of no law which has authorized the secretary of war to make this appointment. There is certainly no statute which directly and expressly confers the power; and the army regulations, which are exhibited as having been adopted by congress in the act of the 2d of March, 1821, declares that agents shall be appointed, but not that they shall be appointed by the secretary of war. If this mode of appointment formed a part of the regulations previous to the revision of September, 1816, that is a fact which might or might not be noticed if averred in the pleadings. The court is not informed of its existence by this demurrer. It must therefore be supposed not to exist, and James Maurice cannot be considered as a regularly appointed agent of fortifications.

§ **13.** *Effect of an irregular appointment to office upon the validity of an official bond.*

This brings us to the question in the cause on which I have felt, and still continue to feel, great difficulty. The appointment of James Maurice having been irregular, is this bond absolutely void, or may it be sustained as a contract entered into by a person not legally an officer, to perform certain duties belonging to an office? If the office had no existence, it has been already stated that a bond to perform its duties generally could create no obligation, but since the office does exist, the condition refers to something certain by which the nature and extent of the undertaking of the obligor may be determined. It is an undertaking that James Maurice shall perform the duties appertaining to the office of agent of fortifications; and this undertaking is in the nature of contract. If this contract does not bind the parties according to its expressed extent, its failure must be ascribed to some legal defect or vice inherent in the instrument. It is contended that the bond is void, because there is an inability on the part of the United States to make any contract not previously directed by statute.

§ **14.** *Right of the government to make contracts. Limits of its power.*

The United States is a government, and, consequently, a body politic and corporate, capable of attaining the objects for which it was created by the means which are necessary for their attainment. This great corporation was ordained and established by the American people, and endowed by them with great powers for important purposes. Its powers are unquestionably limited; but while within those limits, it is a perfect government as any other, having all the faculties and properties belonging to a government, with a perfect right to use them freely, in order to accomplish the objects of its institutions. It will certainly require no argument to prove that one of the means by which some of these objects are to be accomplished is contract; the government, therefore, is capable of contracting, and its contracts may be made in the name of the United States.

The government acts by its agents, but it is neither usual nor necessary to express, in those contracts which merely acknowledge the obligation of an individual to the United States, the name of the agent who was employed in making it. His authority is acknowledged by the individual when he executes the contract, and is acknowledged by the United States when the government asserts any right under that contract. I do not mean to say that there exists any estoppel on either party; I only mean to say that a contract executed by an individual, and received by the government, is *prima facie* evidence that it was entered into between proper parties. So with respect to the subject of the contract.

Without entering on the inquiry respecting the limits which may circumscribe the capacity of the United States to contract, I venture to say that it is co-extensive with the duties and powers of government. Every contract which subserves to the performance of a duty may be rightfully made.

The constitution, which has vested the whole legislative powers of the Union in congress, has declared that the president " shall take care that the laws be faithfully executed." The manner in which a law shall be executed does not always form a part of it; a power, not limited or regulated by the words of the acts, has been given by the legislature to the executive, to construct fortifications; and large sums of money have been appropriated to the object. It is not and cannot be denied that these laws might have been carried into execution by means of contract; yet there is no act of congress expressly authorizing the executive to make any contract in the case. It is useless, and would be tedious, to multiply examples, but many might be given to illustrate the truth of the proposition. It follows, as a necessary consequence, that the duty, and of course the right, to make contracts may flow from an act of congress which does not in terms prescribe this duty; the proposition then is true, that there is a power to contract in every case where it is necessary to the execution of a public duty.

§ 15. *Necessary elements of a contract to which the government is a party.*

It remains to inquire whether it be indispensable to the validity of a contract that it should express the circumstances under which it was made so precisely and distinctly as to show the motives which induced it and the objects to be effected by it. This certainly is often done, and in many cases conduces to a clear understanding of the intention of the parties, and of the obligations which the instrument creates; but it is not universally practiced, would be often inconvenient, and is necessary, I think, only so far as may be requisite to explain the nature of the contract. We know too well that persons intrusted with the public money are often defaulters. It is not, I believe, doubted that the law raises an *assumpsit* to pay the money which the defaulter owes. An overpayment is sometimes made by mistake; is not the receiver liable to the United States? Yet there is no act of congress creating the *assumpsit* in either case. I presume it will not be denied that a declaration charging that the defendant was indebted to the United States for money had and received to their use, and that, being so indebted, he assumed and promised to pay it, would be sufficient without setting forth at large all the circumstances of the character in which, and the objects for which, the money was received. If the law would raise an implied *assumpsit* which would be binding, I cannot conceive that an express *assumpsit* would be less so; nor can I conceive that such express *assumpsit*, more than the implied *assumpsit*, need detail the various circumstances on which its validity might depend. These would be matter of evidence. In any case where an *assumpsit* would be valid, the government may certainly take a bond, and I perceive no reasons why sureties may not also be demanded. It is the duty of the government to collect debts due to it, however they may have accrued; it results from this duty that the means of securing and collecting the public money may be used. Sureties may therefore be required to the bond demanded from the debtor; the instrument itself is an admission that it is given for a debt, and it is contrary to all our received opinions to require that it should show how the debt was contracted. Anything which destroys its validity may undoubtedly be shown in pleading; but a bond given to the United States is, I think, *prima facie* evidence of debt and would be sustained on demurrer.

So if money be committed to the care of any person for a legitimate object, bond and security, on the same principle, may be required with condition that he shall account for it. The jurisdiction of a limited court must undoubtedly appear on the record; but I do not think that the same rule applies to contracts. Infants, *femes covert*, idiots, and persons under duress, are not bound by their contracts. But their disability must be shown by pleading, and it need not appear in any contract that the parties to it are not liable to these disabilities. Every contract which is legal on its face and imports a consideration is supposed to be entered into on valid consideration and to be obligatory, if the parties be ostensibly able, until the contrary is shown; and the same rule applies to a government which is capable of making contracts.

§ 16. *What constitutes an illegal consideration for an official bond.*

It is also contended that this bond is void, because it is entered into on a consideration which is either forbidden by express law, or contrary to the general policy of the law.

The plea refers to the act passed on the 3d of March, 1809, "to amend the several acts for the establishment and regulation of the treasury, war and navy departments." I have already said that I do not consider the prohibition of this act as comprehending agents of fortifications, because they do not belong to the military establishment, nor do their employments relate to it. It is unnecessary to enter into any argument in support of this opinion, because it is of no importance to the point under consideration. The effect, if the act applied to the office, would be to show that the appointment of James Maurice to the office of agent of fortifications was not legal — and that effect is produced by the construction I have given to the constitution. I consider the appointment of James Maurice to the office of agent of fortifications by the secretary of war as invalid; but the question, is the bond void on that account? still remains to be considered. It was undoubtedly intended as an office bond, and was given in the confidence that James Maurice was legally appointed to office. If the suit was instituted to punish him for the neglect of duty, in the nature of non-user, or for any other failure, which could be attributed in any degree to the illegality of his appointment, I should be much disposed to think the plea a bar to the action. But this suit is brought to recover the money of the United States which came to the hands of James Maurice, in virtue of his supposed office, and which he has neither applied to the purpose for which he received it, nor returned to the treasury. In such a case, neither James Maurice, nor those who undertook for him, can claim anything more than positive law affords them.

The plea does not controvert, but must be understood to confess, the material facts charged in the declaration. It must be understood to confess that the money of the United States came to the hands of James Maurice as agent of fortifications; that it was the duty of such agent to disburse it for the use of the United States, in the manner prescribed by the army regulations, or to account for it; that he has failed to do either, and that they were bound for him in this respect. Admitting these things, they say it is a bar to the action brought for the money that his appointment was illegal.

§ 17. *Effect of the illegality of consideration of an official bond on the liability of the sureties.*

If the bond contained no reference to the appointment of James Maurice, as agent of fortifications; if its condition stated only, that certain sums of money had been delivered to him to be disbursed under the discretion of the principal engineer, in the purchase of materials for fortifications, and in the payment of laborers, its obligation, I presume, would not be questioned. It would be a contract which the United States might lawfully make. If, instead of specifying the particular purposes for which the money was received, the condition of a bond refers to a paper which does specify those purposes, I know of no principle of reason or of law which varies the obligation of the instrument from what it would be, if containing that specification within itself. That is certain which may be rendered certain; and an undertaking to perform the duties prescribed in a distinct contract, or in a law, or in any other known paper prescribing those duties, is equivalent to an enumeration of those duties in the body of the contract itself.

This obligation is an undertaking to perform the duties appertaining to the office of agent of fortifications. Those duties were prescribed in the army regulations, and were such as any individual might lawfully undertake to perform. The plea does not allege that the thing to be done was unlawful, nor does it allege that the illegality of the appointment to office constituted any impediment to a performance of the condition of the bond. Were it even improper to disburse the money received in the manner intended by the contract, it could not be improper to return it. There can be nothing unlawful in the engagement to return it. The obligation to return it, as in every other case of money advanced by mistake, is one which, independent of all express contract, would be created by the law itself. So far as respects the receiver himself, he would be bound by law to return the money not disbursed, and if he would be so bound, why may not others be bound with him for his doing that which law and justice oblige him to do?

Admitting the appointment to be irregular, to be contrary to the law and its policy, what is to be the consequence of this irregularity? Does it absolve the person appointed from the legal and moral obligation of accounting for public money which has been placed in his hands in consequence of such appointment? Does it authorize him to apply money so received to his own use? If the policy of the law condemns such appointments, does it also condemn the payment of moneys received under them? Had this subject been brought before the legislature, and the opinion be there entertained that such appointments were illegal, what would have been the probable course? The secretary of war might have been censured; an attempt might have been authorized to make him ultimately responsible for the money advanced under the illegal appointment; but is it credible that the bond would be declared void? Would this have been the policy of those who make the law? Let the course of congress in another case answer this question.

It is declared to be unlawful for any member of congress to be concerned in any contract made on the part of the United States, and all such contracts are declared to be void. What is the consequence of violating this law, and making a contract against its express provisions? A fine is imposed on the violator, but does he keep the money received under the contract? Far from it. The law directs that the money so received shall be forthwith repaid, and in case of refusal or delay, " every person so refusing or delaying, together with his surety or sureties, shall be forthwith prosecuted at law for the recovery of any such sum or sums of money advanced as aforesaid." If, then, this appointment be contrary to the policy of the law, the repayment of the money under it is not, and a suit may, I think, be sustained to coerce such repayment on the bond given for that purpose.

The cases cited by the defendants do not, I think, support the plea. Collins v. Blantern, 2 Wilson, 341, was a bond given, the consideration of which was illegal. It was to compound a prosecution for a criminal offense. It was to induce a witness not to appear and give testimony against a person charged with the commission of a crime. The court determined that the bond was void, and that the illegal consideration might be averred in the plea, though not appearing in the condition. It is only wonderful that this could ever have been doubted.

The case of Paxton v. Popham, 9 East, 408, and the case of Pole v. Harrobin, reported in a note in page 416 of the same volume, are both cases in which bonds were given for the payment of money for the performance of an act which was contrary to law. These cases differ in principle from that at bar. The bond was not given to induce the illegal appointment, or for any purpose in itself unlawful. The appointment had been made, and the object of the bond was to secure the regular disbursement of, or otherwise accounting for public money advanced for a lawful purpose. The bond was not then unlawful, though the appointment was.

The case of Nares and Pepys v. Rolles, 14 East, 510, was a suit on a bond given by a collector and his sureties for the due collection and payment to the receiver-general of certain duties assessed under an act of parliament. The duties were collected but not paid to the receiver-general; in consequence of which the collector was displaced and suit brought against one of the sureties in the bond. The defense was that the duties were not in law demandable, and this defense was founded on an ambiguity in the language of the act. The argument turned chiefly on the words of the statute, but the counsel for the plaintiffs contended also that, supposing the act not to impose the taxes, yet the bond would not be void, for such a security might well be taken, that the duties which were actually collected should not be lost, but might be preserved, to be paid over to those who should be found ultimately entitled to receive the money. It was competent for him to enter into a bond to pay over voluntary payments made to him, although he might not have been able to enforce payment of the rates from those who might refuse.

In answer to this argument, it was said that, unless the act gave authority to assess and collect the duties, he was no collector, and could not be subject to any obligation for not paying money over to the plaintiffs, in that character, which was obtained by extortion. The court seemed inclined to this opinion, but determined that the taxes were imposed and assessed according to law, and, therefore gave judgment for the plaintiffs.

The impression which may, at the first blush, be made by this case will be effaced by an attentive consideration of it. If the money collected was not due by law, the plaintiffs could have no right to receive it, and had, consequently, no cause of action against the defendant. The money sued for was not their money, but the money of the individuals from whom it had been unlawfully collected. The bond to collect and pay over this money to the receiver-general was a bond to do an unlawful act. The contract would have been clearly against law. In giving his opinion on this subject, the chief justice said: "Looking at the condition of this bond, as it appears upon the record, I cannot say that, if the rates were collected without any authority, the collector could be called upon to pay them over, because he would be answerable to the individuals from whom he had received the money, and would be entitled to retain it for his own indemnity."

The case at bar is, in principle, entirely different from that of Nares and Pepys v. Rolles. This is not money obtained illegally from others, and, therefore, returnable to them, but is the money of the United States, drawn out of the treasury. The person holding it is not entitled "to retain it for his own indemnity," against the claims of others, for there are no others who can claim it. The justice of the case requires, I think, very clearly, that the defendants should be liable to the extent of their undertaking, and I do not think the principles of law discharge them from it.

I am, therefore, of opinion that the demurrer to this plea ought to be sustained, and that judgment on it be rendered for the plaintiffs.

KENDALL v. STOKES.

(3 Howard, 87-103. 1844.)

ERROR to the Circuit Court for the District of Columbia.

Opinion by ,TANEY, C. J.

STATEMENT OF FACTS.— The record in this case is very voluminous, and contains a great mass of testimony, and also many incidental questions of law not involving the merits of the case, which were raised and decided in the circuit court, and to which exceptions were taken by the plaintiff in error. But both parties have expressed their desire that the controversy should now be terminated by the judgment of this court; and that the leading principles which must ultimately decide the rights of the parties should now be settled; and that the case should not be disposed of upon any technical or other objections which would leave it open to further litigation. In this view of the subject it is unnecessary to give a detailed statement of the proceedings in the court below. Such a statement would render this opinion needlessly tedious and complicated. We shall be better understood by a brief summary of the pleadings and evidence, together with the particular points upon which our decision turns; leaving unnoticed those parts of the record which can have no influence on the judgment we are about to give, nor vary in any degree the ultimate rights of the parties.

At the time of the trial and verdict in the circuit court, the declaration contained five counts. But after the verdict was rendered, the plaintiffs in that court, with the leave of the court, entered a *nolle prosequi* upon the second, third and fourth, and the judgment was entered on the first and the fifth. It is only of these two last mentioned counts, therefore, that it is necessary to speak. The verdict was a general one for the plaintiffs, and their damages assessed at $11,000.

The first count states that by virtue of certain contracts made with William T. Barry, while he was postmaster-general, and services performed under them, the plaintiffs, on the 1st of May, 1835, were entitled to receive and have allowed to them the sum of $122,000, and that that sum was accordingly credited to them on the books of the postoffice department; and that Amos Kendall, the defendant in the court below, afterwards became postmaster-general, and as such illegally and maliciously caused the items composing the said amount to be suspended on the books of the department, and the plaintiffs to be charged therewith; whereby they were greatly injured, and put to great expenses, and suffered in their business and credit.

The fifth count recites the act of congress of July 2, 1836 (6 Stats. at Large, 665), by which the solicitor of the treasury was authorized to settle and adjust the claims of the plaintiffs for services rendered by them under contracts with William T. Barry, while he was postmaster-general, and which had been suspended by Amos Kendall, then postmaster-general, and to make them such allowances therefor, as, upon a full examination of all the evidence, might seem right and according to principles of equity; and the postmaster-general directed to credit them with whatever sum or sums of money the solicitor should decide to be due to them, for or on account of such service or contract; and after this recital of the act of congress, the plaintiffs proceed to aver that services had been performed by them under contracts with William T. Barry, while he was postmaster-general, on which their pay had been suspended by Amos Kendall, then postmaster-general, and that for these claims the solicitor of the treasury allowed the plaintiffs large sums of money amounting to $162,727.05; that the defendant had notice of the premises, and that it became his duty as postmaster-general to credit the plaintiffs with this sum; but that he illegally and maliciously refused to give the credit, by reason whereof the plaintiffs were subjected to great loss, their credit impaired, and they were obliged to incur heavy expenses in prosecuting their rights, to their damage in the sum of $100,000.

The defendant pleaded not guilty, upon which issue was joined.

At the trial, the plaintiffs offered in evidence the record of the proceedings in the *mandamus* which issued from the circuit court, upon their relation, on the 7th day of June, 1837, commanding the said Amos Kendall to enter the credit for the sum awarded by the solicitor. It is needless to state at large the proceedings in that suit, as they are sufficiently set forth in the report of the case in 12 Pet., 524; the judgment of the circuit court, awarding a peremptory *mandamus*, having been brought by writ of error before the supreme court, and there affirmed at January term, 1838. 12 Pet., 524. Various papers and letters were also offered in evidence by the plaintiffs to show that the allowances mentioned in the declaration had been suspended by the defendant; and that after the award of the solicitor, and before the original *mandamus* issued, he had refused to credit $39,472.47, part of the sum awarded, upon the ground that the items composing it were not a part of the subject-matter referred; and upon which, as the defendant insisted, the solicitor had no right to award. Other papers and letters were also offered, showing that after the judgment of the circuit court awarding a peremptory *mandamus* had been affirmed in the supreme court, the plaintiffs demanded a credit for the abovementioned balance on the 23d of March, 1838; that the defendant declined entering the credit, alleging that a recent change in the postoffice law had placed the books and accounts of the department in the custody of the auditor; and some difficulty having arisen on this point, the circuit court, on the 30th of March, 1838, issued a *mandamus* commanding the postmaster-general to enter the credit on the books of the department; and to this writ the defendant made return on the 3d of April, 1838, that the said credit had been entered by the auditor, who had the legal custody of the books.

The whole of this evidence was objected to by the defendant, but the objection was overruled and the testimony given to the jury. And upon the evidence so offered by the plaintiffs, before any evidence was produced on his part, the defendant moved for the following instruction from the court:

"The defendant, upon each and every of the plaintiffs' said counts, severally and successively prayed the opinion of the court, and their instruction to the jury that the evidence so as aforesaid produced and given on the part of the plaintiffs, so far as the same is competent to sustain such count, is not competent and sufficient to be left to the jury as evidence of any act or acts done or omitted or refused to be done by the defendant, which legally laid him liable to the plaintiffs in this action, under such count, for the consequential damages claimed by the plaintiffs in such count." This instruction was refused, and the defendant excepted.

The question presented to the court by this motion in substance was this: Had the plaintiffs, upon the evidence adduced by them, shown themselves entitled in point of law to maintain their action, for the causes stated in their declaration upon the breaches therein assigned, assuming that the jury believed the testimony to be true?

The instruction asked for was in the nature of a demurrer to the evidence, and in modern practice has, in some of the states, taken the place of it. In the Maryland courts, from which the circuit court borrowed its practice, a prayer of this description, at the time of the cession of the district and for a long time before, was a familiar proceeding, and a demurrer to evidence seldom if ever resorted to. And the refusal of the court was equivalent to an instruction that the plaintiffs had shown such a cause of action as would authorize the jury, if they believed the evidence, to find a verdict in favor of the plaintiffs, and to assess damages against the defendant for the causes of action stated in the declaration.

Now the cause of action stated in the first count is the suspension, by the defendant, of the allowances made by his predecessor in office; and of the recharge of sums with which the plaintiffs had been credited by Mr. Barry, when he was the postmaster-general. And it appeared in evidence, by the proceedings in the *mandamus*, that the plaintiffs being unable to settle with the defendant the dispute between them on the subject, they applied to congress for relief; that upon this application a law was passed, referring the matter to the solicitor of the treasury, with directions that he should inquire into and determine the equity of these claims, and make them such allowances therefor as might seem right, according to the principles of equity; and that the postmaster-general should credit them with whatever sums of money, if any, the solicitor should decide to be due; that the plaintiffs assented to this reference, and offered evidence before the solicitor that they were entitled to the allowances and credits claimed by them; and that, from the conduct of the postmaster-general, in suspending and recharging these allowances and credits, they had been compelled to pay a large amount in discounts and interest, in order to carry on their business; and that the solicitor had finally determined in favor of their claims, and awarded to them the sum hereinbefore mentioned, giving them, as appears in his report to congress, interest on the money withheld from them; and also that, before this suit was brought, they had obtained a credit on the books of the department for the whole sum awarded by the solicitor.

§ **18.** *After an award in his favor and payment of the money awarded, the creditor cannot maintain an action on his original demand on the ground that he is entitled to further damages.*

Assuming, for the sake of the argument, that an action might in the first instance have been sustained against the postmaster-general, can the plaintiffs still support a suit upon the original cause of action? It was not a controversy between the plaintiffs and Amos Kendall, as a private individual, but between them and a public officer acting for and on behalf of the United States. If they had sustained damage, it was the consequence of his act, and the question of damages was necessarily referred with the subject-matter in controversy, out of which that question arose. It was an incident to the principal matters referred, and therefore within the scope of the reference; and it is not material to inquire whether damages for the detention of the money were claimed or not, or allowed or not. In point of fact, however, the plaintiffs did claim interest on the money withheld, as a damage sustained from the conduct of the postmaster-general, and offered proof before the solicitor of the amount of discounts and interest they had been compelled to pay; and, moreover, were allowed in the award a large sum on that account, which was paid to them as well as the principal sum. The question, then, on the first count is, can a party, after a reference, an award, and the receipt of the money awarded, maintain a suit on the original cause of action upon the ground that he had not proved before the referee all the damages he had sustained, or that his damage exceeded the amount which the arbitrator awarded? We think not. The rule on that subject is well settled. It has been decided in many cases, and is clearly stated in Dunn v. Murray, 9 B. & C., 780. The plaintiffs, upon their own showing, therefore, were not entitled to maintain their action on the first count, and the circuit court ought so to have directed the jury.

§ 19. *A public officer is not liable in damages for official acts, not ministerial, done honestly in discharge of his (supposed) duty.*

The judgment upon this count is also liable to another objection equally fatal. The acts complained of were not what the law terms ministerial, but were official acts done by the defendant, in his character as postmaster-general. The declaration, it is true, charges that they were maliciously done, but that was not the ground upon which the circuit court sustained the action either on this count or the fifth. For, among other instructions moved for on behalf of the defendant, the court were requested to direct the jury:

"That if they found from the evidence that the postmaster-general acted from the conviction that he had lawful power and authority, as postmaster-general, to set aside the extra allowances made by his predecessor, and to suspend and recharge the same, and from a conviction that it was his official duty to do so; and if the plaintiffs suffered no injury from such official act but the inconveniences necessarily resulting therefrom, that the defendant was not liable."

This instruction was refused; the court thereby in effect giving the jury to understand, that however correct and praiseworthy the motives of the officer might be, he was still liable to the action, and chargeable with damages.

We are not aware of any case in England or in this country in which it has been held that a public officer, acting to the best of his judgment and from a sense of duty, in a matter of account with an individual, has been held liable to an action for an error of judgment. The postmaster-general had undoubtedly the right to examine into this account, in order to ascertain whether there were any errors in it which he was authorized to correct, and whether the allowances had in fact been made by Mr. Barry; and he had a right to suspend these items until he made his examination and formed his judgment. It repeatedly and unavoidably happens, in transactions with the government, that money due to an individual is withheld from him for a time, and payment suspended, in order to afford an opportunity for a more thorough examination. Sometimes erroneous constructions of the law may lead to the final rejection of a claim in cases where it ought to be allowed. But a public officer is not liable to an action if he falls into error, in a case where the act to be done is not merely a ministerial one, but is one in relation to which it is his duty to exercise judgment and discretion; even although an individual may suffer by his mistake. A contrary principle would indeed be pregnant with the greatest mischiefs. It is unnecessary, we think, to refer to the many cases by which this doctrine has been established. It was fully recognized in the case of Gidley, Ex'r of Holland, v. Lord Palmerston, 7 J. B. Moore, 91; 3 B. & B., 275.

The case in 9 Clark & Finnelly, 251, recently decided in England, in the house of lords, has been much relied on in the argument for the defendant in error. But upon an examination of that case, it will be found that it had been decided by the court of session in Scotland, in a former suit between the same parties, that the act complained of was a mere ministerial act, which the party was bound to perform; and that this judgment had been affirmed in the house of lords. And the action against the party, for refusing to do the act, was maintained, not upon the ground only that it was ministerial, but because it had been decided to be such by the highest judicial tribunal known to the laws of Great Britain. The refusal for which the suit was brought took place after this decision; and the learned lords, by whom the case was decided, held that the act of refusal, under such circumstances, was to be regarded as wilful, and with knowledge; that the refusal to obey the lawful decree of a court of justice was a wrong, for which the party who had sustained injury by it might maintain an action, and recover damages against the wrong-doer. This case, therefore, is in no respect in conflict with the principles above stated; nor with the rule laid down in the case of Gidley v. Lord Palmerston.

In the case before us, the settlement of the accounts of the plaintiffs properly belonged to the postoffice department, of which the defendant was the head. As the law then stood, it was his duty to exercise his judgment upon them. He committed an error in supposing that he had a right to set aside allowances for services rendered upon which his predecessor in office had finally decided. But as the case admits that he acted from a sense of public duty and without malice, his mistake in a matter properly belonging to the department over which he presided can give no cause of action against him.

We proceed to the fifth count. But before we examine the cause of action there stated, it will be proper to advert to the principles settled by this court in the case of the *mandamus* hereinbefore referred to. The court in that case, speaking of the nature and character of the proceeding by *mandamus*, which had been fully argued at the bar, said that it was an action or suit brought in a court of justice, asserting a right, and prosecuted according to the forms of judicial proceeding; and that a party was entitled to it when there was no other adequate remedy; and that although in the case then before them the plaintiffs in the court below might have brought their action against the defendant for damages on account of his refusal to give the credit directed by the act of congress, yet as that remedy might not be adequate to afford redress, they were, as a matter of right, entitled to pursue the remedy by *mandamus*.

§ 20. *A party having elected to bring a particular form of action (mandamus), and succeeded, cannot afterward for the same cause bring another action for damages.*

Now, the former case was between these same parties, and the wrong then complained of by the plaintiffs, as well as in the case before us on the fifth count, was the refusal of the defendant to enter a credit on the books of the postoffice department for the amount awarded by the solicitor. In other words, it was for the refusal to pay them a sum of money to which they were lawfully entitled. The credit on the books was nothing more than the form in which the act of congress, referring the dispute to the solicitor, directed the payment to be made. For the object and effect of that entry was to discharge the plaintiffs from so much money, if on other accounts they were debtors to that amount; and if no other debt was due from them to the United States, the credit entitled them to receive at once from the government the amount credited. The action of *mandamus* was brought to recover it, and the plaintiffs show by their evidence that they did recover it in that suit. The gist of the action in that case was the breach of duty in not entering the credit, and it was assigned by the plaintiffs as their cause of action. The cause of action in the present case is the same; and the breach here assigned, as well as in the former case, is the refusal of the defendant to enter this credit. The evidence to prove the plaintiffs' cause of action is also identical in both actions. Indeed, the record of the proceedings in the *mandamus* is the testimony relied on to show the refusal of the postmaster-general, and the circumstances under which he refused, and the reasons he assigned for it. But where a party has a choice of remedies for a wrong done to him, and he elects one, and proceeds to judgment, and obtains the fruits of his judgment, can he, in any case, afterwards proceed in another suit for the same cause of action? It is true that in the suit by *mandamus* the plaintiffs could recover nothing beyond the amount awarded. But they knew that when they elected the remedy. If the goods of a party are forcibly taken away under circumstances of violence and aggravation, he may bring trespass, and in that form of action recover not only the value of the property, but also what are called vindictive damages — that is, such damages as the jury may think proper to give to punish the wrong-doer. But if instead of an action of trespass he elects to bring trover, where he can recover only the value of the property, it never has been supposed that, after having prosecuted the suit to judgment and received the damages awarded him, he can then bring trespass upon the ground that he could not in the action of trover give evidence of the circumstance of aggravation, which entitled him to demand vindictive damages.

The same principle is involved here. The plaintiffs show that they have sued for and recovered in the *mandamus* suit the full amount of the award; and having recovered the debt, they now bring another suit upon the same cause of action, because in the former one they could not recover damages for the detention of the money. The law does not permit a party to be twice harassed for the same cause of action; nor suffer a plaintiff to proceed in one suit to recover the principal sum of money, and then support another to recover damages for the detention. This principle will be found to be fully recognized in 2 Bl., 880, 831; 5 Co., 61, Sparry's Case; Com. Dig., tit. Action, K., 3. And in the case of Moses *v.* Macferlan, 2 Burr., 1010, Lord Mansfield held that the plaintiff having a right to bring an action of *assumpsit* for money had and received to his use on a special action on the case on an agreement, and having made his election by bringing *assumpsit*, a recovery in that action would bar one on the agreement, although in the latter he could not only recover the money claimed in the action of *assumpsit*, but also the costs and expenses he had been put to. The case before us falls directly within the rule stated by Lord Mansfield.

§ 21. *As a mandamus can only be granted because there is no other adequate remedy at law, an action for damages cannot be afterward sustained for the same cause of action, the two being inconsistent.*

This objection applies with still more force when, as in this instance, the party has proceeded by *mandamus.* The remedy in that form originally was not regarded as an action by the party, but as a prerogative writ commanding the execution of an act, where otherwise justice would be obstructed; and issuing only in cases relating to the public and the government; and it was never issued when the party had any other remedy. It is now regarded as an action by the party on whose relation it is granted, but subject still to this restriction, that it cannot be granted to a party where the law affords him any other adequate means of redress. Whenever, therefore, a *mandamus* is applied for, it is upon the ground that he cannot obtain redress in any other form of proceeding. And to allow him to bring another action for the very same cause after he has obtained the benefit of the *mandamus*, would not only be harassing the defendant with two suits for the same thing, but would be inconsistent with the grounds upon which he asked for the *mandamus*, and inconsistent also with the decision of the court which awarded it. If he had another remedy, which was incomplete and inadequate, he abandoned it by applying for and obtaining the *mandamus*. It is treated both by him and the court as no remedy. Such was obviously the meaning of the supreme court in the opinion delivered in the former suit between these parties, where they speak of the action on the case, and give him the *mandamus* because the other form of action was inadequate to redress the injury, and they would not therefore require the plaintiffs to pursue it. And they speak of the action on the case as an alternative remedy; not as accumulative and in addition to the *mandamus*. In the case in 9 Clark & Finnelly, 251, hereinbefore mentioned upon another point, the attorney-general in his argument said that no other action would lie in any case where the party was entitled to a *mandamus*. And Lord Campbell, in giving his judgment, said that this proposition was not universally true, and at any rate applied only to the original grant of the *mandamus*, and not to the remedy for disobeying it, and that no case had been cited to show that an action would not lie for disobedience to the judgment of the court. This remark upon the proposition stated by the attorney-general shows clearly that in his judgment you could not resort to a *mandamus* and to an action on the case also for the same thing. If the postmaster-general had refused to obey the *mandamus*, then indeed an action on the case might have been maintained against him. But the present suit is not brought on that ground. No question is presented here as to the necessity of pleading a former recovery in bar, nor as to the right to offer it in evidence upon the general issue. The point in the circuit court did not arise upon the pleading of the defendant, nor upon evidence offered by him, but upon the case made by the plaintiffs, in which, by the same evidence that proved their original cause of action, they also proved that they had already sued the defendant upon it and recovered a judgment which had been satisfied before this suit was brought. And, we think, upon such evidence, the instruction first above mentioned ought to have been given on this (the fifth) count, as it appeared by the plaintiffs' own showing that they had already recovered satisfaction for the injury complained of in their declaration.

The case before us is altogether unlike the cases referred to in the argument, where, after a party has been admitted or restored to an office, he has maintained an action of *assumpsit* or case to recover the emoluments which had been received by another, or of which he had been deprived during the time of his exclusion. In those cases the cause of action in the *mandamus* was the exclusion from office; and the suit afterwards brought was to recover the emoluments and profits to which his admission or restoration to office showed him to have been legally entitled. The action of *assumpsit* or case would not have restored him to the office, nor have secured his right to the profits. But, in the case before the court, if this action had been resorted to in the first instance instead of the *mandamus*, the plaintiffs could have recovered the amount due on the award, and the damages arising from its unlawful detention must have been assessed and recovered in the same verdict. Clearly they could not have maintained one action on the case for the amount due, and then brought another to recover the damages; and this, not because both were actions on the case, but because they could not be permitted to harass the defendant with two suits for the same thing, no matter by what name the actions may be technically called, nor whether both are actions on the case or one of them called a *mandamus*.

But, if this action could have been maintained, we think that most of the evidence admitted by the circuit court to enhance the damages ought not to have been received. It consisted chiefly of discounts and interest paid by the plaintiffs before the award of the solicitor, and of expenses on journeys and tavern bills, and fees paid to counsel for prosecuting their claim before congress and the courts. It appears by the record that before this evidence was offered the court had instructed the jury that malice on the part of the defendant was not necessary to support the action; and it appears also that the jury, which found the verdict and assessed the damages, declared that their verdict was not founded on any idea that the defendant did the acts complained of, and for which they gave the damages of $11,000, with any intent other than a desire faithfully to perform the duties of his office of postmaster-general, and to protect the public interests committed to his charge, and that the damages were given on the ground that his acts were illegal, and that the sum given was the amount of the actual damage estimated to have resulted from his illegal acts.

We have already said, that although this action is in form for a tort, yet in substance and in truth it is an action for the non-payment of money. And upon the principles upon which it was supported by the court and decided by the jury, if there had been no proceeding by *mandamus* to bar the action, the legal measure of damages upon the fifth count would undoubtedly have been the amount due on the award, with interest upon it.

The testimony however, appears to have been offered chiefly under the first count, because the items for interest paid, and traveling and tavern expenses, for the most part, bear dates before the award, and also a portion of the fees of counsel. The evidence was certainly inadmissible under this count, since, for the reasons already given, no action could be maintained upon it, if there had been no previous proceeding by *mandamus*, and consequently no damages could be recovered upon it. But independently of this consideration, and even if the action could have been sustained, there are insuperable objections to the admission of this testimony. In the first place, no special damages are laid in the declaration; and in that form of pleading no damages are recoverable but such as the law implies to have accrued from the wrong complained of (1 Chit. Pl., 385); and certainly the law does not imply damages of the description above stated. But we think the evidence was not admissible in any form of pleading. In the case of Hathaway *v.* Barrow, 1 Camp., 151, in an action on the case for a conspiracy to prevent the plaintiff from obtaining his certificate under a commission of bankruptcy, the court refused to receive evidence of extra costs incurred by the plaintiff in a petition before the chancellor. In the case of Jenkins *v.* Biddulph, 4 Bingh., 160, in an action against a sheriff for a false return, the court said they were clearly of opinion that the plaintiff was not entitled to recover the extra costs he had paid; that as between the attorneys and their clients the case might be different, because the attorney might have special instructions, which may warrant him in incurring the extra costs; but that in a case like the one before them the plaintiff could only claim such costs as the prothonotary had taxed. And in the case of Grace v. Morgan, 2 Bingh. N. C., 534, in an action for a vexatious and excessive distress, the plaintiff was not allowed to recover as damages the extra costs in an action of replevin which the plaintiff had brought for the goods distrained; and the case in 1 Stark., 306, in which a contrary principle had been adopted, was overruled.

These were stronger cases for extra costs than the one before us. The admission of the testimony in relation to the largest item in these charges, that is, for interest paid by the plaintiffs, amounting to more than $9,000, is still more objectionable. For it appears from the statement in the exception that the very same account had been laid before the solicitor, and had induced him, as he states in his report to congress, to make the plaintiffs an allowance in his award for interest, amounting to $6,893.93. And to admit this evidence again in this suit was to enable the plaintiffs to recover twice for the same thing; and after having received from the United States what was deemed by the referee a just compensation for this item of damage, to recover it over again from the defendant.

There are several other questions stated in the record, but it is needless to remark upon them, as the opinions already expressed dispose of the whole case. The judgment of the circuit court must be reversed.

MR. JUSTICE McLEAN dissented.

SOUTH v. STATE OF MARYLAND.

(18 Howard, 396–404. 1855.)

ERROR to U. S. Circuit Court, District of Maryland.

Opinion by MR. JUSTICE GRIER.

STATEMENT OF FACTS.—In this case a verdict was rendered for the plaintiff in the court below, and the defendant moved, in arrest of judgment, "that the matters set out in the declaration of the plaintiff are not sufficient, in law, to support the action." If it be found that the court erred in overruling this motion and in entering judgment on the verdict, a consideration of the other points raised on the trial will be unnecessary.

The action is brought on the official bond of South, as sheriff of Washington county. The declaration sets forth the condition of the bond at length. The breach alleged is, in substance, "that while Pottle was engaged about his lawful business, certain evil-disposed persons came about him, hindered and prevented him, threatened his life, with force of arms demanded of him a large sum of money, and imprisoned and detained him for the space of four days, and until he paid them the sum of $2,500 for his enlargement."

That South, the sheriff, being present, the plaintiff, Pottle, applied to him for protection, and requested him to keep the peace of the state of Maryland, he, the said sheriff, having power and authority so to do. That the sheriff neglected and refused to protect and defend the plaintiff, and to keep the peace, wherefore it is charged "the sheriff did not well and truly execute and perform the duties required of him by the laws of said state;" and thereby the said writing obligatory became forfeited, and action accrued to the plaintiff.

This declaration does not charge the sheriff with a breach of his duty in the execution of any writ or process in which Pottle, the real plaintiff in this case, was personally interested, but a neglect or refusal to preserve the public peace, in consequence of which the plaintiff suffered great wrong and injury from the unlawful violence of a mob. It assumes as a postulate that every breach or neglect of a public duty subjects the officer to a civil suit by any individual who, in consequence thereof, has suffered loss or injury; and, consequently, that the sheriff and his sureties are liable to this suit on his bond, because he has not "executed and performed all the duties required of and imposed on him by the laws of the state."

§ 22. *Powers and duties of sheriff are quasi-judicial or ministerial.*

The powers and duties of the sheriff are usually arranged under four distinct classes:

1. In his judicial capacity he formerly held the sheriff's tourn, or county courts, and performed other functions which need not be enumerated.

2. As king's bailiff he seized to the king's use all escheats, forfeitures, waifs, wrecks, estrays, etc.

3. As conservator of the peace in his county or bailiwick, he is the representative of the king or sovereign power of the state for that purpose. He has the care of the county, and, though forbidden by *magna charta* to act as a justice of the peace in trial of criminal cases, he exercises all the authority of that office where the public peace was concerned. He may upon view, without writ or process, commit to prison all persons who break the peace or attempt to break it; he may award process of the peace, and bind any one in recognizance to keep it. He is bound, *ex officio*, to pursue and take all traitors, murderers, felons and other misdoers, and commit them to jail for safe custody. For these purposes he may command the *posse comitatus* or power of the county; and this summons every one over the age of fifteen years is bound to obey, under pain of fine and imprisonment.

4. In his ministerial capacity he is bound to execute all processes issuing from the courts of justice. He is keeper of the county jail, and answerable for the safe-keeping of prisoners. He summons and returns juries, arrests, imprisons, and executes the sentence of the court, etc., etc. 1 Black. Com., 343; 2 Hawk. P. C., ch. 8, § 4, etc.

Originally the office of sheriff could be held by none but men of large estate, who were able to support the retinue of followers which the dignity of his office required, and to answer in damages to those who were injured by the neglect of duty in the performance of his ministerial functions. In more modern times, a bond with sureties supplies the place of personal wealth. The object of these bonds is security, not the imposition of liabilities upon the sheriff, to which he was not subject at common law. The specific enumeration of duties in the bond in this case includes none but those that are classed as ministerial. The general expression, in conclusion, should be construed to include only such other duties of the same kind as were not specially enumerated. To entitle a citizen to sue on this bond to his own use, he must show such a default as would entitle him to recover against the sheriff in an action on the case. When the sheriff is punishable by indictment as for a misdemeanor, in cases of a breach of some public duty, his sureties are not bound to suffer in his place, or to indemnify individuals for the consequences of such a criminal neglect.

§ 23. *Sheriff's duty as conservator of the peace is quasi-judicial. He is liable to indictment.*

It is an undisputed principle of the common law, that for a breach of a public duty an officer is punishable by an indictment; but where he acts ministerially, and is bound to render certain services to individuals, for a compensation in fees or salary, he is liable for acts of misfeasance or non-feasance to the party who is injured by them. The powers and duties of conservator of the peace exercised by the sheriff are not strictly judicial; but he may be said to act as the chief magistrate of his county, wielding the executive power for the preservation of the public peace. It is a public duty, for neglect of which he is amenable to the public, and punishable by indictment only.

§ 24. *Sheriff is liable on his bond only for breach of ministerial duties.*

The history of the law for centuries proves this to be the case. Actions against the sheriff, for a breach of his ministerial duties in the execution of process, are to be found in almost every book of reports. But no instance can be found where a civil action has been sustained against him for his default or misbehavior as conservator of the peace, by those who have suffered injury to their property or persons through the violence of mobs, riots, or insurrections.

In the case of Entick *v.* Carrington, State Trials, vol. 19, page 1062, Lord Camden remarks: "No man ever heard of an action against a conservator of the peace, as such."

The case of Ashby *v.* White, 2 Lord Raym., 938, has been often quoted to show that a sheriff may be liable to a civil action where he has acted in a judicial rather than a ministerial capacity. This was an action brought by a citizen entitled to vote for member of parliament, against the sheriff for refusing his vote at an election. Gould, justice, thought the action would not lie, because the sheriff acted as a judge. Powis, because, though not strictly a judge, he acted *quasi*-judicially. But Holt, C. J., decided that the action would lie: 1. "Because the plaintiff had a right or privilege. 2. That, by the act of the officer, he was hindered from the enjoyment of it. 3. By the finding of the jury the act was done maliciously." The latter cases all concur in the doctrine that, where the officer is held liable to a civil action for acts not simply ministerial, the plaintiff must allege and prove each of these propositions. See Cullen *v.* Morris, 2 Starkie, N. P. C.; Harman *v.* Tappenden, 1 East, 555, etc.

The declaration in the case before us is clearly not within the principles of these decisions. It alleges no special individual right, privilege or franchise in the plaintiff, from the enjoyment of which he has been restrained or hindered by the malicious act of the sheriff; nor does it charge him with any misfeasance or non-feasance in his ministerial capacity, in the execution of any process in which the plaintiff was concerned. Consequently, we are of opinion that the declaration sets forth no sufficient cause of action. The judgment of the circuit court is therefore reversed.

GOULD *v.* HAMMOND.

(Circuit Court for California: 1 McAllister, 235–243. 1857.)

STATEMENT OF FACTS.—Action against the defendant, as collector of the port of San Francisco, to recover damages for an alleged illegal sale of goods. Further facts appear in the opinion of the court.

Opinion by McALLISTER, J.

It appears from the testimony that a report having been made by the warehouse keeper that these goods were in a perishing condition, the defendant as collector directed an examination of them to be made, by two United States appraisers; and upon a report made by them that the goods were in a perishing condition and that an immediate sale was necessary, the defendant ordered the goods to be sold. They were sold at public auction, but only on a day's notice, and at prices considerably less than their real value. The defendant justifies the sale on the ground that the goods were in a perishable condition, and such sale was sanctioned by the act of congress of 6th August, 1846. Dunlop, U. S. Laws, 1106. The language of the *proviso* in the first section of the act enacts, "That all goods of a perishable nature, and all gunpowder, firecrackers, and explosive substances deposited as aforesaid, shall be sold forthwith."

It was not contended that any fraud or other corrupt motive is to be imputed to defendant. But it is urged the goods were not in a perishable condition and the notice of the sale was not duly advertised. There is no doubt that the notice of sale was so brief that nothing short of immediate and pressing necessity could have justified it. But unless the briefness of the notice is to be considered *per se*, in the face of the other testimony in the case, sufficient evidence of fraud or a corrupt motive, we cannot consider that fact as concluding this case. If the law left the sale to the discretion and judgment of the collector, misguided views of duty, an error of judgment, free from corrupt motive, cannot render him liable in this action. If a jury had been impaneled in this case, I would have left the evidence of the briefness of the notice of sale to their consideration as a fact on which they should pass; but the court is unwilling, in a case where fraud is not imputed, to infer it from that fact alone. The perishable condition of the goods had been reported to the defendant by the store-keeper; he thereupon referred the matter to two sworn appraisers, and on their report he ordered the sale. It cannot be deemed practicable for a collector to inspect personally each article of every shipment supposed to be perishable. If he consults with merchants of good character, or with sworn United States appraisers, he will be deemed to have taken the usual and ordinary means of arriving at the true condition of the goods and the necessity of a sale, and the degree of promptitude required. Being *pro hac vice* a judicial officer, the defendant is not liable to an action if he falls into an error, in a case where the act done is not merely ministerial, but one in relation to which his duty is to exercise his judgment and discretion, although an individual may suffer by his mistake. Kendall *v.* Stokes, 3 How., 87.

If a discretion was reposed in him by law the defendant is not punishable, unless it be first proved either that he exercised the power confided in cases not within his jurisdiction, or in a manner not confided to him, as with malice, cruelty or wilful oppression. In Otis *v.* Watkins, 9 Cranch, 355, 356, the court say, "This instruction implies that the collector is liable if he form an incorrect opinion, or if in the opinion of the jury it shall have been made unadvisably or without reasonable care or diligence. But the law exposes his conduct to no such scrutiny." If the jury believed he honestly entertained the opinion under which he acted, although they might deem it incorrect, or without sufficient grounds, he would be entitled to their protection.

§ 25. *Where a statute gives a person discretionary powers, to be exercised by him on his own opinion of the facts, the law constitutes him a judge of those facts.* This does not preclude the proof of malice or other circumstances to impeach the integrity of the transaction. In Martin *v.* Mott, 12 Wheat., 31, it is said, "Whenever a statute gives a discretionary power to any person, to be exercised by him upon his own opinion of certain facts, it is a sound rule of construction that the statute constitutes him the sole and exclusive judge of the existence of those facts." Wilkes *v.* Dinsman, 7 How., 89, 132. It is urged that the discretion of the collector may be abused and perverted to oppressive purposes. This argument will apply to every case in which discretion may have been reposed in an individual. It would be impracticable to carry on the government in all its details without confiding in some instances in the judgment and discretion of public officers; and the numerous decided cases which have enunciated the principles which regulate the responsibility of public officers, in whom a discretion has been reposed by law, establish not only those principles, but the numerous instances in which the legislature have been constrained to impose on officers the duty of doing acts involving on their part the exercise of discretion and judgment. The argument that discretion may be abused is to be addressed to the legislature as to the expediency of imparting any. When it is given it is the duty of the court to see that the legal principles are applied to each case in which a controversy as to its exercise may arise. No better settled principle exists than the one enunciated by foregoing authorities. A contrary one, in the language of Chief Justice Taney, would indeed "be pregnant with the greatest mischief." 3 How., 98. In municipal seizures the party who seizes does so at his peril, with the knowledge that their legality is to be tried by tribunals to which the adjudication of them is awarded. If condemnation follow he is justified; if an acquittal, he must refund in damages for the *tort*, unless he can shelter himself under some statute. The seizure is deemed a ministerial act; hence, various statutory provisions have been passed, enabling the party to protect himself in the event the goods seized are not condemned, by procuring from the court a certificate of probable cause of seizure.

These cases of municipal seizure do not apply to this case. This action is not brought for damages, for the commission of a mere ministerial act. The statute on which defendant relies authorized and required him, as collector, to sell *forthwith* all perishable goods and explosive substances. In the performance of that duty he had to form a judgment as to the condition of the goods, and that judgment must be necessarily based upon the facts. Now we have seen that where a statute gives a person discretionary power to be exercised by him upon his opinion of certain facts, it is a sound construction that the statute constitutes him the sole and exclusive judge of the existence of those facts. Martin *v.* Mott, 12 Wheat., 31. In the case at bar the statute required him to sell forthwith perishable articles. To sell any other would have been an abuse of power. To perform the duty imposed upon him he must, *ex necessitate*, pass upon the question of perishability or explosiveness. How otherwise could the fact have been ascertained? The law provides no other way. His duty was not, as in case of a municipal seizure, to hold the goods to await judicial action; but having them in possession they "shall" be sold "forthwith." How can he sell without ascertaining the condition of the goods? What can he invoke for the examination save his own intellect, the discretion and judgment to which the law had left it? If, when he is impelled by no corrupt motive or negligence so gross as to amount to fraud, the facts on which he acted are to be submitted to a jury in every case in which a party may feel aggrieved, then those facts which the law has confided to the discretion and judgment of the collector will be transferred to juries whose verdicts in different cases might embody different results upon similar statements of facts. It would subject the officer to indefinite liability, and seriously embarrass the government in the execution of the laws; for in a case like the present the validity of the sale and the title of the purchaser of the goods would depend on the opinions of the jury as to the facts acted on by the collector.

It has been urged very strongly that the case of Warne v. Varley, 6 D. & E., 443, is conclusive in favor of the plaintiffs in this case. Now that case simply affirms the distinction between a ministerial and a judicial or *quasi*-judicial act. The action was against defendants for an alleged illegal seizure and detention of goods. The defense was that defendants were appointed under an act of parliament which authorized them to view and search all tanned hides and skins that should be brought to Leadenhall market. That plaintiffs had offered for sale in the market hides which had not after the tanning thereof been well and thoroughly dried, *in the judgments of the defendants*, according to the true intent and meaning of the said act of parliament; wherefore defendants had seized and carried them away until it might be duly tried in manner as directed by said statute; and that they had given due notice to the lord mayor, that triers might be appointed for trying the same according to the statute, etc. The plaintiffs replied that the said skins were dried according to the true intent of the statute, that they had been duly tried by persons appointed by the lord mayor, who determined that the said skins were properly dried, and that said leather had been restored to them. Now, in that case the statute, so far from reposing any discretion, any *quasi-judicial* power in the seizors, expressly excluded them from it by reserving the question of fact to be ascertained by others, to be appointed in the mode prescribed by the statute. The searchers were in the position of those who make a municipal seizure. They were only justified in making seizures in cases deemed legitimate by the appropriate tribunal to which the adjudication of them was confided. The law only authorized them to seize undried leather, within the meaning of the statute; and whether the seizure was legal did not depend upon the judgment or discretion, however honest, of the seizors; but on those of others selected by the law, and subject to whose decision the seizure was made. The act of the former was deemed merely ministerial; that of the latter was *quasi*-judicial. The language of Mr. Justice Lawrence renders it evident that the distinction between the two kinds of acts was kept in view. "It is clear (he says) that, in all cases where a protection is given to a judge, it is incumbent on the party justifying the particular act to show he was acting as a judge.

"In this case the defendants were not acting as judges; they had seized the leather in order to carry it before other persons,— the triers, who were to act as judges." 6 D. & E., 450. It is clear, then, that the seizors were not acting in the exercise of a *quasi*-judicial power; because all discretion as to the condition of the goods was expressly vested out of them, and in others, by the very law under which they themselves acted. Had *those* persons found against the leather, and the owner had sued them, nothing short of a corrupt motive could have rendered *them* liable in damages. It does not appear to the court that the foregoing case conflicts with the principles enunciated by preceding decisions.

§ 26. *Under the act of 1842, section 12, perishable or explosive goods are to be sold forthwith, and shortness of notice does not render the collector liable.*

The second ground taken by plaintiffs is, that they are entitled, independently of all other considerations, to a verdict, because the sale of the goods was not made in conformity to law. The twelfth section of the act of 1842, amended by the act of August, 1846 (Dunlop, 1106), which authorized the sale, applies to two distinct classes of goods. The body of the section refers to one class of goods to be sold, viz., such as have been deposited in the public stores, and shall have remained therein one year without the payment of duties and charges. Such it directs to be appraised by the United States appraisers, and if there be none, then by two respectable merchants appointed and sworn by the collector; and after such appraisement they shall be sold at public auction, on due public notice as prescribed by a general regulation of the treasury department; that at said public sale distinct printed catalogues with the appraised value thereof shall be distributed, and a reasonable opportunity afforded to persons to purchase. The foregoing details are made to protect the sale of the first class of goods; and a neglect of any one essential particular would render a collector liable. These details enumerated in the enacting part of the section are not even inferentially alluded to when the act speaks in its *proviso* of the second class of goods, the perishable and explosive articles. This *proviso* declares that all such shall be sold *forthwith.* It has been urged that the details regulating the sale of the first class of goods apply to the second, mentioned in the *proviso.* The office of a *proviso* is generally either to except something from the enacting clause, or to qualify and restrain its generality, or to exclude some possible ground of misinterpretation of it as extending to cases not intended by the legislature to be brought within its purview. Minis *v.* The United States, 15 Pet., 445. When, therefore, the legislature, as in this case, in the *proviso* declares that all goods of a perishable nature shall be sold forthwith, it expressly exempts such from the provisions of the enacting clause. It seems that when congress directed the immediate sale of the second class of goods they intended to commit the regulation of the sale exclusively to the collector, as no precise rules could be prescribed without the hazard of defeating the whole law in regard to perishable goods. It cannot, therefore, be justly considered that the details of sale enumerated in the body of the twelfth section apply to the second class of goods, referred to in the proviso. The rule of law enunciated by the decisions is well settled. The court cannot relax it. It must be uniform, though it may operate harshly in particular cases. The defendant having honestly exercised his discretion, whatever view may be taken of the erroneous or mistaken manner in which he acted, he cannot be made responsible in this case. Let judgment be entered for the defendant.

§ 27. **Who is an officer.**— An office is a public station or employment, conferred by the appointment of government. The term embraces the ideas of tenure, duration, emolument, and duties. A clerk appointed by the assistant treasurer at Boston, with the approbation of the secretary of the treasury, under the general appropriation act of July 23, 1866 (14 Stat. at Large, 200), is a public officer. His employment was in the public service, he was appointed pursuant to law and his compensation was fixed by law, and his duties were continuing and permanent, not occasional or temporary. And as such officer, in charge of the public moneys, he is indictable under the act of August 6, 1846 (9 Stat. at Large, 59). (MILLER, GRIER and FIELD, JJ., dissented.) United States *v.* Hartwell, 6 Wall., 385.

§ 28. A government office is different from a government contract. The latter from its nature is necessarily limited in its duration and specific in its objects. The terms agreed upon define the rights and obligations of both parties, and neither may depart from them without the assent of the other. *Ibid.*

§ 29. The third section of the act of June 14, 1866, is confined to the officers of banks and banking associations. *Ibid.*

§ 30. Where, under a statute of Wisconsin, the governor entered into a contract with a party appointed by the legislature to make a geological, mineralogical and agricultural survey of the state, by which said party stipulated to perform the duties, and on the part of the state it was stipulated that a certain sum per annum should be paid him, and the contract was to continue for five years, it was held that the employment contracted for was not an office, and the party was not a public officer; and that the repeal of the act providing for said survey could not affect the liability of the state for his compensation under his contract. Hall *v.* Wisconsin, 13 Otto, 5.

§ 31. A surgeon appointed by the commissioner of pensions is not an officer of the United States. United States *v.* Germaine, 9 Otto. 508.

§ 32. The act of congress of March 2, 1863 (12 Stat. at Large, p. 696), provides in the first section that any person in the land or naval forces of the United States, etc., who shall steal, embezzle, etc., any money or other property of the United States, "shall be deemed guilty of a criminal offense, and shall be subject to trial and punishment by court-martial in the manner provided for in the act." In the third section of the act it is provided that any person not in the military or naval forces, etc., committing any of the acts prohibited in the first section, shall forfeit and pay to the United States the sum of $2,000, and, in addition, double damages, etc. A paymaster's clerk in the navy is a person in the land or naval forces of the United States under the first section, and is not liable under the third section to the penalty provided for, but only to actual damages in an action by the United States against him. United States *v.* Bogart,* 3 Ben., 257.

§ 33. A person was appointed clerk at the fractional currency counter of the treasury department in Louisville by the direction and with the approbation of the secretary of the treasury. This appointment constitutes him an officer within the meaning of the constitution of the United States and of the statutes in regard to officers charged with the safe-keeping of the public money. United States *v.* Bloomgart, 2 Ben., 356.

§ 34. **Liability generally.**— The executive officers of the United States are personally liable at law for damages in the ordinary forms of action for illegal official or ministerial acts or omissions to the injury of an individual. United States *v.* Kendall, 5 Cr. C. C., 163.

§ 35. Proof that a sheriff or other public officer acted as such is sufficient to charge him as such. Lawrence *v.* Sherman, 2 McL., 488.

§ 36. Officers of a court who have custody of property seized, pending the suit, are responsible for any loss or injury sustained by want of due diligence. Burke *v.* Trevitt, 1 Mason, 96.

§ 37. An officer is liable for malfeasance where he disposes of the property to the injury of the defendant without complying with the requisites of the law. Corning *v.* Burdick, 4 McL., 133.

§ 38. Where a ministerial officer acts in good faith, he is not liable for exemplary damages for an injury done; but he can claim no further exemption where his acts are clearly against the law. Tracy *v.* Swartwout, 10 Pet., 80.

§ 39. If an officer attach and take possession of personal property of a firm, in Massachusetts, on a writ against one partner who has no equitable interest in such property, he is a trespasser. Cropper *v.* Coburn, 2 Curt., 465.

§ 40. An officer having a warrant against a person in his custody may hold him under it, without informing him that he is arrested upon it. United States *v.* Omeara, 1 Cr. C. C., 165.

§ 41. Money in the hands of an officer can only be reached by the interposition of the court. Reno *v.* Wilson, Hemp., 91.

§ 42. A levy on personal property, shown by the officer's return to be of sufficient value to pay the debt, discharges the defendant, and the plaintiff must look to the officer for his money. Campbell *v.* Pope, Hemp., 271.

§ 43. If a delivery bond is not taken, property levied on is at the risk of the officer; it is his own so far that he may bring an action to recover it, and he is responsible for its forthcoming to answer the execution. *Ibid.*

§ 44. The officer whose duty it is to enforce legally the claims of the United States against delinquents may, for the benefit of the government, exercise a reasonable discretion in the management and compromise of suits. United States *v.* Hudson, 3 McL., 156.

§ 45. The officer levying an attachment upon property is the agent of both plaintiff and defendant and may be liable to either. Starr *v.* Moore, 3 McL., 354.

§ 46. Every public officer is required to perform all duties which are strictly official, although they may be required by laws passed after he comes into office, and may be cumulative upon his original duties, and although his compensation therefor be wholly inadequate. Andrews v. United States, 2 Story, 202.

§ 47. Where a statute with regard to process is directory to the court or to the clerk, and not to the sheriff, the latter is bound to obey the writ as he receives it; but as the indorsement of the true species of the action upon the writ is required by the act of assembly of Virginia, that the sheriff may see whether bail is to be demanded or not, he must be judge himself, and act at his peril.   United States v. Mundel,* 6 Call (Va.), 246.

§ 48. Acts after expiration of term.— A sale of land by a marshal on a *venditioni exponas,* after he is removed from office, and a new marshal appointed and qualified, is not void: and such sale being returned to the court and confirmed by it on motion, and a deed ordered to be made to the purchaser at the sale, by the new marshal, such sale being made, is valid. Lessee of Doolittle v. Bryan, 14 How., 565.

§ 49. At common law, if a sheriff seize goods on execution, and go out of office before the sale thereof is completed, he may proceed to sell them.   Kent v. Roberts, 2 Story, 591.

§ 50. It seems that where an attachment is made by a sheriff, who resigns his office before execution issued, he is not the proper officer to levy it.   *Ibid.*

§ 51. Presumptions in favor of acts.— Where a statute confides a discretion to an officer, a party dealing with him in good faith may assume that the discretion is properly exercised, and if the discretion is vested in a superior officer while the transaction is with the subordinate, the contractor may assume that the discretion has been properly exercised, and that the subordinate is acting in accordance with his superior's orders. The contract need not be in writing in case of military exigencies.   In such cases the only duty of the quartermaster is to procure the needed article on the most reasonable terms, and in the most expeditious way. (DRAKE, C. J., dissented.)   Thompson v. United States,* 9 Ct. Cl., 187.

§ 52. An officer will always be presumed to have done his duty.   Corning v. Burdick, 4 McL., 133.

§ 53. Public officers, when acting under the scope of their duties, must be presumed to have fulfilled every requisite which the discharge of their duty demands.   Russell v. Beebe, Hemp., 704.

§ 54. Official duty is presumed to have been regularly performed.   United States v. Humason, 5 Saw., 587.

§ 55. It is to be presumed, *prima facie,* that a sworn officer has discharged his duty faithfully.   Dunlop v. Munroe, 1 Cr. C. C., 536.

§ 56. The presumption is, until the contrary is made to appear, that a public officer has done his duty.   Alvord v. United States, 13 Blatch., 279.

§ 57. Acts of public officers which presuppose the existence of other acts to make them legally operative are presumptive proof of the latter.   An order of sale set forth that a claim had been allowed by the administrator, but was silent as to its approval by the judge.   The judge who made the order of sale was the judge to approve the claim.   The order was held to be presumptive proof of the requisite approval.   Cornett v. Williams, 20 Wall., 226.

§ 58. Officers are presumed to have done their duty.   Cofield v. McClelland, 16 Wall., 331.

§ 59. Upon the presumption that the officers of the government performed their duty, the conclusion of the court of claims that the proceeds of certain cotton, belonging to the claimant, had been paid into the treasury, and that the claimant was entitled to judgment, was affirmed.   (DAVIS, SWAYNE and MILLER, JJ., dissented.)   United States v. Crusell, 14 Wall., 1.

§ 60. If an officer prove that he acted as a public officer, he is presumed to have been duly appointed or elected until the contrary appear.   It is not necessary for him to produce the certificate of his election.   Dayton v. Wyoming National Bank,* 1 Wyom. T'y, 268.

§ 61. The acts of a public officer to whom a public duty is assigned, within the sphere of that duty, are *prima facie* taken to be within his power.   But the force of this presumption must, from the nature of things, vary with the circumstances.   And where, as in this case, a grant purports to have been made by a governor of California under Mexican rule, within a few weeks of the time when the government of the territory passed from his hands, and "during the very heat and conflict of the struggle in which his power was overthrown," where the evidence that the formalities required by law were observed is imperfect and unsatisfactory and rests wholly in parol, where it does not appear that any preliminary inquiries were made as to the point on which he is supposed to have exceeded his authority, and where the situation of the granting officer, and the mode in which he exercised his authority in other cases, at or about the period when the grant purports to have been issued, suggest the suspicion of carelessness, if not recklessness, in the exercise of his powers,—under all these circumstances the presumption loses much of its force, if it be not entirely repelled.   United States v. Cambuston, 7 Saw., 575.

§ **62.** The continental congress having in 1776 and 1777 passed resolves to borrow money on loan-office certificates, and that a loan office be established in and a commissioner appointed by each of the states respectively, it was held that a person would be presumed to have been the loan commissioner who appeared to have come into possession of certificates from the governor of his state, and to have issued them for value, the interest on such certificates, and both principal and interest of others similar, having been paid by the treasurer of the United States, while the transactions were recent, without objection. Ward v. United States,* 19 Law Rep., 621.

§ **63.** The general principle is "that the public acts of public officers, purporting to be exercised in an official capacity and by public authority, shall not be presumed to be usurped; but that a legitimate authority had been previously conferred or subsequently ratified." This principle has been applied to Spanish titles, but the reasons which grew out of the powers of the Spanish monarch, and his vicegerents in the new world, which called for the application of the principle, do not exist in regard to the territorial or departmental governors of California and the relations which subsisted between them and the government of Mexico. Their power to grant even vacant lands was restricted, and could be legally exercised only when in conformity with the provisions of the colonization decree of 1824 and the regulations of 1828. Their power to alienate the cattle and other fruits of labor, belonging to the neophytes of missions, is not matter of presumption. Den v. Hill, McAl., 480.

§ **64.** A person cannot, by mere declarations made subsequently, invalidate his own deed or official act. United States v. Collins, 1 Woods, 499.

§ **65.** Where an officer, without the creditor's consent, makes a valuation of goods without taking an inventory, such valuation is to be considered *prima facie* as fair and just, and the burden of proof is on the officer to establish the contrary; but it does not operate as an estoppel. Pierce v. Strickland, 2 Story, 292.

§ **66.** Where a public officer is charged with conspiracy or fraud in the discharge of his duties, the presumption of law in favor of his innocence will prevail against circumstances of suspicion; but it may be overcome by proof of previous delinquencies of a similar nature. Bottomley v. United States, 1 Story, 135.

§ **67. Loss of money or property.**— Where a loss of money by an assistant paymaster has been clearly shown to be without his fault or neglect, and without the slightest suspicion of fraud or collusion, but the amount of the loss was not positively proven, and could only be by the testimony of the claimant himself, but circumstances concurred in fixing the amount, the officer was held to be entitled to relief, under the disbursing officers' act. Clark v. United States,* 11 Ct. Cl., 698.

§ **68.** Where a paymaster had on hand certain money of the United States, which he made into a package, and delivery to an orderly in his office to take to a designated depository where his official deposits were kept, and the package was either stolen from or by said orderly, it was held that the paymaster was at fault, and negligent in intrusting such a sum of money to an orderly, instead of depositing it himself, or sending it by his clerk, and therefore was not entitled to relief under the act of May 9, 1866 (14 Stat. at L., 44; R. S., §§ 1059, 1062). Holman v. United States,* 11 Ct. Cl., 642.

§ **69.** Where a paymaster in paying certain accounts drew checks, which his clerk raised in amount, and thus embezzled a sum of money, which the paymaster afterwards paid to the United States, because he had been suspended from duty and his pay and allowances stopped, and was liable to be court-martialed and dismissed the service, *held*, that the funds were not in his possession or charge, and he did not lose them by capture or otherwise, and that the act of May 9, 1866 (14 Stat. at L., p. 44), only afforded relief against the loss of specific things, and not against loss by forgeries committed by employees or others, for which he had recourse against the forger and the depositary. *Held*, further, that his application was too late, being made after payment to the government. Hall v. United States,* 9 Ct. Cl., 270.

§ **70.** The claimant was a captain of engineers, and in charge of the work for the improvement of the mouth of the Mississippi, and the money appropriated for that purpose was under his control. Having to pay off the hands, and for that purpose to leave New Orleans early in the morning, he drew his check the night before, had it cashed and placed the money in the safe in his office, of which the chief clerk had the key, and directed the clerk to be in the office the next morning when he had to leave by the boat, so that his assistant could get the money. The clerk was in the office when the claimant assumed control, and had borne for three years a good reputation. The safe being broken open and the clerk gone when the money was called for, and the money being taken, the claimant was allowed a credit for the amount under the act of May 9, 1866 (14 Stat. at L., p. 44). Howell v. United States,* 7 Ct. Cl., 512.

§ **71.** A paymaster of volunteers, during the war, drew $70,000 to pay troops and put it in his trunk in the room, near the bed, in which he slept. During the night the room was entered by burglars and the money taken. The officer promptly reported his loss and subsequently a small portion of the money was recovered. It was held that there was no bad faith or dishonest purpose in the case; that the care and diligence exercised were of a high degree, and such as a careful, cautious and prudent man would have exercised in the discharge of a high public trust, or in a matter of private interest; that therefore the money was lost while the petitioner was in the line of his duty, and without his fault or neglect, and that under the act of May 9, 1866 (14 Stat. at L., p. 44), he was entitled to a credit for the same. Malone v. United States,* 5 Ct. Cl., 486.

§ 72. Where money of the government is lost, without any carelessness, neglect or want of caution on the part of the officer in whose custody it was, he is, under the act of congress, entitled to a credit for such amount lost. Whittelsey v. United States,* 5 Ct. Cl., 452.

§ 73. Where a paymaster in the United States army, without his fault or neglect, was robbed of money of the government in his hands, and the greater part was subsequently recovered, it was held that the act of May 9, 1866 (14 Stat. at L., p. 44), was not confined to losses which had occurred previous to its passage, but was prospective in its operation, and that under it the officer suffering such loss was entitled to a credit for the same, including the reward offered for the capture of the thieves and the recovery of the money. Glenn v. United States,* 4 Ct. Cl., 501.

§ 74. An officer is not allowed credit for money stolen from him, under the act of May 9, 1866 (14 Stat. at L., p. 44), upon his own testimony alone, where there are disinterested parties fully cognizant of the circumstances connected with the loss. Pattee v. United States,* 8 Ct. Cl., 397.

§ 75. Where an officer had failed to pay over public moneys received by him, as required by the acts of congress and treasury regulations, and they were still in his hands when they were seized by the agents of the Confederate States, he is liable to an action on his bond for said money. (The CHIEF JUSTICE and CLIFFORD, J., dissented.) Bevans v. United States, 13 Wall., 56; Halliburton v. United States, 13 Wall., 63. Whether such forcible taking from one entirely free from fault would not work a discharge of such officer though he had given bond, quære. Bevans v. United States, 13 Wall., 56.

§ 76. Where a mandate has issued from the supreme court of the United States to a district court, reversing its judgment, with directions to cause restitution to be made to appellants of what they had been compelled to pay under the decree of the district court, and the marshal had answered to the order of the district court, under the mandate, that he had, pursuant to instructions from the interior department, deposited part of the fund in a bank which had since failed, it was held that if the money had been deposited in the bank, pursuant to instructions from the proper authority, he was exonerated. In that event the proper certificate should be given to the petitioners, and they must be left to seek redress in the appropriate manner. Ex parte Morris, 9 Wall., 605.

§ 77. An officer of the government holding its money or property is not justified in paying to an insurrectionary government, which only demands it by ordinance or draft, but exercises no force or threat of personal violence to himself or property in the enforcement of its illegal orders. United States v. Keehler, 9 Wall., 83.

§ 78. A postmaster at Salem, North Carolina, had in his hands $330 of postoffice money, belonging to the United States, at the breaking out of the rebellion. At the same time the United States was indebted to one Clemmens, a mail contractor in that region, for postal service in a sum exceeding $300. He had been directed to pay money he might have to Clemmens, upon production of proper orders from the postoffice department. After the war broke out he paid the money to Clemmens, upon an order drawn by the postoffice department of the Confederate States, under an act of the Confederate congress. Held, in an action upon his official bond, that this payment constituted no defense to the action. Ibid.

§ 79. A receiver of public moneys was sued on his bond, and in defense to said action offered to prove that he was beset by some person or persons to him unknown, and thrown down, and, against all defense that he could make, was gagged and bound, and the moneys described in the complaint, violently and without his fault taken from him and carried away. It was held that the evidence offered constituted no defense. Boyden v. United States, 13 Wall., 17.

§ 80. An officer in the army, a commissary of subsistence, had in his possession certain money of the United States, which he disbursed, except a small amount. His vouchers were captured by the enemy together with the remainder of said money. The return of the vouchers being prevented by the unintermitting duty of the officer and his clerk, he was held entitled to a credit under the act of March 9, 1866, for the amount of the captured vouchers and money. Murphy v. United States,* 3 Ct. Cl., 212.

§ 81. An officer in the army, in possession of funds of the government, had locked them up in a chest in the same building where other disbursing officers kept the funds of the United States intrusted to their care. The place was captured by a raiding party of rebels and the funds were lost. As the claimant had shown that the loss was without his fault or neglect, he was held entitled to a credit with the proper accounting officers, under the act of May 9, 1866, for the sum so lost. Prime v. United States,* 3 Ct. Cl., 209.

§ 82. Moneys in the hands of a disbursing officer of the United States, deposited with an assistant treasurer of the United States under the act of congress, are none the less moneys of the United States than they were before being deposited. The officer is bound to account for them to his superior officer, but if he shows that he has deposited them with a designated depositary, and not withdrawn them, he does account for them, and such a showing is a complete defense to an action against him by the United States for such moneys. The officer cannot sue the depositary for such money. If he has paid it the second time into the treasury of the United States, that circumstance alone cannot create in favor of plaintiff a right of action which did not exist. Morgan v. Van Dyck,* 11 Int. Rev. Rec., 45.

§ 83. Officers and other persons charged with the safe-keeping, transfer and disbursement of the public moneys are forbidden by law to loan any portion under any circumstances, and every such act is an embezzlement. United States v. Hartwell,* 12 Int. Rev. Rec., 50.

§ 84. The felonious taking and carrying away the public money in the custody of a receiver of public moneys, without any fault or negligence on his part, does not discharge him and his sureties, and cannot be set up as a defense to an action on his official bond. United States v. Prescott, 3 How., 578.

§ 85. Where an appointment to office is irregular — is contrary to law and its policy — this does not absolve the person so appointed from the moral and legal obligation to account for public money which has been placed in his hands in consequence of such appointment. United States v. Maurice, 2 Marsh., 96.

§ 86. Protected by writ.— Where an officer or tribunal possesses jurisdiction over the subject-matter upon which judgment is passed, with power to issue process to enforce the judgment, and the process issued is regular on its face, showing no departure from the law, or defect of jurisdiction over the person or property affected, the process will, in such case, give entire protection to the ministerial officer in its regular enforcement, against any prosecutions by the party aggrieved, although serious errors were committed by the officer or tribunal in reaching the conclusion or judgment on which the process issued. Erskine v. Hohnbach, 14 Wall., 613.

§ 87. When an officer is directed by the process or order of a court to seize certain specific property described in the writ, he has no discretion, but must seize the property described. And if the court issuing the writ had jurisdiction, in the case before it, to issue that process, and it was a valid process when placed in the officer's hands, and in the execution of it he kept himself strictly within the mandatory clause of the process, then such writ or process is a complete protection to him, not only in the court which issued it, but in all other courts. But where the process directs the officer to levy upon the property of one of the parties to the litigation, sufficient to satisfy the demand, the officer must use his judgment and discretion in ascertaining that the property on which he proposes to levy is the property of the person against whom the writ is directed, and by law subject to be taken under the writ, and as to the quantity necessary to be seized, and he is liable to any person injured by his erroneous action, and the court can afford him no protection against the party injured. Buck v. Colbath, 8 Wall., 334.

§ 88. A federal court will protect an officer in executing its process, and discharge him upon *habeas corpus*, not only when he is held in state custody under a law which seeks expressly to punish him for executing a law or process of the United States, but also when he is in such custody under a law of the state, applying to all persons equally, where it appears he is justified for the act done, because "done in pursuance of a law of the United States, or of a process of a court or judge of the same." United States v. Jailer of Fayette County, 2 Abb., 265.

§ 89. If a messenger takes goods of another, under a warrant to take possession of the alleged bankrupt's effects, he is liable to the party injured upon his official bond. He may take the goods of the bankrupt, no matter in whose hands he may find them. *In re* Muller, Deady, 513.

§ 90. An order of a state judge to discharge a debtor from imprisonment, by virtue of an execution from a court of the United States, affords no protection or defense for the sheriff or jailer who discharged him, if the judge in making the orders exceeded his jurisdiction. Thus, where a debtor had been arrested by the marshal under a ca. sa., and afterwards was ordered to be discharged by the judges of a state court upon his application and compliance with the Pennsylvania insolvent law, the sheriff who discharged him was held liable in an action against him for escape. Darst v. Duncan,* 2 Law Rep., 357; 2 Law Rep., 246.

§ 91. An officer who is charged in a state court with malicious shooting cannot be discharged on *habeas corpus*, unless the evidence shows that the shooting was done in order to enable the officer to execute the process in his hands. United States *v.* Weeden, 2 Flip., 76.

§ 92. When it appears that the officer is actually innocent of the crime imputed, and was faithful in all that he really did, he is not obliged, to entitle him to a discharge upon *habeas corpus*, to show that he was justified by his process in doing the very thing imputed to him and for which he is in confinement. *Ibid.*

§ 93. An officer cannot justify under a *fi. fa.* without producing it. United States *v.* Baker, 1 Cr. C. C., 263.

§ 94. It is not necessary that a peace-officer should have a warrant to suppress an affray. United States *v.* Pignell, 1 Cr. C. C., 310.

§ 95. In an action of trespass against the marshal of the District of Columbia for levying a distress for a militia fine, it is only necessary for him, in his justification, to prove those facts which give jurisdiction to the military court; and that it was regularly constituted and imposed the fine. / Slade *v.* Minor, 2 Cr. C. C., 139.

§ 96. If the subject-matter is within the jurisdiction of the magistrate, and the execution regular on its face, the officer executing the same cannot be held liable as a trespasser. Smith *v.* Miles, Hemp., 34.

§ 97. **Must act with care and diligence.**—An officer is bound to use that care and diligence in the discharge of his duties that a conscientious and prudent man, acting under a just sense of his obligation. would exercise under the circumstances of the particular case. United States *v.* Baldridge, 11 Fed. R., 552.

§ 98. Statutory provisions designed to secure order, system and dispatch in proceedings, and by a disregard of which the rights of parties interested cannot be injuriously affected, are not usually regarded as mandatory, unless accompanied by negative words importing that the acts required shall not be done in any other manner or time than that designated. But when the requisitions prescribed are intended for the protection of the citizen, and to prevent a sacrifice of his property, and by a disregard of which his rights might be and generally would be injuriously affected, they are not directory but mandatory. The power of the officer in all such cases is limited by the manner and conditions prescribed for its exercise. French *v.* Edwards, 13 Wall., 506.

§ 99. The general rule of official obligation, as imposed by law, is that the officer shall perform the duties of his office honestly, faithfully and to the best of his ability. This is substantially the rule by which the common law measures the responsibility of those whose official duties require them to have the custody of property, public or private. But the legislature can change the common law rule of responsibility. A bond given by the officer, with an unqualified condition to account for and pay over public moneys, enlarges the implied obligation of the receiving officer, and deprives him of defenses which are available to an ordinary bailee. He is liable in the case of theft or robbery of the funds, but not when they have been destroyed by an overruling necessity, or taken from him by a public enemy, without any fault or neglect on his part. (SWAYNE, MILLER and STRONG, JJ., dissented.) United States *v.* Thomas, 15 Wall., 837.

§ 100. A ministerial officer, in a case in which it is his duty to act, cannot be made a trespasser. The duties of a collector of internal revenue are ministerial, and where an assessment duly certified is handed to him, he is protected in the collection of the taxes, whether the assessor has acted properly or not. Haffin *v.* Mason, 15 Wall., 671.

§ 101. **Measure of damages.**—Where the law requires absolutely a ministerial act to be done by a public officer, and he neglects or refuses to do such act, he may be compelled to respond in damages to the extent of the injury arising from his conduct. A mistake as to his duty and honest intentions will not excuse the offender. Amy *v.* The Supervisors, 11 Wall., 136.

§ 102. Where an action is brought for an injury done in the discharge of an official duty, the damages are measured generally by the extent of that injury. Bispham *v.* Taylor,* 2 McL., 408.

§ 103. Where an officer is sued for any official misfeasance, the plaintiff can recover only his actual loss arising therefrom. Pierce *v.* Strickland, 2 Story, 292.

§ 104. **Arrest.**—Where an officer, lawfully endeavoring to arrest a person, is set upon and violently resisted by him, and is obliged to take the life of the party resisting, he is held justified. United States *v.* Jailer of Fayette County, 2 Abb., 265.

§ 105. In arresting a person, an officer should make his purpose known, unless the circumstances are such as to render it obvious. If the warrant is demanded it should be produced. In the case of a known officer, the explanation must follow the arrest, and the exhibition of the warrant after the authority of the officer has been acknowledged, and his power over his prisoner acquiesced in. If the officer is not known as such he should show his authority or warrant before making the arrest. *Ibid.*

§ 106. A constable, having a warrant to arrest a man for assault and battery, has a right to break open the door of the offender's dwelling-house to arrest him. United States v. Faw, 1 Cr. C. C., 487.

§ 107. Congress, in passing a law suspending the writ of *habeas corpus*, may provide that the officer effecting an arrest without legal warrant shall not be liable in an action. It seems that the suspension of the writ itself practically legalizes arrests made in obedience to the order or authority of the officer to whom that power is committed. McCall v. McDowell, Deady, 233.

§ 108. Under the common law an officer of the law who has legal process in his hands is bound to execute it according to the mandate of the writ. He is authorized to summons as many persons as may be necessary to assist him in the performance of his legal duties. If he is resisted he must overcome such resistance by the use of such force as may be necessary for him to execute his duty. If necessary, the law authorizes him to resort to extreme measures, and if the resisting party is killed in the struggle the homicide is justifiable. A known officer, in making an arrest, is not bound to exhibit his warrant and read it to a defendant before he secures him, if he resists; if no resistance is shown, he should upon demand show his warrant. One who is not a known officer ought to show and read his warrant, if required, but the neglect of this duty does not make the officer a trespasser *ab initio*, if the party subject to arrest had notice of the warrant and was aware of its contents. If a defendant, without a deadly weapon, or manifestation of excessive violence, makes resistance, an officer is not justified in shooting him; but if he has a deadly weapon and manifests a purpose to use it if arrested, the officer is not bound to wait for him to have an opportunity to do so. If the defendant has ceased his resistance and manifests a willingness to submit, and the officer kills him, he is guilty of manslaughter, and if the blood had time to cool, of murder. An officer has no right to shoot a party attempting to escape, if the warrant is for a misdemeanor; otherwise in cases of felony. If the process is illegal and void on its face, or is against the wrong party, or its execution is attempted out of the district, the officer is not protected. United States v. Rice, 1 Hughes, 560.

§ 109. Individuals must take notice of the powers of government officials. Hawkins v. United States, 6 Otto, 689.

§ 110. Taking insufficient security.— Under the statute of Indiana providing for the replevy of an execution. a replevin bond operates as a judgment, and must be with one or more sufficient freehold sureties. Of the sufficiency of the sureties the officer serving the execution must judge, and if he take a bond with insufficient sureties he is liable to the plaintiff in the amount of the difference between the value of the judgment and the value of the security at the time the bond was executed. Bispham v. Taylor.* 2 McL., 409.

§ 111. A levee board authorized to make contracts for work, and to issue bonds to be negotiated at a rate of discount not greater than ten per cent., may make a contract at a specified rate per cubic yard, payable in bonds at ninety cents on the dollar, and might issue the bonds direct to the contractors. Hemingway v. Stansell, 16 Otto, 399.

§ 112. County officers.— Where an act of the legislature of Wisconsin directed a vote of the people of a certain county to be taken as to whether or not they would have a subscription in aid of a railroad, and authorized certain persons, entitled a board of commissioners, to borrow money on the credit of the county and to issue its bonds therefor, such persons are the agents of the people for the special purpose and not county officers in any proper sense. An officer of the county is one by whom the county performs its usual political functions — its functions of government. Sheboygan Co. v. Parker, 3 Wall., 93.

§ 113. Escape.— In an action on the case against an officer for a negligent escape on mesne process, the damages may be less than the whole debt; the question is one for the jury. Duryee v. Webb.* 16 Conn., 552.

§ 114. A sheriff is liable personally for the escape of an insane prisoner as much as any other prisoner. Hazard v. Hazard, 1 Paine, 295.

§ 115. On an action for an escape, the sheriff cannot take advantage of an irregularity in the process which does not render it void. Spafford v. Goodell, 3 McL., 97.

§ 116. An escape on final process subjects the sheriff to damages to the amount of the injury received by the plaintiff. *Ibid.*

§ 117. In Michigan, although imprisonment for debt is abolished, yet where a debtor acts fraudulently, or is about to act, he may be arrested. And after such arrest, the sheriff, if he permits him to escape, is liable to an action for an escape. Mewster v. Spalding, 6 McL., 24.

§ 118. Deputies and assistants.— The legal relation between public officers and their sworn assistants, even when they are acting directly in connection, is generally not that of master and servant, or principal and agent; and the liability of the official superior for defaults of his assistants arises only in case of his own misconduct and neglect. United States v. Collier, 3 Blatch. 325.

§ 119. An objection was made that a warrant, citation and monition was not signed by the clerk of the court. It was attested by the judge, sealed with the seal of the court, and signed by the deputy clerk. *Held* sufficient. In general, a deputy of a ministerial officer can do every act which his principal might do. The Confiscation Cases, 20 Wall., 92.

§ 120. A sheriff is responsible for the acts of his deputy in making a levy and sale under an execution. Clute *v.* Goodell,* 2 McL., 193.

§ 121. Public officers are not responsible for the fraudulent acts of their clerks, if they show that the embezzlement or misconduct was not attributable to their negligence. United States *v.* Broadhead,* 3 Law Rep., 95.

§ 122. A government officer, in this case a quartermaster, who was empowered to appoint subordinates, cannot delegate such power of appointment to another. Burroughs *v.* United States,* 4 Ct. Cl., 558.

§ 123. The deputy of a marshal is a sworn officer, known to the law, and he may return, as deputy, the process served by him. Spafford *v.* Goodell, 3 McL., 97.

§ 124. The service of a summons, by a deputy marshal, the day after the new marshal has filed his bond and taken the oath, the process having before been in the hands of the deputy, is good. But this does not apply to the service of an execution. Stewart *v.* Hamilton, 4 McL., 534.

§ 125. **Purchasing agents.**— It seems that the official care and custody of a purchasing agent of the government is not ended by the delivery of the property purchased to a carrier of his own choosing for transportation, but continues till the property comes into the official custody of some other government agent or official. Tyson *v.* United States,* 4 Ct. Cl., 389.

§ 126. The declarations of a public agent that he has power to act are not evidence of his authority. James *v.* Stookey, 1 Wash., 331.

§ 127. **State officers.**—A suit may be maintained against an officer of the state to restrain him from invading the rights of the complainant secured by the constitution and laws of the United States. Hancock *v.* Walsh, 3 Woods, 351.

§ 128. A federal court cannot compel officers of a state, by injunction, to execute the laws of the state. McCauley *v.* Kellogg, 2 Woods, 13.

§ 129. A court of equity can enjoin officers of a state from acting under a void law. Bancroft *v.* Thayer, 5 Saw., 502.

§ 130. Requirements by United States courts of state officers must be in conformity with state statutes. Such officers cannot be called on to do more than by the law of the state they have the right to do. United States *v.* County Court of Knox County, 1 McC., 608.

§ 131. **Trial of right to office.**— Under section 2010, Revised Statutes, the cases in which the circuit courts of the United States have jurisdiction are limited to those in which it shall appear that the sole question touching the title to office arises out of the denial of the right to vote to citizens who so offered to vote, on account of race, color, or previous condition of servitude, and that the jurisdiction is only given to the extent of determining the rights of the parties to such office, by reason of the denial of the right guarantied by the fifteenth amendment to the constitution of the United States. Johnson *v.* Jumel, 3 Woods, 69.

§ 132. Section 2010, Revised Statutes, gave no jurisdiction to the federal courts to enable a party to regain an office, to which he had a title established by an election, and from which he had been subsequently ejected. *Ibid.*

§ 133. **Captured property.**— No agent of the treasury department was justified in receiving, after the 30th of June, 1865, any captured property, unless theretofore surrendered; much less was he warranted in making any capture of unsurrendered cotton after that date. McLeod *v.* Calicott,* 2 Am. L. T. (U. S.) Rep., 118; 10 Int. Rev. Rec., 94.

§ 134. A special supervising agent of the United States taking property, as captured property, under color of law, or under a mistake as to the character of the property, is not liable for such act in an action for trespass. *Ibid.*

§ 135. **Minors may hold ministerial offices** that call for the exercise of skill and diligence only. They are not eligible to offices which concern the administration of justice. The office of notary public is a ministerial one, and there being nothing in the constitution and statutes of Indiana making infants ineligible to such office, an infant can hold it in Indiana. United States *v.* Bixby, 9 Fed. R., 78.

§ 136. **Where money is in custodia legis,** the officer holding it is the mere hand of the court; his possession is the possession of the court; to interfere with it is to invade the jurisdiction of the court, and an officer so situated is bound by the orders and judgments of the court, and can make no disposition of the money without the consent of his own court, express or implied. *In re* Cunningham,* 9 Cent. L. J., 208.

§ 137. The fourteenth amendment to the constitution of the United States created a disability to hold office, to be removed by a two-thirds vote of each house of congress, and to be made operative in other cases by the legislation of congress in its ordinary course. Thus a judge holding office in the state of Virginia, who was one to whom the prohibition to hold office applied, was not removed by the direct and immediate effect of the prohibition in such amendment, but legislation was necessary to effect such removal, and his sentence of a prisoner tried in his court was lawful. Griffin's Case, Chase's Dec., 364; *In re* Griffin, 2 Am. L. T. (U. S.) Rep., 93.

§ 138. It is not competent for any officer of the government to donate or remit taxes due from the citizen, under the laws passed by congress for the collection of revenue. United States *v.* Roelle, 6 Rep., 559.

§ 139. Discretion.— Where an act declares that certain officers may, if advisable, do a certain thing, whenever the public interest or individual rights call for its exercise, the language used, though permissive in form, is, in fact, peremptory. In all such cases it is held that the intent of the legislature. which is the test, was not to devolve a mere discretion, but to impose a "positive and absolute duty." Supervisors *v.* United States, 4 Wall., 435.

§ 140. Warrant officers are included in the terms "said officers" in the third section of the act of April, 21, 1806 (2 Stat. at L., p. 390). Johnson *v.* United States,* 2 Ct. Cl., 167.

§ 141. How far government bound by acts of.— It is no defense to a surety on a distiller's bond that the breach of the bond occurred with the knowledge and assent of the agents of the government. The government is not responsible for the laches or wrongful acts of its officers, and enters into no contract with such surety that its officers shall perform their duties. Hart *v.* United States, 5 Otto, 316.

§ 142. The agents of the government do not bind the government when their powers are transcended. United States *v.* City Bank, 6 McL., 130.

§ 143. No officer of the United States has authority to enter into a submission in their behalf which shall be binding on them unless the power is given by a special act of congress. United States *v.* Ames, 1 Woodb. & M., 76.

§ 144. Officers of the United States holding public money, as the money of the United States, are accountable only to the United States, and are not liable at the suit of an individual on account of having such money in their hands. Vasse *v.* Comegyss, 2 Cr. C. C., 564.

§ 145. Money in the hands of a sheriff cannot be levied on nor applied to an execution against the plaintiff. Reno *v.* Wilson, Hemp., 91.

§ 146. A public officer who buys a bill of exchange for public use, and agrees to pay for it when it should be duly honored, is not personally responsible. Stone *v.* Mason, 2 Cr. C. C., 431.

§ 147. A public agent of the government, contracting for the use of government, is not personally liable, although the contract be under his seal. Hodgson *v.* Dexter, 1 Cr. C. C., 109.

§ 148. Whenever a contract or engagement made by a public officer is connected with a subject fairly within the scope of his authority, it shall be considered to have been made officially and in his public character, unless the contrary appears by satisfactory evidence of an absolute and unqualified engagement to be personally liable. Parks *v.* Ross, 11 How., 362.

§ 149. An agent of the United States does not bind his principal by his declarations unless clearly acting within his authority and empowered to make them. United States *v.* Martin, 2 Paine, 68.

§ 150. It is too clear to be controverted, that where a public agent acts in the line of his duty, and by legal authority, his contracts made on account of the government are public, and not personal. They inure to the benefit of, and are obligatory on, the government, not the officer. Hodgson *v.* Dexter, 1 Cr., 345.

§ 151. Cotton purchased within the Confederate lines in pursuance of an agreement with an agent of the treasury department, under the act of July 2, 1864, was seized by a naval officer, and detained, the orders of the department regulating such traffic not having been received by him. Upon the receipt of said orders the cotton was delivered to the claimant, shipped to New York, and sold, the market in the meanwhile having greatly declined. *Held*, neither the government nor the officer was liable, the officer having acted in the line of his duty, and the government not being responsible for laches, if any, in transmitting orders. Burnside *v.* United States,* 8 Ct. Cl., 367.

§ 152. Although a private agent, acting in violation of specific instructions, yet within the scope of his general authority, may bind his principal, the rule as to the effect of the like act of a public agent is otherwise. Individuals as well as courts must take notice of the extent of authority conferred by law upon a person acting in an official capacity, and the rule applies in such a case, that ignorance of the law furnishes no excuse. Whiteside *v.* United States, 8 Otto, 247.

§ 153. Torts committed by an officer do not render the government liable on an implied *assumpsit. Ibid.*

§ 154. If an officer, without just cause or lawful authority, takes or destroys the property of a citizen, though he act by color of his office, he is liable in damages to the injured party.

But where, in carrying out his general instructions, he must act on his judgment, and exercise discretion, his conduct is viewed with liberality. And, although there may have been no precedent authority for the particular act, if it is adopted by the government, the government alone is responsible. Wiggins v. United States,* 3 Ct. Cl., 412.

§ 155. There is no express authority given by law to any officer of the government to draw or accept bills of exchange. Whenever, in conducting any of the fiscal affairs of the government, the drawing a bill of exchange is the appropriate means of doing what the department or officer has a right to do, then he can draw and bind the government in doing so. But the obligation resting on him to perform that duty, and his right and authority to effect such an object, is open to inquiry, and if they be found wanting, or if they be forbidden by express statute, then the draft or acceptance is not binding on the government. The Floyd Acceptances, 7 Wall., 666.

§ 156. Principals in the case of private agents are in many cases bound by the acts and declarations of their agents, even when done or made without authority, if it appear that the act was done or declaration was made by the agent in the course of his regular employment; but the government or public authority is not bound in such a case unless it manifestly appears that the agent was acting within the scope of his authority, or that he had been held out as having authority to do the act or make the declaration for or on behalf of the public authorities. Hawkins v. United States, 6 Otto, 689.

§ 157. Where commissioners employed and authorized by the public to sell and make contracts for the sale of lands in the city of Washington had made contracts with certain parties, who had advanced a considerable sum of money, to convey certain of the lots which they had contracted for, to persons named in their orders, and, supposing that such parties had not yet received titles to land equal in value to the sum advanced, had told the plaintiff that if he would obtain an order from said parties for certain lots they should be conveyed to him, but afterwards discovering that lots had been already conveyed to the amount of the whole sum advanced, had given notice to the plaintiff of this fact, offering, however, to convey to him the lots in question on his paying for them at the rate expressed in their contract with said parties advancing said sum of money, in a suit nominally against said commissioners, but in fact against the United States, wherein plaintiff contended that the defendants, in their public character, having misinformed him as to the state of accounts between them and said parties so advancing said sum of money, thereby induced him to relinquish a demand against the latter, and sought to have discounted from a judgment which they had obtained against him for the use of the United States a sum equal to the principal and interest of the debt lost, it was held that the communication made by the commissioners to the plaintiff being altogether gratuitous, and not being within the sphere of their official duties, the United States could not be injured by it. Lee v. Munroe,* 7 Cr., 366.

§ 158. When the object and purpose of an agency is to create an indebtedness on the part of the United States, then such agency can only be authorized by that branch of the government whose function it is to pledge the public credit, and whose duty it will be to provide for this as for all other public indebtedness. The acts of congress having provided for the purchase of military supplies and organized a corps of officers called the purchasing department, and such purchasing department being afterwards abolished and the duties thereof required to be performed by the officers of the quartermaster's department, such officers are the only military purchasing agents contemplated by the statutes, and can alone bind the government by express contracts for such purpose. (CASEY, C. J., dissented.) Reeside v. United States,* 2 Ct. Cl., 1; Burton v. United States,* 2 Ct. Cl., 223.

§ 159. Where congress had authorized the construction of a mint in California, not to exceed in cost a certain sum, the law-making power was here the government, and the executive officers its agents, and no act of theirs could bind the principal for a greater sum than that fixed by the statute. Curtis v. United States,* 3 Ct. Cl., 144.

§ 160. An officer of the United States had no power to make a lease of part of the public land in California, after the treaty of Guadalupe Hidalgo and prior to the admission of California into the Union; and such lease, though approved by the general commanding, and subsequently ratified by the secretary of the interior, is void. Friedman v. Goodwin, 1 McAl., 142.

§ 161. An agreement between the consul-general for the Ottoman government in the city of New York, with a manufacturing company, by which the latter agreed to pay the former commissions for services in effecting the sale of fire-arms to the Turkish government, is an agreement for the sale and purchase of the official influence of an officer of a government, and is against public policy and void. Oscanyan v. Winchester Repeating Arms Co., 15 Blatch., 79.

§ 162. The United States is not liable to a defendant for the wrongful conduct of its agents. United States v. Wickersham, 10 Fed. R., 505.

§ 163. A state is not bound by the acts of its agents, unless it manifestly appears that they are acting within the extent of their authority, and individuals, as well as courts, must take notice of the nature and extent of the authority conferred by law upon a person acting in an official capacity. Bancroft v. Thayer, 5 Saw., 509.

§ 164. Unless money is in the hands of an officer of the government authorized to receive it, it is not in the hands of the government. Carver v. United States.* 16 Ct. Cl., 381.

§ 165. The government cannot set up the wrongful act of its officers to relieve it from its legal liabilities. Bank of Boston v. United States,* 10 Ct. Cl., 544.

§ 166. The government is not responsible for the mistakes of its agents either in matters of law or of fact. McElrath v. United States,* 12 Ct. Cl., 216.

§ 167. Money is recoverable by the government which was paid out by its agents, under the mistake of law that the person to whom it was paid was an officer of the government, and entitled to it. Ibid.

§ 168. Where the agents of the government illegally sell the property of a person, and apply the proceeds to the payment of a fine illegally imposed on him, the owner can recover, and the measure of damages is the money paid over and held by the government. Devlin v. United States,* 12 Ct. Cl.. 272.

§ 169. The acts of an agent of the government not harmful to a distiller give him no right of action against the government. Finch v. United States,* 12 Ct. Cl., 404.

§ 170. A public officer in charge of public property, exposed to the weather, has authority to procure tarpaulins for the protection of such property, if necessary and proper, and the government is liable therefor. Holton v. United States.* 15 Ct. Cl., 290.

§ 171. If a public agent fails in his duty, it gives a party injured no right of action against the government. Hence, when an officer removes a buoy marking a dangerous obstruction in a harbor, and a vessel in the employ of the goverment runs upon it and is lost, the owner has no cause of action against the government. Flushing Ferry Co. v. United States,* 6 Ct. Cl.. 7.

§ 172. A special agent of the government, clothed with no general powers, has no power to bind the government by a contract outside his powers. So where a special treasury agent sold cotton, employing an auctioneer, the government is bound by no warranty of quantity, express or implied. Bennett v. United States,* 5 Ct. Cl., 100.

§ 173. An agent of the government can bind it only while acting strictly within the limits of his authority. Ryan v. United States,* 8 Ct. Cl., 274.

§ 174. An officer empowered to equip men at a cost not above a certain price has discretion as to the price to be paid for each article needed. Garrison v. United States, 7 Wall., 692.

§ 175. The government is not responsible for the acts of a government agent acting outside the scope of his authority. So where a treasury agent sells captured cotton and pays the proceeds to a claimant who is not the owner, and does not pay the same into the treasury, as he should do, the government is not liable to the real owner of the cotton for the proceeds. Spencer v. United States,* 8 Ct. Cl., 293.

§ 176. A mere special agent of the government, with defined powers, cannot bind the government when he exceeds them. So where the subscription agent of the government advertises government obligations for sale, his representation that they are payable in gold does not bind the government. Savage v. United States,* 8 Ct. Cl., 538.

§ 177. A contractor dealing with the government is chargeable with notice of all statutory limitations placed upon the powers of public officers, but there is a difference between those powers expressly defined by statute and those which rest upon the discretion confided by law to an officer. Where a statute expressly defines the power it is notice to all the world; but where it confides a discretion to an officer, the party dealing with him in good faith may assume that the discretion is properly exercised. If the discretion be vested in a superior, while the transaction is with his subordinate, the contractor may assume that the discretion has been properly exercised, and that the subordinate is acting in accordance with his superior's orders. Thompson v. United States,* 9 Ct. Cl., 197.

§ 178. The United States is not liable for the wrongful conduct of its agents in the management of the property of a third person. Wickersham v. United States, 10 Fed. R., 510.

§ 179. A special treasury agent is an agent of strictly limited powers, and every step taken by him beyond such powers is unlawful and does not bind the government. Noble v. United States,* 11 Ct. Cl., 620.

§ 180. Sheriff.—The provision of the statute of California that the sheriff shall sell for delinquent taxes only the smallest quantity of the property which any purchaser will take and pay the judgment and costs is intended for the protection of the tax payer, and it is incumbent upon the officer to afford the opportunity to buyers to take such quantity as will suffice to pay the judgment and costs, and not to offer the whole tract assessed at once to the highest bidder. A recital in the sheriff's deed that he sold the land described to the "highest bidder " and for the largest sum bid for said property is evidence against the grantee and parties claiming under him, and shows that the directions to sell only the smallest quantity were disregarded. (MILLER, J., dissented.) French v. Edwards, 13 Wall., 506.

§ 181. When a sheriff produces a prisoner in court under a writ of *habeas corpus*, his duties as custodian cease, until the order of the court clothing him with new duties and responsibilities. In the meantime the safe-keeping of the prisoner is entirely under the control and direction of the court, and if the prisoner escape from custody during such time, the sheriff is not responsible. Barth v. Clise, 12 Wall., 400.

§ 182. By an act of the legislature of Mississippi provision was made for the police court of any county, through which a certain railroad should be located, to subscribe for stock, if the sense of the people, obtained through an election, was in favor of it, and authority was given to levy a special tax if the vote was for the subscription. The sheriff of the county, who was *ex officio* tax collector, was required, before he entered on the discharge of the duties imposed on him by this legislation, to execute a bond, payable to the president of the board of police, and his successors, conditioned to safely keep and pay over to his order all moneys collected by virtue of the tax thus levied. The county voted the subscription, the tax was levied and collected. The police court failed to make the subscription, and the controversy arising with the railroad company resulted in litigation. This was compromised, and the railroad company agreed to release all claim for liability on account of stock voted for by the county, if the police board would pay over the amount collected by the sheriff. The president of the board accordingly, by draft, directed the sheriff to pay the money, but the sheriff would not pay it, alleging that the stock had been illegally subscribed for. *Held,* that the sheriff's duty was obedience, and that it was no part of his business to sit in judgment on the proceedings of the board of police, nor could he constitute himself an arbiter to settle the differences that had arisen, or might arise, between the county, the tax payers, and the company, growing out of the vote to subscribe stock, and the refusal to make the subscription. And the sheriff's omission to give bond could not affect his liability. Bell v. Railroad Company, 4 Wall., 598.

§ 183. A sheriff executing the process of a court having jurisdiction of the case in which it is issued is protected by the writ, when keeping himself strictly within its mandatory clause. Where a state court has jurisdiction of a cause in all respects until it is terminated by proceedings in bankruptcy, but the fact putting an end to its jurisdiction does not appear by its own record, and consequently is one of which the sheriff cannot, by legal possibility, have official notice, he is bound to obey the order of the court to which he is responsible. Conner v. Long, 14 Otto, 228.

§ 184. Where a sheriff in one state sells goods under the order of a court, while proceedings in bankruptcy, of which he has no notice, are pending against the owner in another state, and before notice received he has paid over the proceeds, he is not liable for them. *Ibid.*

§ 185. A creditor recovered judgments in the state courts against his debtor, who was afterwards thrown into bankruptcy upon the petition of another creditor. While the executions on the above judgments were in the hands of the sheriff the petitioning creditor obtained from the district court an injunction directed to the judgment creditor and the sheriff, restraining them from disposing of the property of said bankrupt until the further order of the court. Subsequently, on the petition of the judgment creditor, this injunction was modified, allowing the sheriff to sell the property levied on, and directing him to pay the proceeds into the district court to await its further orders. *Held,* in a suit by the judgment creditor against the sheriff, for not paying the money to him upon his executions instead of paying it into court, that the sheriff was not liable. The directions of the plaintiff will not only excuse the sheriff from his general duty, but ordinarily he is bound to obey such directions. O'Brien v. Weld, 2 Otto, 81.

§ 186. When a sheriff receives an execution on which costs are due a clerk, and fails to make them when practicable, the sheriff becomes responsible; nor will the order of the plaintiff in execution vary the case as to the costs, whatever may be the effect on the debt. Lewis v. Hamilton,* Hemp., 21.

§ 187. Where an under-sheriff attached certain goods without a schedule, and made return thereof as of the value of $7,000, and obtained a receiptor therefor with the consent of the plaintiff's attorney, and afterward, by leave of the state court, amended his return by reducing the sum to $2,200, the actual value of the goods, it was held that it was within the discretion of the court to allow such an amendment, it being a case of pure mistake. Pierce v. Strickland, 2 Story. 292.

§ 188. If a sheriff fail to use ordinary vigilance to keep goods levied upon safely, and they are lost through his negligence, he is liable. Starr v. Taylor, 3 McL., 542.

§ 189. The sheriff levying an attachment on goods is the agent of both parties, and liable to either. *Ibid.*

§ 190. A sheriff who receives, as jailer, a person arrested by the marshal, is bound to keep the prisoner under all the responsibilities, as if he had been arrested under state process. Spafford *v.* Goodell, 3 McL., 97.

§ 191. Under the act of congress of January 6, 1800, the sheriff of a county is bound to take a bond for the limits, as provided by the state laws, from a prisoner confined on process from the federal courts, and false imprisonment would lie on his refusal. United States *v.* Noah, 1 Paine, 368.

§ 192. After a prisoner has been enlarged upon a limit bond, the sheriff can confine him again only on the bail's becoming insufficient. He cannot accept a surrender of him — certainly after an assignment of the bond. *Ibid.*

§ 193. A sheriff having a writ of foreign attachment, issued according to the laws of New Jersey, proceeded to levy the same on property of the defendant in the attachment. After the attachment was issued, the plaintiff took the promissory notes of the defendant for his debt, payable at a future time, but no notice of this adjustment was given to the sheriff, nor was the suit on which the attachment issued discontinued. The defendant brought replevin for the property attached, the sheriff having refused to redeliver it. *Held*, that the sheriff was not responsible for levying the attachment for the debt so satisfied or for refusing to redeliver the property so attached. Livingston *v.* Smith, 5 Pet., 90.

§ 194. By the laws of Alabama, where property is taken in execution, if the sheriff does not make the money, the plaintiff is allowed to suggest to the court that the money might have been made with due diligence, and thereupon the court is directed to frame an issue in order to try the fact. Chapman *v.* Smith, 16 How., 114.

§ 195. Whether a sheriff, holding a vessel under a writ of attachment from a state court, can rightfully refuse to permit a marshal to take possession of her, to enforce a paramount lien, and whether the marshal can properly proceed to execute his precept by force, in same manner as against unlawful resistance by a private individual, *quære*. The Gazelle, 1 Spr., 378.

§ 196. The sheriff having in his hands a *fi. fa.*, and having received money for the defendant in the same under an execution in which the defendant was plaintiff, levied on the money in his hands and paid the same to the plaintiff in the *fi. fa. Held*, that under the law of Virginia, it was the duty of the sheriff to have the money made under the *fi. fa.* in the court on the return day of the writ, and that he was not justified in paying over the same. Turner *v.* Fendall, 1 Cr., 117.

§ 197. Where a deputy sheriff has sold property under a defective execution, the principal is chargeable, he having sanctioned the transaction. Lawrence *v.* Sherman, 2 McL., 488.

§ 198. Certain creditors began an action in attachment in Indiana, against certain defendants, and the sheriff levied the attachment on a lot of lumber. Afterwards the plaintiffs and defendants in the attachment proceeding agreed that a third party should take possession of the property attached, sell the same, and apply the proceeds to the plaintiff's debt. The sheriff permitted said party to take possession, sell, etc., and subsequently it was agreed between the parties, no other creditor having then become a party to the proceedings, that the suit should be dismissed. But by neglect the same was not done, and the relator in the present suit filed his complaint, affidavit and bond, while the record showed that the suit in attachment was pending. The court found that the property was subject to the lien of the said under-filing creditor's attachment, and ordered it to be sold to pay his debt. The sheriff failing to deliver the property to his successor in office for execution, the relator brought suit against the sheriff and his sureties. The court not being informed of said agreement to dismiss, it was held that the sheriff was liable, but as to the amount of damages, whether they should be nominal, or the *pro rata* share of the property had there been no agreement to dismiss, there was no decision. State of Indiana *v.* Baldwin, 6 Fed. R., 80.

§ 199. Under section 196, Code of Civil Procedure of Wyoming, Laws 1869, a sheriff is liable to the plaintiff in replevin, where the property has been delivered to the plaintiff, in adequate damages for the illegal detention, not vindictive damages for the wrongful taking, where such taking was wrongful. Dayton *v.* Wyoming National Bank,* 1 Wyom. T'y, 263.

§ 200. A sheriff of a state court is under no obligation to serve a writ of *habeas corpus* when he knows that the persons having custody of prisoners named in the writ are deputy marshals, and hold the prisoners under the authority of the United States, and incurs no liability in refusing to do so. His return of the fact that the prisoners were so held is a complete justification for not serving the writ. If the writ were the ordinary writ of *habeas corpus* requiring the deputy marshals to produce the prisoners, etc., it would have been the duty of those officers to take the persons before the judge, if not as a matter of legal obligation, as a courtesy due authorities of another jurisdiction. But where the writ was under the extraordinary Ohio law of 1856, requiring the officer to whom it was directed to take the prisoners, the deputy marshals had the right to resist the attempt to rescue the prisoners from their custody. *Ex parte* Sifford,* 5 Am. L. Reg., 659.

II. Resignation.

SUMMARY — *Town officers under law of Illinois*, §§ 201, 202.—*At common law and under Michigan statute*, § 203.

§ 201. Under the law of Illinois, town officers hold their offices until their successors have qualified; and where they have resigned, and their resignations have been accepted, they are not relieved from the responsibilities of their offices until such qualification. Badger *v.* United States, § 204.

§ 202. Under the laws of Illinois, the supervisor, town clerk and justices of the peace of a town constitute a board of auditors, not less than three being a quorum, to examine and audit town accounts. The relators, having recovered two judgments against a town, presented to the board a sworn statement that the judgments were just and unpaid, and delivered to and filed with the clerk of the town a certified copy of said judgments, but the board neglected and refused to audit them, and the relators applied for a *mandamus*. The answer of the respondents stating that the supervisor, town clerk and two of the justices had resigned and their resignation been accepted, leaving only two of the board in office, upon demurrer it was held that town officers hold their offices until their successors have qualified; and where they have resigned, and their resignations have been accepted, they are not relieved from the responsibilities of their offices until such qualification, and that a peremptory *mandamus* should issue. *Ibid.*

§ 203. At common law public officers cannot escape the responsibilities of their offices until their resignations have been accepted by the proper authority or their successors have been appointed; and in Michigan no contrary rule has been adopted; but the common law rule seems to be confirmed by the statutes of the state, so far as their intent can be gathered from their specific provisions. So where a person had recovered a judgment against a township, and, the proper township officers having refused to take any steps to levy a tax for the payment of said judgment, had filed a petition for a *mandamus*, the return setting up the resignation of said officers, *held*, that their resignations not having been accepted, a peremptory *mandamus* would issue. Edwards *v.* United States, §§ 205-9.

[NOTES.— See §§ 210-219.]

BADGER *v.* UNITED STATES.

(3 Otto, 599-605. 1876.)

ERROR to U. S. Circuit Court, Northern District of Illinois.

STATEMENT OF FACTS.— The relators filed a petition for a *mandamus* to compel the board of auditors to audit and allow two judgments against the town of Amboy. The board consisted of the supervisor, town clerk and justices of the peace, who, it was alleged, refused to audit the judgments, and a part of the board had pretended to resign, etc. Further facts appear in the opinion.

Opinion by MR. JUSTICE HUNT.

No part of the answer, in our judgment, requires consideration except that which raises the point of the legality of the resignation of the parties named. If they had ceased to be officers of the town when the *mandamus* was issued, there may be difficulty in maintaining the order awarding a peremptory *mandamus* against them. If they were then such officers, the case presents no difficulty. The alleged resignations of the supervisors and town clerk were accepted by the justices of the town; but their successors had not been qualified, nor, indeed, had they been chosen when the petition was filed. Does a supervisor, town clerk or justice of the peace of the state of Illinois cease to be an officer when his resignation is tendered to and accepted by a justice of the peace, or does he continue in office until his successor is chosen and qualified?

§ 204. *Under the township organization laws of Illinois, supervisors, town clerks, justices of the peace, etc., hold their offices until their successors are qualified.*

By the common law, as well as by the statutes of the United States and the laws of most of the states, when the term of office to which one is elected or appointed expires, his power to perform its duties ceases. People *v.* Tilman, 8 Abb. Pr., 359; 30 Barb., 193. This is the general rule. The term of office of a district attorney of the United States is fixed by statute at four years. When this four years comes round, his right or power to perform the duties of the office is at an end as completely as if he had never held the office. R. S., sec. 769. A judge of the court of appeals of the state of New York, or a justice of the supreme court, is elected for a term of fourteen years, and takes his seat on the 1st day of January following his election. When the 14th of January thereafter is reached he ceases to be a judicial officer, and can perform no one duty pertaining to the office. Whether a successor has been elected, or whether he has qualified, does not enter into the question. As to certain town officers, the rule is different. 1 R. S. (N. Y.), 340, sec. 30.

The system of the state of Illinois seems to be organized upon a different principle. Thus, the supreme court consists of seven judges, who are required to possess certain qualifications of age and of residence, and who are elected for the term of nine years (Code of Illinois, 1874, pp. 69, 70), at which time it is provided that the "term of office shall expire." Circuit judges in like manner are elected for a term of six years. Id., p. 701. County judges and county clerks, probate judges and state's attorneys, are elected for the term of four years. Id., pp. 71, 72.

As to all of these officers, including judges, it is provided in the constitution of Illinois that "they shall hold their offices until their successors shall be qualified." Id., p. 73, sec. 32. They may thus hold their officers much longer than the term for which they are elected. The provisions as to town officers are of the same character. It is enacted (art. 7, sec. 61, p. 1075) that, at the town meeting in April of each year, there shall be elected in each town one supervisor and one town clerk, who shall hold their offices for one year, and until their successors are elected and qualified, and such justices of the peace as are provided by law.

Of justices of the peace, it is enacted that there shall be elected in each town not less than two nor more than five (depending upon the population of the town), who shall hold their offices "for four years, or until their successors are elected and qualified." P. 637, sec. 1. The qualifying so often spoken of is defined as to town officers by article 9, section 85:

"Qualifying. Every person elected or appointed to the office of supervisor, town clerk, etc., before he enters upon the duties of his office, and within ten days after he shall be notified of his election or appointment, shall take and subscribe, before some justice of the peace or town clerk, the oath or affirmation of office prescribed by the constitution, which shall, within eight days thereafter, be filed in the office of the town clerk."

Thus far it would seem plain that the office of a supervisor or town clerk could not be terminated until his successor subscribed and filed his oath of office, and that when the supervisor and town clerk before us supposed that their offices were at an end by their resignations, they were in error.

There are two other provisions, which, it is supposed, have some bearing upon the point we are considering. Section 97 (p. 1079) provides that whenever a vacancy occurs in a town office by death, resignation, removal from the town or other cause, the justices may make an appointment which shall continue during the unexpired term, and until others are elected or appointed in their places. By section 100 the justices of the town may, for sufficient cause shown to them, accept the resignation of any town officer, and notice thereof shall immediately be given to the town clerk.

A similar provision as to the elective officers of a higher grade is found in the statutes. By chapter 46, section 124 *et seq.* (p. 466), it is provided that resignations of elective offices may be made to the officer authorized to fill the vacancy or to order an election to fill it, and the various events which may cause a vacancy are defined. Governors, judges, clerks of courts, etc., are specifically referred to.

The provision as to these officers and as to the town offices are parts of the same system. The resignations may be made to and accepted by the officers named; but, to become perfect, they depend upon and must be followed by an additional fact, to wit, the appointment of a successor, and his qualification. When it is said in the statute that the resignation may be thus accepted, it is like to the expiration of the term of office. In form the office is thereby ended, but to make it effectual it must be followed by the qualification of a successor.

Section 92 (p. 1078) is also referred to: "Town officers, except as otherwise provided, shall hold their offices for one year, and until others are elected or appointed in their places and are qualified." The term "otherwise provided" has reference to the original term fixed by law, and not to resignations or vacancies. Thus, justices hold for four years, supervisors and constables for one year; and should there be created or found to exist a town officer, and no provision be made as to the duration of his office, this section is intended to meet the case by fixing one year as such term. It has nothing to do with the case before us, further than it reiterates the rule everywhere found in the statutes of Illinois, that such person shall serve not only for one year, but until his successor shall qualify.

People *ex rel.* Williamson v. McHenry, 52 N. Y., 374, was the case of a *quo warranto* to test the title to the office of collector of the town of Flatbush, Kings county, New York. The defendant was elected such collector on the 5th day of April, 1870. On the 4th day of April, 1871, the relator was elected collector of the same town, but did not take or file an oath of office or execute the bond to the supervisors of the town. The board of supervisors recognized the defendant as the legal collector, and delivered to him the warrant for the collection of the taxes of 1871. To settle the dispute, the relator brought the suit referred to. The attempt of the defendant to sustain himself under an act of the legislature, extending the term of office of the collector of Kings county to three years, failed. The court held the act to be unconstitutional as to existing collectors. The defendant, however, succeeded in retaining the office, and had judgment that he was the legal collector; for the reason, that, although the relator was legally elected, he had failed to take the oath of office. The statute of New York as to town officers was in substance the same as that of the state of Illinois. It was as follows: "Town officers shall hold their offices for one year, and until others are chosen or appointed in their places, and have qualified."

In 6 Bissell, 308, is found the opinion of Judge Blodgett in the case we have before us. He holds that a resignation does not relieve a supervisor or town clerk from the responsibilities of his office until a successor is appointed. We think such is the law.

In People *v.* Hopson, 1 Den., 574, and in People *v.* Nostrand, 46 N. Y., 382, it was said that when a person sets up a title to property by virtue of an office, and comes into court to recover it, he must show an unquestionable right. It is not enough that he is an officer *de facto*, that he merely acts in the office; but he must be an officer *de jure*, and have a right to act. So, we think, where a person being in an office seeks to prevent the performance of its duties to a creditor of the town, by a hasty resignation, he must see that he resigns not only *de facto*, but *de jure*; that he resigns his office not only, but that a successor is appointed. An attempt to create a vacancy at a time when such action is fatal to the creditor will not be helped out by the aid of the courts. *Judgment affirmed.*

EDWARDS *v.* UNITED STATES.

(13 Otto, 471–479. 1880.)

ERROR to U. S. Circuit Court, Western District of Michigan.

Opinion by MR. JUSTICE BRADLEY.

STATEMENT OF FACTS.— William F. Thompson, on the 5th day of September, 1874, recovered a judgment in the court below against the township of St. Joseph, in the county of Berrien, Michigan, for the sum of $17,327.86 besides costs.

By the laws of Michigan an execution cannot be issued against a township upon a judgment, but it is to be "levied and collected as other township charges;" and when collected to "be paid by the township treasurer to the person to whom the same shall have been adjudged." Comp. Laws of 1871, sec. 6630. The mode of raising money by taxation in townships is prescribed in sections 992 and 997, which make it the duty of the township clerk, on or before the first day of October of each year, to make and deliver to the supervisor of the township a certified copy of all statements on file, or of record in his office, of moneys proposed to be raised therein by taxation for all purposes; and it is made the duty of the supervisor, on or before the second Monday of said month, to deliver such statements to the clerk of the board of supervisors of the county, to be laid by him before the board at its annual meeting. At this meeting the board is required to direct the several amounts to be raised by any township, which appear by the certified statements to be authorized by law, to be spread upon the assessment roll of the proper township, together with its due proportion of the county and state taxes. The whole is then certified and delivered by the clerk of the board to the town. supervisor, whose duty it is to make the individual assessment to the various tax payers of the township in proportion to the estimate and valuation of their property. The assessment roll is then delivered to the town treasurer for collection.

The judgment in the present case not being paid, and the township officers having refused to take any steps to levy the requisite tax for the purpose, the United States, on the relation of Thompson, on the 11th of October, 1876, filed a petition for a *mandamus* against Edward M. Edwards, supervisor of the township of St. Joseph, in which he set forth the judgment and alleged that, on the 26th of September, 1876, he caused a certified transcript of the judgment to be served on the township clerk, with proper notice and demand; and on the 27th of September, 1876, he caused a similar transcript, notice and demand to be served on Edwards, the supervisor. The petition further alleged that these officers refused to do anything in the premises, the clerk pretending to have resigned his office. An alternative *mandamus* was issued · commanding Edwards, as supervisor of the township, forthwith to deliver to the clerk of the board of supervisors of the county a statement of the claim of relator under and by virtue of the judgment.

Edwards duly filed a return stating that he was not supervisor, and had no authority to perform the acts required of him; that at the general election of April 3, 1876, he was duly elected supervisor, and qualified and entered upon his office, and continued in office until the 7th of June, 1876, when he resigned; that his resignation was in writing as follows:

"To the township board of the township of St. Joseph, county of Berrien, state of Michigan: I hereby tender my resignation of the office of supervisor of this township. St. Joseph, June 7, 1876.

(Signed)   "EDWARD M. EDWARDS."

That this written resignation was delivered to and filed by the township clerk on the same day; that since then he, Edwards, had not been supervisor, nor had he acted as such, or had charge of the records or papers of the office. He further stated in his return that the township clerk had never delivered to him any certified copy of any statement of the moneys to be raised by taxation, either for the purpose of paying the claim of the relator, or for any other purpose. To this return the relator demurred. The demurrer was sustained and a peremptory *mandamus* awarded. Edwards sued out this writ of error.

If we could take notice of the affidavits annexed to the petition for *mandamus*, we should not have much difficulty in drawing the conclusion that the pretended resignations of the clerk and supervisor were either simulated or made for the purpose of evading compulsory performance of their duties. But the return being demurred to must be taken as true, and the affidavits cannot be considered. The only question to decide, therefore, is whether the facts set forth in the return exhibit a good and sufficient answer to the alternative writ; whether, in other words, they show such a completed resignation on the part of Edwards as amounts to a deposition of his office of supervisor of the township. This is the issue made by the parties, and it is an issue of law. The plaintiff in error insists that having done all that he could do to discharge himself from the office, by filing a written resignation with the township clerk, his resignation was complete. The defendant in error insists that a resignation is not complete until it is accepted by the proper authority. The question then is narrowed down to this: Was the resignation complete without an acceptance of it, or something tantamount thereto, such as the appointment of a successor?

§ 205. *At common law it is the rule that one who accepts a municipal office cannot denude himself of it until his resignation is accepted or his successor appointed.*

As civil officers are appointed for the purpose of exercising the functions and carrying on the operations of government, and maintaining public order, a political organization would seem to be imperfect which should allow the depositaries of its power to throw off their responsibilities at their own pleasure. This certainly was not the doctrine of the common law. In England a person elected to a municipal office was obliged to accept it and perform its duties, and he subjected himself to a penalty by refusal. An office was regarded as a burden which the appointee was bound, in the interest of the community and of good government, to bear. And from this it followed of course, that, after an office was conferred and assumed, it could not be laid down without the consent of the appointing power. This was required in order that the public interests might suffer no inconvenience for the want of public servants to execute the laws. See 1 Kyd, Corporations, ch. 3, sec. 4; Willcock, Corporations, pp. 129, 238, 239; Grant, Corporations, pp. 221, 223, 268; 1 Dillon, Mun. Corp., sec. 163; Rex v. Bower, 1 Barn. & Cres., 585; Rex v. Burder, 4 T. R., 778; Rex v. Lone, 2 Stra., 920; Rex v. Jones, id., 1146; Hoke v. Henderson, 4 Dev. (N. C.) L., 1; Van Orsdall v. Hazard, 3 Hill (N. Y.), 243; State v. Ferguson, 31 N. J. L., 107. This acceptance may be manifested either by a formal declaration, or by the appointment of a successor. "To complete a resignation," says Mr. Willcock, "it is necessary that the corporation manifest their acceptance of the offer to resign, which may be done by an entry in the public books, or electing another person to fill the place, treating it as vacant." Willcock, Corporations, 239.

§ 206. —— *in Michigan the common-law rule of the tenure of municipal office is in force.*

In this country, where offices of honor and emolument are commonly more eagerly sought after than shunned, a contrary doctrine with regard to such offices, and, in some states, with regard to offices in general, may have obtained; but we must assume that the common-law rule prevails unless the contrary be shown. In Michigan we do not find that any contrary rule has been adopted; on the contrary, the common-law rule seems to be confirmed by the statutes of the state, so far as their intent can be gathered from their specific provisions. By section 690 of the Compiled Laws of 1871, if any person elected to a township office (except that of justice), of whom an oath is required, and who is not exempt by law, shall not qualify within ten days, he is subjected to a penalty of $10. By sections 691, 693, resignations of officers elected at township meetings must be in writing, addressed to the township board, who is authorized to make temporary appointments to fill vacancies. The township board is composed of the supervisor, the two justices of the peace whose term of office will soonest expire, and the township clerk, any three of whom constitute a quorum. Sec. 706. Resignations of other officers are directed to be made generally to the officer or officers who appointed them, or who may be authorized by law to order a special election to fill the vacancy. Sec. 615. These provisions indicate a general intention in conformity with the principles of the common law. They make the acceptance of a township office a duty, and they direct resignations of office generally to be made to those officers who are empowered either to fill the vacancy themselves, or to call an immediate election for that purpose,—the controlling object being to provide against the public detriment which would ensue from the continued or prolonged vacancy of a public office. The same intention is manifested by section 649, which prescribes the term of office of township officers as follows: "Each of the officers elected at such meetings [that is, the annual meetings of the township], except justices, commissioners of highways and school inspectors, shall hold his office for one year, *and until his successor shall be elected and duly qualified.*" Here is manifested the same desire to prevent a hiatus in the offices. There is nothing in the spirit of this legislation to indicate that the common-law rule is discarded in Michigan.

§ 207. *Statutes of Michigan concerning tenure of office.*

Section 617 of the Compiled Laws declares that "every office shall become vacant on the happening of either of the following events before the expiration of the term of such office: "First, the death of the incumbent; second, his resignation; third, his removal from office," etc. But it is nowhere declared when a resignation shall become complete. This is left to be determined upon general principles. And in view of the manifest spirit and intent of the laws above cited, it seems to us apparent that the common-law requirement — namely, that a resignation must be accepted before it can be regarded as complete — was not intended to be abrogated. To hold it to be abrogated would enable every office-holder to throw off his official character at will, and leave the community unprotected. We do not think that this was the intent of the law.

§ 208. *Cases cited.*

The plaintiff in error has referred us to several authorities to show that in this country the doctrine that a resignation to be complete must be accepted does not prevail. But whilst this seems to be the rule in some states, it is not the case in all. In many states the common-law rule continues to prevail. In Hoke v. Henderson, *supra*, decided in 1832, Mr. Chief Justice Ruffin, speaking for the supreme court of North Carolina, said: "An officer may certainly resign, but without acceptance his resignation is nothing, and he remains in office. It is not true that an office is held at the will of either party. It is held at the will of both. Generally resignations are accepted; and that has been so much a matter of course with respect to lucrative offices as to have grown into a common notion that to resign is a matter of right. But it is otherwise. The public has a right to the services of all the citizens, and may demand them in all civil departments as well as in the military. Hence there are on our statute book several acts to compel men to serve in offices. Every man is obliged, upon a general principle, after entering upon his office, to discharge the duties of it while he continues in office, and he cannot lay it down until the public, or those to whom the authority is confided, are satisfied that the office is in a proper state to be left and the officer discharged." P. 29. Similar views were expressed by Mr. Justice Cowen in 1842 in Van Orsdall v. Hazard, *supra*, and many common-law authorities on the subject were referred to. The supreme court of New Jersey maintained the same doctrine in 1864 in an able opinion delivered by the present learned chief justice, in the case of State v. Ferguson, *supra*. Speaking of the officer in question (an overseer of highways), the chief justice said: "If he possess this power to resign at pleasure, it would seem to follow, as an inevitable consequence, that he cannot be compelled to accept the office. But the books seem to furnish no warrant for this doctrine. To refuse an office in a public corporation connected with local jurisdiction was a common-law offense, and punishable by indictment." After reviewing the authorities cited to the contrary, particularly that in 1 McLean, 509, the chief justice concludes: "I do not think any of the other cases relied upon on the argument sustain in the least degree the doctrine, but on the contrary they all imply that the resignation, to be effectual, must be accepted."

In Gates v. Delaware County, 12 Ia., 405, referred to and much relied on by the plaintiff in error, whilst the court asserts that acceptance is not necessary, it nevertheless finds that there was, in fact, an acceptance in that case. The county judge, to whom the superintendent of schools addressed his resignation, indorsed it "Resignation," and filed it in his office of the date specified; which act, under the circumstances, was considered by the court an acceptance. This case, therefore, cannot be regarded as definitively settling the doctrine even in Iowa.

Much reliance is also placed on the decision of Mr. Justice McLean in the circuit court in United States v. Wright, 1 McLean, 509, where Wright was sued as surety on a collector's bond for delinquency committed by the collector after he had sent his resignation to the president, but before it was accepted. Mr. Justice McLean held that the resignation was complete when received and that the defendant was not liable. In announcing his decision he used this broad language: "There can be no doubt that a civil officer has a right to resign his office at pleasure, and it is not in the power of the executive to compel him to remain in office." Mr. Chief Justice Beasley, of New Jersey, in commenting upon this language in State v. Ferguson, already cited, justly observes: "It is hardly to be supposed that it was the intention of the judge to apply this remark to the class of officers who are elected by the people and whose services are absolutely necessary to carry on local government; or that it was the purpose to brush away with a breath the doctrine of the common law, deeply rooted in public policy, upon the subject. However true the proposition may be as applied to the facts then before the circuit court, it is clearly inconsistent with all previous decisions, if extended over the class of officers where responsibility is the subject of consideration."

But conceding that the law in some of the states is as contended for by the plaintiff in error,—and he cites cases to this purpose decided in Alabama, Indiana, California and Nevada,—and conceding that Mr. Justice McLean's decision may have been correct in the particular case before him, the question is, what is the law of Michigan? and we think it has been shown that the common-law rule is in force in that state.

Now, in the present case, it is true that the defendant in his return avers that he resigned his office on the 7th of June, 1876. But he does not stop here. He goes on to show precisely what he did do. His whole return on this branch of the subject is as follows:

"That, at the general election of April 3, 1876, this respondent was duly elected the supervisor of said township of St. Joseph, and on April 8, 1876, respondent qualified and entered upon his office as such supervisor. That respondent continued in said office of supervisor until the 7th day of June, 1876, when this respondent resigned his office as such supervisor. That such resignation was in writing, of which the following is a true copy:

"'To the township board of the township of St. Joseph, county of Berrien, and state of Michigan: I hereby tender my resignation of the office of supervisor of this township. St. Joseph, June 7, 1876. Edward M. Edwards.'

"That said writing, of which the above is a copy, was signed by this respondent, and, after being so signed, was by respondent delivered to and filed by the township clerk of said township of St. Joseph, and that said writing was so delivered to and filed by said township clerk on the 7th day of June, 1876. That since said 7th day of June, 1876, this respondent has not been the supervisor of said township of St. Joseph. That he has not acted or assumed to act as such supervisor in any particular. That respondent has not, since said June 7, 1876, had charge of any of the records or papers of said office of supervisor."

It does not appear that the resignation was ever acted upon by the township board, or that it was ever presented to or seen by them, or that the board was ever convened after the resignation was filed. According to the common-law rule, the resignation would not be complete, so as to take effect in vacating the office, until it was presented to the township board, and either accepted by them or acted upon by making a new appointment. A new appointment would probably be necessary in this case, because the township board was not the original appointing power. The supervisor is not their officer, representative or appointee. They only represent the township in exercising the power, vested in them, of filling a vacancy when it occurs. This makes them the proper body to receive the resignation, because they are the functionaries whose duty it is to act upon it.

We think, therefore, that the return made to the alternative *mandamus* did not sufficiently show that the defendant had ceased to be supervisor of the township.

§ 209. *A party who has made a return to an alternative mandamus cannot plead a want of notice.*

Other excuses for not obeying the *mandamus* are propounded in the return, as follows:

"Respondent further says that he has never had served upon him in the cause in which said alternative writ issued any process, notice, or paper of any kind, except said alternative writ.

"And respondent further shows that the township clerk of said township of St. Joseph has never made and delivered to respondent any certified copy of any statement on file or of record in his office of the moneys to be raised by taxation, either for the purpose of paying the alleged claim of the relator or for any other purpose, and no statement whatever of the clerk of said township with reference to the amount of money to be raised for township purposes has ever been delivered to respondent."

The plea of non-service of any other notice than the writ is inadmissible. The appearance of the defendant and the actual making of the return are a sufficient answer to it. Non-service may be good ground for a motion to set aside proceedings based on supposed service, but is not a good return to the writ.

The excuse that the clerk did not deliver to the defendant a certified statement is evasive. Why did he not do so? Was there collusion between them as stated in the petition for *mandamus?* The defendant does not state that the clerk refused to deliver him a statement; nor that he, the defendant, applied to the clerk for one. His own act, in repudiating his office, might well have prevented the clerk from delivering a statement to him. It is to be presumed that, on re-assuming his duties, the clerk will recognize his official character and furnish the requisite statement. But if the clerk should refuse, it would still be the defendant's duty as supervisor to see that the claim of the relator, which is a fixed and indisputable liability of the township, and has been duly presented, is placed before the board of supervisors, and put in the way of payment by means of taxation.

We think the return was insufficient and the demurrer was well taken.

Judgment affirmed.

§ 210. **Resignation** by an officer does not oust the jurisdiction of the court to proceed against him by attachment for misconduct while in office; and this rule applies to a deputy marshal. The Bark Laurens, Abb. Adm., 508 (§§ 260-66); 7 N. Y. Leg. Obs., 174.

§ 210a. A resignation of a municipal officer not accepted by the proper authority is invalid. It seems that it is competent on the trial of an application for a *mandamus* to prove that the resignation of a clerk was simulated and fraudulent. Thompson v. United States, 13 Otto, 480.

§ **211.** The appointment, after the cause is at issue, of a successor to an officer who has attempted to resign cannot be given in evidence unless it be pleaded *puis darrein continuance. Ibid.*

§ **212.** In Illinois a town officer remains in office, though he resign, until his successor is elected or appointed and qualified. United States *v.* Badger, 6 Biss., 308.

§ **213.** When an officer has the right of resignation, he is not guilty of contempt if he resigns rather than obey a writ of *mandamus.* But under the Tennessee constitution of 1870 it is provided that "every officer shall hold his office until his successor is elected or appointed and qualified." By virtue of this provision, though an officer resigns and creates a vacancy *sub modo,* which authorizes the election or appointment of a successor, he cannot abandon his office until that successor is qualified; and he is guilty of a contempt if he fails to obey a writ of *mandamus.* United States *v.* Justices of Lauderdale County, 10 Fed. R., 460.

§ **214.** A civil officer has at any time a right to resign his office, and after his resignation has been received at the proper department his surety is not bound for his faithful performance. United States *v.* Wright, 1 McL., 509.

§ **215.** When the resignation of a surveyor of customs took effect, there arose a disability under the twenty-second section of the act of March 2, 1799 (1 Stat., 644), which put an end to the authority of his deputy to act further as such. Resignation of Office,* 14 Op. Att'y Gen'l, 259.

§ **216.** The resignation of an officer while insane is a mere nullity, which is not made valid by acceptance. His re-appointment is not necessary to restore him to his position; the 'acceptance of his resignation, being made upon misapprehension of the facts, may be recalled, as for the mere correction of error, without consulting the senate. Kavanagh's Case,* 10 Op. Att'y Gen'l, 239.

§ **217.** That a public office may be vacated by resignation is established by long and familiar practice, and is recognized by express provision of law. Nor can there be any doubt that a resignation may be effected by the concurrence of the officer and the appointing power; its essential elements are an intent to resign on the one side and an acceptance on the other. It may be either in writing or by parol, expressly or by implication. To perfect a resignation nothing more is necessary than that the proper authority manifest in some way its acceptance of the offer to resign. It then becomes effectual, and operates to relieve the incumbent either immediately or on the day specially fixed according to its terms. An offer to resign is revocable prior to acceptance; after acceptance and before it has taken effect it may be modified, or withdrawn by consent of both parties, but this control extends no further. When a resignation once takes effect the official relations of the incumbent are *ipso facto* dissolved; he has no longer any right to, or hold upon, the office. Resignation of Office,* 14 Op. Att'y Gen'l, 259.

§ **218.** A resignation placed in the hands of a superior officer to be forwarded in a certain event is a valid resignation if forwarded upon the stipulated contingency. That the resignation was without date is not material. Mimmack *v.* United States, 7 Otto, 426.

§ **219.** Where the president has accepted the resignation of an officer of the army, his subsequent revocation of his acceptance does not re-instate the officer. Nothing short of a new nomination by the president and confirmation by the senate can re-instate him. *Ibid.*

III. Appointment and Removal.

Summary — *Appointment complete, when,* § 220. — *Affixing seal a ministerial act,* § 221. — *Appointment revocable, when,* § 222. — *When acts of heads of departments examinable,* § 223. — *Officers in military and naval service,* § 224. — *Where the term of office is fixed by law,* § 225. — *During recess of senate,* § 226. — *Appointments by circuit justices,* § 227.

§ **220.** An appointment to an office, which is the sole act of the president, is completely evidenced, when it is shown that he has done everything to be performed by him. The last act is the signature to the commission. The commission is complete when the seal of the United States has been affixed to it by the secretary of state. Transmission of the commission is not necessary to constitute the appointment. And where the appointee is not an officer removable at the will of the executive, withholding his commission is contrary to law. Marbury *v.* Madison, §§ 228-37.

§ **221.** The affixing of the great seal by the secretary of state to a commission signed by the president is a ministerial act to be performed under the authority of law, and not under the direction of the executive. *Ibid.*

§ **222.** Where an officer is removable at the will of the executive, the circumstance which completes his appointment is of no concern, because the act is at any time revocable; and the commission may be arrested if still in the office. But when the officer is not so removable, the appointment is not revocable and cannot be annulled. *Ibid.*

§ 223. Where the heads of departments are the political or confidential agents of the executive, merely to execute the will of the president, or rather to act in cases in which the executive possesses a constitutional or legal discretion, their acts are only politically examinable. But where a specific duty is assigned by law, and individual rights depend upon the performance of that duty, an individual, who considers himself injured, has a right to resort to the laws of his country for a remedy. *Ibid.*

§ 224. The president of the United States, by and with the advice and consent of the senate, may displace officers in the military or naval service of the United States, by appointment of others in their places. The fifth section of the act of July 13, 1866, ch. 176 (14 Stat., 92), does not withdraw such power. Blake *v.* United States, §§ 238–40.

§ 225. Where the law fixes the term for which an office is to be held there is no power of removal, except as a consequence of impeachment; but where the law does not fix the term of office, it is held at the pleasure of the appointing power. The office of assessor of internal revenue is so held, and the appointment being made by the president of the United States by and with the advice and consent of the senate, while in the absence of legislation and precedent it would be held that the president alone had no power to remove the appointee, by the action of the first congress, and the uniform practice of the government down to this controversy, the president's power of removal has been practically admitted and acted upon, and must be held to exist. Nor does the tenure-of-office act, which was passed after the defendant had been removed from office, but whilst he was in the possession of the office, affect his right to the same; he was without legal right and an intruder. United States *u.* Avery, §§ 241–46.

§ 226. The president is authorized by section 2, article 2, of the constitution of the United States, and by section 1769, United States Revised Statutes, to fill all vacancies which "may happen during the recess of the senate." This phrase is construed to mean "vacancies which may happen to exist during the recess of the senate," without regard to when they first arose. *In re* Farrow, §§ 247–48.

§ 227. Section 793, United States Revised Statutes, provides that "in case of a vacancy in the office of district attorney or marshal within any circuit, the circuit justice of such circuit may fill the same, and the person appointed by him shall serve until an appointment is made by the president, and the appointee is duly qualified, and no longer." Under this section the circuit justice may fill the vacancy, and the appointee holds until the president appoints the same or some other person. The term under the circuit justice then ceases, and the appointee of the president holds from that time on. The statute does not oust the power of the president to appoint under section 2, article 2, of the constitution, and section 1769, United States Revised Statutes. *Ibid.*

[NOTES.— See §§ 249–256.]

MARBURY *v.* MADISON.

(1 Cranch, 137–180. 1803.)

Opinion by MARSHALL, C. J.

STATEMENT OF FACTS.— At the last term, on the affidavits then read and filed with the clerk, a rule was granted in this case, requiring the secretary of state to show cause why a *mandamus* should not issue, directing him to deliver to William Marbury his commission as a justice of the peace for the county of Washington, in the District of Columbia.

No cause has been shown, and the present motion is for a *mandamus.* The peculiar delicacy of this case, the novelty of some of its circumstances, and the real difficulty attending the points which occur in it, require a complete exposition of the principles on which the opinion to be given by the court is founded. These principles have been on the side of the applicant very ably argued at the bar. In rendering the opinion of the court there will be some departure in form, though not in substance, from the points stated in that argument.

In the order in which the court has viewed this subject, the following questions have been considered and decided: 1st. Has the applicant a right to the commission he demands? 2d. If he has a right, and that right has been violated, do the laws of his country afford him a remedy? 3d. If they do afford him a remedy, is it a *mandamus* issuing from this court?

The first object of inquiry is, 1st. Has the applicant a right to the commission he demands? His right originates in an act of congress passed in February, 1801 (2 Stats. at Large, 103), concerning the District of Columbia. After dividing the District into two counties, the eleventh section of this law enacts "that there shall be appointed in and for each of the said counties, such number of discreet persons to be justices of the peace as the president of the United States shall, from time to time, think expedient, to continue in office for five years.

It appears from the affidavits that, in compliance with this law, a commission for William Marbury, as a justice of the peace for the county of Washington, was signed by John Adams, then president of the United States, after which the seal of the United States was affixed to it; but the commission has never reached the person for whom it was made out.

§ 228. *What constitutes an appointment to office, so as to vest the office.*

In order to determine whether he is entitled to this commission, it becomes necessary to inquire whether he has been appointed to the office. For if he has been appointed, the law continues him in office for five years, and he is entitled to the possession of those evidences of office, which being completed became his property. The second section of the second article of the constitution declares that "the president shall nominate, and; by and with the advice and consent of the senate, shall appoint ambassadors, other public ministers and consuls, and all other officers of the United States whose appointments are not otherwise provided for." The third section declares that "he shall commission all the officers of the United States."

An act of congress directs the secretary of state to keep the seal of the United States, "to make out and record" and affix the said seal to all civil commissions to officers of the United States, to be appointed by the president, by and with the consent of the senate, or by the president alone; provided, that the said seal shall not be affixed to any commission before the same shall have been signed by the president of the United States."

These are the clauses of the constitution and laws of the United States which affect this part of the case. They seem to contemplate three distinct operations:

1st. The nomination. This is the sole act of the president, and is completely voluntary.

2d. The appointment. This is also the act of the president, and is also a voluntary act, though it can only be performed by and with the advice and consent of the senate.

§ 229. *Commissioning officers.*

3d. The commission. To grant a commission to a person appointed might, perhaps, be deemed a duty enjoined by the constitution. "He shall," says that instrument, "commission all the officers of the United States."

The acts of appointing to office, and commissioning the person appointed, can scarcely be considered as one and the same; since the power to perform them is given in two separate and distinct sections of the constitution. The distinction between the appointment and the commission will be rendered more apparent by adverting to that provision in the second section of the second article of the constitution which authorizes congress "to vest, by law, the appointment of such inferior officers, as they think proper, in the president alone, in the courts of law, or in the heads of departments;" thus contemplating cases where the law may direct the president to commission an officer appointed by the courts, or by the heads of departments. In such a case, to issue a commission would be apparently a duty distinct from the appointment, the performance of which perhaps could not legally be refused.

Although that clause of the constitution which requires the president to commission all the officers of the United States may never have been applied to officers appointed otherwise than by himself, yet it would be difficult to deny the legislative power to apply it to such cases. Of consequence, the constitutional distinction between the appointment to an office and the commission of an officer who has been appointed remains the same as if in practice the president had commissioned officers appointed by an authority other than his own.

It follows, too, from the existence of this distinction, that if an appointment was to be evidenced by any public act, other than the commission, the performance of such public act would create the officer; and if he was not removable at the will of the president, would either give him a right to his commission, or enable him to perform the duties without it.

These observations are premised solely for the purpose of rendering more intelligible those which apply more directly to the particular case under consideration. This is an appointment made by the president, by and with the advice and consent of the senate, and is evidenced by no act but the commission itself. In such a case, therefore, the commission and the appointment seem inseparable; it being almost impossible to show an appointment otherwise than by proving the existence of a commission; still the commission is not necessarily the appointment, though conclusive evidence of it.

But at what stage does it amount to this conclusive evidence? The answer to this question seems an obvious one. The appointment, being the sole act of the president, must be completely evidenced when it is shown that he has done everything to be performed by him. Should the commission, instead of being evidence of an appointment, even be considered as constituting the appointment itself, still it would be made when the last act to be done by the president was performed, or, at furthest, when the commission was complete.

The last act to be done by the president is the signature of the commission. He has then acted on the advice and consent of the senate to his own nomination. The time for deliberation has then passed. He has decided. His judgment, on the advice and consent of the senate concurring with his nomination, has been made, and the officer is appointed. This appointment is evidenced by an open, unequivocal act; and, being the last act required from the person making it, necessarily excludes the idea of its being, so far as respects the appointment, an inchoate and incomplete transaction.

Some point of time must be taken when the power of the executive over an officer, not removable at his will, must cease. That point of time must be when the constitutional power of appointment has been exercised. And this power has been exercised when the last act, required from the person possessing the power, has been performed. This last act is the signature of the commission. This idea seems to have prevailed with the legislature, when the act passed converting the department of foreign affairs into the department of state. By that act it is enacted that the secretary of state shall keep the seal of the United States, "and shall make out and record, and shall affix the said seal to, all civil commissions to officers of the United States, to be appointed by the president;" "provided, that the said seal shall not be affixed to any commission before the same shall have been signed by the president of the United States; nor to any other instrument or act, without the special warrant of the president therefor."

§ 230. *The affixing of the great seal by the secretary of state to the commissions of public officers is a ministerial act, to be performed under the authority of law, and not under the direction of the executive.*

The signature is a warrant for affixing the great seal to the commission; and the great seal is only to be affixed to an instrument which is complete. It attests, by an act supposed to be of public notoriety, the verity of the presidential signature. It is never to be affixed till the commission is signed, because the signature, which gives force and effect to the commission, is conclusive evidence that the appointment is made. The commission being signed, the subsequent duty of the secretary of state is prescribed by law, and not to be guided by the will of the president. He is to affix the seal of the United States to the commission, and is to record it.

This is not a proceeding which may be varied, if the judgment of the executive shall suggest one more eligible; but is a precise course accurately marked out by law, and is to be strictly pursued. It is the duty of the secretary of state to conform to the law, and in this he is an officer of the United States, bound to obey the laws. He acts, in this respect, as has been very properly stated at the bar, under the authority of law, and not by the instructions of the president. It is a ministerial act which the law enjoins on a particular officer for a particular purpose.

§ 231. *After the commission of a public officer is signed by the president and sealed by the secretary of state the appointment to office is complete. Transmission of the commission is no part of the appointment.*

If it should be supposed that the solemnity of affixing the seal is necessary not only to the validity of the commission, but even to the completion of an appointment, still when the seal is affixed the appointment is made, and the commission is valid. No other solemnity is required by law; no other act is to be performed on the part of government. All that the executive can do to invest the person with his office is done; and unless the appointment be then made, the executive cannot make one with the co-operation of others.

After searching anxiously for the principles on which a contrary opinion may be supported, none have been found which appear of sufficient force to maintain the opposite doctrine. Such as the imagination of the court could suggest have been very deliberately examined, and after allowing them all the weight which it appears possible to give them, they do not shake the opinion which has been formed. In considering this question, it has been conjectured that the commission may have been assimilated to a deed, to the validity of which delivery is essential. This idea is founded on the supposition that the commission is not merely evidence of an appointment, but is itself the actual appointment; a supposition by no means unquestionable. But for the purpose of examining this objection fairly, let it be conceded that the principle claimed for its support is established.

The appointment being, under the constitution, to be made by the president personally, the delivery of the deed of appointment, if necessary to its completion, must be made by the president also. It is not necessary that the delivery should be made personally to the grantee of the office; it never is so made. The law would seem to contemplate that it should be made to the secretary of state, since it directs the secretary to affix the seal to the commission after it shall have been signed by the president. If, then, the act of livery be necessary to give validity to the commission, it has been delivered when executed and given to the secretary for the purpose of being sealed, recorded, and transmitted to the party.

But in all cases of letters-patent, certain solemnities are required by law, which solemnities are the evidences of the validity of the instrument. A formal delivery to the person is not among them. In cases of commissions, the sign-manual of the president, and the seal of the United States, are those solemnities. This objection, therefore, does not touch the case. It has also occurred as possible, and barely possible, that the transmission of the commission, and the acceptance thereof, might be deemed necessary to complete the right of the plaintiff.

The transmission of the commission is a practice directed by convenience, but not by law. It cannot, therefore, be necessary to constitute the appointment which must precede it, and which is the mere act of the president. If the executive required that every person appointed to an office should himself take means to procure his commission, the appointment would not be the less valid on that account. The appointment is the sole act of the president; the transmission of the commission is the sole act of the officer to whom that duty is assigned, and may be accelerated or retarded by circumstances which can have no influence on the appointment. A commission is transmitted to a person already appointed; not to a person to be appointed or not, as the letter inclosing the commission should happen to get into the postoffice and reach him in safety, or to miscarry.

§ 232. *The possession of the original commission is not necessary to a possession of the office.*

It may have some tendency to elucidate this point to inquire whether the possession of the original commission be indispensably necessary to authorize a person, appointed to any office, to perform the duties of that office. If it was necessary, then a loss of the commission would lose the office. Not only negligence, but accident or fraud, fire or theft, might deprive an individual of his office. In such a case, I presume, it could not be doubted but that a copy from the record of the office of the secretary of state would be, to every intent and purpose, equal to the original. The act of congress has expressly made it so. To give that copy validity, it would not be necessary to prove that the original had been transmitted and afterwards lost. The copy would be complete evidence that the original had existed, and that the appointment had been made, but not that the original had been transmitted. If indeed it should appear that the original had been mislaid in the office of state, that circumstance would not affect the operation of the copy. When all the requisites have been performed which authorize a recording officer to record any instrument whatever, and the order for that purpose has been given, the instrument is, in law, considered as recorded, although the manual labor of inserting it in a book kept for that purpose may not have been performed.

In the case of commissions, the law orders the secretary of state to record them. When, therefore, they are signed and sealed the order for their being recorded is given; and whether inserted in the book or not, they are in law recorded. A copy of this record is declared equal to the original, and the fees to be paid by a person requiring a copy are ascertained by law. Can a keeper of a public record erase therefrom a commission which has been recorded?

Or can he refuse a copy thereof to a person demanding it on the terms prescribed by law? Such a copy would, equally with the original, authorize the justice of peace to proceed in the performance of his duty, because it would, equally with the original, attest his appointment.

If the transmission of a commission be not considered as necessary to give validity to an appointment, still less is its acceptance. The appointment is the sole act of the president; the acceptance is the sole act of the officer, and is, in plain common sense, posterior to the appointment. As he may resign, so may he refuse to accept, but neither the one nor the other is capable of rendering the appointment a nonentity. That this is the understanding of the government is apparent from the whole tenor of its conduct.

A commission bears date, and the salary of the officer commences from his appointment, not from the transmission or acceptance of his commission. When a person appointed to any office refuses to accept that office the successor is nominated in the place of the person who has declined to accept, and not in the place of the person who had been previously in office, and had created the original vacancy. It is, therefore, decidedly the opinion of the court, that, when a commission has been signed by the president, the appointment is made; and that the commission is complete when the seal of the United States has been affixed to it by the secretary of state.

§ 233. *The executive of the United States has no right, after the appointment of an officer who is removable at will, to withhold his commission.*

Where an officer is removable at the will of the executive the circumstance which completes his appointment is of no concern, because the act is at any time revocable; and the commission may be arrested, if still in the office. But when the officer is not removable at the will of the executive the appointment is not revocable, and cannot be annulled. It has conferred legal rights which cannot be resumed. The discretion of the executive is to be exercised until the appointment has been made. But having once made the appointment his power over the office is terminated in all cases where by law the officer is not removable by him. The right to the office is then in the person appointed, and he has the absolute, unconditional power of accepting or rejecting it.

Mr. Marbury, then, since his commission was signed by the president and sealed by the secretary of state, was appointed; and as the law creating the office gave the officer a right to hold for five years, independent of the executive, the appointment was not revocable, but vested in the officer legal rights, which are protected by the laws of his country. To withhold his commission, therefore, is an act deemed by the court not warranted by law, but violative of a vested legal right.

§ 234. *Under the law every wrong has its appropriate remedy.*

This brings us to the second inquiry, which is, secondly. If he has a right, and that right has been violated, do the laws of his country afford him a remedy? The very essence of civil liberty certainly consists in the right of every individual to claim the protection of the laws whenever he receives an injury. One of the first duties of government is to afford that protection. In Great Britain the king himself is sued in the respectful form of a petition, and he never fails to comply with the judgment of his court.

In the third volume of his Commentaries, page 23, Blackstone states two cases in which a remedy is afforded by mere operation of law. "In all other cases," he says, "it is a general and indisputable rule, that where there is a legal right there is also a legal remedy by suit, or action at law, whenever that right is invaded." And afterwards, page 109 of the same volume, he says, "I am next to consider such injuries as are cognizable by the courts of the common law. And herein I shall for the present only remark that all possible injuries whatsoever that did not fall within the exclusive cognizance of either the ecclesiastical, military or maritime tribunals, are, for that very reason, within the cognizance of the common law courts of justice; for it is a settled and invariable principle in the laws of England, that every right, when withheld, must have a remedy, and every injury its proper redress."

The government of the United States has been emphatically termed a government of laws and not of men. It will certainly cease to deserve this high appellation if the laws furnish no remedy for the violation of a vested legal right. If this obloquy is to be cast on the jurisprudence of our country it must arise from the peculiar character of the case. It behooves us, then, to inquire whether there be in its composition any ingredient which shall exempt it from legal investigation, or exclude the injured party from legal redress. In pursuing this inquiry the first question which presents itself is whether this can be arranged with that class of cases which come under the description of *damnum absque injuria;* a loss without an injury. This description of cases never has been considered, and it is believed never can be considered, as comprehending offices of trust, of honor or of profit. The office of justice of peace in the District of Columbia is such an office; it is therefore worthy of the attention and guardianship of the laws. It has received that attention and guardianship. It has been created by special act of congress, and has been secured, so far as the laws can give security, to the person appointed to fill it, for five years. It is not, then, on account of the worthlessness of the thing pursued, that the injured party can be alleged to be without remedy.

Is it in the nature of the transaction? Is the act of delivering or withholding a commission to be considered as a mere political act, belonging to the executive department alone, for the performance of which entire confidence is placed by our constitution in the supreme executive, and for any misconduct respecting which the injured individual has no remedy? That there may be such cases is not to be questioned, but that every act of duty, to be performed in any of the great departments of government, constitutes such a case, is not to be admitted.

By the act concerning invalids, passed in June, 1794 (vol. 3, p. 112; 1 Stats. at Large, 392), the secretary of war is ordered to place on the pension list all persons whose names are contained in a report previously made by him to congress. If he should refuse to do so, would the wounded veteran be without remedy? Is it to be contended that where the law in precise terms directs the performance of an act, in which an individual is interested, the law is incapable of securing obedience to its mandate? Is it on account of the character of the person against whom the complaint is made? Is it to be contended that the heads of departments are not amenable to the laws of their country?

Whatever the practice on particular occasions may be, the theory of this principle will certainly never be maintained. No act of the legislature confers so extraordinary a privilege, nor can it derive countenance from the doctrines of the common law. After stating that personal injury from the king to a subject is presumed to be impossible, Blackstone (vol. 3, p. 255) says, "but injuries to the rights of property can scarcely be committed by the crown without the intervention of its officers, for whom the law, in matters of right,

9)

entertains no respect or delicacy, but furnishes various methods of detecting the errors and misconduct of those agents by whom the king has been deceived and induced to do a temporary injustice."

By the act passed in 1796, authorizing the sale of the lands above the mouth of Kentucky river (vol. 3, p. 299; 1 Stats. at Large, 464), the purchaser, on paying his purchase money, becomes completely entitled to the property purchased, and on producing to the secretary of state the receipt of the treasurer upon a certificate required by the law, the president of the United States is authorized to grant him a patent. It is further enacted that all patents shall be countersigned by the secretary of state and recorded in his office. If the secretary of state should choose to withhold this patent, or, the patent being lost, should refuse a copy of it, can it be imagined that the law furnishes to the injured person no remedy?

It is not believed that any person whatever would attempt to maintain such a proposition. It follows, then, that the question, whether the legality of an act of the head of a department be examinable in a court of justice or not, must always depend on the nature of that act. If some acts be examinable and others not, there must be some rule of law to guide the court in the exercise of its jurisdiction. In some instances there may be difficulty in applying the rule to particular cases, but there cannot, it is believed, be much difficulty in laying down the rule.

By the constitution of the United States the president is invested with certain important political powers, in the exercise of which he is to use his own discretion, and is accountable only to his country in his political character, and to his own conscience. To aid him in the performance of these duties he is authorized to appoint certain officers who act by his authority and in conformity with his orders.

In such cases their acts are his acts; and whatever opinion may be entertained of the manner in which executive discretion may be used, still there exists, and can exist, no power to control that discretion. The subjects are political. They respect the nation, not individual rights, and being intrusted to the executive, the decision of the executive is conclusive. The application of this remark will be perceived by adverting to the act of congress for establishing the department of foreign affairs. This officer, as his duties were prescribed by that act, is to conform precisely to the will of the president. He is the mere organ by whom that will is communicated. The acts of such an officer, as an officer, can never be examinable by the courts.

But when the legislature proceeds to impose on that officer other duties; when he is directed peremptorily to perform certain acts; when the rights of individuals are dependent on the performance of those acts, he is so far the officer of the law, is amenable to the laws for his conduct, and cannot at his discretion sport away the vested rights of others. The conclusion from this reasoning is, that where the heads of departments are the political or confidential agents of the executive, merely to execute the will of the president, or rather to act in cases in which the executive possesses a constitutional or legal discretion, nothing can be more perfectly clear than that their acts are only politically examinable. But where a specific duty is assigned by law, and individual rights depend upon the performance of that duty, it seems equally clear that the individual who considers himself injured has a right to resort to the laws of his country for a remedy.

If this be the rule, let us inquire how it applies to the case under the consideration of the court. The power of nominating to the senate, and the power of appointing the person nominated, are political powers to be exercised by the president according to his own discretion. When he has made an appointment, he has exercised his whole power, and his discretion has been completely applied to the case. If by law the officer be removable at the will of the president, then a new appointment may be immediately made, and the rights of the officer are terminated. But as a fact which has existed cannot be made never to have existed, the appointment cannot be annihilated; and, consequently, if the officer is by law not removable at the will of the president, the rights he has acquired are protected by the law, and are not resumable by the president. They cannot be extinguished by executive authority, and he has the privilege of asserting them in like manner as if they had been derived from any other source.

The question whether a right has vested or not is, in its nature, judicial, and must be tried by the judicial authority. If, for example, Mr. Marbury had taken the oaths of a magistrate, and proceeded to act as one, in consequence of which a suit had been instituted against him, in which his defense had depended on his being a magistrate, the validity of his appointment must have been determined by judicial authority. So, if he conceives that, by virtue of his appointment, he has a legal right either to the commission which has been made out for him, or to a copy of that commission, it is equally a question examinable in a court, and the decision of the court upon it must depend on the opinion entertained of his appointment. That question has been discussed, and the opinion is that the latest point of time which can be taken as that at which the appointment was complete, and evidenced, was when, after the signature of the president, the seal of the United States was affixed to the commission.

It is then the opinion of the court, 1st. That by signing the commission of Mr. Marbury the president of the United States appointed him a justice of peace for the county of Washington, in the District of Columbia; and that the seal of the United States, affixed thereto by the secretary of state, is conclusive testimony of the verity of the signature, and of the completion of the appointment; and that the appointment conferred on him a legal right to the office for the space of five years. 2d. That, having this legal title to the office, he has a consequent right to the commission; a refusal to deliver which is a plain violation of that right, for which the laws of his country afford him a remedy.

§ 235. *Nature of the writ of mandamus.*

It remains to be inquired whether, 3d. He is entitled to the remedy for which he applies. This depends on, 1st. The nature of the writ applied for; and, 2d. The power of this court.

1st. The nature of the writ. Blackstone, in the third volume of his Commentaries, page 110, defines a *mandamus* to be "a command issuing in the king's name from the court of king's bench, and directed to any person, corporation, or inferior court of judicature within the king's dominions, requiring them to do some particular thing therein specified, which appertains to their office and duty, and which the court of king's bench has previously determined, or at least supposes, to be consonant to right and justice."

Lord Mansfield, in 3 Burrow, 1266, in the case of The King v. Barker *et al.*, states, with much precision and explicitness, the cases in which this writ may be used. "Whenever," says that very able judge, "there is a right to execute an office, perform a service, or exercise a franchise (more especially if it be in a matter of public concern, or attended with profit), and a person is kept out of possession, or dispossessed of such right, and has no other specific legal remedy, this court ought to assist by *mandamus*, upon reasons of justice, as the writ expresses, and upon reasons of public policy, to preserve peace, order and good government." In the same case he says, "this writ ought to be used upon all occasions where the law has established no specific remedy, and where in justice and good government there ought to be one."

In addition to the authorities now particularly cited, many others were relied on at the bar, which show how far the practice has conformed to the general doctrines that have been just quoted. This writ, if awarded, would be directed to an officer of government, and its mandate to him would be, to use the words of Blackstone, "to do a particular thing therein specified, which appertains to his office and duty, and which the court has previously determined, or at least supposes, to be consonant to right and justice." Or, in the words of Lord Mansfield, the applicant, in this case, has a right to execute an office of public concern, and is kept out of possession of that right.

These circumstances certainly concur in this case. Still, to render the *mandamus* a proper remedy, the officer to whom it is to be directed must be one to whom, on legal principles, such writ may be directed; and the person applying for it must be without any other specific and legal remedy.

1st. With respect to the officer to whom it would be directed. The intimate political relation subsisting between the president of the United States and the heads of departments necessarily renders any legal investigation of the acts of one of those high officers peculiarly irksome, as well as delicate; and excites some hesitation with respect to the propriety of entering into such investigation. Impressions are often received without much reflection or examination, and it is not wonderful that, in such a case as this, the assertion, by an individual, of his legal claims in a court of justice, to which claims it is the duty of that court to attend, should at first view be considered by some as an attempt to intrude into the cabinet, and to intermeddle with the prerogatives of the executive.

It is scarcely necessary for the court to disclaim all pretensions to such a jurisdiction. An extravagance so absurd and excessive could not have been entertained for a moment. The province of the court is, solely, to decide on the rights of individuals, not to inquire how the executive, or executive officers, perform duties in which they have a discretion. Questions in their nature political, or which are, by the constitution and laws, submitted to the executive, can never be made in this court.

But, if this be not such a question; if, so far from being an intrusion into the secrets of the cabinet, it respects a paper which, according to law, is upon record, and to a copy of which the law gives a right, on the payment of ten cents; if it be no intermeddling with a subject over which the executive can be considered as having exercised any control,— what is there in the exalted station of the officer which shall bar a citizen from asserting, in a court of justice, his legal rights, or shall forbid a court to listen to the claim, or to issue a *mandamus*, directing the performance of a duty, not depending on executive discretion, but on particular acts of congress, and the general principles of law?

If one of the heads of departments commits any illegal act, under color of his office, by which an individual sustains an injury, it cannot be pretended that his office alone exempts him from being sued in the ordinary mode of proceeding, and being compelled to obey the judgment of the law. How, then, can his office exempt him from this particular mode of deciding on the legality of his conduct, if the case be such a case as would, were any other individual the party complained of, authorize the process?

It is not by the office of the person to whom the writ is directed, but the nature of the thing to be done, that the propriety or impropriety of issuing a *mandamus* is to be determined. Where the head of a department acts in a case in which executive discretion is to be exercised; in which he is the mere organ of executive will, it is again repeated, that any application to a court to control, in any respect, his conduct would be rejected without hesitation.

But where he is directed by law to do a certain act affecting the absolute rights of individuals, in the performance of which he is not placed under the particular direction of the president, and the performance of which the president cannot lawfully forbid, and therefore is never presumed to have forbidden,— as, for example, to record a commission, or a patent for land, which has received all the legal solemnities; or to give a copy of such record,— in such cases, it is not perceived on what ground the courts of the country are further excused from the duty of giving judgment that right be done to an injured individual, than if the same services were to be performed by a person not the head of a department.

This opinion seems not now, for the first time, to be taken up in this country. It must be well recollected that in 1792 (1 Stats. at Large, 243) an act passed, directing the secretary at war to place on the pension list such disabled officers and soldiers as should be reported to him, by the circuit courts, which act, so far as the duty was imposed on the courts, was deemed unconstitutional; but some of the judges, thinking that the law might be executed by them in the character of commissioners, proceeded to act, and to report in that character.

This law being deemed unconstitutional at the circuits was repealed, and a different system was established; but the question whether those persons who had been reported by the judges, as commissioners, were entitled, in consequence of that report, to be placed on the pension list, was a legal question, properly determinable in the courts, although the act of placing such persons on the list was to be performed by the head of a department.

That this question might be properly settled, congress passed an act in February, 1793 (1 Stats. at Large, 324), making it the duty of the secretary of war, in conjunction with the attorney-general, to take such measures as might be necessary to obtain an adjudication of the supreme court of the United States on the validity of any such rights, claimed under the act aforesaid. After the passage of this act, a *mandamus* was moved for, to be directed to the secretary of war, commanding him to place on the pension list a person stating himself to be on the report of the judges.

There is, therefore, much reason to believe that this mode of trying the legal right of the complainant was deemed by the head of the department, and by the highest law officer of the United States, the most proper which could be selected for the purpose. When the subject was brought before the court, the decision was, not that a *mandamus* would not lie to the head of a department directing him to perform the act, enjoined by law, in the performance of which an individual had a vested interest, but that a *mandamus* ought not to issue in that case; the decision necessarily to be made if the report of the commissioners did not confer on the applicant a legal right. The judgment, in that case, is understood to have decided the merits of all claims of that description; and the persons, on the report of the commissioners, found it necessary to pursue the mode prescribed by the law subsequent to that which had been deemed unconstitutional, in order to place themselves on the pension list. The doctrine, therefore, now advanced, is by no means a novel one. It is true that the *mandamus*, now moved for, is not for the performance of an act expressly enjoined by statute.

It is to deliver a commission, on which subject the acts of congress are silent. This difference is not considered as affecting the case. It has already been stated that the applicant has, to that commission, a vested legal right, of which the executive cannot deprive him. He has been appointed to an office from which he is not removable at the will of the executive, and, being so appointed, he has a right to the commission which the secretary has received from the president for his use. The act of congress does not indeed order the secretary of state to send it to him, but it is placed in his hands for the person entitled to it, and cannot be more lawfully withheld by him than by any other person.

It was at first doubted whether the action of *detinue* was not a specific legal remedy for the commission which has been withheld from Mr. Marbury; in which case a *mandamus* would be improper. But this doubt has yielded to the consideration that the judgment in *detinue* is for the thing itself, or its value. The value of a public office not to be sold is incapable of being ascertained, and the applicant has a right to the office itself, or to nothing. He will obtain the office by obtaining the commission, or a copy of it from the record.

§ 236. *Congress cannot give any original jurisdiction to the supreme court. Its original jurisdiction is derived from the constitution.*

This, then, is a plain case for a *mandamus*, either to deliver the commission or a copy of it from the record, and it only remains to be inquired, whether it can issue from this court. The act to establish the judicial courts of the United States authorizes the supreme court " to issue writs of *mandamus*, in cases warranted by the principles and usages of law, to any courts appointed, or persons holding office, under the authority of the United States."

The secretary of state, being a person holding an office under the authority of the United States, is precisely within the letter of the description, and if this court is not authorized to issue a writ of *mandamus* to such an officer, it must be because the law is unconstitutional, and therefore absolutely incapable of conferring the authority, and assigning the duties which its words purport to confer and assign.

The constitution vests the whole judicial power of the United States in one supreme court, and such inferior courts as congress shall, from time to time, ordain and establish. This power is expressly extended to all cases arising under the laws of the United States, and, consequently, in some form may be exercised over the present case, because the right claimed is given by a law of the United States. In the distribution of this power it is declared that "the supreme court shall have original jurisdiction in all cases affecting ambassadors, other public ministers and consuls, and those in which a state shall be a party. In all other cases the supreme court shall have appellate jurisdiction."

It has been insisted, at the bar, that as the original grant of jurisdiction, to the supreme and inferior courts is general, and the clause assigning original jurisdiction to the supreme court contains no negative or restrictive words, the power remains to the legislature to assign original jurisdiction to that court in other cases than those specified in the article which has been recited; provided those cases belong to the judicial power of the United States.

If it had been intended to leave it in the discretion of the legislature to apportion the judicial power between the supreme and inferior courts according to the will of that body, it would certainly have been useless to have proceeded further than to have defined the judicial power, and the tribunals in which it should be vested. The subsequent part of the section is mere surplusage — is entirely without meaning — if such is to be the construction. If congress remains at liberty to give this court appellate jurisdiction, where the constitution has declared their jurisdiction shall be original, and original jurisdiction where the constitution has declared it shall be appellate, the distribution of jurisdiction made in the constitution is form without substance.

Affirmative words are often, in their operation, negative of other objects than those affirmed; and, in this case, a negative or exclusive sense must be given to them or they have no operation at all. It cannot be presumed that any clause in the constitution is intended to be without effect, and therefore such a construction is inadmissible unless the words require it. If the solicitude of the convention respecting our peace with foreign powers induced a provision that the supreme court should take original jurisdiction in cases which might be supposed to affect them, yet the clause would have proceeded no further than to provide for such cases if no further restriction on the powers of congress had been intended. That they should have appellate jurisdiction in all other cases, with such exceptions as congress might make, is no restriction unless the words be deemed exclusive of original jurisdiction.

When an instrument organizing fundamentally a judicial system divides it into one supreme and so many inferior courts as the legislature may ordain and establish, then enumerates its powers and proceeds so far to distribute them as to define the jurisdiction of the supreme court by declaring the cases in which it shall take original jurisdiction, and that in others it shall take appellate jurisdiction, the plain import of the words seems to be that in one class of cases its jurisdiction is original and not appellate; in the other it is appellate and not original. If any other construction would render the clause inoperative, that is an additional reason for rejecting such other construction and for adhering to their obvious meaning.

§ 237. *The issue of a mandamus is the exercise of original jurisdiction which cannot be conferred by congress.*

To enable this court, then, to issue a *mandamus*, it must be shown to be an exercise of appellate jurisdiction, or to be necessary to enable them to exercise appellate jurisdiction. It has been stated at the bar that the appellate jurisdiction may be exercised in a variety of forms, and that if it be the will of the legislature that a *mandamus* should be used for that purpose, that will must be obeyed. This is true, yet the jurisdiction must be appellate, not original. It is the essential criterion of appellate jurisdiction that it revises and corrects the proceedings in a cause already instituted, and does not create that cause. Although, therefore, a *mandamus* may be directed to courts, yet to issue such a writ to an officer for the delivery of a paper is in effect the same as to sustain an original action for that paper, and therefore seems not to belong to appellate but to original jurisdiction. Neither is it necessary, in such a case as this, to enable the court to exercise its appellate jurisdiction.

The authority, therefore, given to the supreme court by the act establishing the judicial courts of the United States, to issue writs of *mandamus* to public officers, appears not to be warranted by the constitution, and it becomes necessary to inquire whether a jurisdiction so conferred can be exercised. The question whether an act repugnant to the constitution can become the law of the land is a question deeply interesting to the United States, but, happily, not of an intricacy proportioned to its interest. It seems only necessary to recognize certain principles supposed to have been long and well established to decide it.

That the people have an original right to establish, for their future government, such principles as in their opinion shall most conduce to their own happiness, is the basis on which the whole American fabric has been erected. The exercise of this original right is a very great exertion; nor can it, or ought it to be, frequently repeated. The principles, therefore, so established are deemed fundamental; and as the authority from which they proceed is supreme and can seldom act, they are designed to be permanent. This original and supreme will organizes the government and assigns to different departments their respective powers. It may either stop here, or establish certain limits not to be transcended by those departments.

The government of the United States is of the latter description. The powers of the legislature are defined and limited, and, that those limits may not be mistaken or forgotten, the constitution is written. To what purpose are powers limited and to what purpose is that limitation committed to writing, if these limits may at any time be passed by those intended to be restrained? The distinction between a government with limited and unlimited powers is abolished if those limits do not confine the persons on whom they are imposed, and if acts prohibited and acts allowed are of equal obligation. It is a proposition too plain to be contested that the constitution controls any legislative act repugnant to it, or that the legislature may alter the constitution by an ordinary act.

Between these alternatives there is no middle ground. The constitution is either a superior paramount law, unchangeable by ordinary means, or it is on a level with ordinary legislative acts, and, like other acts, is alterable when the legislature shall please to alter it. If the former part of the alternative be true, then a legislative act contrary to the constitution is not law; if the latter part be true, then written constitutions are absurd attempts, on the part of the people, to limit a power in its own nature illimitable. Certainly all those who have framed written constitutions contemplate them as forming the fundamental and paramount law of the nation, and, consequently, the theory of every such government must be, that an act of the legislature, repugnant to the constitution, is void.

This theory is essentially attached to a written constitution, and is consequently to be considered, by this court, as one of the fundamental principles of our society. It is not, therefore, to be lost sight of in the further consideration of this subject. If an act of the legislature, repugnant to the constitution, is void, does it, notwithstanding its invalidity, bind the courts, and oblige them to give it effect? Or, in other words, though it be not law, does it constitute a rule as operative as if it was a law? This would be to overthrow in fact what was established in theory; and would seem, at first view, an absurdity too gross to be insisted on. It shall, however, receive a more attentive consideration.

It is emphatically the province and duty of the judicial department to say what the law is. Those who apply the rule to particular cases must of necessity expound and interpret that rule. If two laws conflict with each other, the courts must decide on the operation of each. So if a law be in opposition to the constitution; if both the law and the constitution apply to a particular case, so that the court must either decide that case conformably to the law, disregarding the constitution, or conformably to the constitution, disregarding the law, the court must determine which of these conflicting rules governs the case. This is of the very essence of judicial duty.

If, then, the courts are to regard the constitution, and the constitution is superior to any ordinary act of the legislature, the constitution, and not such ordinary act, must govern the case to which they both apply. Those, then, who controvert the principle that the constitution is to be considered, in court, as a paramount law, are reduced to the necessity of maintaining that courts must close their eyes on the constitution, and see only the law.

This doctrine would subvert the very foundation of all written constitutions. It would declare that an act which, according to the principles and theory of our government, is entirely void, is yet, in practice, completely obligatory. It would declare that if the legislature shall do what is expressly forbidden, such act, notwithstanding the express prohibition, is in reality effectual. It would be giving to the legislature a practical and real omnipotence, with the same breath which professes to restrict their powers within narrow limits. It is prescribing limits, and declaring that those limits may be passed at pleasure.

That it thus reduces to nothing what we have deemed the greatest improvement on political institutions, a written constitution, would of itself be sufficient, in America, where written constitutions have been viewed with so much reverence, for rejecting the construction. But the peculiar expressions of the constitution of the United States furnish additional arguments in favor of its rejection.

The judicial power of the United States is extended to all cases arising under the constitution. Could it be the intention of those who gave this power, to say that in using it the constitution should not be looked into? That a case arising under the constitution should be decided without examining the instrument under which it arises? This is too extravagant to be maintained. In some cases, then, the constitution must be looked into by the judges. And if they can open it at all, what part of it are they forbidden to read or to obey?

There are many other parts of the constitution which serve to illustrate this subject. It is declared that "no tax or duty shall be laid on articles exported from any state." Suppose a duty on the export of cotton, of tobacco, or of flour; and a suit instituted to recover it. Ought judgment to be rendered in such a case? ought the judges to close their eyes on the constitution, and only see the law?

The constitution declares "that no bill of attainder or *ex post facto* law shall be passed." If, however, such a bill should be passed, and a person should be prosecuted under it, must the court condemn to death those victims whom the constitution endeavors to preserve?

"No person," says the constitution, "shall be convicted of treason unless on the testimony of two witnesses to the same overt act, or on confession in open court." Here the language of the constitution is addressed especially to the courts. It prescribes, directly for them, a rule of evidence not to be departed from. If the legislature should change that rule, and declare one witness, or a confession out of court, sufficient for conviction, must the constitutional principle yield to the legislative act?

From these, and many other selections which might be made, it is apparent that the framers of the constitution contemplated that instrument as a rule for the government of courts as well as of the legislature. Why otherwise does it direct the judges to take an oath to support it? This oath certainly applies in an especial manner to their conduct in their official character. How immoral to impose it on them if they were to be used as the instruments, and the knowing instruments, for violating what they swear to support!

The oath of office, too, imposed by the legislature, is completely demonstrative of the legislative opinion on this subject. It is in these words: "I do solemnly swear that I will administer justice without respect to persons, and do equal right to the poor and to the rich; and that I will faithfully and impartially discharge all the duties incumbent on me as ——, according to the best of my abilities and understanding, agreeably to the constitution and laws of the United States."

Why does a judge swear to discharge his duties agreeably to the constitution of the United States if that constitution forms no rule for his government — if it is closed upon him, and cannot be inspected by him? If such be the real state of things, this is worse than solemn mockery. To prescribe or to take this oath becomes equally a crime.

It is also not entirely unworthy of observation that in declaring what shall be the supreme law of the land the constitution itself is first mentioned; and not the laws of the United States generally, but those only which shall be made in pursuance of the constitution, have that rank. Thus, the particular phraseology of the constitution of the United States confirms and strengthens the principle, supposed to be essential to all written constitutions, that a law repugnant to the constitution is void; and that courts, as well as other departments, are bound by that instrument.

The rule must be discharged.

BLAKE v. UNITED STATES.

(13 Otto, 227-237. 1880.)

APPEAL from the Court of Claims.

STATEMENT OF FACTS.— Blake, being a post-chaplain, addressed a communication to the secretary of war, which was construed as his resignation. It appeared, also, that at the time of the so-called resignation he was insane, in the opinion of his military superiors. His resignation was accepted and his successor was appointed. Blake sought to recall his resignation, and brought this suit to recover the amount of salary due to him upon the theory that he had not resigned. The judgment of the court was against him, and he appealed.

Opinion by MR. JUSTICE HARLAN.

The claim of Blake is placed upon the ground that before, at the date of, and after the letter addressed to the secretary of war, which was treated as his resignation, he was insane in a sense that rendered him irresponsible for his acts, and consequently that his supposed resignation was inoperative and did not have the effect to vacate his office.

§ **238.** *The appointment by the president of the successor of an army officer proprio vigore operates a dismissal of the incumbent.*

Did the appointment of Gilmore, by and with the advice and consent of the senate, to the post-chaplaincy held by Blake, operate, *proprio vigore*, to discharge the latter from the service, and invest the former with the rights and privileges belonging to that office? If this question be answered in the affirmative, it will not be necessary to inquire whether Blake was, at the date of the letter of December 24, 1868, in such condition of mind as to enable him to perform, in a legal sense, the act of resigning his office; or, whether the acceptance of his resignation, followed by the appointment of his successor, by the president, by and with the advice and consent of the senate, is not, in view of the relations of the several departments of the government to each other, conclusive in this collateral proceeding as to the fact of a valid effectual resignation.

From the organization of the government, under the present constitution, to the commencement of the recent war for the suppression of the rebellion, the power of the president, in the absence of statutory regulations, to dismiss from the service an officer of the army or navy was not questioned in any adjudged case or by any department of the government.

Upon the general question of the right to remove from office, as incident to the power to appoint, *Ex parte* Hennen, 13 Pet., 259, is instructive. That case involved the authority of a district judge of the United States to remove a clerk and appoint some one in his place. The court, among other things, said: "All offices, the tenure of which is not fixed by the constitution or limited by law, must be held either during good behavior or (which is the same thing in contemplation of law) during the life of the incumbent, or must be held at the will and discretion of some department of the government, and subject to removal at pleasure.

"It cannot for a moment be admitted that it was the intention of the constitution that those offices which are denominated inferior offices should be held during life. And if removable at pleasure, by whom is such removal to be made? In the absence of all constitutional provision or statutory regulation, it would seem to be a sound and necessary rule to consider the power of removal as incident to the power of appointment. This power of removal from office was a subject much disputed, and upon which a great diversity of opinion was entertained, in the early history of this government. This related, however, to the power of the president to remove officers appointed with the concurrence of the senate; and the great question was whether the removal was to be by the president alone, or with the concurrence of the senate, both constituting the appointing power. No one denied the power of the president and senate jointly to remove, where the tenure of the office was not fixed by the constitution; which was a full recognition of the principle that the power of removal was incident to the power of appointment. But it was very early adopted, as the practical construction of the constitution, that this power was vested in the president alone. And such would appear to have been the legislative construction of the constitution." 1 Kent, Com., 309; 2 Story, Const. (4th ed.), secs. 1537–1540, and notes; 2 Marshall, Life of Washington, 162; Sergeant, Const. Law, 372; Rawle, Const., ch. 14.

§ **239.** *Cases cited.*

During the administration of President Tyler, the question was propounded by the secretary of the navy to Attorney-General Legaré, whether the president could strike an officer from the rolls, without a trial by a court-martial, after a decision in that officer's favor by a court of inquiry ordered for the investigation of his conduct. His response was: "Whatever I might have thought of the power of removal from office, if the subject were *res integra*, it is now too late to dispute the settled construction of 1789: It is according to that construction, from the very nature of executive power, absolute in the president, subject only to his responsibility to the country (his constituents) for a breach of such a vast and solemn trust. 3 Story, Com. Const., 397, sec. 1538. It is obvious that if necessity is a sufficient ground for such a concession in regard to officers in the civil service, the argument applies *a multo fortiori* to the military and naval departments. . . . I have no doubt, therefore, that the president had the constitutional power to do what he did, and that the officer in question is not in the service of the United States." The same views were expressed by subsequent attorneys-general. 4 Opin., 1; 6 id., 4; 8 id., 233; 12 id., 424; 15 id., 421.

In Du Barry's Case, 4 id., 612, Attorney-General Clifford said that the attempt to limit the exercise of the power of removal to the executive officers in the civil service found no support in the language of the constitution nor in any judicial decision; and that there was no foundation in the constitution for any distinction in this regard between civil and military officers.

In Lansing's Case, 6 id., 4, the question arose as to the power of the president, in his discretion, to remove a military storekeeper. Attorney-General Cushing said: "Conceding, however, that military storekeepers are officers, or, at least, quasi officers, of the army, it does not follow that they are not subject to be deprived of their commission at the will of the president.

"I am not aware of any ground of distinction in this respect, so far as regards the strict question of law, between officers of the army and any other officers of the government. As a general rule, with the exception of judicial officers only, they all hold their commissions by the same tenure in this respect. Reasons of a special nature may be deemed to exist why the rule should not be applied to military in the same way as it is to civil officers, but the legal applicability to both classes of officers is, it is conceived, the settled construction of the constitution. It is no answer to this doctrine to say that officers of the army are subject to be deprived of their commissions by the decision of a court-martial. So are civil officers by impeachment. The difference between the two cases is in the form and mode of trial, not in the principle, which leaves unimpaired in both cases alike the whole constitutional power of the president.

"It seems unnecessary in this case to recapitulate in detail the elements of constitutional construction and historical induction by which this doctrine has been established as the public law of the United States. I observe only that, so far as regards the question of abstract power, I know of nothing essential in the grounds of legal conclusion, which have been so thoroughly explored at different times in respect of civil officers, which does not apply to officers of the army."

The same officer, subsequently, when required to consider this question, said that "the power has been exercised in many cases with approbation, express or implied, of the senate, and without challenge by any legislative act of congress. And it is expressly reserved in every commission of the officers, both of the navy and army." 8 Opin., 231.

Such was the established practice in the executive department, and such the recognized power of the president up to the passage of the act of July 17, 1862, chapter 200 (12 Stat., 596), entitled " An act to define the pay and emoluments of certain officers of the army, and for other purposes," the seventeenth section of which provides that " the president of the United States be, and hereby is; authorized and requested to dismiss and discharge from the military service, either in the army, navy, marine corps or volunteer force, any officer for any cause which, in his judgment, either renders such officer unsuitable for, or whose dismission would promote, the public service."

In reference to that act Attorney-General Devens (15 Opin., 421) said, with much reason, that so far as it " gives authority to the president, it is simply declaratory of the long-established law. It is probable that the force of the act is to be found in the word ' requested,' by which it was intended to re-enforce strongly this power in the hands of the president at a great crisis of the state."

The act of March 3, 1865, chapter 79 (13 Stat., 489), provides that, in case any officer of the military or naval service, thereafter dismissed by the authority of the president, shall make application in writing for a trial, setting forth, under oath, that he has been wrongfully and unjustly dismissed, " the president shall, as soon as the necessities of the service may permit, convene a court-martial to try such officer on the charges on which he was dismissed. And if such court-martial shall not award dismissal or death as the punishment of such officer, the order of dismissal shall be void. And if the court-martial aforesaid shall not be convened for the trial of such officer within six months from the presentation of his application for trial, the sentence of dismissal shall be void."

§ 240. *Construction of the statute of July 17, 1866, chapter 177 (14 Stat., 92).*

Thus, so far as legislative enactments are concerned, stood the law in reference to dismissals of army or naval officers, by the president, until the passage of the army appropriation act of July 17, 1866, chapter 176 (14 Stat., 92), the fifth section of which is as follows:

" That section 17 of an act entitled ' An act to define the pay and emoluments of certain officers of the army,' approved July 17, 1862, and a resolution entitled ' A resolution to authorize the president to assign the command of troops in the same field, or department, to officers of the same grade, without regard to seniority,' approved April 4, 1862, be, and the same are, hereby repealed. And no officer in the military or naval service shall, in time of peace, be dismissed from the service, except upon and in pursuance of the sentence of a court-martial to that effect, or in commutation thereof."

Two constructions may be placed upon the last clause of that section without doing violence to the words used. Giving them a literal interpretation, it may be construed to mean that, although the tenure of army and naval officers is not fixed by the constitution, they shall not, in time of peace, be dismissed from the service, under any circumstances, or for any cause, or by any authority whatever, except in pursuance of the sentence of a court-martial to that effect, or in commutation thereof. Or, in view of the connection in which the clause appears,— following, as it does, one in the same section repealing provisions touching the dismissal of officers by the president, alone, and to assignments, by him, of the command of troops, without regard to seniority of officers,— it may be held to mean that, whereas, under the act of July 17,

1862, as well as before its passage, the president, alone, was authorized to dismiss an army or naval officer from the service for any cause which, in his judgment, either rendered such officer unsuitable for, or whose dismissal would promote, the public service, he alone shall not, thereafter, in time of peace, exercise such power of dismissal, except in pursuance of a court-martial sentence to that effect, or in commutation thereof. Although this question is not free from difficulty, we are of opinion that the latter is the true construction of the act. That section originated in the senate as an amendment of the army appropriation bill which had previously passed the house of representatives. Cong. Globe, 39th Congress, pp. 3254, 3405, 3575 and 3589. It is supposed to have been suggested by the serious differences existing, or which were apprehended, between the legislative and executive branches of the government in reference to the enforcement, in the states lately in rebellion, of the reconstruction acts of congress. Most, if not all, of the senior officers of the army enjoyed, as we may know from the public history of that period, the confidence of the political organization then controlling the legislative branch of the government. It was believed that, within the limits of the authority conferred by statute, they would carry out the policy of congress, as indicated in the reconstruction acts, and suppress all attempts to treat them as unconstitutional and void, or to overthrow them by force. Hence, by way of preparation for the conflict then apprehended between the executive and legislative departments as to the enforcement of those acts, congress, by the fifth section of the act of July 13, 1866, repealed not only the seventeenth section of the act of July 17, 1862, but also the resolution of April 4, 1862, which authorized the president, whenever military operations required the presence of two or more officers of the same grade, in the same field or department, to assign the command without regard to seniority of rank. In furtherance, as we suppose, of the objects of that legislation, was the second section of the army appropriation act of March 2, 1867, chapter 170 (14 Stat., 486), establishing the headquarters of the general of the army at Washington, requiring all orders and instructions relating to military operations issued by the president or secretary of war to be issued through that officer, and, in case of his inability, through the next in rank, and declaring that the general of the army "shall not be removed, suspended, or relieved from command, or assigned to duty elsewhere than at said headquarters, except at his own request, without the previous approval of the senate, and any orders or instructions relating to military operations issued contrary to the requirements of this section shall be null and void; and any officer who shall issue orders or instructions contrary to the provisions of this section shall be deemed guilty of a misdemeanor in office," etc.

Our conclusion is that there was no purpose, by the fifth section of the act of July 13, 1866, to withdraw from the president the power, with the advice and consent of the senate, to supersede an officer in the military or naval service by the appointment of some one in his place. If the power of the president and senate, in this regard, could be constitutionally subjected to restrictions by statute (as to which we express no opinion), it is sufficient for the present case to say that congress did not intend by that section to impose them. It is, in substance and effect, nothing more than a declaration that the power theretofore exercised by the president, without the concurrence of the senate, of summarily dismissing or discharging officers of the army or the navy whenever in his judgment the interest of the service required it to be done, shall not exist, or be exercised, *in time of peace*, except in pursuance of the sentence of a court-martial, or in commutation thereof. There was, as we think, no intention to deny or restrict the power of the president, by and with the advice and consent of the senate, to displace them by the appointment of others in their places.

It results that the appointment of Gilmore, with the advice and consent of the senate, to the office held by Blake, operated in law to supersede the latter, who thereby, in virtue of the new appointment, ceased to be an officer in the army from and after, at least, the date at which that appointment took effect,—and this without reference to Blake's mental capacity to understand what was a resignation. He was, consequently, not entitled to pay as post-chaplain after July 2, 1870, from which date his successor took rank. Having ceased to be an officer in the army, he could not again become a post-chaplain, except upon a new appointment, by and with the advice and consent of the senate. Mimmack *v.* United States, 97 U. S., 426.

As to that portion of the claim covering the period between April 28, 1869, and July 2, 1870, it is only necessary to say that, even were it conceded that the appellant did not cease to be an officer in the army by reason of the acceptance of his resignation, tendered when he was mentally incapable of understanding the nature and effect of such an act, he cannot recover in this action. His claim for salary during the above period accrued more than six years, and the disability of insanity ceased more than three years before the commencement of this action. The government pleads the statute of limitations, and it must be sustained. Congress alone can give him the relief which he seeks.

Judgment affirmed.

UNITED STATES *v.* AVERY.

(Circuit Court for California: Deady, 204-215. 1867.)

STATEMENT OF FACTS.—Information in the nature of a *quo warranto*, to oust the defendant from the office of assessor of internal revenue. The relator was appointed during the recess of the senate, and, after qualifying, demanded the books and papers belonging to the office.

Opinion by DEADY, J.

The constitution provides that the president "shall nominate, and, by and with the advice and consent of the senate, shall appoint ambassadors, other public ministers, and consuls, judge of the supreme court, and all other officers of the United States whose appointments are not. herein otherwise provided for, and which shall be established by law. But the congress may by law vest the appointment of such inferior officers, as they think proper, in the president alone, in the courts of law, or in the heads of departments."

Section 2 of the internal revenue act of July 1, 1862 (12 Stat., 433), creates the office in controversy and provides for the appointment of the incumbent. The material words of the section are these: "That the president of the United States be, and he is hereby, authorized . . . to nominate, and by and with the advice and consent of the senate to appoint, an assessor . . . for each such district, who shall be resident within the same." Upon these provisions of the constitution and statute, and the.facts found in this case, arises the question, did the commission to Bigler, in conjunction with his subsequent qualification and demand upon the defendant, operate, in contemplation of law, to remove the defendant from the office of assessor of the fourth district?

§ 241. *By the act creating the office of assessor of internal revenue, the incumbent holds during the pleasure of the appointing power; this is true of all cases where the law does not fix the term of office.*

By the terms of the act under which the defendant was appointed, there is no limitation upon the tenure of the office, and the constitution is silent upon the subject, except as to judicial offices. The defendant not having any fixed term in the office must be considered as holding it at the pleasure of the appointing power. I admit that, to my mind, this conclusion is not a necessary one; for, from the premises, it appears equally logical to conclude that the defendant is entitled to hold the office during good behavior. But this question is not now open to argument in this court. In *Ex parte* Hennen, 13 Pet., 258–9, it was expressly decided by the supreme court that when the law does not fix the term of office, it is held at the pleasure of the appointing power. In that case a clerk of a district court had been removed by the judge of the court, and there could be no question but that the removal was made by the appointing power. In this case the appointing power is the president and senate, acting concurrently, and the alleged removal is the act of the president alone. Had the president this power as the law was at the time of the commission to Bigler? No case in which the question has been directly decided has been cited in the argument, and I am not aware that any exists. The case of Hennen, *supra*, states the historic fact that, at an early day in the existence of the national government, it was "much disputed" whether the power of removal was in the president and senate or in the president alone, and that, by both practical and legislative construction, it was assumed and acted upon that the power was in the president alone. But the court did not actually decide that this construction of the constitution was warranted by its language, and the question was not really before them for adjudication; yet it cannot be denied that in some measure the court gave its sanction to this doctrine. They speak of "its having become the settled and well understood construction of the constitution that the power of removal was vested in the president alone in such cases, although the appointment of the officer was by the president and senate."

In the case of The United States *v.* Guthrie, 17 How., 284, the power of the president to remove an officer, appointed with the advice and consent of the senate, was called in question but not decided. The act of congress creating the office of judge in the territory of Minnesota had provided that the incumbent thereof should hold for four years. The president removed the relator before the expiration of his term, and *mandamus* was brought against the defendant — the secretary of the treasury — to compel him to pay the relator his salary. A majority of the court, avoiding the decision of the main question — the power of removal — decided that the remedy was not well taken, and dismissed the application for the writ. Mr. Justice McLean delivered a dissenting opinion, in which he discusses the president's power of removal at great length. As to the particular case then before the court, he maintained that the removal was not only unauthorized, but contrary to law. He says: "If congress have the power to create the territorial courts, of which no one doubts, it has the power to fix the tenure of office. This being done, the president has no power to remove a territorial judge, more than he has to repeal a law."

§ 242. *Congress, having the power to create an office, may prescribe the term for which it may be holden; and in such case there is no power of removal except by impeachment.*

This conclusion appears to me both just and legal. Congress, having the power to create an office, may prescribe the term for which it shall be holden, or whether it shall be holden at pleasure. In the former case there is no power of removal anywhere, except as a consequence of impeachment. If the president alone, or the president and senate in conjunction, were allowed to make removals in such cases, it would be equivalent to allowing him or them "to repeal a law."

But in that case there was a fixed term of office, while in the case of the defendant Avery no term is provided for, but the incumbent holds at the pleasure of the appointing power. Upon the real question in this case, had the president the power to remove the defendant without the consent of the senate? Justice McLean argues for the negative, but seems to think that the power had been "too long established and exercised to be now questioned." Referring to the controversy in congress upon the subject, upon the passage of the act creating the department of foreign affairs, in 1789, he says: " There was great contrariety of opinion in congress on this power. With the experience we now have in regard to its exercise, there is great doubt whether the most enlightened statesman would not come to a different conclusion. The attorney-general calls this a constitutional power. There is no such power given in the constitution. It is presumed to be in the president from the power of appointment. This presumption, I think, is unwise and illogical. The reasoning is, the president and senate appoint to office; therefore, the president may remove from office. Now the argument would be legitimate if the power to remove were inferred to be the same that appoints. . . . If the power to remove from office be inferred from the power to appoint, both the elements of the appointing power are necessarily included. The constitution has declared what shall be the executive power ,to appoint, and by consequence the same power should be exercised in a removal. But this power of removal has been, *perhaps*, too long established and exercised to be now questioned. The voluntary action of the senate and the president would be necessary to change the practice; and as this would require the relinquishment of a power by one of the parties to be exercised in conjunction with the other, it can hardly be expected."

So far as adjudged cases are concerned, this is all that can be found bearing upon the subject. Among the elementary writers the question is discussed by Kent and Story. The former (1 Kent's Com., 309–10), after stating the opinion of the Federalist, pending the ratification of the constitution, that "the consent of the senate would be necessary to displace as well as to appoint," and referring to the different construction given to the constitution by the first congress, says: " This amounted to a legislative construction of the constitution, and it has ever since been acquiesced in and acted upon as of decisive authority in the case. . . . This question has never been made the subject of judicial discussion, and the construction given to the constitution in 1789 has continued to rest on this loose, incidental declaratory opinion of congress, and the sense and practice of the government since that time. It is, however, a striking fact in the constitutional history of our government, that a power so transcendant as that is, which places at the disposal of the president alone the tenure of every executive office appointed by the president and senate, should depend upon inference merely, and should have been gratuitously declared by the first congress in opposition to the high authority of the Federalist, and should have been supported or acquiesced in by some of those distinguished men who questioned or denied the power of congress even to incorporate a national bank."

Story (2 Com., § 1538) says: "The power to nominate does not naturally or necessarily include the power to remove; and if the power to appoint does include it, then the latter belongs conjointly to the executive and the senate. In short, under such circumstances, the removal takes place in virtue of the new appointment by mere operation of law. It results, and is not separable, from the appointment itself." After stating the arguments on both sides of the question, and referring to the legislative construction in favor of the executive power, by the congress in 1789, the distinguished commentator concludes (§ 1543): "That the final decision of this question so made was greatly influenced by the exalted character of the president then in office was asserted at the time, and has always been believed. Yet the doctrine was opposed as well as supported by the highest talents and patriotism of the country. The public, however, acquiesced in this decision, and it constitutes, perhaps, the most extraordinary case in the history of a government, of a power conferred by implication on the executive by the assent of a bare majority of congress, which has not been questioned on many other occasions." And again (§ 1544), "whether the prediction of the original advocates of the executive power, or those of the opposers of it, are likely, in the future progress of the government, to be realized, must be left to the sober judgment of the community, and to the impartial award of time. If there has been any aberration from the true constitutional exposition of the power of removal (which the reader must decide for himself), it will be difficult, and perhaps impracticable, after forty years' experience, to recall the practice to the correct theory. But, at all events, it will be a consolation to those who love the Union, and honor a devotion to the patriotic discharge of duty, that in regard to inferior offices (which appellation probably includes ninety-nine out of a hundred of the lucrative offices of the government), the remedy for any permanent abuse is still within the power of congress by the simple expedient of requiring the consent of the senate to removals in such cases."

§ 243. *Where the appointing power is in the president and senate concurrently, the president alone has no power to remove, in the absence of legislation and precedent.*

The constitution does not expressly provide for removal from office, otherwise than as the legal effect or consequence of "impeachment for, and conviction of, treason, bribery or other high crimes and misdemeanors." Art. 11, § 4. If the power of direct removal from office is to be attributed to any department of the government, as a necessary to some express power, my minds inclines to the conclusion that, upon the language of the constitution, such power can only be attributed to the appointing power. The appointing power in this case is the president and senate, acting concurrently. In the absence of legislation and precedent, I think it should be held that the president alone had no power to remove the defendant, and that, consequently, the commission of Bigler was a void act — there being then no vacancy in the office in question, and the president having no power to create such a vacancy.

§ 244. —— *but it is held that the president's power of removal is practically admitted by the uniform practice of the government.*

But by the action of the first congress, and the uniform practice of the government down to the time when this controversy arose, the president's power of removal had been practically admitted and acted upon. The subject is one which, in my judgment, properly belongs to congress to regulate, rather than the courts. It is a legislative or political question, and not a judicial one. Heretofore, the supreme court has regarded the action of congress in the premises and subsequent practice, as establishing or evidencing a regulation of the subject which it was not at liberty to ignore or disregard. Such considerations, at this late day, should have even more force in this court of inferior jurisdiction. It is true that many of the wisest and best men of the republic have always regarded the construction given to the constitution by the congress of 1789 as unwise and impolitic, and I think subsequent events have vindicated the correctness of their opinion. But in this government the people must learn by experience, and within the constitutional limits of legislative action and judgment, they must be free, through their representation in congress assembled, to conduct the administration of their government uncontrolled by the courts. In the progress of time, it has been found or deemed that the unqualified power of removal from office by the president works injuriously, and congress has interfered to control and regulate the exercise of that power by the passage of what is known as " The Tenure of Office Bill." In the passage of this act by congress it must have been assumed, and as I think correctly, that the constitution left the subject of direct removals from office to be regulated by the legislative power. In the great debate which occurred in the senate on this subject in 1835, Mr. Clay, Mr. Webster and Mr. Calhoun, all agreed in maintaining that the constitution did not give the president the power of removal, and that the power was properly subject to legislative control and regulation.

From Mr. Calhoun's speech on this occasion I quote as follows: " If the power to dismiss is possessed by the executive, he must hold it in one or two modes; either by an express grant of the power in the constitution, or as a power necessary and proper to execute some power expressly granted by that instrument. All the powers under the constitution may be classed under one or the other of these heads; there is no intermediate class. The first question then is, has the president the power in question by any express grant in the constitution? He who affirms he has is bound to show it. That instrument is in the hands of every member. The portion containing the delegation of power to the president is short; it is comprised in a few sentences. I ask senators to open the constitution, to examine it, and to find, if they can, any authority of the president to dismiss any public officer. None such can be found. The constitution has been carefully examined, and no one pretends to have found such a grant. Well then, as there is none such, if it exists at all it must be as a power necessary and proper to execute some granted power; but if it exists in that character it belongs to congress and not the executive. I venture not the assertion hastily; I speak on the authority of the constitution itself — an express and unequivocal authority which cannot be denied nor contradicted. Hear what that sacred instrument says: ' Congress shall have power to make all laws which shall be necessary and proper for carrying into execution the foregoing powers (those granted to congress itself), and all other powers vested by this constitution in the government of the United States or in any department or officer thereof.' Mark the fullness of the expression, congress shall have power to make all laws, not only to carry into effect the powers exclusively delegated to itself, but those delegated to the government or any department or officer thereof; comprehending, of course, the power to pass laws necessary and proper to carry into effect the powers expressly granted to the executive department. It follows, that, to whatever express grant of power to the executive the power of dismissal may be supposed to attach; whether to that of seeing the laws faithfully executed, or to the still more comprehensive grant, as contended for by some, vesting executive power in the president, the mere fact that it is a power appurtenant to another power, and necessary to carry it into effect, transfers it, by the provisions of the constitution cited, from the executive to congress, and places it under its control, to be regulated in the manner which it may judge best.

"Such are the arguments by which I have been forced to conclude that the power of dismissing is not lodged in the president, but is subject to be controlled and regulated by congress. I say forced, because I have been compelled to the conclusion in spite of my previous impressions; relying upon the early decision of the question, and the long acquiescence in that decision."

§ 245. *The constitution vests the power of removal in congress; but congress having for three-fourths of a century conceded the power to the executive, the court will not rule to the contrary.*

To the force of this argument I think nothing can be added. It amounts to demonstration. The power is with congress to regulate removals from office. Congress, by early action and long acquiescence, has allowed, if not authorized, the president to make removals without the consent of the senate in each particular case. The question being one of the exercise of a political power which is within the power of congress to control and regulate, I do not deem it meet or proper for this court, at this late day, to assert by its judgment that all the presidents, from Washington to the present, have, in making removals from office, acted without authority or right in the premises.

As the law and long established usage stood at the time of the commission to Bigler, the power of removal must be conceded to the executive by the courts. Congress had practically so conceded it for three-fourths of a century. In the determination of political questions the courts are subordinate to the political department of the government. In *Ex parte* Hennen, *supra*, the supreme court, without deciding the question, expressed a strong opinion that so well established a practice upon such a subject could not be disregarded by the court, even at that early day.

§ 246. *On quo warranto to eject a party from an office, the defendant may yield the controversy at any time pending the proceeding by surrendering the office to a party entitled to receive it. This step may be taken by a plea puis darrein continuance. In such case the plaintiff will recover costs.*

A supplemental answer has been filed in this case, stating the facts as found by the court since the demand upon the defendant by Bigler. This answer was filed subject to the defendant's right to plead these facts at the time. I think the answer may be filed, and that the matter set forth is material. It is a plea *puis darrein continuance* — good at common law and under the code. From it it appears that the defendant had relinquished the office to the United States and delivered the books and papers to an officer duly authorized to receive them. At any time before trial the defendant may yield the controversy and surrender the office. This terminates the controversy, except as to costs, and for these judgment must be given in favor of the United States.

One other question made by the learned counsel for the defendant remains to be noticed. The tenure of office bill, which is understood to have become a law on March 3, provides, as appears from a newspaper report read in court by counsel, that a person holding office by the consent of the senate shall only be removed by the concurrence of that body. Assuming this to be the correct reading of the tenure of office act, I cannot bring my mind to agree with counsel for the defendant — that the defendant, at the passage of this act, *held* the office in contemplation of law. True, he was in the office, as the information alleges, but without legal right. At that time, so far as he can be said to have held the office, it was not by virtue of his appointment by and with the advice and consent of the senate, but rather as an intruder, and without legal right.

Judgment for the plaintiff for its costs and disbursements.

IN RE FARROW.

(Circuit Court for Georgia: 8 Federal Reporter, 112–117. 1880.)

STATEMENT OF FACTS.— Farrow claims the office of district attorney of Georgia, under an appointment by a United States circuit justice, and Bigby under an appointment by the president, which had not been acted on by the senate.

Opinion by WOODS, J.

It is claimed by counsel for Farrow that the appointment by the president of Bigby was, under the facts of the case, beyond his constitutional power, and he cites the third paragraph of section 2, article 2, of the constitution of the United States, which declares: "The president shall have power to fill up all vacancies that may happen during the recess of the senate, by granting commissions which shall expire at the end of their next session." He also relies upon section 1769, United States Revised Statutes, which declares: "The president is authorized to fill all vacancies which may happen during the recess of the senate, by reason of death or resignation or expiration of term of office, granting commissions which shall expire at the end of their next session thereafter." The contention is that the vacancy in the office of district attorney, which the president has undertaken to fill by the appointment of Bigby, did not happen during the recess of the senate, and therefore the power to fill it does not reside in the president.

On the other hand it is claimed that the phrase "vacancies that may happen during the recess of the senate," when properly construed, means "vacancies which may happen to exist during the recess of the senate." In support of this latter view the practice of the executive department of the government for nearly sixty years is invoked, and the concurring opinions of ten of the distinguished jurists who have filled the office of attorney-general of the United States are cited.

§ 247. *Power of the president to fill vacancies.*

The first opinion given upon this point is that of Mr. William Wirt, attorney-general under President Monroe (1 Op., 631), in which he argues for the construction claimed in support of the president's action in this case. He says: "In reason, it seems to me perfectly immaterial when the vacancy first arose, for, whether it arose during the session of the senate or during their recess, it equally requires to be filled. The constitution does not look to the moment of the origin of the vacancy, but to the state of things at the point of time at which the president is called on to act. Is the senate in session? Then he must make a nomination to that body. Is it in recess? Then the president must fill the vacancy by a temporary commission. This seems to me the only construction of the constitution which is compatible with its spirit, reason and purpose, while at the same time it offers no violence to its language, and these are, I think, the governing points to which all sound construction looks."

This opinion of Attorney-General Wirt was concurred in by Mr. Roger B. Taney, attorney-general under President Jackson. See his opinion dated July 19, 1832 (2 Op., 525). Mr. Taney says in construing that clause of the constitution under consideration: "It was intended to provide for those vacancies which might arise from accident, and the contingencies to which human affairs must always be liable; and if it falls out that from death, inadvertence or mistake, an office required by law to be filled is, in recess, found to be vacant, then a vacancy has happened during the recess and the president may fill it. This appears to be the common sense and the natural import of the words used. They mean the same thing as if the constitution had said 'if there happen to be any vacancies during the recess.'"

It is not necessary to quote from the opinions upon this question of the other distinguished jurists who have filled the office of attorney-general. I simply refer to them. They are the opinions of Mr. Hugh S. Legare, dated October 22, 1841 (3 Op., 673); of Mr. John Y. Mason, dated August 10, 1846 (4 Op., 523); of Mr. Caleb Cushing, dated May 25, 1855 (7 Op., 186); of Mr. Edward Bates, dated October 15, 1862 (10 Op., 356); of Mr. James Speed, dated March 25, 1865 (11 Op., 179); of Mr. Henry Stanberry, dated August 30, 1866 (12 Op., 32); and of Mr. William M. Evarts, dated August 17, 1868 (12 Op., 449). I also refer to the well-considered and conclusive opinion of the present attorney-general, Mr. Devens.

These opinions exhaust all that can be said on the subject. They were rendered upon the call of the executive department, and under the obligation of the oath of office, and are entitled to the highest consideration. In his opinion Mr. Bates says the power to fill vacancies which occur during the recess has been sanctioned, so far as he knows and believes, by the unbroken acquiescence of the senate. It is true, individual members of the senate have disputed the power, but not the senate itself. Congress has recognized the power by section 2 of the act of February 9, 1863 (R. S., § 1761), which declares: "No money shall be paid from the treasury as salary to any person appointed, during the recess of the senate, to fill a vacancy in any existing office, if the vacancy existed while the senate was in session, and was by law required to be filled by and with the advice and consent of the senate, until such appointee has been confirmed by the senate."

The only authority relied on to support the other view is the case decided by the late Judge Cadwallader, the learned and able United States district judge for the eastern district of Pennsylvania. It is no disparagement to Judge Cadwallader to say that his opinion, unsupported by any other, ought not to be held to outweigh the authority of the great number which are cited in support of the opposite view, and of the practice of the executive department for nearly sixty years, the acquiescence of the senate therein, and the recognition of the power claimed by both houses of congress. I therefore shall hold that the president had constitutional power to make the appointment of Bigby, notwithstanding the fact that the vacancy filled by his appointment first happened when the senate was in session.

§ **248.** *Limitation of the power of the circuit justice to appoint district attorneys.*

The point, however, most strenuously urged in behalf of Farrow is that, the circuit justice having appointed him to fill the vacancy occasioned by the expiration of his own term of office, there was no vacancy to fill, and the president could not, therefore, appoint Bigby to fill a vacancy which did not exist. This claim brings up for consideration the proper construction of section 793, United States Revised Statutes. That section provides: " In case of a vacancy in the office of district attorney or marshal within any circuit, the circuit justice of such circuit may fill the same, and the person appointed by him shall serve until an appointment is made by the president and the appointee is duly qualified and no longer."

The result of this claim is that an appointment made by the circuit justice takes away the power of the president to appoint. In other words, that the power conferred by this section is precisely the same, in all respects, as that conferred on the president by the third clause of section 2, article 2, of the constitution, and section 1769, United States Revised Statutes, *supra.* That is to say that congress has given the president and the circuit justice the power to fill the same office at the same time, and that the appointee holds for the same length of time under the appointment of either; that whether the appointment is to be made by the president or the circuit justice depends on which is swifter to act; that the power to appoint depends on the result of a scramble between the president of the United States and a justice of the supreme court. Such, it seems to me, could not have been the purpose of congress in enacting section 793. A glance at the section shows its object. It was not to enable the circuit justice to oust the power of the president to appoint, but to authorize him to fill the vacancy until the president should act and no longer. The section expressly declares the term for which the appointee of the circuit justice shall serve, namely, until an appointment is made by the president. As soon as such appointment is made his term under the circuit justice ends, and there is a vacancy in the office, which is simultaneously filled by the appointment which creates it. To say that the power given the circuit justice, to fill a vacancy until the president appoints, precludes the president from making the appointment, is, it seems to me, a very unwarranted construction of the statute. The meaning is clear. No paraphrase can make it clearer. The circuit justice may fill the vacancy, and the appointee holds under him until the president appoints the same or some other person. The term under the circuit justice then ceases, and the appointee holds, from that time on, under the appointment of the president.

My conclusion is, therefore, that, upon the agreed facts, the term of Farrow, under the appointment of the circuit justice, ended as soon as the president appointed Bigby and he was duly qualified, and that Bigby is entitled to the possession of the office.

§ 249. **In general.**— Where the appointing power is in the president and senate concurrently, the president alone has no power to remove, in the absence of legislation and precedent. But it is held that the president's power of removal is practically admitted by the uniform practice of the government. The constitution vests the power of removal in congress; but congress having, for three-fourths of a century, conceded the power to the executive, the court will not rule to the contrary. United States v. Avery, Deady, 204.

§ 250. It is a general rule of law that, in appointments and removals by the president, when the removal is not by direct discharge, but merely by operation of a new commission, the virtue of the old commission ceases only when a sufficient notice of the new commission is given to the outgoing officer. Duration of Commissions,* 6 Op. Att'y Gen'l, 87.

§ 251. The president cannot make a temporary appointment to fill a vacancy not happening during a recess of the senate; thus, if a vacancy happens during a session of the senate, and no regular appointment is made, a temporary appointment cannot be made during the ensuing recess. Case of the District Attorney,* 7 Am. L. Reg. (N. S.), 786.

§ 252. When an appointee has received a commission from the president, taken the oath of office, and given the requisite bond, the present incumbent is superseded and his removal is complete. United States v. Bank of Arkansas, Hemp., 460.

§ 253. The office of minister to Venezuela by the adjournment of congress, without the senate having acted upon the nomination of a person as such minister, by the operation of the third section of the act of March 2, 1867, known as the tenure of civil office act, passes into "abeyance" as described and defined in that section. Whether the office subsists and is vacant, or the office itself is abrogated while this "abeyance" continues, is a question of verbal rather than of substantial distinctions. Case of the Office of Minister to Venezuela,* 12 Op. Att'y Gen'l, 457.

§ 254. When a vacancy happens in an office during the recess of the senate, and the senate fails to act upon an appointment made at its next session, but adjourns without action, such office remains in abeyance till filled by appointment by and with the consent of the senate, and the president alone has not the right to fill such office during its abeyance. Ibid.

§ 255. Where an office was created and took effect during a session of the senate, and a subsequent session of congress passed without the office being filled, held, that the president could not make a valid appointment to such office in the recess of the senate. Schenk v. Peay, 1 Dill., 267; 1 Ch. L. N., 363; 10 Int. Rev. Rec., 54.

§ 256. Vacancies in offices known to exist during the session of the senate cannot be filled by executive appointment in the recess of that body. Hence, where Florida and Iowa were admitted as states while the senate was sitting, upon a subsequent adjournment the president had no authority to appoint district judges, attorneys and marshals, having failed to take action within the proper time. Appointment of Judges, etc., for Florida and Iowa,* 4 Op. Att'y Gen'l, 361.

IV. UNITED STATES MARSHAL.

SUMMARY — *Deputy marshal*, § 257. — *Money coming to hands of deputy*, § 258. — *Acts after expiration of term*, § 259.

§ 257. A deputy marshal is an officer of the court, amenable to its jurisdiction for malfeasance in office by summary order or attachment for contempt. The marshal is personally answerable under the terms of rule 41 of the supreme court and of the rules of the district court, to pay moneys attached by him forthwith into court, and the responsibility of the deputy is no less stringent. The Bark Laurens, §§ 260–66.

§ 258. If money comes properly, in the course of his official duties, into the hands of a deputy marshal, the marshal is immediately liable for it. Ibid.

§ 259. A marshal cannot, after he is removed from office, sell lands levied on by him before his removal, but the removal is not completely effected till notice is actually received by him. All sales made by him previous to such notice are valid; all made after such notice are void. Bowerbank v. Morris, § 267.

[NOTES.—See §§ 268–333.]

THE BARK LAURENS.

(District Court for New York: Abbott's Admiralty, 508–518. 1849.)

STATEMENT OF FACTS.— The Bark Laurens was libeled for being engaged in the slave trade, and an application was made to require the United States marshal and his deputy to pay into court $20,000 in specie found on board.

Opinion by BETTS, J.

An order was granted by the court on the 21st inst., on motion of the United States attorney, that the marshal of this district forthwith pay into court the sum of money attached by him in the above-entitled cause. The hearing of the matter was deferred at the instance of the marshal until yesterday. The order of the court was served on William H. Peck, chief deputy of the marshal, and, concurrently with the motion against the marshal, the district attorney moves for an order that the said deputy pay the aforesaid money into court, or that an attachment issue against him. It is objected on the part of the marshal that no proof is made of personal service on him of the order of court, and, on the part of the deputy, that no order has been granted directing him personally to pay the money into court.

§ 260. *Practice in obtaining an attachment to bring a party before the court to answer upon matters touching a civil suit.*

In order to lay a foundation for a peremptory attachment, it is incumbent on the applicant to show that his preliminary proceedings have all been strictly correct. United States *v.* Caldwell, 2 Dall., 333. But the same rigor is not necessary to obtain an attachment to bring a party before the court to answer upon matters touching a civil suit. In such cases, the first proceedings may be by order that the accused party show cause why he should not be punished for the alleged misconduct; or an attachment may be issued to bring him before the court to answer for the misconduct (2 R. S., 536, § 6), and the practice of the state court governs this court when not otherwise regulated by its own specific rules. Circuit Ct. Rules, 102; Dist. Ct. Rules, 340.

The material question is whether a proper cause is shown for the interposition of the court against the marshal or deputy, by process of attachment in the first instance, or by an order that they show cause why an attachment for contempt of court, because of misconduct in office, shall not issue against them.

Thus far the cases of the marshal and deputy have been considered as depending upon a principle common to both. Upon the facts brought out, however, by the depositions read in court, it seems proper to separate them at this point, and to dispose of each case on its special circumstances.

It appears that a monition and attachment against the bark Laurens, her tackle and apparel, furniture, appurtenances, guns, and goods and effects found on board, and $20,000 in specie, was delivered to the marshal on March 15, 1848. He deputed William H. Peck, J. S. Smith, Joseph Thompson, or either of them, to execute the process, and the same day it was served by Smith and Thompson by the arrest of the vessel and the specie. The specie was taken by Mr. Thompson to the Mechanics' Banking Association in this city, and left there subject to the order of Eli Moore, the marshal, and, as Mr. Thompson deposes, on special deposit, according to his understanding.

The deputy, Peck, states in his affidavit that the specie attached was estimated at $18,992, and no more, consisting of $1,000 in silver, and several kegs of doubloons and half doubloons,— gold pieces of a foreign currency. The $1,000 in silver were afterwards by his direction placed to his credit by the cashier, and the gold coin was sold and the proceeds also passed to his credit in the bank. He says he has disbursed a portion of these moneys for the official services of the office, and that the total sum he has received in his official capacity, including these moneys, amounts to $133,000, or thereabouts, and that he has disbursed and expended for and on behalf of the marshal during that period the sum of $126,000, or thereabouts, leaving about $7,000 in his hands, which he states he is ready to account for and pay over to the marshal. He farther says he resigned his office of deputy marshal on the 23d inst. The resignation was made after these proceedings were initiated and notice thereof had been served on him.

On these facts the counsel for Mr. Peck takes the following objections to the competency of the court to enforce an order, or issue an attachment against him:

That if the moneys in the cause came to the hands of the deputy, they were in judgment of the law received by the marshal, and the deputy is not answerable for them by summary order of the court, nor by suit at law. That the remedy of the parties interested in the moneys must be taken against the marshal alone. That a deputy marshal is not an officer of the court amenable to the authority of the court by way of attachment for misconduct or malversation in his office. That Mr. Peck is now no longer deputy marshal and therefore in no way under the supervisory authority of the court in respect to his transactions when in office.

A subsidiary exception is taken that the specie cannot be regarded as money in the hands of the marshal, but only as cargo in his custody for safe-keeping until the final decision and disposition of the cause, and accordingly not subject to be brought into court. A farther point was taken under the terms of the act of congress of March 3, 1817, that an attachment cannot be awarded for not paying the money into court, but only on the refusal or neglect of the officer to pay it into an incorporated bank of the state to the credit of the court.

1. The main defense against this proceeding was placed on the first position, that a deputy marshal is not an officer of the court, in such a sense as to render him directly amenable to its supervision, and subject to attachment for not paying over money received by him *virtute officii*.

§ 261. *A deputy marshal is subject to the same summary remedy in respect to moneys held by him officially that the marshal is himself.*

Whatever may be the rule at common law in respect to the direct liability of deputy sheriffs to suitors for moneys collected by process of court, it seems to me there is no ground for question under the act of congress of March 3, 1817 (3 U. S. Stats., 395), that a deputy marshal is subject to the same summary remedy in respect to moneys held by him officially that the marshal is himself.

The United States circuit and district courts are directed, by section 1 of the act, to cause all moneys, being subject to their order, to be deposited in bank; and section 2 provides that all moneys which shall be received by the officers thereof in causes pending in court shall be immediately deposited in bank to the name and credit of the court; and section 4 directs that, if any clerk of such court, or officer thereof, having received any such moneys as aforesaid, shall refuse or neglect to obey the order of such court for depositing the same as aforesaid, such clerk or other officer shall be forthwith proceeded against by attachment for contempt. 3 U. S. Stats., 395. If the court were called upon to expound the language of the statute for the first time, there would seem to be no reasonable ground for not giving it its full, plain and natural import, and applying it to every grade of officers carrying into execution the powers of the courts, and receiving moneys under their process or by their direction.

Chief Justice Marshall clearly considered the law as embracing deputy marshals; for in The United States *v.* Man, 2 Brock., 1, he awarded an attachment against a deputy marshal to compel the payment of money into court, collected on execution. No question was raised in that case as to the just liability of that officer to this form of procedure. This was in 1822. In 1844 the point was raised in the sixth circuit, and Mr. Justice McLean, on a careful consideration of the statute, decided that the deputy marshal is an officer of the court, and subject to its power as such, and that he may be compelled by attachment to pay over money collected by him *virtute officii*. The judge remarked that it would be disreputable to the court and to the institutions of justice, if, in such case, the court could not afford a summary remedy against one of its officers. In that case, too, the deputy had received a portion of the money when he had no authority to receive it, the execution having been returned; and the court held he was responsible for it, although the marshal was not. Bagley *v.* Gates, 3 McLean, 465.

If the money had come properly, in the course of his official duty, into the hands of the deputy, the marshal would immediately be liable for it. Judge McLean holds thàt the deputy is no less so for that cause. And it seems to be the rule in Massachusetts, not only that the sheriff is liable for the acts of his deputy done *colore officii*, but that such liability is consequent upon that of the deputy for the same acts. In Knowlton *v.* Bartlett, 1 Pick., 275, a deputy sheriff attached money, after the process was *functus officio*, and embezzled it. The court held the sheriff liable, because the act was done under color of office. The same doctrines are declared by Parsons, C. J., in Marshall *v.* Hosmer, 4 Mass., 63, and Bond *v.* Ward, 7 id., 127; and all the cases go upon the assumption of the personal liability of the deputy for the acts for which the sheriff was made responsible. In South Carolina the sheriff has been held liable to attachment for moneys paid a clerk in his office, embezzled by the clerk afterwards. Abercrombie *v.* Marshall, 2 Bay, 9; Carter *v.* Ken, id., 112.

§ 262. *The United States possess ample authority to prescribe rules in relation to the collection and disposition of moneys obtained under their process or order, and to compel the observance of such rules by attachment.*

Independent of the statute referred to, the courts of the United States, under their inherent powers and their right to regulate their own process, possess ample authority to prescribe rules in relation to the collection and disposition of moneys obtained under their process or order, and to compel the observance of such rules by attachment. Bac. Abr., tit. Attachment, A.; Com. Dig., Day's ed., tit. Attachment for Contempt of Court, note 1; 3 Durn. & E., 351; 2 R. S., 523, § 1. Such rules are prescribed by the supreme court and by this court.

§ 263. *The marshal would be personally responsible for failure to pay moneys attached by him forthwith into court; and the responsibility of the deputy is no less stringent.*

In my opinion the deputy marshal is an officer of this court, amenable to its jurisdiction for malfeasance in office by summary order or attachment for contempt. The marshal would be personally answerable under the terms of rule 41 of the supreme court, and of rule 158 of this court, for failing to pay moneys attached by him forthwith into court; and the responsibility of the deputy is no less stringent. So, also, under the practice of the supreme court of this state, the sheriff is subject to attachment for not paying moneys collected by him on process to the party, or into court, although no demand is made on him therefor. Brewster *v.* Van Ness, 18 Johns., 133.

§ 264. *Resignation by an officer does not oust the jurisdiction of the court to proceed against him by attachment for misconduct while in office; and this rule applies to a deputy marshal.*

2. It is earnestly contended that the resignation of his office by the deputy, on the 23d inst., ousts the jurisdiction of the court over him. This is upon the assumption that the authority of the court, by attachment, cannot be exercised over any one except he be at the time an officer of the court. This doctrine is correct as to executory acts. The court could have no power to compel the deputy to resume his office, or to proceed hereafter in the execution of his duties. But this principle does not touch that of the rightful authority of the court in respect to acts and omissions of its officers while acting as officers. The power of the court to afford a remedy against sheriffs by attachment, after they leave office, for malversation or neglect of duty in office, is one constantly exercised, and has never been questioned.

In February term, 1810, the supreme court of New York awarded an attachment against a late sheriff, for not returning a *fi. fa.* delivered to one of his deputies in 1797, to bring him into court to answer on oath to interrogatories. Brockway v. Wilbur, 5 Johns., 356. He was afterwards discharged on account of laches of the party prosecuting, the process having been delivered to a deputy more than fourteen years previously. The People v. Gilliland, 7 Johns., 555. Equally direct are the cases of Brewster v. Van Ness, 18 Johns., 133; The People v. Brower, 6 Cow., 41, and The People v. Evans, 4 Hill, 71. It is presumed the argument would not be advanced, that the marshal, in this case, if the money in question came into his hands, could exempt himself from these summary proceedings by resigning his office. The deputy, as an officer of the court, stands on the same footing. He is compellable to answer to the court for abuse of its process or other contempt of court whilst acting as its officer. The proceeding by attachment does not affect him as an officer, but individually. It is not against him in the character of one now acting in office, but to compel him to complete and carry out his official duties in doing something he had neglected and omitted, and because of malversation, whilst an officer, in retaining in his hands moneys received by him when in office, and by color of his office. The law empowers the court to act directly upon the office of a deputy marshal for misconduct committed by him in office by removing him. This court had drawn an order in execution of that power removing this deputy from office, when informed of his resignation; but that mode of punishment would in no way affect the civil rights and remedies of suitors against him for embezzling their moneys collected by him, nor the power of the court to inflict punishment by way of fine on him for such malconduct.

§ 265. *Where foreign coin is seized by a marshal, he must pay it into court; he cannot treat it as cargo.*

3. I cannot assent to the doctrine set up in the third point raised in behalf of the deputy, that this specie was merely cargo, which he is not bound to bring into court or deposit in bank. The foreign coins mentioned in the depositions, comprising the large sum in question, were all legal currency under our laws. They were money, the same as coin of the United States mint. By the laws of this state, the sheriff can levy on money or bank bills, and must return and pay them as so much money collected. 2 R. S., 290; Allen on Sheriffs, 159. The case of Knowlton v. Bartlett, 1 Pick., 271, was that of money levied on and embezzled by the deputy sheriff. The process in his hands was a mesne attachment, the same in effect as the attachment and monition issued in this

cause. There was no necessity for changing the character of the property taken. It was already money; and the officer was bound to pay it into court as such.

§ 266. *Notwithstanding the statute requires moneys received by officers to be deposited in bank, the court may require payment into court, the deposit to be made by the clerks.*

4. It is contended that this proceeding is not supported by the act of congress of 1817, as it demands the payment of the moneys into court, whilst the statute directs that they shall be deposited in an incorporated bank of the state to the credit of the court. This is only a different phraseology for the same act and the same result. The purport and object of the motion is to place the moneys under control of the court for the protection of the parties litigant; and the order might be modified so as to conform to the language of the statute, if that were necessary. The act of April 18, 1814 (3 U. S. Stats., 127), directed the deposit of moneys paid into court in an incorporated bank, to be designated by the court. The act of March 3, 1817 (3 U. S. Stats., 395), appointed the branches of the United States Bank such depositaries, still leaving it to the courts to designate state banks when no branch of the United States Bank was convenient. On the termination of the charter of the United States Bank, this court designated incorporated banks in this city for that purpose. The Bank of the State of New York, the Manhattan Bank and the Bank of New York are the only ones appointed. Section 2 of the act of 1817 requires the moneys to be deposited in the name and to the credit of the court. The marshal may, undoubtedly, if he elects so to do, proceed directly to the appointed bank and place money collected by him in deposit in that form, provided the bank will accept it from him. But it is manifest that an orderly and accurate method of conducting this business, and keeping the accounts so that all parties in interest can acquire the information they need in respect to deposits, and so that the funds shall be emphatically in public keeping, is indispensable. The courts in this district require, to that end, that the moneys be paid into court, to be deposited by the clerks, under the title of the cause to which they appertain. The court, as such, keeps no bank account, and there is no general deposit of moneys to its credit. Every deposit is specific and special, to the credit of the cause out of which the money arises. No part of such money can be drawn out but by order of the court, entered on the minutes, signed by the judge, and then checked for by the clerk. Those minutes and records are open to inspection by all persons in interest. If, then, the money is, in the first instance, carried by the marshal to the bank, it will be necessary to redeposit it under the order of the court, in the manner provided for keeping the accounts, and for its safe and correct disbursement.

Upon the law of the case, I am clearly of the opinion that the United States attorney is entitled to compel Peck, the deputy, to pay the money in question into court, under penalty of attachment for contempt.

There is, however, undoubtedly some want of formal steps to entitle him to a peremptory order to that effect. No order has been served personally on Peck which he has disobeyed, and he is not, accordingly, put in a state of contumacy as yet before the court. Sufficient, however, is shown upon his own affidavit to satisfy the court that he was apprised of the proceedings, and to · justify an order or an attachment against him, to bring him before the court to answer.

It is accordingly directed that the United States attorney may take an order on Peck, that he forthwith pay into court the moneys in question or at his election he may have an attachment to bring Mr. Peck into court to answer interrogatories on the subject-matter.

It is not made to appear, upon the proofs submitted to me, that the marshal has personally been guilty of any delinquency. He is answerable for the acts of his deputy done *colore officii* (The People *v.* Dunning, 1 Wend., 16; Clute *v.* Goodell, 2 McLean, 193), although without his knowledge or recognition (McIntyre *v.* Trumbull, 7 Johns., 35; Walden *v.* Davidson, 15 Wend., 575); and in respect to moneys so collected or taken by the deputy, the party entitled to them can have his remedy by process of attachment against the marshal personally. The People *v.* Brower, 6 Cow., 41.

There is some want of complete formality in this instance, as to the proofs necessary to found a motion for a peremptory attachment; and one for the purpose of bringing the marshal before the court to answer is unnecessary, as he presents his own affidavit and that of Mr. Thompson, showing cause in excuse of himself. The excusatory matter set up will not protect him against an attachment, unless it appears that Peck obtained possession of the money tortiously and in fraud of the marshal's rights. The court cannot, upon the statements laid before it, imply that Mr. Peck so acquired the money; and the marshal may be compelled to answer on interrogatories, whether the late deputy had not adequate powers in this behalf to take upon himself the possession and control of the money.

As the evidence of the preliminary steps does not entitle the applicant now to a peremptory attachment, and as there does not appear to have been any personal delinquency on the part of the marshal, I shall direct that an order be entered for him to pay the money into court on or before the first day of May next. or that an attachment issue against him. .

BOWERBANK *v.* MORRIS.

(Circuit Court for Pennsylvania: Wallace, C. C., 118–183. 1801.)

STATEMENT OF FACTS.— Rule to show cause why sales made by Hall, marshal, should not be set aside. A commission to Smith as Hall's successor was issued March 28, and accepted April 4, and Smith gave notice to Hall on April 10. The sales in question were made by Hall on writs of *venditioni exponas* before March 28, before April 4, before April 10 and after that date. On April 10, Smith gave bond and took the oath of office.

Opinion by TILGHMAN, J.

By the act of congress of the 24th of September, 1789 (1 Laws U. S., 67, sec. 28), it was provided "that every marshal or his deputy, when removed from office, or when the term of office is expired, shall have power to execute all such precepts as may be in their hands respectively at the time of such removal or expiration of office." If this act had remained in force, it is clear that John Hall might have gone on to sell all the lands mentioned in the *venditioni exponas;* because that would have been an execution of the precept which was in his hands at the time of his removal.

§ 267. *A marshal is not removed by the appointment of his successor until he receives notice of such removal, and all his acts up to time of receiving such notice are valid.* (a)

But by the act passed the 7th of May, 1800 (5 Laws U. S., 145, sec. 3),

(a) A marshal, under the twenty-eighth section of the act of September 24, 1789, when he is removed from office, or his term has expired, may execute all precepts in his hands at the

it is enacted: "That where a marshal shall take in execution any lands, tenements or hereditaments, and shall die or be removed from office, or the term of his commission expire before sale, or other final disposition of the same; in every such case the like process shall issue to the succeeding marshal, and the same proceedings shall be had as if such former marshal had not died or been removed, or the term of his commission had not expired." What were the reasons which induced the legislature to make the restrictions of the marshal's power in cases of precepts ordering the sale of lands, it is unnecessary for us to inquire: we are bound by the law as it is written. The intention of the act is plain; if a marshal is removed before he has actually sold the land, he shall not proceed to make the sale, but a new writ shall issue to his successor. But when shall he be said to be removed? A removal from office may be either express, that is, by a notification by order of the president of the United States that an officer is removed; or implied, by the appointment of another person to the same office. But in either case, the removal is not completely effected till notice actually received by the person removed. This construction of the act of the 7th of May, 1800, avoids all inconveniences and is warranted by well established principles. In general, all persons who act by authority derived from others may proceed to execute business until notice of the revocation of their authority; and their acts between the time of revocation of their power and of their receiving notice of such revocation are held good; and with regard to a sheriff in particular, it was held in the case of Boucher v. Wiseman, Cro. El., 440 (cited in 4 Bac. Ab., 446), that the execution of a *fi. fa.* by a sheriff after a writ of discharge had issued to remove him from his office, but before notice of such writ of discharge, was good.

The marshals in many districts of the United States live so remote from the seat of government that a considerable time must elapse before notice can be received; and it cannot be supposed that it was intended to injure *bona fide* purchasers who may have paid their money at marshals' sales before it was possible to know the marshal was removed. As to those sales which had not actually taken place when Mr. Hall received notice of Smith's appointment, I am of opinion they cannot be supported by the doctrine of relation. A sale is a term well understood. When the marshal has struck off the land to the highest bidder, he has made the sale. But if he only puts the land up, and then adjourns the sale to some other time, it cannot be said he has made the sale. And if he receives notice of his removal before the time adjourned to arrives, it would be directly contrary to the provisions of the act of congress if he were to proceed to make the sale. I am therefore of opinion that all sales made by Mr. Hall, the late marshal, after he received notice of the commission to Mr. Smith, the present marshal, which is stated to have happened on the 4th April last, were contrary to law and must be set aside.

Opinion by GRIFFITH, J.

The act for establishing the judicial courts of the United States, passed the 24th September, 1789, creates the office of a marshal, designates his powers and fixes the tenure of his commission. By the twenty-seventh section (1 vol. Laws U. S., p. 65) it is enacted: "That a marshal shall be appointed, in and

---

time of such removal or expiration of office. But under the third section of the act of May 7, 1800, where he has levied on lands but not sold the same, when he is removed or his term expires, his successor in office must sell them. And a sale of lands by the marshal after his removal, although he is not notified of it, is void. Overton v. Gorham,* 2 McL., 509.

for each district, for the term of four years, but shall be removable from office at pleasure, whose duty it shall be to attend," etc. "And to execute throughout the district all lawful precepts," etc. "And before he enters on the duties of his office he shall become bound for the faithful performance," etc., "and shall take the following oath," etc. By the twenty-eighth section: "In causes where the marshal or his deputy shall be a party the writs and precepts therein shall be directed to such disinterested person as the court may appoint. And in case of the death of any marshal, his deputy or deputies shall continue in office, unless otherwise specially removed, and shall execute the same in the name of the deceased until another marshal shall be appointed and sworn. And every marshal or his deputy, when removed from office, or when the term for which the marshal is appointed shall expire, shall have power notwithstanding to execute all such precepts as may be in their hands respectively at the time of such removal or expiration of office."

By this act every marshal is to be appointed for four years, but is removable from office at pleasure; it was provided that the execution of all precepts in his hands at his death shall be executed by his deputy until a new marshal sworn; or if at the expiration of four years, when his office ceases by its own limitation, or at the time of his removal from office, precepts are in his hands, they shall be proceeded upon by himself or his deputy. Had the law remained so this question now debated could not have arisen; for a *venditioni exponas* being a precept within the meaning of the law, the ex-marshal Hall would have been right in making the sales in question.

But for reasons best known to the legislature of the United States it was enacted on the 7th May, 1800 (5 vol. Laws U. S., 146), "that whenever a marshal shall sell any lands, tenements or hereditaments by virtue of process from a court of the United States, and shall die or be removed from office, or the term of his commission expire before a deed shall be executed for the same by him to the purchaser, in every such case the purchaser may apply to the court," etc. "And where a marshal shall take in execution any lands, tenements or hereditaments, and shall die, or be removed from office, or the term of his commission expire before sale, or other final disposition made of the same, in every such case the like process shall issue to the succeeding marshal, and the same proceeding shall be had as if such former marshal had not died or been removed, or the term of his commission had not expired."

The only cases, then, where an old marshal, going out of office by efflux of time or removal, is restrained from proceeding on process in his hands is when, having taken lands in execution, he has sold and made no deed, or has not sold; in both these cases the new marshal shall, by order of the court, make a deed, or by new process proceed to sale.

All sales made after Hall was, in law, removed from his office are void, and must be set aside. The notion of protecting sales actually made after a removal, by giving them a fictitious relation to the time of seizure or taking them in execution by the marshal, would defeat the very terms and evident intention of the law. Nothing can be plainer than that the unsold lands are to be sold by a new writ, and by the new marshal. It can make no difference that, as in this case, the sales are begun. Each sale on the adjourned days, though under the same execution or authority, is a distinct sale, at a different time, of a different property, and it may be to a different purchaser and for a different price. It is, therefore, quite absurd to maintain that a sale made on the 4th April to A. was made to A. on the 27th of February. The act of congress speaks of sales, and I do not see how the common law doctrine of relation is at all brought in. If a sheriff seizes goods in execution, and afterwards a *supersedeas* comes, he may proceed; for an execution once begun shall proceed, as the expression is in the case cited from 4 Term, 411–12. But why? Because the *supersedeas* is too late; the property was divested from the debtor; it is in the officer; the sheriff has authority to sell. But in this case a previous law says that where he has taken property in execution, and is removed before sale, he shall not sell, but the new marshal proceed with the execution.

The only question then is, " At what time was John Hall removed from his office." The expiration of the office by death or limitation of the term, or a direct notice of dismission, are certain events; but removal by the pleasure of the president, effected merely by a new appointment, necessarily refers to some act or acts to be performed by the person having the power of appointment and removal.

There can be no question, I apprehend, but that the president may, by a proper act of office, remove a marshal without a new appointment. But this would not supersede him until he had notice of such declaration of the president's pleasure, and only from the time of notice; the office then would be vacant. That is not the kind of removal in this case. The removal here is effected by a new appointment; or, as his honor the chief judge observes, it is an implied removal by the commissioning another to the office. The president does not remove the old marshal by a discharge, and then proceed to make a new appointment, but he leaves the old marshal to proceed in the duties of his office until certain acts are done relative to a new one, which amount to a removal. What are these?

1st. He nominates a new one to the senate, and the senate concur. Did he stop there, no one would say the old officer was removed. He may or may not appoint the other. 2d. He signs a commission for the new officer. Did he keep this in his pocket, no one will say that the old marshal is removed; the very withholding it is an expression of his pleasure for so long, that the new one shall not take, and the old one continue. 3d. He delivers the commission or patent to the new officer. If he refuses it, or sends it back, there is no new appointment, no officer. It has not been contended that the commission to Shee, which he refused, superseded Hall. 4th. The new commission must be accepted and shown to the old marshal, or other notice of it given to him, before he can be said to be removed from his office by the will or pleasure of the president. There is then a new patentee, and a proper discharge of the old marshal. I do not go the length of saying the new marshal must be sworn in (though Mr. Levy's argument was very strong), but he must accept and give notice by showing his commission or otherways, to his predecessor; and from that time he must be considered as the officer, though before he " enters on the duties of his office " he must be sworn in. In the case of an implied removal, by the appointment and acceptance of another, nothing is more reasonable than that all acts done by the predecessor before notice of his removal should be valid; or in other words, that until such notice the removal of the principal is not complete. The reasons assigned by his honor the chief judge are very strong.

This case is not to be distinguished from other cases of revocable authority. The president, by the commission to Hall, gave him authority to do all acts as marshal, until he revoked that authority. Now it is settled law that " Where a man makes an actual revocation of an authority, and, before notice, the other executes his authority, the revocation being without notice, is no revocation " (16 Vin. Ab., 4, pl. 7; Vivion v. Wild, 2 Brownl., 291); as where an arbitrator makes award before notice, though after the countermand, the award is good; or the attorney in fact makes livery on a feoffment after countermand, but before notice, the estate passes. ·

By the demise of the king, at common law, all commissions were at an end; yet in the case of Crew v. Vernon, Cro. Car., 97, where a commission had issued to examine witnesses, and the commissioners began the examination the day after the demise of the king, it was held, " That all the depositions taken before notice of the demise to the commissioners should stand; though it was allowed in that case that the demise of the king determined the commission, and it was said that if the demise before notice were to avoid acts done under commissions from the crown, then many trials at *nisi prius* and attainders upon gaol deliveries after the demise would be avoided, which, it was agreed, were good before notice."

" Defendant in assize pleaded recovery before commissioners; plaintiff replied that after the said commission, and before judgment given by those commissioners, another commission issued; and judgment was given for the defendant, the plaintiff not having alleged that the first commissioners had notice before; for the second commission to some purposes has relation to the date, yet acts done under the first commission, before notice, are good; so adjudged 34 Ass., pl. 8."

" An attachment was issued before the demise of Charles II., but executed three days after, without notice; the return, however, of *cepi corpus* was made after notice,' and then proceedings for the contempt; yet because the service was before notice of the demise, that, and the return and all subsequent proceedings, were held good. Burch v. Maypowder, 1 Vern., 400."

" A commission was granted to examine witnesses at Algiers; the plaintiff died before execution of the commission, by which the suit abated, and of course the commission was at an end; yet the depositions being taken by the commissioners before notice of the death, they stood." Thompson's Case, 3 P. Wms., 194.

There are determinations on this very question upon the office of sheriff of England. Sheriffs there are nominated by the chancellor and other great officers to the king, who, if he approves, appoints one for the county, and issues a patent or commission; but it has never been held that notwithstanding the new appointment and patent made out, yet the office of the old one continues until a discharge or notice of the new patent is given to him; and this, not upon any statutable provision, but upon a lawful construction of what amounts to a removal of the old officer, and when, to the purposes of avoiding his acts, he is removed by the appointment of a new one.

" False imprisonment was brought against St. John; he pleaded that at the time he was sheriff of Wiltshire, and took the plaintiff by a *capias*. The plaintiff replied that one Earnley was sheriff, and traversed that St. John was sheriff; the defendant rejoined that he was sheriff all the year before, and had no notice of the patent to Earnley, and had received no discharge of himself; and on demurrer, the defendant had judgment, because all acts which he hath done as sheriff, are good in law till he has received his discharge, or has perfect notice of the new sheriff. Mo., 186, pl. 338; St. John's Case, cited 19 Vin., 451, pl. 3."

In Westby's Case, 3 Rep., 71, the ancient sheriff is not discharged till three things are done, viz.: the patent to the new sheriff, the writ of discharge, which is notice to the old sheriff, and the delivery of the prisoners, etc. The case cited by his honor, the chief judge, Boucher v. Wiseman, Cro. El., 440, was this: " Action on the case against Wiseman, because the plaintiff had recovered £100 against Pynder, and the defendant, as sheriff, levied £28 by *fieri facias*, and had not returned the writ or paid the money. Plea, not guilty. On evidence to the jury it was proved that the writ was delivered the 9th November to Cowell, his under-sheriff, and the same day he made execution, but the defendant, the sheriff, proved that a writ of discharge was delivered to him the same day, dated the 6th November. But because he did not prove that he had notice of this writ of discharge before the execution served, the court held clearly that he was yet sheriff, and chargeable to the plaintiff's action."

" A *ca. sa.* was awarded to Clifton, then sheriff: a new patent was made to Kircombe, and before notice Clifton arrested A., and left him in execution. Kircombe died, and then Fitz was made sheriff, who let A.'go. The question was, if this was a good arrest by Clifton; for if not, then it was no escape." The court held clearly, that the arrest was good, and it was an escape; for Sir J. Clifton remained sheriff until the new patent is showed to him, so as he may have notice of his discharge; and if in the meantime between the sealing of the new patent and the showing it to him he keeps a county court, it is good." Fitz's Case, Cro. Eliz., 12.

The true time, then, of the " removal of a marshal by the pleasure of the president," where the removal is not by a direct discharge or vacating of the office, but merely by the operation of a new commission or appointment, is when notice is given to the old marshal of the new commission by the president, or the showing of the commission to him by the officer, or other perfect notice. In the case stated it is agreed that Hall had notice of the new commission and acceptance by Smith on the 4th of April last. I agree, therefore, with his honor, the chief judge, that all sales by Hall previous to the notice are valid, but all sales after that day are void, and a new writ of sale must issue to the new marshal, Smith. .

§ 268. **Contracts by.**— If the marshal rents a building in his custody without an order of the court, he is liable for all damages resulting to the owner. Perrin v. Epping,* Chase's Dec., 430.

§ 269. A marshal has no authority in law to appoint auctioneers to conduct judicial sales, at the expense of the government or of private parties, without the consent of the parties for whose benefit the services are performed. The Tubal Cain, The Annie Deas, Bl. Pr. Cas., 847.

§ 270. A marshal cannot contract for repairs not absolutely necessary to the preservation of a vessel while in his custody. It is his duty simply to keep the vessel as he receives her. The Sultana, Brown's Adm., 35.

§ 271. **Executions.**— The marshal is not bound to hold an execution the sixty days it might run before making a return; the presumption that the officer performed his duty is not overcome by the fact that he returned the process the day he received it. Bassett v. Orr, 7 Biss., 297.

§ 272. **Delivery bond.**— Under the statute of Ohio, a delivery bond was given to the marshal for property replevied. In such a case it is discretionary with the marshal to deliver the property in bulk or as the party is ready to remove it. Where his return shows only a partial delivery, it is conclusive of the facts set forth, and cannot be collaterally impeached, and as to the property in the marshal's possession, the sheriff has no right to disturb or in any way to interfere with it. Crane v. McCoy, 1 Bond, 422.

§ 273. **Custody of prisoners.**— A marshal or deputy marshal having prisoners in lawful custody has a right to use all necessary force to retain them in custody, and in case of an open, undisguised attempt to rescue them by force, he is justified in killing the assailants if that be necessary to retain possession of the prisoners. *Ex parte* Sifford,* 5 Am. L. Reg., 659.

§ 274. **Bailiffs.**—A marshal has authority to appoint a bailiff to execute a particular process. In states where a sheriff may, by writing, empower any person to execute original or mesne process, a United States marshal may, under section 7 of the act of July 29, 1861 (12 Stat. at L., 282), do the same. United States v. Jailer of Fayette County, 2 Abb., 265.

§ 275. A marshal may appoint a bailiff and authorize him to do a particular act or duty. When so appointed, and engaged in the performance of the act, the bailiff is the deputy of the marshal; not the general deputy, it is true, but the special deputy. In re Crittenden, 2 Flip., 212.

§ 276. **The presentation of a false account for fees** by a deputy marshal to the marshal for approval is a presentation to an officer within the meaning of section 5438, Revised Statutes, providing for the punishment of presenting to an officer a false claim against the government. United States v. Strobach, 4 Woods, 592.

§ 277. **An action on the case will not lie against the executors** of a deceased marshal, where executions had been placed in his hands, and false returns made on some of them and imperfect and insufficient entries made on others. United States v. Daniel, 6 How., 11.

§ 278. **Taking bail.**—The marshal is bound to take sufficient bail for the appearance of the defendant, in all cases, except in the actions of trespass on the case mentioned in the third section of the Maryland act of 1715, chapter 46, and he is the judge of its sufficiency. Winter v. Simonton, 2 Cr. C. C., 585.

§ 279. In the district of Connecticut, the marshal may, upon an attachment for debt, without a mittimus, commit the defendant to prison for want of bail. Palmer v. Allen, 7 Cr., 550.

§ 280. **Order to produce prisoner.**—The marshal, being called upon by the court to bring before them any defendant arrested by him upon any original writ or mesne process, according to the tenor of his return, and failing so to do, will, on motion, be amerced to the amount of the debt, or damages and costs, and judgment will be enforced therefor, nisi, the second day of the next term. Winter v. Simonton, 2 Cr. C. C., 585.

§ 281. **Failure to sell property.**—If the sheriff or marshal seizes property in execution and neglects to sell it, and is sued for his neglect, the plaintiff shall recover damages to the amount of what the property would have produced had he sold it. Dunlap v. West,* 2 Hayw. (N. C.), 346.

§ 282. On a replevy bond the marshal is required to take one or more sufficient freehold sureties, otherwise he will be liable. Bispham v. Taylor, 2 McL., 355.

§ 283. **Where bonds are made payable to the marshal** of a court, he has a right to collect them. In such case the marshal must be considered as a trustee for the creditor. Wallis v. Thornton, 2 Marsh., 422.

§ 284. **False return.**—After a rule on the marshal to return a ca. sa., issued against the defendants, and the return of the marshal that the plaintiff had directed him not to serve the writ on one defendant, and that the other could not be found, the court have nothing more to do with the rule; if the marshal has misconducted himself the remedy is an action for a false return. Segourney v. Ingraham, 2 Wash., 336.

§ 285. **Arrears of taxes on property sold.**—The marshal who sells certain property under a venditioni exponas has no power to pay the tax collector the arrears of taxes on the property sold out of the proceeds of other property sold under the same writ. Bleeker v. Bond, 4 Wash., 322.

§ 286. **Custody of goods libeled.**—The practice in New York of giving the custody of goods libeled to the marshal is erroneous; the collector is legally entitled to the keeping of the property. Jewels of the Princess of Orange,* 2 Op. Att'y Gen'l, 496.

§ 287. **Act as to alien enemies.**—The marshals of the several districts are the proper officers to execute the orders of the president, under the act relative to alien enemies. Lockington v. Smith, Pet. C. C., 466.

§ 288. **Order to bring money into court.**—After the marshal is commanded by the writ to bring money, the proceeds of a sale, into court, he may pay it to the plaintiff on the execution, on his responsibility, for the right of the plaintiff to receive it. Wartman v. Conyngham, Pet. C. C., 341.

§ 289. **The marshal of the District of Columbia** is not a county or corporation officer; he has the powers of a sheriff in executing the laws of the United States, but is not bound to perform all the duties of a sheriff under the state laws. Ex parte Ringgold, 8 Cr. C. C., 86.

§ 290. The marshal of the District of Columbia and his sureties are liable to account for all common-law fines and forfeitures received by the marshal, whether on execution or otherwise. United States v. Williams, 5 Cr. C. C., 619.

§ 291. The marshal of the District of Columbia is not liable for fines which he has no means of collecting. Levy Court v. Ringgold, 2 Cr. C. C., 659.

§ 292. The marshal has no right to expend the funds of the levy court of Washington County, D. C., in the repair of the jail without their order. Ibid.

§ 293. The "act concerning the District of Columbia," passed March 8, 1801, does not require the marshal to apply to the district attorney for executions in cases of fines levied by the federal circuit court, and make him liable for neglecting to do so, if no execution issued. The Levy Court of Washington County v. Ringgold, 5 Pet., 451.

§ 294. Summary remedy against.—Under a statute of Mississippi, relating to sheriffs, a summary process against a marshal might be resorted to in order to enforce the payment of a debt, interest and costs, for which he was liable by reason of his default; that the courts of the United States could not enforce the payment of a penalty imposed by the state laws in addition to the money due on the execution; that a marshal and his sureties could not be proceeded against, jointly, in this summary way, but they must be sued as directed by the act of congress. Gwin v. Barton, 6 How., 7.

§ 295. A statute of the state of Mississippi, passed February 15, 1828, provided that if a sheriff should fail to pay over to the plaintiff money collected by execution, the amount collected, with twenty-five per cent. damages and eight per cent. interest, might be recovered against such sheriff and his sureties by motion before the court to which such execution was returnable. A marshal, in that state, and his sureties cannot be proceeded against, jointly, in this summary manner, but they must be sued as directed by the act of congress. But the marshal himself was always liable to an attachment, under which he could be compelled to bring the money into court; and by the process act of congress of May, 1828, was also liable, in Mississippi, to have a judgment entered against himself by motion. Gwin v. Breedlove, 2 How., 29.

§ 296. Care of property.—The marshal is bound, when a seizure of property is made by him, to use due and reasonable diligence to keep it safe, and to protect it from injury, but he is not authorized to insure it, unless under some authority of the owner. Burke v. Brig M. P. Rich, 1 Cliff., 509.

§ 297. It is a great irregularity for the marshal to keep property or the proceeds thereof in his own hands, or to distribute the same among the parties entitled, without a special order from the court; but such an irregularity may be cured by the assent and ratification of all the parties interested, if there be no mala fides. The Collector, 6 Wheat., 194.

§ 298. The responsibility of a marshal for the safe keeping of alcohol seized by him is in nowise affected by the fact that, at a period subsequent to its seizure by him, a collector of internal revenue claimed that the property had been at all times in his possession, under entry for deposit in a United States bonded warehouse, where the property seized, if constructively in the possession of the collector, was found in an exposed position on a wharf, and not in charge of any person claiming to represent said collector, or claiming that it was in his custody under bond. The United States v. Three Hundred Barrels of Alcohol, 1 Ben., 72; 8 Int. Rev. Rec., 105.

§ 299. Commitment to jail.—When there is an order of commitment to a county jailer, and the marshal has executed the mittimus, he has no further control over the prisoner, and is not responsible for any escape from prison. For certain purposes and to certain intents the state jail, lawfully used by the United States, may be deemed to be the jail of the United States, and that keeper to be the keeper of the United States. United States v. Harden, 10 Fed. R., 802; 4 Hughes, 455.

§ 300. The marshal must deliver a copy of the mittimus to the jailer as his authority to hold the prisoner, and the original warrant, with due entry of service, must be returned to the proper officer. A jailer ought never to receive a prisoner into his custody without some written authority, except under the order of a court in session. When the marshal or his deputies have arrested a person, and there is urgent necessity to commit him to jail, they ought to furnish a copy of the warrant to the jailer and a written statement of the causes which induce the necessity of such commitment. Where a marshal arrests a defendant on a capias, he has power to take a recognizance of bail as sheriffs do, and if defendant fails to give bail he may commit to a jailer, but he ought to give the jailer a written statement of his authority. This is not an absolute commitment, as the marshal can take the prisoner out of custody to bring him into court. Ibid.

§ 301. In bankruptcy.—It is the duty of a marshal under a warrant in bankruptcy, directing him to take possession of all the property and effects of the bankrupt, etc., to collect and hold possession until the assignee is appointed, or the property released by some order of court. This duty is not limited to such property as he finds in the actual possession of the bankrupt, but extends to property of the bankrupt wherever found. But he does this on his own responsibility for not only a faithful but a correct judgment in deciding what property to seize. He is liable to suit if by mistake he takes possession of property not liable to seizure under his warrant. Sharpe v. Doyle, 12 Otto, 686.

§ 302. A marshal directed by a provisional warrant to seize the effects of a bankrupt is liable to the injured party if he seizes property belonging to other than the bankrupt. *In re* Marks,* 2 N. B. R., 575.

§ 803. The marshal has the authority, under a warrant issued under section 40 of the bankrupt law, to hold possession of property claimed by others than the bankrupt, when once in possession, and to take possession of property not in the possession of the bankrupt, whether indemnified or not. If indemnified it is his duty to do so. His authority is as complete in the one ´case as in the other, but with indemnity he is bound to exercise his authority; without it, he may exercise it or not, at his option. *In re* Briggs,* 3 N. B. R., 638.

§ 804. In the execution of admiralty process in rem, the officer should take actual and manifest possession, and hold in such manner that inquirers and observers may learn, or see, that he has such possession. The Hibernia, 1 Spr., 78.

§ 805. Conflict of authority.—A bill in chancery which recites that the complainants had ˎrecovered a judgment at law in a court of the United States, upon which an execution had issued and been levied upon certain property by the marshal; that another person, claiming to hold the property levied upon by virtue of some fraudulent deed of trust, had obtained a process from a state court, by which the sheriff had taken the property out of the hands of the marshal; and praying that the property be sold, cannot be sustained. There is a remedy at law in such a case; the marshal might have brought trespass against the sheriff, or applied to the federal court for an attachment. Knox v. Smith, 4 How., 298.

§ 806. A marshal exceeds his authority in taking a prisoner from the custody of the sheriff. He should make a return of the fact that the prisoner was held in custody for a violation of state law. United States v. Wells,* 15 Int. Rev. Rec., 56.

§ 807. Where a sheriff claims to have had custody of a vessel, under process issued by a state court, at the time that the marshal undertook to seize her under process of a district court of the United States, he can bring the facts before the court, whose officer he is, and that court will protect his custody, or he may apply to the federal court by petition, praying it to instruct its officer to withdraw from the vessel. It is very doubtful if he has the power, by making himself a party to proceedings *in rem* in the federal court, to bring proceedings pending in a state tribunal before the court for adjudication as to their validity. The Steamer Circassian, 1 Ben., 128.

§ 808. The court will not dictate to the marshal what return he shall make to process in his hands. He must make his return at his peril, and any person injured by it may have his legal remedy for such return. Wortman v. Conyngham, Pet. C. C., 241.

§ 809. The marshal is responsible for the execution of process, and should be left free to state what he does in the premises, subject to his responsibility under the law. The court will not direct him to amend his return. The Steamer Circassian, 1 Ben., 128.

§ 810. Money in hand.—A marshal has the right, primarily, to retain money in his hands, the proceeds of sale of goods sold under execution and claimed by another than the judgment debtor, until the determination of a suit against him by such claimant. And in the case of a verbal motion for an order to deposit the money in court, in a suit upon a creditor's bill, there being no allegation that the funds were not safe in the marshal's hands, supported by affidavit, nor that the notice of the motion was served on him, and no evidence of collusion between the claimant of the property and the marshal, nor that the marshal was not responsible, the court refused to grant such an order. Day v. Emerson, 5 Biss., 56.

§ 811. The marshal is personally answerable under the terms of rule 41 of the supreme court, and of rule 158 of the district court of the United States for the southern district of New York, for failing to pay moneys attached by him forthwith into court; and the responsibility of the deputy is no less stringent. The Bark Laurens, Abb. Adm., 508; United States v. The Brig Lawrence, 7 N. Y. Leg. Obs., 174.

§ 812. Acts after expiration of term.—A marshal has the power to amend his return to process after his office has expired. Until a true return be made, the process, under the act of September 24, 1789 (1 U. S. Stat. at Large, 88), must be regarded as still in the hands of the outgoing marshal. Cushing v. Laird, 4 Ben., 70.

§ 813. A marshal whose time has expired is, for the performance of certain duties, still an officer. United States v. Strobach, 4 Woods, 592.

§ 814. If the marshal die, is removed from office, or his commission expires, he has no power to sell if he has made a levy, but another execution must issue to his successor. Stewart v. Hamilton, 4 McL., 534.

§ 815. A marshal, like a sheriff, is bound, after the expiration of his term of office, to complete an execution which has come to his hands during his term; and an execution is never completed until the money is made and paid over to the plaintiff, if it is practicable to make it. McFarland v. Gwin, 3 How., 717.

§ 816. The removal of a marshal before he has sold real estate on execution in his hands destroys his right to proceed; and a sale of land after such removal is null and void.   United States v. Bank of Arkansas, Hemp., 460.

§ 817. The removal of a marshal would not affect his right to sell personal property in his possession and for which he is answerable. *Ibid.*

§ 818. Deputy.—A person was regularly appointed by a late marshal, and duly sworn as a deputy, but no return was made by the marshal to the district judge of the appointment. Such omission held not to affect the legality of the service of subpoenas nor the right of the deputy to his fees. Wintermute v. Smith, 1 Bond., 210.

§ 819. A deputy marshal is an officer of the United States, authorized to serve process, and resistance to him is prohibited by the twenty-second section of act of April 30, 1790 (1 U. S. Stat. at Large, 117). United States v. Tinklepaugh, 3 Blatch., 425.

§ 820. A prison-bounds bond may be assigned by a deputy marshal. Scott v. Wise, 1 Cr. C. C., 473.

§ 821. A sale of treasury notes by a marshal for currency, at eight per cent. premium, and a payment of his deputy in such currency, is a violation of the law. United States v. Patterson, 3 McL., 53.

§ 822. Where a writ of *ca. resp.* comes to the hands of a deputy marshal, who arrests the debtor, and the debtor thereupon pays to the deputy the amount of the debt for which he was sued, and the officer discharges the debtor from custody and returns the writ, "debt and costs satisfied," this is not an official act which binds the principal. The deputy marshal is a mere ministerial officer, and he has no right to adjust the debt and make himself responsible to the plaintiff. He is bound to pursue the mandate of the writ, and that requires him to arrest the debtor and take bail. The discharge of the debtor from custody without taking bail is a misfeasance in office for which his principal, the marshal, is responsible; but he is only responsible to the extent of the injury done to the plaintiff. If the return of the deputy shows that no bail was taken, and the plaintiff, by taking out other process, could have secured his debt, the loss of the debt to the plaintiff is not the necessary legal consequence of the conduct of the deputy, and no injury, in a legal sense, is done to the plaintiff. United States v. Moore, 2 Marsh., 317.

§ 823. A plaintiff has a right to direct a deputy marshal to receive a certain description of money in satisfaction of an execution; but the deputy then acts as agent of the plaintiff and not of the marshal. If, therefore, the plaintiff, when he does this, gives to the deputy marshal other instructions, which are disobeyed, the marshal himself is not responsible, but the plaintiff must look to the deputy. Gwin v. Buchanan, 4 How., 1.

§ 824. A deputy marshal is an officer of the court, amenable to its jurisdiction for malfeasance in office by summary order or attachment for contempt. The Bark Laurens, Abb. Adm., 508; United States v. The Brig Lawrence, 7 N. Y. Leg. Obs., 174.

§ 825. A marshal is answerable for the acts of his deputy done *colore officii* although without his knowledge or recognition; and in respect to moneys collected or taken by the deputy, the party entitled to them can have his remedy by process of attachment against the marshal personally. The Bark Laurens, Abb. Adm., 508; United States v. The Brig Lawrence, 7 N. Y. Leg. Obs., 174.

§ 826. A marshal is responsible for the defaults and misfeasances of his deputies, but the keeper of a state jail is neither in fact nor in law his deputy, and the marshal is not liable for the escape of a prisoner committed to the custody of such keeper. Randolph v. Donaldson,* 9 Cr., 76.

§ 827. A marshal may appoint a deputy to perform a particular service upon general principles; and under section 788 of the Revised Statutes, where by the laws of a state a sheriff may appoint a person to perform a special service, the marshal has the same authority. Such appointee is an officer *de facto*, and a person summoned by him cannot dispute his authority for the reason that he has not taken the oath of office. Hyman v. Chales,* 12 Fed. R., 855.

§ 828. A marshal is responsible for the acts of his deputies while acting in the line of their duty, but beyond this he is not responsible. Where a deputy received the principal part of the amount due on a judgment, after the return of the execution, when he had no authority to receive it, the marshal cannot be held responsible. But as the deputy has received the money under the assumed authority of the process of the court, he may be ordered to pay it over to the plaintiff, and in case of his refusal so to do he may be attached. Bagley v. Yates,* 3 McL., 465.

§ 829. A marshal is answerable for the misconduct of his deputy. If the deputy, who served a writ of replevin and took the statutory bond, erased the name of the principal without the direction of some one having authority, he violated a plain duty and his principal is liable. But if the attorney for the plaintiff gives such directions to the deputy as are calculated to mislead him, the marshal is not chargeable. So, where the deputy marshal took a bond offered by the defendant, signed by himself and a surety, to the plaintiff's attorney, who objected to the surety and stated that the bond would be satisfactory with a certain surety's name on it, but that he would not have the plaintiff on the bond at all, and the deputy, after the bond had been executed by the proposed surety, told the plaintiff that his name was not desired on the bond at all, and the plaintiff, in the deputy's presence, erased his name, thus rendering the bond void, it was held that if the erasure was found by the jury to have been made in consequence of the direction of the attorney, the marshal would not be liable. Rogers v. The Marshal, 1 Wall., 644.

§ **880.** A marshal may depute a person specially to execute a process or arrest a vessel. The Tug E. W. Gorgas, 10 Ben., 460.

§ **881.** Under the laws of New York, a sheriff or under-sheriff, by instrument in writing, may depute persons to do particular acts, which term includes the service of writs, and a marshal of a court of the United States has the same power. *Ibid.*

§ **882. Powers of a sheriff.**— Under section 788, Revised Statutes, the marshals in each state, in executing the laws of the United States, have the same powers as sheriffs in executing the laws of the state. United States v. Harden, 10 Fed. R., 802; 4 Hughes, 455.

§ **883.** It seems that by virtue of section 788 of the Revised Statutes, which is a re-enactment of statutes 1861, chapter 25, section 7 (12 Stat., p. 282), and that again a re-enactment of statutes 1795, chapter 36, section 9 (1 Stat., p. 425), marshals have such powers as sheriffs had on the 29th day of July, 1861, the date of the passage of said act of 1861, and such powers are not affected by a restrictive state statute passed in 1877. Such acts of congress are, however, empowering and not restrictive statutes, and it is not within their purview to take away or limit the powers of important executive officers. The Tug E. W. Gorgas, 10 Ben., 460.

V. MISCELLANEOUS.

§ **884. Failure to take oath.**— Under the ordinance of the constitution of Missouri, popularly called the "ousting ordinance," providing for the taking of an oath of loyalty by officers of the state, or of a municipal corporation, and vacating the offices of those who failed to do so, the officers of the city of Ste Genevieve having failed to take the prescribed oath, their official existence came to an end. Welch v. Ste Genevieve, 10 Am. L. Reg. (N. S.), 513; 1 Dill., 130; 14 Int. Rev. Rec., 93.

§ **885.** Where a notary public falsely and corruptly certifies to the execution of a deed by a party not before him, he is liable in damages to the purchaser of property under such deed, but not to his grantee or assignee. Ware v. Brown, 2 Bond, 267.

§ **886. Wrongful acts.**— Where gold certificates were taken to the sub-treasury to be exchanged for gold, and, upon a representation that it was necessary, were left over night for examination, and the officer receiving said certificates treated them as though received from a party indebted to him for government funds lent said party, and canceled and transmitted them to Washington, the government is not relieved of its obligation incurred to the owner of the certificates to pay their amount in coin, by the wrongful act of its officer subsequent to the receipt of said certificates. Bank of Boston v. United States, 10 Ct. Cl., 519; United States v. State Bank, 6 Otto, 30.

§ **887.** The collector of a port is liable where goods, deposited in a warehouse under the act of August 6, 1846 (9 U. S. Stat. at Large, 53), are lost in consequence of his personal negligence. Such negligence cannot be inferred from the mere loss of the goods. He is not liable for the negligence of his subordinates. *Quere,* whether in an action against the storekeeper or subordinate officer in charge of the goods, his negligence could be inferred from their loss. Brissac v. Lawrence, 2 Blatch., 121.

§ **888.** The secretary of war had no authority in 1818, under any act of congress, or the army regulations, to appoint an agent of fortifications. United States v. Maurice, 2 Marsh, 97 (§§ 8–17).

§ **889. Commissioners or board of supervisors** of a county, in the exercise of their general powers as such, have no authority to subscribe stock to railroads, and bind the people of the county to pay bonds issued for that purpose, without special authority conferred upon them by the legislature. Sheboygan Co. v. Parker, 3 Wall., 93.

§ **840.** The presentation of a false claim against the government to a district or circuit court for approval is a presentation of such claim to an officer in the civil service of the United States, within the meaning of section 5438, Revised Statutes. United States v. Strobach, 4 Woods, 592.

§ **841.** A commissioner has no authority to make the warrant issued by him returnable before another commissioner. *In re* Crittenden, 2 Flip., 212.

§ 342. The power given to pilot commissioners by the act of the legislature of Oregon of October 28, 1868, to examine pilots, and grant or refuse them licenses, cannot be delegated. The California, 1 Saw., 596.

§ 343. Tax commissioners.— An act of congress of July 20, 1868 (15 Stats. at Large, 123), declaring "that the acts and proceedings which have been had or performed by any two of the tax commissioners, in and for the state of Arkansas, shall have the same force and effect as if had and performed by all three of said commissioners," does not give validity to the acts of two commissioners unless there were three commissioners in office. Schenk v. Peay, 1 Dill., 267; 1 Ch. L. N., 363; 10 Int. Rev. Rec., 54.

§ 344. The shipping commissioner has the power to appoint clerks and deputies. under section 4505, Revised Statutes. In re Accounts of the Shipping Commissioner of the Port of New York, 16 Blatch., 93.

§ 345. A magistrate is a person intrusted with power, as a public civil officer. Gordon v. Hobart, 2 Sumn., 401.

§ 346. An overseer of a road in Virginia, who has not been notified of his appointment, is not liable to the penalty of the act of Virginia of January 5, 1786. United States v. Custis, 1 Cr. C. C., 417.

§ 347. A justice of the peace in the District of Columbia is not an officer, judicial or executive, of the government of the United States, and is liable to militia duty. Wise v. Withers, 1 Cr. C. C., 262.

§ 348. A judgment against an officer cannot be binding upon the state as a matter adjudicated between the state and the plaintiff. Adams v. Bradley, 5 Saw., 217.

§ 349. The publication of advertisements by the superintendent of Indian affairs for Oregon in two newspapers, when such publication was authorized by the general order signed by the commissioner of Indian affairs and directed by the predecessor of the superintendent, was held to be authorized by the secretary of interior under section 3828 of the Revised Statutes, and the expense was allowed as a credit to said superintendent. United States v. Odeneal,* 7 Saw.. 431.

§ 350. A levee board being incorporated by a statute of the state of Mississippi, and the offices of commissioners, secretary and treasurer of said board being abolished by a subsequent act of the legislature, and the auditor of public accounts and the treasurer of the state being constituted and appointed the levee board by said act, "it being the intent and purpose of this act to substitute the auditor of the state and the treasurer thereof, ex officio, as such commissioners, secretary and treasurer" of said board, etc., it was held that the statute, while it abolished the offices of the commissioners who previously constituted the bond, did not dissolve or extinguish the corporation, but merely substituted the state treasurer and the auditor of accounts as the members of that corporation, and that a suit having been commenced against the old board could be prosecuted against the new one, and that a motion to dismiss the bill because the levee board had been abolished should be overruled, and that the treasurer and auditor describing themselves by their individual names as treasurer and auditor respectively, and also as ex officio the levee board, could appeal from a final decree in said suit. Hemingway v. Stansell, 16 Otto, 399.

§ 351. Under the acts of congress the postmaster-general has power to discontinue a postoffice, notwithstanding the postmaster has been appointed by the president, by and with the advice and consent of the senate; the incumbent accepting the appointment subject to the legal contingency that the postoffice may be discontinued. In such event he ceases to be postmaster, because there is no longer a postoffice at the place. Ware v. United States, 4 Wall., 617.

§ 352. An appointment of a judge, by a military governor of Louisiana, during the war is purely military, and is subject to revocation whenever in the judgment of the military governor it is either necessary or expedient. When the constitution was adopted during the war, under military orders, and Hahn was elected governor, he had as military governor the same right as his predecessor to revoke the appointment. If the situation was changed, and the civil constitution of the state was in full operation, independent of military control, the authority derived from the appointment of the military governor ceased of necessity. Handlin v. Wickliffe, 12 Wall., 173.

§ 353. Custom-house officers have an inchoate interest in a forfeiture upon a seizure, but it may be defeated by a remission by the secretary of the treasury. They cannot be said to have a vested right upon condemnation, but their interest continues conditional, and the condemnation only ascertains and determines the fact, on which the right is consummated, should no remission take place. Such a remission, in an action against a marshal for failure to levy a venditioni exponas, was said to operate as a supersedeas to the execution, and the marshal was held not liable. United States v. Morris,* 10 Wheat., 246.

§ **354. Judicial functions.**— The act of congress of 2d March, 1867, supplementary to the several former acts abolishing imprisonment for debt, in its concluding words provides, "but all such proceedings shall be had before some one of the commissioners appointed by the United States circuit court to take bail and affidavits." The objection that these words confer an independent judicial function, and that congress cannot constitutionally make such a function exercisable by any officer who is not appointed by the president with the consent of the senate, cannot prevail. *In re* Russell *v.* Thomas,* 10 N. B. R., 14; 10 Phila., 289.

§ **355.** The action of two out of three commissioners, to all of whom was confided a power to be exercised, cannot be upheld when the third took no part in the transaction, and was ignorant of what was done, gave no implied assent, and was neither consulted by them, nor had any opportunity to exert his legitimate influence in the determination of the course to be pursued. Peay *v.* Schenck, 1 Woolw., 175.

§ **356.** Where the law required a board of three commissioners, and the third commissioner, although nominated and confirmed, did not qualify or enter upon the duties of his office, there was no board of commissioners in existence. *Ibid.*

§ **357. Under the organic law of the territory of Utah** the territorial attorney-general and not the district attorney of the United States is the proper person to prosecute offenses against the laws of the territory. Snow *v.* United States,* 18 Wall., 317.

§ **358.** The territorial marshal of Utah is not a federal officer, and his bailiwick being co-extensive with the territory, he is not therefore a township, district or county officer. He is included amongst "all officers not herein otherwise provided for," and must be nominated, and, by and with the advice and consent of the legislative council, appointed by the governor. (Organic Act, sec. 7.) The Utah statute providing for the election of a marshal by vote of both houses of the legislative assembly, so far as it conflicts with the organic act, is null and void. One commissioned as marshal by the governor, therefore, will be recognized as *de facto* territorial marshal, rather than one elected by the legislative assembly. Duncan *v.* McAllister,* 1 Utah T'y, 81.

§ **359. A collector of internal revenue** cannot revise nor refuse to enforce an assessment regularly made by the assessor in the exercise of the latter's jurisdiction. The duties of the collector in the enforcement of the tax assessed are purely ministerial. Erskine *v.* Hohnbach, 14 Wall., 618.

§ **360. Special treasury agents** charged with the duty of collecting "abandoned or captured property" were required to pay into the treasury of the United States the proceeds of property sold by them as abandoned or captured, and they transcended their powers when they assumed to surrender such property which came into their hands, or to distribute its proceeds after sale to those claiming them. But where these duties were disregarded, and the proceeds paid to persons falsely pretending to be the owners of the property, the real owner has no right of action against the government on account of such wrongful act of said agents. Spencer *v.* United States,* 8 Ct. Cl., 288.

§ **361. A receiver of public money** is individually responsible for all money received in his public capacity. And when the action against him is for money had and received, and the account charges money and stock, it is held that stock is receivable as money at par, and that where the balance claimed is reduced by the verdict of the jury, which is for money only, below the amount of cash claimed, the just inference is that the stock balance has been extinguished by the vouchers produced on the trial in the court below. Walton *v.* United States,* 9 Wheat., 651.

§ **362. The officers of the quartermaster's department** at Key West had no right during the war to hire for the United States premises, the title to which was invalid by circumstances known to the officers at the time the lease was made. And the United States did not become by such action of said officers parties to the lease nor liable thereupon. (PECK, J., dissented.) Filor *v.* United States,* 8 Ct. Cl., 25.

§ **363.** An acting assistant quartermaster at Key West cannot bind the United States to a lease of premises for the use of the quartermaster's department, or any branch of it, without the approval of the quartermaster-general. Until such approval, his action fixes no liability on the government. It matters not that such lease was approved by the commanding officer at Key West. Nor can the unauthorized acts of such officers estop the government from insisting on their invalidity, however beneficial they may have proved. Filor *v.* United States, 9 Wall., 45.

§ **364. Pay and expenses.**— If the duties and services of an appointee by the secretary of the navy turn out to be more onerous, important and expensive than was contemplated when the contract between him and the secretary was made, they nevertheless cannot change that contract, but they afford a good reason for modifying it or making a new one, or for the exercise of the secretary's discretion in making allowances to meet these unexpected contingencies. United States *v.* McCall,* Gilp., 563.

§ 365. The items in an account of an agent suspended by one secretary of the navy may be allowed by a subsequent one, but once allowed, they cannot afterwards be brought into question by the United States. *Ibid.*

§ 366. A United States commissioner is a magistrate of the government, exercising functions of the highest importance to the administration of justice. He is an examining and committing magistrate, bound to hear complaints of the commission of offenses against the laws of the United States in his district, to cause the offender to be arrested, to examine into the matters charged, to summon witnesses for the government and for the accused, and to commit for trial or discharge from arrest according as the evidence tends or fails to support the accusation. United States *v.* Schumann, 2 Abb., 523; 7 Saw., 489.

§ 367. While a charge is under investigation before either the commissioner or the grand jury, the district attorney has no absolute power over the case. His duty requires him to attend the sessions of the grand jury, to advise that body upon points desired, to examine witnesses, and to draw indictments when directed. But he cannot control the action of that body. After indictment, and before trial, his authority may be said to be absolute. He can enter a *nolle prosequi*, even without the consent of the court. After trial has commenced, he can do so with the consent of the defendant. United States *v.* Schumann, 2 Abb., 523; 7 Saw., 439.

§ 368. United States commissioners are not conservators of the peace and have no control of police regulations in their districts except where express powers are conferred by a statute of the United States. Their powers and duties are confined in criminal matters to those necessarily exercised as examining and committing magistrates, and within this jurisdiction they must conform, as near as may be, to the forms and procedure required by law of justices of the peace. The powers and duties of a commissioner are co-extensive with the limits of the judicial district in which he is appointed, and he may commit a prisoner to the jailer of the county in which the United States court is held, but it is best to commit to the jailer of the county of residence, that the prisoner may have convenient opportunity of procuring bail. If the commitment be to the last-mentioned jail without any qualification, the commissioner has no further control over the prisoner except to admit him to bail. Under a statute of the state of North Carolina, justices of the peace have power to let to bail persons committed to prison charged with crime not capital, and the recognizance must be filed with the clerk of the court of trial. Commissioners have similar powers in United States cases. When a prisoner desires to give bail, the commissioner need not go to the jail, but may issue a warrant to the marshal or his deputy to bring the prisoner before him at some convenient place for the purpose of accepting bail. United States *v.* Harden, 10 Fed. R., 802; 4 Hughes, 455.

§ 369. A navy agent may at the time of being such be also an acting purser. There is no law which prohibits a person from holding two offices at the same time. United States *v.* White, Taney, 152.

§ 370. The office of navy agent had no existence prior to the passage of the act of March 3, 1809. Under the act of 1809, the phrase "permanent agents" signifies those appointed by the president with the advice and consent of the senate. And a navy agent appointed by the president with the advice and consent of the senate is such a permanent agent, whether he is a foreign or domestic agent, and his compensation is regulated by said act. Armstrong *v.* United States,* Gilp., 399.

§ 371. A superintendent of Indian affairs has a right, under section 3828 of the Revised Statutes, to advertise for proposals to furnish supplies, in newspapers in which he was authorized to publish such advertisements, by a general order made and issued by the secretary of the interior and signed by the commissioner of Indian affairs, and directed to the predecessor of such superintendent. And the expense of such advertisements must be allowed such superintendent in his accounts. United States *v.* Odeneal, 10 Fed. R., 616; 7 Saw., 451.

§ 372. An Indian agent cannot exceed the limit of an amount which he was authorized to expend in the erection of an agency house, and if he does so exceed his instructions the loss must fall on him, although his disbursements were made with economy. United States *v.* Duval,* Gilp., 856.

§ 373. An Indian agent cannot charge the United States for money expended on land reserved to the Indians, and upon their credit. *Ibid.*

§ 374. A sub-Indian agent cannot draw drafts so as to charge the United States. Jackson *v.* United States,* 1 Ct. Cl., 260; Fremont *v.* United States,* 2 Ct. Cl., 461.

§ 375. The statute of Nevada in regard to the duties of the attorney-general, defining them to be to appear and defend the interests of the state in those cases where the state may be rightfully sued, may make it desirable that he should appear and defend officers of the state or even others where the interests of the state may be affected; but it does not authorize parties to sue the state nor does his appearance confer jurisdiction to determine the rights of the state, and the state is not concluded by a judgment in any such case. Adams *v.* Bradley, 5 Saw., 217.

§ **376. Compensation.**— A suit cannot be maintained by an agent employed by a marshal for services rendered in taking care of a bankrupt's estate. If the marshal fraudulently refuses to pay his agent for such services he may apply to a court of bankruptcy for relief. Rumsey *v.* Wolcott,* 1 Wyom. T'y, 259. See FEES AND SALARIES.

§ **377.** An agent not appointed under the act of congress of March 3, 1809, but appointed under a general authority, lawfully exercised by the secretary of the navy, to appoint agents of the department, is not, properly speaking, a navy agent nor an officer of the United States, but the agent of the secretary or his department, and his duties and compensation must be regulated by the agreement between him and the secretary. United States *v.* McCall,* Gilp., 563.

§ **378.** A person was appointed a special agent of the interior department without compensation, except such fees as were then or might thereafter be authorized by said department, to collect and pay over to the Indians, whose attorney he was, their claims for military services. As it does not appear that he was appointed in pursuance of any law of congress, or that his compensation was fixed by law, but that he was to be paid out of funds collected for the Indians as the secretary of the interior might allow, his appointment being limited in its duration and specific in its objects, he did not become by such appointment, or by a bond given by him for the faithful performance of his duties, an officer within the meaning of the sixteenth section of the act of 1846. Case of J. W. Wright,* 13 Op. Att'y Gen'l, 588.

§ **379.** In a suit against a deputy postmaster on his bond, to recover amount due upon certain quarterly accounts, the defendant, in his rejoinder to plaintiff's replication, averred that, but for the unlawful discontinuance of the postoffice, mailable matter would have passed through sufficient to have authorized an allowance of commissions at the rate of $2,000 per annum, and that said commissions so wrongfully withheld from him exceeded the balance claimed by the United States. The plaintiff demurred. *Held,* that the admission that the commissions were wrongfully withheld meant that the defendant was wrongfully prevented from earning commissions; that defendant's claim was a claim for damages for such wrongful prevention; that no commissions could have been earned in this case, and that the department possessed no authority to make any other allowance; and further, that, as a claim for damages, defendant's claim was required to be presented to the auditor of the postoffice, and not having been so presented and disallowed, it could not be sustained, unless it appeared that the defendant was then in possession of vouchers not before in his power to procure, and that he was prevented from presenting the claim for credit to the auditor by unavoidable accident. Ware *v.* United States, 4 Wall., 617.

§ **380.** In an action against an officer of the army to recover money for which he has failed to account, to enable him to obtain credit for extra compensation for disbursements made, or for extra services performed by him, he must show that such disbursements or such services were such as were not ordinarily attached to the duties of his office, and that such disbursements were made, or such services performed, under the sanction of the government, or under circumstances of peculiar emergency, such as rendered the extra labor and responsibility assumed by said officer necessary. United States *v.* Ripley,* 7 Pet., 18.

§ **381.** A navy agent is entitled to compensation for the distribution of stores furnished by the government, and not purchased by him; to a reasonable charge for clerk hire; to damages entailed by reason of the protest of drafts not paid, under a mistake of fact, by the government, and to compensation for articles purchased by him and received by the government, although purchased without authority, but not for services after the revocation of his appointment, or the expenses of his return trip home. Armstrong *v.* United States,* Gilp., 399.

§ **382.** The secretary of the board of commissioners of the navy hospital fund was held to be entitled to compensation beyond his salary for services outside of his regular duties as secretary, such as commissions on money disbursed by him of a fund under the control of the board. And the approval of his claim by the board of commissioners was not an indispensable preliminary to his setting it up against a demand of the United States. United States *v.* Fillebrown,* 7 Pet., 28.

§ **383.** The relator recovered upon a writ of *quo warranto,* and a judgment of ouster was rendered against the defendant. A writ of error was sued out, and bond given operating as a *supersedeas.* The relator applied for a *mandamus,* which was refused. The writ of error being dismissed, and the judgment of ouster being enforced, the relator was installed in office. He then sued on the bond to recover the portion of salary received by the defendant while he was in office. *Held,* that he was entitled to judgment, and that the measure of damages was the amount of salary so received by the defendant. United States *v.* Addison,* 6 Wall., 291.

§ **384.** When a charge is prohibited to a public agent by the law it cannot be allowed, but where there is no such prohibition, but the objection or defect is the want of express authority for it, and it is therefore not a subject of strict legal right, yet if it is supported by a clear equity arising from a *bona fide* performance of a service, or the *bona fide* expenditure of money for the public service, there is a discretion properly and necessarily vested in the head of the proper department to allow the charge. Whenever and wherever the head of a department, in the exercise of his discretion, may refuse the allowance, and the court and jury before whom the case shall come for trial think that he ought to have made the allowance, they may do it. United States v. Duval,* Gilp., 356.

§ 385. An Indian agent who acts as a commissioner in negotiating a treaty, at the request of the secretary of war, and not volunteering his services, is entitled to compensation for such extra service. *Ibid.*

§ 386. A paymaster of the marine corps, under the act of 1814, was entitled to a certain sum in lieu of all emoluments, and was not entitled to the pay, etc., of a major of cavalry. United States v. Kuhn,* 4 Cr. C. C., 401.

§ 387. A clerk in the navy department, who has, for years, under the direction of the department, performed certain duties in the payment of pensioners and in navy disbursements, for which he has received, during the greater part of that time, extra compensation in addition to his pay, but which extra compensation was, upon the settlement of his accounts, refused him for the latter period of his services, is, in an action by the United States against him for the balance charged against him, entitled to credit for such services. United States v. Macdaniel,* 7 Pet., 1.

§ 388. Where an agent appointed by the secretary of the navy under his general authority had his compensation fixed by his contract with the secretary, and having found his duties more onerous, important and expensive than contemplated, had made charges in his accounts rendered to the secretary for an increased allowance, which items in his account were suspended, but afterwards allowed by a subsequent secretary, and he had upon the faith of this change of contract gone on to render his service and to disburse his money in the public service, the inquiry as to his compensation is not confined to the terms of his original contract, but is extended to the right of the succeeding secretary to make a new contract or arrangement with the agent, whether he has done so, the discretion exercised by said secretary, and whether he was too liberal or not in the terms he gave to his agent. United States v. McCall,* Gilp., 568.

§ 389. Accounts.— In an action on an Indian agent's bond, the agent was allowed credit in his account for the price of telegraphic messages paid in good faith, without notice of price agreed upon between the government and the telegraph company, also for price paid interpreters in good faith under instructions previously given, at the rate of $500 a year, without knowledge of the change in the law fixing their compensation at $400 a year, and for salary from the time he actually went to work for the government. United States v. Roberts,* 10 Fed. R., 540.

§ 390. A receiver of public moneys at a local land office is not entitled, when sued on his official bond, to set off against the government a rejected account for unauthorized clerk hire, fuel, lights, and for transmitting money to the proper government depositary. His claim for office rent may, under circumstances, be allowed as an equitable credit under the act of March 3, 1797. United States v. Lowe,* 1 Dill., 585.

§ 391. Under the fourth section of the act of congress of 3d of March, 1797, no claim for a credit shall be admitted upon the trial, in suits between the United States and individuals, except such as have been presented to the accounting officers of the treasury, and by them disallowed in whole or in part. United States v. Duval,* Gilp., 356.

§ 392. A marshal who, in taking the census, advances money to pay his deputies, after attempting to obtain it from the government, may retain the amount thus paid, out of public money in his hands, although the government has paid the deputies a second time, it having had previous notice of the payment by the marshal. United States v. Ten Eyk,* 4 McL., 119.

§ 393. Marshals, like other officers, are required to render their accounts quarter-yearly to the accounting officers, with the vouchers necessary to the correct and prompt settlement thereof, within the time prescribed by law. In an action by the United States on an official bond, claims for credit cannot be admitted unless they have been duly presented to the accounting officers of the treasury, and have been by them disallowed. Watkins v. United States, 9 Wall., 759.

§ 394. The account of every revenue officer made up and adjusted by the officers of the United States is *prima facie* evidence of the amount due by such revenue officer to the government, subject, however, to be corrected by competent evidence. United States v. Gaussen, 19 Wall., 198.

§ 395. Accounts rendered by a revenue officer to the government are competent evidence against his surety in a suit on official bond. *Ibid.*

§ **396.** The agent of the United States must act as strictly within his authority as the agent of an individual. He has no claim on the government for expenditures exceeding the sum limited by his instructions. United States v. Duval, Gilp., 376.

§ **397.** In an action by the United States against a disbursing officer or agent, or other individual, for the recovery of moneys claimed of him, the defendant is entitled, on the trial, to the allowance of all equitable demands of his against the United States, if the same have been submitted to the proper accounting officers of the government, and disallowed by them. United States v. Collier, 3 Blatch., 325.

§ **398.** Where the treasury department have made up several accounts against a collector, one after suit brought against him, stating as balance due the department more than was found due, and a payment was received from the defendant, overpaying the principal found due on the account as it then stood, the department has no right to restate the account, and claim interest on the amount due the United States, when the suit was brought to augment the account. The first section of the act of March 3, 1797 (1 U. S. Stat. at Large, 512), has no application to such collector. *Ibid.*

§ **399.** An officer of the government cannot pay moneys of the United States to a creditor of the United States without an order from the proper department, and such voluntary payment cannot be pleaded by such officer as a defense, nor as an equitable set-off to a suit on his bond. United States v. Keehler, 9 Wall., 83.

§ **400. Disbursements** for purchases of clothing, groceries, stores, etc., may be directed by the navy department to be made by the navy agent at navy yards where there was such an officer stationed, or by the purser assigned to that station. Strong v. United States, 6 Wall., 788.

§ **401.** Unofficial letters of subordinate officers of the treasury are not admissible in evidence, in suits against disbursing officers, to contradict or explain the official adjustment of accounts as shown in the duly certified transcripts. *Ibid.*

§ **402.** Disbursing agents are required to settle their receipts and disbursements with the accounting officers of the treasury, and their private books are inadmissible to control that official adjustment. *Ibid.*

§ **403.** Under the acts of congress (5th, 6th and 10th sections of act of August 6, 1846, 9 U. S. Stat. at Large, 59; act of March 3, 1857, 11 U. S. Stat. at Large 249; act of July 17, 1862, 12 U. S. Stat. at Large, 593; act of May 2, 1866, 14 U. S. Stat. at Large, 41; and act of June 14, 1866 14 U. S. Stat. at Large, 64), and circulars of the treasury department of May 27, 1857, October 27. 1862, and of November 10, 1866, an assistant treasurer of the United States is not liable to a disbursing officer for moneys of the United States deposited with him. The disbursing officer may check upon such fund in favor of persons to whom payment is to be made pursuant to law and instructions, but said fund remains the money of the United States. Nor does the fact that such disbursing officer has a second time paid into the treasury of the United States the moneys so deposited create any liability on the part of said assistant treasurer, or give said disbursing officer any right of action against him. Morgan v. Van Dyck,* 7 Blatch., 147.

§ **404.** Under the act of March 27, 1804, the commandant of a navy yard was not required to make navy disbursements. United States v. Macdaniel,* 7 Pet., 1.

§ **405.** Where an officer of the government has money committed to his charge, with a duty of disbursing or paying it out as occasion may require, he cannot be charged with interest on such money until it is shown that he has failed to pay when such occasion required him to do so, or has failed to account, when required by the government, or to pay over or transfer the money on some lawful order. United States v. Denvir, 10 Otto, 536.

§ **406.** The surveyors of public lands are disbursing officers under the provisions of the act of congress. Farrar v. United States, 5 Pet., 373.

§ **407. Army officers.**—It seems that a subordinate military officer, acting in obedience to the orders of his superior, is not liable for an unlawful arrest. If liable, his liability cannot be extended beyond his delivery of the prisoner to the provost marshal. And under section 1 of the act of May 11, 1866 (14 Stat., 46), a military officer is protected by the order of the commander of the department, district or place within which the arrest was made from liability for such arrest. In this case the subordinate officer, acting in obedience to a general order of his department commander, was held not liable, but the commanding officer, not being shown to have acted in obedience to the order of any military superior, was held liable. McCall v. McDowell, Deady, 233.

§ **408.** An officer in command of a military station upon a United States military reservation has an equal right with town and village governments to impound and dispose, by settled rules and regulations, of animals running at large, and at least to retain possession of them until the owner of them enters into some satisfactory and binding arrangement or agreement in reference to the same. And a subordinate officer, taking such property in pursuance of the general orders of the officer in command, is not liable to the owner thereof. Brown v. Ilges,* 1 Wyom. T'y, 202.

§ 409. The destruction of cotton, under the orders of the rebel military authorities, for the purpose of preventing it from falling into the hands of the federal army, was an act of war upon the part of the military forces of the rebellion, for which the person executing such military orders was relieved from civil responsibility at the suit of the owner voluntarily residing at the time within the lines of the insurrection. Whether redress could be denied one who was to be deemed an enemy solely by reason of residence, pending the struggle in the insurrectionary district, but who was in fact a loyal citizen, quære. Ford v. Surget,* 18 Alb. L. J., 493.

§ 410. Certain army officers seized whisky in what they claimed was Indian country, when it was not Indian country, and where they were without authority. Their belief that they had authority constitutes no defense to an action of trespass against them. Whatever may be the rule in time of war and in the presence of actual hostilities, military officers can no more protect themselves than civilians in time of peace by orders emanating from a source which is itself without authority. Bates v. Clark, 5 Otto, 204.

§ 411. Under the eighth section of the act of 1838 (5 U. S. Stat. at Large, 212), a military force, by orders of the secretary of war, under instructions from the president, was placed at different points on the northern frontier "to prevent the violation and to enforce the due execution" of the act. The defendant, an officer in the army, was ordered on such duty, with instructions faithfully to execute the purposes of the act. Under such orders the defendant took possession of a vessel loaded with arms and munitions of war intended for the insurgents in Canada, though the vessel herself was not destined to pass the frontier. The vessel was wrecked and destroyed by a storm on the same night. Held, that though the officer had not the power of seizure of property, which the civil officers mentioned in the first section of the act had, he could, at least when necessary, take property as a precautionary measure to prevent an intended violation of the act, and detain it until an officer having the power to seize and hold it for the purpose of proceeding with it in the manner directed might be procured and act in the matter. And it not appearing that the loss of the vessel was in consequence of any want of ordinary care on his part, he was not liable for it. Stoughton v. Dimick, 3 Blatch., 356; 8 L. Rep., 557; 29 Vt., 535.

§ 412. An assistant quartermaster has no authority to lease lands for the use of his department, though he acted under direction of a military commander who approved his acts. The quartermaster-general only had power to approve such lease so as to make it binding, and without his approval the government is bound no more than it would have been had there been no agreement; and as the premises were so occupied during the rebellion, no action is maintainable therefor in the court of claims. Filor v. United States, 9 Wall., 48.

§ 413. Term of office.— Where an officer is appointed for a definite term, congress has no power to extend the term after the appointment; a renomination and concurrence by the senate would be necessary. Case of the District Attorney,* 7 Am. L. Reg. (N. S.), 786.

§ 414. Where a person holds an office during good behavior, with a fixed salary and certain fees annexed thereto, the tenure of the office cannot be altered without impairing the obligation of a contract. Allen v. McKeen, 1 Sumn., 276.

§ 415. The "tenure of civil office act" does not extend the term of any office the duration of which is limited by law. The term of office of a district attorney expires during the cession of the senate. A nomination to the office is sent to the senate, but it adjourns without action. A vacancy thus existing during the recess of the senate, the president can grant a commission to expire at the end of the next session of the senate, to fill this vacancy. Case of Pennsylvania District Attorney,* 12 Op. Att'y Gen'l, 469.

§ 416. As regards offices established under the government of the United States, the right of an incumbent of an office to continue therein after the expiration of his term, until the appointment of his successor, depends altogether on whether congress has provided that he may so continue; and where the legislature has not authorized the officer to hold over, his incumbency ceases at the end of his term. It seems, that even where an officer is authorized to thus hold over, his resignation, if accepted, would relieve him from official responsibility and discharge him from the office, though a successor were not appointed when the resignation took effect. Resignation of Office,* 14 Op. Att'y Gen'l, 259.

§ 417. Where a person is commissioned to hold the office of register "during the term of four years from the 2d day of March, 1845," his term includes the 2d March, 1849. The word "from" always excludes the day of date. Best v. Polk, 18 Wall., 112.

§ 418. All officers, except those in the judicial department, hold their offices during pleasure, and the president of the United States has power to remove them. Gratiot v. United States,* 1 Ct. Cl., 258.

§ 419. By the act creating the office of assessor of internal revenue, the incumbent holds during the pleasure of the appointing power; this is true of all cases where the law does not fix the term of office. United States v. Avery, Deady, 204.

§ 420. Congress, having the power to create an office, may prescribe the term for which it may be holden; and in such case there is no power of removal except by impeachment. *Ibid.*

§ 421. The district attorney in prize cases acts in his character as prosecuting officer. The Anna, The Annie Deas, The Revere, Bl. Pr. Cas., 387.

§ 422. The attorney for the United States is by law official master of suits prosecuted by the United States in the prize court, and has authority, at his discretion, to offer or withhold from the consideration of the court any particular of testimony relative to a prize suit in prosecution in court. The Peterhoff, Bl. Pr. Cas., 463.

§ 423. It is the duty of the district attorney to prosecute all suits, civil or criminal, in which the United States is concerned, within his district, and the court will not recognize such a suit as legally before them unless instituted and prosecuted by the district attorney. United States v. McAvoy, 4 Blatch., 418; 18 How. Pr., 380; United States v. Doughty, 7 Blatch., 424.

§ 424. The court has no power to require the appearance of the United States; he is not so far the officer of the court that the court can compel him to perform an official act of that kind. Fifth National Bank v. Long, 7 Biss., 502.

§ 425. It is within the power of the district attorney to have witnesses recognized to appear at the trial when he doubts whether they will be [present without such recognizance. United States v. Durling, 4 Biss., 509.

§ 426. The officers in the district attorney's office cannot compromise a case arising under the internal revenue law, such suit having been commenced. No compromise is effectual without the concurrence of the commissioner of internal revenue, the secretary of the treasury and the attorney-general. United States v. A Quantity of Distilled Spirits, 4 Ben., 349.

§ 427. The district attorney represents the United States, and the correspondence between him and the attorney-general is confidential in its nature and cannot be cited by third persons. United States v. Six Lots of Ground, 1 Woods, 234.

§ 428. The district attorney has exclusive control over and direction of the prosecution of offenders until they come under the control of the court, but after the case has become subject to judicial control, the district attorney acts with the express assent or tacit acquiescence of the court. United States v. Corrie,* 23 Law Rop., 145.

§ 429. Section 1030, Revised Statutes, directs that " no writ is necessary to bring into court any prisoner or person in custody, or for remanding from the court into custody, but the same shall be done on the order of the court or district attorney." This statute may be regarded a\ restrictive, and intended to exclude all officers of the government not mentioned. United States v. Harden, 10 Fed. R., 803; 4 Hughes, 455.

§ 430. It is not the official duty of a district attorney of the United States to attend on the examination, by a magistrate of a state, of a complaint preferred by an officer of the army against a citizen for violation of an act of congress; or to leave the place of his residence to assist such officer of the army in procuring evidence or otherwise preparing the case. District Attorney,* 6 Op. Att'y Gen'l, 218.

§ 431. By the practice of the United States courts, the public prosecutor represents the government in prosecutions, and protects its interests without advice from the court. Preliminary accusations of crime are submitted to his examination, and it is a part of his duty to determine whether the public interest requires that the testimony of an accomplice should be received; and in general, he must determine whether the conduct of the accomplice, in case he is received as a witness, and examined, was such as constitutes a compliance with the legal conditions which give him an equitable right to the executive clemency. United States v. Hartwell,* 12 Int. Rev. Rec., 50.

§ 432. The district attorney is the recognized officer of the government, through whom alone the court can have communication with the executive authorities of the government. United States v. Blaisdell, 8 Ben., 132; 9 Int. Rev. Rec., 82.

§ 433. The district attorney is the regular officer of the government, having charge of all its legal proceedings within his district, subject only to the general direction and supervision of the attorney-general. When other counsel are employed in these proceedings, it is to aid him in their management, not to assume his authority or direct his conduct. The Pueblo Case, 4 Saw., 553.

§ 434. A proceeding instituted by the district attorney for the benefit of the United States in his own name, though irregular, is not invalid. Benton v. Woolsey, 12 Pet., 27.

§ 435. A district attorney of the United States is liable for money actually received by him, or which has been lost by his unwarranted neglect; but he is not answerable for the default, inattention or frauds of the marshal. United States v. Ingersoll, Crabbe, 135.

§ 436. A federal district attorney has power, under the control of the court, at any time before a jury is impaneled, to enter a *nolle prosequi.* United States v. Stowell, 2 Curt., 153.

§ 437. When the decree of a judge raises a presumption against the jurisdiction of the courts of the United States, in cases of captures, it will not be improper for the district attorney to cause the necessary depositions to be taken *de bene esse*, to be used by the executive in case the appellant does not prosecute his appeal or the decree be affirmed. Capture within the United States,* 1 Op. Att'y Gen'l, 39.

§ 438. A district attorney of the United States may assure a counterfeiter who shall disclose his accomplices, and produce the plates and counterfeited paper, of a pardon; but the mere disclosure is not enough. Assurance of Pardon,* 1 Op. Att'y Gen'l, 77.

§ 439. It is the duty of United States district attorneys to attend all the courts of their respective districts when thereunto required by the government, whether such courts be state or federal. Duties of District Attorneys,* 2 Op. Att'y Gen'l, 818.

§ 440. The attorney of the United States for the District of Columbia is not bound, by the second section of the Maryland act of 1795, to order writs of *ca. sa.* for fines, etc., on the application of the marshal; nor can the marshal order them without the authority of the district attorney, who has a discretion in that respect which the marshal has no right to control. Levy Court v. Ringgold, 2 Cr. C. C., 659.

§ 441. There is no act of congress imposing upon the attorney of the United States for the District of Columbia the special duties imposed upon the attorney-general of Maryland and his deputies by the statutes of Maryland. *Ibid.*

§ 442. The district attorney of the District of Columbia is specially charged with the prosecution of all delinquents for crimes and offenses; and these duties do not end with the judgment or order of the court. He is bound to provide the marshal with all necessary process to carry into execution the judgment of the court. This falls within his general superintending authority over the prosecution. The Levy Court of Washington County v. Ringgold, 5 Pet., 451.

§ 443. No delivery of property on bail can legally be made in cases where the United States are a party, without due notice to the district attorney that he may have a hearing before the court. *Ex parte* Robbins, 2 Gall., 820.

§ 444. Acts of a de facto officer are valid so far as they concern the public, or the rights of third persons who have an interest in the things done. County of Ralls v. Douglass, 15 Otto 728.

§ 445. The acts of public officers, appointed or elected, are valid as to third persons, and cannot be questioned collaterally although they fail to observe the positive prescriptions of law to give a bond or take an oath before entering upon the exercise of their duties. But the decisions in relation to the acts of officers *de facto* are restricted to those who hold office under some degree of notoriety, or are in the exercise of continuous official acts, or are in possession of a place which has the character of a public office. Merchants called in by the collector to estimate the value of merchandise take no rank as public officers, and as to them the statute (act of March 2, 1799, sec. 20, 1 U. S. Stats. at Large, 641) is mandatory, and their acts without the sanction of an oath are void. Vaecari v. Maxwell, 8 Blatch., 368.

§ 446. One who was appointed to an office without authority, and who never performed any official duty as such officer, and never had the reputation of being such officer, is not an officer *de jure* or *de facto*. Schenk v. Peay, 1 Dill., 267; 1 Ch. L. N., 368; 10 Int. Rev. Rec., 54.

§ 447. A person convicted by a judge *de facto*, acting under color of officer, though not *de jure*, and detained in custody in pursuance of his sentence, cannot properly be discharged upon *habeas corpus*. Griffin's Case, Chase's Dec., 864; *In re* Griffin, 2 Am. L. T. (U. S.) Rep., 93.

§ 448. An appraiser is a *quasi* judge or legislative referee. If such an office has been even colorably created, and the incumbent has discharged *de facto* its duties, his acts, so far as the public or third persons are concerned, are as valid as if they were the acts of an appraiser *de jure*. Gibb v. Washington, 1 McAl., 430.

§ 449. Persons appointed as judges, under an act of the state of Oregon, of constitutionally created and existing courts, and acting as such judges, although the act authorizing said appointment be unconstitutional, and the appointees under it therefore not judges *de jure*, are nevertheless judges *de facto*, and their acts, while so in office, are held valid and binding as to third persons. And it appearing that the petitioner has been convicted of an offense charged against him in a court having jurisdiction of the subject-matter and the person, held by at least a *de facto* judge, he is not restrained of his liberty or adjudged to lose his life, so far as the court can inquire, without due process of law, and his petition for a *habeas corpus* is denied. *In re* Ah Lee, 5 Fed. R., 899; 6 Saw., 410.

§ 450. Where a person is the acting secretary of a territory, though not regularly appointed, a public obligation created by debts which would have been binding on the government if made by a regular secretary cannot lawfully or justly be repudiated on the mere ground that the secretary's title to the office was defective. The acts of an officer *de facto* are always held to be good where the public or third parties are concerned. The legality of his appointment can never be inquired into except upon *quo warranto* or some other proceeding to oust him, or else in a suit brought or defended by himself, which brings the very question whether he was an officer *de jure* directly in issue. Officers de Facto,* 9 Op. Att'y Gen'l, 482.

§ 451. If officers are elected, though irregularly, under a city charter, and are exercising powers thereunder, they are officers *de facto*, and their acts respecting the public are valid; but when a town organization is without legislative authority, the officers elected are neither officers *de jure* nor *de facto*. Welch v. Ste Genevieve, 10 Am. L. Reg. (N. S.), 512; 1 Dill., 130; 14 Int. Rev. Rec., 93.

§ 452. Where a marshal of the United States in Utah served the process in a suit for the foreclosure of a mortgage, made the sale under the decree, and executed a deed for the premises to the purchaser, under the understanding of the law then held, that he was the proper officer to perform such services, his acts were valid as being those of an officer *de facto*, although it was afterwards held by the supreme court of the United States that his authority extended only to cases where the United States were concerned. Hussey v. Smith, 9 Otto, 20.

OFFICIAL BONDS.

See BONDS.

OHIO.

See STATES.

OHIO RIVER.

See WATER-COURSES.

OPENING AND CLOSING.

See PRACTICE.

OPTIONS.

See CONTRACTS.

ORDERS.

See PRACTICE.

ORDINANCE OF 1787.

See CONSTITUTION AND LAWS.

ORDINANCES.

See CORPORATIONS.

OREGON.

See STATES.

OREGON LAND TITLES.

See LAND.

OYER.

See PLEADING.

OYSTER BEDS.

See CONSTITUTION AND LAWS; FISHERIES.

PARDON AND AMNESTY.

See CRIMES; WAR.

PAROL EVIDENCE.

See EVIDENCE.

PARTIES.

See PRACTICE.

PARTNERSHIP.*

[In Bankruptcy, see DEBTOR AND CREDITOR.]

I. FORMATION. WHAT CONSTITUTES.

SUMMARY — *Participation in profits,* §§ 1, 2, 4.— *By operation of law,* § 3.— *Statements and declarations,* §§ 5, 6.

§ 1. Participation in the profits of a business does not necessarily make one liable as a partner, but the fact of such participation is to be treated as presumptive evidence of a partnership. *In re* Francis. §§ 7, 8.

---

*Edited by CHARLES R. DARLING, ESQ., of the Boston Bar.

§ 2. By the terms of a written agreement between F. and a certain firm F. agreed to advance to the firm a certain sum of money and to keep the firm books, the firm to pay him twelve per cent. interest on the money (that being the highest legal rate of interest), and a certain proportion of the profits, but not less than a certain sum per month, as compensation for keeping the books. In a proceeding to hold F. as a partner for the debts of the firm, B., one of the partners, testified that F. was an actual partner as to the profits, though not in the losses, but that this fact did not appear in the written agreement because he held a clerkship in a bank which did not allow its employees to be engaged in any outside business. It appeared that once during the absence of B., F. had assumed control of the business without claiming to have any special authorization, although at the trial he produced a power of attorney under which he claimed to have acted. After the failure of the concern he made active efforts to induce the creditors to settle, making promises to one of them indicating some authority in the premises. The sum guarantied him as compensation for keeping the books seemed to be a fair compensation of itself, and the additional agreement for a percentage of the profits was apparently intended as a device to cover up a usurious loan or a partnership. In view of these circumstances, *held*, that the weight of evidence was in favor of the conclusion that F. was a partner, but if the evidence should be considered as evenly balanced, he should still be held as a partner, as the presumption of partnership, arising from participation in the profits, put the burden of proof upon him. *Ibid.*

§ 3. A partnership may arise between parties as to third persons by mere operation of law against the intention of the parties, but a partnership *inter sese* can exist only when such is the actual intention of the parties. Hazard *v.* Hazard, §§ 9–11.

§ 4. Mere participation in the profits will not make parties partners *inter sese*, unless they so intend it. Where, therefore, A. agreed with B. to run the latter's factories for a certain proportion of the profits of the business, it was held that there was no partnership as between the parties themselves, and that B. could not maintain a bill against A. for an account. *Ibid.*

§ 5. One not actually a partner will not render himself liable as such merely by stating to individuals that he is, if those seeking to hold him could not have known of such statements when they dealt with the firm. Benedict *v.* Davis, §§ 12–15.

§ 6. To rebut such statements as evidence of a partnership in fact, the contract made between the parties may be shown. *Ibid.*

[NOTES.— See §§ 16–62.]

IN RE FRANCIS.

(District Court for Oregon: 2 Sawyer, 286–301. 1872.)

Opinion by DEADY, J.

STATEMENT OF FACTS.— On October 29, 1872, the firm of Walter Brothers filed their petition in this court, alleging that at and between the dates hereinafter mentioned, W. W. Francis and W. A. Buchanan were partners, doing business at Portland, under the name and style of " W. A. Buchanan," and praying that said "firm and its members" be adjudged bankrupts for the following causes:

I. That said firm on September 10, 1871, made their promissory note, payable nine months after date, to the order of the petitioners, for $200, with interest at one per centum per month; and that on and after June 10, 1871, they fraudulently stopped payment of said note during a period of fourteen days.

II. That there is due the petitioners from said firm the sum of $500.29, the same being a balance of account for goods sold said firm between November 1, 1871, and October 1, 1872.

III. That on September 15, 1872, said firm, being then insolvent, paid $250 to a creditor thereof, to wit, Field & Frie, of San Francisco, with the intent to thereby give a preference to such creditor, and to defeat and delay the operation of the bankrupt act.

Buchanan made default, but on November 6, Francis answered, denying in effect that he was a partner with Buchanan in any of the alleged transactions or indebtedness. On November 12 and 13 the issue was tried by the court without a jury, and reserved for decision. The following facts are admitted or satisfactorily proven:

I. That the matters stated in the opinion, except as to the allegation of partnership between Francis' and Buchanan, are true.

II. That on January 24, 1871, Paul Richter and W. A. Buchanan were doing business as furniture dealers and upholsterers, under the firm name of Paul Richter & Co., and that on said day said firm made an agreement in writing with said Francis, to the effect following:

1. Francis agrees to advance said Richter & Co. the sum of $3,000 "in all before June, 1871, and to also keep the books of the firm for one year from said date," unless agreement terminated in the meantime.

2. Richter & Co. agree to pay Francis interest monthly at the rate of twelve per centum per annum upon said $3,000, and any further sum which he may advance to them, and also, "as remuneration for keeping the books of the firm, a sum equal to one-sixth of the net profits of the firm which shall be made during the year 1871."

3. If Francis is absent from the city, a deduction in proportion to the length of such absence to be made from his remuneration.

4. Agreement may be terminated at the pleasure of either party, on giving the other notice in writing, in which case the amount then due Francis to "be repaid in notes of firm of $1,000 each," payable at intervals of sixty and thirty days after such notice, with interest at the rate of twelve per centum per annum; and if agreement terminated before end of year 1871, Francis to be paid as compensation for keeping books a fair sum, "not less than $45 per month."

III. On August 1, 1871, Richter retired from the firm, and said written agreement was modified by a verbal one, then made between B. and F., to the effect that the latter should receive one-fourth of the net profits of the business for keeping the books, but not less than $25 per month, profits or no profits.

IV. For the five months ending December 31, 1871. Francis' share of the profits amounted to $389, $250 of which was added to the $3,000 due him, and a new note, payable on demand, taken by him for the amount, with interest at the rate aforesaid, signed W. A. Buchanan; but during the year 1872 the business made no profits.

V. Francis advanced the sum of $3,000 as per agreement, in January, 1871, and the $250 left in the business as aforesaid, and kept the books until September, 1872, during which time he loaned W. A. Buchanan, to be used in the business, from $2,000 to $2,500, on current account, which was secured by sufficient collaterals, and received from the business for all the money so advanced and loaned, interest monthly at the rate aforesaid, and $25 per month.

· VI. Francis was not known by the creditors of W. A. Buchanan to be a partner in the business, nor did he, during the time of his employment therein, volunteer any direction or advice in the conduct of it, except for a few weeks in 1872, while Buchanan was absent from the city, when he took into his custody the daily receipts of sales, and in some instances directed the salesman whom to credit and whom not; but during this time he had written authority from W. A. Buchanan to act as his agent, which authority, however, was not exhibited to said salesman, or any one else, so far as appears, until it was produced on the trial.

VII. That Buchanan was adjudged a bankrupt, individually, on the petition of one of his creditors, in this court on October 28; and that the liabilities incurred in the business at the time of such adjudication amounted to $13,000 or $14,000, and that Francis' claim against Buchanan for money loaned and advanced the business was at that time $5,200 or $5,300.

Upon this state of facts, counsel for the petitioners insist that, as to third persons, the law conclusively presumes that Francis was a partner in the firm of W. A. Buchanan, and therefore he is liable for its acts of bankruptcy and debts.

§ 7. *Participation in profits is only prima facie evidence that the party participating is a partner. Authorities reviewed.*

Under what circumstances a person not ostensibly a partner is nevertheless liable as one is a vexed question. In the language of a distinguished commentator, " The cases on this subject are not easily reconciled, nor is the language used in relation to it always admissible, or indeed intelligible." Parsons on Part., 66. And again (Id., 92), " The many cases cited in the notes to this chapter exhibit in strong light the difficulty, if not impossibility, of drawing from the decisions any definite principle or rule applicable with certainty to the question, ' Who are partners as to third persons?' "

In Waugh v. Carver, 2 H. Bl., 235, cited as the leading case on this subject (1 Smith's L. C., 831), L. Ch. J. Eyre held that while, upon the facts, the Carvers and Geslier were not partners *inter se*, and did not intend to be, still they were such as to third persons, because, by the arrangement between them, they agreed " to take a moiety of the profits of each other's business generally and indefinitely, as they should arise, at certain times agreed upon;" and upon the alleged authority of Grace v. Smith, 2 W. Bl., 998, he laid down the rule as follows: " He who takes a moiety of all the profits indefinitely shall, by operation of law, be made liable to losses, if losses arise, upon the principle that, by taking a part of the profits, he takes from the creditors a part of that fund which is the proper security to them for the payment of their debts." But in Grace v. Smith, *supra*, Ch. J. DeGrey says: " Every man who has a share of the profits of a trade ought also to bear his share of the loss. And if any one takes part of the profits, he takes part of that fund upon which the creditor of the trader relies for his payment. . . . I think the true criterion is to inquire whether Smith agreed to share the profits with Robinson, or whether he only relied upon these profits as a fund of payment."

It will be observed that this latter case makes no distinction between sharing the profits definitely or indefinitely, the point for which it was cited in Waugh v. Carver, *supra*, but does make an entirely different distinction, that is, between sharing in the profits of a trade or relying upon them for payment, in both of which cases the degree of indefiniteness may be the same. Again, the reason given in the distinction taken in Grace v. Smith is not sufficient, because, in point of fact, a person who shares in the profit of a trade, or receives such profits in payment, equally diminishes the fund on which the creditors rely.

In *Ex parte* Rowlandson, 1 Rose, 91, Lord Eldon said: " The ground was settled, that if a man as the reward for his labor chooses to stipulate for an interest in the profits in the business, instead of a sum proportionate to those profits, he is, as to third persons, a partner."

In *Ex parte* Hamper, 17 Ves., 403, he said: " The cases have gone to this nicety, upon a distinction so thin, that I cannot state it as established, upon due consideration, that if a trader agrees to pay another person for his labor in the concern a sum of money, even in proportion to the profits, equal to a certain share, that will not make him a partner; but if he has specific interest in the profits themselves as profits, he is a partner. . . . It is clearly settled, though I regret it, that if a man stipulates that, as the reward of his labor, he shall have not a specific interest in the business, but a given sum of money, even in proportion to a given quantum of the profits, that will not make him a partner; but if he agrees for a part of the profits, as such, giving him a right to an account, though having no property in the capital, he is, as to third persons, a partner."

These *dicta* of Lord Eldon have been very much deferred to by the courts and the profession. Parsons says: "We have reason to believe that for many years, in various parts of this country, numerous contracts of this kind have been drawn, carefully using the language which Eldon is supposed to have made safe by the distinction he asserted. Nor is it difficult to account for this. For, to say nothing of the immense authority of so eminent a judge, his words, so understood, supply a clear, simple and easily applicable rule for the avoidance of a great danger. They tell the lawyer who would draw a contract of this kind how, by a mere formula, he can guard his clients from a great uncertainty, the inconvenience of which might otherwise suffice to prevent the proposed arrangement. As a convenient rule, much may be said of it; but as an accurate one, it must be spoken of very differently."

" It is indeed remarkable that a rule or a distinction to which Lord Eldon strongly objects, not merely 'doubting,' but positively affirming his dislike, and which he lays down, as he says, under the constraint of irresistible authority, should since have been generally adopted, not so much on his authority as on his assertion of preceding authority, when in point of fact no such authority can be found, or, so far as any accessible evidence goes, can now be believed to have existed."

The criterion for determining whether the agreement makes a case of compensation or partnership as to third persons differs in these cases (*Ex parte* Rowlandson and *Ex parte* Hamper) from the one asserted in Waugh v. Carver, that he who participates in the profits of a trade, indefinitely, is liable as a partner, because he takes from the fund upon which the creditors rely; and the only reason given for the distinction between the liability of the person who contracts to take a sum equal to a share of the profits of a trade and one who stipulates for a share of such profits, as profits, is that the latter has a right to an account, and therefore he is liable as a partner. And this reason has been since asserted and relied on by courts and writers. 3 Kent's Com., 25, note b; Champion v. Bostwick, 18 Wend., 184; Heimstreet v. Howland, 5 Denio, 68; Deny v. Cabot, 6 Met., 92.

In reference to these, Bisset on Part., 14, says: "Some of the writers, and even some of the judicial authorities on this subject, appear to think they have surmounted the difficulty by confining the rule of liability to the cases where the party would have a right to an account of the profits; but to this it may be answered, that in all cases where a person is to be paid for his services by a sum proportioned to the profits, he must be entitled to an account of the profits. If not, how is he to ascertain that he has what he has stipulated for? . . . The distinction between the cases where a participation in the profits has been held to make a man liable as a partner, and those where it has been held not to make him so liable, is, certainly, at least as Lord Eldon has given expression to that distinction, so thin that it does not seem possible from the most careful consideration of it to arrive at any clear, general conclusion; nor does Mr. Justice Story's attempt to reconcile the repugnancy of the various decided cases and to bring them, as he says, 'into harmony with each other, as well as with common sense,' appear to be very successful. If the matter were *res integra*, a plain and intelligible rule, and one, too, which would not be at variance with anything in the cases decided previously to *Ex parte* Hamper, 17 Ves., 403, would be, that those whose share of the returns of the business or adventure consisted wholly of the profits of the stock, or partly of the profits of the stock and partly of the wages of labor, should be held liable as partners; but those whose share of the said returns consisted wholly of the wages of labor, or the interest of money lent, or a certain fixed annuity, and who had no control or voice as principals in the management of the business or adventure, should not be held liable as partners."

In discussing this supposed test of liability as a partner — the right to an account of the profits of the business — Parsons on Part., 92, says: "Undoubtedly every partner has a right to an account of the profits; but the converse is not true, that every one who has such a right is a partner. There are many ways in which a man may represent another, and in that right be entitled to an account without being liable as a partner."

Hickman *v.* Cox and Wheatcroft, 91 E. C. L., 523, is a comparatively late English case, 1860, in which the rules given in the cases above cited seem to have treated as erroneous or unintelligible. The case was this:

Smith & Son, prior to 1850, carried on business at the Stanton Iron Works, as iron-masters and merchants, and, being involved and indebted to the defendants and others, executed a composition deed transferring their property and business to certain trustees, in trust, that they would carry on the business in the name of the Stanton Iron Co., and after paying expenses and interest on a certain mortgage, whenever and as often as the net income amounted to a shilling on the pound of the indebtedness, to divide the same among the creditors in proportion to their claims, and when these were discharged to reconvey the property to Smith & Son. The deed was executed by the trustees and creditors, who thereby released the debtors. In 1855 the plaintiff, who was the proprietor of the Grafton Iron Ore Works, drew three bills for upwards of thirteen hundred pounds, for ore furnished the Stanton Iron Co., which were accepted by James Haywood, one of the trustees, "per procuration, the Stanton Iron Co." Afterwards the works passed into the hands of the mortgagee, and ceased to be carried on under the composition deed, when the plaintiff brought suit against the defendants as acceptors of the bills, on the ground that the creditors under the deed were partners in the business of the Stanton Iron Co., because the same was conducted by their agents, the trustees, and they had stipulated to take the profits thereof.

At Trinity term, 1856, the plaintiff had judgment in the court of common pleas, the court holding on the authority of Owen *v.* Body, 5 Ad. & E., 28, and Janes *v.* Whitbread, 11 C. B., 406, that the creditors executing this deed became partners in the trade agreed to be carried on thereunder. On appeal the case was argued in the Ex. Ch. in February, 1857, and judgment reserved until November, when the judgment of the common pleas was affirmed — three judges for and three against. On appeal to the house of lords the decision was reversed (99 E. C. L., 47). The six judges who heard the argument in the house of lords delivered opinions *seriatim*, and were equally divided on the question, "Are the defendants liable upon the bills of exchange?"

The lord chancellor, Campbell, and the law lords, Brougham, Cranworth,

Wensleydale and Chelmsford, delivered opinions to the effect that the defendants were not partners.   •

In the course of the opinions delivered, the supposed rule that participation
in the profits of a trading concern makes one liable as a partner was questioned and commented upon freely. Blackburn, J., who was for holding the
defendants as partners, said: " The phrase, taking the profits as such, is not a
happy one, and there is some difficulty at times in defining what it means; but
I think, at all events, it means this: It is not possible, according to the common
law, to cause a trading concern to be carried on upon the terms that the advantages of a partnership, including the participation in profits and partnership lien and security over the assets of the firm, shall belong to those who
have but a limited liability."

Whightman, J., who was for reversal, said: " It is said that a person who
shares in net profits is a partner. That may be so in some cases, but not in
all; and it may be material to consider in what sense the words 'sharing in
the profits' are used. In the present case, I greatly doubt whether the creditor who merely obtains payment of a debt incurred in the business, by being
paid the exact amount of his debt, and no more, out of the profits of the business, can be said to share the profits."

Pollock, C. B., who was of the same mind, said: " The question then arises,
whether the interest which the creditors had in the profits to be made by the
carrying on of the business under the deed was such as to make them partners in respect to third persons. . . . If a firm were in difficulties, and a
person proposed to assist them by a loan of money, engaging to receive payments out of the profits only, and to make no claim in the event of there being
no profits, but stipulating that one-half of the profits should be applied as they
arose in payment of his debt, and that he should have power to see that this
was done — would he thereby become a partner, and liable for all debts contracted subsequently to this arrangement? On this very simple state of facts
there may possibly arise a difference of opinion; but I think a large majority
of all lawyers and commercial men would decide at once that assistance so
offered and so accepted would not make the lender of the money a partner as
to third persons. If he took a warrant of attorney, entitling him to enter
up judgment at his pleasure, and sweep away, in payment of his demand, capital, debts, profits and everything, he certainly would not be a partner; but as
is said, if he limits his claim to be paid out of the profits only, his limited right
to payment creates an unlimited liability. I think, my lords, there must be
some fallacy in this; the conclusion, to my mind, appears so unjust and absurd,
and so much at variance with natural equity."

Lord Cranworth said: " Would they (the creditors) have become partners
in the concern carried on by the trustees merely because they passively assented to its being carried on upon the terms that the net income, i. e., the net
profits, should be applied on discharge of their demands? I think not. It was
argued that, as they would be interested in the profits, therefore they would
be partners. But this is a fallacy. It is often said that the test, or one of the
tests, whether a person, not ostensibly a partner, is nevertheless in contemplation of law a partner, is whether he is entitled to participate in the profits.
This, no doubt, is in general a sufficiently accurate test; for a right to participate in the profits affords cogent, often conclusive, evidence that the trade in
which the profits have been made was carried on in part for or behalf of the
person setting up such a claim. But the real ground of the liability is that the

trade has been carried on by persons acting on his behalf. When that is the case, he is liable to the trade obligations, and entitled to its profits, or to a share of them. It is not strictly correct to say that his right to share the profits makes him liable to the debts of the trade. The correct mode of stating the proposition is to say that the same thing that entitles him to the one makes him liable to the other, namely, the fact that the trade has been carried on in his behalf, *i. e.*, that he stood in the relation of principal towards the persons acting ostensibly as the traders, by whom the liabilities have been incurred, and under whose management the profits have been made."

Lord Wensleydale said: " A man who orders another to carry on a trade, whether in his own name or not, to buy and sell, and to pay over all the profits to him, is undoubtedly the principal, and the person so employed is the agent; and the principal is liable for the agent's contracts in the course of his employment. So if two or more agree that they should carry on a trade and share the profits of it each is a principal, and each is an agent for the other, and each is bound by the other's contracts in carrying on the trade, as much as a single principal would be by the act of an agent who was to give the whole of his profits to his employer. Hence, it becomes a test of the liability of one for the contracts of another, that he is to recover the whole or a part of the profits arising from that contract, by virtue of the agreement made at the time of the employment. I believe this is the true principle of partnership liability. Perhaps the maxim, that he who takes the profits ought to bear the loss, often stated in the earlier cases on this subject (Waugh *v.* Carver, etc.), is only the consequence, not the cause, why a man is liable as a partner."

From the general conclusion reached in this case, that the defendants were not partners in the Stanton Iron Co., simply because they were to receive the net profits of the business, and from the opinion expressed in the H. of L., I think it is clear that the decision set aside the arbitrary rule, that indefinite or other participation in profits necessarily made one liable as a partner under any circumstances, but the fact of such participation is to be treated as evidence, more or less cogent, according to the circumstances, of a partnership.

Following the final decision in Hickman *v.* Cox & Wheatcroft, *supra*, and in consonance with the views therein expressed, the English parliament recently passed an act (28 and 29 Vic., ch. 86) which provides, among other things, that a loan to a person engaged in trade, upon a written contract that the lender shall receive a rate of interest in proportion to profits, or a share of the profits, shall not itself constitute the lender a partner; nor shall a contract to remunerate a servant or agent of a person engaged in trade by a share of the profits, of itself render such servant or agent liable as a partner. In noticing this act, Parsons on Part., 93, says:

" We will add our hope and our belief that the courts of this country will regard this statute rather as declaratory of the law merchant in respect to partnership than as changing that law, and will apply to cases which come before them the principles upon which the statute is founded."

The American cases on this subject are also conflicting, but the weight and tendency of authority appears to be in favor of the doctrine " that a mere promise to pay out of the profits a sum of money, as a specific proportion of the profits, does not necessarily constitute the payee a partner, and gives him no interest in the profits, and no right to the profits, but only a personal claim against the promisor for such money, or for such a share of profits, after they

are ascertained and may be divided." Parsons on Part., 70. In Berthold *v.*
Goldsmith, 24 How., 542 (AGENCY, §§ 614–15), Mr. Justice Clifford, speaking
for the court, says: "Actual participation in the profits as principal, we think,
creates a partnership as between the parties and third persons, whatever may
be their intentions in that behalf, and notwithstanding the dormant partner
was not expected to participate in the loss beyond the amount of the profits."
In support of this proposition, the cases of Waugh *v.* Carver and Grace *v.*
Smith, *supra*, are cited, together with the rule announced therein, that he who
has a share of the profits ought to bear his share of the loss. But the opinion
goes on to say: "That rule, however, has no application whatever to a case of
special service or agency, when the employee has no power as a partner in the
firm, and no interest in the profits as property, but is simply employed as a
servant or special agent, and is to receive a given sum out of the profits, or a
proportion of the same, as a compensation for his services." In other words,
the participation in the profits which will make one liable to third persons as a
partner is a participation as a partner, or, in the language of the opinion, as
principal — and that is the fact to be ascertained. In that case the court held
that a person who negotiated the sale of goods for another, under a contract
to have half the profits and a certain compensation in any event, was not a
partner as to such sales.

Mr. Justice Story believes that the true doctrine upon this subject is that a
participation in the profits is presumptive proof that the participant is a partner, and sufficient proof in the absence of all other opposing circumstances.
Story on Part., sec. 38.

§ 8. *Evidence on question of partnership considered in the light of preceding
doctrine.*

Having reached this conclusion, I cannot, upon the facts so far stated, conclude that Francis is liable as a partner with Buchanan. For although he
participated in the profits of the trade, the agreement and circumstances under
which such participation took place are sufficient to modify the presumption
of law that he did so as a partner or principal, and so leave it in doubt whether
he took such profits only as a compensation for money loaned and services
rendered or otherwise.

It then becomes necessary to inquire further and ascertain whether, upon
the whole evidence, Francis was in fact a partner or not. Buchanan, being
called as a witness by the petitioners, testified that Francis was an actual partner in the firm of Richter & Co., and also in that of W. A. Buchanan, so far
as the profits were concerned, but not in the losses, and that the written and
verbal agreement aforesaid, and the manner of keeping the books, and the
written authority to Francis to act as his agent, by which it appeared that
Francis only loaned money to Richter & Co. and to W. A. Buchanan for a
certain interest, and kept their books for a share of the profits with a guaranty of a certain sum per month, were all a mere pretense and device, not intended to wrong any one engaged in business with said firms, but merely to
conceal the fact of such partnership from Francis' employer, the Bank of
British Columbia, it being contrary to the rules of such bank that their employees should be engaged in other business.

Francis, being called as a witness on his own behalf, testified that he was
not a partner in the concern, unless the agreement made him one, that it
truly stated his relations to the parties and the business, and that he desired

such relations to be kept secret, but did not state why. He also admitted that he was a clerk in the bank aforesaid, during the period covered by these transactions.

Paul Richter, called as a witness by the petitioners, testified that it was his understanding that Francis was a partner in the firm of Richter & Co., but he had no direct knowledge on the subject.

Dr. Cardwell, called by the petitioners, testified that after Buchanan was adjudged a bankrupt, Francis urged him to agree to a settlement for fifty cents on the dollar, and he then said that if witness would so settle he would never hear of a $600 note made by witness as an accommodation to B., and which Francis then held as collateral security for money loaned B. on account, and that B. considered their debts confidential, and would pay them dollar for dollar.

Here is a direct conflict between the testimony of the two persons who ought to know better than any one else what was the real relation between them concerning this business. Resort must, then, be had to the circumstances and other proofs of the case to ascertain the truth of the matter. Buchanan, so far as can be seen, has no pecuniary interest in the question. Francis has a large one. Buchanan may have some personal feeling against Francis, regarding him as one who, in the language of counsel, has sucked the sap out of the business; or, as the leonine partner in what the Roman lawyers called *societas leonina*, in allusion to the fable of the lion — who, having entered into a hunting partnership with the other beasts of the forest, appropriated to himself all the prey. Be this as it may, he did not impress me as a witness who was inimical in his feelings towards Francis. He stated that he did not first disclose the fact of partnership. His testimony was direct and positive, and went into details of conversations between himself and Francis, with the circumstances of time and place, that gave it the semblance of probability and truth.

On the contrary, Francis' testimony was brief, somewhat ambiguous — as that he was not a partner unless his agreement made him one — and consisted mainly of general denials.

Again, the fact of Francis' employment in the bank furnishes a motive, reason or inducement to disguise a partnership with this cloak of a loan of money and hiring of services.

The interest which Francis took in having the creditors settle at fifty cents on the dollar may have been prompted by mere friendship for Buchanan, but the fact that he assured Cardwell that in such event his debt would be paid in full, or he would never hear of his note again, indicates a concern, knowledge and authority in the premises that we might expect of a person interested in the matter otherwise than as a mere creditor.

When Francis exercised the direct authority in the business that he did in the absence of Buchanan, although he had a secret writing appointing him agent, he did not deem it necessary to show it to the salesman or any one else, but proceeded to take the cash into his own custody from the till, daily, and direct who to credit and who not, with all the authority of a partner. The salesman, Mr. Lewis, does not seem to have had any question or doubt about his right to do so, independent of the writing, which he never saw or knew of, until it was produced in court.

Richter's testimony goes to establish the partnership. The particulars of the transaction do not appear to have been disclosed to him by either B. or F.

But from all that he observed during the six or seven months that he was an active partner in the concern, he regarded and treated Francis as a partner in the profits at least, although not in the capital stock. As to what B. told Richter, I do not consider it, because B.'s declarations upon the question of the existence of the partnership are not evidence against Francis.

It does not directly appear from the evidence what was a reasonable compensation for keeping the books. It was assumed by counsel for the petitioners, and not questioned by opposing counsel, that $25 per month was a fair compensation, and the conclusion appears probable. Now, if Francis was simply employed to keep books, what inducement was there for Buchanan to agree to give him any interest in the profits of the business, or any other compensation beyond the $25 per month, which he was guarantied and paid, profits or no profits? The money put into the concern, if a loan, was drawing the highest legal rate of interest, independent of the compensation paid as book-keeper.

This single circumstance indicates that this arrangement was either a device to cover up a partnership in the profits or a usurious loan. As it is not unlawful to be a dormant or secret partner in a trading business, and it is to loan money at usurious interest, the court ought to infer that the contingent and extra compensation for keeping the books was a device whereby Francis was to be admitted to a share in the profits as a partner.

All these circumstances considered, I think the weight of the testimony is in favor of the conclusion that Francis was a partner in the firm of W. A. Buchanan. But if, as contended by counsel for respondent, the evidence was evenly balanced, effect being given to the fact that Francis did participate in the profits, the same conclusion would follow.

As has been shown, a participation in the profits, in fact, is presumptive proof of partnership, and sufficient proof unless overcome by other circumstances. Story on Part., sec. 38. It being admitted that Francis participated in the profits of the concern, and the circumstances of the agreement, at least, leaving it in doubt whether such participation was as partner or employee, the burden of proof is upon him to overcome the presumption that such profits were received by him as a partner.

HAZARD v. HAZARD.

(Circuit Court for Rhode Island: 1 Story, 371–376. 1840.)

STATEMENT OF FACTS.— Bill in equity for the settlement of the accounts of an asserted partnership between the plaintiff and the defendant, and for a decree for payment of the balance due to the plaintiff, etc. The answer denied the partnership, and stated expressly that no partnership was intended between the parties; but that the defendant was by an informal written instrument annexed to the bill, and which was admitted to be the true agreement between the parties, to have a certain portion of the profits of the business in lieu of and as a compensation for his services.

The written instrument was not signed, but was in the following terms, and was in the handwriting of the defendant: "Benjamin Hazard agrees with Thomas R. Hazard to run his two factories, situated on Rocky Brook, on the following terms, viz.: The said Benjamin Hazard agrees to devote his whole time, excepting his attendance of religious meetings, exclusively to the management of the concerns of said factories, and to take the machinery in the order it is at present in and return it in like order at the expiration of this agreement. In consideration of which the said T. R. Hazard agrees to allow him one-fourth of the profits of the business for the first year, and one-third of the profits for each year after, until the expiration of this agreement, *which is to be the sole reward of the said B. Hazard's services.* And Thomas R. Hazard agrees on his part to purchase the stock and attend to the sale of the goods, without any charges for his personal services and time excepting the actual expenses necessarily incurred. All stock and articles of any description, bills, etc., paid by Thomas R. Hazard are to be credited to the said T. R. H., and the proceeds of the goods are to be delivered and charged to him in the factory books. And the said Thomas R. Hazard agrees to furnish a horse and wagon to do the business of the factory, which is to be kept at the expense of the factory, and returned of equal value at the expiration of this agreement. It is to be understood that Benjamin Hazard is to have no control over or profits arising from the rents, etc., of the houses and lands adjoining the factories. Thomas R. Hazard is to charge no rent for the factories, which, with the dam, water-wheels, running gear, etc., is to be kept in running repair, and the expenses charged to the factory." The agreement has no date, but it is admitted that it was made in December, 1825, and the factories were carried on under it for four years, until about December, 1829. The business being then found unprofitable, it was discontinued by the consent of both parties.

Opinion by STORY, J.

In the view which I take of this case, it is wholly unnecessary to go into the examination of several collateral matters which are stated in the bill and answer and evidence, and which have been adverted to at the argument. The only question which it appears to me is now before the court for consideration is whether, under and in virtue of the informal agreement in December, 1825, there was constituted a partnership between the parties for carrying on the factories. If there was, then there ought to be an interlocutory decree for an account. If there was not, then the bill ought to be dismissed; for although in positive terms it does not (as doubtless it ought) aver a partnership, yet the whole structure and frame of the bill is formed to this aspect of the case, and the bill would be unintelligible without it.

§ 9. *Partnership as to third persons may arise by operation of law, but as between the parties themselves only when such is the actual intention.*

Now, upon the point whether there was a partnership or not between these parties in the factory business, under the agreement, it is necessary to take notice of a well-known distinction between cases where, as to third persons, there is held to be a partnership, and cases where there is a partnership between the parties themselves. The former may arise between the parties by mere operation of law against the intention of the parties; whereas, the latter exists only when such is the actual intention of the parties. Thus, if A. and B. should agree to carry on any business for their joint profit, and to divide the profits equally between them, but B. should bear all the losses and should agree that there should be no partnership between them, as to third persons dealing with the firm they would be held partners, although *inter sese* they would be held not to be partners. This distinction is often taken in the authorities. It was very fully discussed and recognized in Carver *v.* Waugh, 2 H. Bl., 235; Cheap *v.* Cramond, 4 Barn. & Ald., 663; Peacock *v.* Peacock, 16 Ves., 49; *Ex parte* Hamper, 17 Ves., 404; *Ex parte* Hodgkinson, 19 Ves., 291; *Ex parte* Langdale, 18 Ves., 300; Tench *v.* Tench, 6 Madd., 145, note; Hesketh *v.* Blanchard, 4 East, 144; Muzzy *v.* Whitney, 10 Johns., 226; Dob *v.* Halsey, 16 Johns., 34.

§ 10. *Mere participation in profits will not make parties partners inter sese.* The question before us is not as to the liability to third persons, but it is solely whether between themselves the agreement was intended to create and did create a partnership. I have looked over the agreement carefully, and my opinion is that no partnership whatsoever was intended between the parties; but that Benjamin Hazard was to be employed as a mere superintendent, and not as a partner, and was to be paid the stipulated portion of the profits for his services as superintendent. This, it is said in the agreement, was to be the *sole* reward of his services; and if there were no profits, then he was to submit to lose the value of his services. It is not anywhere said in the agreement that the parties are to be partners in the business; nor that Benjamin Hazard is to pay any part of the losses. But language is used from which, I think, it may fairly be inferred as the full understanding of the parties, that the whole capital stock was to be held by T. R. Hazard, as his sole and exclusive property, and that the stock was to be furnished by him, and the proceeds thereof was to be delivered and sold by him and charged to him as his individual property, and debts and credits. Now, if this be so, there is no pretense to say that the parties intended a partnership. A mere participation in the profits will not make the parties partners *inter sese*, whatever it may do as to third persons, unless they so intend it. If A. agrees to give B. one-third of the profits of a particular transaction in business for his labor and services therein, that may make both liable to third persons as partners, but not as between themselves. This was the very point adjudged in Hesketh *v.* Blanchard, 4 East, 144, where Lord Ellenborough said, " The distinction taken in Waugh *v.* Carver and others applies to this case. *Quoad* third persons it was a partnership, for the plaintiff was to share half the profits. But, as between themselves, it was only an agreement for so much as a compensation for the plaintiff's trouble and for lending R. his credit." The same doctrine was fully recognized in Muzzey *v.* Whitney, 10 Johns., 226.

§ 11. *Distinction between cases of partnership as to third persons and cases of mere agency.*

It is not necessary, in the present case, to decide whether Benjamin Hazard was, under the agreement, a partner as to third persons. That question may be left for decision until it shall properly arise in judgment. And before it is decided it might be necessary to examine a very nice and curious class of cases, standing certainly upon a very thin distinction, if it is a clearly discernible distinction, between cases of partnership as to third persons, and cases of mere agency, where the remuneration is to be by a portion of the profits. This distinction is alluded to by Lord Eldon in *Ex parte* Hamper, 17 Ves., 404, and by Lord Chief Justice Abbott in Cheap *v.* Cramond, 4 Barn. & Ald., 663, 670. In the latter case the chief justice said: " Such an agreement is perfectly distinct from the cases put in the argument before us, of remuneration made to a traveler or other clerk or agent (in proportion to the profits), by a portion of the sums received by the master or principal, in lieu of a fixed salary, which is only a mode of payment adopted to increase or secure exertion." It was also acted upon in Muzzey *v.* Whitney, 10 Johns., 226; Dry *v.* Boswell, 1 Camp., 329; Wish *v.* Small, id., note; Benjamin *v.* Porteus, 2 H. Bl., 590; and Wilkinson *v.* Frazier, 4 Esp., 182; and Mair *v.* Glennie, 4 Maule & Selw., 240, 244.

My judgment is that in the present case the parties never intended any partnership in the capital stock, but a mere participation of interest in the profits; and that the one-third or one-fourth of the profits allowed by the agreement to Benjamin Hazard was merely a mode of paying him as agent for his superintendency of the factories. In this view, I think the bill ought to be dismissed with costs.

BENEDICT v. DAVIS.

(Circuit Court for Indiana: 2 McLean, 347–353. 1841.)

Opinion of the COURT.

STATEMENT OF FACTS.— This action is brought against the defendants to recover from them, as the representatives of Davis, a partner in the house of Allison & Co. The jury found for the defendants, and a motion for a new trial was made on the following grounds:

First. The jury should have been instructed that Davis, having held himself as a partner to the world, was liable as such. *Second.* Evidence was given to the jury in regard to the contract between Davis and the Allisons, which should have been excluded. *Third.* The weight of the evidence was in favor of the plaintiffs.

Among other evidence conducing to show a partnership between Davis and the Allisons, several witnesses stated that the former represented himself to them, both before and after the purchase of the goods for the price of which this action was brought, as a partner. And it is insisted that, on this ground alone, he is chargeable as a partner. That where an individual holds himself out as a partner he is liable as such, though, in fact, he had no interest in the partnership concern.

§ 12. *Doctrine as to interest in profits creating a partnership.*

The doctrine of partnership, though pretty well defined, does not seem, on some points, to have been settled on sound principles. It is laid down that if an individual, as a compensation for his labor, agrees to receive a part of the profits, he will be liable as a partner; and yet if he is to receive a certain sum of money in proportion to a given quantum of the profits, he is not so liable. Now although this is the established doctrine, in the language of Lord Eldon, in reason it would seem to be impossible to say that, as to third persons, they are not equally partners. *Ex parte* Rowlandson, 1 Rose, 39; *Ex parte* Watson, 10 Ves., 461.

§ 13. *One who lends his name to a partnership thereby becomes liable as a partner.*

Where a person lends his name to a partnership, though, in fact, he has no interest in it, he is liable as a partner. And this rule is founded upon general policy. Waugh v. Carver, 2 H. Bl., 235; Gow on Part., 23. To create responsibility as a nominal partner, the allowed use of the name on bills of parcels used by the firm seems to be sufficient, notwithstanding that the creditor was originally ignorant of the introduction of the name. Gow, 23; Young v. Axtell, 1 Esp. N. P. C., 29; 1 Serg. & R., 338.

§ 14. *One not actually a partner will not render himself liable as such by representations to individuals of which the creditor could have known nothing.*

In the case under consideration the declarations of Davis, in regard to his being a partner, as proved, were made at, and in the neighborhood of, Laporte, in Indiana, to residents of that place; the bills were not made out against

Davis as a partner, nor was there any evidence conducing to prove that the plaintiffs had any knowledge that he represented himself to be a partner, or that the plaintiffs, who are citizens of New York, gave credit to the Allisons on his account. And it is important to inquire whether, from this state of facts, he can be held responsible as a partner.

The counsel for the plaintiffs earnestly contends that Davis is liable on the above evidence, though it be, in fact, clear that he had no partnership interest. That this liability does not depend on the credit given by the plaintiffs to him at the time the goods were sold, nor on their having a knowledge of his having held himself out as a partner, but upon the fact of his having so represented himself. In this view of the case, if there be a liability, it arises from general policy that an individual shall be held bound where, by holding himself out to the world as a partner, he has given the influence of his name to the firm. That a contrary doctrine would enable an individual to practice a fraud upon all who gave credit to the firm.

Before a reference is made to adjudged cases on this point, it may be proper to remark that it is difficult to perceive how a fraud can have been practiced on the plaintiffs, if, at the time they sold the goods, they had no knowledge of Davis as being connected with the firm, or as representing himself to be connected with it. It is clear that, under such circumstances, his name or credit could not have operated on the plaintiffs, or in any way influenced their conduct. Such a fraud seems to be too refined for legal comprehension or action.

It may be readily admitted that positive proof of knowledge of the above facts, by the plaintiffs, is not necessary to establish the liability of Davis; but such facts must be proved as to authorize the jury to infer this knowledge. This inference might well be drawn from the fact that the name of Davis was published as a partner in a newspaper, or inserted in a sign over the door of the house in which the goods were kept and sold, or that the bills were made out against him as a partner. But not one of these facts are proved in this case.

In the case of Vice v. Lady Anson, 7 Barn. & Cres., 409, Lord Tenterden said the plaintiff, at the time when he supplied the goods, did not know that the defendant either had, or thought she had, any interest in the mine. He did not, therefore, supply the goods on her credit. The fact of her having thought that she had such an interest, that being wholly unknown to the plaintiff at the time when he supplied the goods, will not make her liable for those goods. Her having expressed an opinion in private letters and society that she was interested might be *prima facie* evidence that she had an interest; but the other facts in the case show that she had not any interest. This case is more fully reported in 3 Car. & Payne, 19, and, also, the decision of the court in bank on a motion to set aside the nonsuit which was overruled.

In the case of Dickinson v. Valpy, 10 Barn. & Cres., 128, Mr. Justice Park said if it could have been proved that the defendant had held himself out to be a partner, not " to the world," for that is a loose expression, but to the plaintiff himself, or under such circumstances of publicity as to satisfy a jury that the plaintiff knew of it, and believed him to be a partner, he would be liable to the plaintiff in all transactions in which he engaged, and gave credit to the defendant, upon the faith of his being such partner. .

In Chitty on Bills (ed. 1839), 43, it is said if a person represents himself to be a partner, though, in fact, he was not so, and thereby induce a person to give credit to a concern, he will be liable as a partner; but the representation must be by himself, or by some third person by his authority; and it must be general and public, or to the particular creditor, for a representation only to one or more persons which the creditor never heard of could not mislead him, and he has no right to avail himself of it, in order to fix a party, who, in fact, was not a partner. These authorities show that, independently of the proof of the fact of partnership, there was no such holding out by Davis to the public or to the plaintiffs as to make him liable as a partner, and that the court did not mistake the law in their charge to the jury.

§ 15. *To rebut the inference of partnership arising from statements made, the contract between the parties may be shown.*

The motion for a new trial cannot be granted on the second ground. The complaint here is, that illegal evidence was admitted to show the contract between Davis and the Allisons, in regard to his advance to them of $500, the amount of which he was to receive in goods at cost. This evidence was introduced by the defendants to rebut and explain the evidence of a partnership given by the plaintiffs. The terms of the contract were repeated by the parties in the presence of the witness, before one of the Allisons, who purchased the goods, left Laporte for that purpose.

Now, it is true this contract was made without the knowledge of the plaintiffs, but in this respect it stands upon the same footing as the evidence to prove a partnership. And as they had no knowledge of the one they can complain of no surprise as to the other. In every view the evidence to prove this contract was legal. Whether it was fraudulently entered into or not was a matter for the jury.

That the weight of evidence, as to the proof of partnership, was with the plaintiffs, must be admitted. At least this is my view on the subject. But the preponderance is not such as to authorize the court to set aside the verdict and give a new trial. To authorize this it is not enough that the court differ, in their opinion of the evidence, from the jury. There was some impeachment of two or three of the witnesses from the facts proved and the circumstances of the case. The jury had the facts fully before them, and gave such weight to the witnesses as they believed them to be entitled to. Under all the circumstances we are not convinced that the rules of law, and the purposes of justice, require a new trial, and the motion is overruled.

§ 16. **In general.**— Community of profit constitutes the true criterion whereby to ascertain whether any given agreement for carrying on a trade or business is one of partnership. As a general rule, whenever two or more persons agree that each shall contribute capital or labor, or both. for the purpose of carrying on a trade or business, and that the profits shall be received on joint account and be subsequently apportioned among all, they will be considered as partners with respect to third persons, even though they may have expressly stipulated to the contrary between themselves. Bigelow *v.* Elliot,* 1 Cliff., 28.

§ 17. It is not necessary to constitute a partnership that there should be any property constituting the capital stock jointly owned by the partners; but the capital may consist of the mere use of property owned by the individual partners separately, and it is sufficient to constitute the relation that.they have agreed to share the profits and losses arising from the use of property or skill either separately or combined. *Ibid.*

§ 18. The participation in the profits which will make one liable to third persons as a partner is a participation as a partner or principal. A participation in the profits as a compensation for money loaned or services rendered does not constitute one a partner or render him liable to third persons, but if the participation in the profits of a concern be admitted, and the circumstances of the agreement leave it in doubt whether such participation was as partner or employee, the burden of proof is upon the party so participating to overcome the presumption that such profits were received by him as a partner. *In re* Francis,* 7 N. B. R., 359.

§ 19. A contract between three persons to operate a "mining property as a company" creates a partnership between them from date, and makes each of them liable for debts incurred in prosecuting the enterprise, notwithstanding it is agreed that there shall be no division of profits until two of the parties are reimbursed from the proceeds for money expended in the purchase of two-thirds of the property from the third party, and the cost of improving it. Bybee v. Hawkett.* 12 Fed. R., 649.

§ 20. A court of admiralty has no jurisdiction of a contract of partnership in the earnings of a ship. A contract of partnership is where parties join together their money, goods, labor or skill, for the purposes of trade or gain, and where there is a community of profits. Where two parties agreed together, one to contribute a steamboat to carry freight, passengers, etc., the other to contribute the good-will of an established line, together with his care, skill and experience, and to have general management of the business, etc., the receipts, after paying expenses, and a certain specified sum to each of the parties, to be divided between them equally, the agreement was held to be one of partnership and not a charter-party. Ward v. Thompson, 22 How., 330.

§ 21. Partnership is a contract between two or more persons to place their money, effects, labor and skill, or some one or all of them, in business, with the understanding that there shall be a community of profits between them. Community of interest does not necessarily constitute a partnership; but where there is a community of interest in the capital stock, and also a community of interest in the profit and loss, then there is a partnership. Both of these ingredients, however, need not concur to establish a partnership. Actual participation in the profits as principal creates a partnership as between the parties' and third persons, whatever may be their intention in that behalf, and notwithstanding the dormant partner was not expected to participate in the loss beyond the amount of the profits. But where a person is employed as a special agent or servant, and is to receive a given sum out of the profits, or a proportion of the same, for his services, and his relation is known to the party dealing with him, there is no partnership. Berthold v. Goldsmith. 24 How., 536.

§ 22. An obligation joint in its terms does not constitute the obligors partners, nor the contract a partnership engagement. Nor does the fact that the obligors were partners constitute the agreement a partnership contract. *In re* Miller,* 1 N. Y. Leg. Obs., 38.

§ 23. A parol agreement to become copartners in the business of purchasing and selling lands and lumber in the state of Maine is a parol contract respecting an interest in lands, and void by the statute of frauds, so that it will not be enforced by a court of equity. Smith v. Burnham, 3 Sumn., 435.

§ 24. A mere joint proprietorship of property, or joint contract, does not render the persons concerned copartners. The partnership relationship, though not limited to mercantile transactions, necessarily depends upon a mutual interest between the parties in the profit and loss of the concern; either by an actual sharing of profits or an expectation of them. *In re* Miller,* 1 N. Y. Leg. Obs., 88.

§ 25. One venture or transaction in which two parties have an interest will not make them technical partners requiring a bill in equity for adjusting their accounts. Marsh v. Northwestern National Ins. Co., 3 Biss., 351.

§ 26. If two persons make a loan jointly, it will not constitute them partners so as to require the doctrine of survivorship to be enforced. In such case, if one of the persons dies, the survivor may maintain an action to recover the money, but, after the death of both, a settlement may properly be made with the executor of the one who died first, and he may maintain an action upon notes given in such settlement for the balance found due. Catlin v. Underhill,* 4 McL., 387.

§ 27. To constitute a partnership there must be a community of interest — a participation in profit and loss — and this joint interest must continue to the time of the sale of the property. Felichy v. Hamilton,* 1 Wash., 492.

§ 28. This joint interest in the whole is what constitutes the liability of all for the contracts of one. *Ibid.*

§ 29. Where a party is held out as a partner by another, it is not necessary, to make them partners as to third persons who have given them credit on the strength of their being partners, that there should be either community of interest or participation in the profits; but knowledge or notice of his being so held out must be brought home to the party, or there must be proof of circumstances which will authorize a court to presume notice to make him liable as a partner. *In re* Jewett, 15 N. B. R., 126; 7 Biss., 328.

§ 30. Instances.— A., B. and C., under an agreement to furnish the outlay and share in the profit and loss equally, bought property for the purpose of selling again; sold some lots and built on another out of common funds. Then A. and B. with common funds bought out C.

B. went into bankruptcy. *Held*, upon a bill by A. against B.'s assignees, that this was a partnership adventure, and that A. and B.'s assignee held the title to the real estate subject to such rights and liabilities as accrued to A. and B. at the time of the commencement of the bankruptcy proceedings; that it was necessary to adjust the partnership dealings up to such time and ascertain the exact interest of each; and that A. had a lien upon the property to protect him until the partnership creditors were paid. Thrall *v.* Crampton, 9 Ben., 218.

§ 81. The owner of a tug and the owner of a barge agreed that they should be employed in carrying freight, the earnings, after the payment of expenses, to be divided in a certain proportion. *Held*, that the parties were partners. The servants employed on either vessel were the servants of the association, and persons injured by the negligence of such servants have a right of action against either partner. Bowas *v.* The Pioneer Tow Line, 2 Saw., 21.

§ 32. An association or joint stock company, with a capital stock divided into shares, was formed for the purpose of dealing in real estate, and the title to all property bought was conveyed to certain trustees in trust for the benefit of the shareholders, with power to make sales and do all acts necessary or proper to carry into effect the objects of the association, and with a provision for dividing the lands and money after lands enough had been sold to pay the purchase price and all other charges. The interest of one of the shareholders having been sold on execution against him individually, *held*, that the association was a partnership, and that the law governing the rights of individual creditors of a partner must determine the rights of the purchaser at the execution sale. Clagett *v.* Kilbourne,* 1 Black, 846.

§ 38. Such purchaser takes the same interest in the property that the judgment debtor would have upon a final adjustment of the accounts of the partnership. He cannot sue in ejectment; his remedy is to go into equity and call for an account, and thus entitle himself to the interest of the judgment debtor, if any, after the settlement of the partnership liabilities. The fact that the property consists of real estate does not alter the matter. Real property belonging to a partnership is treated in equity as part of the partnership fund, and is disposed of and distributed the same as personal assets. *Ibid.*

§ 34. An association of separate owners of several steamboats into a joint concern, to run their vessels upon the Hudson river, and to collect and receive the earnings of the boats in a common fund, out of which the expenses of all the boats are to be paid, is no more than a private copartnership in a particular business; and each member of the association is responsible individually for his acts or contracts in the business of the common concern. The Steamboat Swallow, Olc., 334.

§ 35. Where various parties are owners of a boat, and are engaged in the transportation of freight for hire, although they are tenants in common as to the boat itself, they are copartners as to the business of the boat, the freighting, etc. Russell *v.* The Minnesota Outfit,* 1 Minn., 162.

§ 36. Where A. and B. purchased a ship and her cargo, on account of themselves and C. and D., in equal third parts, and it was agreed among the parties that C. should go as master and supercargo, the outward cargo to be consigned to C., and A. and B. made all the advances both for ship and cargo, and were constituted the agents and factors in New York for the several parties, and the return cargo was to be consigned to them for sale on account of the concern, *held*, that the parties interested in this adventure could not be considered partners, but must be deemed tenants in common, and not to be governed by the law of partnership. DeWolf *v.* Howland, 2 Paine, 356.

§ 37. A. and B. were tenants in common with C. and D. of a ship in certain proportions, and purchased a cargo, by agreement, on their account in the like proportions for a voyage, and consigned the same to the master for sale and returns; it was held that they were tenants in common of the cargo and not partners. Jackson *v.* Robinson, 3 Mason, 138.

§ 38. Where A. and B. agreed to carry on two stores separately, each on his own capital, credit and responsibility, neither to be in any way answerable for the engagements of the other, and there was to be participation in the profits but not in the losses, *held*, that, whether or not there was a partnership as to third persons, there was not *inter sese*, and that one could maintain an action at law against the other for goods sold or money loaned by plaintiff to defendant. Jordan *v.* Wilkins,* 3 Wash., 110.

§ 39. *A fortiori* such action could be maintained under a supplementary agreement destroying the community of profits. *Ibid.*

§ 40. Agreements by which seamen are to receive for their services a share of the profits of the voyage are not partnerships, but contracts of hiring, and the shares so agreed upon are wages, and are recoverable as such; and this is so whether the compensation is to be made in kind or in money. Reed *v.* Hussey, Bl. & How., 525.

§ 41. W., being owner of a steamboat, agreed with T. that he might run the boat during two sailing seasons. The boat was to be under the control of T., and he was to appoint all the officers and crew of the boat except the clerk. The clerk was to be under the control of

W., and to make reports to him of the receipts and expenditures of the boat. The receipts were to be applied, 1st, to the payment of the boat's expenses; 2d, to her insurance; 3d, to the payment of $6,000 to W., and the balance to be divided between W. and T. T. was to be allowed $300 per annum for his services as agent of the boat. It was held that although by this agreement the parties became partners after a certain event in the profits of the business of the boat, they were not partners to such an extent as to oust the admiralty court of jurisdiction in a cause for the recovery of damages for a breach of the agreement. Ward v. Thompson, Newb., 95.

§ 42. An agreement was entered into between M. & S., a firm in one city, and H., a certain party in another, under which the latter bought several cargoes of wheat and shipped them to the former, they paying for the same, and the profits or losses were equally divided. A certain cargo was bought under such agreement with funds advanced by a bank, to F., the cashier of which, H., gave a draft upon M. & S., with the bill of lading of such wheat and a certificate of insurance. The draft, bill of lading and certificate of insurance were forwarded, and the draft was paid by M. & S., who received the bill of lading and certificate of insurance. H., mistaking the purport of a dispatch from M. & S., gave notice to the insurance company that the insurance was canceled, but the certificate had already been delivered to F. Held, that the purchase and shipment of each cargo was a separate venture, and that H. acquired no interest as a partner with M. & S., in any of the cargoes; that he had no authority to cancel or give notice of cancellation of the policy of insurance while it was in the hands of a bona fide holder entitled to payment of loss, if any. And that the certificate, being then in the hands of M. & S., as assignees of F., they could, upon a loss of the cargo, sustain a libel for the insurance. Marsh v. Northwestern National Ins. Co., 3 Biss., 351.

§ 43. A entered into a contract with B., whereby A. undertook to carry on the butchering business for B. at B.'s establishment, "as his agent and salesman to purchase cattle, slaughter them and sell the beef, and to do all acts necessary in reference thereto;" "the offal, feet and the commission on hides, and the usual slaughter-house perquisites," were to go to B., and A. was to receive "in lieu of wages or other compensation, all he" could "make over and above the current price of cattle after deducting all expenses." A. was to account daily to B., and pay over to him all moneys received until B. was fully reimbursed for the stock and expenses. Held, that the agreement did not create a partnership. In re Blumenthal,* 18 N. B. R., 555.

§ 44. Although A. may be interested with B. in his interest in a partnership consisting of B. and two others, that does not make him a member of the latter partnership. Bybee v. Hawkett,* 12 Fed. R., 649.

§ 45. W. was an experienced merchant, but without means. B. and P. each had some money which they were willing to risk in a mercantile enterprise, but did not intend to render themselves liable for the debts of the concern should it prove unsuccessful; to avoid this they advanced the money to purchase the stock of merchandise, the business to be carried on in W.'s name alone, giving to them the option to share in the profits if successful, or if not successful, then to receive back the amount advanced with ten per cent. interest. P. becoming dissatisfied demanded a settlement, when B. executed his note to him for the balance due him, which was afterwards made. B., upon the business being broken up, took what was left of the goods as a creditor. Shortly afterwards the petitioners filed their petition in bankruptcy against W., B. and P. Held, that without an election on the part of B. and P. to share in the profits, there was no partnership between W., B. and P. in the meaning of the bankrupt law, although they might be liable to creditors as having by their acts justified such creditors in believing that they were partners. Moore v. Walton,* 9 N. B. R., 402.

§ 46. Where cattle were delivered to certain parties by the owner to be herded, for a certain time, upon an agreement that after the expiration of the time the owner should sell them, and, after deducting their valuation when delivered, divide the remainder of the proceeds with said parties, it was held that there was no partnership, since there was no community of loss, community of title, community of expenses, nor a common right to dispose of the property. Beckwith v. Talbot,* 2 Colo. T'y, 639.

§ 47. A lay or share in the proceeds or catchings of a whaling voyage does not create a partnership in the profits of the voyage, but is in the nature of seamen's wages, and governed by the same rules. Coffin v. Jenkins, 3 Story, 108.

§ 48. A trust was constituted by deed, to purchase bonds, from a fund to be raised by subscription. The subscribers received certificates, payable to bearer, entitling the holder to participate in the distribution of the profits and proceeds of the trust investments by a drawing in a mode set out in the deed. Held, that the certificate holders were not partners. Johnson v. Lewis, 2 McC., 479.

§ 49. A contract between a dispatch company and various railroad companies for a through rate on goods, shipped from St. Louis to New York, to be divided between themselves upon the basis of the distance the goods were carried by each road, and providing for periodical accountings and settlements, does not constitute them partners *inter sese* or as to third persons. Insurance Co. *v.* Railroad Co., 14 Otto, 146.

§ 50. Two firms, Warner, Dickson & McElrath, and Anderson & Co., entered into an agreement in respect to the peach business, by which moneys, the proceeds of the sales of peaches, were deposited to the credit of Warner, Dickson, McElrath & Co., to keep them separate from money on deposit in the same bank to the credit of Warner, Dickson & McElrath. *Held,* that this agreement did not constitute a partnership between the members of the two firms; and a petition in bankruptcy filed by the holder of checks, signed by Anderson in the name of Warner, Dickson, McElrath & Co., against the members of both firms, was dismissed. *In re* Warner,* 7 N. B. R., 47.

§ 51. In the case of joint patentees, where no agreement of copartnership exists, the relation of copartners does not result from their connection as joint patentees; nor where one joint owner transfers his undivided interest does his assignee become the partner of his coproprietor. Pitts *v.* Hall, 3 Blatch., 201.

§ 52. A joint interest in a patent does not make those interested partners. Parkhurst *v.* Kinsman, 1 Blatch., 488.

§ 53. Proof of partnership.— In an action brought against several defendants as partners, to recover the price of a saw-mill, the answer of the only one who appeared and defended admitted that he and the other defendants " were interested together in the business " of manufacturing lumber and intended to procure a saw-mill, but denied that they or either of them applied to plaintiff to purchase a saw-mill. *Held,* that this language of the answer, in connection with uncontradicted evidence that the mill was at the time of the alleged sale in the possession and use of the defendants, and with the language of a letter referring to the partnership, justified the court in saying, in the charge to the jury, that the existence of the partnership was conceded. Porter *v.* Graves,* 14 Otto, 171.

§ 54. Partnership may be proved by parol as well as by written evidence; and an authority or ratification from one partner to another to bind the firm need not be in writing. Moran *v.* Prather, 23 Wall., 492.

§ 55. Where the question before the jury was whether or not one of the defendants was a partner in a commercial firm, it was proper for the court to exclude the declarations made by the defendant in the absence of the plaintiffs. It was also proper not to confine the attention of the jury to declarations made at one particular time in the presence of one of the plaintiffs, but to allow all similar declarations to be given in evidence, so that the jury could judge of the entire question of the existence of the partnership. Teller *v.* Patten, 20 How., 125.

§ 56. The plaintiff, assignee of a bankrupt, claimed that a partnership formerly existing between said bankrupt and others was dissolved prior to a certain transaction. The defendants insisted that it continued down to the close of the business involving said transaction, and offered in evidence the declarations of the former partners of the bankrupt touching the points in controversy. *Held,* that such testimony was properly excluded; the partners should have been called as witnesses. Nudd *v.* Burrows, 1 Otto, 426.

§ 57. To prove a partnership parol evidence cannot be given of the contents of printed cards bearing their joint names, nor are the cards themselves evidence unless traced to the defendant. Nor can general reputation of partnership be given in evidence. Wilson *v.* Colman, 1 Cr. C. C., 408.

§ 58. The allegation of a partnership between the master and mate of a vessel is not sustained by proof that the mate shipped for a share of the profits, unattended by other circumstances, and without proof of what that share was to be. The Crusader, 1 Ware, 437.

§ 59. The acknowledgment of a debt by one partner will bind another partner after the partnership is proved; but it is not sufficient or proper to be given in evidence to prove a partnership. Corps *v.* Robinson, 2 Wash., 388.

§ 60. The question of partnership or no partnership in the case of persons not ostensibly partners is one of fact; the old rule of the common law, that participation in the profits is *ipso facto* conclusive of a partnership, is not the law to-day, but such participation is strong evidence of a partnership. *In re* Ward,* 2 Flip., 462.

§ 61. Evidence that one of two persons sought to be charged as partners procured a loan for the other to use in a cotton speculation, and that the latter gratuitously promised that he would give him a share of the profits, if he made any, not mentioning any definite share or amount, is not sufficient evidence of a partnership to require the submission of the question to the jury. Pleasants *v.* Fant,* 22 Wall., 116.

§ 62. On an issue of partnership, an offer to pay the partnership note, if the holder would take property, is evidence; and also that the defendant said the note was signed by his partner. Thomas *v.* Wolcott, 4 McL., 365.

II. Partnership Property.

SUMMARY — *Real estate; judgment lien,* § 63. — *Conveyance by survivor for benefit of creditors,* § 64.

§ 63. Partnership real estate is to be treated as personalty so far as is necessary to secure the payment of the firm debts and advances made by the partners respectively, but for every other purpose it remains subject to the principles and laws applicable to real estate. Thus a judgment against a partnership for a partnership debt is a lien on the partnership real estate. *In re* Codding, §§ 65, 66.

§ 64. If a surviving partner conveys all the firm property to a trustee for the benefit of creditors of the firm, purchasers from the trustee of partnership real estate can, by bill in equity, compel one in whom the legal title to an undivided half of the real estate has vested by the will of the deceased partner to convey such title to them. Shanks *v.* Klein, §§ 67, 68.

[NOTES. — See §§ 69-92.]

IN RE CODDING.

(District Court for Pennsylvania: 9 Federal Reporter, 849–851. 1881.)

Opinion by ACHESON, J.

STATEMENT OF FACTS. — This contest is over a fund realized from the real estate of the bankrupts, sold by the assignee divested of liens. The claimants are Lawrence Butler and Matthew Jackson, two judgment creditors of the bankrupt firm, on the one hand, and, on the other, the assignee in bankruptcy. The judgments are not assailed as unlawful preferences, but it is denied that they were liens against the real estate; and therefore the assignee claims the fund for the benefit of the general creditors of the firm.

No exceptions having been filed to the register's findings of fact, their correctness will be assumed. These findings are substantially as follows: John A. Codding and Chauncey S. Russell, the bankrupts, composed the firm of Codding & Russell. The said real estate was owned and held by the bankrupts, as copartners, for partnership purposes and as partnership property. The judgment of Lawrence Butler was entered against "Codding, Russell & Co." (a name by which the firm was formerly designated), upon a judgment note signed "Codding, Russell & Co." The judgment of Matthew Jackson was entered against "Codding & Russell," upon a judgment note signed "Codding & Russell." The consideration of each note was money loaned to and used by the partnership. Both partners participated in giving the notes, and the judgments thereon were each entered at the suggestion of both the partners.

§ 65. *How far and under what limitations real estate purchased with partnership funds and brought into a firm is to be treated as personalty.*

Any question growing out of the Butler judgment note having been entered up in the old firm name may be dismissed from the case; for the Jackson judgment alone, under the rule which prevails in this court to allow interest on a judgment down to the time of distribution, would absorb the whole fund; and Jackson does not question the lien of Butler's judgment, or his right to be paid out of the proceeds of sale. The question upon which the case turns is whether a judgment against a partnership, for a partnership debt, entered by confession of the firm, and at the suggestion of all the partners, is a lien against the partnership real estate. The register held that it was not, and he awarded the fund to the assignee in bankruptcy. The decision of the register rests exclusively upon the assumption that partnership real estate is personalty, and therefore not the subject of a judgment lien. But the doctrine that partnership real estate is to be treated as personalty is not to be pushed too far. Real estate brought into a firm as stock is not converted absolutely and for all purposes. The conversion manifestly has its limitations. For example, partnership real estate unquestionably is governed by the statute of frauds. Again, to pass the title each partner is required to join in the conveyance. Story, Part., § 94; Parsons, Part., § 377.

§ 66. *Partnership real estate is subject to a lien of a judgment against the partnership for a partnership debt.*

I suppose no one would seriously maintain that on an execution against a firm a constable could seize and sell their real estate. It was held in Foster's Appeal, 74 Pa. St., 391, that after payment of the firm debts and the advances made by the surviving partner, the remaining share of a deceased partner in partnership real estate passed, not to his personal representatives, but to the widow and heirs. Conversion of partnership real estate is allowed to secure, in the interest of the partners themselves, the payment of the firm debts and advances made by the partners respectively. Id. Therefore, the true doctrine, as I conceive, is that in so far as may be necessary to attain those ends, partnership real estate is to be treated as personalty, but for every other purpose it remains real estate, and is subject to the principles and laws applicable to that species of property. Why, then, is partnership real estate not bound by the lien of a judgment against the partnership for a partnership debt, especially where such judgment is entered by confession of the firm and at the instance of all the partners? From a very early period it has been the settled law of Pennsylvania that a judgment is a lien on every kind of right,—on every sort of beneficial interest,— in real estate, vested in the debtor at the time of the judgment. Caskhuff *v.* Anderson, 3 Binn., 9; Troubat & H., §§ 58, 778; Price, Liens, 277.

The general creditors of a firm are preferred in the distribution of firm assets wholly by virtue of the equities of the partners, and not on account of any equities of their own. They themselves have no lien upon the partnership property. What right, therefore, have they, or an assignee in bankruptcy who represents them, to gainsay the lien of a judgment upon the partnership real estate, where that judgment is for a firm debt, and was entered against the partnership by the confession of the firm? The validity of a mortgage given by partners upon partnership real estate was distinctly recognized in Lancaster Bank *v.* Myley, 13 Pa. St., 544. But if the partners may incumber their real estate by mortgage, why may they not do so by judgment? Undoubtedly it was the intention of Codding & Russell to give Butler and Jackson judgment liens, and I am at a loss to see upon what principle that intention is to be frustrated by the assignee in bankruptcy, who stands, in this matter, in no better position than the bankrupts themselves.

While, perhaps, the precise question now before me has not been judicially determined, yet in more than one case the validity of such judgment liens, it would seem, has been assumed. Overholt's Appeal, 12 Pa. St., 222; Erwin's Appeal, 39 Pa. St., 535. And it is said by Mr. Price, in his work on liens, that a judgment for a firm debt would bind the real estate of the firm. Price, Liens, 280, 281. And now, December 21, 1881, the exceptions to the register's report are sustained; and it is ordered that the fund for distribution be applied first to the payment of the judgment of Lawrence Butler, and the residue to the judgment of Matthew Jackson, and that the assignee pay the fund to said judgment creditors in accordance with this decree.

SHANKS v. KLEIN.

(14 Otto, 18–24. 1881.)

APPEAL from U. S. Circuit Court, District of Mississippi.

Opinion by MR. JUSTICE MILLER.

STATEMENT OF FACTS.— This is a bill in chancery filed by John A. Klein and others against David C. Shanks, executor of the last will and testament of Joseph H. Johnston.

The substance of the bill is, that in the life-time of Johnston there existed between him and Shepperd Brown a partnership, the style of which was Brown & Johnston; that their principal place of business was at Vicksburg, in the state of Mississippi, where they had a banking-house; that they had branches and connections with other men in business at other places, among which was New Orleans; that they dealt largely in the purchase and sale of real estate, of which they had a large amount in value on hand at the outbreak of the recent civil war; that this real estate was in different parcels and localities, and was bought and paid for by partnership money, and held as partnership property for the general uses of the partnership business; and that early in the war, namely, in 1863, Johnston died in the state of Virginia, where he then resided, leaving a will by which all his property, including his interest in the partnership, became vested in Shanks, who was appointed his executor.

It seems that both Brown and Johnston were absent from Mississippi and from New Orleans during the war,— the one being in Virginia and the other in Georgia. Upon the cessation of hostilities, Brown returned to New Orleans, and visited Vicksburg to look after the business of the firm of Brown & Johnston, and the other firms with which that was connected. Finding that suits had been commenced by creditors of the firm against him as surviving partner, and, in some instances, attachments levied, he became satisfied that unless he adopted some mode of disposing of the partnership property and applying its proceeds to the payment of the debts in their just order, the whole would be wasted or a few active creditors would absorb it all. Under these circumstances, acting by advice of counsel, he executed a deed conveying all the property of the firm of Brown & Johnston to John A. Klein, in trust for the creditors of that partnership, and providing that the surplus, if any, should be for the use of the partners and their heirs or devisees. Klein accepted the trust, and pursuant thereto paid debts with the lands, or with the proceeds of the sale of them.

There is an allegation that Shanks, while acting as executor, and about the time the deed of trust was made, had an interview with Brown, and being fully informed of the condition of the affairs of the partnership, expressed his approval of what Brown intended to do. This is denied in the answer, and some testimony is taken on the subject. Other questions of bad faith on the part of Brown are raised. But in the view which we take of the case, the record establishes that Brown acted in good faith, and did the best that could be done for the creditors of the partnership and for those interested in its property.

It appears that after all this property had been sold to purchasers in good faith, Shanks, as executor of Johnston's will, instituted actions of ejectment against them. They thereupon filed this bill to enjoin him from further prosecuting the actions, and compel him to convey the legal title to the real estate which came to him by the will of his testator. A decree was rendered in conformity with the prayer of the bill, and Shanks appealed.

Being satisfied, as already stated, of the fairness and honesty of the proceedings of Brown and Klein and of the purchasers from them, and waiving as of no consequence, in regard to the principal point in the case, the allegation of Shanks' concurrence in or ratification of Brown's action, we proceed to consider the question as to the power or authority of Brown, the surviving partner, to bind Shanks by the conveyance to Klein, and by the sales thereunder made.

§ 67. *Contention of counsel.*

There is no doubt that in the present case all the real estate which is the subject of this controversy is to be treated as partnership property, bought and held for partnership purposes within the rule of equity on that subject. Nor is it denied by the counsel who have so ably argued the case for the appellant that the equity of the creditors of the partnership to have their debts paid out of this property is superior to that of the devisee of Johnston. Their contention is that this right could only be enforced by proceedings in a court of justice, and that no power existed in Brown, the surviving partner, to convey the legal title vested in Shanks by the will of Johnston, nor even to make a contract for the sale of the real estate which a court will enforce against Shanks as the holder of that title.

Counsel for the appellees, while conceding that neither the deed of Brown to Klein, nor of Klein to his vendees, conveyed the legal title of the undivided moiety which was originally in Johnston, maintain that Brown, as surviving partner, had, for the purpose of paying the debts of the partnership, power to sell and transfer the equitable interest or right of the partnership, and of both partners, in the real estate; that the trust deed which he made to Klein was effectual for that purpose, and that by Klein's sales to the other appellees they became invested with this equitable title and the right to compel Shanks to convey the legal title.

One of the learned counsel for the appellant concedes that at the present day the doctrine of the English court of chancery "extends to the treating of the realty as personalty for all purposes, and gives the personal representatives of the deceased partner the land as personalty, to the exclusion of the heir," and that the principle has "acquired a firm foothold in English equity jurisprudence, that partnership real estate is in fact in all cases, and to all intents and purposes, personalty." He maintains, however, that the principle has not been carried so far in the courts of America; that the extent of the doctrine is that the creditors of the partnership and the surviving partner have a lien on the real estate of the partnership for debts due by the firm, and for any balance found due to either partner on a final settlement of the partnership transactions; and that the right of the surviving partner, and of the creditors through him, is no *more than a lien*, which cannot be asserted by a sale, as if the property were personal, but to the enforcement of which a resort to a court of equity is necessary.

§ 68. *The equitable right of the surviving partner in partnership real estate is something more than a lien. It is an interest in the property, giving him the right to sell it to pay partnership debts, and the purchaser the right to enforce a conveyance of the legal title from the holder thereof. Authorities reviewed.*

We think that the error which lies at the foundation of this argument is in

the assumption that the equitable right of the surviving partner and the creditors is nothing but a lien.

It is not necessary to decide here that it is not a lien in the strict sense of
that word, for if it be a lien in any sense it is also something more.

It is an equitable *right* accompanied *by an equitable title*. It is an *interest
in the property* which courts of chancery will recognize and support. What
is that right? Not only that the court will, when necessary, see that the real
estate so situated is appropriated to the satisfaction of the partnership debts,
but that for that purpose, and to that extent, it shall be treated as personal
property of the partnership, and like other personal property pass under the
control of the surviving partner. This control extends to the right to sell it,
or so much of it as may be necessary to pay the partnership debts, or to satisfy the just claims of the surviving partner.

It is beyond question that such is the doctrine of the English court of chancery, as stated by counsel for appellant. As this result was reached in that
court without the aid of any statute, it is authority of very great weight in
the inquiry as to the true equity doctrine on the subject. We think, also, that
the preponderance of authority in the American courts is on the same side
of the question.

In the case of Dyer *v.* Clark, 5 Metc. (Mass.), 562, that eminent jurist, Chief
Justice Shaw, while using the word "lien" in reference to the rights now in
controversy, asks, "What are the true equitable rights of the partners as resulting from their presumed intentions in such real estate? Is not the share
of each pledged to the other, and has not each an equitable lien on the estate,
requiring that it shall be held and appropriated, first, to pay the joint debts,
then to repay the partner who advanced the capital, before it shall be applied
to the separate use of either of the partners? The creditors have an interest
indirectly in the same appropriation; not because they have any lien, legal or
equitable (2 Story, Eq., sec. 1253), upon the property itself; but on the equitable principle that the real estate so held shall be deemed to constitute a part
of the fund from which their debts are to be paid before it can be legally or
honestly diverted to the private use of the parties. Suppose this trust is not
implied, what would be the condition of the parties?" etc. "But treating it
as a trust, the rights of all the parties will be preserved." It is clear that in
the view thus announced the right of the creditors is something more than an
ordinary lien.

In Delmonico *v.* Guillaume, 2 Sandf. (N. Y.) Ch., 366, where the precise
question arose which we have in the present case, the vice-chancellor held that
"Peter A. Delmonico, as the surviving partner, became entitled to the Brooklyn farm, and as between himself and the heir of John he had an absolute
right to dispose of it, for the payment of the debts of the firm, in the same
manner as if it had been personal estate." In so deciding he followed the
English authorities, and cited Fereday *v.* Wightwick, 1 Russ. & M., 45; Phillips
v. Phillips, 1 Myl. & K., 649; Brown *v.* Brown, 3 id., 443; Cookson *v.* Cookson, 8 Sim., 529; Townshend *v.* Devaynes, 11 id., 498, note.

In Andrews' Heirs *v.* Brown's Adm'r, 21 Ala., 437, the supreme court said
that, "inasmuch as the real estate is considered as personal for the purpose of
paying the debts of the firm, and the surviving partner is charged with the
duty of paying these debts, it must of necessity follow that he has the right in
equity to dispose of the real estate for this purpose, for it would never do to
charge him with the duty of paying the debts and at the same time take from

him the means of doing it. Therefore, although he cannot by his deed pass the legal title which descended to the heir of the deceased partner, yet as the heir holds the title in trust to pay the debts and the survivor is charged with this duty, his deed will convey the equity to the purchaser, and through it he may call on the heir for the legal title and compel him to convey it."

In Dupuy v. Leavenworth, 17 Cal., 262, Chief Justice Field, in the name of the court, said: "In the view of equity it is immaterial in whose name the legal title of the property stands,— whether in the individual name of the copartner or in the ·joint names of all; it is first subject to the payment of the partnership debts, and is then to be distributed among the copartners according to their respective rights. The possessor of the legal title in such case holds the property in trust for the purposes of the copartnership. Each partner has an equitable interest in the property until such purposes are accomplished. Upon dissolution of the copartnership by the death of one of its members, the surviving partner, who is charged with the duty of paying the debts, can dispose of this equitable interest, and the purchaser can compel the heirs at law of the deceased partner to perfect the purchase by conveyance of the legal title."

If the case could be held to be one which should be governed by the decisions of the courts of Mississippi because the principle is to be regarded as a rule of property, which we neither admit nor deny, the result would still be the same.

In one of the earliest cases on that subject in the high court of errors and appeals of that state (Markham v. Merritt, 8 Miss., 437), Chief Justice Sharkey, in delivering the opinion of the court, concurs in the general doctrine that "when land is held by a firm, and is essential to the purposes and objects of the partnership, then it is regarded as a part of the joint stock, and will be regarded in equity as a chattel." A careful examination of the Mississippi cases cited by counsel has disclosed nothing in contravention of this doctrine or in denial of the authority of the surviving partner to dispose of such property for the payment of the debts of the partnership.

We are of opinion, therefore, that the purchasers from Klein acquired the equitable title of the real estate conveyed to him by Brown; that they had a right to the aid of a court of chancery to compel Shanks to convey the legal title to the undivided half of the land, vested in him by the will of Johnston.

Decree affirmed.

§ 69. In general.—The interest of a partner in a trade-mark is of too intangible and shadowy a character to be the subject of sale under a decree of a court of chancery. Taylor v. Bemis, 4 Biss., 406.

§ 70. A court of equity should know, before making a decree for the sale of the interest of a partner, that there is some tangible interest which can be sold, which will be of some value. *Ibid.*

§ 71. Where a partnership has been proved to exist, oral evidence may be admitted to prove that the factory in which the partners carried on their business, and upon which they expended their money, was a part of the capital stock contributed by them; and the oral evidence being clear and undisputed, and admitted to be true, the property in question is to be treated in bankruptcy as the property of the firm; if on no other ground, then clearly on that of part performance. *In re* Farmer,* 18 N. B. R., 207.

§ 72. When deemed individual and when firm property.—Property purchased by a member of a firm for his own account, and not claimed by the other partners, is individual and not firm property. Sedgwick v. Place, 12 Blatch., 163.

§ 73. In the absence of fraud and breach of trust, property purchased with partnership funds does not of necessity become partnership property, if that is not the intention of the parties. Hoxie v. Carr,* 1 Sumn,. 173.

165

§ 74. But, in the absence of controlling circumstances, the fact that payment for property purchased is made out of partnership funds, especially if the property is needed for the use of the partnership and is so used, will be decisive that it was intended as partnership property. *Ibid.*

§ 75. Premises used by partners for the purpose of carrying on their trade *prima facie* form part of the partnership property. But this presumption may be rebutted. Osborn *v.* McBride.* 16 N. B. R., 22.

§ 76. Real property purchased with money belonging to a firm is in equity *prima facie* firm property. Patrick *v.* Central Bank, 1 Dill., 803.

§ 77. In the absence of proof of its purchase with partnership funds for partnership purposes, real property standing in the names of several persons is deemed to be held by them as joint tenants or as tenants in common, and none of the several owners possesses authority to sell or bind the interest of his co-owners. Thompson *v.* Bowman,* 6 Wall., 316.

§ 78. Where a complainant files a bill, claiming for himself and others certain tracts of land purchased in partnership, to sustain the suit it is enough to show that the land was purchased by the partnership funds, without specifying the amount contributed by each partner. Piatt *v.* Oliver, 2 McL., 267.

§ 79. —— purchased by partner with funds of firm.— Where land is purchased by one partner in his own name with the partnership funds and is used for partnership purposes, the law raises an implied trust in favor of the firm, and parol evidence is admissible to establish such a trust. Scruggs *v.* Russell,* McCahon, 39.

§ 80. Real estate, settled by a partner on his wife, is liable to the debts of the firm, when it appears that it was improperly purchased with the assets of the firm. But neither the wife, nor her executors if she be dead, can be sued *in personam* for the value of such property. Phipps *v.* Sedgwick, 5 Otto, 3.

§ 81. A resulting trust will arise where lands have been purchased by one partner and paid for out of the funds of the partnership. Philips *v.* Crammond, 2 Wash., 441.

§ 82. If a partner fraudulently or improperly, without the consent of his copartners, applies partnership funds to the purchase of real estate or other property, taken in his own name and for his own use, his copartners may, if they can distinctly trace the investment, follow it, and treat it as trust property held for the benefit of the firm by the partner or any one in whose hands it may be, except a *bona fide* purchaser for value. Kelley *v.* Greenleaf,* 3 Story, 98.

§ 83. Where partnership funds were thus invested by one of the partners in mortgaged real estate, and such partner subsequently died, *held*, that the real estate would be sold at the suit of the surviving partner, and the proceeds be applied first to the discharge of the mortgage and the residue to the discharge of the debt due from the partner to the firm. *Ibid.*

§ 84. —— considered as personalty.— Real estate held by partners, either as capital stock for partnership purposes or as purchased with partnership means, is for the purpose of paying the debts due by the partnership, or the balance due its members, considered as personal assets of the partnership, the legal title being vested in the partners as tenants in common, in trust for the creditors and members of the firm as stated in the articles of copartnership. And upon the death of one of the members, the legal title descends to his heirs or devisees as tenants in common with the survivors upon the same trusts. Kleine *v.* Shanks,* 3 Cent. L. J., 799.

§ 85. When real estate is purchased for partnership purposes and on partnership account, it will be regarded as partnership property, no matter in whose name the title may stand, and will be treated for most purposes as personalty in equity. Hoxie *v.* Carr,* 1 Sumn., 173.

§ 86. It seems that it will be considered in equity as personalty, as between the personal representatives of a deceased partner and his heir or devisee. *Ibid.*

§ 87. Lands bought and held for partnership purposes, whether standing in the name of one or both partners, are considered in equity as partnership property, and stand on the same footing as personal property. Lyman *v.* Lyman,* 2 Paine, 11.

§ 88. Real estate may be purchased with partnership funds for the individual account of the partners, but if the intention was to hold it as partnership property equity treats it as personalty of the partnership, and as against a judgment creditor of one member of the firm, it is first subject to the payment of the firm debts. Marrett *v.* Murphy,* 1 Cent. L. J., 554; 11 N. B. R., 181.

§ 89. Real property belonging to a partnership is treated in equity as part of the partnership fund, and is disposed of and distributed the same as personal assets. Clagett *v.* Kilbourne,* 1 Black, 346.

§ 90. Real estate of a partnership, although considered in equity as personal property for most purposes, cannot be transferred by one of the partners the same as personalty. The mode of conveyance of real estate is not affected by the general law of partnership. Platt *v.* Oliver,* 3 McL., 27.

§ 91. —— bona fide purchaser of.— If a purchaser of real estate has actual or constructive notice at the time of the purchase that it is partnership property, it will be chargeable in his hands with the payment of the partnership debts, even though he has no notice of the existence of the debts. If the purchaser has no notice that it is partnership property, he will be exonerated to the extent of the purchase money already paid, and the balance unpaid will be chargeable the same as the real estate itself would be. Hoxie *v.* Carr,* 1 Sumn., 173.

§ 92. Where the deed under which purchasers of real estate derived title described the property as "heretofore owned by " a certain company, and one of the members of that company was at the time of the purchase in possession of the property and holding out the other, *held*, that the purchasers were put upon inquiry as to whether it was not partnership property. *Ibid.*

III. Power of Partner to Bind the Firm.

SUMMARY — *In general; dormant partners,* § 93.— *Misapplication of funds,* § 94.— *Signing in individual name,* §§ 95, 96.— *Application of funds to separate debt,* § 97.— *Assignment for creditors,* §§ 98, 99.— *By deed,* § 100.— *Real property,* § 101.— *Assignment of debts,* § 102.— *Act in violation of law,* § 103.— *Conversion,* §§ 104–107.— *Use of name after dissolution,* § 108.— *Admissions after dissolution,* § 109.— *Appearance to suit,* § 110.

§ 93. An active partner binds the firm by transactions within the ordinary scope of the partnership business, such as, in case of an ordinary mercantile partnership, signing and indorsing notes and bills in the name of the firm and obtaining discounts, notwithstanding any private restrictions on his powers, which are unknown to those dealing with him; and this principle applies as well to dormant as to ostensible partnerships. Winship *v.* United States Bank, §§ 111–118.

§ 94. The fact that the partner misapplies funds so procured by him will not defeat a recovery unless the plaintiffs were parties or privy to the misapplication. *Ibid.*

§ 95. Generally, if one member of a firm draws a bill or a note in his own name, he only will be bound and not the firm, although it is a partnership transaction; but this rule does not hold where there is a dormant partner, unknown to the creditor, nor when such bills or notes have been customarily drawn as firm paper and the other partners have so treated them. *In re* Warren, §§ 119–124.

§ 96. When partners sign a bill or note in their several names and not in that of the firm, it seems that it will be treated as partnership paper, if it is in fact on partnership account. *Ibid.*

§ 97. The funds of a partnership cannot be applied by one partner to the discharge of his separate debt without the assent, express or implied, of the other partner. In such case it makes no difference that the separate creditor had no knowledge, at the time, that the fund was partnership property; the partnership may, nevertheless, reassert its claim to it. Rogers *v.* Batchelor, §§ 125, 126.

§ 98. A partner has power to bind his copartners by a general conveyance of the effects of the partnership, not including real estate, for the benefit of the firm creditors, whether the conveyance be made directly or through the intervention of trustees. Anderson *v.* Tompkins, §§ 127–131.

§ 99. An objection to such conveyance that it prefers certain creditors, and that the copartner had a right to be consulted about that matter, is not available, if the latter was absent in a foreign country and the business was being conducted by the partner who made the conveyance. *Ibid.*

§ 100. The rule that one partner cannot bind another by deed does not go so far as to vitiate a conveyance by deed of property which is transferable by delivery without deed. *Ibid.*

§ 101. Real property conveyed to a firm, or to partners in trust for a firm, is held by them as tenants in common, and neither party can convey more than his undivided interest. *Ibid.*

§ 102. An assignment by one partner of debts which are assignable at law is valid, and is not vitiated by being made under seal. As to book accounts (which are not assignable at law, but are so in equity), if successive assignments are made by each of the partners separately, the prior equity should prevail, and the accounts will therefore pass by the first deed. *Ibid.*

§ 103. A tort or an act in violation of a particular statute law, and attended with a forfeiture, is not within the proper scope and business of a partnership entered into for lawful purposes. Where, therefore, one of two partners, in the absence and without the knowledge of his copartner, loaned money on usurious interest and received certain steamships as security, and afterwards refused, upon demand, to surrender possession of the steamships, held, that the other partner did not by such facts alone become liable in trover for the steamships, no demand being made upon him, and he not being shown to be connected with the transaction in any way, although under the usury law the plaintiff was entitled to a return of the ships. Graham v. Meyer, §§ 182–185.

§ 104. If a firm, acting through one of the partners, while engaged in the regular course of business of the firm, innocently or wrongfully appropriates property other than money, or what has the quality of money, and sells it and receives and uses in its business the proceeds, or, without a sale, uses it in the firm's business, the firm is liable for conversion; and it is wholly immaterial that all or any of the members of the firm were ignorant of the wrong committed, or innocent of any wrongful intent. In re Ketchum, §§ 186–148.

§ 105. If money is thus received and used by a firm, through the fraud of one of the partners, the liability of the firm therefor will depend upon whether the innocent partner has an individual equity by reason of which the firm should not, on account of his rights and for his protection, be held liable, viz., that he has received the money as a payment upon a balance due from his copartner on account of the partnership business, or has in some way parted with value, or will suffer some injury from relying on the apparent title made by his copartner's actual possession of the money. Ibid.

§ 106. One of two partners in a firm of stock brokers, who attended to all the financial affairs of the firm, and who in his individual capacity acted as agent for a third person, being intrusted by the latter with the possession of certain stocks belonging to him, and being empowered to draw on his bank account, in violation of his trust drew checks against said bank account and deposited them to the credit of the firm, sold certain of the stocks intrusted to him and deposited the proceeds in the bank account of the firm, and hypothecated others of the stocks for loans made to the firm. No entry of these transactions or of anything to show an indebtedness of the firm to such third person was made on the firm books until after the failure of the firm, and the other partner was entirely ignorant of the transactions. Held, that the firm was liable for the amount of the checks and hypothecated stocks on the ground that they were to be regarded as chattels converted by the firm; and that, as to the proceeds of the stocks sold, while the same rule does not apply in the case of money as in the case of chattels, the firm was liable for them too, both because the innocent partner appeared to have no equity to avail himself of the protection accorded to one who receives money in ignorance that it does not belong to the party paying it, not having parted with value or altered his position in reliance on it, especially as the state of the accounts between the partners at the time of the deposits did not appear, and because the innocent partner, having given his copartner unrestricted authority to raise money for the firm without exercising any supervision over him, should be held bound by his acts in doing so. Ibid.

§ 107. The fact that the guilty partner, after making the deposits to the firm's credit, drew out money for his own private use, would be no defense, especially if he drew money for purposes forbidden by the partnership articles. Ibid.

§ 108. After the dissolution of a partnership the partnership name cannot be used by either partner in the creation of a new contract. The name cannot be used in giving a note for a debt due by the late firm, and authority granted to one partner to settle all demands by or against the firm does not warrant the giving of such a note. Lockwood v. Comstock, § 144.

§ 109. The admission of a partner after dissolution is not evidence against the firm. Bispham v. Patterson, §§ 145–148.

§ 110. After dissolution of a copartnership, one of the partners has no authority to enter an appearance in a suit brought against the firm for other partners who do not reside in the state where the suit is brought and have not been served with process; and a judgment against all the partners, founded on such an appearance, can be questioned by those not served in a suit brought thereon in another state. (WAITE, C. J., STRONG and HUNT, JJ., dissented.) Hall v. Lanning, §§ 149–151.

[NOTES.—See §§ 152–194.]

WINSHIP v. UNITED STATES BANK.

(5 Peters, 529–580. 1831.)

ERROR to U. S. Circuit Court, District of Massachusetts.

Opinion by MARSHALL, C. J.

STATEMENT OF FACTS.—This was an action brought in the court for the first circuit and district for Massachusetts against John Winship, Amos Binney and John Binney, merchants and partners, trading under the name and firm of John Winship, as indorser of several promissory notes, made by Samuel Jacques, Jr. At the trial the maker was called by the plaintiffs and sworn. He was objected to by the defendants as an interested witness, an instrument being produced purporting to be a release, in the name of John Winship, of all liability of the maker on the said notes. The operation of the said instrument as a release of the notes in suit was controverted by the plaintiffs. It is unnecessary to state the instrument, or to discuss the question arising on it, or on the competency of the witness, because the court is divided on the effect of the instrument and on the competency of the witness.

The witness testified that he knew from general reputation that the defendant, John Winship, was concerned with the other defendants, Amos and John Binney, in the soap and candle business; that Winship avowed the part- nership; that he had dealings with Winship soon after its commencement, and supplied him with rosin, for which he sometimes gave a note signed John Winship, which the witness always took on the credit of the Binneys. Winship and the witness were in the habit of lending their names to each other, and Winship always represented that the notes made or indorsed by the witness for his accommodation were for the use of the firm.

Several other witnesses were examined on the part of the plaintiff to prove the partnership, whose testimony was rendered unimportant by the production of the articles themselves. The defendants exhibited them, and they are in the following words:

"The memorandum of an agreement made this 25th day of September, 1817, between Amos Binney and John Binney, of Boston, county of Suffolk, and John Winship, of Charlestown, county of Middlesex, all in the common-wealth of Massachusetts, for the manufacture of soap and candles, witnesseth:

"That the said Amos and John Binney agree to furnish for the above purpose the sum or capital stock of $10,000, at such times as may be wanted to purchase stock or materials for carrying on the aforesaid manufacture; and the said John Winship agrees, on his part, to conduct and superintend the manufactory, and to pay his whole and undivided attention to the business; to manufacture, or cause to be manufactured, every article in the best possible manner, and to use his utmost skill and exertions to promote the interest of the establishment, under the name and firm of John Winship, and without any charge for his personal labors, and to keep a fair and regular set of books and accounts, open and subject at all times to the inspection of the parties interested in the concern, and annually, on the 1st day of October of each year, to make and exhibit a statement of the state of the business, the amount of purchases and sales, and the profits, if any, of the business, that have been made; the expenses of conducting the business and the profits to be divided in the following manner: to say, from the profits is to be paid interest for the capital stock of $10,000, at the rate of six per centum per annum, all expenses of rent, labor, transportation, fuel and utensils, that it may be necessary to purchase or have, and the remainder of the profits, if any, to be equally divided between the said Winship and Binneys, one-half thereof to the said John Winship, and the other half to A. and J. Binney; and, in case no profit should be made, but a loss, then the loss is to be borne and sustained one-half by the said A. and J. Binney, and the other half by the said John Winship.

"The agreement to continue in force for two years from the 1st day of October next ensuing, and then for a further term, provided all parties agree thereto. And to the true and faithful performance of the foregoing conditions, each party bind themselves to the other in the penal sum of $10,000." On the back of which were receipts signed by the said Winship, acknowledging that he had received of Amos Binney $1,000, on the 6th of September, 1817, and $4,000 on the 9th of October, 1817; and on the 27th of December, 1827, he had in his hands $10,000, as said Amos' proportion of the capital; and that he had received of John Binney $2,500 on the 1st of October, 1817, and $500 on the 3d of November, 1817, and $500 on the 17th of November, 1817, and $1,500 on the 13th of June, 1820, and on the 2d of June, 1821, he had in his hands $10,000, as said John's proportion of the capital stock.

They also gave in evidence a bond given by said Winship to said Amos, on the 25th of September, 1817, in the penal sum of $10,000, with the condition following:

"The conditions of this obligation are such, that whereas the above bounden John Winship has this day made an agreement with Amos Binney and John Binney, both of Boston aforesaid, for the purpose of carrying on a manufactory of soap and candles, on joint account of the parties aforesaid; and whereas the said A. Binney hath engaged to indorse the notes given by the said John Winship, for the purchase of stock and raw materials for manufacturing, when necessary to purchase on a credit, and in consideration of which the said John Winship hath engaged not to indorse the notes, paper, or become in any manner responsible or security for any person or persons other than the said Amos Binney, for the term of two years from the 1st day of October, 1817.

"Now, therefore, if the said John Winship shall faithfully observe the conditions, and wholly abstain from becoming the surety or indorser of any person to any amount other than the same Amos Binney for the aforesaid term of two years from the 1st day of October, 1817, then this obligation to be void and of no effect; otherwise to remain in full force and virtue."

The defendants also produced witnesses whose testimony furnished some foundation for the presumption that the money arising from the notes, on which the suits were brought, was not applied by Winship to the purposes of the firm. Other testimony led to the belief that a part, if not the whole, of the money was so applied. All the notes in suit were discounted by and applied to the credit of John Winship.

The testimony being closed, the counsel for the defendant insisted: 1. "That the said copartnership between them was, in contemplation of law, a secret copartnership, and did not authorize the giving of credit to any other name than that of the said Winship." But to this the counsel for the plaintiffs did then and there insist, before the said court, that this was an open or avowed and not a secret copartnership. And the presiding justice of the said court did state his opinion to the jury on this point, as follows: "That, according to his understanding of the common meaning of 'secret partnership,' those were deemed secret where the existence of certain persons as partners was not avowed or made known to the public by any of the partners. That, where the partners were all publicly known, whether this was done by all the partners, or by one only, it was no longer a secret partnership; for, secret partnership was generally used in contradistinction to notorious and open partnership; that whether the business was carried on in the name and firm of one partner only, or of him and company, would in this respect make no difference; that, if it was the intention of the Binneys that their names should be concealed, and the business of the firm was to be carried on in the name of Winship only; and yet that Winship, against their wishes, in the course of the business of the firm, publicly did avow and make known to the partnership, so that it became notorious who were the partners, such partnership could not, in the common sense of the terms, be deemed any longer a secret partnership; that, if 'secret' in any sense, it was under such circumstances, using the terms in a peculiar sense. That, however, nothing important in this case turned upon the meaning or definition of the terms 'secret partnership,' since the case must be decided on the principles of law applicable to such partnership, as this was in fact proved to be. That there was no stipulation for secrecy as to the Binneys being partners, on the face of the original articles of copartnership; and when those articles, by their own limitation, expired, the question what the partnership was, and how it was carried on for the future, whether upon the same terms as were contained in the original articles or otherwise, was matter of fact from the whole evidence; that, if the evidence was believed, Winship constantly avowed the partnership, and that the Binneys were his partners in the soap and candle manufactory business, and obtained credit thereby."

But he left the jury to judge for themselves as to the evidence.

Second exception. And the said counsel of the defendants did then and there further insist that the said jury had a right to infer from the evidence aforesaid, notwithstanding the entries of the shipments in the invoice book kept by said Winship, that the said Amos Binney and John Binney had no knowledge thereof, and therefore could not be presumed to have adopted or ratified the conduct of said Winship making said shipments. But the presiding judge did then and there instruct the jury as follows:

"That whether the said Amos and John Binney, or either of them, knew of the said entries or not, was matter of fact for the consideration of the jury, upon all the circumstances of the case. That, ordinarily, the presumption was, that all the parties had access to the partnership books, and might know the contents thereof. But this was a mere presumption from the ordinary course of business, and might be rebutted by any circumstances whatsoever, which, either positively or presumptively, repelled any inference of access; such, for instance, as the distance of place in the course of business of the particular partnership, or any other circumstances raising a presumption of non-access."

And he left the jury to draw their own conclusion as to the knowledge of the Binneys of the entries in the partnership books, from the whole evidence in the case.

Third exception. And the said counsel of the defendants did then and there further insist that, by the tenor of the said recited articles of agreement and bond, the said Winship had no right or authority to raise money on the credit of the said firm, or to bind the firm by his signature, for the purpose of borrowing money. But the presiding judge did then and there instruct the jury as follows:

"That if the particular terms of the articles of copartnership were not known to the public, or to persons dealing with the firm in the course of the business thereof, they had a right to deal with the firm in respect to the business thereof, upon the general principles and presumptions of limited partnership of a like nature; and that any secret and special restrictions contained in such articles of copartnership, varying the general rights and authorities of partners in such limited partnerships, and of which they are ignorant, did not affect them. That the case of Livingston v. Roosevelt, 4 Johns., 251, had been cited by the defendants' counsel as containing the true principles of law on this subject; and this court agreed to the law, as to limited partnership, as therein held by the court. That it was not denied by the defendants' counsel, and was asserted in that case, that it was within the scope and authority of partners generally, in limited partnerships, to make and indorse notes, and to obtain advances and credits for the business and benefit of the firm; and, if such was in fact the ordinary course and usage of trade, the authority must be presumed to exist. The court knew of no rule established to the contrary. That the authority of one partner in limited partnerships did not extend to bind the other partners in transactions, or for purposes, beyond the scope and object of such partnerships. That, in the present articles of copartnership, Winship was in effect constituted the active partner, and had general authority given him to transact the business of the firm. That he had, so far as respects third persons, dealing with and trusting the firm, and ignorant of any of the restrictions in such articles, authority to bind the firm, to the same extent and in the same manner as partners in limited partnerships of a like nature usually possess in the business or for the objects within the general scope of such a firm.

" That the articles limited the partnership to a particular period, after which it expired, unless the parties chose to give it a future existence. That no new written articles were proved in the case, and the terms and circumstances under which it was subsequently carried on were matters to be decided upon the whole evidence. The fair presumption was, that it was subsequently carried on, on the same terms as before, unless other facts repelled that presumption. That the bond executed at the time of the execution of the articles ought to be considered as a part of the same transaction and contract."

And the said counsel of the defendants did then and there further request the said court to instruct the said jury as follows, to wit:

1. That, if upon the whole evidence, they are satisfied that the copartnership, proved to have existed between the defendants, under the name of John Winship, was known or understood by the plaintiffs to be limited to the manufacturing of soap and candles, they must find a verdict for the defendants, unless they are also satisfied that these notes were given in the ordinary course of the copartnership business, or that the moneys obtained upon them went directly to the use of the firm, with the consent of Amos Binney and John Binney; and that, if they are satisfied that any part of these moneys did go to the use of the firm with such consent, that then they must find a verdict for the plaintiffs for such part only, and not for the residue. And,

2. That if they are also satisfied that the Messrs. Binneys furnished Winship with sufficient capital and credit for carrying on the business of the firm, no such consent can be implied from the mere fact that Winship applied these moneys, or any part of them, to the payment of partnership debts.

But the presiding judge refused to give the instructions first prayed for unless with the following limitations, explanations and qualifications, namely: " That the defendants as copartners are bound to pay the notes sued on, or money borrowed or advanced, unless the indorsements of the same notes and the borrowing of such money was, in the ordinary course of the business of the firm, for the use, and on account, of the firm. But, if the said Winship offered the notes for discount as notes of the firm and for their account, and he was intrusted by the partnership, as the active partner, to conduct the ordinary business of the firm, and the discount of such indorsed notes was within such business, then, if the plaintiffs discounted the notes upon the faith of such notes being so offered by the said Winship and as binding on the firm, the plaintiffs were entitled to recover, although Winship should have subsequently misapplied the funds received from the discount of said notes, if the plaintiffs were not parties or privies thereto, or of any such intention. And if Winship borrowed money or procured any advances on the credit and for the use of the firm, and for purposes connected with the business of the firm, in like manner and under like circumstances, and money was lent or advanced on the faith and credit of the partnership, the money so borrowed and advanced bound the partnership, and they were liable to pay therefor, although the same had been subsequently misapplied by Winship, the lender not being party or privy thereto, or of any such intention.

And with these limitations, explanations and qualifications, he gave the instructions so first prayed for. And the presiding judge gave the instruction secondly prayed for, according to the tenor thereof. To these opinions and decisions of the court the defendants excepted. A verdict was found for the plaintiffs and judgment entered thereon, which is brought before this court by writ of error.

The exceptions will now be considered. All must admit that the opinion asked in the first instance by the counsel for the defendant in the circuit court ought not to have been given. That court was required to decide on the fact as well as law of the case, and to say, on the whole testimony, that it did not warrant giving credit to any other name than that of John Winship. But, though this prayer is clearly not sustainable, the counsel for the plaintiff in error contends that the instructions actually given were erroneous.

§ 111. *A secret partnership is where the existence of certain persons as partners is not avowed or made public.*

The first part of the charge turns chiefly upon the definition of a secret partnership, which is believed to be correct; but the judge proceeds to say that, if incorrect, it would have no influence on the cause; and adds: " that the case must be decided on the principles of law applicable to such a partnership as this was, in fact, proved to be;" " that when the original articles expired by their own limitation, the question what the partnership was and how it was carried on for the future, whether upon the same terms as were contained in the original article or otherwise, was matter of fact from the whole evidence."

The error supposed to be committed in this opinion is in the declaration that nothing important in this case turned on the meaning or definition of the terms " secret partnership." This is not laid down as an abstract proposition universally true, but as being true in this particular case. The articles were produced, and the judge declared that the case must depend on the principles of law applicable to such a partnership as this was in fact. This instruction could not, we think, injure the plaintiff in error. Its impropriety is supposed to be made apparent by considering it in connection with the third exception.

§ 112. *Secret restrictions on the powers of a partner do not affect third persons. A partner will bind his copartner by making or indorsing notes, if that is within the general scope of the partnership business.*

The second instruction appears to be unexceptionable, and the counsel for the plaintiff in error is understood not to object to it. The third instruction asked in the circuit court goes to the construction of the articles of copartnership. The plaintiff in error contends that those articles gave Winship no au-

173

thority to raise money on the credit of the firm, or to bind it by his signature for the purpose of borrowing money.

The instruction given was, that if the particular terms of the articles were unknown to the public, they had a right to deal with the firm in respect to the business thereof, upon the general principles and presumptions of limited partnerships of a like nature, and that any special restrictions did not affect them; that, in such partnerships, it was within the general authority of the partners to make and indorse notes and to obtain advances and credits for the business and benefit of the firm; and if such was the general usage of trade, the authority must be presumed to exist, but that it did not extend to transactions beyond the scope and object of the copartnership. That, in the present articles, Winship was, in effect, constituted the active partner, and has general authority to transact the business of the firm, and a right to bind the firm, in transacting its ordinary business with persons ignorant of any private restriction, to the same extent that partners in such limited partnerships usually possess.

The amount of the charge is, that if Winship and the two Binneys composed a joint company for carrying on the soap and candle business, of which Winship was the acting partner, he might borrow money for the business on the credit of the company, in the manner usually practiced in such partnerships, notwithstanding any secret restriction on his powers, in any agreement between the parties, provided such restriction was unknown to the lender.

The counsel for the plaintiff in error has objected to this instruction with great force of reasoning. He contends, very truly, that, in fact, scarcely any unlimited partnerships exist. They are more or less extensive; they may extend to many or to few objects, but all are in some degree limited. That the liability of a partner arises from pledging his name, if his name is introduced into the firm, or from receiving profits if he is a secret partner. No man can be pledged but by himself. If he is to be bound by another, that other must derive authority from him. The power of an agent is limited by the authority given him; and if he transcends that authority, the act cannot affect his principal; he acts no longer as an agent. The same principle applies to partners. One binds the others so far only as he is the agent of the others.

If the truth of these propositions be admitted, yet their influence on the case may be questioned. Partnerships for commercial purposes, for trading with the world, for buying and selling from and to a great number of individuals, are necessarily governed by many general principles, which are known to the public, which subserve the purpose of justice, and which society is concerned in sustaining. One of these is, that a man who shares in the profit, although his name may not be in the firm, is responsible for all its debts. Another, more applicable to the subject under consideration, is, that a partner, certainly the acting partner, has power to transact the whole business of the firm, whatever that may be, and consequently to bind his partners in such transactions, as entirely as himself. This is a general power, essential to the well conducting of business, which is implied in the existence of a partnership. When, then, a partnership is formed for a particular purpose, it is understood to be in itself a grant of power to the acting members of the company to transact its business in the usual way. If that business be to buy and sell, then the individual buys and sells for the company, and every person with whom he trades in the way of its business has a right to consider him as the company, whoever may compose it. It is usual to buy and sell on credit; and if it be so, the partner who purchases on credit in the name of the firm must bind the firm. This is a general authority held out to the world, to which the world has a right to trust. The articles of copartnership are perhaps never published. They are rarely, if ever, seen, except by the partners themselves. The stipulations they may contain are to regulate the conduct and rights of the parties as between themselves. The trading world, with whom the company is in perpetual intercourse, cannot individually examine these articles, but must trust to the general powers contained in all partnerships. The acting partners are identified with the company, and have power to conduct its usual business in the usual way. This power is conferred by entering into the partnership, and is perhaps never to be found in the articles. If it is to be restrained, fair dealing requires that the restriction should be made known. These stipulations may bind the partners, but ought not to affect those to whom they are unknown, and who trust to the general and well-established commercial law. 2 Hen. Black., 235; 17 Ves., 412; Gow on Part., 17.

§ 113. *The responsibility of an open partner and a secret or dormant partner is the same. It depends on general principles of commercial law, not on articles of partnership.*

The counsel for the plaintiff in error supposes that, though these principles may be applicable to an open avowed partnership, they are inapplicable to one that is secret.

Can this distinction be maintained? If it could, there would be a difference between the responsibility of a dormant partner and one whose name was to the articles. But their responsibility, in all partnership transactions, is admitted to be the same. Those who trade with a firm on the credit of individuals whom they believe to be members of it take upon themselves the hazard that their belief is well founded. If they are mistaken, they must submit to the consequences of their mistake; if their belief be verified by the fact, their claims on the partners who were not ostensible are as valid as on those whose names are in the firm. This distinction seems to be founded on the idea that, if partners are not openly named, the resort to them must be connected with some knowledge of the secret stipulations between the partners, which may be inserted in the articles. But this certainly is not correct. The responsibility of unavowed partners depends on the general principles of commercial law, not on the particular stipulation of the articles.

It has been supposed that the principles laid down in the third instruction, respecting these secret restrictions, are inconsistent with the opinion declared in the first; that in this case, where the articles were before the court, the question whether this was in its origin a secret or an avowed partnership had become unimportant. If this inconsistency really existed, it would not affect the law of the case, unless the judge had laid down principles in the one or the other instruction which might affect the party injuriously. But it does not exist. The two instructions were given on different views of the subject, and apply to different objects. The first respected the parties to the firm, and their liability, whether they were or were not known as members of it; the last applies to secret restrictions on the partners, which change the power held out to the world by the law of partnership. The meaning of the terms " secret partnership," or the question whether this did or did not come within the definition of a secret partnership, might be unimportant; and yet the question whether a private agreement between the partners, limiting their responsibility, was known to a person trusting the firm might be very important.

175

§ 114. *Authority to make and indorse notes and to raise money. Construction of partnership articles.*

The proposition of the defendants in the circuit court was that Winship had no right or authority to raise money on the credit of the firm, or to bind the firm by his signature for the purpose of borrowing money.

This can scarcely be considered as a general question. In the actual state of the commercial world it is perhaps impossible to conduct the business of any company without credit. Large purchases are occasionally made on credit; and it is a question of convenience to be adjusted by the parties, whether the credit shall be given by the vendor or obtained at the bank. If the vendor receives a note he may discount it at the bank. If, for example, the notes given by Winship to Jacques for rosin to carry on his manufacture, which have been mentioned by the witness, had been discounted in bank, it would not have been distinguishable from money borrowed in any other form. The judge said that if it was within the scope and authority of partners generally, in limited partnerships, to make and indorse notes, and to obtain advances and credits for the business and benefit of the firm, and if such was in fact the ordinary course and usage of trade, the authority must be presumed to exist. Whether this was the fact or not was left to the jury.

Does anything in the articles of agreement restrain this general authority? The articles state the object of the company to be the manufacture of soap and candles; the capital stock to be $10,000, which sum is to be paid in by Amos and John Binney; John Winship to conduct and superintend the manufactory; the name of the firm to be John Winship; the profit and loss to be divided. They are silent on the subject of borrowing money. If the fact that the Binneys advanced $10,000 for the stock in trade implied a restriction on the power of the manager to carry on the business on credit, it would be implied in almost every case.

But the bond given by Winship to Amos Binney, which is admitted by the judge to constitute a part of the partnership agreement, is supposed to contain this restriction. The condition of the bond recites that " whereas Amos Binney had engaged to indorse the notes given by the said John Winship for the purchase of stock and raw materials for manufacturing, when necessary to purchase on credit, in consideration of which the said John Winship hath engaged not to indorse the notes, paper, or become in any manner responsible or security for any person or persons other than the said Amos Binney." " Now if the said John Winship shall faithfully observe the conditions, and wholly abstain from becoming the surety or indorser of any person, to any amount, other than the said Amos Binney, then," etc.

The agreement recited, but not inserted in this condition, that Amos Binney would indorse the notes of Winship when it should be necessary to purchase on credit, while it implies that the power was incident to the act of partnership, was not in itself a positive restriction on that power. The affirmative engagement on the part of Amos Binney that he will indorse is not a prohibition on Winship to obtain any other indorser. The exigencies of trade might require the negotiation of a note in the absence of Mr. Binney, and this may have been a motive for leaving this subject to the discretion of the acting partner. If he has abused this confidence the loss must fall where it always falls when a partner, acting within his authority, injures his copartners. If, then, the agreement between Amos Binney and John Winship contains nothing more than is recited in the condition, it contains no inhibition on Winship to negotiate notes in the ordinary course of business. The restriction on Winship is not in this recital, but in his engagement expressed in the condition of the bond.

He engages not to indorse the notes, paper, or become in any manner responsible or security for any person or persons other than the said Binney. The obvious import of this engagement is that Winship will not make himself responsible for another. Had he made an accommodation note for Jacques it would have been as much a violation of this agreement as if he had indorsed it. The undertaking is not to indorse notes for another. But this note is indorsed for himself. It is negotiated in bank in the name of the firm, and the money is carried to the credit of the firm. Had not Winship misapplied this money, no question would have arisen concerning the liability of his-partners on this note. The stipulation in the bond, not to indorse or to become security for another, would not have barred the action. But, be this as it may, this stipulation between the parties is a secret restriction on a power given by commercial law and usage, generally known and understood; which is obligatory on the parties, but ought not to affect those from whom it is concealed.

§ 115. *Where notes are offered by the active partner and discounted by a bank in the usual course of business, the other partners are liable on his indorsement, although the active partner may have afterward misapplied the proceeds of such notes.*

The counsel for the defendants in the circuit court then prayed an instruction to the jury, that if they were satisfied that the partnership was known to the plaintiffs to be limited to the soap and candle business, they must find for the defendants; unless they were also satisfied that these notes were given in the ordinary course of the partnership business, or that the moneys obtained upon them went directly to the use of the firm with the consent of Amos Binney and John Binney; and that if they are satisfied that any part of these moneys did go to the use of the firm with such consent, that then they must find a verdict for such part only; and not for the residue.

This instruction was not given as asked; but was given with "limitations, explanations and qualifications." The judge instructed the jury, in substance, that the defendants were not bound to pay the notes sued on, unless the indorsements thereon were in the ordinary course of the business of the firm, for the use and on account of the firm; but if they were satisfied that the notes were so offered and discounted, and that the said Winship was intrusted by the partnership, as the active partner, to conduct the ordinary business of the firm, and the discount of such indorsed notes was within such business, then the plaintiffs were entitled to recover, although Winship should have subsequently misapplied the funds, received from the discount of said notes, if the plaintiffs were not parties or privies thereto, or of any such intention.

The plaintiffs in error contend that the instruction ought to have been given, as prayed, without any qualification whatever. The instruction required is that, although the jury should be satisfied that the money went to the use of the firm, they should find for the defendants; unless they should be also satisfied that the consent of Amos and John Binney was given to its being so applied. That is, that a note discounted by the acting and ostensible partner of a firm for the use of a firm, the money arising from which was applied to that use, could not be recovered from the firm, by the holder, unless the application was made with the consent of all the partners.

The counsel for the plaintiffs in error is too intelligent to maintain this as a general proposition. He must confine it to this particular case. He is understood as contending that, under the secret restrictions contained in the bond given by Winship to Amos Binney, Winship was restrained from discounting these notes even for the use of the firm; and that no application of the money to the purposes of the copartnership could cure this original want of authority and create a liability which the note itself did not create, unless such application was made with the consent of all the partners. So understood, it is a repetition of the matter for which the third exception was taken, and is disposed of with that exception. The instruction, therefore, ought not to have been given as prayed. Still, if the court has erred in the instruction actually given, that error ought to be corrected. That instruction is, that if the notes were offered in the usual course of business for the firm, by the partner intrusted to conduct its business, and were so discounted, and if such discount was within such business, then the subsequent misapplication of the money, the holders not being parties or privies thereto, or of such intention, would not deprive them of their right of action against the copartnership.

We think this opinion entirely correct. It only affirms the common principle that the misapplication of funds raised by authority cannot affect the person from whom those funds are obtained.

We think there is no error in the opinions given by the judge to the jury, the court being divided on the competency of Samuel Jacques as a witness. The judgment is affirmed, with costs, and damages at the rate of six per centum per annum, by a divided court.

Dissenting opinion by MR. JUSTICE BALDWIN.

The plaintiffs sued in this case as the indorsees of six promissory notes drawn by James Jacques and indorsed by John Winship, which came to their hands as the discounters thereof, being offered by John Winship, and the proceeds thereof placed to his credit in the bank. They were not notes indorsed to the plaintiffs in payment, or as collateral security for the payment of an antecedent debt, or the performance of any pre-existing contract. The bank are prohibited in their charter from dealing in goods, unless for the sale of such as are pledged for the payment of debts. 4 Laws U. S., 43 (3 Stats. at Large, 272). Ninth fundamental article of the charter of the bank.

§ 116. *Discount of commercial paper; nature of the transaction and liabilities arising therefrom.*

This was not, then, the case of goods sold by plaintiffs to defendants, as partners, on the faith of the partnership in the course of their business. Neither is it a case of money previously lent, and a note or bill indorsed over in payment or security. The case finds, and the circuit court considered it a case of discount, which is a purchase of the note on stipulated and well-known terms. The purchase or discount of a note is a contract wholly unconnected with the objects, uses or application of the money paid. A party who sells a bill or note incurs no liability to the discounter by the mere contract of discount, where he does not indorse it; nor does the discounter who pays for the discounted bill or note in other bills and notes, without indorsement, guaranty their payment. The contract is one of sale; and in the absence of fraud or misrepresentation, the rights of the parties are tested exclusively by the only contract which the nature of the case imports — of sale and purchase as of any other article in market.

Where a purchase is made or money borrowed on partnership account, an immediate debt is created; a note or bill given or indorsed is for payment of the existing debt; and if not paid, the debt remains, unless the bill or note has been accepted as payment. So if the bill or note is given as collateral security. And the law is the same whether one or all the partners do the act; there is an antecedent debt binding on all, or an indemnity to be provided; the obligation is not impaired by giving or transferring an ineffectual security. But the present case is wholly different. The defendants owed no antecedent debt to the bank for which these notes were transferred to them. They were neither offered nor accepted as payment or indemnity; but sold by Winship, and purchased by the bank at their value. The value is, in my opinion, to be ascertained with reference to the names on the bill, who are the parties to the contract, and, in my view of the law, the only parties. The bank bought from John Winship the promise of James Jacques, guarantied by Winship, on known conditions. This distinction between passing or pledging a note in payment, and discounting it, has been wholly overlooked in the opinion of the circuit court; and the case seems to have been considered throughout as governed by the same rules which apply to purchases, loans, and other partnership engagements. The case before them was a pure case of discount, which is governed by its own principles; which, in my opinion, would have produced a different result in the cause, had they been laid down to the jury.

These principles are fully illustrated and established in their various bearings on cases which have been adjudicated, and laid down in terms too clear not to be understood. 15 East, 10, 11; Doug., 654, note; 3 Ves. Jr., 368; 10 Ves. Jr., 204; 3 Durnf. & East, 757; 1 Lord Ray., 442; 2 Com. R., 57, S. C.; 1 Cranch, 192; 6 Cranch, 264; 1 Wash. C. C. R., 156, 321, 328, 399; 3 Wash. C. C., 266; 9 Johns., 310; Burke's Cases in Bankruptcy, 114, 170; 3 Mad., 129; 1 Esp. N. P., 448. I do not refer to the latter case because it ought to be any authority in this court, but because it shows that Lord Kenyon, who dissented from the court of king's bench, in 1790, in the case quoted from 3 Durnf. & East, 757, came to the same opinion in 1796. Neither do I rely on elementary writers who lay down the same positions, but on the adjudged cases, which seem to me to be the safest guides to the law. *Satius est petere fontes, quam sectari rivulos.* 10 Coke, 118.

Resting on these authorities, I shall consider the case on the evidence as one of discount, not of loan, purchase, or any other pre-existing liability. As the evidence of Jacques proves that these notes were accommodation, and not notes of business; as Mr. Harris, the discount clerk, testifies that all the notes were discounted at Winship's request, and the proceeds passed to his credit; that it is easy to distinguish accommodation notes from others; and that he considered these in suit to be of that description; and that the bank had frequently discounted notes drawn by Winship, and indorsed by Amos Binney; and Mr. Parker, one of the directors of the bank, testified that, when the bank discounted these notes, it was understood that Amos and John Binney were bound by them. Witness understood that they were bound as partners in the soap and candle business, not general partners. Did not know as to John Binney, whether plaintiff considered him answerable, but they did so consider Amos Binney; that a number of notes of this kind were discounted, while other notes indorsed by Amos Binney were in bank; that Amos and John Binney were engaged in large business as merchants, and witness does not know that any one ever supposed defendants to be partners, except in the manufacture of soap and candles.

I cannot do injustice to the plaintiffs by founding my opinion on this testimony. Mr. Parker was present at the making of the contract of discount of these notes; he was one of the agents of the bank in making it, and a party to it, as a member of the corporation, directly interested. His evidence is the solemn admission on oath of a party to the contract, and ought to be taken as true. The defendants have a right to its full benefit as explanatory of the nature, terms and circumstances under which it was made. Mr. Harris, the discount clerk, was the appropriate agent of the bank in consummating the contract of discount, by paying to Winship the proceeds of the discounted notes; and I cannot err in saying, from the record, that these were the only witnesses examined at the trial touching the discount of these notes; the only contract, in my opinion, which the law raises between the plaintiffs and defendants. What, then, was the obligation which this contract of discount, as proved by Harris and Parker, imposed on Amos and John Binney, by the bank's purchasing these notes at the request of John Winship, and paying or passing the proceeds to his credit?

§ 117. *The indorsee of an accommodation note who seeks to hold liable a person whose name does not appear on the note must prove that such person had authorized the negotiation of the note or afterward ratified it.*

The notes were accommodation, so understood by the plaintiffs, and discounted as such. The bank, then, knew that they were not what they purported to be; they are set forth in the record, are all drawn for value received, and thus bear a falsehood on their face known to the bank. Such notes, Mr. Harris says, are easily distinguishable from notes of business, and the bank did not discount them as representing a purchase, a loan, or any preexisting obligation by Jacques to pay the amount to Winship, but as the lending of his name by Jacques to Winship to enable him to raise money by the sale of the notes. There was in this respect no fraud on the bank. They knew they were not purchasing notes given and indorsed in the usual course of business. They did not come to their hands as innocent indorsers, taking them to be what they imported to be, for value received. The bank are purchasers, it is true, for a valuable consideration, but not innocent or without notice. They took the notes with a known taint on their very face, which can only be effaced by some subsequent indorsee or holder who takes them in the course of business without notice, and takes them between the payor and payee as having been given for value received. But the plaintiffs have become the indorsees by discount, knowing that by the acknowledged principles of commercial law, as between the original parties in all their relations, Winship was the drawer and Jacques the indorser. As between them and the bank, their relations were the same; whether the notes were of business or accommodation, they were liable in the capacities they respectively assumed on the face of the notes. When the discounter or the indorsee of an accommodation note, known by him to be such, seeks to recover the amount from a person whose name does not appear on the note, he must prove that the person charged had made himself a party to the note, had authorized its negotiation or transfer previously, or afterwards assented to, ratified or adopted the indorsement as his own. Had there been no previous connection between the Binneys and Winship, and the Binneys had procured the discount from the bank without their indorsement, they would be no more answerable to the bank than by receiving payment of a check. On the face of these notes the Binneys are strangers to the bank. The contract of discount which they made with Winship does not, *per se*, create one with the Binneys. Being accommodation notes, they were discounted as such; that is, as the notes of Winship indorsed by Jacques; for such is the acknowledged character of such notes in the commercial world. The line separating business from accommodation paper is clearly defined by law and usage. There is the same difference between the indorser of a note known not to be what it purports to be, and one which represents a real debt from the drawer to the drawee, as between the purchasers of real estate with or without notice of an incumbrance or the defect of title, so far as respects their standing in courts of justice, in relation to third persons, not parties to the contract. Those who purchase in good faith, without notice of fraud, and pay their money, confiding in the face of the transaction, ignorant of anything which can affect its legal or equitable character, are entitled to the protection of all courts as their most favored parties.

A peculiar sanctity is thrown round the obligation of negotiable paper, actually negotiated in the usual course of business, and in the hands of an innocent holder, for a valuable consideration, without notice. Every presumption which the law can raise is in favor of such a holder whether he receives the note in payment or by discount. It becomes divested of this peculiar obligation when the paper in its original concoction or negotiation becomes divested of these attributes and remains in the hands of a holder who has a knowledge of all the circumstances attending both. I know of no decision of any court, no principle of law nor usage of merchants which confounds the distinction between these two kinds of paper in the hands of indorsees, with or without notice; it is too well established to require support from argument or authority. The same distinction exists in paper negotiated after it is due, or partnership notes given for the private debt of a partner. Notice is the distinguishing criterion in all these cases, and settles the question as to the burden of proof. So I find the law laid down by the supreme court of Massachusetts in the case of The Manufacturing & Mechanics' Bank *v.* Winship, 5 Pick., 11. The suit was brought on an accommodation note drawn by John Winship to Jacques or order, indorsed by him and discounted by the plaintiffs in the usual course of banking business. The chief justice charged the jury that the burden of proof was in the plaintiffs; and that if no proof was given by them that the money was raised for the business of the firm at the manufactory, the jury should find the fact for the defendants. In giving judgment for the defendants the court affirmed the charge of the chief justice as to the burden of proving the note to have been given on partnership account being on the bank; that no recovery could be had against the partners so long as it remained doubtful whether they have or have not made the contract declared upon; that from the fact of the note being found to be an accommodation one between Winship and Jacques, it would seem more likely that it related to the private concerns of Winship than to those of the partners; at any rate, the uncertainty resting on the face of the note would still continue. The plaintiffs knew or might have known that Winship was openly engaged in commercial speculations which were wholly unconnected with the business of the manufactory, and that his signature might relate to one concern as well as another. If, therefore, they meant that the note should be enforced against the partnership, they should have ascertained that the signature of Winship was intended for the signature of the firm. But they made no such inquiry, and it does not appear that Winship or Jacques ever made any representation to that effect. And although it appears that the plaintiffs supposed the Binneys would be answerable because they were partners with Winship in the manufactory, yet they gave no intimation whatever to the parties to the note to be discounted that such was their understanding of the contract.

There are few courts whose opinions may be more safely confided in, as to the rules of the common law; there is none whose authority I feel more bound to respect, as to the common law of Massachusetts, than its highest judicial tribunal. The law of the state where a contract is made and carried into effect seems to me to be the law which must control its obligation; and until evidence of the common law of that state, more imposing than the solemn decision of its supreme court, is furnished me, I feel it my duty to respect and adopt it; believing that, in doing so, I violate no principle which has ever been sanctioned by this court. In some particulars the evidence in the cause referred to was more favorable to the bank than in this. The note was discounted at the bank, on the belief that the Binneys were liable as partners of the manufactory at Charlestown only. This was found by the jury; but it was not found, and there appears to have been no evidence, that the bank or its officers knew the note to be an accommodation one.

The judgment of the court was on the fact being so found, not on its being known to the plaintiffs.

In this case, the notice is brought home to the plaintiffs by the evidence of their discount clerk. Mr. Parker, the director, does not say the note was discounted on the belief that the Binneys were liable as partners; all he says on that subject is, when the bank discounted these notes, it was understood the Binneys were bound by them. He immediately corrects this, and says he does not know, as to John Binney, whether plaintiffs considered him answerable; but they did so consider Amos Binney. This is certainly very lame evidence of the notes being discounted on the credit of both Amos and John Binney; and much weaker than the fact found by the jury in the other case. The bank had notice of the course of business between Winship and Amos Binney, by his indorsing Winship's notes, and the bank discounting them. The Binneys were in good credit; and being reputed wealthy, it was not to be presumed they would borrow credit from Jacques. These circumstances ought to have put the bank on inquiry, as Binney was a customer residing in the place. The court placed no reliance on these circumstances, or on the fact of the notes being discounted with the knowledge that they were notes of accommodation.

§ 118. *Distinction between dormant and open partners and their respective liabilities. Authorities reviewed.*

Nor did the court, in my opinion, correctly define the difference between a dormant and an open partnership. It seems to me to be this: where the names of the partners do or do not appear in their accounts, their advertisements, or their paper; where the business is carried on in the name of all, it is open; but if any are kept back, it is dormant; that the knowledge which the public may have is not the test, when it is acquired from the acts or declarations of the acting, avowed partners; it may enable them to reach the dormant one, if the transaction is one in which he had an interest, but does not alter its nature. The partnership remains dormant as to all whose names do not appear on its transactions. The dormant, the sleeping, inactive partner may be known by reputation, or the declaration of his copartner, but these do not make him an avowed or active one without the avowal and pledge of his name or paper. If credit is given to the other names on the faith of such reputation or representation, the persons so trusting must do it at the risk of suffering, if their information is not true. The declarations of one of a firm are not evidence of another person's being a partner, in any particular transaction, unless a previous connection is established, which gives him authority to bind by his acknowledgment, or proof given of subsequent assent; reputation is not *per se* evidence, unless brought home to the party charged; then his silence may be deemed acquiescence or assent. 11 Serg. & R., 362; 2 Wash. C. C. R., 388, 390; 14 Johns., 215; 3 Caines, 92; 10 East, 264; 5 Pick., 415, 417; 1 Gall., 635, 638, 640.

The language of some of the cases is, that it is rather on the ground of agency than partnership resulting from the community of interest in the subject-matter of the contract. The principle which makes a dormant partner liable is this: having an interest in the profits which are a part of the funds to which a creditor looks for payment, he shall be bound. 2 Black. Rep., 1000; 2 Hen. Black., 247; 4 East, 144; 16 Johns., 40; 2 Nott & M'Cord, 427, 429; 1 Hen. Black., 45, etc. As his name is not pledged, his liability arises only from his interest (16 East, 174, 175); and the burden of proving such interest is on the party suing. The language of the court in 2 Nott & M'Cord, 429, is very emphatic: "To charge defendant as partner, one of two things is necessary; either he must have permitted his name to be used as one of the firm, thereby holding it out as a security to the community, or he must have participated in the profits." As the Binneys never pledged their names on these notes, they were not discounted on their faith. There is, then, wanting in this case that fact on which the power of one partner to bind the firm by negotiable paper is created — the use of the names. The plaintiff who seeks to make those parties to a note whose names do not give it currency or credit must make them parties by affirmative proof of an interest in profits, previous authority or subsequent recognition. It is true that, when a dormant partner is discovered, he is liable; but then he must be shown to be one by an interest in the subject-matter of the note. Till this is brought home to him he is no party to it. I know of no authority for saying that the mere existence of a partnership composed of names not avowed or pledged to the public makes them, when discovered, liable for any other than contracts in which they have an interest; one who suffers his name to be used on paper is liable as a partner, though there is in fact no existing partnership; but the man who does not suffer his name to be used or pledged is bound only by virtue of his interest.

This furnishes, I apprehend, the true distinction between dormant and open partnerships; and that it does not depend on the knowledge which the public may have, or the representation made by the contracting partner when he is giving or negotiating a note. The reason which makes a note drawn or indorsed by one partner in the joint name, though for his own use, binding on the firm in the hands of an innocent holder, is because it has been taken on the faith of his name. 3 Kent, Com., 18. The case of Van Reimsdyk v. Kane shows the importance attached to the names of the partners appearing on a bill. One partner was authorized by the others to take up money on the credit of the partnership concern, and draw bills therefor on a house at A. He took up money, drew a bill directing it to be charged on the account of all the partners, but it was signed by himself alone; the court held that the representative of a deceased partner was ·liable in equity to a payee who trusted his money on the faith of the joint credit, but expressed themselves with great doubt and caution as to the liability of the partners at law. 1 Gall., 630.

It seems to me that the circumstance which would excite a doubt in that case would remove it in this. But when all the names are not used, the reason and the law cease together. Where the liability attaches to the name, proof of the signature is enough; where it depends on the mere participation of the profits, that must be proved by the holder; as he claims to hold persons bound whose names were not held out on the paper as inducements to take it, he must show that the law has placed their names upon it. In proving a partnership assignment, it must appear that the party making it had a right to sign the name of the firm and that his act is the act of all the partners. 5 Cranch, 300. A party claiming the money due on a note indorsed to him in the name of the firm must show the indorsement to be made in the name of the firm by a person duly authorized. 7 Wheat., 669. The case of Leroy v. Johnson, in this court (2 Pet., 186), was this: Hoffman and Johnson were partners, under the firm of Hoffman & Johnson; so advertised in the papers, so publicly known, and so carried on under articles of partnership. Hoffman drew a bill on London, in Alexandria, in his own name, which the plaintiff, residing in New York, purchased from Hoffman. The bill was drawn to raise money to pay a note of the firm, and sent to New York by Johnson for the purpose of selling it. Not succeeding, Hoffman went on, and, assisted by letters of recommendation from merchants of Baltimore, negotiated the bill, and with the proceeds paid a partnership note. The circuit court of the district were asked to instruct the jury: 1. That on the evidence of partnership, and the application of the proceeds of the bill to partnership purposes; 2. That if the bill was drawn with reference to the business of the concern; 3. That if the name of Jacob Hoffman was sometimes used in relation to the business of the firm, that the bill was drawn in his name, and so negotiated for the firm, and to pay their debts,— that the plaintiff was entitled to recover. These instructions were refused, and judgment rendered for the defendant, which was affirmed, this court holding it indispensable for the plaintiff to prove that the name of Hoffman was used in the transaction as the name of the firm, and that the parties so traded and carried on their business; that the jury would be well warranted from the facts of the case in believing that Hoffman dealt in his individual name, and on his sole responsibility, without even an allusion to the partnership; though the bill was drawn for partnership purposes, with the knowledge of Johnson, and by him sent to New York for sale, and the proceeds applied in good faith. The attention of the court was not drawn to the distinction between notes discounted and those received in payment, nor was the bill in question an accommodation one. There was no fraud in the transaction as between the partners. It was drawn, negotiated, and the proceeds applied with the consent of both, and the aid of letters of recommendation. It came to the hands of the holder by fair purchase in market, in the usual and regular way of business, yet Johnson was not bound; his name was not on the bill; the plaintiff did not prove it to be the name of the firm in the particular transaction, though Hoffman's name was sometimes used alone in partnership transactions.

If, in addition to these defects in the plaintiff's case, it had appeared that the bill drawn in the name of Hoffman had been one of accommodation, known to Le Roy to be so, and purchased as such, without the knowledge of Johnson of its having been drawn or negotiated, or the application of its proceeds to partnership purposes, and with a knowledge by Mr. Le Roy, derived from his having been in the frequent habit of discounting bills drawn by one and discounted by the other, understanding there was a special partnership between them, it is not presuming too much to think that this court would have deemed these circumstances strong presumptive proof and reasonable notice of their accustomed mode of raising money, for partnership purposes, by discount; and that a known accommodation note, drawn by a stranger, and indorsed by Hoffman alone, was not a partnership note, when offered by him for discount, without the name of Johnson. It would seem to me to furnish the very case which this court, in delivering their opinion in Le Roy v. Johnson, make a proviso of the liability of the members of a firm whose names appear on a bill negotiated and in the hands of an indorsee. The court say: A bill drawn or accepted by a firm, by their usual name and style, is presumed to be on their joint account and authority, and that third persons are not bound to inquire whether it was so done or not, " unless the contrary be shown, and that the persons with whom the partner deals had notice or reason to believe that the former was acting on his separate account." This restriction to the liability of partners, whose names appear on a joint note in the hands of an indorsee, to whom the faith of a partnership is publicly pledged, seems to me conclusive in a case circumstanced·like this; where the agents, who effect the discount of the note in question for the bank, prove distinctly their own knowledge of the nature, extent and objects of the partnership, the mode adopted to raise funds for the firm in the same bank, and of these notes being for the accommodation of Winship and his receiving the proceeds.

Under the circumstances of this case, I cannot consider the plaintiffs as innocent indorsees of the negotiable paper of a firm actually negotiated by them on its pledged credit without notice or reason to believe that Winship was acting on his separate account. The testimony of Harris is conclusive on my mind to prove that the officers of the bank perfectly understood the nature of the transaction; that the notes were not discounted on any representation made by Winship, or on the belief that they were the notes of the firm. The bank may have thought the Binneys, or one of them, liable; but, according to the testimony of Parker, could not have believed the indorsement to represent a regular and authorized partnership transaction. The statement of Mr. Parker was at first that they understood the Binneys were liable, but he afterwards corrected himself, and said he did not know, as to John Binney, whether the plaintiffs considered him so answerable, but that they so considered Amos Binney. They evidently thought Amos liable because he had been in the habit of indorsing Winship's notes, but could by no possibility have believed Amos and John liable as partners under the signature of Winship, when one of the directors who made the discount could not say that the bank ever considered John Binney to be liable.

Finding, on a careful examination of the charge of the circuit court, that none of the restrictions and qualifications of the liability of a dormant partner, whose name does not appear in an indorsement of an accommodation note, discounted under unknown circumstances of suspicion, have been laid down or explained to the jury, I am constrained to say that it is erroneous, and that the judgment ought to be reversed. I cannot, on a subject so important as this, silently dissent from the opinion of the court, when my judgment has been made up on what seems to me the best established principles of commercial law; nor can I consent to overrule a decision of the supreme court of the state where this contract was made, executed and enforced, without the highest possible evidence of their having been mistaken in their judicial exposition of their common law.

IN RE WARREN.

(District Court for Maine: Daveis, 320–328. 1847.)

Opinion by WARE, J.

STATEMENT OF FACTS.—In the spring of 1834, Warren and Brown formed a partnership for carrying on the business of attorneys and counselors at law. There were no written articles of partnership, but the understanding between them was that it was to be confined to their professional business. Without any additional agreement, they began soon after buying and selling timber lands. There was no formal agreement as to the terms on which this business was to be carried on, but they do not appear originally to have contemplated a general partnership in land transactions, and probably did not anticipate the extent to which their speculations were eventually carried. It was understood between them that either might purchase, but that the other was not bound to take a share in the purchase without his own consent to each particular purchase, but when both parties assented to the purchase they were to share in equal portions in the profit or loss. According to the usage of the time, they sometimes purchased and sold lands directly, and sometimes pre-emption bonds or contracts for the sale of lands.

This land business was commenced in the fall of 1834, and was continued on an extensive scale through the ensuing winter and summer, until the period of speculation was over. Though they did not contemplate originally a general partnership, and each was considered at liberty to purchase and sell on his own private account, there were in fact no timber lands purchased by either, except what were taken on joint account. When they commenced the business, they gave their joint notes, signing separately and not the partnership name, but more frequently the securities, for the convenience of negotiation, were in the form of bills of exchange, drawn by one and accepted by the other. It was not long, however, before the name of the firm was freely used in these land securities; at first, it seems, by Brown, but not objected to by Warren. This trade in timber lands appears to have led to the lumbering business, in which they seem to have been engaged in the same way without any special partnership agreement. Whatever may have been the private intentions of the parties, it seems that they must have soon come to be considered, and dealt with by others, as a firm. A list of notes or bills of exchange is produced, taken from the books of Warren, more than sixty in number, commencing with the spring of 1836, and continued to the fall of 1839, growing out of land and lumber transactions, in which the name of the firm is used as promisor, drawer, acceptor and indorser for various amounts, from small sums up to two, three, and five thousand dollars, and in the whole exceeding $50,000. It is quite impossible that such an amount of business, continued for such a length of time, could have been done in the partnership name without its being generally understood that a partnership in the business existed. Third persons must have dealt with them and given them credit on that understanding.

The earliest land transaction in which they were engaged was with Thacher and Parker. This was an obligation of Thacher and Parker to convey to them twelve thousand and forty acres of land at the price of $2 an acre, part to be paid in cash and part on credit of one, two and three years, provided satisfactory security was given in sixty days. This obligation is in the handwriting of Warren, and the obligation runs to them in their partnership name; so that from the very commencement of their speculations, whatever may have been the private intentions of the parties, the business was transacted in a way that must have led those who dealt with them to suppose that a partnership existed, and that the trade was on partnership account. Between the parties themselves, in the earlier part of their speculations, each purchase was treated as a separate and independent transaction, and, when the land was sold, the parties settled it and divided the profits and loss. But this was a private affair between themselves, and not known to third persons with whom they dealt.

§ 119. *There may be a partnership in a single transaction.*

A partnership may exist in a single transaction as well as in a series. Story on Partnership, § 21; Pothier, Contrat de Société, No. 54; 3 Kent's Com., 30. If there is a joint purchase, with a view to a joint sale and a communion of profit and loss, it is a partnership trade, although it is confined to a single thing. Dig., 17, 2, 5. Now every purchase was made with a view to a joint sale on joint account, so that, without any general agreement for a partnership, they were, in law, partners in every purchase, and, by the habit of buying and selling in this way, they held themselves out to the public as general partners in the business.

§ 120. *There may be a partnership in buying and selling lands. As to third persons it may be proved by parol.*

There may be a partnership in buying and selling lands as well as in ordinary commercial business. 21 Me., 418, Dudley v. Littlefield; Story on Partnership, § 23. And so far as the rights of third persons are involved, it is not perceived why it may not be proved by the same evidence. To give full effect in law to the partnership between the partners themselves, it seems to be necessary that the articles be in writing. For if the partnership is by parol only, and one of the partners makes a purchase in his own name, but intended for the benefit of the firm, the other, on the mere ground of the partnership, that being by parol, cannot take advantage of the contract, for, if he could, he would acquire an interest in lands by parol, directly in opposition to the statute of frauds. 3 Sumn., 435, 471 (Eq., §§ 174–79), Smith v. Burnham. But this is only between themselves. Third persons, dealing with them, are not affected by any private arrangements between the partners unknown to them. If they hold themselves out to the public as partners, those who deal with them have a right so to regard them, and they will be bound as partners.

It appears to me that there is abundant evidence to prove a partnership in their land speculations, as to third persons. Their very first contract was in the name of the firm, and every succeeding one, whether made in form in the name of the firm or not, was adopted by them and taken on joint account. Though the securities they gave in their earlier transactions were not given in the partnership name, yet when they gave their joint note, or one drew a bill and the other accepted it, it was as well understood to be a partnership transaction as if the name of the firm had been used. But the business having been transacted in this way, a question arises of some difficulty, whether, on the bankruptcy or insolvency of the partners, these debts are to be placed to the partnership account, or are a charge on the separate estates of the partners.

§ 121. *A firm is not generally bound by the separate note or bill of a partner, though it is known to be on partnership account. This rule does not apply where there is a dormant partner.*

By the general rule of law, if one member of a firm makes his separate note, or draws a bill of exchange in his own name, he will be bound, and not the firm, although it is on account and for the benefit of the partnership. Story on Partnership, §§ 124, 127. The general reason by which this decision is vindicated is, that the creditor, by accepting the separate security of the individual partner, is supposed to have elected to take that in preference to the security of the firm. As the decision proceeds on the ground of a supposed choice in the creditor, it does not hold in cases where it appears that no choice could have been made; and consequently, where there is a dormant partner, and not known to the creditor, if the contract is for the benefit of the partnership, he will be bound, although he is not named.

§ 122. *Where a partner's bills have been habitually recognized by the firm as binding it, the debt will be held as a partnership debt.*

And for the same reason, where one of the partners has been in the habit of drawing and indorsing bills and notes in his own name, for the use and benefit of the firm, if it appears that the other partners have treated such signature as binding on the firm, the name of the partner will be held as standing for that of the firm, and be binding upon them. So it was ruled in the case of The South Carolina Bank *v.* Case, 8 Barn. & Cresw., 427; Story on Partnership, § 142. The creditor will be held as trusting not the partner alone but the firm. It is not therefore universally true, when a contract appears on its face to be the separate contract of one partner, that it will not be binding on the firm, if it is understood to be, and is in fact, for their benefit. The presumption that arises from the form of the security, that the separate name of the partner was taken from choice, may be overcome by proof that no such election was. made. The true and more general principle seems to be, that when the intention of the contracting parties is that the firm shall be bound, and the contract is within the scope of the partnership business, the contract will bind the firm in whatever form it may be made.

§ 123. *Liability of the firm when both partners become individually bound as drawers and acceptors of bills.*

But when a partnership consists of two persons, and they both sign a note or bill with their individual names and not by the name of the firm, or one draws a bill and the other accepts it, if it be in fact for a joint or partnership object, there would seem to be strong reasons for putting it, in the marshaling of securities, to the partnership account. Indeed, it has been held that if two persons, who are not partners, unite in drawing a bill of exchange, they are to be considered as partners in that bill. It is said that the public are to infer their relation to each other from the face of the paper. 3 Kent's Com., 30; Carvick *v.* Vickery, Doug., 653, note. And a like decision has been made on a joint and several promissory note, so that a demand or notice to one is a demand or notice to both, though perhaps the weight of authority is, where the parties are not in fact partners, the other way. Story on Promissory Notes, § 239, note; Story on Bills of Exchange, § 197. But where two persons, who are partners, unite in drawing a bill or making a note, though they sign their several names and not that of the firm, if it is in fact for partnership purposes, I am not aware that it has been decided that such a note or bill is not to be treated throughout as a partnership security; that a demand or notice to one is not a demand or notice to both, or that a creditor holding such a security would not have, in the administration of assets, a preference against the joint estate, over the separate creditors of the partners. The general language of elementary writers leads to the conclusion that such a note or bill is to be treated for all purposes as strictly a partnership security. The reason for so doing, in the marshaling of assets and securities, is certainly very strong. The fruits of the contract have gone to increase the social fund, and there is a natural equity in allowing the creditor a preference against that fund which his contract has contributed to augment.

§ 124. *Equity rule for distributing assets of partnerships and the separate assets of partners. The rule in bankruptcy.*

On the dissolution of a partnership, in cases of insolvency, the rule in equity is, that the partnership creditors have a preferred claim against the partnership assets over the separate creditors of the partners, and the separate creditors of the individual partners have a like preference over the partnership creditors, against the separate assets. The principle is, that each class of creditors is thrown on that fund to which he has given credit, and which he has contributed to enrich, and neither class can come on the other estate until the appropriate creditors of that estate have been fully satisfied. 3 Kent's Com., 64, 5, note. The same general rule holds in bankruptcy. In England it is indeed, in bankruptcy, qualified by some exceptions partly founded on technical reasoning, and partly on some supposed convenience, but certainly not standing on any plain and intelligible rule of equity or justice. Story on Partnership, §§ 377, 381; Eden on Bankruptcy, §§ 170, 175.

The rule of distribution, established in the general jurisprudence of courts of equity, has been incorporated in express terms into our bankrupt law. The fourteenth section directs that after the expenses and disbursements of the assignee are fully paid, the whole of which are a charge on the whole property, "the net proceeds of the joint estate shall be appropriated to pay the creditors of the company, and the net proceeds of the separate estate of each partner shall be appropriated to his separate creditors; and the balance, if any, of each estate, after paying the debts primarily chargeable upon it, shall be carried to the other estate." The language of the law is clear and explicit, and the only question left is, which are partnership and which separate creditors? I have already expressed my opinion that the speculations in land were, from the beginning, on partnership account, and in whatever form the securities were given, the presumption is that credit was given to the firm. That presumption, however, may be overcome by proof that credit was in fact given to the individual. partners.

ROGERS *v.* BATCHELOR.

(12 Peters, 221-234.   1838.)

Opinion by MR. JUSTICE STORY.

STATEMENT OF FACTS.— This cause comes before us on a writ of error to the district court of the district of Mississippi. The original action was debt, brought by the plaintiffs in error (Rogers & Sons) against Abel H. Buckholts, upon the following writing obligatory: "Natchez, Mississippi, $3,288.03. On the 1st day of April next we promise to pay N. Rogers & Sons, or order, $3,288.03, value received, with interest from date. Witness our hands and seals, this 1st day of January, 1824. Jno. Richards, [seal.] A. H. Buckholts, [seal.]" Upon such an instrument, by the laws of Mississippi, one of the parties may be sued alone; and, accordingly, Richards was no party to the suit. Upon the plea of payment issue was joined; and, pending the proceedings, Buckholts died, and his administrators were made parties; and upon the trial a verdict was found for the defendants for the sum of $1,826.74, being the balance due to them upon certain set-offs set up at the trial. A bill of exceptions was taken at the trial by the plaintiffs; and judgment having passed for the defendants, the present writ of error has been brought to revise that judgment.

By the bill of exceptions it appears that the defendants set up as a set-off an account headed " Dr. Messrs. N. Rogers & Sons in account current to 1st of April, 1830, with John Richards & Co.   Cr.," on the debit side of which account were the two following items which constituted the grounds of the objections which have been made at the argument: " To cash, $1,450.46." " To our acceptance of your draft, payable at six months, $3,000." To support their case the defendants offered the testimony of one Rowan, who testified to a conversation had in his presence, in the year 1830, between Buckholts and one of the plaintiffs, relative to their accounts; that the accounts then before them were accounts made out by Rogers & Sons, between themselves and Richards and Buckholts, and John Richards & Co., and John Richards and Lambert & Brothers in account with John Richards & Co., Richards and Buckholts, and John Richards; and an account made out by Buckholts between Richards and Buckholts, and Rogers & Sons. In the conversation relative to these accounts Buckholts asked Rogers if the several items charged in his account had not been received, and Rogers admitted they had been. Among other items so admitted were the above items of $1,450.46 and $3,000. In the conversation about the item of $1,450.46, Rogers admitted that sum had been received by Rogers & Sons from Lambert & Brothers, in New York; and that it was part of the proceeds of seventy-four bales of cotton shipped by Richards and Buckholts to Lambert & Brothers. Very little was said about the item of $3,000. Something was said between Buckholts and Rogers about the right to apply moneys to the payment of John Richards' private debts; Buckholts contending that he had no right so to do, and Rogers that he had; but which particular item of payment the witness did not understand. This was all the evidence of payment introduced by the defendants to support the above two items of $1,450.46, and $3,000. The witness stated that he had understood that John Richards had once failed before he went into partnership with Buckholts. It was admitted by the defendants that the item of $3,000 was for a bill of exchange, drawn in 1825 by Rogers & Sons on John Richards alone.

The plaintiffs then introduced a letter written by John Richards to the plaintiffs, dated at Natchez, June 6, 1825 (and which is in the record), containing statements relative to a shipment of seventy-eight bales of cotton made to Lambert & Co., and to certain payments which, the letter says, " we have left in the hands of Messrs. Lambert Brothers & Co., to be divided among you and them." It then enumerates $8,550, "intended to pay my own debts;" and on account of Richards & Co., $3,000. It then adds that the sum of

$654.55 had been that day sent to New Orleans to purchase exchange on New York, to be forwarded and go to the payment of John Richards & Co.'s debt to plaintiffs, and Messrs. Lambert Brothers & Co.

Upon this evidence the plaintiffs requested the court to charge the jury that the defendants were not entitled, upon the evidence before them, to the item of $1,450.46, as an offset to the plaintiffs' claim; and also that the defendants were not entitled, upon the evidence before the jury, to the item of the $3,000 as an offset, which charge the court refused to give, and in our judgment very properly refused to give, as it involved the determination of matter of fact properly belonging to the province of the jury.

The defendants then requested the court to charge the jury as follows: "First, that if the jury believe the offset of $1,450 was the proceeds of cotton of Richards and Buckholts, or John Richards & Co., shipped on their joint accounts, then it is a legal offset to a joint debt, and cannot be applied to an individual debt of John Richards, without proof that Buckholts was himself consulted and agreed to it. Second, that if the jury believed that the draft of $3,000 was paid by Richards and Buckholts or John Richards & Co., or out of the effects of either of those firms, with the knowledge of Rogers & Sons, then in law it is a legal offset to the joint debt of the said Richards and Buckholts, or John Richards & Co., and cannot be applied to the private debt of either partner without the consent of the other partner. Third, that the letter of John Richards, read in this case, is not evidence against Buckholts, unless the jury believe that Buckholts knew of the letter, and sanctioned its contents." The court gave the charge as requested; and the present bill of exceptions has brought before us for consideration the propriety of each of these instructions.

§ 125. *One partner cannot lawfully apply partnership funds to the payment of his separate debt, and it makes no difference that the separate creditor had no notice that there was a misappropriation of partnership assets.*

The first instruction raises these questions, whether the funds of a partnership can be rightfully applied by one partner to the discharge of his own separate pre-existing debt, without the assent, express or implied, of the other partner; and whether it makes any difference, in such a case, that the separate creditor had no knowledge at the time of the fact of the fund being partnership property. We are of opinion in the negative on both questions. The implied authority of each partner to dispose of the partnership funds strictly and rightfully extends only to the business and transactions of the partnership itself; and any disposition of those funds by any partner beyond such purposes is an excess of his authority as partner, and a misappropriation of those funds, for which the partner is responsible to the partnership; though in the case of *bona fide* purchasers without notice, for a valuable consideration, the partnership may be bound by such acts. Whatever acts, therefore, are done by any partner, in regard to partnership property or contracts, beyond the scope and objects of the partnership, must, in general, in order to bind the partnership, be derived from some further authority, express or implied, conferred upon such partner beyond that resulting from his character as partner. Such is the general principle; and, in our judgment, it is founded in good sense and reason. One man ought not to be permitted to dispose of the property, or to bind the rights of another, unless the latter has authorized the act. In the case of a partner paying his own separate debt out of the partnership funds, it is manifest that it is a violation of his duty and of the right

191

of his partners unless they have assented to it. The act is an illegal conversion of the funds; and the separate creditor can have no better title to the funds than the partner himself had.

Does it make any difference that the separate creditor had no knowledge at the time that there was a misappropriation of the partnership funds? We think not. If he had such knowledge, undoubtedly he would be guilty of gross fraud, not only in morals, but in law. That was expressly decided in Shirreff v. Wilks, 1 East, 48; and indeed seems too plain upon principle to admit of any serious doubt. But we do not think that such knowledge is an essential ingredient in such a case. The true question is, whether the title to the property has passed from the partnership to the separate creditor. If it has not, then the partnership may reassert their claim to it in the hands of such creditor. The case of Ridley v. Taylor, 13 East, 175, has been supposed to inculcate a different and more modified doctrine. But, upon a close examination, it will be found to have turned upon its own peculiar circumstances. Lord Ellenborough, in that case, admitted that one partner could not pledge the partnership property for his own separate debt, and if he could not do such an act of a limited nature, it is somewhat difficult to see how he could do an act of a higher nature, and sell the property. And his judgment seems to have been greatly influenced by the consideration that the creditor in that case might fairly presume that the partner was the real owner of the partnership security; and that there was an absence of all the evidence (which existed and might have been produced) to show that the other partner did not know and had not authorized the act. If it had appeared from any evidence that the act was unknown to or unauthorized by the other partners, it is very far from being clear that the case could have been decided in favor of the separate creditor; for his lordship seems to have put the case upon the ground that either actual covin in the creditor should be shown, or that there should be pregnant evidence that the act was unauthorized by the other partners. The case of Green v. Deakin, 2 Starkie, 347, before Lord Ellenborough, seems to have proceeded upon the ground that fraud or knowledge by the separate creditor was not a necessary ingredient. In the recent case, *Ex parte* Goulding, cited in Collyer on Partnership, 283, 284, the vice-chancellor (Sir John Leach) seems to have adopted the broad ground upon which we are disposed to place the doctrine. Upon the appeal, his decision was confirmed by Lord Lyndhurst. Upon that occasion his lordship said: "No principle can be more clear than that where a partner and a creditor enter into a contract on a separate account, the partner cannot pledge the partnership funds or give the partnership acceptances in discharge of this contract so as to bind the firm." There was no pretense in that case of any fraud on the part of the separate creditor; and Lord Lyndhurst seems to have put his judgment upon the ground that, unless the other partner assented to the transaction, he was not bound; and that it was the duty of the creditor to ascertain whether there was such assent or not.

The same question has been discussed in the American courts on various occasions. In Dob v. Halsey, 16 Johns., 34, it was held by the court that one partner could not apply partnership property to the payment of his own separate debt, without the assent of the other partners. On that occasion, Mr. Chief Justice Spencer stated the difference between the decision in New York and those in England to be merely this: that in New York the court required the separate creditor, who had obtained the partnership paper for the private debt of one of the partners, to show the assent of the whole firm to be bound; and that in England the burden of proof was on the other partners to show their want of knowledge or dissent. The learned judge added: "I can perceive no substantial difference, whether the note of a firm be taken for a private debt of one of the partners by a separate creditor of a partner, pledging the security of the firm, and taking the property of the firm, upon a purchase of one of the partners, to pay his private debt. In both cases the act is equally injurious to the other partners. It is taking their common property to pay a private debt of one of the partners." The same doctrine has been, on various occasions, fully recognized in the supreme court of the same state. And we need do no more than refer to one of the latest, the case of Everingham v. Ensworth, 7 Wend., 326. Indeed, it had been fully considered long before in Livingston v. Roosevelt, 4 Johns., 251.

It is true that the precise point now before us does not appear to have received any direct adjudication; for in all the cases above mentioned there was a known application of the funds or securities of the partnership to the payment of the separate debt. But we think that the true principle to be extracted from the authorities is that one partner cannot apply the partnership funds or securities to the discharge of his own private debt without their consent; and that without their consent their title to the property is not divested in favor of such separate creditor, whether he knew it to be partnership property or not. In short, his right depends, not upon his knowledge that it was partnership property, but upon the fact whether the other partners had assented to such disposition of it or not.

If we are right in the preceding views, they completely dispose of the second instruction. The point there put involves the additional ingredient that the separate debt and draft of Richards for the $3,000 was, with the knowledge of the plaintiffs (Rogers & Sons), paid out of the partnership funds; and if so, then, unless that payment was assented to by the other partner, it was clearly invalid and not binding upon him. It is true that the draft of $3,000 was drawn on Richards alone; and therefore it cannot be presumed that the plaintiffs had knowledge that it was accepted by the partnership or paid out of the partnership funds. But the question was left, and properly left, to the jury to say whether the plaintiffs had such knowledge; and if they had, unless the other partner consented, the payment would be a fraud upon the partnership. With the question, whether the jury have drawn a right conclusion, it is not for us to intermeddle. It was a matter fairly before them upon the evidence; and the decision upon matters of fact was their peculiar province.

§ 126. *No presumption that partner knows of contents of letter written by copartner.*

The third instruction admits of no real controversy. The letter purports to be written by Richards alone, and not in the name of the firm or by the orders of the firm. It embraces topics belonging to his own private affairs, as well as to those of the firm. Under such circumstances, not being written in the name of the firm, it cannot be presumed that the other partner had knowledge of its contents, and sanctioned them, unless some proof to that effect was offered to the jury. If the other partner did not know of the letter, or sanction its contents, it is plain that he ought not to be bound by them; and such was the instruction given to the jury.

Upon the whole, our opinion is that the judgment of the court below ought to be affirmed, with six per cent. interest, and costs.

ANDERSON v. TOMPKINS.

(Circuit Court for Virginia: 1 Marshall, 456–465. 1820.)

Opinion by MARSHALL, C. J.

STATEMENT OF FACTS.— This suit is brought to establish a deed made by Adam Murray, a partner of the house of Tompkins & Murray, in November, 1819, while in England, conveying his moiety of the property of that house to certain creditors of the firm.

On the 29th of April, 1819, Murray had embarked for England, leaving all the effects of the company in the hands of John Tompkins, the partner remaining in this country, who continued, for a short time, to conduct the business of the concern. The pressure of their affairs was such that in May the house stopped payment, and Tompkins, for himself and his partner, conveyed all the effects of the company, and also the separate property of himself and partner, to trustees for the payment, first, of certain creditors named in the deed, and then of those who should bring in their claims, the American creditors within sixty days, the foreign creditors within six months. As the deed under which the plaintiffs claim can operate on that property only which is not conveyed by the first, it will be proper first to inquire into the legal extent of the deed made by Tompkins.

That deed, as has been already stated, purports to convey the whole property of the concern and the private property of the partners. That property consisted of the effects of the partnership for sale of real property and of debts. I shall consider the deed in its application to each of these subjects.

§ 127. _One partner can convey the partnership effects other than real estate to secure firm creditors._

First. The goods in possession for sale. The convenience of trade requires that each acting partner should have the entire control and disposition of this subject. It would destroy copartnerships entirely if the co-operation of all the partners were necessary to dispose of a yard of cloth. It is therefore laid down in all the books which treat on commercial transactions, that with respect to all articles to be sold for the benefit of the concern, each partner, though the others be within reach, has, in the course of trade, an absolute right to dispose of the whole. "Each," says Watson, "has a power to dispose of the whole of the partnership effects." This is a general rule resulting from the nature of the estate, and from the objects for which men associate in trade. They are joint tenants, without the right of survivorship; they are seized _per mi et per tout_, and they associate together for objects which require that the whole powers of the partnership should reside in each partner who is present and acting.

These general doctrines are universal and have not been controverted in this case; but it is contended that they do not authorize the deed made by Tompkins, because, 1st, this is not an act in the course of trade, but is a disposition of the whole subject, and a dissolution of the partnership.

2d. It is a preference to particular creditors, in making which Murray ought to be consulted.

3d. It is by deed. It will be readily conceded that a fraudulent sale, whether made by deed or otherwise, would pass nothing to a vendee concerned in the fraud. But, with this exception, I feel much difficulty in setting any other limits to the power of a partner in disposing of the effects of the company purchased for sale. He may sell a yard, a piece, a bale, or any number of bales. He may sell the whole of any article, or of any number of articles. This power would certainly not be exercised in the presence of a partner without consulting him; and if it were so exercised, slight circumstances would be sufficient to render the transaction suspicious, and, perhaps, to fix on it the imputation of fraud. In this respect every case must depend on its own circumstances. But with respect to the power, in a case perfectly fair, I can perceive no ground on which it is to be questioned.

But this power, it is said, is limited to the course of trade. What is understood by the course of trade? Is it that which is actually done every day, or is it that which may be done whenever the occasion for doing it presents itself? There are small traders who scarcely ever in practice sell a piece of cloth uncut, or a cask of spirits. But may not a partner in such a store sell a piece of cloth or a cask of spirits? His power extends to the sale of the article, and the course of trade does not limit him as to quantity. So with respect to larger concerns. By the course of trade is understood dealing in an article in which the company is accustomed to deal, and dealing in that article for the company. Tompkins & Murray sold goods. A sale of goods was in the course of their trade, and within the power of either partner. A fair sale, then, of all or of a part of the goods was within the power vested in a partner.

The reasoning applies with increased force when we consider the situation of these partners. The one was on a voyage to Europe, the other in possession of all the partnership effects for sale. The absent partner could have no agency in the sale of them. He could not be consulted. He could not give an opinion. In leaving the country he must have intended to confide all its business to the partner who remained, for the purpose of transacting it.

Had this, then, been a sale for money, or on credit, no person, I think, could have doubted its obligation. I can perceive no distinction in law, in reason, or in justice, between such a sale and the transaction which has taken place. A merchant may rightfully sell to his creditor, as well as for money. He may give goods in payment of a debt. If he may thus pay a small creditor, he may thus pay a large one. The *quantum* of debt, or of goods sold, cannot alter the right. Neither does it, as I conceive, affect the power, that these goods were conveyed to trustees to be sold by them. The mode of sale must, I think, depend on circumstances. Should goods be delivered to trustees, for sale, without necessity, the transaction would be examined with scrutinizing eyes, and might, under some circumstances, be impeached. But if the necessity be apparent, if the act is justified by its motives, if the mode of sale be such as the circumstances require, I cannot say that the partner has exceeded his power.

This is denominated a destruction of the partnership subject, and a dissolution of the partnership. But how is it a destruction of the subject? Can this appellation be bestowed on the application of the joint property to the payment of the debts of the company? How is it a dissolution of the partnership? A partnership is an association to carry on business jointly. This association may be formed for the future, before any goods are acquired. It may continue after the whole of a particular purchase has been sold. But either partner had a right to dissolve this partnership. The act, however, of applying the means of carrying on their business to the payment of their debts might suspend the operations of the company, but did not dissolve the contract under which their operations were to be conducted.

§ 128. *A partner has a right to be consulted on the making of a conveyance of partnership effects giving preference to certain creditors; but in case of his absence from the country the want of such a consultation will not invalidate the conveyance.*

Second. It is said that Murray had a right to be consulted on giving a preference to creditors. It is true, Murray had a right to be consulted. Had he been present, he ought to have been consulted. The act ought to have been, and probably would have been, a joint act. But Murray was not present. He had left the country and could not be consulted. He had, by leaving the country, confided everything which respected their joint business to Tompkins, who was under the necessity of acting alone.

§ 129. *A partner cannot bind his copartners by deed; but the mere adding a seal to an instrument conveying property which might be conveyed by parol will not invalidate the transfer.*

Third. It is said this transfer of property is by a deed, and that one partner has no right to bind another by deed. For this a case is cited which I believe has never been questioned in England or in this country. Harrison v. Jackson, 7 Durnf. & East, 207.

I am not, and never have been, satisfied with the extent to which this doctrine has been carried. The particular point decided in it is certainly to be sustained on technical reasoning, and perhaps ought not to be controverted. I do not mean to controvert it. That was an action of covenant on a deed, and if the instrument was not the deed of the defendants, the action could not be sustained. It was decided not to be the deed of the defendants, and I submit to the decision. No action can be sustained against the partner, who has not executed the instrument, on the deed of his copartner. No action can be sustained against the partner which rests on the validity of such a deed, as to the person who has not executed it. This principle is settled. But I cannot admit its application in a case where the property may be transferred by delivery under a parol contract, where the right of sale is absolute and the change of property is consummated by delivery. I cannot admit that a sale so consummated is annulled by the circumstance that it is attested by, or that the trusts under which it is made are described in, a deed. No case goes thus far, and I think such a decision could not be sustained on principle.

The power of applying all the goods on hand for sale to the payment of the partnership debts is, I think, a power created by the partnership, and the exercise of it must be regulated by circumstances. In extraordinary cases an extraordinary use of power must be made. What is called the course of trade is not confined to the most usual way of doing business in the usual state of things. In the absence of one of the partners, in a case of admitted and urgent necessity, the power to sell may be exercised by the partner who is present, and who must act alone, in such manner as the case requires, provided it be exercised fairly. In this case the fairness of the transaction is not impeached, and, certainly, upon its face, is not impeachable.

So far, then, as respects the partnership effects which were delivered, I have never, from the first opening of the cause, entertained a moment's doubt.

§ 130. *Real property held by a firm is held by the members thereof as tenants in common, and neither can convey more than his undivided interest.*

Second. The next subject to be considered is the real property comprehended in this deed. Real property, whether held in partnership or otherwise, can be conveyed only by deed, executed in the manner prescribed by statute. This deed can convey no more title at law than is in the person who executed it. Property conveyed to a firm, or to partners in trust for a firm, is held by them as tenants in common, and neither party can convey more than his undivided interest.

In this case, where the legal estate was in Tompkins, the whole property passes at law by his deed. Where the legal estate was in Murray, the whole property passes at law by his deed. Where the legal estate was in Tompkins & Murray, the property passes in moieties by their several deeds. I do not think that the superior equity of either party is such as to control the legal estate or the disposition made by law of the subject.

Where the legal estate is in trustees for the use of Tompkins & Murray the title does not pass at law by either deed, and I have greatly doubted whether the first deed ought not to be preferred. I have, however, come to the opinion that this trust ought to follow the nature of the estate at law, and where the trustees have not conveyed before the subsequent deed was executed, that the title to this property likewise should pass in moieties.

§ 131. *Debts assignable at law are assignable by the deed of one copartner. In case of successive assignments by each of two partners separately of debts which are assignable only in equity, the prior assignment will prevail over the subsequent one.*

The last subject to be considered is the debts due to the partnership. The right of one of the partners to assign debts which are assignable at law is admitted, provided that assignment be made in the usual way. The assignment, then, of these debts, is as valid a transaction as the sale of goods on hand, if it be not contaminated with the seal. I should not suppose, on the principle settled in 7 Durnf. & East, that an action could be maintained on this assignment. But I am not satisfied that it does not pass the assignable paper which the partner had a legal right to assign. I rather think it does.

A question of more difficulty respects the book debts. This is a part of the subject on which I have entertained, and still entertain, great doubts. The deed does not pass these debts at law. They are not assignable at law, but they are assignable in equity, and a court of equity sustains their assignment. At law, the assignment is only a power to collect and appropriate, and that power is revocable. So far as collections were made under it before it was revoked, I can have no doubt that the money collected was in the trustees. With respect to debts not collected I have felt great doubts. I consider the power to collect as a contract which could not be enforced at law. But as Mr. Murray could not convey this property at law, and could only convey it in equity, I have supposed that the prior equity must be sustained, and that these debts also pass by the deed of Tompkins.

The opinion of the court, then, is that the plaintiffs have a right to a decree for a sale of all the real property contained in the deed made by Adam Murray, the legal title to which was in Adam Murray, and to a moiety of the real property, the title to which was in Tompkins & Murray, or in trustees for their benefit; and that the residue of the property passes to the trustees in the deed executed by John Tompkins.

GRAHAM v. MEYER.

(Circuit Court for New York: 4 Blatchford, 129–185. 1858.)

STATEMENT OF FACTS.— Trover for the value of certain steamships, valued at $400,000, and which it was claimed had been conveyed to the firm of Meyer & Stucken as security for a usurious loan made by the firm to plaintiff. This action was against Meyer alone. The plaintiff had also brought a suit in equity against Stucken to recover the vessels. In this action defendant was held to bail in the sum of $360,000. He now moves to be discharged on common bail, or for a reduction of the amount, and also that plaintiff be compelled to elect which of his two suits he will prosecute.

Opinion by INGERSOLL, J.

The transaction out of which this suit arose is said to have taken place in the city of New York; and as, by the laws of the state of New York, all conveyances for the security of a usurious loan of money are absolutely void, and the party making a conveyance of personal property for the security of a usurious loan of money has a right to proceed, in an action of trover, against the party receiving the property as security, if he converts it to his use, it follows, as the defendant is charged in the affidavit with making the usurious loan, with receiving the steamships as a security for such usurious loan, and with refusing to deliver them up to the plaintiff, upon a demand being made for the same, that there is a good cause of action shown in the affidavit; and, if the allegations in the affidavit are true, the plaintiff has a right to require that the defendant be held to bail. An order was thereupon made to hold him to bail; and, as disinterested witnesses swore that the steamships were worth the sum of $360,000, the defendant was ordered to be held to bail in that amount.

The facts upon which the motion now made in respect to bail is founded admit of little or no doubt. On the 5th of December, 1855, the defendant and · one Stucken were in partnership, under the name of Meyer & Stucken. They have ever since been, and now are, in partnership. At the last mentioned date the defendant was in Europe. For some considerable time before then he had been in Europe, and he continued to be there from the 5th of December, 1855, to about the middle of October, 1857. On the 5th of December, 1855, Stucken advanced to the plaintiff a sum of money amounting to at least $80,000. On the same day he took an absolute bill of sale of the ships in question, in the name of Meyer & Stucken, and took possession of the same with the consent of the plaintiff. The transaction purported to be an absolute sale of the steamships, upon a valuable consideration paid. The plaintiff insists that it·was, in reality, a usurious loan of money, and that the ships were transferred as a security merely for such usurious loan of money. Stucken insists that there was no loan, and that the transaction was an absolute sale of the ships, for a valuable and adequate consideration paid. In considering the motion now made, ĺ I will assume that the transaction between the plaintiff and Stucken was a usurious loan of money; that the transfer of the steamships was, in reality, merely a security for such loan of money; and that Stucken would be liable to the plaintiff, in action of trover, for the value of the ships. I do this merely for the purposes of this case, and without intending to intimate what, in my opinion, was the true nature of the transaction between the plaintiff and Stucken, as there is no necessity for me to determine what its true nature was to dispose of the motion now under consideration. The question then is presented — would the defendant, upon this assumption, upon the facts as they now appear, be liable to such action?

The ships were sold by Stucken in the month of May, 1856, for $180,000, he before that having been obliged to pay about $70,000 to satisfy certain liens upon them. Up to the time of commencement of this suit the defendant never, to his knowledge, saw the plaintiff, and never personally made any loan of any kind to him, or had any transaction or dealing with him. No demand has ever been made personally on the defendant to deliver the steamships to the plaintiff, or to account for the same to the plaintiff, or to pay the value of the same to him. The defendant was not consulted in reference to the transaction between the plaintiff and Stucken, and the contract between them was negotiated and concluded when the defendant was absent in Europe, and he had no knowledge in reference thereto. The defendant knew nothing of any usurious transactions between the plaintiff and Stucken, if any took place. There is no evidence that, prior to the commencement of the plaintiff's suit, the defendant was ever informed that the plaintiff claimed that the transaction between him and Stucken was a usurious one. The defendant never authorized any usurious transaction between his partner, Stucken, and the plaintiff; and, as he knew nothing of any usurious transaction between the plaintiff and his partner, Stucken, at the time it took place, and as there is no evidence that he ever was, prior to the commencement of the plaintiff's suit, informed of any such usurious transaction, it cannot with truth be said that he ever ratified any such usurious transaction, if, in point of fact, it ever existed.

§ **132.** *A tort committed by one partner will not bind the partnership, nor the other partner unless he adopted it, or it be within the scope and business of the partnership.*

What the particular terms were of the articles of copartnership between the defendant and Stucken does not appear. We know, however, that it was a partnership for a lawful purpose. It is to be presumed, therefore, that the articles were such as ordinarily exist between partners engaged in lawful business. By such articles, one partner does not authorize the other to engage in unlawful business. The law of New York makes it unlawful to loan money at a usurious rate of interest. The law declares that all conveyances made to secure any usurious loan shall be absolutely void, and that no title shall be transferred by any such conveyance. It also declares that, when the party borrowing goes into a court of equity to recover back the property conveyed as security for the loan, he shall not be obliged to tender or pay the actual amount received, and that he may ask for equity without offering to do equity. The transaction, as claimed by the plaintiff, between him and Stucken, was, therefore, an unlawful one, disastrous in its consequences, and highly prejudical to the interest of the defendant, if he is to be bound by it; and the partnership articles cannot be invoked to authorize Stucken to make the defendant liable for a tort committed by Stucken, either in his own name individually, or in the name of the copartnership.

§ **133.** *To make one partner liable for his copartner's violation of law, it must appear that he authorized or ratified it.*

A tort committed by one partner will not bind the partnership or the other copartner, unless it be either authorized or adopted by the firm, or be within the proper scope and business of the partnership. Story on Partnership, sec. 168. A tort, an act in violation of a particular statute law, and attended with a forfeiture, is not within the proper scope and business of a partnership entered into for lawful purposes. Therefore, to make the defendant liable in an action of tort, for this violation of law on the part of Stucken, it must be made to appear, by some other evidence, that he either authorized it or ratified it. It has already been shown that he never authorized it; and as, up to the time of the commencement of this suit, there is no evidence that he was informed of any violation of law, he could not have ratified any violation at law. Collyer, in his Treatise on Partnership (p. 252, ed. of 1854), says, that if one of two bankers in partnership commits usury, the innocent partner should not be liable to an action for penalties or damages. By the laws of New York, a usurious loan is unlawful, and the penalty of the forfeiture of the goods attempted to be conveyed as security therefor is prescribed as a consequence.

§ 184. *A demand upon and refusal by one partner is not a conversion by the other partner, but only evidence of such conversion.*

Where one having an apparent right to convey personal property executes a conveyance of it to a partnership, and the same is taken possession of by one of two partners, a demand by the true owner having the right of possession, upon one of the copartners, and a refusal by him, is evidence of a conversion by the other copartner. Nisbet *v.* Patton, 4 Rawle, 120; Mitchell *v.* Williams, 4 Hill, 13. But such a demand and refusal is not a conversion by the other copartner. It is not only evidence of a conversion, not conclusive evidence, but *prima facie* merely, which may be rebutted by other evidence; and, when it is rebutted, it will not be effective to show that there has been a conversion by such other copartner.

This view of the motion now under consideration settles the question that the defendant should not be held to bail to answer the demand in this suit. An order must, therefore, be entered, vacating the order heretofore made, holding him to bail in the sum of $360,000, and that he be discharged on common bail.

§ 185. *A party will not be compelled to elect between a suit at law and a bill in equity filed by him touching the same matter.*

In June, 1856, the plaintiff brought his suit in equity against Stucken and other parties, for the recovery of the ships in question, or the value thereof. The defendant was not made a party to that suit in equity. He was out of the country when it was instituted, and could not be served with the subpœna. There was a prayer, however, in the bill, that he might be made a party, should he return to this country. He has never been made a party.

A motion is now made by the defendant that the plaintiff be compelled to elect which suit to pursue, whether the suit in equity or the suit at law; and that all proceedings in the other be stayed until the final determination of the suit elected to be pursued. When a suit in equity and a suit at law are pending between the same parties, for the same matter, cause and thing, one cannot be pleaded in bar or in abatement of the other. But, notwithstanding this, the court of equity will sometimes order a stay of proceedings in one, until the other is determined.

The defendant in this suit is not a party to the suit in equity. His interest cannot be affected by the determination in that suit. A determination against the plaintiff in that suit will not deprive him of the right to pursue the defendant in this. The determination in that case can have no effect upon this. The motion to compel the plaintiff to elect which suit to pursue, and that the proceedings in the other may be stayed, must, therefore, be denied.

IN RE KETCHUM.

(District Court for New York: 1 Federal Reporter, 815–888. 1880.)

Opinion by CHOATE, J.

STATEMENT OF FACTS.— This is a proceeding to expunge two proofs of debt made and filed by Morris Ketchum. The bankrupts, Franklin M. Ketchum and Thomas Belknap, Jr., were partners, composing the firm of Ketchum & Belknap, and they were adjudicated bankrupts on the petition of Ketchum, one of the partners, filed August 31, 1878. They did business as stock-brokers, in the city of New York, down to the 24th of July, 1878, when they failed. The proofs of debt now objected to were sworn to by Morris Ketchum and filed July 30, 1879. One is for the sum of $8,612.37, alleged to be due "upon an account stated between deponent and said Ketchum & Belknap, of which account a copy is hereto annexed." Annexed to the proof is an account showing sundry items of cash debit and credit between the dates of June 2. 1875, and July 24, 1878, with a balance struck July 24, 1878, to the credit of Morris Ketchum, of $8,549.21, to which interest is added to August 31, 1878, making in all the sum mentioned in the proof of debt, $8,612.37. The second proof of debt is for $27,080.69, alleged to be due as "the proceeds of certain stocks and securities which the said Ketchum & Belknap held for this deponent, and belonging to him, which were sold and disposed of by the said Ketchum & Belknap, and said proceeds appropriated to their own use."

There is little or no dispute about the facts. The firm of Ketchum & Belknap was in business from some time in the year 1871 to the time of their failure, except for a period of about eight months after the panic of 1873, when they suspended business. The partner Ketchum had a seat in the stock board, and attended almost exclusively to buying and selling stocks for customers, and other business of the firm out of the office. Belknap attended almost exclusively to the business in the office, the financial affairs of the firm, the raising of money, the drawing of checks, and the charge of the bank account. For several years prior to the failure this alleged creditor, Morris Ketchum, who was the father of Ketchum, the bankrupt, employed the bankrupt Belknap, individually, as his agent and attorney to attend to some parts of his business. He intrusted to Belknap, individually, for safe keeping, large amounts of stocks and securities, which Belknap kept in a tin box, of which he retained the key. The box was deposited in a safe in the office of the firm, to which safe both the partners had access.

Morris Ketchum also kept a deposit account with the Fourth National Bank of New York city, and Belknap individually acted as his attorney in drawing out moneys from this account, upon checks signed by him, in the name of Morris Ketchum. This part of the business done by him for Morris Ketchum was transacted under a power of attorney, executed before the formation of the firm, which authorized Thomas Belknap, Jr., and Franklin M. Ketchum, severally, to draw and indorse checks and drafts. This power was in fact not acted on by Franklin M. Ketchum, but by Belknap alone. Belknap had no authority, as between himself and Morris Ketchum, to draw out any money from the bank, except for the proper use and benefit of Morris Ketchum, nor had he any authority to use or dispose of said stocks and securities except by order of Morris Ketchum. Belknap, without the knowledge or consent of Morris Ketchum, from time to time drew checks, in Morris Ketchum's name, against this bank account for various sums of money, and deposited said checks to the credit of the firm of Ketchum & Belknap in the same bank, where they also kept their bank account. These transactions were wholly without the knowledge of Franklin M. Ketchum until after the failure of the firm, when Belknap informed his partner and Morris Ketchum of the fact that he had misappropriated these funds to the use of the firm by depositing them in their bank account.

Belknap, also, without the knowledge or consent of Morris Ketchum, or of his partner, Franklin M. Ketchum, sold and disposed of some of the stocks and securities belonging to Morris Ketchum, in his possession, and deposited the proceeds of them in the bank account of the firm, and used others of these stocks and securities by hypothecating them with the Fourth National Bank for loans to the firm; and, at the time of the failure of the firm, some of the stocks thus hypothecated were still held by the bank as security for such loans. The proof of debt first above stated, being the balance of an alleged account, consists wholly of moneys thus transferred by means of checks drawn as aforesaid from the account of Morris Ketchum to the account of the firm. The proof of debt second above stated is for the value of the securities so sold, and their proceeds deposited in the firm's bank account, and of those hypothecated with the bank as security for its loans to the firm. At the time of the failure the firm was largely indebted to the bank for overdrafts, besides the secured debt above stated.

After the failure and before the filing of the petition in bankruptcy, Belknap made entries in the books of the firm crediting Morris Ketchum with the amounts of the several checks misapplied by him as aforesaid, and also entered upon the books of the firm, as of the date of July 24, 1878, a credit of Morris Ketchum "for sundry stocks and bonds, $26,822.50." It is not shown when these entries were made, except that they were in August, 1878, and before the filing of the petition in bankruptcy by Franklin M. Ketchum. In the schedule of debts annexed to his petition the bankrupt Ketchum included the following as unsecured claims of Morris Ketchum: "Sales of sundry stocks and bonds belonging to said Morris Ketchum, and which Ketchum & Belknap were unable to return credited at market value, on July 24, 1878, $26,822.50; interest to August 31, 1878, $198.19." "Balance of book account, receipts and payments of money on July 24, 1878, $8,549.21; interest to August 31, 1878, $63.16." Another unsecured claim of Morris Ketchum is included, as to which no claim of Morris Ketchum is raised, with the exception of the entries thus made in the books of the firm.

After the failure and the insertion of these items in this schedule of the firm debts, nothing was done by either partner, so far as the evidence shows, by way of adoption by the firm of these contested claims, nor was any account rendered by the firm to Morris Ketchum, or any agreement made between him and the firm in respect to said moneys so received by the firm, or in respect to said securities, other than such as may be, if any, implied by law from the foregoing facts. Franklin M. Ketchum testified that, at the time he inserted these items in the schedule, he knew of the entries made in the books by Belknap, and he put these claims in the schedule because he believed the firm to be liable for the money and stocks to Morris Ketchum. It also appeared by the evidence, that, at the time of making the schedule, Franklin M. Ketchum knew, by the confession of Belknap, that the money and the stocks had been wrongfully used by Belknap, and that the proceeds had gone into the bank account of the firm. Belknap drew from the firm bank account for his own use, and for the use of the firm, at all times indiscriminately, and there is no proof that he individually used the money thus wrongfully paid in, except so far as it may be inferred from this indiscriminate drawing on the bank account, which was partly for his own private stock speculations, which were in violation of the partnership agreement; and, at the time of the failure, he was largely indebted to the firm, and his frauds caused, or largely contributed to cause, the failure of the firm.

There is no evidence whatever of an account stated as to the money taken from the private bank account of Morris Ketchum and deposited in the bank account of the firm. No account, such as is annexed to the first proof of debt, and which is a copy of the account made up by Belknap in the firm's book, was, so far as appears, ever rendered to Morris Ketchum or assented to by him. Without such assent to the account, either express or implied by failure to object to it upon its being rendered, there can be no account stated. Therefore, if there be any liability of the firm for these moneys, the same is misdescribed in the proof of debt. The question of liability, however, has been argued upon the facts proved, with little regard to form, and if a firm liability exists the proof may be amended, or a new proof, according to the fact, may be filed. So in regard to the second proof of debt, so far as regards the securities sold by Belknap, it is clearly stated untruly in the proof of debt that they were held and sold by the firm. As to those securities the liability of the firm, if there is any, arises not from the improper sale of the securities, which was Belknap's individual act, but from the receipt of the money and its subsequent use by the firm. And in this respect, also, if the claim is sustained, the proof may be amended or a new proof filed.

§ 136. *Rule in case of loans made to partner, where the moneys are used for the purposes of the partnership.*

The questions that arise are different as to the money taken from the private bank account, the stocks pledged to the bank for a loan to the firm, and the proceeds of the stocks deposited in the firm's bank account. Upon the argument a large number of cases have been cited, illustrative of the rules of law as to loans made to a partner, where the moneys are by him used for the purposes of the partnership. As to this whole class of cases the rules of law are well settled, but they afford little or no aid in determining the questions that arise where the money or the property used by the firm is brought in through the fraud of one of the partners in abusing the trust confided to him by a third party.

Where a third party loans money to a partner on his individual credit, his putting that money into the firm creates no contract between the firm and the lender, for the very obvious reason that it was the lender's intention to lend the money to the individual partner, and, as in such a case the money is lent without any restriction as to its use, the borrower may do what he likes with it, and what he does with it is no longer any concern of the lender; and, of course, it makes no difference whatever that the borrower's copartner happens to know, when the borrower pays it into the firm, that he has borrowed it even for the purpose of lending it to the firm.

If a partner, in applying for a loan, however, acts therein as a partner and for his firm, then the firm will owe the money to the lender, even though he did not, at the time, know that the borrower was acting for his firm. At any rate, if he chooses to treat the firm as the borrower, he may do so as in any other case of an undisclosed principal acting through an agent. But it is unnecessary to refer especially to this class of cases, because the principles that govern the present case are not those that relate to the lending of money unattended by fraud or breach of trust.

§ 137. *Contention of contesting creditors.*

It is claimed by the learned counsel for the contesting creditors that the rule of law is well settled that where a partner, coming into the possession of money by the abuse of his individual trust, or duty to a third person, puts that money into the firm without any knowledge of the fraud on the part of his copartners, no obligation arises on the part of the firm to pay back the money to the party who, as against the partner so wrongfully paying it in, could demand it; that, though the guilty partner is liable to the person wronged, the firm is not liable; that, though the party wronged, if he can trace the money distinguishable from other moneys in the hands of the firm, may follow and recover it as his specific property, yet that he cannot maintain an action, as for a debt, or as for money had and received, against the firm for it, if, as in this case, the money is spent and gone.

§ 138. *Circumstances under which a partnership is liable to a third party whose money or property one of the partners has received and appropriated to the use of the partnership.*

There are some points in regard to the liability of a firm for the misappropriation of the property of a third party well settled; thus, if the firm has assumed, or is properly chargeable with, any duty in the safe-keeping of the property, the firm is liable for its misappropriation by one partner, although done without the knowledge of the other partners. This rule rests on the familiar principle that, within the scope of the partnership business, each partner is the agent of the firm, and the act of each partner, whether in making a contract or in performing or failing to perform a duty imposed on the firm by contract, is the act of all. And, where one of the partners is employed in a transaction or matter of business fairly within the scope of the business undertaken to be transacted by the firm, the fact that he was specially trusted by the customer, or that the business was transacted, so far as the firm was concerned, exclusively by him, and without the knowledge of the copartners, will not, in itself, make the transaction an individual transaction.

The question is one, in every case, of fact and of the intention of the parties, the principle being that, if the business was fairly, as between the partners themselves, a firm matter, in the benefits of which, under the copartnership agreement, they were entitled to share, or if the customer, in fact, employed the partner as a member of the firm, engaged in the business, to which the particular transaction belonged, and was justified in so doing by the nature of the business of the firm, as publicly exhibited, then the transaction is a firm transaction, and in every such case the firm must make good all unauthorized intermeddling with the customer's property, by either partner, in violation of the duty which the firm, or he on behalf of the firm, has assumed with regard to the property.

And it seems that the employment of a member of the firm, carrying on a particular kind of business, as, for instance, that of a stock-broker, or a solicitor in a matter fairly within the line of business done by the firm, though the form of the employment, so far as correspondence or personal intercourse with the customer or client is concerned, is with one of the partners only, and it is induced by relations of special friendship with or confidence in him, yet it is presumed to be, as a matter of fact, an employment of him as a member of the firm, thus throwing the burden of showing that the employment was really intended to be personal on the firm, if they deny their liability. Willett *v.* Chambers, Cowp., 814; Devaynes *v.* Noble; Clayton's Case, 1 Mer., 575; Baring's Case, 1 Nev., 611; De Rebeque *v.* Barclay, 23 Beav., 107.

§ **139.** *Liability of firm for conversion of chattels by partner.*

These, and other similar cases which might be cited, rest on the basis of a violation by the firm of a duty assumed by the firm, under an employment made with, or which, under the circumstances, the firm cannot deny was made with it. They are not, properly, cases of a firm getting into its possession the property of another party by the tortious act of one of the partners; but from the admitted principles of the law of partnership, there would seem to be no question that a firm would be liable in trover for the conversion of personal property other than money, or what, by the law merchant, passes for money, under the same circumstances under which an individual would be liable in that form of action.

Each partner being the agent of the firm in the transaction of its business, the firm is liable for the tort of either of its members, if, under the same circumstances, any other principal would be so liable; that is, if the principal has authorized the particular act, or has adopted it, and taken the benefit of it, or, without special authorization, it was done by the agent in the course of and as part of his employment. The test of liability for trover or conversion of chattels is the unauthorized exercise of such dominion over them as is inconsistent with the rights of the true owner. Bryce *v.* Buckway, 81 N. Y., 490; Heald *v.* Carey, 11 C. B., 977; Cobb *v.* Dows, 10 N. Y., 335; Helbery *v.* Hatten, 2 H. & C., 822.

That the sale or hypothecating of chattels, without authority, is a conversion, is too clear to need authority; and it is wholly immaterial whether the unauthorized sale or pledge, or other act of conversion, was knowingly wrongful, or, in fact, wholly innocent — done under a mistake as to the title or the right of the party making the sale or pledge. (Same cases.) That ignorance of the fact that the property belongs to another, and the want of intent to commit a trespass upon it, constitutes no defense to an action of trover, is in conformity with the rule of the common law that no man can (with certain exceptions not here needful to notice) be deprived of his property without his own consent, and that his permitting another to have the possession of his chattels does not carry with it such an *indicium* of title as authorizes or justifies any other party, dealing with the party so in possession, to rely upon that possession as evidence of title. Ballard *v.* Burgett, 40 N. Y., 314.

The owner may estop himself by declarations, oral or written, creating or importing an apparent title on which parties dealing with the person may rely. This, however, is only where, upon the principles of estoppel *in pais*, the prevention of possible or intended frauds makes it necessary in favor of persons parting with value, or altering their condition for the worse by reason of the reliance on the declarations that the title shall be held to pass. Moore *v.* Metropolitan Bank, 55 N. Y., 41.

Clearly then, with this exception of a case of estoppel, all the world deals with chattels, wherever found, at the peril of liability for trover, if in fact they belong to another, or the party dealing with them has in fact no right to them. If one is misled by another's possession and apparent ownership of them it is his misfortune, for which the owner is not responsible, and which constitutes no legal defense to a claim for their conversion.

If, therefore, a firm, acting through an agent or one of the partners, while engaged in the regular course of the business of the firm, innocently or wrongfully appropriates chattels, other than money or what has the quality of money, and sells it, and receives and uses in its business the proceeds, or, without a sale, uses it in the firm's business, the firm is liable for conversion, and it is wholly immaterial that all or any of the members of the firm were ignorant of the wrong committed or innocent of any wrongful intent. But, when the thing misappropriated is money, other considerations arise growing out of the nature of money.

§ **140.** *Money has no ear-mark, and title to it passes by delivery. Scope and application of the rule.*

It is a maxim of the common law that money has no ear-mark. The peculiarity of money, as distinguished from other chattels, is that the title to it passes by delivery, and any one taking it without notice of any other title to it may safely rely on the title of the party in possession of it. This is essential to its beneficial use as money, and any private mischiefs that may result from the principle are outweighed by the public and general good resulting from its use. Yet the maxim that money has no ear-mark was very early held not to prevent the owner of property wrongfully converted into money from tracing and recovering it, if the money had been again invested by itself in other property, although in the meantime it had been in the form of money in the possession of the wrong-doer.

Thus, in Whitcomb v. Jacob, 1 Salk., 160 (9 Ann.), it was ruled that, if one employs a factor and "intrusts him with the disposal of merchandise, and the factor receives the money and dies indebted in debts of a higher nature, and it appears, by evidence, that this money was vested in other goods and remains unpaid, those goods shall be taken as part of the merchant's estate and not the factor's; but if the factor have the money, it shall be looked upon as the factor's estate, and must first answer the debts of his superior creditor, etc., for, in regard that money has no ear-mark, equity cannot follow that in behalf of him that employed the factor." See, also, Scott v. Surman, Willes, 400.

Modern decisions, however, have so far modified or defined, in its application, the ancient doctrine that money cannot be traced when mingled with other moneys, that it is now established that the owner of property which has been disposed of without his authority can recover the proceeds if the same can be traced as a part of a particular fund or lot of money, or as part of a deposit of money in bank, though mingled in such fund or deposit with other money, or into whatever form or new investment the proceeds may be carried, whether of money or property, provided that the rights of third parties have not intervened. And it is the settled rule of courts of law, as well as of courts of equity, that, "where property is tortiously disposed of by one intrusted with it, the title of the owner of the property so misappropriated attaches to the proceeds, whatever may be their form, whether money or anything else; that the substitute for the original thing follows the nature of the thing itself so long as it can be ascertained to be such." Taylor v. Plumer, 3 M. & S., 573; Small v. Atwood, 1 Younge, 537; Pennell v. Deffell, 4 De G., McN. & G., 386; Frith v. Cartland, 2 H. & M., 241; Van Allen v. American Nat. Bank, 1.

Except as against persons who have parted with value for the money which was the proceeds of the property, the title of the former owner of the property to the money remains unaffected so long as he can trace it.

Money, of course, is lost to the owner, and cannot be recovered, or the receiver held liable for its value, if he took it in good faith, without notice of any other title, in payment of a debt, or for the purchase of property, or for other valuable consideration. But this is the limit of the distinction between money and other chattels. See Clarke *v.* Shee, Cowp., 200. And in this case the learned counsel for the opposing creditors concedes that if Morris Ketchum's money still remained in the bank deposit of the firm he could recover it.

It is not very obvious why, if the firm is not liable to an action for money after they had used it, they can justly or consistently be held obliged to restore it if they have not used it, because, if the mode in which they took it does not give them such an equity in it as will enable them to hold it against the true owner, their use of it in their business would seem to give them no new equity or right in it, but would seem, on the contrary, to subject them to an action for money had and received for having disposed of another's money without authority, if it be, indeed, the case that it was still his so that he could recover it *in specie.*

§ 141. *Equity of innocent partner in respect of money held in trust by his copartner but misappropriated by him and paid into the firm. Cases reviewed.*

But the real question after all is whether the circumstances under which the money came to the hands of the firm were such that Franklin M. Ketchum, as the copartner of Belknap, acquired an equity in it or right to keep it as being apparently Belknap's money, contributed to the firm by him, which ought to prevent a suit for the recovery against the firm. As to Belknap, or the firm, if his interest in the firm were alone to be considered, it is clear that a suit could be maintained. The only possible equity of Franklin M. Ketchum in the money, upon its being paid into the firm by Belknap, which will take the case out of the general rule that would allow it to be recovered by the owner, grows out of the nature of money as stated above. This equity must be based on the fact that Belknap paid it in in the form of money, and, therefore, that his copartner had the right to rely on Belknap's possession of it as evidence of its being in fact his money; for this is the only distinction that can be drawn between money and other personal property in such a case. In other words, did Franklin M. Ketchum, so far as it was received on his behalf, receive it in payment of a debt or for some other valuable consideration?

The counsel for the opposing creditor relies chiefly on two cases, which, it is claimed, establish the general position that if one partner misapplies trust funds in his hands by paying them into the firm, without knowledge of the fraud on the part of his copartner, the firm is not thereby rendered liable to an action to recover the money. These cases are: *Ex parte* Apsey, 3 Bro. C. C., 265, and Jacques *v.* Marquand, 6 Cow., 497.

The case of *Ex parte* Apsey was before Lord Chancellor Thurlow, and decided in 1791. The report is very brief, and shows the following facts: On the 11th of February, 1790, a commission of bankruptcy issued against one Toey. The petitioner Apsey and Edward Allen were chosen his assignees. Edward Allen and James Allen were partners in business, and in April, 1791, a joint commission in bankruptcy was issued against them. Edward Allen, before the issue of the commission against himself and his partner, received money as assignee of Toey, which he had paid and applied in discharge of the debts of his firm, and otherwise used in their firm business. The question was whether Apsey, as assignee of Toey, could prove for the money so used by the firm of Edward and James Allen against their joint estate. Proof was refused, and upon petition to the lord chancellor the decision was sustained. Counsel for the petitioner cited the cases of Boardman v. Mosman, 1 Bro. C. C., 68, and *Ex parte* Clones, 2 Bro. C. C., 595. But the lord chancellor said: "In the latter of these cases the partners had agreed to consolidate the separate debts which made the difference. Here one, by abusing his trust, advances the money to the partnership. That will not raise a contract between the partnership and the person whose money it is."

That the firm will be liable to an action to recover the money where the other partner knew of the source from which the money paid in was derived, and that it belonged to or was charged with a trust in favor of another party, on the ground that one who aids in the perpetration of a fraud will be equally responsible with the principal wrong-doer, is sufficiently obvious, but it has been frequently so ruled. Vanderwich v. Summerel, 2 Wash. C. C., 41; Hutchinson v. Smith, 7 Paige, 33; *Ex parte* Walsin, E. & B., 414; Smith v. Jameson, 5 T. R., 601.

It would be no answer to the owner of the money who, waiving the tort, sued for money lent, or money had and received to his use, that what was paid in was money, or that money has no ear-mark, and that it went in payment of the balance due from the partner paying it to his copartner. This was precisely how the proceeds of plaintiff's property had been applied, as between the copartners, in Vanderwich v. Summerel, *ut supra*, but with knowledge of the other copartner, and he was compelled to account for it.

But it is entirely consistent with the case of *Ex parte* Apsey that the innocent partner knew of the advance of the money to the firm by his copartner, though he did not know of the breach of trust committed by him in paying it in. It is also wholly consistent with that decision that the innocent partner assented to and accepted this payment of money, and relied upon its being the proper money of his copartner, and acted upon such reliance in his dealings with his copartner, subsequent to the advance of the money to the firm.

If these facts existed, on which the report is silent, but which, perhaps, may be inferred, upon the general presumption that a merchant keeps himself informed as to his own business affairs, then there is a view of the case which gives the innocent partner an equity to deny his liability for the money, although his firm had the use of it. In such a case, especially if the partner paying in the money is indebted to his copartner on the firm accounts, the innocent copartner may, perhaps, say to the real owner of the money: "It is true this was your money and my firm has received it, and given no consideration for it as a firm, but I received it from the hands of my copartner as money. The law allowed me to rely on his possession of it as proof that it was his own money. I did so. I applied it in our accounts, to the discharge of his indebtedness to me, on firm account. I forbore to press him to make good his account. I have dealt with him ever since with the same reliance and belief that it was his money. I have kept him as my partner, which I might not otherwise have done. I have given him credit, and now, if you reclaim the money as yours, I shall be injured and put in a worse position for having relied on his possession as proof of his title, which, by law, I had a right to do, and must, by the law, be protected in doing."

In other words, if, in the case supposed, the innocent copartner has an individual equity, by reason of which the firm should not, on account of his rights, and for his protection, be held liable for the receipt and appropriation to itself, without consideration, of another man's money, it must be exactly that equity which any other party receiving it as money could plead on his behalf, as against the owner, to wit, that he has received it in payment of a debt, or for the purchase of something of value, which he has parted with in exchange for it, or that he will suffer some injury by reason of his relying on the apparent title made by the actual possession of it, which injury may be equivalent to the parting with value. For, as pointed out above, and illustrated by the authorities cited, money is, in all things, a chattel, and subject to the law which governs other chattels, except so far as it has the peculiar attribute of money in carrying its title by delivery from hand to hand, and that exception is only made on grounds of public policy for the protection of those who take it as money.

The case of *Ex parte* Apsey, therefore, if it can stand as an authority consistently with more recent decisions, is not an authority for the position that the firm of Ketchum and Belknap could defend against a suit by Morris Ketchum for his money misappropriated by Belknap to the use of the firm, since here it is clearly proved that Franklin M. Ketchum did not even know, till the fraud itself was discovered by him after the failure, that his partner, Belknap, had paid in the money at all. It appears by the proofs that Belknap had exclusive charge of the financial affairs of the firm, and the raising of money for its use; that he alone kept the books; that Franklin M. Ketchum never examined the books or knew what was in them; that the only entries of these transactions in the books until after the failure, when Belknap wrote them up, was the memorandum of the deposits made in the bank account of the firm in its check-book, where were minuted, among other sums deposited, these sums in question, against some of which were placed the initials " M. K.," denoting to Belknap that it was Morris Ketchum's money, but with nothing to show whether the sums deposited were moneys borrowed or received for debts due the firm or belonging to the individual partners. Nor, so far as appears, was Belknap ever credited in his account on the firm's books with these sums as money contributed by him. Nor does it appear how his account stood at the time these advances by him to the use of the firm were made.

Thus, a more complete case of the total want of those elements which are necessary to make out an equity on Franklin M. Ketchum's part to this money, on the ground that he, as between himself and his copartner, took it as money, could not well be made out.

If it is suggested that the mere payment of money into the firm operated *ipso facto*, and, because it was money, as a discharge of that amount of the indebtedness of Belknap to his copartner, whether the copartner knew of it or not, and whether he consented to it or not, it may be answered, so far as this case is concerned, that it is not proved that Belknap was then indebted to his copartner in account; but if the parties desire to have the true state of that account appear in case of an appeal, leave will be given to show the facts. But another answer is, that to hold that payment of the money in, without the knowledge and consent of the copartner, operates, because it is money that is paid in, as a payment, would simply be to apply to the case blindly, and without regard to its reason and nature, the maxim that money has no ear-mark.

As above pointed out, this rule goes no further than this in protecting the receiver of money and extinguishing the former title: that the title changes only where the money is received as money, with the *bona fide* belief on the part of the receiver that it was the money of the party paying it. Clearly, Franklin M. Ketchum, if his rights as an individual in his relations to his co-partner are considered — and it will be observed those are the only rights entitled to consideration — was not such a receiver of this money. It must not be lost sight of in this matter that if the firm is not liable for the money received and used by the firm, through Belknap, with full notice of the rights of Morris Ketchum in it, it is an exception from the well-settled rules of the law of partnership, which, for strong reasons of public policy and justice, make the act of one partner in the course of the firm's business the act of all, and the knowledge of the one partner, in the like case, the knowledge of all; and the equity of the innocent partner which is strong enough to countervail and override this well-settled and just rule of law must be a real equity, based on the actual existence of facts which would render the application of the ordinary rule of law in the particular case inequitable and unjust.

The suggestion, in *Ex parte* Apsey, that no contract arises, cannot be understood as basing the objection merely on the circumstance that there is no promise to repay the money on the part of the firm, but simply that, upon the case made, no implied promise is raised by law; for the action for money had and received, as is well settled, does not rest on privity of contract. It lies wherever one man has, or has received, money which, *ex æquo et bono*, he ought to repay. The common case of money paid under mistake of fact is a good illustration of this; and where trover will lie for the conversion of property, and it has been turned into money, the owner may waive the tort, and bring his action for money had and received. In such a case the law implies a contract to repay, where the party has no equity to retain the money or the proceeds of property. Scott *v.* Surman, Willes, 404; Mason *v.* Waite, 17 Mass., 563.

What is meant by the suggestion of the learned chāncellor is, therefore, simply that the case was not one in which the law would imply a promise to repay the money. The views above expressed, as to the necessity of the receiver of money having given a valuable consideration of some kind in order to hold it, or protect himself against an action for it if spent, and as to the true distinction between money and other chattels, are confirmed by the case of Lime Rock Bank *v.* Plimpton, 17 Pick., 160.

The case of Marsh *v.* Keating, 1 Bing. N. C., 198, cannot, I think, be distinguished in principle from the present case. One Fauntleroy, a partner of the defendants, by means of a forged power of attorney, procured the transfer of the plaintiff's stock and sold the same, and paid the proceeds into the bank account of the firm. He kept the pass-book of the bank in his own custody, and took measures to prevent the deposit from being entered in a book called "the house-book," which was accessible to the defendants, and which, in the due course of their business, should have shown the deposit also.

By this and other devices he concealed entirely from his copartners the receipt of the money, and afterwards checked it out himself and used it for his own purposes. In the pass-book it was entered "cash per Fauntleroy." The defendants reposed great confidence in Fauntleroy, and allowed him almost exclusively to attend to the banking business. This and other forgeries being discovered long afterward, and Fauntleroy having been executed for some other forgery, the plaintiff sued defendants, his surviving partners, to recover the money paid into the bank. They were shown to be wholly guiltless of the fraud, and to have had no use of the money, except that it had been paid into their bank in the usual course of their banking business by Fauntleroy. No entry of the money appeared in any of the books of the firm except the pass-book, and that they never saw, and never in fact knew of the deposit. The defendants were held liable on the ground that the firm received the plaintiff's money and had it under their control by being paid into their bank account; that the fraud of their partner, Fauntleroy, afforded no answer to the plaintiff's claim, after the money had once come into their power. The court say: "It must be admitted that they were so far imposed upon by the acts of their partner as to be ignorant that the sum above mentioned was the produce of the plaintiff's stock; but it is equally clear that the defendants might have discovered the payment of the money, and the source from which it was derived, if they had used the ordinary diligence of men of business. If they had not the actual knowledge they had all the means of knowledge, and there is no principle of law upon which they can succeed in protecting themselves from responsibility in a case wherein, if actual knowledge was necessary, they might have acquired it by using the ordinary diligence which their calling requires."

The case of *Ex parte* Apsey is not cited, but is consistent with the case of Marsh *v.* Keating, that if the defendants had known of the payment into the bank, and, using ordinary diligence, had not discovered the fraud, and had been in fact misled, by the payment being made in money, into believing that the money was Fauntleroy's, and had, in reliance thereon, dealt with him as their copartner accordingly, and applied it to his account, that they might have been relieved.

The case discloses that the plaintiff was a customer of the defendants' firm, but the liability of the defendants is not rested at all on any fiduciary relation between the firm and the plaintiff, as respects her stocks, but wholly, as it seems, on the receipt of her money.

The case also suggests another ground on which the firm of Ketchum & Belknap must be held liable; that, as Franklin M. Ketchum deliberately left to his copartner all that part of the business which related to the raising of money, he is chargeable with the knowledge of all such facts as he might, with ordinary diligence in attending to his business, have discovered. He constituted Belknap his agent to raise money for the firm. It seems reasonable that he should be held liable, civilly, of course, for what Belknap did in that respect; at least, so far as he might, with reasonable diligence, have discovered the facts. He did not seek to know what Belknap did, or how or where he got money for the firm. The rule laid down in Marsh *v.* Keating, for such a case, is the only safe rule of business, since, if the rule were otherwise, partners might purposely keep themselves ignorant of what their partners did, in order to avail themselves of their frauds by reason of their ignorance, and it would be almost impossible to detect such a fraud. Equity helps the diligent. The rule is, also, in accordance with the principle that pervades the law of principal and agent, that the principal is liable, civilly, for the acts of his agent, done in the conduct of his business.

The other case relied on by the opposing creditor is Jacques *v.* Marquand, 6 Cow., 497. In that case one member of a firm had misappropriated the plaintiff's property, which he had held upon a special trust, and had used the proceeds in paying debts of the firm; and he pleaded, in abatement, that the other partner was not joined as a defendant. The evidence showed that

Paulding, the defendant's copartner, lived in New Orleans, and the defendant in New York, and Paulding knew nothing of the transaction. The court cited *Ex parte* Apsey for support of the general proposition, which the opposing creditors maintain here, that the payment of money into the firm by the guilty partner does not raise an implied contract to repay on the part of the firm. The distinction above pointed out between this case and Apsey's case existed in Jacques *v.* Marquand, but it was not adverted to by the court. The real point in the case, however, was not whether the firm was liable, but whether Marquand was individually liable. The firm might be liable, and yet Marquand, as the actual wrong-doer, who first misappropriated the money, might still continue individually liable. But, so far as the *dicta* of the learned judge are inconsistent with the views herein expressed, as applicable to the present case, I am unable to concur in them. The case has been several times cited and distinguished, but the precise case seems not to have arisen again. Whitaker *v.* Brown, 16 Wend., 509; Hutchinson *v.* Smith, 7 Paige, 33; Willett *v.* Stringer, 17 Abb. N. S., 155. The chancellor, in Whitaker *v.* Brown, seems to take pains to restrict the authority of Jacques *v.* Marquand to the precise point that the defense of non-joinder was not good, and the later cases in which it is cited certainly add nothing to its authority.

§ 142. *Liability of firm not affected by the fact that guilty partner drew the money out after depositing it.*

The point made by the opposing creditors, that Franklin M. Ketchum, or the firm, is not liable because Belknap, after the deposit of these moneys, drew out all or some of them for his own personal uses, is untenable. If, by the receipt of the money, the firm was made chargeable with it, it is no answer that the firm was afterwards robbed of it, or a part of it; much less that a member of the firm, being authorized to draw checks on the firm's bank account, abused that authority by drawing for purposes not authorized by the agreement between the partners. If any authority is needed for this proposition, the case of Marsh *v.* Keating, cited above, which was a much harder case than this for the deceived partner, is sufficient.

§ 143. *Summing up.   Distinction noted between paying money into the firm and appropriating checks and securities to the use of the firm.*

The claims, therefore, of Morris Ketchum, set forth in the proofs of debt, those proofs being properly amended, unless amendment shall be waived, must be sustained on the ground that Franklin M. Ketchum, the innocent partner, on the facts proved, appears to have no equity to avail himself of the payment of the money to the firm, as a payment between himself and his copartner of money in settlement or adjustment of any balance due to him on account of the partnership business, or as a payment of money to him upon any consideration whatever, in receiving which he relied upon his copartner's possession as proof of ownership.

They must also be sustained on the further ground that Franklin M. Ketchum gave his copartner full and unrestricted authority to raise more money for the use of the firm, without exercising any supervision over his acts in that respect, and without inquiring or seeking to discover how and from what sources his copartner raised money for the firm; that, therefore, he is liable by the law of principal and agent for the acts of his agent done in the performance of this agency, whether in the making of contracts or in the tortious intermeddling with the property of others, including money, at least to the extent to which he could, by reasonable inquiry, have ascertained the truth; and in this case the circumstances warrant the inference that a very slight attention on his part to the business would have discovered to him the source from which the money came.

But, while the entire claims must be sustained on these grounds, it is evident that the transfer of the money from Morris Ketchum's bank account, and the hypothecating of his securities for a loan to the firm, must be sustained on other grounds. These were not, either in form or substance, payments of money into the firm by Belknap within the rule in Apsey's case, whatever may be the extent and limits of that rule.

The checks drawn against Morris Ketchum's bank account have, by consent of counsel, been produced since the argument, and it appears that they were checks signed "Morris Ketchum, per T. Belknap, Jr.,*Attorney," and payable to the order of "Ketchum & Belknap."

The deposit of these checks with other funds in the bank was an act of Belknap in the regular course of the business of the firm. Franklin M. Ketchum, as a partner, is clearly chargeable with notice of the form of the deposit and of the form of the checks deposited, for that deposit was unquestionably a firm transaction, and the checks on their face do not import any title to the money in Belknap. On the contrary, they show that up to the very moment of the deposit the money deposited was Morris Ketchum's money. All that the papers on their face and the acts of Belknap purport to show is that Morris Ketchum had this money in the Fourth National Bank, and that it was his own money, and that Belknap, by drawing the check, represented that he had authority from Morris Ketchum to draw it out and pay it into the firm of Ketchum & Belknap, but whether as a loan or as a gift, or in payment of a debt due to the firm, neither the papers nor the account show at all.

While, therefore, if Franklin M. Ketchum had seen the checks, he might possibly have been misled into believing that Morris Ketchum had given Belknap authority to draw out the money and pay it into the firm, it would have been his own folly; and it would not have been any proper inference to be drawn from the facts if he had concluded that the money had in any way become Belknap's. If Belknap had deceived him as to his authority, so far as the form of the check imports authority, it would have been clearly his misfortune and would not have affected Morris Ketchum's rights. Besides, there was no payment of money to the firm till the check was collected, and this was done by the firm. In fact, both deposits were in the same bank, and the transaction was a transfer from the account of one depositor to that of the other. That transfer was effected after or simultaneously with the deposit of the checks.

That the deposit of the checks by Belknap was a firm transaction, done by him as a partner, and not by him as an individual, is too plain for argument. By that very act, and as an inseparable part of it, and not before it, in order of time, the money of Morris Ketchum was appropriated to the use of the firm. It is impossible to say that the deposit was an act of the firm and the transfer of the money was not. The two things may be abstractly considered as separate acts, but they were in reality one act, and the firm cannot take the benefit of the one without being responsible for the other.

The case thus differs from the case of the proceeds of the securities sold and the money afterwards paid in. In that case Belknap individually converted the property into money, and then, having the money in hand, paid it in. Here Belknap never had the money, or what purported to be the money, held by him as his own, but he held what purported to show that the money belonged to the firm, or to Morris Ketchum, himself; and the firm, not Belknap individually, converted the money, and appropriated it to their own use. If the checks had been drawn by Morris Ketchum, payable to Belknap's order, and by him indorsed to the firm, there might be some ground for holding that the firm received money from Belknap; but on these facts they received what did not purport to be his money, and cannot, as to this part of the case, invoke in their defense the rule that they are not liable to repay money paid in by a partner, which in fact belongs, without the knowledge of the other partner, to a third party.

Similar considerations apply to the stocks hypothecated to the bank for a loan. The raising of money by a loan was a firm transaction, especially committed by the firm to Belknap. He pledged certain securities, which may be assumed to be in such form that they passed by delivery. He presented them to the bank in this form. Nothing else appears as to any representation of title. The borrowing and the pledge were one act. The firm converted the securities by hypothecating them. One of the partners, as a member of the firm, handed them to the bank as securities of the firm.

The transaction did not purport on its face that the securities were Belknap's, but rather that they were the firm's. If Franklin M. Ketchum had been present and witnessed the transaction there would have been no more reason for him to conclude that they were Belknap's than that they were the firm's. The ordinary presumption that a man knows his own business, and, therefore, that he knew the firm owned no such property, cannot be drawn in this case, because, on the proofs, Franklin M. Ketchum knew and sought to know nothing of the financial affairs of the firm. He left all that to Belknap. The firm bought and sold and held in their own right stocks. For aught that Franklin M. Ketchum knew, Belknap might have bought these stocks for the firm. The circumstances were not such, if they had been known to him, as to justify any inference that the securities were contributed to the firm by Belknap. I see no reason, therefore, why the firm should not be held liable for the conversion of these securities.

It is unnecessary to consider the further question raised and argued, whether the entry of these claims as debts in the bankrupt's schedules were such an adoption of them as would alone make the firm liable. The proofs of debt may be amended conformably to this opinion, then stand as valid claims.

LOCKWOOD v. COMSTOCK.

(Circuit Court for Michigan: 4 McLean, 383, 384. 1848.)

Opinion of the Court.

STATEMENT OF FACTS.— This is a motion for a new trial reserved for a full bench. The suit was brought by plaintiff, as indorsee of two promissory notes, dated September 1, 1839, against defendants, as makers, under the firm of Charles Bissell & Co. It was in evidence that the firm was dissolved October 29, 1838, of which payees had personal notice prior to the making of the notes. They were given for a debt due by the firm by Bissell, without any authority from Comstock to use the partnership name. The following advertisement of the dissolution of the partnership was published in the Daily Advertiser, of Detroit, a paper of general circulation, October 31, 1838: "Dissolution." "The copartnership heretofore existing under the firm of

Charles Bissell & Co. is this day dissolved by mutual consent. The business will hereafter be continued by Charles Bissell, who is duly authorized to settle all demands in favor or against said firm." "Detroit, October 29, 1838. Signed, Charles Bissell, H. II. Comstock."

It is argued, 1. That the dissolution of the partnership put an end to the power of Bissell to use the partnership name. Bell v. Morrison, 1 Pet., 370; Gillet v. Atwood, 2 Doug.; Story on Partnership, 458, 472-4; Gow, 253-4. Second ground. That the terms in which the dissolution was announced to the public did not authorize Bissell to use the name of his former partner.

§ 144. *After dissolution of a partnership neither partner can bind the other in a new contract by note or otherwise.*

The question is well settled in this country that, after the dissolution of a partnership, the partnership name cannot be used by either partner in the creation of a new contract. That power existed during the partnership, but its dissolution terminated it. The name cannot be used in giving a note for a debt due by the late firm. For that would be a new contract, variant from that which was entered into during the partnership. This power to use the name of Comstock was clearly not given in the notice of dissolution. It authorized Bissell, who continued the business, "to settle all demands in favor or against said firm." But it did not authorize him to use the name of his late partner in entering into a new contract. To settle was to ascertain the balance due and pay it, but not to give a note or any other obligation. The motion for a new trial is granted.

BISPHAM v. PATTERSON.

(Circuit Court for Indiana: 2 McLean, 87-92. 1840.)

Opinion of the Court.

STATEMENT OF FACTS.— This is an action of *assumpsit*, brought against the defendants as partners. The writ was served on Patterson, but the marshal returned *non est* as to Walter.

The plaintiff introduced, as evidence, the letter of Patterson acknowledging the justice of the account on which the action was brought. This was objected to as evidence, on the ground that the letter was written after the dissolution of the partnership, and that it is not, therefore, evidence to establish a partnership demand. But the circuit judge observed that the evidence would be received as competent, and the point would be considered, if necessary, on a motion for a new trial.

The jury found a verdict for the plaintiff, and the question of the admissibility of the evidence is now brought before the court on a motion to set aside the verdict.

§ 145. *Declaration made by one of several joint parties jointly interested is evidence against all.*

It is a general principle that, in a civil suit by or against several persons, who are proved to have a joint interest in the decision, a declaration made by one of those persons, concerning a material fact within his knowledge, is evidence against him and against all who are parties with him in the suit. 1 Phil. Ev., 92; 11 East, 589.

§ 146. *Admission by partner is evidence to bind the firm.*

So, in an action by several partners, the admission by one is evidence against all. 1 Maule & Selw., 249. And where an action is brought against partners,

215

the fact of partnership being proved, the admissions of any one of the defendants is evidence to charge the firm. 1 Phil. Ev., 92; 1 Stark. N. P., 6, 81; 4 Conn., 338; 15 John., 409; 2 Wash., 6, 390; 2 Har. & John., 474, 477; 3 J. J. Marsh., 498, 500.

§ 147. *In England admission by partner after dissolution is competent evidence against the other partners. This is correct on principle.*

And in England it is held that the admission of a partner, though not a party to the suit, is evidence against another partner, who is sued as to joint contracts, during the partnership, whether made after the determination of the partnership or before. 1 Phil. Ev., 93; 1 Taunt., 104; 2 Doug., 661; 2 H. Black., 340; 2 John., 667; 1 Gall., 630; 1 Barn. & Cres., 169; 2 Barn. & Cres., 29; 2 Bing., 306; Cady *v.* Chepherd, 11 Rich., 400. And, in the case of Pritchard *v.* Draper, 1 Russ. & Mylne, 191, which was decided by Lord Brougham, it was held that, though the admission of one of the partners be not only made after the dissolution, but be of a payment which was made to him after the dissolution, the evidence may be received to bind the other partner. No rule of evidence seems to be better settled in the English courts than this, and it is conceived to be settled on sound principles.

The dissolution of the partnership cannot affect the relation which the firm bears to its creditors. The individuals composing it are liable as partners; and, if they are thus bound, why should not the demand be established by the same evidence as before the dissolution? The partnership continues in all its force, as it regards the particular transaction; and it would seem to be an anomaly that the act of the parties, defendants, should change the rule of evidence on which their liability is to be established.

It is argued, that it would be dangerous to the interests of partners, if, after the dissolution, the admissions of one, in relation to a prior and partnership transaction, should be evidence against the firm. That on this ground it would be in the power of each individual that composed the late firm to make it responsible for his private debts.

If there be any force in this argument, it goes against the principle which admits the confessions of one partner as evidence to bind the others during the partnership. Now, this rule is believed to be nowhere controverted. It has been found safe in practice. But, if there be danger in receiving the admissions of a late partner, as evidence, in relation to a partnership transaction, the danger must be much greater to receive such admissions, as evidence, during the partnership.

In the latter case, the admissions may go to create an obligation on the firm for an individual transaction; whilst the former can only relate to transactions prior to the dissolution. Admissions, under such circumstances, could rarely, if ever, go to prejudice the rights of the late firm. A *bona fide* individual transaction, originally, could not easily, by the confession of a late partner, be established against the firm. The danger consists in the power of the individual, at the time of the transaction, to give it a form which shall bind the firm.

§ 148. *By the weight of American authority the admissions of one of a firm made after dissolution cannot bind a former partner.*

But this is a question to be decided by the force of authority, and not of reason. The weight of American authority is against the English rule on this subject. In the cases of Hackley *v.* Patrick, 3 John., 536; Walden *v.* Sherburne, 15 John., 409; Shelton *v.* Cooke, 3 Mun., 191; Walker *v.* Duberry,

1 Marsh., 189; 9 Cowan, 57; Baker *v.* Stackpole, 9 Cowan, 420, 434; Chardon *v.* Calder & Co., 2 Const. Rep. (South Carolina), 685; White *v.* The Union Ins. Co., 1 Nott & M'Cord, 561; Fisher's Ex'rs *v.* Tucker's Ex'rs, 1 McCord's Ch., 171–2; Ward *v.* Howell *et al.*, 5 Har. & John., 60; 2 Black, 372, the rule seems to be settled that, after the dissolution, the admission of a partner is not evidence to charge the late firm.

And, in the case of Clementson *v.* Williams, 8 Cranch, 72, the court held that the acknowledgment of one partner, after the dissolution of the partnership, is not sufficient to take a case out of the statute of limitations. And, in the case of Bell *v.* Morrison, 1 Pet., 373, the court held that, after a dissolution of partnership, no partner can create a cause of action against the other partners, except by a new authority, communicated to him for that purpose. It is wholly immaterial what is the consideration which is to raise such cause of action; whether it be supposed a pre-existing debt of the partnership, or any auxiliary consideration, which might prove beneficial to them. Unless adopted by them, they are not bound by it.

The case of Bell *v.* Morrison presented the question whether, after the dissolution, the acknowledgment of a partner took the case out of the statute of limitations; but Mr. Justice Story, who delivered the opinion of the court, considers the case very much at large, and takes occasion to say that the New York doctrine was well founded. He, it is true, remarks that, whether the confessions of a late partner can, for any purpose, be admitted as evidence to charge the firm, was a question not before the court, though it had been discussed by the counsel on both sides; but, as its determination was not necessary in the case, it would not be decided. But the course of his reasoning has so direct a bearing on this question, and so clearly shows the view of the court, that unless we close our eyes, we cannot escape from the effects of it.

I have read this opinion more than once, under the strongest conviction in favor of the English rule, and with a sincere desire to follow it, but the language of the opinion is so decisive and authoritative that I am forced to adopt the New York rule. The court do not, in technical language, adjudge that the admissions of a late partner cannot be received as evidence, but they say that the New York rule is a sound one, and they sustain its reasonableness and propriety. And this rule was shown to be the foundation of all the American decisions on the question.

I looked to this opinion with the more earnestness, as my brother Story, in the case cited from Gallison, had followed the English rule; the judgment in which case was taken to the supreme court and affirmed. This point, however, though made, does not seem to have been expressly decided by the supreme court. There were several other points on which the case turned, but it is difficult to perceive how the judgment could have been affirmed, without ruling this point.

A distinction is drawn by the supreme court between receiving the admissions of a late partner to take the partnership debt out of the statute, and as merely evidence of the debt. That to take a case out of the statute a new obligation must be imposed on the late firm, which cannot be done by the acknowledgments of a late partner.

In England, it is said, the courts on recent occasions have been in the habit of considering that the effect of an acknowledgment of the debt, made by the defendant, is to create a fresh promise, and not to revive the promise which is barred by the statute. 1 Phil. Ev., 138; Tanner *v.* Smart, 6 Barn. & Cres.,

606.   But a contrary doctrine is held in Pittam *v.* Foster, 1 Barn. & Cres., 248; Hunt *v.* Parker, 1 Barn. & Ald., 93; Ayton *v.* Bolt, 4 Bing., 105; 3 Bing., 329, 638.

In the cases of Shelton *v.* Cocke, 3 Mun., 191, and Smith *v.* Ludlow, 6 John., 267, it was held that the admission of a debt by one of several partners, made after the dissolution, will take the debt, so admitted, out of the statute of limitations, though the original debt cannot be so proved.

In the case of Fisher's Ex'rs *v.* Tucker's Representatives, 1 McCord's Ch., 169, the court say, the admission or promise of a surviving partner will not even take the debt out of the statute of limitations, as to the estate of the deceased partner; much less would it prove an original debt.

Amidst this conflict of authority I yield my conviction in favor of the English rule to the authority of the case of Bell *v.* Morrison.   The verdict is set aside and a new trial granted.

HALL *v.* LANNING.

(1 Otto, 160-171. 1875.)

ERROR to U. S. Circuit Court, Northern District of Illinois.

Opinion by MR. JUSTICE BRADLEY.

STATEMENT OF FACTS.— The question to be decided in this case is whether, after the dissolution of a copartnership, one of the partners in a suit brought against the firm has authority to enter an appearance for the other partners who do not reside in the state where the suit is brought, and have not been served with process; and, if not, whether a judgment against all the partners, founded on such an appearance, can be questioned by those not served with process in a suit brought thereon in another state.

§ 149. *Jurisdiction of court of another state to render a judgment relied on is always open to inquiry.*

We recently had occasion, in the case of Thompson *v.* Whitman, 18 Wall., 457 (JUDG., §§ 1131-33), to restate the rule that the jurisdiction of a foreign court over the person or the subject-matter embraced in the judgment or decree of such court is always open to inquiry; and that, in this respect, the court of another state is to be regarded as a foreign court.   We further held, in that case, that the record of such a judgment does not estop the parties from demanding such an inquiry.   The cases bearing upon the subject having been examined and distinguished on that occasion, it is not necessary to examine them again, except as they may throw light on the special question involved in this cause.   In the subsequent case of Knowles *v.* The Gas-Light Co., 19 Wall., 58 (JUDG., §§ 1137-38), we further held, in direct line with the decision in Thompson *v.* Whitman, that the record of a judgment showing service of process on the defendant could be contradicted and disproved.

§ 150. *A member of a partnership residing in one state cannot be rendered personally liable in a suit brought in another state against him and his copartners, in which suit he is not but his copartners are served with process, although the law of the latter state authorizes judgment against him.*

It is sought to distinguish the present case from those referred to, on the ground that the relation of partnership confers upon each partner authority, even after dissolution, to appear for his copartners in a suit brought against the firm, though they are not served with process, and have no notice of the suit.   In support of this proposition, so far as relates to any such authority after dissolution of the partnership, we are not referred to any authority directly in point; but reliance is placed on the powers of partners in general, and on that class of cases which affirm the right of each partner, after a dissolution of the firm, to settle up its business.   But, in our view, appearance to a suit is a very different thing from those ordinary acts which appertain to a general settlement of business, such as receipt and payment of money, giving acquittances, and the like.   If a suit be brought against all the partners, and only one of them be served with process, he may undoubtedly, in his own defense, show, if he can, that the firm is not liable, and to this end defend the suit.   But to hold that the other partners, or persons charged as such, who have not been served with process, will be bound by the judgment in such a case, which shall conclude them as well on the question whether they were partners or not when the debt was incurred as on that of the validity of the debt, would, as it seems to us, be carrying the power of a partner, after a dissolution of the partnership, to an unnecessary and unreasonable extent.

The law, indeed, does not seem entirely clear that a partner may enter an appearance for his copartners without special authority, even during the continuance of the firm.   It is well known that by the English practice, in an action on any joint contract, whether entered into by partners or others, if any defendant cannot be found, the plaintiff must proceed to outlawry against him before he can prosecute the action; and then he declares separately against those served with process, and obtains a separate judgment against them, but no judgment except that of outlawry against the defendant not found.   1 Chitty's Plead., 42; Tidd's Prac., ch. vii, p. 423, 9th ed.   A shorter method by *distringas* in place of outlawry has been provided by some modern statutes, but founded on the same principle.   Now, it seems strange that this cumbrous and dilatory proceeding should be necessary in the case of partners, if one partner has a general authority to appear in court for his copartners.   On the basis of such an authority, had it existed, the courts, in the long lapse of time, ought to have found some means of making service on one answer for service on all.   But this was never done.   In this country it is true, as will presently be shown, legislation to this end (applicable, however, to all joint debtors) has been adopted; but it is generally conceded that a judgment based on such service has full and complete effect only as against those who are actually served.   Further reference to this subject will be made hereafter.

It must be conceded, however, that the general authority of one partner to appear to an action on behalf of his copartners, during the continuance of the firm, has been asserted by several text-writers.   Gow on Partn., 163; Collyer on Partn., sec. 441; Parsons on Partn., 174, note.   But the assertion is based on somewhat slender authority.   We find it first laid down in Gow, who refers to a *dictum* of Sergeant Dampier, made in the course of argument (7 T. R., 207), and to the case of Morley *v.* Strombong, 3 Bos. & Pull., 254, where the court refused to discharge partnership goods taken on a *distringas* to compel the appearance of an absent partner, unless the partner who was served would enter an appearance for him.   As to this case, it may be said that it is not improbable that the home partner had express authority to appear in suits for his copartner; for, in a subsequent case (Goldsmith *v.* Levy, 4 Taunt., 299), a *distringas*, issued under the same circumstances, *was* discharged where the home partner made affidavit that the goods were his own, and that he had no authority to appear for his copartner.   These seem to be the only authorities relied on.

But, as said before, these authorities, and one or two American cases which follow them, refer only to appearances entered whilst the partnership was subsisting; and it is pertinent also to add that they only refer to the validity and effect of judgments in the state or country in which they are rendered.

Domestic judgments, undoubtedly (as was shown in Thompson *v.* Whitman), stand, in this respect, on a different footing from foreign judgments. If regular on their face, and if appearance has been duly entered for the defendant by a responsible attorney, though no process has been served and no appearance authorized, they will not necessarily be set aside; but the defendant will sometimes be left to his remedy against the attorney in an action for damages; otherwise, as has been argued, the plaintiff might lose his security by the act of an officer of the court. Denton *v.* Noyes, 6 Johns., 296; Grazebrook *v.* McCreedie, 9 Wend., 437. But even in this case it is the more usual course to suspend proceedings on the judgment, and allow the defendants to plead to the merits, and prove any just defense to the action. In any other state, however, except that in which the judgment was rendered (as decided by us in the cases before referred to), the facts could be shown, notwithstanding the recitals of the record; and the judgment would be regarded as null and void for want of jurisdiction of the person.

So, where an appearance has been entered by authority of one of several copartners on behalf of all, it may well be that the courts of the same jurisdiction will be slow to set aside the judgment, unless it clearly appears that injustice has been done; and will rather leave the party who has been injured by an unauthorized appearance to his action for damages.

There are many other cases in which a judgment may be good within the jurisdiction in which it was rendered so far as to bind the debtor's property there found, without personal service of process, or appearance of the defendant; as in foreign attachments, process of outlawry, and proceedings *in rem.*

Another class of cases is that of joint debtors, before alluded to. In most of the states legislative acts have been passed, called joint-debtor acts, which, as a substitute for outlawry, provide that if process be issued against several joint debtors or partners, and served on one or more of them, and the others cannot be found, the plaintiff may proceed against those served, and, if successful, have judgment against all. Various effects and consequences are attributed to such judgments in the states in which they are rendered. They are generally held to bind the common property of the joint debtors, as well as the separate property of those served with process, when such property is situated in the state, but not the separate property of those not served; and, whilst they are binding personally on the former, they are regarded as either not personally binding at all, or only *prima facie* binding, on the latter. Under the joint-debtor act of New York, it was formerly held by the courts of that state that such a judgment is valid and binding on an absent defendant as *prima facie* evidence of a debt, reserving to him the right to enter into the merits, and show that he ought not to have been charged.

The validity of a judgment rendered under this New York law, when prosecuted in another state against one of the defendants who resided in the latter state, and was not served with process, though charged as a copartner of a defendant residing in New York, who was served, was brought in question in this court in December term, 1850, in the case of D'Arcy *v.* Ketchum, 11 How., 165. It was there contended that by the constitution of the United States, and the act of congress passed May 26, 1790, in relation to the proof and effect of judgments in other states, the judgment in question ought to have the same force and effect in every other state which it had in New York. But this court decided that the act of congress was intended to prescribe only the effect of judgments where the court by which they were rendered had jurisdiction; and that, by international law, a judgment rendered in one state, assuming to bind the person of a citizen of another, was void within the foreign state, if the defendant had not been served with process, or voluntarily made defense, because neither the legislative jurisdiction nor that of the courts of justice had binding force.

This decision is an authority which we recognized in Thompson v. Whitman and in Knowles v. Gas-Light Co., before cited, and which we adhere to as founded on the soundest principles of law; and, in view of this decision, it is manifest that many of the authorities which declare the effect of a domestic judgment, in cases where process has not been served on one or all of the defendants, and where those not served have not authorized any appearance and do not reside in the state, can have little influence as to the effect to be given to such a judgment in another state.

§ 151. *One copartner has no implied authority, after dissolution of the copartnership, to appear for or enter the appearance of any of the other partners, in a suit against the copartnership.*

It appearing to be settled law, therefore, that a member of a partnership firm, residing in one state, cannot be rendered personally liable in a suit brought in another state against him and his copartners, although the latter be duly served with process, and although the law of the state where the suit is brought authorizes judgment to be rendered against him, the case stands on the simple and naked question, whether his copartners, after a dissolution of the partnership, can without his consent and authority involve him in suits brought against the firm by voluntarily entering an appearance for him.

We are of opinion that no authority can be found to maintain the affirmative of this question. In the case of Bell v. Morrison, 1 Pet., 351, this court decided, upon elaborate examination, that, after a dissolution of the partnership, one partner cannot by his admissions or promises bind his former copartners. Appearance to a suit is certainly quite as grave an act as the acknowledgment of a debt.

It is well settled by numberless cases, that, even before dissolution, one partner cannot confess judgment, or submit to arbitration so as to bind his copartners. Stead v. Salt, 3 Bing., 101; Adams v. Bankart, 1 Cromp., Mees. & R., 681; Karthaus v. Ferrer, 1 Pet., 222, and cases referred to in Story on Part., sec. 114; 1 Amer. Lead. Cas. (5th ed.), 556; Freeman on Judgments, sec. 232; Collyer on Part., secs. 469, 470, and notes; Parsons on Part., 179, note. It is equally well settled, that, after dissolution, one partner cannot bind his copartners by new contracts or securities, or impose upon them a fresh liability. Story on Part., sec. 322; Adams v. Bankart, *supra.*

Appearance to a suit does impose a fresh liability. If there is no doubt of the validity of the demand, it places that demand in a position to be made a debt of record. If there is doubt of it, it renders the defendant liable to have it adjudicated against him, when, perhaps, he has a good defense to it.

On principle, therefore, it is difficult to see how, after a dissolution, one partner can claim implied authority to appear for his copartners in a suit brought against the firm. It may, in some instances, be convenient that one partner should have such authority; and, when such authority is desirable, it can easily be conferred, either in the articles of partnership or in the terms of dissolution. But, as a general thing, one can hardly conceive of a more dangerous power to be left in the hands of the several partners after the partnership connection between them is terminated, or one more calculated to inspire a constant dread of impending evil, than that of accepting service of process for their former associates, and of rendering them liable, without their knowledge, to the chances of litigation which they have no power of defending.

Few cases can be found in which the precise question has been raised. The attempt to exercise such a power does not appear to have been often made. Had it been, the question would certainly have found its way in the reports; for a number of cases have come up in which the power of a partner to appear for his copartners during the continuance of the partnership has been discussed. The point was raised in Phelps v. Brewer, 9 Cush., 390; but the court, being of opinion that the power does not exist even pending the partnership, did not find it necessary to consider the effect of a dissolution upon it.

In Alabama, where a law was passed making service of process on one partner binding upon all, it was expressly decided, after quite an elaborate argument, that such service was not sufficient after a dissolution of the partnership, and that acknowledgment of service by one partner on behalf of all was also inoperative as against the other partners. Duncan v. Tombeckbee Bank, 4 Port., 184; Demott v. Swaim's Adm., 5 Stew. & Port., 293. .

In the case of Loomis & Co. v. Pearson & McMichael, Harper (S. C.), 470, it was decided that, after a dissolution of partnership, one partner cannot appear for the other, although it is true that it had been previously decided by the same court, in Haslet v. Street et al., 2 McCord, 311, that no such authority exists even during the continuance of the partnership.

But the absence of authorities, as before remarked, is strong evidence that no such power exists. In our judgment the defendant Lybrand had a right, for the purpose of invalidating the judgment as to him, to prove the matter set up by him in his offer at the trial; and for the refusal of the court to admit the evidence the judgment should be reversed, with directions to award a venire de novo.

Judgment reversed.

WAITE, C. J., and JUSTICES STRONG and HUNT, dissented.

§ 152. **In general.**—One partner, during the continuance of the partnership, cannot bind the other partner to a submission of the interests of both to arbitration; but he might bind himself, so as to submit his own interests to such decision. Karthaus v. Ferrer, 1 Pet., 222.

§ 153. A written contract by one of two joint partners, made in his own name, does not bind the other partner, although the money obtained thereby is brought into the joint concern. Smith v. Hoffman, 2 Cr. C. C., 651.

§ 154. The rest of the members of a copartnery cannot engage the firm in another partnership, so as to bind a member who was not privy or consenting to it. Tabb's Adm'rs v. Gist, 6 Call (Va.), 279; also, 1 Marsh., 83.

§ 155. But his privity may be presumed from circumstances; and, at any rate, his remaining silent and not dissenting, after he knows of the new establishment, will be considered as acquiescence. Moreover, if it could be proved that he had withdrawn from the old firm before the establishment of the new, he would, by such acquiescence, still be responsible for the transactions of the new; especially if it was generally understood by other people that the old firm was united with the new. *Ibid.*

§ 156. Any violation of the internal revenue laws incurring a penalty, committed by a partner in the course of the partnership business, is, in legal contemplation, the act of all the partners; and each is liable to pay the penalty. United States v. Thomasson, 4 Biss., 99.

§ 157. The acts of one member of a firm in subscribing and swearing to an entry of goods under the act of March 8, 1863 (12 Stat. at Large, 737), are the acts of the firm.   United States v. Baker, 5 Ben., 25.

§ 158. A bank will not be protected in charging up the individual note or check of a member of a firm to the partnership account, in pursuance of such partner's direction, accompanied by the statement that the note or check represents a partnership transaction, unless such statement turns out to be true.   A partner has no power to bind the firm by such statement. Coote v. Bank of the United States,* 3 Cr. C. C., 95.

§ 159. A copartnership may exist in the purchase and sale of real property, and each member of the copartnership may contract for the sale or other disposition of its entire property, though for technical reasons the legal title vested in all the copartners can only be transferred by their joint act.   Thompson v. Bowman,* 6 Wall., 316.

§ 160. Where a partnership owns stock in a corporation it is not necessary that each member of said partnership should be present at a meeting of stockholders of said corporation and participate in the deliberations to bind the firm.   One partner has the power to represent that stock in all matters which relate to it in the usual management of the business of the firm of which he is a member.   Notice of a stockholders' meeting given to one partner is notice to all, and he may waive notice, and if he participates in the actions of such meeting, the other members of the firm are estopped from denying notice.   Kenton Furnace Railroad & Manuf'g Co. v. McAlpine, 5 Fed. R., 737.

§ 161. An assignment was made by a debtor for the benefit of his creditors to two attorneys-at-law, who were partners in their business, as trustees; one of them assented to the assignment at the time, the other being absent.   It was held that the latter must be presumed to assent also, unless upon notice he refused to accept the trust, and notified it to the debtor; and especially if he and his partner proceeded to act under the assignment by a private conditional agreement between them as to giving a priority to certain attachments made by them in favor of certain creditors, which agreement was unknown to the debtor.   Gordon v. Coolidge, 1 Sumn., 537.

§ 162. By sealed instruments.— A release under the seal of one of the copartners is a sufficient release of a joint right of action.   Beltzhoover v. Stockton, 4 Cr. C. C., 695.

§ 163. A partner has no implied authority to bind his copartner by deed.   United States v. Astley,* 3 Wash., 508.

§ 164. If a partner who has express authority from his copartner to bind the firm by deed or bond executes a bond in his own name for a firm indebtedness, the original liability of the firm will be extinguished and the signing partner will alone be liable on the bond.   Ibid.

§ 165. A mortgage executed by one partner in the name of the firm, the testatum clause setting forth that said firm, by said partner, had thereto set their hands and seals, said partner alone signing and sealing the document, is the act of the firm, if the other partners of the firm authorized the one executing the mortgage to do so, and after its execution, with full knowledge, acquiesced in what he had done.   Gibson v. Warden, 14 Wall., 244.

§ 166. In an action of covenant against two partners, upon a plea putting the execution of the agreement sued upon in issue, in the absence of some special authority to such partner signing to execute a sealed instrument, the other partner is not liable.   Hobson v. Porter,* 2 Colo. T'y, 28.

§ 167. A transportation bond for the removal of spirits, in which the blanks were filled in after the signature of the parties, was ratified and delivered by one of two partners with the remark that it was "all right."   On the faith of it the collector issued a permit for the removal of the spirits, and they were delivered to the firm.   Held, that the act of the partner in a firm transaction was binding on the firm, and that if said partner ratified and adopted the bond, it was the act of the firm and obligatory on them.   United States v. Turner, 2 Bond, 379.

§ 168. It is a well settled rule, though a very technical one, that one partner cannot bind his copartners by deed.   And it is equally well settled that one partner may dispose of the personal property of the firm.   One partner may bind his copartner by deed, if the latter is present and assent to it.   The seal of one partner, with the assent of the copartner, will bind the firm.   Anthony v. Butler, 13 Pet., 423.

§ 169. By negotiable instruments.— Each partner in a mercantile partnership has authority to bind the other members of the firm by drawing or accepting bills of exchange in the name of the firm.   Persons taking such paper are not bound to inquire or assure themselves as to whether the partner is acting on partnership account; they may presume that if they have no reason to suppose the contrary.   Le Roy v. Johnson,* 2 Pet., 186.

§ 170. A partner in a strictly farming partnership cannot bind his copartners by drawing bills of exchange in the name of the firm, but if farming is not their sole business, but they also carry on a saw-mill for manufacturing purposes, or engage in general trade, he may so bind them.   Kimbro v. Bullitt,* 22 How., 256.

§ 171. The right of one accepting, on account of a firm, bills of exchange drawn by one of the partners, to recover against the firm, cannot be affected by the fact that the drawer applied the money to an unlawful purpose. *Ibid.*

§ 172. If a partner draws notes in the name of the firm, payable to himself, and then indorses them to a third party for a personal and not a partnership consideration, the first indorsee cannot maintain an action upon them against the firm, if he knew that the notes were antedated. But if the first indorsee passes them away to a second indorsee before the maturity of the notes, in the due course of business, and the second indorsee has no knowledge of the circumstances of their execution and first indorsement, he may be entitled to recover against the firm, although the partner who drew the notes committed a fraud by antedating them. But if the second indorsee received the notes after their maturity, or out of the ordinary course of business, or under circumstances which authorize an inference that he had knowledge of the fraud in their execution or first indorsement, he cannot recover. Smyth *v.* Strader, 4 How., 404.

§ 173. Although where one partner gives notes in the firm name, which are indorsed by an accommodation indorser and subsequently taken up by him, the partnership is liable to said indorser for the amount of said notes, though given for the payment of such partner's individual contribution to the stock of the partnership, and consequently a fraud upon the other partner, yet where the circumstances are such that the accommodation indorser should have known of the fraud, or was affected with notice of it, the firm is not liable. *In re* Dunkle,* 7 N. B. R., 107.

§ 174. Where one partner gives notes in the firm name, and applies the proceeds to his individual indebtedness, such use of the firm credit is unauthorized and fraudulent as to the other partner; but the notes being drawn apparently in the course of partnership dealing, and without notice of the facts from which the holder is bound to infer that they were made without authority, or that a misapplication of them was contemplated, such holder is a *bona fide* holder of them, and entitled to their allowance as debts against the bankrupt partnership. Bush *v.* Crawford,* 7 N. B. R., 299; 9 Phil., 392.

§ 175. A., a member of a firm, applied to B. to indorse his notes. Upon inquiry by B., A. stated that the notes were to be used in payment of goods purchased by the firm. Upon B.'s suggestion new notes were drawn in the name of the firm, which B. indorsed, and was subsequently required to take up. Instead of using these notes in the partnership business, A. applied them to the payment of his individual indebtedness. There being no evidence of *mala fides* in B., it was held that the firm was liable. *Ibid.*

§ 176. —— indorsement.—Where one partner indorses a note in the name of the firm, evidence that such partner had no authority to do so, under the articles of copartnership of said firm, is inadmissible (1) where the indorsement is made in pursuance of a previous understanding between the firm and the maker of the note, and the evidence shows that the partner indorsing said note was advised by his partner to indorse the parcel of notes which contained the one in controversy, although blanks in the note were left to be filled up by the maker; and (2) where the holder of the note has no knowledge of the contents of the articles of copartnership, nor of any fact or circumstance showing or tending to show that the indorsement was made without authority, but is a *bona fide* holder for value. Michigan Bank *v.* Eldred, 9 Wall., 544.

§ 177. The act of a partner outside the scope of the partnership business will not bind the firm. Accordingly where a partner applied for and obtained a loan, in one case for the use of his brother, and in the other to pay a debt of an old firm, and gave as security notes made to the firm (but in which, in fact, the firm had no interest) and indorsed by him in the name of the firm, *held*, that the other partners were not bound by such indorsement. Newman *v.* Richardson,* 9 Fed. R., 865.

§ 178. Where a note was indorsed in a firm name, by one member thereof, and the transaction showed on its face that the indorsement was only an accommodation indorsement, it appearing that the other member of the firm did not consent to said indorsement, *held*, that the note could not be proved against the partnership in bankruptcy. *In re* Irving,* 17 N. B. R., 22.

§ 179. —— in name of one partner.—If a partner draws a bill in his own name against the account of his copartners, and the proceeds inure to their benefit, they will be held responsible in equity for the amount of the bill. Van Reimsdyk *v.* Kane,* 1 Gall., 630.

§ 180. If no original authority to draw were given, but subsequently the whole transaction were ratified by all the partners, such ratification would be equivalent to original authority. *Ibid.*

§ 181. If a check upon a bank be drawn in the name of one of a firm only, it cannot be charged to the firm, unless drawn by authority of the firm, although used and applied in the business of the firm; and the promise of one partner, individually, to make good an overdraft, does not bind the firm. Patriotic Bank *v.* Coot, 3 Cr. C. C., 169.

§ 182. In order to charge B. upon a bill drawn by A. in his own name, it is necessary to prove that A. and B. carried on business in partnership under the firm name of A. *Prima facie* it is the sole bill of A. Nicholson *v.* Patton, 2 Cr. C. C., 164.

§ 183. Money deposited in a bank in the name of a firm cannot be drawn out by the individual check of one of the firm in his own name only; and if the bank pay such a check out of the joint funds, it can only justify itself by showing that the money thus drawn out was applied to the use of the firm. Coote *v.* Bank of the United States, 3 Cr. C. C., 50.

§ 184. It is no excuse for a bank, in paying out the joint funds of a firm upon the individual check of one of the partners, that the individual partner who drew the check told the bank officer that it was drawn on the joint account, and drawn in his individual name by mistake, and directed him to pay it and any others of the like kind which he might draw out of the joint funds. *Ibid.*

§ 185. If one partner, in a voyage on joint account, be authorized by the others to take up money on the credit of the whole concern, and draws bills therefor on a house at Amsterdam, and the partner take up money and draw a bill for the same, directing it to be charged to the account of all the partners, but it is signed by himself only, it seems such a bill is binding on all the partners; at least equity will enforce payment thereof against all the partners in favor of the payee of the bill, who has trusted the money on the faith of the joint credit. Van Reimsdyk *v.* Kane, 1 Gall., 630.

§ 186. —— for partner's individual debt.— Where one partner had given notes of the firm for his separate debt, which were fraudulent as to the other partner and constituted no claim against the partnership, the subsequent recognition of such notes by the latter, or promise to pay them as acts of the firm, would render them partnership debts. But where an agreement of dissolution was made, and the defrauded partner agreed to pay the other, upon retiring, a specific sum, a part of which was to be appropriated to the payment of said notes, there was no ratification of them, and they could not be proved against the partnership estate in bankruptcy; but the effect of such agreement was to make such partner so agreeing a separate debtor in equity from its date for the amount of said notes, without any merger of the former relation of the partner giving them, who also continues a separate debtor. *In re* Dunkle,* 7 N. B. R., 107.

§ 187. Where G., being a member of the firms of S. M. & Co. and D. & Co., drew a bill of exchange in the name of the former firm upon the latter firm, payable to himself, accepted it in the name of D. & Co. and then negotiated it for value before maturity to an innocent third person, *held,* that the latter could recover thereon, although the bill was drawn to secure an individual debt and not on account of the firm of D. & Co. or any indebtedness of theirs. Babcock *v.* Stone,* 3 McL., 172.

§ 188. By assignment.— A general assignment is valid for future liabilities, as well as for debts due, if the parties so intend; and one partner may sign and seal such an assignment for the firm, and it will bind the partnership, as a release of the debt. Halsey *v.* Fairbanks, 4 Mason, 206.

§ 189. Where various parties are tenants in common of a steamboat and partners in the business of carrying freight, and one of the part-owners of said boat incurs a debt for freighting, which the captain, another part-owner, authorized to transact the business of the boat, with assent and authority of a majority of the owners, but without the knowledge of the said debtor, assigns to a third person, it was held that the assignment was valid, and the assignee was authorized to sue in his own name. Russell *v.* The Minnesota Outfit,* 1 Minn., 162.

§ 190. Transfers of reservations by assignees, whose assignments express them as a firm, are not valid when executed by one member thereof, but only when executed by them all, unless the partner assigning exhibit authority to assign from all. But where the reservee assigned to a firm, as to "M. W. Perry & Co.," and the transfer by the firm was signed in that manner, the assignment is valid. Transfers of Creek Reservations,* 3 Op. Att'y Gen'l, 423.

§ 191. Whatever acts are done by any partner in regard to partnership property, or contracts beyond the scope and objects of the partnership, must in general, in order to bind the partnership, be derived from some authority, express or implied, conferred upon such partner beyond that resulting from his character as partner. A general assignment, if it does not dissolve a partnership, at least takes away the right of disposing of the effects from the partners, and if made by one partner against the known wishes of the other, is a fraud upon him and invalid; if made without his knowledge it is presumptively so. If one partner has left the country he must be considered as having vested in the other implied authority to act in all matters for the benefit of the firm, and an assignment under such circumstances, if fairly made, and beneficial to the interests of the company, will be sustained. But if the partner has not left the country, but is only absent from the place where the business is carried on, and in another city, where he may be communicated with or personally seen in a few days, his assent is essential to the validity of the assignment. Bowen *v.* Clark, 5 Am. L. Reg., 203; 1 Biss., 128.

§ 192. An assignment of copartnership effects in the name of the firm by one of the copartners for the benefit of particular creditors is valid. Harrison *v.* Sterry, 5 Cr., 289.

§ 193. By fraudulent acts.— An agreement to sell an individual partner certain articles for his individual use and consumption, to be paid for out of partnership goods of the firm of which he is a member, without the knowledge, assent or approval of his copartners, is fraudulent and void as to them. To uphold such an agreement, the party selling must show the assent, express or implied, of the other partners to it. Taylor *v.* Rasch,* 5 N. B. R., 299.

§ 194. Where goods are in the custody of a partnership for sale on commission, and one or more of the partners make false and fraudulent representations as to the party to whom they are to be sold, the partnership is liable, if, in consequence of such representations, the plaintiff consents to the sale to that party and the sale is accordingly made. Castle *v.* Bullard, 23 How., 172.

IV. RIGHTS, DUTIES AND LIABILITIES OF PARTNERS.

SUMMARY — *Partnership in developing an invention,* §§ 195, 196.— *Illegal partnership; right to an accounting,* §§ 197-199.— *Opening settlement,* § 200.

§ 195. In case of a partnership formed for the purpose of perfecting and patenting an invention under articles providing, among other things, that any improvement or modification of the invention made by either party shall inure to the benefit of both, if one partner, upon the discovery of an important improvement, whether made by him or his copartner, has it patented in the joint names of himself and a third party, the patentees will be liable to the copartner for an undivided half in the patent and the profits. Ambler *v.* Whipple, §§ 201–204.

§ 196. The copartner in such case cannot be held to have abandoned the enterprise by leaving the city where it was to be prosecuted for a week or two, nor would his bad character, drunkenness or dishonesty justify the other partner in treating the partnership as at an end of his own motion, whatever effect they might have as the basis of a suit for dissolution.   *Ibid.*

§ 197. Plaintiff and defendant formed a partnership to buy up soldiers' claims to land warrants, a traffic which was made illegal by act of congress. After carrying on the business for some time and when all the claims thus illegally purchased had been converted into land warrants and all the warrants sold or located, plaintiff brought suit to set aside a contract made with defendant to sell to the latter his interest in the business and for an account and division of profits. *Held,* that the rule of public policy against enforcing illegal contracts did not extend so far as to enable a partner to withhold from his copartner the latter's share of the profits of the business, under circumstances like the present, and was no bar to the present suit. Brooks *v.* Martin, §§ 205-208.

§ 198. A., B. and C. were partners in buying up soldiers' claims to land warrants. A. advanced the money necessary to carry on the business, but took no active part in the management, B. having almost exclusive control thereof, in pursuance of an understanding to that effect, and by which he was to represent A. so as to give him a preponderating influence over C. B. was also A.'s brother-in-law. The business, after they had ceased buying up claims, as they did after a time, consisted in obtaining warrants and disposing of the latter, or the lands located under them, and this was done at a long distance from A.'s residence. A. having agreed with B. to sell out to him his interest in the business, *held,* upon a suit brought by A. to set aside the agreement on the ground of fraud, that, whether or not the relation of partner and partner is of itself one of those fiduciary relations which require of the parties more than ordinary fairness and candor in dealing with one another, the relation in this case was, at any rate, of that character, and, it appearing that the business had been very prosperous; that A.'s share of the profits would probably be $30,000 as matters then stood; that B. concealed this condition of the business from A., and, as the consideration for the purchase, merely agreed to assume the debts of the firm, and perhaps paid a small account previously owing to A., the contract should be annulled. *Ibid.*

§ 199. In order to sustain a sale between persons occupying such relations to each other, it must be made to appear, first, that the price paid approximates reasonably near to a fair and adequate consideration for the thing purchased; and, second, that all the information, in the possession of the purchaser, which was necessary to enable the seller to form a sound judgment of the value of the thing sold, was communicated to the latter. *Ibid.*

§ 200. A settlement of partnership accounts made during the life-time of one of the partners will not be opened and a re-settlement ordered at the instance of his executor, unless it appears that errors were committed or imposition practiced. Where the principal errors complained of consisted of alleged overcharges for commissions and insurance and similar matters, but it appeared that the deceased partner had originally approved the charges and afterwards allowed them in the settlement understandingly, the court refused to open the settlement. Brydie v. Miller, §§ 209–12.
[NOTES.—See §§ 213–236.]

AMBLER v. WHIPPLE.

(20 Wallace, 546–559. 1874.)

APPEAL from the Supreme Court of the District of Columbia.

STATEMENT OF FACTS.— Ambler and Whipple were in partnership in getting up an invention for the manufacture of gas, the former being the inventor and the latter the capitalist and business manager. Ambler filed a bill charging that Whipple had defrauded him by patenting one of his inventions in connection with Dickerson, who pretended to be himself the inventor. The bill prayed for a discovery and account of profits made on the pirated invention, and for compensation and damages. The answer of Whipple denied the availability of Ambler's inventions, made charges against him of gross misconduct, alleged that Dickerson had made the real invention himself, and admitted that he had entered into partnership with him in it. There was a cross-bill, and a supplemental bill, and much contradictory testimony. Further facts appear in the opinion. The bill was dismissed.

Opinion by MR. JUSTICE MILLER,

It is to be observed that neither party prays for a dissolution of the partnership. Indeed, the bill and cross-bill, and the answers to both, proceed upon principles which do not recognize the partnership as existing. The complainant seems to imply that by reason of Whipple's course of conduct he is remitted to all his rights as the inventor, and claims that being the sole inventor of the successful machine he is entitled to all the benefit of it. Whipple assumes that by his purchase from Ambler, and Ambler's misconduct, that the partnership has been dissolved, and he has succeeded to all its rights, if they are of any value.

The testimony is voluminous and contradictory. In the view we shall take of the case, while the decision will mainly turn on these questions of fact, we shall only state the effect which the testimony has had upon our minds without referring to it in detail.

§ 201. *An agreement containing mutual releases, signed by one party and not by the other, is not obligatory on the party who did not sign it.*

1. If the complainant really released or sold his interest in the partnership business, or in the patent of Whipple and Ambler, his case is at an end, and we will, therefore, consider that question first. The instrument of writing dated September 24, 1869, is supposed to have that effect. There is no doubt that the language of the instrument is sufficient for the purpose for which it was intended, but it wants the signature of Ambler. Nor is it pretended that he ever signed it or any copy of it. It is clearly on its face a paper which requires the signature of both parties to make it binding on either. The releases and assignments are mutual, and each is the consideration of the other, and it requires no great penetration to see that it was drawn in the interest of Whipple, who signed it, and not in the interest of Ambler, who did not sign it.

But it is argued that the paper was procured from Whipple by Martin, the agent of Ambler, at Ambler's request, and was signed by Whipple and delivered to Martin; that Martin delivered it to Ambler, who received a copy of it without objection, and promised to sign it. Admitting all this to be true, it is very clear that both parties intended to have a written instrument signed by each as the evidence of any contract they might make on that subject, and neither considered any contract concluded until it was fully executed. Under these circumstances Ambler had a right to decline to sign the paper, and until he signed he was not bound by it. It was not drawn by him, nor at his dictation. It was first signed by Whipple, and drawn up by him or in his presence, and made to suit his purposes. It is idle to say that because Ambler took a copy of it from Martin to examine he became a party to it, though he never signed it.

Further, we are of opinion, notwithstanding Martin's declaration that he acted on Ambler's suggestion, that he was throughout the whole affair acting for Whipple, and governed solely by his interest. This transaction does not, in our opinion, establish any release or transfer of Ambler's interest in the partnership concern.

§ 202. *Partnership enterprise not abandoned by short absence.*

2. Nor is there any such evidence of abandonment of the enterprise on the part of Ambler as to justify the court in holding that he had lost or forfeited his rights in the venture. It is true that about the middle of August he left Washington City for a week or two, but when he returned he found himself excluded from the workshops and from all participation in Whipple's plans, and it seems probable he was by Whipple's authority forbidden to go there before he left the city. It is unreasonable to call this a voluntary abandonment of the enterprise.

§ 203. *Though bad conduct of one partner might authorize a court to decree a dissolution of a partnership, it does not justify the other party in treating it as at an end.*

3. What weight would be given to the charges of bad character, drunkenness and dishonesty in a suit by Whipple to dissolve the partnership we need not here state. If all that is charged were proved in such a suit it would make a strong case for relief, on such terms as equity might impose for the protection of both parties. But they did not authorize Whipple, of his own motion, to treat the partnership as ended and take to himself all the benefits of their joint labors and joint property. It seems also to be a fair inference from the pleadings and other circumstances, that Whipple must have known of Ambler's conviction for felony *before* he entered into the agreement with him. We are, therefore, of opinion that the case shows nothing which deprives Ambler of his rights under the original contract with Whipple.

§ 204. *A contract between partners, that future improvements on patented inventions shall inure to the advantage of both, makes the partner patenting improvements a trustee for the other.*

4. We are also of opinion that Whipple is chargeable as trustee for Ambler with one-half of all that has been realized or may be realized from the use of the patent to Whipple and Ambler and the patent to Whipple and Dickerson. This conclusion we rest upon the sixth article of the agreement between Whipple and Ambler. This article provides that any improvement or modification of the invention which may be made by either party, in this country or any other, for which a patent may be obtained, shall inure to the joint

benefit of both. In the peculiarly close and confidential relation which the parties assumed toward each other in regard to an invention which both understood to be imperfect, undeveloped, and the subject of future trial and experiment, this provision was eminently wise and necessary. And since Whipple was, by the assignment of Ambler, invested with the legal title of the patent and chief conduct of the affairs of the partnership, he was under a peculiar obligation of good faith as both partner and trustee of Ambler.

Notwithstanding the bills, cross-bills and supplemental bills, set up both by the patent to Whipple and Ambler and the patent to Whipple and Dickerson, No. 95,665, and another issued to them pending the suit, No. 102,662, which are charged by Ambler to be all covered by his invention, and by the others to be totally distinct, none of these patents are found in the record. It is impossible, therefore, for this court to give any *conclusive* opinion or judgment as to how far they are identical, or how far there may be distinctive features, under which the whole or some part of the two latter patents might be sustained. We base our decree on other principles.

We are satisfied, from the testimony in the case, that the results of the experiments conducted by Ambler and Whipple in their joint enterprise developed the practicability of success in obtaining the object of their pursuit; that these experiments disclosed the fact that while they had mainly relied on the effect of heat by steam, applied to petroleum indirectly by encompassing the vessel in which the petroleum was, by the steam let into an outer chamber, it was found that it was necessary to introduce the steam into the vessel, thus bringing it into direct contact with the petroleum.

Whether Ambler had seen this as clearly as Whipple is not very well or satisfactorily shown. But it is proved to our entire satisfaction that when Whipple saw this point, and that through it success was within his reach, he immediately recognized its great value. This experiment was made at the same shops, with the same machines, and in the same pursuit, which for three months had engaged the active energies of both Ambler and Whipple. The weight of evidence is that Ambler was present and assisting, but this is denied by other witnesses.

What is clear to us is that as soon as Whipple recognized the value of this discovery he made up his mind to be rid of Ambler. The undisputed facts of the case, taken in connection with much other testimony of a direct character, convince us that Whipple, in violation of his trust to Ambler and in fraud of his rights, deliberately entered upon a scheme by which Ambler was to be deprived of the benefits resulting from success in their joint experiments. That in pursuit of this scheme he called in Dickerson, who, without having invented anything, and in a remarkably short space of time, procured letters-patent to issue to himself and Whipple which embraced the results of Ambler's discoveries and experiments, whether they embraced anything else or not.

For all that has come to Whipple's hands, for all that is included in the patents to him and Dickerson, he is, under the terms of the sixth article of the agreement, a trustee for Ambler to the extent of one-half, and must be so charged and held to account in this proceeding.

As to Dickerson, while he is not a trustee under that article, we are of opinion that he has so far knowingly connected himself with and aided in the fraud on Ambler that he cannot resist Ambler's right to an undivided half of both the patents to Dickerson and Whipple, and of the profits made or to be

made out of them. What rights or remedies he may have against Whipple
we do not decide.

The result of these views is that the decree of the supreme court of the District must be reversed; that a decree must be entered in that court declaring Whipple and Dickerson to hold in trust for the benefit of Ambler to the extent of one-half the two patents issued to them, mentioned in the pleadings as 95,665 and 102,662; that an accounting be had as to the profits realized by them, or either of them, from the use or sale, or otherwise, arising from said patents, and for such other and further proceedings as may be in conformity to this opinion.

BROOKS *v.* MARTIN.

(2 Wallace, 70–87. 1863.)

APPEAL from U. S. Circuit Court, District of Wisconsin.

STATEMENT OF FACTS.— The plaintiff and defendant and one Field had formed a partnership for the ostensible purpose of buying up soldiers' land warrants issued under act of congress of February, 1847, and locating them on the public lands. Martin, the complainant below, who was a banker in New Orleans, and a brother-in-law of Brooks, furnished the money, and Brooks was the active manager in charge of the business. The complainant, Martin, filed his bill in equity in the circuit court of Wisconsin to set aside a contract of sale of his interest to his partner, Brooks, and for an account and division of the profits, alleging that Brooks, who had charge of the business, had purchased his interest by means of a concealment of the true state of the affairs of the partnership, and by false representations. Brooks denied the fraud, and further set up as a defense that the partnership had been formed for an illegal purpose; that while the ostensible object was to buy up soldiers' land warrants, the real object was to buy up soldiers' claims before any warrant had been issued by the government, in direct violation of the act of congress. The evidence supported this latter allegation, but further showed that where a claim had been thus bought before the issuing of a warrant, a warrant had subsequently issued and the title of the partnership had thus become valid.

The consideration paid by defendant for the plaintiff's interest in the business was the former's assumption of the debts of the firm, amounting to $45,000, and a payment, as he alleged, of $3,000 to plaintiff, but, as plaintiff testified, merely the payment of half of another account already due to plaintiff from defendant.

§ 205. *A partnership formed to buy up soldiers' claims before the issue of the land warrants by the government is illegal, under act of congress.*

Opinion by MR. JUSTICE MILLER.

We think that, in point of fact, the allegation of the answer — that the traffic in which this firm engaged was the buying up of soldiers' *claims*, before any scrip or land warrants were issued, and not the purchase and sale of bounty land warrants and scrip — is true. We have as little doubt that the traffic was illegal. Undoubtedly, the main object of the ninth section of the act of February 11, 1847, was to protect the soldier against improvident contracts of the precise character of those developed in this record. It was a wise and humane policy, and no court could hesitate to enforce it, in a case which called for its application. If a soldier, who had thus sold his claim to Brooks, Field

& Co., had refused to perform his contract, or to do any act which was necessary to give them the full benefit of their purchase, no court would have compelled him to do it, or given them any relief against him. And if they had, by any such means, got possession of the land warrant or scrip of a soldier, no court would have refused, in a proper suit, to compel them to deliver up such land warrant or scrip to the soldier. Or, if Brooks, after the signing of these articles of partnership, had said to Martin, "I refuse to proceed with this partnership, because the purpose of it is illegal," Martin would have been entirely without remedy. If, on the other hand, he had said to Martin, "I have bought one hundred soldiers' claims, for which I have agreed to pay a certain sum, which I require you to advance according to your agreement," Martin might have refused to comply with such a demand, and no court would have given either of his partners any remedy for such a refusal. To this extent go the cases of Russell *v.* Wheeler, 17 Mass., 281; Sheffner *v.* Gordon, 12 East, 304; Belding *v.* Pitkin, 2 Caines, 149, and the others cited by counsel for appellant, and no further.

§ 206. *Where partnership has acquired valid title to money and property, one partner cannot defeat an account and settlement by alleging illegal purpose of partnership. Authorities reviewed.*

All the cases here supposed, however, differ materially from the one now before us. When the bill in the present case was filed, all the claims of soldiers thus illegally purchased by the partnership, with money advanced by complainant, had been converted into land warrants, and all the warrants had been sold or located. The original defect in the purchase had, in many cases, been cured by the assignment of the warrant by the soldier after its issue. A large proportion of the lands so located had also been sold, and the money paid for some of it, and notes and mortgages given for the remainder. There were then in the hands of defendant, lands, money, notes and mortgages, the results of the partnership business, the original capital for which plaintiff had advanced. It is to have an account of these funds, and a division of these proceeds, that this bill is filed. Does it lie in the mouth of the partner who has, by fraudulent means, obtained possession and control of all these funds, to refuse to do equity to his other partners, because of the wrong originally done or intended to the soldier? It is difficult to perceive how the statute, enacted for the benefit of the soldier, is to be rendered any more effective by leaving all this in the hands of Brooks, instead of requiring him to execute justice as between himself and his partner; or what rule of public morals will be weakened by compelling him to do so? The title to the lands is not rendered void by the statute. It interposes no obstacle to the collection of the notes and mortgages. The transactions which were illegal have become accomplished facts, and cannot be affected by any action of the court in this case.

In Sharp *v.* Taylor, 2 Phillips' Ch., 801, a case in the English chancery, the plaintiff and defendant were partners in a vessel, which, being American built, could not be registered in Great Britain, according to the navigation laws of that kingdom. Nor could the owners, who were British subjects, residing in England, have her registered in the United States. They undertook to violate the laws of both countries by having her falsely registered in Charleston, South Carolina, as owned by a citizen and resident of that place. In this condition, she made several trips, which were profitable; and the defendant, colluding with Robertson, the American agent in whose name the vessel had been registered, refused to account with plaintiff for his share of the profits, or to acknowledge his interest in the ship.   When plaintiff brought his suit in chancery in England the defendant set up the illegality of the traffic, and the violation of the navigation laws of both governments, as precluding the court from granting any relief, on the same principle that is contended for by the defendant in the present case.   It will be at once perceived that the principle is the same in both cases, and that the analogy in the facts is so close that any rule on the subject which should govern the one ought also to control the other.   The case was decided by Lord Chancellor Cottenham, and from his opinion we make the following extracts: " The answer to the objection appears to me to be this,— that the plaintiff does not ask to enforce any agreement adverse to the provisions of the act of parliament.   He is not seeking compensation and payment for an illegal voyage.   That matter was disposed of when Taylor." (the defendant) " received the money ; and plaintiff is now only seeking payment for his share of the realized profits. . . .   As between these two, can this supposed evasion of the law be set up as a defense by one against the otherwise clear title of the other?   Can one of two partners possess himself of the property of the firm, and be permitted to retain it, if he can show that, in realizing it, some provision or some act of parliament has been violated or neglected? . . .   The answer to this, as to the former case, will be that the transaction alleged to be illegal is completed and closed, and will not be in any manner affected by what the court is asked to do between the parties. . .   The difference between enforcing illegal contracts and asserting title to money which has arisen from them is distinctly taken in Tenant v. Elliot, 1 Bos. & Pul., 3, and Farmer v. Russell, id., 29, and recognized and approved by Sir William Grant in Thomson v. Thomson, 7 Ves., 473."

These cases are all reviewed in the opinion of this court in the case of McBlair v. Gibbes, 17 How., 232 (CONTRACTS, §§ 457–58), and the language here quoted from the principal case is there referred to with approbation.   We are quite satisfied that the doctrine thus announced is sound, and that it is directly applicable to the case before us.

. § 207. *Query, whether the relation of partner with copartner is in all cases fiduciary, so that the purchase by one of the other's interest will be avoided, if not free from all suspicion of unfairness.*

The plaintiff alleges in his bill that on the 28th day of June, 1848, he sold his interest in the partnership business to the defendant Brooks ; that in making the sale he was overreached by the fraud of Brooks, who, by concealment of what he knew, and false representations in what he professed to tell, took advantage of the embarrassed financial condition of plaintiff, and his ignorance of the partnership business, and procured from him the sale for a consideration totally disproportioned to the real value of his interest in the concern.   The defendant admits the purchase of plaintiff's interest, but denies the fraud, and insists that the transaction was in all respects fair and honest.   The issue thus generally stated here is the one mainly contested in the case ; and so contested that a record of a thousand printed pages is mostly filled with testimony on this subject.

· If the parties are to be regarded in this transaction as holding towards each other no different relations from those which ordinarily attend buyer and seller, and as, therefore, under no special obligation to deal conscientiously with each other, we are satisfied that no such fraud is proven as would justify a court in setting aside an executed contract.   But there *are* relations of trust and confidence which one man may occupy towards another, either personally or in regard to the particular property which is the subject of the contract, which impose upon him a special and peculiar obligation to deal with the other person towards whom he stands so related, with a candor, a fairness and a refusal to avail himself of any advantage of superior information 'or other favorable circumstance, not required by courts of justice in the usual business transactions of life. It is contended that the relation of Brooks towards Martin was of this character; and before we can dispose of the question of fraud it is necessary to determine whether the claim thus set up is well founded; and if it is, what are the principles upon which courts of equity determine the validity of contracts between parties so situated. It is argued that the partnership existing between the parties constitutes of itself a relation which calls for the application of the principles which we have alluded to; and Judge Story, in recapitulating the confidential relations to which they are appropriate (Equity Jurisprudence, § 323), mentions partner and partner as one of them. It is not necessary to decide here whether, in all cases, a sale by one partner to another of his interest in the partnership concern will be scrutinized with the same closeness which is applied to fiduciary relations generally; for there are special circumstances in this case which bring it clearly within the rules applicable to that class of cases.

§ 208. *Partner in charge of the business is under special obligation to make no concealment in purchasing the interest of his copartner.*

1. The defendant was not only the partner of plaintiff, but he was his special agent in the management of the business. The bill alleges that he had a power of attorney from plaintiff, authorizing him to represent, on all occasions, the interest of plaintiff in the conduct of the affairs of the firm; and although this is denied in the answer, and is not proven, the answer *does* state that at the time the partnership was formed it was distinctly agreed between plaintiff and defendant that the latter was to have the full and exclusive control of the business, and should so far represent the plaintiff as to give defendant a preponderating influence in the management of the partnership over Mr. Field, the third partner. The record leaves no doubt that he acted throughout in accordance with this agreement.

2. It is abundantly established by the testimony that, within some two or three months after the partnership was formed, the parties closed their operations in New Orleans, after having invested over $50,000, advanced by Martin, in the purchase of soldiers' claims; and that thenceforth very little was done in the way of purchasing claims or warrants. That Brooks then came to Washington to procure the warrants to be issued, and Field went to Wisconsin to seek a market for their sale. From that time forward Brooks and Field had the entire management of the business, mainly under the direction of Brooks; and none of it was conducted in New Orleans save the purchase of five or six warrants made by Brooks on Martin's suggestion, nor were any reports made of the business to Martin.

Brooks and Field thus managed the entire concern, at a distance of near two thousand miles from Martin, and, as we think the testimony shows, without consulting him in any way, and with very little regard for his large interest in the business. Under these circumstances Brooks must be held to have been not only the partner, but the special agent of Martin; and the purchase made by him of Martin's interest must be tested by the rules which govern such transactions as between principal and agent.

What are these rules? "On the whole, the doctrine may be generally stated, that wherever confidence is reposed, and one party has it in his power, in a secret manner, for his own advantage, to sacrifice those interests which he is bound to protect, he will not be permitted to hold any such advantage." 1 Story's Equity, § 323. Or, to speak more specifically, "if a partner who exclusively superintends the business and accounts of the concern, by concealment of the true state of the accounts and business, purchase the share of the other partner for an inadequate price, by means of such concealment, the purchase will be held void." Id., § 220.

Speaking of a purchase by a trustee from his *cestui que trust*, Lord Chancellor Eldon says, in the case of Coles *v.* Trecothick, 9 Vesey, 234, that though permitted, it is a transaction of great delicacy, and which the court will watch with the utmost diligence; so much, that it is very hazardous for a trustee to engage in such a transaction. "A trustee may buy from the *cestui que trust*, provided there is a distinct and clear contract, ascertained to be such after a jealous and scrupulous examination of all the circumstances; provided the *cestui que trust* intended the trustee should buy; and there is no fraud, no concealment, no advantage taken by the trustee of information acquired by him in the character of trustee. I admit," he says, "it is a difficult case to make out, wherever it is contended that the exception prevails." This has long been regarded as a leading case, and the above remarks have been often cited by other courts with approbation. We think them fully applicable to a purchase by an agent from his principal of the property committed to his agency. See, also, Michoud *v.* Girod, 4 How., 503; Bailey *v.* Teakle, 2 Brockenborough, 51-54; Hunter *v.* Atkyns, 3 Mylne & K., 113; Maddeford *v.* Austwick, 1 Simons, 89.

We lay down, then, as applicable to the case before us, and to all others of like character, that, in order to sustain such a sale, it must be made to appear, first, that the price paid approximates reasonably near to a fair and adequate consideration for the thing purchased; and, second, that all the information in possession of the purchaser, which was necessary to enable the seller to form a sound judgment of the value of what he sold, should have been communicated by the former to the latter.

In regard to the adequacy of the price, it is obvious that Brooks did not pay to Martin anything which he was not bound to pay before the sale was made, or assume any obligation under which he did not already rest; nor did Martin receive anything which Brooks did not then owe him, or his promise to do anything for which Brooks was not previously bound. The only matter in which their relations were changed was, that Martin sold to Brooks his share of the profits of the business, and Brooks assumed to bear all Martin's share of the losses.

So the condition of the partnership business, at this time, shows a balance of $15,000 of profits, all of which was cash, or funds equal to cash. It further appears that there were on hand and unsold over forty-five thousand acres of land, which, at the government rate of $1.25 an acre, gives an aggregate value of $57,000. Add this to the $15,000 above mentioned, and we have $72,000 as the probable profits of the partnership venture, at the time of this sale.

It is said that the danger that soldiers would seek to reclaim the warrants, or the lands on which they had been located, under the provisions of the act of 1847, already mentioned, must have detracted largely from the amount which any prudent man would have given for Martin's interest in the concern.

This danger was, however, a very remote and improbable one, and must have so appeared, when we consider that these claims have been bought from young men scattered over the different states of the Union, with no means of ascertaining where the warrants were located, or in whom the title was vested; and that the amount, in each case separately, was not worth the trouble and expense of the search and subsequent litigation. But while these considerations might have some weight, if the question of adequate price were otherwise in doubt, they can go but a little way to establish that point, in the circumstances of the present case.

Martin's share of the profits was $30,000, for which Brooks gave him substantially nothing. Was Martin placed by Brooks in possession of all the information known to himself, and which was necessary to enable Martin to form a sound judgment of the value of what he was selling?

But we are not left alone to this negative and inferential testimony on the subject. We have letters from Brooks to the Fields, written before the sale was made, in which he urges that all remittances shall be made to him at Washington, showing from the allusions in them to a proposed remittance to Martin, and to Lake & Co., who were Martin's correspondents in New York, that his intention was that no remittance should be made to Martin. When we consider that the letter of June 20th was written at a moment when he was expecting in a few days an interview with Martin, which he had himself suggested, and that he was no doubt then contemplating the very purchase which he made at the interview, and that he knew that Lake was the other partner in the firm of Martin & Co., we look upon it as remarkable, pointing clearly to one conclusion, namely, a determination to keep from Martin all the funds of the concern and all information of its condition, in order that he might perform the *operation* of buying Martin's interest at a sacrifice.

We are of opinion from a careful examination of the testimony that Brooks occupied towards Martin a relation of confidence and trust, being his partner, his agent and his brother-in-law, and having also entire control of the partnership business; that he took advantage of this position to conceal from Martin the prosperous condition of the concern, and purchased from him his interest for a price totally disproportioned to its real value; and that, under such circumstances, it is the unquestionable duty of a court of chancery to set aside the contract of sale.

Decree affirmed with costs.

MR. JUSTICE CATRON dissented.

BRYDIE v. MILLER.

(Circuit Court for Virginia: 1 Marshall, 147-155. 1809.)

Opinion by MARSHALL, C. J.

STATEMENT OF FACTS.— The object of this suit is to open an account which was settled between the parties in the life-time of the testator of the plaintiff, and to have a re-settlement of all the transactions of M'Clure, Brydie & Co.

§ 209. *An account settled is binding in the absence of mistake or imposition.*

It is the right of every individual to exercise his own judgment on his own affairs, and to arrange them in such a manner as his own will may dictate. Where this arrangement is made under the fair exercise of judgment, without imposition, and with a requisite knowledge of the subject, it is certainly conclusive, unless the arrangement be in its nature alterable at the will of the person who has made it.

It is a necessary consequence of this right, that an individual who has settled his accounts with another and arranged the transactions between them in a manner which receives the full and free assent of his mind has a right to consider those transactions closed, and is consequently bound so to consider them. That which might before have been a matter of controversy is adjusted by mutual consent, and claims which might have been uncertain are reduced to certainty. It is no objection to this adjustment that some sacrifice may have been made. The party had a right to make the sacrifice. He had a right to balance in his own mind the advantages of the settlement against its disadvantages, and if, in his judgment, the former preponderated, no other individual has a right to say that he was mistaken, and that, therefore, transactions which he had closed shall remain open.

It follows that an account settled between two individuals, each exercising his own free judgment on every part of it, is binding on both as to all the items of that account. Mistakes may be corrected, omissions may be supplied, impositions may be relieved against, but a principle, understood, considered and agreed upon by a party in a situation fairly to exercise his own judgment and to act in conformity with that judgment, must bind himself and his representatives in and out of court. To controvert those principles would be to question the right of a man of full age and sound mind to manage his own property and to insist on transferring that right to another.

That Mr. Brydie was capable of acting for himself; that he had a full knowledge of the subject into the adjustment of which he entered; that his judgment was exercised free from undue influence of any kind, is not denied; certainly is not disproved. It is said that his health was too delicate for laborious research or execution. Should this be admitted, he had clerks to perform what was too toilsome for himself, and the subject to be settled had long been familiar to him. In such a case, it surely must be necessary to show that items have been introduced which were not understood before his own settlement shall be subverted.

§ 210. *Overcharges in an account settled cannot afterwards be objected to when they were allowed in the settlement understandingly and had been previously acquiesced in. Inspection of documents. Right to copies.*

Great errors are alleged to exist in the settlement. Errors so great and so manifest that the court ought to correct them. An inquiry into this allegation will now be made. The first error alleged is in the premiums of insurance. M'Clure, Brydie & Co. directed the tobacco to be insured at a specified price, and Miller, Hart & Co. insured that tobacco at a higher price. Miller, Hart & Co. held three-fourths of the the interest of M'Clure, Brydie & Co., and insist that, under the terms of the copartnership, they had a right to insure upon the principles upon which they acted.

To simplify the question, I will suppose Miller, Hart & Co. to have misconstrued articles, and that the point, if depending on them alone, would be decided in favor of the plaintiff. It remains to inquire whether Brydie has not completely sanctioned this act.

Accounts of sales exhibiting the premiums paid for insurance were regularly received. Of consequence, their conduct on this subject was completely understood by Mr. Brydie. It does not appear, nor is it alleged, that he ever expressed any dissatisfaction at this proceeding. On the contrary, by receiving these accounts, and entering the balances without objection, he tacitly and impliedly sanctioned the principle on which Miller, Hart & Co. had acted. It gave them his authority to proceed in the same line of conduct. Had the case stopped here, it would have been going very far to say that Mr. Brydie might, after the business was closed, charge Miller, Hart & Co. with the extra premium they had paid for insurance, under the impression, very justifiably entertained, that he approved their conduct. But the case does not stop here. A full settlement afterwards takes place, and Mr. Brydie, with a full knowledge of the fact, admits this item of charge. To controvert it now, unless it could be proved that some imposition was practiced on him, would be to deny the right of an intelligent merchant to settle and close any one of his accounts.

I do not mention the circumstance of Mr. Brydie's taking credit for this extra insurance in the cases of lost and damaged cargoes, because there may be some question about the fact, and because I do not think the case requires the aid of that fact. To afford a pretext for revising this item, it ought to be shown that some imposition was practiced on Mr. Brydie. For this purpose, it is alleged in the bill that Miller, Hart & Co. did not pay these premiums in reality, but stood insurers themselves. This allegation is totally unsupported and is positively denied in the answer. It is therefore to be considered as untrue.

But the plaintiff requires that authenticated copies of all the policies of insurance should be transmitted to this country. The defendants refuse to accede to this demand, and declare their readiness to exhibit the policies to any person whom the plaintiff may employ to inspect them. The policies are said to be so numerous as to form too bulky a package to be sent without necessity. They transmit copies of the particular policies, specifically required by the plaintiff.

Had this account never been settled, or was any circumstance in proof which might give countenance to the allegation of fraud made in the bill, the court would not hastily overrule the demand for the production of the policies. But the account had been settled. Mr. Brydie has been satisfied that these premiums have been actually paid, and there is no single circumstance in the case to warrant the suspicion which has been expressed. The demand, then, that authentic copies of the policies should be transmitted to this country is most unreasonable. It is founded on nothing which has a semblance of right. If this subject could be closed now, I should feel no difficulty on this part of the case. But as an account is to be taken. I shall leave the plaintiffs at liberty to demand a view of the policies in London.

The second error to be corrected is the item of £3 3s. on each hogshead of a cargo sold to Holder for risk of damage on the tobacco. The reasoning applied to the preceding claim applies to this, and need not be repeated. It is apparent on the face of the account of sales, and was, consequently, understood by Mr. Brydie. But it is contended that this was not a conclusive statement. It was a conjectural allowance dependent on a subsequent statement.

This allegation is not supported, and there is no reason to believe it correct. Had this been the fact, Mr. Brydie would have required evidence of the actual damage on the final settlement of the account. His settling the account without charging this item is proof that he considered the arrangement as having been definitely made with Holder, and was satisfied with it. If in this he was deceived, the deposition of Holder ought to have been taken by the plaintiffs in order to prove the fact.

The third error, a correction of which has been required, is an extra charge of commissions and of interest. In the articles of copartnership, Miller, Hart & Co. stipulate to do the business in London on the same terms on which they had done the business for Alexander Brydie & Co. Consequently they were bound to be content with the same commissions, and to keep an interest account on the same principles.

The bill charges a departure from this stipulation. This allegation also is in express and unequivocal terms denied in the answer. Alexander Brydie was the acting partner, in this country, of Alexander Brydie & Co., and of M'Clure, Brydie & Co. Consequently he understood perfectly the commissions charged by Miller, Hart & Co. to each of these firms. He never complained of their commissions, but impliedly approved them; first, by admitting the accounts, and afterwards, by making a final settlement, which acknowledged their correctness.

The plaintiff does not pretend to show that the commissions charged M'Clure, Brydie & Co. vary from those charged Alexander Brydie & Co., but shows that different commissions have been charged M'Clure, Brydie & Co. for different cargoes, sold at different places, and under different circumstances, with all of which Alexander Brydie was perfectly satisfied. The interest account is not so clear, and I do not so well understand it. If the plaintiff can show a positive error in it, I shall permit him to do so. But the whole weight of proof lies with him.

A fourth error charged against Miller, Hart & Co. is, premiums paid for insurance against fire. But this item is in express terms allowed by Brydie, and was afterwards admitted by him in the settlement.

A fifth error is, an allowance of 10s. per cwt., on four hundred hogsheads of tobacco purchased for Keymer, M'Taggert & Co. at £3 per cwt. Keymer, M'Taggert & Co. alleged that their orders had been disobeyed, and refused to receive this tobacco. Miller, Hart & Co. made a compromise and agreed to receive 50s. instead of 60s. per cwt. Alexander Brydie says he does not think they were bound to make this concession, but, believing they acted for the best, he acquiesces in it, and will cheerfully bear his proportion of the loss.

Alexander Brydie might certainly have refused to accede to this compromise, in which case Miller, Hart & Co. would have stood in the place of Keymer, M'Taggert & Co., and must have paid whatever sum that company was liable for. But, although Alexander Brydie might have withheld his assent, he was not bound to withhold it. He was at liberty to accept or reject the compromise. With a full knowledge of the subject he chose to accept it. Who shall reverse his decision and say that, against his will, he shall go on with the contest, and risk almost the whole cargo on the liability of Keymer, M'Taggert & Co. to pay 60s. per hundred for the tobacco?

It is alleged that this compromise was not actually made, but this allegation is not supported by even the semblance of probability, and, if the plaintiffs rely on it, they ought to have taken the testimony, which was in their power, to establish the fact. A sixth error is a credit taken in the books for £1,800, a variance between the London and Virginia books. This allegation is expressly denied in the answer, and is not proved. I understand the answer as accounting for the alleged error of £2,000 in favor of M'Clure.

§ 211. *Acquiescence in settlement renders it binding on party not signing.*
In objection to the account which was settled, it is alleged that M'Clure signed it for himself only, not for his partners. That Miller and Hart were

not bound, and, therefore, Brydie ought not to be bound. Whenever Miller and Hart signified their acquiescence in this account, it became obligatory on them, even supposing that their silence did not render it obligatory. But whatever force might arise from this circumstance, if Miller and Hart had never signified their acquiescence in the settlement, and Brydie had alleged this fact and brought a bill on that account to have a resettlement, it can have no force when Miller and Hart appear to have approved the settlement, and are not put upon the proof of that fact by the allegation that they had not assented to it.

§ 212. *Upon bill for resettlement of partnership accounts, defendant need not set forth the original settled account.*

It has been also contended that Miller, Hart & Co. ought to have set forth the settled account, if they relied upon it as a bar to the resettlement which is demanded in the bill.

If this bill had been brought for a settlement of accounts, without admitting a former settlement, this observation would be correct. The defendant ought not to be, and most certainly would not be, admitted to plead a former settlement in bar, without showing that former settlement. But this bill admits a former settlement, which must be in possession of the plaintiffs. It is therefore not essential that the defendants should exhibit it, nor have they ever been required to exhibit it. The original has been produced and read in court. That it cannot longer be produced is not the fault of either party; each party is, I presume, possessed of copies. If, on this part of the case, any difficulty should arise, the court will interfere so far as may be necessary.

The errors alleged in the former settlement have been considered. If there was nothing further in the case, I could not hesitate to dismiss the bill. But the parties agree that some accounts between them still remain open. Of these, an account is, of course, to be taken. If, during the pendency of this account, the plaintiff chooses to inspect the policies in London, he is at liberty to do so, and if there is any one case in which Miller, Hart & Co. have themselves stood insurers, he is at liberty to bring the circumstances of that case before the court. He may also take depositions to show any imposition on Alexander Brydie, and he may show to the commissioner any positive error in the interest account, but he is not at liberty to open the settlement on any point agreed to by Alexander Brydie, unless he can prove fraud or misrepresentation in obtaining that agreement.

§ 213. A partner is not entitled to compensation for his services either before or after dissolution, in the absence of a special agreement entitling him to it. Lyman v. Lyman,* 2 Paine, 11.

§ 214. Right of partner to manage firm business.— If two are jointly concerned in a particular adventure, the one authorized to dispose of the property may appropriate the whole proceeds to his own use, and make himself the debtor to the other for a moiety; or he may hold the money for the joint account, and subject his associate to all the risks which may attend it. Hourquebie v. Girard, 2 Wash., 212.

§ 215. Plaintiff and defendant engaged in a joint adventure, the management of the affair being placed in the hands of the defendant, who was in command of the vessel in which the shipment was made. Held, that being a joint adventure, the plaintiff had no right to order, but only to advise, as to the disposition of the property, and that the defendant having exchanged the property for bills on the French government, instead of for cash or produce as directed by the letter of the plaintiff, was not responsible for the loss occasioned thereby, having acted in good faith. Lyles v. Styles, 2 Wash., 224.

§ 216. The law gives to each partner a lien upon the joint effects of the partnership for any excess over his partner which he has contributed to their joint business, or to preserve their joint property. Wilson v. Davis,* 1 Mont. T'y, 183.

§ 217. Of retiring partner.— Partnership property is responsible for what is due to a partner retiring, and if not enough to satisfy the claim, each member is liable for the residue in a ratio with his interest. Perkins v. Currier, 3 Woodb. & M., 69.

§ 218. Where one member of a firm withdraws, the dealing of creditors with the remaining partner, selling him goods, giving him fresh credit, and permitting such goods to be mingled with the old stock, does not release the retiring member from liability for the firm's indebtedness, or sanction the appropriation by him of the moneys he took out of the firm, so as to deprive them of the right to follow those moneys, if it be found that the remaining assets were insufficient to pay their debts in full. In re Sauthoff,* 5 Cent. L. J., 364; 16 N. B. R., 181.

§ 219. Partners are liable for the torts of each other committed in the course of partnership business. Stockwell v. United States, 3 Cliff., 284.

§ 220. When one partner a trustee for the other — Patents.— A copartnership was formed between A., a man of inventive genius, and B., a man of business and of capital, for the purpose of experimenting with and bringing to perfection a certain invention. By the sixth article of the agreement it was provided that any improvement, etc., should inure to the joint benefit. B., by the assignment of A., was invested with the legal title of the patent, and chief conduct of the affairs of the partnership. Subsequent'y B. endeavored to get rid of A., under circumstances which indicated that he intended to deprive him of the benefits resulting from success in their joint experiments, and in pursuance of such scheme called in D., who, without having invented anything, and in a remarkably short space of time, procured letters patent to issue to himself and B., which embraced the results of A.'s discoveries and experiments, whether they embraced anything else or not. Held, that B. was chargeable, under the sixth article of the agreement between A. and B., as trustee for A., with one-half of all that had been realized or might be realized from the use of the patent to B. and A., and the patent to B. and D. As to D., while he was not a trustee under the said article, he had so far knowingly connected himself with, and aided in the fraud on A., that he could not resist A.'s right to an undivided half of both the patents to B. and D., and of the profits made or to be made out of them. Ambler v. Whipple, 20 Wall., 546.

§ 221. Forfeiture of interest in firm.— A partner, by failing to contribute his share of the partnership fund, does not, in ordinary cases, forfeit the interest which he already has in the firm. Especially is this so where no extraordinary emergency exists requiring such payment. Piatt v. Oliver,* 3 McL., 27.

§ 222. Interest on partnership accounts.— A partner is not liable to pay interest on partnership accounts, before settlement and balance struck. Dexter v. Arnold, 3 Mason, 284.

§ 223. Liability for firm debts.— The stockholders of an unincorporated banking company are individually liable in equity to the holders of the notes of the company, issued while they were stockholders, notwithstanding an article of their association declares that the joint stock or property of the company should alone be responsible for the debts and engagements of the company, and that no person who might deal with the company, or to whom they should become indebted, should, on any pretense whatever, have recourse against the separate property of any present or future member of the company, or against their persons, further than might be necessary to secure the faithful application of the funds thereof to the purposes to which, by those articles, they were liable. Each stockholder, notwithstanding such article, is liable to the full extent of all the notes outstanding in the hands of creditors of the company, which were issued while he was a stockholder. Riggs v. Swann,* 3 Cr. C. C., 183.

§ 224. It is a principle of the law of partnership, that a contract made by copartners is several as well as joint, and the assumpsit is made by all and by each. It is obligatory on all and on each of the partners. Barry v. Foyles, 1 Pet., 311.

§ 225. The responsibility of one partner for the contracts of another is not solely on the ground of the credit being given to all. Felichy v. Hamilton,* 1 Wash., 492.

§ 226. In 1784 two brothers, who were engaged in trading and boating on the Connecticut river, orally agreed upon a partnership, it being understood that all their property should be in common, and that each should be at liberty to do any kind of business he might see fit on joint account. This connection continued until 1820, and in the meantime their business grew to considerable proportions, including a variety of transactions, such as building and dealing in vessels, the purchase of land, and of stock in bridge and turnpike companies. Deeds and other evidences of title were taken in the names of both or either indiscriminately. Held, that the partnership was a general and unlimited one, that all their property of every description was partnership property, including land belonging to one of them before the partnership and upon which buildings were erected with the joint funds, and legacies received by one of them and the wife of the other and applied to the use of the partnership; and that losses sustained by the transactions of either, however ill advised, must be borne by both, so long as there was no fraud shown. Lyman v. Lyman,* 2 Paine, 11.

§ **227.** Upon a bill for an accounting, *held,* that the plaintiff was entitled to have a sale of the real estate made to wind up the partnership, although defendant desired to have each retain what real estate he had, the difference in values to be so held by a corresponding charge and credit. *Ibid.*

§ **228.** Each having been in possession of different portions of the real estate, by tacit consent, for eight years after dissolution, *held,* that, owing to the extraordinary character of the case, each should be allowed for improvements made upon such real estate during that time, contrary to the usual rule applicable to partnerships. *Ibid.*

§ **229.** An agreement purporting to create a partnership, to continue a certain number of years from date, provided that one of the parties should obtain the lease of a certain railroad in his own name, but for the joint account of all; that he should manage it at a monthly salary for their mutual benefit; that the others should furnish the money necessary for the purpose and be reimbursed with interest out of the annual net profits; that after such repayment of the capital and interest, the net profits should be equally divided, and that all losses should be borne equally. *Held,* that the postponement of a division of profits until the capital advanced should be refunded to the partners advancing it did not defer or affect the liability of the partners for debts contracted in the prosecution of the business, but that the managing partner, as well as the others, became liable for such debts from the start. Beauregard *v.* Case,[*] 1 Otto, 134.

§ **230.** Such a partnership is, under the Louisiana law, termed an "ordinary" as distinguished from a "commercial" partnership. Under that law in such a partnership each partner is only bound individually for his share of the partnership debts; but, to that extent, a debt contracted by one partner, even without authority from the others, binds them, if it is proved that the partnership was benefited by the transaction. *Ibid.*

§ **231.** In an action against a partnership in Louisiana praying a judgment against all the defendants *in solido* for the whole amount of the debt, if the evidence shows an ordinary, as distinguished from a commercial, partnership, the verdict and judgment may be against each defendant for his proportional share only, and they will not be vitiated by the variance from the prayer of the petition. *Ibid.*

§ **232.** Where a member of a firm is discharged in bankruptcy, upon his individual petition, such discharge does not release him from partnership debts, without any proceedings to declare the partnership bankrupt. Hudgins *v.* Lane,[*] 11 N. B. R., 462.

§ **233. Partnership note — Consideration as to new member.—** Where A. agreed to sell B. and C. certain property, and D. afterward entered into copartnership with B. and C., and a conveyance was made of said property to B., C. & D., and their note given for a certain amount, which said parties alleged was given partly in consideration of a further agreement entered into between A. and said B., C. & D., it was held upon their claiming that there was no consideration for D.'s becoming a joint promisor in said note, except said subsequent agreement, that he was a partner of B. and C. and a joint owner with them of the property for which the debt had been contracted, and that a consideration moving to his copromisors was enough to support his promise independent of said subsequent agreement. Philpot *v.* Gruninger, 14 Wall., 570.

§ **234. As to mines.—** If tenants in common of a mine unite in working it, being practically forced by circumstances into a partnership in working the mine, but not becoming partners as to the ownership of it, one may buy up the interest of a second without becoming answerable therefor to the others. The rule that forbids a partner from deriving any private advantage from his position as partner has no application to such a case. First Nat. Bank *v.* Bissell,[*] 2 MoC., 73.

§ **235. Distribution of stock.—** Partners cannot distribute among themselves any part of the stock in trade to the prejudice of creditors. But when a distribution is made with the assent of the creditors the act is not fraudulent. Wilkinson *v.* Yale, 6 McL., 16.

V. DISSOLUTION AND CHANGE IN FIRM. SURVIVING PARTNERS.

SUMMARY — *Notice,* §§ 237, 238.— *Surviving partner; abatement and revival,* §§ 239, 240.— *Acceptance of new firm as debtor,* §§ 241, 242.— *Liability of estate of deceased partner,* § 243. *Profits from other partnerships,* § 244.— *Dissolution of law partnership; death of partner; suit for an accounting,* §§ 245-247.

§ **236.** Notice of dissolution of a partnership published in the public papers is conclusive upon all persons who have had no previous dealings with the firm. Shurlds *v.* Tilson, §§ 248, 249.

§ **237.** Notice of dissolution of a partnership by publication in a newspaper is not indispensable to protect a retiring partner against one who has not had previous dealings with the firm. Other public notice may be sufficient. Lovejoy v. Spafford, §§ 250-252.

§ 238. In an action brought on an acceptance given in the name of a dissolved firm by the continuing partner, seeking to hold the retired partner, it appeared that the defendant firm was located at Davenport, Iowa, and the acceptance was given at Read's Landing, Wisconsin, for the price of lumber bought of plaintiffs there; that the firm had been dissolved several months previously, and the business was thereafter carried on in the name of the continuing partner alone; that actual notice had been given to those who had dealt with the firm previously; there was no evidence that the firm had ever transacted any business before at Read's Landing, or at Eau Claire, which was near by. Held, that it was error to exclude evidence offered by defendant to show that it was generally known along the Mississippi river that the dissolution had taken place, to show to whom, to what extent and in what manner notice had been given; that all the lumber dealers in Davenport were notified and knew of the dissolution; and that, just before the draft in question was given, notice was given to nearly all the lumber dealers in Eau Claire and vicinity, although such evidence was not offered to prove actual notice to plaintiffs. Ibid.

§ 239. In case of the death of a member of a firm, leaving his copartners surviving him, during the pendency of a suit against the partnership, the suit does not abate, but, upon suggestion of the death of one, it will proceed against the others; and there is nothing in the nature of a bill in equity to restrain the infringement of letters patent, and praying for an account of profits arising from such infringement, to withdraw the case from the operation of the general rule. Troy Iron & Nail Factory v. Winslow, §§ 253-255.

§ 240. Such a suit cannot be revived against the executor of the deceased copartner, at least unless it is shown that the surviving partners are insolvent, or that the partnership assets are not sufficient to satisfy the demand, as, without such showing, creditors of a partnership have no right to proceed against the estate of a deceased copartner. Ibid.

§ 241. In 1871 the banking firm of J. C. & Co. was dissolved and a new firm formed under the same name, two members of the old firm, including defendant's testator, retiring and being succeeded by two new members. The liabilities of the old firm were assumed by the new, and it was agreed that the retiring partners should be relieved from liability. In 1873 the new firm failed and went into bankruptcy, and among its debts, published in the proceedings, was an account due plaintiff's intestate as depositor, he having made the deposits in 1869, and having disappeared in 1870. This debt was proved in the bankruptcy proceedings in 1873 and dividends accepted on it afterwards. The defendant's testator died in 1877, and no claim was made on him during his life-time on account of the deposits. In 1878 a demand was made on defendant, who denied any liability, and no steps were taken to enforce the demand. In 1879 the bankrupt estate was wound up; plaintiff participated in a distribution of stocks made to the creditors, and sold the stocks so received at private sale without notice to defendant. Upon these facts, held, that as the representative of plaintiff's intestate was notified by the bankruptcy proceedings of the dissolution of the old firm and of the assumption of the debt by the new firm, proof of the debt in the bankruptcy proceedings, coupled with the omission to make any claim upon the retired partner during his life, and with the lapse of time occurring before any demand was made on his estate, justified the inference that the new firm was adopted as the debtor in lieu of the old, and therefore plaintiff could not maintain a claim for an unsatisfied balance of the debt against the defendant. Regester v. Dodge, §§ 256-260.

§ 242. Held, also, that plaintiff was barred from obtaining any relief in equity by the consideration that his failure to make a claim upon the defendant or his testator until the bankrupt estate was nearly wound up resulted in the loss to the defendant of the opportunity to make a claim upon the bankrupt estate, and by the further consideration that defendant may have chosen to keep the stock received from the bankrupt estate instead of selling it, and should have been allowed the option to do so. Ibid.

§ 243. A partnership agreement fixed no definite period for the continuance of the partnership, but provided that, in the event of the death of either party, the copartnership "shall not on that account dissolve, but the interest of such deceased party may be continued and represented by the legal representatives of said deceased party, or otherwise disposed of by them." The will of one of the partners, who died during the continuance of the partnership, provided that the testator's share or interest in the partnership "shall not cease, nor said partnership be determined, by reason of my death," but that such share and interest "shall continue and be kept up and represented by the executor of this my will, in my stead, until such time as, in his judgment, it shall be most advantageous for my estate to sell out and settle up and close up" the said share and interest, "and to that end I do hereby fully authorize and empower and direct the executor of this my will to hold, manage and represent" such share or interest, "for the benefit and use of those who shall be entitled to my estate, until such time as, in his discretion and judgment, it shall be most advantageous to sell or close and settle the same." The testator then provided for a sister, and then devised the residue of his estate to certain persons, "subject to the foregoing provisions and to dower." *Held*, that his general estate did not become liable for debts of the partnership contracted after his death. Cook *v.* Rogers, §§ 261-263.

§ 244. Such debts held not payable out of profits derived by the estate from other partnerships, as to which the will made similar provisions, it not appearing, however, that the partnership articles provided for the continuance of the partnerships, and it not appearing whether such partnerships were solvent or insolvent, or whether there were any outstanding debts against them. *Ibid.*

§ 245. An agreement was made between the members of a law firm to dissolve the partnership, but to continue it for the purpose of closing up the business then on hand. Afterwards a further agreement provided that in case of the death of either partner, the fees collected for unfinished business should be divided between the survivors and the representatives of the deceased partner in certain specified proportions. One of the partners having died, his executor brought a bill in equity against the survivors for discovery and an account. *Held*, that the bill could be maintained, although there was still unfinished business of the old firm on hand, and fees uncertain in amount were yet to be collected; that the decree properly allowed a recovery of a due proportion of the fees already collected, and reserved consideration of fees yet to be earned until after they should be earned. Denver *v.* Roane, §§ 264-266.

§ 246. In such case the surviving partners are not entitled to any extra allowance for their services in closing up the unfinished business. *Ibid.*

§ 247. The executor of the deceased partner can recover nothing on account of fees received in a case from which the testator during his life-time personally withdrew and had his name stricken from the record, denouncing the claim to the court as a corrupt one. *Ibid.*

[NOTES.— See §§ 267-333.]

SHURLDS *v.* TILSON.

(Circuit Court for Illinois: 2 McLean, 458-461. 1841.)

Opinion of the COURT.

STATEMENT OF FACTS.— This action is brought by the plaintiff, as assignee of certain bills or promissory notes which purported to be signed by the defendants and dated the 8th of May, 1839, and the 23d of July following. The defendants were partners in merchandising at Quincy, in this state, until the 19th of April, 1839, when their partnership was dissolved, of which notice was given at the above date in a newspaper published at Quincy. Both the defendants resided at that place.

The plaintiff is a citizen of St. Louis, in Missouri. From the indorsements on the bill it would seem that this suit is brought for the benefit of the Bank of St. Louis. It is not pretended that either the bank or the plaintiff had any dealings with the defendants during their partnership. And the only question is, whether such notice of the dissolution of the partnership has been given to exonerate Tilson from liability on the bills. They were drawn by his late partner, Pitkin, and signed in the name of the partnership.

§ 248. *Two kinds of notice of dissolution of partnership. Without one kind dissolution not effective, even as to strangers. English authorities. Publication in the Gazette.*

There are two modes of giving notice of the dissolution of a partnership, which shall put it out of the power of either partner to bind the other. The first is a special notice, by circular or otherwise, of the dissolution, to those persons with whom the partnership had had dealings. This is the safer and more advisable course. And until this notice be given, either expressly or constructively, the partnership may be still bound after the dissolution. And the partners are bound, where the act purports to be a partnership act, without notice, whether it be done with a customer or a stranger.

The second mode of giving notice is by a publication in a gazette. This publication of the dissolution is admissible as evidence, but Mr. Gow, in his Treatise on Partnership, page 280, says that it is of little avail unless it be shown that the party entitled to notice was in the habit of reading the Gazette. Godfrey v. Turnbull, 1 Esp. N. P. C., 371; Leeson v. Halt, 1 Starkie, N. P. C., 186. He says, indeed, that an advertisement in a common newspaper is not even admissible, without proof that the party took in the paper. In the case above cited from 1 Starkie, Lord Ellenborough said that he would receive evidence of the advertisement in the gazette, but that, unless it were proved that the party was in the habit of reading the Gazette, the evidence would be of little avail. And his lordship was of opinion that the advertisement in the Times was not admissible at all, without proof that it was taken in by the party. From these remarks it would seem that the Gazette was the paper in which such notices usually appeared or were required to be published, and, therefore, a notice published in that was admissible in evidence on a different principle from a notice in the Times.

In the case of Jenkins v. Bizard, 1 Starkie, 418, the notice in the Gazette being read, the defendants proved that a similar advertisement had been inserted once in the Morning Chronicle, and, also, that the plaintiffs took in the latter paper. Lord Ellenborough was of opinion that it was admissible, and referred to a case where a party was sought to be affected with notice of an advertisement contained in a weekly provincial paper; in that case the paper was not only delivered at the house, but the party was seen to read it. Upon the whole his lordship submitted the evidence to the jury, and informed them that it was for them to say whether, under all the circumstances, the plaintiffs had notice. He, at the same time, remarked it would be a more prudent course to send circulars to all with whom the parties had dealings.

The court of king's bench, however, have recently decided in the case of Wright v. Pulham, 2 Chitt., 121, that notice in the Gazette is notice to all the world of the dissolution of a partnership. In that case it did not appear that the party had had actual notice of the dissolution. This decision conflicts with some of the *nisi prius* decisions above cited, and, of course, overrules them. And from this decision the law seems to be now settled in England, although the report of the case is very short and unsatisfactory, that a publication in the Gazette is sufficient notice of the dissolution of a partnership. And that the question there now is, not whether notice was, in fact, given to the party, but whether it was published in the Gazette. It is known that newspapers are sold in London by the carriers, and not delivered to subscribers as in this country. This, however, can make no difference as to the publication of the notice.

§ 249. *Published notice conclusive upon persons who have had no previous dealings with the firm, but not upon others.*

In the case of Lansing v. Ten Eyck, 2 John., 300, it was held that a notice of the dissolution in the public papers is conclusive upon all persons who have had no previous dealings with a copartnership. But as to such persons as have had dealings with a copartnership it is not so to be considered, unless, under the circumstances, it appears satisfactory to the jury that it operated as a notice. Bristol v. Sprague, 7 Wend. Rep., 423; Graves v. Merry, 6 Cowen, 701; 6 John. Rep., 147, 148; Mowatt v. Howland, 3 Day, 353; Martin v. Walton, 1 McCord, 16.

Prudence requires, when an individual by his act assumes the right to bind another, that some inquiry should be made into his power to do so. And even to a stranger, and especially a bank, to whom the bill was negotiated. It would seem not to impose an unreasonable diligence to inquire whether a partnership, which formerly existed, is still subsisting. The court instructed the jury that if they shall find there was, in good faith, a dissolution of the copartnership between the defendants, and that notice was published of the same, on the 19th of April, in a newspaper of general circulation, at Quincy, it was sufficient to discharge Tilson from liability in this action.

LOVEJOY v. SPAFFORD.

(3 Otto, 430–442. 1876.)

Error to U. S. Circuit Court, District of Minnesota.

Opinion by Mr. Justice Hunt.

Statement of Facts.— The action was by the holder of two drafts dated September 27, 1870, drawn by J. B. Shaw upon J. B. Shaw & Co., and accepted in the name of J. B. Shaw & Co. The object of the action was to charge Lovejoy as a partner. The firm of J. B. Shaw & Co. was formed on the 15th day of April, 1868; transacted a lumber business at Davenport, Iowa, and continued until the 12th day of May, 1870, when it was dissolved by an instrument in writing. In fact, Lovejoy was not a member of the firm of J. B. Shaw & Co., nor was there in existence such a firm when the drafts were accepted in its name. The acceptance in the firm name was a fraud on the part of Shaw.

The questions arising upon the bill of exceptions grow out of the sufficiency of the notice of the dissolution of the firm given by the retiring member.

Formal notice was given to all those who had previously dealt with the firm. It does not appear whether there had been any change of signs, nor whether the firm had any external sign.

No evidence was given that notice of the dissolution was published in any newspaper; and it was proved that two daily papers were published in Davenport at the time of the dissolution. After that time the business was carried on in the name of J. B. Shaw alone.

Prior to the present transaction, the plaintiffs, in discounting its paper, had heard of the firm, and who were its members. They testified that they had no information of the dissolution till some time after its occurrence. The drafts in suit were given for lumber sold by the plaintiffs and by one Mead, were drawn by Shaw, and accepted by him in the name of the firm at Read's Landing, where the lumber was sold. There was no evidence that the firm had ever had any other transaction at Eau Claire or Read's Landing. No evidence was given of the relative position of the places in question; but from the maps and gazetteers we learn that Eau Claire is in the interior of the state of Wisconsin, and distant several hundred miles from Davenport, in the state of Iowa. Read's Landing is not far from Eau Claire.

The case was tried by the circuit court upon the theory that, to discharge a member of a firm from the claim of one who had had no dealing with it prior to its dissolution, but who knew of its existence and who were its members, it was necessary that the latter should have received actual notice of the dissolution, or that notice should be published in a newspaper at the place of business. This doctrine was not announced in terms, but such was the result of the trial. Either of these notices were held to be sufficient; but it was held that, without one of them, the retiring member could not protect himself. In terms, the holding of the judge was, that there must be either actual notice or public notice; and it will be seen from the offers and exclusions presently to be stated, that this public notice could mean only a newspaper publication.

Thus the witness Barnard, after testifying that he had been in business at Davenport prior to May 12, 1870, until the time of the trial; that he had business relations with all the lumber dealers at that place, and knew them all; and that he knew of the dissolution when it occurred,—was then asked whether or not it was generally known at Davenport at the time the firm was dissolved that such dissolution had taken place. To which the plaintiffs objected, on the ground that the same was incompetent and immaterial; which objection was sustained, and the defendant Lovejoy excepted, and his exception was noted.

Defendants' counsel then asked the witness: "State whether or not it was generally known at this time along the river that this dissolution had taken place." To which plaintiffs made the same objections as before; and the objection was sustained, and an exception taken by defendant Lovejoy, and noted.

Defendants' counsel then asked the witness: "Did you at or near the time of the dissolution communicate the fact that it had occurred to any persons other than the plaintiffs; and, if so, to whom, and in what manner?" To which the plaintiffs made the same objection as before; which objection was sustained, and an exception was taken and noted for the defendant Lovejoy.

Counsel for defendant Lovejoy stated, in connection with the questions to the witness Barnard, that he did not expect to prove actual notice of the dissolution to the plaintiffs, or to the persons who sold the lumber.

John C. Spetzler was sworn as a witness in behalf of the defendant, and testified that in May, 1870, he was in the employment of J. B. Shaw & Co., in their yards at Davenport, as salesman; that the business was conducted after the dissolution by Shaw, in the name of J. B. Shaw.

The defendant proposed to prove by the witness that the dissolution, immediately upon its occurrence, was a matter of general repute and knowledge in the city of Davenport, where the firm did business, and that all lumber dealers in Davenport were informed of it. To which plaintiff objected, on the grounds that the same was incompetent and immaterial; which objection was sustained. To which the defendant Lovejoy excepted, and his exception was noted.

Sumner W. Farnham, not a partner, was sworn on behalf of the defendant, and testified that, in September, 1870, and before the transaction in question, he visited Eau Claire in company with J. B. Shaw; was there two or three days and called on the lumber dealers of that place. The witness was then asked whether on that occasion he or Shaw gave any notice to the lumber dealers at Eau Claire of the dissolution of the firm of J. B. Shaw & Co. If so, to whom and in what manner?

To which the plaintiffs objected, on the grounds that the same was incompetent and immaterial, unless the defendant proposed to prove actual notice to plaintiffs, or to those who sold the lumber, or notice by publication in a newspaper. The objection was sustained by the court; and the defendant Lovejoy excepted, and his exception was noted.

The defendant then offered to prove by this witness, that, while he and Shaw were at Eau Claire on this occasion, and before the sale of the rafts in question, the said Shaw, in the presence of the witness, notified all, or nearly all, of the lumber dealers in Eau Claire, where plaintiffs then lived and did business, and in the vicinity, that the firm of J. B. Shaw & Co. had dissolved, and that Farnham & Co. had sold out to Shaw.

To which the plaintiffs objected, on the grounds that the same was immaterial and incompetent, unless the defendant proposes to show actual notice to the plaintiffs, or to those who sold the lumber; which objection was sustained, and the defendant Lovejoy excepted, and his exception was noted.

§ 250. *Notice required in case of dissolution of a partnership. Review of authorities.*

In Pratt v. Page, 32 Vt., 11, cited as an important case, it was held that, to entitle a plaintiff to recover in a case like the present, these facts must appear: 1. The claimant must have known at the time of making his contract that there had been a partnership. 2. That he did not then know of its dissolution. 3. That he supposed he was entering into a contract with the company when he made it. In the court below the plaintiff recovered, on the ground of want of sufficient notice of dissolution; but in the appellate court that question was not reached.

In City Bank of Brooklyn v. McChesney, 20 N. Y., 240, the bank having had previous knowledge of the existence of the firm of Dearborn & Co., of which the defendant, McChesney, was a member, discounted a note made in the firm name, but after the partnership was in fact dissolved, without knowledge or information on the part of the bank; it was held, there being no publication of dissolution, that the retiring partner was liable. The court makes no examination of the law, but adopts as the basis of its judgment the opinion of Senator Verplanck in Vernon v. Manhattan Company, 22 Wend., 183.

In that case Senator Verplanck made use of this language: "Now, following out this principle, how is a person, once known as a partner, to prevent that inducement to false credit to his former associates which may arise after the withdrawal of his funds, from the continued use of credit which he assisted to obtain? How shall he entitle himself to be exempted from future liability on their account? The natural reply is, he must take all the means in his power to prevent such false credit being given. It is impossible for him to give direct notice of his withdrawal to every man who may have seen the name of his former firm, or have accidentally received its check or note. No man is held to impossibilities. But he does all he can do in such a case by withdrawing all the exterior indications of partnership, and giving public notice of dissolution in the manner usual in the community where he resides. He may have obtained credit for his copartnership by making his own interest in it known, through the course of trade. So far as those are concerned who have had no direct intercourse with the firm, he does all that is in his power to prevent the continuance and abuse of such credit, if he uses the same sort of means to put an end to that credit which may have caused it. But there are persons with whom he or his partners may have transacted business in the copartnership name and received credit from. To such persons he has given more than a general notice of the partnership; for he has directly or indirectly ratified the acts of the house, and confirmed the credit that may have been given, either wholly or in part, upon his own account. He knows, or has it in his power to know, who are the persons with whom such dealings have been had. Public policy, then, and natural justice, alike demand that he should give personal and special notice of the withdrawal of his responsibility to every one who had before received personal and special notice, either by words or acts, of his actual responsibility and interest in the copartnership. Justice requires that the severance of the united credit should be made as notorious as was the union itself. This is accomplished by the rule that persons having had particular dealings with the firm should have particular notice of the dissolution or alteration, but that a general notice, by advertisement or otherwise, should be sufficient for those who know the firm only by general reputation." Both the senator and the chancellor, and the court in McChesney's case, agree in the opinion that persons who merely take or receive for discount the paper of a firm are not to be deemed dealers with the firm, so as to be entitled to actual notice.

In Bristol v. Sprague, 8 Wend., 423, which was an action against a retired partner upon a note made after the dissolution, Nelson, J., says, "It is well settled that one partner may bind another after dissolution of the firm, if the payee or holder of the note is not chargeable with notice, express or constructive, of the disolution of the partnership (6 Johns., 144; 6 Cowen, 701); and that such notice must be specially communicated to those who had been customers of the firm, and as to all others by publication in some newspaper in the county, or in some other public and notorious manner."

In Ketcham v. Clark, 7 Johns., 147, Van Ness, J., said, "In England it seems to be necessary that notice should be given in a particular newspaper, the 'London Gazette,' but we have no such usage or rule here. I think, however, we ought at least to go so far as to say that public notice must be given in a newspaper of the city or county where the partnership business was carried on, or in some other way public notice of the dissolution must be given. The reasonableness of it may, perhaps, become a question of fact in the particular case."

Mr. Parsons, in his Treatise on Partnership, pp. 412, 413, gives this rule: "In respect to persons who have had dealings with the firm, it will be necessary to show either notice to them of a dissolution or actual knowledge on their part, or at least adequate means of knowledge of the fact. As to those who have not been dealers, a retiring partner can exonerate himself from liability by publishing notice of the dissolution, or by showing knowledge of the fact." He adds: "A considerable lapse of time between the retirement and the contracting the new debt would, of course, go far to show that it was not, or should not have been, contracted on the credit of the retiring partners."

Mr. Justice Story, in his work on Partnership, says the retiring partner "will not be liable to mere strangers who have no knowledge of the persons who compose the firm, for the future debts and liabilities of the firm, notwithstanding his omission to give public notice of his retirement, for it cannot be truly said, in such cases, that any credit is given to the retiring partner by such strangers." Sec. 160. In a note he discusses the doctrine as laid down by Bell and Gow, and adheres to the rule as above announced.

Mr. Watson says that to dealers actual notice must be given; as to strangers, he says, "An advertisement in the 'London Gazette' is the most usual and advisable method of giving notice of a dissolution to the public at large." Watson on Part., 385.

In his Commentaries on the Law of Scotland, Professor Bell, in speaking of a notice to dealers, says, "An obvious change of firm is notice, for it puts the creditor on his guard to inquire, as at first. So the alteration of checks or notes, or of invoices, is good notice to creditors using those checks or invoices." As to notices to strangers, he says, "As it is impossible to give actual notice to all the world, the law seems to be satisfied with the 'Gazette's' advertisement, accompanied by a notice in the newspaper of the place of the company's trade, or such other fair means taken as may publish as widely as possible the fact of dissolution." The "Gazette" notice he holds to be one circumstance to be left to the jury. 2 Bell's Com., 640, 641.

In Wardwell *v.* Haight, 2 Barb. S. C., 549, 552, Edmonds, J., says, "The notice must be a reasonable one. It need not be in a newspaper. It may be in some other public and notorious manner. But whether in a newspaper or otherwise, it must, so far as strangers and persons not dealers with the firm are concerned, be public and notorious, so as to put the public on its guard."

§ 251. *Notice of dissolution, to protect a retiring partner as to persons who have not previously dealt with the firm, must be a reasonable one. It need not be either actual notice to plaintiff, or publication in a newspaper.*

In view of these authorities, we are of the opinion that the rule adopted by the judge on the trial of this cause was too rigid. We think it is not an absolute, inflexible rule, that there must be a publication in a newspaper to protect a retiring partner. That is one of the circumstances contributing to or forming the general notice required. It is an important one; but it is not the only or an indispensable one. Any means that, in the language of Mr. Bell, are fair means to publish as widely as possible the fact of dissolution; or which, in the words of Judge Edmunds, are public and notorious to put the public on its guard; or, in the words of Judge Nelson, notice in any other public or notorious manner; or, in the language of Mr. Verplanck, notice by advertisement or otherwise, or by withdrawing the exterior indications of partnership and giving notice in the manner usual in the community where he resides,— are means and circumstances proper to be considered on the question of notice.

§ 252. *It is competent, as evidence of notice of dissolution, to prove that the fact had been made known to most dealers in that vicinity.*

When, therefore, the defendant proved that actual notice had been given to all those who had dealt with the firm; that all subsequent business was carried on in the name of the remaining partner only, thus making a marked change in the presentation of the firm; when the claimants received and obtained the draft at a distance of several hundred miles from the place where the firm did business, and there was no evidence that the firm had ever before transacted any business in that place,— we think the evidence offered should not have been excluded. When the defendant offered to prove that it was generally known along the Mississippi river that the dissolution had taken place, and offered evidence showing to whom, to what extent, and in what manner, notice had been given; that all the lumber dealers in Davenport were notified and knew of the dissolution; that at Eau Claire, on the occasion of the transaction in question, and before the drafts were made, notice was there given to all, or nearly all, of the lumber dealers in that place that the firm had been dissolved,— we think the evidence was competent to go before the jury.

The question is not exclusively whether the holders of the paper did in fact receive information of the dissolution. If they did, they certainly cannot recover against a retired partner. But if they had no actual notice, the question is still one of duty and diligence on the part of the withdrawing partner. If he did all that the law requires, he is exempt, although the notice did not reach the holders. The judge held peremptorily that there must be either actual notice or public notice,— in effect that it must be through a newspaper,— and excluded other evidence tending to show a public and notorious disavowal. In this we think he erred.

He refused to admit evidence which would have sustained the fifth request to charge, that, if the notice was so generally communicated to the business men of Eau Claire as to be likely to come to the claimants' knowledge, the jury are at liberty to find such knowledge. In this we think he erred.

Without prescribing the precise rule which should have been laid down, we are of the opinion that the errors in the rulings were of so grave a character that a new trial must be ordered.

<h3 style="text-align:center">TROY IRON AND NAIL FACTORY v. WINSLOW.</h3>

(Circuit Court for New York: 11 Blatchford, 513–519. 1874.)

Opinion by WOODRUFF, J.

STATEMENT OF FACTS.— A suit was begun, and has hitherto been prosecuted, against Erastus Corning, John F. Winslow and James Horner, doing business as copartners, and, as such copartners, being the proprietors of, and carrying on their business at, what was known as the Albany Iron Works, for an injunction to restrain the use by them of a machine for which the complainant held letters patent theretofore granted to Henry Burden, and to compel the said defendants to account for and pay to the complainant the profits realized by the defendants from the use of the said machine by them at the works aforesaid. The complainant had an interlocutory decree therein, declaring the rights of the complainant, awarding an injunction, and decreeing that the defendants account for such gains and profits. For the purposes of such accounting, a reference was ordered, to ascertain the amount of such gains and profits, such accounting was had, and the master's report filed. Exceptions to such report were filed and were argued, and the opinion of the court upon the exceptions has been filed (6 Blatchf., 328), but no final decree has been entered. Afterwards, Erastus Corning, one of the defendants, died, leaving a last will and testament, wherein he appoints Erastus Corning, Junior, executor. Thereupon, the complainant, preparatory to a final decree, and with a view to an appeal therefrom, moved this court that the said executor be substituted as defendant in the place of his testator, and that the cause proceed against such executor, and the other defendants in the suit, "in the same manner that it would proceed were the said Erastus Corning, deceased, still living." That motion was denied. The complainant has now filed a bill of revivor, setting out the proceedings in such suit, alleging its abatement by the death of the said Erastus Corning, and praying that the same be revived against the said executor, etc. The executor has answered, and, by stipulation, the parties have agreed upon certain facts, and the case has been brought to a hearing upon pleadings and proofs.

§ 253. *Where a patent has been infringed by a partnership, the profits, considered as a trust fund, constitute a partnership liability for which the partnership is bound, and which is in its nature ex contractu.*

Upon consideration of the facts disclosed by the pleadings and proofs, in substance as above recited, I adhere to the views which governed the decision of the motion heretofore made in the principal cause. The theory of the case made by the complainant, and by the proofs, etc., is, that the original defendants, as copartners, by the unlawful use of the invention, the exclusive right to the use of which was vested in the complainant, have realized gains and profits which rightfully and in equity belong to the complainant; that in equity they were liable to be treated as trustees, receiving those profits to the use and for the benefit of the complainant; and that the defendants were, therefore, in equity, debtors of the complainant to the amount of such gains and profits. No question of damages sustained by the complainant by the wrong done arises in such case. When the original bill was filed, and when the decretal order was made, the law did not permit the recovery of damages in such a suit. To recover damages, a patentee must go to a court of law, treat the defendants as tort-feasors, and establish his damages, which, being proved, might be recovered, whether the defendants had made any profits by their infringement of the patent or not. The subsequent alteration of the law by a statute which enables the complainant in a suit in equity to recover damages does not apply to this case nor affect the present litigation. The original defendants then, as copartners in the business of manufacturing, etc., have received gains and profits, for which they have been required to account to the complainant, and for which he is entitled to ask a final decree. Those gains and profits constitute a debt due by the copartnership to the complainant. The liability is, in equity, in its nature, *ex contractu*, and a copartnership liability or obligation.

§ 254. *Upon the death of one of several partners, defendants, the suit does not abate.*

On the death of Erastus Corning his two copartners survived him. The copartnership property became, on such decree, vested in them, and the copartnership liabilities devolved upon them, as survivors. The suit, therefore, did not abate. Nothing was necessary but a suggestion of the death of Erastus Corning, and the suit would thereupon proceed against the others. This is a familiar elementary principle, and there is nothing in an equity suit founded on letters patent, and a prayer for an account of the profits arising from the infringement thereof, which withdraws this case from its operation. The fact that the infringement was a tortious act, and the original defendants were tort-feasors, and might have been so treated, will not help the complainant. He did not so treat them, and, so far as the tortious nature of the defendants' acts gave character to the defendants or their liability, the inference is the other way. As tort-feasors, they may have been severally liable, and, being so, it would be even more plain that the suit did not abate, and that the survivors are separately liable.

§ 255. *A creditor of a partnership cannot proceed against the estate of a deceased partner while the surviving partners are solvent. English cases reviewed and criticised.*

There is no allegation or claim that those survivors are not solvent, or that the copartnership assets are not entirely sufficient for the satisfaction of the complainant's demand. Some modern English cases have held that a creditor of a copartnership may proceed in equity against the survivors and the representatives of a deceased copartner, in the same suit, for the recovery of a copartnership debt, and indicate that this may be done without first resorting to the copartnership fund or the surviving partners, and without showing that they are insolvent. See Wilkinson v. Henderson, 1 Mylne & K., 582; Devaynes v. Noble, 2 Russ. & M., 495. In other cases, the creditor was held entitled to pursue the estate of the deceased where the survivors had become bankrupt, and without reference to the state of the accounts between the partners or the fund in the hands of the assignees of the bankrupt survivors. See Devaynes *v.* Noble, 1 Meriv., 529; Vulliamy *v.* Noble, 3 id., 592. The case of Wilkinson *v.* Henderson is pointed in its declaration that, in a suit in equity by a creditor of the copartnership against the representatives of a deceased partner and the survivor, the complainant is entitled to satisfaction out of the assets of the deceased, although it be not shown that the surviving partner is insolvent; and it was held that, in that suit, no decree could be made against the surviving partner, but against the assets of the deceased only, because the liability of such survivor was at law, and when that was the case, equity could not even render a decree against such survivor and the representatives of the deceased jointly, but the decree must be against the estate of the deceased alone. The decision was by the master of the rolls, and his opinion does not, it seems to me, very satisfactorily meet the grounds upon which the contrary doctrine rests. The copartnership property is the primary fund for the payment of the copartnership debts. That fund has passed to, and the title therein has become vested in, the survivors, and in their hands it is held in equity in trust for the payment of those debts. At law, confessedly, the representatives of the deceased are not liable at all, and the survivors are solely liable, and there is, in ordinary cases, no reason for going into equity until legal remedies have been exhausted, or, at least, until it is shown that they will be unavailing; and this latter consideration has the same force, in an original suit in equity, to charge the copartnership with a debt as if the original remedy was at law. *Non constat,* that a decree against the survivors, and, through them, to reach the fund presumptively in their hands, will not be completely effectual. They hold, and are legally entitled exclusively to hold, in this case, the very fund which the complainant seeks to recover. No case is cited showing that the doctrine somewhat loosely, as I think, indicated in the English cases above referred to has been adopted or followed in this country, and, so far as I have observed, the rule is held otherwise and in conformity with what I have already above stated.

Where it is shown that the survivors are insolvent, then, indeed, the court of equity will entertain a bill to charge the separate estate of the deceased partner, and, under statutes which limit the time for the presentation of claims to an estate in course of settlement and distribution before a surrogate or in courts of probate, and which statutes authorize and require that all claims be so presented, they may, perhaps, be received and allowed, lest they be barred pending a litigation with the survivors (Camp *v.* Grant, 21 Conn., 41); but, waiving such possible qualifications, it is held that the creditors of the copartnership have no claim, even in equity, to payment out of the estate of the deceased partner, unless the surviving partners are insolvent, nor even then, as held in some cases, and by law-writers, though not without conflict of decision, until the separate creditors of the deceased are satisfied. The United States bankrupt law, section 36, makes a like provision. Surely this case is not to be incumbered by an endeavor to marshal the assets of the deceased copartner, the defendants' testator. Thus, in Trustees, etc., *v.* Lawrence, 11 Paige, 80, the chancellor notices that there are some recent cases in England in conflict with the decisions in this country, and hold that a creditor of a copartnership cannot file a bill in equity against the representatives of a deceased copartner without showing that the survivors are insolvent, or showing some other ground of necessity for such a proceeding. The case of

Wilder *v.* Keeler, 3 Paige, 167, proceeds upon the like principle, and upon the necessity, as the case may be, of marshaling the assets in favor of creditors of the separate estate of the decedent. The case of The Trustees, etc., *v.* Lawrence was considered further on appeal to the court of errors (2 Denio, 577), the recent English cases were reviewed, and the decree of the chancellor was unanimously affirmed. Numerous cases in this country are cited to show that the doctrine upon which alone the decision seems to have been placed in England, viz., that the liability of copartners is joint and several, is not sustained in this country so as to warrant any such conclusion as was drawn therefrom. That their liability is not solely joint, in such sense that the death of a copartner terminates his liability, so that his estate can, in no event, be charged, must be conceded, but it is not several in such sense that a several action, either at law or in equity, can be maintained against his representatives on mere proof of a copartnership liability.

Thus, in Sturges *v.* Beach, 1 Conn., 509, it is said that it is only on the failure of the survivors that the estate of the deceased can be made liable in equity. In Alsop *v.* Mather, 8 Conn., 584, apparently overlooking some of the cases already decided in England, it is said that " there is no case in England or in this country, in law or in equity, of pursuing the effects of a deceased partner while the surviving partner is solvent." The same rule is affirmed in the opinion of the court in Filley *v.* Phelps, 18 Conn., 294. The cases of Lang *v.* Keppele, 1 Binn., 123; Caldwell *v.* Stillman, 1 Rawle, 212, and Hubble *v.* Perrin, 3 Ham. (Ohio), 287, are cited to the same effect. The cases of Van Reimsdyk *v.* Kane, by Mr. Justice Story, 1 Gall., 371 (Eq., §§ 919–29), and Pendleton *v.* Phelps, 4 Day, 481, in the circuit courts of the United States, affirm the same rule, and so does the case of Bennett *v.* Woolfolk, 15 Geo., 213. In the opinion of the court in Bloodgood *v.* Bruen, 4 Seld., 362, 371, the same doctrine is positively stated, and it is declared that, until the insolvency of the copartner, no cause of action exists against the estate of the deceased, and that it is by such insolvency the cause of action accrues against such estate, and, therefore, that the statute of limitations does not begin to run in favor of the estate until the cause of action has so accrued. So late as the year 1858, the subject was again considered in the court of appeals of this state, after the enactment of our code of procedure (which, however, has no application to suits in equity in the federal courts, under the fifth section of the act of congress of June 1, 1872, 17 U. S. Stat. at Large, 197). In that case, the court again review the cases in England, above adverted to, and collate most of the cases in this country above mentioned, and hold that the personal representatives of a deceased partner cannot be joined as a party defendant with the surviving partner, in an action for a partnership debt, where the complaint does not show the complainant's inability to procure satisfaction from the survivor. The bill herein must be dismissed, with costs.

REGESTER *v.* DODGE.

(Circuit Court for New York: 19 Blatchford, 79–89. 1881.)

Opinion by BENEDICT, J.

STATEMENT OF FACTS.— In this case I have listened to a re-argument, and have re-examined the question upon which, as I suppose, the case turns, and my opinion remains unchanged, that the plaintiff is not entitled to recover.

The earnestness of the contention made in behalf of the plaintiff has impelled me to state at length the reasons for my conclusions.

The action is a suit in equity brought by the administrator of David Regester, who disappeared in the year 1870, and is supposed to be dead, against Harry E. Dodge, executor of Edward Dodge, for the purpose of charging the estate of Edward Dodge with the amount of certain deposits of money made by David Regester, in the year 1869, with the firm of Jay Cooke & Co., of Philadelphia, of which firm Edward Dodge was then a member. ·

The material facts are as follows: At the time of the deposits in question, the banking firm of Jay Cooke & Co., of Philadelphia, was composed of William G. Morehead, Henry D. Cooke, Pitt Cooke, George C. Thomas, Harry C. Fahnestock, John W. Sexton and Edward Dodge. This firm dissolved January 1, 1871. John W. Sexton and Edward Dodge then retired from the business, and a new firm was formed, consisting of the remaining members of the old firm, and two new members, Jay Cooke, Jr., and James A. Carhart. The new firm succeeded to the business of the old firm, the account with the retiring members was made up and settled, and the new firm then assumed all the obligations of the old firm, and agreed that the liability of the retiring members therefor should be terminated.

The new firm continued business until November 26, 1873, when it was adjudged bankrupt. Among the debts of the new firm, published in the bankruptcy proceedings of that firm, was the debt here sued on. In June, 1873, this debt was, without objection, proved as a debt of the new firm in the bankruptcy proceedings of that firm by the representative of David Regester.

Upon this debt so proved dividends were from time to time declared out of the assets of the new firm of Jay Cooke & Co., and the same were received by the representative of David Regester. In the year 1879 the estate of the new firm was wound up under the direction of the trustees, in accordance with the provisions of the bankrupt law, and the stocks then constituting the assets of the new firm were distributed among the creditors of that firm in pursuance of a scheme assented to by the creditors. Edward Dodge died in 1877. During his life-time no claim of liability for the deposits in question was made upon him in any form so far as appears. In September, 1878, and prior to the distribution of the stocks by the trustees of the new firm, payment of this debt was demanded by the representative of David Regester of the executor of Edward Dodge, who then denied the existence of the debt as a liability of Edward Dodge. Thereafter the representative of David Regester participated in the distribution of the stocks belonging to the new firm of Jay Cooke & Co., made by the trustees thereof, and, as a creditor of that firm, received sundry shares of various stocks, which he forthwith, and on June 12, 1879, sold at private sale without notice to the executor of Edward Dodge. The amount of the cash dividends received from the estate of the new firm, together with the amount realized from the sale of the stocks distributed by direction of the trustees of that firm, not being equal to the amount of the deposits made in 1869 by David Regester, this action is brought by his representative to charge the estate of Edward Dodge with the deficiency.

The law of the case is not doubtful. By the deposits made in 1869 with the old firm of Jay Cooke & Co., Edward Dodge, then a member of that firm, became liable for the amount thereof. That liability continues unless facts be shown from which an intention on the part of the creditor to accept the liability of the new firm in lieu of the liability of the old firm can be fairly inferred. The question, therefore, is whether the facts above stated are sufficient to warrant the conclusion that the liability of the new firm was so accepted by the plaintiff.

§ 256. *Slight evidence is sufficient to establish the fact that a creditor of an old firm whose debts have been assumed by a new firm has accepted such new firm as his debtor. Novation of the debt. Cases cited.*

In disposing of questions of this character courts have frequently held that when the dissolution of an old firm has occurred, and a new firm has agreed to assume the liabilities of the old firm, but slight circumstances are required to justify finding an intention on the part of a creditor of the old firm, who has notice of the dissolution and of the agreement by the new firm to accept the liability of the new firm in place of the liability of the old. In *Ex parte* Williams, Buck, 13, the court, speaking of such a case, say: "A very little will do." In *In re* Smith, Knight & Co., L. R., 4 Ch. App., 671, Lord Justice Giffard says: "There is no doubt whatever, that if you have an old firm, and either a new partner is taken into it, or a new firm constituted, and the assets are taken over by that new firm, and the customer, knowing all these circumstances, afterwards goes on and deals with the new firm, you infer from slight circumstances an assent on his part to accept the new firm as his debtors." In *In re* Family Endowment Soc., L. R., 5 Ch. App., 118, speaking of a case very like the present, it was said that very slight evidence would be required to establish that the creditor had taken the liability of the new firm instead of the old.

§ 257. *Failure of creditor to object upon being notified of purpose to release retiring partner and to substitute new firm as debtor, as evidence of assent to such arrangement.*

What, then, are the circumstances in this case tending to show assent by the plaintiff to the novation of the debt sued on? In the first place it will be observed that, from the time of the publication of this debt as a debt of the new firm of Jay Cooke & Co., the creditor — and the representative of David Regester was then the creditor, authorized to collect and discharge the debt — knew that the old firm of Jay Cooke & Co. had dissolved; that Edward Dodge and John W. Sexton had retired from the business; that a new firm had been formed, containing members who were not members of the old firm; and that such new firm had agreed to assume all the liabilities of the old firm. The creditor is also chargeable with knowledge that the purpose of this agreement made by the new firm was to relieve the outgoing parties from their liability for the debts of the old firm. The nature of the agreement itself disclosed that to be its object.

This knowledge on the part of the creditor is not without significance in ascertaining his intention. If it had been the intention of the creditor to maintain intact the then existing liability of the retired partner, such an intention would naturally have evoked from the creditor, when he came to deal with the new firm, in respect to this debt, some positive expression of a purpose to avoid a substitution of the liability of the new firm in place of the liability of the old. The proofs here fail to show that any expression of such a purpose in any form escaped from this creditor.

§ 258. *Lapse of time as a proof of the acceptance of the new firm and release of the old as debtor.*

The next circumstance deserving attention is the time which elapsed before any attempt was made to enforce the debt as a subsisting liability of Edward

Dodge. The deposits sued on came to be known at the time of the bankruptcy of the new firm of Jay Cooke & Co., in 1873. Edward Dodge lived until 1877 without the suggestion of a continuing liability on his part for this debt from any source. There is no evidence that he was insolvent or absent; and the omission to make a claim upon him in his life-time, the other members of the old firm being insolvent, is hardly consistent with the position now assumed, that there was no intention to accept the liability of the new firm in lieu of the old. Furthermore, no claim was made on the executor of Edward Dodge until September, 1878, when the estate of the new firm of Jay Cooke & Co. was substantially wound up, which seems to indicate that the making of the demand upon the executor of Edward Dodge had some connection with the result of the bankruptcy proceedings of the new firm, and gives rise to the suggestion that the intention to maintain a liability on the part of Edward Dodge was an afterthought.

In cases of this description, delay in asserting the liability of an outgoing partner, when coupled with a dealing with the new firm, has often been deemed to be a circumstance tending to show an intention to discharge the liability of the old. In *In re* Smith, Knight & Co., already cited, it is said that the time which has elapsed may be most material.

§ 259. *Proving debt in bankruptcy against a firm as evidence of acceptance of such firm as the debtor and consequent release of retiring partners of the old firm. Cases cited.*

The next circumstance deserving attention is of more significance. Indeed, it is one that in some of the cases has been considered to be of itself conclusive. This circumstance is, that when the existence of these deposits was disclosed in the bankruptcy proceedings of the new firm, the creditor, knowing that he was dealing in respect to the assets of a new firm which had agreed to assume the debts of the old firm for the purpose of extinguishing the liability of the old firm, adopted the new firm as his debtors for this very debt. This he did in the most formal way, by proving the deposits made by David Regester with the old firm as a debt of the new firm. The proof was not of a liability by reason of property or money received by the new firm, to be applied to the discharge of debts of the old firm; but the original deposits were proved as a ground of liability. This adoption of the new firm as the debtors, coupled with the omission, during the life-time of the retired partner, to indicate, by word or deed, the existence of a liability on his part for the debt in question, and coupled with the lapse of time that occurred before the liability of the retired partner's estate was asserted, appear to me to be sufficient, according to the requirements of the cases already cited, to justify the inference that the new firm was adopted as debtor with the intention that the liability of that firm was to stand in place of the liability of the old.

In some of the adjudged cases less proof than is here presented has been considered sufficient to warrant a similar inference.

In Hart *v.* Alexander, 2 Mees. & Wels., 489, Follett, *arguendo*, says that if the creditor, by some positive act, adopts a new firm as his debtor, the retired partner is discharged. And Lord Abinger, in giving judgment, states, as the result of the cases, that, if a new partner comes in, and an account is accepted in which the new partner is made liable for the balance, that discharges the old firm, as both cannot be held liable at once for the same debt.

In *In re* Medical Invalid and General Life Assurance Soc., Spencer's Case, 24 L. T. R., 455, the circumstance that the new company and the customer had treated each other as insurer and insured was held to be "complete evidence of novation."

In *In re* Smith, Knight & Co., already cited, the case was made by the master of the rolls to turn upon the question whether the company had been adopted as debtor. He says: "I am of the opinion that Gibson & Co. thus adopted the company as their debtors. It is useless to go into the cases, because it is admitted that very small circumstances are sufficient to establish such adoption." The decision of the master of the rolls in that case was reversed by the court of appeal upon the ground that the circumstance from which the master of the rolls found that there had been an adoption of the company as debtor was not sufficient to warrant that conclusion; but there was no dissent from the proposition of the master of the rolls that an adoption of the company as debtor by the creditor, with knowledge, was a fact decisive of the case.

In Kerwan v. Kerwan, 2 Cromp. & Mees., 627, the opinions of Lyndhurst and Bolland proceed upon the assumption that the consent of the creditor to take the new firm as debtors would be conclusive. In Brown v. Gordon, 16 Beav., 309, great stress is laid upon a fact, which appears in this case also, that the partners had settled with each other, treating the debt as a debt of the new firm.

The conclusion that a novation of the debt in question was effected, and the liability of Edward Dodge therefore extinguished, is not at variance with any of the cases upon which the plaintiff relies. In Harris v. Farwell, 15 Beav., 31, the creditor proved against the new firm an original obligation of the new firm, based upon money paid the new firm to the use of the creditor. The case is made to turn upon the particular form of the proof of debt. In Hall v. Jones, 56 Ala., 493, it is said: "Proof, if made, that the accounts against the old firm were restated against the new, would be strong evidence from which an agreement" (to release the retired partner) "might be inferred." In principle, that is this case. The debt due from the old firm of Jay Cooke & Co. was by the creditor restated against a new firm, and that for the purpose of sharing in the distribution of the estate of a firm known to be in nowise liable for the debt, except by reason of an agreement to assume it, made for the purpose of releasing their retired partner from liability.

In Heath v. Hall, 4 Taunt., 326, the case put is that of proving the joint debt in the bankruptcy proceeding of one of two joint debtors, and suing the other debtor in an action at law. This is not such a case. In Devaynes v. Noble, Sleech's Case, 1 Meriv., 563, the question decided was whether delaying for the space of eight months after the death of one partner, and meanwhile accepting part of the debt from the surviving partners, who were liable for the whole, was evidence of the transfer of the credit to the surviving partners.

In Daniel v. Cross, 3 Ves., 277, the only act done, as stated by the court, was receiving interest from the surviving partners. In Harris v. Lindsay, 4 Wash., 100, the liability of the outgoing partner was clearly shown to have been extinguished, and so the court decided. In the same case (id., 273) it is said that no delay to pursue the outgoing partner, which falls short of an agreement, express or implied, to take the paying partner as a debtor, will discharge the retiring partner; and the decisive question is stated to be whether the plaintiff had conformed to the agreement made between the parties at the dissolution, and the decisive fact considered to be that the paying partner was to be credited with the notes when paid. In the present case we have an express adoption of a new and different firm as the debtors, and a credit to that firm of part payment of the debt.

It is not seen that any difference arises from the circumstance that the acquiescence in the arrangement made between the old firm and the new, for a transfer of the liability of the old debts to the new firm, occurred after the new firm had become bankrupt, and not before. No inference is created by that delay, because David Regester, the depositor, disappeared before the new firm was formed, and the existence of the deposits was not known until the bankruptcy. The representative of David Regester, upon learning of the debt and of the agreement by the new firm to assume it, had the right to take the benefit of that agreement, and to accept the new firm as debtors in place of the old firm. The acts and omissions under consideration were, in law and in fact, those of the creditor, and so they have been treated here.

§ 260. *Right of retired member in equity to be notified and otherwise enabled to secure himself against loss.*

I now proceed to consider this case in another aspect, which, as it seems to me, is also fatal to the plaintiff's claim. The suit is in equity. The plaintiff applies for equitable relief, but his claim is inequitable. This plainly appears. In 1873, when the new firm of Jay Cooke & Co. went into bankruptcy, and the plaintiff was called on to act in respect to the debt sued on, it was open to him at once to assert the liability of Edward Dodge for the debt in question. Had he then done so, and had the liability of Edward Dodge been then established, a right on the part of Edward Dodge to become a creditor of the new firm in the bankruptcy proceeding would have arisen. This was a substantial right lost to Edward Dodge by unexcused delay on the part of the plaintiff. Still more, if, instead of dealing with this debt as an existing liability of the new firm alone, the liability of Edward Dodge had been asserted and maintained before the estate of Jay Cooke & Co. was wound up, those shares of stock which the plaintiff received for this debt would have passed to Edward Dodge or his representative, with, of course, the election to sell or to hold them. It is obvious that the distribution of those stocks was not made for the purpose of enabling the creditors to turn them at once into money. That could have been done by the assignee in bankruptcy. The object of the distribution was to give the creditors an election to sell or to hold those stocks. This, too, was a substantial benefit. Its value in this case appears by the fact that the stocks distributed to the plaintiff as creditor of the new firm are now equal in value to the debt proved against the new firm by the plaintiff. The plaintiff has seen fit, without any cause assigned, to adopt a course by which the right to vote as a creditor in the bankruptcy proceeding was lost to Edward Dodge, and his representative deprived of the power to secure his estate against loss.

Having, without cause, delayed asserting the liability of the outgoing partners during a period of some five years, whereby the party was deprived of an opportunity to take part in the bankruptcy proceedings of Jay Cooke & Co., and to reimburse himself from the estate of that firm, the plaintiff cannot now ask a court of equity to exercise its power in his behalf. The right here claimed is an equitable right only, and it may, therefore, be met by equitable circumstances. *Ex parte* Kendall, 17 Ves., 522.

I have not overlooked the fact that the defendant did at one time make demand on the representative of Edward Dodge for the payment of the debt now sued on. But this demand was not made until 1878, when the distribution of the estate of Jay Cooke & Co. had been determined upon, and, when made, it was not enforced; on the contrary, the defendant's denial of liability was apparently acceded to, for the plaintiff commenced no suit at that time, and after that time received the stocks distributed by the trustees of Jay Cooke & Co., and sold them at private sale without notice.

Attention should also be called to the fact that the plaintiff makes no tender of the stocks he so received. He who asks equity must do equity. If, at this late day, the estate of Edward Dodge is to be charged with the debt in question, equity demands of the plaintiff that he transfer to the estate of Edward Dodge the stocks which Edward Dodge would have been entitled to receive if his liability had been asserted in his life-time. The plaintiff does not do this. All that he offers is to credit the amount of the cash dividends and the proceeds of the private sale of those stocks. Manifestly, in view of the evidence respecting the value of those stocks, it would not be for his advantage to make tender of them now. But only in that way can he do equity. Failing to do this, his prayer cannot be granted.

Let an order be entered dismissing the bill, with costs.

COOK v. ROGERS' ADMINISTRATOR.

(Circuit Court for Ohio: 8 Federal Reporter, 69–79. 1880.)

Opinion by SWING, J.

STATEMENT OF FACTS.— This suit is brought to recover of the defendant the amount of two promissory notes — the first, given by the Sectional Dock Company to the order of Thomas P. Morse & Co., for $12,000, dated June 4, 1873, and payable at ninety days; the second, given by Thomas P. Morse and John D. Daggett to the Sectional Dock Company, for $4,000, dated April 4, 1873, and payable at ninety days,— both of which were indorsed, and of which it is alleged that the plaintiff is now the holder and owner.

The petition alleges, in substance, that on the 17th day of November, 1857, Rowland Ellis, Jr., Patrick Rogers, John Daggett, Thomas Morse and Mary Thomas formed a copartnership in the city of St. Louis, in the state of Missouri, for the purpose of carrying on the business of docking and repairing steamboats and other vessels in said city; that it was provided in the articles of copartnership that in the event of the death of either party to said agreement said copartnership should not be dissolved, but the interest of said deceased partner should be continued and represented by the legal representatives of said deceased partner; that the name should be "The Sectional Dock Company;" that said copartnership carried on business under said agreement until the 5th day of December, 1870, when said Patrick Rogers died in the city of Cincinnati, leaving a will, which was duly admitted to probate in Hamilton county, Ohio; that by the terms of said will, Robert C. Rogers was appointed executor of his estate, and was directed to continue the interest of decedent in the said Sectional Dock Company, at St. Louis, until the same could be disposed of; that said Robert C. Rogers did continue the said business as executor, representing the interests of the estate of said Patrick Rogers in said partnership until his death, when the defendant, Joseph Rogers, was appointed administrator of said estate, with the will annexed; that said Robert C. Rogers, as executor of said Patrick Rogers, deceased, took possession, by virtue of the will of said Patrick Rogers, of the interest of said estate in the Sectional Dry Dock Company, at St. Louis, and of the Marine Railway & Dry Dock Company, of Cincinnati, and of the Louisville & Cincinnati Mail

Line Company, and that he collected dividends therefrom, and that the estate realized large sums of money from the second and third properties so mentioned, and still holds interests therein undisturbed, and that whatever sums have been realized by said estate from either of said properties is liable for the debts contracted in carrying on the others, and especially for the claims sued on in this case; that by the laws of the state of Missouri, where said copartnership was formed and where the notes were executed, the liability of partners is joint and several, and therefore each partner is liable separately upon a debt of said firm.

To this petition the defendant has filed an answer containing three separate defenses, the second of which is only necessary to be noticed, and is as follows:

" For a further defense to said first cause of action, he says it is true that prior to the 5th day of December, 1870, said Patrick Rogers was a partner in the copartnership known by the name of the Sectional Dry Dock Company named in the petition.

" He says it is true that the persons named in the petition entered into written articles of copartnership on said 17th day of November, 1857, and that said written articles of copartnership contained the following provision, to wit: ' It is further agreed that, in the event of the death of either party to this agreement, this copartnership shall not on that account dissolve, but the interest of such deceased party may be continued and represented by the legal representatives of said deceased party, or otherwise disposed of by them.'

" He says that this is the only agreement relating to said partnership. He admits the death of Patrick Rogers, the execution and probate of his will, and the appointment of Robert C. Rogers as executor, and of defendant as administrator, with the will annexed; that the only clause in said will authorizing the continuance of said copartnership after the testator's death is as follows: ' It is my will and direction that my share and interest as one of the partners in the Louisville & Cincinnati Mail Line Company, and also my share and interest as one of the partners in the Marine Railway & Dry Dock Company, of Cincinnati, and also my share and interest as one of the partners in the Sectional Dry Dock Company, of St. Louis, Missouri, shall not cease nor said partnership be determined by reason of my death, but that my share and interest in each of said partnerships shall continue and be kept up and represented by the executor of this my will, in my stead, until such time as in his judgment it shall be most advantageous for my estate to sell out or settle up and close the said shares and interests respectively, and to that end I do hereby fully authorize, empower and direct the executor of this my will to hold, manage and represent all my shares and interests in said companies, respectively, for the benefit and use of those who shall be entitled to my estate, until such time as in his discretion and judgment it shall be most advantageous for my estate to sell or close and settle the same, and then to sell out my shares and interests in said companies, or either of them, or settle and close the same by agreement with the partners, whichever he considers best, and upon such terms and for such price as he shall deem proper and sufficient.' "

A similar provision is made in said will as to the testator's share of stock in the Niles Works.

Said will next makes provision for the testator's sister, Letitia McNamara, and then follows the residuary clause in said will, as follows:

" Subject to the foregoing provisions, and to the dower, distributive share, and allowance for my wife provided by law, I give and devise to each of my five children, Robert, Sarah, Thomas, Joseph, and Fenton, one-sixth part, respectively, of all the residue of my estate, to them and their respective heirs, subject, however, to the following deductions: From the share of Robert, $6,750, being the amount heretofore advanced to him by me; from the share of Sarah, $6,750, being the amount advanced to her; and the other and remaining equal one-sixth part thereof, less the sum of $5,000 heretofore advanced to my deceased daughter, Mary, I give and devise to my said son, Thomas, and his heirs, to hold the same in trust for the two children of my said deceased daughter, Mary, until they become of age, and upon their becoming of age to convey to each, respectively, the equal one-half of said one-sixth part of my estate, and in the meantime to apply the income of their respective shares to their proper education and maintenance, so far as necessary, and the surplus, if any, to invest and hold upon the same trust and use."

Said will also provides for the payment of the testator's debts, and authorizes his executor to spend money to purchase, for the benefit of his estate, the fee-simple title to the Merchants' Hotel property, in Cincinnati, and to complete all contracts of the testator for the purchase or sale of real estate; that the clauses of said will quoted and referred to are all the parts of said will relating to the disposition of the testator's estate. And the defendant says that the said executor had no power, under said will, to invest any part of the estate of said testator, in said copartnership, the Sectional Dock Company, except that which was so invested in the life-time of said testator, and that said will does not render the estate of the testator not already invested in said partnership liable to the payment of any debts of said partnership contracted after said testator's death. He says that said will limits the responsibility of said testator's estate for debts of said partnership to be contracted after his (said testator's) death to that part of said estate already embarked in said partnership at the death of said testator, and he denies that said estate is liable to the plaintiff beyond the amount of its property and assets embarked in said copartnership. To this point the plaintiff demurs generally. Two questions are involved in the determination of this demurrer: *First.* By virtue of the contract of partnership and the provisions of the will, did the general estate of the testator become liable for debts contracted by the partnership after the death of the testator? *Second.* If it did not, did that part of the estate belonging to and arising out of other partnerships, which it is claimed the executors were authorized to continue, become liable for the debts of this partnership?

§ 261. *Provision in partnership articles against dissolution by death of partner. Construction and effect of.*

Did this liability of the general estate arise out of the terms of the agreement creating the partnership? The agreement was not for any definite number of years; there could be no question, therefore, that the death of either partner, of itself, would dissolve the partnership; but, even if it had stipulated for duration of a particular period, the death of either partner within that period would have worked its dissolution, unless expressly stipulated that it should not have that effect.

This agreement provides simply against that result by saying that "in the event of the death of either party to this agreement this copartnership shall not, on that account, be dissolved, but the interest of such deceased party may be continued and represented by the legal representative of said deceased party, or otherwise disposed of by them." It does not provide that it shall be continued notwithstanding the death, but that it may be. There is no binding obligation upon the part of Patrick Rogers that this copartnership should continue after his death; it does not in terms fix and extend any liability upon him or his estate after his death. And it seems to me very clear that if he had died intestate, and his administrator had undertaken to have carried on this partnership with the general assets of the estate, he could not, under this clause, have been justified in doing so. It would have been the exercise of a discretion and power which, as against the individual creditors and the heirs of the intestate, could not have been supported.

§ 262. —— *similar provision in will. General direction to executor to continue business does not render general assets of estate liable.*

Does, then, the will, in connection with this agreement, or without it, give such power as to make his general estate liable? The clause of the will by which it is claimed this result is produced is: "It is my will and direction that my share and interest as one of the partners in the Louisville & Cincinnati Mail Line Company, and also my share and interest as one of the partners in the Marine Railway & Dry Dock Company, and also my share and interest in the Sectional Dry Dock Company, of St. Louis, Missouri, shall not cease, nor said partnership be determined, by reason of my death, but that my share and interest in each shall continue and be kept up and represented by the executor of this my will, in my stead, until such time as in his judgment it shall be most advantageous for my estate to sell out and settle up and close up the said shares and interests respectively. And to that 'end I do hereby fully authorize and empower and direct the executor of this my will to hold, manage and represent all my shares and interest in said companies respectively, for the benefit and use of those who shall be entitled to my estate, until such time as in his discretion and judgment it shall be most advantageous to sell or close and settle the same, and then to sell out my said shares and interest in said companies, or either of them, or settle and close the same by agreement with the partners, whichever he considers best, and upon such terms and for such price as he shall deem proper and sufficient."

The testator then provides for a sister, and then provides that "subject to the foregoing provisions, and to the dower, distributive share, and allowances for my wife provided by law, I give and devise to each of my five children, Robert, Sarah, Thomas, Joseph and Fenton, one-sixth of all the residue of my estate," and to the children of a deceased daughter one-sixth, subject to certain deductions to be made to some of them for advance payments he had made.

So far as the authority to carry on these several partnerships is provided for by this will, it speaks of his shares and interests in them, and they are to be continued and kept up and represented by the executor until such time as shall be most advantageous to sell them and settle them up; not to continue the business of these firms generally and indefinitely by the use of his general assets, but only to continue the interests which he then had in them, and that only to such times as they could be most advantageously sold or closed up. But if it were doubtful, from the language used in this clause, whether the testator intended to limit the carrying on of this business to the funds already embarked in it, the residuary clause of the will, when taken in connection with this, seems to show such intention, for this disposes of all the balance of his property to his children and grandchildren.

Mr. Lindley, in his work on Partnership, 1105, says: "It is now, however, clearly settled that the extent of the liability of the testator's estate does not exceed the amount authorized by him to be employed in the trade or business directed by him to be carried on." And again, on the same page, he says: "A general direction to carry on a business in which a testator was engaged does not authorize the employment for that business of more of his assets than was embarked in that business when he dies." Justice Story, in delivering the opinion of the supreme court of the United States in Burwell v. Mandeville, 2 How., 560–577 (Est. of Dec., §§ 1650–54), says: "And this leads us to remark that nothing but the most clear and unambiguous language, demonstrating in the most positive manner that the testator intends to make his general assets liable for all debts contracted in the continued trade, would justify the court in arriving at such a conclusion, from the manifest inconvenience thereof, and the utter impossibility of paying off the legacies bequeathed by the testator's will, or distributing the residue of his estate, without, in effect, saying at the same time that the payments may all be recalled if the trade should become unsuccessful or ruinous. Such a result would ordinarily be at war with the testator's intention in bequeathing such legacies and residue, and would or might postpone the settlement of the estate for half a century, or until long after the trade or continued partnership should terminate."

Mr. Parsons, in his work on Partnership, treats the continued partnership as a new partnership, and on page 454 says: "So the creditors of the new partnership have no claim whatever upon and no interest in the general assets of the deceased, or any part of them, but that which he expressly placed in the new partnership." And to the same effect is the doctrine of *Ex parte* Garland, 10 Ves., 109, 110; Pitkin v. Pitkin, 7 Conn., 307; and Lucht, Adm'r, v. Behrens, 28 O. S., 231.

I think, therefore, that neither by the agreement nor will does the law make the general assets of the estate liable for the debts of this partnership contracted after the death of the testator.

§ 263. *Debts of one partnership continued after death of partner not payable from profits derived from others continued in same manner.*

Does, then, the provision of the will in regard to the other partnerships, and the fact that the executor collected dividends, and that the estate has derived large sums of money from them, make such incomes liable for the debts contracted after the death of the testator by this particular partnership? There may be more difficulty in this proposition, but it seems to me that it can hardly be maintained. It is true that, for the time being, the shares and interest in these partnerships are placed in the management of the executor; but they are separate and distinct partnerships — separate and distinct in their formations and purposes, composed, so far as we know, of separate and distinct members, and there is nothing in the pleadings which shows that by their articles of co-partnership there was any provision by which they should be continued, not-withstanding the death of any of its members. Neither is there anything in the pleadings which shows that these partnerships are solvent or insolvent, or whether there may be outstanding debts against them. If they are insolvent, or there be debts of them unpaid, it would be more equitable that the separate income of each should be applied to the payment of its separate indebtedness. But, aside from this, the provisions of the will are that the shares and interest of the testator in them should be continued, not generally, but until they could be most advantageously disposed of and settled up. And, although the term "kept up" is used by the testator, it does not seem from the will that it was the intent of the testator that they should be kept up by his general estate, or by taking the profits and dividends arising from either and appropriating them to the payment of the losses and debts of the other. And, unless it was his intent that this should be done, I do not think that the mere fact that there had been some dividends received by the estate of a deceased partner from one or more of these partnerships would entitle a creditor to a judgment against his estate upon an indebtedness contracted by another partnership long after his death. Parsons on Part., 454; *Ex parte* Garland, 10 Vesey, 109, 110. Persons dealing with partnerships are presumed to look to the partnerships themselves, and not to the estates of its deceased members, for the payment of debts contracted after such decease.

I think, therefore, that upon this ground the demurrer cannot be sustained. The demurrer is therefore overruled.

DENVER v. ROANE.

(9 Otto, 855–861. 1878.)

APPEAL from the Supreme Court of the District of Columbia.

Opinion by MR. JUSTICE STRONG.

STATEMENT OF FACTS.— The bill filed in this case was not an ordinary bill for the settlement of partnership accounts. James Hughes, the complainant's testator, and James W. Denver and Charles F. Peck were in partnership as attorneys and counselors-at-law from 1866 until the 18th of March, 1869. On that day it was agreed between them virtually that the general partnership should terminate; that thereafter no new business should be received in partnership, and that any coming to the firm through the mails should be equitably divided. The agreement, however, contained a stipulation that the business of the firm theretofore received and then in hand should be closed up as rapidly as possible by the members of the firm "as partners, under their original terms of association and in the firm name."

Soon after, on the 13th of August, 1869, a further agreement was made to the effect that in case of the death of any one of the partners, his heirs or personal representatives, or their duly authorized agent, should receive one-third of the fees in cases nearly finished, and twenty-five per cent in other partnership cases. Denver acceded to this second agreement, with the understanding that before any such division should be made, at any time, all partnership obligations should be first satisfied, proposing no new terms, only stating the legal effect. We think this was a closed contract.

It is upon these two agreements the bill is founded. Hughes died on the 21st of October, 1873, and Roane, the executor of his will, has brought the present suit for a discovery, and to recover from the surviving partners the share of the testator in the fees received by them out of the partnership business which remained unfinished when the general partnership was dissolved. A decree having been entered against the defendants in the court below, they have appealed to this court, and have assigned numerous errors. Of most of them it will be necessary to say but little, and, indeed, in regard to most of them there has been hardly any controversy between the parties during the argument.

§ 264. *Representatives of deceased law partner may maintain suit against survivors for discovery and an account, notwithstanding agreement as to closing up unfinished business and the fact that all the business is not yet closed up.*

It is first insisted by the appellant that the court below had no competency or jurisdiction to entertain a bill for such relief as is prayed for, nor to give such a decree as the court gave, whereby it attempts to settle and close the affairs of a partnership by decreeing specific sums as legally due, and if so demandable at law, and providing for the further continuance of the partnership and collection by virtue of its decree of other like sums until the business of the partnership may end. Such is the first assignment of error. The objection misapprehends the nature of the case made by the bill, overlooks the facts, and does not state accurately the decree. That a bill in equity may be maintained by the personal representatives of a deceased partner against the survivors to compel an account, so far as an account is possible, and for a discovery of the partnership property which came to their hands, is undeniable, and such was the object of the present bill. When the firm was dissolved in March, 1869, for general purposes, the agreement of dissolution stipulated that, as to the business then in hand, the members of the firm should continue partners and should close it up. What that business was the present defendants only could know, after the death of Hughes, for it was then left in their hands, and they only could know what fees had been received on account of it. A bill for discovery, as well as for distribution of the fees received, was, therefore, plainly within the province of a court of equity. And as the partners had agreed, as they did by the agreement of August, 1869, to divide those fees in certain proportions, it was quite competent for the court to enforce fulfillment of the contract, so far as was possible when the decree was made. The court did not attempt to make a complete settlement of the affairs of the partnership. In the nature of the case that was impossible. Some of the partnership business remained unfinished, and fees uncertain in amount were yet to be collected. But so far as fees had been collected, the right to immediate distribution was complete. The agreement did not contemplate that all the fees collected might be held by the surviving partners until all the partnership business should be brought to an end, and it was, therefore, quite proper to reserve consideration of the fees yet to be received after they shall have been earned.

§ 265. *Surviving partner of a firm of lawyers is not entitled to an extra allowance for services in closing up the business, when an agreement has been made as to the division of fees in case of death. Quære, whether law partnership is different from any other in respect to such allowances.*

An objection raised by several other assignments of error (particularly the sixth, seventh, eighth, ninth, eighteenth and nineteenth) is, in substance, that the court erred in applying to a partnership between lawyers and claim agents the principles of the law of commercial partnerships, in regard to the modes of settlement of the same after the death of a partner, and in regard to the neglect of the business of such a firm by a partner; that by the decree no compensation is allowed to the survivors for carrying on the unfinished business, but that they are required to continue it as well for themselves as for the benefit of the deceased partner's estate. We think these objections to the decree ought not to be sustained. We are not convinced that during his life Hughes (except perhaps in reference to a single case in charge of the firm) was guilty of such neglect or violation of his duty to his partners as should deprive him or his personal representative of a right to share in the profits of the partnership. In regard to the work done and the fees received after his death, the parties, by their agreements, prescribed the rule for determining their rights as against each other. Having jointly undertaken the business intrusted to the partnership, all the parties were under obligation to conduct it to the end. This duty they owed to the clients and to each other. And as to the unfinished business remaining with the firm on the 18th day of March, 1869, the duty continued. The agreement provided for that. Now in reference to this duty the law is clear. " As there is an implied obligation on every partner to exercise due diligence and skill, and to devote his services and labors for the promotion of the common benefit of the concern, it follows that he must do it without any rewards or compensation, unless there be an express stipulation for compensation." Story, Partn., secs. 182, 331; Caldwell v. Leiber, 7 Paige (N. Y.), 483. So it is held that where partnerships are equal, as was true in the present case, and there is no stipulation in the partnership agreement for compensation to a surviving partner for settling up the partnership business, he is entitled to no compensation. Brown v. McFarlam, Executor, 41 Pa. St., 129; Beatty v. Wray, 19 id., 516; Johnson v. Hartshorne, 52 N. Y., 173. This is the rule in regard to what are commonly called commercial partnerships, and the authorities cited refer to those. There may possibly be some reason for applying a different rule to cases of winding up partnerships between lawyers and other professional men, where the profits of the firm are the result solely of professional skill and labor. No adjudicated cases, however, with which we are acquainted recognize any such distinction. And in the present case, as we have said, the parties made arrangements for the work and results of work after the death of any of their number. The agreement of August 13, 1869, provided that in case of the death of any partner, one-third of the fees in cases nearly finished, and one-quarter of the fees in other partnership cases, should belong to the representatives of the decedent. Of course it was contemplated that the surviving partners should finish the work, and that no allowance should be made to them beyond the share of the fees specified in the agreement.

§ 266. *Where one of a firm of lawyers refuses to take any part in a case and withdraws his name, neither he nor his administrator is entitled to any part of the fee as against either his copartners or the client.*

The most important objection to the decree which has been urged by the appellant is that it adjudged to the complainant one-third of the fee collected by the defendants in the case of Gazaway B. Lamar against the United States, including the claim of D. A. Martin. That case was in charge of the firm before the agreement of March 18, 1869, was made, and was commenced in 1868. It was, therefore, one of the cases within the purview of the agreement of August 13, 1869. Hughes' name appeared on the record as attorney and counsel with the appellants for the claimant. But on the 9th of January, 1873, he came into court and asked that his name be erased as such attorney, and that he have leave to withdraw his appearance and sever his connection with the cause. His motion was allowed, and his appearance was then withdrawn. The appellants, however, went on with the case. Briefs were filed for the claimant on the 21st of March and the 22d of April, 1873, the case was argued on the 20th of May, and on the 2d of June next following the court entered a judgment for the claimant. An appeal was then taken to this court, which was subsequently dismissed. After the withdrawal of his appearance and the severance of his connection with the cause, Hughes took no part in prosecuting the claim, neither in the court of claims nor in the supreme court, and he paid no attention to it. He quarreled with Lamar, and about the time he withdrew from the cause he denounced the claim privately to one of the judges of the court of claims as altogether without merit and a fraudulent case, or words to that effect, and said that he had decided not to be involved in a case of so scandalous a character, and for so worthless or unworthy a client. In regard to the question of fees in the case the judge testifies "he declined to have any interest in the case, or to take fees, because he believed the case was a corrupt one and not likely to succeed, and that he would not lose much by his withdrawal from the case."

The question presented by this state of facts is whether, inasmuch as the case was afterwards conducted by the appellants to final success, and they received a fee from Lamar, the claimant, Hughes, would be entitled to any part of the fee were he now living. If not, certainly his personal representative cannot be now. The recovery of the claim was undertaken by the firm without any agreement respecting fees. By undertaking it the firm and each member of it assumed to conduct the case to a final conclusion, and with all fidelity to the client. Such was the contract of Hughes with Lamar, as completely as if he had been the sole attorney and counsel employed. And as the contract was entire, he could not have abandoned it after a partial performance, and still have held the other party bound. Much less could he have accompanied his abandonment by denouncing the honesty of the claim to one of the judges of the court whose province it was to find the facts and adjudicate upon its merits, and yet claim compensation for services rendered. Such conduct on his part was not merely a renunciation of his engagement to the client. It was a flagrant breach of professional duty. It was not in his power to refuse performance of his part of the implied contract with Lamar, take action hostile to the claim, and still hold Lamar bound. Certainly he could not hold Lamar directly liable. And we do not perceive that, in equity, his situation is any better because he had contracted with the client jointly with his copartners.

If, then, by abandoning the case and denouncing it as fraudulent, he lost all the right which he had against Lamar, how can he claim from his copartners any of the compensation they obtained for conducting the case after his abandonment to final success? His action was a breach of his duty to those partners, as well as of his obligation to Lamar. By the agreement of copartnership he had undertaken to share in the labor, and to promote the common interests of the firm, and that was the foundation of his right to share in its earnings. It may be that mere neglect of his duty would not have extinguished that right, but a repudiation of his obligations, refusing to act as a partner, or to perform the functions of a partner, is quite a different thing. It may well be considered as a repudiation of the partnership. It was said in Wilson *v.* Johnstone, 16 Eq. Ca. Abr., 606, "He who acts so as to treat the articles as a nullity as it regards his own obligations cannot complain if they are so treated for all purposes." It may, therefore, very justly be held that by his action Hughes became a stranger to the case, and repudiated any relation he had previously held to it as a partner in the firm. The partnership ceased as respects that claim. The other partners who continued to attend to the case could charge the client nothing for his services, for as the contract was contingent on success, nothing was due to any partner until success was attained. They certainly could claim nothing for services rendered by him after he severed his connection with the case, for he rendered none; and if he had any just claim on a *quantum meruit* for services rendered before, it was against Lamar, and not against his copartners.

We think, therefore, the decree of the court below was erroneous, in so far as it allowed to the complainant any part of the fee collected from Lamar or from Martin, who owned a part of what was recovered in the Lamar suit. We discover no other fault in the decree, but for this the case must be sent back for correction.

The decree of the supreme court of the District will be reversed, and the record remitted with instructions to enter another decree in conformity with this opinion; and it is so ordered.

§ 267. **How effected.**— If one of two partners interested in a patent assign his interest in the patent to a third party, such assignment works a dissolution of the partnership and the parties interested in the patent are left simply to their rights under it. Parkhurst v. Kinsman, 1 Blatch., 498.

§ 268. In Illinois certain formalities are necessary to the dissolution of a special partnership. If they be not complied with the dissolution does not take effect as to creditors, and the partnership still continues. *In re* Terry, 5 Biss., 110.

§ 269. Where several persons owning land jointly were sought to be held as partners upon a contract made by one of them with a broker to pay him a certain commission to sell the land, and evidence was offered of admissions made by such alleged partner after the land had been sold, *held*, that the evidence was incompetent upon the ground that the partnership, if any, was dissolved by the sale of the land, and after dissolution the admissions of a partner do not bind the firm. Thompson v. Bowman,* 6 Wall., 316.

§ 270. On the formation of a partnership between A. and B., real estate belonging to A. was put into the business at an estimated value, each partner was credited on the books with half of that amount, and B. became indebted to A. in a corresponding sum. No conveyance of the half interest was made to B., but A. gave him an acknowledgment in writing that one-half of the property was held in trust for him, and B. gave back a mortgage to secure the agreed price. The property, which was a brewery situated in Japan, was sold under a decree, made in a suit brought by B., dissolving the partnership, and, as there was apparently no one in the country besides A. and B. who wished to engage in the brewing business, and B. had no means, A. was the only bidder at the sale and bid in the property at a very low figure, the result being to leave B. indebted to A., when, if the property had brought what it was worth, there would have been something coming to B. *Held*, upon appeal from the decree ordering a sale, that the property was partnership property, and that the only proper mode of winding up the partnership was by a sale of it; that if B. had any ground of complaint regarding the manner of conducting the sale, such complaint could not be considered except upon appeal from other decrees made subsequent to that appealed from. Wiegand v. Copeland,* 7 Saw., 442.

§ 271. —— **by war.**— Though the war of the rebellion commenced as to certain states, including Louisiana, on April 19, 1861, yet it was not until August 16, 1861, that all commercial intercourse between the states at war was interdicted and became unlawful; and a partnership between citizens of the states at war was not dissolved *ipso facto* until that day, and an acceptance of a bill of exchange before August 16, 1861, bound all the members of the firm. Matthews v. McStea, 1 Otto, 7.

§ 272. A partnership between the citizens of two belligerent states is dissolved by war. A citizen residing in a hostile country should return as soon as possible, and if he holds partnership relations with citizens of such hostile country should sever them, dispose of his interest and withdraw his effects, for if suffered to remain in the hostile country his property or interest becomes impressed with the national character of the belligerent where it is situated. Prize courts usually apply these rules as to partnership effects of citizens or neutrals suffered to remain in the enemy country. The share of a citizen in a ship sailing under the enemy's flag, which he had opportunity to dispose of, is therefore subject to capture and condemnation. And where the cargo is the property of the same owners, it is subject to the same rule. The William Bagaley, 5 Wall., 377.

§ 273. A declaration of war, or commencement of actual hostilities, which is equivalent thereto, between two nations, *ipso facto* dissolves the partnership relations existing between citizens of the hostile states. Planters' Bank v. St. John, 1 Woods, 585.

§ 274. Where a member of a partnership in one of the insurgent states removed within the federal lines, adhering to the United States, all partnership relations between him and the members of said firm who remained in the insurgent states were dissolved, whether the latter engaged in the rebellion or not. It was not in the power of the parties to continue the partnership. It was void, and no notice of dissolution was necessary. *Ibid.*

§ 275. —— by decree in bankruptcy.— A decree in bankruptcy against a member of a firm dissolves the partnership, and the assignee becomes tenant in common with the solvent partner. The property remains in the hands of the surviving or solvent partner, clothed with a trust, to be applied by him to the discharge of the partnership obligations, and to account to the representatives of the bankrupt partner for his share of the surplus. *In re* Norcross,* 5 Law Rep., 124; 1 N. Y. Leg. Obs., 100.

§ 276. When fraudulent.— Where a firm was confessedly insolvent, and one member, for a consideration, retired, leaving the other member in custody of the goods, with power to collect claims due from customers, said remaining member assuming the payment of liabilities of the firm, and the dissolution was advertised, *held*, that it became competent for a court of equity, under section 2 of chapter 175 of the code of Virginia, to avoid the transfer and to take charge of and administer the effects according to the equities of the case. Johnson *v.* Straus, 4 Hughes, 621.

§ 277. One partner may transfer his interest in a firm to his copartner, but such transfer may be impeached by bill in equity brought by the partnership creditors, and the court may, upon a proper showing, set it aside, with a view to a sale and distribution of the proceeds according to equity. *Ibid.*

§ 278. Rights, duties and liabilities of surviving partner.— The surviving partner has the control and management of the partnership real estate for the purpose of satisfying the trusts which rest upon it. He may rent it and receive the rents, may sell it and receive the purchase money, and convey to the purchaser, not only the legal and equitable title in himself, but the equitable title which he holds as trustee as surviving partner, and if the sale be a fair and *bona fide* one and for a fair consideration, the court will compel the party holding the legal title under the deceased partner to convey such legal title to the holder of the equitable title, and thereby make the title complete. Kleine *v.* Shanks,* 8 Cent. L. J., 799.

§ 279. Upon the death of a member of a firm, the surviving member has the right to control the assets of the firm, including stock in a corporation, and represent the same until the final and complete closing up of the old company. If a new partner is introduced into the company and obtains an interest in the stock by its being carried into the new company as an asset, then either partner may represent it. If it does not become part of the assets of the new firm, the relation of the surviving partner of the old firm to it, as assets of the old firm, is unchanged. Kenton Furnace Railroad & Manuf'g Co. *v.* McAlpin, 5 Fed. R., 737.

§ 280. If one of two partners has authority, after the dissolution of the firm, to collect the debts, and he opens a new account with a debtor of the firm, charging him with the balance due to the firm and giving him credits for payments and goods received, and there is found a balance in his favor, this balance is due to the bankrupt and not to the firm. Oxley *v.* Willis, 1 Cr. C. C., 436.

§ 281. By the dissolution of a partnership, provision being made in the articles of dissolution for the payment, equally, of all the creditors of the firm, by the partner who purchases the interest of the retiring partner, and continues the business, such partner is a trustee for the creditors of the firm; and a subsequent assignment, by such partner, of the partnership effects, preferring certain creditors to others, and contrary to the stipulation in the articles of dissolution, is fraudulent and void. Marsh *v.* Bennett, 5 McL., 117.

§ 282. In the absence of fraudulent intent, partners may dissolve a partnership, sever their interest in the property, or one partner sell out his interest to the other, and the partner continuing the business and owning the goods may claim his exemption as though no partnership had existed, although at the time of dissolution the liabilities of the partnership far exceeded their assets. *In re* Bjornstad,* 18 N. B. R., 282.

§ 283. A sole surviving partner can make a valid transfer by deed of trust in the nature of a mortgage of personal property, belonging to the partnership, to secure the payment of a partnership debt. Bohler *v.* Tappan,* 1 McC., 184.

§ 284. In the case of the death of one partner, his representatives have a right to require the survivor to apply the joint property to pay the joint debts; and if he becomes bankrupt, the joint creditors may insist that this shall be done. *In re* Clap, 2 Low., 168.

§ 285. The administrator of a deceased partner has no right to claim a debt due to the partnership. It is the right of the surviving partner to settle up the concerns of the firm. Wickliffe *v.* Eve, 17 How., 468.

§ 286. Where a partner buys his copartner's interest and binds himself to appropriate the goods on hand to the payment of the debts of the firm, he becomes a trustee for the other partner and for the creditors. Sedam *v.* Williams, 4 McL., 51.

§ 287. When a partnership was dissolved, and while it was in liquidation, the liquidating partner bought with his own means, in the firm name, under which he was then doing business alone, certain cotton which was subsequently captured and sold; he was held to be the owner, and entitled to the proceeds, in a suit brought by him before the court of claims. Low v. United States,* 7 Ct. Cl., 515.

§ 288. A decree in favor of the representatives of a deceased partner against surviving partners should not charge defendants with the value of the assets at the exact time of the decedent's death, but only with such sum as the assets would, by reasonable diligence in closing up the partnership affairs, produce. Moore v. Huntington,* 17 Wall., 417.

§ 289. Neither should defendants be charged with the value of partnership real estate the title to which is left in the decedent's heirs. Ibid.

§ 290. —— as to negotiable or other instruments.— Where a firm has failed, and a member in conducting the settlement of the affairs of the company gives a note payable to himself on demand after date, with interest and indorsed by him, and no demand was made until nearly five years after date, it was held that the private estate of the indorser, in bankruptcy, was not liable for the amount. In re Grant,* 6 Law Rep., 158.

§ 291. If the holder and payee of the note of a firm upon its becoming worn exchanges it for another note, signed in the firm name, after the death of one of the partners, with no intention of changing the original liability, the new note will not in bankruptcy be construed as the separate note of the surviving partner who signed it, but the amount may be proved as a claim against the joint estate of the partners. In re Clap,* 2 Low., 226.

§ 292. In this country, although the law is different in England, after dissolution neither partner can bind the other by a note or bill. But where a note was thus given by a partner who was authorized to settle all demands by or against the firm, and his copartner afterwards agreed to pay the note, held, that the latter was bound by his ratification if not otherwise. Draper v. Bissel,* 3 McL., 275.

§ 293. Where the course of business between a factor and his principals was for the principals, upon shipments of goods, to draw bills for the estimated value thereof, which the factor would pay, although he had not sold the goods, and charge interest on the advances thus made, held, that shipments made by a surviving partner, after the death of the other partner, could not be applied by the factor to the liquidation of the general indebtedness of the principals to him at the time of the dissolution by death, but must be applied first to meet bills drawn upon the credit of such shipments, and the surplus only applied to the general indebtedness. Dick v. Laird,* 5 Cr. C. C., 328.

§ 294. But if the bills thus drawn by the surviving partner and paid by the factor exceed the net proceeds of the cargoes shipped after the dissolution of the firm, the excess is not chargeable to the estate of the firm, but to the survivor only, it not being competent for him to charge the estate of the firm by drawing bills after the dissolution. Ibid..

§ 295. Where one partner receives authority by the advertisement, giving notice of the dissolution of the firm, to settle all accounts for and against the firm, it is bound by his settlements, though he may not be authorized to give a new instrument for the payment of the amount. Draper v. Bissel,* 3 McL., 275.

§ 296. One member of a dissolved partnership cannot be held upon a bill of exchange drawn by another member in his individual name after the dissolution, although the proceeds of the bill went to pay debts of the firm which the drawer had assumed upon dissolution, and although notice of the dissolution was not given. Le Roy v. Johnson,* 2 Pet., 186.

§ 297. Rights of creditors.— Partnerships are often dissolved on terms agreed upon by the members, and the terms enforced by the courts, as between themselves. But the rights of creditors are not affected by such arrangement. Hudgins v. Lane,* 11 N. B. R., 462.

§ 298. —— to follow assets in hands of new firm.— Where officers of a bank are members of a partnership which becomes largely indebted to the bank, and such officers assign their interest in the firm to others, who, with the remaining members of the firm, form a new company assuming the debts of the old, and issue stock which is disposed of to other persons, the receiver of the bank cannot follow the property of the old firm and subject it in the hands of the new firm to a trust in favor of the bank, on the ground of its being the product of the money of the bank wrongfully taken by the partners, especially where such money due the bank has been intermingled with other funds of the firm so that no specific property purchased therewith can be identified. Case v. Beauregard,* 1 Woods, 125. See §§ 356-60.

§ 299. A member of a firm having bought out the interest of his partner in the partnership, and agreed to pay the debts of the firm, carried on the business for over a year, replenishing the stock of goods, mingling old and new together, and selling from both indifferently, so that it was impossible to tell which goods had belonged to the partnership and which not. He was adjudicated a bankrupt. Held, that the assets in the hands of his assignee, arising from a sale of the goods, should be regarded as belonging to said bankrupt's individual estate, and liable, in the first instance, to the payment of his individual debts in full, before any portion could be applied to the payment of the debts of the former partnership. *In re* Montgomery, 3 Ben., 565.

§ 800. Lien — Mortgage — Assignment.—The firm of A. & B. owned real estate as a part of their partnership property. It was agreed between them and C. that B. should sell all his interest in the partnership assets to C., who was thereupon to form a new partnership with A. B. made a conveyance accordingly, executing to C. a deed of an undivided half of the real estate, subject to a savings bank mortgage which had been made by the firm. C. mortgaged this half back to B. to secure the purchase price, and his agreement to pay B.'s shares of the debts of the old firm; also agreeing that the property so conveyed to him by B. should be subject to the payment of the debts of the old firm as fully as before. A. & C. on the same day formed a new firm, each partner contributing his interest in the assets of the old firm. The new firm mortgaged the real estate to D., subject to B.'s mortgage. The firm of A. & C. afterwards went into bankruptcy, the mortgages to B. and D. being both unpaid, but the debts of the old firm being mostly paid. Upon a petition brought by D. against B., praying that D.'s mortgage be declared a superior lien to B.'s, and upon a petition by the assignees in bankruptcy of A. & C. against B., praying that his mortgage lien be postponed to the payment of the debts of A. & C. and the adjustment of the accounts between the partners, it was *held:* 1. That the real estate, being partnership property, was to be treated in equity as if it were personal estate. 2. That a sale of the interest of one partner in partnership property conveys only his interest in the surplus, if any, which may remain after the payment of the partnership debts and the discharge of the liabilities of the partners *inter sese;* for the property and effects of a partnership belong to the firm and not to the partners, each of whom is entitled only to a share of what may remain after the payment of the partnership debts and after a settlement of the accounts between the partners. 3. That the right or equity, that such an interest, when sold, is subject to the payment of partnership debts, is to be enforced only by the remaining partner. Partnership creditors have no specific lien upon partnership property, and the equity that partnership property must be used to pay partnership debts is to be worked out through the partners. Partnership creditors have no lien upon partnership property which has, *bona fide,* been transmuted by the partners into separate estate, or which has been sold in good faith upon dissolution of the partnership, by the retiring partner to the remaining partner, or which has been sold in good faith by one partner to a third person with the consent of the other partner. If the remaining partner waives or abandons his right to have such property subjected to the payment of partnership debts, the creditors have no remedy against the property which has been sold if the sale is free from fraud. 4. That such a mortgage by a partner of his interest in real estate, known by the mortgagee to be partnership property, to secure an individual debt, is not a mortgage of a specific part of the real estate, but of his interest in the portion mortgaged after the payment of the partnership debts and the settlement of the partnership accounts between the partners. This interest is not available to the mortgagee until the firm debts have been paid and the partnership accounts discharged if the other partner chooses to assert his equity, or if subsequent partnership mortgagees, who have a specific lien upon the mortgaged property, assert their priority. 5. That if the mortgage to B. had been a mortgage of the interest of C. in the new firm, it would have been subject to the debts of the new firm, provided the other partner or his assignees in bankruptcy had not waived their equity. 6. That upon the facts in this case, the mortgage was to be regarded as a mortgage back to B. of the same partnership interest in the old firm which was conveyed to C., and not of C.'s interest in the new firm. This mortgage was subject to the payment of the debts of the old firm if A. had chosen to assert his equity, but neither A. nor his assignees in bankruptcy were now claiming any equity for that purpose. 7. It appearing that, by agreement of all the parties, for the purpose of enabling A. & C. to make a larger savings bank mortgage, B. and D. had released their mortgages, and that A. & C. had then made a new savings bank mortgage, that C. then made a new mortgage to B. upon the undivided half of the real estate to secure the unpaid portion of the purchase price, and that subject to that mortgage A. & C. made a mortgage to D., it was held that the mortgage given to B. was, so far as A. and the subsequent mortgage was concerned, a continuation of the same security which was originally given to B., and the assignees of A. would have no superior equities to those which A. himself had, and he could not have asserted a right to have the new mortgage subject to the partnership debts of the new firm. Beecher *v.* Stevens,* 43 Conn., 587.

§ 801. Power of partners to bind each other after.—The acknowledgment of a debt by one partner, after a dissolution of the copartnership, is not sufficient to take the case out of the statute as to the other partners. Bell *v.* Morrison, 1 Pet., 351.

§ 802. A dissolution of partnership puts an end to the authority of one partner to bind the other; it operates as a revocation of all power to create new contracts, and the right of partners, as such, can extend no further than to settle the partnership concerns already existing and distribute the remaining funds, and this right may be restrained by the delegation of this authority to one partner. *Ibid.*

§ 803. After a dissolution of a partnership no partner can create a cause of action against the other partners, except by a new authority communicated to him for that purpose. *Ibid.*

§ 804. After the dissolution of a partnership, one partner has no power to bind the late firm by giving a note for a partnership debt. Draper *v.* Bissel,* 3 McL., 275.

§ 805. If a firm, after dissolution, puts a debt owing to it at the *disposal* of one of the partners, the latter may assign it to secure a private debt of his own, and such assignment will be conclusive on him and enable the assignee to recover the debt in equity. McLanahan *v.* Ellery,* 3 Mason, 269.

§ 806. A bill of exchange drawn upon a firm but not accepted until after its dissolution, and then by one partner only, binds only the partner who accepts it. Tombeckbee Bank *v.* Dumell,* 5 Mason, 56.

§ 807. **New firm is not liable for debts of old.**— Where a sale is made to two persons and they afterwards take in a third partner, an action for the price of the goods cannot be maintained against the three, counting on a sale by the two to the three and the *assumpsit* of the company to the plaintiff. Atwood *v.* Lockhart,* 4 McL., 350.

§ 808. If goods be consigned by the plaintiff to K. & G. for sale, and be sold by them and the proceeds of the sale received by them, and B. becomes a partner with K. & G. under the name of K., G. & Co., the new firm is not liable to the plaintiff for the proceeds of the sales of those goods unless they come to the use of the new firm, who, in consideration thereof, promised to pay the same to the plaintiff. Edmondson *v.* Barrell, 2 Cr. C. C., 228.

§ 809. **Property of deceased partner allowed to remain.**— A partner dying, by his will appointed his copartner executor, and devised to him in trust the residue of his estate, etc., and authorized him to employ and use in business the estate and property given him in trust till required for distribution. *Held,* that the residue was the portion of the estate said copartner was authorized to use, and he was still bound to pay the debts and wind up the business in the usual way. Nor did the fact that he retained the testator's property and did business thereon, and so notified some of his creditors, affect the right of a creditor, who had not been notified, to be paid out of the joint estate, upon the bankruptcy of said surviving partner. *Quære,* whether notice would have made any difference. *In re* Clap, 2 Low., 168.

§ 810. W., who was engaged in mercantile business, died leaving a will, which directed that all his capital and interest in said concern should be continued therein, and should be chargeable for its debts and liabilities, but his other estate should not be so chargeable. And further, that the profits of said concern should be divided between persons named in said will. The firm afterwards having become bankrupt, *held,* that the property of deceased not embarked in the partnership enterprise was not liable for its debts, and that the dividends of profits being honestly and fairly made, and not diminishing the capital, nor withdrawing what was necessary to pay the debts of the firm, could not be recovered of the legatees by the assignee in bankruptcy of the firm. Jones *v.* Walker, 13 Otto, 444.

§ 811. Representatives of deceased partners are liable to their beneficiaries for any deviation from duty in permitting assets to remain in the partnership. Hoyt *v.* Sprague, 13 Otto, 613.

§ 812. The death of a partner dissolves the firm, but the liability of a deceased partner, as well as his interest in the profits of the concern, may by contract be extended beyond his death. Scholefield *v.* Eichelberger, 7 Pet., 586.

§ 813. Where the representative of a deceased partner allows the interest of his decedent, or a guardian allows the interest of his ward in such decedent's estate, to be used in the business by the surviving partner, and thereby loses his lien upon the partnership property, he does not thereby become a creditor of the new firm, and cannot come into concourse with the creditors thereof, but the property of the firm is first subject to the claims of such creditors, and after they are satisfied, the representative's right to have an account against the surviving partner remains as before. And as the representative ceases to have a lien, as against subsequent creditors, the beneficiaries of the deceased partner's estate can have none. Hoyt *v.* Sprague, 13 Otto. 613.

§ 814. The administrators of deceased partners have the power, if they see fit, unless restrained by their beneficiaries, to allow the estate of their deceased intestates to be continued in the business of the partnership; and if it is continued by their allowance and consent, the property becomes liable to the partnership debts subsequently incurred as well as to prior debts; but with this qualification, that the property which remains unchanged is still subject to the partnership lien in preference to after-incurred debts; whilst new property which, in the course of business, takes the place of the old, is not subject to said lien in preference to such debts. *Ibid.*

§ 815. Although by the general rule of law, every partnership is dissolved by the death of one of the partners, where the articles of copartnership do not stipulate otherwise, yet either one may, by his will, provide for the continuance of the partnership after his death; and in making this provision, he may bind his whole estate or only that portion of it already embarked in the partnership. But it will require the most clear and unambiguous language, demonstrating in the most positive manner that the testator intended to make his general assets liable for all debts contracted in the continued trade after his death, to justify the court in arriving at such a conclusion. Burwell *v.* Mandeville's Executor, 2 How., 560.

§ 316. **Rights and liabilities of retiring partners.**— Where a partner retires from a partnership, but suffers his name to be retained in the new firm, he is responsible to a creditor, the holder of a note, who takes it without actual notice of the dissolution, even though a notice thereof was published in the newspapers. He may be proceeded against in bankruptcy, by the creditor, as a member of the firm. Whether an estoppel ought to apply where the creditor has not been misled, that is, where he has had actual notice, *quere. In re* Krueger, 5 N. B. R., 439; 2 Low., 66.

§ 317. Where a partner transferred his interest in partnership assets to the other partner, and said remaining partner agreed to apply said assets to the payment of the firm debts, and afterwards, before paying said firm debts, filed his petition in bankruptcy, upon the petition of the retiring partner, asking that he be made a party to the proceedings, and that the firm be adjudicated bankrupt, to the end that the firm assets should be applied to the payment of the firm debts, *held*, that he was not estopped by said transfer from saying that they were partnership assets, (1) because, as between himself and the firm creditors, he could not estop himself by any dealings with the other partner from any duty he owed those creditors; and (2) because the assets were pledged to the payment of said firm debts, and that the remaining partner was only a trustee for the benefit of the creditors, to convert the assets and pay the debts of the firm. *In re* Gorham, 9 Biss., 23.

§ 318. Upon the dissolution of a mercantile firm, if it be agreed that the acting partner shall take the effects and pay all the debts of the firm, and this be known to the creditor of the firm, he cannot, with a good conscience, take a lien on the joint effects for new advances made by him to the acting partner on his own individual account, so as to exhaust the joint effects, and leave the retiring partner liable for the old joint debt. McClean's Executors *v.* Miller, 2 Cr. C. C., 620.

§ 819. The rights of partnership creditors cannot be altered by any private agreement which the partners may choose to make with each other upon dissolution. Although the partnership effects are by such agreement to be retained exclusively by one of the partners who is also to discharge the debts, the recourse of the creditors against the retiring partner remains unchanged, unless by some positive act which directly or by a fair inference amounts to an agreement to discharge him. Harris *v.* Lindsay,* 4 Wash., 98, 271.

§ 820. Indulgence granted by a creditor would not amount to such agreement. But if, with full knowledge of the agreement between the partners, that one is to retain the effects and pay the debts, a creditor shall enter into a totally new contract with such partner, by which the nature of the partnership debt is wholly changed so as to become a different debt from that which the retiring partner was bound to pay, or such as to subject him to a different kind of responsibility, such new contract will amount to an acceptance by the creditor of the paying partner as his debtor, and to a discharge of the other. *Ibid.*

§ 321. Accordingly, where a retiring partner, who assumed the debts of the firm, formed successively two new partnerships, each of which had dealings with and became indebted to a creditor of the old firm, and after the dissolution of the last firm he settled with such creditor for the indebtedness of the three firms, giving notes for the aggregate amount, divided into three parts, neither of which answered to the balance due by either house, and the creditor gave a receipt by which he agreed to give the maker of the notes credit for them when they should be paid, *held*, that the other member of the original firm was discharged. *Ibid.*

§ 822. —— notice.— A firm was dissolved, two of the members retired, and a new firm was formed, consisting of the remaining members of the old firm and two new members. The new firm then assumed all the obligations of the old firm and agreed that the liabilities of the retiring members should be terminated. Subsequently the new firm was adjudicated bankrupt. Among the debts of the new firm published in the bankruptcy proceedings was a certain debt of the old firm. This debt was proved without objection as a debt of the new firm by the representative of the creditor. Dividends were declared and received by said representative. The estate of the new firm was subsequently wound up, and certain stocks constituting the assets were distributed among the creditors of the firm in pursuance of a scheme assented to by such creditors. During the life-time of one of the retired members of the old firm, no claim for liability was made upon him for said debt, but prior to the distribution of stocks, payment was demanded of the executor of said retired partner, who denied his testator's liability. Thereafter the representative of said creditor participated in the distribution of stocks, which he sold without notice to the executor of said retired partner. The amount received by the representative of said creditor not being equal to the debt, he sued the estate of said retired partner for the deficiency. *Held*, that the plaintiff knowing that the old firm was dissolved, and that the new firm had assumed the liabilities of the old, was chargeable with knowledge that the outgoing members were to be relieved from liability, and that if it had been his intention to maintain intact the then existing liability of the retired partner, he should have given some positive expression of such purpose when he came to deal with the new firm in respect to the debt. That the lapse of time, the omission to make a claim upon said retired partner in his life-time, the other members of the old firm being insolvent, and making no demand on the executor of said partner until the estate of the new firm was substantially wound up, is hardly consistent with the position assumed, that there was no intention to accept the liability of the new firm in lieu of the old. That by proving the debt in the bankruptcy proceedings of the new firm, the plaintiff adopted the new firm as his debtors. And that by adopting a course by which the right to vote as a creditor in the bankruptcy proceeding was lost to said retired partner and his executor, deprived of the power to secure his estate against loss, the plaintiff had acted in such a manner as to render his claim to relief inequitable. Regester *v.* Dodge, 19 Blatch., 79.

§ 823. —— social partnership.— In a social partnership, where an absolute community of property with right of survivorship on the one hand, and care, by the community, of every member through life, on the other, is the fundamental and pervading principle, if one member be unjustly expelled by a usurped though unquestioned authority, not having under the clear terms of the association any right to expel him, the court will not oblige him to return to the association (there not being on its part an offer of full and satisfactory reconciliation and reception), but will interfere with the fundamental and pervading principle; and though the expelled member brought nothing into the community, will give to him, for himself, a separate and individual part of the property. And where payment for the party's services at the ordinary rate of services like his, during the years he was a member, would give him more than his numerical proportion or share of the whole capital stock, and where the question of profits was a little obscure, the court regarding this as the simplest and most natural justice, gave to him his numerical share or proportion of the whole capital stock, from whatever source arising, as the same existed at the time he was expelled, irrespective of the amount which he found in the association when he became a member. Nachtrieb *v.* The Harmony Settlement, 3 Wall. Jr., 66. Reversed, Baker *v.* Nachtrieb, 19 How., 126.

§ 824. To what extent partnership continues.— A partnership, although dissolved, still continues for the purpose of liquidation and partition of gains, and under the law of Louisiana the partners may be sued at the domicile of the partnership for such purposes. Goodrich *v.* Hunton, 2 Woods, 137.

§ 825. C. and S., partners, entered into an agreement reciting that the partnership was dissolved, the dissolution to date from the date of the agreement, "except so far as it may be necessary to continue the same for the final liquidation and settlement of the business thereof." C., by said agreement, sold to S. his interest in the partnership assets, and S. was to apply said property and the proceeds thereof to the payment of the partnership debts and the necessary expenses of carrying on the business. *Held*, that whatever effect this agreement had to dissolve the partnership as to future business, and debts contracted thereafter, it had no such effect as respected the partnership property in which C. theretofore had an interest, or the partnership debts named in that agreement, or as respected proceedings under the bankruptcy act to affect such partnership property. The case is not one where the transfer of the interest of the retiring partner is absolute, and the remaining partner agrees to pay and assume the debts. In the present case C. took from S. an express agreement that the partnership property assigned, and its proceeds, should be applied by S. to pay the partnership debts, and the agreement by S. was to pay those debts with that property. Therefore there was no dissolution of the partnership or transfer to S. until and unless the debts were first paid. *In re* Shepard, 3 Ben., 347.

§ 826. Notice.— Where R. and C., who had been doing business as partners under the firm name of R. & Son, divided their stock in trade and afterwards carried on business in separate establishments, but each using the old firm name, *held*, that they continued to be partners as to one who had previously dealt with them, and dealt with them, or one of them, thereafter, unless public or personal notice of dissolution was brought home to such person. Moline Wagon Co. *v.* Rummell,[*] 2 McC., 307.

§ 827. Special agreements between partners.— Dissolutions of partnerships upon terms agreed upon will be enforced as between the parties, but will not be allowed to affect the rights of creditors. Hudgins *v.* Lane, 2 Hughes, 361.

§ 828. Where one partner dissolves a copartnership, he cannot demand of the other to carry out the stipulations of the articles which made the copartnership, which provide that the excess of funds either has contributed to the firm is to be paid by the company out of the net earnings. A sale of the property should be made, to give each his due rights in the partnership assets. Wilson *v.* Davis,* 1 Mont. T'y, 188.

§ 329. A partner sold his interest in a firm to his copartner and another, and the paper writing or bill of sale executed by him contained this clause: "and it is further understood by the parties of the second part, that the above sale is made subject to any indebtedness made by the purchase of the before mentioned goods, wares and merchandise, by Jennings & Phelps and Phelps & Clasen, for which reference is made to an account of liabilities on the 1st day of April, 1867." *Held,* that the vendees took the goods charged in their hands with a liability to pay the debts mentioned out of those goods. *It seems* that such clause meant a promise on the part of the vendees to pay all such debts of the two firms as were created by the purchase of any of the goods conveyed by the bill of sale, and which should be found in account of liabilities taken on the 1st of April, 1867. Phelps *v.* Clasen, Woolw., 204.

§ 330. If an outgoing partner takes an obligation from the continuing partners to assume and pay the debts of the firm, and to "relieve" him from any and all claims, an action can be maintained thereon against the obligors upon their failure to pay the debts, although the obligee has not been compelled to pay any of them, and has, in fact, been discharged in bankruptcy. Hood *v.* Spencer,* 4 McL., 168.

§ 331. An agreement dissolving a partnership between A. and B., who under the partnership carried on two stores, a jewelry and a hardware store, provided that B. should have "the goods in the jewelry store and all the debts due that store, as a compensation in lieu of profits arising from the whole business." *Held,* under this clause, that B. could not maintain a claim to any profits of the jewelry store not existing in debts or goods. Finley *v.* Lynn,* 6 Cr., 238.

§ 332. The same agreement gave to A. all the debts due to the hardware store, and required him to assume all debts due from the concern. *Held,* that he was entitled to a debt due from the jewelry store to the hardware store. *Ibid.*

§ 333. An agreement of dissolution of a partnership existing between A. and B. provided that A. should indemnify B. against "all claims and demands upon the concern." An indemnity bond, afterwards executed in pursuance of this agreement, embraced in its language a debt owing by B. prior to the partnership, and which it was agreed, at the time of the formation of the partnership, that the partnership should assume. *Held,* that there was not such a repugnancy between the dissolution agreement and the bond as to justify the court in reforming the latter at the suit of A. *Ibid.*

VI. PRIVATE AND PARTNERSHIP CREDITORS.

SUMMARY — *Right of private creditor to attach property,* § 334.— *Garnishing firm debtor on suit against partner,* § 335.— *Rights of creditors derivative,* §§ 336-338.— *Creditors' liens,* §§ 339-343.— *Fraud in transfer,* § 344.— *Surviving partner's use of assets,* §§ 345, 346.— *Equity where new rights have attached,* § 347.— *Creditors of new and old firms,* §§ 848, 349.— *Retiring partner; homestead,* §§ 350-352.

§ 334. A separate creditor of a partner can only take and sell the interest of the debtor in the partnership property, being his share upon a division of the surplus after the partnership debts are paid. Such creditor may, however, attach the partnership property, and the debtor has any available interest therein, and a bill in equity to recover property so attached and to restrain the attaching officer, not averring that there are any partnership debts or that the partner sued has not an ultimate interest in the property, cannot be maintained. Peck *v.* Schultz, § 853.

§ 335. A separate creditor of a partner can only subject to the payment of his claim such interest in the firm property as his debtor may be found to have on a partnership accounting. Where, therefore, in an action against the firm of A. & B., one having in his hands funds of the firm of A. & C. was summoned as trustee, C. not being joined and nothing appearing as to the solvency of the firm of A. & C., or as to the state of the accounts between A. & C., *held,* that the trustee must be discharged. Lyndon *v.* Gorham, §§ 354, 355.

§ 336. The equity of partnership creditors to have the partnership property applied to the payment of the debts in preference to the individual debts of the partners is a derivative one, which is worked out through the equity of the partners themselves, and if the latter are not in a position to enforce it, the partnership creditors cannot. In the case of simple contract creditors, it is essential to obtaining relief that the property should be within the control of the court and in course of administration, brought there by the bankruptcy of the firm, or by an assignment, or by the creation of a trust in some mode.   Case *v.* Beauregard, §§ 856-860.

§ 837. If, before the interposition of the court is asked, the property has ceased to belong to the partnership, and by a *bona fide* transfer it has become the several property either of one partner or of a third person, the equities of the partners are extinguished, and consequently the derivative equities of the creditors are at an end.   *Ibid.*

§ 838. Where two of three partners, engaged in operating a railroad under a lease of it, transferred their interests *bona fide* to pay individual debts, and the remaining partner and the successors to the title of the transferees afterwards executed an act of fusion by which all the rights of the parties became vested in the railroad company, *held*, that a creditor of the partnership could not thereafter maintain a bill in equity, alleging the insolvency of the partnership and its original members, to have the property so transferred, subjected to the payment of its claim.   *Ibid.*

§ 839. The general creditors of a firm, before levy and seizure, have not, as such creditors, any specific lien on the assets of the firm, but the preference of the company creditors over the separate creditors in the distribution of the joint assets arises from and must be worked out through the rights of the partners to insist upon such application.   Tracy *v.* Walker, §§ 861-865.

§ 840. The partners may relinquish their rights to each other or to third persons, or they may enforce them in a court of equity for their own benefit, or become the instruments by which creditors may, in like manner, enforce them.   *Ibid.*

§ 841. When the primary right of partners to apply the partnership property to the extinguishment of the company debts is gone, the right of partnership creditors to compel such application is also gone.   *Ibid.*

§ 842. The right of one partner to appropriate the joint assets to the separate creditors, by consent of the other partner, does not depend upon the solvency of the firm.   *Ibid.*

§ 843. A partner sold his interest in the firm business and assets to his copartner, the latter agreeing to give him a bond of indemnity against the liabilities of the firm.   The continuing partner did not give the bond, but was allowed, nevertheless, to retain absolute control of the stock and assets, and to pay company and private debts from the proceeds, without objection or interference on the part of the retiring partner.   *Held*, that, under such circumstances, a private creditor of the continuing partner who received a transfer of part of the stock and assets in payment of his claim should be protected, as against a firm creditor, if such private creditor acted in good faith.   *Ibid.*

§ 844. It appearing that the continuing partner made false representations as to his solvency to the complainant, a firm creditor, and thus gained time to dispose of the property to his private creditor, a relative, that the value of the assets transferred exceeded the amount of the debt due to the transferee, and that the excess of assets was afterwards used in payment or compromise of debts of the firm, and the transaction not being satisfactorily explained by the transferee, *held*, that the transfer would be held fraudulent as to such excess and the transferee charged to that extent.   *Ibid.*

§ 845. If a surviving partner, with the acquiescence of the personal representatives of the deceased partner, uses the firm property to continue the business on his own account and in his own name, and no proceedings are taken by partnership creditors to wind up the business and apply the partnership assets to the payment of their claims, any application of such assets made by such survivor in the course of the business, in good faith, in payment of his individual debts, will be valid and effectual, and cannot be treated as a fraud in law upon the partnership creditors.   Fitzpatrick *v.* Flannagan, §§ 866-871.

§ 846. The firm of A. & B. was insolvent during the whole period of its existence, and A., by whose death the partnership was dissolved, before his death drew from the partnership more than his interest in it and was indebted to it.   After A.'s death, B. continued the business without objection on the part of A.'s personal representatives, sold from and replenished the stock of goods, and applied the assets indiscriminately to the payment of debts of the late firm and debts contracted by him in the subsequent course of business, paying as much at least on account of partnership debts as he realized from partnership assets.   After a time, in order to repay certain money borrowed by him and used to pay partnership debts, he made a transfer of the entire stock of goods at a fair valuation to a relative of the lender, upon an agreement by the transferee to apply the balance of the price agreed to be paid, over and above the amount of the loan, to the payment of other debts of the concern.   *Held*, that this transfer was not fraudulent in law as to creditors of the late partnership, and, in the absence of an actual intent to defraud, furnished no ground for an attachment upon an affidavit, in an action against B. as surviving partner, alleging that he had disposed of his property to defraud his creditors.   *Ibid.*

§ 847. The equity of a retiring partner, who has assigned his interest in the firm assets to the continuing partner upon an agreement by the latter to become responsible for the firm debts, to compel the application of the firm assets to the payment of the firm debts, if it exist at all, cannot exist where new rights have attached by reason of the change of interests, as where rights of individual creditors have accrued, or where the continuing partner or the new firm has disposed of the property, or there are creditors of the new firm. Crane *v.* Morrison, §§ 872-875.

§ 848. A partnership existing between A. and B. was dissolved, each partner taking one of two mills composing the partnership property, and each assuming the debts contracted in respect to the mill of which he became the separate owner. B. afterwards claimed the right to rescind the dissolution agreement on the ground of A.'s failure to pay the debts assumed by him, but before such claim was made and before A.'s default, A. had taken in a new partner and conveyed to him an interest in his mill for a price agreed upon. A creditor of the old firm attached the personal property at the mill, and subsequently the new firm went into bankruptcy. In an action by the assignee in bankruptcy to recover the attached property, *held,* that any equity of B.'s to have property received by A. applied in payment of the debts of the old firm assumed by A.. and *a fortiori* any such equity of the creditors of the old firm, was lost upon A.'s taking in the new partner; that the right acquired by the attachment was only a right to subject the interest of A. in the property after payment of the debts of the new firm; that such right would be protected in the bankruptcy proceedings, and that the assignee was entitled to the property. *Ibid.*

§ 849. In such case the fact that B. had filed a bill in equity in another court against A.. the latter's partner, and the attaching creditor, praying for an accounting of the copartnership affairs and that a receiver had been appointed in such suit, *held* not to affect the case, it appearing that the receiver was not in possession of the property, but that it was held by the sheriff under the attachment. *Ibid.*

§ 850. Partnership assets, improperly withdrawn by one of the partners upon retiring from the firm, may be pursued by a firm creditor and subjected to the payment of his claim, although they have been invested in a homestead. *In re* Sauthoff, §§ 876-880.

§ 851. If a retiring partner takes out a portion of the assets of the firm for his individual use, he must do so without impairing the fund to which the firm creditors have a right in equity to look for payment of their claims; and it must be made clearly to appear that such remaining fund is ample. The fact that the partners believed that enough remained to pay the partnership debts, if such belief was a mistaken one, will be no defense. *Ibid.*

§ 852. Subsequent dealings of the creditors with the continuing partner, selling him goods, giving him fresh credit, and permitting such goods to be mingled with the old stock, will not estop them from asserting a claim on the property withdrawn on the ground that they have ratified the transaction between the continuing and retiring partner. *Ibid.*

[NOTES.—See §§ 381-421.]

PECK *v.* SCHULTZE.

(Circuit Court for Massachusetts: 1 Holmes, 28-30. 1870.)

Opinion by SHEPLEY, J.

STATEMENT OF FACTS.—The bill of complaint alleges that the complainants are copartners under the name and style of A. M. Peck & Co.; that they are the owners of a large quantity of domestic liquors; that the defendant, George L. Andrews, the marshal of the United States for the district of Massachusetts, has attached the liquors upon a writ in favor of Emil Schultze and Robert Sailer against Albert M. Peck, claiming that the liquors were the property of said Peck; that he unjustly detains the liquors and threatens to remove them from complainants' store. Complainants pray for a decree that Andrews may return the liquors, and for an injunction to restrain him from further interfering with said property.

§ 353. *On execution against a copartner in favor of an individual creditor, only the partner's interest in the surplus of the partnership property after the payment of the partnership debts can be taken.*

By the rules of law as formerly held in England, the sheriff, under an execution against one of two copartners, took the partnership effects and sold the moiety of the debtor, treating the property as if owned by tenants in common.

Heydon *v.* Heydon, 1 Salk., 392; Jacky *v.* Butler, 2 Ld. Raym., 871. The law is now well settled in England, that a separate creditor can only take and sell the interest of the debtor in the partnership property, being his share upon a division of the surplus, after the partnership debts are paid. Fox *v.* Hanbury, Cowp., 445; Taylor *v.* Fields, 4 Ves., 396. This latter rule is the one now more generally adopted in the United States.

The rule in Massachusetts, giving a priority to the partnership creditor in such cases, was settled in the case of Pierce *v.* Jackson, 6 Mass., 242, and has been uniformly followed since. Allen *v.* Wells, 22 Pick., 450. The effect of this rule, that the only attachable interest of one of the copartners at the suit of a separate creditor is the surplus of the joint estate that may remain after the discharge of all the joint demands upon it, necessarily creates a preference in favor of the partnership creditors in the application of the partnership property.

§ **353a.** *A partner's interest in the firm property, subject to the payment of the firm debts, is attachable by his individual creditor; and in order to avoid such attachment it must be shown that, by reason of firm debts or otherwise, there is no interest to sell.*

The creditor of the individual partner may attach his interest in the partnership property; but the attaching officer will be bound in the application of the property, or its proceeds on execution, to give priority to the partnership creditor.

In the case of Cropper *v.* Coburn, 2 Curt., 465, the complainants, forming a partnership under the style of Hemsley & Cropper, brought their bill in equity against a creditor of one of the parties and the officer who had attached the property of the firm for a private debt and liability of Francis Hemsley, one of the partners. The bill in that case alleged that large claims and debts and liabilities were outstanding against the firm of Hemsley & Cropper, and more than sufficient to absorb all the partnership property of said firm and the interest of said Hemsley in said copartnership; and that, after the payment of said partnership debts, no surplus or interest would remain to the credit of said Hemsley, and that the merchandise attached was required to pay and discharge the debts and liabilities of the copartnership.

The demurrer to this bill was overruled on the ground that, as the allegations in the bill were admitted by the demurrer, it appeared that the partner against whom the suit was brought had no ultimate interest in the partnership property. As the validity of the attachment must depend upon the debtor's having such an interest in the property that something would pass by a sale of his interest on execution, and in this instance there was no interest to sell, it follows that, by the rule of law established in Massachusetts, there was no interest to attach.

The bill of complaint in this case does not contain any averments that there are any partnership liabilities, or that the assets of the firm are needed to satisfy the claims of partnership creditors; nor is there any averment that the partner against whom the suit is brought has not an ultimate interest in the partnership property and a share of the surplus which may remain after the payment of partnership debts and liabilities. If he has such an interest, it may lawfully be attached and sold on execution.

The bill in this case does not present a case for relief in equity, and the demurrer is sustained. Bill dismissed without prejudice, and with costs for defendants.

LYNDON v. GORHAM.

(Circuit Court for Rhode Island: 1 Gallison, 366–371. 1812.)

STATEMENT OF FACTS.— The trustee had effects in his hands, the property of the firm of Gorham & Lawrence, but not of Gorham & Greene, or of either of them separately.

§ 854. *A debtor of a partnership cannot be held as trustee for the several or joint debt of one of the partners, it not appearing whether the partnership is solvent or what the extent of the partner's interest is.*

Opinion by STORY, J.

In order to adjudge the trustee responsible in this suit, it must be decided that the funds of one partnership may be applied to the payment of the debts of another partnership, upon the mere proof that the principal debtor has an interest in each firm. If this be correct, it will follow that a separate creditor of one partner will have greater equitable, as well as legal, rights than the partner himself has. The general rule undoubtedly is, that the interest of each partner in the partnership funds is only what remains after the partnership accounts are taken; and unless upon such an account the partner be a creditor of the fund, he is entitled to nothing. And if the partnership be insolvent, the same effect follows. West v. Skip, 1 Ves., 240; Doddington v. Hallett, 1 Ves., 497; Fox v. Hanbury, Cowp., 445. Now the party sued as a trustee in this suit is a total stranger to both partnerships. There is nothing before the court from which it can ascertain the situation of the partnership, whether solvent or not, whether Gorham be a creditor on the fund or not, and if a creditor, what is his proportion of interest. If, therefore, the trustee be held, it must be from some stubborn rule of law which rides over all these difficulties. I know of no such rule.

§ 354a. *A sale of partnership property upon execution against one of the partners does not convey an indefeasible title in a moiety of the property. It conveys merely the unascertained interest of the partner therein.*

I have the authority of Lord Hardwicke and Lord Mansfield, in the cases above cited, for holding that a creditor cannot be in a better situation than the partner himself, as to his right upon the joint funds; and their opinions are fully corroborated by more recent authorities. But I have been pressed with the common case of a separate execution against the tangible partnership property, in which it is said that the moiety of the judgment debtor may be sold on the execution. There are certainly decisions which countenance this opinion, and perhaps it may be considered that at law the sheriff has a right to seize such property in execution. Heydon v. Heydon, 1 Salk., 392; Backhurst v. Clinchard, 1 Show., 173; Jacky v. Butler, 2 Lord Ray., 871; Eddie v. Davidson, Doug., 650; Parker v. Parker, 3 Bos. & Pull., 288; Chapman v. Koops, 3 Bos. & Pull., 289; Morley v. Strombom, 3 Bos. & Pull., 254. But still it by no means follows that he can sell and convey an indefeasible title to a purchaser of a moiety of the property. He may sell the interest of the partner therein, but he sells it *cum onere;* and although the parties may be driven into a court of equity to ascertain their respective rights, yet if upon the whole it appears that the judgment debtor had a nominal interest only in the fund, I do not think that the authorities which are cited show that a greater interest can be conveyed under the execution, and if the partnership be insolvent, that any interest can be conveyed. In Fox v. Hanbury, Cowp., 445, Lord Mansfield says, "no person deriving under a partner can be in a better condition than

279

the partner himself;" and he cites with approbation the opinion of Lord Hard-wicke, in Skip *v.* Harwood, from his manuscript note. "If a creditor of one partner take out execution against the partnership effects, he can only have the undivided share of his debtor, and must take it in the same manner the debtor himself had it, and subject to the rights of the other partner." The same doc-trine is explicitly avowed in the court of exchequer, in Field *v.* ———, 4 Ves. jun., 396, where the court say, "the right of the separate creditor under the execution depends upon the interest each partner has in the joint property. With respect to that, we are of opinion that the *corpus* of the partnership effects is joint property, and neither partner separately has anything in that *corpus;* but the interest of each is only his share of what remains after the partnership accounts are taken." *Vide* The King *v.* Sanderson, Wightwick, 50; Waters *v.* Taylor, 2 Ves. & Beames, 299. And in Pierce *v.* Jackson, 6 Mass. Rep., 242, which, since the argument, I have had an opportunity of consulting, these principles seem fully adopted. In that case the court held that a creditor of a partnership was entitled to payment before a creditor of one partner only, although the latter had made the first attachment.

§ **355.** *Difference between ordinary attachment or levy on execution and trustee process. Latter in nature of bill in equity.*

The case then put by counsel, admitting it to apply to the present, does not prove all that it was supposed to do. But it will be recollected that in such case the other partner has his remedy at law as well as in equity; that he may bring his action against the sheriff, if he sell more than the debtor's moiety. In the present suit, no such remedy lies. If the trustee be adjudged responsible in this suit, there would seem to be a complete severance of the partnership debt; at all events he could be held as a debtor to the partner-ship, only for the remaining moiety. And it may be doubtful, if the judg-ment creditor could be obliged to refund, when the money had been adjudged to him by the regular judgment of the court; at all events, in states where no court of equity exists, the case would be attended with many embarrassments. I consider that the present is a process in the nature of a bill in equity, to reach the funds of a debtor, and subject to all the liens and equities between the original parties; and in order to do complete justice, it is necessary that all proper parties should be before the court. If the other partner had been sued as a trustee, and upon his disclosure it had clearly appeared that the partnership was solvent and that Gorham was a creditor to the fund, some of the difficulty of the case would have been obviated. Perhaps even then it might deserve consideration, how far the separate funds of one partner should, under this process, be applied in the first instance to discharge debts of a part-nership, which was not shown to be insolvent, nor the partner a debtor thereto. However I give no opinion on this point. In the present case I am satisfied that the trustee ought not to be charged.

I feel pleasure in adding, that my present opinion is fully supported by the decision of the supreme court of Massachusetts, in Fisk *v.* Herrick, 6 Mass., 271.

Let the trustee be discharged with costs.

By the statute of Rhode Island (1 Rhode Island Laws, 208), a foreign at-tachment issues only in cases where the debtor resides out of the state, or con-ceals himself therein; and by section 3, "if it shall appear by the oath of the person or persons, who have been served with the copy of any writ as afore-said, that he or they have not any of the personal estate of the defendant in their hands, that then such action shall be dismissed, and the person who shall appear to defend such suit shall recover his costs."

CASE v. BEAUREGARD.

(9 Otto, 119–180. 1878.)

APPEAL from U. S. Circuit Court, District of Louisiana.

STATEMENT OF FACTS.— Beauregard, May and Graham were partners in a lease of a railroad, and the firm became heavily indebted to the First National Bank of New Orleans, of which Case afterward became the receiver. On the 8th May, 1867, Graham assigned his interest in the partnership to the Fourth National Bank of New York; on the 16th of that month May assigned his interest to the United States, who, on the 31st October, 1867, transferred that interest to Binder, Bonneval and Hernandez. On the 15th October, 1867, the lease was surrendered, and a fusion arrangement made for carrying on the business of the railroad company. On the 10th July, 1869, this bill was filed by Case, as receiver of the First National Bank of New Orleans, claiming the sum of $237,000.89, as due to the bank from the partnership. The bill was dismissed and Case appealed. Further facts appear in the opinion of the court.

Opinion by MR. JUSTICE STRONG.

The object of this bill is to follow and subject to the payment of a partnership debt property which formerly belonged to the partnership, but which, before the bill was filed, had been transferred to the defendants. There is little if any controversy respecting the facts, and little in regard to the principles of equity invoked by the complainant. The important question is, whether those principles are applicable to the facts of the case.

§ 356. *The equity or "privilege" of the creditor of a partnership is derivative.*

No doubt the effects of a partnership belong to it so long as it continues in existence, and not to the individuals who compose it. The right of each partner extends only to a share of what may remain after payment of the debts of the firm and the settlement of its accounts. Growing out of this right, or rather included in it, is the right to have the partnership property applied to the payment of the partnership debts in preference to those of any individual partner. This is an equity the partners have as between themselves, and in certain circumstances it inures to the benefit of the creditors of the firm. The latter are said to have a privilege or preference, sometimes loosely denominated a lien, to have the debts due to them paid out of the assets of a firm in course of liquidation to the exclusion of the creditors of its several members. Their equity, however, is a derivative one. It is not held or enforceable in their own right. It is practically a subrogation to the equity of the individual partner, to be made effective only through him. Hence, if he is not in a condition to enforce it, the creditors of the firm cannot be. Rice *v.* Barnard, 20 Vt., 479; Appeal of the York County Bank, 32 Pa. St., 446. But so long as the equity of the partner remains in him, so long as he retains an interest in the firm assets as a partner, a court of equity will allow the creditors of the firm to avail themselves of his equity, and enforce through it the application of those assets primarily to payment of the debts due them whenever the property comes under its administration.

§ **357.** *In order to enforce the rights of simple contract creditors of a partnership against partnership property, the property must be at the time in course of administration.*

It is indispensable, however, to such relief, when the creditors are, as in.the present case, simple contract creditors, that the partnership property should be within the control of the court and in the course of administration, brought there by the bankruptcy of the firm, or by an assignment, or by the creation of a trust in some mode. This is because neither the partners nor the joint creditors have any specific lien, nor is there any trust that can be enforced until the property has passed *in custodiam legis.* Other property can be followed only after a judgment at law has been obtained and an execution has proved fruitless.

§ **358.** *The lien or "privilege" of a creditor of a partnership may be defeated by a bona fide transfer of the property to third persons before the creditor's claim is asserted.*

So if, before the interposition of the court is asked, the property has ceased to belong to the partnership, if by a *bona fide* transfer it has become the several property either of one partner or of a third person, the equities of the partners are extinguished, and consequently the derivative equities of the creditors are at an end. It is, therefore, always essential to any preferential right of the creditors that there shall be property owned by the partnership when the claim for preference is sought to be enforced. Thus, in *Ex parte* Ruffin, 6 Ves., 119, where from a partnership of two persons one retired, assigning the partnership property to the other, and taking a bond for the value and a covenant of indemnity against debts, it was ruled by Lord Eldon that the joint creditors had no equity attaching upon partnership effects, even remaining in specie. And such has been the rule generally accepted ever since, with the single qualification that the assignment of the retiring partner is not *mala fide.* Kimball *v.* Thompson, 13 Met. (Mass.), 283; Allen *v.* The Centre Valley Co., 21 Conn., 130; Ladd *v.* Griswold, 9 Ill., 25; Smith *v.* Edwards, 7 Humph. (Tenn.), 106; Robb *v.* Mudge, 14 Gray (Mass.), 534; Baker's Appeal, 21 Pa. St., 76; Sigler & Richey *v.* Knox County Bank, 8 Ohio St., 511; Wilcox *v.* Kellogg, 11 Ohio, 394.

The joint estate is converted into the separate estate of the assignee by force of the contract of assignment. And it makes no difference whether the retiring partner sells to the other partner or to a third person, or whether the sale is made by him or under a judgment against him. In either case his equity is gone. These principles are settled by very abundant authorities.

§ **359.** *Application of the preceding principles to the facts of the case.*

It remains, therefore, only to consider whether, in view of the rules thus settled and of the facts of this case, the complainant, through any one of the partners, has a right to follow the specific property which formerly belonged to the partnership, and compel its application to the payment of the debt due from the firm to the bank of which he is the receiver. The partnership, while it was in existence, was composed of three persons, May, Graham and Beauregard, but it had ceased to exist before this suit was commenced. It was entirely insolvent, and all the partnership effects had been transferred to others for valuable considerations. None of the property was ever within the jurisdiction of the court for administration.

On the 8th of May, 1867, Graham, one of the partners, assigned all his right and interest in any property and effects of the partnership, and whatever he might be entitled to under the articles thereof, together with all debts due to him from the partnership or any member thereof, to the Fourth National Bank of the city of New York. By subsequent assignments, made on the 14th and 16th of May, 1869, May, the second partner, transferred all his interest in the partnership property to the United States, and by the same instruments transferred to the United States, by virtue of a power of attorney which he held, the interest of Graham. On the 21st of August, 1867, the United States sold and transferred their interest obtained from May and Graham in all the partnership property, including real estate, to Alexander Bonneval, Joseph Hernandez and George Binder. On the 15th of October next following, an act of fusion was executed between the New Orleans & Carrollton Railroad Company, Beauregard, Bonneval, Hernandez and Binder, by which the rights of all the parties became vested in the railroad company, subject to the debts and liabilities of the company, whether due or claimed from the lessee or the stockholders.

The effect of these transfers and act of fusion was very clearly to convert the partnership property into property held in severalty, or, at least, to terminate the equity of any partner to require the application thereof to the payment of the joint debts. Hence if, as we have seen, the equity of the partnership creditors can be worked out only through the equity of the partners, there was no such equity of the partners, or any one of them, as is now claimed, in 1869, when this bill was filed. No one of the partners could then insist that the property should be applied first to the satisfaction of the joint debts, for his interest in the partnership and its assets had ceased. Baker's Appeal, 21 Pa. St., 823. That was a case where a firm had consisted of five brothers. Two of them withdrew, disposing of their interest in the partnership estate and effects to the other three, the latter agreeing to pay the debts of the firm. Some time after, one of the remaining three sold his interest in the partnership property to one of the remaining two partners. The two remaining, after contracting debts, made an assignment of their partnership property to pay the debts of the last firm composed of the two; and it was held that the creditors of the first two firms had no right to claim any portion of the fund last assigned, and that it was distributable exclusively among the creditors of the last firm. So in McNutt v. Strayhorn & Hobson, 39 id., 269, it was ruled that though the general rule is that the equities of the creditors are to be worked out through the equities of the partners, yet where the property is parted with by sale severally made, and neither partner has dominion or possession, there is nothing through which the equities of the creditors can work, and, therefore, there is no case for the application of the rule. See, also, Coover's Appeal, 29 id., 9. Unless, therefore, the conveyances of the partners in this case and the act of fusion were fraudulent, the bank of which the complainant is receiver has no claim upon the property now held by the New Orleans & Carrollton Railroad Company, arising out of the facts that it is a creditor of the partnership, and was such a creditor when the property belonged to the firm.

The bill, it is true, charges that the several transfers of the partners were illegal and fraudulent, without specifying wherein the fraud consisted. The charge seems to be only a legal conclusion from the fact that some of the transfers were made for the payment of the private debts of the assignors. Conceding such to have been the case, it was a fraud upon the other partners, if a fraud at all, rather than upon the joint creditors,— a fraud which those partners could waive, and which was subsequently waived by the act of fusion. Besides, that act made provision for some of the debts of the partnership. And it has been ruled that where one of two partners, with the consent of the other, sells and conveys one-half of the effects of the firm to a third person, and the other partner afterwards sells and conveys the other half to the same person, such sale and conveyances are not *prima facie* void, as against creditors of the firm, but are *prima facie* valid against all the world, and can be set aside by the creditors of the firm only by proof that the transactions were fraudulent as against them. Kimball *v.* Thompson, 13 Metc. (Mass.), 283; Flach *v.* Charron, 29 Md., 311. A similar doctrine is asserted in some of the other cases we have cited; and see 21 Conn., 130. In the present case we find no such proof. We discover nothing to impeach the *bona fides* of the transaction by which the property became vested in the railroad company.

§ 360. *The Louisiana law as to the rights of partnership creditors.*

Thus far we have considered the case without reference to the provisions of the Louisiana code, upon which the appellant relies. Article 2823 of the code is as follows: " The partnership property is liable to the creditors of the partnership in preference to those of the individual partner." We do not perceive that this provision differs materially from the general rule of equity we have stated. It creates no specific lien upon partnership property which continues after the property has ceased to belong to the partnership. It does not forbid *bona fide* conversion by the partners of the joint property into rights in severalty, held by third persons. It relates to partnership property alone, and gives a rule for marshaling such property between creditors. Concede that it gives to joint creditors a privilege, while the property belongs to the partnership, there is no subject upon which it can act when the joint ownership of the partners has ceased. Article 3244 of the code declares that privileges become extinct " by the extinction of the thing subject to the privilege."

What we have said is sufficient for a determination of the case. If it be urged, as was barely intimated during the argument, that the property sought to be followed belongs in equity to the bank, or is clothed with a trust for the bank because it was purchased with the bank's money, the answer is plain. There is no satisfactory evidence that it was thus purchased. It cannot be identified as the subject to the acquisition of which money belonging to the bank was applied.

The bank has, therefore, no specific claim upon the property, nor is there any trust which a court of equity can enforce; and, it was well said by the circuit justice, that, without some constituted trust or lien, " a creditor has only the right to prosecute his claim in the ordinary courts of law, and have it adjudicated before he can pursue the property of his debtor by a direct proceeding " in equity.   *Decree affirmed.*

TRACY *v.* WALKER.

(Circuit Court for Ohio: 1 Flippin, 41–48. 1861.)

Opinion by WILLSON, J.

STATEMENT OF FACTS.— This cause was heard upon bill, answers, replication, exhibits and testimony. The complainants are judgment creditors of the late firm of Walker & Ouland, of the city of Tiffin, Ohio. They seek, by this proceeding, to subject certain equities in the hands of some of the defendants to the payment of their judgment. The leading facts disclosed by the record are not controverted.

In the fall of 1856, the defendants, Walker & Ouland, were a mercantile firm of good credit doing business at Tiffin. They had purchased goods of the complainants, from time to time, for cash and on deferred payments. One of their notes, for $570.41, matured on the 15th of May, 1857, and was protested for non-payment. The complainants, becoming anxious about the safety of their claim, immediately called upon Walker for security, but failed to obtain it. On the 3d day of June, 1857, they again attempted to obtain security, and for that purpose sent their agent to Tiffin. Walker then and there made an exhibit of the affairs of the concern to this agent, in which he represented the assets at his disposal to be worth $54,500, and the liabilities of the firm of Walker & Ouland not to exceed $13,000, leaving an excess of assets over liabilities in his hands of $41,500. Upon this representation the paper was renewed without security.

On the same day, to wit, the 3d of June, 1857, Walker sold and transferred all of the aforesaid property and assets to his father-in-law, Josiah Hedges, and other relations, in payment of his own individual liabilities.

It appears that, some time in the spring of 1857, Ouland sold to his partner his entire interest in the property and effects of the firm, and in retiring from the concern took Walker's agreement to furnish him a bond of indemnity with good security, against the liabilities of the firm, which bond of indemnity has never been given.

It further appears that the complainants obtained judgment against Walker & Ouland in this court at the July term, 1857, for $684.25 damages, upon said renewed note. Execution was issued on the judgment in January, 1859, and duly returned by the marshal, but he found no goods, chattels, lands or tenements of either Walker or Ouland on which to levy. The judgment remains wholly unsatisfied, and it is conceded that both Walker and Ouland are insolvent.

It is insisted by the complainants: 1st. That the creditors of the firm of Walker & Ouland have an equitable lien upon the property and assets of the partnership, and that such property cannot be diverted to the payment of the individual debts of the partners, to the prejudice of the creditors of the firm. 2d. That if such lien shall be held not to exist, it is nevertheless insisted that the sale by Walker to Hedges and others was, in fact, fraudulent, and therefore void.

§ 361. *Mercantile partners joint tenants. Lien of partners on the assets, existing and subsequent, of the firm.*

Mercantile partners are joint tenants in the copartnership stock and effects. Each has a *specific lien* upon the assets. This lien is not only applied to the property and effects brought into the concern at its organization, but also to everything coming in lieu thereof, during the continuance, or after the determination of the partnership. Upon a dissolution, the lien of the individual members of the firm continues, as well for the indemnity of each as for his proportion of the surplus.

§ 362. *Strictly, firm creditors have no lien on firm assets, but their rights are worked out through the equity of the partners.*

But, in strict law, creditors have no lien upon the partnership property for their debts. It is only worked out through the equity of the partners, over the whole funds, in a court of chancery. That the company property should first be liable for the company debts, and that joint creditors should have a priority or privilege of payment before separate creditors, are rights which the law secures to each and all the members of the firm. They may relinquish these rights to one and the other, or to third persons, or they may enforce them in a court of equity for their own benefit, or become the instruments by which creditors may, in like manner, enforce them for the benefit of creditors.

Hence, when the primary rights of partners to apply the partnership property to the extinguishment of the company debts is gone, the right of the partnership creditors to enforce the application of the property of the firm to the payment of their debts is also gone. That the general creditors of a firm before levy or seizure have not, as such creditors, any specific lien on the assets of the firm, and that the preference of the company creditors over the separate creditors in the distribution of the joint assets arises from, and must be worked out through, the rights of the partners to insist upon such application, are principles now too well established to admit of question. Sigler & Richey v. Knox Co. Bank, 8 O. S. R., 511; 5 id., 101, 516; 11 O. R., 399; Ruffin, *Ex parte*, 6 Ves. Jr., 126–9; Williams, *Ex parte*, 11 id., 2; Hoxie v. Carr, 1 Sumn., 181; Story on Part., § 357 *et seq.*

§ **363.** *Mere insolvency does not deprive partners of their control over the property.*

Nor does the right of appropriation of the joint assets to the separate creditors by consent of the other partner depend upon the solvency of the firm. "Mere insolvency, as commonly understood, *no fraud intervening*, will not deprive partners of their legal control over the property, and their right to sell and dispose of it as to them shall seem just and proper." A contrary rule would produce incalculable mischief and great inconvenience, and would be attended with absolute injustice to *bona fide* purchasers of such property. But it is said that in this case the legal right, title and interest of Ouland in the partnership effects never passed to Walker, inasmuch as the latter failed to comply with his agreement to give bond with surety against the company debts. And the objection is put on the ground that the agreement between the parties was executory.

The case of *Ex parte* Rowlandson, Rose, 416, would seem to sustain this doctrine. In that case, after a dissolution and assignment of the partnership effects to one of the partners, a bill was filed by the retiring partner against the other, alleging *fraud* in the non-performance of the articles of dissolution, and praying an injunction and receiver, which was ordered. It was held that such interference of the court, arising from the non-performance of the articles, restored the property to its original character as joint property, unless the plaintiff in equity by his conduct rendered nugatory the effect of such interference. But in Young v. Keighly, 15 Ves., 558, where the agreement to convert separate into joint property was only in part performed, the court treated the conversion as complete.

§ **364.** *Retiring partner cannot follow firm assets into hands of bona fide purchaser from continuing partner.*

It seems just and reasonable that where the retiring partner thus sells and transfers all his interest in the joint property to his copartner, who then assumes exclusive control over it and disposes of it to *bona fide* purchasers, he should not be permitted to follow such property in the hands of third persons, but should be remitted to his action at law for a breach of the agreement.

As between the partners themselves, when the property has not changed hands, a court of equity will always interpose and protect one of them against the fraudulent contract or fraudulent conduct of the other, and for that purpose will appoint a receiver and finally adjust the affairs of the partnership. But what are the facts of the case in this regard?

In the spring of 1857 Ouland sold to Walker his interest in the concern, including the goods in the store and the entire assets. Walker took exclusive possession and exercised absolute control over them. He traded them off on his own account, paid company and private debts from their proceeds, *without objection or interference on the part of Ouland.* So far as his dealing with third persons was concerned, they had a right to treat and regard such property as his own, and they should be protected in the purchase of it when made in good faith, unless such purchase was tainted with fraud.

§ **365.** *Actual fraud on part of private creditor renders him chargeable as against firm creditor to the extent of the assets fraudulently received.*

And this brings us to the consideration of the other branch of the case, to wit: Was the transfer of the property from Walker to Hedges and others attended by such circumstances of *fraud* as to vitiate the sale of the property or any part of it? When Pratt, the plaintiffs' agent, called upon Walker for security, early in June, 1857, the latter evidently made false statements as to his solvency. By these false representations he obtained a renewal of the note, and thereby gained sufficient time to dispose of the property in question to his father-in-law, without any hindrance from the plaintiffs, by attachment proceedings or otherwise.

The individual indebtedness of Walker to Josiah Hedges on the 3d of June, 1857, is alleged to have been $10,608. On that day Walker assigned and delivered to Hedges certain of his book accounts, amounting to $865.53, and also put into Hedges' possession goods in the store valued at $12,385.55, of which amount it is claimed $9,742.55 were applied in payment of the indebtedness of Walker to Hedges.

It appears from the testimony of Pratt, that on the 5th of June, 1857, finding Walker's store and stock of goods in the possession of Hedges, he called upon the latter for an explanation of the transfer. In his testimony, in relation to this interview, Pratt declares that he [Hedges] said, " the goods in the store all belonged to him — that he had *bought* them of Walker. I asked him the consideration, and he replied that Walker owed him a great deal more than he could get out of the goods, and that the indebtedness was for money borrowed a long time ago."

It further appears that afterward Walker disposed of a portion of the goods thus held by Hedges to Reed, Jenrings & Co., and other creditors, in compromise or payment of the debts of Walker & Ouland, and that the goods so disposed of amounted to $2,643.

The effect of this transaction, so far as the $2,643 worth of goods is concerned, was a direct fraud on the complainants. The legal representatives of Josiah Hedges have failed to explain the transaction upon any ground consistent with fair dealing. An inventory of the goods was made at the time of the alleged transfer, and a bill of sale to Hedges was drawn up and executed by Walker. These papers have not been produced in evidence. Their non-production forces upon us the conviction that the goods, to the amount of $2,643 at least, were covered up by Hedges either to defraud the complainants or to hinder and delay them in the collection of their debt, and to enable

Walker to force a compromise with his creditors on terms favorable to himself.

In the celebrated case of Chesterfield *v.* Jansen, 2 Ves., 155, Lord Hardwicke, after remarking that a court of equity has an undoubted jurisdiction to relieve against every species of fraud, declares that to be fraud which may be collected and inferred in the consideration of a court of equity, from the nature and circumstances of the transaction, as being *an imposition and deceit on other persons not parties to the fraudulent agreement.*

Without impinging the application of the $9,743.55 to the payment of Hedges' debt, or inquiring into the validity of the sales made by Walker to Baldwin and other defendants, it is sufficient to answer the purposes of equity in this suit to charge the estate of Josiah Hedges for the payment of the complainants' judgment and costs, and this, in consideration of the fraudulent conduct of the parties in relation to the $2,643 worth of goods taken by Hedges in excess of his claim. A decree will be entered accordingly.

FITZPATRICK *v.* FLANNAGAN.

(16 Otto, 648–660. 1882.)

ERROR to U. S. Circuit Court, District of Mississippi.

Opinion by MR. JUSTICE MATTHEWS.

STATEMENT OF FACTS.—This is an action of *assumpsit* commenced by Charles M. Flannagan and George M. Flannagan, copartners, doing business under the firm name and style of C. M. & G. M. Flannagan, by the issuing of a writ of attachment, according to the practice as prescribed by the law of Mississippi, they being citizens of Missouri. The process of attachment was founded on an affidavit, which set forth that John J. Fitzpatrick, as the surviving partner of the firm of Fitzpatrick Brothers, composed of himself and his brother James C. Fitzpatrick, deceased, was the legal owner of the partnership property; that he, as such survivor, was indebted to the plaintiffs in several sums, evidenced by partnership obligations, as well as in a sum of $6,000, for a debt contracted by James C. Fitzpatrick and Eugene A. Forbes, then partners under the name of Forbes & Fitzpatrick, and which had, on the dissolution of that firm, by the retirement of Forbes, been assumed by the firm of Fitzpatrick Brothers, which debt was evidenced by the promissory note of Forbes & Fitzpatrick, held by the plaintiffs. The whole indebtedness, for which suit was brought, was alleged to amount to $15,936.55. The affidavit then charged that "the said John J. Fitzpatrick has property or rights in action which he conceals and unjustly refuses to apply to the payment of his debts, and that he has assigned or disposed of, or is about to assign or dispose of, his property or rights in action, or some part thereof, with intent to defraud his creditors, or give an unfair preference to some of them; and that he has converted, or is about to convert, his property into money, or evidences of debt, with which to place it beyond the reach of his creditors." And suggesting that John McGinty, Edward McGinty and George M. Klein, cashier of the Mississippi Valley Bank, are indebted to him, or have property of his in their hands, etc., the affidavit prays for a summons against them as garnishees.

The statutory bond having been given, a writ of attachment was issued, which the marshal returned as served by levying upon and taking possession of certain personal property, according to an inventory attached, as the property of the defendant; and that afterward Edward McGinty, having made claim that he was the owner of the property attached, and the same having been valued, and a claimant's bond given and accepted, he had turned said goods over to said McGinty, and had summoned the defendant and the garnishees.

The defendant then, in due time, filed a plea in abatement to the writ, denying the several grounds thereof as alleged in the affidavit; and on the same day the plaintiffs, by leave of court, filed an amendment to the affidavit, setting forth "that the firm of Fitzpatrick Brothers, composed of defendant and James C. Fitzpatrick, deceased, and of which he is the surviving partner, fraudulently contracted the debt or incurred the obligation for which suit has been brought." The granting of this leave to amend the affidavit was objected to by the defendant, and is the subject of an exception, and assigned for error. But section 1483 of the code of Mississippi of 1871 expressly authorizes amendments to defective affidavits, and we see no objection on principle, under such a provision, to an amendment adding a new ground for the attachment. There was no claim on the part of the defendant of being taken by surprise or put to any disadvantage by reason of the amendment, and we fail to perceive how, in any way, he could have been prejudiced. In point of fact, he immediately filed his plea in abatement, traversing the additional allegations of the amendment; and the cause being at issue upon the pleas in abatement was submitted to a jury, according to the practice authorized by the statute. There was a verdict finding "that the attachment herein was rightfully sued out;" and the defendant thereupon had leave to plead to the merits, and filed with a plea of *non assumpsit* several special pleas, which it is not necessary now to notice. The cause having upon these issues been tried by a jury, there was a verdict for the plaintiff, whereon judgment was rendered. The present writ brings up for review these proceedings and judgment, errors being assigned upon bills of exception duly taken to the rulings of the court upon both trials.

Upon the trial of the issues of fact arising upon the pleas in abatement, evidence was introduced, as appears by the bill of exceptions, by the respective parties, tending to prove the following state of facts:

In March, 1878, the defendant purchased the interest of Forbes in the firm of Forbes & Fitzpatrick, wholesale grocers, and formed with the latter person the partnership of Fitzpatrick Brothers, which, by the terms of the purchase, assumed the liabilities of Forbes & Fitzpatrick, including, among others, about $15,000 due to the plaintiffs. These liabilities, as was afterwards ascertained, exceeded the value of the assets of the original firm. James C. Fitzpatrick died in September, 1878, leaving in the hands of the defendant, as surviving partner, the partnership property, and the concern insolvent. The defendant continued the business, sold out in part the old stock, purchased other goods to replenish it to the amount of more than $12,000, partly on credit, partly for cash, putting the goods indiscriminately in stock with those on hand. The firm of Fitzpatrick Brothers, during its existence, paid part of the debt due to the plaintiffs, assumed by it, and contracted with them, for goods bought and money loaned, an indebtedness for about the same amount as that paid. The deceased partner, before his death, had drawn out of the partnership more than his interest therein, and was indebted to it. On December 3, 1878, the defendant, being very much pressed to pay some maturing bills to the Mississippi Valley Bank, being debts created by the firm of Fitzpatrick Brothers, borrowed $5,700 from John McGinty, giving his note, at one day's date, verbally promising to repay the amount speedily out of the assets of the late firm. This money was used by him in paying partnership debts. Fitzpatrick Brothers owed John McGinty, besides, two notes, one for $2,500, and one for $5,200. Being unable to repay the borrowed money to John McGinty, the defendant, on December 19, 1878, sold to Edward McGinty, a relative of John McGinty, his entire stock of goods, amounting to $6,633.46, at cost and ten per cent. added, and the partnership accounts, amounting to $10,222.06, for which Edward McGinty paid $8,200 in cash, and assumed to pay obligations due in part from Fitzpatrick Brothers, and in part from the defendant, for commercial debts contracted by him since the death of his partner, to the amount of $6,974.16. This price was the full and fair value for the goods and accounts, and in fact Edward McGinty paid out several thousand dollars more on the debts assumed than he had collected out of the assets transferred.

This sale to Edward McGinty was made with the knowledge of John McGinty, who, in fact, advanced the money to complete it, Edward being without means, and upon an understanding that the money should be paid to John McGinty on account of the debts due to him; and accordingly the $8,200 cash was returned to him in payment of the two notes for $2,500 and $5,700, respectively. Immediately after the sale, Fitzpatrick was employed by Edward McGinty as a clerk to carry on the business, at a salary of $2,500 per annum, and shortly afterwards a partnership between them was advertised. The assets of the firm of Fitzpatrick Brothers on hand at the time of the death of James C. Fitzpatrick, together with after-acquired goods and moneys, were applied indiscriminately by the defendant to the payment of debts of the firm, and of those contracted by him in the subsequent course of business; and it appeared that he had paid as much at least on account of partnership debts as he had realized from partnership assets, and that he had applied all the proceeds of the business, after paying its necessary expenses, to the payment of the debts of the late firm, and of his own, contracted in carrying on the business as surviving partner.

The second issue, upon the pleas in abatement, was upon the allegation of the affidavit that " the defendant has assigned and disposed of, or was then about to assign or dispose of, his property or rights in action, or some part thereof, with intent to defraud his creditors, or give an unfair preference to some of them."

Upon the first branch of this issue — whether the defendant had disposed of any of his property with intent to defraud his creditors — the court charged the jury as follows:

" If you shall find from the evidence that the defendant sold or transferred any of the property or assets of the late firm of Fitzpatrick Brothers, with intent to prevent the creditors of the firm of Fitzpatrick Brothers, or any of them, from collecting their debts, such sale or disposition will sustain this ground of attachment. It was the duty of the defendant, as such surviving partner, to apply all of the assets of the firm to the payment of the debts due by the firm; and if he appropriated any part of them to the payment of his individual debts, it was a fraud upon the firm creditors, whether he so considered it or not, and, if established by the proof, will sustain this ground of attachment, as the law will presume that he intended the natural result of his act. The defendant being liable for the debts of the firm, could not, by borrowing money and paying the debts of the firm, create himself a creditor of the firm, or subrogate himself to the rights of the creditors as paid." And to the giving of this instruction an exception was taken.

§ 366. *Quære, whether an allegation, in an affidavit for an attachment, that defendant has disposed of his property to defraud his creditors, is supported by proof of disposing of the property of a dissolved firm to defraud firm creditors.*
The ground on which this part of the charge appears to rest is, that a surviving partner, although invested with the legal title to the partnership property, on the dissolution of the firm, by the death of his copartner, is not the beneficial owner, but a mere trustee to liquidate the partnership affairs, by selling the assets and applying them to the payment of the partnership debts; that the continuance of the business by means of the partnership assets is a breach of that trust, and, if it results in diverting any of the partnership property from the creditors of the firm, is a fraud upon them. And yet, upon that supposition, it deserves consideration, whether the allegation made in the affidavit as the ground of the attachment — that the defendant has disposed of his own property to defraud his creditors — can be supported by proof of a disposition of property belonging to the firm, in order to defraud the creditors of the firm; especially, in view of the result that, if the attachment is sustained, it not only subjects the partnership property, but also takes the individual property of the defendant, from individual creditors, for the payment of the firm debts. The writ runs against his individual property alone, and upon the sole ground that he has sought fraudulently to withdraw it from the claims of his individual creditors. This incongruity is sufficient, at least, strongly to suggest the suspicion that the proceeding itself, and the grounds on which it has been sustained, are based upon a misconception of the law which governs the case.

And this will be confirmed by a critical examination of the charge.

Upon the state of the evidence, as disclosed by the bill of exceptions, the jury may have found that the defendant, as surviving partner, with the assent, either express or tacit, of the personal representatives of his deceased copartner, had been left in possession of the firm property, for the purpose of continuing the business; that, in doing so, in good faith he raised money upon the individual credit given him, by reason of his possession and control of property, which he was allowed to deal with as his own, and applied it to the purpose of paying the debts due from the firm of which he was the surviving partner; and yet felt compelled, under this charge, to find that an appropriation out of the property which had come to him as such survivor, to repay such a loan, without any actual fraudulent intent, would be a fraud in law upon every creditor of the partnership, justifying a seizure, on attachment for that cause, of all his property, whether formerly belonging to the partnership, or since acquired, and that although his individual additions to his stock in trade were, at least, equal to what had been taken for the payment of individual debts.

It is fair to consider this charge, although not so qualified, in connection with the facts, in reference to which there was evidence, that the firm of Fitzpatrick Brothers, and its individual members, were insolvent, in the sense of not being able to pay their debts, during the whole period of its existence, and the additional fact that the deceased partner had before his death drawn from the partnership more than his interest therein, and was indebted to the firm.

§ 367. *Limitations upon the right of a partnership creditor to be paid out of firm assets.*
The legal right of a partnership creditor to subject the partnership prop-

erty to the payment of his debt consists simply in the right to reduce his claim to judgment, and to sell the goods of his debtors on execution. His right to appropriate the partnership property specifically to the payment of his debt, in equity, in preference to creditors of an individual partner, is derived through the other partner, whose original right it is to have the partnership assets applied to the payment of partnership obligations. And this equity of the creditors subsists as long as that of the partner, through which it is derived, remains; that is, so long as the partner himself "retains an interest in the firm assets, as a partner, a court of equity will allow the creditors of the firm to avail themselves of his equity, and enforce through it the application of those assets primarily to payment of the debts due them, whenever the property comes under its administration." Such was the language of this court in Case v. Beauregard, 99 U. S., 119 (§§ 356–60, *supra*), in which Mr. Justice Strong, delivering its opinion, continued as follows: "It is indispensable, however, to such relief, when the creditors are, as in the present case, simple-contract creditors, that the partnership property should be within the control of the court, and in the course of administration brought there by the bankruptcy of the firm, or by an assignment, or by the creation of a trust in some mode. This is because neither the partners nor the joint creditors have any specific lien, nor is there any trust that can be enforced until the property has passed *in custodiam legis*." Hence it follows that, " if before the interposition of the court is asked the property has ceased to belong to the partnership, if by a *bona fide* transfer it has become the several property either of one partner or of a third person, the equities of the partners are extinguished, and consequently the derivative equities of the creditors are at an end." In that case it was held, in respect to a firm admitted to be insolvent, that transfers made by the individual partners of their interest in the partnership property converted that property into individual property, terminated the equity of any partner to require the application thereof to the payment of the joint debts, and constituted a bar to a bill in equity filed by a partnership creditor to subject it to the payment of his debt, the relief prayed for being grounded on the claim that these transfers were in fraud of his rights as a creditor of the firm.

Another case between the same parties came again for consideration before the court, which reaffirmed the decision, and held that in such a case the bill might be properly filed by a creditor without first reducing his claim to judgment. Case v. Beauregard, 101 U. S., 688.

The same doctrine has been fully sanctioned by the supreme court of Mississippi in Schmidlapp v. Currie, 55 Miss., 597, where it is said that " the doctrine that firm assets must first be applied to the payment of firm debts, and individual property to individual debts, is only a principle of administration adopted by the courts where, from any cause, they are called upon to wind up the firm business, and find that the members have made no valid disposition of or charges upon its assets. Thus, where, upon a dissolution of the firm by death, or limitation, or bankruptcy, or from any other cause, the courts are called upon to wind up the concern, they adopt and enforce the principle stated; but the principle itself springs alone out of the obligation to do justice between the partners." In that case one of two partners, but with the assent of the other, and without any fraudulent intent, transferred the whole business and stock of the firm to a third person in payment of an individual debt. A creditor of the partnership sued out a writ of attachment against them, and caused it to be levied on the goods in the possession of the purchaser, upon the ground that the transfer of the firm goods in satisfaction of the individual debt of one of the partners was fraudulent and void as against firm creditors. The right to do so was denied.

The same principle applies in case of a dissolution of the partnership. "It is competent," says Mr. Justice Story (Partnership, sec. 358), "for the partners, in cases of a voluntary dissolution, to agree that the joint property of the partnership shall belong to one of them; and if this agreement be *bona fide* and for a valuable consideration, it will transfer the whole property to such partner wholly free from the claims of the joint creditors. The like result will arise from any stipulation to the same effect, in the original articles of copartnership, in cases of a dissolution by death or by any other personal incapacity."

§ 368. *Surviving partner may use firm assets to pay his private debts, so long as neither the partnership creditors nor the representatives of the deceased partner take any steps to liquidate the affairs of the partnership.*

And in case of dissolution by the death of one of the partners without any previous agreement as to the mode of liquidation, the only difference is, that the joint creditor may, at his election, institute proceedings by filing a bill in equity against the personal representatives of the deceased partner, and the survivors, to wind up the partnership business, to marshal the assets, and appropriate the partnership property to the payment of the joint debts. Story on Partnership, secs. 347, 362. Although in Mississippi it is denied that a court of equity has jurisdiction to entertain a suit on behalf of a firm creditor at large against a partnership, whether it be an existing one, or one that has ceased by limitation or by the withdrawal or death of one of the partners. Roach *v.* Brannon, 57 Miss., 490; Freeman *v.* Stewart, 41 id., 138.

And unless a partnership creditor, or the personal representatives of the deceased partner, commence such a proceeding, to liquidate the affairs of the partnership, there is nothing to prevent the surviving partner from dealing with the partnership property as his own, and, acting in good faith, to make valid dispositions of it. Locke *v.* Lewis, 124 Mass., 1. And if, in like good faith, with the acquiescence of the personal representatives of the deceased partner, he uses the firm property, to continue the business on his own account and in his own name, he does it without other liability than to be held accountable to the estate of his deceased partner for a share of the profits; or, as we have seen, upon a bill filed for that purpose, by the personal representatives of the deceased partner or a partnership creditor, to wind up the firm business and apply its assets to the payment of its debts. Any intermediate disposition of the property, made in good faith, even although it may have been specifically a part of the partnership assets, and even if it has been applied to the payment of his individual obligations, will be valid and effectual; and, without circumstances showing an actual intention to defraud, cannot be treated as a fraud in law upon partnership creditors. Accordingly, in Roach *v.* Brannon, 57 Miss., 490, the supreme court of Mississippi said: "If, then, a firm creditor may sue out and levy an attachment upon firm assets in the hands of a surviving partner, upon what grounds must he proceed? Must he aver and prove one of the specific grounds of attachment laid down in the statute, or will it be sufficient to show that the surviving partner is acting in violation of that *quasi* trust imposed upon him by law for the benefit of firm creditors? We have no hesitation in saying that he must bring his case strictly within the letter of the statute."

§ 369. *Right of an insolvent debtor to prefer creditors in Mississippi.* The next assignment of error is based on an exception to the following instruction, being in continuation of that just considered:

"5th. The latter clause of this issue is as to whether or not the disposition made by the defendant of the assets was with the intention of giving an unfair preference to some of his creditors over others. It is difficult to determine what particular acts will constitute such preference. I am of the opinion that the legislature meant something by this expression, but it has never been construed by the supreme court of the state. In the absence of such construction, I will instruct you that when a debtor is insolvent, and knows that he will be unable for a great length of time to pay all his debts, and disposes of his means to one or more of his creditors, to the exclusion of others, and with the design that those unpaid shall remain so, it will constitute an unfair preference within the meaning of this clause of the statute. You will, therefore, apply this rule to the facts in proof under this issue."

The language of the Mississippi code of 1871, describing one of the grounds for which an attachment might issue, was that "the debtor has assigned or disposed of, or is about to assign or dispose of, his property or rights in action, or some part thereof, with intent to defraud his creditors-or give an unfair preference to some of them." Code of 1871, sec. 1420. This provision, it is said, so far as it relates to an "unfair preference," was first introduced into the statutes of the state by the code of 1857, article 2, page 372. It is said by the supreme court of Mississippi, in Eldridge *v.* Phillipson, 58 Miss., 270, that "the right of a debtor, insolvent or in failing circumstances, to give a preference to one or more of his creditors, if it be *bona fide* and with no intent to secure a benefit to himself, is a firmly established rule in the jurisprudence of this state," and many cases are cited, occurring both before and after the adoption of the code of 1857, in support of the statement. It was well settled, therefore, that whatever else the prohibition against unfair preferences might be supposed to include, it certainly did not make all preferences illegal. But the necessary result of preferring one or more creditors by a debtor unable to pay all would be that the rest should remain unpaid, and for an indefinite length of time; and as the preference is supposed to have been designed, it could well be said, in every such case, that the debtor making it also designed its natural and expected consequences. It follows, therefore, if the part of the charge of the court now under examination be correct, that all preferences are unfair, and, being unfair, are illegal,— a conclusion which we have seen is opposed to the settled law of Mississippi.

In the case just referred to, of Eldridge *v.* Phillipson, the question was presented directly for decision for the first time to the supreme court of that state. It was then decided that no preference could be held to be unfair which, tested by the rules of law, is legal; and that as to be illegal it must be fraudulent, and as all fraudulent dispositions of his property by a debtor are prohibited in other words, the clause relating to unfair preferences is mere surplusage. This construction is confirmed by the fact that the words in question have been omitted from the code of 1880 by the legislature of Mississippi.

In our opinion, this interpretation of the statute is correct, and we accordingly adopt it. The ruling of the circuit court to the contrary we adjudge, therefore, to be erroneous.

§ **370.** *A rule of estoppel.*

The cause came on for further trial upon the issues raised by the pleas to the merits. Besides the general issue, the defendant pleaded, as to the note for $6,000 made by Forbes & Fitzpatrick, the defense of the statute of frauds; that the alleged promise was not in writing; and, also, that the sole consideration therefor was the sale to him by Forbes of his interest to the partnership of Forbes & Fitzpatrick; and that the promise to pay the same, as one of the debts of that firm, was procured from him by means of false and fraudulent misrepresentations made to him by Forbes as to the value of that interest.

On the trial, as appears from the bill of exceptions, there was evidence tending to show that, although the original assumption by the firm of Fitzpatrick Brothers of the debts of Forbes & Fitzpatrick was verbal, yet, that afterwards it was repeated in writing in sundry letters by the defendant, written after he had full knowledge of the character and condition of the assets, property and business which he had purchased from Forbes.

The court instructed the jury as follows: "The plea of the defendant alleges, as to the $6,000 note of Forbes & Fitzpatrick, that its payment was assumed as part consideration of a purchase by him from Eugene A. Forbes, and that said purchase was made on fraudulent misrepresentations as to the character and value of the things sold. If you believe this, and that the defendant was thereby injured, you will deduct from said note the amount of his damages by reason of such misrepresentations, unless you shall find that the defendant, after he had a full knowledge of the misrepresentations, continued to recognize his liability to plaintiffs, and promised to pay after he had acquired such knowledge, in which case he will be estopped to make such defense."

To this portion of the charge an exception was taken, and instructions of an opposite tenor asked to be given, which were refused, but which it is not necessary to notice specially, as they are directly negatived by the instruction given, and are disposed of if that be correct. And of its correctness we have no doubt. A subsequent promise, with full knowledge of the facts, is certainly equivalent to an original promise made under similar circumstances; and no one, acting with full knowledge, can justly say that he has been deceived by false representations. *Volenti non fit injuria.*

§ **371.** *A rule of practice in Mississippi.*

We are advised that, according to the practice in Mississippi, as authorized by its statutes (Code of Miss. of 1880, sec. 2434), which, by sections 914 and 915, Revised Statutes, are adopted as the practice of the circuit court of the United States in that district, the proceeding which resulted in the verdict sustaining the attachment, and the verdict and judgment on the merits of the cause of action, are separate, and consequently may be separately considered on error. The judgment on the plea in abatement is not final in the sense that it may be reviewed before the final determination of the cause; but a writ of error upon the final judgment brings up the whole record, and subjects to review all the proceedings in the cause. As we find no error in the personal judgment against the defendant, ascertaining the existence and amount of the debt due from him, and awarding execution therefor, the same will be affirmed; - but the judgment overruling the pleas in abatement and sustaining the attachment must be reversed, and the cause remanded with instructions to set aside the verdict upon the issues arising upon the pleas in abatement of the writ of attachment, and to grant a new trial thereof.

Judgment accordingly.

CRANE v. MORRISON.

(District Court for California: 4 Sawyer, 188–148. 1876.)

Opinion by HOFFMAN, J.

In the case of Henry C. Hyde v. Lewis Baker, Jr., this court had occasion incidentally to consider what are the rights of a retiring partner who has assigned his interest in the firm assets to a remaining partner upon an agreement by the latter to become responsible for the firm debts.

§ 372. *Equity of retiring partner to have assets applied in payment of firm debts is lost where new rights have attached.*

There seemed to be much reason for holding with Mr. J. Allen in Menagh v. Whitwell, 52 N. Y., 157–8, that even where there was no express stipulation for the application of the joint assets to the payment of the joint debts, the same equity might exist in favor of the retiring partner to compel such application as he would have had as continuing partner. But this equity cannot exist where new rights have attached by reason of the change of interests, as where rights of individual creditors have accrued, or where the continuing partners or the new firm have disposed of the property, or there are creditors of the new firm. 9 Cush., 553; 14 Gray, 534; Dimon v. Hazard, 32 N. Y., 65.

STATEMENT OF FACTS.— It appears in the case at bar, that on the 2d of July, 1875. the firm of Jessup & Stevens, composed of William H. Jessup and Russell Stevens, was dissolved by mutual consent, and public notice given thereof by advertisement. The firm property was divided between the partners, Stevens retaining the Cobb Mountain saw-mill property, and Jessup the flour-mill property in Lake county. Each of the partners agreed to assume and pay and save the other harmless from the debts contracted in respect of the property of which he became the separate owner.

Stevens having failed to comply with this latter part of the agreement within the time prescribed, Jessup notified him that he had rescinded the contract. In the meantime, and before any default on the part of Stevens to fulfill his contract had occurred, he had entered into a partnership with one Marshall to run the Cobb Mountain saw-mill, and had conveyed to him one-third of that property for $10,000, $1,000 to be paid in cash, and the remainder in the manner specified in the agreement.

On or about the 17th September, 1875, the defendant, Morrison, commenced an action against Stevens and Jessup on a promissory note for $600, made by Stevens and indorsed by Jessup. The consideration for this note was the payment (in effect) by Morrison of a firm debt due by the former firm of Stevens & Jessup to one Mills.

On the same day, an attachment was levied by Morrison's direction on the property now in dispute. The property seized consisted chiefly of lumber at the Cobb Mountain saw-mill, and claimed by and in the possession of the new firm of Stevens & Marshall. It still remains in the possession of the sheriff (the defendant Ingram), who holds it under that attachment.

On the 29th December, 1876, Stevens & Marshall were adjudged bankrupts, and their assignee brings this suit to recover the property referred to.

It does not very clearly appear whether the property was seized as the property of Stevens, or that of Stevens & Jessup, or that of Stevens & Marshall. The right to hold it seems to be defended on three grounds:

1. That by the rescission by Jessup of the contract between him and Stevens the property which had been divided between them and converted into the

separate property of each was reconverted into joint property, and became liable for the joint debts of the dissolved firm, of which debts the promissory note signed by Stevens and indorsed by Jessup was one.

2. That as some of the property was the joint property of the firm of Stevens & Marshall, the separate creditor of Stevens had a right to seize and sell his interest in the firm; *i. e.*, the balance that might be due after payment of the joint debts.

3. That the property was in part at least the separate property of Stevens, and, therefore, liable for his debts.

§ 373. *A dissolution of a partnership and a division of the partnership assets converts those assets into separate property of the partners, and, on formation of a new firm, the creditors of such firm are to be preferred to creditors of the old.*

1. It seems to me unquestionable that the agreement between Stevens and Jessup operated not only a dissolution of the partnership, but a conversion of the firm property assigned to each partner into the separate property of the partner to whom it was assigned. Whatever lien or equity Jessup might have enforced to compel the application by Stevens of his share of the joint assets so converted into his separate property to the payment of those of the joint debts which he had assumed (a point upon which it is unnecessary to express an opinion), it is plain that Jessup would have had no such right as against the creditors of the new firm, or any assignee of Stevens for value. Before default made by Stevens or notice of rescission by Jessup, the latter had sold a third interest in the property to Marshall, with whom he had entered into partnership, the partners holding the whole property as joint assets in the proportion of their respective interests.

The adverse and paramount right of Marshall, and of the creditors of Stevens & Marshall, had therefore attached, and Jessup had no longer any right or lien, equitable or otherwise, upon the property, for the payment of the joint debts of the former firm. *A fortiori* the property which had thus become the property of the new firm, and primarily liable for its debts, could not be taken to satisfy the claim of a joint creditor of the extinct firm, even admitting Morrison to have been such. On the bankruptcy of the firm of Stevens & Marshall, their joint property passed to the assignee in bankruptcy, to be applied to the satisfaction of their joint debts. The balance (after satisfying those debts and adjusting the accounts between the partners) which may be due to Stevens would alone be subject to Morrison's attachment. As the firm is admitted to be insolvent, no such balance can be looked for.

§ 374. *The right of separate creditors of partners to levy on the firm property is subject to the right of firm creditors to have their debts satisfied first, and in equity or bankruptcy the rights of the latter will be enforced accordingly.*

2. It is claimed that Morrison, as the separate creditor of Stevens, had a right to seize all the property of the firm of Stevens & Marshall, although he can sell only the defendant partner's interest, and that the sheriff thereby became tenant in common with the other partner. In the case of Osborn, Assignee, etc., *v.* McBride, 3 Sawyer, 590, this court had occasion to consider a question nearly similar. In that case, several judgments had been obtained against each of two partners, for separate debts, and several executions issued. The interests of both partners in the firm assets had been separately sold on execution, and bought by the defendant in the suit brought by the assignee in bankruptcy of the firm.

It was held that "the sale on execution, of either or both of the partners' interests, in satisfaction of a separate debt, gave to the purchaser only an interest in the assets which might remain after the payment of the partnership debts. The fact that he purchased the interests of both the partners, sold on separate executions, can have no effect to enlarge the interest of either, acquired on the separate sale of that interest. He took merely a right to an account, and can now hold the partnership assets only subject to that account, and in entire subordination to the joint creditors."

It was further held that partnership debts have in equity and by the bankrupt act an inherent priority of claim, to be discharged out of partnership property, and as between a firm and its creditors the title of the former is not divested by any separate transfers to strangers, by one or all of the partners, in payment of their individual debts, or by proceedings against them separately with reference to their individual interests; and when there has been no transfer by the firm, and the property remains in specie and capable of being levied upon, it may be followed in the hands of those claiming by such transfers or proceedings, and may be levied on by a judgment creditor of the firm. Menagh v. Whitwell, 52 N. Y., 149.

But even admitting that the rights here attributed to the creditor may be doubtful, and that his remedy is to be sought in equity, there can be no doubt that where the separate creditor of a partner has taken partnership property in execution for his separate debt, the other partners may file their bill against the separate creditor, the debtor partner and the sheriff, praying a general account of the partnership, and the payment of what is due them, and that the debtor and sheriff may be enjoined from proceeding under the execution and selling the stock and effects; and, a court of equity will give relief accordingly, and the same relief is given in favor of the assignees in bankruptcy. Collyer on Partnership, sec. 831; Taylor v. Field, Wats. Partnership, p. 100; 15 Ves., 559; 4 Ves., 396; and see Osborn v. McBride, 3 Saw., 590.

§ 375. *Appointment of receiver of property which is in possession of the sheriff in another suit will not preclude an assignee in bankruptcy from recovering the property from the sheriff.*

It is urged that Jessup has filed his bill in the fourth district court in this state, against Stevens, Marshall and the defendant Morrison, praying for an accounting of the copartnership affairs of Jessup & Stevens, and for the appointment of a receiver; and that a receiver has been appointed whose possession cannot now be divested. To this it is a sufficient answer to say that the receiver is not in possession; the property sued for is in the possession of the sheriff, who holds under the attachment levied in the suit brought by defendant Morrison.

On the whole I am of opinion that the property levied on by Morrison was the firm property of the bankrupts, Stevens & Marshall, and that their assignee is entitled to the possession of it for the purpose of converting it into cash, and satisfying the joint creditors of that firm. The right of Morrison under his attachment to any balance that may be due Stevens, after satisfying the joint creditors, will be duly protected by the court.

IN RE SAUTHOFF.

(District Court for Wisconsin: 8 Bissell, 85–48. 1877.)

STATEMENT OF FACTS.— Sauthoff and Olson were partners in business, and upon the dissolution, January 27, 1876, Olson retired and Sauthoff continued in the business, paying to Olson certain sums in money, and in the notes and accounts of the partnership and in his own notes, and assuming the debts of the firm. In March, 1876, Olson bought a homestead. In April Sauthoff became insolvent, and soon afterward proceedings in bankruptcy were instituted against the partnership. The assignee seeks to subject to the payment of the firm debts the means withdrawn by Olson from the assets of the partnership, and as much of them as were devoted to the purchase of the homestead.

Opinion by DYER, J.

In a case where a copartnership which is indebted has been dissolved, the retiring partner withdrawing, on transfer of his interests, a portion of the assets or capital, and the transaction being followed at a not remote period by the insolvency of the member assuming the debts and continuing the business, it is the duty of the court, when called to consider the rights and liabilities of the parties, to look cautiously into the facts, with a view to the discovery of any possible fraud, and the correction of any wrong that may have resulted to creditors.

§ 376. *Partnership creditors have an absolute priority of claim upon the partnership property for the payment of their demands.*

The principle is elementary that in equity partnership creditors have an absolute priority of claim upon the partnership property for the payment of their demands, and that the interest of each individual partner is his share of the surplus after payment of the partnership debts. To such an extent has this rule been carried that it has been held that where a partner sells his interest to a stranger, or it is sold upon execution against him, his right to have the partnership debts paid, and his liability therefor discharged out of the property, are not divested by the sale, and that such a sale gives to the purchaser only such an interest in the assets as may remain after the payment of partnership debts. Menagh v. Whitewell, 52 N. Y., 146; Osborn v. McBride, 16 N. B. R., 22. The sale of partnership property by one of a firm of commercial partners on the eve of his insolvency will be set aside. Saloy v. Albrecht, 17 La. Ann., 75.

The appropriation by an insolvent firm of partnership property to the payment of the individual debts of one partner is not simply void, but is fraudulent, and avoids the deed of assignment. Wilson v. Robertson, 21 N. Y., 587.

§ 377. *Bona fide dissolution, unaccompanied by improper withdrawal of assets, is unassailable, but otherwise if a scheme for enabling partner to appropriate assets which should be applied to pay partnership debts.*

Admitting the full force of these principles, it is also true that they are not so enforced as to operate against or affect a dissolution of copartnership made in good faith, and which is unaccompanied by any improper withdrawal of assets beyond the reach of creditors.

"Tue right of copartners upon dissolution to transfer the joint property to one of the firm is clear and unquestionable. The effect of such a transfer as between the partners is to vest the legal title to the property in the individual partner, with a right to use and dispose of it as his separate estate. . . . If in such transfer there is no fraud and collusion between the copartners, for the purpose of defeating the rights of the joint creditors, and the transaction is made in good faith upon dissolution, and for the purpose of closing the affairs of the partnership, the joint property thereby becomes separate estate, with all the rights and incidents, both in law and equity, which properly attach thereto." Howe v. Lawrence, 9 Cush., 555.

These are principles applicable to a case where one partner retires and the other takes the entire property and assets; and they are substantially reiterated in Sage v. Chollar, 21 Barb., 596, and in Waterman v. Hunt, 2 R. I., 298. See, also, Dimon v. Hazard, 32 N. Y., 65. Where, however, the circumstances of the case show that the dissolution of the partnership is a fraud, as if it be an incident to a scheme for giving one creditor a preference, or for enabling a member of the firm wrongfully to appropriate assets which should be applied in payment of partnership debts, or where the conversion of joint into separate assets is a result contemplated, and is the motive, or one of the motives, of the act of dissolving the firm, the act may be avoided by the joint creditors. In re Waite & Crocker, 1 N. B. R., 373.

§ 878. *The right of partnership creditors to follow assets of a partnership that has been dissolved and subject them, although invested by the retiring partner in a homestead.*

The correctness of the ruling in In re Boothroyd & Gibbs, 14 N. B. R., 223, cannot be questioned, namely: "That the purchase by an insolvent trader of a homestead upon the eve of bankruptcy, with knowledge of his insolvent condition and for the purpose of placing the property beyond the reach of process, is a legal fraud, which no court should hesitate to hold void as to creditors." Advancing a step further, where a copartnership is insolvent, or is possessed of assets not more than adequate for the payment of debts, one member of the firm cannot, upon retiring, rightfully withdraw beyond the reach of creditors and to their injury a portion of the assets or property, and make a personal appropriation of those assets by putting them in the shape of a homestead.

Under such circumstances, though it takes the form of a homestead, the property is as much within the reach of a court of equity as before; and no such change in its form or character can give it new sacredness or endow its possessor with new privileges in its ownership or use.

§ 879. *If a retiring partner takes out a portion of the assets of the firm for his individual use, he must do so without impairing fund for payment of partnership creditors. Mistake of judgment will not protect him.*

Keeping in view the principles thus stated, the question now is, whether, upon the facts, the transaction between Sauthoff and Olson is one which must be condemned as a fraud in fact or law upon their creditors.

Without referring in detail to the circumstances bearing upon the point, it may be first stated that the evidence does not show that there was any actual intended fraud in the act of dissolution. Although the interest of the retiring partner, based upon the estimated value of their assets, was greatly exaggerated, I think the intent of the parties in dissolving their business relations, as disclosed by the testimony, was honest, and that positive bad faith is not to be imputed.

Admitting this to be true, the question still remains, whether their actual pecuniary condition was such as to justify the withdrawal by Olson of the assets which were taken by him when the partnership was dissolved. The amount so withdrawn was $2,400. He took $2,650 in book accounts. Of these he collected $1,400, and returned the balance to the assignee. It is true that the $1,000 paid him in cash by Sauthoff was then raised by loan or pledge, as collateral security, of a mortgage on Sauthoff's homestead, held by his brother. But, subsequently, the holder of that mortgage, as such security, having obtained judgment against Sauthoff for the $1,000, it was held by this court that Sauthoff's brother, as the assignor of the mortgage, stood in the position of a surety, and was entitled as such to protection; and, there having been an execution levy under the judgment upon Sauthoff's stock, it was ordered that the $1,000 be paid in full from the general fund; so that, ultimately, it came from the assets of the concern, and to that extent, in fact, diminished them. Now, the question is, keeping in view the rights of creditors, was the actual pecuniary condition of this firm such as to entitle the retiring partner to appropriate the amount of their assets which he in fact received, and to place them in the form of exempt property?

In settling this question the principle we must apply is, that if a retiring partner takes out a portion of the assets of the firm for his individual use, he must do so without impairing the fund to which the creditors have the right in equity to look for payment; and it must be made clearly to appear that such remaining fund is ample. If such partner receives more than his interest in the surplus after payment of the firm indebtedness, equity must treat it as a wrong to creditors, and this equity cannot be avoided by the fact that the partners believed that enough remained to pay the partnership debts, if, in fact, after making such appropriation in favor of one or both partners, the remaining assets prove insufficient.

The results to be reached one way or the other in this case depend, of course, upon what shall be the determination as to the sufficiency of the assets of the firm left by Olson for the payment of the partnership debts. On their face, the book accounts of the firm amounted to between nine thousand and ten thousand dollars, and this was the value placed upon them by the parties. But that they erred greatly in judgment is demonstrated by the fact that only about $2,800 of the accounts have thus far proved of any value, and of this amount the assignee has received about $1,400, the bankrupt Olson retaining the balance. What further moneys may be derived from such of the accounts as are uncollected is not now known.

Concerning the value of the stock of goods of which the parties were possessed at the time of the dissolution, it is quite impossible upon the present testimony to arrive at a satisfactory conclusion. Complications in this connection arise because of the fact that no distinction has been preserved in the bankruptcy proceedings between the debts of the firm and those incurred by Sauthoff subsequently to the dissolution. Goods purchased by Sauthoff on his individual credit were mingled with the original stock, debts were paid by him from the common fund, without regard to those contracted by the firm and those contracted by himself, the sale made by the assignee included goods on hand at the dissolution and those purchased subsequently, and, so far as distribution has been made, no distinction has been observed between the firm creditors and the subsequent individual creditors of Sauthoff.

Of course, no part of the moneys which it may be determined Olson should restore can rightfully be used in the payment of individual liabilities incurred by Sauthoff subsequently to the dissolution. And, in view of the necessity of ascertaining with accuracy the value of the assets of Sauthoff & Olson at the time the copartnership was dissolved, I shall direct a further reference to take testimony upon that question. Having settled the principles upon which the rights of the parties are to 'be determined, upon the coming in of that testimony it can be ascertained what amount, if any, should be restored to the fund by Olson for application upon the partnership indebtedness.

§ 380. *Subsequent dealings with the remaining partner will not estop creditors from enforcing their claims against the assets withdrawn by a retiring partner.*

It has been urged by counsel for respondent that, by their course of dealing with Sauthoff, selling him goods, giving him fresh credit and permitting such goods to be mingled with the old stock, the creditors must be held to have ratified the transaction between Sauthoff and Olson, and are now estopped from asserting a claim upon the property withdrawn by the latter from the assets of the firm. But it cannot be claimed that the action of the creditors operated to release Olson from liability for the firm indebtedness, and I fail to see how their subsequent dealing with Sauthoff so far sanctioned the appropriation by Olson of the moneys he took out of the firm as now to deprive them, if it shall be found that the remaining assets were insufficient to pay their debts in full, of the right to follow those moneys.

The present order will be that the case be referred to the register to take testimony and ascertain what was the fair actual value of the assets of the firm of Sauthoff & Olson at the time of the dissolution of that firm, the value of the stock in trade, fixtures and book accounts to be separately stated; also, to ascertain what proportion of the stock of goods sold by the assignee was held by the firm at the time of dissolution, and what was the amount and value of the goods purchased by Sauthoff on his individual account subsequent to the dissolution.

§ 881. **In general.**—The rule is, that partnership creditors shall, in the first instance, be satisfied from the partnership estate; and separate or private creditors of the individual partners from the separate and private estate of the partners with whom they have made private and individual contracts; and that the private and individual property of the partners shall not be applied in extinguishment of partnership debts until the separate and individual creditors of the respective partners shall be paid. Murrill *v.* Neill, 8 How., 4M.

§ 882. The general rule in bankruptcy is, that the property of partnerships is first to be applied to the discharge of the partnership debts, and the surplus only is to be applied to the individual debts of any one partner. But if it be necessary, in order to make a final settlement of all claims, the court may take upon itself the administration as well of the partnership estate as of the estate of the partners. Parker *v.* Muggridge, 2 Story, 334.

§ 883. Partnership debts must first be paid out of partnership property, and the individual debts out of the individual property. But where by a *bona fide* transaction the property ceases to be partnership property, and becomes individual property, it is not liable first to partnership debts. *Quere*, whether it should not be first applied in bankruptcy to the payment of the bankrupt's individual debts. *In re* Wiley, 4 Biss., 214.

§ 884. A. and B., partners, agreed with C. in writing signed by them individually, and purporting on its face to be a joint and several agreement, by which agreement certain bills of lading were to be delivered by C. to said partners, and they were to account to him for the proceeds of the bills of lading, and for the insurance money received as such proceeds, until certain drafts accepted by C. were provided for, the bills of lading having been held by him as security for such acceptances. The goods were lost at sea, having been insured by said partnership in the name of one partner. The partnership became insolvent, and an assignment was made by A. and B. of their partnership and individual estate for the benefit of creditors. *Held*, that C. had the right to come in first as a creditor of each of the partners individually, and afterwards to come in upon the surplus, if any, of the partnership estate, after the payment of the partnership debts. Drake *v.* Taylor, 6 Blatch., 14.

§ 885. Where an administrator of an estate appropriates the funds of the estate to the use of a firm of which he is a member, and his copartner is cognizant of the transaction, the firm becomes chargeable as trustees for the amount thus loaned to the firm by said partner as

PRIVATE AND PARTNERSHIP CREDITORS. §§ 886-400.

administrator. Where the administrator dies and the firm becomes bankrupt, the administratrix *de bonis non* may prove a claim for such funds against the estate of the partnership and of the deceased administrator. *In re* Jordan, 2 Fed. R., 819.

§ 886. In equity, and under the fourteenth section of the bankrupt law, partnership creditors are entitled to payment out of partnership assets to the exclusion of separate creditors. Collins *v.* Hood, 4 McL., 186.

§ 887. Where a partner withdraws from a firm, without any formal dissolution, the remaining partner takes the assets clothed with a trust in favor of the firm creditors, and upon his subsequent bankruptcy his individual creditors have no claim on those assets as against the firm creditors. Jones *v.* Newsom, 7 Biss., 321.

§ 888. The natural presumption, where a partner pays a sum of money to his private creditor, who is also a creditor of the firm, is that he means to pay it on his private accounts, unless circumstances vary this presumption. Gass *v.* Stinson, 8 Sumn., 98.

§ 889. On dissolution of a partnership in case of insolvency, the rule in equity is that the partnership creditors have a preferred claim against the partnership assets over the separate creditors of the partners, and the separate creditors of the individual partners have a like preference over the partnership creditors against the separate assets. This rule is incorporated in the provisions of the bankrupt law. *In re* Warren, Dav., 320 (§§ 119-24).

§ 890. **Private creditors.—** The proceeds of sale of the individual property of a partner are individual assets, and must be first applied to the payment of the individual debts of such partner. *In re* Estes, 6 Saw., 459.

§ 891. —— **United States as creditor.—** Where it was alleged that A. and B. were partners, and after A.'s death his executors appropriated partnership property to the payment of taxes on his estate and in expenses of administration, he being at the time of his death insolvent and indebted to the United States in judgments and otherwise, which judgments were a lien on the real estate of A., the lien of the United States and their priority of payment were not thereby affected, but they could enforce the judgments notwithstanding the acts of the administrators. United States *v.* Duncan, 4 McL., 607.

§ 892. Where partnership property is not sufficient to pay the debts of the firm, the priority of the United States does not reach the undivided interest of one of the partners in the partnership effects if he is indebted to the United States. But when it has become his separate, individual property, the rule would be different. The true test is whether the property belonged to the partnership or the individual. *Ibid.*

§ 893. Where the United States has a claim against a partnership composed partly of foreign and partly of resident members, and the resident members become bankrupt, it is entitled to a priority of payment out of the separate estate of such resident partners. United States *v.* Lewis,* 13 N. B. R., 33.

§ 894. Where a partnership firm, being indebted to the United States for duties, makes an assignment of all their effects for the payment of their debts, for which the social fund is inadequate, this is an act of insolvency *quoad* the social fund, under the act of congress, which gives the United States the preference to other creditors "in all cases of insolvency." United States *v.* Shelton, 1 Marsh., 517.

§ 895. The priority of the United States does not extend so as to take the property of a partner from partnership effects, to pay a separate debt due by such partner to the United States, when the partnership effects are not sufficient to satisfy the creditors of the partnership. United States *v.* Hack, 8 Pet., 271.

§ 896. —— **how far entitled to partnership assets.—** Judgment against an individual partner is a lien against the real estate of the partnership, subject to the payment of the firm debts, and subject to the equities of his partners. Johnson *v.* Rogers,* 15 N. B. R., 1.

§ 897. Where the interest of a partner in the joint assets of a firm is levied on, and sold under an execution, the purchaser acquires only an interest in the assets which remain after the payment of the partnership debts. The fact that he purchased the interest of both partners sold on separate executions can have no effect to enlarge the interest of either acquired on the separate sale of that interest. His rights are in subordination to the claims of the joint creditors. Osborn *v.* McBride, 16 N. B. R., 22; 3 Saw., 590.

§ 898. The rule that prefers partnership property to the payment of partnership debts is for the benefit of partners, and they may waive it. *Held*, that they did waive it by giving their notes, and a mortgage upon the partnership property to secure them, notwithstanding the debts for which the notes were given were the individual debts of the partners; and that such mortgage was good in bankruptcy. *In re* Kahley, 3 Ch. Leg. N., 85; 2 Biss., 383.

§ 899. If goods are delivered to a consignee to sell, and are taken to pay his debt, the seizure cannot be justified on the ground that he was a partner, for partnership assets cannot be taken for separate debts. Merrill *v.* Rinker, 1 Bald., 528.

§ 400. A levy of execution against a partner upon the joint property, real or personal, of
303

the partnership is a levy upon the interest only of the judgment debtor, if any, after payment of all the partnership debts and other charges thereon. The purchaser at such execution sale takes merely the unascertained interest in the property which the judgment debtor would have upon final adjustment of the partnership accounts. The sale does not transfer any part of the joint property to the purchaser, so as to enable him to take it from the other partners, for instance, in case of real estate, to maintain ejectment for it. Clagett v. Kilbourne,* 1 Black, 346.

§ 401. It is a rule too well settled to be now called in question, that the interest of each partner in the partnership property is his share in the surplus, after the partnership debts are paid; and that surplus, only, is liable for the separate debts of such partner. United States v. Hack, 8 Pet., 271.

§ 402. Where one partner becomes bankrupt, his assignee can take that portion of the partnership assets, only, which would belong to the bankrupt after the payment of all the partnership debts, and the solvent partner has a lien upon the partnership assets for all the partnership debts, and also for his own share thereof, before the separate creditors of the bankrupt can come in and take anything. Parker v. Muggridge, 2 Story, 334.

§ 403. Partnership creditors.— Where a firm carries on business in two different places under different partnership names, if all the partners are the same they are the same firm, and the assets of both nominal firms are equally applicable to the payment of all the creditors. In re Williams,* 3 Woods, 493.

§ 404. A person who sell goods to a partner, knowing that they are for his own separate use, has no right to charge them to the firm. Gullat v. Tucker,* 2 Cr. C. C., 83.

§ 405. —— claims of against partner's separate estate.— Query: Whether under the bankrupt act the creditors of a partnership can be allowed to prove claims against the separate estate of one of the partners to receive dividends, in concurrence with the separate creditors of the partner, when there is no joint estate and no living solvent partner? If there be any joint fund, however small, such proof cannot be allowed, although such fund may have been created by the separate creditors purchasing some of the partnership assets, actually worthless, for the purpose of creating it; for if there be a joint fund, the court cannot, under the statute, look behind the fact, to inquire how it has been produced. In re Marwick, Dav., 229.

§ 406. —— rights of, as to assignees.— Where a partnership firm assign their interest in the partnership property subject to a stipulation for the payment of the partnership debts, a creditor of the partnership cannot maintain a bill against the assignees to obtain a direct appropriation of that property to the payment of the firm debts, unless it be shown that the assignment was intended to defraud the creditors. Case v. Beauregard,* 1 Woods, 125.

§ 407. —— exemptions.— Partners cannot have an exemption of household and kitchen furniture out of property belonging to a bankrupt partnership. In re Corbett, 5 Saw., 206.

§ 408. Partnership effects in the hands of the assignee in bankruptcy are charged with a trust or equitable lien in favor of joint creditors, and the partners have only separate interests in the surplus, and cannot claim any particular article as exempt. There is a decided distinction between a partner and a tenant in common, in claiming such exemption. Ibid.

§ 409. —— lien of.— Where partners, acting in good faith, whether before or after the dissolution of the firm, convert the joint into separate property in whole or in part, the creditors are bound by that action, because their lien depends upon that of the partner himself, and if he has in good faith relinquished it they cannot revive it. In re Clap, 2 Low., 168.

§ 410. Partnership debts constitute a lien or equitable charge upon whatever partnership property existed at the time of the dissolution of the firm. Fiske v. Gould,* 12 Fed. R., 372.

§ 411. Where a partnership has not gone into liquidation, a simple contract creditor of the firm cannot maintain a suit to subject partnership assets, no trust having been declared. Case v. Beauregard,* 1 Woods, 125. See §§ 356-60.

§ 412. One partner may, with the consent of the other partners, assign his interest in the firm to pay an individual debt. The partners in such case have an equity to have the property subjected to the payment of the partnership debts, and to this equity the partnership creditors may be subrogated, unless the partners themselves waive it. The creditors as such have no lien on the property. They can only operate through the lien of the partners, and if this be given up they are without remedy, unless they can show fraud. Ibid.

§ 413. Upon the dissolution of a partnership each partner has a lien upon the partnership effects, as well for his indemnity against the joint debts as for his proportion of the surplus. But the creditors of the partnership, as such, have no lien upon the partnership effects for their debts. Their equity is the equity of the partners, and is to be worked out through the rights of the latter. Hoxie v. Carr,* 1 Sumn., 173.

§ 414. —— what fraud on.— If a surviving partner mingles his own goods with those of the partnership, so that they cannot be distinguished, an appropriation to the payment of his individual debts of the mingled stock to the extent of a value no greater than would be allowed in equity to individual creditors, in marshaling the assets for distribution between them and the creditors of the partnership, is not in any view a fraud upon the latter. McGinty v. Flannagan,* 16 Otto, 661.

§ 415. A *bona fide* sale for valuable consideration, by one partner to another, of all the partnership effects, vests the sole title in the latter as his separate estate; but if there be want of good faith sufficient to raise a presumption of fraud, equity will declare the assignment void. The insolvency of the firm and of the members, and even a knowledge of such insolvency by the partners, does not make the transaction void; but where only five days intervene between the transfer and the filing of a petition in bankruptcy by the partner to whom the property was transferred, the conclusion is almost irresistible that the bankrupt had in contemplation the filing of the petition at the very time he accepted the transfer, and the transfer is void as to joint creditors. *In re* Byrne,* 7 Am. L. Reg. (N. S.), 499.

§ 416. Where two partners divided their stock in trade and afterwards carried on separate establishments, but each continued to use the firm name, *held*, that if a dissolution was not effected by such arrangement, a mortgage given by one of them on that part of the assets falling to him in the division, to secure an individual debt, was void as to the firm creditors; and, whether a dissolution was effected or not, such mortgage was fraudulent and void as to such creditors, if intended by the parties to prevent, hinder or delay them in the collection of their claims. Moline Wagon Co. *v.* Rummell,* 2 McC., 307.

§ 417. Where a copartnership is insolvent, or is possessed of assets not more than adequate for the payment of debts, one member of the firm cannot, upon retiring, rightfully withdraw beyond the reach of creditors, and to their injury, a portion of the assets or property, and make a personal application of those assets by putting them in the shape of a homestead. Such property is as much within the reach of a court of equity as before. *In re* Sauthoff, 5 Cent. L. J., 364; 16 N. B. R., 181. See §§ 874-80.

§ 418. A transfer by a partner of his firm property to the other partners is not such a transfer as constitutes a fraud upon the creditors of the firm, or hinders or delays creditors, or constitutes a preference contrary to the provisions of the bankrupt act, particularly when the firm, or members composing it, are solvent. *In re* Munn, 7 N. B. R., 468; 8 Biss., 442.

§ 419. Equity will not sustain an agreement between partners, if the firm be at the time insolvent, by which the whole property and effects of the firm are transferred to one member; the effect being to defeat the equitable preference of the firm creditors, and to give the separate creditors of the partner accepting such transfer a preference to the creditors of the company. Collins *v.* Hood, 4 McL., 186.

§ 420. When partners are in fact insolvent they should be considered in equity as holding the partnership effects in trust for the benefit of the firm creditors, and that they cannot, by a transfer of the interest of one to the other, defeat this trust. *In re* Cook, 4 Ch. Leg. N., 1; 3 Biss., 122.

§ 421. A sale by one partner to his copartner, when the firm is insolvent and upon the eve of bankruptcy, which, if upheld, would operate to apply the property of the retiring partner to the payment of the individual debts of the partner purchasing, is presumptively fraudulent as to the firm creditors, and the courts will set aside such sale and distribute the property as firm property to the payment of the firm debts. If the legal effect of such transfer would be to change the order of payment, and prefer the private creditors over the firm creditors, it is void as creating a preference contrary to the provisions of the bankrupt act, section 35. *Ibid.*

VII. ACTIONS.

1. *Between Partners.*

§ 422. In general.—A state court is the proper tribunal for settling the affairs of a partnership between partners. The rights of partners, as respects each other, will not be adjudicated as an out-branch of a proceeding in bankruptcy. *In re* Lathrop, 5 Ben., 199.

§ 423. Where a party claims to be a partner in a lot of cattle with one who, as he believes, denies his interest, he should come to an understanding with the latter at once, and bring his suit for breach of partnership agreement; but after lying by for four years, all the time under the belief that he is not recognized as a partner, and until his alleged partner is dead, he cannot set up a claim to be regarded as a partner. Rice *v.* Martin, 7 Saw., 837.

§ 424. A promissory note given by one member of a commercial company to another member, for the use of the company, will sustain an action at law by the promisee in his own name against the maker, notwithstanding both parties were partners in that company, and the money when recovered would belong to the company. Van Ness *v.* Forrest, 8 Cr., 80.

§ 425. If one of three joint defendants pay the whole debt upon a joint execution for a debt contracted by them jointly, in a transaction in which they were partners, he cannot, at law, recover from the other partners their respective proportions of the whole debt which he has thus paid. Riggs v. Stewart, 2 Cr. C. C., 171.

§ 426. S. and H. were partners. Upon a settlement of accounts in a chancery suit, it was ascertained what the assets, debts and estimated surplus were; it was ascertained further that S. owed H. on account of transactions of the firm a certain amount exceeding said surplus, but there was no final decree ascertaining the clear assets of the firm, and requiring S. to pay any finally ascertained sum to H. In a suit by G. against said firm as guarantors of a debt due by R., a decree was rendered directing the payment by said firm of an ascertained deficiency remaining after recourse against R., and the same was paid out of the social assets. S. subsequently went into bankruptcy, and H. claimed a lien upon the individual estate of S. by right of subrogation to G. for half of the debt paid out of said firm assets. It was held that if, in the suit for settlement, a final balance had been found due from S. to H., and a decree rendered requiring S. to pay such balance to H.; and afterwards, upon the decree of this debt to G., H. had paid it out of his individual means, then H. might have had a right of subrogation for half against S.'s individual estate, but that such debt having been paid out of social assets, H. had no right to be subrogated to the rights of G. In re Smith,[*] 16 N. B. R., 113.

§ 427. For services.—A partner cannot maintain an action at law against his copartners to recover for services rendered the partnership. Taylor v. Smith,[*] 3 Cr. C. C., 241.

§ 428. Evidence.—In an action at law by one partner against another, the partnership book kept by the defendant is not evidence against the plaintiff, although it has been in his possession. Sutton v. Mandeville, 1 Cr. C. C., 2.

§ 429. Action at law before final settlement.—Until there is a final settlement and adjustment of all accounts between partners, and a balance struck, one partner is not permitted to sue the others either at law or in equity for money paid by him on account of the partnership. Held, accordingly, that a suit in equity could not be maintained by a partner against his copartners to recover a sum which, it appeared from a statement signed by defendants, the plaintiff was entitled to be credited with, it clearly appearing from the statement itself that it was not intended as a final settlement, and the bill not seeking an accounting and final settlement. Halderman v. Halderman,[*] Hemp., 559.

§ 430. An action at law will lie for a balance found, on final accounting, to be due by the firm to one of the partners. Whether a bill in equity will lie in such case, quære. Ibid.

§ 431. If the connection in a joint adventure terminate in a sale of the property, and one appropriates the proceeds to his own use, and charges himself with the proportion due to his associate in the adventure, an action on the case will lie by the part owner for his portion. Aliter, if the connection does not terminate with the sale, in which case account rendered must be brought. Hourquebie v. Girard, 2 Wash., 212.

§ 432. One partner cannot maintain an action at law against his copartner unless there has been an express promise to pay a balance ascertained upon settlement of accounts to be due. Pote v. Philips,[*] 5 Cr. C. C., 154.

§ 433. Items of partnership account cannot be recovered in a suit at law by one partner against the other if the joint concerns have not been settled. The accounts current rendered by each to the other are admissible in evidence to show by the admissions of the parties that the items are not items of partnership account. Barry v. Barry, 3 Cr. C. C., 120.

§ 434. An action at law will not lie between partners on a partnership transaction until a balance is struck, and the defendant promises to pay it. Goldsborough v. McWilliams,[*] 2 Cr. C. C., 401.

§ 435. For an accounting.—An accounting between partners cannot be had on affidavits on an interlocutory motion; it must be had in the orderly progress of a suit. Wilkinson v. Tilden,[*] 9 Fed. R., 683.

§ 436. Upon a bill for a partnership accounting and to have lands of the partnership sold, the court can enforce a sale of lands outside of the district by obliging the parties to convey. Lyman v. Lyman,[*] 2 Paine, 11.

§ 437. A mercantile firm being desirous of obtaining title to certain valuable property upon which they held a mortgage for much less than its value, a scheme was devised by which, with the connivance of the debtor, they should obtain judgment for more than the actual amount of their claim, in fraud of the rights of other creditors of the mortgagor, and buy the property in on foreclosure. The partner to whom was intrusted the management of the affair, instead of obtaining title to the property for the firm, secured it for himself, whereupon one of his copartners sued to compel him to account. Held, that the purchase of real estate was outside the scope of the partnership business, and, both for that reason and because the transaction was a corrupt one, in carrying out which no aid could be derived from a court of equity, the bill could not be maintained. Wheeler v. Sage,* 1 Wall., 518.

§ 438. The old action of account, which has almost totally fallen into disuse, cannot be maintained against a dormant partner who has had nothing to do with conducting the business. Spear v. Newell,* 2 Paine, 267.

§ 439. The fact that a balance of stock on hand has been sold to a new company, of which defendant is a member, will not render him liable to an action. Ibid.

§ 440. Where plaintiff and defendant entered into an agreement to buy and sell real estate and divide the profits, plaintiff to furnish the capital, which was to be refunded with interest, and defendant to perform the labor, and defendant, after refusing to sell a certain piece of land which had been bought and the title put in his name, until it deteriorated in value, conveyed it to plaintiff, held, that plaintiff could maintain a bill in equity to have the real estate sold and the loss or profit, if there should be a profit, divided; the difference between the purchase price of the land, with interest and expenses, and the sale price, to constitute the profit or loss. Olcott v. Wing,* 4 McL., 15.

§ 441. If the books and papers of a firm have been destroyed or suppressed, false entries made in them, or no entries made by the partner who has charge of them to his debit, with a view to fraud, the injured partner may support a specific charge by his own affidavit, but not by one which specifies no amount under any particular item. Askew v. Odenheimer,* 1 Bald., 380.

§ 442. On bill by the fraudulent partner for an account, the master may charge him on any evidence which is competent or admissible as proof of the item; he cannot hold the injured partner to such a degree of proof as would justify a charge, under ordinary circumstances, against a customer or partner; there must, however, be some proof. Ibid.

§ 443. Where the plaintiff sued for a certain amount as his share of the profits resulting from a joint or copartnership transaction, and the only issue raised by the pleadings was whether or not plaintiff and defendant were jointly interested in the contract and plaintiff entitled to one-half the profits, and no accounting was asked for, none is necessary, and there is no occasion for a reference. McCormick v. Largey,* 1 Mont. T'y, 158.

§ 444. To enjoin.— In a suit to enjoin a retired partner from enforcing a claim against the new firm, accruing subsequent to his retirement, on the ground that, after collecting the claims and paying the debts of the old firm, a statement of the accounts between the old and new firm showed a balance, exceeding the amount of defendant's claim, in favor of the new firm, held, that a correct computation showed the balance to be on the other side, and that an injunction should be denied. Nixdorff v. Smith,* 16 Pet., 182.

§ 445. Upon bill for a partnership accounting, a sale of stock threatened by defendant may be restrained temporarily on the ground that the injury to plaintiff would be irreparable. Wilkinson v. Tilden,* 9 Fed. R., 683.

§ 446. Equity will interfere by injunction to restrain one partner from violating the rights of his copartner, even when a dissolution of the partnership is not necessarily contemplated. Marble Co. v. Ripley, 10 Wall., 339.

§ 447. For dissolution.— Bad character, drunkenness and dishonesty on the part of a partner, if proved, make a strong case for relief, on such terms as equity may impose for the protection of both parties, in a suit by the other partner to dissolve the partnership, but they do not authorize him of his own motion to treat the partnership as ended, and to take to himself all the benefits of the joint labors and joint property. Ambler v. Whipple, 20 Wall., 546.

§ 448. Necessary parties in suit to settle.— Creditors are not necessary or proper parties to a suit between partners to wind up the partnership. Hoxie v. Carr,* 1 Sumn., 173.

§ 449. If, in a bill to wind up a partnership, certain of the original partners are not joined, and to join them as defendants would oust the jurisdiction of the court, and the successors to the plaintiff (but not the obligations) of certain of the original partners are joined, there being no charge of fraudulent confederacy in the bill, the bill should be dismissed, both on account of the non-joinder and misjoinder. Bank v. Carrollton Railroad,* 11 Wall., 624.

§ 450. In a suit to settle the affairs of a copartnership, all the partners or their representatives are necessary parties. Gray v. Larrimore, 2 Abb., 542.

2. By and against Partners.

§ 451. In name of one partner, when maintainable.— When each of two partners is in the habit of taking to different parts of the country, for sale, articles belonging to the firm, which when taken are charged to the person taking them, and he is considered accountable to the firm for them, held, that although there is no absolute sale of the property to the person taking it, it is in his custody and control, and he is a trustee of it, accountable to the firm, and can maintain an action for its loss in his own name. Myers v. Cottrill, 5 Biss., 465.

§ 452. Where a member of a partnership makes an individual contract with a third person, he may sue thereon in his own name notwithstanding the correspondence is conducted through the firm and he had agreed to give his copartners an interest in the contract. Law v. Cross, 1 Black, 533.

§ 453. Where a contract is made and the work under it done by a certain person, the fact that he had a partner interested in the profits of the contract does not make it necessary that such partner should be a party to a suit upon the contract. Simpson v. Baker, 2 Black, 581.

§ 454. Against one partner.— H. drew a bill of exchange on "B. & Co.," which B., one of the firm, accepted for the accommodation of H., without restriction, and without the knowledge or consent of his partners. and not in the course of the partnership business, by writing the name of the firm on the bill. Held, that a recovery could be had against B., as sole acceptor, under a count in the declaration stating the bill to have been drawn on B. & Co., and to have been accepted by B. by the name and style of B. & Co., by writing the name of B. & Co. thereon. City Bank of Columbus v. Beach, 1 Blatch.. 438.

§ 455. —— effect on firm.— Under a separate commission of bankruptcy against one partner, only his interest in the joint effects passes. Harrison v. Sterry, 5 Cr., 289.

§ 456. —— when bar to further action.— Under the common law rule a judgment against one partner on a partnership note merges the note in the judgment, and the judgment is a bar to an action against the others, though they were dormant partners, and this fact was unknown to the plaintiff when the action was commenced. But by the statute of the state of Michigan, known as the joint debtor act, the common law rule is changed, and a judgment may be obtained against one of several joint debtors, and the demand against the others not sued is not merged in the judgment against the one brought into court. Under this statute, a judgment against one partner in Michigan is not a bar to a suit against the others, in the same state, and, giving the judgment the same effect and operation in other states, it is no bar to such a suit in such states. Mason v. Eldred, 6 Wall., 231.

§ 457. Where a judgment has been obtained against one of two partners on a joint promise, an action at law against the partners cannot be maintained on the same ground. Sedam v. Williams, 4 McL., 51.

§ 458. A judgment against one partner, in a suit against him and two other copartners, merges the instrument on which the action was founded, and such judgment may be pleaded in bar to an action on the instrument against one or all of the partners. Woodworth v. Spaffords, 2 McL., 168.

§ 459. —— levy on firm property.— A court of equity will enjoin the levy of an execution against one partner on property of the firm in which it is admitted he has no interest which can pass by a sale. Cropper v. Coburn, 2 Curt., 465.

§ 460. A purchaser under an execution against one partner becomes a tenant in common with the other partners in an undivided share of the land purchased subject to all the rights of the other partners. Until the partnership debts are paid, he can have no claim but on the separate interest of the individual partner in the residue. Gilmore v. North American Land Co., Pet. C. C., 460.

§ 461. Under an execution against a member of a firm individually, the sheriff may seize the goods of the firm and sell the defendant's moiety therein, in which case the vendee will be tenant in common with the other partner. United States v. Williams,* 4 McL., 236.

§ 462. Unless the officer levying the execution can make an arrangement satisfactory to himself, he has a right to take the whole of the goods into his possession until the sale. Ibid.

§ 463. Name.— In an action for goods sold by Tibbs & Company, the plaintiffs must prove themselves to be the firm of Tibbs & Company. Tibbs v. Parrott, 1 Cr. C. C., 313.

§ 464. The names of a firm must be proved, but where some evidence has been given on the point the court will leave it with the jury. Varnum v. Campbell, 1 McL., 313.

§ 465. Offset.— Although one partner is bound singly to pay the whole of a partnership debt, unless he compels the plaintiff by a proper plea to join his partner, yet he cannot when sued alone offset a debt due to the partnership, as he is not entitled to the whole of a partnership debt. Jordan v. Wilkins,* 3 Wash., 110.

§ 466. In an action to recover for labor in packing pork, held, that the defendant might show, under the general issue and a plea of payment, that plaintiff was a partner in a commission house to which defendant had consigned the pork, and that the house owed defendant for the proceeds of sales of the pork an amount exceeding plaintiff's claim; and that such facts if proved would be a defense. Buckingham v. Burgess,* 3 McL., 364.

§ 467. One who obtains employment by representing himself to be a partner in a certain concern thereby renders his claim for services subject to an offset which would be good against a partner in the concern, whether or not he is in fact a partner. Buckingham *v.* Burgess,* 3 McL., 364, 549.

§ 468. Creditor's remedy after death of partner.— Upon the death of a partner, a partnership creditor may, at his option, proceed at law against the surviving partner, or go at once into equity against the representatives of the deceased partner, and in such equity suit he may and should join the surviving partner, as well as the representatives of another deceased partner. Nelson *v.* Hill,* 5 How., 127.

§ 469. Where such deceased partner was a member of two firms, the creditors of both may join in the same bill and make the other partners of both firms, or their representatives, parties defendant, so that a proper accounting may be had. *Ibid.*

§ 470. Jurisdiction.— Although the probate courts in a state may have ample power to direct the application of copartnership property to the payment of the debts of the firm, yet a partnership creditor who is a citizen of another state is not compelled to go into the state tribunals for the purpose of asserting his rights to such property, but he may proceed in equity in the federal courts, the marshaling of such assets being one of the original subjects of equity jurisdiction. Fiske *v.* Gould,* 12 Fed. R., 372.

§ 471. Against firm on note of partner.— If a person advance money to a partnership on the note of an individual member, knowing it is to be used for firm purposes, he cannot sue the other partner. If, in ignorance of the fact that it is to be so used, he advances money on such a note, and subsequently sues the individual partner, he cannot afterwards sue the other partner. *In re* Herrick,* 13 N. B. R., 312.

§ 472. Against firm by representatives of deceased partner.—Declarations of a deceased partner as to the extent of his interest in the partnership, not made in the immediate presence of his copartners, cannot, in a suit by his representatives against his copartners, overcome the sworn statements of the defendants in answers responsive to the allegations of the bill. Moore *v.* Huntington,* 17 Wall., 417.

§ 473. A suit against surviving partners by the administratrix of a deceased partner, alleging the plaintiff to be sole heir as well as administratrix, may be sustained in favor of plaintiff as administratrix, although there are other heirs who are not joined. *Ibid.*

§ 474. Pleading and practice.—Where two parties are sued as partners, and the separate answer of one alleges, as new matter in defense, that the defendants were for a short time associated in business under said firm name, but that one furnished all the capital stock, and by special agreement was to be liable for all debts incurred, and that the other, the party answering, was to receive one-third of the profits in compensation for his services, and that plaintiff had actual knowledge of said agreement while in the employment of said partnership, it was held that the new matter was insufficient, as it stated facts which legally constituted a partnership, and that, in order that the special agreement should affect the plaintiff, it was necessary to aver that plaintiff had notice or actual knowledge of such agreement before the liability alleged in the complaint accrued. The allegation that plaintiff had such knowledge while in the employment of said partnership was too vague. Lomme *v.* Kintzing.* 1 Mont. T'y, 290.

§ 475. In an action on a promissory note by a firm, no affidavit by the defendants having been filed, denying their signatures, it was held unnecessary to prove the partnership of the plaintiffs, the defendants, by their remissness, having admitted that. Pratt *v.* Willard, 6 McL., 27.

§ 476. Where the contract shows that the defendants are liable jointly, it is not necessary to allege or prove a partnership. Kendall *v.* Freeman, 2 McL., 189.

§ 477. If goods sold belonged to a partnership at the time of sale, the action must be brought in the name of all the partners, although the defendant was ignorant of the partnership. Bennett *v.* Scott, 1 Cr. C. C., 330.

§ 478. In a declaration upon a bill of exchange, payable to L., F. & Co., all the persons composing the firm must be named, with an averment that they were joint partners or joint traders under the name and firm of L., F. & Co., otherwise the bill of exchange cannot be received in evidence. Lapeyre *v.* Gales, 2 Cr. C. C., 291.

§ 479. In general, in a bill in equity, the answer of one co-defendant is no evidence against another. But this rule does not apply to the case where the defendants are all partners in the same transaction, for in such case the answer or confession of either is evidence against the others. Van Reimsdyk *v.* Kane,* 1 Gall., 630.

§ 480. Where, upon a submission by one partner of all matters in controversy between the partnership and the person entering into the agreement of reference, an award was made directing the payment of money, in an action on the bond to abide by the award, the breach assigned was that the partner who agreed to the reference did not pay, etc. This is a sufficient assignment of a breach, as he only who agreed to the reference was bound to pay. Karthaus *v.* Ferrer, 1 Pet., 222.

§ 481. The declaration in an action against one partner only never gives notice of the claim being on a partnership transaction. The proceeding is always as if the party sued were the sole contracting party; and if the declaration were to show a partnership contract, the judgment against the single partner could not be sustained. Barry v. Foyles, 1 Pet., 811.

§ 482. Where suit is brought upon a partnership transaction, against one of the partners, and the declaration stated a contract with the partner who is sued, and gave no notice that it was made by him with another person, evidence of a joint *assumpsit* may be given in support of a declaration; and the want of notice has never been considered as justifying an exception to such evidence at the trial. *Ibid.*

§ 483. The rule that the answer of one defendant in equity is no evidence against a co-defendant does not apply when the defendants are partners. Van Reimsdyk v. Kane,* 1 Gall., 630.

§ 484. —— necessary parties.— The representatives of a deceased partner need not be made parties to a bill filed by the surviving partner, as they have no claim until the partnership debts are paid, and then it is upon the surviving partner or his representatives. Pagan v. Sparks, 2 Wash., 325.

§ 485. Evidence.— A partnership debt may be given in evidence to support a several *assumpsit* by one of the partners. Elmondson v. Barrell, 2 Cr. C. C., 228.

§ 486. The interest of a copartnership cannot be given in evidence on an averment of individual interest, nor an averment of the interest of a company be supported by a special contract relating to the interest of an individual. Grave v. Boston Marine Ins. Co., 2 Cr., 419.

§ 487. Until a *prima facie* case of partnership is established, the declarations of one of the alleged partners that the other is a partner are inadmissible. Pleasants v. Fant,* 22 Wall., 116.

§ 488. A deed signed "H., D. & Co." is admissible in evidence as the deed of the firm upon proof of the concurrence of its members not signing it. Darst v. Roth,* 4 Wash., 471.

§ 489. Parties cannot give their private conversations or correspondence, with one another or their agent, to rebut proof that they were partners of a third person, or held themselves out to the public as such. Freeborn v. Smith, 2 Wall., 160.

§ 490. Where the evidence shows that a note executed by a member of a firm, in the firm name, was given in settlement of an account for goods sold to said firm, the testimony of a person that said party executing the note was a member of the firm when the goods were bought should be admitted. Buck v. Smith,* 2 Colo. T'y. 500.

§ 491. Miscellaneous.— Partnership property was attached by the marshal, and afterwards released, upon the defendants filing a bond with sureties to pay the amount of the judgment that might be recovered against them in the suit in which said attachment issued. The suit being afterwards dismissed against two of the partners upon their plea to the jurisdiction of the court, and judgment recovered against the administrator of the third partner, an objection that the judgment recovered was not such as described in the bond, it was held that any judgment which would have bound the property, if it had remained under attachment, would bind the obligors in the bond, in a case where the suit was commenced against the partnership upon a partnership contract, and the property attached was partnership property. Inbusch v. Farwell, 1 Black, 566.

§ 492. Where a suit was brought against a partnership, and one partner pleaded an adjudication of bankruptcy, and the court directed a stay of proceedings as to him, and rendered judgment for the plaintiff to be enforced against the partnership property, and the individual property of the other partner, it was held that, if error, it was such as neither appellant could complain of. Lomme v. Kintzing,* 1 Mont. T'y, 290.

3. Against Estates and Representatives of Deceased Partners.

§ 493. The payment of a bill of exchange may be enforced in equity against the executors of a deceased partner, or joint contractor, when the survivors are insolvent. Van Reimsdyk v. Kane,* 1 Gall., 630.

§ 494. In such case no decree need be had against the survivors if their insolvency is apparent. *Ibid.*

§ 495. Witnesses.— One partner, who is jointly liable with the others, is a good witness against them in a bill in equity. *Ibid.*

§ 496. Pleading.— A bill to charge the executors of a deceased partner with a partnership debt must expressly charge an insolvency of the survivor. Van Reimsdyk v. Kane, 1 Gall., 871.

§ 497. —— necessary parties.—To a bill in equity brought against the estate of a deceased partner to recover a debt due from the firm, the surviving partners should be made parties. If they are out of the jurisdiction the court may dispense with their being made parties, but it is a matter in the sound discretion of the court whether, under all the circumstances, it ought to do so or not. Vose v. Philbrook,* 8 Story, 335.

VIII. LIMITED PARTNERSHIPS.

SUMMARY — *Payment of share in merchandise,* § 498. — *Certificate,* § 499. — *Liability of special partner,* § 500. — *Custom of general-partners,* § 501.

§ 498. Under the provision of 1 Revised Statutes of New York, 764, section 2, relating to limited partnerships, requiring the special partner to contribute his share of the capital "in actual cash payment," and granting him an exemption from liability beyond the fund "so contributed by him," and requiring a certificate to be filed stating the amount contributed by each special partner, accompanied by an affidavit stating that the sums specified in the certificate to have been so contributed "have been actually and in good faith paid in cash," if part of a special partner's contribution to the capital stock is made in merchandise he will not be entitled to any of the benefits of the act, although the certificate states the facts as they are. *In re* Merrill, §§ 502–505.

§ 499. A provision of the statute, requiring the certificate to state "the amount of capital which each special partner shall have contributed to the common stock," is not satisfied by a certificate that the special partner had contributed "$1,000 in cash and *about* $3,000 of effects and property, the exact amount of which is yet to be ascertained." *Ibid.*

§ 500. A provision of a statute regulating limited partnerships, that the general partners only shall be authorized to transact business and to bind the firm, does not enable the general partners to bind the special partner by transactions beyond the scope of the partnership business. Taylor v. Rasch, §§ 506, 507.

§ 501. The scope of the business of a limited partnership, as specified in the partnership articles, cannot be changed or enlarged, so as to affect the special partner, by any departure therefrom by the general partners, no matter how common or long continued, if not consented to or known and acquiesced in by the special partner. *Ibid.*

[NOTES.— See §§ 508–513.]

IN RE MERRILL.

(Circuit Court for New York: 12 Blatchford, 221–225. 1874.)

Opinion by WOODRUFF, J.

STATEMENT OF FACTS.— The firm of Merrill, Wilder & Co. were charged by a creditor with having committed acts of bankruptcy, and in the petition it was averred that the firm was composed of William G. Merrill, David Wilder, Villars Merrill, Junior, and George J. Letchworth, all general partners therein. The application for a decree adjudging them bankrupts was resisted by Letchworth, only on the ground that he was not, and had never been, a general partner, but was only a special partner in the firm, and that the copartnership was a limited copartnership, formed under the provisions of the statutes of the state of New York, wherein he was in nowise liable for the debts of the firm otherwise or beyond the capital he had contributed to the common stock. The district court held him to be a general partner, and adjudged all the partners bankrupt, and that adjudication Letchworth seeks to review and reverse in this court. His petition of review states the facts upon which the adjudication proceeded, and, as the allegations of the petition are not denied, they are to be deemed admitted for the purposes of the review.

The only facts which I deem it material to notice, and upon which the petition will be disposed of, are, that the parties attempted to form a limited partnership in which Letchworth should share in the profits of the business to be carried on, and have the immunities which the statutes authorizing such copartnerships allow, and yet not contribute, nor be bound to contribute, his share of the capital in cash.   They entered into articles of copartnership containing numerous details touching the business to be carried on, stipulating that each of the four partners should share equally in the profits and losses of the business.   The consideration for which Letchworth was to be thus admitted to membership in the firm, and permitted to share the profits, was that he should contribute to the common stock $1,000 in cash, and, in addition thereto, "the entire inventory on hand, of the effects and property belonging to him, lately owned and used by M. Alden, deceased, and said Letchworth, supposed to be about $8,000."   To carry their purpose into effect they signed and filed, as required by the statute, a "certificate of limited partnership" (so entitled), in which, among other proper particulars, it was certified that "the said William G. Merrill, David Wilder and Villars Merrill, Jr., shall be the general partners, and the said George Letchworth shall be a special partner, and has contributed to the common stock $1,000 in cash and about $8,000 of effects and property, the exact amount of which is yet to be ascertained."   To this certificate was annexed the affidavit of William G. Merrill that Letchworth "has actually contributed the sum of $1,000 in cash to the common stock of the said firm, and has paid in the same in good faith."

§ 502. *New York statute as to limited partnerships.*

The statute under which the parties attempted to establish a limited partnership (1 R. S. of N. Y., 764, § 2) provides that such partnerships may consist of general partners, responsible as general partners now are by law, and "of one or more persons who shall contribute *in actual cash payments*, a specific sum, as capital, to the common stock, who shall be called special partners, and who shall not be liable for the debts of the partnership, beyond *the fund so contributed* by him or them to the capital."   It then requires that the certificate to be filed shall, among other things, state "the amount of capital which each special partner shall have contributed to the common stock," and that there shall be filed with the certificate an affidavit "stating that *the sums specified in the certificate to have been contributed by each of the special partners to the common stock* have been actually and in good faith paid in cash."

§ 503. *Contribution of goods in the formation of a limited partnership, when the statute requires cash, will make the partners general partners, although the certificate states the facts.*

It is quite certain that the copartnership which these parties attempted to establish was not such as this statute provides for.   They doubtless acted with most entire fairness and integrity.   They no doubt supposed that what they did sufficiently satisfied the reason and intent of the statute, so long as, in their published notice, they informed the world that the capital contributed by Letchworth to the common stock was *not* actually paid in cash, but consisted in part of property, the amount of which was not yet ascertained.   But this was not in compliance with the statute, and neither they nor the court are to entertain the inquiry, whether a statute authorizing just such a partnership as they entered into, and securing to Letchworth immunity for the debts of the firm, would not be a better statute than the legislature have seen fit to enact.   In general, all who share the profits of the business of a copartnership are liable to its creditors for all of its debts.   The statute permits the formation of a copartnership in which, as to one or more of the members, there shall be an exemption from liability beyond the fund "contributed by him or them to the capital."   The express condition of that immunity is that

that fund be contributed in actual cash payments. The expression "fund so contributed," which fund is made the limit of the liability of special partners, imports contributed "in cash." It was, of course, competent for the legislature to have authorized such partnership, and to have permitted the special partner to contribute property or goods at a just valuation, but they have not done so. So it was competent to have permitted a contribution of part cash and part goods or other property, but for reasons concerning which we are hardly at liberty to speculate, this was not done.

§ 504. *Parties who claim under a statute which derogates from the general rule of law must show a strict compliance.*

We are bound by the statute, and the parties cannot claim under the statute, which derogates from the general rule of law, without showing a strict compliance with the statute. They cannot be permitted to say that it was just as well for the firm and for its creditors to have a contribution of goods at their fair value as to have cash. The legislature saw fit to require that he who contributed capital to be employed in the joint business, to be the basis or consideration of his participation in the profits, should, in order to the limitation of his liability for debts, pay all of that contribution in money, before the partnership should be deemed formed; that that money should be under the exclusive control of the general partners; that they should be at liberty to invest or employ it as in their discretion they saw fit, for the benefit of the firm and its creditors; and that no one should be permitted to share profits on the basis of a contribution of goods or property, and yet be entitled to limit his liability for debts. It is unnecessary to vindicate the statute, and yet it is pertinent to inquire — can a person be permitted, under such a statute, to put in $100 cash, and a stock of goods estimated at $50,000, be permitted to share profits on the basis of a contribution of $50,100, to capital, and yet be not liable for the debts?

§ 505. *Necessity that the statement of the amount contributed to the capital stock shall be specific.*

I am decidedly of opinion that the parties failed to establish a limited partnership, and that they were always general partners. I may add, further, that an express provision of the statute, that the certificate filed shall state "the amount of capital which each special partner shall have contributed to the common stock," was not satisfied by a certificate that Letchworth had contributed "$1,000 in cash and *about* $8,000 of effects and property, the exact amount of which is yet to be ascertained."

For these reasons the decision of the district court was correct. Whether the other ground of the decision was so or not it is unnecessary to inquire. The adjudication is affirmed, with costs.

TAYLOR *v.* RASCH.

(Circuit Court for Michigan: 1 Flippin, 883–888. 1874.)

Opinion by LONGYEAR, J.

STATEMENT OF FACTS.— The firm of Tillman, Sillsbee & Company was a limited partnership, and was composed of William Tillman and Charles E. Sillsbee as general partners, and John S. Newberry as special partner.· Whatever the proofs show as to the general partners being parties to the arrangement for exchange of patronage between them and the defendants, or as to what the particular character of that transaction was, one thing is certain, and that is, there is no proof or pretense that the special partner was in any way privy to the arrangement, or knew of it, or in any way assented to it.

§ 506. *The capital of a special partner in a limited partnership is protected against contracts out of the scope of the business made by the general partners.*

It is contended, however, that by the statutes of Michigan the general partners had authority to bind the firm. The statute referred to is as follows: "Section 3. The general partners only shall be authorized to transact business, to sign for the partnership, and to bind the same." 1 Compiled Laws of 1871, p. 520, sec. 1569. The effect of the statute is simply to exclude the special partner from active participation in the business of the firm; and as to the general partners, it confers no authority upon them to transact business, sign for the partnership, and to bind the same in any manner, or to any extent whatever, beyond the purposes and scope of the partnership. Therefore, conceding that the arrangement in question was made with the general partners, as claimed in the answer, if it was not within the scope and purposes of the partnership, it was wholly unauthorized, and therefore void. This brings us to the second and only remaining issue made by the answer.

The scope and purposes of the partnership are specified in the articles as follows:

2d. "That the general nature of the business to be transacted by said partnership is the purchase, sale and manufacture of all kinds and descriptions of furniture, chairs, upholstering, furnishing and upholstered goods, lumber, and all kinds of articles, merchandise, tools and machinery, used in such manufactures."

Surely it does not require argument to show that a contract for the purchase of clothing for the individual general partners, or otherwise, does not come within "the general nature of the business to be transacted by said partnership," as specified in the articles.

§ 507. *Usage of general partners in limited partnership to engage in transactions beyond the scope of the partnership articles cannot affect a special partner not aware of and not assenting to such usage.*

But it was contended that such had been the usual course of business of the firm, and proofs were adduced tending to show that such was the fact; and it was argued that, therefore, the defendants had a right to assume that the transaction was within the scope of the partnership. The articles of copartnership were duly filed and published as required by the statute, and all persons dealing with the firm were bound to take notice of, and were chargeable with knowledge of their contents. No departure by the general partners, no matter how common or long continued, if not consented to or known and acquiesced in by the special partner, could have the effect to change or enlarge the scope of the business as specified in the articles. To hold the contrary would be to disregard plain provisions of law for the protection of special partners and the public, and would make a limited partnership one of extreme hazard to the special partner.

In the opinion of this court, overruling the demurrer to the bill, it was shown that a general partnership could not be made liable upon a contract by an individual partner out of the scope of the partnership business. The same principle of law that protects general partners from liability in such cases protects the capital of special partners in a limited partnership. Troubat on Limited Partnership, sec. 377.

It results that the complainant is entitled to a decree against the defendants for the balance of the account of Tillman, Sillsbee & Co. against them over and above the $50 actually paid to the firm by one of its employees on account of defendants, together with interest on such balance from and after the date of the last item in the account, viz., June 8, 1870, and for costs.

The balance of the account as alleged in the bill and admitted by the answer was.... $473 25
Interest from June 8, 1870, to date, October 19, 1874, four years, four months, eleven
days 144 47
                                                                                       ———————
      Total $617 72

Decreed accordingly.

§ 508. What constitutes.— Partnerships are divided into general and limited; the former is where the parties are partners in all their commercial business; the latter, where it is limited to some one or more branches and does not include all the business of the partners. United States Bank v. Binney,* 5 Mason, 176.

§ 509. An agreement between owners of vessels to form a line for carrying passengers and freight between New York and San Francisco is but a contract for a limited partnership, and the remedy for the breach of it is in the common-law courts. Vandewater v. Mills, 19 How., 82.

§ 510. Notice — Articles of partnership.— All persons dealing with a limited partnership are bound to take notice of the articles of partnership when duly filed and published according to law, and are chargeable with knowledge of their contents. Taylor v. Rasch, 1 Cent. L. J., 555; 11 N. B. R., 91. See §§ 506–7.

§ 511. —— dissolution.— In publishing notice of the dissolution of a limited partnership before the time named in the certificate of its formation, pursuant to the provisions of the statute of New York (1 R. S., 767, § 24), requiring such notice to be published "once in each week for four weeks," when any day of the week is taken for the first publication, the same day of the week must be taken for each of the succeeding publications. Successive publications at irregular intervals, held not to be good simply because, by dividing the time covered by the publications, beginning with the date of the first, into periods of seven days each, it appeared that one publication was made during each of those periods, although five publications were thus made and more than four weeks elapsed between the first and the last. In re King,* 5 Ben., 453.

§ 512. Under the laws of New York, special partners must contribute in cash a specific sum to the common stock of a partnership, and the certificate must state the amounts each special partner has contributed, and the affidavit must state that such sums have been paid in cash. A certificate that the special partner has contributed a certain amount in cash, and a certain amount in goods, is not within the statute, and in such a case he is a general partner and liable as such. In re Merrill, 13 N. B. R., 91. See §§ 502–5.

§ 513. A general partnership cannot be made liable upon a contract by an individual partner out of the scope of the partnership business. The same principle of law that protects general partners from liability in such cases protects the capital of special partners in a limited partnership. No departure by the general partners, no matter how common or long continued, if not consented to, or known and acquiesced in by the special partner, can change or enlarge the scope of the business as specified in the articles. Taylor v. Rasch, 1 Cent. L. J., 555; 11 N. B. R., 91. See §§ 506–7.

IX. MISCELLANEOUS.

§ 514. Dormant partners — Secret partnership.— One may be a dormant partner although the style "& Co." is used in the firm name. Metcalf v. Officer,* 1 McC., 825.

§ 515. A secret partnership is where the existence of certain persons as partners is not avowed or made known to the public by any of the partners; even if some of the partners intend to be such secretly and their names are disclosed against their will, it is no longer a secret partnership. United States Bank v. Binney,* 5 Mason, 176. See Winship v. United States Bank, 5 Pet., 559.

§ 516. The liability of a secret partner arises from his being one of the contracting parties, and being benefited by the profits of the contract, so that to charge a secret partner for debts contracted in the name of the firm, it is necessary to show that such debts were contracted in the name and business of the firm, or that the secret partner had an interest in the contract or profits. *In re* Munn, 7 N. B. R., 468; 8 Biss., 442.

§ 517. The firm of Munn & Scott, together with several others, were engaged in carrying on the elevator business, at various elevators, as partners in receiving, storing and shipping grain, the profits being divided. The business was carried on under the name of Munn & Scott. The two parties, Munn and Scott, continued to do business outside of the elevator business in their firm name. Certain notes were given by Munn & Scott, and for non-payment of these within fourteen days a petition was filed in bankruptcy against the various parties engaged in the elevator business under such name. *Held,* that all the members of the elevator firm, except those whose names were used, were silent or dormant partners, and only liable as such; and, as it appeared that the proceeds of the notes did not go to the use of the firm of which they were members, and that they were not given for the benefit of the firm, or in the business of that firm, they had shown a sufficient reason for not voluntarily paying the notes described before their liability should be judicially determined; and that the suspension of payment for fourteen days was not an act of bankruptcy within the meaning of the bankrupt act. *Ibid.*

§ 518. A secret partner is not liable unless money, obtained by the discount of a note which he has not signed, comes to the use of the secret partnership. Bank of Alexandria *v.* Mandeville, 1 Cr. C. C., 575.

§ 519. An action of debt, under the Virginia law, may be maintained upon a promissory note against a secret partner who has not signed it. *Ibid.*

§ 520. General reputation, while not admissible to prove a partnership, is admissible to show that one of the partners, in a partnership otherwise proved, was a dormant, and not an ostensible, partner. Metcalf *v.* Officer,* 1 McC., 325.

§ 521. It was agreed between A. and B. that A. should furnish a certain amount of goods to stock a store, which B. was to conduct as the sole person interested in the business; that B. should be at liberty, if he chose, to furnish additional goods; that the net profits of the business should be divided equally between them; A. to be entitled to an accounting from B., and to have the right to sell any goods in the store, with certain exceptions, to his friends and customers. The business was carried on as designed, A. and B. in fact furnishing goods in about equal amounts, and B. was ostensibly the sole person interested in the business. *Held,* that A. was liable as a partner to third persons dealing with B. Bigelow *v.* Elliot,* 1 Cliff., 28.

§ 522. A. and B., by virtue of a private agreement, became partners as to third parties. The contract specified no firm name, but allowed each partner to purchase goods on his own individual credit and designated B. to transact the business, while the connection of A. with the concern was kept secret. B. having given his note for certain goods bought by him, *held,* that, while no recovery could be had against A. on the note, B. not having used his own name as a firm name or intended to bind any one but himself, yet the note was not, under the circumstances, to be considered as payment, even under the Massachusetts rule making the giving of a negotiable promissory note *prima facie* evidence of payment under ordinary circumstances, and that a recovery could be had against A. on the general counts, upon surrendering the note. Palmer *v.* Elliott,* 1 Cliff., 63.

§ 523. **Assignment.**— Where partners assigned the partnership property in trust for certain purposes, and submitted their affairs to arbitration for the purpose of an accounting to be made in conformity with such assignment, the arbitrator cannot make an award inconsistent therewith. McCormick *v.* Gray, 13 How., 27.

§ 524. —— **fraudulent stipulation in.**— A provisional stipulation in a deed of assignment, coercing the creditors of a partnership "to delay their suits" against the firm or else forfeit their claims upon the fund assigned, is fraudulent. Marsh *v.* Bennett, 5 McL., 117.

§ 525. —— **of partner's interest — Rights of assignee.**— Where one member of a firm had sold to a third person an interest in the concern upon certain payments to be made, it was held that such partner could not, by such agreement to sell, compel his partners to accept the vendee as a member of the firm. McNamara *v.* Gaylord, 1 Bond, 302.

§ 526. The assignee of a bankrupt surviving partner succeeds to the rights of the bankrupt as such surviving partner. Loveridge *v.* Larned,* 7 Fed. R., 294.

§ 527. The assignee of a partner's interest in the partnership obtains only an equity to share in the surplus, if any, of the firm property after settlement of the partnership accounts. This rule applies in all cases, whatever may be the nature of the partnership property, as, for instance, in case it is a lease of a railroad, and however broad may be the language of the assignment. To a bill to enforce such an assignment, therefore, all the partners should be made parties. Bank *v.* Carrollton Railroad,* 11 Wall., 624.

§ 528. An assignee of an interest in a partnership, under an assignment of part of the partners, not consented to by the others, is not a partner, and cannot dissolve the partnership or maintain a suit for an accounting; but after dissolution he may maintain such suit, although one of the defendants had no notice or knowledge of his interest. Mathewson v. Clarke,* 6 How., 122.

§ 529. The assignee of an assignee of a copartner's interest in a firm formed for the purchase and sale of lands may maintain a bill in equity against the other partners and the agent of the concern to discover the quantity purchased and sold, and for an account and distribution of the proceeds. Pendleton v. Wambersie,* 4 Cr., 73.

§ 530. Partnership settlement — Accounts — Indemnity.— In a settlement made between two partners residing in different countries, through a third person as agent, one of them was credited with a certain agreed sum to cover a liability which he was under for the firm as surety on certain custom-house bonds. Afterwards, by the death of such partner and the e'ection of the government to take a joint judgment on the bonds, his estate was exonerated. *Held*, that the settlement would not be opened so as to allow the other partner to recover back one-half of the money. Bispham v. Price,* 15 How., 162.

§ 531. A paper containing mutual releases and assignments, each the consideration of the other, was prepared by one partner and signed by him; the other partner received a copy without objection, and promised to sign it, but did not. Until said partner had signed the paper he was not bound by it. Ambler v. Whipple, 20 Wall., 546.

§ 532. If the exception from the operation of a statute of limitations of merchants' accounts applies to the accounts of partners *inter sess* in any case, yet it does not include their stated accounts. Bispham v. Price,* 15 How., 162.

§ 533. To constitute a settled account between partners, all parties must consent to it, and this consent must be either express or implied; and in the absence of an account thus settled, an action of *indebitatus assumpsit* will not lie. Lamalere v. Caze,* 1 Wash., 486.

§ 534. In stating a partnership account, if one partner has had sole charge of the business, he should be charged with the total capital and the proceeds of sales, and credited with the cost of goods disposed of by him and which are included in the capital. Gunnell v. Bird,* 10 Wall., 304.

§ 535. If a partner who has committed frauds on the firm agrees to indemnify the injured party to his satisfaction, by an assignment of all the partnership effects, such assignment will be construed liberally in favor of the latter, and will be reformed in equity so as to meet the intention of the parties. Askew v. Odenheimer,* 1 Bald., 380.

§ 536. Expenses, special agreements as to.— Where a partnership agreement provided that one of the partners should be entitled to a certain share of the net profits of the business after deducting . . . "the actual expenses that may appertain to the goods themselves," it was held that those terms included taxes, clerk hire and advertising. They are as much a part of the actual expenses appertaining to the goods as storage commission or insurance, Foster v. Goddard — Goddard v. Foster, 1 Black, 506.

§ 537. Where the families of partners were supported out of the common fund, there being an understanding that no charge was to be made for family expenses, *held*, that this included expenses of children during their minority, but not advances made to them after coming of age. Salaries paid to children as clerks, after coming of age, *held* to be a proper charge against the partnership. Lyman v. Lyman,* 2 Paine, 11.

§ 538. A stipulation in partnership articles, that each partner shall pay his own individual expenses, *held* not to include expenses when traveling on the business of the firm. Withers v. Withers,* 8 Pet., 355.

§ 539. Contracts against public policy.— Where a party signed an administration bond as surety of one of the partners of a mercantile firm, who was administrator, at the request of the members of the firm, and upon their joint representation that they intended to make the administration a matter of partnership business, to take possession of the assets of the intestate, and share as partners in the gains and losses of the administration, so that in signing the bond he became surety for the partnership, and not merely of the partner who was administrator, the transaction was against the policy of the law, and illegal, inasmuch as administration is a trust, and to permit the appropriation of administration assets by a mercantile firm is a breach of trust. The contract cannot therefore be enforced, and a loss sustained by such surety upon the bond cannot be recovered from the firm. Forsyth v. Woods, 11 Wall., 484.

§ 540. Liability of firm on separate obligations of members.— Where money was borrowed by certain parties as copartners upon a note signed by such partners individually, but the money was borrowed for the benefit of the firm, and was so used, the liability created is a firm liability. *In re* Thomas, 6 Cent. L. J., 151; 8 Biss., 189.

§ 541. In single transaction — Parol proof.— A partnership may exist in a single transaction as well as in a series. *In re* Warren, Dav., 320 (§§ 119-24).

§ 542. There may be a partnership in buying and selling lands, and, so far as third persons are concerned, it may be proved by parol. *Ibid.*

§ 543. **Claim of firm against separate estate of member.**— If funds of a partnership come into the hands of one of the partners as treasurer of the company, the company, in case of the partner's insolvency, is upon the footing of a separate creditor and entitled to repayment of the funds out of his separate estate. Brown v. Curtis,* 5 Mason, 421.

§ 544. **Notes of partnership.**— Goods were bought by an individual and he gave his note for them. After the note became due he formed a partnership, the goods were put into the firm business, and, by agreement between the partners and the holder of the note, the words "and company" were added to the signature to make the note a company note. *Held*, that the company was bound. Crum v. Abbott,* 2 McL., 283.

§ 545. The personal note of a partner given for a partnership debt is not a payment but a renewal, if so intended by the parties. Loveridge v. Larned,* 7 Fed. R., 294.

§ 546. **Firm name.**— If partnership articles omit to provide for a firm name, but the partners adopt a name, which they use in their transactions generally and by which they are known, such name becomes the legitimate firm name, no less so than if it had been inserted in the partnership articles. Under such circumstances, the fact that the firm's bank account is kept in the name of one of the members, and that they stipulate to raise money for the firm upon the paper of one indorsed by the other, or in such other shape as should be found suitable, does not justify the assumption that the individual name of either partner is or can be used as the firm name. Le Roy v. Johnson,* 2 Pet., 186.

§ 547. Where the name of one partner is used as the firm name, the plaintiff, in order to hold the firm upon the signature of such partner, must show that the name was used upon the occasion in question as the firm name. A bank, for instance, which has discounted notes so signed must show that the notes were offered as notes binding the firm, or that the discounts were made for the benefit and in the course of business of the firm. It is not sufficient to show merely that the bank acted upon the belief that the notes bound the firm; nor is the mere fact that the discounts so procured were applied to the use of the firm conclusive that they were procured on account of the firm, although a strong circumstance tending to show it. United States Bank v. Binney,* 5 Mason, 176.

§ 548. **Partner's knowledge of firm's business, presumptions as to.**— In a civil suit by the United States to recover of two members of a firm double the value of goods illegally imported, under the statute of 1823, the knowledge of one member of a firm that the goods were subject to duties raises the presumption of knowledge of such fact on the part of the other members of the firm; and if they have received the goods and disposed of them in the usual course of business, and the profits are divided, a jury is authorized to find that they received them knowing that they were illegally imported and liable to seizure. (FIELD, J., dissented.) Stockwell v. United States, 13 Wall., 531; S. C., 13 Int. Rev. Rec., 88.

§ 549. It is presumed that all partners have access to the partnership books and know their contents, but the presumption may be rebutted. Winship v. United States Bank, 5 Pet., 529 (§§ 111–18).

§ 550. A partner will not be presumed to have knowledge of the contents of a letter written by his copartner in his own name relating to both private and firm matters. Rogers v. Batchelor, 12 Pet., 221 (§§ 125–26).

§ 551. **Continuation of partnership after term limited.**— Where a partnership expires by limitation, but the business is still carried on, without any change in the circumstances, or in the expressions of the articles, it must still be considered as conducted on its original principles, and as a continuing partnership. Robertson v. Miller, 1 Marsh., 466.

§ 552. If a partnership is continued beyond the term limited in the partnership articles it is presumed to be continued on the same terms as before in respect to its being a limited or general partnership. Whether or not it is, however, is a matter of evidence. United States Bank v. Binney,* 5 Mason, 176.

§ 553. **Miscellaneous.**— A judgment was confessed by a partnership and an assignment of goods made to the plaintiffs to secure the judgment. Afterwards one of the partners had the judgment set aside as to him, because the partner confessing had no power to bind him by such confession. The assignment was held void. On motion of the plaintiffs, the judgment was also set aside as to the other partners, and suit brought on the original notes. *Held*, that the judgment was properly vacated as to the remaining partners, because it had been released as to one, and because the goods assigned to secure the judgment had been taken from the assignee by a previous mortgagee. Clark v. Bowen, 22 How., 270.

§ 554. The whole arrangement to secure the debt being annulled, the original indebtedness stood revived and was properly enforced by judgment. *Ibid.*

§ 555. An undertaking by all the members of a firm is not necessarily the contract of a firm. Forsyth v. Woods, 11 Wall., 484.

§ 556. Where a mortgage had been given to one partner to secure a debt of a firm, and after the failure of the firm and an assignment of the debt, one of the partners entered into an arrangement with the debtor, without the consent of the assignees, by which he took negotiable notes for the debt payable on time, and afterward he assigned the mortgage to the other partner, who was not a party to the arrangement, it was held that the mortgage was not extinguished. Osborne v. Benson, 5 Mason, 157.

§ 557. Where money belonging to A. and C., arising out of a joint transaction between them, has, with the knowledge by B. of the interest of A. in the same, been placed by the agent of A. and C. to the credit of B. and C., who are partners, and C. is indebted to his partner, B., B. cannot apply the money of A. to the credit of C. in satisfaction of his claim upon him. Vanderwick v. Summerl, 2 Wash., 41.

§ 558. A separate and express promise by one copartner to pay a debt of the firm is not a promise to pay the debt of another within the statute of frauds, although judgment for the same debt had been recovered against the other partner; and forbearance to arrest this other partner, at the request of the former, is a good consideration to support his promise. Rice v. Barry,* 2 Cr. C. C., 447.

§ 559. The signature of a firm to a paper reciting only the name of one of the partners binds the firm. George v. Tate, 12 Otto, 564.

§ 560. If, in the course of the business of a firm, a clerk is in the habit of signing the name of the firm to transportation bonds for the removal of spirits, without objection, and impliedly with their consent and approbation, and they apply for and obtain permits from the collector, from time to time, for such removal of spirits, it may be fairly inferred that he had the requisite authority, and the signing is obligatory on the members of the firm. United States v. Turner, 2 Bond, 879.

§ 561. Any partner in a firm may be the agent of a third person in drawing bills in favor of the firm, for advances made to such third person, under an express authority. Baring v. Lyman, 1 Story, 396.

§ 562. A firm may negotiate its own paper to one partner, and the latter will thereby become the owner thereof. So, a firm may take a separate negotiable security from one of its partners, and hold and use the same for its own purposes. A fortiori, where he acts as the agent of third persons. Ibid.

PARTNERSHIP ESTATES.

See ESTATES OF DECEDENTS.

PARTITION.

See LAND.

PASSENGERS.

See CARRIERS; TORTS.

PATENTS.

See volume 25.

PAYMASTER.

See WAR.

PAYMENT AND SETTLEMENT.

I. In General. What Constitutes Payment.

Summary — *By note*, §§ 1-8, 6.— *Check on a bank*, §§ 4, 5.

§ 1. Contrary to the doctrine of the common law, the rule in Massachusetts is, that whenever a party bound to a simple contract debt gives his own negotiable security for it, whether it be a bill of exchange or promissory note, it is presumed as a matter of fact, in the absence of any circumstances to indicate a contrary intention of the parties, that the bill or note was given and received in satisfaction and discharge of the pre-existing debt. If there is, however, any deception or fraud in the giving of the new security, or if it was accepted without a full knowledge of the facts, or under a misapprehension of the rights of the parties, the plaintiff or libelant is not bound by the acceptance of the note, but may tender it back or produce it at the trial, to be canceled, and seek his remedy on the original contract. Baker *v.* Draper, § 7.

§ 2. A receipt of payment by note is not conclusive, but only *prima facie* evidence of the payment of the debt, and such evidence may always be explained by other extraneous circumstances showing the intention of the parties when the receipt was given, and that there was in fact no actual payment of the debt. Moore *v.* Newbury, §§ 8, 9.

§ 8. A receipt in the following terms: "Received payment by note," does not extinguish the debt or the lien of the original security, unless there is evidence of a manifest intention to take the note as sole security. *Ibid.*

§ 4. A check on a bank which is not paying specie, drawn by A. in favor of B., on account of a debt due from the bank to the former, is not payment of A.'s debt to B., although exchanged at the bank by B. for a certificate of deposit, unless A. and B. so agreed. Downey *v.* Hicks, §§ 10-12.

§ 5. An admission by A., after the maturity of the certificate, that he is liable to make it good, conduces to prove that neither the check nor the certificate was taken in payment, and evidence of such an admission is admissible in suit by B. against A. for the original debt. *Ibid.*

§ 6. The taking of a promissory note of one of two joint debtors, and acknowledging receipt of payment on the bottom of the account, is *prima facie* payment, and in the absence of evidence showing a contrary intention of the parties will be deemed payment. Palmer *v.* Priest, § 13.

[Notes.— See §§ 14-186.]

BAKER v. DRAPER.

(Circuit Court for Massachusetts: 1 Clifford, 420-425. 1860.)

Suit *in personam* for supplies. Answer, payment by promissory note. The note was brought into court and tendered to respondents.

Opinion by Clifford, J.

It is insisted by the respondents on this state of the case that the note was accepted by the libelants in payment of the bills for the supplies in question, and therefore that the suit cannot be maintained. On the part of the libelants it is denied that they ever received the note in payment, and they insist that the whole case shows that it was not so agreed or intended by the parties.

§ 7. *Unless so intended, a note does not extinguish a debt.*

At common law a promissory note given for a simple contract debt does not operate as a discharge of the original obligation or constitute a payment of the original debt unless it affirmatively appears from the evidence that such was the intention of the parties at the time it was given. Holt, C. J., said in Clark *v.* Mundall, 1 Salk., 124, that a bill shall never go in discharge of a precedent debt except it be a part of the contract that it should be so. Such bill or note of the debtor himself or of a third party, say the supreme court in Downey *v.* Hicks, 14 How., 249, is never considered payment of a precedent debt unless there is a special agreement to that effect. Where persons were indebted to a bank, and gave their promissory notes for the amount of the debt, it was held by the same court that the mere acceptance of the notes by the bank did not necessarily operate as a satisfaction; and whether or not there was an agreement at the time to receive them as payment, or whether the circumstances attending the transaction warranted such an inference, was a question of fact for the jury. Lyman *v.* The Bank of the United States, 12 How., 225. Satisfaction of the pre-existing debt, as distinguished from an actual payment, must always arise from the agreement of the parties and not from the new security given for that purpose, which only operates as the consideration for the agreement. Hence the agreement must always be proved, and cannot be implied by law in a case where there are no facts or circumstances from which it may reasonably be inferred. James *v.* Hackley, 16 Johns., 277; Peter *v.* Beverly, 10 Pet., 567 (Est. of Dec., §§ 345–50); Whitleck *v.* Van Ness, 11 Johns., 414; Callagher *v.* Roberts, 2 Wash., 191.

But the courts of this state have adopted a different rule, and the question in this case must be governed by the rules of law which prevail in the jurisdiction where the transaction took place. Whenever a party bound to a simple contract debt in this state gives his own negotiable security for it, whether it be a bill of exchange or promissory note, it is presumed as a matter of fact, in the absence of any circumstances to indicate a contrary intention of the parties, that the bill or note was given and received in satisfaction and discharge of the pre-existing debt. That rule was adopted at a very early period in the history of the state, and has been followed by such repeated decisions that it must be regarded here as the settled law upon the subject. Very little embarrassment results from the practice, as was remarked by this court in another case, so long as the application of the principle is kept within the bounds which the rule itself announces. Properly understood, most or all of the cases admit that it is a presumption of fact and not of law, and that it may be controlled by any circumstances which show that such was not the intention of the parties to the contract. When the rule was first adopted it was placed upon the ground that, if an action could be maintained for the original debt, the debtor might also be sued by an innocent indorsee of the bill or note, and thus be compelled to pay the debt twice; and that is the principal reason assigned for the rule at the present time. Wherever the doctrine prevails, the new security is regarded in all respects as a substitute for the first promise, and the reasons assigned for its adoption show that it ought to be very cautiously applied in all cases where the remedy upon the new security is not as effectual and comprehensive as upon the one for which it was substituted. Mr. Greenleaf says, where the debtor's own negotiable bill or note is given for a pre-existing debt, it is *prima facie* evidence of payment, but is still open to inquiry by the jury. To the same effect also are the remarks of Shaw, Ch. J., in the case of Fowler *v.* Bush, 21 Pick., 230. He says the rule here differs from that of the common law, only in determining what shall be presumed to be the intent of the parties, from the fact of giving and accepting a negotiable note for a simple contract debt. Without further evidence of intent, we construe it, says the learned judge, to be payment, but the common law deems it to be collateral security. But this presumption may be controlled by other evidence, and when ascertained such intent shall govern.

All of the cases upon the subject, in point of fact, agree that the giving and accepting of such a security is only presumptive evidence of the intent to extinguish the prior simple contract debt, which, like other presumptions of fact, is liable to be repelled by the circumstances. Courts of justice in this state and in Maine, where alone this rule prevails, have often had occasion to inquire and determine what circumstances are, and what are not, sufficient to repel this presumption. In the course of the numerous decisions upon the subject they have established certain general principles, to which it may be useful to refer. If there is any deception or fraud in the giving of the new security, or if it was accepted without a full knowledge of the facts, or under a misapprehension of the rights of the parties, the plaintiff or libelant, as the case may be, is not bound by the acceptance of the note, but may tender it back or produce it at the trial, to be canceled, and seek his remedy on the original contract. So also, if, when the note was taken, he supposed the maker was the only person bound for the goods, and that he was not changing the parties, but only taking a new security from the same party, then it is clear, say the supreme court of this state in French v. Price, 24 Pick., 22, that the original contract is not so far extinguished as to prevent a resort to it after new parties are discovered. Where negotiable paper had been taken for a pre-existing debt, Shepley, Ch. J., in Fowler *v.* Ludwig, 34 Me., 461, held that if the paper was not binding on all the parties previously liable, or, if the paper of a third party was received not expressly in payment, the presumption that it was so accepted might be considered as repelled. Similar views were also expressed in the case of Melledge v. The Boston Iron Co., 5 Cush., 170, where it was held, that when the promissory note given is not the obligation of all the parties who are liable for the simple contract debt, and *a fortiori* when the note is that of a third person, and if regarded as in satisfaction, would wholly discharge the liability of the party previously liable, the presumption, if it exists at all, is of much less weight.

Applying these principles to the present case, there can be no doubt what the result must be on the state of facts disclosed in the evidence. Testimony was introduced by the libelants tending to show, as matter of fact, that the note was not accepted as payment, but was received only as a convenient mode of adjusting the accounts; and the book-keeper testifies expressly that it was not so accepted, and that he made the transfers on the books without the authority or knowledge of the libelants. Whether so or not, and wholly irrespective of that evidence, I am of the opinion, from the circumstances of the case, that the libelants did not understandingly and with a full knowledge of all the material facts accept the note in satisfaction and discharge of the parties to whom the original credit was given; and there is much reason to conclude from the evidence, that there was a want of good faith on the part of the maker of the note in negotiating the transaction. His clerk went to the counting-room of the libelants with the note already prepared; and when the maker of it sent the clerk, he must have known that the libelants supposed him to be owner of one-half part of the bark, else he could not have expected that the proposition would have been accepted; and he well knew at the same time that he had conveyed his interest to another person. Another bills for repairs against the bark was settled on the same day in the same manner, and a conveyance was also made by him of certain real estate. Whether he owned any other property does not appear, but it does appear that he suspended payment shortly afterwards, and that he was insolvent. Taking all of the circumstances together, it is clear that the defense set up in the answer cannot prevail. The decree of the district court is, therefore, affirmed, with costs.

MOORE v. NEWBURY.

(Circuit Court for Michigan: 6 McLean, 472–478. 1855.)

Opinion by WILKINS, J.

STATEMENT OF FACTS.— The clerk of the libelants, invested with a general authority to collect debts, presented a bill for the amount claimed, to the respondent, on the 22d of May last, 1854, and demanded payment. The respondent, not denying the accuracy of the account, stated that he was not able at the time to make payment. At a subsequent interview, the clerk renewed his application, expressed his willingness to take a negotiable note for the amount, if a certain individual, whom he named, would join in the same, and that then he would extend to the respondent the time desired, but that if this proposition was rejected he would be compelled to attach the vessel.

The note indicated was procured by the respondent, received by the clerk, and the account adjusted by a receipt, given in this language:

"Received payment by note.   "MOORE & FOOTE,
                                           "By G. F. BAGLEY, Clerk."

This note, being indorsed by the libelants, was, on the same day, cashed at a broker's office, and not being paid at maturity was returned to them; it is now exhibited in court and offered to be canceled.

This libel is exhibited on the original account. The answer alleges payment and denies the existence of the maritime lien. Such being the facts, two questions are presented:

1st. Was the original debt extinguished by the note?

If not, 2dly. Does the transaction show an abandonment or waiver of the lien?

§ 8. *A receipt of payment by note is only prima facie evidence of payment.* The circuit court for the United States for this district, in Allen *v.* King, 4 McLean, 128 (BILLS AND NOTES, §§ 1041–47), and in Weed *v.* Snow, 3 McLean, 265, has settled the law for this court, namely, that a receipt of payment by note is not conclusive, but only *prima facie* evidence of the payment of the debt, and that such evidence may always be explained by other extraneous circumstances, showing the intention of the parties when the receipt was given, and that there was in fact no actual payment of the debt. This renders unnecessary the consideration of the conflicting decisions in other states. This court will follow the rulings of the circuit, as long as they are unreversed by the supreme court of the United States. Most of the cases cited were considered in Allen *v.* King, and there is nothing in this receipt which takes it out of the ruling in that case.

Here there is no proof of an agreement that the note should discharge the pre-existing debt, and no proof that it should not so operate. Our judgment must rest on the intention, as manifested by the conversation and conduct of the parties at the time. The receipt, unexplained, as in De Graff *v.* Moffat, cited by the respondent's proctor, would have been conclusive.

The proofs exhibit these facts: The master was not able or not willing to pay when the account was first presented. He did not contest the sum due. But he wanted time as a convenience to himself. The agent or clerk was willing to give time on certain conditions. With this spirit of accommodation the note in question was procured and received. The statement of the clerk that, unless the proposed arrangement was acceded to, the vessel should at once be attached, can, by no fair principle of construction, be held to signify his design to receive the note as absolute payment and an extinguishment of the debt. Moreover, it appears that the agent was only authorized to collect debts. He had no power to exchange securities, especially a higher for one of less grade,— a security *in rem* for one merely *in personam*. Such power is not necessarily implied in a simple agency to collect. And certainly the cashing of the note by the broker was solely on the strength of the contract of indorsement. Had the intrinsic credit of the drawers been sufficient, the face of the obligation would have been otherwise.

§ 9. "*Received payment by note*" *does not extinguish the debt or the lien of the original account, unless there is evidence of a manifest intention to take the note as sole security.*

Holding, therefore, that the note, independently, was not a satisfaction of the debt, the only question remaining is, Was the lien abandoned by the libelants receiving the note, and thus recognizing the act of the clerk?

It is to be observed that, as the transaction took place in Chicago, the libelants did not, in fact receive the note, but only the money raised by its discount, when it was too late for them to disavow or repudiate the transaction.

Where materials are furnished a vessel, the credit is given either to the owner, the captain, or to the ship, and the law creates a lien on the latter. Such lien, however, may be waived, either at the time the materials are furnished, or be abandoned by a subsequent agreement, expressed or implied, on the part of the creditor. He may, at his option, look to other security, and if so, no lien attaches to the ship.

In the case of De Graff v. Moffat, so confidently relied upon, the contract, at the time it was entered into by the parties, *embraced a credit by the notes of the respondent.* After the libelant had closed his proofs, the respondent introduced in evidence a settlement between the parties — an account current in the handwriting of the libelant — in which sundry promissory notes were credited and admitted as cash. This account was balanced, and for the sum remaining due a receipt in full was given, being expressed at the foot of the account as a payment by note, which was not produced or offered for cancellation. No evidence was introduced showing any understanding modifying or contradicting this receipt, and it was, of course, held, as in Allen v. King, *prima facie* evidence of payment. Besides, the original agreement, as shown by the account, certainly waived all lien upon the vessel.

Although a note under certain circumstances will not operate as an extinguishment of the debt, yet, when the creditor accompanies the act of receiving it in payment with the manifest *intention* to take it as his sole security, and not to look to the ship, such intention, clearly expressed or certainly implied, operates as the abandonment of the lien which the law gave him. Such an intention was not manifested in this case. There was no understanding to release the vessel. It is true that she was not yet attached by process; and it is true that the clerk threatened it; but it is alike true that, at that interview between the clerk and the respondent, *all the latter wanted was further time to pay the debt.* The former wanted the money due; and under these circumstances the note was given and taken.

But if the note was not taken with the understanding that it was absolute payment, can it be inferred that it was received as additional security? If it was, it would not help the respondent's defense. He pleads payment, and relies upon a change of securities. The note was not a higher security than the ship. Why, then, collateral, or why a change? There can be but one answer. The note was received to raise the money at the time for the mutual accommodation of the clerk and the respondent, by placing the former in possession of funds which he *then* needed, and extended to the latter further time to meet an acknowledged obligation then due. This intention of the parties is too obvious to be disregarded or overlooked. The one did not receive the note in discharge of the lien; the other did not give it with such an understanding. The intention must govern. The note was to be payment, if paid at maturity; if unpaid, all the relations of the parties as to the vessel and the debt remained unchanged. The circumstance, so ingeniously pressed, that the note was cashed, and the libelants thereby received the amount of the lien (which then ceased and could not be revived), does not materially vary the transaction, or exhibit a different intention. The note gave thirty days' time to the respondent. Until that time elapsed, the vessel could not be attached. Why? Certainly not because the debt was paid, or the lien waived, but because the note and its discount evidenced an understanding to await its maturity, and the default of the makers to meet it.

It was in proof that the note was discounted on the indorsement of the libelants. That it was never paid by the respondents, but by the former, fully appears by their present possession. The witness stated that the note was returned by the indorsees, who had cashed it in May last, and that the libelants were charged with the amount in their account current with the broker. In other words, the note, when due, was lifted by the libelants.

In cases of this description the material-man is not to be deprived of any of his remedies, except upon the most conclusive proof that exclusive credit has been given to other security than the owner, the master, or the ship. Looking to either of the former, to the exclusion of the latter, releases the lien, but must be clearly established. In no case will either be released, unless such was the manifest intention of the party. The maritime law guards, with most scrupulous care, its various subjects. The material-man, the furnisher of supplies, and the mariner are equally protected.

That credit was originally extended to the vessel in this case is not questioned. The schedule appended to the answer reads:

"Steamboat Fashion,

"To MOORE & FOOTE, Dr.

" To merchandise rendered on account."

To this the receipt is attached upon which the defense is based. So that the lien was in existence and recognized the day the note was given. There is no proof that it was ever waived — no proof of an intention to waive it.

The court was forcibly impressed during the hearing with the fact that the instrument was negotiable, and had been discounted, and that, therefore, as the libelants had received the money, their relation to the vessel had ceased. But the subsequent production of the note, and its tender for cancellation, removed all difficulty as to sustaining the lien. This note is not now outstanding. No innocent indorsee can be affected by the decree, nor can it be discovered how sustaining the libel on the principle stated will peril vessels hereafter by secret liens. The purchaser of a ship or any vessel afloat purchases with a presumed knowledge of the existing legal responsibilities. The note and the lien cannot both be sustained. While the one is still current as cash, or outstanding, the other is without force or vitality; but if the former is itself dead and as waste paper, the legal existence of the latter is not impaired. Here the ship contracted the debt. That debt never has been paid. The note was but a promise to pay — a broken promise. It was made and accepted with the sole view to an extension of time. Certainly in this tribunal, as a court of equity, the respondent cannot complain of being dealt with inequitably by a decree enforcing payment of the debt of the boat from the boat — a debt not denied either in its character or amount.

Decree for the entire claim and costs, and the cancellation of the note on payment of the decree.

DOWNEY v. HICKS.

(14 Howard, 240-253. 1852.)

Opinion by McLEAN, J.

STATEMENT OF FACTS.— This case was brought before us by a writ of error to the circuit court for the southern district of Mississippi.

An action of *assumpsit* was commenced by the plaintiff on a note for $456, and a large sum for the hire of slaves.

The declaration contained ten counts, to which the defendant pleaded *non assumpsit*, the statute of limitations, and payment, on all of which issues were joined. The jury "found for the defendant upon the issues joined as to the within note of $456, and the within account." This finding, it is contended, is imperfect, irresponsive to the issues, and does not dispose of the whole matter submitted by the pleadings.

§ 10. *A verdict for defendant on issues joined as to note and account, though informal, is good.*

A verdict is bad if it varies from the issue in a substantial matter, or if it finds only a part of that which is in issue; and though the court may give form to a general finding, so as to make it harmonize with the issue, yet if it appears that the finding is different from the issue, or is confined to a part only of the matter in issue, no judgment can be rendered upon the verdict. Patterson v. United States, 2 Wheat., 221. The verdict rendered was informal, but there was sufficient to authorize the court to enter it in form. The matter in controversy was the note stated and the hire of the negroes, the amount claimed for which was stated in an account; and on both these the jury found for the defendant on the issues joined. We think this was sufficient.

§ 11. *If a release of a witness be given in evidence without exception for want of proof of execution that objection is waived.*

Andrew Arnold, a copartner of the testator, was offered as a witness, and being objected to on the ground of interest, a release was given in evidence, which on its face appeared to be duly executed; on which the witness was sworn. Objection is made that the execution of the release was not proved. The answer to this is, that there was no exception taken to the paper on that ground.

From the facts, it appears that Joseph T. Hicks, now represented by his executrix, was indebted to the plaintiff on the 10th January, 1839, on a settle-

324

ment, $9,799.89, for the hire of negroes, which John R. Hicks, the friend of Downey, received in a certificate of deposit from the Mississippi Railroad Bank, situated at Natchez, payable on the 1st of November ensuing, for which he executed a receipt. He was not authorized to act as the agent of Downey, but he acted as his friend in the business. Being assured by his brother Joseph T. Hicks and others that the bank was good (and as a reason for this opinion it was stated that wealthy men had an interest in the bank), and as eight per cent. interest was paid for deposits, the certificate was preferred, believing it would be satisfactory to the plaintiff. At the time of this transaction, the bank was indebted to Joseph T. Hicks and Arnold, for labor on the railroad, a sum exceeding $20,000. The mode of payment was by drawing a check on the bank for several claims, and then crediting on the books of the bank, as a deposit, the sum due to each claimant.

In February ensuing, when John R. Hicks returned to North Carolina, where he and the plaintiff resided, he handed over to Downey the certificate of deposit, who received it, saying he would have preferred the gold and silver; but said nothing further in repudiation or confirmation of the act of Hicks. In a letter dated the 3d of March, 1839, from J. T. Hicks and Arnold to the bank, they say: "We have ever entertained the kindest feeling towards your institution, and every disposition of indulgence to the utmost of our ability. The time has now arrived when ruin awaits us, from a total inability to use your post-notes to meet our engagements;" and they proposed to take some money and negroes for the money due them from the bank, or to take the whole in negroes, if the money could not be paid.

For a short time after the date of the certificate of deposit the bank continued to pay small notes in specie, but evidence was given conducing to show it was unable to meet its engagements, and that in a short time it failed. Suit was brought by Downey against the bank on the certificate of deposit, in the spring of 1840; and also for other sums, due him from Hicks and Arnold, by arrangements with them. But nothing could be recovered from the bank.

Evidence was offered with the view of showing that Downey considered the certificate of deposit as good, and that he said he could not complain of Hicks in receiving the certificate, as he had received a similar one on his own account.

Evidence was also given to show that on the 11th of March, 1840, Joseph T. Hicks and Arnold admitted the certificate of deposit was given as collateral security, and that they considered themselves bound to pay the debt due the plaintiff, including the certificate of deposit, and other demands. Evidence was also given to explain this conversation as referring exclusively to other demands, not including the certificate of deposit.

The testimony being closed, the plaintiff prayed the court to instruct the jury: 1. That the acceptance by the plaintiff of the certificate of deposit for a precedent debt due him by Hicks, or Hicks and Arnold, was no payment or extinguishment of such debt, unless there was an express agreement to accept it as such payment; and to take the risk of the solvency of the bank.

2. That the certificate of a bank due at a future day, like the note of any third person, if given for a pre-existing debt, is not payment and discharge thereof, unless specially agreed to be so taken; and if a receipt in full be given, it is still a question of fact for the jury to decide, whether there was such an agrement or not; and that unless the certificate be afterwards paid by the bank, it is *prima facie* no satisfaction of the pre-existing debt.

3. That if the jury believe, from the evidence, that Hicks and Arnold, or Hicks, after the maturity of the certificate, admitted their liability to make it good, such admission is evidence that the certificate was not taken as payment absolutely, but as conditional payment only, and that they had notice of all the facts necessary to hold them responsible.

The court charged the jury that "an agent is bound to act in accordance with his authority, to make his acts binding on his principal. If the agent exceeds his authority, his principal is not bound by his act, so exceeding his authority, unless the principal afterwards ratify his acts. If a principal, after he is informed what his agent has done, ratify his acts, he is bound by the acts of his agents, although the agent may not have had any authority to do the act so ratified at the time it was done. An act done as an agent by one having no authority is obligatory on his principal; if, in a reasonable time after he is fully informed of what has been done, he does not object thereto, he is presumed to ratify the acts, and is bound thereby."

That "if Downey received the certificate, conditioned that he would receive the money in discharge of the debt, if the bank should pay it, then Downey was bound to use reasonable diligence to collect the money due on the certificate. Reasonable diligence consists in such exertions as a prudent man would use in his own case in the collection of the certificate; and if Downey failed to use such diligence to collect the money, the defendants are not liable, and the jury should find for the defendant."

§ 12. *A check on a bank which is not paying specie is not payment of an existing debt, unless the parties so agree.*

In ordinary transactions, a check on a specie-paying bank, payable on demand, is payment. And, if the holder of the check present it to the bank and direct the amount to be placed to his credit as a deposit, and the bank should fail, the loss would be the depositor's. The deposit was at his option and for his benefit. But the transaction of Downey and Hicks was not of this character. Doctor Hicks, who acted for Downey, was not authorized to make the arrangement; he acted, in his own language, "without authority, as the friend of the plaintiff." There was no money, in fact, deposited in the bank. It was indebted to J. T. Hicks and Arnold, who were in partnership, in a large sum; and, to pay Downey, Hicks drew a check for the amount, which was charged to his account in bank, and a certificate of deposit for the same amount was given to Downey. This arrangement was strongly recommended by the debtor, Hicks, to his brother, the friend of Downey. Eight per cent. was allowed on the certificate of deposit, which was payable in ten months.

A note of the debtor himself, or of a third party, is never considered as a payment of a precedent debt, unless there be a special agreement to that effect. Had Downey received the certificate of deposit himself, it could not have been considered a payment unless it was so agreed. The transaction, in fact, was only a dealing with credits. No money was drawn from the bank, or deposited in it. By the certificate, the credit of the bank was given in addition to the credit of the original debtor. Such a transaction, without a special agreement to receive the certificate in payment, would make it a collateral security only. A receipt for the amount, executed at the time, would not affect the question. In this view, it was error in the court not to give the first and second instructions asked by the plaintiff, unless the charge given substantially embraced the points stated.

In the charge given it is nowhere stated that, to make the certificate of deposit a payment, there must be an agreement to that effect. The jury are informed that, where an agent exceeds his authority, or acts without authority, the principal is not bound, unless he ratify such acts. But the jury are not informed what amounts to a ratification. They are told where acts are done, of which the principal is informed, if he does not in a reasonable time object thereto, he is presumed to ratify the acts, and is bound thereby.

This, in all probability, misled the jury. Doctor Hicks, in receiving the certificate of deposit, did not pretend that he was authorized to receive it,—much less that he was authorized to receive it as payment. The receipt of the certificate, under such circumstances, by Downey, without any express agreement on the subject, could not operate as payment. In this respect, therefore, unless such an agreement was shown and connected with this part of the charge, it was erroneous.

The jury were instructed that, if the certificate was received on condition that the deposit, if paid by the bank, should be applied as payment, Downey was bound to use reasonable diligence. But the jury were not informed what that kind of diligence was, except "that it consisted in such exertions as a prudent man would use in his own case in the collection of the certificate." Where a note is received as collateral security, and this certificate of deposit is only the obligation of the bank, and does not in principle, in this respect, differ from a note, the holder is not bound to active diligence. If the note have an indorser, and it matures in his hands, he may be bound to take such steps as shall charge the indorser, as a bank is bound where a note is sent to it for collection. But he is not bound to bring suit. He is only chargeable with a negligence which shall operate to the injury of the owner of the paper.

As in less than three months from the date of the certificate of deposit by the showing of the defendant, the post-notes of the bank answered him no valuable purpose in satisfying the demands against him, there is no ground to allege that the defendant suffered by any want of diligence in the plaintiff. The bank was insolvent, if not when the certificate was given, before it became due. The above instruction was erroneous.

We think the court erred, also, in refusing to give the third instruction, as prayed by the plaintiff. If the evidence showed, after the maturity of the certificate, that Hicks and Arnold, or Hicks, admitted their liability to make it good, the jury should have been told by the court that if they believed such an admission was made, it conduced to prove that the certificate was not taken in payment.

For the above reasons the judgment of the circuit court is reversed, and the cause is remanded for further proceedings.

Justices DANIEL and GRIER dissented.

PALMER v. PRIEST.

(District Court for Massachusetts: 1 Sprague, 512–514. 1860.)

Opinion by SPRAGUE, J.

STATEMENT OF FACTS.— This is a suit by material-men against the owners of a vessel for repairs. It appears that the two defendants, Priest and Dodd, were the owners, and that the repairs were done on the credit of the vessel and owners. Priest was the ship's husband, but the libelant did not originally trust to him alone. The account bears date July 15, 1856, on which date the negotiable promissory note of Priest was given, and the account was receipted by a writing at the foot, "Received Payment," and was signed by the libelants. The note was payable six months from date, and by the indorsement seems to have been negotiated, but is now produced by the libelants ready to be delivered up to the respondents.

Was the account paid and the original claim discharged by the taking of the note? If it was, the libelants can have their remedy only on the note. If it was not, they may sue on the original account, and the respondents are liable in this suit.

In Page v. Hubbard, 1 Sprague, 335, I had occasion to consider the Massachusetts doctrine upon this subject. The facts of that case, however, were different from the present. There the builder had a lien upon the vessel — here no lien is set up, or mentioned in the pleadings, and this suit is in personam. There, too, the receipt given stated only that the notes were taken on account; here the receipt states that payment had been received. These differences are quite material. As to the first ground of difference, the general principle stated in the case of Page et al. v. Hubbard et al. might indeed cover the present, viz., that when the taking of the note would not materially affect the rights of the creditor, but merely substitute a second promise for the first, both being by the same parties, there it might be presumed that it was the intention of the parties that the first should be extinguished; but that, if it would materially affect the right of the creditor, such ought not to be the presumption. This would seem also to apply to a case where there were other persons liable for the original debt, besides the person who signed the note, and in this case, if nothing appeared but the giving of the note by Priest, I should have great hesitation in saying that it would discharge the original claim of the creditors against both their debtors, and compel them to rely on one only, especially as it does not appear that Dodd has paid anything to Priest, or would now be in any worse condition, if liable to the libelants, than he would have been, if that note had never been given. It would seem from the case of French v. Price, 24 Pick., 13, and other cases there referred to, that the supreme court of Massachusetts were inclined to hold that knowingly taking the note of one of several debtors would prima facie discharge the others. In the case now before me, there is an express declaration made by the creditors, at the time they received the note, that it was received in payment of a pre-existing debt. This declaration was in writing, being a receipt signed by them and delivered to Priest. If that declaration were literally true, it would certainly discharge the original claim.

In Sheehy v. Mandeville, 6 Cranch, 253 (BILLS AND NOTES, §§ 1406–7), a plea that a note was given "for and in discharge of" a pre-existing claim of goods sold and delivered was held good, although, as the court viewed it, it was the note of one of two debtors.

In Kearslake v. Morgan, 5 T. R., 213, a plea that the negotiable note of the defendant was given to and received by the plaintiff "for and on account of" the sums of money previously owing from the defendant to the plaintiff was held good. But in that case the note was not produced, and might have been in the hands of an indorsee. Where, then, it appears to the court that the note of a sole debtor, or of one of several debtors, or of a third person, was by mutual agreement taken in discharge or payment of a pre-existing debt, the original claim is thereby extinguished, and the creditor can rely only on the note.

§ **13.** *The taking of a promissory note of one of two joint debtors, and acknowledging receipt of payment on the bottom of the account, is prima facie payment.*

The receipt in this case is evidence that such was the agreement between these parties. It is not necessarily conclusive. It may be controlled, either by direct evidence or by circumstances. But here there is neither direct evidence nor any circumstance in any degree impairing the force of the receipt, and the libelants have therein declared that the note was received in payment. This is more direct and positive than in the Barque Chusan, 2 Story, 457, where the receipt was of a note "*for the above amount*," or in Butts *v.* Dean, 2 Met., 77, where the receipt was "*for balance of account to date.*"

Libel dismissed.

§ **14. What admissible to support plea of payment.**—If a debt has in whole or in part been paid; or has been extinguished by any means, as by a contract of a superior nature; or has been released; or if the debt be not in conscience due; or has by some means been satisfied, so that it cannot be conscientiously demanded, these facts may be given in evidence under the plea of payment. Latapee *v.* Pecholier, 2 Wash., 180.

§ **15.** Upon the plea of payment to debt on bond, it is competent for the defendant to give in evidence that wheat was delivered to the plaintiff, on account of the bond, at a certain price; and that the defendant assigned sundry debts to the plaintiff, part of which were collected by the plaintiff, and part lost by his indulgence or negligence. Buddicum *v.* Kirk, 3 Cr., 293.

§ **16.** Upon suit brought by a foreign creditor in a domestic forum, a plea by the defendant of a discharge in bankruptcy, as payment of the debt, is good. Ruiz *v.* Eickerman, 5 Fed. R., 790; 2 McC., 259; 12 Cent. L. J., 60.

§ **17.** A payment which might have been pleaded to the original *sci. fa.* to revive a judgment cannot be given in evidence on a second *sci. fa.* Wilson *v.* Hurst, Pet. C. C., 441.

§ **18.** By the practice and laws of Pennsylvania, any evidence may be given under the plea of payment which proves that, *ex æquo et bono*, the debt claimed ought not to be paid. Latapee *v.* Pecholier, 2 Wash., 180.

§ **19. Payment by note.**—It is a settled doctrine that the acceptance of a negotiable promissory note for an antecedent debt will not extinguish the debt, unless it is expressly agreed that it is received as payment. Peter *v.* Beverly, 10 Pet., 532; Allen *v.* King, 4 McL., 128; Beers *v.* Knapp, 5 Ben., 104; Bank of the United States *v.* Daniel, 2 Pet., 32.

§ **20.** A note is not payment unless received as such; or unless the party, by his after-conduct, make it his own. Maze *v.* Miller,* 1 Wash., 329.

§ **21.** At common law, a promissory note given for a simple contract debt does not operate as discharge of the original obligation, or constitute a payment of the original debt, unless it affirmatively appears that such was the intention of the parties at the time it was given. Kimball *v.* Ship Anna Kimball, 2 Cliff., 4.

§ **22.** By the common law, a simple contract debt is not extinguished by the taking of a new security for it, unless the security be of a higher nature, as an instrument under seal, or unless it be agreed to be received in satisfaction of the debt. The Betsy and Rhoda, Dav., 112.

§ **23.** By the commercial law, a negotiable promissory note received in payment of a pre-existing debt, *bona fide*, and without notice, is not subject in the hands of the holder to the equities between the original parties, although it be an accommodation note, though the rule in the state of New York be otherwise; but the acceptance of such note as payment, on the express assurance of the assignor that it was business paper and not accommodation, does not amount to a payment and extinguishment of the original indebtedness. Crosby *v.* Lane,* 14 Law Rep., 452.

§ **24.** If the assignor of a note represents, at the time of transferring the note, that the parties to it are of high credit and responsibility, such parties being non-residents and unknown to the creditor, and if in point of fact such representations are not true, and circumstances indicate a knowledge on the part of the debtor that their credit and responsibility were doubtful, receiving the note on such representation does not extinguish the original debt. The creditor on returning the note protested for non-payment, or as dishonored, or offering it to the assignor in court on trial, may maintain an action on the original debt. *Ibid.*

§ **25.** Action for goods sold and delivered in Virginia. The plaintiff sold to the defendant a quantity of salt, and afterwards received from him a promissory note payable at a future day, which was indorsed by the vendee of the goods, the defendant. The note being protested, suit was instituted against the vendee, as indorser of the note, and a judgment was obtained in his favor on the ground that, by the laws of Virginia, an action could not be maintained against the indorser of a promissory note until after judgment had been obtained against the drawer and proof of his insolvency. This suit was then brought on the original contract. *Held*, that it could be maintained, and that, although the indorser of the note, the defendant, is entitled to the benefit of the note, yet as it was not an extinguishment of the original debt, there was no absolute necessity to prove an offer of the note before the institution of the suit against him as vendee of the goods. Clark *v.* Young, 1 Cr., 181.

§ 26. Where a worthless promissory note is imposed upon the vendor as part of the cash payment, it would seem that, if any fraud has been practiced on the vendor by the vendee, the amount of the note still remained a lien upon the land for which it was given. Shelton *v.* Tiffin, 6 How., 163.

§ 27. An agreement of one partner to pay a note against his copartner by entering a credit on a note which he holds against the payee, and a charge is made on the books of the firm against the partner for whom the payment is made, and he delivers to his partner other paper as a payment, it is a payment to the payee of the note, although a credit was not indorsed on the note to be credited, until after the lapse of some months. Gwathney *v.* McLane, 3 McL., 871.

§ 28. If the vendor of property accept a note or bill in satisfaction of his debt he cannot sue his original debtor, provided there was no fraud or unfairness on the part of the vendee. Parker *v.* United States, Pet. C. C., 262.

§ 29. Upon a guaranty to the plaintiff of all notes of A., which he should indorse, to the amount of $10,000, the plaintiff indorsed notes of A. to the stipulated amount at several banks; and when the notes became due they were taken up at the banks, and new notes, signed by A., and B., his partner, and indorsed, were received by the banks in their stead. It was held that by such substitution the old notes were extinguished, and the guaranty did not apply. Russell *v.* Perkins, 1 Mason, 368.

§ 30. Circumstances may show that a note was given and received in payment of an account. Riley *v.* Anderson, 2 McL., 589.

§ 31. Where higher security is given by a debtor, *prima facie* the law presumes it intended as an extinguishment of the debt; *aliter*, where it is the bond of a third person. United States *v.* Lyman, 1 Mason, 482.

§ 32. A surety who gives his own note for the debt for which he is contingently liable, such note being received as payment, satisfies the original contract, and fulfills the requirements of section 19 of the bankrupt act. *In re* Morrill, 2 Saw., 356.

§ 33. A promissory note given and received for and in discharge of an open account is a bar to an action on the open account, although the note be not paid. Sheehy *v.* Mandeville, 6 Cr., 253.

§ 34. Where a subscription is made to a public institution, and a note is afterwards given in satisfaction of the subscription, such subscription must be considered as settled. Every presumption is in favor of the transaction, and the court will not go behind it in bankruptcy proceedings instituted against the subscriber years after the subscription was made. Sturgis *v.* Colby, 2 Flip., 168.

§ 35. Generally, the taking of a note is treated as conditional payment only. Risher *v.* The Frolic,* 1 Woods, 98.

§ 36. A note will operate as an extinguishment of the debt if so intended by the parties *Ibid.*

§ 37. And where a party accepted a note bearing a higher rate of interest than the account, and gave a receipt acknowledging payment, it was held that the note was received in payment. *Ibid.*

§ 38. An action cannot be maintained on an original contract for goods sold and delivered, by a person who has received a note as conditional payment, and has passed away that note. Harris *v.* Johnston, 3 Cr., 311.

§ 39. —— In admiralty.— The presumption of the local law will not be enforced in the admiralty against a seaman who receives of the owners of the vessel their negotiable note for his wages. Such a note will not be held to be an extinguishment of the claim for wages, nor of the seaman's lien against the ship, unless it is distinctly stated to him at the time that such will be the effect, and the note is accompanied by some additional security or advantage to the seaman as a compensation for his renouncing his lien on the vessel. The Betsy and Rhoda, Dav., 112.

§ 40. Where the libelants, being ship-chandlers, furnished materials to the barque Chusan while in New York, and took therefor the promissory note of one of the owners, and gave a receipt, it was held that the matter was governed by the *lex loci*, by which a note taken for a debt is only conditional payment until it is duly paid. The Barque Chusan, 2 Story, 455.

§ 41. —— of debtor.— Where persons were indebted to a bank, and gave their promissory notes for the amount of the debt, the mere acceptance of the notes by the bank did not necessarily operate as a satisfaction; and whether or not there was an agreement at the time to receive them in satisfaction, or whether the circumstances attending the transaction warranted such an inference, were questions for the jury. Lyman v. Bank of the United States, 12 How., 225.

§ 42. Where a written contract, with respect to labor to be performed, specified that payment was to be made in "cash or its equivalent," part payment was made in cash and a note given for the balance. Held, that the giving of the note was not a payment of such balance; that the non-payment of the note remitted the payee to all his rights, and caused the taking of the note to operate merely as a giving of credit. Lawrence v. Morrisania Steamboat Co., 12 Fed. R., 850 ; 9 Fed. R., 208.

§ 43. —— of third person.— The note of a third person, given and received in payment of the debt of another, is a valid contract, and operates to extinguish or discharge the original debt, and a note given by a partner for a debt of the firm is, as to such debt, the note of a third person. But to constitute an absolute payment of a pre-existing debt by a promissory note, there must be an agreement to receive it as such, and the burden of proof is upon the party alleging this fact. In re Parker, 11 Fed. R., 397; 6 Saw., 248.

§ 44. The note of a debtor of a third person is not payment of the debt for which it is given, unless expressly accepted as such. In re Ouimette, 1 Saw., 47.

§ 45. A creditor who receives the note of a third person as payment of the debt, "if such note is collectible," thereby binds himself to sue upon the note, if necessary to its collection. Ibid.

§ 46. Where bills of exchange are transmitted by a debtor to his creditor to be sold, and the debtor directs the creditor to credit him with the proceeds; and the creditor sells the bills, partly for cash and partly for negotiable notes, and gives the debtor credit in his books for the amount in two distinct items, first, for the notes, and second, for the balance in cash, this is a mere provisional payment, and if the notes be not paid, he may recur to his original claim, unless, by his subsequent conduct, he converts the provisional payment into an absolute payment. Hamilton v. Cunningham, 2 Marsh., 350.

§ 47. If the landlord take a single bill of a third person for the amount of rent due from his tenant, and give time of payment to the third person until he fail, this is good evidence to support the plea of no-rent arrear. Josse v. Shultz, 1 Cr. C. C., 185.

§ 48. He who receives any note upon which third persons are responsible, as a conditional payment of a debt due to himself, is bound to use due diligence to collect it of the parties thereto at maturity, otherwise by his laches the debt will be discharged. Douglass v. Reynolds, 7 Pet., 113.

§ 49. The taking of a note for a pre-existing debt from the indorser imposes an obligation on the holder to demand payment when the money is due, and give notice of non-payment. If he fail in this, he makes the note his own. Allen v. King, 4 McL., 128.

§ 50. Where a note was received, the proceeds to be applied in discharge of a debt, if demand be not made and notice given to the indorser at the proper time, so as to charge him, the indorsee makes the note his own, in discharge of the debt. Ibid.

§ 51. —— Maryland rule.— In Maryland a due bill or promissory note given for a debt does not discharge the original debt nor extinguish the remedy upon it. Reppert v. Robinson, Taney, 492.

§ 52. —— Maine rule.— By the law of Maine, if a negotiable security be given for a pre-existing simple contract debt, the legal presumption is that it is received in payment, and that it is an extinguishment of the original cause of action; but this presumption is liable to be controlled by proof to the contrary. The Betsy and Rhoda, Dav., 112.

§ 53. In Massachusetts and Maine, when a promissory note is taken for a debt, the presumption arises that it was taken in payment of the debt; this presumption, however, may be overcome by evidence showing the contrary intention of the parties. But at common law there is no presumption that the taking of negotiable paper extinguishes the debt for which it was taken. Carter v. Townsend, 1 Cliff., 1.

§ 54. —— Massachusetts rule.— A note taken on a simple contract debt in Massachusetts is presumed to be taken in payment, but the presumption may be rebutted. ·Hudson v. Bradley,* 3 Cliff., 184.

§ 55. If a debt is secured by lien, and negotiable promissory notes are taken for a portion of the debt, the mere fact of the existence of the lien is sufficient to repel the presumption arising under the Massachusetts rule that the notes were taken in payment. Hence, in such case, the notes being surrendered upon action brought, the lien may be enforced for the whole amount of the debt. Page v. Hubbard, 1 Spr., 335.

§ 56. The rule in Massachusetts is, that if a party who is bound to the payment of a simple contract debt gives his own promissory note for the debt, the presumption, in the absence of any proof to the contrary, is that such note was accepted by the creditor in satisfaction and discharge of the pre-existing debt; but such presumption is one of fact only, and may be rebutted and controlled by any evidence showing that such was not the intention of the parties; and when it appears that the note was not the obligation of all the parties who were liable for the original debt, or that the note was that of a third party, and if held to be in satisfaction would wholly discharge the party previously liable, the presumption, if it exist at all, may be repelled by slight circumstances evidencing a contrary intention. Where a note of a third party was taken, but no settlement was made at the time, and the account was not receipted, *held*, that the circumstances were sufficient evidence of such contrary intention to rebut the presumption. Hudson *v.* Bradley,* 2 Cliff., 130.

§ 57. The rule in Massachusetts, that when a debtor gives his own negotiable bill or note for a pre-existing debt, it is *prima facie* evidence of payment, does not apply where the bill or note is accepted in ignorance of the facts, or under any misapprehension of the rights of the parties. So if the paper accepted is not binding upon all the parties previously liable, it is held that the presumption of payment may be considered as repelled. If the transaction is tainted with fraud, or if it appears that there was any concealment, misapprehension or unfairness in giving or passing the new security, proof of such facts, or any one of them, will be sufficient to repel the presumption, and to entitle the creditor to recover upon the original contract. Palmer *v.* Elliot, 1 Cliff., 68.

§ 58. Although the rule in Massachusetts is, that wherever a party bound to a simple contract debt gives his own negotiable security for it, the presumption is that the bill or note was given and received in satisfaction of the pre-existing debt, this presumption is not a conclusive one, but may be controverted by any circumstances which show that such was not the intention of the parties. Thus where notes were given by the charterers of a ship to the owner, covering a portion of the charter money, the agreement being that, if the notes fell due before the ship returned, the owner was to take them up or renew them, and if the ship got in before the notes fell due, he was to return them or deduct the amount from the charter money, *held*, that the notes were not given or received in payment, but as an accommodation to the owner. Kimball *v.* Ship Anna Kimball, 2 Cliff., 4.

§ 59. By the general commercial law, a promissory note does not discharge the debt for which it is given, unless such be the express agreement of the parties; it only operates to extend until its maturity the period for the payment of the debt. The rule in Massachusetts, however, is, that when a note is given for a simple debt, the presumption is that the note was given and received in satisfaction of the debt; but this presumption may be repelled by circumstances showing that such was not the intention of the parties. Where notes, given for a portion of the charter money, were drawn so as to mature near the time of the anticipated arrival of the ship, and, according to the statement of the broker who made the arrangement, were given for the accommodation of the ship-owner, and were to be held over or renewed in case they fell due before the arrival, *held*, that these circumstances were sufficient to repel any presumption, under the Massachusetts law, that the notes were taken in payment of the claim for the charter money. The Kimball, 3 Wall., 37.

§ 60. By draft — Bill of exchange.— An accepted draft is not to be held payment of an indorsed note unless it is expressly agreed that it should be so received. Cooper *v.* Gibbs, 4 McL., 396.

§ 61. Bills purchased and remitted to pay a foreign debt may be given in evidence as payment, if purchased and remitted before the writ was served on the defendant. Fairfax *v.* Fairfax, 2 Cr. C. C., 25.

§ 62. A bill of exchange is not, in general, to be considered as a satisfaction of a pre-existing debt, unless it be paid or accepted as such; nor, if remitted conditionally, unless the debtor sustain injury by the laches of the creditor who received it. Gallagher *v.* Roberts, 2 Wash., 191.

§ 63. Taking a bill of exchange is, at most, only *prima facie* evidence of a satisfaction and extinguishment of an antecedent debt. *Quære:* How far even this is to be relied on as a general presumption in foreign states? Wallace *v.* Agry, 4 Mason, 336.

§ 64. A bill of exchange remitted in payment of a debt due to the person to whom it is sent, where the amount of the bill is lost by the negligence of such person, is to be considered as payment of the debt. Roberts *v.* Gallagher,* 1 Wash., 156.

§ 65. Where a creditor receives a draft drawn by his debtor on a third person, taking the same in payment of his account, and gives a receipt in full, it is a novation of the debt, which is extinguished with all its accessory rights and privileges. Underwriters' Wrecking Co. *v.* The Katie, 3 Woods, 182.

§ 66. A master of a vessel, being obliged to borrow money in a foreign port to pay for repairs and necessary expenses of the vessel, drew drafts on the owners for the amount borrowed. *Held*, that in the absence of proof showing that the drafts were received as payment, they were only a conditional payment and did not discharge the original debt. The Emily Souder, 17 Wall., 666.

§ 67. If a bill of exchange be taken in payment as a discharge of a pre-existing debt, or in such manner as imports an intention of the creditor to take the risk of the bill on himself, the original debt is thereby discharged. Brown *v.* Jackson, 2 Wash., 24.

§ 68. A draft of a third person does not discharge the original consideration, unless it is received unconditionally as payment. Slocomb *v.* Lurty, Gilp., 431.

§ 69. If a debtor remit a bill of exchange to his creditor in payment of the debt, and he receives it as such, and credits the debtor, it is payment, and he can only sue the debtor as indorser; and if he neglect to present it in time for acceptance and payment, and to give notice of its dishonor, he makes the debt his own, whether the drawer had funds in the hands of the drawee or not. Denniston *v.* Imbrie,* 3 Wash., 396.

§ 70. Where a bill of exchange is sent to a creditor in payment of a debt, and through the negligence of the creditor the amount of the bill is lost, the bill is to be deemed payment; but if the bill was sent to the creditor, as agent, to be collected, he would only be liable in damages for his negligence. Roberts *v.* Gallagher,* 1 Wash., 156.

§ 71. By check, order, etc.— The simple drawing of a check and delivery thereof to the payee, without presentation, acceptance or payment, does not transfer the fund drawn on, to the amount of the check, from the drawer to the holder of the check, or operate as an appropriation *pro tanto* of the fund in the hands of the drawee. Strain *v.* Gourdin, 2 Woods, 380.

§ 72. A collector of the customs is not authorized to receive anything in payment of a duty bond but the lawful money of the United States, or foreign gold or silver coins made current by law. If he receives a check upon a bank, this is not payment of the bond until the check is paid. United States *v.* Williams, 1 Ware, 175.

§ 73. A check drawn by the defendant in favor of the plaintiff, or bearer, with the bank's canceling mark upon it, and produced by the defendant, is not evidence of money paid to the plaintiff, although it appear by the plaintiff's evidence that when payment was demanded the defendant said he had paid it by such a check, and although he produces his own checkbook, with a memorandum corresponding with the check, with the additional words "for rent." Lowe *v.* McClery, 3 Cr. C. C., 254.

§ 74. Where the payer is requested to remit his check by mail, such check so forwarded is a valid payment, although the agent making the request had no special instructions, the receipt of the money being within the scope of his duties. Tayloe *v.* Merchants', etc., Ins. Company, 9 How., 390.

§ 75. An order payable out of a particular fund is not payment. Governor of Virginia *v.* Turner,* 1 Cr. C. C., 261.

§ 76. Where sharesmen in a fishing voyage, their cruise being completed, and they having gone on another voyage, sent orders in writing to the owners of the vessel they had just quitted to pay their shares to M., and M. gave a written order to pay the money to S., which was done, and S. afterwards failed while the money was in his possession, *held*, that, as to the owners, it was a payment by them of the respective shares of the seamen, although the orders were not negotiable. Crowell *v.* Knight, 2 Low., 307.

§ 77. By bond.— A receipt of a bond of a third person "in part pay" of a precedent debt is conclusive evidence of payment to that extent, although the obligor was insolvent at the time the receipt was given. Muir *v.* Geiger,* 1 Cr. C. C., 323.

§ 78. The official bond given by a receiver of public moneys does not extinguish the simple contract debt arising from a balance of account due from him to the United States. Walton *v.* United States, 9 Wheat., 651.

§ 79. An action of *assumpsit* for the balance of account, and an action of debt upon the bond against the principal and sureties, may be maintained at the same time. *Ibid.*

§ 80. Where the consideration of a bond has failed, it cannot be pleaded as payment. Wilson *v.* Hurst,* Pet. C. C., 441.

§ 81. Bonds assigned to be applied to the discharge of a debt for which a suit is brought, although they are not returned to the assignor, cannot be given in evidence on the plea of payment, it being proved that the consideration of the bonds had failed, and that they had been acknowledged by the assignor to be of no value. *Ibid.*

§ 82. By levy and seizure.— A writ of *fi. fa.* returned executed, that is, levied upon the property, is a discharge of the debt as to the debtor, unless, by actual sale of the property seized, the value should appear to be insufficient to discharge the debt. Until that appears the plaintiff cannot have a new execution. Smith *v.* Bank of Columbia, 4 Cr. C. C., 143.

§ 83. A levy is said to be a satisfaction of the debt if the property be of sufficient amount.

And this is said to be the case though the property should be wasted by the negligence of the officer. Starr v. Moore, 3 McL., 354.

§ 84. Where an attachment is laid upon goods, and they are lost through the negligence of the sheriff, the defendant may set up the levy as a satisfaction, if the value of the goods be equal to the amount of the judgment. Starr v. Taylor, 3 McL., 542.

§ 85. Where a res is seized by a judicial process for a debt which carries with it a jus in re, as between a debtor and creditor, the destruction of the seized property, without the fault of the debtor, works a payment of the debt to the extent of the value. Where third parties voluntarily join the seizing creditor in his proceeding, and unite, so to speak, in the seizure, also asserting claims which carry with them liens, the destruction of the property without fault of the debtor works a payment of their respective claims to the extent of the value of the property destroyed in the order of the priority of their claims, the same as if the property had been sold and the proceeds applied in payment of the claims. So held, where a ship, libeled, and condemned to be sold, sank while in the hands of the marshal, and became a wreck. Gill v. Packard, 4 Woods, 270.

§ 86. By deposit of money with third person.— If a debtor deposit money for his creditor with a third person, and the creditor assent thereto, or give the depositary a new credit upon the footing of such deposit, the original debtor is discharged. Swift v. Hathaway, 1 Gall., 417.

§ 87. By discontinuance.— Under a plea of payment, proof of the discontinuance of the suit cannot be given in evidence. Latapee v. Pecholier, 2 Wash., 180.

§ 88. A voluntary discontinuance by a party plaintiff is not satisfaction of the debt or cause of action. Bingham v. Wilkins, Crabbe, 50.

§ 89. By mail.— Where money is remitted by mail, by the direction of the creditor, to pay a debt, it goes at the risk of the creditor, and if lost on the way, it nevertheless operates as a payment of the debt. Selman & Son v. Dunn,* 10 West. L. J., 459.

§ 90. Payment of partnership note by note of surviving partner.— The personal note or bond of a partner given for partnership notes taken up by him operates not as payment, but as a renewal of the firm note, if such be the intention of the parties. Loveridge v. Larned, 7 Fed. R., 294.

§ 91. Where a partnership is dissolved by the death of one partner, and a firm note held by a creditor is exchanged for one given by the remaining partner in the firm name, such exchange will not operate as a payment of the joint debt, and create a separate debt by the surviving partner, unless it was intended to do so by the parties. In re Clapp, 2 Low., 226.

§ 92. Forged and worthless paper — Confederate bonds.— The plaintiff, having drawn his check on the Bank of North Carolina, in the usual form, for the full amount there on deposit in his name, accepted, as part payment, coupon bonds which were issued by the state of North Carolina in aid of the rebellion. Held, that such bonds, having a value in the business transactions of the country, were a valid medium for the payment and satisfaction of a bona fide debt when accepted by the creditor as such. Holleman v. Dewey,* 2 Hughes, 341.

§ 93. Where a bank, in which the bonds for customs were left for collection under the authority of the government, discounted for the principal obligor certain notes for the payment of these bonds, and the proceeds were carried to the credit of the United States by the bank, in discharge of the bonds, and it turned out that the indorsements on the notes were forgeries practiced by the principal, it was held that the bonds were discharged, and there was no remedy in equity to acquire a priority on the assets of the principal. United States v. Rousmanier, 2 Mason, 373.

§ 94. A person who sells a note is always understood as affirming that it is what it purports to be, to wit, a genuine note; if it is not what it purports to be, it is nothing, and if given in payment of an antecedent debt, it is no payment. Semmes v. Wilson, 5 Cr. C. C., 285.

§ 95. —— of a bank, when good payment to such bank.— In general, a payment received in forged paper or in base coin is not good; and, if there be no negligence in the party, he may recover back the consideration paid for them or sue upon his original demand. But this principle does not apply to a payment made bona fide to a bank in its own notes, which are received as cash, and afterwards discovered to be forged. United States Bank v. Bank of Georgia, 10 Wheat., 333.

§ 96. In case of a payment upon a general account made bona fide to a bank in its own notes, which are received as cash, and afterwards discovered to be forged, an action may be maintained by the party paying the notes if there is a balance due him from the bank upon their general account, either upon an insimul computassent or as for money had and received. Ibid.

§ 97. The mere offer of a master to pay a seaman's wages is not necessarily an admission that the wages are due and payable. The Martha, Bl. & How., 151.

§ 98. **Payment by government to wrong person — Effect on rightful claimant.** — A requisition and warrant issued in favor of A. are not discharged by payment wrongfully made to another person. Effect of an Erroneous Payment of a Treasury Warrant,[*] 4 Op. Att'y Gen'l, 398.

§ 99. The payment of a liquidated demand against the government to a person not authorized to receive it does not relieve the government from responsibility to make payment to the proper claimant. Effect of Erroneous Payments at the Treasury,[*] 5 Op. Att'y Gen'l, 183.

§ 100. If accounting officers err, designedly or by mistake, in making payments, the loss must fall on the United States. *Ibid.*

§ 101. Where a payment has been made illegally at the treasury of the United States, on account of some specific appropriation, that does not prevent payment out of the same appropriation to the rightful party when he does appear. Gigo's Case,[*] 8 Op. Att'y Gen'l, 377.

§ 102. **Presumption of payment from lapse of time.** — Where the statute of limitations does not apply, lapse of time affords a presumption against the justice of the claim, which is entitled to weight by a court or jury. Patterson v. Phillips, Hemp., 69. See LIMITATIONS.

§ 103. Where a debt has remained due and payable for sixteen years, the law holds such lapse of time as *prima facie* ,evidence of payment, regardless of the statute of limitations; and after the lapse of twenty years, the presumption of payment becomes conclusive. Didlake v. Robb, 1 Woods, 680.

§ 104. W., living in Virginia, draws a bill of exchange, in November, 1775, on R. & Co., merchants in London, which was duly protested in June, 1776. W. died in 1777 or 1778. Payment was not demanded of the representative of W. until 1819, when suit was instituted on the protested bill. *Quære:* Does the doctrine of presumption of payment, arising from lapse of time, which is applicable to sealed instruments, apply to a bill of exchange? If it does, such presumption is merely *prima facie*, and the holder may rebut it by accounting for the time which has been permitted to elapse, and by showing the improbability that the debt has been paid. Should this presumption be rebutted, still the plaintiff shall only recover legal interest from the assertion of his claim. Hopkirk v. Page, 2 Marsh., 20.

§ 105. A presumption that the purchase money for land has been paid to the proprietaries cannot arise from length of time, when the claimant of the land does not produce a patent or show that a patent was issued for the land. Conn v. Penn, Pet. C. C., 496.

§ 106. The presumption of payment from lapse of time may be rebutted by circumstances, which are for the consideration of the jury; but when a petitioner seeks to have a *supersedeas* of a commission in bankruptcy revoked, in order to allow him to prove debts against which there is a *prima facie* presumption of payment, he must satisfy the court that he has a fair and reasonable expectation of rebutting the presumption, if the opportunity is afforded him. *In re* Morris' Estate, Crabbe, 70.

§ 107. —— **mortgages.** — No presumption of payment against the mortgagee or his assigns in possession can arise from lapse of time, where the mortgagor became insolvent and died before the mortgage debt became due, leaving no personal representatives, and none but collateral heirs, and his alienee also became insolvent, removed from the state before foreclosure, and never returned. Brobst v. Brock, 10 Wall., 519.

§ 108. In respect to the mortgagee, who is seeking to foreclose the equity of redemption, the general rule is, that where the mortgagor has been permitted to retain possession, the mortgagee will, after a length of time, be presumed to have been discharged by payment of the money or by a release, unless circumstances can be shown sufficiently strong to repel the presumption, as payment of interest, a promise to pay, or an acknowledgment by the mortgagor that the mortgage is still existing. Hughes v. Edwards, 9 Wheat., 489.

§ 109. The presumption of payment of a mortgage arises, where no interest on it has been paid for twenty years. But the relation of vendor and vendee must exist to authorize such a presumption. Lessee of Ransdale v. Grove, 4 McL., 282.

§ 110. —— **bonds.** — After the lapse of twenty years, a presumption of payment of a bond or note arises; and, under peculiar circumstances, it may arise on a shorter time. Denniston v. McKeen, 2 McL., 253.

§ 111. In an action upon a bond, payable by instalments, the jury may, and ought to, presume payment of any instalment payable more than twenty years before the commencement of the suit, and may presume payment of an instalment payable nineteen years and ten months before the commencement of the suit. Miller v. Evans, 2 Cr. C. C., 72.

§ 112. The equitable rule of limitation applied to bonds, where there has been no demand for twenty years, is a mere presumption of payment, not an absolute limitation. The Postmaster-General v. Rice, Gilp., 554.

§ 113. Twenty years creates a presumption of payment of a bond, if no interest has been paid in that time. If a shorter period is relied upon, the presumption should be fortified by circumstances. Goldhawk v. Duane, 2 Wash., 323.

§ 114. To authorize a presumption of payment of a bond, twenty years must have elapsed, exclusive of the period of the disability of the holder to sue for the same. Dunlop v. Ball, 2 Cr., 180.

§ 115. There is no presumption of payment of a bond held by an alien enemy during a war. But it is not so clear that upon a bond dated in 1778, and on which suit was not brought until 1802, the same length of time after the removal of the disability is necessary to raise the presumption of payment as would be required if the bond had borne date at the time of such removal. Ibid.

§ 116. —— against the government.— Presumption of payment from lapse of time cannot be raised against the government. United States v. Williams, 4 McL., 567.

§ 117. The statute of limitations does not run against the government, nor is it chargeable with delays so as to raise a presumption of payment. United States v. Williams, 5 McL., 133.

§ 118. —— in admiralty.— A forbearance to sue for nine months, even if the libelant was on the spot and the vessel within the power of the court during that time, does not raise a presumption of payment, either in the admiralty or any other court. Holmes v. The Lodemia, Crabbe, 434.

§ 119. Payment by deed.— If a creditor accepts a deed of land in payment of a debt it is a bar to an action for the debt, and if the title be defective the creditor must look to his warranty. Miller v. Young, 2 Cr. C. C., 53.

§ 120. Where judgment has been rendered against a defendant who has subsequently conveyed real estate to the plaintiff, he is entitled, under a plea of payment to a sci. fa. issued to revive the original judgment, to a credit for the value of the property at the date of the conveyance. United States v. Thompson, Gilp., 614.

§ 121. By devise.— It is a general rule that a devise of land is not a satisfaction or part performance of an agreement to pay money. Bryant v. Hunter, 3 Wash., 48.

§ 122. By chattels.— In action for breach of contract the court cannot, unless empowered by statutory provision, compel the plaintiff to accept as part payment, or in mitigation of damages, the property the non-delivery of which occasioned the suit, if tendered in open court by the defendant. Colby v. Reed, 9 Otto, 560.

§ 123. Where the defendant sets up as a defense that certain collaterals assigned to the plaintiff were accepted by the latter in satisfaction of the debt, and not as collateral security, he must clearly establish the truth of his allegation. Where the written assignment states that the property was assigned "as collateral security," and the face value of the collaterals is less than the amount of the debt, such facts tend strongly to show the intrinsic improbability that any agreement was made that the collaterals were to be taken in satisfaction of the debt, and will control in the absence of direct proof that they were so taken. Brown v. Hiatt, 1 Dill., 372.

§ 124. Where a creditor wrongfully takes and carries away personal property belonging to his debtor, no part of the debt due him is thereby extinguished, for a debt cannot be extinguished by a credit or set-off arising from unliquidated damages for a trespass. Palmer v. Burnside, 1 Woods, 179.

§ 125. Miscellaneous.— A court of equity will not appropriate a sum of money paid for the extension and renewal of a note as a payment on the indebtedness of the maker, unless the complainant's bill shows a case of usury and prays relief on that ground. McNamara v. Condon, 2 McAl., 364.

§ 126. A payment made to the mortgagee, after an assignment of the mortgage, but before the mortgagor has notice of it, is good against the assignee. Hubbard v. Turner, 2 McL., 519.

§ 127. Where a suit may be prosecuted by the drawer of a bill of exchange, in the name of the payees for the benefit of the drawer, payment of the bill by the drawer to the payees is no bar. Davis v. McConnell, 3 McL., 391.

§ 128. If money is to be paid, or any other act to be done, on a certain day and at a certain place, the legal time of performance is the last convenient hour of the day for transacting business. But if the parties meet at any part of the day, a tender and refusal at the time of the meeting are sufficient. Savary v. Goe, 3 Wash., 140.

§ 129. Where a suit was brought for a balance of account for advances made at Boston, upon goods consigned to the plaintiffs at Trieste, and sold by them at a great loss, it was held that the balance was not payable at Trieste but at Boston, and, therefore, the balance was to be estimated in damages at the par and not at the rate of exchange. Grant v. Healey, 3 Sumn., 523; 2 L. Rep., 113.

§ 130. The comptroller of the treasury has a right to direct the marshal to whom he shall pay money received upon execution. and a payment according to such directions is good; and it seems he may avail himself of it upon the trial, without having submitted it as a claim to the accounting officers of the treasury. United States v. Giles, 9 Cr., 212.

§ 181. A promissory note, given as collateral or counter security for a note borrowed, is not discharged or vacated by the borrower's discharging or taking up the borrowed note with funds furnished by the lender. Smith v. Johnson, 2 Cr. C. C., 645.

§ 182. Where, by a contract between American citizens, a payment is to be made in a foreign country, the intention of the parties must govern the form of payment. Searight v. Calbraith, 4 Dall., 325.

§ 183. A citizen of North Carolina, being indebted to a citizen of Pennsylvania at the time of the breaking out of the late rebellion, was compelled to pay, by proceedings under an act of the self-styled Confederate congress for the sequestration of the estates of alien enemies, the amount of such indebtedness to the receiver appointed under the sequestration act. *Held*, that such payment was in no sense a payment and satisfaction of the debt due the citizen of the loyal state. Shortridge v. Macon, 1 Abb., 58; Chase's Dec., 136.

§ 184. Legal and equitable assets were in the hands of an administrator, he being also commissioner to sell the real estate of a deceased person; and by a decree of the court of chancery he was directed to make payment of debts due by the intestate out of the funds in his hands, without directing in what manner the two funds should be applied. Payments were made under this decree to the creditors by the administrator and commissioner, without his stating, or in any way making known, whether the same were made from the legal or equitable assets. A balance remaining in his hands, unpaid to those entitled to the same, the sureties of the administrator, after his decease, claimed to have the whole of the payments made under the decree credited to the legal assets, in order to obtain a discharge from their liability for the due administration of the legal assets. It was held that their principal having failed to designate the fund out of which the payments were made, they could not do so. Backhouse v. Patton, 5 Pet., 160.

§ 185. The proceeds of certain property seized under the confiscation act were by order of the court turned over to the clerk of the court, who in turn deposited them to his credit, as clerk, in the bank of S., having been notified by the interior department that such bank had been designated by the secretary of the treasury as a depository of public money. Judgment in the condemnation suit was rendered in favor of the owner of the property, but in the meantime the bank had failed. Upon suit by the owner against the United States, *held*, that the depositing of the proceeds in the above manner was not a payment into the treasury, and hence the government was not liable for the amount lost by the failure of the bank. Branch v. United States,* 12 Ct. Cl., 281.

§ 186. A. and B. shipped a cargo of goods for C., but consigned them to D., the partner of E. Before the arrival of the goods, D. died, C. became bankrupt, and the defendant, under a power of attorney from E., took possession of them, sold them and remitted part of the proceeds to E., at the same time informing A. and B. of his having taken possession of the goods; and when he remitted in part their proceeds to E. he advised A. and B. of such remittances, who approved of the whole of his proceedings. *Held*, that the defendant did not become the agent of the shippers, but was the agent of E.; and that any remittances made to E., of which advice was not given by the defendant to A. and B. that they were for the proceeds of the goods, were not payments to A. and B. Holt v. Dorsey, 1 Wash., 396.

II. APPLICATION OF PAYMENTS.

SUMMARY — *General rule*, §§ 187, 147.— *When the law will apply*, § 188.— *By a receipt*, § 139.— *Voluntary payments*, §§ 140, 141.— *Proceeds of a judicial sale*, §§ 142, 143.— *Payment by administrator*, § 144.— *Running accounts*, §§ 138, 145, 146, 149-153.— *Payment to treasury department*, § 148.

§ 187. When a debtor makes payment to a creditor to whom he is indebted in several sums and on various accounts, as by note, bond, and book account, he has a right to direct to what account or what debt the payment shall be appropriated. If the debtor pays generally on account, the creditor may make the appropriation. But the application, whether made by the debtor or creditor, must be made at the time of the payment. United States v. Bradbury, §§ 154-158.

§ 188. If no appropriation is made by either party at the time the payment is made, neither debtor nor creditor is permitted to go back afterwards and apply the payment, but the law intervenes and makes the application according to its own notions of justice between the parties. In cases of open running accounts, where there have been a number of successive charges and payments, the law applies these payments to the extinguishment of the debits in the order of time in which they stand in the account, each payment being appropriated to the extinguishment of the oldest charge on the debtor side of the account. *Ibid.*

§ 139. When the appropriation of a payment is made by a receipt, it is by the creditor and not by the debtor that it is made. He executes the instrument and the words are his; and if the debtor takes the receipt without objection, he will be considered as consenting to the application thus made by the creditor, and it will be binding upon him unless he has been overreached by fraud or surprise. *Ibid.*

§ 140. The rule as to voluntary payments is that the debtor may direct the application of such payments upon one of several debts due from him to the creditor. Nichols *v.* Knowles, § 159.

§ 141. A voluntary payment within the meaning of this rule is one made by the debtor on his own motion and without any compulsory process. A payment made upon execution does not fall within the rule. *Ibid.*

§ 142. Where, under the statute of Minnesota, a chattel mortgage is placed in the hands of the sheriff with orders to seize and sell the mortgaged property for the purpose of paying the mortgage debt, the sale is made by virtue of legal proceedings, and the proceeds of the sale are in no sense voluntary payments, the application of which the debtor is authorized to direct; but inasmuch as the mortgage does not direct how the proceeds shall be applied, the creditor has the right to apply them to the payment of any of the debts secured by the mortgage. *Ibid.*

§ 143. Where some of the notes secured by chattel mortgage were also secured by the indorsement of a third party, it may be inferred that the parties intended to apply the proceeds of the sale of mortgaged property first to the notes not otherwise secured, so as to give the creditor the full benefit of all of his security. *Ibid.*

§ 144. In case of payments made by an administrator of an insolvent estate, all such payments must be deemed to be made on general account, and *pro rata* towards the extinguishment of all the debts due to the creditor. The United States, as creditor, having priority by law in such cases does not change the rule. The duty of the administrator is the same. United States *v.* Wardwell, §§ 160–163.

§ 145. In cases of running accounts, where debits and credits are made at different times, the payments are to be deemed as made towards items antecedently due, in the order of time in which they stand in the account. *Ibid.*

§ 146. The case of the United States furnishes no exception to this rule in cases of running accounts. All payments are deemed to be made on general account. *Ibid.*

§ 147. In case of payments by a debtor to a creditor the debtor has a right to direct the application of them, and if he does not the creditor may apply them as he pleases. *Ibid.*

§ 148. In case of payments to the treasury department of the United States, the officers of that department have not a right to make any application of such payments against the will of the debtor or of his administrator. *Ibid.*

§ 149. In an action on a long running account between the parties, of notes, acceptances, etc., if the debtor transfer a note or draft to the plaintiff, which is due at a future day, and give no direction on what claim the money when collected shall be applied, the creditor may apply it before action, and in case of his failure so to do the court may at the trial. Whetmore *v.* Murdock, §§ 164–167.

§ 150. The true application of such money is to such of the claims as seem most proper under all the circumstances; as, to one not bearing interest if others do; one not secured if others are; one owned in his own right if others are not; and finally, if none of these exist, to the oldest demand. *Ibid.*

§ 151. But if one of the claims is not due when the draft is received, or is supposed to be otherwise secured before the money is collected on this draft, or if the creditor, when it is collected, credits it generally and informs the assignees beforehand that when received it will reduce their general balance so much, the money should be applied to the oldest demand, or be considered as applied generally to the whole account by the creditor when he received it. *Ibid.*

§ 152. If notes are given, as in the other case between these parties, to secure acceptances, and are found against by a jury for want of consideration or fraud, the money, when actually paid on the acceptance before the suit, may be recovered as not merged by those notes. But the sum received by the creditor on the draft cannot be applied first to such demand. when the debtor did not so direct, nor the creditor so enter it, but both resorted to what they considered other security for the payment of what might be so advanced on those acceptances. *Ibid.*

§ 153. Money not paid for a principal before action brought cannot be recovered by the surety as money paid, unless on a special promise to pay it previously; and if that promise is found to be fraudulent, the money actually paid after the suit may be recovered, but only in a separate, subsequent action. *Ibid.*

[NOTES.— See §§ 168–223.]

UNITED STATES *v.* BRADBURY.

(District Court for Maine: Daveis, 146–154. 1841.)

STATEMENT OF FACTS.— This was an action upon the official bond of Bradbury as postmaster. He had held the office from 1831, and in January, 1838, gave a new bond. which is the one in question. When he gave the new bond he owed $465.60, and paid on the same day $227.91, and took a receipt therefor, which stated the amount paid to include all previous dues back to October 1, 1836. He ceased to be postmaster on the 30th of September, 1838, and it appeared that he had paid in three payments amounts corresponding with the sums for which he was debited. There was a verdict for the penalty, and now a motion is made for a new trial.

§ 154. *The rule as to appropriation of payments when a debtor owes several sums and on various accounts.*

Opinion by WARE, J.

The instruction to the jury was, that when a debtor makes payment to a creditor, to whom he is indebted in several sums and on various accounts, as by note, bond, and book account, he has a right to direct to what account or what debt the payment shall be appropriated. This is a rule which arises out of the nature of the act. The payment is the act of the debtor, and he has a natural right to determine the quality of his own act, that is, to make the appropriation of his own money. If the debtor pays generally on account, this right results to the creditor: he may then make the appropriation, and apply it to the payment of which debt he chooses. But the imputation, whether made by the debtor or creditor, must be made at the time of payment; *in re presenti, hoc est statim, atque solutum est.* Dig., 46, 3, 1.

§ 155. *When the law will intervene and apply the payments.*

If not then made, it is not permitted to either party to go back afterwards and apply the payment, but the law intervenes, and makes the application according to its own notions of justice, between the parties.

§ 156. *The rule of open and running accounts.*

In cases of open, running accounts, where there have been a number of successive charges and payments, from time to time, if neither of the parties has imputed these payments to extinguish any particular charges in the account, the law applies them to the payment of the debits in the order of time in which they stand in the account, each payment being appropriated to the extinguishment of the oldest charge on the debtor side of the account. Such was the direction to the jury, and, as a general rule, this is too well established to be brought into doubt. United States *v.* Kirkpatrick, 9 Wheat., 720 (BONDS, §§ 419–22); Postmaster-General *v.* Furber, 4 Mason, 333; United States *v.* Wardwell, 5 Mason, 82 (§§ 160–63, *infra*); Clayton's Case, 1 Merivale, 572.

§ 157. *The rule of the Roman law.*

The Roman law, from which our rules for the imputation of general and unappropriated payments are in part derived, looks generally to the interest of the debtor, and is governed by what may be presumed to have been the will of a prudent and discreet man, if his attention had been particularly called to the subject; *quod verisimile videretur diligentem debitorem admonitu ita suum negotium gesturum fuisse.* Dig., 46, 3, 97.

When there were several debts, and the payments were general, the law imputed it to a debt which the debtor owed on his own account rather than to one for which he was liable as surety; to one which bore interest before one which did not; to a debt secured by mortgage, or by sureties, rather than to one which was not; to one having a penalty attached to it rather than to one which had none; and, generally, to extinguish the debt which was most onerous to the debtor. It proceeded upon this principle, that, as the right of making the appropriation belongs of right to the debtor in the first instance, when none is made by either party and it is left to be made by the law, that ought to look to the supposed will of the debtor rather than that of the creditor. But, if the debts were all of the same character, this preference was abandoned, for, though the debtor, on some accounts, may have an interest in extinguishing the more recent rather than the more ancient debts, the law adopted the more equitable rule between the parties, and applied the payment to the oldest. *Si nihil eorum interveniat, vetustior contractus ante solvitur.* Digest, 46, 3, 97 and 5; Pothier des Obligations. Nos. 565, 571; Toullier, Droit Civil, Vol. 7, Nos. 173, 186. In this rule, therefore, the common and civil law agree, and the rule itself has its foundation in principles of natural justice. There was then no error in the instruction given to the jury in laying down the principles of law applicable to the general question, independent of the specialties belonging to the particular case.

The only question which can be considered as fairly open is, whether there is in this case such an appropriation of the payments made by the debtor as will take it out of the common rule. It is contended that there was, and that this, as a fact, may be justly inferred from the circumstances under which the payments were made and from the receipts which were taken.

The bond bears date January 26, 1838. Bradbury remained postmaster for three quarters after, and, at the end of each quarter, paid the amount of postage which had accrued during the quarter and took a receipt for the sum, which described it as " being the amount due from him to the United States for the quarter ending," etc., " as shown by his account current, including all previous dues." It is argued that this receipt makes an appropriation of the payment first to extinguish the debt which accrued the past quarter, and that the excess only, if any there were, was to be applied towards paying the old balance; and that such was the intention of the debtor is a just inference from the fact that each payment was the precise amount of postage which had accrued during the preceding quarter. Undoubtedly it was the right of the defendant to have the money so applied if he chose to make the application. But, to carry this intention into effect, it must be made known in a clear and intelligible manner, either by positive directions or by circumstances equivalent to a direct order. The fact that the payments were in each case precisely equal to the postage of the preceding quarters does, undoubtedly, raise a strong presumption that they were intended to be applied to the extinguishment of that part of the debt. In the case of Marryatt v. White, 2 Starkie, 101, Lord Ellenborough seemed to consider this circumstance as conclusive in a case which in its leading features resembles the present. That was an action on a promissory note, against the surety, given to secure the payment for flour to be afterwards delivered to the principal on the note. He was, at the time, indebted to the plaintiff for goods previously delivered. There was, therefore, an open running account. By the usage of trade a credit was allowed of three months, and if payment was sooner made the debtor was entitled to a discount. Lord Ellenborough observed " that the payment of the exact amount of goods previously delivered is irrefragable evidence to show that the sum was intended in payment of those goods, and the payment of sums within the time allowed for discount, and *on which discount has been allowed*, affords a strong inference, in the absence of proof to the contrary, that it was made in relief of the surety."

It will be observed that this case, in one important circumstance, differs from the case at bar. A discount was, by usage, allowed when payment was made before the expiration of the credit, and on some of the payments a discount was, in fact, allowed. This conclusively proved that the imputation was to the new and not to the old debt; because if it had been applied to the old account no discount could have been claimed. Two circumstances here concurred to indicate the intention of the debtor, but one of which exists in the present case. That, it is true, Lord Ellenborough seems to have considered as conclusive when standing alone and unconnected with any circumstances contributing either to confirm or weaken the presumption.

As a universal proposition this will perhaps be found to be not wholly free from difficulty. But in the present case it does not stand alone; a receipt was taken and an appropriation of the payment may be made by the form of the receipt. Manning *v.* Westerne, 2 Vern., 607. Does this receipt, in its legal construction, make the appropriation which is contended for? In its terms it professes to be for the amount of the last quarter, including the previous dues. This form of expression seems to contemplate the whole debt due as one mass, and to impute the payment to the aggregate. The language of the receipt also implies that it is in satisfaction of the whole debt — the old balance, if any there was, as well as the last quarterly charge. It appears to me that the legal and proper import of the words renders it a payment on the general account; and if so, the law applies it to extinguish the oldest debits, leaving the last quarter unsatisfied.

§ 158. *When an appropriation is made by a receipt it is the creditor who makes it.*

But if the receipt admitted the construction for which the defendant's counsel contends, it would not relieve his case. When the appropriation of a payment is made by a receipt, it is by the creditor and not by the debtor that it is made. He executes the instrument, and the words are his. If the debtor objects to the appropriation, he may require a receipt in a different form, or he may by his own act impute the payment to the extinguishment of a different debt; for he is not bound, provided he objects, by the imputation of the creditor. But he must object at the time, and if he takes it without objection he will be considered as consenting to the application made by the creditor, and it will be binding upon him unless he has been overreached by fraud or surprise. Pothier des Obligations, No. 566, Part 3, ch. 1, art. 8. Now, if it had been the intention of the agent of the postoffice to impute the payment · to the last quarter, to the exclusion of the antecedent balance, and this had been done in terms ever so precise, it would not have been binding on the United States, because it would have been in direct opposition to the law. Nothing can be clearer, both in principle and authority, than that a public agent, acting under the authority of law, cannot bind the government when he exceeds his powers, or when his act is repugnant to the law. Johnson *v.* United States, 5 Mason, 425. The agent who gave the receipt had no authority to impute the payment to any particular part of the debt, for this had been already done by law. By the act of July 2, 1836 (ch. 270, § 37), it is provided, when a new bond has been given by a postmaster, and there is an unpaid balance remaining against him, "that payments made subsequent to the execution of the new bond by said postmaster shall be applied first to discharge any balance which may be due on the old bond, unless he shall at the time of payment expressly direct them to be applied to the credit of his new account." The construction of a receipt is therefore wholly immaterial, unless it be shown by other evidence that a receipt in this form was specially required by the debtor, or that the appropriation might be considered as his act. But there was no evidence of this kind in the case. In whatever point of view this case is considered, it appears to me that judgment must be for the United States.

Another question remains, and that is, for what sum the parties on this bond are liable. The whole balance due and now claimed is $227.78. If the payment made at the time when the bond was executed be imputed upon the debt which accrued back to October, 1836, then the whole of the old balance will be of more than two years' standing, and by the act of congress of 1825, chapter 275, section 3 (Story's ed.), the sureties of a postmaster are not liable for any default which occurred more than two years before the suit was brought. This period of limitation had passed before the date of the writ. The receipt expressly imputes the payment upon that part of the debt. But, as has been already observed, when an appropriation is made by a receipt, it is *prima facie* the act of the creditor. It can only be construed to be the act of the debtor when it appears by other evidence that he required the receipt in that particular form. But if it be taken as the act of the agent of the general post-office, he had no authority to make the appropriation. It was already made by a general law. The bond, however, by its terms, is made to operate only prospectively. The condition is that, "if the said Bradbury shall well and truly execute the duties of said office, etc., and shall pay the balance of all moneys that *shall* come into his hands, etc., and shall faithfully account with the United States for all moneys, etc., which he shall receive," etc. The bond, therefore, can have no retroactive effect to render the parties liable for antecedent defaults. Now the whole amount of postage which accrued after the date of the bond was $157, and for this amount, and this only, are the parties in this action liable.

Judgment for the penalty, and execution to be issued for $157 and interest from the date of the service of the writ, December 31, 1839.

NICHOLS v. KNOWLES.

(Circuit Court for Minnesota: 3 McCrary, 477–479. 1881.)

STATEMENT OF FACTS.— Suit on two of a series of five notes which were originally secured by mortgage. When the first note matured the property was sold under a power in the mortgage, and, contrary to directions from defendant, the proceeds of the sale were applied on the two notes last due. The notes first due were secured by the indorsement of a third party.

§ 159. *Rule as to voluntary payments, and payments made on execution.*

Opinion by McCRARY, J.

The rule as to voluntary payments is that the debtor may direct the application of such payments upon one of several debts due from him to the creditor. Tayloe v. Sandiford, 7 Wheat., 13. Does this rule apply to the present case? A voluntary payment, within the meaning of this rule, is one made by the debtor on his own motion, and without any compulsory process. A payment made upon execution does not fall within the rule. When, under the statute of Minnesota, a chattel mortgage is placed in the hands of the sheriff with orders to seize and sell the mortgaged property for the purpose of paying the mortgaged debt, the sale is made by virtue of legal proceedings, and the proceeds of the sale are in no sense voluntary payments, the application of which the debtor is authorized to direct.

If the debtor could not direct the application of the payments, could the creditor? It is strongly urged by counsel for defendant that neither party could direct a particular application, and that the law will apply the proceeds of the sale *pro rata* upon all the notes. Inasmuch, however, as the mortgage does not direct how the proceeds of the sale of the mortgaged property shall be applied, and since there are no circumstances from which it can be inferred that a *pro rata* application was intended by the parties, I hold that the creditor had the right to apply the proceeds to the payment of any of the debts secured by the mortgage. Gaston *v.* Barney, 11 Ohio St., 506. This view is much strengthened by the fact that some of the notes were secured by the indorsement of a third party as well as by the chattel mortgage, from which it may be inferred that the parties intended to apply the proceeds of the sale of mortgaged property first to the notes not otherwise secured, so as to give the creditor the full benefit of all his security. Stamford Bank *v.* Benedict, 15 Ct., 437; Martin *v.* Pope, 6 Ala., 532; Matthews *v.* Switzler, 46 Mo., 301; Field *v.* Holland, 6 Cranch, 8; Schuelenberg & Beockler *v.* Martin, 1 McCrary, 348 (Conv., §§ 765–67). Judgment for plaintiff.

UNITED STATES *v.* WARDWELL.

(Circuit Court for Rhode Island: 5 Mason, 82–94. 1828.)

STATEMENT OF FACTS.— Proceeding by bill in equity against the administrators of the principal and surety on a naval purser's bond. It appeared from the evidence that Bourne was appointed naval purser on the 14th of April, 1814, and gave two bonds to the United States, one for $10,000, on the 14th of April, 1814, with Abel Jones and Stephen Price as sureties, and the other for $25,000, on the 30th of April, 1817, with Price, Dale and Johnson as sureties. That on the 30th April, 1817, a balance was found due to the United States, amounting to $7,560.86, and a further balance on the 10th of November, 1823, of $31,556.88, in the whole amounting to $39,117.14. Bourne died in office on the 10th of November, 1823. Howe, his administrator, paid to the United States $4,968.42, on account of moneys due them, each party claiming the right to apply the money to either account, Howe wishing to apply the same in part payment of the first balance of $7,560.86, whereas the United States contended that it should be applied in satisfaction of the last indebtedness.

Opinion by STORY, J.

There is no controversy as to the facts in this case; and the whole resolves itself into mere questions of law. I pass over all the grounds insisted upon by way of laches on the part of the officers of the government, for the decisions of the supreme court have fully settled them.

§ 160. *Where a new bond is required by law, and such is given, the latter is a substitute for the old bond, and the sureties on it are discharged.*

The first ground insisted on by way of defense is, that the act of 1817, chapter 197, is a complete discharge of the first bond as to all sums received

after the second bond was executed. The statutes provides, " that every person now in service, or who may hereafter be appointed, shall, *instead of the
bond required by the act* to which this is a supplement, enter into a bond with
two or more sufficient sureties, in the penalty of $25,000 conditioned for the
faithful discharge of all his duties as purser in the navy of the United States,
which sureties shall be approved," etc. My opinion is that the argument is well
founded. The new bond is to be given *instead of*, that is, in the place or
room of, the old bond, and not in addition to the latter. It is a complete substitute for, and not a supplementary security to, the former. To construe the
act otherwise would be a plain departure from the meaning of the terms, and,
as I think, also from its true object and intent. From the time the second
bond was given, I am therefore of opinion that the first bond was *functus
officio* as to future responsibilities for future advances.

§ 161. *A debtor has generally the right to direct the application of his payments.*

Then as to the payment made to the district attorney by the administrator
of Bourne. Generally speaking, the debtor has a right to make the application of payments as he chooses; if he omits so to do, the creditor, having different debts, may make the application to which he pleases. If neither party
makes any application, the law will adjust it by its own notions of the equity
and justice of the particular case. It is plain that the officers of the treasury
department had no power to make an absolute application of the present payment by the administrator to the liquidation of the last balance, unless the
law justifies it upon general principles. If either party had a right to direct
the application, it was the administrator of Bourne; and if applied according
to his direction, it goes to the reduction of the first balance.

§ 162. —— *quære, whether this privilege of the debtor passes to his administrator.*

But I doubt, exceedingly, whether an administrator is subrogated in this
respect to all the rights which the debtor himself would have if living. Especially do I doubt it in case the estate is insolvent. When a debtor here dies
insolvent, all his estate is distributable among his creditors, *pro rata*, with the
exception of certain privileged creditors having priorities, such as the United
States, the state. and creditors for charges of the last sickness, and of the
funeral of the party. In such cases of administration, it seems to me that all
the demands of each creditor form one consolidated debt, and that the payments made are to be *pro rata* upon the whole, to be applied in the same way
towards the discharge of the whole. The administrator has no right, at the
instance or for the benefit of third persons, to direct the payment to be applied on account of any particular debt. He is bound to pay on all debts a
pro rata sum. If this be so as to ordinary creditors, the circumstance that
the United States have a priority does not change the duty imposed by law ;
for if the assets are not sufficient to pay all the debts due to the United States,
the same reason applies, that is, that the payment shall be *pro rata* on all.
The administrator acts not for himself, nor for sureties, nor upon personal
preferences, but as a trustee for the benefit of all the creditors *pari passu.*
And I think the law requires him, in the execution of the trust, to distribute
the burthen and the benefits equally among all the creditors without preferences, and without prejudice to the rights of any sureties. Upon these principles my opinion is, that the sum paid by the administrator ought to be
applied as of right to both balances, discharging each *pro rata* in the propor-

tion which the respective amounts bear to the whole sum paid. Perris *v.* Roberts, 1 Vern., 34, proceeded on principles which afford a just analogy.

§ 163. *Where payments are applied to a running account made up of several items, those oldest in point of time must be the first to be extinguished.*

But another ground of defense supersedes, or rather renders the former unimportant. It appears that the accounts of the treasury have run on, from time to time, ever since his first appointment, charging him with advances made, and crediting him with disbursements. Balances have been struck from time to time; and the balances have been again carried forward to the debit side of the new accounts. It is, therefore, the common case of a running account where there are various debits and credits on each side, and the question is, in such a posture of things, where there has been no specific application made of any payments, by either party, to any specific items, how the payments thus passed into general account are to be deemed, in point of law, to have been applied. My opinion is that they are to be considered as applied in discharge of the items antecedently due in the order of time in which they stand in the account.

This is the natural, and, as I think, the legal result of carrying the credits into general account. The doctrine of Clayton's Case, 1 Merivale, 572, 604, 608, is directly in point, and stands upon irresistible reasoning. It is confirmed, if confirmation were necessary, by Bodenham *v.* Purchas, 2 Barn. & Ald., 39; Simson *v.* Cooke, 1 Bing., 452, and Simson *v.* Ingham, 2 Barn. & Cresw., 65. The case of United States *v.* January & Patterson, 7 Cranch, 572 (Bonds, § 595), has been supposed to justify a different doctrine. It appears to me that such is not the true explanation of that case. It turned wholly upon its own particular circumstances, and the charge of the circuit court, which, with reference to the facts, the supreme court thought erroneous. The questions then were, (1) whether the supervisor had any right to make a special application of any prior payments, made on general account, and if he had, then, (2) whether the promise of the supervisor to make a particular application of the payments, after they had been passed into general account, was, *per se*, an application of such payments, unless followed by some positive act of appropriation. The supreme court decided both points against the defendant, and overruled the contrary decision of the circuit court. The case of The United States *v.* Nicoll, 12 Wheat., 505 (Bonds, §§ 671–73), in which The United States *v.* January & Patterson is recognized, turned upon entirely distinct considerations. There the United States were supposed to have a right, like any other creditor, to apply payments made by the debtor to any account where the debtor himself had made no application.

I have had occasion to consider this point in the case of The Postmaster-General *v.* Furber (Maine), 1827, and to the opinion there given I deliberately adhere. In truth, the same point was substantially decided by the supreme court in the case of The United States *v.* Kirkpatrick, 9 Wheat., 720 (Bonds, §§ 419–22), and further discussion of it would seem to be unnecessary.

My judgment is that, as the credits carried into the general account of Bourne, for disbursements since the second bond was given, far exceed those due by him to the United States, the parties to the first bond are discharged from any responsibility thereon. The bill must therefore be dismissed.

WHETMORE v. MURDOCK.

(Circuit Court for Massachusetts: 3 Woodbury & Minot, 390–399. 1847.)

STATEMENT OF FACTS.— This was an action on a running account between the parties, and among the credits was an acceptance transferred by defendant to plaintiffs. The jury were instructed to apply this credit to the oldest of plaintiffs' demands, and after a verdict in their favor plaintiffs moved for a new trial, on the ground of misdirection. Further facts appear in the opinion of the court.

§ 164. *Rule as to the application of a general payment where there are several different debts.*

Opinion by WOODBURY, J.

There is no doubt that if there be a payment of money by a debtor, without any special application of it to one of several debts, the creditor before the suit, or the court, if not done by him before, may at the trial apply it in such way as seems most equitable and proper, under all the circumstances of the case. *Recipitur in modum recipientis.* 23 Pick., 473; 2 N. H., 193; 5 Metc., 268; 3 Metc., 536; Pitman on Principal and Surety, 158; Boody v. United States, 1 Woodb. & M., 150 (BONDS, §§ 433–38).

Some cases hold that the creditor, in such an event, may, when receiving the money, apply it to any legal claim then due. 2 Strange, 1194; 1 Taunt., 564; 2 N. H., 196; 11 Metc., 184.

I am not prepared to say that this power may not exist in the creditor, though it would look more just to confine his application to the claim seeming to be indicated by the reason and justice of the case, when these are strong for one of the debts due, rather than for another. That is, it should be applied to the claim implied, if there be any implication.

But if no such reason is found to exist here, it would seem probable that the creditor here had, in fact, before the action, applied the money received on the draft to the account generally. It is so entered on the exhibit annexed to the writ, and beside this, he wrote to these assignees, that, when collected, it would reduce the general balance due to them so much. In that exhibit the acceptances when made were charged in the account to the defendant, as they are in the action.

Supposing, then, that they were rightfully charged in that manner, and were recoverable in this action, if due and paid before the trial, though not due when the action was brought, then, under this aspect, the result would be much the same as under the ruling of the judge, though it would be reached in a different form, and would rest on a different fact and principle.

But supposing that this view be questionable, or that the creditor should not in equity apply the money generally to the account, when a demand like this in the present case exists, which it is supposed has strong claims to be first extinguished by it, the inquiry becomes necessary, whether any such claim existed here stronger than in favor of the oldest debt, to which the judge ordered the payment to be applied first.

What is the demand which it is contended here should possess a preference? It is for the money advanced by the plaintiffs to meet their acceptance, secured by notes of the defendant, but which notes the jury have found in the other case to be void. In the first place such a demand is not of the strongest character, the security taken for it having been pronounced invalid by a jury. But still, as the defense there went rather to the security itself than the original debt, and as a note in Massachusetts is not considered to merge the orig-ignal consideration (Leland *v.* The Medora, and Brown *v.* Noyes, 2 Woodb. & M., 92, 75), I think the money advanced on the acceptances constitutes still a legal claim to be paid some way by the defendant, and which may be enforced against him at law.

It was included in the account annexed here by the plaintiffs, and should, therefore, have been allowed by the jury in the verdict, if it could be, when not actually paid till after the action was instituted. But more of this after ascertaining whether the ruling as to the credit of the money received was legal. We have seen already that this demand, instead of standing with strong features now in its favor, has been at least in bad company, and the security for it avoided.

In the next place, does the debtor appear to have indicated in any way a wish to have it extinguished specially by the money collected by the plaintiffs, although he may not expressly have ordered it to be so applied? For if he did, *solvitur in modum solventis.* Mills *v.* Fowkes, 5 Bingh., N. S., 455.

There was no evidence whatever of such a desire on the part of the debtor, but, on the contrary, the draft had been transferred to the plaintiffs, probably in June, 1836, near the time of its date, some weeks before those acceptances existed, and still longer before the substituted notes for them were given in the latter part of August.

Nor was the money received on this draft before or at the time the accept-ances fell due in September; but more than a month after, October 30, 1846. Not only did the debtor give no indication that he wished this money thus applied, but the creditors gave none before the suit.

The creditors, when receiving it, did not apply it specially to the payment of what had been advanced on the acceptances, or to the notes executed there-for, but proceeded to trial afterwards to recover those very notes in Novem-ber, 1846, and continued to hold to secure their payment since the last of August, the special attachment made on the writ in that action, rather than the draft and money. This attachment furnished a good reason why the creditor did not, when the draft was received, or when the money was after-wards collected on it, mean to apply either in discharge of the consideration of these notes. And this course of procuring other security for those notes, and by an attachment by co-operation of the debtor in recovering them on de-mand, is decisive evidence that both the debtor and creditor did not mean to apply this draft, or the proceeds of it, specially to discharge what should be paid by the plaintiffs on the acceptances, which they were then trying to se-cure in another way. Both at that time gave strong indications of a desire to obtain different security for them and eventual payment from other sources.

§ **165.** *Circumstances which may control a creditor or a court in applying a general payment to one of several debts.*

But though in this view neither the debtor nor creditor made a special ap-plication of the money collected to this particular demand, nor either of them did anything showing a desire for such an application, but rather the reverse, it is contended that certain circumstances exist in connection with a debt itself, which sometimes show it to be equitable to apply a payment to one debt rather than another. Upham *v.* Lefavour, 11 Metc., 184. Thus assuredly it might be equitable for the court or the creditors, if one demand was on in-terest and another not, to make the application of the money received to the latter, in the first instance. Pothier, Oblig., n. 530; 9 Cowen, 773; 3 Sumn., 98, 111; 1 Story, Eq. Jur., § 459. But all here in law drew interest alike.

So, if one demand was secured and another not, it might be equitable to make the application first to the latter. 6 Cranch, 8, 10; 1 Mason, C. C., 324; 2 Maule & Selw., 318; 5 Taunt., 596. This last rule would exclude the present demand, as at the trial, as well as at the time of the receipt of the money on the draft, it was supposed to be secured by a special attachment of property. So it might be just to apply it to the debt in the creditor's own right, if one be *in autre droit.* 12 Mass., 321. Or to a debt similar in character with the payment, in amount or otherwise. 11 Mass., 300; 5 Taunt., 596. In the present instance at the trial, I do not see that any of these circumstances existed which rendered it probable that the parties meant there should be any specific application of this sum, collected by the plaintiffs in October, to this, rather than the other claims.

§ 166. *When a payment may be applied to the oldest debt.*

Nor do I perceive any strong equitable consideration to require the application then to be made to this particular demand. In this situation the rule long existing and well established is that adopted at the trial, to make the application first to the oldest demands. Boody *v.* United States, 1 Woodb. & Min., 150; Hilton *v.* Burle, 2 N. H., 193; 2 Maule & Selw., 18; 5 Taunt., 597; 2 Barn. & Ald., 39; 1 Merivale, 572.

Nor is this course arbitrary and inequitable, but rests on a like foundation with the other rules, where the debtor says nothing. It must be presumed, if there be no other equity to settle the question, to intend to pay first what has been longest due, and about which there has been most forbearance on the one side and neglect on the other, and which is the nearest being lost or barred by the statute of limitations.

§ 167. *Nothing can be recovered which was not due when the writ was served. In the absence of a contract to the contrary the debt of the drawer to the acceptor of a bill is not due till the bill is paid.*

The only remaining question is, whether the payments made· on account of the acceptances, if not included in the verdict, ought to have been, and a new trial be proper, so as to have them included. If not included, I think that, as before intimated, the plaintiffs are entitled to recover them in some suit, but whether in this or not is questionable. The money had not been actually paid when this suit was instituted, but it had been agreed to be paid at the time of the acceptances. The notes were taken to secure the acceptances. At first they were payable at a future day, like the acceptances, but were afterwards changed to be payable on demand, and the change was legal so far as respects the mere alteration of time.

Does this imply an alteration of the time at which the defendant was to become liable to the plaintiffs for the acceptances, so as to make them a debt or obligation *in presenti,* as between the plaintiffs and defendant, the former being bound to pay them, and thus agreed to do it, at all events, and hence the defendant might undertake to secure and pay them forthwith? If it did, in that view, the verdict should have embraced their amounts unless the fraud extended to them, as well as the note, the defendant having thus undertaken, before this action was brought, to secure and pay for the acceptances forthwith.

But if the acceptances were regarded only as liabilities not due when this suit was brought, and nothing had been done by the parties to make them, as between the parties, a debt incurred by the plaintiffs for the defendant, which the latter was to secure and pay *in presenti*, then some doubt would exist if an action could lie by the plaintiffs till they were paid. There would be an obligation on the defendant to indemnify them when the suit was brought, though actual payment was not made before the suit, but only before the trial.

This would constitute a strong equity to recover for them in that action, but it might not be strictly legal. Perhaps, to be thus legal, it must be apparent that the parties changed the time of paying the acceptances, as well as of the note. The presumption, for the purpose of this motion, may be considered in favor of such a change. But if so, was not this change void? The presumption may be, if the new agreement as to time was void in regard to the note or security, it was as to the acceptance, and at best left them as they stood before.

If the plaintiffs insist otherwise, or that the amount can be allowed here, even if the new agreement was void, and the actual payment of the acceptances not made till after this suit was brought, these questions must be argued further. And if it be deemed material to have the fraud specifically settled by a jury, in respect to any change of time in paying the acceptances, or if the counsel for the assignees wish to put it to another jury, that the change in the time of payment was fraudulent towards other creditors, and if so, insist that without such change these acceptances cannot be received as between these parties but by a suit brought after they fell due as originally given, and after their actual payment, it is doubtful whether we ought not to examine further the last position, and if for the defendant, to allow another jury to pass on this point of fraud as to the acceptances not before made in his suit. But the natural inference being that any fraud in the new agreement was void as to the acceptances no less than the note, and it being apparent, on now looking to the minutes on which the amount of the verdict was computed, that these acceptances were not included, contrary to the impression heretofore made, we must hear the counsel further, whether they can be allowed in this action on a new trial, or the plaintiffs must bring a new suit for them instituted since they were actually paid. The point becomes important, as property is attached in this action which may prove sufficient to pay their whole amount, whereas if not recoverable here, but only in another action, the payment of them will not be in full, but only *pro rata* with other creditors out of other funds.

The general rule doubtless is, that nothing can be recovered which was not due at the time the writ was served. Kerr *v.* Dick, 2 Chitty, 11. Before the term closed at an adjourned session in April, 1848, the plaintiff moved to have the verdict set aside, or reformed so as to include the amount paid on the acceptances. The motion was argued by the same counsel, but no new cases were cited in its support. The court overruled it for these reasons.

There was no evidence at the trial that the acceptances, independent of the second note, were agreed to be payable on demand. The jury, therefore, passed an opinion on the notes and found them to be fraudulent and void. This is the most favorable view for the plaintiffs, because, if the agreement extended to the acceptances, as well as the notes, it must as to the former be considered void as well as to the latter.

The acceptances would then stand as originally, and as thus they were not due when this action was instituted, they cannot be included in the verdict, either by amendment or a new trial. But at the same time they should not be barred by the present verdict and judgment on it, as the jury have not passed any opinion on the acceptances. We will, therefore, give a special judgment on the verdict, expressly excluding the acceptances as not decided on, or let the plaintiffs withdraw them from the declaration without* prejudice, in order that they may be proved before the commissioner of insolvency, or be sued in new action, if not obliged to be so proved.

§ 168. In general.—The general doctrine as to the application of payments is, that if the debtor fail to apply them the creditor may do so. If both fail, the law will make the application as the principles of justice shall require. United States v. Linn, 2 McL., 501; Postmaster-General v. Norvell, Gilp., 106; Gordon v. Hobart, 2 Story, 243; Cremer v. Higginson, 1 Mason, 323.

§ 169. The right of appropriation is one strictly existing between the original parties; and no third person has any authority to insist upon an appropriation of such money in his own favor, where neither the debtor nor the creditor has made or required any such appropriation. Gordon v. Hobart, 2 Story, 243.

§ 170. Where a debtor pays money, he may dictate the mode of its application at his pleasure, for the reason that he might have withheld the payment altogether. If he gives security, he gives it for such debts as he agrees to have it applied to; if payment is made generally, or security given without restriction, the creditor has the right of appropriation. Ex parte Howard National Bank, 2 Low., 487.

§ 171. In general, the debtor has the right to make the appropriation of payments; if he omits, the creditor may make it; but neither party has a right to make an appropriation after the controversy has arisen. United States v. Kirkpatrick, 9 Wheat., 720.

§ 172. The doctrines of the common law as to the appropriation of indefinite payments, generally, have been borrowed from the Roman law. Gass v. Stinson, 3 Sumn., 99.

§ 173. Advances made on account generally, for work done under several distinct contracts, some of which have not been completed, must be applied in the first place to the extinguishment of the amounts due on the contracts which have been completed, and not of those which have not been completed. McDowell v. Blackstone Canal Co.,* 5 Mason, 11.

§ 174. Where a general payment has been made some years after expiration of the bond, the payment must be applied to discharge, pro tanto, the general balance. United States v. Linn, 2 McL., 501.

§ 175. A., an agent, drew two drafts for $4,000 each, and one for $2,000, on his principal, B., all of which were discounted at a bank. B. refused to accept the drafts, but was finally adjudged liable for the two drafts of $4,000 each, but not for the draft of $2,000. A. having assigned to the bank his claim against B. in trust to apply the proceeds in payment of all his debts to the bank, a suit was brought thereon and referred to arbitrators, who awarded a certain sum, which was paid by B. to the bank accordingly. Upon suit subsequently brought by the bank against B. on the drafts, held, that the terms of the assignment must govern the appropriation of the payment, and that A.'s debts to the bank being the three drafts before mentioned, the payment was to be appropriated upon them pro rata, four-fifths to the two drafts of $4,000, and one-fifth to the draft of $2,000. Farmers' and Mechanics' Bank v. Stickney,* 8 Law Rep., 161.

§ 176. A material-man who had extensive claims against a vessel, his account extending over a considerable period of time, some of the items of which were maritime and some were not, received cash for part of the amount due him, and notes for the balance. Held, that the cash payment must be applied to the extinguishment of that portion of the debt which was not maritime. The Schooner D. B. Steelman, 5 Hughes, 210.

§ 177. By the debtor.—A person owing money under distinct contracts has a right to apply his payments to whichever debt he may choose, and this power may be exercised without any express directions given at the time. Tayloe v. Sandiford, 7 Wheat., 13.

§ 178. An act of congress (act of March 3, 1797) declares that where a revenue officer, indebted to the United States, shall become insolvent, the debt due to the United States shall first be satisfied and that this priority shall extend to cases where a debtor, not having sufficient property to pay all his debts, shall make a voluntary assignment thereof. Held, that although this act gives to a debt due to the United States a priority over debts to individuals, it does not give to one part of a debt due to the United States a priority over any other part of it; nor does it vest the property absolutely in the United States, though it gives them a right to pursue it for the purpose of appropriating it in payment; nor does it affect the right of the debtor to apply a payment of money in his hands to either a bond debt, or a debt due by open account by him to the government. Therefore, where a collector of the revenue at a port had given bond with sureties in the penalty of $10,000 for the faithful discharge of his official duties, and, being largely indebted to the United States, had made a deed of his property for their benefit, but previously thereto had transferred $10,000 to his sureties, and directed them to apply that money to their exoneration, and the sureties accordingly did so apply it, by paying it into the treasury, and receiving from the treasury their obligation, without any knowledge at the treasury that the money so paid had been transferred by the collector himself to his sureties, it was adjudged that by applying that payment to the extinguishment of the bond the sureties were discharged. United States v. Cochran, 2 Marsh., 274.

§ 179. In making payments on debts due for monthly wages, the debtor may apply the payments to either or any of the debts, but he must do so at the time of payment, and by some act, word, or other means, notify the creditor of such application. The Pioneer, Deady, 72.

§ 180. By the creditor.— If the debtor, at the time of payment, does not direct to which account the payment shall be applied, the creditor may at any time apply it to which account he pleases. Mayor of Alexandria v. Patten,* 4 Cr., 317.

§ 181. A creditor may apply payments in his discretion when the debtor fails to give any direction, but if the creditor makes the appropriation he cannot change it afterwards. Offutt v. King, 1 MacArth., 312.

§ 182. Where the owners of a whaling vessel advance money during the voyage to the master, who is also a part owner, there being nothing to show whether the money was advanced on account of his earnings as master or on account of his interest as part owner, held, that they might properly appropriate the advance payments to the master's lay. Hazard v. Howland, 2 Spr., 68.

§ 183. The law will apply a payment in the way most beneficial to the creditor, and therefore to the debt least secured. T., the holder of the bonds of a certain company, recovered two judgments against the company, one for interest on said bonds and the other for the principal, the former standing on a footing of equality with another judgment recovered by other creditors against the company, the latter being subsequent to such judgment. The property of the company had been insured for the benefit of the holder of said bonds, and by the terms of the policy the loss was payable to the trustee. The property having been destroyed by fire, T., under a power of attorney from such trustee, collected $43,000 insurance money and applied the same to his last judgment. Held, that the application was properly made. Coons v. Tome, 9 Fed. R., 532.

§ 184. A creditor holding several notes, all of which are due, upon receiving a payment from the maker, with instructions to apply the same on the debt or notes due, is not obliged to make the application so as to pay, as far as it will do so, certain notes in full, leaving the others wholly unpaid, but may indorse such payment in equal amounts upon all the notes, and thus protect them from the bar of the statute of limitations. Jackson v. Burke, 1 Dill., 311.

§ 185. Under a statute which merely prevents a recovery by suit of more than ten per cent. per annum where there is no agreement in writing, but does not otherwise prohibit higher rates of interest, money paid on account by a debtor may be applied by the creditor to the payment of an account stated, which includes interest in excess of ten per cent., if there be no appropriation by the debtor. Marye v. Strouse, 6 Saw., 204.

§ 186. If a bank discount a note, knowing it was the intention of the party offering it that the proceeds should be applied to the discharge of a particular note held by the bank, those proceeds cannot be applied by the bank to the discharge of any other note. Bank of Alexandria v. Saunders, 2 Cr. C. C., 183.

§ 187. M. and R. had become, by separate engagements, liable to make up any deficiency of the proceeds of property assigned to the plaintiffs to pay the debts of another, for equal portions of which they were also liable as indorsers. After the deficiency was ascertained, an account was rendered, in which the proceeds of the sale were credited to both M. and R. R. having become insolvent, the court refused to permit the plaintiffs to apply the proceeds of the property to discharge the whole of R.'s engagement, and to claim the whole deficiency from M., the plaintiffs having applied the proceeds in the first instance to the discharge of both debts. Bank of North America v. Meredith, 2 Wash., 47.

§ 188. If a creditor takes a security, by deed of trust, of personal property, for a debt due to him by an indorsed promissory note, and the debtor becomes tenant of the creditor, and rent is in arrear, and the creditor, who is landlord, distrains the goods conveyed to the trustee, as security for the payment of the note, and the same goods are sold under the distress, and the proceeds paid over to the landlord, he is bound to apply the proceeds to the payment of the note, although the goods were found on the premises, at the time of the distress, the same being there, by the consent of the landlord, as security for the note; and these facts are ad.

missible in evidence, on the part of the defendant, who is sued as indorser of the note. Bank of the United States v. Smith, 4 Cr. C. C., 712.

§ 189. Where debts of different dignities are due to a creditor of the estate of an intestate, and no specific application of the payment made by an administrator is directed by him, if the creditor applies the payment to either of his debts by some unequivocal act, his right to do so cannot be questioned. *Quære:* Whether the application must be made by the creditor at the time or within a reasonable time afterwards? Backhouse v. Patton, 5 Pet., 160.

§ 190. The law appropriates payments to the claims having the poorest security, and prefers lawful to unlawful claims; but it seems that the creditor may apply a payment upon an unlawful contract. The Pioneer, Deady, 72.

§ 191. It seems that the creditor cannot elect to what debt to apply an indefinite payment, except where it is utterly indifferent to the debtor to which it is applied. Gass v. Stinson, 3 Sumn., 99.

§ 192. —— after action commenced.— When the creditor is left to make the application, it seems that he may make it after an action is commenced. The Pioneer, Deady, 72.

§ 193. Secured and unsecured debts.— Where a party owes two debts, one secured by a lien and the other not, a payment not applied by either the debtor or the creditor will be applied by the law to the debt secured by the lien. The Ship Antarctic, 1 Spr., 206.

§ 194. A. mortgaged certain property to B. to secure a loan of $3,000. Subsequently there were various business transactions between them and various notes received by B. from A., no specific application of which by the mortgagor was shown; it was held, under the circumstances, that the notes were not to be applied to the payment of the $3,000. Gordon v. Hobart, 2 Story, 243.

§ 195. If a creditor has several debts, some of which are secured by mortgage, and some not, it is gross negligence to unite them all in a single suit at law, and so take a single judgment therefor; and if in such case the execution issuing on the judgment is satisfied in part only, a court of equity will apply the moneys received on the execution in the first instance to extinguish such parts of the debt and judgment as were not secured by mortgage. Williams v. Reed, 3 Mason, 405.

§ 196. If both the debtor and creditor have failed to make application of payments, a court of equity may in its discretion apply them to the unsecured debts, although such debts form items in a running account the first or oldest items of which are secured by mortgage. Schuelenburg v. Martin, 1 McC., 348.

§ 197. The rule that where a creditor has two distinct debts, and money is paid him generally, without specific appropriation, the payment must be applied in the way most beneficial to the debtor, does not apply to a running account, and require a creditor to satisfy first all those items for which he has no lien. To such an account the general rule applies, that, if there is no appropriation at the time, the law will apply the payments to the items in the order of their dates. (The Antarctic, 1 Spr., 206, distinguished.) The A. R. Dunlap, 1 Low., 350.

§ 198. If neither the debtor nor the creditor has made an application of the payments, the court will apply them to the debts for which the security is most precarious, it being equitable that the whole debt should be paid. Field v. Holland, 6 Cr., 8.

§ 199. Running accounts.— In cases of long and running accounts, where balances are adjusted merely for the purpose of making rests, the law will apply payments to extinguish the debts, according to the priority of time. United States v. Kirkpatrick, 9 Wheat., 720.

§ 200. Where a running account is kept at the postoffice department between the United States and a postmaster, in which all postages are charged to him, and credit is given for all payments as they are successively made, this amounts to an election by the creditor to apply the payments as they are successively made to the extinguishment of preceding balances. Jones v. United States, 7 How., 681.

§ 201. In the case of running accounts between parties, with various items of debit and credit on both sides, occurring at different times, each item of payment or credit is to be applied, in the absence of any special appropriation, in extinguishment of the earliest items of debt then actually due, and constituting *debitum in præsenti.* Gass v. Stinson, 3 Sumn., 99.

§ 202. When there is a running account between parties, every item on either side, whether for pay, services or otherwise, ending in a debt, is to be deemed a credit in favor of the party *pro tanto. Ibid.*

§ 203. The settlement of quarterly accounts at the treasury, running on in a continued series, is not conclusive. The officers of the treasury cannot, by an exercise of their discretion, enlarge or restrict the obligation of the collector's bond. Much less can they, by the mere fact of keeping an account current in which debits and credits are entered as they occur, and without any express appropriation of payments, affect the rights of sureties. United States v. Eckford, 1 How., 250.

§ 204. In the case of a running account of separate items, as for monthly wages due, general payments are presumed to have been made in discharge of the earlier items of the account. The Pioneer, Deady, 72.

§ 205. Where there are items of debt and credit in a running account between the postmaster-general and the deputy postmasters, in the absence of any specific appropriation by either party the credits are to be applied to the discharge of the debits antecedently due in the order of the account. Postmaster-General v. Furber, 4 Mason, 333.

§ 206. Where payments are made from time to time, to apply generally on an open account, it is such an appropriation as to leave no particular item due, but only the balance after deducting the payments. But if this were not so, equity would not permit an appropriation of a payment, made subsequent to the execution of a trust deed by the debtor, to items of subsequent indebtedness, for the mere purpose of leaving an apparent indebtedness at the date of the deed of trust, in order to raise a presumption that such deed was executed in fraud of creditors. Offutt v. King, 1 MacArth., 312.

§ 207. The debtor, if he pleases, has the right to make the appropriation of payments; if he omits it, the creditor may make it; if both omit it, the law will apply the payments according to its own notions of justice. And in cases of running accounts between the parties, unless there are some particular circumstances to vary the rule, the payments ought to be applied to extinguish the debts according to the priority of time. Leef v. Goodwin, Taney, 460.

§ 208. **Interest and principal.**— Payments should be applied to extinguish the interest and then the principal. Russell v. Lucas, Hemp., 91.

§ 209. The correct rule as to interest is that the creditor shall calculate interest whenever a payment is made. To this extent the payment is first to be applied, and if it exceed the interest due, the balance is to be applied to diminish the principal. This rule is equally applicable, whether the debt be one which expressly draws interest, or on which interest is given as damages. Story v. Livingston, 13 Pet., 359.

§ 210. **As between different sureties.**— A debtor cannot appropriate a payment in such a manner as to affect the relative liability or rights of his different sureties without their assent. Postmaster-General v. Norvell, Gilp., 106.

§ 211. Where a public officer has given different bonds with different sureties, his payments must be so appropriated as to give each bond credits for the moneys respectively due, collected and paid under it. *Ibid.*

§ 212. Where a collector is continued in office for more than one term, payments by him into the treasury of moneys accruing and received in the second term should not be applied to the extinguishment of a balance apparently due at the end of the first term. Payment made in a subsequent term of moneys received on duty bonds or otherwise, which remain charged to the collector as of the preceding official term, should be so applied. United States v. Eckford, 1 How., 250.

§ 213. As between different sureties, the court will apply the payments so as to avoid injustice. United States v. Linn, 2 McL., 501.

§ 214. A payment is to be applied to the oldest debt if the debtor gives no directions; and it must be proved that the payment came from receipts accruing under a second bond, if that is relied on against the propriety of applying it to any other balance whatever still due under a prior bond. Boody v. United States, 1 Woodb. & M., 150.

§ 215. Where a public officer has given successive official bonds with different sureties, moneys received subsequent to the execution of the latter cannot, before it is discharged, be applied to the payment of the former. Postmaster-General v. Norvell, Gilp., 106.

§ 216. When a collector of revenue has given two bonds for his official conduct at different times with different sureties, a promise by the supervisor to apply his payments exclusively to the discharge of the first bond, although some of the payments were for money collected and paid after the second bond was given, does not bind the United States, and does not amount to an application of the payments to the first bond. United States v. January, 7 Cr., 572.

§ 217. Where there is a general assignment of a debtor's property for the benefit of creditors, and the priority of the United States attaches, they having various debts due by bonds, with different sureties, all payments made by the assignees are to be applied *pro rata* to all the debts of the United States, and the latter are not at liberty to apply the payments in any other manner without the consent of all parties in interest. United States v. Amory, 5 Mason, 455.

§ 218. When a question arises between liabilities of securities on different bonds of different dates, the general doctrine of the application of payment does not apply. Myers v. United States, 1 McL., 493.

§ 219. The government cannot apply money received by a receiver of public moneys, and paid over, after the date of the bond, in discharge of a previous defalcation, to the prejudice of the new sureties. *Ibid.*

§ 220. **Payments by a partner.**—The natural presumption is that a partner paying a sum of money to his private creditor, who is also a creditor of the partnership, means to pay it on his private account, unless circumstances vary this presumption. Gass *v.* Stinson, 3 Sumn., 99.

§ 221. *Quære*, if the payments and credits made by one partner after a dissolution of the partnership and joint agency, and after a new individual agency in him, can be applied to the extinguishment of a debt of the partnership, unless circumstances justify the presumption that the partnership debt has been adopted as his individual debt. *Ibid.*

§ 222. Where, during a long period of mercantile intercourse between the principal and factor, it appeared that the principal was permitted, upon shipments of tobacco, to draw bills for the estimated value thereof, which bills the factor was in the habit of accepting and paying, whether the cargoes were or were not sold; the factor being generally in advance, and charging interest upon his advances, and giving credit for interest upon the net proceeds of the cargoes, shipments made after dissolution of the firm of the principal by the death of one of the partners to the factor (upon the credit of which shipments bills were drawn by the surviving partner according to the usual course of their former dealings) were held to have been made according to such usual course, and were not to be applied to the liquidation of the general debt due by the principal to the factor at the time of the dissolution, but were to be applied, in the first place, to meet the bills drawn upon the credit of such shipments; and the surplus only, if any, to be applied to the liquidation of the general balance due by the principal to the factor. But if the bills thus drawn by the surviving partner and paid by the factor exceeded the net proceeds of the cargoes thus shipped after the dissolution of the firm, the excess was not chargeable to the estate of the firm, but to the survivor only; it not being competent for him to charge the estate of the firm by drawing bills after dissolution. Dick *v.* Laird, 5 Cr. C. C., 838.

III. Recovery Back.

Summary — *Mistake*, §§ 223, 224. — *Duress*, §§ 225, 228. — *Protest*, § 226. — *Legal compulsion*, § 227.

§ 223. In an equitable action to recover back money paid under a mistake, the plaintiff must show that he is equitably entitled to the money; and if by his delay to give notice of the discovery of the mistake the defendant loses his remedy over against another party, no recovery can be had. United States *v.* The Union National Bank, §§ 229, 230.

§ 224. In the application of this rule no exception is made in favor of the United States. Thus, where a United States sub-treasurer gave notice to the defendant on the discovery of the mistake, and demanded payment, but subsequently withdrew the notice, *held*, that assuming that he was the proper person to give the notice, and demand payment of the defendant, he was also the proper party to withdraw that notice, and that the defendant, having relied upon the withdrawal of such notice until he had lost his remedy over, was released from all liability on account of the money paid him under mistake. *Ibid.*

§ 225. To constitute the coercion or duress which will be regarded as sufficient to make a payment involuntary, there must be some actual or threatened exercise of power possessed, or believed to be possessed, by the party exacting or receiving the payment over the person or property of another, from which the latter has no other means of immediate relief than by making the payment. Thus, where the Confederate government by public notice prohibited the exportation of cotton, except upon the condition that the exporter should sell to them an equal amount for the benefit of the Confederate government, and the plaintiff, an exporter, fearing that if he did otherwise his cotton would be confiscated, complied with the condition, receiving a permit to export his cotton upon payment of such sum as they might demand, took advantage of this privilege and redeemed the cotton, paying the sum demanded, *held*, that there was no such coercion or duress as to make the payment involuntary. Radich *v.* Hutchins, § 231.

§ 226. An action does not lie to recover back moneys claimed without right, if the payment was made voluntarily, and with a full knowledge of the facts upon which the claim was predicated. It is not enough that the payment was made under protest. The payment must have been compulsory; that is, it must have been made under coercion, actual or legal, in order to authorize the party paying to recover it back. Ocean Steam Navigation Co. *v.* Tappan, §§ 232, 233.

§ 227. Money paid upon a demand, to prevent the seizure of property, which can only take place by judicial proceedings, where the party paying may have his day in court and defeat the proceeding, is not paid under legal compulsion, and cannot be recovered back, although paid under protest. Thus where a passenger tax, exacted under a New York statute, was paid under protest, in order to avoid the accumulation of penalties provided by the statute in case of refusal to pay, and the statute was afterwards declared to be unconstitutional by the supreme court of the United States, *held*, that the payments thus exacted could not be recovered back. *Ibid.*

§ 228. Where there is a detention of personal property by private bailees, money illegally exacted as the price of its release may be recovered back. Accordingly, where a carrier, having agreed to carry goods to a certain place for a certain sum, refused to deliver the goods at their destination except upon the payment of a larger sum, which was paid by the owner in order to obtain possession of his goods, *held*, that the payment was not a voluntary one, and the amount in excess of the stipulated freight might be recovered back, as paid under duress. Tutt v. Ide, §§ 234, 285.

[Notes.—See §§ 236–255.]

UNITED STATES v. UNION NATIONAL BANK.

(District Court for New York: 10 Benedict, 408–410. 1879.)

Opinion by Choate, J.

Statement of Facts.— This is a motion for a new trial for error of law in directing a verdict for the defendant. It was not attempted on the argument to sustain the action, except as an action for money paid under a mistake of fact.

§ 229. *The United States is bound by the same rules of equity that affect other plaintiffs.*

Assuming that all the elements of such a cause of action once existed, a question which it is unnecessary now to examine, yet I see no reason why the United States should be exempted from the general rule applicable to any other party who is entitled to maintain such an action, that they shall not, by their delay after the discovery of the mistake, lead the party liable to them into further loss, as, for instance, the loss of a remedy over against another party. This is an equitable action, and the plaintiff can only recover on showing that it is equitably entitled to the money.

§ 230. *Where notice of a mistake is given and withdrawn by a competent agent, the defendant is released from the effect of such mistake.*

The duty of promptly notifying the defendant, on discovery of the mistake, is conceded by the plaintiff's counsel; but it is claimed that the notice from the sub-treasurer was a performance of this duty. The discovery by the United States of the alleged mistake before that notice was given cannot, I think, be denied. Assuming that the sub-treasurer was the proper person to give the notice, and demand payment of the defendant, he was also the proper party to withdraw that notice, and I think it is clear that what took place after the notice was given was equivalent to a withdrawal of the notice, on which the bank had a right to rely, and did rely, until it lost all remedy over against Polhemus and Jackson; and after that, only, was the claim renewed by commencement of this action. I think this is a claim in respect to which laches may be imputed to the United States, and that on the ground of laches and entire want of equity in the claim on the undisputed facts, the direction of a verdict for the defendant was right. See United States v. Cooke, 5 Am. L. T., 166.

Motion denied.

RADICH v. HUTCHINS.

(5 Otto, 210–214. 1877.)

ERROR to U. S. Circuit Court, Eastern District of Texas.

Opinion by MR. JUSTICE FIELD.

STATEMENT OF FACTS.— If at the time the transaction took place which has given rise to the present action the plaintiff was a subject of the emperor of Russia, as he alleges, that fact cannot affect the decision of the case, or any question presented for our consideration. He was then a resident of the state of Texas and engaged in business there. As a foreigner domiciled in the country, he was bound to obey all the laws of the United States not immediately relating to citizenship, and was equally amenable with citizens to the penalties prescribed for their infraction. He owed allegiance to the government of the country so long as he resided within its limits, and can claim no exemption from the statutes passed to punish treason or the giving of aid and comfort to the insurgent states. The law on this subject is well settled and universally recognized. Carlisle v. United States, 16 Wall., 147.

The case presented by the petition is without merit.

The substance of the complaint is that the defendants, as officers of the Confederate government, by a public notice, had prohibited the exportation of cotton from the state of Texas to Mexico, except upon condition that the exporter should sell to them an equal amount for the benefit of the Confederate government; and that the plaintiff, being the owner of cotton which he desired to export, and fearing that if he attempted to export it without such permit it would be seized and confiscated by the armed forces of that government, complied with the condition, and obtained a permit from the officers to export two hundred and twenty-five bales, and sold to them an equal amount for the Confederate government, obtaining at the same time the privilege of redeeming the cotton sold, and receiving a permit to export it, upon payment of such sum as they might demand; that he took advantage of this privilege and redeemed the cotton, paying in money and goods the sum mentioned in the petition.

§ 231. *What is necessary to constitute such coercion or duress as to make a payment or other contract involuntary.*

There is nothing in these allegations showing that the defendants subjected the plaintiff to any coercion or duress, which would justify an action against them, either for the return of the money paid, or for the value of the goods delivered in place of the money, or for damages of any kind. There is no averment that either of the defendants ever made, or attempted to make, any seizure of the cotton, or that either of them was an impressing or other officer, exercising or claiming to exercise any power for its seizure; or had anything to do with the command or operations of the armed forces of the insurgents in the state of Texas. All that is directly charged against them is the publication of a notice that the exportation of cotton was forbidden, except on permits from the cotton office. The armed force is not stated to have been under the direction of that office. The whole proceeding set forth in the petition was a voluntary one by the plaintiff. He applied to the cotton office and sold the cotton subsequently redeemed. It is not pretended that either of the defendants made any application for its purchase.

To constitute the coercion or duress which will be regarded as sufficient to make a payment involuntary,— treating now the redemption of the cotton as made in money, goods being taken as equivalent for a part of the amount,—

there must be some actual or threatened exercise of power possessed, or believed to be possessed, by the party exacting or receiving the payment over the person or property of another, from which the latter has no other means of immediate relief than by making the payment. As stated by the court of appeals of Maryland, the doctrine established by the authorities is, that "a payment is not to be regarded as compulsory unless made to emancipate the person or property from an actual and existing duress imposed upon it by the party to whom the money is paid." Mayor and City Council of Baltimore *v.* Lefferman, 4 Gill (Md.), 425; Brumagim *v.* Tillinghast, 18 Cal., 265; Mays *v.* Cincinnati, 1 Ohio St., 268.

Tested by these cases, the allegation of coercion or duress becomes frivolous. It is plain that the plaintiff entered voluntarily upon the negotiation with the defendants, and subsequently paid the redemption money without any constraint which would in law change the voluntary character of the payment. Such being the case, the transaction is one which is fatally tainted. The sale of the cotton was to the Confederate States; the money paid and goods delivered for its redemption were for the benefit of those states, to assist them in their war against the government and authority of the United States. The money paid and the goods delivered constituted, therefore, nothing less than a direct contribution to the support of the insurgents; they gave aid and comfort to the enemy. No demand arising out of such a transaction can have any standing in the courts of the Union.

At this time, also, it was the declared policy of the United States to prevent all intercourse between the insurgent states and the loyal states, and also between them and foreign countries, and thus to cut off from the insurgents the means of prolonging the existing war. In pursuance of this policy the ports and coasts of those states were blockaded, commerce with their inhabitants was prohibited, except as specially authorized under regulations of the treasury department, and property which eluded the blockade was subject to seizure and condemnation. The attention of the authorities was specially directed to prevent the exportation of cotton, upon which the insurgents chiefly relied to obtain the means for the continuance of their struggle. The plaintiff alleges that he paid money and delivered goods to the defendants for the use of the Confederate government, in order to obtain permission to violate this policy and legislation, and now he modestly asks that he should be allowed in the courts of the United States to recover damages from them because they took what he offered for the permission. The demurrer was properly sustained. *Judgment affirmed.*

OCEANIC STEAM NAVIGATION COMPANY *v.* TAPPAN.

(Circuit Court for New York: 16 Blatchford, 296–302. 1879.)

Opinion by WALLACE, J.

STATEMENT OF FACTS.— This action is brought to recover moneys alleged to have been illegally exacted by the defendant, the chamberlain of the city of New York, and to whom the plaintiff paid the sum involved, under protest. The moneys were collected by the defendant under color of the provisions of acts of the legislature of the state of New York, by which, in effect, a tax was imposed upon alien passengers arriving in vessels at the port of New York, to be collected of the master or owner of the ship by which they were landed. These acts, since the payment of the moneys in suit, have been declared unconstitutional by the supreme court of the United States, as in conflict with the clause of the constitution of the United States which delegates to congress the right to regulate commerce with foreign nations. Henderson *v.* The Mayor, 92 U. S., 259 (CONST., §§ 1336–42). Since the payment of the moneys, however, congress has passed an act (Act of June 19, 1878; 20 U. S. Stat. at Large, 177) which declares that the acts of every state and municipal officer or corporation of the several states, in the collection of these moneys, shall be valid, and that no action shall be maintained against such officer or corporation for the recovery of such moneys. The defense of the action is placed upon two grounds — first, that the moneys were paid voluntarily; and second, that the validating act of congress precludes a recovery by the plaintiff.

§ 232. *Money paid voluntarily, though under protest, if claimed without right and with a full knowledge of the facts, cannot be recovered back; the payment must have been compulsory.*

An action does not lie to recover back moneys claimed without right, if the payment was made voluntarily, and with a full knowledge of the facts upon which the claim was predicated. It is not enough that payment was made under protest by the party paying. The payment must have been compulsory; that is, it must have been made under coercion, actual or legal, in order to authorize the party paying to recover it back. In the absence of such coercion, the person of whom the payment is demanded must refuse the demand; and he will not be permitted, with knowledge that the claim is illegal and unwarranted, to make payment without resistance, where resistance is lawful and possible, and afterwards to select his own time to bring an action for restoration, when, possibly, his adversary has lost the evidence to sustain the claim. Where, however, the demandant is in a position to seize or detain the property of him against whom the claim is made, without a resort to judicial proceedings, in which the validity of the claim may be contested, and payment is made under protest, to release the property from such seizure or detention, the party paying can recover back his payment.

The commutation moneys paid by the plaintiff were paid to relieve the plaintiff from an accumulation of penalties, the collection of which could only be enforced by judicial proceedings. The statute required the plaintiff, within twenty-four hours after the arrival of its vessel at the port of New York, to report in writing to the mayor of the city the number, names, places of birth and last legal residence of each alien passenger, and, in case of failure, imposed a penalty of $75 for each passenger not reported. The statute also directed the mayor, by an indorsement to be made on such report, to require the owner of the vessel to execute a several bond, with sureties, in a penalty of $300, for each passenger included in the report, to indemnify and save harmless the commissioners of emigration, and each and every city, town or county in the state, against all expenses which might necessarily be incurred for the care and support of such passenger. The statute also enacted that such owner might commute for the bonds so required, within three days after the landing of such passengers, by paying to the chamberlain of the city of New York the sum of $1.50 for each and every passenger reported according to law, and that the receipt of such sum should be deemed full and sufficient discharge from the requirements of giving bond. In case of neglect or refusal to give the bonds required within twenty-four hours after landing passengers, the statute imposed a penalty upon the owner or consignee of the vessel, of $500 for each passenger landed.

The penalties given by the act were to be sued for and recovered by the commissioners of emigration, in any court having jurisdiction of such actions, under a general statute of the state respecting claims against vessels, such an action could be commenced by the seizure of the vessel by attachment, upon giving security to indemnify the owner. Briefly stated, the plaintiff's position was this — if it failed to report, it was liable to a penalty of $75 for each alien passenger; if it did report, it was required to pay $1.50 for each passenger, by way of commutation, or was liable, if required by the mayor, to give onerous bonds, and, in default, to pay a penalty of $500 for each bond withheld; and the penalties, in either case, were a lien upon the vessel, collectible by an action at law, wherein, upon giving security for the indemnity of the vessel owner, an attachment against the vessel might be obtained and the vessel seized.

Palpably, the statute was framed to coerce the payment of the commutation moneys. If they were not paid, the owner of the vessel was made liable to an accumulation of penalties, which would aggregate an enormous sum, and which, if collected, would ordinarily bankrupt the ship-owner. Naturally, rather than incur the hazard of such disastrous consequences, the ship-owner would pay in preference to abiding the contingencies of litigation. The hardship of the particular case, however, cannot change the rule of law. The penalties imposed in lieu of the commutation money could only be collected by suit in a court of law, where the corporation against which they were claimed could have its day and all the protection which the courts afford to suitors; and a payment made under such a state of facts is not made under legal coercion. The party paying is bound to know the law and to assume that it will be correctly administered by the tribunal which is to decide the controversy. The rule is well stated in Benson v. Monroe, 7 Cush., 125, which was a case to recover head money, under a statute similar to the one here, and was precisely likely the present case, except that attachment had been obtained, and the vessel seized under them, to recover the penalties. The plaintiffs thereupon paid the commutation money under protest, and brought suit to recover it back; and the court said: "They should have contested the demand made on them, in the suit that was instituted against them, and having voluntarily adjusted that demand, and relieved their vessel from seizure, with a full knowledge, or means of knowledge, of all the facts of their case, they cannot now be permitted to disturb that adjustment."

It is stated in general terms, in some of the decisions, that where money is paid to a public officer, upon an unlawful demand, to save the person paying from the infliction, under color of authority, of great or irreparable injury, from which he can only be saved by making the payment, such payment is made under an urgent and immediate necessity and may be recovered back. But it will be found that none of these decisions were in cases where the injury apprehended by the party paying could only be inflicted by the decision of a court in favor of the validity of the claim made against him. There cannot be an immediate and urgent necessity for the payment of a demand which can only be enforced by the decision of a court of justice. The case of Benson v. Monroe, and that of Cunningham v. Boston, 16 Gray, 468, are directly in point, as deciding that the apprehension of the recovery of heavy penalties by suit, in case the demand for a small sum is not complied with, does not take the case out of the general rule.

The case of Cunningham v. Monroe, 15 Gray, 471, cited for the plaintiff, was one where the payment was made under circumstances amounting to duress *de facto*, which were emphasized, in the opinion of the court, as distinguishing it from Cunningham *v.* Boston. There are cases in the books where payments have been extorted by threats of criminal or civil proceedings, and the party paying the demand has been permitted to recover back, but these were cases where the facts were held to constitute actual duress, of which the threats were an incident.

In reaching this conclusion I have not adverted to the fact that the mayor never required the bonds to be executed by the plaintiff, by the indorsement upon the reports, which the statute directs. The moneys were paid by the plaintiff to escape the penalties imposed for neglect to execute the bonds, and not the penalties for failing to make the report required by the act. Until the mayor's indorsement these penalties could not accrue. The plaintiff, without waiting to ascertain whether or not the mayor would take the action required to subject the plaintiff to the penalties, paid the commutation moneys, upon the assumption that the mayor would take such action at some future time. Within the recent decision of the supreme court of the United States in Railroad Co. *v.* Commissioners, 98 U. S., 541, this circumstance should defeat the plaintiff. That case holds that, where a warrant was in the hands of an officer, for the collection of a tax, which authorized him to seize the property of the plaintiff, and no actual attèmpt to execute the warrant had been made, but the plaintiff, assuming that a seizure would be made, went to the treasurer and paid the tax under protest, setting forth in the protest the illegality of the tax, and stating that a suit would be brought to recover back the payment, the payment was not compulsory, in a legal sense, and could not, therefore, be recovered back.

I have preferred, however, to rest the decision upon this branch of the case upon the broad ground that money paid upon a demand, to prevent the seizure of property, which can only take place by judicial proceedings, where the party paying may have his day in court and defeat the proceeding, is not paid under legal compulsion, and cannot be recovered back, although paid under protest. Mayor of Baltimore *v.* Lefferman, 4 Gill, 425; Town Council of Cahaba *v.* Burnett, 34 Ala., 400; Cook *v.* City of Boston, 9 Allen, 393; Taylor *v.* Board of Health, 31 Penn. St., 73; Mays *v.* Cincinnati, 1 Ohio St., 268.

§ 233. *A passenger tax levied under a New York statute, paid voluntarily but under protest, cannot be recovered back though the act be invalid.*

Having thus reached a conclusion which must dispose of this case adversely to the plaintiff, it is not necessary to pass upon the question presented by the defense, which rests on the effect of the act of congress declaring that the acts of the defendant in collecting the moneys in suit shall be valid, and declaring that no action shall be maintained to recover back the money. It would be indecorous to adjudge an act of congress unconstitutional, when it is not necessary to do so in the disposition of the controversy before the court. It is proper, however, to say, that, to sustain the validity of this act, it will be necessary to decide that it is within the authority of congress to legalize the action of officers of a state in collecting moneys under a law of the state, which, because it was unconstitutional, conferred no authority whatever to act under it; and I am not aware of any legislative validating act containing such a vigorous and radical measure of relief, which has been the subject of judicial exposition. Unless the act can be sustained as a validating act, it would seem that the clause which declares that no action shall be maintained to recover back the moneys collected must be ineffectual, because it would deprive the plaintiff of a right of action, which is a vested right of property, without due process of law. Judgment is ordered for the defendant.

TUTT v. IDE.

(Circuit Court for New York: 8 Blatchford, 249–255. 1855.)

STATEMENT OF FACTS.—A common carrier agreed to transport and deliver goods at a stipulated rate of freight, and then refused to deliver except upon the payment of a higher rate. This was paid by the consignee to obtain possession of the goods, and suit was brought for the overcharge. There was a demurrer to the declaration.

Opinion by HALL, J.

It was insisted by the defendants upon the argument that the plaintiffs paid the excess which they seek to recover back without legal coercion,—not by mistake, but with full a knowledge of the facts; and that the payment was therefore voluntary, and could not be recovered back. On the other hand, the plaintiffs insisted that the payment was compulsory, and that they were entitled to recover back the excess beyond the sum due under the contract, which was paid by them to obtain possession of their goods.

§ 234. *Money paid to a common carrier, beyond the sum to which he is entitled, in order to obtain possession of the goods, may be recovered back by the owner as money paid under duress.*

It was conceded by the counsel for the defendants that the case of Astley v. Reynolds, 2 Str., 915, was in point as an authority for the plaintiffs; but he insisted that that case had been overruled by the courts of this state, and that the rule of law in this state was well established, and was directly opposed to the doctrines of that case.

The earliest case cited to sustain this position is that of Hall v. Shultz, 4 Johns., 240. The case of Astley v. Reynolds, and also the case of Knibbs v. Hall, 1 Esp., 84, in which the principle of the case of Astley v. Reynolds was said to have been overruled, were referred to in that case. But Spencer, J., in delivering the opinion of the court, without adverting to the case of Bates v. The New York Ins. Co., 3 Johns. Cas., 238, which will be hereafter referred to, and " without undertaking to pronounce between the cases cited " (Astley v. Reynolds and Knibbs v. Hall), declared that the case then before him differed materially from both.

In the case then under consideration the defendants had purchased the lands of the plaintiff on execution, under a verbal agreement to convey them to him on the repayment of the amount advanced, with interest, and a reasonable compensation for the defendants' trouble. Afterwards, when the plaintiff applied to have the agreement reduced to writing, they required him to execute an agreement in which the compensation for their trouble was fixed at $300, which was deemed extortionate and unjust. The agreement was executed, and the $300 subsequently paid, and the conveyance to the plaintiff made; and he then brought his action to recover back the $300. In concluding his opinion Mr. Justice Spencer said: " On the ground that there existed no legal right on the part of the plaintiff to demand or enforce a conveyance, that he must be considered in the light of any other purchaser, and that the defendants might make their own terms, and that the plaintiff has voluntarily, and with his eyes open, fixed the compensation claimed by the defendants, and paid them the money, he can have no claim to call on the court to aid him in getting rid of what he conceives an unconscientious advantage. But if there did exist a legal remedy to enforce a reconveyance, as the measure of the defendants' claim to compensation rested in arbitrary discretion, the plaintiff, by voluntarily acceding to the terms proposed by the defendants, has lost any right to call on a jury to relieve him from an allowance deliberately fixed by himself." It is, I think, quite clear that this case of Hall v. Shultz does not overrule the case of Astley v. Reynolds, or the case of Bates v. The New York Ins. Co., above referred to; and I think the same remark applies to the cases, cited by the defendants' counsel, of Ripley v. Gelston, 9 Johns., 201; Clarke v. Dutcher, 9 Cowen, 681; Supervisors of Onondaga v. Briggs, 2 Denio, 39, 40; Wyman v. Farnsworth, 3 Barb., 371; and Elliott v. Swartwout, 10 Pet., 137.

The manuscript opinion of Mr. Justice Nelson, in the case of Converse v. Coit, appears to favor, if it does not directly sanction, the position assumed by the defendants. But on looking into the bill of exceptions in that case, it appears that the flour on which the excessive charges for freight were demanded and paid had been delivered two or three days prior to such payment; and that there was no formal demand made of the flour, and no refusal to deliver it up, and no threat made of detaining the flour because of a refusal to pay. The question now raised was not presented in that case, and therefore the decision therein is not an authority for the position assumed by the defendants in this case.

§ 235. *Where there is duress of personal property, by seizure or detention by public officers or private bailees, money illegally exacted as the price of its release may be recovered back. Cases cited.*

The case of Astley v. Reynolds was decided by the king's bench, in Michaelmas term, 5 Geo. 2 (1732). It is admitted that if that case is to be followed, the question presented by the demurrer must be decided in favor of the plaintiffs. But it is contended, as before stated, that Astley v. Reynolds has been overruled by the supreme court of this state in the cases before cited. Those cases have been fully considered, and, having reached the conclusion that they have not expressly overruled the case in 2 Strange, I now propose to refer to other cases in the courts of this and other states and in England which are supposed to bear directly upon this question.

In Bates v. The New York Ins. Co., 3 Johns. Cas., 238, decided in 1802, the plaintiff had purchased from one Norman Butler fifty shares of the stock of the defendants, subject to some future calls. Those calls were paid by the plaintiff, and he became entitled to a transfer of the stock upon the books of the company. The defendants refused to transfer this stock to the plaintiff until the plaintiff paid a debt due to them from Butler, the original owner of the shares. This the plaintiff paid. He afterwards brought his action to recover it back; and the court held, after a verdict taken subject to the opinion of the court upon the facts stated, that the plaintiff was not liable for the payment of $465 of the amount paid by him to procure the transfer, and that he was therefore entitled to recover back that amount in an action for money had and received. Thompson, J., delivered the opinion of the court, and referred with approbation to Astley v. Reynolds, and to Irving v. Wilson, 4 T. R., 485, and also to Munt v. Stokes, id., 561, in which he said the principles of the case of Astley v. Reynolds were fully recognized and adopted.

In Fleetwood v. The City of New York, 2 Sandf., 479, Mr. Justice Sandford refers with approbation to the case of Chase v. Dwinal, 7 Greenl., 134, and says: " There are cases of duress of personal property in which payments for its relief are deemed involuntary, and the money may be recovered back. Most of these cases have arisen upon seizures of goods under revenue or excise laws, and by public officers acting under process or warrant of law. The principle has been extended occasionally to cases where bailees or others, who came into the possession of goods lawfully, have exacted more than was due before they would relinquish such possession. It is founded upon the movable and perishable character of the property, and the uncertainty of a personal remedy against the wrong-doer."

The general rule undoubtedly is that this action for money had and received, being an equitable action, lies whenever money has been received by the defendant, which, *ex æquo et bono*, belongs to the plaintiff. Buel *v.* Boughton, 2 Denio, 91.

In the case of Chase *v.* Dwinal, 7 Greenl., 134, it was held that money paid to liberate a raft of lumber, detained in order to exact an illegal toll, might be recovered back. Weston, J., in delivering the opinion of the court, refers to the remark of Spencer, J., in Hall *v.* Shultz, that Astley *v.* Reynolds had been overruled by Lord Kenyon in Knibbs *v.* Hall, and says: " There " (in Knibbs *v.* Hall) " the plaintiff had paid, as he insisted, five guineas more rent than could have been rightfully claimed of him, to avoid a distress which was threatened. Lord Kenyon held this to be a voluntary payment and not upon compulsion, as the party might have protected himself from a wrongful distress by replevin. His lordship does not advert to the case of Astley *v.* Reynolds; and subsequently, in Cartwright *v.* Rowley, before cited " (from 2 Esp., 723), " he refers, with approbation, to an action within his recollection, for money had and received, brought against the steward of a manor, to recover money paid for producing at a trial some deeds and court rolls, for which he had charged extravagantly. It was urged that the payment was voluntary; but, it appearing that the party could not do without the deeds, and that the money was paid through the urgency of the case, the action was sustained."

In Chase *v.* Taylor, 4 Harr. & Johns., 54, it was held that money improperly demanded as a condition of the release of a ship pledged to the party receiving the money might be recovered back in an action for money had and received.

The cases of Alston *v.* Durant, 2 Strobhart, 257, and Richardson *v.* Duncan, 3 N. H., 508, are also strongly comfirmatory of the case of Astley *v.* Reynolds, and other cases of a similar character are to be found in the reports of the different states.

In respect to the English cases, it may be observed that the decision in Astley *v.* Reynolds, made in the king's bench sitting *in banco*, ought not to be considered as overruled by a *nisi prius* decision, though made by a judge of such distinguished ability and learning as Lord Kenyon. But the case of Astley *v.* Reynolds and not that of Knibbs *v.* Hall has, since the decision of Lord Kenyon, been followed in England.

In 1827, in Shaw *v.* Woodcock, 7 Barn. & Cress., 73, it was held by Lord Chief Justice Tenterden and Justices Bayley, Holroyd and Littledale, of the king's bench, that a payment made in order to obtain possession of goods or property to which a party was entitled, and of which he could not otherwise obtain possession at the time, was a compulsory and not a voluntary payment, and might be recovered back. In 1844, in the case of Parker v. The Great Western Railway Co., 7 Mann. & Gr., 253, it was held by the court of common pleas in England, Chief Justice Tindal delivering the judgment of the court, that money paid by the plaintiff to a common carrier, to obtain possession of the plaintiff's goods, beyond the amount to which the carrier was entitled, might be recovered back; such payment not being considered as a voluntary payment. And this doctrine I understand to have been again acted upon in the court of exchequer in Parker v. The Bristol & Exeter Railway Co., 7 Eng. L. & Eq., 528, in the year 1851.

I am entirely satisfied, as well upon the authority of these cases as upon principle, that the payment alleged in the count demurred to cannot be held to have been a voluntary payment. The demurrer is, therefore, overruled.

§ 236. Mistake.—Money paid under a mutual mistake of fact may be recovered back. Negligence or delay in making the demand or bringing the action, however, may defeat the right of action, if by reason of such delay the other party has suffered any loss or damage. United States v. National Park Bank of New York, 6 Fed. R., 852.

§ 237. It seems that money paid under ignorance of the law cannot be recovered back. Washington v. Barber, 5 Cr. C. C., 157.

§ 238. Money paid with knowledge of the facts, but under a mistake of law, cannot be recovered back. Lamborn v. County Commissioners, 7 Otto, 181.

§ 239. Duress—Involuntary payment.—While an illegal demand paid under duress of real property may be recovered back, to make it a case of payment under compulsion there must be an illegal demand coupled with a present power or authority in the person making such demand to sell or dispose of the property if payment is not made as demanded. A mere cloud upon the title, or a threat to create one, does not produce such compulsion. The Mariposa Co. v. Bowman, Deady, 228.

§ 240. Where money is paid upon a wrongful demand, to save the party paying from some great or irreparable mischief or damage, from which he could not be saved but by the payment of the sum wrongfully demanded, it can be recovered back. Corkle v. Maxwell,* 3 Blatch., 413.

§ 241. Payments made without protest, under peremptory orders of a superior officer, are in no sense voluntary, and may be recovered back if illegally exacted. Accordingly where a collector of customs, having received a peremptory order from the commissioner of customs requiring him to account for all fees, accounted for and paid into the treasury, without protest, all moneys collected by him as duties, whereas, as a matter of right, he was entitled to a percentage thereof as fees, held, that he was entitled to recover the fees paid into the treasury, or such portion thereof as was not barred by the statute of limitations. United States v. Lawson, 11 Otto, 164; United States v. Ellsworth, id., 170.

§ 242. When the payment has been obtained by fraud or by oppression or by extortion, or when it has been made to secure a right which the party paying was entitled to without such payment, and which right was withheld by the party receiving the payment until such payment was made, such payment was not voluntary, and the money can be recovered back. Corkle v. Maxwell,* 3 Blatch., 413.

§ 243.* Money paid as a bonus under a license to traffic in cotton in the insurrectionary states during the late rebellion, such bonus being required by the regulations established by the president and secretary of the treasury, cannot be recovered back on the ground that the fee or bonus exacted was illegal, and was paid under compulsion; for, independently of the question whether the president and secretary exceeded their powers in exacting the fee, permission to engage in the trade on the conditions imposed was applied for voluntarily and the bonus was voluntarily paid, thus precluding any recovery back as for money paid under compulsion. Hamilton v. Dillon, 21 Wall., 73.

§ 244. Illegal contract.— Where money has been paid by one party in part performance of an illegal contract, not malum in se, the other party not having performed the contract or any part of it, and both parties having abandoned the illegal agreement before it was consummated, the money may be recovered back. Spring Co. v. Knowlton, 13 Otto, 49.

§ 245. Money paid under an illegal contract cannot at common law be recovered; and where a statute gives the right to recover it back, a pending suit brought to enforce that right falls with the repeal of the statute. Kimbro v. Colgate, 5 Blatch., 229.

§ 246. Illegal demand.— The corporation of Washington has no right to require a keeper of a livery-stable to take and pay for a license to keep the same; but if it be taken, and paid for, and enjoyed, the money paid for it cannot be recovered back. Washington v. Barber, 5 Cr. C. C., 157.

§ 247. If a payment be freely and voluntarily made it cannot be recovered back, although made upon a demand which could not be enforced at law. Corkle v. Maxwell,* 3 Blatch., 413.

§ 248. The secretary of the treasury, upon application of A., the owner, designated a certain store as a warehouse for the storing of dutiable merchandise, under the warehouse act of August 6, 1846 (9 U. S. Stat, at L., 53). Subsequently the secretary issued a circular requiring owners or occupants of warehouses similar to A.'s to pay monthly to the collector a sum equivalent to the salary of an inspector, or, at their option, to pay monthly to the collector one-half storage at the rates charged in stores owned by the United States. A., being required to elect before any goods were placed in his store, adopted the mode of paying the inspector's salary. After paying for several years the sums thus exacted, A. brought suit to recover back the several sums so paid, on the ground that there was no law authorizing the secretary to demand such payments, and that the payments were not voluntary. Held, that regardless of any legal right on the part of the government to demand the payments, they could not be recovered back, as A. had enjoyed the privilege, granted by the secretary, of keeping a warehouse for dutiable goods, in return for which the payments had been made, and therefore A. was precluded from any recovery. Ibid.

§ 249. Where the collector insisted upon either having the goods appraised at the value at the time of shipment, the consequence of which would have been an addition of so much to the invoice price as to subject the importer to a penalty; or to allow the importer to voluntarily make the addition to the invoice price and so escape the penalty, and the importer chose the latter course, this was not such a voluntary payment of duties on his part as to debar him from bringing an action against the collector to recover the excess thus illegally exacted. Maxwell v. Griswold, 10 How., 242.

§ 250. —— payment under protest.— A collector is generally liable in an action to recover back an excess of duties paid to him as collector, when the duties have been illegally demanded, and a protest of the illegality has been made at the time of payment, or notice given that the party means to contest the claim. Nor is there any doubt that a like action generally lies, where the excess of duties has been paid under a mistake of fact, and notice thereof has been given to the collector before he has paid over the money to the government. Bend v. Hoyt. 13 Pet., 263.

§ 251. Upon the refusal of the secretary of the treasury to redeem certain treasury notes, in gold, the holder received, under protest, legal tender notes in payment, delivered up the treasury notes to be canceled, and brought suit to recover the difference, at the time of payment, between the legal tender notes and a like amount in gold. Held, that the legal tender notes were a payment in full, regardless of the question whether or not such a medium was a legal tender in payment of such notes, inasmuch as the protest being unauthorized by law, there was an unqualified surrender and payment of the treasury notes. Savage v. United States, 2 Otto, 382; 8 Ch. Leg. N., 369.

§ 252. —— taxes.— Payment of money not made by reason of fraud, mistake of fact, or duress, is voluntary and cannot be recovered back. Accordingly where lands, sold for taxes and bid in by the county, were afterwards redeemed by the trustee of the owner, held, that the money thus voluntarily paid into the county treasury could not be recovered back, it having been decided in the meantime that the taxes for which the lands were sold were illegal, such lands not being taxable. Lamborn v. County Commissioners, 7 Otto, 181.

§ 253. In order to recover back money paid on an illegal demand under protest, there must have been at the time of the payment an urgent necessity amounting to compulsion. A payment of delinquent taxes illegally assessed, before any active steps have been taken to enforce their collection, accompanied by a general protest against the illegality of the charges and a notice that suit would be commenced to recover back the full amount that was paid, is voluntary and cannot be recovered back as made under compulsion. Railroad Co. v. Commissioners, 8 Otto, 541.

§ 254. Miscellaneous.— Money paid as a fee to an attorney, by an insolvent person, for necessary services, cannot be recovered back by the assignee in bankruptcy, there being no fraud intended or effected upon the bankrupt act; but fees paid, after the filing of the petition, for services in opposing the petition in bankruptcy, may be recovered back in part, if in excess of what the court in the exercise of its discretion may be disposed to allow as a reasonable compensation for such services. Triplet v. Hauley, 1 Dill., 217.

§ 255. If the acceptor of a bill pays a bona fide holder, he cannot recover the money from him because an indorsement was forged. His acceptance admits that he has funds of the drawer who would be liable to the holder for the amount of the bill. Hortsman v. Henshaw, 11 How., 177.

IV. Tender.

§ 256. What constitutes tender.—Upon a plea of tender, it is not sufficient to prove that the defendant asked the plaintiff if he would take the money, and said he was ready to pay it, and would give his check for it. Ladd v. Patten,* 1 Cr. C. C., 263.

§ 257. A cargo of iron having been injured by the carelessness of the ship-owner, the consignee made repeated offers, before suit brought, to pay the balance of the freight, deducting the loss occasioned by the injury, to be ascertained by arbitration, or by a sale of the damaged iron at auction, but they were refused and the whole amount of freight demanded. Afterwards a sale of the damaged iron took place, with notice to the agents of the vessel, and the amount of the loss was in that way ascertained; but no offer was made to pay the balance thus ascertained until the filing of the answer to the libel of the ship-owner. Held, that because of the offers and refusals that had previously taken place, the case must be regarded in admiralty as standing upon the same footing as if a tender had been made after the sale. Dedekam v. Vose, 3 Blatch., 44.

§ 258. —— must be unconditional.—A tender of money upon condition of receiving change and 'a receipt in full for rent is not a legal tender. Perkins v. Beck,* 4 Cr. C. C., 68.

§ 259. A tender must be unconditional. Ibid.

§ 260. A conditional tender, in the absence of an express stipulation contemplating the condition, will not entitle the party making the tender to demand a release. B. agreed with his debtor, A., to accept and receive an assignment of a contract entered into by C., for the payment of $21,112 to A. for lands, "towards the discharge of his debt," the same to be ascertained by an award, and if the sum of $21,112 should exceed the amount of the award, that he, B., would pay the excess to A. By the award, the excess of the sum of $21,112 beyond the debt due by A. to B. was ascertained to be £494 6s. 7d. Virginia currency. A. afterwards tendered to B. a deed of assignment of the contract, upon condition that he would first sign, seal and deliver on the same day a release of all claims and demands upon him, A. B. refused to execute and deliver the release before the assignment of the contract, and the assignment was then withheld by A. Upon suit brought by A. for the excess as shown by the award, held, that the tender of the assignment, on condition that the release should be first executed, was not in compliance with the agreement, and that he could not recover. Hepburn v. Auld,* 1 Cr., 321.

§ 261. Must be kept good.—To have the effect of stopping interest or costs, a tender of payment must be kept good; and it ceases to have that effect when the money is used for other purposes. Bissell v. Heyward, 6 Otto, 580.

§ 262. The money should be deposited or in some manner set apart or appropriated for the purpose of the tender. Ibid.

§ 263. When unnecessary — Waiver.—Where a party declares that he will not receive money about to be tendered, the money need not be produced. Barker v. Parkenhorn, 2 Wash., 142.

§ 264. Any one bound to do a particular thing must either do it or offer to do it, and if no objections are made he must show he made the tender in a regular manner; but this is not necessary if the other party by his conduct dispenses with a regular tender, as by a previous refusal to accept it, etc. After an offer of performance and a refusal of acceptance, it is not in the power of the opposite party to say that he who made the offer would not or could not have done what he declared himself ready to do. Blight v. Ashley, Pet. C. C., 15.

§ 265. A party who, by reason of his residence in the south during the late rebellion, had been prevented from paying the yearly premiums as required for the continuance of the insurance policy on his life, wrote, upon the termination of hostilities, to the insurers, whose place of business was in Pennsylvania, making inquiry as to what steps he must take to continue his insurance. They replied that his insurance was forfeited by non-payment of the premium in 1861, the first year of the war, and that they would not revive it. Held, that this reply dispensed with an actual tender of the unpaid premiums, and the question of his right to have the insurance continued must be determined as if the premiums had been tendered with interest. Bird v. Penn Mutual Life Ins. Co.,* 11 Phil., 485; 1 Law & Eq. Rep., 505.

§ 266. Where a tender of performance or payment is necessary to the establishment of a right against another party, it will be considered as waived when it is reasonably certain that it will be refused. Accordingly where land was sold for taxes by commissioners, under the acts of congress of June 7, 1862, and February 6, 1863, and the proof showed that the commissioners had established and uniformly followed a general rule, under which they refused to receive, on property which had been advertised for sale, from any one but the owner or a party in interest, in person, the amount chargeable upon said property, held, that such rule dispensed with the necessity of a tender, since a tender by the proper agent of the property owner would have been of no avail; and that the sale of such property under such rule was unauthorized, and conferred no title on the purchaser. United States *v.* Lee, 16 Otto, 196.

§ 267. **Rights of plaintiff on plea of tender.**— The plaintiff, upon a plea of tender, cannot take out the money and proceed for more. Alexandria *v.* Patten, 1 Cr. C. C., 294.

§ 268. **In admiralty.**— The doctrine of courts of admiralty on the subject of tender is less stringent than that of common-law courts; admiralty courts look to the substance and good faith of the transaction, rather than to technical forms of proceeding. Dedekam *v.* Vose, 3 Blatch., 44.

§ 269. —— **effect of.**— A tender admits a liability in admiralty, and decree must be rendered for amount tendered, although if no tender had been made, no recovery might have been had. Cain *v.* Garfield, 1 Low., 483.

§ 270. **Miscellaneous.**— In a suit to recover money paid in advance on the purchase of a horse, which was to be forfeited if the balance was not paid by a certain day, it is incumbent on plaintiff to prove a tender within the time, or that he attended at the defendant's house on the last day, ready to pay, and that defendant was not there; if no place was agreed upon, then it was the duty of the plaintiff to use reasonable endeavors to find· defendant. Bayley *v.* Duvall,* 1 Cr. C. C., 283.

§ 271. A mere attempt to negotiate a compromise of a claim at an amount specified, unaccompanied with a tender or direct offer to pay such amount, does not operate as an equitable bar to costs. The H. B. Foster, Abb. Adm., 222.

§ 272. The demand, by a creditor, of payment in a certain species of coin, does not dispense with the obligation, on the debtor, to make tender agreeably to his own sense of the law and the contract. Searight *v.* Calbraith, 4 Dall., 325.

V. ACCORD AND SATISFACTION.

§ 273. **What constitutes.**— A creditor took a number of notes of smaller amounts in lieu of one note for a larger sum, in order to bring the notes within the jurisdiction of a justice of the peace. *Held*, that the new notes created a new indebtedness and were an accord and satisfaction of the old note. *In re* Dixon, 2 McC., 556.

§ 274. A debtor delivered certain property to trustees in satisfaction of the debts due his various creditors, upon a mutual agreement among the creditors to receive the property as a discharge of his indebtedness. *Held*, that there was a valid accord and satisfaction, which was good as against the indorsee of a promissory note, payable on demand, given originally to one of the parties to the said agreement by the debtor, it not appearing that the note was indorsed before said accord and satisfaction was made. Bartlett *v.* Rogers, 3 Saw., 62.

§ 275. Where congress has paid in full a doubtful claim presented with full knowledge of all the facts, such payment will be deemed to have been paid and received by accord in satisfaction and will be final and conclusive. Thus, where a sailing master in the navy became insane and remained in a private asylum for twenty-seven years, during which time he was supposed to be dead and was dropped from the navy register, but after his decease his friends applied to congress for half pay during the period of his insanity, the granting of such request by congress is such a settlement of their demands upon the government as to preclude them from prosecuting any further claim on the ground of mistake of law in the first application to congress by which half pay only was demanded, whereas the master or his representatives were entitled by law to full pay. Rush's Case,* 2 Ct. Cl., 167.

§ 276. An assignment of debts and balances of accounts cannot be pleaded as an accord and satisfaction to an action of debt on a bond. Buddicum *v.* Kirk, 3 Cr., 293.

§ 277. **An accord must be executed.** An executory agreement is not an accord and satisfaction. Accordingly, where a city agreed to issue its bonds to a contractor embarrassed in carrying out his contract, upon the consideration that the contractor would release the city from all liabilities on the contract, but letters of credit were issued instead of bonds, *held*, that the city having failed to carry out its agreement could not avail itself of the release; that the agreement was an executory agreement for an accord and satisfaction, and all performance on the part of the city having failed, the agreement to release was left without obligatory force. City of Memphis *v.* Brown, 20 Wall., 289.

§ 278. An accord must be executed before it can amount to satisfaction. An unperformed agreement is not sufficient, and cannot be pleaded in bar. United States *v.* Clarke,* Hemp., 315.

§ 279. **How pleaded.**— Accord and satisfaction occurring after issue formed in a suit must be pleaded *puis darrein continuance* if the party would avail himself of it. Good *v.* Davis, Hemp., 16.

VI. Receipts.

§ 280. A receipt is only prima facie evidence of payment, and may be explained, varied or contradicted by parol or other extraneous testimony. Weed *v.* Snow,* 3 McL., 265.

§ 281. A receipt for so much is only evidence of payment, and may be explained by parol or other evidence. Maze *v.* Miller,* 1 Wash., 328.

§ 282. A receipt of payment by a note is only *prima facie* evidence of payment, which may always be explained by other testimony. Moore *v.* The Steamboat Fashion, Newb., 49.

§ 283. But unexplained, such receipt is conclusive, and the party against whom it is produced must establish its character if he wishes to avoid its legitimate effect. *Ibid.*

§ 284. If payment acknowledged in a receipt turn out to be a note, or bill, or the like, and if the same were not paid or received in satisfaction, and turn out unproductive, it is no payment. In order to make such note or bill a payment, it is necessary that it be received in satisfaction, and the receiver to run all risks, or where the receiver has made it his own by neglecting to give notice. Maze *v.* Miller,* 1 Wash., 328.

§ 285. A receipt in full is only *prima facie* evidence of what it purports to be; and if clearly proved to have been obtained by fraud, mistake or ignorance of the rights of the party, it will be examined into and corrected in a court of law, as well as in a court of equity ; but if such evidence is not given, the presumption in favor of the validity of the instrument will prevail. Thompson *v.* Faussat, Pet. C. C., 182.

§ 286. A receipt in full on a settled account is not conclusive on the parties, but it is merely *prima facie* evidence of what it purports to be, and may be opened, if it be unfairly obtained. or be given under a mistake of facts or of the legal rights of the party complaining, for the correction of such errors as may be made out by proof. But if it be the result of a compromise, it is binding. Lawrence *v.* The Schuylkill Navigation Co., 4 Wash., 563.

§ 287. By seaman.— A settlement between the master of a vessel and a seaman of a claim for damages by the latter against the former for assault and battery, evidenced by a receipt, will not operate as an acquittance of the master, unless it appear that the seaman was free from constraint, and at liberty to exercise his deliberate judgment, and also that the satisfaction was reasonable. Where such a receipt was for " twenty-five cents for assault and battery, in full for all dues and demands," and was signed by the seaman in the cabin in the presence of the master and mate, no release from the shipping articles being given him until after he had signed the receipt, the master thus being at liberty to compel him to continue on the voyage in case the receipt had not been signed, instead of releasing him as the seaman desired, *held,* that the receipt under the circumstances was no bar to the seaman's claim for damages. Mitchell *v.* Pratt, Taney, 448.

§ 288. The receipt of a collector acknowledging payment is *prima facie* evidence, but not conclusive of the fact of payment. Johnson *v.* United States, 5 Mason, 425.

§ 289. A receipt of a collector upon a duty bond, acknowledging payment and satisfaction of the bond, does not operate as an estoppel. It is open to explanation, and is no bar to a suit on the bond if it be not paid. United States *v.* Williams, 1 Ware, 175.

§ 290. Operation of, confined to that for which they are given.— A contractor, who, having furnished for the erection of an arsenal a large quantity of stone, a portion of which is rejected by the government, receives payment for the amount of stone actually used, and gives a receipt for the payment of such specific number of yards, is not thereby concluded from seeking payment for the stone not embraced in the receipt. Kerchner *v.* United States,* 7 Ct. Cl., 579.

§ 291. By attorney for money paid by himself as attorney to himself as administrator.— Administrators upon an estate who were appointed in the Cherokee nation had a right to maintain a suit or prosecute a claim for money in the District of Columbia, and a payment to a person acting under a power of attorney from them would have been valid ; but where this person, instead of receiving the money under his power of attorney, took out letters of administration then in the District of Columbia, and then signed a receipt as attorney for money paid by himself as administrator to himself as attorney for the Cherokee administrators, this receipt is good, and the surety upon his administration bond is not responsible to the Cherokee heirs. Mackey *v.* Coxe, 18 How., 100.

VII. Settlement and Release.

§ 292. A covenant, under seal, to come to a settlement within a limited time and to pay the balance which might be found due, is merely collateral and cannot be pleaded as an extinguishment of a simple contract debt. the period within which the settlement was to be made having elapsed before the commencement of the suit, and the plea not averring that any such settlement had been made. Baits v. Peters, 9 Wheat., 556.

§ 293. **Settlement binding as an accord and satisfaction — Subsequent attempt at arbitration.** — A board of levee commissioners effected a settlement with contractors for work done upon certain levees, by which a certain sum, based upon measurements and estimates made by the engineer of the board, was paid, and a receipt given in full for all demands. Subsequently, the contractors claiming that injustice had been done them by the settlement, an agreement was entered into reciting the former settlement and the receipt acknowledging the same, the complaint of the contractors, and stipulating that a board of arbitrators, consisting of engineers appointed in a designated manner, should measure all the work done and render to the parties to the agreement an estimate of the amount due to the contractors, if any, according to the original contracts: that if such estimate should differ from the sum paid by the terms of the former settlement, the difference should be paid or refunded as the case might be; that in the adjustment of all questions pertaining to measurement the contractors should have the privilege of introducing all proper evidence, the board to have the privilege of rebutting that evidence. A dispute occurring as to the admissibility of testimony proposed to be offered and the acceptance of the third arbitrator, the contractors abandoned the arbitration and brought suit for the balance claimed to be their due. *Held*, that the claim could not be enforced, as the prior settlement bound both parties as an accord and satisfaction; that the arbitrament was an agreement to open that settlement only to the extent of correcting errors, if any, in the measurement of the work, and that the proposed arbitrament having failed without the fault of the board the settlement stood. Hemingway v. Stansell,* 16 Otto, 399.

§ 294. **Effect of non-compliance with terms of settlement.** — Where a controverted case was, by agreement of the parties, entered settled, and the terms of the settlement were that the debtor should pay by a limited day, and the creditor agreed to receive a less sum than that for which he had obtained a judgment, and the debtor failed to pay on the day limited, the original judgment became revived in full force. Early v. Rogers, 16 How., 599.

§ 295. **Based upon false statements.** — Where the treasurer of a corporation furnishes, with intent to deceive, a false statement of a contractor's account with the corporation, any settlement made upon the faith of such statement will be set aside. James v. Atlantic Delaine Co., 3 Cliff., 622.

§ 296. **In ignorance of rights.** — A., being indebted to B., took out a policy of insurance on his life for $3,000 and assigned the same to B. to secure his debt of $70; B. agreeing, in case of the receipt by him of the insurance money, to pay to the wife of A., his heirs and assigns, one-third of the amount of the policy. A. dying shortly after the issuing of the policy, B. received the amount of the policy, paying over one-third thereof to A.'s widow. The court, having found the policy of $3,000 to cover a debt of $70 to be a mere wager, *held*, that the receipt of the one-third of the insurance money by the widow did not conclude her as a settlement of the matter or prevent her recovering the balance of the amount of the policy, it being obvious that she was ignorant of the full extent of her rights, that she acted hastily and without due consideration. Cammack v. Lewis, 15 Wall., 643.

§ 297. **By seamen.** — Where libel is brought against the owner of a vessel by a seaman for wages, a clandestine settlement effected by the owner with the seaman will not prevent the latter's proctor from prosecuting the suit for costs, the seaman having received merely the amount of his wages without costs. Collins v. Nickerson, 1 Spr., 126.

§ 298. Where a seaman, after suit brought, effects a settlement with the master for damages for a tort of the latter, such settlement will be upheld, although made by the seaman in the absence of his proctor, if made fairly and understandingly and the consideration paid appears to be adequate. Brooks v. Snell, 1 Spr., 48.

§ 299. **Release, effect of.** — A release covering the whole subject-matter of the claim, and not tainted with fraud, is conclusive. Perkins v. Fourniquet,* 14 How., 813.

§ 300. If the accounts between the parties are impeached, and a release has been obtained, executed by one of the parties, in a case depending before a court of chancery, the release will not prevent the court from looking into the settlements; and the release in such a case is entitled to no greater force in a court of equity than the settlement of the account on which it was given. Kelsey v. Hobby, 16 Pet., 269.

§ 301. Bond by the defendant, executor of R., to the plaintiff, his co-executor, conditioned to pay a sum of money, which is in his hands as assets, to the plaintiff, for the use of the proper and legal heirs of R., to whom it belongs. R. left two sons, A. and B., to whom he devised his estate. A., by an instrument reciting the bond, and that the money belongs to him and B., assigns and releases all his right in and to the same, for a valuable consideration. The release of A. cannot be pleaded as such, because A., equitably entitled to only one-half of the money, could not release the bond; but it may be given in evidence to prove payment of his half of the debt. The acknowledgment of B. of the defendant's accounts, showing that his interest in the bond had been discharged, may be given in evidence by the defendant, to prove payment. Campbell *v.* Hamilton, 4 Wash., 93.

§ 302. —— cannot be enlarged beyond its intended scope.— M., an attorney, having claims against the government for legal services under two different contracts, rendered a specific account for one of them. After some personal negotiations he wrote a letter accepting the verbal offer of the secretary of the treasury to pay him a reduced amount in compromise and settlement of the balance claimed by him on the account rendered. The letter, after directing the amount to be sent by check, concluded: "And this letter may thereupon be taken as a full release and discharge of all claims under the said account or under the said contract." The secretary indorsed upon the account his approval "on the terms and conditions specified in the written memorandum," and referred the matter to a subordinate officer for examination and settlement. The memorandum stated that the amount allowed was "in full of all claims and demands upon the government under the aforesaid contract, or any other contract," etc., "and said letter is hereby accepted as a full release and discharge by said M. of all indebtedness whatsoever from the United States to him." No notice of this memorandum was given to M., and the check was sent as directed in the letter. *Held,* that this memorandum at most only amounted to a direction to a subordinate officer to procure a general release before paying the money; that an official memorandum of a secretary is not a matter of record of which the public or persons dealing with the department are bound to take notice, and could in no way extend M.'s specific release of one indebtedness to a full release of all indebtedness whatsoever. Mellen *v.* United States,* 13 Ct. Cl., 71.

§ 303. —— duress — Undue advantage.— If a release is executed, and a settlement is made of a particular item in an account for which suit has been brought, and in which the party has been arrested, the settlement having been confined to the claim for the damages for which suit was brought, the mere circumstances of the defendant being detained by the process issued to recover the amount claimed would be no objection to the validity of the agreement and the release. But if, while under detention for want of special bail, a release was obtained of other matters than those embraced in the suit, and much more important in amount, and which had been insisted on for years in the suit previously instituted, then in the course of proceeding, neither the circumstances under which the release was taken, and the account connected with it settled, nor the contents of the papers, entitle them to any consideration in equity. Kelsey *v.* Hobby, 16 Pet., 269.

§ 304. An agreement by the plaintiff to release the defendant upon his executing a deed is a good defense in *assumpsit,* the deed being executed. Bartleman *v.* Douglass, 1 Cr. C. C., 450.

§ 305. Miscellaneous.— In equity, where a creditor agrees to receive specific articles in satisfaction of a debt, even although it be a debt upon bond, secured by mortgage, he will be held to the performance of his agreement, provided the agreement is not inequitable in its terms and effect; that there is a valuable consideration for such agreement, and that there is a readiness to perform and an absence of laches on the part of the debtor. Very *v.* Levy, 13 How., 345.

§ 306. C. was in possession of two drafts drawn by K. upon G. and accepted by him for the accommodation of K. C. pledged these drafts to the Farmers' Bank of Virginia, as collateral security for a debt which he owed to the bank. The drafts not being paid at maturity, the bank sued both Groves and King, and recovered judgments against them, which were liens upon their property. C. and K. then agreed that if C. were to purchase K.'s property at a certain sum, he would return his drafts to him and free him from the bank. To this agreement G. was a witness, and the purchase was accordingly made. C. and the bank then agreed that the bank should give him time, and he should give additional collateral security to the bank and mortgage his property; first reducing the liens of prior mortgages down to a certain sum. The bank was, moreover, to surrender the collateral securities previously received. The mortgage was made by C. and the collateral securities surrendered to him by the bank. After this the bank had no right to prosecute the judgment which it had obtained against G. By the first agreement made between K. and C., to which G. was privy, C. exonerated G., as far as it was in his power; and in consequence of the second agreement between C. and the bank, C. became re-invested with the whole control of the matter, and his previous exoneration of G. became immediately operative. G. was, therefore, entirely discharged from all responsibility. The failure of C. to comply with his contract with the bank did not prevent this exoneration of G. from being effectual. Farmers' Bank of Virginia *v.* Groves, 12 How., 51.

VIII. Compromise.

§ 307. In general.— To sustain a settlement as a compromise of doubtful claims without any other consideration, the doubt must be such as a person of ordinary intelligence, familiar with the class of things which is the subject of the settlement, might be expected to entertain. City of Memphis *v.* Brown, 6 West. Jur., 495; 11 Am. L. Reg. (N. S.), 629; 1 Flip., 188.

§ 308. Where the amount of a debt due from the government is a matter of dispute between the government and the claimant, and the latter finally accepts the balance of the account as made out on the basis contended for by the government, and gives a receipt in full, such settlement concludes him from making any further demand. United States *v.* Clyde, 13 Wall., 35.

§ 309. An agreement made in a spirit of peace and compromise, for the settlement of unadjusted demands, will not, when executed with due caution, after deliberate consideration by parties of intelligence and business experience, be questioned in a court of equity. On the contrary it is the duty of the court to uphold such an agreement, and protect and enforce the rights of both parties under it. May *v.* Le Claire, 11 Wall., 217.

§ 310. Offer of compromise — Effect of.— A mere offer of compromise, by which a creditor deducts a certain amount from his bill, will not prejudice his right of recovery, especially where the debtor refuses to pay the balance after making such deduction. West *v.* Smith, 11 Otto, 263.

§ 311. Offers of compromise to pay a sum of money by the way of compromise, as a general rule, are not admissible against the party making the offer; but if admitted such offers are open to explanation, no matter whether it was by letter or by oral communication. *Ibid.*

§ 312. By implication.—Payment for one thing is not necessarily payment for another, provided the two things are so distinct as to form *per se* independent causes of action; but where a contractor, having been delayed for several years in the fulfillment of his contract by changes made in the plan of the work, puts in a claim for extra labor and effects a compromise in regard to such claim, he cannot afterwards maintain a suit for delay, insurance on his buildings, and tools, rent, interest on his capital, etc., such things being incident to the things already compromised and paid for. Swift *v.* United States,* 14 Ct. Cl., 208.

§ 313. No general rule of compromises by implication exists in favor of the government; hence, to establish a compromise, there must be an agreement to that effect. Thus, where a dispute having arisen between a contractor and the quartermaster-general as to the value of horses delivered under contract, the quartermaster directed his officers to pay a part of the contract price as a compromise, but they negligently pay the amount as directed without exacting a release from the contractor for the balance of the contract price, *held*, that there was no compromise by implication, and that the contractor was not precluded from bringing suit for the balance of his claim. Wilcox *v.* United States,* 7 Ct. Cl., 586.

§ 314. Party claiming benefit of, must show performance.— A party cannot avail himself of the conditions of a compromise unless he can show a performance of its terms on his part. Accordingly where, by the terms of a compromise, certain notes were to be delivered up upon the payment of a prescribed amount, at the time and in the manner set forth in the agreement, but nothing was ever paid or tendered, nor anything ever done in fulfillment of the agreement, *held*, that such compromise was no defense to an action brought for the full face of the notes. Brown *v.* Spofford, 5 Otto, 474.

§ 315. Under protest — Duress.— Where a party without force or intimidation, and with a full knowledge of all the facts of the case, accepts on account of an unliquidated and controverted demand a sum less than what he claims and believes to be due him, and agrees to accept that sum in full satisfaction, he cannot avoid his act on the ground of duress, and make a further demand. A provost guard having forcibly entered the office of parties having a claim against the government, and having seized their vouchers, business papers and private books of account and carried the same before a military commission appointed to report on unsettled claims, the commission indorsed on the vouchers the amount allowed by it, deducting a considerable sum from the claim. The commission also withheld the vouchers until the claimants signed a receipt or agreement providing that the payment of the amount allowed by the commission should be payment in full of all the claimants' demands against the United States, which was done by the latter under protest to obtain possession of their vouchers. Subsequently the claimants received payment of the amount allowed by the commission, from the quartermaster, making no formal objection or protest. They were required to and did sign a receipt acknowledging the receipt of such reduced amounts "in full of the above account." *Held*, that such payment and receipt was a compromise and settlement in full, obtained without duress, and unaffected by the probability that the claimants were constrained to accept the reduced amount by the fear that bankruptcy would result from a refusal of the sum offered, and the consequent delay in obtaining the money due them. United States v. Child & Co., 12 Wall., 232.

§ 816. With one debtor, does not affect other debtors.— Where a creditor, having obtained a decree against several defendants, compromises with some of them by taking fifty cents on the dollar, such compromise does not operate as a surrender of any of his rights as to the other defendants, or release them from any of their liabilities under the decree. Molyneaux v. Marsh, 1 Woods, 452.

§ 817. Sum less than debt received as payment in full.— Upon the plea of payment to an action of debt upon a bond conditioned to pay $500, evidence may be received of the payment of a smaller sum, with an acknowledgment by the plaintiff that it was in full of all demands; and from such evidence, if uncontradicted, the jury may and ought to infer payment of the whole. Henderson v. Moore, 5 Cr., 11.

§ 818. Where a creditor, having full power and privilege to acquire information, agrees to accept, and actually receives, a less sum than the amount of his debt, there being no fraud on the part of the debtor, such agreement and acceptance is binding upon him. The binding force of the settlement does not depend upon ultimate results or the correctness of the judgment exercised by the creditor in the transaction. A , doubting the solvency of a certain bank, his debtor, accepted the offer of the latter to pay twenty-five per cent. of its indebtedness, and received that proportion of his claim as payment in full. Subsequently the bank proved able to pay larger dividends, some creditors receiving the entire amount of their claims. *Held*, that A. was precluded by his compromise and settlement from demanding anything further from the bank or its assets. *In re* Bank of North Carolina,[*] 19 N. B. R., 314.

§ 819. An agreement to take a part of the debt for the whole, when the whole is due, as *nudum pactum*, is of no legal obligation. A. entered into a contract with the government to furnish muskets. The inspection of the muskets, when delivered, being delayed, the price of such muskets fell in the meantime, and the contract was referred by the government to a commission. A. then made a proposition as a compromise in order to obtain money, which, not being accepted, he made a reduced offer, which the commission accepted. *Held*, in accordance with the above principle, that A.'s last offer was not binding upon him, and, moreover, that the officers' refusal of the adjudication of A.'s claim, to which he was entitled, thus forcing from him the proposal he made as the only means of obtaining any part of the money due him, which he needed to meet his engagements for the guns, was legal duress, which voided the transaction made under it. Ramsdell v. United States,[*] 2 Ct. Cl., 508.

§ 820. Although, at common law, the payment of a less sum is not a sufficient consideration for an agreement to discharge a greater, under the code of Tennessee such contracts will be enforced when performed in good faith according to the intention of the parties. But an agreement by a debtor to deliver in satisfaction of a large sum his notes or money for a less sum will not operate as a discharge, although there be a consideration for the agreement, unless it be fully and fairly performed both as to time and amount. City of Memphis v. Brown, 6 West. Jur., 495; 1 Flip., 188.

§ 821. Composition with creditors.— It is generally true, in cases of composition, that the debtor who agrees to pay a less sum in the discharge of a contract, must pay punctually; for, until performance, the creditor is not bound. The reason is obvious; the creditor has the sole right of modifying the first contract, and of prescribing the conditions of its discharge. If the agreement stipulates for partial payments, and the debtor fails to pay, the condition to take part is broken, the second contract forfeited, and is no bar to the original cause of action. Clarke v. White, 12 Pet., 178.

§ 822. In composition for a debt, by which one party agreed to deliver goods to the amount of seventy per cent., in satisfaction of a debt exceeding $10,000, and omitted to deliver within $1.41 of the amount, the mistake was too trivial to deserve notice. *Ibid.*

§ 823. —— claim for negotiating— Fraud.— Upon suit brought upon a promissory note given by the debtor, defendant, to plaintiff, the agent of one of defendant's creditors, for his services in effecting a compromise between defendant and his creditors, the court instructed the jury: 1st. That if the note was obtained from defendant by the threat of plaintiff to interfere and defeat defendant's proposed compromise unless defendant would give plaintiff this note, as a bonus to him, then said note was void in the hands of plaintiff as against defendant. 2d. That if it was expected or understood between plaintiff and defendant that plaintiff was not to disclose to other creditors the fact that he was specially retained by defendant, but was to urge the compromise, giving other creditors to understand that he was only acting in the interest of creditors, then the note was void. 3d. That if the plaintiff was, by his agreement with his firm, authorized to accept compensation from debtors for securing compromises in which the firm, upon certain conditions, were to share, the result of such an arrangement might be to give his firm an undue preference over other creditors, and no contract to that end between plaintiff and a debtor could be enforced in a court of justice. Bullene v. Blain, 6 Biss., 22.

§ 324. —— obtained by fraudulent concealments.— A compromise entered into between a debtor and his creditors, by which the latter agree to accept a portion of the amount their due, in full settlement of their claims, may be treated as void, if brought about by the misrepresentations or fraudulent concealments of the former as to his means and ability to pay. The same is true, although the misrepresentations or concealments were made by an agent of the debtor in effecting the compromise, however innocent such agent may have been, provided that the real state of the facts at the time was known to the debtor. Elfelt v. Snow. 2 Saw., 94.

§ 325. Agreement to pay one creditor more than others — Validity thereof — Effect if fulfilled.— A creditor who, after having joined with other creditors in executing a composition deed discharging their common debtor, brings an action against such debtor on the original indebtedness, on the ground that the composition deed was procured by the misrepresentations and fraudulent concealments of the latter, is not precluded from asserting his claims by the fact that, by an agreement entered into previous to the composition deed, he received, unbeknown to the other creditors, a sum of money in excess of that stipulated in the deed. Ibid.

§ 326. The rule, that if a debtor, in compounding with his creditors, secretly promises to give to one more than to the others, in order to induce him to sign the instrument of composition, it is void, only applies to cases where the creditors are supposed mutually to agree with each other, as well as with the debtor. But when each creditor is separately compounded with, this principle of mutuality and equality does not apply. White v. Clarke, 5 Cr. C. C., 102.

§ 327. If, upon failure or insolvency, one creditor goes into a contract of general composition common to the others, at the same time having an underhand agreement with the debtor to receive a large per cent., such agreement is fraudulent and void. Clarke v. White, 12 Pet., 178.

§ 328. Where a debtor attempted to settle with his creditors at fifty cents on the dollar, but one creditor refused to sign the composition unless the debtor would give his note for ten per cent. more, thus making such creditor's share in the settlement sixty cents on the dollar, held, in an action by the debtor to recover such extra ten per cent. paid the creditor, to be a good defense that the composition itself was fraudulent, and that in making the settlement misrepresentations had been made and assets concealed by the debtor. Armstrong v. Mechanics' National Bank, 6 Biss.. 520.

§ 329. By seamen.— Where, after libel filed by seamen for wages, one of their number accepts, with the advice of his proctor, a certain sum in full settlement, such settlement will not be disturbed. The Hermon, 1 Low., 515.

PEDIGREE.

See EVIDENCE.

PENAL STATUTES.

See CONSTITUTION AND LAWS.

PENALTIES AND FORFEITURES.

[See INFORMERS; MARITIME LAW; REVENUE; WAR.]

I. IN GENERAL, §§ 1-82.
II. ACTIONS AND PROCEDURE, §§ 83-155.
III. SEIZURE, §§ 156-175.

IV. DISTRIBUTION OF PROCEEDS, §§ 176-194.
V. REMISSION AND PARDON, §§ 195-242.

I. IN GENERAL.

§ 1. **When property forfeited vests in government.**— Forfeitures made absolute by statute relate back to the time of the commission of the wrongful acts which the statute prohibits. In such case the title to the thing forfeited vests immediately in the government; but where more than one remedy is given and the government has an election to proceed for the forfeiture, or in some other way not involving a forfeiture, the title to the property does not vest in the United States prior to the seizure, or the performance of some other act which amounts to such an election. United States v. Sixty-Four Barrels of Distilled Spirits, 3 Cliff., 308.

§ 2. The court below instructed the jury, in the case at bar, that, if the goods were fraudulently entered, it was no matter in whose possession they were when seized, or whether the United States had made an election between the penalties, and that the forfeiture took place when the fraud, if any, was committed, and the seller of the goods could convey no title to the purchaser. This instruction was right in respect to the sixty-eighth section of the act of 1799, as the penalty is the forfeiture without an alternative of their value; but wrong as the instruction applies to the sixty-sixth section of same act, as the forfeiture under it is either the goods or their value. Caldwell v. The United States, 8 How., 366.

§ 3. When the act has been done which the law declares to work a forfeiture of the property, the right of the government to seize the property and assert the forfeiture attaches at once, and may be pursued by the government whenever and in whose hands soever that property may be found. Thacher's Distilled Spirits, 18 Otto, 679.

§ 4. When property is forfeited it does not vest in the government until after a seizure, which then relates back to the time of the forfeiture. Clark v. Protection Ins. Co., 1 Story, 109.

§ 5. In point of law, no duties, as such, can legally accrue upon the importation of prohibited goods. They are not entitled to entry at the custom-house, or to be bonded; they are *ipso facto* forfeited by the mere act of importation. McLane v. United States, 6 Pet., 404.

§ 6. Where a statute denounces a forfeiture of property as the penalty for the commission of an offense, if the denunciation is in direct terms, and not in the alternative, that is, if the statute does not say that the forfeiture shall be of the property or its value, the forfeiture takes place at the time the offense was committed, and operates as a statutory transfer of the right of property to the government. United States v. Stevenson, 3 Ben., 119; United States v. One Copper Still, 8 Biss., 270.

§ 7. Whether or not a forfeiture is to take effect upon the happening of the act or only after due process of law depends upon the intention of congress, as evidenced by the language of the statute. Where such intention is uncertain the rules of the common law governing such cases may be resorted to. The Kate Heron. 6 Saw., 106.

§ 8. —— **bona fide purchasers.**— The title of the wrong-doer remains undisturbed until there is a condemnation, and then the forfeiture relates back to the wrongful act, if there is no alternative remedy, and to the seizure if there is, in which latter case it does not overreach the title of an innocent purchaser whose interest was acquired after the commission of the wrongful acts, but before the condemnation. United States v. Sixty-Four Barrels of Distilled Spirits, 3 Cliff., 303.

§ 9. It is a settled principle of the law that where a statute declares a forfeiture to be the penalty for a violation of law, the forfeiture takes place *eo instanter* the offense is committed. The title vests in the United States, and cannot afterwards be transferred even to a *bona fide* purchaser by the wrong-doer. United States v. One Hundred Barrels Spirits, 1 Dill., 49.

§ 10. Where the forfeiture is made absolute by statute, the decree of condemnation, when entered, relates back to the time of the commission of the wrongful acts, and takes date from the wrongful acts, and not from the date of the sentence or decree. Hence the purchase of goods before seizure by an innocent purchaser, without notice that they are forfeited under the statute, will not protect such purchaser, nor relieve the goods from forfeiture in his hands. Henderson's Distilled Spirits, 14 Wall., 44.

§ 11. A *bona fide* purchaser of the whole interest in a vessel, subsequent to a forfeiture incurred under the sixteenth section of the act of congress of December 31, 1792, by the sale or transfer to an alien of any interest in an American registered vessel, is not within the proviso of that section, and such purchase will not prevent the forfeiture, as said forfeiture takes place at the moment of the sale or transfer to an alien, and any subsequent judgment of forfeiture relates back to that time. The Florenzo, Bl. & How., 52.

§ 12. A purchase of goods which have become forfeited to the United States will not purge the forfeiture, when the purchase has been made under a full knowledge of the facts, or of such facts as were sufficient to put the party on inquiry. Brig Ploughboy,* 1 Gall., 41.

§ 13. Property which has become forfeited to the United States, and afterwards, and before seizure, while remaining in the possession of the vendor, is sold to a *bona fide* purchaser for a valuable consideration, without notice, will be protected in the hands of such purchaser against the claim of the United States. Brig Mars,* 1 Gall., 191. Reversed, United States v. The Brigantine Mars, 8 Cr., 418.

§ 14. Where congress declares a forfeiture for violation of its laws, such forfeiture is absolute. Hence where goods are seized as forfeited and proceeded against, it is of no avail for claimants to urge that they were *bona fide* purchasers, having made advances in good faith upon the goods in question before seizure. Boyd v. United States, 14 Blatch., 317.

§ 15. The forfeiture of goods for the violation of the non-intercourse act of March 1, 1809, takes place upon the commission of the offense, and avoids a subsequent sale to an innocent purchaser, although there may have been a regular permit for landing the goods, and although the duties may have been paid. United States v. One Thousand Nine Hundred and Sixty Bags of Coffee, 8 Cr., 398.

§ 16. In a proceeding *in rem* to ascertain a forfeiture it is not material whether the statute declares that the property shall be forfeited, or that the offender shall forfeit it. In either case, the date of the offense is the time to which the forfeiture relates. United States v. Fifty-Six Barrels of Whisky, 6 Am. L. Reg. (N. S.), 32; 1 Abb., 93.

§ 17. Where a statute in direct terms denounces a forfeiture of property as a penalty, the forfeiture takes place at the time the offense is committed, and operates as a statutory transfer of the right of property to the government. Therefore, in a proceeding for the condemnation of property, the fact that such property has passed into the hands of a *bona fide* purchaser before the commencement of the suit will not avail the claimant. *Ibid.*

§ 18. When the law denounces an absolute forfeiture as the consequence of an act, the title of the United States accrues when the prohibited act is done, and holds as against an innocent purchaser. The Mary Celeste, 2 Low., 354.

§ 19. Forfeitures are always deemed odious in law, and courts will insist upon the forfeiture being made clearly apparent before enforcing it. Mt. Diablo M. & M. Co. v. Callison, 5 Saw., 439.

§ 20. —— Interest of mortgagee.— Property was seized as forfeited to the United States for violation of the revenue laws, and suit brought to enforce the forfeiture. Upon motion made by certain parties to bond a portion of the property in the hands of the marshal, as to which property they were mortgagees by a mortgage given before the forfeiture was incurred, *held*, that, as it was the offending thing that was forfeited, the entire right of property of all the world in the thing was cut off, and not merely the mortgagor's right of property therein, and that the motion must therefore be denied. All the Distilled Spirits, etc., 2 Ben., 483.

§ 21. Not attachable by private creditors after commission of act which works forfeiture.— A vessel was seized as forfeited under the act of May 22, 1794. At the time of the service of the munition by the marshal, the vessel was in the custody of a sheriff, under a process of attachment issued from a state court. *Held*, that whenever the forfeiture is made absolute by an act of congress, the forfeiture attaches at the time the wrongful act is committed, the owner is divested of all title *eo instanti*, and the same becomes vested in the United States; and, consequently, that the seizure by the marshal was a valid one, because the vessel, at the time of the attachment, was not attachable for the debts of the former owner, the property in such vessel having already vested in the United States. United States v. Reindeer, 2 Cliff., 57.

§ 22. A levy on the property forfeited under the act of congress of December 31, 1792, under an execution against an alien purchaser, previous to the prosecution of the forfeiture, will not prevent the forfeiture. The Florenzo, Bl. & How., 52.

§ 23. Claims of seamen, etc., when preferred to claim of government.— A forfeiture under the act of congress of December 31, 1792, does not avoid the lien of seamen and material-men existing at the time of forfeiture. *Ibid.*

§ 24. The claims of seamen for wages, and of material-men for supplies, where the parties were innocent of all knowledge of, or participation in, the illegal voyage, are preferred to the claim of forfeiture on the part of the government. The St. Jago de Cuba, 9 Wheat., 409.

§ 25. **Property when forfeited by acts of persons other than owners.**— A forfeiture for the embezzlement of wines, etc., under section 5 of the act of April 20, 1818, is incurred only by the act of the owner, and not of a mere stranger or the inspectors of the revenue. Six Hundred and Fifty-one Chests of Tea v. United States, 1 Paine, 499.

§ 26. The spirit of the revenue laws is not to create a forfeiture of property, except for acts of the owner attended with fraud, misconduct or negligence. *Ibid.*

§ 27. A capture made by citizens of the United States of property belonging to the subjects of a country in amity with the United States is unlawful, and in case of such unlawful capture, the property of the lawful owner cannot be forfeited for a violation of the revenue laws of the United States by the captors, or by persons who have rescued the property from their possession. The Bello Corrunes, 6 Wheat., 152.

§ 28. Under a piratical capture, the property of the original owners cannot be forfeited for the misconduct of the captors in violating the municipal laws of the country where the vessel seized by them is carried. The Josefa Segunda, 5 Wheat., 388.

§ 29. The owner of goods cannot forfeit them by an act done without his consent or connivance, or that of some person employed or trusted by him. Peisch v. Ware, 4 Cr., 347.

§ 30. The acts of April 18, 1818, and May 15, 1820 (3 U. S. Stat. at Large, 432, 602), which provide that the ports of the United States shall be closed against every British vessel coming from a port closed against the United States, and that every vessel so excluded which shall enter a port of the United States shall be forfeited, apply only to a voluntary entry by the act of the owner or master of the vessel, or of their agents. The Waterloo, Bl. & How., 114.

§ 31. Hence, an entry by a derelict vessel, brought in by salvors, without the consent of her owner or master, or of their agents, does not work a forfeiture under those acts. *Ibid.*

§ 32. **Ignorance of law will relieve from forfeiture, when.**— The act of March 3, 1855, regulating the carriage of passengers in steamships and other vessels, and imposing penalties and punishments for contravention, is made applicable to ship abroad in sixty days in Europe, and six months in other ports of the world, and requires notice of the act to be given in all foreign ports through the department of state. *Held,* that where such notice had failed to be given in such foreign port, and the owner or master of a vessel had thus unconsciously offended, it was a proper case for remission of forfeiture and for pardon of the master. The Passenger Ship Law, * 7 Op. Att'y Gen'l, 489.

§ 33. The embargo law was passed December 22, 1807. A vessel cleared from a southern port January 15, 1808, and that evening the collector received the information of the passage of the law, and gave public notice of it. It appearing that the owners or master of the vessel were ignorant of the passage of the law, prior to her sailing, and the vessel having been seized for the violation, it was held no good cause for forfeiture, and she was restored. The Ship Cotton Planter, 1 Paine, 23.

§ 34. **Repeal of law while action pending thereunder.**— If the law under which the sentence of condemnation was pronounced be repealed after sentence in the court below, and before final decree in the appellate court, no sentence of condemnation can be pronounced, unless some special provision be made for that purpose by the statute. Yeaton v. United States, 5 Cr., 281.

§ 35. A mere penalty never vests, but remains executory; and there can be no vested right in it until it has been reduced to a judgment. Hence, if an action brought for a penalty created by statute is pending at the time of the repeal of such statute, it cannot be further prosecuted. Union Iron Co. v. Pierce, 4 Biss., 327.

§ 36. The fourth section of the act of congress, approved February 12, 1793 (1 U. S. Stat. at Large, 302), entitled "An act respecting fugitives escaping from justice, and persons escaping from the service of their masters," is repealed, so far as relates to the penalty, by the act of September 18, 1850 (9 Stat. at Large, 462), entitled "An act to amend, and supplementary to, the above act." Therefore, where an action for the recovery of the penalty prescribed in the act of 1793 was pending at the time of the repeal, such repeal is a bar to the action. Norris v. Crocker, 13 How., 429.

§ 37. **Embargo act — Vessel only, not cargo, may be seized.**— The authority given in the eleventh section of the embargo act of April, 1808 (2 Stat. at Large, 499), to collectors of the customs to detain any vessel ostensibly bound with a cargo to some other port of the United States, whenever in their opinion the intention is to violate or evade any of the provisions of the embargo acts, extends only to the seizure of the vessel. Slocum v. Mayberry.* 2 Wheat., 1.

§ 38. The owner has a right to the cargo, and if withheld from him by an officer he may maintain replevin therefor in a state court. *Ibid.*

§ 39. **Violation of registry acts.**— A transfer of a registered vessel of the United States, to a foreign subject, in a foreign port, for the purpose of evading the revenue laws of the foreign country, with an understanding that it is to be afterwards reconveyed to the former owner, works a forfeiture of the vessel, under the sixteenth section of the ship registry act of December 31, 1792, unless the transfer is made known in the manner prescribed by the seventh section of that act. A registered vessel which continues to use its register after such a transfer is liable to forfeiture under the twenty-seventh section of the act, as using a register without being actually entitled to the benefit thereof. The Margaret, 9 Wheat., 421.

§ 40. **Fraudulent intent, when necessary to incur forfeiture.**— To subject goods to forfeiture, for a false valuation, it must be accompanied by a fraudulent intent and design. United States v. 14 Packages of Pins, Gilp., 235.

§ 41. Courts will not inflict penalties for such violations of the penal laws as are unintentional. The Brig William Gray, 1 Paine, 16.

§ 42. Under a libel against a vessel as forfeited for removing timber from public lands in Florida, in violation of a federal statute, it was held that the forfeiture could not be enforced except upon averment in the libel, and proof, that the acts charged as a public offense were done by the master of the vessel wilfully, or with knowledge of their culpability. The Schooner Cherokee,* 13 N. Y. Leg. Obs., 83.

§ 43. It was a proper instruction to the jury that, under an information filed against goods suspected of being fraudulently imported, they were not restricted in the condemnation of the goods to any entered goods which they found to be undervalued; but that they might find either the whole package or the invoice forfeited, though containing other goods correctly valued, provided they should find that such package or invoice had been made up with intent to defraud the government. Buckley v. United States, 4 How., 251.

§ 44. No one incurs the penalty under section 4 of the act of congress of 1793, for hindering or obstructing an arrest, who does not act knowingly. Driskill v. Parrish, 3 McL., 631; 10 L. Rep., 393.

§ 45. Penal statutes not authorizing indictments have never been considered within the rule of the criminal law, that no man is punishable unless he has been guilty both of a criminal act or omission, and a criminal or unlawful intent. United States v. Thomasson, 4 Biss., 99.

§ 46. **Forfeitures for piracy.**— Under the act of congress of March 3, 1819, to protect the commerce of the United States, and punish the crime of piracy, any armed vessel may be seized and brought in; or any vessel, the crew whereof may be armed, and which shall have attempted or commited any piratical aggression, search, restraint, depredation or seizure upon any vessel, and such offending vessel may be condemned and sold, the proceeds whereof to be distributed between the United States and the captors, at the discretion of the court. Harmony v. United States, 2 How., 210.

§ 47. **Duties paid on false valuation no protection against forfeiture.**— If invoices of goods were fraudulently made by a false valuation to evade or defraud the revenue, the fact that they were entered, and the duties having been paid or secured at the custom-house in New York upon these invoices, was no bar to the information for the forfeiture of the goods to the United States. It can never be permitted, that a party who perpetrates a fraud upon the custom-house, and thereby enters his goods upon false invoices and false valuations, and gets a regular delivery thereof upon payment of such duties as such false invoices and false valuation require, can avail himself of that very fraud to defeat the purposes of justice. Wood v. United States, 16 Pet., 342.

§ 48. **There can be but one penalty for the same act,** in hindering an arrest of one or many fugitives from labor, under the act of congress of 1793; and so of harboring one or many at the same time. Driskill v. Parrish, 3 McL., 631; 10 L. Rep., 393.

§ 49. A person who has been convicted and punished by fine and imprisonment for smuggling goods on shore, in violation of the provisions of the act of August 30, 1842, is not liable to an action to recover the penalty imposed by the statute of March 2, 1799, for landing them without a permit, the act complained of in the two cases being the same. United States v. Hoffman,* 4 N. Y. Leg. Obs., 8.

§ 50. **Penalty, when waived.**— The receipt of dog tax after suit brought is a waiver of the penalty. Boswell v. Washington, 2 Cr. C. C., 18.

§ 51. Where a seaman has misconducted himself and is discharged, but has been afterwards received again on board, his services accepted, and his wages allowed in his account, such misconduct cannot be alleged as a ground of forfeiture against him, though the shipping articles contain a clause that the re-instating of an offending seaman shall not be a waiver of the forfeiture. Lang v. Holbrook, Crabbe, 179.

§ 52. Any right may be waived, and, where that right is a severe penal forfeiture, a waiver will be considered with favor to the offender. Ibid.

§ 53. **Limitations.**— Under the consular act of 1803, the penalty of $500 for not depositing the ship's register with the consul, on arrival in a foreign port, must be sued for within two years, the limitation prescribed by the act of 1790, it not being a revenue law within the meaning of the act of 1804. Parsons v. Hunter. 2 Sumn., 419.

§ 54. The provisions of the thirty-first section of the act of congress of April 30, 1790, by which prosecutions on penal statutes are limited, is general in its provisions, so that they extend to penalties imposed after as well as before the act, and also to actions of debt, as well as to informations and indictments. Adams v. Woods, 2 Cr., 336.

§ 55. The two years' limitation of suits for penalties contained in the thirty-second section of the crimes act of April 30, 1790 (1 U. S. Stat. at Large, 119), is repealed by implication by the fourth section of the act of February 28, 1839 (5 U. S. Stat. at Large, 332), which extends the time five years. Stimpson v. Pond, 2 Curt., 502.

§ 56. Forfeiture strictly construed.— The rule that provisions for forfeiture are regarded with disfavor and construed with strictness, and that courts of equity will lean against their enforcement, is true when applied to cases of contract, and the forfeiture relates to a matter admitting of compensation or restoration; but there can be no leaning of the court against a forfeiture which is intended to secure the construction of a work, such as the building of a railroad, in which the public is interested, where compensation cannot be made for the default of the party, nor where the forfeiture is imposed by positive law. Farnsworth v. Minnesota & Pacific Railroad Co., 2 Otto, 49.

§ 57. A statute of Connecticut requires the president and secretary of each corporation to make an annual certificate showing the condition of the affairs of the corporation, as nearly as the same can be ascertained, on the 1st day of January or July next preceding the time of making such certificate, stating the amount of paid capital, the cash value of its credits, the amount of its debts, and the name and number of shares of each stockholder, which certificate it is required shall be deposited on or before the 15th of February or of August, with the town clerk, who shall record the same. The statute also provides that such an officer, whether president or secretary, if he intentionally neglects or refuses to comply with that requirement, and perform the duty therein specified, shall be liable to an action founded on the statute for all debts of such corporation contracted during the period of such neglect or refusal. Held, in an action brought against the president of a corporation, that the statute is penal and must be strictly construed; that an officer was not liable for debts due and unpaid during the period of his neglect or refusal to comply with the terms of the statute, if they were actually contracted before such neglect, etc. Steam Engine Co. v. Hubbard, 11 Otto, 188.

§ 58. Equity never lends its aid to the enforcement of a forfeiture or penalty, or anything in the nature of either. Marshall v. Vicksburg, 15 Wall., 146.

§ 59. A court of equity may not decree a forfeiture. It will relieve against a penalty, but not against stipulated damages. Goesele v. Bimeler, 5 McL., 223.

§ 60. —— relief will be granted, when.— Where the articles of agreement of a private stock company provide for the forfeiture of the stock of stockholders in case of non-payment of assessments, but provide no express mode by which the forfeiture is to be established, a court of equity will relieve where the forfeited stock has not been distributed among the shareholders or sold as provided by the articles, no rights of property having become vested in such case. Walker v. Ogden, 1 Biss., 287.

§ 61. Fine for contempt of court.— Where a fine was imposed by a federal court for contempt of court, and the offending party committed until the fine should be paid, held, upon application of the prisoner for discharge on the ground that he was unable to pay the fine, (1) that the court would not exercise or claim the power invoked unless the president should disclaim all right and power as a part of his constitutional prerogative to grant relief by pardon; (2) that the case was not beyond the pardoning power of the president, because the court in imposing the fine directed it to be paid to the plaintiffs towards the reimbursement of their expenses in the suit; (3) that if the right to the fine should be regarded as a vested private right in the plaintiffs in the suit, existing in the shape of a judgment, the court would have no right to discharge it. In re Mullee, 7 Blatch., 23.

§ 62. Miscellaneous.— Wine and spirits saved from a wreck and landed are not liable to forfeiture because unaccompanied with such marks and certificates as are required by law; nor because they were removed without the consent of the collector, before the quantity and quality were ascertained, and the duties paid. Peisch v. Ware, 4 Cr., 347.

§ 63. If a vessel be driven by stress of weather to the West Indies, and the cargo there detained by the government of the place, this is such a casualty as comes within the exception of "dangers of the seas" in the condition of an embargo bond. United States v. Hall, 6 Cr., 171.

§ 64. Under the third section of the act of January 9, 1808, the return cargo is not affected with forfeiture. The Brig Short Staple and Cargo, 1 Gall., 104.

§ 65. Forfeiture under the act of March 15, 1820, attaches to the cargo on board at the time the vessel enters or attempts to enter our ports; and not to any cargo subsequently taken on board, though on board at the time of the seizure. United States *v.* An Open Boat, 5 Mason, 232.

§ 66. The statute of 1794, prohibiting the fitting out any ship, etc., for the service of any foreign prince or states, to cruise against the subjects, etc., of any other foreign prince or states, does not apply to any new government, unless it has been acknowledged by the United States, or by the government of the country to which such new state belonged. And a plea which sets up a forfeiture under that act, in fitting out a ship to cruise against such new state, must aver such recognition, or it is bad. Gelston *v.* Hoyt, 3 Wheat., 246.

§ 67. Under the eighth section of the coasting act of February 18, 1793, a coasting vessel is not forfeited for proceeding on a foreign voyage, if such vessel has not actually left the port from which she intended to proceed on a foreign voyage. The forfeiture does not attach until the vessel has quitted such port, with an intent to proceed on such voyage. Schooner Friendship and Cargo, 1 Gall., 45.

§ 68. The clerk of a paymaster in the navy is a "person in the naval forces of the United States" within the meaning of the act of March 2, 1863, section 1 (12 Stat. at Large), and hence is not liable to the penalty provided in the third section of such act for those persons not in the military or naval forces who shall steal or embezzle . . . "any money or property of the United States." United States *v.* Bogart, 3 Ben., 257.

§ 69. The statute of 1857 prohibits the importation of indecent or obscene articles, prints, etc., and makes any "invoice or package" of imported goods containing such articles liable to forfeiture, the indecent articles to be destroyed and the others to be sold. An information was filed against a case of stereoscopic slides as being "indecent and obscene articles," praying that the same might be condemned under the statute and destroyed. The jury found that the case contained fifty-nine stereoscopic slides that were indecent, but that the rest were not indecent or obscene. *Held,* that under the pleadings only the fifty-nine articles could be condemned, and that the remainder must be acquitted: that the verdict that the case contained the two kinds of slides did not warrant a condemnation under the above law, as the court had no judicial knowledge that a "case" was always a "package." United States *v.* One Case of Stereoscopic Slides, 1 Spr., 467.

§ 70. A provision in the law or constitution of a state that "there shall be no imprisonment for debt" should be construed to refer to debts arising upon contract express or implied, and hence not to extend to and prohibit imprisonment upon a judgment for a statute penalty. United States *v.* Walsh, 1 Abb., 66; Deady, 281.

§ 71. An agent appointed by the secretary of the navy for the preservation of timber on the public lands of Florida informed of and seized quantities of timber which had been removed from such lands by trespassers. The timber had been hewn into beam pieces for ship-building before its seizure. It was libeled, condemned and appropriated by the United States. The agent claimed one-half of the value of the timber so seized and condemned, as informer, under the act of March 2, 1831 (4 Stat. at Large, 472). *Held,* that the timber in question in its improved condition was as much the property of the United States as it was before the trespassers took it into their possession; that no right was acquired in the timber by the wrong-doer in whose possession it was found by the agent, capable of being forfeited, and hence the improved value of the timber was not a penalty or forfeiture incurred under the provisions of this act. Thistle *v.* United States,* Dev., 131.

§ 72. The tenth section of the Virginia act of December 21, 1792, provides that "it shall not be lawful for any person to export," etc., "any cask of flour marked condemned by an inspector, . . . on pain of forfeiting," etc. The fifteenth section of the same act provides that "if any person, after any cask of flour shall be branded 'condemned,' shall unpack and repack," etc., "shall forfeit and pay," etc. *Held,* that the word "condemned" must be branded on the cask or it is neither within the fifteenth nor the tenth section of the act. Cloud *v.* Hewitt,* 3 Cr. C. C., 199.

§ 73. The United States cannot be regarded as trustee for officers who, if the penalty in a forfeiture case had been collected, would have been entitled to a share of it. United States *v.* Morris,* 1 Paine, 209.

§ 74. Wines, the produce of France, imported into the United States before the non-intercourse act, re-exported to a Danish island, there sold to a merchant of that place, and thence exported to New Orleans during the operation of that act of congress, were liable to forfeiture under that law. The Schooner Hoppet *v.* United States, 7 Cr., 389.

§ 75. Spirits, wines and teas are not subject to seizure, under the forty-third section of the collection law, which declares, that "if any chest," etc., "shall be found in the possession of any person, unaccompanied with such marks and certificates, it shall be presumptive evidence that the same is liable to forfeiture," unless the certificates and marks are both wanting. 651 Chests of Tea *v.* United States, 1 Paine, 499.

§ 76. If a defendant has incurred a forfeiture, and seeks to avail himself of a defense granted to him by a subsequent law, to which he was not entitled at the time when the act, for which the penalty is given, was performed, he must take it subject to such terms and conditions as the legislature, at the time it passed the beneficial law, or at any future time, might please to prescribe. United States v. Hall, 2 Wash., 366.

§ 77. The penalty of not less than $100, provided in the fifth section of the act of August 29, 1842 (5 U. S. Stat. at Large, 544), for the offense of marking the word " patent " on unpatented articles, is a penalty of $100 and no more. Stimpson v. Pond, 2 Curt., 502.

§ 78. The words of a law imposing a forfeiture or penalty shall not be construed to embrace a case not within the parts of the law which prohibit the act done, or direct the performance of an act by the omission of which the penalty or forfeiture is incurred. United States v. Twenty-four Coils of Cordage, Bald., 502.

§ 79. A marshal of the United States who pays to his deputies and assistants, in taking the census, less than the funds, or their equivalent, which he may have received from the government for that purpose, is liable to a penalty of $500, under the act of March 3, 1839. United States v. Patterson, 3 McL., 53.

§ 80. The law which is in force at the time of the entry and presentment of the invoice is that which must control the proceedings and forfeiture in consequence thereof. Forfeitures,* 2 Op. Att'y Gen'l, 358.

§ 81. Where a lease of a wharf provided for a penalty "in case the right to collect wharf-age or rents should be defeated permanently through the instrumentality or with the aid of the mayor and council of the city," held, that the penalty was not incurred by a quarantine embargo laid with the consent of the lessee, nor by an ordinance of the city which he himself had caused to be passed because he thought it would be beneficial to him, although both resulted in his injury. Marshall v. Vicksburg, 15 Wall., 146.

§ 82. The fines mentioned in the second section of the act of March 3, 1801 (2 Stat. at L., 115), are such only as accrued by law, in whole or in part, to the government. United States v. Simms,* 1 Cr., 252.

II. Actions and Procedure.

SUMMARY — Where no form of action is provided, § 83.— Debt proper at common law, § 84.— Under steamboat act of 1852, §§ 85, 86.— Jurisdiction, § 87.— Qui tam actions; complaint; signing by district attorney; undertaking for damages, §§ 88, 89.

§ 83. When an act is declared to be unlawful by statute, and a penalty is prescribed, a person who violates the law may be proceeded against by indictment, or by an action of debt, if no mode of suing for the penalty is specially provided by the statute. United States v. Bougher, §§ 90-92.

§ 84. At common law, debt is the proper action to recover a pecuniary penalty imposed by statute. Ibid.

§ 85. The forty-first section of the steamboat act of 1852, declaring that "all penalties imposed by this act may be recovered in an action of debt by any person who will sue therefor," does not preclude the United States from suing for a penalty in an action of debt. Ibid.

§ 86. The right to sue under the provisions of the steamboat act of 1852, as an informer, being limited to a person, the United States cannot sue in that character. Ibid.

§ 87. The ninth section of the judiciary act of 1789, relating to the jurisdiction of the district court, establishes the right of the United States to sue in the district courts for penalties where the matter in dispute amounts to $100 exclusive of costs. Ibid.

§ 88. Actions to recover a forfeiture or penalty by an informer under sections 3490-3493, Revised Statutes United States, are qui tam actions, and the complaints need not be signed by the United States district attorney. Although the action is required to be brought in the name of the United States, and cannot be withdrawn or discontinued without the consent of the district attorney and the judge, it is still otherwise under the control of the informer. United States v. Griswold, §§ 93-96.

§ 89. In a qui tam action, brought by an informer to recover a forfeiture or penalty, the United States is so far the plaintiff that no undertaking to answer in damages for the arrest can be required by the defendant. Ibid.

[NOTES. — See §§ 97-155.]

UNITED STATES v. BOUGHER.

(District Court for Ohio: 6 McLean, 277–282. 1854.)

Opinion by LEAVITT, J.

STATEMENT OF FACTS.— This is an action of debt prosecuted in the name of the United States. The declaration avers, in substance, that the defendant, being the master of a steamboat used for the transportation of passengers on the Ohio and Mississippi rivers, employed a pilot to serve on his boat without being licensed for that purpose as required by law, and that thereby he has incurred a penalty of $100.

A demurrer has been filed to the declaration; and it is insisted in argument that the United States cannot maintain an action of debt for the penalty, and that it can only be recovered in a suit brought by an informer.

The tenth subdivision of the ninth section of the act of the 13th of August, 1852, to amend the act "to provide for the better security of the lives of passengers on board of vessels propelled in whole or in part by steam" (Pamphlet Laws U. S., 1 Session, 32 Congress, p. 61), declares that "it shall be unlawful for any person to employ, or any person to serve as, an engineer or pilot on any steamboat" used for the conveyance of passengers, who has not procured a license from the proper inspectors for that purpose; and it provides that any one violating this provision shall forfeit $100 for each offense. The forty-first section of the act just referred to provides that "all penalties imposed by this act may be recovered in an action of debt by any person who will sue therefor in any court of the United States." This is the only provision of the statute relating to the manner of enforcing the penalty for employing an unlicensed pilot or serving as an unlicensed engineer. It is true the first section of the act provides that the owner of a steamboat, for the offense of permitting a boat to be navigated, with passengers on board, without complying with the terms of the act, shall be subject to the penalties contained in the second section of the act of July, A. D. 1838. But it is very clear this provision cannot, on any just principle of interpretation, include or apply to the case set out in the declaration in this action. And it is equally clear that this action is not sustainable upon the eleventh section of the act of 1838, which enacts that penalties imposed by that act may be sued for and recovered, in the name of the United States, in the district or circuit court of the proper district. That provision is restricted in its terms to offenses created by the act of 1838, and cannot be held to extend to those created by the subsequent act, although in its title the latter statute purports to be an amendment of the former. It was doubtless competent for congress, in the act of 1852, to have declared that all penalties incurred under it should be prosecuted in accordance with the eleventh section of the act of 1838. But, having failed to do so, it would violate all settled rules for the construction of penal statutes to hold that the provisions of that section can be transferred to and made a part of the act of 1852. The first section of the latter act, adopting the provisions of the act of 1838, and prescribing the manner of prosecuting for violations of the act, must be restricted to the cases specified in that section. These, as before noticed, include only offenses by the *owner* of a steamboat, in fitting out and navigating the same, without complying with the requirements of the statute. Violations of the statute in the service or the employment of unlicensed pilots or engineers are not specified in the first section of the act of 1852. In reference to the manner of enforcing the penalty against the defendant for the offense set out in the declaration, the act of 1838 must be wholly excluded from the consideration of the court.

Having thus referred to the statutory enactments relating to this subject, the question raised on this demurrer is, whether the United States can sue in debt for the penalty which it is alleged the defendant has incurred, under the forty-first section of the act of 1852, before cited. The right to sue under this provision is limited to a person; and it is clear that the government, in its sovereign capacity, is not a *person* to whom this right attaches.

§ 90. *The provision of a statute authorizing an informer to sue for a penalty does not exclude the right of the government to proceed against the offender in an action of debt.*

It was strenuously insisted in the argument, that under the provisions of the statute referred to, if the United States could not maintain this action, as an informer, it could not be sustained on any other basis. In other words, that as the forty-first section of the act of 1852 provided that all penalties imposed by the act may be recovered in an action of debt by any person who will sue therefor, in any court of the United States, every other mode of enforcing a penalty under the act is prohibited. On the other hand, it was contended by the counsel for the government, that this is merely a cumulative provision, not intended to abridge or deny the right of the government to proceed in any other mode known to the law, and usually resorted to in practice, but to sanction a remedy deemed necessary to the efficient enforcement of the law, and one which could exist only by express legislative enactment. The latter view is the one adopted by this court, as best suited to carry into effect the intention of the law, and not in conflict with either the provisions of the statute or any just principles of construction. It is most obvious that the requirements of the statute in relation to steamboats would have been wholly inefficient if the enforcement of its penal provisions had been referred solely to the action or interposition of common informers. Such, clearly, was not the intention of congress in the provision referred to, giving an informer the right in all cases arising under the statute to prosecute for the penalties.

The words of the statute are merely permissive to an informer to sue, and do not import that that is the sole remedy for its violation. This is also inferable by a reference to the first section of the act of 1852, from which it will be seen, as to one class of offenses, the penalties provided and the mode of proceeding authorized in the eleventh section of the act of 1838 are expressly adopted.

The right of the United States to prosecute for violations of the act of 1852 is, therefore, in no way affected by the provision securing to an informer a right to sue for the penalties incurred under it. It is most obvious that it was not designed to restrict the manner of prosecuting for a penalty to one particular form of proceeding, but as authorizing a supplemental or additional remedy.

§ 91. *At common law an action of debt is the proper mode of enforcing a penalty by the government.*

In this view, the only remaining inquiry is, whether the United States can maintain the action of debt, for the penalty for the alleged offense, without an express statutory provision authorizing such mode of procedure. On this point no authorities were adduced in the argument, nor have I been able to recur to any bearing directly upon it. I suppose, however, that it is hardly a controvertible proposition, that upon the facts alleged in the declaration the defendant could have been prosecuted by indictment, although the statute does not authorize it in terms. The statute makes it an offense for any one to employ an engineer or pilot on a steamboat, or for any person to serve in such capacity, without a license, and subjects the party offending to a penalty of $100. It is silent as to the manner of prosecuting for penalties, except that the forty-first section confers upon an informer a right to sue in debt, in any case arising under the statute in which a penalty has been incurred. But if no one chooses to avail himself of this right by instituting a suit, the guilty person may be proceeded against by indictment. In all cases when an act is declared to be unlawful, and a punishment or penalty is annexed to the doing of the act, it pertains to the sovereignty of the state, through the agency of ·the judicial department, to punish it by indictment; and it does not require any express statutory authority as the warrant for such a proceeding. Is it not equally clear, upon the same principle, that if the government chooses to waive the right of proceeding in this way, and to adopt the milder form of an action of debt for the penalty, it is competent to do so? It is a long settled principle of the common law, that the action of debt is maintainable to recover a pecuniary penalty imposed by a statute, and when such a penalty is incurred by a violation of a statute of the United States, it accrues to the government, and may be sued for in its name; and it certainly can constitute no just ground of complaint on the part of the person implicated, that he is called upon to answer for the violation of a law, in a civil suit, instead of being arraigned for it, upon the finding of a grand jury.

§ 92. *Right of the United States to sue for a penalty given by the judiciary act of 1789, section 9.*

In addition to these views, it may be stated that the right of the United States to sue in this court, for the penalty alleged to have been incurred by the defendant, and the competency of the court to entertain the jurisdiction of the case, may be deduced from the clause in the ninth section of the judiciary act of 1789, relating to the jurisdiction of the district court; which declares that said court shall have cognizance of all suits at common law, where the United States sue, and the matter in dispute amounts, exclusive of costs, to the sum of $100. 1 vol. L. U. S., page 77. This case certainly meets all the conditions of this clause. It is a suit at common law, brought by the United States, and the matter in dispute amounts to $100. Demurrer overruled.

UNITED STATES *v.* GRISWOLD.

(District Court for Oregon: 5 Sawyer, 25–31. 1877.)

Opinion by DEADY, J.

STATEMENT OF FACTS.—This action was brought by B. F. Dowell, as well for himself as the United States, upon section 3490 of the Revised Statutes, to recover from the defendant the sum of $40,096.66 alleged to be due the United States; for that the said defendant caused to be made and presented for payment at the treasury of the United States false and fictitious claims, purporting to be claims for supplies furnished on account of the Oregon Indian war of 1854, to the amount of $19,048.83; and also used false vouchers, rolls, etc., and combined with another for the purpose of obtaining the payment of such claims, by means of which he received from the treasury of the United States the said sum of $19,048.83 in payment of the same. The complaint was verified by the oath of the informer, and signed by Messrs.

Gibbs and Stearns and B. F. Dowell, attorneys of this court, as "attorneys for the plaintiff," and was filed May 30, 1877.

On June 2, the district judge, upon the application of "Mr. Addison C. Gibbs, of counsel for the plaintiff," under section 3492 of the Revised Statutes, and upon said complaint so verified, made an order for the arrest of the defendant, and fixed his bail thereon at the sum of $10,000, to be given in the manner and with the effect provided in sections 108-9 of the Oregon Civil Code. Upon this order a writ of arrest was issued by the clerk, upon which the defendant, on June 4, was arrested and gave bail as therein provided. Afterwards the defendant moved to strike the complaint from the files, because it was not signed by the district attorney nor any one authorized to represent the United States, and for his discharge and the exoneration of his bail because there was no affidavit filed prior to the issuing of the writ, nor undertaking filed before the arrest was made.

§ 93. *Actions to recover a forfeiture or penalty by an informer, under sections 3490–3493, are qui tam actions, and the complaints need not be signed by the United States district attorney.*

By the Revised Statutes (sec. 5438), it is declared to be a crime punishable by fine and imprisonment to make or present for payment any false or fictitious claims against the United States, or, to that end, to make or use any false voucher, etc., or to combine with any person to obtain payment from the United States of any such claim. Section 3490 provides that if any person not in the military or naval forces of the United States shall do or commit any of the acts prohibited by section 5438, aforesaid, such person "shall forfeit and pay to the United States the sum of two thousand dollars," together with "double the amount of damages which the United States may have sustained by reason of the doing or committing such act," to be recovered in one action with the costs thereof. Section 3491 gives the district court within whose jurisdictional limits the person doing or committing such act shall be found, jurisdiction of such action; and provides that the same "may be brought and carried on by any person, as well for himself as the United States," . . . "at the sole cost and charge of such person, and shall be in the name of the United States, but shall not be withdrawn or discontinued without the consent, in writing, of the judge of the court and the district attorney, first filed in the case, setting forth their reasons for such consent." Section 3492 makes it the duty of the several district attorneys to be diligent to ascertain any violations of said section 3490 by persons found within their respective districts, "and to cause them to be proceeded against in due form of law for the recovery of such forfeiture and damages;" and provides that "such person may be arrested and held to bail in such sum as the district judge may order, not exceeding the sum of two thousand dollars, and twice the amount of the damages sworn to, in the affidavit of the person bringing the suit." Section 3493 provides that "The person bringing said suit and prosecuting it to final judgment shall be entitled to receive one-half the amount . . . he shall recover and collect; and the other half shall belong to and be paid over to the United States;" and such person shall "receive to his own use all the costs the court may award against the defendant," as in actions between private parties; but he "shall be liable for all costs incurred by himself in the case, and shall have no claim therefor on the United States."

These sections of the Revised Statutes are substantially taken from the act of March 2, 1863 (12 Stat., 696), entitled "An act to prevent and punish frauds upon the United States." The action — improperly called a "suit" — thereby authorized to be "brought and carried on by any person as well for himself as the United States," is the action called at common law *qui tam*, because the plaintiff therein described himself as one — *qui tam pro domino Rege quam pro se ipso in hac parte sequitur* — who as well for the king as for himself sues in this matter. When, as in this case, a statute imposed a penalty for the commission of an act, and also gave such penalty in part to whoever would sue for it, and the remainder to the king or other public use, the action to recover such penalty, if brought by a private person, was brought in his own name and subject to his control. Although a judgment obtained therein was for the benefit of the king or other public use as well as the plaintiff, yet the action was, to all intents and purposes, the private action of the latter. 3 Black., 160; 1 Bac. Ab., Ac., *q. t.*

The fact that this action is required to be brought in the name of the United States and that it cannot be withdrawn or discontinued without the consent of the district attorney and the judge, it is still otherwise under the control of the informer. It is still an action which by the express authority of the statute may "be brought and carried on" — commenced and conducted — "by any person, as well for himself as the United States." The power to commence and conduct this action necessarily implies the right to do so, and to employ attorneys for that purpose, irrespective of the district attorney. The statute has authorized Dowell to bring this action and conduct it at his own cost. Although the United States is the plaintiff, Dowell is its authorized representative, and not the district attorney, who is not authorized or required to act or interfere in the matter, otherwise than as expressly provided by the statute. For all purposes except the discontinuance of the action the attorney employed by the informer to commence and conduct the same is the attorney of the United States therein. Neither does the fact that the district attorney is required to be diligent to enforce the statute against persons violating it make him the attorney of the United States in this action. Although it is his duty "to be diligent in inquiring into any violations" of the statute and to bring actions therefor in the name and for the benefit of the United States, he may not, and therefore congress has provided this alternative, that every person who will may do the same thing, "as well for himself as the United States;" and whichever — the informer or the district attorney — first commences an action for a particular violation of the statute thereby excludes the other from so doing. 3 Black., 160.

Neither does the provision in section 771 of the Revised Statutes, which makes it the duty of the "district attorney to prosecute in his district . . . all civil actions in which the United States are concerned," authorize or require him to act as attorney for the plaintiff in this action. This section is general in its terms and necessarily qualified and restrained by the sections above cited which relate to the commencement and conduct of this particular action. For that matter the United States is concerned in all *qui tam* actions, whether brought in its own name or that of a private person, because it is entitled to a share of the penalty or forfeiture that may be recovered therein. But the rule of law is, and the practice always has been, that a *qui tam* action is the action of the party who brings it, and the sovereign, however much concerned in the result of it, has no right to interfere with the conduct of it except as specially provided by statute.

As has been shown, this is a *qui tam* action. The statute authorizing it imposes no restraint upon the power of the party bringing it, except that he shall bring it in the name of the United States, and shall not dismiss it without the consent of its district attorney and the judge. Subject to these qualifications, he may proceed as if the action was in name as well as in fact his own, which certainly implies the right to select and employ counsel to commence and conduct it.

§ 94. *The complaint in a qui tam action may be subscribed by the attorney of the informer who sues.*

The complaint being subscribed by attorneys of this court as attorneys for the plaintiff, the presumption is that they were employed by the person who brings this suit to conduct it. This being so, such attorneys are the attorneys of the plaintiff, and the complaint is duly subscribed by the attorney of the party plaintiff within the requirement of section 79 of the Oregon Civil Code, and is therefore not liable to be stricken out. When the statute authorized Dowell to bring and conduct this action in the name of the United States it necessarily authorized him to employ attorneys for that purpose, and thereupon the persons so employed became and are the attorneys of the United States for that purpose. The motion to discharge the defendant from the arrest, or, more properly, "to vacate the writ of arrest (see sec. 128, Or. Civ. Code), is based upon the assumption that by virtue of sections 914 and 915 — particularly the latter — the law of the state (sec. 107, Civ. Code) regulates and controls the allowance and issuing of a writ of arrest, and therefore the writ in this case was improperly issued, because there was no prior undertaking or affidavit as provided in said section 107.

§ 95. *If a complaint in a qui tam action is verified by the affidavit of the informer, plaintiff, the defendant may be arrested upon it.*

As to the affidavit, the complaint contains all the facts necessary to authorize an arrest, and it is verified by the oath of Dowell. Such a complaint is an affidavit, and may be used in the case whenever an affidavit as to such facts is required. In United States *v.* Walsh, 1 Deady, 293, which was an action upon a statute for a penalty, this court held: "Where the cause of action is sufficiently set forth in the complaint, and the cause of action and arrest are identical, there is no necessity for an additional or separate affidavit to authorize an arrest." Here the cause of action and arrest are identical, and the verified complaint, as to the facts stated therein, is an affidavit. Neff *v.* Pennoyer, 3 Saw., 292.

Before proceeding to consider the objection as to the undertaking, it is proper to state that section 915, *supra*, upon which counsel for the motion seems to rely, does not appear to apply to the case of an arrest. Briefly, it provides that plaintiffs in the United States courts shall be entitled to the remedies by "attachment or other process against the property of the defendant," allowed by the laws of the state for the courts thereof, such plaintiff first furnishing the preliminary affidavits or proofs and security required by such state laws. As will be seen, the operation of this section is confined to the remedy by attachment or other process — probably like process — only against the property of the defendant and not against his person.

§ 96. *In a qui tam action the United States is so far the plaintiff that no undertaking to answer in damages for the arrest can be required by the defendant.*

Section 914, *supra*, requires in effect that the mode of proceeding in this action "shall conform as near as may be" to the mode of proceeding in like cases in the state courts. This is a general direction, and only intended to secure uniformity in the practice in the national and state courts, in civil actions at law, as far as practicable. Indianapolis v. Horst, 93 U. S., 300. But when congress has specially prescribed the mode of proceeding it does not apply. Now, section 3492, having specially provided that the defendant in this action might be arrested, and held to bail by the district judge, without requiring the plaintiff, or any one for it, to give any undertaking or security for costs or damages, the most reasonable inference is that it was not intended that any should be given. Besides, it is a settled rule of construction, that the general words of a statute do not include the government or affect its rights, unless such purpose be clear and indisputable upon the face of the act. Jones v. United States, 1 N. & H., 383; United States v. Weise, 2 Wall. Jr., 72; Bright, Fed. Dig., 843. This was a well established rule of the common law, founded upon considerations of public policy, and, therefore, it was said, that an act of parliament did not bind the king, unless particularly named therein. 1 Black., 185. Under this rule, a statute of the state requiring a plaintiff to give an undertaking for costs and damages before procuring an arrest does not include the United States. The motions are denied.

§ 97. Jurisdiction of courts.— United States district courts have exclusive jurisdiction of forfeitures. Hall v. Warren, 2 McL., 332.

§ 98. The federal courts have exclusive cognizance of all seizures authorized by congress to be made on land or water for a breach of its laws, and may enforce by summary process the redelivery of the thing forfeited, in case the same has been taken by state authority out of the hands of a United States officer. Slocum v. Mayberry,* 2 Wheat., 1.

§ 99. The courts of the United States have an exclusive cognizance of questions of forfeiture upon all seizures made under the laws of the United States; and it is not competent for a state court to entertain or decide such questions of forfeiture. If a sentence of condemnation be definitely pronounced by the proper court of the United States, it is conclusive that a forfeiture is incurred; if a sentence of acquittal, it is equally conclusive against the forfeiture; and in either case the question cannot be again litigated in any common law forum. Gelston v. Hoyt, 3 Wheat., 246.

§ 100. —— state courts.— In suits for penalties incurred under the act of congress of August 2, 1813 (2 U. S. Stat. at Large, 611), giving a moiety to the United States and the other moiety to the collector or informer, the state courts have jurisdiction. Stearns v. United States, 2 Paine, 300.

§ 101. The act of congress of August 2, 1813 (2 U. S. Stat. at Large, 611), giving to the state courts jurisdiction in certain specified cases of penalties, incurred under the laws of the United States, must be considered pro tanto a repeal of the judiciary act of 1789, whereby exclusive original jurisdiction of the same was given to the United States district courts. Ibid.

§ 102. —— justice of the peace.— Fines, penalties and forfeitures, under by-laws of the corporation of Washington, D. C., not exceeding $50, are recoverable before a justice of the peace. Ex parte Reed, 4 Cr. C. C., 582.

§ 103. —— chancery.— A court of chancery is not the proper tribunal to enforce a forfeiture, the remedy being at law. Horsburg v. Baker, 1 Pet., 232.

§ 104. Nature of action.— Actions for penalties, being founded upon the implied contract which every person enters into with the state, to observe its laws, are civil actions both in form and substance. Stearns v. United States, 2 Paine, 300.

§ 105. When debt will lie.— The action of debt lies for a statutory penalty, because the sum demanded is certain, but though in form ex contractu it is founded in fact upon a tort. The necessity of establishing a joint liability in such cases does not therefore exist; it is sufficient if the liability of any of the defendants be shown; judgment may be entered against them and in favor of the others, whose complicity in the offense, for which the penalty is prescribed, is not proved, precisely as though the action were in form as well as in substance ex delicto. Chaffee & Co. v. United States, 18 Wall., 516.

§ 106. An action of debt to recover a penalty is a "civil cause" within the meaning of the ninth section of the judiciary act, from which a writ of error lies from the district court to the circuit court of the United States. Jacob v. United States, 1 Marsh., 520.

§ 107. A fine or a penalty incurred by the breach of a by-law of the corporation of Washington, D. C., is a debt and recoverable as such. *Ex parte* Reed, 4 Cr. C. C., 582.

§ 108. At common law, debt is a proper action to recover a pecuniary penalty imposed by statute. United States *v.* Bougher, 6 McL., 277.

§ 109. When a penalty is given by statute, and no remedy for its recovery is expressly provided, debt will lie. United States *v.* Willets, 5 Ben., 220.

§ 110. Where a statute gives a penalty, and no particular remedy is prescribed for enforcing it, an action of debt may be brought to recover it. The debt to the government arises when the penalty is incurred by the commission of the act prohibited by the statute. *In re* Rosey, 6 Ben., 507.

§ 111. **When qui tam action will lie.**—In an action for a penalty under the Virginia act of December 21, 1792, "regulating the inspection of flour and bread," it is not necessary that the United States should be nominally a plaintiff, as it may be recovered in an action *qui tam.* Cloud *v.* Hewitt,* 3 Cr. C. C., 199.

§ 112. A *qui tam* action will not lie for the penalty of the by-law of March 30, 1813, of the corporation of Washington, D. C. Washington *v.* Eaton, 4 Cr. C. C., 852.

§ 113. The eighth section of the act of February 28, 1799, in relation to prosecutions upon a penal statute, by an informer, contemplates an action in the name of the informer, as well as in the name of the United States, to the use, in whole or in part, of an informer. The Steamboat Planter, Newb., 262.

§ 114. **By information.**—When a statute creates a new offense and affixes a specific pecuniary penalty, appropriating one-half thereof to the informer, it adopts by necessary implication those remedies which appropriately belong to the common informer, and by which alone he can prosecute for the same. And, although there be no informer, and the government is entitled to judgment for the whole, the action must be brought by information as though there were an informer, and not by indictment. United States *v.* Tilden,* 21 Law Rep., 598.

§ 115. **By indictment or suit at law.**—In proceedings by libel against a steamboat to recover a penalty incurred under the act of congress of the 7th July, 1838, the corporation owning the boat appeared as claimants, and the decree was rendered that the owners of the steamboat forfeit and pay to the United States the sum of $500; and that the boat be sold, etc. *Held,* upon appeal, that the penalty of $500 could not be recovered from the owners in an admiralty proceeding by libel; that the mode of proceeding to recover the penalty from them was by suit or indictment, proceeded in according to the forms of the common law, as this was the mode of proceeding provided for in the eleventh section of the above act. Virginia & Maryland Steam Navigation Co. *v.* United States, Taney, 418.

§ 116. When an act is declared to be unlawful by statute, and a penalty is prescribed, a person who violates the law may be proceeded against by indictment, or by an action of debt, if no mode of suing for the penalty is specially provided by the statute. United States *v.* Bougher, 6 McL., 277.

§ 117. If a statute prescribes a particular mode of enforcing payment of a penalty it must be pursued, and indictment will not lie. United States *v.* Ellis, 1 Cr. C. C., 125.

§ 118. An indictment will not lie, under the Virginia act, for suffering gaming in the defendant's house, because the act has given an action of debt to the informer. United States *v.* Gadsby, 1 Cr. C. C., 55.

§ 119. **Forfeiture of lands and franchises by legislative action.**—A forfeiture of an interest in lands and connected franchises, granted for the construction of a public work, may be declared by the state for non-compliance with the conditions annexed to their grant or to their possession, when the forfeiture is provided by statute, without judicial proceedings to ascertain and determine the failure of the grantee to perform the conditions. Where land and franchises are thus held, any public assertion by legislative act of the ownership of the state, after default of the grantee, such as an act resuming control of them, and appropriating them to particular uses, or granting them to others to carry out the original object, will be equally effectual and operative. Farnsworth *v.* Minnesota & Pacific Railroad Co., 2 Otto, 49.

§ 120. **Abatement of action.**—At common law an action for a penalty abates on the death of the defendant. Jones *v.* Van Zandt, 4 McL., 604.

§ 121. **Trial by jury.**—In all cases of seizures which are not of admiralty cognizance, the claimants of the property seized as forfeited are entitled to trial by jury; and a provision in an act of congress that "the proceedings to enforce said forfeiture of said property shall be in the nature of a proceeding *in rem* in the circuit or district courts of the United States for the district where such forfeiture is made," cannot take away the constitutional right of claimants to trial by jury. United States *v.* 130 Barrels of Whisky, 1 Bond, 587.

§ 122. **Pleading, practice and procedure.**— In an action of debt on a penal statute the existence of the statute on which based must be made in the declaration by direct allegation as matter of fact. The mere assertion of a conclusion of law, as that by force of a statute an action has accrued, is insufficient. United States v. Batchelder,* 9 Int. Rev. Rec., 97.

§ 123. An objection to the want of a seizure prior to the allowance of the libel is not properly a plea to the jurisdiction of the court, and is not waived by filing a claim. The Schooner Silver Spring, 1 Spr., 551; 17 Law Rep., 264.

§ 124. The institution of penal suits on behalf of the government by stipulation or compromise is an objectionable practice, and not looked upon with favor by the courts. United States v. Brig Henry, 4 Blatch., 359.

§ 125. In an action for the penalty for altering the inspector's marks on barrels of flour, it is necessary to set out the marks and how altered. Cloud v. Hewitt,* 3 Cr. C. C., 199.

§ 126. The rule relieving a defendant from the necessity of answering any allegation or interrogatory contained in the libel, which will expose him to any prosecution or punishment for crime, or for any penalty or any forfeiture of his property for any penal offense, extends to corporations as well as to individuals. Pollock v. Steamboat Laura, 5 Fed. R., 133.

§ 127. In an action under the statute of February 12, 1793, containing separate counts for harboring slaves and obstructing claimants, several penalties cannot be recovered for the same act, whatever may be the number of persons affected by the course of the defendent, nor can the same act be separated into distinct charges. Driskell v. Parish,* 10 Law Rep., 395.

. § 128. A libel for a statute forfeiture should substantially agree with the terms of the statute; otherwise it is bad. The Schooner Betsy, 1 Mason, 354.

§ 129. A warrant to recover the penalty of a by-law must name the plaintiffs by their corporate name, and must describe the offense with reasonable certainty. Barney v. Washington City, 1 Cr. C. C., 248.

§ 130. In an action for penalties given by statute the complainant must not only state the acts of omission or commission by which they are claimed, but that they were omitted or done contrary to the form of the statute in such cases made and provided. Briscol v. Hinman,* 10 Int. Rev. Rec., 53.

§ 131. If a declaration for a statute penalty conclude "against the form of the statutes," when it is founded on a single statute, it is good on error. Kenrick v. United States, 1 Gall., 268.

§ 132. In an action or information to recover a fine or penalty under a statute, it is sufficient if the conclusion is contrary to the act of congress in such cases made and provided. United States v. Babson, 1 Ware, 450.

§ 133. In debt for the double value under section 3 of the embargo act, January 9, 1808, it is not necessary to allege the particular articles which composed the cargo; nor that the owner was knowingly concerned in the illegal voyage. Cross v. United States, 1 Gall., 26.

§ 134. An information for a statute forfeiture should conclude against the form of the statute, or at least refer to some subsisting statute authorizing the forfeiture. A mere conclusion of an information against the form of a statute will not cure the defect of material averments to show that a forfeiture has accrued. The Sloop Nancy, 1 Gall., 67.

§ 135. If two penal offenses be described in one count, and one penalty only sought, after verdict the declaration will be supported. Smith v. United States, 1 Gall., 261.

§ 136. In debt for the penalty of double value, under the embargo act of January 9, 1808, it need not be averred in the declaration that the vessel and cargo had not been and could not be seized for the offense. *Ibid.*

§ 137. In debt for a penalty brought in the name of "the United States of America," if the verdict find that the party is indebted "to the United States," without saying "of America," it is sufficient. *Ibid.*

§ 138. If a declaration on a penal statute do not conclude against the form of the statute, it is a fatal omission on error. Alleging "whereby, and by force of such act," the defendant had forfeited, etc., is not sufficient. Sears v. United States, 1 Gall., 257.

§ 139. *It seems* that a declaration on a penal statute need not specify the uses to which the forfeiture inures; and if it allege it to be "to the uses expressed in said statute," where several statutes have been before mentioned, and no one of them is the statute which expresses such uses, it is not fatal on error. *Ibid.*

§ 140. A conclusion of a declaration of debt for a penalty under a statute, "against the law in such case made and provided," is not a conclusion against the form of the statute, and is bad on error. Smith v. United States, 1 Gall., 261.

§ 141. —— **parties.**— Under section 4610, Revised Statutes United States, which provides that "all penalties and forfeitures imposed by this title, for the recovery whereof no specified mode is hereinbefore provided, may be recovered, with costs, in any circuit court of the United States, at the suit of any district attorney of the United States or any person by information to any district attorney," etc., *held*, that a civil suit for the penalties imposed by section 4609, Revised Statutes United States, was properly brought in the name of the United States.   United States *v.* Kellum, 19 Blatch., 872.

§ 142. An action for a forfeiture or penalty must be brought in the name of the government, and not of a private person, unless some other mode is expressly provided by statute. Matthews *v.* Offley, 8 Sumn., 115.

§ 143. The forty-first section of the steamboat act of 1852, declaring that "all penalties imposed by this act may be recovered in an action of debt by any person who will sue therefor," does not preclude the United States from suing for a penalty in an action of debt.   United States *v.* Bougher, 6 McL., 277.

§ 144. The acts of congress of the 27th of February, 1801 (2 Stat. at L., 108), and 3d of March, 1801 (2 Stat. at L., 115), did not enable the United States to sue in its own name to recover a penalty for an offense committed in that part of the District of Columbia ceded by Virginia, which by the law of Virginia went to the informer.   United States *v.* Simms,* 1 Cr., 252.

§ 145. The penalty imposed by section 11 of the copyright act of February 8, 1831 (4 U. S. Stats. at Large, 438), for putting the imprint of a copyright upon a work not legally copyrighted, and given by the act to "the person who shall sue for the same," cannot be recovered in the name of more than one person.   Ferrett *v.* Atwill, 1 Blatch., 151; 4 N. Y. Leg. Obs., 215.

§ 146. —— burden of proof — Evidence.— Where the *onus probandi* is thrown on the claimant, in an instance or revenue cause, by a *prima facie* case made out on the part of the prosecutor, and the claimant fails to explain the difficulties of the case, by the production of papers and other evidence, which must be in his possession or under his control, condemnation follows from the defects of testimony on the part of the claimant.   The Luminary, 8 Wheat., 407.

§ 147. In proceedings under a penal statute the right to a decree of forfeiture must be made out *strictissimi juris.* · No presumptions or conclusions are allowable, unfavorable to the claimants, unless based on clear and indisputable facts, and sustained and demanded by the positive and explicit requirements of the law.   United States *v.* Steamboat Henry C. Homeyer, 2 Bond, 217.

§ 148. One who asserts that another has forfeited a legal right secured to him in due form of law, for the purpose of defeating his enjoyment of that right, must make out the point clearly and satisfactorily, because the law does not favor an abandonment, and throws upon the party who seeks to obtain the benefit of a forfeiture the burden of proving it beyond all reasonable question.   McCormick *v.* Seymour, 2 Blatch., 240.

§ 149. In suits for penalties or forfeitures, where a *prima facie* case is made out by the government, the burden of explanation is thrown upon the claimant.   The Governor Cushman, 1 Biss., 490.

§ 150. A party who offers an excuse for violating a penal statute must make out the *vis major* under which he shelters himself, so as to leave no reasonable doubt of his innocence. The Brig Struggle, 9 Cr., 71.

§ 151. The fourth section of the act of 1820, referring to the act of 1818, and that referring again to the revenue acts of the United States, as to the mode of suing for and recovering penalties and forfeitures, does not, by implication, adopt the seventy-first section of the collection act of 1799, as to the *onus probandi* being thrown on the claimant on seizures under the act.   The Schooner Abigail, 3 Mason, 331.

§ 152. No individual should be punished for a violation of law which inflicts a forfeiture of property, unless the offense shall be established beyond a reasonable doubt.   This is a rule which governs a jury in all criminal prosecutions, and the rule is no less proper for the government of the court when exercising a maritime jurisdiction.   United States *v.* The Brig Burdett, 9 Pet., 682.

§ 153. On an information for forfeiture of goods, subject to *ad valorem* duty, the appraisement of the public appraisers is a necessary and preparatory proceeding, and is *prima facie* evidence.   United States *v.* Fourteen Packages of Pins, Gilp., 235.

§ 154. An inft rmer who receives one-half the penalty on conviction is, notwithstanding, a competent witness.   United States *v.* Patterson, 8 McL., 299.

§ 155. An officer of the customs who has assisted in the seizure of goods for violation of the revenue laws is a competent witness on a suit for the forfeiture of such goods.   United States *v.* Twenty-five Cases of Cloths, Crabbe, 356.

III. Seizure.

[See MARITIME LAW; REVENUE.]

§ 156. Validity of — What constitutes.— A seizure to be valid must be open, visible, continuous and persisted in until the property seized is transferred to the custody of the law. A superior physical force is not necessary to be employed if there is a voluntary acquiescence in the seizure and dispossession; but the parties must understand that they are dispossessed and no longer at liberty to exercise dominion on board the ship. The Josefa Segunda,* 10 Wheat., 312.

§ 157. A seizure to be effectual must be followed by subsequent prosecution or proceedings. A seizure voluntarily abandoned loses all its validity·and becomes a complete nullity. Ibid.

§ 158. By seizure, in the ninth section of the act of congress of 1799 (1 Stat. at Large, 76), is meant any taking possession of the thing forfeited by virtue of a warrant or other legal authority, for the purpose of enabling the proper court to inquire into, and to adjudicate upon, the cause of forfeiture. The Washington,* 7 Law Rep. (N. S.), 497.

§ 159. Before property can be condemned upon a forfeiture, in rem, there must be a seizure; and this seizure must be alleged. Evidence of communications between the collector of the port, the secretary of the treasury and the district attorney, and the filing of the libel by the district attorney, in conformity with the instructions of the collector, in connection with the fact that the vessel was, at the time, in the collection district, and that this was known to the collector, does not constitute a sufficient seizure. The Schooner Silver Spring, 1 Spr., 551; 17 Law Rep., 264.

§ 160. —— single act, not continuous.—A seizure to enforce a forfeiture is a single act and not continuous. Hence, where a state statute provided for the giving of information, as to the seizure of a boat or vessel unlawfully used in dragging clams, "to two justices of the peace of the county where such seizure shall have been made, held, that the literal seizure of the vessel having taken place in a certain county, only the justices of that county could take jurisdiction of the case, and that the conveyance of the vessel, by the persons making the seizure, into another county, where the same was brought to land, did not continue the seizure into such county, so as to give the justices thereof jurisdiction of the case under the statute. Thompson v. Whitman, 18 Wall., 457.

§ 161. —— how determined.— The question whether the seizure of a vessel as forfeited to the United States is rightful or tortious belongs exclusively to the federal courts, and can only be determined by the final decree of such courts in all cases where some law authorizes a seizure of the subject. In the absence of any such law the rule would not apply. Slocum v. Mayberry,* 2 Wheat., 1.

§ 162. Who may make.— Under the act of March 2, 1807 (2 Stat. at L., 428), providing for the forfeiture of vessels or cargoes seized for being engaged in the slave trade, the seizure may be made by any person, but the forfeiture is by the terms of the act for the use of the United States, and the officer or person making the seizure is entitled to no share therein. The Josefa Segunda,* 10 Wheat., 312.

§ 163. At common law any person may, at his peril, seize for a forfeiture to the government, and if the government adopt his seizure, and the property is condemned, he is justified. By the act of February 18, 1793, officers of the revenue are authorized to make seizures of any ship or goods for any breach of the laws of the United States. Gelston v. Hoyt, 3 Wheat., 246.

§ 164. Any citizen may seize any property forfeited to the use of the government, either by the municipal law or as a prize of war, in order to enforce the forfeiture; and it depends upon the government whether it will act upon the seizure; if it proceeds to enforce the forfeiture by legal process, this is sufficient confirmation of the seizure. The Caledoniana, 4 Wheat., 100.

§ 165. Where and how must be made ·to give jurisdiction.— To authorize any district court of the United States to adjudicate upon a cause of forfeiture of a ship, such ship must be taken possession of, or seized by the process of the court; and to give such court jurisdiction ,to adjudicate upon the cause of forfeiture, the first seizure or taking possession, by some one having legal authority, must be made within the limits of the district in which the court is established, unless the first seizure is made upon the high seas, in which case the ship must be brought within such limits. The Washington,* 7 Law Rep. (N. S.), 497.

§ 166. A seizure by the marshal, upon a warrant issued by the court, is sufficient, under the ninth section ·of the act of congress of 1799 (1 Stat. at Large, 76), to enable the court to adjudicate upon a cause of forfeiture, unless there has been a prior legal seizure in some other district, or a seizure on the high seas, and the property brought into some other district. A seizure by a custom-house officer is not an essential prerequisite to give the court authority judicially to inquire into the cause of forfeiture. *Ibid.*

§ 167. **Refusal of seizing officer to ascertain the forfeiture — Remedy of claimant.**— If the seizing officer should refuse to institute proceedings to ascertain the forfeiture of the vessel seized, the district court may, upon the application of the aggrieved party, compel the officer to proceed to adjudication, or to abandon the seizure. And if the seizure be finally adjudged wrongful, and without reasonable cause, he may proceed, at his election, by a suit at common law, or in the admiralty, for damages for the illegal act. Slocum *v.* Mayberry,* 2 Wheat., 1.

§ 168. **Property seized and bonded can only be seized for subsequent acts.**— Where property is seized as forfeited to the government, and is bonded and returned to the claimants, the lien of the government thereon is gone, and it is entirely free from liability to further seizure for the causes assigned for the forfeiture; but, like any other property, it may be forfeited if subsequent cause therefor arise, and such forfeiture would be solely by reason of such subsequent cause, and would in no manner affect the claim of the government in the proceeding in which it was bonded. United States *v.* Eighteen Barrels of High Wines, 8 Blatch., 475.

§ 169. **Liability of party making seizure — Justification.**— A plea alleging a seizure for a forfeiture as a justification should not only state the facts relied on to establish the forfeiture, but aver that thereby the property became and was actually forfeited, and was seized as forfeited. Gelston *v.* Hoyt, 3 Wheat., 246.

§ 170. If a suit be brought against the seizing officer for a supposed trespass while the suit for the forfeiture is depending, the fact of such pendency may be pleaded in abatement or a temporary bar of the action. If after a decree of condemnation, then that fact may be pleaded as a bar; if after an acquittal, with a certificate of a reasonable cause of seizure, then that may be pleaded as a bar. If after an acquittal, without such certificate, then the officer is without any justification for the seizure, and it is definitely settled to be a tortious act. If to an action of trespass in a state court for a seizure, the seizing officer plead the fact of forfeiture in his defense without averring a *lis pendens*, or a condemnation, or an acquittal, with a certificate of reasonable cause of seizure, the plea is bad; for it attempts to put in issue the question of forfeiture in a state court. *Ibid.*

§ 171. Property was seized by a collector of internal revenue for an alleged violation of the internal revenue laws, and was libeled for forfeiture in the United States district court, the cause tried, verdict given for the claimant, and certificate of probable cause granted. Upon suit brought by the claimant against the collector to recover the value of the property so seized and never returned to him, *held*, that a certificate of probable cause is no defense in such an action unless the collector shall have forthwith returned the seized goods to the claimant. Smith *v.* Averill,* 10 Int. Rev. Rec., 139.

§ 172. A plea justifying a seizure and detention by virtue of the seventh section of the act of 1794, under the express instructions of the president, must aver that the naval or military force of that government was employed for that purpose, and that the seizor belonged to the force so employed. The seventh section of the act was not intended to apply except to cases where a seizure or detention could not be enforced by the ordinary power, and there was a necessity, in the opinion of the president, to employ naval or military power for this purpose. Gelston *v.* Hoyt, 3 Wheat., 246.

§ 173. Where a seizure is made for a supposed forfeiture, under a law of the United States, no action of trespass lies in any common law tribunal until a final decree is pronounced upon the proceeding *in rem* to enforce such forfeiture; for it depends upon the final decree of the court proceeding *in rem* whether such seizure is to be deemed rightful or tortious, and the action, if brought before such decree is made, is brought too soon. *Ibid.*

§ 174. **Certificate of probable cause, when given.**— The seizure of a vessel, which, under a cod-fishing license, had incidentally caught mackerel, is a municipal seizure expressly provided for by acts of congress as justifiable, if a certificate of probable cause is given; and a certificate of probable cause will be given, if the officer making the seizure acts in good faith, and has reasonable grounds to suppose that the law has been violated. United States *v.* Schooner Reindeer,* 14 Law Rep., 285.

§ 175. Constructive seizure, evidenced by stipulation of counsel, is sufficient to authorize an order for a certificate of probable cause of seizure under the eighty-ninth section of the act of congress of March 2, 1799 (1 U. S. Stat. at Large, 696). United States *v.* Brig Henry, 4 Blatch., 359.

IV. DISTRIBUTION OF PROCEEDS.

SUMMARY — *In general*, § 176. — *Acts of 1799 and 1846*, § 177. — *Disputes as to shares, where decided*, § 178.

§ 176. The proper practice, under the act of March 2, 1867 (14 Stat. at L., 546), is for the court to cause the money in court for fines, penalties or forfeitures, to be paid to the collector, to be by him, after proper deductions have been made, paid into the treasury and distributed under the directions of the secretary of the treasury to the persons and in the proportions prescribed by the court. United States v. George, §§ 179–181.

§ 177. The act of August 6, 1846, contains no provisions giving, to any person, any share of any forfeiture for the violation of that act, and no provision respecting the disposition of the proceeds of such forfeiture. The provisions of the act of 1799 refer solely to forfeitures for a breach of the act itself, but the act of March 2, 1867, applies to the proceeds of all forfeitures incurred under the provisions of any laws relating to the customs, and hence applies to and controls the disposition of forfeitures under the act of 1846. *Ibid.*

§ 178. The court having custody of a fund derived from forfeitures or penalties is the proper forum to entertain and decide disputes as to shares in the fund, and to direct how it shall be distributed, and to what persons, under the act of 1867, under the directions of the secretary of the treasury as a ministerial officer. *Ibid.*

[NOTES. — See §§ 182–194.]

UNITED STATES v. GEORGE.

(Circuit Court for New York: 6 Blatchford, 87–47. 1868.)

STATEMENT OF FACTS. — A judgment had been rendered against George for a large sum of money for penalties incurred by a violation of laws governing duties on imports. A claim was made for a share by a person professing to be the informer through whom the forfeiture had been secured.

Opinion by BLATCHFORD, J.

The first section of the act of March 2, 1867 (14 U. S. Stat. at Large, 546), provides that, "from the proceeds of fines, penalties and forfeitures, incurred under the provisions of the laws relating to the customs, there shall be deducted such charges and expenses as are, by law, in each case, authorized to be deducted, and, in addition, in case of the forfeiture of important merchandise of a greater value than $500, on which duties have not been paid, or, in case of a release thereof, upon payment of its appraised value, or of any fine or composition in money, there shall also be deducted an amount equivalent to the duties in coin upon such merchandise (including the additional duties, if any), which shall be credited in the accounts of the collector, as duties received, and the residue of the proceeds aforesaid shall be paid into the treasury of the United States, and distributed under the direction of the secretary of the treasury, in the manner following, to wit: one-half to the United States; one-fourth to the person giving the information which has led to the seizure, or to the recovery of the fine or penalty, and, if there be no informer other than the collector, naval officer or surveyor, then to the officer making the seizure; and the remaining one-fourth to be equally divided between the collector, naval officer and surveyor, or such of them as are appointed for the district in which the seizure has been made, or the fine or penalty incurred, or, if there be only a collector, then to such collector." The section then provides for a different distribution where the information is given by the officer of a revenue cutter. The fourth section of the act repeals specially two sections of two former acts, relating to matters not involving any question arising in this case, and also repeals "all other laws, or parts of laws, inconsistent with, or supplied by, the provisions of this act," and then provides that "the secretary of the treasury shall prescribe all needful regulations to carry out and enforce the provisions of this act."

§ 179. *Terms and construction of the act of congress of March 2, 1799, relative to fines, forfeitures, etc., and of other acts on the same subject.*

These provisions of the act of 1867 are, to some extent, a substitute for provisions contained in the eighty-ninth, ninetieth and ninety-first sections of the act of March 2, 1799 (1 U. S. Stat. at Large, 695–697). The eighty-ninth section authorizes the collector, within whose district a seizure is made, or a forfeiture is incurred, for any breach of that act, to receive from the court in which a trial is had of any issue of fact, in any suit founded on any such breach, the sum recovered, after deducting all proper charges, to be allowed by the court, and requires him, on receipt thereof, to pay and distribute the same, without delay, according to law. The ninetieth section requires that the proceeds of sales of property condemned by virtue of the act, and not previously bonded, shall, after deducting all proper charges allowed by the court, be paid by it to the collector of the district in which the seizure or forfeiture took place, as directed in the eighty-ninth section. The ninety-first section provides that all fines, penalties and forfeitures recovered by virtue of the act (and not otherwise appropriated), "shall, after deducting all proper costs and charges, be disposed of as follows: one moiety shall be for the use of the United States, and be paid into the treasury thereof, by the collector receiving the same; the other moiety shall be divided between, and paid in equal proportions to, the collector, and naval officer of the district, and surveyor of the port, wherein the same shall have been incurred, or to such of the said officers as there may be in the said district; and, in districts where only one of the said officers shall have been established, the said moiety shall be given to such officer; provided, nevertheless, that, in all cases where such penalties, fines and forfeitures shall be recovered in pursuance of information given to such collector by any person other than the naval officer or surveyor of the district, the one-half of such moiety shall be given to such informer, and the remainder thereof shall be disposed of between the collector, naval officer, and surveyor, or surveyors, in manner aforesaid." The section then provides for a different distribution where any fines, forfeitures or penalties incurred by virtue of the act are recovered in consequence of any information given by any officer of a revenue cutter. By the seventh section of the act of May 28, 1830 (4 U. S. Stat. at Large, 411), it is provided that all forfeitures incurred under that act shall be distributed according to the provisions of the act of March 2, 1799. The first section of the act of March 3, 1863 (12 U. S. Stat. at Large, 738), provides that property forfeited under that section, or its value, shall be disposed of as other forfeitures for violations of the revenue laws. The act of 1846, which is the only act claimed to have been violated in the present case, contains no provision giving any share to any person of any forfeiture for a violation of that act, and no provision respecting the disposition of the proceeds of such forfeiture. I have been unable to find any provision by statute respecting the disposition of the proceeds of a forfeiture under the act of 1846, or respecting shares in the same, except the provision in the act of 1867. The provisions of the act of 1799 refer solely to forfeitures for a breach of that act itself. The act of 1867, however, applies to the proceeds of all forfeitures incurred under the provisions of any laws relating to the customs. The act of 1846 is a law relating to the customs.

On comparing the provisions of the act of 1799 with those of the act of 1867, in the particulars above recited, the following results appear: In respect to the channel of distribution by the former act, the court is to pay the net amount remaining, after the deduction of proper charges, to the collector of the district, and he is to "pay and distribute the same without delay according to law;" by the latter act it is not provided to whom the court shall pay the net amount, but it is provided that the net amount shall "be paid into the treasury of the United States, and distributed under the direction of the secretary of the treasury," in the proportions and to the persons designated by the act, the act not stating by whom it shall be paid into the treasury. The secretary of the treasury is required by the latter act to distribute the amount according to law quite as much as the collector is required by the former act to distribute the amount according to law. The amount is required by the former act to be distributed under the direction of the collector quite as much as it is required by the latter act to be distributed under the direction of the secretary of the treasury. The provision in the latter act, that the secretary of the treasury shall prescribe all needful regulations to carry out and enforce the provisions of the act (the second and third sections of which relate to the seizure of books and papers in cases of fraud on the revenue, and to the enforcement of liens for freight on imported merchandise in the custody of officers of the customs), gives to the secretary no greater power, in respect to prescribing regulations in reference to the distribution of the proceeds of forfeitures, than the collector had in the same respect, under the former act, in subordination to his superior officers, or than the secretary himself had under that act. The fourth section of the act of 1867 only repeals laws and parts of laws that are inconsistent with, or supplied by, the provisions of the act of 1867. In respect to forfeitures for breaches of the act of 1799, the provision of that act which requires the payment by the court to the collector of the net proceeds of such forfeitures, is not inconsistent with, or supplied by, any provision of the act of 1867. In respect to such net proceeds, the proper construction of the act of 1867 is, that the court is still to pay to the collector, under the eighty-ninth and ninetieth sections of the act of 1799, the amount recovered, after deducting all proper charges allowed by the court. The collector is then to deduct, in proper cases, the amount representing duties named in the act of 1867, and any other lawful charges, and is to pay the residue into the treasury of the United States. There is nothing in the act of 1867 which takes away the right given to the collector by the act of 1799 to receive from the court the proceeds of forfeitures for breaches of that act. So, also, with regard to forfeitures under the acts of 1830 and 1863, and under any other acts which adopt the mode of disposition of forfeitures prescribed by the act of 1799.

In regard to the duties mentioned in the act of 1867, the collector is the proper person, and the only proper person, to ascertain the proper amount representing the duties, and it is impossible that that amount can be, as the act of 1867 requires, "credited in the accounts of the collector, as duties received," unless the collector receives the amount, so as to credit the United States with it in his accounts, as duties received. I think that the act of 1867 intends that the collector shall receive from the court the whole amount, and not merely an amount equal to the duties. The act evidently recognizes the then existing practice, and assumes that the collector will receive from the court the proceeds, less the lawful charges and expenses which the court may allow to be deducted from the proceeds while in court, and, in substance, provides that he shall ascertain the duties, if any, and retain them, and then, instead of distributing the balance himself, shall pay it into the treasury of the United States. And there is no reason for any different mode of procedure in the case of a forfeiture for a violation of the warehousing act of 1846, nor is there anything in the act of 1867 to indicate that the collector is not to receive the proceeds of such a forfeiture. There may be duties to be ascertained and retained by the collector in cases under the act of 1846, quite as much as in cases under the act of 1799, or under any other customs act. The effect of the change made by the act of 1867, in regard to the channel of distribution, is merely to substitute the treasury of the United States for the coffers of the collector as a place of deposit for the money, when nothing is left to be done in regard to it but to distribute it, and to substitute the secretary of the treasury for the collector as the ministerial agent of distribution. In regard to the distributees, both acts give the same quantum, one-half, to the United States; the act of 1799 divides the other half equally among the collector, the naval officer and the surveyor, except that, where some person other than the naval officer or the surveyor is informer to the collector, such informer receives a moiety of such other half, and the other moiety thereof is divided equally among the collector, the naval officer and the surveyor; the act of 1867 gives one-fourth of the whole to the informer, and, if there be no informer other than the collector, the naval officer or the surveyor, then to the officer making the seizure, and directs that the remaining one-fourth shall be equally divided among the collector, the naval officer and the surveyor. Where an officer of a revenue cutter is the informer, the distributees and their shares are the same under the two acts.

Such being the state of the law on this subject, and the money before named being in court, in this case, D. Henry Burtnett presents a petition to this court, setting forth that he is the person who gave the information which led to the recovery in this case; that he claims an interest, as informer, in said money; that five other persons, named Davis, Webster, Wiggin, Giles and Hefflin, also claim to have given information of the character aforesaid, and claim to be informers herein; and that the petitioner has served notice of his claim as such informer on the collector and on the United States attorney. The prayer of the petition is that the court will refer it to a commissioner of the court, to take proof of the facts and of the respective claims and rights of the several persons claiming to be the informers herein, as such claimants, and report the same to this court, with his opinion thereon, as to who is or are the informer or informers herein. Notice of the presentation of the petition has been served on the United States attorney, and on the collector, and on the other persons named as claiming to be informers. It is contended on the part of the petitioner that the court has jurisdiction to determine the question as to who is or are the person or persons entitled, as informer or informers, to share in the money. The attorney for the United States denies the jurisdiction of the court and contends that, under the act of 1867, the secretary of the treasury has the exclusive power to determine who is the informer. On the part of the petitioner it is urged that, independently of the act of 1867, the court has inherent jurisdiction to determine all claims to moneys which are in court, and that such jurisdiction is not taken away by the act of 1867; that, under the act of 1799, and kindred acts, it has always been held by the courts of the United States that they have jurisdiction to examine and decide contested claims to the proceeds of forfeitures under the act, while such proceeds are still in court, and to direct in what manner they shall be distributed; that, it having been so held in respect to the act of 1799, there is nothing in the act of 1867 taking away or affecting such jurisdiction; that the act of 1867 confers no authority on the secretary of the treasury to determine or adjudicate who the informer is in case of a dispute; that, in such a case, a resort must be had to a proper judicial tribunal; that the secretary of the treasury has no judicial functions; and that the act of 1867 merely makes him, instead of the collector, the ministerial officer for paying over the money to such persons as the proper judicial tribunal declares are entitled to it under that act.

§ 180. *The proper practice under the act of 1867 is for the court to cause the money in court for fines, penalties or forfeitures to be paid to the collector, to be by him, after proper deductions have been made, paid into the treasury and distributed under the directions of the secretary of the treasury to the persons and in the proportions prescribed by the court.*

A similar question came before the circuit court of the United States for the district of New Jersey, in 1824, in the case of Westcot *v.* Bradford, 4 Wash., 492. In that case there was a forfeiture decreed by the district court for New Jersey of certain property for violations of the act of 1799. While the proceeds of the forfeiture were in that court, Bradford presented to it a petition setting forth that the condemnation took place in pursuance of information given by him to the collector, and praying for the payment to him of the informer's share,— one-quarter,— given by the ninety-first section of the act. The district court made a decree establishing the claim of Bradford as informer, and directing that the money in court be paid to the then collector, to be disposed of by him as directed by the decree. The decree disposed, finally, of the whole fund remaining in court, as concerned all the parties interested in it,— the United States, the collector who made the seizure and the informer,— leaving nothing to be done but to execute the decree. The collector appealed to the circuit court from the decree. The circuit court held that the petition of Bradford was an original suit from the decree in which an appeal would lie. An objection was taken in the circuit court to the power of the district court to direct a distribution of the proceeds of the forfeiture remaining in court. This objection was put on the ground that the eighty-ninth section of the act of 1799, which authorized the collector to receive from the court, or its officer, the sums recovered, after deducting costs and charges, and enjoined upon him the duty of making the distribution, was imperative on the court, and ousted its general jurisdiction to make the distribution. But the court (Mr. Justice Washington delivering the opinion) held that the eighty-ninth section merely pointed out the officer who was to receive the money from the court and who was to distribute it where no dispute existed respecting the distribution; that the jurisdiction of the court to examine into contested claims to the money while under its control, and to direct the collector in what manner it was to be distributed, was not taken away or even impliedly affected; and that if, upon general principles, this could be questioned, the point was directly settled in the case of Jones *v.* Shore, 1 Wheat., 462. The decree of the district court was affirmed so far as it directed how the funds in court should be distributed.

In the case of Jones *v.* Shore, the fund was in the circuit court as the proceeds of a penalty or forfeiture, under the embargo act of December 22, 1807 (2 U. S. Stats. at Large, 451), and was required by the sixth section of the act of January 9, 1808 (id., 454), to be distributed and accounted for in the manner prescribed by the act of 1799. A contest as to shares in the fund was brought before the circuit court. The case went to the supreme court on a division of opinion. That court directed that the money in the circuit court be paid to the collector, with directions to him as to how he should distribute it. This was in 1816.

In the case of McLane v. The United States, 5 Pet., 404, the supreme court say: "Where a sentence of condemnation has been finally pronounced in a case of seizure, the court, as an incident to the possession of the principal cause, has a right to proceed to decree a distribution of the proceeds, according to the terms prescribed by law; and it is a familiar practice to institute proceedings of this nature wherever a doubt occurs as to the rights of the parties who are entitled to share in the distribution." The same doctrine was held in The Josefa Segunda, 10 Wheat., 312, 323, 324.

In Hooper v. Fifty-one Casks of Brandy, Daveis, 271, the district court for Maine (Ware, J.) entertained the petition of an informer for a share of the proceeds of a forfeiture incurred under the act of 1799, the collector and surveyor being the adverse parties, and sustained the claim of the informer. The court, in its opinion, expressly upholds its jurisdiction on the authority of the cases in 4 Washington and 6 Peters.

In the case of The United States v. Fifty Thousand Cigars, Ex parte Smith (vol. 2 Internal Revenue Record, page 108), the district court for Massachusetts (Lowell, J.) entertained petitions filed by several persons claiming shares, as informers, in the proceeds, in court, of forfeitures incurred under the act of 1799, and made a decree that one of them was entitled, as informer, to one-fourth of the fund.

§ 181. *The court having custody of a fund derived from forfeitures or penalties is the proper forum in which should be settled the claims of informers and others to that fund.*

This jurisdiction being well established, there is nothing in the act of 1867 which takes it away, or which confers on the secretary of the treasury any more power to decide disputed claims to the fund than the collector had under the act of 1799. The judicial tribunal which•has the custody of the fund is the proper forum to entertain and decide disputes as to shares in the fund, and to direct how it shall be distributed, and to what persons, under the act of 1867, under the direction of the secretary of the treasury, as a ministerial officer.

To this end it is proper to refer the matter to a commissioner of the court, for the taking of testimony on the part of all parties concerned, and for a report. On the coming in of the report, the court will make such decree as is warranted by the facts, in regard to the subject-matter of the petition, and will direct the money to be paid over to the collector, and to be by him, subject to the provisions of the act of 1867, paid into the treasury of the United States, and to be then distributed, under the direction of the secretary of the treasury, to the persons, and in the proportions, prescribed by the decree of this court. The hearing before the commissioner will be on notice to all parties having any claim to the fund.

§ 182. **By whom distributed.**— "Fines" imposed for obstructing officers of the custom, as well as "penalties," under the act of March 2, 1799, are to be received and distributed by the collector of the customs. *Ex parte* Marquand, 2 Gall., 552.

§ 183. **Interest of United States.**— Upon the seizure and condemnation of a vessel for violation of the act of congress of February 28, 1806, "to suspend the commercial intercourse between the United States and certain parts of the island of San Domingo," the United States are interested only in one-half of the forfeiture. United States *v.* Yeaton, 3 Cr. C, C., 73.

§ 184. **Collectors, rights of.**— No officer of the customs is debarred from receiving a distributive share of fines, penalties and forfeitures, by the act of February 11, 1846, allowed by previous laws, in consequence of having received his maximum of compensation allowed by the law. Hooper *v.* Fifty-one Casks of Brandy, Dav., 370; 6 N. Y. Leg. Obs., 302.

§ 185. What is received by the officers of the customs for forfeitures constitutes no part of the emoluments to which the limitation of the maximum is applied. *Ibid.*

§ 186. The acts of 1802, March, 1822 and 1838, regulating the compensation of collectors of the port, do not deprive such officers of their shares in fines, penalties and forfeitures. They are allowed to claim such shares in addition to the annual compensation. Hoyt *v.* United States, 10 How., 109.

§ 187. Whatever is reserved to the government out of a forfeiture is reserved as well for the seizing officer as for itself; and is distributed accordingly. The government has no authority under its existing laws to release the collector's share as such, and yet to retain to itself the other part of the forfeiture. McLane *v.* United States, 6 Pet., 404.

§ 188. —— **when vacating office before judgment or forfeiture.**— A collector of the customs, who makes a seizure of goods for an asserted forfeiture, and before the proceedings *in rem* are consummated by a sentence of condemnation is removed from office, acquires an inchoate right by the seizure, which by the subsequent decree of condemnation gives him an absolute vested right to his share of the forfeiture under the collection act of March, 1799. Van Ness *v.* Buel, 4 Wheat., 74.

§ 189. A bond was given to J. S., the collector of the district of Petersburg, Va., under the second section of the embargo act of December 22, 1807, and the bond being forfeited, suit was instituted upon it in the district court by the collector. Before judgment was obtained J. S. died, and T. S., his deputy collector, continued in the discharge of the duties of the office until December 14, 1811. On November 30, 1811, judgment was rendered for the penalty of the bond against one of the co-obligors. On November 26, 1811, J. J. was appointed collector for the same port, but did not qualify until the 14th of December, 1811. The defendant obtained a writ of error to the judgment of the district court, and the judgment of the district court was affirmed in the court above. The amount of the penalty of the bond was then paid into the circuit court, and thereupon T. S., executor of J. S., filed his petition, claiming a moiety of the amount so paid, which the law directed to be distributed among the revenue officers of the district where the penalty was incurred. *Held,* that the proportion of the penalty given to the collector belonged to the collector who was in office when the bond was given, and who had prosecuted it to judgment, and not to the collector who happened to be in office when the money was paid. United States *v.* Jones, 1 Marsh., 285.

§ 190. The personal representatives of a deceased collector and surveyor, who was such at the time of the seizure being made, or prosecution or suit commenced, and not his successor in office, are entitled to that portion of fines, forfeitures and penalties, which is, by law, to be distributed among the revenue officers of the district where they were incurred. And where there was no naval officer in the district, the division was adjudged to be made in equal proportions between the collector and surveyor. Jones *v.* Shore, 1 Wheat., 462.

§ 191. **Officers of revenue cutter.**— It is not necessary that the officers of a revenue cutter should, when they give the information against a vessel for a violation of the non-intercourse law, make a claim for a part of the forfeiture; or that they should take any part in the prosecution of the case, to entitle them to a portion of the proceeds. Sawyer *v.* Steele, 3 Wash., 464.

§ 192. **Informers.**— In an admiralty seizure cause, the court cannot award a proportion of the proceeds of the property condemned to informers, unless the case be within some statute provision. But it will allow compensation for expenses incurred in securing and preserving the property. *Ex parte* Cahoon, 2 Mason, 85.

§ 193. **Inspector entitled to informer's share, when.**— When a seizure is made by a collector under the collection act of March 8, 1799, in pursuance of information given by an inspector of the customs, the inspector is entitled to the informer's share of the forfeiture. Hooper *v.* Fifty-one Casks of Brandy, Dav., 370; 6 N. Y. Leg. Obs., 302.

§ 194. **Waiver of right to share.**— The consent of the plaintiffs, in an action of *indebitatus assumpsit,* for one-half a forfeiture incurred by a violation of the non-intercourse law, that the vessel should be sent from the district of Delaware to the district of Pennsylvania, or a disavowal by them of having instituted this suit, does not constitute a waiver of their right to their share of the forfeiture. Sawyer *v.* Steele, 3 Wash., 464.

V. REMISSION AND PARDON.

SUMMARY — *After judgment.* § 195; *right of informer under act of 1866,* § 196.— *Before judgment,* § 197.— *By the secretary of the treasury,* §§ 198–201.— *Conviction and pardon a bar to suit,* §§ 202, 203.

§ 195. The president's power to pardon and remit fines and penalties, after a judgment ordering a portion of a fine to be paid to a private citizen as informer, is limited to a remission of the share of the government only, and is inoperative to divest an interest vested by such judgment in the citizen. United States v. Harris, §§ 204, 205.

§ 196. Prior to the amended internal revenue act of 1866 (14 Stat. at L., 146), the interest of an informer in a judgment, procured upon his information, for a fine or penalty, vested immediately upon the rendering of the judgment in his favor, and the change made by the above act does not affect the rights of an informer vested before its passage. *Ibid.*

§ 197. It seems that before judgment rendered in a suit for a fine or penalty, where the prosecution is wholly in the name of the United States, the president has the power to pardon and remit the fine notwithstanding the interest of an informer in the suit. *Ibid.*

§ 198. Under section 5294, Revised Statutes United States, the secretary of the treasury has power to remit fines or penalties provided for in laws relating to steam vessels, or discontinue any prosecution to recover penalties denounced in such laws, and thus cut off the rights of an informer, except where the informer's share of the penalty shall have been determined by a court of competent jurisdiction prior to the application for the remission of the penalty. The provisions of the above section are valid and not unconstitutional as infringing on the pardoning power vested in the president. The Laura, §§ 206–208.

§ 199. Congress having power to impose a penalty may provide for its remission by vesting the power in the secretary of the treasury of remitting a fine or penalty, or of discontinuing a suit for its enforcement. *Ibid.*

§ 200. The power of the secretary of the treasury under section 5294, Revised Statutes United States, to remit a fine or penalty after suit brought, is not restricted to cases where the suit is by the United States and under the control of its officers, nor is the power of the secretary to discontinue prosecutions limited to prosecutions brought by the United States. *Ibid.*

§ 201. Within the meaning of section 5294, Revised Statutes United States, which provides that "all rights granted to informers by such laws shall be subject to the secretary's power of remission," a libelant is none the less an informer because he sues in his own name, and is entitled to the whole penalty. The object of the statute was to provide in favor of the party incurring the penalty a mode of mitigating it, and the mischief sought to be remedied is the same whoever is to receive the penalty. *Ibid.*

§ 202. A conviction for conspiracy to defraud the revenue under section 5440, Revised Statutes United States, is a bar to a civil suit for penalties for the same acts under section 3296, Revised Statutes United States. United States v. McKee, §§ 209, 210.

§ 203. A pardon by the president for an offense is a bar to a civil suit for a penalty incurred by the same acts which constituted the offense for which the pardon was granted. *Ibid.*

[NOTES.— See §§ 211–242.]

UNITED STATES v. HARRIS.

(District Court for Kentucky: 1 Abbott, 110–119. 1866.)

Opinion by BALLARD, J.

STATEMENT OF FACTS.— On March 15, 1866, J. G. Harris was convicted of having in his possession merchandise subject to duty for the purpose of selling the same with the design of avoiding the payment of duties imposed thereon, and also of the offense of selling cigars, not being the manufacturer thereof, upon which the duties imposed by law had not been paid, with the knowledge thereof.

On the same day, the court rendered judgment against the convict, that he pay a fine to the United States of $500 on account of the first offense, and $100 for the second offense, in all $600. On the motion of the district attorney, the convict was not committed to prison until the fine should be paid, but a *capias* was awarded against him.

On the next day, March 16, John M. Hewitt was, by the judgment of the court, ascertained to be the first informer of the matters whereby the fine imposed on account of the first offense was incurred, and the judgment rendered on the day previous was so far modified that one moiety of said fine, to wit, $250, was adjudged to be for the use of said Hewitt, and the remainder for the use of the United States.

On April 15th, the president of the United States, by his deed of pardon. which recites that the said Harris had been "sentenced to pay a fine of $600," remitted to him the payment of two-thirds of the same.

The marshal, who at this time had in his hands said *capias*, assuming that the pardon was fully effective to discharge, according to its tenor, the defendant from the payment of $400 of said fine, and that the defendant had a right, under the laws of the state of Kentucky, which have been adopted by the United States, to replevy the judgment, allowed the defendant to give his bond, with Walter C. Whittaker and others, sureties, dated May 14th, whereby the parties undertook to pay, three months after date, $253, with interest from date. This sum is just equal to one-third of the fine and the costs of prosecution. This bond was subsequently satisfied by the payment into court, on December 17, of $261.40.

And now R. M. Moseby, the assignee of the informer, has moved the court that the whole sum adjudged to the informer by the judgment of March 16, 1866, be paid to him out of the fund in court, with interest from May 14th, the date of the replevin bond. This motion assumes for its basis that the president had no right to remit any portion of the fine previously adjudged to the informer, and that the informer is, therefore, entitled to his whole share, just as if no remission had taken place.

§ 204. *Power of the president to remit fines.*

The question presented by this motion is an exceedingly interesting and important one. It involves a consideration of the power of the president, under the constitution of the United States, to remit fines, and, so far as I am informed, it has never been determined by either the supreme court or by any circuit court of the United States. I would, therefore, gladly avoid its decision if I could; but every view which I take of the motion submitted only confirms me in the conviction that the question suggested is directly involved, and that its determination can in no way be shunned. But whilst I approach its consideration with unfeigned diffidence, fully impressed with the responsibility which every judge must feel when he is obliged to determine any matter concerning the limit which the constitution has imposed on any department of the government, I have no disposition to shrink from the performance of a duty which I conceive is clearly enjoined on me. Without, therefore, any further apology, I proceed to announce the conclusion to which I have arrived, and to assign some of the reasons on which it is founded.

By section 41 of the act of June 30, 1864, commonly called the internal revenue act, under which this conviction was had, it is provided that "all fines, penalties and forfeitures which may be incurred or imposed by virtue of this act shall he sued for and recovered in the name of the United States, in any proper form of action, or by any appropriate form of proceeding; . . . and when not otherwise or differently provided for, one moiety thereof shall be to the use of the United States, and the other moiety to the use of the person, to be ascertained by the judgment of the court, who shall first inform of the cause, matter or thing whereby any such fine, penalty or forfeiture was incurred." A similar provision is also to be found in section 179.

It has already been stated that by judgment of this court, rendered March 16, 1866, John M. Hewitt was ascertained to be the person who first informed of the matter, whereby the fine of $500 was incurred, and that one moiety thereof was then adjudged to him. Did this judgment so vest this moiety in him that it could not be, or rather was not, divested or impaired by the pardon of the president? This is the question which I now proceed to consider. By section 2 of article II of the constitution of the United States it is declared that "the president . . . shall have power to grant reprieves and pardons for offenses against the United States, except in cases of impeachment." This language is less explicit than that employed in the constitution of Kentucky, and in the constitutions of other states, to confer a like power on the governor. In this, and in other states, the governor is expressly empowered to remit fines and forfeitures, as well as to grant reprieves and pardons. But although this difference of language might have led to a difference of construction in respect to the extent of the power intended to be conferred, and might have resulted in denying to the president the power of remitting either fines or forfeitures, such, in fact, has not been its effect, for it may be considered as settled that the power of pardon in the president embraces all offenses against the United States, except cases of impeachment, and includes the power of remitting fines, penalties and forfeitures. 2 Story, Const., § 1504; United States v. Lancaster, 4 Wash., 66; United States v. Wilson, 7 Pet., 161; Ex parte Wells, 18 How., 307.

Conceding, however, that the power of pardon includes the right to remit fines and penalties, still, to understand the extent to which it may be exercised by the president, we must look to the extent of this prerogative rightfully belonging to the executive of that nation whose language we speak, and whose principles of jurisprudence the people of the United States brought with them as colonists, and established here. If the terms "pardon," "habeas corpus," "bill of attainder," "ex post facto," and other terms used in the constitution, had a well known meaning in that language, and in that system of jurisprudence, the conclusion is irresistible that the convention which framed the constitution had reference to that meaning when it employed them, and that the people accepted them in that sense when they ratified the work of the convention. But this proposition, impregnable as it seems to be in the light of mere abstract reasoning, is doubly fortified by judicial decisions. Calder v. Bull, 3 Dall., 390 (CONST., §§ 582–99); Watson v. Mercer, 8 Pet., 110 (CONST., §§ 1849–51); Carpenter v. Pennsylvania, 17 How., 463 (CONST., §§ 600–602); United States v. Wilson, 7 Pet., 160. Indeed, the supreme court, in the last case cited, speaking in reference to the very matter we have now before us,— that is, the extent of the power of the president to grant pardons,— says : . " As this power has been exercised from time immemorial by the executive of that nation whose language is our language, and to whose judicial institutions ours bear a close resemblance, we adopt these principles respecting the operation and effect of a pardon."

It follows from this reasoning, and from these authorities, that if the king of England cannot, under his prerogative of pardon, remit, after judgment, the share of a fine given by law to an informer, it is not within the power of the president to do it under the constitution of the United States. Indeed, it would seem absurd to suppose that either the framers of the constitution, or the people who ratified it, intended to confer on the president a power, in this respect, larger than that possessed by the sovereign of Great Britain.

Now I find that the English authorities are uniform to the effect that the king cannot make pardon to the injury or loss of others; that he cannot, by his act of grace, give away that which belongs to another; that he cannot divest a vested interest; in short, that, after an action popular, brought *tam pro domino rege quam pro se ipso* according to any statute, he may discharge his own share as well after as before judgment, but that, after judgment, he cannot remit the part of the informer, because in the language of the law, this share of the informer is, by the judgment, vested in him. 3 Coke, Inst., ch. 105, 236–238; 2 Hawkins, Pl. of the Crown, ch. 37, 553; 11 Coke, 65, d, 66, a (Foster's Case); Vin. Abr., tit. Prerogative, n, a, 7; 5 Comyn, Dig., tit. Pardons, 245, citing Strange, 1272; Parker, 289; Crocker, 9, 199.

The authorities in the United States are to the same effect, though, as I have already said, the precise question here presented has never been decided. United States v. Lancaster, 4 Wash., 64; State v. Simpson, 1 Bailey, 378; State v. Williams, 1 Nott & McC., 26; Matter of Flourney, 1 Kelley, 606; State v. Farley, 8 Blackf., 229; State v. McO'Blenis, 21 Mo., 272; *Ex parte* McDonald, 2 Whart., 440; Duncan v. Commonwealth, 4 Serg. & R., 451; Playford v. Commonwealth, 4 Barr, 144; The Hallen and Cargo, 1 Mason, 431. In some of these cases it is expressly stated that by the common law of England, the king, in the exercise of his prerogative of pardon, cannot remit either the share or fine awarded to an informer by the judgment of a court, or the costs of prosecution when they are adjudged to the officers of the court, and it is held that this limit also attaches to the power of pardon conferred on the governors of states by their several constitutions.

§ **205.** *After judgment ordering a portion of a fine to be paid to a private citizen, a remission by the president does not affect such portion.*

Following the mandate of the authorities, my conclusion is, that a proper interpretation of the constitution limits the power of pardon confided to the president, after a judgment ordering a portion of a fine to be paid to a private citizen, to a remission of the share of the government only, and that it is inoperative to divest an interest vested by such judgment in a citizen. What the president may do before judgment, it is, perhaps, not proper for me, in this case, to say; but when the prosecution is wholly in the name of the United States, I see nothing in the foregoing authorities which would deny him complete power over the whole case; for although the cases of Jones v. Shore, 1 Wheat., 670, and Van Ness v. Buell, 4 id., 74, suggests that the informer has a right which attaches on seizure, or at least on the institution of a prosecution, they admit that this right is only inchoate and is not consummated or vested until judgment.

I have not overlooked the decision of the supreme court in the case of The United States v. Morris, 10 Wheat., 246, in which it is held that the secretary of the treasury, under the power conferred on him by the act of 1797, to remit fines, penalties and forfeitures, may remit, after judgment, the share of the informer, as well as the share of the United States. But it will be seen by reference to the opinion of the court, that they regard this power, conferred by act of congress on the secretary, as materially distinguishable from the power of pardon conferred on the president by the constitution. The secretary, by the terms of the act, can remit only where the penalty "shall have been incurred without wilful negligence or any intention of fraud;" and is, therefore, authorized to administer a sort of equitable relief,— that is, to relieve where in justice and equity no penalty should be paid. But the power of the president proceeds on no such principle. He may pardon whom he will, and wholly without respect to the moral guilt or innocence of the legal offender. Moreover, the court rest their decision on the ground that the statute expressly confers on the secretary the power claimed; and recognizing the maxim *cujus est donare ejus est disponere*, they consider that there can be no question that congress, which gives the right to the informer, may, in its discretion, provide upon what conditions it may be enjoyed or taken away.

Nor have I overlooked the provisions of section 9 of the amended internal revenue act of 1866 (14 Stat. at L., 146), which assert that "it is hereby declared to be the true intent and meaning of the present and all previous provisions of internal revenue acts granting shares to informers, that no right accrues to or is vested in any informer in any case until the fine, penalty or forfeiture in such case is fixed by judgment or compromise and the amount or proceeds shall have been paid, when the informer shall become entitled to his legal share of the sum adjudged or agreed upon and received."

Whatever may be the effect of these provisions in cases arising under this act, it is manifest they cannot affect rights vested previous to their adoption under the law as it then existed. If more was meant by these provisions than to change existing laws; if they were intended to furnish to the courts a rule for the interpretation of previous statutes, I cannot admit their binding force to this extent. It is the province of congress to make laws, not interpret them. Their interpretation, when made, is confided by the constitution to the judiciary.

Nor has the decision of the court of appeals of this state, in the case of Rout v. Freemster, 7 J. J. Marsh., 132, escaped my attention. That decision has been understood by some to hold that the governor may remit the share of the citizen in a fine. It will, however, be seen that the case goes only to this extent, that the governor may remit the whole fine, including the portion given by law to the commonwealth's attorney, because by the terms of the statute he is entitled to nothing until the fine is collected. But if the decisions of the courts in this state are to control my decision in this case, it may be well to refer to the case of Frazier v. Commonwealth, 12 B. Mon., 369, in which it is held that when the governor remits less than half of the fine, or more than half, the part not remitted, to the extent of not more than half, should be paid to the attorney of the commonwealth. This is an express authority for giving the whole of the fine collected in this case to the informer.

It is due to the president to say that it is very apparent, from the terms of the pardon granted by him, he was not aware that any portion of the fine adjudged against the convict had been ordered to be paid to an informer. If he was furnished with a copy of the judgment at all, it must have been a copy of that rendered March 15, which, as we have seen, adjudged the whole fine to the United States. If he had seen the judgment as it was modified by the order of the next day, which adjudged $250 to be for the use of John M. Hewitt, informer, it is not probable that he would have attempted to impair his right; for I find, by consulting the opinions of the attorney-general of the United States, that the power of the president to remit the share of an informer after judgment has never been expressly affirmed, but, on the contrary, frequently doubted, and often denied. .

Let judgment be entered: That out of the money in the registry of the court, in this case, there be paid to the assignee of the informer $258.87, which is the amount of the sum heretofore adjudged to the informer, with interest from the date of the replevin bond, May 14, until the day the money was paid into the registry of the court.

THE LAURA.

(Circuit Court for New York: 19 Blatchford, 562–572. 1881.)

STATEMENT OF FACTS.— The steamer Laura violated the law by carrying on two trips between New York and Bridgeport more passengers than the law allowed. A libel was filed against her by an informer, and on application to the secretary of the treasury the penalty was remitted. The district court dismissed the libel in accordance with the orders of the secretary of the treasury, and the libelant appealed to this court.

Opinion by BLATCHFORD, J.

This suit is founded on sections 4465 and 4469 of the Revised Statutes. The former section provides as follows: " It shall not be lawful to take on board of any steamer a greater number of passengers than is stated in the certificate of inspection; and for every violation of this provision the master or owner shall be liable, to any person suing for the same, to forfeit the amount of passage money and ten dollars for each passenger beyond the number allowed." The latter section provides that the penalties imposed by the former section "shall be a lien upon the vessel, . . . but a bond may, as provided in other cases, be given to secure the satisfaction of the judgment." The provisions of section 5294, under which the warrant of remission in this case was granted, are as follows: " The secretary of the treasury may, upon application therefor, remit or mitigate any fine or penalty provided for in laws relating to steam vessels, or discontinue any prosecution to recover penalties denounced in such laws, excepting the penalty of imprisonment, or of removal from office, upon such terms as he, in his discretion, shall think proper; and all rights granted to informers by such laws shall be held subject to the secretary's power of remission, except in cases where the claims of any informer to the share of any penalty shall have been determined by a court of competent jurisdiction, prior to the application for the remission of the penalty; and the secretary shall have authority to ascertain the facts upon all such applications, in such manner and under such regulations as he may deem proper." Title 52 of the Revised Statutes, in which sections 4465 and 4469 are found, is entitled "Regulation of Steam Vessels." Those sections and section 5294 were originally enacted as part of the act of February 28, 1871, entitled "An act to provide for the better security of life on board of vessels propelled in whole or in part by steam, and for other purposes" (16 U. S. Stat. at Large, 440), section 4465 being a part of section 48 of that act, and section 4469 being a part of section 49, and section 5294 being, in substance, section 64.

§ 206. *The power of the president to pardon offenses is not infringed by the power conferred on the secretary of the treasury to remit penalties under Revised Statutes, section 5294.*

It is contended for the libelant that the warrant of remission is void and of no effect, because section 5294 is unconstitutional, in that it infringes on the pardoning power vested in the president. The constitution (art. 2, sec. 2) provides that the president "shall have power to grant reprieves and pardons for offenses against the United States, except in cases of impeachment." It is contended that this power is exclusive, and that congress cannot lawfully grant to the secretary of the treasury the power conferred on him by section 5294.

The power of the president to pardon has always been construed to extend to the remission of fines, penalties and forfeitures accruing to the United States for offenses against the United States. 1 Opinions of Attorneys-General, 418. In United States v. Lancaster, 4 Wash. C. C. R., 64, a vessel had been seized by the collector and libeled for forfeiture for a violation of the embargo laws, and released on a bond for her value. She was condemned as forfeited, and a suit was brought by the United States on the bond. Afterwards, the president remitted to the defendant all the right and interest of the United States in and to said bond, and required all proceedings on the part of the United States to be forthwith discontinued. The question arose in the suit whether the pardon of the president affected the rights of the officers of the customs to the moiety of the forfeiture. It was held that the terms of the pardon were such as to remit only the interest of the United States, and not the rights of the officers. The question as to the power of the president, by pardon, to defeat the inchoate rights of the officers, was not passed upon. In United States v. Morris, 10 Wheaton, 246, it was held that the interest of officers of the customs in forfeitures was subordinate to the authority of the secretary of the treasury, under section 1 of the act of March 3, 1797 (1 U. S. Stat. at Large, 506), (now sec. 5292 of the Revised Statutes) to remit them. In the case of a vessel condemned as forfeited to the United States for a violation of the slave trade act, the president was advised to remit only the interest of the United States, on the ground that his pardon could not defeat the vested rights of the seizing officer. 4 Opinions of Attorneys-General, 533. On the question whether the president had the power to pardon offenses committed by the owners or masters of steam vessels in respect to the transportation of passengers, in violation of certain statutes, he was advised that he had such power; and the question whether he had authority to remit, by pardon, a penalty accruing to individuals was suggested, but not discussed. 6 id., 393.

In the case of a vessel arrested for violating a statute in regard to the transportation of passengers, a remission being applied for to the secretary of the treasury, under section 1 of the act of March 3, 1797, the question occurred whether the case came within the pardoning power of the president. The secretary was advised (1) that the president had power to pardon the imprisonment, fines and forfeitures imposed for violating the provisions in regard to space for, and number of, passengers, unless, perhaps, as regarded a forfeiture the right of which had duly vested in the custom-house officers or others except the United States; (2) that it was doubtful whether the president had power to remit such forfeiture; (3) that the secretary of the treasury had power to remit all forfeitures of vessels for carrying an excess of passengers; (4) that the president had power to pardon in all cases of vessels libeled by reason of liens on them for penalties imposed by the statute; (5) that the secretary of the treasury had the concurrent power to remit in the last named cases, but any doubt could be cured by the authority of the president, as no interest but that of the United States was affected; (6) that, as the act of 1797 afforded the means of judicial investigation as to the question of remission, it was more convenient, in cases of seizures, and prosecutions instituted, by officers of the customs, to dispose of that class of seizures in that way than to refer them to the unaided discretion of the president. 6 id., 488. In United States v. Harris, 1 Abbott's U. S. Rep., 110, a person was convicted and fined for violating the internal revenue law. Afterwards, the court adjudged that H. was the informer, and that one-half of the fine should be for his use, and the remainder for the use of the United States. Afterwards, the president, by a pardon, remitted to the defendant the payment of two-thirds of the fine. One-third of the fine, with interest, was paid into court. The informer claimed, and was allowed by the court, therefrom the whole sum adjudged to him, on the ground that the president had no right to remit any of the part of the fine so adjudged to the informer, and that he was entitled to the whole of such part, as if there had been no remission. The conviction was under a statute (act of June 30, 1864, § 41; 13 U. S. Stat. at Large, 239) which provided that all suits for fines under it should be in the name of the United States. The court remarked that, where the prosecution was wholly in the name of the United States, it saw nothing in any of the authorities which denied to the president the power, by pardon, to remit the interest of an informer, before judgment.

The view urged by the libelant is, that the power of the president to pardon is exclusive; that no part of it can be exercised by any one else without infringing on the power of the president; that, if the secretary of the treasury can pardon without the president's concurrence, he may grant pardons which the president would refuse; that, if congress can authorize the secretary to grant pardons, it can itself grant them and prescribe the terms and conditions under which they shall be granted; and that if it can authorize the secretary to remit penalties incurred under the statute in question, it can authorize him, or any one else, to remit the punishment of any offense, and can so legislate that after the president has refused to grant a pardon it can still be granted under authority conferred by congress. In support of this view, the case of Ex parte Garland, 4 Wall., 333 (CONST., §§ 619–37), is cited, as holding that the power of the president to pardon is unlimited, extending to every offense known to the law, and not subject to legislative control, and that congress can neither limit the effect of such pardon nor exclude from its exercise any class of offenders. The case of United States v. Klein, 13 Wall., 128, is also referred to, as holding that congress cannot impair the effect of a pardon, because that would be to infringe the constitutional power of the president.

There is not, in this case, any question raised as to the effect of a pardon which has been granted by the president, as there was in Ex parte Garland and in United States v. Klein. The question is not as to any restriction of the pardoning power of the president. It is not claimed that the secretary alone could remit this forfeiture and that the president could not. The practice of the government, as is seen from the citations, has been to regard the power of the secretary to remit penalties and forfeitures of the character of those in the present case as a valid power in concurrence with the power of the president to pardon in the same cases. The existence of the power in the secretary is not regarded as interfering with the pardoning power of the president. The decision in United States v. Morris, 10 Wheat., 246, that the secretary's remission of the entire forfeiture, the vessel having been seized as forfeited to the United States, and prosecuted in the name of the United States and condemned, had the effect to extinguish the interest of the officers of the customs in the property, necessarily recognized the fact that the power of the secretary to remit was a valid power and did not infringe on the pardoning power of the president. A power in the secretary to remit penalties and forfeitures has existed by statute since 1790, and has never been regarded as invalid because of the existence of the power in the president to remit, by pardon, the same penalties and forfeitures.   Even assuming, then, that the president could discharge, by pardon, the interest of the libelant in the forfeiture of this vessel, it does not seem that the secretary could not be lawfully authorized to discharge it.

But it may well be doubted whether the president's power of pardon extends to taking away the interest given by the statute to the libelant.   If so, then there is no power of pardon to be interfered with by the remission of the secretary.   The statute gives nothing to the United States.   It does not authorize any prosecution by the United States by indictment or by civil suit. It imposes a penalty, which is made a lien on the vessel, for doing what it declares it shall not be lawful to do, but the penalty is declared to be a pecuniary liability, not to the United States, but to any one who will sue for it. It is wholly to such person.   While the unlawful act which gives rise to the suit, if to be called an offense, is one denounced by a statute of the United States, yet it may well be doubted whether it is an offense *against* the United States, in the sense of the constitution; and still more, whether, if the United States could sue for the penalty, which is given to "any person suing for the same," there is any offense against the United States which can be pardoned by the president, beyond what is involved in such right of the United States to sue.

The power, however, of the president, to pardon has never been construed to extend to taking away such rights as the statute in this case vests in the libelant, where they have been asserted by a suit brought by an informer in his own name, and where they belong wholly to him, and the United States have no share in the penalty.   The case of United States *v.* Harris, *supra*, refers to the power of the president over the whole case, before judgment, as existing only where the prosecution is wholly in the name of the United States.

§ 207. *Congress, having power to impose a penalty, may provide for its remission.*

There is, therefore, nothing in the existence of the pardoning power which affects the present case.   This being so, there can be no doubt that congress, which created the penalty, could provide any method of remitting it.

The next question is as to the construction of section 5294.   It is contended for the libelant that that section does not give to the secretary power to remit a penalty after a suit has been brought by a private person to recover it.   The matter is a very plain one.   The power extends to "any fine or penalty," that is, to all fines and penalties.   It includes those given to individuals as well as those given to the United States.   Probably, because of a doubt whether the pardoning power of the president could reach all cases, and because cases proper for remission would arise, the power of remission was confided to the secretary, to be exercised on an ascertainment of facts, with the restrictions, however, that the power should not extend to remitting the penalty of imprisonment or of removal from office, or to affecting the rights of informers after they had been judicially determined before the application for remission. It is contended that the power to remit is restricted by the statute, after suit, to cases where the suit is by the United States and under the control of its officers.   It is also contended that the power given to remit applies only to cases before suit is brought, and that the power to discontinue prosecutions is limited to prosecutions brought by the United States. These views do not seem well founded. The statute covers the remission of "any" fine or penalty, and although, under the words "discontinue any prosecution," the secretary should be held to be restricted to discontinuing prosecutions in the name of the United States, yet he may remit any penalty. The limitation of the power of discontinuing prosecutions does not restrict the power of remission. A prosecution may be discontinued without remitting the penalty, and there may be reasons for doing so. But no reason is perceived why the power to "discontinue any prosecution" does not include a suit like the present. There is nothing in section 5294 to suggest that the power of remission or of discontinuance was not intended to be as broad as the imposition of penalties, except as to the particular matters specially excepted.

§ 208. *One who sues for a penalty under sections 4465, 4469, Revised Statutes, is an informer.*

It is argued that the libelant is not an informer, within section 5294, because he is not a person on whose information the United States bring suit. But this is too restricted a meaning of the word. When the section speaks of "rights granted to informers by such laws," it means rights granted to individuals and not to the United States. The libelant is none the less an informer because he sues in his own name and is entitled to the whole penalty. The object of the statute was to provide in favor of the party incurring the penalty a mode of mitigating it, and the mischief sought to be remedied was the same whoever was to receive the penalty. In section 976, the person to whom the whole of a penalty in a penal statute is directed to accrue, and who sues for it in his own name, is called an informer. The suggestion that in section 5294 only a person who is entitled to part of a penalty is an informer is too narrow a view. If a person has the whole of a penalty he has all its shares, and his claims are fairly included within the words "the claims of any informer to the share of any penalty." A person may be an informer without being a "plaintiff on a penal statute," in the sense of section 975, but a "plaintiff on a penal statute," such as the libelant is, is an informer within section 5294.

The fact that by section 41 of the act of August 30, 1852 (10 U. S. Stat. at Large, 75), in regard to steam vessels, all the penalties imposed by it were given to any person who would sue for them, and that no power of remission of penalties was given by that act, has no tendency to show that under the act of 1871 all penalties, some of which are to go wholly to the informer, and some partly to the informer and partly to the United States, are not within the power of remission given to the secretary.

The warrant of remission must be held to be a complete discharge of the penalties and the passage money sued for in this case, and there must be a decree dismissing the libel, and directing the clerk of this court to pay out to the proctor for the libelant his portion of the taxed costs of the libelant in the district court, on deposit herein, and to distribute the remainder thereof among the officers of the district court entitled thereto, and ordering that the libelant pay to the claimant its costs in this court to be taxed.

UNITED STATES v. McKEE.

(Circuit Court for Missouri: 4 Dillon, 128-131. 1877.)

Opinion by MILLER, J.

STATEMENT OF FACTS.— This is a civil action brought by the government against William McKee, to recover the liability which section 3296 of the Revised Statutes denounces, of double the amount of taxes of which the United States had been defrauded by the unlawful removal of whisky from the distilleries of divers persons, at different times, within this district. The petition charges that in all these removals the defendant, in the language of the statute, aided and abetted.

To each and all of these charges defendant made two defenses. 1. That he has been indicted in this court, convicted and punished for the same offenses. 2. That for these offenses he has been pardoned by the president, and he exhibits a copy of the pardon with his plea.

To this answer the plaintiff demurs.

In determining the sufficiency of both these defenses, it is necessary to ascertain clearly the nature of the offense charged in the indictment for which the defendant has been punished; for if it is the same offense, as defined by law, for which he is now prosecuted, and is also for the same transactions, our laws forbid that he or any one else shall be twice punished for the same crime or misdemeanor.

In the former trial he was indicted for a conspiracy to defraud the government of the United States out of taxes due on whisky distilled by the several parties mentioned, and that in pursuit of that conspiracy other parties than defendant — who were his co-conspirators — did unlawfully remove said whisky.

§ 209. *A conviction for conspiring to defraud the revenue, under Revised Statutes, section 5440, is a bar to a civil suit for penalties for the same acts under Revised Statutes, section 3296.*

It thus appears that the whisky was actually removed; that by this removal the government was defrauded of its taxes; that defendant was one of the several persons who conspired together to do this act, though it was not charged that he personally took part in the acts of removal.

In the present case, while he is not charged with a conspiracy by that name, he is charged with aiding and abetting this same removal, and, if convicted, will be punished for the same removals. We are all of opinion that his joining the conspiracy, of which the purpose was to remove the whisky, was aiding and abetting the removal which was effected by means of that conspiracy.

How can a man more effectually aid an unlawful act than ·by counseling and advising its execution, and giving his influence to its support, and the best energies of his mind to devise the safest and surest means of its accomplishment? If three men agree to compass the death of another, and one of them puts their joint purpose into effect, do not the other two aid and abet the murder? and is not such an agreement also a conspiracy to murder the victim? We are, therefore, of opinion that if the specific acts of removal on which this suit is brought are the same which were proved in the indictment, the former judgment and conviction is a bar to the present action; and we are also of opinion that the allegations of the answer are sufficient averments that they are the same. If the counsel for the United States thinks they are not the same he can take issue on that plea, and have the issue tried.

§ 210. *A pardon by the president for an offense is a bar to a civil suit for a penalty for the same acts.*

Little need be said about the plea of pardon, because if the indictment and sentence of McKee were for the same offenses, both in law and in fact, for which this action is brought, it is conceded that the pardon is also a bar to the civil suit. If it is not conceded, we have no doubt that it is so. As it stands in connection with the averments of the answer, we hold it to be a good plea. Whether it would be a good bar to an action for acts not included in that prosecution, but of the same character, we need not now decide, though I have, personally, a strong opinion that it would be. The demurrer is overruled.

DILLON, J., concurs.

§ 211. **Pardon by president — Extent and effect of.** — Whether the pardoning power of the president extends to the barring of private inchoate interests in suits for penalties and forfeitures, *quære?* United States *v.* Lancaster,[*] 4 Wash., 64.

§ 212. The president's remission of a fine or penalty, imposed upon a conviction for an offense against the postoffice laws, is of no effect if the fine has been paid before the granting of the remission. In such case the money cannot be refunded without an appropriation by congress. Smith's Case,[*] 10 Op. Att'y Gen'l, 1.

§ 213. The power of the president to pardon "offenses against the United States" does not extend to forfeitures enforced by proceedings *in rem.* Nor can the president afford relief against a judgment entered upon a bond accepted by the court as a substitute for the thing seized. Case of Steamboat Minnesota,[*] 11 Op. Att'y Gen'l, 122.

§ 214. A pardon granted by the president, after reciting that it, being made known to him that proceedings are still pending against said L. on a bond given which was forfeited in consequence of a violation of the embargo law, proceeded to remit "all the interest of the United States in the penalty or forfeiture of said bond, so far forth as the said L. is concerned therein, willing and requiring all further proceedings in the case, on behalf of the United States, to be forthwith discontinued and discharged." *Held,* that only the interest of the United States, and not that of the custom-house officers in a moiety of the penalty, was remitted or affected by the pardon. United States *v.* Lancaster.[*] 4 Wash., 64.

§ 215. Where a party sentenced to fine and imprisonment in a criminal prosecution, for conspiracy to defraud the United States of its revenue, is pardoned by the president of the conspiracy, such pardon cannot embrace any other offense for which separate penalties and punishments are prescribed. *In re* Weimer,[*] 7 Rep., 38.

§ 216. **Remission by secretary of the treasury.** — The object of vesting a remitting power in the secretary of the treasury is to relieve in cases where courts are bound to inflict penalties. Under the collection laws courts must decide "according to the law," which means that if the fact which works a forfeiture be proved, the court must decide without reference to the innocence of the person to whom the forfeited article belongs. United States *v.* Morris,[*] 1 Paine, 209.

§ 217. The secretary of the treasury has no power to remit penalties except as provided by law. If he recites his authority under a special act, and remits in pursuance of that act, the remission, if unsupported by such act, cannot be supported under the general act of March, 1797. The Margaretta and Cargo, 2 Gall., 515.

§ 218. The power conferred on the secretary of the treasury by the act of January 2, 1813, to remit any fine incurred by any importer of goods, wares and merchandise from Great Britain, which were shipped between the 23d of June and December 23, 1812, if it appeared to the satisfaction of the secretary, upon petition of the claimants, that the property was, *bona fide,* owned by a citizen or citizens of the United States, extended to the case of a joint interest between citizens of the United States and Great Britain, and might rightfully be exercised in favor of such joint owners, being citizens of the United States. Gallego *v.* United States, 1 Marsh., 439.

§ 219. Under the act of February 27, 1813, the secretary of the treasury has no authority to remit the penalties for goods subsequently imported contrary to the non-importation acts. The Margaretta and Cargo, 2 Gall., 515.

§ 220. —— **cannot remit part.** — Under the act of February 27, 1813, the secretary of the treasury has no authority to make a remission of part only of the property forfeited. If he remit at all, he is bound to remit *in toto. Ibid.*

§ 221. —— before libel filed — Collector must restore. — A remission of a forfeiture by the secretary of the treasury, under the act of March 3, 1797, chapter 13, granted before a libel or information has been filed, operates directly to revest the right of property and possession in the petitioner, and the collector on his presenting the warrant of remission is bound to restore it. The Palo Alto,* Dav., 343; 6 N. Y. Leg. Obs., 262.

§ 222. But after the filing of a libel or information, the property is in the custody of the law, and the collector is the keeper of the court. The *remittitur* being filed in court is a bar to further proceedings to enforce the forfeiture, and the court will direct the suit to be dismissed and issue a precept to restore the property. But the property being in the custody of the court, the collector cannot restore the possession without an order of the court. *Ibid.*

§ 223. Interest of collectors, informers and others, how affected by. — Neither under the act of 1797, nor the act of 1813, has the secretary of the treasury any authority to remit the collector's share of the forfeited property, nor any part of it *eo nomine.* The Margaretta and Cargo, 2 Gall., 515.

§ 224. The secretary of the treasury has power, under the act for the mitigation and remission of forfeitures, to remit as well the moiety or share allowed to individuals as the part belonging to the government. United States v. Morris,* 1 Paine, 209.

§ 225. A decree of condemnation or judgment in a suit for a forfeiture has not the effect so to vest or consummate the rights of individuals as to secure them against the exercise of the power of remission possessed by the secretary of the treasury. *Ibid.*

§ 226. There is no analogy between the power of the secretary to remit forfeitures and the power of the king to pardon in England, or the pardoning power of the president in this country. The principle upon which is founded the rule, that a pardon will not be allowed to interfere with or defeat a private interest which had attached on the commission of the act which was pardoned, can have no application to the case of a forfeiture remitted by the secretary of the treasury, as the same authority, an act of congress, which gives the right to a part of the forfeiture also declares how it shall be asserted and in what way it may be defeated. The right of an individual to a part of the forfeiture is contingent in its very inception. *Ibid.*

§ 227. —— at what stage of proceedings may be exercised. — The act of April 3, 1797, authorizes the secretary to remit the interest of officers in forfeitures in certain cases after suit brought and before judgment. United States v. Lancaster,* 4 Wash., 64.

§ 228. No limit is prescribed in any of the acts of congress to the secretary's power to remit forfeitures, as to the time when it shall be exercised, other than that it must be during the prosecution. A prosecution is not at an end so long as an execution be necessary to produce the fruits of it. Hence, the secretary may certainly remit a forfeiture at any time before execution. United States v. Morris,* 1 Paine, 209.

§ 229. Where a seizure has been made, it seems that the power of the secretary to remit the forfeiture does not cease until the penalty has been collected and distributed. *Ibid.*

§ 230. The secretary of the treasury has authority, under the remission act of March 3, 1797, to remit a forfeiture or penalty accruing under the revenue laws, at any time, before or after a final sentence of condemnation or judgment for the penalty, until the money is actually paid over to the collector for distribution; and such remission extends to the shares of the forfeiture or penalty to which the officers of the customs are entitled, as well as to the interest of the United States. United States v. Morris, 10 Wheat., 246.

§ 231. Under section 5294, Revised Statutes United States, the power of the secretary of the treasury to remit or mitigate penalties extends as well and as fully to penalties given to the person suing for the same as to those given to the United States, or one-half to the government and one-half to the informer, and is exercisable as well after as before suit brought, if the claim of the informer has not been actually determined by the court, as this power of remission given to the secretary by congress is not a power to pardon, but is simply a restriction, limitation or condition annexed to the grant of the penalty. Pollock v. Steamboat Laura, 5 Fed. R., 133.

§ 232. After a final decree of condemnation unappealed from, in a cause of seizure by a collector for a breach of the revenue laws, the secretary of the treasury has no authority to remit the collector's share of the forfeiture. It is a vested and absolute right. The Brig Hollen and Cargo, 1 Mason, 431.

§ 233. Until final judgment no part of a forfeiture vests absolutely in the collector; but after a final judgment, his share vests absolutely and cannot be remitted. The Margaretta and Cargo, 2 Gall., 515.

§ 234. Conditional remission. — If the remission of a forfeiture by the secretary of the treasury under the act of March 3, 1797, be on the payment of costs, this is a condition precedent, and the remission is inoperative until the costs are paid. The Palo Alto,* Dav., 343.

§ 235. Where the secretary has remitted a forfeiture on the payment of costs, a tender of the costs, after a reasonable time allowed for taxing them, is equivalent to actual payment to revest the right of property and possession. A neglect of the collector, reasonably to furnish the attorney with the costs of seizure and custody, will not defeat or suspend the right of the claimant to the possession of the property. *Ibid.*

§ 286. The ship Good Friends, and her cargo of British merchandise, owned by Stephen Girard, a citizen of the United States, was seized by the collector of the Delaware district on April 19, 1812, for a violation of the non-intercourse laws of the United States, then in force. The ship and cargo were condemned as forfeited in the district and circuit court of the Delaware district. On July 29, 1813, congress passed an "act for the relief of the owners of the Good Friends," etc., and a remission of the forfeiture was granted by the secretary of the treasury under the authority of that act, with the exception of a sum equal to double the duties imposed by an act of congress, passed July 1, 1812. The collector was entitled to one moiety of the whole amount reserved by the secretary of the treasury as the condition of the remission. McLane *v.* United States, 6 Pet., 404.

§ 287. **May be revoked, when.**—The secretary has the power, after a *remittitur* has been granted and communicated to the claimant, to revoke the warrant, and if the remission of the forfeiture be free and unconditional, the power of revocation continues after the *remittitur* is filed and an order of restoration passed, and until the precept is finally executed by a delivery of the property into the possession of the claimant. The Palo Alto,* Dav., 343.

§ 288. —— **when remission is conditional.**—If the remission of a forfeiture by the secretary of the treasury be conditional, he has no power to revoke it after the condition has been performed, whether the possession of the goods has been delivered to the claimant or not. *Ibid.*

§ 289. After the remission of a forfeiture by the secretary of the treasury has been made known to the claimant, a revocation of the remission by the former is inoperative until the knowledge of it is brought home to the claimant; and in case the remission be conditional, if the condition be performed before he has notice of the revocation, the rights of the claimant become fixed, and the remission is irrevocable. *Ibid.*

§ 240. **Order of restoration may be demanded by claimant.**—The order of restoration, made by the court pursuant to a remission of a forfeiture by the secretary of the treasury, is not properly a judicial but a ministerial act. It is the remission of the secretary that restores the right of property and possession, and the order of the court, carrying that into effect, may be demanded by the claimant *ex debito justitiæ. Ibid.*

§ 241. **A motion made under section 1020 of the Revised Statutes, to remit the penalty** of a forfeited recognizance, on the ground that the party bound to appear was, when called, in the custody of a state officer, under a warrant issued out of a state court on a criminal charge, was denied on the ground that the question could be best determined on the trial of the action which had been brought upon the forfeited recognizance. United States *v.* Stricker, 12 Blatch., 389.

§ 242. **By state.**—The state of Maryland in 1836 passed a law directing a subscription of $3,000,000 to be made to the capital stock of the Baltimore & Ohio Railroad Company with the following proviso: "That if the said company shall not locate the said road in the manner provided for in this act, then, and in that case, they shall forfeit $1,000,000 to the state of Maryland for the use of Washington county." In March, 1841, the state passed another act, repealing so much of the prior act as made it the duty of the company to construct the road by the route therein prescribed, remitting and releasing the penalty and directing the discontinuance of any suit brought to recover the same. The proviso was a measure of state policy, which it had a right to change, if the policy was afterwards discovered to be erroneous, and neither the commissioners nor the county nor any one of its citizens acquired any separate or private interest under it which could be maintained in a court of justice. It was a penalty inflicted upon the company as a punishment for disobeying the law, and the assent of the company to it as a supplemental charter is not sufficient to deprive it of the character of a penalty. Maryland *v.* Baltimore & Ohio R. Co., 3 How., 534.

PENDING ACTION.

See NOTICE; PRACTICE.

PENITENTIARY.

See CRIMES.

PENNSYLVANIA.

See STATES.

PENSIONS AND BOUNTIES.

[See CONSTITUTION AND LAWS, §§ 484-495; CRIMES.]

§ 1. The right to give pensions and bounties is implied from the power to raise and support armies. United States v. Fairchilds, 1 Abb., 74; 1 Am. L. T., 58.

§ 2. This power to give pensions authorizes congress to guard by appropriate penalties the pensions and bounties awarded to soldiers against pension agents or others who would divert them from the beneficiary. Hence, sections 12 and 13 of the pension act of July 4, 1864 (13 Stat. at Large, 389), providing for the punishment of any attorney or agent demanding or receiving a greater compensation than that prescribed, etc., are valid and constitutional. *Ibid.*

§ 3. **Offenses under the law — Power of congress.** — It is competent for congress to pass laws securing to pensioners the enjoyment of their pensions, and to protect the fund both before and after it reaches their hands, and to this end may declare the embezzlement by a guardian of money which came to his hands as pension money for his wards to be a crime against the United States, and as such punishable in the United States courts. United States v. Hall, 8 Otto, 343.

§ 4. The last clause of the thirteenth section of the pension act of July 4, 1864 (13 Stat. at Large), providing for the punishment of any attorney or agent wrongfully withholding from a pensioner or other claimant the whole or any part of the pension or claim allowed and due such pensioner or claimant, etc., is not limited in its operation to pensions granted under that act, but extends to pensions granted under an act subsequently passed. United States v. Chaffee, 4 Ben., 330. In an indictment for presenting for payment a false and fraudulent claim for pension moneys, it is not sufficient to allege the offense in the words of the statute. The facts constituting the offense should be set out with such certainty as to apprise the defendant of what is intended to be proved against him, to the end that he may prepare his defense and plead the judgment as a bar to any subsequent prosecution for the same offense. United States v. Goggin, 1 Fed. R., 49; 9 Biss., 269.

§ 5. The provisions of the act of congress for the punishment of frauds on the government (act of March 3, 1823; 3 Stat. at Large, 771) will support an indictment for the transmission of false affidavits and declarations to the pension office, in support of applications for bounty land warrants. United States v. Bickford, 4 Blatch., 337; 12 Law Rep. (N. S.), 278.

§ 6. Upon the trial it is not necessary to prove a transmission by the hand of the prisoner. Assistance in procuring the papers for transmission by another is sufficient. *Ibid.*

§ 7. Congress, having the right to grant pensions and bounties for the support of meritorious soldiers and sailors, may by all suitable laws guard the fund thus devoted from being diverted from its object by either the craft or the extortion of unscrupulous agents. The two powers are co-extensive in congress. Hence the act of July 4, 1864 (13 Stat. at Large, 387), prescribing the fees of pension agents and providing penalties for receiving greater fees than those prescribed, is constitutional. United States v. Marks,* 2 Abb., 531. See CONSTITUTION AND LAWS, §§ 482-95.

§ 8. Section 13 of the pension act of July 4, 1864, provides "that any agent or attorney who shall, directly or indirectly, demand or receive any greater compensation for his services under this act than is prescribed in the preceding section of this act," etc., shall be subject to a certain penalty. The provision herein contained as to a penalty can only be applied in case of services rendered in procuring pensions granted under this act, and has no application whatever to the procuration of pensions under the act of 1862, although the provisions as to penalties in the latter act were expressly repealed by the act of 1864. *Ibid.*

§ 9. **Widows of soldiers of the Revolution.** — A widow of a soldier of the Revolutionary war married subsequent to 1800. She received a pension under the act of February 3, 1853 (10 Stat. at L., 154), commencing, under a decision of the secretary of the interior, on the 3d day of February, 1853. Claiming that the pension should have commenced on the 4th of March, 1848, in accordance with the provisions of the act of that date (9 Stat. at L., 265), granting pensions to widows of soldiers of the Revolution married prior to 1800, she brought suit for her pension from the 4th day of March, 1848, to the 3d day of February, 1853. *Held,* that the act of 1853 referred to the act of 1848, and adopted its provisions as to the rate, duration and commencement of the pensions it grants, and for that reason the pension should commence in 1848 instead of 1853, and that she was entitled to recover. Alexander v. United States,* 4 Ct. Cl., 218; Clark v. United States,* 1 Ct. Cl., 179.

§ 10. The widow of a soldier of the Revolution, having remarried since his death, is entitled under the act of August 23, 1842, to the pension given by the act of July 7, 1838, as well during the period of her second coverture as during her widowhood, occasioned by the death of her second husband, provided that she be a widow at the time she makes the application. Poucher v. United States,* 1 Ct. Cl., 207.

§ 11. The act of June 4, 1832, granting Revolutionary pensions, provides that when a female pensioner shall die, leaving children, the amount due at the time of her death shall be paid to her representatives for the benefit of her children; and "that on the death of any pensioner, male or female, leaving children, the amount due may be paid to any one, or each of them, as they may prefer, without the intervention of an administrator." Held, that the word children in these provisions embraces the grandchildren of a deceased pensioner, whether their parents died before or after his decease. (DANIEL, CURTIS and CAMPBELL, JJ., dissented.) Walton v. Cotton.* 19 How., 355.

§ 12. Under the act of February 28, 1853, granting pensions to widows of Revolutionary soldiers, who were married subsequently to January, A. D. 1800, "in the same manner as those who were married before that date," the widows therein designated take the pension provided from the date of the passage of the act, and not, as the widows married prior to 1800, from 1848, the date of the act granting pensions to the latter. The phrase "in the same manner" refers to the mode in which the pension must be obtained by the adjudication of the commissioner of pensions, and to the rules, regulations and prescriptions provided by law for the government of the commissioner and pension agents, and for the payment of pensions. United States v. Alexander,* 12 Wall., 177.

§ 13. Widows.— Where a pension is provided for a widow for the services of her husband as an officer in the navy of the United States, by a special act of congress, and a general act, passed the same day, provides a pension for widows of officers who have died in the naval service, such widow, having elected to take under the general law, and having taken under the same, although taken under protest, by receiving the same did not prejudice her claim under the resolution of the same date, and cannot take under the special act. Decatur v. Paulding, 14 Pet., 497.

§ 14. A claim for a Revolutionary land warrant must be presented to the secretary of the interior, and not to the court of claims. Chamberlain v. United States,* 17 Ct. Cl., 681.

§ 15. A deserter from the army who was re-instated, without trial, upon condition of serving out the time lost by such desertion, and having done so was honorably discharged, is entitled to bounty notwithstanding the desertion. United States v. Kelley,* 15 Wall., 34.

§ 16. Soldiers' Home.— The statutes relating to the Soldiers' Home (R. S. U. S., §§ 4814, 4819) recognize two classes of beneficiaries: 1st, soldiers who while in service contributed voluntarily or involuntarily to its support; 2d, soldiers who did not contribute. Those who contributed have a right of membership without surrendering their pensions to the institution; those who did not contribute may become members by surrendering their pensions. Bowen v. United States,* 14 Ct. Cl., 162.

§ 17. Section 4820, Revised Statutes of United States, provides that "the fact that one to whom a pension has been granted for wounds or disability received in the military service has not contributed to the funds of the Soldiers' Home, shall not preclude him from admission thereto. But all such pensioners shall surrender their pensions to the Soldiers' Home during the time they remain there and voluntarily receive its benefits." The meaning of this section is clear and obvious, viz., that only those invalid pensioners who have not contributed to the funds of the "Home" are bound to surrender to it their pensions while enjoying its benefit. Such being the case, the courts cannot look, for an interpretation, back of the Revised Statutes to the statutes which have been revised and embodied therein. United States v. Bowen,* 10 Otto, 508.

§ 18. The commissioner of pensions is not the head of a department within the meaning of the second section of article 2 of the constitution of the United States, which prescribes by whom officers of the United States shall be appointed. United States v. Germaine, 9 Otto, 508.

§ 19. The construction given to statutes relating to pensions by the commissioner of pensions is entitled to great consideration by the courts of the United States in interpreting such statutes. Bowen v. United States,* 14 Ct. Cl., 162.

§ 20. The certificate of the commissioner of pensions is prima facie evidence of title to a pension and of all the facts that make the title. Alexander v. United States,* 4 Ct. Cl., 218.

§ 21. Half pay under act of 1780.— A claim for the half pay granted by the resolution of congress of October, 1780, is barred by not being presented at the treasury by the 27th of March, 1794, according to section 1 of the act of March 27, 1792 (1 Stat., 245). It is also barred by section 1 of the act of February 12, 1798, if not presented at the treasury before May 1, 1794, as it is a claim upon the United States for services. Chamberlain v. United States.* 17 Ct. Cl., 631.

§ 22. **Pension of a deceased pensioner.**— A claim on the United States for the pension due a decedent must be prosecuted by the administrator, and not by the heirs, as it is personal estate. *Ibid.*

§ 28. The representatives of a person entitled to a pension under the act of May 15, 1828, but who never obtained its allowance or any adjudication in his favor, have no claim for the money after his death. Thatcher v. United States.* 12 Law Rep. (N. S.), 82.

§ 24. Under a general act, like that of 1828, no person becomes a pensioner so as to leave "arrears of pension," within the meaning of the acts of congress upon the subject, until after such adjudication in his favor by the secretary of the treasury. *Ibid.*

§ 25. **Accrued pensions not assets.**— The Revised Statutes provide (section 4718) that an accrued pension shall not be considered as a part of the assets of the estate of a deceased pensioner. This provision is applicable to and governs the act of January 25, 1879 (1 Supplmt. R. S., p. 395, ch. 23), which provides for the ascertainment and allowance of "arrears of pension," but does not use the term "accrued pensions." Donnelly v. United States,* 17 Ct. Cl., 105.

§ 26. A pensioner having applied for arrears under the act of January 25, 1879, the commissioner allowed the claim and issued the usual certificate, but before payment the pensioner died. *Held,* that the issuing of the certificate did not create a debt against the government which survived to the administrator of the pensioner. *Ibid.*

§ 27. **Who entitled — Acts of officers conclusive.**— The whole matter of ascertaining, determining and certifying who is lawfully entitled to a pension on account of military service is confided to certain executive officers, and not to the judiciary, and no right to a pension is fixed until those officers declare it to be; and if they decide against the right there is no appeal except to congress. So held in suit brought upon a pension claim which had been rejected by the commissioner of pensions. Daily v. United States,* 17 Ct. Cl., 144.

§ 28. **Surgeons of regiments** were not included in the resolution of congress of October 21, 1780, providing that "the officers who shall continue in the service to the end of the war shall be entitled to half pay during life." Thatcher v. United States,* 12 Law Rep. (N. S.), 82.

§ 29. **Pension agent — Bond.**— The approval by the secretary of the interior of a new bond of a pension agent, without an accounting by the agent, is not such an acceptance of the new bond as will cancel the liability of the sureties on the old bond, where, upon a settlement of his accounts, it appears that at the time of giving the new bond the agent was in default. United States v. Haynes, 9 Ben., 23.

§ 80. **Adopted and illegitimate children.**— Under the act of March 4, 1814 (3 Stat. at Large, 103), an adopted child is not entitled to a pension; but an illegitimate child, which, by intermarriage of the parents, and acknowledgment as their child, becomes legitimatized by the law of the state in which the parents reside, is entitled to a pension if the father dies in the naval service and the mother marries again. United States v. Skam, 5 Cr. C. C., 367.

§ 81. **By the act of March 3, 1819** (3 Stat. at Large, 514), a new requisite is prescribed to the validity of pensions, viz., the biennial affidavit of continued disability to be given by two surgeons. The repeal of that act in 1832 (4 Stat. at Large, 599) was prospective only, and could not restore to the pension roll any one who had been dropped from it for non-compliance with the said condition. Williams v. United States,* 10 Law Rep. (N. S.), 631.

§ 82. **Navy agents.**— There is no such distinct office known to the constitution and laws of the United States as navy pension agent; hence it is competent for the secretary of the navy to require the navy agents to pay these pensions; and having done so, the sureties of the navy agent are responsible for the faithful performance of that service. United States v. Cutter, 2 Curt., 617.

PERILS OF THE SEA.

See Carriers; Insurance.

PERJURY.

See Crimes.

PERPETUITY.

See CONSTITUTION AND LAWS; ESTATES OF DECEDENTS; USES AND TRUSTS.

PERSONAL PROPERTY.

See PROPERTY.

PETITION, RIGHT OF.

See CONSTITUTION AND LAWS.

PILOTS AND PILOTAGE.

See CONSTITUTION AND LAWS; MARITIME LAW.

PIRACY.

See CRIMES.

PLEADING.

See *post.*

PLEADING AND EVIDENCE.

See EVIDENCE.

PLEA IN ABATEMENT.

See PLEADING; PRACTICE.

PLEAS.

See PLEADING.

PLEDGE.

See BAILMENT.

PLENE ADMINISTRAVIT.

See ESTATES OF DECEDENTS; PLEADING.

POLICE POWERS.

[See Constitution and Laws.]

§ 1. In general.—The police power of a state extends to the protection of the lives, limbs, health, comfort and quiet of all persons, and the protection of all property within the state, and hence to the making of all regulations promotive of domestic order, morals, health and safety. Railroad Co. v. Husen, 5 Otto, 465.

§ 2. Under its police powers a state may regulate the conduct of its citizens towards each other, and the manner in which each shall use his own property, when such regulation is necessary for the public good. Included in these powers is that to regulate warehouses, and in so doing to fix a maximum of charge to be made for services rendered, accommodations furnished, etc. Munn v. Illinois, 4 Otto, 113.

§ 3. The court were inclined to regard with favor the following definition: Every law comes within the description of a regulation of police which concerns the welfare of the whole people of a state or any individual within it; whether it relates to their rights or their duties; whether it respects them as men or as citizens of the state, in their public or private relations; whether it relates to the rights of persons or property of the whole people of a state or of any individual within it; and whose operation was within the territorial limits of the state and upon the persons and things within its jurisdiction. City of New York v. Miln, 11 Pet., 102.

§ 4. The supreme police power of a state is one of the different means used by sovereignty to accomplish that great object, the good of the state, and is either national or municipal, in the confined application of that word to corporations and cities. Police powers and sovereign powers are the same, the former being considered so many particular rights under that name or word, collectively placed in the hands of the sovereign. Passenger Cases, 7 How., 283.

§ 5. The legislature having granted an exclusive right, and that branch or organ of the government possessing the police power with reference to the subject-matter of the right granted permits and acknowledges the exercise of the right as harmless, the right is so vested that neither the legislature nor the people have power to abrogate it. Crescent City, etc., Co. v. Butchers' Union, etc., Co., 9 Fed. R., 743.

§ 6. State acts in conflict with powers of congress.—The police powers of a state cannot be so exercised as to practically assume the powers conferred upon congress by the constitution. For example, a state cannot exercise its police powers over the interstate transportation of articles and subjects of commerce. Railroad Co. v. Husen, 5 Otto, 465.

§ 7. The statute of Missouri, prohibiting the importation of any Texas, Mexican or Indian cattle into the state, between the first day of March and the first day of November in each year, is not a quarantine nor inspection law, nor otherwise within the police powers of the the state, but is in conflict with that clause of the constitution of the United States ordaining that "congress shall have power to regulate commerce with foreign nations, and among the several states and with the Indian tribes." Ibid.

§ 8. The patent laws passed by congress do not in any way displace or restrict the police powers of a state. Hence, it is competent for a state to exact a license fee for the sale of patented articles as well as of those not patented. Webber v. Virginia, 13 Otto, 347.

§ 9. The twenty-ninth section of the internal revenue act of March 2, 1867 (14 Stat. at Large, 484), prohibiting the sale of certain kinds of oil, or oil unable to undergo a certain fire test, is plainly a police regulation, relating exclusively to the internal trade of the states, and as such can only have effect where the legislative authority of congress excludes territorially all state legislation, as, for example, in the District of Columbia. Within state limits it can have no constitutional operation. United States v. Dewitt, 9 Wall., 41.

§ 10. A state statute, providing a summary proceeding to remove intruders on Indian lands, is a police regulation and not unconstitutional. State of New York v. Dibble, 21 How., 366.

§ 11. State regulations of commerce are not valid as an exercise of police powers. Thus an Alabama statute, requiring steamboat owners, before leaving the waters of the state at Mobile, to file with the probate judge a written statement containing the name of the vessel, and of the owners, etc., etc., held, to be in conflict with the constitution and laws of the United States, and therefore void. Sinnot v. Davenport, 22 How., 227.

§ 12. A state may exclude from its limits paupers and convicts of other countries, persons incurably diseased, and others likely to become a burden upon its resources. It may, perhaps, exclude persons whose presence would be dangerous to its established institutions. But there its power ends. Whatever is done by way of exclusion beyond this must come from the general government. That government alone can determine what aliens shall be permitted to land within the United States and upon what conditions they shall be permitted to remain. Ah Kow v. Nunan, 5 Saw., 552.

§ 13. The police power of the state extends to all matters relating to the internal government of the state, and the administration of its laws which have not been surrendered to the general government, and embraces regulations affecting the health, good order, morals, peace and safety of society. This police power may be exercised by precautionary measures against the increase of crime or pauperism, or the spread of infectious diseases from persons coming from other countries. Thus, the state may entirely exclude convicts, lepers and persons afflicted with incurable disease; may refuse admission to paupers, idiots, lunatics and others, who from physical causes are likely to become a charge upon the public, until security is afforded that they will not become such a charge; and may isolate the temporarily diseased until the danger of contagion is gone. *In re* Ah Fong, 3 Saw., 144.

§ 14. But the extent of the power of the state to exclude a foreigner from its territory is limited by the right in which it has its origin — the right of self-defense. Whatever outside of the legitimate exercise of this right affects the intercourse of foreigners with our people, their immigration to this country and residence therein, is exclusively within the jurisdiction of the general government, and is not subject to state control or interference. Accordingly, a statute of California preventing the landing of foreigners who are "lunatic, idiotic, deaf, dumb, blind, crippled or infirm," or who are or have been paupers, etc., held to be beyond the police power of the state, as to prohibit the landing of blind or crippled people, etc., without regard to their present ability to support themselves, is to prohibit immigration. *Ibid.*

§ 15. Each state has exclusive control over all matters pertaining to its own internal police. It can establish and regulate ferries across its rivers, control the moving of vessels in harbors within its borders, and enact health and inspection laws which, by quarantine or otherwise, may operate on persons brought within its jurisdiction in the course of commercial operations. It has the same undeniable and unlimited jurisdiction over all persons and things, within its territorial limits, as any foreign nation, where that jurisdiction is not surrendered or restrained by the constitution of the United States. All those powers which relate mainly to municipal law, or what may be called internal police, not being restrained by or surrendered to the federal government,— the authority of a state in relation to these is complete, unqualified and exclusive. King *v.* American Transportation Co., 1 Flip., 1.

§ 16. State legislatures have an undoubted right to make all police regulations which they may deem necessary (not inconsistent with constitutional restrictions) for the preservation of the public health, good order, morals and intelligence, but they cannot under pretense of a police regulation interfere with the fundamental privileges and immunities of American citizens. Thus where the legislature of Louisiana granted to an incorporated society the exclusive privilege of keeping cattle landings, stockyards and slaughter houses in and about the city of New Orleans, and prohibited all others from keeping such establishments, *held*, that the grant of such exclusive privilege violated the rights of others desiring to keep such establishments, and willing to conform to all police regulations adopted for the public health, safety and comfort, and that such grant could not be sustained under the power to make police regulations. The Slaughter House Case, 1 Woods, 21; Live Stock, etc., Association *v.* Crescent City, etc., Co., 1 Abb., 388. But see Slaughter House Cases, 16 Wall., 36 (CONST., §§ 752–801).

§ 17. As a measure of police regulation a law prohibiting the manufacture and sale of intoxicating liquors ·is not repugnant to the constitution of the United States. Beer Co. *v.* Massachusetts, 7 Otto, 25.

§ 18. While a state may pass sanitary laws, and laws for the protection of life, liberty, health, or property within its borders; while it may prevent persons and animals suffering under contagious or infectious diseases from entering the state, and for the purpose of self-protection establish quarantine, and reasonable inspection laws, it may not interfere with transportation into or through the state beyond what is absolutely necessary for its self-protection. Railroad Co. *v.* Husen, 5 Otto, 465.

§ 19. Persons are not the subject of commerce, and not being imported goods, they do not fall within the reasoning founded upon the construction of the power given to congress to regulate commerce, and the prohibition of the states from imposing a duty on imported goods. Accordingly, the legislature of New York, having passed an act requiring the master of every vessel arriving in New York from any foreign port, or from a port of any of the states of the United States other than New York, under certain penalties prescribed in the law, within twenty-four hours after his arrival, to make a report in writing, containing the names, ages and last legal settlement of every person who had been on board the vessel commanded by him during the voyage, *held*, that this act was not a regulation of commerce, but of police; and that being so, it was passed in the exercise of a power which rightfully belonged to the state. City of New York *v.* Miln, 11 Pet., 102.

§ 20. The act of New York of 1824, above referred to, being intended to protect New York against the importation of foreign paupers, was an internal police regulation and constitutional. *Ibid.*

§ 21. It is not within the police powers of a state to impose taxes upon alien passengers arriving in the ports of that state. Passenger Cases, 7 How., 283.

§ 22. **Miscellaneous.** — A state may, under its police power, impose special assessments for levee purposes and the like. A special assessment for such a purpose is not a tax in the strict legal sense of that word, and hence it has been uniformly held that the usual constitutional provisions, requiring the burdens of taxation to be equally distributed, and requiring an equal and uniform valuation of all property for purposes of taxation, have relation to taxation for general state and county purposes, and are not limitations on the exercise of the police power, and do not inhibit special local assessments, when the fund raised is expended for the improvement of the property taxed. Boro v. Phillips County, 4 Dill., 216.

§ 23. An ordinance declaring that every male person imprisoned in the county jail, under the judgment of any court having jurisdiction in criminal cases in the city and county, shall, immediately upon his arrival at the jail, have the hair of his head cut or clipped to a uniform length of one inch from the scalp thereof, cannot be upheld either as a measure of discipline or as a sanitary regulation. Ah Kow v. Nunan, 5 Saw., 552.

§ 24. All rights granted by charter to corporations are subject to the police powers of the state when exercised in behalf of the public health or morals. The legislature cannot, by any contract, divest itself of the power to provide for these objects. Beer Co. v. Massachusetts, 7 Otto, 25.

§ 25. It seems that the power to impose a license fee or tax may be supported as an exercise of the police power. Railway Co. v. Philadelphia, 11 Otto, 528.

§ 26. The legislature of a state cannot bargain away its police power. Hence a charter to a company, authorizing them to conduct a lottery for a certain number of years, is nothing more than a license to enjoy the privilege on the terms named for the specified time, unless it be sooner abrogated by the sovereign power of the state for the general good. Stone v. Mississippi, 11 Otto, 814.

POLICY OF INSURANCE

See INSURANCE.

POLITICAL QUESTIONS.

See COURTS; GOVERNMENT.

POLYGAMY.

See CRIMES; DOMESTIC RELATIONS.

POSSESSION.

See LAND; LIMITATIONS.

POSTMASTER.

See BONDS; POSTOFFICE.

POSTMASTER-GENERAL.

See GOVERNMENT; POSTOFFICE.

POST-NUPTIAL SETTLEMENT.

See DOMESTIC RELATIONS; FRAUD.

POSTOFFICE.

[See BONDS; CRIMES; GOVERNMENT.]

I. IN GENERAL, §§ 1-61.
II. POSTOFFICE DEPARTMENT, §§ 62-85.
III. POSTMASTERS, §§ 86-140.

IV. CONTRACTS FOR CARRYING THE MAIL, §§ 141-181.

I. IN GENERAL.

SUMMARY — *Powers of congress: non-mailable matter*, §§ 1-8.

§ 1. The power vested in congress to establish postoffices and post-roads embraces not merely the designation of the routes over which the mail shall be carried, but the regulation of the entire postal system of the country, and under and by virtue of this power congress may designate what shall be carried, and determine what shall be included. *Ex parte* Jackson, §§ 9-12.

§ 2. Letters and sealed packages subject to letter postage are as fully guarded from examination, except as to their outward form and weight, as if they were retained by the parties forwarding them in their own domiciles, and can only be opened and examined under warrant issued under oath or affirmation, particularly describing the thing to be seized. The constitutional guaranty of the right of the people to be secure in their papers against unreasonable searches and seizures extends to their papers thus closed against inspection wherever they may be. *Ibid.*

§ 3. No regulations can be enforced against the transportation of printed matter in the mail, which is open to examination, so as to interfere in any manner with the freedom of the press. If, therefore, printed matter be excluded from the mails, its transportation in any other way cannot be forbidden by congress. *Ibid.*

§ 4. Regulations, excluding matter from the mail, may be enforced as to letters or sealed packages subject to letter postage, upon competent evidence of their violation, obtained from the parties receiving the letters or packages, or from others cognizant of the facts. As to objectionable printed matter, open to examination, the regulations may be enforced in some cases by the direct action of the officers of the postal service, as where the postage is not prepaid, etc., or where the object is exposed and shows unmistakably that it is prohibited, as in the case of an obscene picture or print. *Ibid.*

§ 5. In the enforcement of laws and regulations excluding matter from the mails, a distinction is to be made between different kinds of mail matter — between what is intended to be kept free from inspection, such as letters and sealed packages subject to letter postage, and what is open to inspection, such as newspapers, magazines, etc., purposely left in a condition to be examined. *Ibid.*

§ 6. An act of congress providing for the punishment of persons who send through the mails lottery circulars is constitutional. *Ibid.*

§ 7. Under section 8894, Revised Statutes United States, providing that "no letter or circular concerning lotteries, so-called gift concerts, or other similar enterprises, offering prizes, or concerning schemes devised and intended to deceive and defraud the public for the purpose of obtaining money under false pretenses, shall be carried in the mail," a postmaster is not authorized to detain and refuse to deliver letters addressed to lottery companies or their secretaries. The above section was intended to apply only to letters posted in the interest of lottery companies for the purpose of attracting custom, and not to letters addressed to such companies by persons having no interest therein; but if this were otherwise the postmaster would still be unauthorized to detain letters upon the mere suspicion that they contained unmailable matter, the act having provided no machinery for the arrest and detention of such letters. Commerford v. Thompson, §§ 13, 14.

§ 8. When letters actually belonging to a lottery company are withheld by a postmaster, an injunction to restrain the latter from detaining them will be refused, as a court of equity will not aid in promoting schemes contrary to public policy. *Ibid.*

[NOTES.— See §§ 15-62.]

EX PARTE JACKSON.

(6 Otto, 727-737. 1877.)

PETITION for writs of *habeas corpus* and *certiorari*.

STATEMENT OF FACTS.—Jackson was indicted for sending by mail circulars concerning an illegal lottery in violation of the act of congress. Having been convicted, he was fined $100, and ordered to be imprisoned until the fine should be paid. He applied for a *habeas corpus*, alleging that his imprisonment was unlawful. Further facts appear in the opinion of the court.

§ 9. *What is included in the power of congress to establish postoffices and post-roads.*

Opinion by MR. JUSTICE FIELD.

The power vested in congress "to establish postoffices and post-roads" has been practically construed, since the foundation of the government, to authorize, not merely the designation of the routes over which the mail shall be carried, and the offices where letters and other documents shall be received to be distributed or forwarded, but the carriage of the mail, and all measures necessary to secure its safe and speedy transit, and the prompt delivery of its contents. The validity of legislation prescribing what should be carried, and its weight and form, and the charges to which it should be subjected, has never been questioned. What should be mailable has varied at different times, changing with the facility of transportation over the post-roads. At one time only letters, newspapers, magazines, pamphlets and other printed matter, not exceeding eight ounces in weight, were carried; afterwards books were added to the list; and now small packages of merchandise, not exceeding a prescribed weight, as well as books and printed matter of all kinds, are transported in the mail. The power possessed by congress embraces the regulation of the entire postal system of the country. The right to designate what shall be carried necessarily involves the right to determine what shall be excluded. The difficulty attending the subject arises, not from the want of power in congress to prescribe regulations as to what shall constitute mail matter, but from the necessity of enforcing them consistently with rights reserved to the people of far greater importance than the transportation of the mail. In their enforcement, a distinction is to be made between different kinds of mail matter,—between what is intended to be kept free from inspection, such as letters, and sealed packages subject to letter postage; and what is open to inspection, such as newspapers, magazines, pamphlets and other printed matter, purposely left in a condition to be examined. Letters and sealed packages of this kind in the mail are as fully guarded from examination and inspection, except as to their outward form and weight, as if they were retained by the parties forwarding them in their own domiciles. The constitutional guaranty of the right of the people to be secure in their papers against unreasonable searches and seizures extends to their papers, thus closed against inspection, wherever they may be. Whilst in the mail, they can only be opened and examined under like warrant, issued upon similar oath or affirmation, particularly describing the thing to be seized, as is required when papers are subjected to search in one's own household. No law of congress can place in the hands of officials connected with the postal service any authority to invade the secrecy of letters and such sealed packages in the mail; and all regulations adopted as to mail matters of this kind must be in subordination to the great principle embodied in the fourth amendment of the constitution.

Nor can any regulations be enforced against the transportation of printed matter in the mail, which is open to examination, so as to interfere in any manner with the freedom of the press. Liberty of circulating is as essential to that freedom as liberty of publishing; indeed, without the circulation, the publication would be of little value. If, therefore, printed matter be excluded from the mails, its transportation in any other way cannot be forbidden by congress.

In 1836, the question as to the power of congress to exclude publications from the mail was discussed in the senate; and the prevailing opinion of its members, as expressed in debate, was against the existence of the power. President Jackson, in his annual message of the previous year, had referred to the attempted circulation through the mail of inflammatory appeals, addressed to the passions of the slaves, in prints, and in various publications, tending to stimulate them to insurrection; and suggested to congress the propriety of passing a law prohibiting, under severe penalties, such circulation of "incendiary publications" in the southern states. In the senate, that portion of the message was referred to a select committee, of which Mr. Calhoun was chairman; and he made an elaborate report on the subject, in which he contended that it belonged to the states, and not to congress, to determine what is and what is not calculated to disturb their security, and that to hold otherwise would be fatal to the states; for if congress might determine what papers were incendiary, and as such prohibit their circulation through the mail, it might also determine what were not incendiary, and enforce their circulation. Whilst, therefore, condemning in the strongest terms the circulation of the publications, he insisted that congress had not the power to pass a law prohibiting their transmission through the mail, on the ground that it would abridge the liberty of the press. "To understand," he said, "more fully the extent of the control which the right of prohibiting circulation through the mail would give to the government over the press, it must be borne in mind that the power of congress over the postoffice and the mail is an exclusive power. It must also be remembered that congress, in the exercise of this power, may declare any road or navigable water to be a post-road; and that, by the act of 1825, it is provided ' that no stage, or other vehicle which regularly performs trips on a post-road, or on a road parallel to it, shall carry letters.' The same provision extends to packets, boats, or other vessels on navigable waters. Like provision may be extended to newspapers and pamphlets, which, if it be admitted that congress has the right to discriminate, in reference to their character, what papers shall or what shall not be transmitted by the mail, would subject the freedom of the press, on all subjects, political, moral and religious, completely to its will and pleasure. It would in fact, in some respects, more effectually control the freedom of the press than any sedition law, however severe its penalties." Mr. Calhoun, at the same time, contended that when a state had pronounced certain publications to be dangerous to its peace, and prohibited their circulation, it was the duty of congress to respect its laws and co-operate in their enforcement; and whilst, therefore, congress could not prohibit the transmission of the incendiary documents through the mails, it could prevent their delivery by the postmasters in the states where their circulation was forbidden. In the discussion upon the bill reported by him, similar views against the power of congress were expressed by other senators, who did not concur in the opinion that the delivery of papers could be prevented when their transmission was permitted.

§ 10. *What congress can and what it cannot forbid to be transported outside the mails.*

Great reliance is placed by the petitioner upon these views, coming, as they did in many instances, from men alike distinguished as jurists and statesmen. But it is evident that they were founded upon the assumption that it was competent for congress to prohibit the transportation of newspapers and pamphlets over postal-routes in any other way than by mail; and of course it would follow that if, with such a prohibition, the transportation in the mail could also be forbidden, the circulation of the documents would be destroyed, and a fatal blow given to the freedom of the press. But we do not think that congress possesses the power to prevent the transportation in other ways, as merchandise, of matter which it excludes from the mails. To give efficiency to its regulations and prevent rival postal systems, it may perhaps prohibit the carriage by others for hire, over postal-routes, of articles which legitimately constitute mail matter, in the sense in which those terms were used when the constitution was adopted, consisting of letters, and of newspapers and pamphlets, when not sent as merchandise; but further than this its power of prohibition cannot extend.

Whilst regulations excluding matter from the mail cannot be enforced in a way which would require or permit an examination into letters, or sealed packages subject to letter postage, without warrant, issued upon oath or affirmation, in the search for prohibited matter, they may be enforced upon competent evidence of their violation obtained in other ways: as from the parties receiving the letters or packages, or from agents depositing them in the post-office, or others cognizant of the facts. And as to objectionable printed matter, which is open to examination, the regulations may be enforced in a similar way, by the imposition of penalties for their violation through the courts, and, in some cases, by the direct action of the officers of the postal service. In many instances, those officers can act upon their own inspection, and, from the nature of the case, must act without other proof; as where the postage is not prepaid, or where there is an excess of weight over the amount prescribed, or where the object is exposed, and shows unmistakably that it is prohibited, as in the case of an obscene picture or print. In such cases, no difficulty arises, and no principle is violated, in excluding the prohibited articles or refusing to forward them. The evidence respecting them is seen by every one, and is in its nature conclusive.

§ 11. *Powers of congress to exclude from the mails matters injurious to public morals.*

In excluding various articles from the mail, the object of congress has not been to interfere with the freedom of the press, or with any other rights of the people; but to refuse its facilities for the distribution of matter deemed injurious to the public morals. Thus, by the act of March 3, 1873, congress declared "that no obscene, lewd, or lascivious book, pamphlet, picture, paper, print, or other publication of an indecent character, or any article or thing designed or intended for the prevention of conception or procuring of abortion, nor any article or thing intended or adapted for any indecent or immoral use or nature, nor any written or printed card, circular, book, pamphlet, advertisement, or notice of any kind, giving information, directly or indirectly, where, or how, or of whom, or by what means, either of the things before mentioned may be obtained or made, nor any letter upon the envelope of which, or postal-card upon which, indecent or scurrilous epithets may be written or printed, shall be carried in the mail; and any person who shall knowingly deposit, or cause to be deposited, for mailing or delivery, any of the hereinbefore mentioned articles or things, . . . shall be deemed guilty of a misdemeanor, and, on conviction thereof, shall, for every offense, be fined not less than $100, nor more than $5,000, or imprisonment at hard labor not less than one year nor more than ten years, or both, in the discretion of the judge."

§ 12. *An act of congress punishing persons who send through the mails lottery circulars is constitutional.*

All that congress meant by this act was that the mail should not be used to transport such corrupting publications and articles, and that any one who attempted to use it for that purpose should be punished. The same inhibition has been extended to circulars concerning lotteries,— institutions which are supposed to have a demoralizing influence upon the people. There is no question before us as to the evidence upon which the conviction of the petitioner was had; nor does it appear whether the envelope in which the prohibited circular was deposited in the mail was sealed or left open for examination. The only question for our determination relates to the constitutionality of the act; and of that we have no doubt.

The commitment of the petitioner to the county jail, until his fine was paid, was within the discretion of the court under the statute.

As there is an exemplified copy of the record of the petitioner's indictment and conviction accompanying the petition, the merits of his case have been considered at his request upon this application; and as we are of opinion that his imprisonment is legal, no object would be subserved by issuing the writs; they are therefore denied.

COMMERFORD v. THOMPSON.

(Circuit Court for Kentucky: 2 Flippin, 611–620. 1880.)

STATEMENT OF FACTS.— Bill asking an injunction restraining defendant, who is postmaster at Louisville, Kentucky, from detaining plaintiff's letters. The answer sets up as a justification the orders of the postmaster-general, upon the ground that the correspondence in question was illegal, relating to unlawful lotteries.

Opinion by BROWN, J.

Few intelligent persons will deny that lottery gambling is a vice which merits the reprobation visited upon it by almost all the enlightened legislatures of modern times. The moral sense of the community long since pronounced against it, and the eloquent denunciations of Mr. Justice Catron, in the case of The State v. Smith, 2 Yerg., will touch a responsive chord in the breast of every honest man. The recent report of the postmaster-general to the house of representatives sets forth with startling emphasis the systematic deceptions, and often deliberate swindling, practiced by the promoters of these and kindred enterprises, and his efforts to purge his department of all complicity in their doings challenges the approval of public opinion.

At the same time courts are bound to administer the law as they find it, and are often powerless to remedy evils, the existence of which is fully admitted. The toleration or inhibition of lotteries is a matter exclusively within the control of the several states, and congress can do no more than to deny them the use of the national mails for the propagation of their schemes. But while there is undoubtedly power to prescribe what shall or what shall not be carried by post (*Ex parte* Jackson, 96 U. S., 727, 732; §§ 9–12, *supra*), the mails are, *prima facie*, intended for the service of every person desiring to use them, and a monopoly of this species of commerce is secured to the postoffice department. Sec. 3982. It is then scarcely necessary to say that the officers of the department are the agents of the public in the performance of this service, and that no postmaster, whether acting under the instructions of the postmaster-general or not, can lawfully refuse to deliver letters addressed to his office, unless specific authority for so doing is found in some act of congress. Indeed the unlawful detention of letters by a postmaster is denounced by sections 3890 and 3891, and a violation of his duty to deliver mail matter is made punishable by fine and imprisonment.

§ 13. *Under section 3894, Revised Statutes, a postmaster is not authorized to detain letters addressed to the secretary of a lottery company.*

Authority for the detention of the complainant's letters by the defendant in this case is claimed to exist under the following section of the Revised Statutes:

"Section 3894. No letter or circular concerning lotteries, so-called gift concerts, or other similar enterprises offering prizes, or concerning schemes devised and intended to deceive and defraud the public or for the purpose of obtaining money under false pretenses, shall be carried in the mail. Any person who shall knowingly deposit or send anything to be conveyed by mail in violation of this section, shall be punishable by a fine of not more than $500 nor less than $100 with costs of prosecution."

Counsel for the government have based their whole defense upon the applicability of this section to the case under consideration. Whether it was intended to apply only to mail matter, posted in the interest of lottery companies, gift concerts and other similar enterprises, by their managers or agents, for the purpose of attracting custom, or equally to letters addressed to such companies, is the main question in this case. Its solution depends largely upon the construction to be put upon the word "concerning." It is obvious that this word was not intended to be used in its broadest sense of "pertaining to or relative to," as such construction would include every letter of which the enterprises mentioned in the section were wholly or in part the subject; comprising not only letters written in the interest of these enterprises, but letters of inquiry, letters seeking legal advice, letters written for the purpose of suppressing their business, and even the correspondence carried on between the defendant and the general postoffice in this case. This certainly was not the intention of congress.

The word "circular," we think, affords a clue to the meaning of the section. This word obviously refers to circulars sent out by lottery companies for the purpose of advertising their schemes, and the word "letter" used in connection with it, under the rule of *ejusdem generis*, imports letters of similar character, and mailed for a like purpose. It was evidently the intention of congress to strike at the root of the lottery system, by inhibiting to them the use of the mails for the publication of their schemes, and to fix a penalty for such use; but the imposition of such penalty upon the writers of letters, addressed to the promoters of the enterprises, mentioned in this section, might result in great injustice, as many of these men purport to be engaged in a perfectly legitimate business, and the letters might be written by persons wholly ignorant of the true nature of the enterprise and with a perfectly innocent intent. The act is not only in derogation of the common law, but is penal in its character, and should therefore receive a strict construction.

This section was evidently intended for the punishment of the guilty promoters of these impostures, but in other sections congress has provided, not for the punishment, but for the protection of their victims, by requiring registered letters and money-orders to be returned to the writers under such regulations as the postmaster-general may prescribe. Sections 3929 and 4041. No penalty is in express terms affixed to the senders of these letters, and we think it would be a forced construction of the law to apply the penalties of section 3894 to them. Obviously sections 3929 and 4041 will not justify the act of the defendant in this case, as the Commonwealth Distribution Company is not fraudulent, but is apparently legalized by the law of the state (at least this was assumed upon the argument); and there is no averment in the answer that the letters are registered, or contain money-orders, nor is there an allegation of a compliance by the defendant with the requirements of these sections; indeed it was admitted upon the argument that the act of the defendant could not be justified unless 3894 covered the case.

But we think the act of the defendant in detaining these letters was unauthorized for another reason. The act declares certain letters unmailable, but provides no machinery for their arrest and detention, probably because no such machinery is possible, except by resort to the courts, without a violation of the constitutional guaranty of the right of the people to be secure in their papers against unreasonable searches and seizures. *Ex parte* Jackson, 97 U. S., 733. The act simply provides for the imposition of a fine upon the person mailing them. We think this method of enforcing the statute is exclusive, at least of any such remedy as the detention of letters upon a mere suspicion, though I would not say that a postmaster might not lawfully refuse to receive letters *known* to him (by the statements of those mailing them or otherwise) to contain unmailable matter. It is a cardinal rule in the construction of statutes, that where a new offense is created and a penalty is prescribed for it, or a new right is given, and specific relief provided for the violation of such right, the punishment or remedy is confined to that given by the statute. Sedgwick on Statutory Law, 94. In this construction I concur in the opinion of Mr. Attorney-General Devens, of April 30, 1878.

§ **14.** *Where letters actually belong to a lottery company, an injunction to restrain the postmaster from detaining them will be refused, because a court of equity will not aid in promoting schemes contrary to public policy.*

But, conceding that the act of the defendant in detaining these letters was unauthorized, and that the complainant might maintain an action at law for damages, it does not necessarily follow that he is entitled to an injunction. The writ of injunction does not issue as a matter of course, even if the complainant has made out a technical right to relief. "An application to a court of chancery for the exercise of its prohibitory powers of restrictive energies must come recommended by the dictates of conscience and be sanctioned by the clearest principles of justice." The granting of an application is largely a matter of discretion, and is addressed to the conscience of the chancellor acting in view of all the circumstances connected with the case. A party seeking this extraordinary remedy must come into court with clean hands, and show not only that his claim is valid by the strict letter of the law, but that in justice and equity he is entitled to this particular mode of relief.

In the case of The Maryland Savings Institution *v.* Schroeder, 8 Gill &

Johns., 93, the depositor of a sum weekly in a savings institution, which he was entitled to withdraw at pleasure, agreed with and requested the institution to convert and invest his deposits permanently into the stock of said company. Upon the conversion he received increased dividends and participated in its entire profits. The institution became insolvent, and receiving in the course of its settlement with its debtors its own certificates of deposit in payment, which would absorb all available funds, the depositor, on the ground that a conversion of his money into stock was in violation of the charter of the company, applied for an injunction. It was held that, whether the charter authorized it or not, he was not entitled to the restraining power of the court. In delivering the opinion, the court observed: " The object of the injunction appears to have been, and its effect and operation are, to prevent the officers of the corporation from paying the special depositors or receiving their certificates of deposit in the payment of debts due to the institution. How far it is warranted by the principles of equity and conscience in such its operation upon their rights and interest, it is the duty of this court now to examine and declare; and we think that, in a court of conscience at least, but little doubt can be entertained upon the subject. It is an unyielding and inflexible principle of the court of chancery, that he who seeks equity ought to be prepared to do equity. Before, therefore, the complainant can enlist the countenance of a court of equity in his favor he must be prepared to render to these depositors that full measure of justice which the principles of equity and conscience demand at his hand."

It was said in Bolsey v. McKim, 7 Harr. & J., 468, that there was no case in which a court of equity ever granted a perpetual injunction to a complainant to protect him in the enjoyment of a naked legal right which he or those under whom he claims have stipulated by deed not to exercise. " Legal rights are to be asserted by legal means, and in such cases courts of equity never lend their aid where justice and equity do not imperiously demand it." In Kneedler v. Lane, 3 Grant's Cases, 523, an injunction had been issued against the officers of enrolling boards to restrain them from proceeding further with the drafting of soldiers under the conscription act of March 3, 1863, upon the ground that the act was unconstitutional. In a subsequent argument of the case, this decision was overruled, and the act pronounced constitutional. But it was further held that even if the act had been unconstitutional the court ought not to have granted an injunction. In delivering the opinion, Mr. Justice Strong observed: " I had no doubt then, and I have none now, that these bills do not present a proper case for the interference of a court of equity by an injunction, even if the act of congress were unconstitutional. The facts charged exhibit no case for the intervention of a court of equity. No chancellor ever enjoined in such a case, and I think it has never before been supposed that he has any jurisdiction over such wrong, if it be a wrong. As these complainants ask to be restrained, . . . no one has ventured to assert that every civil wrong may be restrained by injunction, and that a judge sitting in equity can enjoin against any act that a common law court and jury can redress." See, also, Kerr on Injunctions, p. 6; 2 Story, Eq., § 959; Tucker v. Carpenter, Hemps., 440; Cassaday v. Cavenor, 37 Ia., 300; Jones v. The City of Newark. 3 Stock., 452; Cobb v. Smith, 16 Wis., 661; Bonaparte v. The Camden & Amboy Railroad Co., Bald., 218.

In Edwards v. The Allouez Mining Co., 38 Mich., 46, an injunction was denied to restrain a corporation from encroaching upon the land of a riparian proprietor and polluting the stream in front, upon the ground that he had bought the lands upon speculation knowing of the encroachments, and had tried to sell it to the corporation at an exorbitant price. The comments of Mr. Justice Cooley are pertinent in this connection: " Wherever one keeps within the limits of the lawful action, he is certainly entitled to the protection of the law, whether his motives are commendable or not; but, if he demands more than the strict rules of law can give him, his motives may become important. In general, it must be assumed that the rules of common law will give adequate redress for any injury, and when the litigant avers that under the circumstances of his particular case they do not, and that, therefore, the gracious ear of equity should incline to hear his complaint, it may not be amiss to inquire how he came to be placed in such circumstances."

Let us apply these principles to the case under consideration. The answer avers, and for the purposes of this case it must be taken as true, that all of said letters are letters and communications about and concerning a lottery known as the Commonwealth Distribution Company, and that all of said letters are intended to be received by said company, and are its exclusive property. The word "concerning," as used in this answer, must be taken in the sense in which it was intended by the pleader, and as meaning that the letters detained belonged to the Distribution Company, and related to the business carried on by that company. It is fair to presume that this company is seeking them in furtherance of its business as a lottery; indeed, in the bill they are expressly averred to be of the value of over $5,000, and in their brief complainants' counsel admit that these are in fact orders for tickets. Now, congress has placed upon all this class of enterprises the stamp of its disapproval. It has denounced it by legislation, as far reaching as its constitutional power permitted, as contrary to public policy. We think that a court of equity ought not to lend its aid, directly or indirectly, to schemes which congress has thus characterized. Suppose the defendant had detained letters and circulars mailed by this company, and the complainant had filed a bill, confessing the character of the letters, to enjoin her action upon the ground that the section only imposed a penalty, and did not in terms authorize the detention of letters ; we think a court of equity would not hesitate to refuse its aid thus sought for an unlawful purpose. The case under consideration is but one remove from this. In all human probability the letters detained here were written not only in furtherance of the lottery business (Dwight v. Brewster, 1 Pick., 50), but are to be answered, and in answering them complainant will be guilty of a clear violation of the law. Had he replied to the answer, and made it appear that the letters had no connection with the lottery business, he might have been entitled to the protection of a court of equity. But the pleadings fail to show a moral obligation on the part of this court to relieve him. In any light in which this case can be viewed, it is impossible to avoid the conclusion that the court is required to lend its aid to a scheme, condemned alike by congress and by public opinion. Complainant should be left to his remedy at law.

An order will therefore be entered dismissing the bill.

§ 15. **Powers of congress.**— The power vested in congress to establish postoffices and post-roads must be construed to authorize not merely the designation of the routes over which the mail shall be carried and the offices where letters and other documents shall be received to be distributed or forwarded, but to embrace the regulation of the entire postal system of the country, the right to designate what shall be carried, and to determine what shall be excluded. *Ex parte Jackson*, 6 Otto, 727; 17 Alb. L. J., 448; 10 Ch. Leg. N., 807. See §§ 9–12.

§ 16. An act regulating the rate of postage on mail matter is not unconstitutional by reason of its having originated in the senate instead of the house of representatives, as a bill establishing a rate of postage is not a bill "for raising revenue," within the meaning of that clause in the constitution of the United States providing that "all bills for raising revenue shall originate in the house of representatives." United States v. James, 13 Blatch., 207.

§ 17. —— freedom of the press.—No regulations can be enforced against the transportation of printed matter in the mail which is open to examination, so as to interfere in any manner with the freedom of the press. Liberty of circulating is as essential to that freedom as liberty of publishing. If, therefore, printed matter be excluded from the mails, its transportation in any other way cannot be forbidden by congress. Ex parte Jackson, 6 Otto, 727; 17 Alb. L. J., 448; 10 Ch. Leg. N., 807.

§ 18. Penalties for violation of postal laws.—The act of March 3, 1845, regulating the rates of postage and providing penalties for infractions of the postal laws, is a revenue law within the meaning of the act of May 31, 1844, pertaining to writs of error and appeals. United States v. Bromley,* 12 How., 88.

§ 19. —— for failure to deliver mail.—Before a person can be subject to the penalty of $150, under the thirteenth section of the act of 1845, for failing to deliver letters as prescribed in the sixth section of the postoffice act of 1825, the letters, for the non-delivery of which the penalty is sought to be imposed, must have been brought by him, or intrusted to his care, or within his power; and in a case where he has no knowledge of it, and could not obtain such knowledge by the exercise of reasonable diligence, he is not responsible. United States v. Beaty,* Hemp., 487.

§ 20. Express knowledge on the part of a defendant need not be proved, but it is essential to show such facts and circumstances as render it probable that he obtained that knowledge, or by the use of ordinary and reasonable diligence could have done so, so as to authorize the jury to presume it. Ibid.

§ 21. The master, captain, manager or owner are not responsible, under the act of 1845, for the conduct of the clerk of the boat in the matter of failing to deliver a letter, where they are ignorant of the existence of such letter, or could not obtain a knowledge of it by the use of reasonable diligence; and the diligence required by the law is not the utmost of which the case is susceptible; but only such as rational men employ in their own affairs. Ibid.

§ 22. —— for unlawfully carrying mail.—A passenger in a railroad car or steamboat passing over the post-road or route, carrying a letter without the knowledge or consent of the owner of the car or steamboat, or any of his agents or servants, does not render such owner liable to the penalty provided by the nineteenth section of the act of March 3, 1825. Nor is the person who sends such letter by such passenger liable to the penalty provided by the twenty-fourth section of said act, unless the owner of the car or steamboat is liable to the penalty provided by the nineteenth section of said act. United States v. Kimball,* 7 Law Rep., 32; 1 West. L. J., 399.

§ 23. It is not a violation of the postal laws for an express company to receive and transmit, in the usual course of its business, a package in a letter envelope, unstamped, containing a sum of money and a letter relating thereto, receiving the usual rate of payment for transmitting such a sum of money. United States v. United States Express Co.,* 5 Biss., 91.

§ 24. It was the intention of congress in the act of March 3, 1845, to permit a party who transmitted any article of property or money, by an express company or otherwise, to send at the same time and by the same mode of conveyance, although it might be beween cities where there was a post-route, and where the United States mail was carried, a letter of advice merely relating to the money or property thus sent. Ibid.

§ 25. Under the act of March 3, 1825, chapter 275, which provides that "if any person concerned in carrying the mail of the United States shall collect, receive or carry any letter or packet, etc., every such offender shall forfeit and pay, for every such offense, a sum not exceeding $50," a carrier may carry and deliver to the person named a package containing nothing but executions. The word "packet," as used in the act, must be construed to mean packet of letters. United States v. Chaloner,* 1 Ware, 214.

§ 26. Under the act of congress of March 3, 1825, the carrier of letters in a package is not liable to the penalty provided by such act unless he knew that the package contained letters. United States v. Adams & Co.,* 1 West. L. J., 315.

§ 27. Where an express company had positively refused to carry letters, and had instructed its agents not to carry letters, held, that such company was not liable under the act of March 3, 1825, for the wrongful acts of its agents in carrying letters without the knowledge or sanction of the company. Ibid.

§ 28. A person who sends a packet of letters by a passenger in a railroad car over a post-road, without the knowledge and against the consent of the owners of the car and their agents, is not subject to the penalty imposed by the nineteenth section of the act of congress of March 3, 1825. United States *v.* Pomeroy,* 8 N. Y. Leg. Obs.,· 148.

§ 29. If a passenger in a railroad car or steamboat carry letters over a post-road, without the knowledge of the proprietor of such car or steamboat, or of any of his servants, such proprietor is not liable under the nineteenth section of the act of March 8, 1825, and the proprietor of the car or steamboat not being liable under the nineteenth section, the sender of the letters is subject to no penalty under the twenty-fourth section of the same act; but if a party be openly engaged in carrying letters over the post-roads of the United States, and the railroad company be notified of this fact by one of the agents of the postoffice department, and by public advertisement, such company will be liable to the statute penalty for carrying such party carrying letters. And the company being thus liable under the nineteenth section, the person employing such party as agent to carry letters becomes liable under the twenty-fourth section. United States *v.* Hall,* 9 Am. L. Reg., 282.

§ 30. **Private letter carriers.**— The third section of the statute of 1827, which enacts that no person shall set up any foot or horse post for the conveyance of letters or packets upon any post-road, cannot be construed so as to prohibit the setting up of a post by railroad car or steamboat. United States *v.* Kimball,* 7 Law Rep., 32.

§ 31. The acts of congress of March 2, 1827, section 3, forbidding all persons other than the postmaster-general, or his agents, from setting up any foot or horse post for the conveyance of letters, etc., upon any post-road then or thereafter established, and of March 3, 1845, section 9, forbidding the establishment of any private express for the conveyance of letters, etc., from a city, town or place to another city, town or place, between which the mail is regularly transported, prohibit the business of private letter carriers on mail-routes, but not that of private letter carriers within the limits of a post-town. United States *v.* Kochersperger,* 9 Am. L. Reg., 145.

§ 32. A portion of the citizens of Brooklyn, unwilling to be served by the legal carrier, and desirous to appoint one of their choice, associated themselves together, and gave a standing order to the postmaster that he should deliver all their letters and papers to a person by them designated, which the postmaster refused to do. *Held*, that such combination on the part of the citizens was a palpable effort to evade the law and pervert it from the purpose for which it was made; and that although any man is at liberty to have his mail delivered at the office to himself, his family, clerk, servant or friend, a person who intends to make the carrying of letters his regular business, or part of his business, and to do it periodically, for hire, in opposition to the public carrier, is legally incapable of receiving authority to take letters out of the postoffice for that purpose, no matter what credentials he may have; whether it be a joint order from all his employers, or a separate order from each one; a permanent standing order, or an order renewed every day. Letter Carriers,* 9 Op. Att'y Gen'l, 161.

§ 33. **Franking privilege.**— Letters from the proper officers of banking associations employed as depositaries of public moneys, under the fifty-fourth section of the national currency act of February 25, 1863, upon business arising from their employment as depositaries, although certified by them to be on official business, are not transmissible through the mail, free of postage, to the treasury department, under the act to amend the laws relating to the postoffice department, approved March 3, 1863 (12 Stats., 701). National Banking Associations,* 11 Op. Att'y Gen'l, 23.

§ 34. The heads of bureaus in the executive departments may frank official papers for transportation in the mails, free of postage, under the postal act of March 3, 1863 (12 Stat., 708), by the impression of a stamp, or by the use of an engraved signature, as well as by writing the name. The Franking Privilege,* 11 Op. Att'y Gen'l, 31.

§ 35. The head of a bureau, having the right to frank packages for free transmission by mail, by the use of a stamp, cannot, for the purpose of facilitating the prompt transaction of public business, delegate the power to another, who under his direction shall stamp documents with his engraved frank; such stamping must be done by his own hand. Exercise of the Franking Privilege,* 11 Op. Att'y Gen'l, 35.

§ 36. **Postal money-orders.**— It is not the intent of the act of June 8, 1872, that the remitter of a postal money-order should be able to revoke the order or demand back his money against the objection of the payee. He cannot obtain repayment of the money deposited unless he produces the order. The payee of the money-order is entitled to the money upon demand, and upon complying with the statutes and regulations of the postoffice department, notwithstanding the protest of the remitter, and the remitter of the money-order cannot forbid the payment of it by any notice to the office at which it is made payable before it has been paid. Money Orders,* 14 Op. Att'y Gen'l, 119.

§ 37. **Obstruction of vehicle carrying mail.**— The right of the United States to have the mails carried over roads recognized as mail-routes is paramount to all other claims. Hence, a person. although holding a writ of possession from a state court against a railroad company, cannot obstruct the passage of a train carrying mails over the land thus placed in his possession without making himself liable under section 3995, Revised Statutes United States. United States *v.* De Mott, 3 Fed. R., 478.

§ 88. **Adoption of route.**— To "adopt" a route for the transportation of the mail means to take the steps necessary to cause the mail to be transported over that route. That is the sense of the resolution of congress of May 24, 1828 (4 Stats. at Large, 322). Rhodes *v.* United States,* Dev., 47.

§ 89. **What constitutes mailable matter.**— A written order for merchandise, folded in the form of a letter, but not sealed, is mailable matter within the meaning of the act of March 3, 1815, and the conveyance of such an order by the steward of a steamboat subjects the offender to the penalty prescribed by such act. United States *v.* Bromley,* 12 How., 88.

§ 40. —— **dutiable articles in mails.**— It is unlawful to transmit from a foreign country a dutiable article by mail in a sealed envelope. And though neither the sender nor receiver had any intention to defraud the government of its revenue, such article upon its arrival is liable to seizure by the customs officers; and upon such seizure the owner can only redeem it by payment of the appraised value as prescribed by the statute. Von.Cotzhausen *v.* Nazro,* 8 Rep., 645.

§ 41. **Letter postage — What constitutes a newspaper.**— A publication to be a newspaper, within the meaning of the thirteenth section of the act of 1825, concerning the general postoffice, must be published for everybody's use, in numbers, with regularity, or something approaching it; must convey news, not mere dissertation and discussion, or literary and poetical miscellanies; must be in sheets and in a cheap form. Postage,* 4 Op. Att'y Gen'l, 10.

§ 42. Under the act of March 3, 1845, establishing rates of postage for newspapers, magazines, etc., to entitle any publication to the privilege of a newspaper, its main object and purpose must be the dissemination of intelligence of passing events; it must be issued in numbers consisting of not more than two sheets, the superficies of which do not exceed one thousand nine hundred inches, at short stated intervals of not more than one month. The main object and purpose of the publication must be to disseminate intelligence of passing events; but the employment of a portion of its columns in publishing essays or compositions of a moral, political or literary character is not inconsistent with this leading and general object. Rates of Postage,* 4 Op. Att'y Gen'l, 407.

§ 43. —— **what marks on newspaper wrapper subject it to.**— A letter or initial upon the wrapper of a newspaper is not a "writing or memorandum" within the meaning of the act of March 3, 1825 (4 Stats. at Large, 105, 111), authorizing postmasters to collect letter postage on newspapers within which, on which, or on the wrapper of which, any writing or memorandum appears besides the name of the person to whom it is directed. And a postmaster who detains such newspaper, refusing to deliver it up to the person to whom it is directed, until full letter postage is paid, is liable in an action of trover in a state court for the conversion to which such unlawful detention is equivalent. Teal *v.* Felton, 12 How., 284.

§ 44. **Remedy to compel delivery of letters.**— An injunction will not be granted to prohibit a postmaster from refusing to deliver letters, and other matter addressed through the mail, on which has been prepaid postage, to the party to whom they are directed. The proper remedy is by *mandamus* or replevin. Boardman *v.* Thompson,* 12 Fed. R., 675.

§ 45. **Owner of bonds stolen and sent through the mail may maintain replevin, when.**— Bonds belonging to plaintiff were stolen from a bank and deposited in a postoffice for transmission through the mails; but as the addressee could not be found they were returned, and the postmaster, under instructions from the postoffice department, detained them, subject to such legal action as might be taken by the bank. *Held*, that as the bonds were not, while thus held by the postmaster, ordinary mail matter for transmission by mail, they were subject to replevin at the suit of plaintiff. Wylie *v.* Pearson,* 11 Fed. R., 61.

§ 46. **Privilege of writer to reclaim letter in transitu.**— B., a member of the firm of P., B. & Co., of San Francisco, applied to the postmaster-general for an order to the deputy-postmaster of the city of New York, that all the correspondence of the firm in San Francisco addressed to their several agents in the Atlantic and western states, and daily expected in New York by the steamer bringing the mails from San Francisco, should be delivered to him, B. *Held*, that the writer of a letter has no such general property in it as to entitle him in every case to reclaim it while *in transitu.* Stoppage of Letters,* 7 Op. Att'y Gen'l, 76.

§ 47. It seems that cases may occur in which the postmaster-general may lawfully authorize the writer of a letter to reclaim it *in transitu*, upon satisfactory proof that he is the writer of it, and that adequate legal cause of stoppage exists; but if this can be done, it must be upon specific proof applied to the particular emergency. *Ibid.*

§ 48. **Suppression of letters calculated to cheat and defraud the public, and of objectionable mail matter.**— In the enforcement of the regulations of congress, as to what shall constitute mail matter, and what shall be excluded therefrom, a distinction is to be made between different kinds of mail matter; between what is intended to be kept free from inspection, such as letters and sealed packages subject to letter postage; and what is open to inspection, such as newspapers, magazines, pamphlets and other printed matter, purposely left in a condition to be examined. Letters and sealed packages of this kind in the mail are as fully guarded from examination and inspection, except as to their outward form and weight, as if they were retained by the parties forwarding them in their own domiciles, and can only be opened and examined under like warrant issued upon similar oath or affirmation, particularly describing the thing to be seized, as is required when papers are subjected to search in one's own household. The constitutional guaranty against unreasonable searches and seizures extends to such letters and sealed packages in the mails. *Ex parte* Jackson, 6 Otto, 727; 17 Alb. L. J., 448; 10 Ch. Leg. N., 307.

§ 49. Although regulations excluding matter from the mail, cannot be enforced in a way which would require or permit an examination into letters or sealed packages, subject to letter postage, without warrant issued upon oath or affirmation, in the search for prohibited matter, they may be enforced upon competent evidence of their violation obtained in other ways, as from the parties receiving the letters or packages, or from their agents or others cognizant of the facts. And as to objectionable printed matter which is open to examination, the regulations may be enforced in a similar way by the imposition of penalties for their violation through the courts; and in some cases by the direct action of the officers of the postal service, as where the object is exposed and shows unmistakably that it is prohibited, as in the case of an obscene picture or print. *Ibid.*

§ 50. Where parties are engaged in practicing a gross fraud upon the public through the agency of the mails, it is competent for the postmaster-general to adopt measures or issue instructions to the end of preventing the postal service from being made a means for the accomplishment of the unlawful purpose; but to justify the adoption of preventive measures, the evidence of the dishonest scheme and fraudulent intent ought to be very clear. A lottery firm doing business, under the name of Murry, Eddy & Co., at Covington, Kentucky, a town on the Ohio river, directly opposite Cincinnati, received mail and had a box in the postoffice at both these points. A new lottery firm was organized in the latter place under the same style, Murry, Eddy & Co., which issued *fac-similes* of the circulars and tickets of the other firm, for the evident purpose of deceiving the public. As to whether the department could withhold letters addressed to Murry, Eddy & Co., directed to the proper box of the Cincinnati firm, *held*, that the department could not interfere with the delivery of letters merely with a view to protect one party from damage consequential upon the use of its name, style or trademark; but that such interference was warranted, if necessary for the protection of the public. Case of Murry, Eddy & Co.,* 12 Op. Att'y Gen'l, 399.

§ 51. The postoffice department has the power to make regulations which will prevent the service from being prostituted to purposes of fraud, and hence may order the non-delivery of letters addressed to any person under a name which is known to have been assumed as part of a system intended to cheat and defraud the public. But the fraudulent intent ought to be very clear, for the department is not invested with any authority to carry on an extended inquiry into the private affairs of persons who receive letters by mail. The mere misnomer of a man is not sufficient grounds for saying that the name is fictitious; neither is a firm an imaginary one because the style of it has no reference to the names of its members; nor can a letter be stopped on the sole ground that it is addressed to a person whose employment is immoral. Case of Emory & Co.,* 9 Op. Att'y Gen'l. 454.

§ 52. **Mail of debtor not subject to attachment.**— A postmaster has no authority to comply with the demand of the sheriff for the delivery of letters to him, upon an attachment levied at the suit of creditors of the party to whom the letters are addressed. Delivery of Letters,* 12 Op. Att'y Gen'l, 186.

§ 53. **Adverse claimants, rights of to mail.**— Letters addressed to business firms that had gone out of existence were claimed, at their destination, by different persons who once composed such firms. The postmaster-general having given to the local postmaster having custody of the letters, directions upon the subject which were not satisfactory to some of the contending parties, a suit was instituted in the state court to determine the rights of the parties, and an order obtained enjoining the postmaster from delivering the letters in accordance with the instructions of the postmaster-general. The attorney-general advised that the postmaster be directed to retain the letters, and to deliver them to the parties who should be finally ascertained by the court to be legally entitled to them. Delivery of Letters,* 13 Op. Att'y Gen'l. 395.

§ 54. Where letters are addressed to a young lady over eighteen years of age, but under twenty-one, and are claimed both by herself and her guardian, it is the better course for the postmaster to deliver the letters to the young lady, as she is the person to whom the letters are addressed, and thus answers the description in the postoffice laws, particularly section 22 of the act of March 3, 1825 (4 Stat., 108), and section 32 of the act of July 2, 1836 (5 Stat., 87), and sections 58 and 59 in the regulations made by the postoffice department. Delivery of Letters,* 18 Op. Att'y Gen'l, 481.

§ 55. Where a letter is directed to A., care of B., the postmaster may, in the absence of any demand by A., deliver the letter to B.; but if A. claim the letter and demand possession of it, the postmaster cannot lawfully deliver it to B. A prohibition by B., in conflict with a demand by A., must be disregarded by the postmaster. Delivery of Letters,* 12 Op. Att'y Gen'l, 136.

§ 56. Chief clerk of postoffice department not entitled to commissions in addition to salary.— The rules and regulations of the postoffice department having provided that the division of finance shall be under the superintendence of the chief clerk, who shall be treasurer of the department, held, that the chief clerk, receiving a stated salary as such, was not entitled to commissions or other extra pay for services performed by him as treasurer, such duties being incumbent on him by virtue of his office of chief clerk. United States v. Brown,* 9 How., 487.

§ 57. Miscellaneous.— The United States are creditors of a delinquent postmaster and his sureties, against whom a judgment has been entered, within the meaning of an act of the Illinois legislature, which provides that all conveyances which are not filed are void against creditors. And on this ground a conveyance of property by the parties to a postmaster's bond, the deed not having been left for record until after the defalcation occurred, was held void. Rose v. Prentiss, 4 McL., 106.

§ 58. Under a compact entered into between the federal government and the state of Ohio, by which the Cumberland road was surrendered to the control of the state, subject to certain restrictions, among which was one to the effect that no toll should be collected for the passage of any stage or coach conveying the United States mail, held, that a toll charged upon passengers traveling in the mail stages, without being charged, also upon passengers traveling in other stages, is against the contract, and not collectible. Neil v. State of Ohio, 3 How., 720.

§ 59. It rests altogether in the discretion of the postmaster-general to determine at what hours the mail shall leave particular places and arrive at others, and to determine whether it shall leave the same place only once a day or more frequently; hence the state, under the above contract, cannot complain of the frequency of the departure of carriages carrying mail as an abuse of the privilege of the United States; but the unnecessary division of the mail bags amongst a number of carriages, in order to evade the payment of tolls, would be such an abuse. Ibid.

§ 60. The act of 1836, chapter 270, section 1, requiring the revenue of the postoffice department to be paid into the treasury, does not require each payment to be carried in by a separate warrant, but they may be carried in quarterly by large covering warrants. Boody v. United States, 1 Woodb. & M., 150.

§ 61. If extra compensation shall have been paid by one postmaster-general, without the sanction of an act of congress, the money so paid may be recovered back. Acts of Postmasters-General,* 3 Op. Att'y Gen'l, 1.

II. POSTOFFICE DEPARTMENT.

§ 62. Scope of powers.— Postmasters-general are merely agents of the government, with limited authority; and none of their acts, except those that are found to be within the scope of their authority and conformable to law, are obligatory upon the government. Contractors with them are chargeable with knowledge of the law, and must be presumed to be acquainted with the extent of their powers, and consequently with any departure from them in respect to contracts for transportation of the mails, and cannot, therefore, legally claim any benefit under acts done in contravention of the law; for such are void from the beginning, and no legal right can be founded upon them. Acts of Postmasters-General,* 3 Op. Att'y Gen'l, 1.

§ 63. Not subject to control of president.— The postmaster-general, in the discharge of those duties which are prescribed by law, is not lawfully subject to the control of the president. United States v. Kendall, 5 Cr. C. C., 163.

§ 64. To require bonds from deputies.— By virtue of the acts of congress relative to the postoffice, making it the duty of the postmaster-general to superintend the department, to regulate the conduct and duties of his deputies, and to collect the moneys received by them for the general postoffice, he is empowered to take bonds to secure the payment of money due, or which may become due, to the general postoffice. Postmaster-General v. Early, 12 Wheat., 186.

§ 65. The postmaster-general has a right to require a bond from a deputy-postmaster, for the faithful performance of the duties of his office, although such bond is not expressly required by law. Postmaster-General *v.* Rice, Gilp., 554.

§ 66. **To make mail contracts.**— The word "temporary," as used in the proviso to the twenty-third section of the act of July 2, 1886, authorizing the postmaster-general to make contracts for temporary service without receiving bids, should not be construed to authorize a discretionary contract for a term extending beyond the time when the next annual letting will take effect, but that the postmaster-general has a discretion within that limit to advertise immediately, or to wait until the time for the usual annual advertisement, except when the exigency arises too late in the contract year for the advertisement and letting to be completed before the beginning of the next year, in which case the right to make temporary contracts extends through the succeeding year. Contracts for Carrying the Mail,* 13 Op. Att'y Gen'l, 478.

§ 67. The postmaster-general is not authorized to make any contracts for the conveyance of mails other than for "temporary" service, except under or in pursuance of bids received after inviting them by advertisement; and if the lowest bidder at an annual letting fails to enter into contract and perform service, the postmaster-general cannot legally contract with the next lowest bidder who will agree to perform the service at his bid for the whole term without re-advertising. *Ibid.*

§ 68. **To fine mail contractors.**— Under the act of June 27, 1848, authorizing and requiring the postmaster-general "to impose fines on contractors, for any unreasonable or unnecessary delay in the departure of mails to and from foreign countries, or in the performance of the trip," the power to impose a fine is limited to the cases and for the causes specified in the act, and does not extend to cases where vessels other than those called for by the contract are used, provided there was no unreasonable delay in the departure of the mails or the performance of the trip. United States *v.* Collins, 4 Blatch., 142.

§ 69. The power of the postmaster-general, under the act of June 27, 1848, to fine a mail contractor, though an administrative power, is so far judicial in its character that it must appear that the officer clothed with the power has assumed to exercise and has in fact exercised it. A letter from the postmaster-general, advising the head of another department to make a deduction from the pay of a contractor, on the ground that an inferior service has been performed, is not the imposition of a fine within the meaning of the above act. *Ibid.*

§ 70. **To establish post-routes.**— In the act of March 3, 1851, section 10, authorizing the postmaster-general "to establish post-routes within the cities or towns," the postmasters of which are appointed by the president, the word "post-routes" is not synonymous with post-roads in the act of 1827. United States *v.* Kochersperger,* 9 Am. L. Reg., 145.

§ 71. The postmaster-general, conformably to the provisions of the act of 1851, and other statutes, having established within the postal district of a city, the postmaster of which was appointed by the president, a local post for the collection and delivery of letters, etc., not carried by mail, issued an order declaring that under the authority conferred by the act of 1851, the streets of the city were established as "post-roads." This order did not make them "post-roads" within the meaning of the act of 1827, or make the business of private letter carriers within the postal district of the city unlawful. *Ibid.*

§ 72. **To discontinue postoffices.**— Although the power to establish postoffices and post-roads is conferred upon congress, the policy of the government has been to delegate the power to designate the places where mails shall be received and delivered to the postmaster-general, and the power to discontinue postoffices is incident to the power to establish them, unless there is some provision in the acts of congress restraining its exercise. Ware *v.* United States.* 4 Wall., 617.

§ 73. Possessing that power, it is lawful for the postmaster-general to exercise it by discontinuing an office, notwithstanding the fact that the postmaster in charge was appointed by the president, by and with the consent of the senate, because such incumbent accepted the appointment subject to the legal contingency that the postoffice might be discontinued. *Ibid.*

§ 74. **To make loans of public money.**— The power of the postmaster-general to make loans of public money must be limited to acts inseparable from the exigencies of the department over which he presides — acts necessarily incident to its regular, legitimate operations. It can never be extended to a right in the postmaster-general to advance money to a postoffice clerk, either as a loan or to purchase stocks or certificates of deposit for the purpose of speculation. United States *v.* Brown,* 9 How., 487.

§ 75. **To correct mistakes of predecessor.**— The act of a postmaster-general in making extra allowances to mail contractors in consequence of alterations made, after the execution of the contract, in the frequency and speed of the conveyances used for transportation, and on account of the increased weight of the mailed matter, are not, where the account is still open, conclusive upon his successor; on the contrary, the latter possesses competent authority to look into such allowances, and where he finds them to have been founded on material errors of law or fact, to correct them as justice shall appear to require. Acts of Postmaster-General,* 8 Op. Att'y Gen'l, 1.

§ 76. The right of the postmaster-general to review the decisions of his predecessor extends to mistakes in matters of fact arising from errors in calculation, but if a credit has been given or an allowance made by his predecessor, which, in his opinion, was wrongful, he must have suit brought. It is no longer a case between one officer's judgment and that of his successor. United States v. Bank of the Metropolis, 15 Pet., 877.

§ 77. To bind successors.— Although postmasters-general have no authority to bind their successors, in matters of purely public concernment, the case is different in respect to transactions with individuals. Their authorized contracts with individuals, when not affected by fraud or material error, are obligatory upon successors, the change of incumbents not in anywise affecting nor impairing the rights of the contractors; but the incapacity to vary the contracts of predecessors in office is occasioned by the obligatory force of the contracts themselves,— a force as operative upon the officer who made them as upon his successors,— and not because they were made by predecessors. Frauds and material errors, however, may as lawfully be inquired into by successors as by him or them who shall have made the contracts. Acts of Postmasters-General,* 8 Op. Att'y Gen'l, 1.

§ 78. To contract for postal-cards before appropriations made by congress.— The authorization and direction contained in the one hundred and seventieth section of the act of June 8, 1872, chapter 335, to furnish and issue " postal-cards to the public, with postage stamps impressed thereon," is not sufficient to warrant the postmaster-general in making a contract for the same before a specific appropriation by congress has been made, without violating the seventh section of the act of July 12, 1870, which provides that no department shall involve the government in any contract for the future payment of money in excess of appropriations for that fiscal year. Postal Cards,* 14 Op. Att'y Gen'l, 107.

§ 79. To allow extra compensation to deputy.— Under the act of June 22, 1854 (10 Stat., 293, 299), authorizing the postmaster-general to allow extra compensation to postmasters in certain cases for extra labor, etc., and the act of July 1, 1864 (13 Stat., 335, sec. 5), providing that " the postmaster-general shall allow to the postmaster a just and reasonable sum for the necessary cost, in whole or in part, of rent, fuel, lights," etc., the allowance of the extra compensation rests in the discretion of the postmaster-general, and the subordinate cannot claim the allowance as a matter of right, nor set up a claim of this nature, once rejected by the postmaster-general, as a set-off in suit by the government on the postmaster's official bond. United States v. Davis, Deady, 294.

§ 80. Under the act of congress of March 8, 1863, which provides, "that whenever, by reason of the presence of a military or naval force near any postoffice, unusual business accrues thereat, the postmaster-general is hereby required to make a special order allowing proportionately reasonable compensation to the postmaster, and for clerical services during the period of such extraordinary business;" the postmaster-general is the sole judge to determine not only whether the exigencies in the case have arisen, but if they have, the manner and extent of the allowance; and it is not competent for court or jury to revise his decision, nor is it re-examinable anywhere else. So held, where, in an action against the principal and his sureties on a postmaster's bond, a set-off was claimed on account of extra and unusual business occasioned by "the presence of a military force," which claim, upon presentation to the postmaster-general, had been disallowed. United States v. Wright, 11 Wall., 648.

§ 81. Re-adjustment of deputy's salary.— After a salary of a postmaster has been fixed it cannot be increased under the act of June 12, 1866, and prior acts, until re-adjusted by the postmaster-general, such re-adjustment being based upon the postmaster's quarterly returns. The re-adjustment is an executive act made necessary by the law in order to perfect any liability of the government. Hence, although the quarterly returns of a postmaster may warrant a re-adjustment of his salary, if the executive officer fails to do his duty by not making it, the government is not bound to pay an increased salary, as the courts cannot enforce rights which are dependent for their existence upon a prior performance, by an executive officer, of duties which he has failed to perform. United States v. McLean, 5 Otto, 750.

§ 82. Performance of ministerial duties may be compelled by mandamus.— The postmaster-general may be compelled by *mandamus* to perform a duty merely ministerial in its character, enjoined upon him by an act of congress, and as to which he has no discretion. So held where the postmaster-general refused to carry to the credit of S. & S., certain mail contractors, amounts allowed by the solicitor of the treasury, who had been appointed to settle and adjust the claims of such contractors by congress, which at the same time directed the postmaster-general to credit S. & S. with whatever sum the solicitor should decide to be due them. Kendall v. United States, 12 Pet., 524.

§ 83. The circuit court of the District of Columbia has authority to issue a *mandamus* to the postmaster-general, commanding him to perform a ministerial duty required by an act of congress, in which the right of an individual is concerned, if that right is clear and he has no other legal specific remedy. United States *v.* Kendall, 5 Cr. C. C., 163.

§ 84. **Discretionary acts not subject to revision.**— The sufficiency of excuses for failures in the delivery of the mails is by the regulations of the department submitted to the discretion of the postmaster-general, and the court of claims has no revisory power over decisions made in the exercise of such discretion. Buckles *v.* United States,* 20 Law Rep., 630.

§ 85. **Liability of.**— A public officer, acting from a sense of duty in a matter where he is required to exercise discretion, is not liable to an action for an error of judgment. Accordingly, where a postmaster-general wrongfully, although in the conscientious discharge of his supposed duty, suspended on the books of the postoffice department credits which had been entered by his predecessor in favor of certain parties, whereby injury resulted to those parties, *held,* that he was not personally liable. Kendall *v.* Stokes, 8 How., 87.

III. Postmasters.

Summary — *Marks on newspaper; letter postage,* §§ 86-88.

§ 86. The thirteenth section of the act of 1825 (4 Stat. at L., 105), provides that "any memorandum which shall be written on a newspaper or other printed paper, pamphlet or magazine, and transmitted by mail, shall be charged with letter postage." The thirtieth section of the same act, providing a penalty for writing on a newspaper, etc., uses the terms "any writing or memorandum." *Held,* that a single letter or initial upon the wrapper of a newspaper is neither a memorandum nor a writing, within the meaning of the above act, and that a postmaster is not authorized to detain a paper thus marked, although a circular from the postoffice department relating to the same subject contains the terms, "marks or signs made in any way." Teal *v.* Felton, §§ 89-93.

§ 87. The postal act of 1825, authorizing postmasters to hold papers having "any writing or memorandum" upon them, reposes in postmasters no discretionary or judicial powers, and the act of a postmaster in arresting the transmission of a paper because of a letter or initial written upon it is purely ministerial, and he can claim no exemption from liability for his illegal detention on the ground that he was called upon to exercise discretion and judgment. *Ibid.*

§ 88. If a person tender to the postmaster the legal postage on mail matter addressed to him, and the postmaster refuses to deliver it, such unlawful detention amounts to conversion, for which trover will lie. *Ibid.*

[Notes.— See §§ 94-140.]

TEAL *v.* FELTON.

(12 Howard, 284-293. 1851.)

Opinion by Mr. Justice Wayne.

Statement of Facts.— This suit was brought in a justice's court to recover from the plaintiff in error the value of a newspaper, received by him as postmaster at Syracuse, which he refused to deliver to the defendant in error, to whom it was addressed. The plaintiff in error had charged the newspaper with letter postage, on account of a letter or initial upon the wrapper of it, distinct from the direction. This the defendant refused to pay, at the same time tendering the lawful postage of a newspaper. The postmaster would not receive it, and retained the paper against the will of the defendant; upon that demand and refusal the suit was brought. The action was trover, and the general issue was pleaded. In the course of the trial, when the defendant in error, who was plaintiff in the suit below, was introducing testimony in support of his case, the defendant objected to a further examination of the case by witnesses, upon the ground that the court had not jurisdiction of the case. The objection having been overruled, the trial of the case was continued; and after the plaintiff had proved that he demanded from the defendant the newspaper, tendering the lawful postage, and that the postmaster refused to deliver it to him, he rested his case.

§ **89.** *Where the decision of the state court necessarily involves a denial of a defense claimed under a law of the United States, the supreme court has jurisdiction on writ of error under the twenty-fifth section of the judiciary act of 1789.*

The defendant below then moved for a nonsuit, which having been denied, he offered in evidence a circular from the postoffice department, of the 4th December, 1846, marked in the record as A, and also the postoffice act of 1845. The case was submitted to a jury. A verdict was rendered by it against the defendant, upon which a judgment was entered. The defendant carried the case to the court of appeals, and the judgment of the lower court was affirmed. It is brought to this court by a writ of error. As the court of appeals could not have adjudicated the case without having denied to the defendant a defense which he claimed under a law of the United States, the case is properly here under the twenty-fifth section of the judiciary act of 1789.

The circular from the postoffice department is as follows: "The wrappers of all such newspapers, pamphlets and magazines, when they have reached their destination, should be carefully removed; and if, upon inspection, they are found to contain any manuscript or memorandum of any kind, either written or stamped, or by marks or signs made in any way, either upon any newspaper, etc., etc., or the wrapper upon which it is inclosed, by which information shall be asked or communicated, except the name of the person to whom it is directed, such newspaper, etc., etc., with the wrapper in which it is inclosed, shall be charged with letter postage by weight."

If the person to whom the newspaper is directed refuses to pay the letter postage, the postmaster is directed to transmit the same to the office whence it came, with a request that the person who sent it may be prosecuted for the penalty of $5, according to the thirtieth section of the act of 1825. Those parts of the thirtieth section mentioned, upon which the circular was issued, and of the thirteenth section of the act directing that a memorandum which shall be written on a newspaper shall be charged with letter postage, are: "If any person shall inclose or conceal a letter or other thing, or any memorandum in writing in a newspaper, pamphlet or magazine, or in any package of newspapers, etc., etc., or make any writing or memorandum thereon, which he shall have delivered in any postoffice or to any person for that purpose, in order that the same may be carried by post, free of letter postage, he shall forfeit the sum of $5 for every such offense, and the letter, newspaper, package, memorandum or other thing shall not be delivered to the person to whom it is directed until the amount of single letter postage is paid for each article of which the package is composed." That part of the thirteenth section of the act mentioned is: "Any memorandum which shall be written on a newspaper or other printed paper, pamphlet or magazine, and transmitted by mail, shall be charged with letter postage." 4 Laws of the United States, 105–111. Those parts of the law of 1845, in a way applicable to this case, are the first and second sections fixing the rates of postage upon letters and newspapers, and the sixteenth section, which defines a newspaper to be a printed publication issued in numbers, consisting of not more than two sheets, and published at short intervals of not more than a month, conveying intelligence of passing events, and the *bona fide* extras and supplements of any such publication. 5 U. S. L., 732, 737.

§ **90.** *A single letter on a wrapper is not "any writing or memorandum" within the postal act of 1825.*

From the evidence in this case, we do not think that the initial or letter upon the wrapper of the newspaper in this case, subjected it either under the thirteenth or thirtieth section of the act of 1825 to letter postage. Why it was placed there, supposing it not to have been accidental, cannot be found out from this record, and it must have been a meaningless mark to the postmaster. It may have excited a suspicion that it was a sign arranged between the person sending it and the person to whom it was directed, to convey information of some sort or other, for which letter postage would have been charged if it had been conveyed in words. The acts forbids a memorandum in the thirteenth section; and in the thirtieth, providing for a penalty, the terms are, "any writing or memorandum," but in neither are found the terms "marks or signs," as used in the circular. No provision is made for such a case. It must be obvious, too, that frauds of that kind cannot be prevented in the transmission of newspapers, without legislation by congress subjecting newspapers, conveyed by mail, to letter postage, whenever there shall be, either upon the newspaper or the wrapper of it, any letter, sign or mark, besides the address of the person to whom it is sent. A single letter or initial upon the wrapper of a newspaper is neither a memorandum nor a writing, in the sense in which either of those terms are ordinarily used, or as we think they are intended to be used, in the thirtieth section of the act. Both mean something in words to convey intelligence, a remembrance for one's self or to another. The act speaks of something concealed in a newspaper or package of newspapers, of a writing or memorandum, from which it may be seen to have been the intention of the sender to convey information clandestinely under the wrapper, or upon it in a form, though not disclosing what it is, which will leave no doubt of his intention.

§ 91. *The postal act of 1825, authorizing postmasters to hold papers with "any writing or memorandum," reposed in them no discretion to determine that a single letter was such.*

The initial in this case does not seem to have been one or the other. It is not a memorandum certainly, and a single letter of the alphabet can convey no other idea than that it belongs to it, unless it is used numerically. This was not a case in which judgment could be used to determine any fact, except by some other evidence than the letter itself. Nor was it one calling for discretion, in the legal acceptation of that term, in respect to officers who are called upon to discharge public duties. What was done by the postmaster was a mere act of his own, and ministerial, as that is understood to be, distinct from judicial. It could not have been the intention of congress to put it in the power of postmasters, upon a mere suspicion raised by a single letter or initial, to arrest the transmission of newspapers from the presses issuing them, or when they were mailed by private hands.

This view of the law disposes also of that point in the argument, claiming for the postmaster an exemption from the suit of the plaintiff, upon the ground that he was called upon, in the act which he did, to exercise discretion and judgment. In Kendall *v.* Stokes, 3 How., 97, 98, will be found this court's exposition upon that subject, with the leading authorities in support of it. The difference between the two must at all times be determined by the law under which an officer is called upon to act, and by the character of the act. It is the law which gives the justification, and nothing less than the law can give irresponsibility to the officer, although he may be acting in good faith under the instructions of his superior of the department to which he belongs. Here the instructions exceed the law, as marks and signs, of themselves, without some knowledge of their meaning, and the intention in the use of them, are, as we have said, neither memoranda nor writings. Tracy v. Swartwout, 10 Pet., 80.

But it is said that the courts of New York had not jurisdiction to try the case. The objection may be better answered by reference to the laws of the United States, in respect to the services to be rendered in the transmission of letters and newspapers by mail, and by the constitution of the United States, than it can by any general reasoning upon the concurrent civil jurisdiction of the courts of the United States, and the courts of the states, or concerning the exclusive jurisdiction given by the constitution to the former.

§ 92. *Where a person tenders to the postmaster the legal postage on mail matter addressed to him, and the postmaster refuses to deliver it, this is a conversion, and suit may be brought.*

The United States undertakes, at fixed rates of postage, to convey letters and newspapers for those to whom they are directed, and the postage may be prepaid by the sender, or be paid when either reach their destination, by the person to whom they are addressed. When tendered by the latter, or by his agent, he has the right to the immediate possession of them, though he has not had before the actual possession. If, then, they be wrongfully withheld for a charge of unlawful postage, it is a conversion, for which suit may be brought.

§ 93. —— *and such suit may be brought in a state court having jurisdiction in trover.*

His right to sue existing, he may sue in any court having civil jurisdiction of such a case, unless for some cause the suit brought is an exception to the general jurisdiction of the court. Now the courts in New York, having jurisdiction in trover, the case in hand can only be excepted from it by such a case as this having been made one of exclusive jurisdiction in the courts of the United States by the constitution of the United States. That such is not the case, we cannot express our view better than Mr. Justice Wright has done in his opinion in this case in the court of appeals. After citing the second section of the third article of the constitution, he adds: " This is a mere grant of jurisdiction to the federal courts, and limits the extent of their power, but without words of exclusion or any attempt to oust the state courts of concurrent jurisdiction in any of the specified cases in which concurrent jurisdiction existed prior to the adoption of the constitution. The apparent object was not to curtail the powers of the state courts, but to define the limits of those granted to the federal judiciary." We will add that the legislation of congress, immediately after the constitution was carried into operation, confirms the conclusion of the learned judge. We find, in the twenty-fifth section of the judiciary act of 1789, under which this case is before us, that such a concurrent jurisdiction in the courts of the states and of the United States was contemplated, for its first provision is for a review of cases adjudicated in the former, " where is drawn in question the validity of a treaty or statute of, or an authority exercised under, the United States, and the decision is against their validity." We are satisfied that this was no error in the decision of the court of appeals in this case, and the same is affirmed by this court.

§ 94. In general.—The mere neglect of a postmaster to reasonably forward a letter does not create a cause of action. The plaintiff must show that damage has been sustained by him by reason of such neglect. Dunlop v. Munroe,* 7 Cr., 242.

§ 95. A postmaster is not bound to keep the money received for postage distinct from his own, nor to deposit it specifically in the name of the United States. Trafton v. United States, 3 Story, 646.

§ 96. The provision of the postoffice law, that a postmaster shall reside at the place where the office is kept, is directory to the postmaster-general; imperative on him, to be sure; but until he acts, although the postmaster may have removed from the neighborhood of the postoffice, he and his sureties are responsible to the department and to individuals injured by any neglect of duty in the office. United States v. Pearce, 2 McL., 14.

§ 97. Where A., being postmaster, gave an official bond to the United States, and subsequently employed B. as his assistant, and the receipts from the postoffice were deposited in their joint names, and an action was brought against A. on his bond, and judgment recovered, but he having subsequently become bankrupt, upon action brought against A. and B., *held*, that the deposit in the joint names of A. and B. did not make them jointly responsible; that there was no privity of contract between B. and the United States, and that even if there were, the former judgment against A. was a bar to the second action. Trafton v. United States, 3 Story, 646.

§ 98. Appointment.— When a postmaster has been nominated to an office by the president, confirmed by the senate, and his commission has been signed by the president, and the seal of the United States affixed thereto, his appointment is complete. The transmission of the commission is not essential to his investiture of the office. Nor would the subsequent death of the president have any effect on that completed act. United States v. Le Baron, 19 How.,78.

§ 99. Amount of diligence required.— A deputy-postmaster is only called upon to exercise, with respect to letters and packages left at his office to be mailed, the same degree of care and diligence which a prudent man would have taken of his own property. Dunlop v. Munroe,* 1 Cr. C. C., 536.

§ 100. The policy of the government of the United States, in respect to the business of the postoffice department, requires that principals and sureties upon the bonds of postmasters shall be held liable at all events. Neither robbery, nor theft, nor misadventure of any kind, except, perhaps, when caused by the action of the government itself, will excuse a postmaster or his sureties. United States v. Morrison,* Chase's Dec., 521.

§ 101. The only exceptions to the above rule are those provided for by acts of congress. The act of 1864 excuses loyal postmasters from losses occasioned by the Confederate forces or rebel guerillas. That of 1865 extends the same relief to cases where the losses are occasioned by armed forces other than those of the so-called Confederate States. *Ibid.*

§ 102. Discontinuance of office — Government money retained for damages.— Upon the discontinuance of a postoffice by the postmaster-general the incumbent ceases to be postmaster; and never having been entitled to any compensation except commissions and receipts from boxes, and those sources of compensation being extinguished upon the discontinuance of the office, he loses nothing to which he is entitled. Ware v. United States,* 4 Wall., 617.

§ 103. In suit by the government on the official bond of a deputy-postmaster, by reason of the refusal of the latter to pay over certain moneys received for postages, as exhibited in his quarterly accounts for the last two quarters preceding the discontinuance of the office, the rejoinder of the defendant that the commissions of the office, if it had not been unlawfully discontinued, would have been sufficient to justify an allowance to the incumbent of a sum greater than the amount retained, and that the commissions were wrongfully withheld from him, amounts to a claim for damages, and not for commissions. To such claim there are two sufficient answers: 1. The compensation of a deputy-postmaster depends upon postage commissions and rental of boxes, and those sources having entirely failed, the department possessed no authority whatever to make any other allowances. 2. The claim being for damages, the court could not sustain it unless the same had been presented to the auditor, and by him disallowed. *Ibid.*

§ 104. Abandonment of office — Failure to make return.— Under the act of March 3, 1825, a postmaster, who leaves office between the beginning and end of a quarter, is liable to a double charge for postage, if he fails to make a return and render his account within one month after the expiration of the quarter. United States v. Roberts,* 9 How., 501.

§ 105. Default — No demand necessary to constitute.— No preliminary demand of payment is necessary to put in default a postmaster omitting to pay over the public funds in his hands at the expiration of each successive quarter of his service; and no proof of such demands having been made is requisite to sustain an action against him. Demand of Payment, etc.,* 4 Op. Att'y Gen'l, 304.

§ 106. Deputy's bond — Acceptance and approval of.— A bond given by a deputy-postmaster speaks only from the time when it reaches the postmaster-general and is accepted by him; it cannot relate back to any earlier date than the time of its acceptance, because it is only after its acceptance that there can be any such holding of the office as the bond was meant to apply to. Thus where a bond recited: "Whereas the said B. is deputy-postmaster at Mobile," etc., and he was in fact postmaster at the date of the bond, but under a previous appointment, the bond must be held to be security for his duties under a new appointment confirmed after its date, but before its delivery to the postmaster-general for approval, and sureties on this bond are liable for defaults of the principal under the new appointment, but not under the old. United States *v.* Le Baron, 19 How., 78.

§ 107. A bond given by a postmaster, with sureties, for the performance of his official duties, does not constitute a binding contract until approved and accepted by the postmaster-general; but the reception and detention of an official bond by the postmaster-general for a considerable time without objection is sufficient evidence of its acceptance; and the return of the bond to the principal obligor, for the purpose of obtaining an additional surety, affords no proof that it has not been accepted, nor does it amount either to a surrender or cancellation of it. Postmaster-General *v.* Norvell, Gilp., 106.

§ 108. —— not vitiated by extension.— A postmaster's official bond, given to secure the faithful performance of official duties and the payment of money of the United States which might come to his hands, is not vitiated as security for the payment of the money stipulated because also extended to the official conduct of the obligor, although such part of said bond may be void as not being authorized by law. Postmaster-General *v.* Early, 12 Wheat., 136.

§ 109. Defenses to suit on.— In suit brought against a postmaster or his sureties on his official bond, to recover money held by him for the government, it is no defense that the money was paid to a mail contractor, a creditor of the government, either voluntarily or by command of the postoffice department of the so-called Confederate States, the defendant having been postmaster in one of the rebellious states and the payment having been made after the outbreak of the rebellion. United States *v.* Keehler, 9 Wall., 83.

§ 110. A postmaster who, disregarding the instructions of the department, makes a payment to a mail contractor without taking the proper receipts and notifying the department, cannot, the contractor having given no credit for the amount of such payment when his accounts with the government were finally settled, be allowed credit for such payment in an action on his official bond. United States *v.* Roberts,* 9 How., 501.

§ 111. Actions against — Evidence.— Deputy-postmasters are civilly liable for the acts of their servants and clerks, but the neglect of the servant or clerk cannot be given in evidence upon a count charging the loss to have been incurred by the neglect of the deputy-postmaster himself. Dunlop *v.* Monroe,* 1 Cr. C. C., 536.

§ 112. The instructions of the postmaster-general to the deputy-postmasters may be given in evidence in an action on the case against a deputy-postmaster for negligence. *Ibid.*

§ 113. Where the issue is taken upon the neglect of the postmaster himself, it is not competent to give in evidence the negligence of his assistant. Dunlop *v.* Munroe,* 7 Cr., 242.

§ 114. —— accounts— Quarterly returns.— Under sections 8 and 15 of the act of July 2, 1836 (5 Stat. at Large, 81, 82), transcripts of the quarterly returns of a postmaster, with the corrections of the auditor of the postoffice department thereon, and of the auditor's accounts based on them, are admissible in evidence in actions upon such postmaster's official bond, though items of credit in dispute do not appear in such transcript. United States *v.* Hodge, 13 How., 478.

§ 115. The provisions of the act of March 3, 1825, substitute a certified statement of the settled account, as evidence in suits against deputy-postmasters, in lieu of the certified copy of the account current, required by the provisions of the act of April 30, 1810. Postmaster-General *v.* Rice, Gilp., 554.

§ 116. —— civil action for money stolen.— An averment that a letter, containing bank-notes, was fraudulently and improperly secreted, withheld and taken in the postoffice by the defendant, the deputy-postmaster, is not a charge of felony, so as to deprive the plaintiff of his civil remedy. Dunlop *v.* Munroe,* 1 Cr. C. C., 536.

§ 117. —— jurisdiction.— The circuit courts of the United States have jurisdiction under the act of March 3, 1815, of suits brought by the postmaster-general, on the official bonds of postmasters, for debts and balances due the general postoffice. Postmaster-General *v.* Early, 12 Wheat., 136.

§ 118. Limitations to actions against deputy-postmasters and their sureties.— The law which limits suits by the postmaster-general against sureties to two years after a default of the principal does not operate in cases of balances unpaid at the end of a quarter, which are subsequently liquidated by the receipts of a succeeding one. Postmaster-General *v.* Norvell, Gilp., 106.

§ 119. The official bonds taken by the postmaster-general from his deputies are valid, and the omission to bring suits on such bonds at the periods prescribed by law, for the defaults of the principal, does not discharge the sureties although injury has resulted to them by reason of such omission. Postmaster-General *v.* Reeder, 4 Wash., 678.

§ 120. Suit must be brought against the sureties of a postmaster within two years from the time the postmaster made default or the statute bars the action against them; and in computing the time, the defalcation is to be counted from the time the law requires the moneys to be paid over, viz., at the end of every three months, and not from the time the postmaster shall fail to pay the draft of the department. Postmaster-General v. Fennell, 1 McL., 217.

§ 121. The provisions of the act of March 3, 1825, releasing the sureties of a deputy-postmaster, where suit is not brought within two years after a default, do not apply to a default which occurred before the passing of the act. Postmaster-General v. Rice, Gilp., 554.

§ 122. General liabilities of sureties.— The bond of a deputy-postmaster being conditioned that he "shall well and truly execute the duties of the said office according to law and the instructions of the postmaster-general," his sureties are liable for his non-compliance with subsequent as well as past laws or orders till his official term expires, if the orders be such as are justified by law. Boody v. United States, 1 Woodb. & M., 150.

§ 123. Subsequently to the giving of a postmaster's bond, with sureties, conditioned that he, the postmaster, should pay over all moneys which should come to his hands for postages to the postmaster-general, acts of congress were passed increasing the rates of postage, and, consequently, the responsibility of the sureties. Held, that as the undertaking of the sureties was general, that all postages should be paid over, and referred to no particular act explaining or limiting the rate of postage, and was not taken under any law defining its extent and operation, the sureties were liable for moneys received by reason of the increased rates of postage; but that it would have been otherwise had the acts of congress enlarged the powers of the postmaster or superadded any new duties whereby he was made the receiver of other moneys than for postages. Postmaster-General v. Munger, 2 Paine, 189.

§ 124. The postmaster-general can employ a deputy-postmaster as agent, to keep money collected by himself or other deputies near, and the sureties of such deputy will be liable on his official bond to the extent of its penalty for any neglect by the deputy as such agent. Boody v. United States, 1 Woodb. & M., 150.

§ 125. The order of the postmaster-general to the postmaster, not to remit the money he may receive, but to retain it to answer his drafts, does not discharge the sureties. Postmaster-General v. Reeder, 4 Wash., 678.

§ 126. —— for stamps furnished principal without prepayment.— The postmaster-general is authorized, by section 3 of the act of congress of March 3, 1851 (9 Stat. at L., 589), to furnish to deputy-postmasters postage stamps or stamped envelopes without exacting payment therefor in advance, and the sureties on a postmaster's bond are responsible for a failure by the postmaster to account for stamps furnished him by the postmaster-general without prepayment. United States v. Mason, 2 Bond, 183.

§ 127. Upon the theory that the statute did not authorize in terms the delivery of postage stamps to a deputy postmaster without prepayment, yet as the bond stipulating for the liability of the sureties is founded upon a good consideration, is executed in good faith, and is not prohibited by law, it is a valid bond, and the sureties are liable for stamps received by their principal as upon a valid common-law contract. Ibid.

§ 128. —— not discharged by new bond taken.— The liability of the sureties on a postmaster's official bond continues as long as the principal continues in office under the appointment or commission which placed him in office at the time the bond was given and until its legal termination. Hence the giving of a new official bond by the postmaster, at the request of the postmaster-general, does not discharge the sureties under the old bond for the past or subsequent defaults of the principal. Postmaster-General v. Reeder, 4 Wash., 678.

§ 129. —— entitled to benefit of bankrupt law.— Although a defaulting postmaster is excluded from the benefit of the bankrupt law, his surety is not, and the latter, being discharged, may plead it in bar of a suit by the government on the postmaster's official bond. United States v. Davis, 3 McL., 483.

§ 130. Sureties not relieved by delay of postmaster-general in bringing suit.— Although the neglect of the postmaster-general to bring suit against a defaulting postmaster within six months after the default has been committed renders him personally liable for the amount due from the defaulter, under the act of April 30, 1810 (2 Stat. at Large, 602), such neglect in no manner affects the liability of the postmaster and his sureties. Dox v. Postmaster-General, 1 Pet., 318.

§ 131. Under the postoffice act of 1810, which provides that each postmaster shall account at the end of every three months, and pay over to the postmaster-general the balance due him, and that, in case of failure so to do, if the postmaster-general shall not bring suit for such balance within six months from the end of the three months, the balance due from the delinquent shall be charged to, and recoverable from, the postmaster-general, held, that the neglect of the postmaster-general to sue for balances due by postmasters within the time prescribed by law, although he thereby is rendered personally chargeable with such balances, is not a discharge of the postmasters or their sureties upon their official bonds; also that an order from the postoffice department, directing a postmaster to retain the balances due until drawn for by the general postoffice, does not operate as such discharge. Locke v. United States, 3 Mason, 446.

§ 132. Rights and liabilities of sureties on different bonds.— A. gave a bond as surety for a postmater, conditioned for the faithful discharge of his duties, and that he should pay over all moneys which should come to his hands for postages to the postmaster-general. Afterwards, the postmaster continuing in office, another bond with different sureties was taken with the same condition. All liabilities on the part of the postmaster incurred before the giving of the second bond having been canceled by payments, it was held, in an action against A., as surety on the first bond, for postages not paid over, that his liability did not cease upon the giving of the second bond for defaults thereafter committed; that the second bond was not a substitute for, or extinguishment of, the first, but additional security; and that equity would consider the two sets of sureties as jointly responsible for defaults occurring after the giving of the second bond. Postmaster-General v. Munger, 2 Paine, 189.

§ 133. A., having been surety on the official bond of B., a postmaster, was released, by the acceptance on the part of the government of a new bond with other sureties, from all liability for defaults of B. committed subsequent to the giving of the new bond. B. was subsequently removed, and, being at the time indebted to the government, suit was brought against A. as surety. Held, that no proof being offered by the government that B. did not have in his possession, at the time the new bond was given, all the moneys of the government with which he was chargeable, the presumption was that B. was not a defaulter, but that he then had in his hands, in accordance with his duty, whatever sum he was chargeable with in favor of the government, and hence, not A., but the sureties on the new bond, were liable for B.'s default. Alvord v. United States, 13 Blatch., 279.

§ 134. Notice to government officials of defalcation does not relieve sureties.— Where defalcation is made by a postmaster, and suit is brought against the sureties on his official bond, it is no defense that the government through its agent, the auditor of the treasury of the postoffice department, had full notice of the defalcation and embezzlement of government funds, and yet neglectfully permitted the said postmaster to retain his office, whereby he was enabled to commit all the default and embezzlement that was not barred by the statute of limitations. Jones v. United States, 18 Wall., 662.

§ 135. Application of payments as affecting sureties.— In an account current between the United States and a postmaster exhibiting an unbroken series of charges against, and credits to, the postmaster from the date of the first item to the close of the account, when the final balance was struck, each payment made by the postmaster in the order of time in which it was made is to be applied to the extinguishment of the preceding quarterly balance against him, and the residue, if any, to be credited to the account of receipts for the quarter within which the payment was made. Thus, where a payment is made, sufficient in amount to satisfy a prior quarterly balance against the postmaster, the default will be extinguished, and by the operation of this principle the defaults will all be thrown on the last quarter of the account. Hence, unless the default appearing in the last quarter of the account is of two years' standing, the sureties cannot claim the protection of the act of March 3, 1825, section 3, providing that suit must be brought against the postmaster and his sureties within two years after default shall be made, or else such sureties shall not be liable. United States v. Kershner, 1 Bond, 432.

§ 136. The lapse of five years between the removal of a postmaster and demand made upon him for balances due from him to the government affords no presumption of the payment of his official bond. Dox v. Postmaster-General, 1 Pet., 318.

§ 137. A payment made by a deputy-postmaster to the postoffice department, without directions as to its application, is to be applied to the oldest debt; and it must be proved that the payment came from receipts accruing under a second bond, if that is relied on against the propriety of applying it to any balance whatever still due on a prior bond. Boody v. United States, 1 Woodb. & M., 150.

§ 138. Where a balance became due from a deputy-postmaster July 20, after the expiration of the previous quarter, and a payment was made as large as all of it but $3.34 on the 12th day of the same month, and a second bond was not taken until the 16th of the same month, the presumption is that the payment was to be applied on the balance due under the first bond, and that the money did not come from accruing receipts under the second appointment, being much larger than their ordinary amount. Ibid.

§ 139. A postmaster having given different bonds with different sureties, his payments must be so appropriated as to give each bond credits for the moneys respectively due, collected and paid under it. The government cannot apply moneys collected by the postmaster after and under the second bond, and on the responsibility of the sureties in the second bond, to the payment of the balance due on moneys collected, and which ought to have been paid by and under the first bond. Postmaster-General v. Norvell, Gilp., 106.

§ 140. Where a running account is kept at the postoffice department between the United States and a postmaster, in which all postages are charged to him, and credit is given for all payments made, this amounts to an election by the creditor to apply the payments, as they are successively made, to the extinguishment of preceding balances; and if, by such application, all defaults occurring more than two years previous to the institution of suit on the postmaster's bond are extinguished, the act of congress of 1825 (4 Stat. at Large, 102), which exonerates the sureties if balances are not sued for within two years after they occur, does not apply. Jones v. United States, 7 How., 681.

IV. Contracts for Carrying the Mail.

§ 141. Proposals for carrying the mails — Notice, sufficiency of.— A notice published by the postoffice department called for proposals for carrying the mails on route No. 43,132, from Portland, Oregon, to Sitka, Alaska. The distance was stated to be fourteen hundred miles; the duty was required to be performed each way once in each month, in safe and suitable steamboats, by way of Port Townsend and San Juan; the time of departure and arrival at each terminus was specified, and ten days was allowed for the passage. It was then added, "Proposals invited to begin at Port Townsend (W. T.), five hundred miles less." Held, that this was sufficient notice, under the act of congress of June 8, 1872 (17 Stat., 313, sec. 243), that proposals were desired for carrying the mail from Port Townsend to Sitka. Garfielde v. United States,* 3 Otto, 242.

§ 142. —— acceptance of, what amounts to — Effect of.— A proposal to carry mails at a certain price, made in response to a legal public notice inviting such proposals, and accepted by the postmaster-general, constitutes a valid contract of the same force and effect as a formal written contract subscribed by the parties. Ibid.

§ 143. The acceptance in writing by the postmaster-general of a written proposal to carry the mails, made in response to a legal and sufficient notice published by the postoffice department, calling for proposals to carry the mails over a certain route, is as obligatory as a formal contract. Ibid.

§ 144. —— withdrawal of.— A person who files a written proposal for carrying the mails may withdraw it at any time before it is accepted by the department, as, until accepted, it is but a mere offer to make a contract coming from one party, and if, after the withdrawal, the other party signifies his willingness to accept, that is but another proposal coming from the opposite side. A withdrawal, however, must be notified. The mere intention to withdraw is not a withdrawal. Proposals for Carrying the Mails,* 9 Op. Att'y Gen'l, 174.

§ 145. A rule of the department, that bids put in shall not be withdrawn after a certain time, whether accepted or not, is of no effect and cannot be enforced without authority of law. Ibid.

§ 146. —— need not be subscribed.— A bid for carrying the mails may be signed by the bidder in such a manner as to bind him by a valid contract, upon its acceptance, without his name appearing at the bottom of the instrument. Ibid.

§ 147. It is a sufficient signing if the name is written by the proper hand, either in the body of the instrument or on the margin, or anywhere else, so that its authenticity and genuineness are sufficiently attested. Ibid.

§ 148. —— combination to prevent bidding, what constitutes.— Upon the receipt of bids for carrying the mails the contract was given to parties who afterwards transferred it to other parties, who were competitors at the original bidding. The latter, being dissatisfied with the contract, asked that the service should be reduced, or that the contract should be abrogated and the route advertised and re-let, basing their claim on the twenty-eighth section of the act of July 2, 1836, which prohibits the postmaster-general from entering into any contract with persons who have combined to prevent bidding for mail contracts, and also provides for the dismissal of any mail contractor so offending. Held, that the section did not apply, as the facts did not show any combination to prevent bidding for the contract. Application of Witherspoon & Saffell,* 9 Op. Att'y Gen'l, 331.

§ 149. —— informal proposals cannot be accepted.— It is not lawful, after once advertising and failing to secure a contractor, to contract with a party who was not a bidder, on a proposition informally submitted for the contract term. Contracts for Carrying the Mail,* 13 Op. Att'y Gen'l, 478.

§ 150. —— drafts, etc., deposited by bidders— When to be returned.— The draft or check deposited by bidders for the transportation of mails, as required by the fourth section of the act of March 3, 1871 (16 Stat., 572), is merely as security for the required bond, and has completed its office, and should be returned to the bidder, in case his bid is accepted, as soon as such bond is filed, no matter how long this may be before the commencement of the service. The drafts or checks deposited by persons who are underbid should be returned to them as soon as the contract is awarded. Checks Deposited by Bidders for Mail Contracts,* 13 Op. Att'y Gen'l, 477.

§ 151. A check or draft drawn on a national bank, and deposited by a party submitting proposals for the transportation of mails with the postmaster-general, together with a letter of credit from the bank, setting forth that he, the said party, is authorized to draw on said bank at sight, in sums to suit his convenience, amounting in the aggregate to a sum equal to the face of the check or draft, is a sufficient compliance, to the extent of that sum, with the requirement of section 4 of the act of March 3, 1871. Transportation of the Mails,* 13 Op. Att'y Gen'l, 534.

§ 152. —— unjust refusal to award contract — Measure of damages. — By section 263 of the regulations of the postoffice department the postmaster-general may wholly discontinue the mail service over a fixed route, in which case the contractor is entitled to one month's extra pay as an indemnity. Where, therefore, the proposal of a contractor having been accepted, the postmaster-general illegally refuses to award the contract, one month's pay must be the measure of damages. Garfielde v. United States,* 3 Otto, 242.

§ 153. Annulment — Discontinuance — Indemnity. — Where a contract for carrying the mails is annulled for repeated failures on the part of the contractor, no extra pay is allowed. The provisions of the three hundred and seventeenth regulation apply only to annulment for other causes. Buckles v. United States,* 20 Law Rep., 630.

§ 154. Upon the breaking out of the civil war the postmaster-general suspended the service on a certain mail route, refusing to annul the contract under which the mail had been carried, holding the contractor liable to renew the service when called upon. Held, this was a discontinuance of the service under the act of 1861, and that the contractor was entitled to the one month's extra pay as provided in such cases. Reeside v. United States,* 8 Wall., 38.

§ 155. The annulment of a contract by act of congress does not destroy the contractor's right to compensation for a voyage begun before the passage of the act. Steamship Co. v. United States,* 13 Otto, 721.

§ 156. Use of vessels in the service not accepted by the department. — Where vessels which have not been accepted by the department are used in the mail service, the contractors are only entitled to "sea postage," and not to the contract price which would have been, allowed them had the service been performed by vessels formally accepted. Ibid.

§ 157. Vessels accepted under one contract used under another. — A contract for carrying mails between San Francisco and China required the service to be performed as designated in the act of 1865, in first-class American sea-going steamships, constructed of the best material, etc., and to be accepted by the postmaster-general. A part of the service was performed without objection by the postmaster-general, in vessels accepted under a second contract under the act of March 2, 1872, which called for all the conditions required by the act of 1865, and superadded other conditions. Held, that the contractor was entitled to recover for such service under the first contract, although performed in vessels accepted only under the second contract. Pacific Mail Steamship Co. v. United States,* 18 Ct. Cl., 30.

§ 158. The Pacific Mail Steamship Company, being already engaged in carrying monthly mails between San Francisco and Japan and China in vessels which had been accepted by the government, entered into a contract with the postmaster-general for the performance of a semi-monthly service over the same route. This contract contained the following: "And the said contractors do further covenant and agree with the United States that the steamships hereafter offered for the service shall be built of iron, and with their engines and machinery shall be wholly of American construction," etc., etc.; and further provided that after acceptance by the postmaster-general they should during the period of service be kept up, by alterations and repairs, fully equal to the best state of steamship improvement attained; "and if not so kept up and maintained, they may be rejected by the postmaster-general as not meeting the requirements of the act of congress authorizing the additional monthly service, and other satisfactory steamships required in their place." Held, that the company was not bound by this contract to carry this additional semi-monthly mail in vessels of the class here described and in no others, but that while exercising due diligence to have as many vessels of that kind as were necessary, in addition to those which had been accepted under the first contract, these last could be used in performing the contract. Steamship Co. v. United States,* 13 Otto, 721.

§ 159. Land-grant railroad company — Power of government to alter compensation — Imposition of extra duties. — The condition of the grant to a "land-grant railroad," that it shall carry the mail over its road at such price as congress may by law direct, applies only to the mere transportation of the mails, and not to other duties and obligations which the road may contract to perform, such as furnishing separate cars warmed and furnished, carrying the mails to and from the postoffice, carrying the agents of the department, etc. When the contract entered into between the postmaster-general and the road imposes such extra duties, and congress enacts that the contract rate of compensation shall be lowered without fixing in express terms the price to be paid for the mere service of carrying the mails as distinct from the other duties, the only course open to the road under such circumstances is to throw up its contract and receive the one month's pay prescribed in case of discontinuance, and fall back upon the simple service of carrying the mail according to the condition of the grant. Chicago & Northwestern R'y Co. v. United States,* 15 Ct. Cl., 232.

§ 160. —— what necessary to constitute a road a land-grant road.— Congress granted land to the state of Wisconsin in trust, to aid in the construction of a certain railroad, upon the condition that the United States mail should be transported over such railroad, under the directions of the postoffice department, at such price as congress might by law direct. The state passed a law granting such lands to a certain company, but stipulating that the title to the lands should vest in said company only as the governor of the state should certify to the secretary of the interior that certain conditions had been fulfilled. The lands were never deeded to the company by the state, but with the consent of congress were disposed of for the benefit of farmers along the line of the proposed road who had mortgaged their farms to aid in the construction of the road. The enterprise having failed, the C. Company purchased all the rights of the prior corporation and completed the road. The latter company having carried the mails under contract entered into for four years, the postoffice department claimed that its road was a "land-grant road" and the compensation subject to the reduction provided for in such cases. Held, 1, that the company actually constructing the road never having received the land or any of the benefits thereof, it could not be bound by the conditions in the original grant; 2, that neither the prior corporation nor the C. company having received or participated in the lands granted to the state, no road constructed by either or both was a "land-grant road," within the meaning of the act of July 12, 1876; 3, that the use in the construction of the road of the mortgage subscriptions of the farmers for whose benefit the lands were finally sold was not such an equitable application of the lands to the construction of the road as to entitle the government to the benefit of the provision of the act of June 8, 1856, relative to postal rates. Chicago, Milwaukee, etc., Railroad Co. v. United States,* 14 Ct. Cl., 125.

§ 161. —— existing contracts with, how far subject to alteration by government.— Under the revised postoffice act of 1872 (17 Stat. at Large, 283), authorizing the postmaster-general to make contracts for the transportation of mails for four years, land-grant roads being neither specially included nor excluded from the operation of the authority, the postmaster-general entered into a contract for four years with a land-grant railroad, which had received lands upon the condition that the United States mails should be carried over such road at such price as congress might by law direct, the price until fixed by law to be determined by the postmaster-general. This contract authorized the postmaster-general to discontinue the service in whole or in part at any time, allowing as a full indemnity to the contractor one month's extra pay on the amount of service dispensed with, and a pro rata compensation for the amount of service retained and continued. Before the expiration of the four years during which the contract was to run, congress reduced the rate of all mail transportation, and made a further reduction in the rate of the land-grant roads. The company protested against the reduction of rates, but still continued to carry the mails, receiving the reduced rates. Held, 1, that even had the road not been a land-grant road, the statute ordering a reduction of the contract rate of compensation would operate as a renunciation of the contract, unless the other party would assent to the reduction, and to that extent enter into a new contract, which the railroad did when it continued to perform and accept payment for its services at the reduced rate; 2, that as a land-grant road it was bound to do service at such rate as congress might by law prescribe, and if the provision of the revised postoffice act was applicable to land-grant roads, it must be construed to have been an authority to the postmaster-general to fix the rate of compensation for periods of four years instead of for shorter or longer periods, but always subject to the original condition of the grant — that congress might fix the price for the service by law. Chicago & Northwestern R'y Co. v. United States,* 15 Ct. Cl., 232.

§ 162. A railroad company which had received from the United States, to aid in the construction of its road, grants of lands to which was attached the condition that the United States mail should be transported over its road, under the direction of the postoffice department, at such price as congress might by law direct, provided that, until such price was fixed by law, the postmaster-general should have the power to determine the same, entered into a contract, in the year 1873, with the postmaster-general to carry the mail for four years, the price agreed upon being in conformity with the provisions of the act of March 3, 1873. After the passage of the act of July 12, 1876, providing for a reduction of ten per centum from the rates allowed by the above act, the postmaster-general issued an order notifying the company of the reduction. To which notice the company replied with a protest against the reduction as in violation of its contract, but still continued to carry the mails. After the passage of the act of June 17, 1878, it received notice of still further reduction in rates, and again protested. *Held*, that it was entitled to recover the full contract price, notwithstanding the reductions provided for subsequent to the date of the contract; that by continuing to carry the mail after notice of proposed reduction, none of its rights were waived, as it had no option, being bound by its contract to perform the service. Chicago & Northwestern R'y Co. *v.* United States, 14 Otto, 680.

§ 163. The act of July 12, 1876, providing for a reduction of rates for railway service, does not apply to or affect a contract for the transportation of mails for a definite term of years, which was in force at the time of its passage, even though the railroad of the contracting company was the subject of a land grant under the provisos of the acts of 1856. Chicago, Milwaukee & St. Paul R'y Co. *v.* United States, 14 Otto, 687.

§ 164. One railroad track may be considered as part of two routes.— Where a railroad company engaged to carry mails of the United States employs its own servants, cars and engines to do so, but uses the track of another company for a portion of its route, it is entitled to consider such hired track as a part of its own road in dealing with the postoffice department, although another company may be carrying mails under another contract over the same track. The Railway Mail Service Cases,* 13 Ct. Cl., 199.

§ 165. A railroad company which operates a main line, and a branch line joining the main line at a point between its termini, may operate two distinct and separate mail-routes over that portion of its main line between one of its termini and the junction formed by the branch line. *Ibid.*

§ 166. Four years' contracts authorized by statute.— Section 3956 of the Revised Statutes of the United States authorize contracts for carrying the mails for a period of four years or less, and this section is not explained, controlled or limited by the provisions of sections 3679 and 3752, the two latter having been taken by the revisors from the acts of 1861 and 1870, whereas the former was taken from the "act to revise, consolidate and amend the statutes relating to the postoffice department," of June 8, 1872. Chicago, Milwaukee, etc., Railroad Co. *v.* United States,* 14 Ct. Cl., 125.

§ 167. Schedule, to what extent it may be changed — Time of arrival at intermediate points.— Under a contract for carrying the mails between Cairo and New Orleans, agreeably to a schedule appended, which regulates the time of arrival and departure at the ends of the route, the contractor cannot be required to deliver the mails at an intermediate point at a particular hour of the day. So long as he arrives at the ends of his route agreeably to the stipulation, it matters not when he passes any particular place between them. Nor does the power given to the postmaster-general by the contract, to "change the schedule," authorize him to fix a time for the arrival at any intermediate point, since that would be not to "change the schedule," but to make a new one. He may accelerate the time or retard it, paying less or more for the service, and this is the extent of his power to "change the schedule." Mail Contract,* 9 Op. Att'y Gen'l, 252.

§ 168. Power of the department to reduce the service and compensation.— The act of March 3, 1857, authorized the postmaster-general "to contract for the conveyance of the entire letter mail from such point on the Mississippi as the contractors may select to San Francisco, for six years, at a cost not exceeding $300,000 per annum for semi-monthly, $450,000 for weekly, or $600,000 for semi-weekly service, to be performed semi-monthly, weekly or semi-weekly at the option of the postmaster-general." In pursuance of this statute a contract was made between the postmaster-general and one B., by which the latter agreed to perform the service semi-weekly for the compensation of $600,000. The contract made no provision for any reduction of the service; nor did it stipulate what should be the pay of the contractor for carrying mails according to any other schedule; nor did it contain the usual covenant reserving to the postmaster-general the power to increase or diminish the service. *Held*, that under this contract and the law above quoted, the postmaster-general had no legal right to reduce the amount of service, and the compensation with it, below what was expressly agreed for. Mail Contract,* 9 Op. Att'y Gen'l, 342.

§ 169. Claim for additional compensation — Waiver — Estoppel.— A mail contractor who had performed extra and additional service in carrying the mail presented his claim to the postmaster-general, who informed him that in case he continued to press such claim, a certain other extra service, having several months to run, would be discontinued, the discontinuance of such extra service resting in the discretion of the postmaster-general. The contractor afterwards presented documents in support of his claim before the second assistant postmaster-general, with whom the business pertaining to this claim had been transacted, but did not otherwise notify the postmaster of his action in pressing his contested claim.

In the meantime the contractor continued to perform the extra service, which the postmaster-general had conditionally threatened to discontinue, and to receive the benefits thereof. *Held*, that, not having directly notified the postmaster-general of his intention to press the disputed claim, he was now estopped from asserting that claim. (NOTT, J., dissented.) Alvord *v.* United States,* 9 Ct. Cl., 500.

§ 170. The presentation of a claim to the second assistant postmaster-general, with whom all the business relating to the claim had previously been transacted, is equivalent in contemplation of law to presenting it to the postmaster-general himself. Plaintiff, by agreement with the postmaster-general, was to receive $14,000 per annum additional for improved service on a certain mail-route. Extra services, not contemplated by the plaintiff, having been required of him, he presented to the postmaster-general a claim for $35,100. The latter replied that the additional compensation of $14,000 had been made in view of these extra services, and that, should the claim for $35,100 be pressed, he would annul the former arrangement for additional pay. Plaintiff continued to receive the $14,000 under such former arrangement, but also pressed his claim for extra services by personal interviews with the second assistant postmaster-general. *Held*, that he had not waived his rights under the latter claim. Alvord *v.* United States,* 5 Otto, 356.

§ 171. Reduction of compensation — Statutory notice — Notice to department — Waiver.— During the continuance of a contract for carrying the mails, which authorized the postmaster-general to discontinue the service in whole or in part at any time, allowing as a full indemnity to the contractor one month's extra pay on the amount of service dispensed with, and a *pro rata* compensation for the amount of service retained and continued, the act of July 12, 1876, was passed, requiring the postmaster-general to reduce the compensation to all railroad companies for the transportation of mails ten per centum per annum from the rates fixed and allowed in the act of March 3, 1873, the rates in the above contract having been calculated on the basis of the conditions and at the rates prescribed in said act of 1873. *Held*, that the statutory directions to the postmaster-general were also a notice to the contractors that the service would be discontinued under the old rates and would be continued, if at all, under the new rates; and that, having continued to carry the mails without objection after such notice, the contractor must be deemed to have acceded to the terms of the new contract. Chicago, Milwaukee, etc., Railroad Co. *v.* United States,* 14 Ct. Cl., 125.

§ 172. Where congress passes an act reducing the rate of compensation to contractors carrying the mails, protest given by such contractors to the postmaster-general is of no effect if they continue to perform service, as notice to him as agent of congress, in face of the statute of congress, is not such notice as to operate in favor of the claimants or bind the government. Chicago & Northwestern R'y Co. *v.* United States,* 15 Ct. Cl., 232.

§ 173. Service begun under a ten years' contract prolonged beyond the contract period — Compensation.— A certain company contracted with the government to transport mails monthly, in round trips, for ten years, between San Francisco, China and Japan. These round trips took, in the ordinary course of navigation, about seventy days each, the last two trips, in which the transportation was begun before the expiration of ten years from the day when the service under the contract commenced, were not finished until after the expiration of ten years from that day. *Held*, in an action to recover the contract compensation for these last two trips, that, as it was a physical impossibility to begin twelve trips in twelve successive months, and to complete them, as twelve round trips of seventy days each, in the same twelve months, congress must therefore have intended that the voyages begun in the last months of the year in which the contract was to expire should be within the contract, although prolonged into another year, and, hence, the company was entitled to recover. Pacific Mail Steamship Co. *v.* United States,* 18 Ct. Cl., 30.

§ 174. Indefinite contract to carry mail has no reference to weight — Extra compensation.— Contracts to carry the mail of the United States, without stipulation as to its weight, include the whole mail accruing between the termini named therein, or coming into it from other routes, according to the arrangements contemplated when they are made; and if justice shall demand extra allowance on account of the increased weight, it must be sought of congress, not of the postmaster-general. Acts of Postmasters-General.* 3 Op. Att'y Gen'l, 1.

§ 175. Acquiescence in settlements works an estoppel.— Acquiescence in settlements by the postoffice department is inferred from the silence of the contractor. His failure to claim in due season the money paid to another estops him from demanding it. Thus repeated adjustments were made, by the postmaster-general, of sums due each of two railroad companies for carrying the mail between certain points. These sums as adjusted by the postmaster-general were received by the two companies without protest for two years, when it was discovered that, by the adjustments made, one of the companies had been receiving pay for mails carried by the other. *Held*, that the injured company was estopped from claiming of the government compensation for carrying the mails for which the other company had already received pay. Railroad Company v. United States, 13 Otto, 703.

§ 176. A certain railroad company carried the mails from A. to B. and thence over the road of another company to C. The postoffice department, in fixing the annual compensation to be paid for the entire service, reached the sum to be paid by estimating the distance from A. to B. at $200 per mile. The amount thus ascertained was paid by the department for the entire service, and was received by the company without objection. After the termination of the service the company brought suit for mail service between B. and C. *Held*, that the sum paid by the department was intended as full payment for the entire service, including the distance from B. to C., and was accepted as such by the claimants, and hence no recovery could be had. Pittsburgh, Cincinnati, etc., R'y Co. v. United States,* 18 Ct. Cl., 814.

§ 177. Under the act of March 8, 1873, the compensation of railroad companies carrying the mails was determined by the average weight of mails per day carried over the whole route, the lower averages receiving a much greater proportionate sum than the higher ones. A company operating a main line, and a branch line forming a junction with the main line, received compensation for all the mail carried between such junction and the terminus of the main line, upon the supposition that all such mail belonged to the same route, whereas a portion of such mail belonged to the route that extended over the entire length of the main line, and the remainder to the route beginning at one of the termini of the main line, and extending to the junction formed by the branch line, and thence over the branch line. *Held*, that although such compensation was erroneous, yet having been accepted without objection, the company could not recover more than the amounts so accepted; but that from the time of exceptions taken by the company to the rate of compensation, it was entitled to the full compensation allowed by statute. The Railway Mail Service Cases,* 13 Ct. Cl., 199.

§ 178. Compensation for constructing road — Construction of contract with reference to.— If one contracts with the department to transport the mail from one given point to another, between which points it is known to the department that no road exists, and to fulfill his contract he must prepare, and in fact makes, a road, the contractor may be compensated by the department for such duty and expense by a sum sufficient to pay him for carrying the mail under such circumstances. Rhodes v. United States,* Dev., 118.

§ 179. R. wrote to the postoffice department offering to carry the mail from Mobile to New Orleans, by way of Pascagoula, thrice a week, for $14,000, adding: "The road from here (Mobile) to Pascagoula to be made by or at the expense of the United States. The road I will be obligated to make . . . for the sum of $4,000, or for $100 per mile." To this the postmaster-general replied that he had decided to accept his proposal to transport the mail by land and water between Mobile and New Orleans, at the rate of $14,000 per annum. According to R.'s offer the road was made by him, whereupon he commenced running the mail. About two months after the completion of the road, R. received notice, by letter, that the department possessed no means to remunerate him. *Held*, 1, that R.'s proposal was in substance to transport the mail by land and water, for $14,000 a year, provided the United States would pay the expense of making the road over the land route, as there was no road in existence; or, 2, that the transaction might be regarded in substance as an offer by the claimants to transport the mail for $18,000 per year, for the first year, and to build the road; 3, that the acceptance by the department of the proposal was an acceptance of the proposal with the conditions upon which it was offered, as they were not excluded by the terms of the acceptance. *Ibid.*

§ 180. Implied contract for additional service.—A contractor entered into an agreement with the postoffice department to carry the mails from H. to W., "in two-horse coaches," semi-weekly, at a certain price. The two-horse coaches specified in the contract becoming insufficient for the service by reason of the bad condition of the roads, and the increase of mail matter, he placed on the route four-horse coach service, notifying the postmaster-general of such change, to which the postmaster objected. *Held*, that there was no implied contract for additional service in carrying the mail, and that nothing could be recovered by the contractor for such increase of service. Huston v. United States,* 22 Law Rep., 52.

§ 181. Additional compensation — Power of court of claims to adjust.— Where one enters into a contract with the government for the transportation of the mails between N. and O., touching at an intermediate point, and between such intermediate point and H., but, having established a direct line without any stoppage between N. and H., by which quicker service may be made, transports mail over the new route, at the request of the postoffice department, relying on congress to make additional appropriations, the department having declined to make any arrangements for additional compensation, congress having referred the claim of the contractor to the court of claims, such court is authorized thereby to adjust the claim of the contractor *ex æquo et bono.* Roberts v. United States,* 2 Otto, 41.

POUNDAGE.

See FEES.

POWERS.

[See ESTATES OF DECEDENTS; CONVEYANCES; USES AND TRUSTS.]

SUMMARY — *Revocation of power of attorney, §§ 1-3, 5.—Power coupled with an interest, § 4.*

§ 1. A letter of attorney may in general be revoked by the party making it, and is revoked by his death. Hunt v. Rousmanier, §§ 6-8.

§ 2. Where a power of attorney forms part of a contract, and is a security for the performance of any act, it is usually made revocable in terms, or, if not so made, is deemed irrevocable in law; but a power of attorney, though irrevocable during the life of the party, becomes, at law, extinct by his death. *Ibid.*

§ 3. If a power be coupled with an interest, it survives the person giving it, and may be executed after his death. *Ibid.*

§ 4. To constitute a power coupled with an interest, there must be an interest in the thing itself, and not merely in the execution of the power. In other words, the power must be engrafted on an estate in the thing. *Ibid.*

§ 5. The general rule that a power of attorney, though irrevocable by the donor during his life, is extinguished by his death, is not affected by the circumstance that testamentary powers are executed after the death of the testator, as the law, in allowing a testamentary disposition of property, not only permits a will to be considered as a conveyance, but gives it an operation not allowed to deeds, which have their effect during the life of the person who executes them. *Ibid.*

[NOTES.— See §§ 9-62.]

HUNT v. ROUSMANIER.

(8 Wheaton, 174-217. 1823.)

APPEAL from U. S. Circuit Court for Rhode Island.

STATEMENT OF FACTS.— Bill in equity and demurrer. Rousmanier obtained a loan from Hunt. He gave his notes therefor, and as security offered a bill of sale or mortgage of the brig Nereus. On the 15th of January, 1820, a power of attorney, authorizing, in case the loan should not be repaid, the sale of three-fourths of said vessel, was executed. It was stipulated therein, that, in the event of the loss of vessel or cargo, the insurance money might be collected by Hunt. A further sum was loaned to R., and a like security taken on the Industry. Rousmanier died insolvent, in May, 1820, having paid $200 on the above notes. Plaintiff took possession of the ships and offered them for sale. Defendants objected, and this bill is to compel defendants to join in the sale. The court sustained the demurrer. Leave to amend the bill was given. The amended bill set forth, in addition, that specific security on the vessels was to be given, that a mortgage was offered, and that counsel advised that the power of attorney was better than a mortgage. The power was executed with the belief and intention to give Hunt security equal to that of a mortgage. In event of refusal of first prayer, a prayer for a sale of the vessels to pay the debt due plaintiff was added. Defendants demurred; demurrer sustained and amended bill dismissed. Plaintiff appealed.

Opinion by MARSHALL, C. J.

The counsel for the appellant objects to the decree of the circuit court on two grounds. He contends, 1. That this power of attorney does, by its own

453

operation, entitle the plaintiff, for the satisfaction of his debt, to the interest of Rousmanier in the Nereus and the Industry. 2. Or, if this be not so, that a court of chancery will, the conveyance being defective, lend its aid to carry the contract into execution, according to the intention of the parties. We will consider, 1. The effect of the power of attorney.

§ **6.** *A simple power, irrevocable during life of donor, extinguished by his death.*

This instrument contains no words of conveyance or of assignment, but is a simple power to sell and convey. As the power of one man to act for another depends on the will and license of that other, the power ceases when the will, or this permission, is withdrawn. The general rule, therefore, is that a letter of attorney may, at any time, be revoked by the party who makes it, and is revoked by his death. But this general rule, which results from the nature of the act, has sustained some modification. Where a letter of attorney forms a part of a contract, and is a security for money, or for the performance of any act which is deemed valuable, it is generally made irrevocable in terms, or, if not so, is deemed irrevocable in law. 2 Esp. N. P., 565. Although a letter of attorney depends, from its nature, on the will of the person making it, and may, in general, be recalled at his will, yet if he binds himself for a consideration in terms, or by the nature of his contract, not to change his will, the law will not permit him to change it. Rousmanier, therefore, could not, during his life, by any act of his own, have revoked this letter of attorney. But does it retain its efficacy after his death? We think it does not. We think it well settled that a power of attorney, though irrevocable during the life of the party, becomes extinct by his death.

This principle is asserted in Littleton, section 66, by Lord Coke, in his commentary on that section, 52, b, and in Willes' Reports, 105, note, and 565. The legal reason of the rule is a plain one. It seems founded on the presumption that the substitute acts by virtue of the authority of his principal, existing at the time the act is performed; and on the manner in which he must execute his authority, as stated in Coombes' Case, 9 Co., 766. In that case it was resolved that "when any has authority as attorney to do any act, he ought to do it in his name who gave the authority." The reason of this resolution is obvious. The title can regularly pass out of the person in whom it is vested only by a conveyance in his own name; and this cannot be executed by another for him, when it could not in law be executed by himself. A conveyance in the name of a person who was dead at the time would be a manifest absurdity.

This general doctrine, that a power must be executed in the name of a person who gives it, a doctrine founded on the nature of the transaction, is most usually engrafted in the power itself. Its usual language is, that the substitute shall do that which he is empowered to do in the name of his principal. He is put in the place and stead of his principal, and is to act in his name. This accustomed form is observed in the instrument under consideration. Hunt is constituted the attorney, and is authorized to make, and execute, a regular bill of sale in the name of Rousmanier. Now, as an authority must be pursued, in order to make the act of the substitute the act of the principal, it is necessary that this bill of sale should be in the name of Rousmanier; and it would be a gross absurdity, that a deed should purport to be executed by him, even by attorney, after his death; for, the attorney is in the place of the principal, capable of doing that alone which the principal might do.

§ *7. A power to A. to sell, engrafted on an estate conveyed to A., is coupled with an interest and survives donor.*

This general rule, that a power ceases with the life of the person giving it, admits of one exception. If a power be coupled with an "interest," it survives the person giving it, and may be executed after his death. As this proposition is laid down too positively in the books to be controverted, it becomes necessary to inquire what is meant by the expression, "a power coupled with an interest." Is it an interest in the subject on which the power is to be exercised, or is it an interest in that which is produced by the exercise of the power? We hold it to be clear that the interest which can protect a power after the death of a person who creates it must be an interest in the thing itself. In other words, the power must be engrafted on an estate in the thing.

The words themselves would seem to import this meaning. "A power coupled with an interest" is a power which accompanies or is connected with an interest. The power and the interest are united in the same person. But if we are to understand by the word "interest" an interest in that which is to be produced by the exercise of the power, then they are never united. The power to produce the interest must be exercised, and by its exercise is extinguished. The power ceases when the interest commences, and therefore cannot, in accurate law language, be said to be "coupled" with it.

But the substantial basis of the opinion of the court on this point is found in the legal reason of the principle. The interest or title in the thing being vested in the person who gives the power, remains in him unless it be conveyed with the power, and can pass out of him only by a regular act in his own name. The act of the substitute, therefore, which in such a case is the act of the principal, to be legally effectual must be in his name, must be such an act as the principal himself would be capable of performing, and which would be valid if performed by him. Such a power necessarily ceases with the life of the person making it. But if the interest or estate passes with the power, and vests in the person by whom the power is to be exercised, such person acts in his own name. The estate, being in him, passes from him by a conveyance in his own name. He is no longer a substitute, acting in the place and name of another, but is a principal acting in his own name, in pursuance of powers which limit his estate. The legal reason which limits a power to the life of the person giving it exists no longer, and the rule ceases with the reason on which it is founded. The intention of the instrument may be effected without violating any legal principle.

This idea may be in some degree illustrated by examples of cases in which the law is clear and which are incompatible with any other exposition of the term "power coupled with an interest." If the word "interest" thus used indicated a title to the proceeds of the sale, and not a title to the thing to be sold, then a power to A. to sell for his own benefit would be a power coupled with an interest; but a power to A. to sell for the benefit of B. would be a naked power, which could be executed only in the life of the person who gave it. Yet for this distinction no legal reason can be assigned. Nor is there any reason for it in justice; for a power to A. to sell for the benefit of B. may be as much a part of the contract on which B. advances his money as if the power had been made to himself. If this were the true exposition of the term, then a power to A. to sell for the use of B., inserted in a conveyance to A.. of the thing to be sold, would not be a power coupled with an interest, and, consequently, could not be exercised after the death of the person making it; while a power to A. to sell and pay a debt to himself, though not accompanied with any conveyance which might vest the title in him, would enable him to make the conveyance and to pass a title not in him, even after the vivifying principle of the power had become extinct. But every day's experience teaches us that the law is not as the first case put would suppose. We know that a power to A. to sell for the benefit of B., engrafted on an estate conveyed to A., may be exercised at any time, and is not affected by the death of the person who created it. It is, then, a power coupled with an interest, although the person to whom it is given has no interest in its exercise. His power is coupled with an interest in the thing, which enables him to execute it in his own name, and is, therefore, not dependent on the life of the person who created it.

¹ The general rule that a power of attorney, though irrevocable by the party during his life, is extinguished by his death, is not affected by the circumstance that testamentary powers are executed after the death of the testator. The law, in allowing a testamentary disposition of property, not only permits a will to be considered as a conveyance, but gives it an operation which is not allowed to deeds, which have their effect during the life of the person who executes them. An estate given by will may take effect at a future time or on a future contingency, and, in the meantime, descends to the heir. The power is, necessarily, to be executed after the death of the person who makes it, and cannot exist during his life. It is the intention that it shall be executed after his death. The conveyance made by the person to whom it is given takes effect by virtue of the will, and the purchaser holds his title under it. Every case of a power given in a will is considered in a court of chancery as a trust for the benefit of the person for whose use the power is made, and as a devise or bequest to that person.

It is then deemed perfectly clear that the power given in this case is a naked power, not coupled with an interest, which, though irrevocable by Rousmanier himself, expired on his death.

§ 8. *Where effect of an instrument has been misunderstood by the parties thereto, equity will relieve.*

It remains to inquire whether the appellant is entitled to the aid of this court to give effect to the intention of the parties, to subject the interest of Rousmanier in the Nereus and Industry to the payment of the money advanced by the plaintiff on the credit of those vessels, the instrument taken for that purpose having totally failed to effect its object. This is the point on which the plaintiff most relies, and is that on which the court has felt most doubt. That the parties intended, the one to give, and the other to receive, an effective security on the two vessels mentioned in the bill, is admitted; and the question is, whether the law of this court will enable it to carry this intent into execution, when the instrument relied on by both parties has failed to accomplish its object.

The respondents insist that there is no defect in the instrument itself; that it contains precisely what it was intended to contain, and is the instrument which was chosen by the parties deliberately, on the advice of counsel, and intended to be the consummation of their agreement. That in such a case the written agreement cannot be varied by parol testimony.

The counsel for the appellant contends, with great force, that the cases in which parol testimony has been rejected are cases in which the agreement itself has been committed to writing, and one of the parties has sought to contradict, explain or vary it by parol evidence. That in this case the agreement is not reduced to writing. The power of attorney does not profess to be the agreement, but is a collateral instrument to enable the party to have the benefit of it, leaving the agreement still in full force, in its original form. That this parol agreement, not being within the statute of frauds, would be enforced by this court if the power of attorney had not been executed; and not being merged in the power ought now to be executed. That the power being incompetent to its object, the court will enforce the agreement against general creditors.

This argument is entitled to, and has received, very deliberate consideration. The first inquiry respects the fact. Does this power of attorney purport to be the agreement? Is it an instrument collateral to the agreement? Or is it an execution of the agreement itself in the form intended by both the parties?

The bill states an offer on the part of Rousmanier to give a mortgage on the vessels, either in the usual form or in the form of an absolute bill of sale, the vendor taking a defeasance; but does not state any agreement for that particular security. The agreement stated in the bill is, generally, that the plaintiff, in addition to the notes of Rousmanier, should have specific security on the vessels; and it alleges that the parties applied to counsel for advice respecting the most desirable mode of taking this security. On a comparison of the advantages and disadvantages of a mortgage, and an irrevocable power of attorney, counsel advised the latter instrument, and assigned reasons for his advice, the validity of which being admitted by the parties, the power of attorney was prepared and executed, and was received by the plaintiff as full security for his loans.

This is the case made by the amended bill; and it appears to the court to be a case in which the notes and power of attorney are admitted to be a complete consummation of the agreement. The thing stipulated was a collateral security on the Nereus and Industry. On advice of counsel this power of attorney was selected and given as that security. We think it a complete execution of that part of the agreement; as complete, though not as safe, an execution of it as a mortgage would have been.

It is contended that the letter of attorney does not contain all the terms of the agreement. Neither would a bill of sale, nor a deed of mortgage, contain them. Neither instrument constitutes the agreement itself, but is that for which the agreement stipulated. The agreement consisted of a loan of money on the part of Hunt, and of notes for its repayment, and of a collateral security on the Nereus and Industry, on the part of Rousmanier. The money was advanced, the notes were given, and this letter of attorney was, on advice of counsel, executed and received as the collateral security which Hunt required. The letter of attorney is as much an execution of that part of the agreement which stipulated a collateral security, as the notes are an execution of that part which stipulated that notes should be given.

But this power, although a complete security during the life of Rousmanier, has been rendered inoperative by his death. The legal character of the security was misunderstood by the parties. They did not suppose that the power would, in law, expire with Rousmanier. The question for the consideration of the court is this: If money be advanced on a general stipulation to give security for its repayment on a specific article; and the parties deliberately, on advice of counsel, agree on a particular instrument, which is executed, but, from a legal quality inherent in its nature, that was unknown to the parties, becomes extinct by the death of one of them, can a court of equity direct a new security of a different character to be given? or direct that to be done which the parties supposed would have been effected by the instrument agreed on between them?

This question has been very elaborately argued, and every case has been cited which could be supposed to bear upon it. No one of these cases decides the very question now before the court. It must depend on the principles to be collected from them. It is a general rule that an agreement in writing, or an instrument carrying an agreement into execution, shall not be varied by parol testimony, stating conversations or circumstances anterior to the written instrument.

This rule is recognized in courts of equity as well as in courts of law; but courts of equity grant relief in cases of fraud and mistake, which cannot be obtained in courts of law. In such cases a court of equity may carry the intention of the parties into execution, where the written agreement fails to express that intention.

In this case there is no ingredient of fraud. Mistake is the sole ground on which the plaintiff comes into court; and that mistake is in the law. The fact is, in all respects, what it was supposed to be. The instrument taken is the instrument intended to be taken. But it is, contrary to the expectation of the parties, extinguished by an event not foreseen nor adverted to, and is, therefore, incapable of effecting the object for which it was given. Does a court of equity, in such a case, substitute a different instrument for that which has failed to effect its object?

In general, the mistakes against which a court of equity relieves are mistakes in fact. The decisions on this subject, though not always very distinctly stated, appear to be founded on some misconception of fact. Yet some of them bear a considerable analogy to that under consideration. Among these is that class of cases in which a joint obligation has been set up in equity against the representatives of a deceased obligor, who were discharged at law. If the principle of these decisions be that the bond was joint from a mere mistake of the law, and that the court will relieve against this mistake on the ground of the pre-existing equity arising from the advance of the money, it must be admitted that they have a strong bearing on the case at bar. But the judges in the courts of equity seem to have placed them on mistake in fact, arising from the ignorance of the draftsman. In Simpson v. Vaughan, 2 Atk., 33, the bond was drawn by the obligor himself, and under circumstances which induced the court to be of opinion that it was intended to be joint and several. In Underhill v. Howard, 10 Ves., 209, 227, Lord Eldon, speaking of cases in which a joint bond has been set up against the representatives of a deceased obligor, says: "The court has inferred, from the nature of the condition and the transaction, that it was made joint by mistake. That is, the instrument is not what the parties intended in fact. They intended a joint and several obligation; the scrivener has, by mistake, prepared a joint obligation."

All the cases in which the court has sustained a joint bond against the representatives of the deceased obligor have turned upon a supposed mistake in drawing the bond. It was not until the case of Sumner v. Powell, 2 Meriv., 36, that anything was said by the judge who determined the cause, from which it might be inferred that relief in these cases would be afforded on any other principle than mistake in fact. In that case the court refused its aid, because there was no equity antecedent to the obligation. In delivering his judgment, the master of the rolls (Sir W. Grant) indicated very clearly an opinion that a prior equitable consideration, received by the deceased, was indispensable to the setting up of a joint obligation against his representatives; and added: "So, where a joint bond has in equity been considered as several, there has been a credit previously given to the different persons who have entered into the obligation."

Had this case gone so far as to decide that "the credit previously given" was the sole ground on which a court of equity would consider a joint bond as several, it would have gone far to show that the equitable obligation remained, and might be enforced after the legal obligation of the instrument had expired. But the case does not go so far. It does not change the principle on which the court had uniformly proceeded, nor discard the idea that relief is to be granted because the obligation was made joint by a mistake in point of fact. The case only decides that this mistake, in point of fact, will not be presumed by the court in a case where no equity existed antecedent to the obligation, where no advantage was received by, and no credit given to, the person against whose estate the instrument is to be set up.

Yet the course of the court seems to be uniform, to presume a mistake in point of fact in every case where a joint obligation has been given, and a benefit has been received by the deceased obligor. No proof of actual mistake is required. The existence of an antecedent equity is sufficient. In cases attended by precisely the same circumstances, so far as respects mistake, relief will be given against the representatives of a deceased obligor, who had received the benefit of the obligation, and refused against the representatives of him who had not received it. Yet the legal obligation is as completely extinguished in the one case as in the other; and the facts stated, in some of the cases in which these decisions have been made, would rather conduce to the opinion that the bond was made joint from ignorance of the legal consequences of a joint obligation, than from any mistake in fact.

The case of Lansdown v. Lansdown (reported in Mosely, 364), if it be law, has no inconsiderable bearing on this cause. The right of the heir at law was contested by a younger member of the family, and the arbitrator to whom the subject was referred decided against him. He executed a deed in compliance with this award, and was afterwards relieved against it, on the principle that he was ignorant of his title.

The case does not suppose this fact, that he was the eldest son, to have been unknown to him; and, if he was ignorant of anything, it was of the law, which gave him, as eldest son, the estate he had conveyed to a younger brother. Yet he was relieved in chancery against this conveyance. There are certainly strong objections to this decision in other respects; but, as a case in which relief has been granted on a mistake in law, it cannot be entirely disregarded.

Although we do not find the naked principle, that relief may be granted on account of ignorance of law, asserted in the books, we find no case in which it has been decided that a plain and acknowledged mistake in law is beyond the reach of equity. In the case of Lord Irnham v. Child, 1 Bro. Ch. Cas., 92, application was made to the chancellor to establish a clause which had been, it was said, agreed upon, but which had been considered by the parties, and excluded from the written instrument by consent. It is true, they excluded the clause from a mistaken opinion that it would make the contract usurious, but they did not believe that the legal effect of the contract was precisely the same as if the clause had been inserted. They weighed the consequences of inserting and omitting the clause, and preferred the latter. That, too, was a case to which the statute applied. Most of the cases which have been cited were within the statute of frauds, and it is not easy to say how much has been the influence of that statute on them.

The case cited by the respondent's counsel from precedents in chancery is not of this description; but it does not appear from that case that the power of attorney was intended or believed to be a lien. In this case, the fact of mistake is placed beyond any controversy. It is averred in the bill, and admitted by the demurrer, that "the powers of attorney were given by the said Rousmanier, and received by the said Hunt, under the belief that they were, and with the intention that they should create a specific lien and security on the said vessels."

We find no case which we think precisely in point; and are unwilling, where the effect of the instrument is acknowledged to have been entirely misunderstood by both parties, to say that a court of equity is incapable of affording relief. The decree of the circuit court is reversed; but as this is a case in which creditors are concerned, the court, instead of giving a final decree on the demurrer in favor of the plaintiff, directs the cause to be remanded, that the circuit court may permit the defendants to withdraw their demurrer and to answer the bill.

§ 9. In executing a power it is not necessary to recite it or refer to it. Its existence and the intent to execute it are sufficient. The intent is matter *in pais* to be collected from all the circumstances. Crane *v.* Morris, 6 Pet., 598.

§ 10. In the case of a naked power not coupled with an interest, the law requires that every prerequisite to the exercise of that power should precede it. Williams *v.* Peyton, 4 Wheat., 77.

§ 11. Where, a power having been given by will, there has been a complete execution of it, and something *ex abundanti* added which is improper and inconsistent with the purpose of the power, the execution is good and only the excess is void; but it is otherwise if there is not a complete execution of the power, where the boundaries between the excess and execution are not distinguishable. Warner *v.* Howell, 3 Wash., 12.

§ 12. Courts always lean in favor of the execution of the power if it can be supported, even though it should disappoint the intention of the person executing the power. *Ibid.*

§ 13. The doctrine that courts in the interpretation of wills are to regard the intention of the testator, and that technical words and set phrases are controlled by that intention, is equally applicable to the execution of powers, especially in regard to their execution by last wills and testaments. But the intention to execute the power must be clear. If it be doubtful, under all the circumstances, that doubt will prevent it from being deemed an execution of the power, although it is not necessary that the intention to execute the power should appear in express terms or by the recitals in the instrument. Blagge *v.* Miles, 1 Story, 426.

§ 14. A naked power or trust must be literally followed and strictly construed. But where a trust deed of land empowered the trustee to convey when a certain railway company wished to "sell" it, and the land was exchanged at the request of said company for its coupon bonds, which were delivered up and canceled, *held*, that the power was strictly and literally followed, and as a sale of lands does not necessarily suppose a sale for cash. Speigle *v.* Meredith, 4 Biss., 120.

§ 15. A limited statutory power must be strictly executed. Charles *v.* Matlock, 3 Cr. C. C., 280.

§ 16. A power supported by a usage is defined and limited by that usage. Evidence of usage may be given to explain what is doubtful, not to contradict what is plain. Merchants' National Bank *v.* State National Bank, 3 Cliff., 205.

§ 17. A power of disposal by will does not of itself enlarge a limited interest. Thus, where a testator divided his estate into shares and devised the interest or income of the shares to certain of his children and relatives "during their respective lives," declaring "they shall have power to dispose of their interest in the estate by will as they see fit," *held*, that the power did not enlarge their life estates into fees. Ward *v.* Amory, 1 Curt., 419.

§ 18. Rights of third persons.—A testatrix devised to A. one-fifth of all her real estate, in trust, for the entire use and benefit of B., during her natural life, the said fifth part to be subject to the absolute disposal of the said B. by her last will and testament, and if the said B. should die without having disposed of the same, then the remainder and reversion was devised to her heirs forever. B. subsequently procured a resolve of the legislature authorizing the sale of a part of the real estate which had been set off to her under the aforesaid will, the proceeds to be invested in other estate, to be held upon the like trusts, and for the same uses and purposes, as the same estate was then holden. The proceeds were accordingly invested in real estate in N. Subsequently B. died, having made her will, by which she bequeathed to E. "my house and land in N., being the same which I purchased of," etc.; and then, by a residuary clause, "all the rest and residue" of her estate she devised to her three daughters. B. had no real estate except what was devised to her by the original will. *Held*, that if the investment by the trustee under the resolve was adopted by the appointees under the power, and the power had been well executed, third persons had no right to interfere and object to it; that the last will and testament of B. was a complete execution of the power in the will of A. Blagge *v.* Miles, 1 Story, 426.

§ 19. Power of sale.— A trust was created by will for the purpose of giving A., a married woman, the separate and exclusive use of land for her life, free from her husband's control. The will also directed the trustees to "lease, demise, let, convey, assure and dispose of" the said property as she might, "by any instrument in writing, order, direct, limit or appoint." In pursuance of this power, A., by deed duly executed, directed that the trustees convey the premises immediately after her demise, as she should have appointed by her last will and testament, and for want thereof, then that her trustees convey the said premises to B. and her heirs. Certain portions of the estate having been sold by the direction of A., subsequent to the execution of the above mentioned deed, *held*, upon her dying intestate, that her power to convey and dispose necessarily included the power to sell, and that having really two distinct powers, the one to sell and the other to dispose of the property in favor of a volunteer, the former, being a power of superior dignity, would override the latter and supersede it, if previously exercised, and therefore that all sales of land made at her direction to actual purchasers for a valuable consideration were effectual as superseding the prior appointment in favor of B. Bowen *v.* Chase, 4 Otto, 812; 8 Otto, 254.

§ 20. But subsequent conveyances, apparently intended merely as means of restoring the property to its original trusts, or of vesting it absolutely in A. herself, freed from the said appointment, *held* to be simply voluntary conveyances, having no paramount effect over the previous appointment in favor of B. *Ibid.*

§ 21. A. devises all his real estate to his son B. and his heirs, and, in case of his death without issue, he orders C., his executors and administrators, to sell the real estate within two years after the son's death, and he bequeaths the proceeds thereof to his brothers and sisters, by name, and their heirs forever, or such of them as shall be living at the death of the son. All the brothers and sisters die, leaving issue. Then C. dies, and afterwards B., the son, dies without issue. Heirs being held to be a word of limitation, and that, as none of the testator's brothers and sisters were alive at the death of B., the devise to them failed to take effect, *quære*, whether a sale by the executors or administrators, under such circumstances, is to be considered as valid in a court of law? But, however this may be, a sale thus made, after the lapse of two years from the death of B., is without authority and conveys no title. Daly *v.* James, 8 Wheat., 495.

§ 22. *Quære*, under what circumstances a court of equity might relieve, in case the trustee should refuse to exercise the power within the prescribed period, or should exercise the same after that period? *Ibid.*

§ 23. A power to C., and his executors or administrators, to sell, may be executed by the executors of the executors of C. *Ibid.*

§ 24. A testator's will contained the following: "I give and bequeath every part of my estate, of every kind whatsoever, to be equally divided (by sale or otherwise as may be deemed best) between my wife and my children, not heretofore named, and their heirs forever, having particular regard to the education of my children not as yet educated." *Held*, that the will did not confer a power on the executors to divide or sell the real property of the estate. Dunlap *v.* Pyle, 5 McL., 322.

§ 25. But supposing that the power to sell was given to the executors, the widow being the only one to take out letters testamentary, this power did not extend to the husband of the executrix, whom she afterwards married, and any sale made by him was void as an attempted execution of the power. *Ibid.*

§ 26. Where a person who held lands as trustee directed by his will that the whole of the property that he might die seized and possessed of, or that might be in anywise belonging to him, should be sold, the executors had power to sell the land held in trust, as well as that belonging to the testator in his own right. Taylor *v.* Benham, 5 How., 233.

§ 27. In such case, where the testator, after directing the payment of a few legacies out of the proceeds, devised the remainder or residue of his estate to various devisees, *held*, that the will was capable of either of two constructions, one considering the testator as devising the proceeds of the lands, and hence their title, to the devisees, subject to a power in the executors, coupled with a trust, to sell them and pay certain legacies; or another, which would consider the power of the executors as one coupled with an interest, and vest the title at once in them for the purpose of selling the lands and discharging the small legacies and debts, but holding the proceeds in trust to be paid over to his devisees for the benefit of the testator's *cestui que trust. Ibid.*

§ 28. Where an executor, by the will, is empowered to sell real estate in the best mode in his judgment, for the interest of the estate, he cannot delegate the power to another. It is a case of special trust and confidence, and is personal to the executor. Pearson *v.* Jamison, 1 McL., 197.

§ 29. Where a sale is made under such circumstances by one to whom the executor has attempted to delegate his power, the heir at law may sell the same estate, the first sale being void. *Ibid.*

§ 30. The act of assembly of Maryland, which authorized the commissioners of the city of Washington to resell lots for default of payment by the first purchaser, contemplates a single resale only, and by that resale the power given by the act is executed. O'Neale *v.* Thornton, 6 Cr., 53.

§ 31. A testator in New York devised real estate to his executors in trust to sell and convey it, and after having converted it into money to divide the proceeds among certain benevolent institutions, but did not empower said executors to receive the rents and profits. *Held*, that, under the fifty-sixth section of the article "Of Uses and Trusts" (1 R. S. of New York, 728), the trust to sell and apply the moneys under the will was simply a power in trust, and that the land followed the law of descents and remained in the heirs, subject to their ownership and control until the execution of the power. Pennoyer *v.* Shelden, 4 Blatch., 316.

§ 32. A. by will devised his real estate to B., his wife, for life or during her widowhood, for the support of herself, her three daughters, and one C., and on the death or remarriage of B. the estate was devised to C. for life, for his support, and that of the three daughters; and after the death or remarriage of B., and the death of C., the estate was devised to the three daughters in fee. Power was given by the will to B., as long she should remain single, and to C. after her death or remarriage, to sell the estate, provided that D. should in writing consent to, and approve of, such sale, the moneys arising from the sale to be invested as D. should direct for the purposes of the will. *Held*, that B. had only a naked power in respect to the disposition of the estate, and that the power could be rightly exercised only by a sale of the estate in fee; and that a lease made by B. was void as a conveyance under the power of sale given in the will, and could only hold as to the extent and duration of the widow's life estate, which being absolute, she could dispose of by lease. Waldron *v.* Chasteney, 2 Blatch., 62.

§ 33. The testator having bequeathed a certain annual allowance to his three younger children, to be paid out of the rents of his real estate, and having by his will disposed of all his property except the reversion of certain land, directs his executors, in case the rents should not be sufficient to pay the allowance, to adopt some mode for raising the deficiency out of the other parts of the estate not devised to his wife. *Held*, that the executors had thereby power to sell the reversion of the lands. Roberdeau *v.* Roberdeau, 1 Cr. C. C., 305.

§ 34. From a power to hire out a slave and receive his wages, the jury cannot infer a power to sell him. Negro Daniel *v.* Kincheloe, 2 Cr. C. C., 295.

§ 35. A power to sell coupled either with an interest or trust survives to the surviving executor. So also if all the trustees or executors in such a case decline to act except one. Taylor *v.* Benham, 5 How., 233.

§ 36. Under a written power to sell upon a contingency a judgment specified in the writing, no duty devolves upon the grantee of the power to issue an execution upon it. Bast *v.* Bank, 11 Otto, 93.

§ 37. Where a testatrix empowered a trustee to sell lands for purposes of re-investment "when the major part of my children shall recommend and advise the same," it was held that the consent of the major part of those living at the time when the sale was made was sufficient. Sohier *v.* Williams, 1 Curt., 479.

§ 38. **Power of appointment.**— A testator made his will, giving annuities to his wife and others, and directing that his executors, or the survivor of them, after the decease of his wife, should provide for the annuitants then living, and dispose of the residue of his property for the use of such charitable institutions as they or he might deem most beneficial to mankind. His wife and three other persons were appointed executors. The three other persons all died during the life-time of the wife, and no appointment was made or attempted to be made during the life-time of the executors. *Held*, that the executors were vested with a mere power of appointment with no special trust attached to it; that the executors, having died before the wife's decease, had no power to make the appointment; and that the conditions annexed by the testator having made the appointment impossible, the charity could not be carried out. Fontain *v.* Ravenal, 17 How., 869.

§ 89. Where a marriage settlement gave a woman the power of appointment to the use of such persons as she might from time to time appoint, during the coverture, by any writing or writings under her hand and seal, attested by three credible witnesses, and she executed a deed which recited that the parties had thereunto set their hands and seals, and which the witnesses attested as having been sealed and delivered, *held* to be a sufficient execution of the power, although the witnesses did not attest the fact of her signing it. Ladd *v.* Ladd, 8 How., 10.

§ 40. Where a marriage settlement recited that the woman was possessed of real and personal estate, which it was agreed should be settled to her sole and separate use, with power to dispose of the same by appointment or devise, and then directed that the trustee should permit her to have, receive, take, and enjoy all the interest, rents and 'profits of the property to her own use, or to that of such persons as she might from time to time appoint during the coverture, or to such persons as she, by her last will and testament, might devise or will the same to, and in default of such appointment or devise, then the estate and premises aforesaid to go to those who might be entitled thereto by legal distribution, *held*, that this deed enabled her to convey the whole fee, under the power, and not merely the annual interest, rents and profits. *Ibid.*

§ 41. A power of appointment by will among such of the children of R. and M., and in such proportions as M. may appoint, is an exclusive power. The right in the distributor to select necessarily implies the power to exclude. Hence, no distributee can say his share is illusory, the distributor not being bound to give him anything. Ingraham *v.* Meade, 8 Wall. Jr., 82.

§ 42. An appointment under a power is an attempt to appoint carried out, and if made by will the intent and its execution are to be sought for through the whole instrument, and if the will contains no expressed intent to exert the power, yet if it may reasonably be gathered from the gifts and directions made that their purpose and object were to execute it, the will must be regarded as an execution. Blake *v.* Hawkins, 8 Otto, 315.

§ 48. **Power to make partition.**— A testator in Mississippi constituted A. a trustee for his children, and gave him full power to dispose of the property devised in the will that might fall to them, and invest the proceeds in such manner as he might think proper for their benefit. The court, without assuming to lay down a general rule on the subject, followed the clearly expressed opinion of the supreme court of Mississippi on the precise point, to the effect that the trustee had power to make partition. Phelps *v.* Harris, 11 Otto, 370.

§ 44. A power to sell and exchange lands includes the power to make partition. *Ibid.*

§ 45. **Relief in equity.**— A., having devised land to four trustees to sell and dispose of the same at private sale, on such terms as to them should seem meet, one of the trustees died, and another removed from the state. A sale of the land to B. was negotiated by the other two, with the assent of the one who was absent. B. paid the agreed consideration, and it was distributed in accordance with the terms of the will among the legatees, the two resident trustees making a conveyance of the lands to B., all of the parties concerned supposing at the time that such a conveyance was a valid execution of the power. The trustees were discharged by the order of the court, and B. subsequently filed a bill praying a specific performance of the contract of sale by the heirs at law (who were also legatees under the will) and their grantees. *Held*, (1) that if the non-execution of a power by trustees is occasioned by a misapprehension of the law, ignorance of the law must have been the sole occasion of the mistake, in order to defeat the interference of a court of equity, and if the case involves other facts which present a case for relief, equity is vigilant to lay hold of them in order to protect rights; (2) that when a power is coupled with a trust, which imposes upon the trustee the duty of executing it, equity will compel its execution in performance of the trust, when its aid is invoked by a person standing in a meritorious relation to the power; (3) that in this case all of the trustees having, in legal effect, negotiated the contract of sale, the purchaser, having performed the contract on his part, is entitled to the aid of the court to compel its completion on the part of the others. Long *v.* Soule,* 22 Int. Rev. Rec., 244; 9 Ch. Leg. N., 83.

§ 46. Although courts of equity may afford relief against the defective execution of a power executed by a party, they cannot afford relief against the defective execution of a power created by law. As where an administrator sells real estate of his intestate without having previously given the proper bond with sureties approved by the judge of probate, the sale is void and equity cannot relieve. Bright v. Boyd, 1 Story, 478.

§ 47. Although a court of chancery will not aid a defective power, it will relieve from a defective execution of a power. Accordingly, where an executor, empowered to convey real estate of testator, acted, in executing the deed, through an attorney authorized to act by an instrument not under seal, *held*, to be a case of defective execution of a power from which equity would relieve. Piatt's Heirs v. McCollough's Heirs, 1 McL., 69.

§ 48. A Connecticut statute authorized the probate court, for reasonable cause, to order the sale of real estate belonging to a minor, on application of his guardian, and to empower him or some other person to make a conveyance of the same. A deed executed under the order of the court, in accordance with this statute, did not refer distinctly to the order of sale nor give its date, the only clause in the deed referring to the order of sale being an averment that the grantor was "authorized by an order of the court of probate for the district of S." to make the conveyance, nor did it show that the notice of sale had been given as required. *Held*, that there was a defective execution of a valid power, but that equity would interfere in favor of the grantee to aid such defective execution, there being no opposing equities. Segee v. Thomas, 3 Blatch., 11.

§ 49. **Deed with power of sale.**—Where by the terms of a deed conveying real estate in trust, to be sold for the benefit of the creditor of the grantor, the trustee is directed to sell the property conveyed by public auction, the trustee is bound to conform to this mode of sale, nor is it competent for him to establish any other, although by doing so he might in reality promote the interests of those for whom he acted. Greenleaf v. Queen, 1 Pet., 188.

§ 50. A temporary injunction will be granted against the sale of mortgaged premises under a power to sell in the conveyance, if the assignee of the mortgagor bought in ignorance of the existence of such a power and the mortgage containing it was not recorded. Platt v. McClure, 3 Woodb. & M., 151.

§ 51. **The administrator** has no estate in the land of his intestate, but a power to sell under the authority of the court. This is not an independent power, to be exercised at discretion, when the exigency in his opinion may require it, but it is conferred by the court in a state of things prescribed by the law. The order of the court is a prerequisite, indispensable to the very existence of the power, and if the law which authorizes the court to make the order be repealed the power to sell can never come into existence. Bank of Hamilton v. Dudley, 2 Pet., 492.

§ 52. **Death ; substituted trustee.**—When a debtor has conveyed to a trustee real estate to be sold for the benefit of creditors, and the trustee dying before the conveyance of the property to a purchaser, another trustee is appointed by the court upon the application of the creditors to execute the trust, in a proceeding relative to the execution of the trust and the conveyance of the estate, it is necessary that the heirs at law of the first trustee shall be parties to the same, as the legal title did not pass to the substituted trustee, by the appointment, but remained in the legal heirs. Greenleaf v. Queen, 1 Pet., 188.

§ 53. **Death of a trustee; power of survivor.**—A testatrix by her will appointed A. and B. trustees and invested them with the whole of the legal estate, to hold the same in trust, to "manage, invest and re-invest the same according to their best discretion," and pay over the income to the three children of the testatrix during their lives, and on their decease, the said A. and B., or their "successors, as trustees," were to appoint three or more persons, who should then be informed of the facts by the trustees, whereupon the said trust fund was to be disposed of and distributed, in accordance with the determination of the said persons, among permanently established and incorporated charitable institutions for the benefit of the poor. *Held*, that, the trustees being invested with the legal estate in order to enable them to discharge the various trusts declared, the power conferred upon them to appoint the donees of the power was a power coupled with an interest, and as such survived the death of one of them and could be executed by the survivor. Lorings v. Marsh, 6 Wall., 337.

§ 54. Courts of equity generally apply to the construction of powers given to executors the principle which applies the construction of other parts of the will to ascertain and carry into execution the intention of the testator. When the power is given to executors, to be executed in their official capacity as executors, and there are no words in the will warranting the conclusion that the testator intended, for safety or some other object, a joint execution of the power, as the office survives, the power ought also to be construed as surviving. And courts of equity will lend their aid to uphold the power, for the purpose of carrying into execution the intention of the testator and preventing the consequences that might result from an extinction of the power. Peter v. Beverly, 10 Pet., 532.

§ 55. To constitute a power so coupled with an interest in executors that it will survive, it is not necessary that they derive a personal benefit from the devise, for a trust will survive, though in no way beneficial to the trustee. It is the possession of the legal estate, or a right in the subject over which the power is to be exercised, that makes the interest in question. And when an executor, guardian, or other trustee, is invested with the rents and profits of land for the use of another, it is still an authority coupled with an interest and survives. *Ibid.*

§ 56. **A power coupled with an interest does not expire** with the death of the person creating it. Hunt *v.* Rousmaniere,* 2 Mason, 244.

§ 57. A naked power does not necessarily expire with the death of the person creating it. It may be such as can only be exercised after the death of such party, as a power to an executor to sell land to pay debts. *Ibid.*

§ 58. A naked power which expires with the death of the party creating it is such as requires the power to be executed in the name and as the act of the grantor and not of the grantee, as a power of attorney to execute an instrument or do other acts in the name of the grantor. *Ibid.*

§ 59. A power of attorney is not coupled with an instrument, though given as collateral security for a debt; and, although irrevocable by the donor during his life, expires upon his death. *Ibid.*

§ 60. Where an agreement is made to lend money, and to take collateral security on property, and by mistake a power of attorney only is taken, and the party dies, equity will relieve the creditor, and enforce the original agreement against the administrators, where the estate is insolvent. *Ibid.*

§ 61. A collateral power expires at the death or bankruptcy of the appointer. *Aliter* with a power complied with an interest. Hence, as a mortgage in Georgia is merely security for a debt, and passes no title, a power of sale in a mortgage given in that state is not a power coupled with an interest, but is merely a collateral power, and cannot be executed after the mortgagor has been adjudged a bankrupt. Lockett *v.* Hill, 1 Woods, 552.

§ 62. Where a power of sale given in a mortgage is limited to a specified time, and the mortgagor fails to execute it within that time, the power is gone forever. *Ibid.*

POWER OF ATTORNEY.

See AGENCY.

PRACTICE.

This subject will be found in a separate volume.

PRACTICE, CRIMINAL

See CRIMES.

PRACTICE IN SUPREME COURT.

See APPEALS AND WRITS OF ERROR.

PRE-EMPTION.

See LAND.

PRESCRIPTION.

See LIMITATIONS.

PRESIDENT.

See GOVERNMENT. Pardoning Power, see CRIMES.

PRESUMPTIONS.

See EVIDENCE.

PRESUMPTION OF PAYMENT.

See LIMITATIONS.

PRINCIPAL AND AGENT.

See AGENCY.

PRINCIPAL AND SURETY.

See BILLS AND NOTES; BONDS; CONTRACTS.

PRIORITY OF UNITED STATES.

See GOVERNMENT.

PRISONERS.

See CRIMES.

PRISONERS OF WAR.

See WAR.

PRIVATE CARRIERS.

See CARRIERS.

PRIVATEERS.

See WAR.

PRIVILEGE.

[See COURTS.]

SUMMARY — *Judges*, §§ 1, 3. — *Judges, jurors, witnesses and suitors*, § 2. — *Mode of redress*, § 4. — *Parties*, §§ 5–7.

§ 1. A judge of a state court is privileged from arrest or summons in civil causes while in actual attendance at his court, and while going to or returning from the same. Lyell *v.* Goodwin, §§ 8–12.

§ 2. The privilege of a judge, juror, witness or suitor from arrest while in actual or constructive attendance upon court is not the privilege of the individual but of the public, and is granted to guard the administration of justice, and for this reason it is the duty of the courts to give this privilege their constant protection. *Ibid.*

§ 3. A judge, privileged from arrest, when about to set out on his circuit, is not liable to be served with process of summons. *Ibid.*

§ 4. The mode of redress for a person privileged from arrest, when arrested, is by motion to the court from which the process issued. *Ibid.*

§ 5. Parties and witnesses in attendance in good faith before commissioners, whether with or without a writ of protection, are privileged from arrest or civil process during their attendance, and for a reasonable time in going and returning. Larned *v.* Griffin, §§ 13, 14.

§ 6. A party privileged from arrest on civil process may, if arrested, take advantage of his privilege by motion or by plea in abatement. The privilege secures absolute protection. *Ibid.*

§ 7. A party privileged from arrest who submits to an arrest, makes application to give bail, and enters into a bond to appear, does not thereby waive his privilege, but may assert the same notwithstanding, by motion or plea in abatement. *Ibid.*

[NOTES.—See §§ 15–31.]

LYELL *v.* GOODWIN.

(Circuit Court for Michigan: 4 McLean, 29–44. 1845.

. Opinion by WILKINS, J.

STATEMENT OF FACTS.— A writ of summons having been issued out of this court, and served upon the defendant, the present motion is made by the defendant "That the writ, and the service thereof, and all proceedings thereon, be set aside, quashed and vacated." The defendant sets forth in his affidavit upon which this motion is founded, the following facts, which are not contested:

"That he is now, and for some time has been, one of the justices of the supreme court of this state. That a regular term of said court was, under the provisions of the laws of the state, commenced and held at the city of Detroit, on the first Tuesday of January last past, and which term did not expire until the 27th of March ensuing. That he, the defendant, as one of the justices of the said court, was in attendance upon the said court during and throughout the said term. That the court was in actual session on the 7th of March last, and was adjourned from that day until the 11th of the same month. That on the 20th day of the same month, the deputy marshal of the United States for this district came into the room assigned by the state authorities to the justices of the supreme court, and where the sessions of the said court are held, and while the defendant and two other justices of said court were actually engaged in the performance of judicial duties, and served upon the defendant a writ from this court, commanding the marshal of the district to *summon* the defendant to appear before this court on the first Monday of April ensuing (which was the 7th day of April), to answer unto the plaintiff in this cause, in a plea of trespass on the case, etc., etc. On the day the said writ bears date, viz., the 8th day of March, the defendant was employed in the discharge of his official duties."

By the provision of the state law prescribing the duties of the justices of the supreme court of the state of Michigan, the defendant is the presiding judge of the first judicial circuit of said state. The said circuit comprises the counties of Wayne, Monroe, Macomb, St. Clair, Mackinac and Chippewa; in which counties (excepting the counties of Mackinac and Chippewa), circuit courts are required to be held twice a year by the said presiding judge; the spring term of the Macomb circuit required by law to be held at Mt. Clemens on the first Tuesday of April (which this year was the *first* day of April), and for the county of Monroe, at the city of Monroe, on the second Tuesday of April ensuing, which was the 8th day of April, the day subsequent to the return day of the writ. The city of Monroe is forty miles from Detroit, the present residence of the defendant; and the defendant states in his affidavit, which was made on the 26th of March last, that it was his duty, and he would proceed to the city of Monroe on the 7th of April (the day when he was summoned to appear in this court) to commence and hold the Monroe circuit.

It appears, then, that the writ of summons in this cause was issued on the 8th of March last, served on the 10th, and made returnable on the first Monday, which was the 7th day of April. And it further appears that the supreme court of the state was in session from the first Tuesday of January until the 28th day of March; and that the Macomb circuit, as required by law, was commenced and held on the Tuesday following the adjournment of the court; and that the Monroe circuit, held at the city of Monroe, forty miles from the city of Detroit, the residence of the defendant, was commenced and held by him on the 8th of April, the day after the *return day of the summons* from this court, and continued till the commencement of the St. Clair term, on the fourth Tuesday of April.

Such are the facts, unquestioned by the plaintiff, and such the provisions of the state laws, regulating the circuit courts of the state, which are courts of record, of general jurisdiction, civil and criminal, and conferring upon and demanding of the circuit judge the exercise of high judicial powers in vacation. From these circumstances, two points necessarily arise in the case, the defendant having in his motion preferred the claim of privilege. 1st. The regularity of the writ of summons by the marshal; and, 2d, to what extent the privilege exempts a justice of the supreme court of the state during its existence.

§ 8. *A judge of a state court is privileged from arrest or summons in civil causes while in actual attendance at his court.*

1st. It being conceded by the plaintiff that the defendant was and is a justice of the supreme court of the state, and that this writ *was served* upon him while engaged in the discharge of his judicial duties, *and during his actual attendance upon the court*, the service must, of course, be set aside as irregular. The privilege protecting the defendant while engaged in judicial duty, as well from the service of a summons as from arrest, for although, by the service of a summons, the trouble of entering special bail is avoided, yet the summons as well as the *capias* obliges the defendant to attend the court from which it issues, and exposes the public service to inconvenience and interruption, to prevent which the protection of privilege in all cases, whether that of parliament or of jurors, witnesses or suitors, was created by the common law. The privilege is not the privilege of the individual, but of the public, and is granted to guard the legislation of the country and the administration of justice, and it is the duty of courts to give this privilege their constant protection.

§ 9. *Judicial privilege from arrest or summons in civil actions extends to the proper time of going, staying or returning, etc., as in cases of other privileged persons.*

But, secondly, the privilege to the presiding officer of a court, without whose attendance the court cannot be held, is as extensive as to a suitor or witness or juror of the court; and if public policy, which is the reason of the rule, thus protects these officers and parties, with stronger reason should the rule be applied to those public functionaries composing the highest judicial tribunal of the state. This privilege of the court protects jurors, parties and witnesses from the service of civil process *eundo, morando, et redeundo*, and comprehends protection from arrest by *capias* as well as the service of a summons. In other words, the privilege *protects them from suit* while necessarily going to, staying at, or returning from, the court; private right being suspended in favor of the public good during the period thus comprehended.

Such was the well established principle of the common law of England upon this subject before the statute of 12th and 13th William III., chapter 3. For, antecedent to this statute, members of parliament were not only privileged from arrest, but also from being served with any process out of the courts of law, not only during the sitting of the parliament, but also during the recess within the time of privilege, which was ever liberally construed a reasonable time, *eundo et redeundo*. It was not within the design of this statute to abridge the common-law privilege, which was enjoyed during the sitting of parliament, but to authorize the commencement of suit a certain time after the dissolution or prorogation of parliament. The statute directs the *manner* of bringing the action, viz., by summons or distress infinite to compel a common appearance, but not until after the rising of parliament; and provides — what may be a just construction of the rule in this country — " that the plaintiff is not to be barred by the statute of limitations " in the time consumed by the privilege, but is at liberty to proceed *de novo* after the cessation of privilege, which, being a public right, enjoyed for the benefit of the public, only so far interferes with private right as to secure the public good, on the termination of which the private right recommences, unimpaired by the time of privilege, the statute of limitations ceasing to run when privilege commenced. By this statute, as well as by the common law, which it slightly modified, during the session of parliament *a suit could not be instituted;* and if it had been commenced before, it could not be prosecuted during the session. *Under the provisions of the statute*, the courts authorized an original to be filed against a member of parliament in order to prevent him from taking advantage of the statute of limitations, but no process could be issued upon it; and before this statute, this could not have been done at any time after the rising of parliament, during the continuance of privilege.

In Col. Pitt's Case, 2 Strange, 987, which occurred during the reign of George II., and to which the statute of William applied, and who was arrested two days after the dissolution of the parliament of which he was a member, and before he had time to settle his private affairs in order to return home, it was held upon the third point made in that case, that he should be discharged from the suit upon motion, the institution of the suit within the time of privilege being a breach of the privilege of parliament. All the judges were of opinion that he should be discharged on motion, except two,— the chief baron at first intimating a doubt, but subsequently ordering the entry of common bail to be stricken out, and the party discharged. And the principal question was, whether he should be discharged on common bail, or discharged altogether? It being after the dissolution of parliament, the plaintiff had a right to commence a suit under the statute, and therefore there was a doubt whether he should not be discharged from the arrest on common bail, and the proceedings against him continued. But the judges held that they would not countenance the infraction of the privilege, and therefore discharged him entirely. Mr. Justice Blackstone, who published his commentaries in 1765, *after this decision*, observes, "neither can any member of either house be arrested, or taken into custody, or served with *any process*, without a breach of the privilege of parliament." So that the law, as it stood in England before the statute of William III., or since, extended the priviledge to an *exemption from arrest*, or the *service of civil process* during the time covered by the privilege.

In a recent case in the queen's bench — that of Cassidy v. Stewart, which fully adopts the ruling in Col. Pitt's Case, 40 Eng. Com. Law Rep., 464,— it was held that a *ca. sa.* issued against a member of parliament, although with a direction to be returned *non est investus*, and with the *avowed object of continuing the proceedings of the original suit*, and *not to molest* the defendant with an arrest, was irregular, and that the proceeding should be set aside; Bosanquet, justice, observing, "formerly [before the statute of 12 and 13 William III., chapter 3], the privilege was *exemption from being sued*. Exemption from arrest is recognized in various acts of parliament. The arrest, therefore, would be an illegal act. But if the thing ordered to be done be illegal, the order must also be illegal. But the writ commands the sheriff to do an act, which act, if done by the officer, in obedience to the writ, would be a violation of the privilege, and would throw upon the defendant the trouble and expense of obtaining that discharge to which his privilege entitles him." The same reasoning applies with equal force to a writ of summons issued during the existence of the privilege under the common law. For the latter writ commands an officer of the court to do *an illegal act*, namely, *a breach of privilege*, and where the privilege is exemption from the service of a summons as well as from an arrest, the order to infract it is *as irregular* as the *obedience of the order itself* in the actual service.

§ 10. *The doctrine of privilege generally.*

The doctrine of privilege generally is not peculiar to the common law of England, nor does it spring from the peculiar system of kings, lords and commons. It is as ancient as Edward the Confessor, and is consistent with, nay, necessary to the universal equality established in a republic. It is inseparably connected with the fundamental maxim in all free governments, that where the public exigency renders it necessary for common preservation, private right shall yield to public good. It has been recognized and adopted in its fullest extent in the courts of the United States and in several of the states of this Union.

In Hunt's Case, decided in the circuit court of the United States for the district of Pennsylvania, Judges Washington and Peters both held that the privilege protected a witness at his lodgings while under subpœna, *and directed his discharge.* The motion was made for his discharge from arrest under a *ca. sa.*, the judgment having been rendered before he was subpœnaed as a witness. 4 Dall., 388. In Gergei's Lessee *v.* Irwin, 4 Dall., 107, decided in 1790, the court held that the privilege extended to arrest, *summons, citation*, or other civil process during the necessary attendance to the public business.

In Hays *v.* Shields, a suitor was privileged from being sued by summons while attending to his cause in court, and *eundo et redeundo*. In this case the cause had been tried, and a day had intervened after the delivery of the verdict, when he was served with process, and the court very properly held that they would not nicely scan the time of the return of witnesses, parties, etc., etc., and that the exemption from suit, claimed by the party, was the privilege of the court, and not the privilege of the.party.

The plaintiff in this cause endeavored to establish a distinction between writs of summons and *capias*, which the court held not to be solid, observing that the party's attention to his own business in court is distracted by other objects, and he is not to be subjected to that inconvenience which would be contrary to the wise indulgence of the law. The defendant was, on motion, discharged from the action. This case occurred in 1797, in Pennsylvania. The motion was made by Ross, whose legal eminence was co-extensive with the Union in his day; and the decision pronounced by Addison, justice, as profound a lawyer and as honest a man as ever adorned the bench of this country or England. Were it a modern Pennsylvania decision, I should probably hesitate to give that weight to it, to which its intrinsic merits entitle it, inasmuch as it is now the common parlance of the bar to treat with levity at least the modern decisions of both New York and Pennsylvania. But it is not merely Pennsylvania law, but the common law of England, maintained and enforced. In the argument of the counsel, and the opinion of the judge, we find cited Pitt's Case from Strange, and the common law from its ancient expounders.

In Bolton *v.* Martin, 1 Dall., 296, the defendant, who was a member of the state convention in 1788, was served with a summons. Sargeant, so celebrated as a jurist and a statesman, moved to quash the process, upon his mere suggestion, as an officer of the court, that the defendant was acting in a public capacity, as a member of a legislative body, and was entitled to his privilege. The motion was sustained by Justice Shippen, and the defendant discharged from the action. In this case the attorney-general of the state appeared in support of the motion, the privilege being considered a *public right;* and the whole common-law doctrine of privilege was fully sustained, the court reviewing the history of privilege, and placing it on the true ground, not of exclusive favor to an individual, but of public good. And in 1803, when the supreme court of that state was filled with eminent and profound jurists, it was held (in Miles *v.* McCullough, 1 Binn., 77) that a suitor attending an appeal from the court of another county was privileged from a summons, and discharged from the suit, on motion.

And still more recently, in 1822, in the case of The United States *v.* Edme, where a witness attending before a magistrate to give his deposition under a rule of court was arrested on a *capias* on his return home from the magistrate's office, under a writ from the district court of the United States, in a suit for the recovery of the penalties of an official bond, the supreme court of Pennsylvania discharged him from the arrest, after he had given bail to the marshal, and where the application was made to the court, not by the party himself, who was absent, but by his bail, the court holding that the privilege protected

471

·the witness from suit, while attending under subpœna, and for a reasonable time in returning home; and he was discharged *without the entry of common bail.* This case is to be found in 9 Sargeant and Rawle, 150, and is valuable, not only for the point decided, but for the eloquent exposition, by Mr. Justice Duncan, of the right of privilege, and the constitutional boundaries of the federal and state jurisdiction.

And but a few years ago, in 1836, the *district court in Philadelphia,* in the case of Witherall *v.* Leitsinger, discharged the defendant from a summons (which is tantamount to the dismissal of the suit), he being a suitor in *another* county, and having come into Philadelphia to attend to the taking of a deposition in the pending suit, although the taking of the deposition had been adjourned, and he was about to return. 1 Miles, 237. Although this decision goes greater length than any prior English or American case, yet it exhibits the spirit that courts will not be deterred from a liberal construction of the privilege of the public, by the allegation of private loss or inconvenience. Nor is the extension of the privilege, in this case, more an invasion of private right, than that in the case of Cole *v.* Hawkins, in the court of king's bench (Andrews, 275), where merely serving process upon a party attending to his cause in court, and while he was upon the steps leading into the court, was held *a great contempt* of court, punishable by attachment, and the court compelling the attorney, who purged himself of the contempt by declaring that he had served the writ through *mere inadvertence,* to pay the costs — and discharging the defendant. If the Philadelphia decision in 1836 is calculated to alarm, in its extension of privilege, how much more this adjudication of the court of king's bench, in England, in 1738 — a century previous. Both cases deem the infraction of the privilege a *public wrong,* and, as such, punishable by the court against whose jurisdiction the wrong was committed and whose process was abused.

The courts of New Jersey and Connecticut have followed in the Pennsylvania path, or rather, fearlessly proclaimed the common-law doctrine upon the subject of privilege, recognizing no distinction between a *capias* and a summons, and considering the privilege as the privilege of the court, protecting the administration of justice from interruption and delay. Such is Halsey *v.* Stewart, 1 N. J., 366, where the decision is pronounced by Justice Southard, of the supreme court of the state, recognizing and adopting the Pennsylvania decisions in Dallas; and Cole and Hawkins, in Andrews, 275. Such is Harris *v.* Grantham, 1 Coxe, 142, and King *v.* Coit, 1 Day, 139, where it was held by the supreme court of Connecticut, in 1810, that the party entitled to the privilege might avail himself of it, by a plea abating the writ, which is all the present motion under consideration calls for. Though this decision is based upon a local statute, and so referred to by Judge Smith, who gave the opinion of the court, yet the language of the statute is recited in the opinion, and but repeats the common law provision, "that the party is not to be molested by suit during the sessions of, or going to, or returning from, the general court."

The court had no doubt but that the writ of error served upon the defendant was an invasion of his privilege as a member of the court, and that he had chosen the proper method to take advantage of his privilege, and ordered that the writ abate. Such, also, has been the character of the decisions of the supreme court of the late territory of Michigan in Woodbridge *v.* Cook, decided in 1833, where the defendant was served with a summons while preparing to leave home to attend to his duties as a judge of the supreme court on a distant circuit. The judgment recovered against him in a suit thus irregularly commenced was reversed on error — and this court has repeatedly recognized the same principle in relation to members of the state legislature, allowing the privilege when pleaded, and sustaining the demurrer in a suit commenced by Narr, where the privilege was set forth.

In Massachusetts the same principle has been recognized, and to the same extent. In the case of McNeill, 6 Mass., 245 and 264, it was decided by the supreme court of the state that a suitor to an action pending in court, and during the discussion of a mere question of law by his counsel, could not be arrested on a *ca. sa.* issued on a judgment previously obtained against him in another cause; the court holding that his privilege protected him while " his action was discussing," and ordered him to be discharged.

In all the states of the Union where the question has arisen, the doctrine of the common law has been fully maintained, unless altered and modified by local statute. In New York a cursory examination of their reports would lead to a contrary impression; but I find that the principle is fully recognized.

In the case of Livingston, in 8 John., 350, the supreme court declined interference with an inferior tribunal by *mandamus*, commanding the court of common pleas of a county to proceed in a case against the judge of the court, intimating that a judge is not liable to be proceeded against except by bill in his own court.

In the case of Secor *v.* Bell, 18 John., 52, the question arose in a collateral action of debt brought against the sheriff for an escape of an attorney of the court who had been taken in an execution at the suit of the plaintiffs, and had produced to the sheriff a writ of privilege, upon which the sheriff discharged him from custody, and returned the execution accordingly. Chief Justice Spencer decided that the sheriff had no authority to discharge the attorney, because it was not his province, as a ministerial officer of the court, to take notice of the privilege of an attorney, and that the proper mode to apply the protection of the privilege was by motion in court to discharge him on an affidavit of the facts. And as, by the Revised Statutes of that state, counselors, attorneys and solicitors are made liable to arrest on mesne process, and to be held to bail as other persons, the intimation of the judge, that the motion must be to discharge on common bail, depended upon the local statute of the state; Judge Spencer recognizing the common-law rule by his citation of authority, and consequently the principle in Col. Pitt's case, which exempted jurors, and witnesses, and parties from arrest, and other civil process, and defined the proper mode to be a motion to discharge altogether, and not the writ of privilege.

It is needless to cull from the numerous authorities, other cases; sufficient have already been referred to, to establish these propositions as the common law of England, and the law in the various states of the Union.

§ 11. *To what classes of persons the privilege of exemption from arrest or summons extends.*

1. The privilege extends to suitors, witnesses, jurors and officers, and consequently to the presiding officers of the courts of justice; and protects them, while in attendance upon their public duties, from arrest, summons, or any other civil process.

§ 12. *The proper mode of redress when the privilege of exemption from arrest or summons is invaded.*

2. When the privilege is invaded, the proper mode of redress is by motion

in the court from which the process issued, to set aside the service, and discharge the party, where privilege has been invaded; or, in other words, to *abate the writ.*

Apply these principles to the case under consideration. By provision of the state law, known to the counsel of the plaintiff, who took out the writ, the supreme court, of which he was an attorney, met on the first Tuesday of January last. It did not rise until *Friday,* the 28th of March. By another provision of the state law, the justices of the supreme court are the presiding judges of certain designated circuits; the defendant, Judge Goodwin, being the presiding judge of the first circuit, and required by law to commence the Macomb circuit on the first Tuesday in April; affording him this year *but two legal days* from the close of the supreme court, to prepare for and go to that circuit, and by law also required to attend in succession the Monroe and St. Clair circuits, commencing at Monroe on the second Tuesday of April.

The writ of summons commanded the marshal to summon the defendant, Judge Goodwin, to be and appear in this court on the first Monday of April, to answer the plaintiff; and the law of the state commanded his presence, forty miles from this city, on the day after. He must necessarily obey the law of the state; and his judicial privilege — the same as that which would protect the humblest suitor in the court — protected him from obedience to the summons.

The writ was taken out by an officer of this court, who was also a practitioner in the supreme court, while that court was in session, and made returnable on a day when the defendant was necessarily engaged in going to a court some forty miles distant from his residence. It was served upon the defendant on the 10th of March, while actually engaged in his official duties, and returned on the same day. Now, at what period of time from the commencement of the supreme court, in January, to the adjournment of the St. Clair circuit, two weeks *after* the return day of the writ, did the privilege of the judge cease to protect him from process? Certainly not the 29th and 31st of March, both of which days, according to the reasonable time allowed in Col. Pitt's case, and the case in Yeates, was little enough for preparation to go, and actual going, to the Macomb circuit. And from that time onward, to the close of the St. Clair term, in the beginning of May, there was not a day in which his privilege did not clearly and fully protect him from the service of the writ; and, therefore, the service was illegal, and consequently it was an abuse of the process of *this* court, to take out a writ commanding the marshal to do an *illegal* act; an act which, from the known provisions of the state law, must be illegal within the time in which it was commanded to be done, and, therefore, this writ must be quashed.

This privilege is not exclusive, but general; and is not appropriately obnoxious to condemnation, as invasive of private right. It is an ample shield, covering alike the suitor and the witness, the juror and the judge, and protecting from impediment the administration of justice between man and man. More especially is it essential that the judicial functionary should be thus defended. For the time being, while engaged in the public service, he is divested of self and of private concernment, and, as it were, dedicated in time and mind to the public service. Nor need there be *private* injury as a necessary consequence. There may be a time when the privilege of these functionaries ceases,— when the special duty that sets them apart to the public service has been performed, and their return to private life is clear and unquestioned; when the public interest no longer demands their protection, and the *private* right to their attention can commence, and they be held answerable as any other citizen.

3. In regard to the question of jurisdiction, it is unnecessary to pronounce an opinion, as that question will come up in other cases now pending, and *this* writ is quashed on the ground already considered. But, it may be well observed, that since the argument I have directed an examination by the clerk of the cases instituted since the organization of this court, and the great majority of them state the citizenship of the parties in the original writ, and the few that omit this important allegation are of recent date. By this writ, we are not informed of the character of either plaintiff or defendant. By the affidavits on file. it appears that the defendant is a judge of the highest court in the state, and the plaintiff an inhabitant of the city of Detroit. Now, the judicial act of 1789 *limits* the jurisdiction of the courts of the United States to suits between a citizen of the state where the suit is brought and a citizen of another state, and to cases where an alien is a party; and, to maintain a suit in the circuit court of the United States, "the jurisdiction must appear on the record." This does not appear on the record, *as yet*, in this cause, and the presumption is, that a cause is without the jurisdiction of the court until the contrary appears; and, did the quashing of this writ depend *solely* upon this ground, I would enter more fully into the investigation of the question, notwithstanding the remark of Mr. Justice Taney, in 12 Pet., 64, "that the proper place for the averment in a *writ of right* is the declaration." Was this court asked to discharge a defendant on a writ or a *capias*, where the writ did not disclose the jurisdiction, or the plaintiff's right to the process, it would not be insisted on that the defendant must patiently await the plaintiff's pleasure to aver the jurisdiction of the court in his declaration.

The court direct the writ of summons in the above cause, and the service thereof, and all proceedings thereon, to be set aside and vacated, and the defendant discharged.

LARNED *v.* GRIFFIN.

(Circuit Court for Massachusetts: 12 Federal Reporter, 590-595. 1882.)

Opinion by COLT, J.

STATEMENT OF FACTS. — In this case it appears that the defendant was arrested while in Boston, Massachusetts, in attendance before a commissioner acting under a commission issued out of the superior court for Cook county, Illinois, to take the depositions of certain witnesses in a case pending in that court between the same parties, and for the same cause of action as this suit. The defendant submitted to the arrest, and gave bail. The suit was first brought in the state court and afterwards duly removed here. The only question now before the court is whether the plea in abatement, setting up the privilege of the defendant from arrest, can be sustained. To decide this we must determine — *First*, whether the defendant was privileged from arrest at the time; *second*, whether his remedy can be enforced by a plea in abatement; *third*, whether submitting to the arrest and giving a bail bond is a waiver of the privilege; *fourth*, whether answering to the merits is a waiver of the plea in abatement.

§ 13. *What persons are privileged from arrest or summons, etc.*
It has long been settled that parties and witnesses attending in good faith

any legal tribunal, with or without a writ of protection, are privileged from arrest on civil process during their attendance, and for a reasonable time in going and returning. Thompson's Case, 122 Mass., 428; *In re* Healey, 53 Vt., 694; S. C., Reporter, April 5, 1882; Huddeson *v.* Prizer, 9 Phila., 65; *Ex parte* Hurst, 1 Wash., 186; Juneau Bank *v.* McSpedan, 5 Biss., 64; Bridges *v.* Sheldon, 7 Fed. R., 17, 43; Person *v.* Grier, 66 N. Y., 124; Bacon, Abr., "Privilege, B.," 2; Meekins *v.* Smith, 1 H. Bl., 636; 1 Greenl. Ev., § 316. And this protection extends to the attendance of parties and witnesses before arbitrators, commissioners and examiners. Spence *v.* Stewart, 3 East, 89; Arding *v.* Flower, 8 Term R., 534; Sanford *v.* Chase, 3 Cow., 381; U. S. *v.* Edine, 9 S. & R., 147; Huddeson *v.* Prizer, 9 Phila., 65; Wetherall *v.* Leitsinger, 1 Miles, 237; Bridges *v.* Sheldon, 7 Fed. R., 17, 43; 1 Greenl. Ev., § 317.

It is clear, therefore, that the defendant was privileged from arrest at the time it was made. But whether his remedy is by plea in abatement is less free from doubt. Under the old English rule this immunity was taken advantage of by writ of privilege.

" The only way by which courts of justice could anciently take cognizance of privilege of parliament was by writ of privilege, in the nature of a *supersedeas*, to deliver the party out of custody when arrested in a civil suit. . . . But since the statute of 12 William III., chapter 3, which enacts that no privileged person shall be subject to arrest or imprisonment, it has been held that such arrest is irregular *ab initio*, and that the party may be discharged upon motion." 1 Bl. Comm., 166.

The more modern way in England has been to raise the question either by motion or by plea in abatement. Pitt's Case, 2 Stra., 985; Cameron *v.* Lightfoot, 2 W. Bl., 1190; Meekins *v.* Smith, 1 H. Bl., 636; Randall *v.* Gurney, 3 B. & Ald., 252; Com. Dig., "Abatement," D, 6; 1 Chit. Pl., 443; Davis *v.* Rendlesham, 7 Taunt., 679.

§ 14. *Advantage may be taken of the privilege by motion or by plea in abatement, and the privilege secures absolute protection. Cases cited.*

In this country the right of privilege has been brought before the court in three ways. By motion: *Ex parte* Hurst, 1 Wash., 186; Lyell *v.* Goodwin, 4 McLean, 29, 41; Juneau Bank *v.* McSpedan, 5 Biss., 64; Sanford *v.* Chase, 3 Cow., 381; Seaver *v.* Robinson, 3 Duer, 622; Harris *v.* Grantham, Coxe (N. J.), 142; Starrett's Case, 1 Dall., 356; Hammerskold *v.* Rose, 7 Jones (Law), 629; Hunter *v.* Cleveland, 1 Brev., 168; Henegar *v.* Spangler, 29 Ga., 217. By *habeas corpus:* *Ex parte* McNeil, 6 Mass., 264; Wood *v.* Neale, 5 Gray, 538; May *v.* Shumway, 16 Gray, 86; Richards *v.* Goodson, 2 Va. Cas., 381. By plea in abatement: King *v.* Coit, 4 Day, 130; Case *v.* Rorabacher, 15 Mich., 537; Julio *v.* Bolles, 22 Law Rep., 354; Gilbert *v.* Vanderpool, 15 Johns., 242; Anderson *v.* Rountree, 1 Pin. (Wis.), 115; Chaffee *v.* Jones, 19 Pick., 261, 265; Hoppin *v.* Jenckes, 8 R. I., 453.

It is contended by the plaintiff that the common-law privilege of suitors and witnesses never extended so far as to abate the suit, however different the rule may be in case of members of parliament, ambassadors and attorneys.

Anciently, it would seem, in all cases of privilege, the *supersedeas* which was granted upon a writ of privilege only operated to deliver the party out of custody, and he was still held upon common bail. Long's Case, 2 Mod., 181; Pitt's Case, 2 Stra., 987; 1 Bl. Comm., 166. But after the statute of 12 William III., chapter 3, it was decided in Pitt's Case, 2 Stra., 987, that members of parliament, or those entitled to privilege of parliament, should be discharged absolutely, and not upon common bail. See, also, Cassidy v. Stewart, 4 Scott, N. R., 432; 40 Eng. Com. Law, 450.

The rule, however, with respect to suitors and witnesses wàs still maintained, that while the arrest would be set aside, common bail must be filed,— the suit did not abate. Cameron v. Lightfoot, 2 W. Bl., 1190.

The early decisions in this country are not harmonious. In some of the older cases the rule was followed that the privilege of suitors and witnesses extends no further than exemption from arrest; that service by summons is legal; and that in cases of arrest common bail must be filed, or a general appearance entered. Blight v. Fisher, Pet. C. C., 41; Hunter v. Cleveland, 1 Brev., 16; Taft v. Hoppin, Anthon, N. P., 255; Booraem v. Wheeler, 12 Vt., 311; and the more recent case of Bishop v. Vose, 27 Conn., 1.

In other cases, however, we find the right extended, and a more complete protection afforded suitors and witnesses, the discharge from arrest being absolute, and service by summons held illegal. Hayes v. Shields, 2 Yeates, 222; Miles v. McCullough, 1 Binn., 76; U. S. v. Edme, 9 S. & R., 147; Norris v. Beach, 2 Johns., 294; Sanford v. Chase, 3 Cow., 381; Harris v. Grantham, Coxe (N. J.), 142.

Whatever may have been the earlier view, we have no doubt that the tendency in this country has been to enlarge the right of privilege so as to afford full protection to suitors and witnesses from all $f_o$rms of process of a civil character during their attendance before any judicial tribunal, and for a reasonable time in going and returning. Let us pursue the subject a little further. The case of Blight v. Fisher, Pet. C. C., 41, decided in 1809 by Justice Washington, holding that a service of summons upon a witness is good, is distinctly overruled in the later case of Parker v. Hotchkiss, 1 Wall. Jr., 269, the court stating that the opinion met with the approval of Chief Justice Taney and Justice Grier. See, also, the elaborate opinion in Lyell v. Goodwin, 4 McLean, 29, to the effect that a judge about to start on his circuit is not liable to be served with summons, his privilege being as extensive as that of a suitor or witness or juror of the court. The same view is expressed in Juneau Bank v. McSpedan, 5 Biss., 64; Bridges v. Sheldon, 7 Fed. R., 17, 43.

In the earlier cases in New York a distinction was taken between resident and non-resident suitors and witnesses. In the case of non-residents an absolute discharge was granted. Norris v. Beach, 2 Johns., 294. But in the case of residents common bail had to be given. Bours v. Tuckerman, 7 Johns., 538.

Referring to these two decisions, in Sanford v. Chase, 3 Cow., 381, the court observed: " We adopt the first case; the privilege of a witness should be absolute." In the recent case of Person v. Grier, 66 N. Y., 124, the court declare that any distinction between residents and non-residents is doubtful, and the broad ground is taken that this immunity is one of the necessities of the administration of the justice, and that courts would often be embarrassed if suitors or witnesses, while attending court, could be molested with process. Seaver v. Robinion, 3 Duer, 622; Merrill v. George, 23 How. Pr., 331.

The case of Taft v. Hoppin (1816), Anthon, N. P., 255, which decided that the defendant, a non-resident suitor, should be held upon common bail, was rendered at *nisi prius*, and in view of the prior case of Norris v. Beach, 2 Johns., 294, and of the subsequent decisions in the highest court of the state, it can hardly be deemed authority.

In Pennsylvania, from an early period, complete immunity seems to have been extended to suitors and witnesses. Miles v. McCullough, 1 Binn., 77;

Hayes *v.* Shields, 2 Yeates, 222; United States *v.* Edme, 9 S. & R., 147; Holmes *v.* Nelson, 1 Phila., 217.

"It is alike the privilege of the person and the privilege of the court. It renders the administration of justice free and untrammeled, and protects from improper interference all who are concerned in it," say the court in Huddeson *v.* Prizer, 9 Phila., 65.

In New Jersey, also, a full discharge is granted. Harris *v.* Grantham, Coxe (N. J.), 142.

In Massachusetts it was held by Judge Morton in Julio *v.* Bolles, 22 Law Rep., 354, that a foreign witness was protected from summons. In that case a plea in abatement had been filed, which was demurred to by the plaintiff. In overruling the demurrer the learned judge observes: "If this service was illegal, the jurisdiction fails and the writ should be abated."

In Vermont we are referred by plaintiff's counsel to the case of Booraem *v.* Wheeler, 12 Vt., 311, which holds a plea in abatement bad in the case of a witness arrested while attending court; the court maintaining that it has never been held that a man's property may not be attached, or he be served with a summons, while attending court as a witness or suitor. What is wanted is that the suitor or witness may give uninterrupted attendance at court; that this object is not secured by abating the writ, for the question may not be heard until long after the court he was attending had closed its session. The legal object can be and always has been better secured by the summary proceeding of a motion to the court to release the person for the time being, or by *habeas corpus.*

But the views here expressed of the extent of the privilege of suitors or witnesses are clearly inconsistent with the later case in Vermont of *In re* Healey (1881), 53 Vt., 694, which declares a service by summons upon a witness to be illegal. The court, citing Person *v.* Grier, 66 N. Y., 124, and other cases, remark: "In the case of a non-resident suitor or witness, the weight of authority is to the effect that the immunity is absolute from the service of any process, unless the case is exceptional." And it is further declared that if the writ had been made returnable to that court it would have been dismissed upon motion; the court would not have taken jurisdiction of a party whose rights were thus invaded, for to do so would be in effect a withdrawal of the shield and protection which the law uniformly gives to witnesses.

Whether this plea in abatement shall be sustained or not turns upon the view taken of the extent and character of the privilege to which suitors and witnesses are entitled. If we adopt the older and narrower view, that this is wholly the privilege of the court rather than of the suitor, and therefore a question of judicial discretion rather than of personal right; and further, that while the offender may be punishable for contempt if the arrest is made in the actual or constructive presence of the court,—still the suitor or witness can only ask to have the arrest set aside upon giving common bail, or entering a general appearance; then the suit does not abate, and the present plea is bad. But if we adopt the broader rule, which it appears to us is clearly warranted by the more recent decisions in the federal and state courts, and which in our opinion is necessary to the due administration of justice, that this immunity extends to all kinds of civil process, and affords an absolute protection, then we see no good reason why a plea in abatement is not proper here, as in other cases of privilege where an absolute discharge is granted, and where the plea is held good. See authorities before cited.

The plaintiff contends that the defendant submitted to the arrest, made application to give bail, and entered into a bond, and that this constitutes a waiver of his privilege. We do not think this sound, though we are aware that some cases seem to point in this direction. Fletcher v. Baxter, 2 Aiken (Vt.), 224; Brown v. Getchell, 11 Mass., 11, 14.

The question, however, was directly passed upon in United States v. Edme, 9 S. & R., 147, 149, and it was there decided that the giving of a bail-bond is so far from waiving the privilege, that the court, when they discharge, will order it to be delivered up and canceled.

"It is not esteemed any good ground for presuming a waiver of privilege from arrest, because the person takes the ordinary and most expeditious mode of freeing himself from arrest." Redfield, J., in Washburn v. Phelps, 24 Vt., 506.

It appears in this case that an answer to the merits was filed with the plea in abatement. It has been decided that in Massachusetts the validity of neither is affected by their being pleaded together, and that the plea in abatement is not thereby waived. Fisher v. Fraprie, 125 Mass., 472; O'Loughlin v. Bird, 128 Mass., 600.

Upon the whole we are of the opinion that the plea in abatement should be sustained. Action dismissed.

§ 15. In general.—The privilege of a party or witness to a suit from arrest is one not merely for the benefit of the party and witness, but exists for the purpose of maintaining the dignity, and carrying out the commands, of the court which issues the subpœna, and of promoting public justice; and the order of the court discharging the party from imprisonment will be a conclusive justification of the sheriff in every other court, even in the court which issued the process. In re Kimball, 2 Ben., 38.

§ 16. It is not a contempt of court to serve a person while attending at the court as a party in a cause, or as a witness, with a summons. This privilege extends to exemption from arrest, and no further. Blight v. Fisher, Pet. C. C., 41.

§ 17. It is a contempt of court, however, to serve process, either of summons or capias, in the actual or constructive presence of the court. Ibid.

§ 18. Members of congress are privileged from arrest both on judicial and mesne process, and from the service of a summons or other civil process while in attendance on their public duties. Nones v. Edsall, 1 Wall. Jr., 189.

§ 19. Attendance upon congress as a member of that body does not confer such "privilege" as to entitle a party to have a postponement of his suit as a matter of right; though the court may grant a postponement under particular circumstances, in its discretion, and upon terms. Ibid.

§ 20. Judges.—A summons was served on a judge by leaving a copy at his residence. At the time of the service he was making preparations to leave home on the same or the next day, to meet the court in which he presided. Held, that although privileged from arrest while in the performance of his judicial duties, or traveling to and from his court, he could not claim the privilege against the service when at home and not about to set out on his judicial circuit. Lyell v. Goodwin,* 4 McL., 44.

§ 21. A suitor in a United States circuit court, residing without the circuit, is privileged from the service of a summons. The case of Blight v. Fisher, decided in 1809, in which this privilege was limited to exemption from arrest, overruled. Parker v. Hotchkiss, 1 Wall. Jr., 269.

§ 22. The general rule is that a person illegally in custody at the suit of one party is not privileged from arrest at the suit of another, unless there is some proof of concert or collusion. Union Sugar Refinery v. Mathiesson, 2 Cliff., 304.

§ 23. A bankrupt was arrested while on his way to the register's office for the purpose of being examined, an order having been served upon him commanding him to appear and be examined. Held, that the order was substantially a subpœna, and that, as a witness and as a party to the bankruptcy proceedings, he was privileged from arrest and entitled to the protection of the court. In re Kimball, 2 Ben., 38.

§ 24. A party to a suit having been discharged from arrest by reason of his privilege from arrest as such party may be re-arrested under the same or other process, whenever the privilege ceases. *Ibid.*

§ 25. A petitioner in bankruptcy is privileged from arrest on civil process pending the proceedings in his application for relief under the bankruptcy law.   United States *v.* Dobbins,* 1 Penn. L. J., 9.

§ 26. Petitioners under the bankrupt act are entitled to the same privilege from arrest given to other suitors, and this privilege will be regarded liberally.   Thus, where a petitioner was taken on a *ca. sa.* while on his way to the commissioner's office on business connected with the petition, *held,* that he was privileged from arrest, although at the time of his arrest he had deviated three hundred yards from the straight course from his residence to the office of the commissioner.   *Ex parte* Mifflin,* 1 Penn. L. J., 146.

§ 27. A party to a cause depending for trial is privileged from arrest during the continuance of the court at which the trial will take place.   This privilege extends not only to prevent his arrest when attending the court, and when coming to and returning from it, but while he is at his lodgings.   *Ex parte* Hurst,* 1 Wash., 186.

§ 28. A **witness** is privileged from arrest for a reasonable time to prepare for his departure and return to his home as well as during his actual attendance upon the court.   But the privilege does not extend throughout the term at which the cause is marked for trial; nor will it protect him while engaged in transacting his general private business after he is discharged from the obligation of the subpœna.   Smythe *v.* Banks, 4 Dall., 329.

§ 29. A citizen of another state who, when in attendance on court as a suitor, has been subpœnaed as a witness in another case, is privileged from an arrest in execution issuing from a state court, while at his lodgings; and a sheriff will be indemnified by an order of discharge of a court of competent jurisdiction.   Hurst's Case, 4 Dall., 387.

§ 30. A recommitment of a debtor upon a *ca. sa.* after he has been out for more than a year upon a prison-bounds bond is not a breach of his privilege as a witness and party, bound to attend the court.   *Ex parte* Bill, 8 Cr. C. C., 117.

§ 31. If an attachment, under the Maryland act of 1795, chapter 56, and a *capias ad respondendum,* be both served while the defendant is attending the court as a party in another cause, the attachment will be ordered to be dissolved upon the arrest of the defendant on the *capias,* and the defendant will be discharged from the arrest, because privileged as a suitor in another cause.   McFerran *v.* Wherry, 5 Cr. C. C., 677.

PRIVILEGED COMMUNICATIONS.

See Evidence.

PRIVILEGES AND IMMUNITIES.

See Constitution and Laws.

PRIZE.

See War.

PROBATE COURTS.

See Courts.

PROBATE OF WILL.

See Estates of Decedents.

PROCESS.

See WRITS.

PROCLAMATIONS BY THE PRESIDENT.

See GOVERNMENT; WAR.

PRODUCTION OF BOOKS AND PAPERS.

See EVIDENCE; PRACTICE; REVENUE.

PROFERT.

See PLEADING.

PROHIBITION.

See WRITS.

PROMISSORY NOTES.

See BILLS AND NOTES.

PROPERTY.

§ 1. **In general.**— Property is everything which has an exchangeable value, and the right of property includes the power to dispose of it according to the will of the owner. Labor is property, and as such merits protection. Parrott's Chinese Case, 6 Saw., 849.

§ 2. **Situs.**— Personal property is presumed to follow the person, and in actions for personalty the *lex domicilii*, and not the *lex loci rei sitœ*, as in cases of real or immovable property, governs. Benton v. United States,* 5 Ct. Cl., 692.

§ 3. The fiction of law that the domicile of the owner draws to it the personal estate which he owns. wherever it may happen to be located, yields whenever it is necessary for the purpose of justice that the actual *situs* of the thing should be examined; and always yields to laws for attaching the estates of non-residents, because such laws necessarily assume that property has a *situs* entirely distinct from the owner's domicile. Personal property situated in Illinois was mortgaged in New York. Two days later, before the mortgage could be recorded in Illinois, the property was attached and sold under process issued out of a court of the latter state. *Held*, that as the laws of Illinois required a mortgage to be recorded, the attachment proceedings took precedence of the mortgage, although by the laws of New York no record of the mortgage conveyance was necessary to its validity as against third persons. Green v. Van Buskirk, 7 Wall., 139.

§ 4. Where personal property is sold under attachment proceedings instituted in the state where the property is located, the liability of the property in such proceedings must be determined solely by the law of that state, although the owner of the property as well as the other claimants are domiciled in another state; and where, in another state, a suit is instituted growing out of the attachment proceedings, the law of the state where such proceedings were had must determine their effect, and the title to the property thereunder. Green v. Van Buskirk, 5 Wall., 307.

§ 5. A conveyance of personal property by deed in trust, which deed was duly recorded in the state where all the parties resided, and was valid by the laws of that state, is sufficient to protect the title thereto against subsequent creditors of or purchasers from the grantor, although the parties to the deed have removed to another state, taking the property with them. Bank of the United States v. Lee, 13 Pet., 107.

§ 6. Personal property has no locality. The law of the owner's domicile is to determine the validity of the transfer or alienation thereof, unless there is some positive or customary law of the country where it is found to the contrary. Hence an assignment, lawful and regular in the state where made, of personal property in another state, will bind all persons who have notice of it. Black v. Zacharie, 3 How., 483.

§ 7. **Personalty.**—Unchallenged and continued possession of personal property, with a claim of title to it, is *prima facie* evidence of ownership. Grossmeyer v. United States,* 4 Ct. Cl., 1.

§ 8. Where a party held undisturbed possession of personal property for two years before the same was captured by the military forces of the United States, *held*, to be a sufficient proof of ownership in an action under the "abandoned or captured property act" (12 Stat. at Large, 820). Geilfuss v. United States,* 4 Ct. Cl., 478.

§ 9. Where several persons reside together, and have a joint possession of property, the law casts the actual possession upon the legal owner. Lenox v. Notrebe, Hemp., 225.

§ 10. **A membership in an "Exchange,"** a corporation organized for the purpose of advancing the interests of trade, etc., with the power of holding property to a certain amount for the purposes of the association, is property which passes to the assignee in bankruptcy under sections 5044 and 5046, R. S. U. S., and which the creditors of the bankrupt are entitled to have applied to the payment of their debts. *In re* Warder, 10 Fed. R., 275.

§ 11. **A whale killed and taken into complete possession** is the property of the taker. And where a whale after being killed was anchored by the taker, and, having drifted from its anchorage, was found by other parties, with the anchor still attached, and by them appropriated, *held*, that the original taker might maintain an action for the value of the whale as his property. Bartlett v. Budd, 2 Low., 223.

§ 12. A lease for ninety-nine years, renewable forever, by the common law is only a chattel. McLean v. Rockey, 3 McL., 235.

§ 13. **Movable property of railroad company.**— Under the Illinois constitution of 1870, the rolling stock and other movable property of railroads is personal property; but this does not affect the rule of equity declared in the case of Pennock v. Coe, 23 How., 117, to the effect that whenever a mortgage is made by a railroad company to secure bonds, and the mortgage includes all present and after-acquired property, as soon as the property is acquired the mortgage operates upon it. Scott v. Clinton & Springfield Railroad Co., 6 Biss., 529.

§ 14. **An inchoate title to lands** is property, and comes within the scope of the clause in the treaty ceding Louisiana to the United States, declaring that the rights of the inhabitants "of the ceded territory shall be maintained and protected in the free enjoyment of their liberty, property," etc. Delassus v. United States, 9 Pet., 117.

§ 15. **"Good will,"** as property, may adhere to, or spring out of. corporeal property, but no corporeal property can adhere to it as an incident. Sheldon v. Houghton, 5 Blatch., 285.

§ 16. "Good will," resting upon no legal foundation other than a "courtesy of the trade," is not property within the meaning of the law. Accordingly where a bill in equity alleged that "by the custom of the trade of booksellers and publishers in the United States, when any person or firm engaged in that business has undertaken the publication and sale of a book not the subject of statute copyright, and has actually printed and offered an edition of such book to the public for sale, other persons and firms in the same trade, having respect to the trade priority so acquired in the publication and sale of such book, refrain from entering into competition with such publisher by publishing such book in a rival edition," *held*, that by reason of the above custom, if such existed, the publication of such book did not become a "good will" in the hands of the person or firm so first publishing the same. *Ibid.*

§ 17. **Where a will directs land to be sold** and turned into money, or money to be employed in the purchase of land, courts of equity in dealing with the subject will consider it that species of property into which it is directed to be converted. Peter v. Beverly, 10 Pet., 532.

§ 18. No exception to the rule, that land directed to be sold and turned into money is considered as money from the death of the testator, arises because the period of sale is remote, and the conversion cannot be made until the time arrives. The rule also applies to a bequest of the proceeds of the land to a residuary legatee, unless he has made an election to consider the proceeds as land. Rinehart v. Harrison, Bald., 177.

§ 19. Where a testator by his will devised his real estate to his executors, and directed them to apply the rents and profits to specific purposes until the happening of a certain event, and then to sell it and divide the proceeds among certain residuary legatees, *held*, that the real estate is in equity to be considered as money, from the death of the testator, for all the purposes of the will; and that if any of the residuary legatees who were alive, and capable of taking at the death of the testator, die before the time of sale, their shares go to their next of kin as personal property. Reading *v.* Blackwell, Bald., 166.

§ 20. A clause in a will was as follows: " I give and bequeath to my brother T. C.," an alien, " all the proceeds of my estate, real and personal, which I have herein directed to be sold, to be remitted to him accordingly as the payments are made," etc. *Held*, that the legacy given to T. C. was to be considered as a bequest of personal estate, which he was capable of taking for his own benefit, though an alien. Craig *v.* Leslie, 3 Wheat., 563.

§ 21. **Conquered or ceded territory.**— Although a sovereign who acquires an inhabited territory acquires full dominion over it, this dominion is never supposed to divest the vested rights of individuals to property. The people change their sovereign, but their right to property remains unaffected by the change. Delassus *v.* United States, 9 Pet., 117.

PROTEST.

See BILLS AND NOTES.

PROVISIONAL COURTS AND GOVERNMENTS.

See WAR.

PROXIMATE CAUSE.

See DAMAGES; TORTS.

PUBLICATION.

See WRITS.

PUBLIC ENEMY.

See CARRIERS; WAR.

PUBLIC LANDS.

See LAND.

PUBLIC LAW.

See CONSTITUTION AND LAWS; WAR.

PUBLIC MONEY.

See GOVERNMENT; OFFICERS.

PUBLIC POLICY.

See CONSTITUTION AND LAWS.

PUBLIC PRINTING.

§ 1. The commissioner of patents communicated to the senate a portion of his annual report, and on the ensuing day the same communication was made to the house of representatives. Each house having ordered it printed, the printing was assigned to A. Shortly afterwards the other portion of the report was sent to both houses, and both of them, on the same day, ordered it to be printed, and the printing of it was given to B. *Held*, that whether the two portions of the report constituted one document, and which house passed the order first, were questions requiring the exercise of judgment and discretion in the superintendent of public printing, who had something more than a ministerial duty to perform, and that a writ of *mandamus* would not lie to compel him to deliver the report to A. United States *v.* Saeman, 17 How., 225.

§ 2. The government printing office is not a bureau of any of the executive departments; hence the employees of that office, not being specially enumerated, are not included in the resolution of February 28, 1867 (14 Stat., 569), and consequently are not entitled to additional compensation under that resolution. United States *v.* Allison, 1 Otto, 308.

PUBLIC RECORDS.

§ 1. **Right to copy of.** — Patents are public records, of the contents of which all persons are bound to take notice. Hence, any person is entitled to a copy of a patent on making proper application and tendering the proper fees. Boyden *v.* Burke, 14 How., 575.

§ 2. Any one who will pay the fees is entitled to copies of public records; but if his demand for them is accompanied by insulting language, it may be refused. *Ibid.*

§ 3. But where a second demand is made in a proper manner, unaccompanied with any insulting missive, the government official is not justified in refusing such demand on account of the former misconduct of the applicant, or to enforce an apology by withholding his rights. *Ibid.*

PUEBLO LANDS.

See LAND.

PUIS DARREIN CONTINUANCE.

See PLEADING.

PUNISHMENTS.

See CONSTITUTION AND LAWS; CRIMES.

PURSER OF THE NAVY.

See FEES; OFFICERS; WAR.

PLEADING.*

[For averments of citizenship, see COURTS.]

I. PLEADING AT LAW.

1. *The Declaration.*

a. In General.

SUMMARY — *Variance between writ and declaration*, § 1.— *Venue for trial sufficient*, § 2.— *Venue necessary for every material fact*, § 3.— *Venue in margin sufficient*, § 4.— *Example of good venue*, § 5.— *Count in wrong form of action*, § 6.— *Proper joinder of count improperly framed*, § 7.— *Averment of fact of partnership not always necessary*, § 8.— *Money had and received against joint defendants*, § 9.— *Trover against joint defendants*, § 10.— *Joinder of causes by plaintiff in two capacities*, §§ 11, 12.— *Facts within judicial notice not averred*, § 13.— *Want of formal conclusion*, § 14.— *Averment of act by agent*, § 15.— *Surplusage*, § 16.— *Assumpsit on an agreement improperly sealed*, § 17.— *Averment of citizenship at time of filing declaration*, § 18.— *Averment of title to note in suit*, § 19.— *In suit on note allegation of demand at place of payment not necessary*, § 20.— *Distinction between declarations in debt and in assumpsit*, § 21.— *Declaration for infringement of patent*, § 23.— *Setting out instrument declared on*, § 23.— *Joinder of torts in one count*, § 24.— *Informality in conclusion for damages*, § 25.

§ 1. A variance between writ and declaration should be objected to by plea in abatement, and after a plea of the general issue it is too late for the defendant to take the objection or for the court to notice it. McKenna v. Fisk, §§ 26, 27.

§ 2. In a transitory action it is not necessary to lay in the declaration the true venue, and under a *scilicet* the venue for trial. It is sufficient simply to lay the venue for trial. *Ibid.*

§ 3. A venue is necessary for every material traversable fact; but where none is laid in the declaration the venue in the margin will be sufficient. Cocke v. Kendall, §§ 28, 29.

§ 4. A venue is a formal rather than substantial part of the declaration in a transitory action, and may appear in the margin as well as in the declaration itself. Cage v. Jeffries, §§ 30-32.

§ 5. A declaration on a note dated at Cincinnati, which described the note as dated at Cincinnati, in the state of Ohio, to wit, at Indianapolis, in the state of Indiana, is good, as the words, "in the state of Ohio," may be rejected as surplusage. Especially is this true when it is proved that Cincinnati is in the state of Ohio. Drake v. Fisher, §§ 33, 34.

---

* Edited by FRANK A. FARNHAM, ESQ., of Boston, Massachusetts.

§ 6. A count in *assumpsit* upon a writing obligatory is bad, as debt or covenant would be the appropriate remedy. French *v.* Tunstall, §§ 35, 36.

§ 7. Such a count, however, is still *assumpsit*, and may be joined with a good count of the same kind without producing a misjoinder of actions. *Ibid.*

§ 8. The averment of the fact of partnership is unnecessary when the instrument declared on shows a joint liability of the defendants. Davis *v.* Abbott, § 37.

§ 9. A declaration for money had and received against joint defendants must show that the money was received by them jointly. Simmons *v.* Spencer, §§ 38, 39.

§ 10. A declaration in trover against joint defendants for money received and converted to their own use may be maintained only by showing that the money received and converted in turn by the various defendants was the identical money belonging to the plaintiff. *Ibid.*

§ 11. Joinder of causes of action by a plaintiff in his personal and in his official capacity is a fatal defect at any stage of the suit. Picquet *v.* Swan, §§ 40-42.

§ 12. A plaintiff is suing in his official capacity as administrator when the statement of his right of action, arising under French law, taken in connection with the French law, shows that his right of action is only as administrator. *Ibid.*

§ 13. A declaration depending upon provisions of a municipal charter need not set out the charter, as the latter is within the judical notice of the court. Fauntleroy *v.* Hannibal, § 43.

§ 14. Want of a formal conclusion to the damage of the plaintiff is not an open question on error. Bank *v.* Guttschlick, §§ 44-48.

§ 15. An allegation that a bank made an agreement "through the president and cashier" is sufficient without showing their authority. *Ibid.*

§ 16. Where the cause of action is a refusal to convey lands, allegation in the declaration that plaintiff was evicted will be treated as surplusage. *Ibid.*

§ 17. *Assumpsit* will lie against a bank on a'n agreement sealed not with the corporate seal, but with that of the president and cashier. *Ibid.*

§ 18. Averment that plaintiff is a citizen of a certain state is sufficient without averring that he was when the writ was brought. Thompson *v.* Cook, §§ 49-52.

§ 19. Where title to a note was derived through a firm it is not necessary to aver the names of the partners. *Ibid.*

§ 20. When the note sued on is payable at a certain place the declaration need not allege that a demand was there made. *Ibid.*

§ 21. A declaration in debt upon a simple contract should describe the subject-matter of the debt as in *assumpsit,* and should aver that the defendant *agreed* to pay. The use of the word *promised* would be bad, as this word is indicative of *assumpsit,* and in *assumpsit* a breach is to be alleged, while in debt it is not. Metcalf *v.* Robinson, § 53.

§ 22. A declaration on an infringement of a patent need not aver when the patent was made, nor to whom the application was made, nor that the commissioner had authority to grant the patent. Wilder *v.* McCormick, §§ 54-59.

§ 23. A declaration purporting to set out an instrument according to its import and effect, and really setting it out in its words and figures, is not thereby defective. *Ibid.*

§ 24. Several torts of one kind may be properly joined in one count. *Ibid.*

§ 25. A declaration commencing in case, and concluding with a demand for actual damages, is good. *Ibid.*

[NOTES.— See §§ 60-136.]

McKENNA *v.* FISK.

(1 Howard, 241-250. 1843.)

ERROR to the Circuit Court for the District of Columbia.

Opinion by MR. JUSTICE WAYNE.

STATEMENT OF FACTS.— The declaration in this case contains three counts. It is alleged in the first and third that the defendant, with force and arms, in the county of Washington, seized, took, detained and destroyed the goods and chattels belonging to the plaintiff, and also the shanty or storehouse in which the goods were found, of the value of $2,000. The only difference in the counts is in the specification of the goods destroyed. In the second count the defendant is charged with having, with force and arms, in the county of Wash-ington, broke and entered a certain other shanty or temporary storehouse of the plaintiff, situate and being in the county of Washington. The defendant pleaded not guilty, and issue was joined on that plea.

The plaintiff, on the trial, in support of his case, offered evidence to prove that the defendant, with a large force of armed men, came to the storehouse or shanty of the plaintiff in Alleghany county, Maryland, entered into the same, and took and carried away the goods and chattels stated in the declaration, etc., and other evidence was offered to show the value of the goods. The court refused to permit the evidence to be given to the jury. Upon an exception to this ruling the case is now before this court.

§ 26. *A plea of "not guilty" in an action of trespass waives a variance between the writ and the declaration.*

It was first urged in argument that as the original writ in the case declared that the defendant, with force and arms, etc., broke into the storehouse of the plaintiff, etc., it was such a declaration of the nature of the complaint which the defendant was required to answer that it must be considered as the gist of each count, and that there was such a variance between the counts and the writ that it would abate the writ. Admit that this fault exists, and that the nature of the plaintiff's demand must be mentioned in the writ, that the defendant may know before he appears in court the kind of complaint he is required to answer, and that the declaration afterwards filed, or the writ, or both, shall be deficient in some legal requisite, or shall contain irregularity, informality or mistake which would abate the writ, the defendant is not here in a situation to avail himself of the fault. He has pleaded not guilty. This plea refers to the counts and not to the writ. It puts the plaintiff to prove the material allegations in his declaration, and the defendant assumes by it to contest them. To allow, then, a defendant, after the general issue has been pleaded, to avail himself of any defect or mistake in the writ, or variance or repugnancy between the count and the writ, would be not to try the cause at issue, but would have the effect to take it from the jury and to place it before the court upon a point of pleading which has not been pleaded, and which is unconnected with the merits of the cause. Such mistakes, either in the writ or in a variance between the count and the writ, must be taken advantage of by a plea in abatement. And if the mistake or fault is apparent on the face of the declaration, such as a misstatement of the cause of action, it will be a good cause of demurrer. 3 Black. Com., 301; Com. Dig., Abatement, G., I., 8; Willes, 410; 1 Show., 91; 1 Salk., 212; Duvall *v.* Craig. 2 Wheat., 45, 55. The case, then, is not in a condition to enable the defendant to avail himself of the objection. But is there any such variance in this case? We think not. The writ mentions a trespass with force and arms upon the storehouse of the plaintiff, and the seizure and destruction of goods. This puts the defendant in possession of the complaint against him, or what he will be required to answer before he appears in court. It is but the commencement of the suit, and is sufficient if it advises the defendant of the cause of action, without those particulars which must be set out in the declaration, which, when filed, gives the defendant an opportunity to use any of those defenses or pleas to which he may be entitled by the rules of pleading.

§ 27. *Trespass to personal property is a local action, and venue for trial only need be laid.*

It was also urged that the venue laid in each of the counts was so imperfect that the evidence offered could not be received to support either of them. That it could not be received under the second count, for that was *quare clausum fregit* in the county of Washington, and the evidence proved a local trespass within another jurisdiction or sovereignty; and that it could not be received under the first and third counts, because, though they might be counts for transitory causes of action, it was necessary to lay a venue where the trespass was committed with a *scilicet*, to let in the evidence at any other place of trial. The evidence offered as to the local count was certainly not competent; but that is because the venue is local, and cannot be changed into any other county than where the trespass to the realty was done, and never can be carried out of the sovereignty in which the land is. But it is an established rule that, in transitory actions, a venue is only necessary to be laid to give a place for trial. Such a venue is indispensable; for without, it would not appear in what county the trial was to take place, nor could a jury be summoned to try the issue. Com. Dig., Pleader, C., 20; 1 Cowp., 176, 177; 5 Term R., 620; 2 Lev., 227; Bacon's Ab., Venue, C.; 3 Term R., 378. The venue for trial is a legal fiction devised for the furtherance of justice and cannot be traversed. So that if A. becomes indebted to B., or commits a tort upon his person, or upon his personal property in Paris, an action in either case may be maintained against A. in England, if he is there found, upon a declaration alleging a cause of action to have occurred in an English county, in which the action is laid, without taking notice of the foreign place. 1 Cowp., 177–179. Lord Mansfield said: But, as to transitory actions, there is not a color of doubt but that any action which is transitory may be laid in any county in England, though the matter arises beyond the seas. Mostyn *v.* Fabrigas, 1 Cowp., 161. In Doulson *v.* Matthews and another, 4 D. & East, 503 (a case in all its particulars like this), which was an action for entering the plaintiff's house in Canada, and expelling him, and in which there was a count for taking away his goods, Lord Kenyon nonsuited the plaintiff because the first count was local, and because he had not supported his second count by proof. Buller, J., also said: It is now too late for us to inquire whether it was wise and politic to make a distinction between transitory and local actions; it is sufficient for the courts that the law has settled the distinction, and that an action *quare clausum fregit* is local. We may try actions here which are in their nature transitory, arising out of a transaction abroad, but not such as are in their nature local. In Rafael *v.* Verelst. 2 W. Black., 1055, which was a trespass committed in the dominions of a foreign prince, De Grey, C. J., said: Crimes are in their nature local, and the jurisdiction of crimes is local. And so as to the rights of real property, the subject being fixed and immovable. But personal injuries are of a transitory nature and *sequuntur forum rei*. And though in all declarations of trespass it is laid *contra pacem regis*, yet that is only matter of form and not traversable. The same doctrine in respect to local and transitory actions has been repeatedly affirmed in the courts of the states of this Union. 1 Stra., 646; 2 W. Black., 1070; 1 Cowp., 176; 4 Term Rep., 503–507; Cowp., 587; 6 East, 598, 599; Com. Dig., Action, 177; 1 Cowp., 161, 177, 178, 184, 344; 2 H. Black., 145, 161; Co. Litt., a, n. 1; 3 Term Rep., 616; 7 Term Rep., 243; 1 Saund., n. 2; Glen *v.* Hodges, 9 Johns., 67; Gardner *v.* Thomas, 14 Johns., 134. It then appears from our books that the courts in England have been open in cases of trespass upon real property to foreigners as well as to subjects, and to foreigners against foreigners when found in England, for trespasses committed within the realm and out of the realm, or within or without the king's foreign dominions. And it also appears from the authorities which have been cited, that in a transitory action of trespass it is only necessary to lay a venue for a place of trial, and that such venue is good without stating where the trespass was in fact committed, with a *scilicet* of the county in which the action is brought.

The courts in the District of Columbia have a like jurisdiction in trespass upon personal property with the courts in England and in the states of this Union, and, in the absence of statutory provisions in the trial of them, must apply the same common-law principles which regulate the mode of bringing such actions, the pleadings, and the proof. It is our opinion that the exception taken by the plaintiff to the ruling of the court, in respect to the evidence excluded, must be sustained, and we direct the cause to be remanded for further proceedings.

COCKE v. KENDALL.

(Superior Court of Arkansas Territory: Hempstead, 236–238. 1834.)

Opinion of the COURT.

STATEMENT OF FACTS.— This case comes up on a writ of error to the Pulaski circuit court. The principal grounds relied upon for the reversal of the judgment in the court below are: 1. That there is no place or venue stated in the declaration where the assignment of the writing declared upon was made. 2. That the judgment is rendered for federal money, when it should have been for lawful money of Virginia. 3. That the judgment is for more than was due. 4. That the court erred in sustaining the demurrer to the defendant's first plea, of payment.

These objections will be considered in the order they are stated. And first, as to the want of a sufficient venue. The plaintiff in his declaration states a venue in the margin, and alleges " that on the 6th day of April in the year 1824, in the state of Virginia, to wit, in the county of Pulaski and territory of Arkansas aforesaid, and within the jurisdiction of this court, the defendant, John H. Cocke, by this certain writing obligatory, acknowledged himself to be held and firmly bound unto one John Brown in the sum of $157.75, lawful money of Virginia, etc., to be paid to said Brown six months after the date of said writing obligatory. and that the said Brown, in the day and year last aforesaid, assigned his interest in the aforesaid writing obligatory to the said plaintiff, by writing on the back of said writing obligatory in the words following, to wit: ' I assign,' of which the defendant had notice."

§ 28. *Venue, how laid in the declaration.*

The authorities are abundant to prove the necessity of a venue to every material traversable fact. 6 Com. Digest, tit. Pleader, C., 20; 10 East, 364; 1 Chitty, 307. But when there are several facts the venue stated as to the first will apply to all the sentences connected by the conjunction "and." 1 Chitty, Pl., 307. In the case of Skinner v. Gunton, 1 Saund., 229, it is decided that when the venue is laid for the first matter in the count, all the matter which follows refers to it. In the state of New York it has been decided that where no venue is laid in the body of the declaration (if the action be transitory) the venue in the margin is sufficient. 9 Johns., 81. The courts of Massachusetts have said that the want of venue can only be reached by special demurrer. Briggs v. Nantucket Bank, 5 Mass., 96. These authorities, we think, apply with great force to the case before us. The venue stated in the margin of the declaration alone would be considered sufficient, according to the rule that prevails in most of the states. It is also stated in the body of the count as to the execution of the writing and assignment alleged on the day of its date. The venue, therefore, as to assignment, must be considered the same with that stated for the execution of the writing declared on. We think, without considering the effect of a verdict, that the objection as to venue cannot prevail.

§ 29. *Lawful money of the United States is lawful for all the states.*

The second objection relates to the judgment, which is rendered for money in the usual form. It is insisted that it should have been rendered for lawful money of Virginia, according to the expression used in the writing. This, we think, in substance has been done, as lawful money of the United States would be lawful money of Virginia, or any other state or territory. At all events, the attitude in which the question is now presented would preclude us from reversing the judgment for that cause. The third and fourth errors assigned have not been urged with much seriousness, and indeed they both present questions that have been heretofore settled by this court. Upon the whole, we see no cause for reversing the judgment of the circuit court.

Judgment affirmed.

CAGE v. JEFFRIES.

(Circuit Court for Arkansas: Hempstead, 409–411. 1839.)

Opinion of the COURT.

STATEMENT OF FACTS — This is an action of debt, in which the plaintiff declared as follows, namely:

" James D. Cage, a citizen of and residing in the state of Tennessee, complains of Richard Jeffries, a citizen of and residing in the state of Arkansas, of a plea that he rendered unto him the sum of $539, which to him he owes and from him unjustly detains.

" For that whereas the said defendant, on the 1st day of April, 1837, at the state aforesaid, by his certain writing obligatory, promised to pay," and then proceeds as in the ordinary form.

To this declaration the defendant has filed a special demurrer, and assigned as cause " the uncertainty of the venue laid in the declaration, the averment being that the defendant, at the state aforesaid, by his certain writing obligatory, promised to pay, having previously mentioned the state of Tennessee and the state of Arkansas."

§ 30. *The venue is a formal rather than a substantial part of the declaration.*

In England the general rule respecting laying the venue in declarations was, that every material and traversable fact should be alleged with a venue, as it regulated the summoning the jury, who were anciently always returned from the vicinage on account of their supposed personal knowledge of the matter in dispute. With us venues in statutory actions are of no practical utility (Stephen on Pl., 280 to 292, and cases cited in the notes); and the rule became so modified there that in transitory actions the jurisdiction of the court was not affected by the venue laid, or the entire omission to lay one. Cowper's Rep., 176. Venues, however, have been always considered as a part of the technical form, but not as a substantial part of the declaration. A declaration without a venue, or with a wrong one, may be bad in form by reason of long, immemorial and technical usage (1 Chitty's Pl., 310); but where the jurisdiction of the court depends on the sum in controversy and citizenship of parties, the objection ought not to be allowed.

§ 31. *The venue in the margin will cure an ambiguity in the declaration.*

There does not, however, appear to be any uncertainty in the venue laid in the declaration in this case. The venue, as laid in the margin, is the state of Arkansas, and the state of Tennessee is only mentioned as a part of the description of the plaintiff. The words "state aforesaid" have a general reference to the state of Arkansas in the margin, and not a particular reference to the addition of the plaintiff's name. 1 Chitty's Pl., 305. Where a county is in the margin of a declaration, and the trespass or thing alleged to have been done at D., and it is not shown in what county D.·is, yet it is well enough, because it shall be intended to be in the same county stated in the margin, for a general intendment shall there serve. 3 Wilson, 340; 1 Saund., 308, note 1; 5 Mass., 95.

§ 32. *A special demurrer may be filed in all actions in the federal courts.*

A question has been made as to whether a special demurrer is allowable by the practice of this court. The thirty-second section of the judiciary act of congress of 1789 (1 Story's Laws U. S., 66) expressly gives the right of filing a special demurrer in all actions in the courts of the United States.

Demurrer overruled.

DRAKE v. FISHER.

(Circuit Court for Indiana: 2 McLean, 69-74. 1840.)

Opinion of the Court.

STATEMENT OF FACTS.— This action is brought on several promissory notes, and an objection is made to the introduction of one of the notes in evidence, on the ground that it is not described according to its tenor, or legal effect, in the declaration.

The note is dated at Cincinnati, 12. m. 1., 1837, and the declaration describes it as a note given at Cincinnati, in the state of Ohio, to wit, at Indianapolis, in the state of Indiana. And the plaintiff offered to prove that Cincinnati is in the state of Ohio, as alleged in the declaration. This, however, was not done until the objection was made by the defendant's counsel, but the truth of the allegation is not controverted.

§ 33. *Authorities reviewed as to statement of venue of instrument declared on.*

Several authorities are cited by the defendant's counsel in support of his objection. In the case of Kearney v. King, 2 Barn. & Ad., 301, the declaration stated the note was given at Dublin, to wit, at Westminster, etc.; and at the trial it appeared that the bill was drawn at Dublin, in Ireland. And the court held there was a fatal variance between the proof and the declaration, and a judgment of nonsuit was entered.

This variance was material, as the bill being given in Ireland was payable in Irish currency, which was less valuable than English currency, in which, it appeared from the declaration, the bill was payable. Mr. Justice Bayley said: The court must see upon the face of the record that the bill was drawn in Ireland, and it cannot take notice judicially that a bill drawn at Dublin is drawn at Dublin in Ireland. The instrument, it is said, is set out in the same words and letters as the bill produced. But that is not enough; for it must be set out the same in substance and in legal operation, which is not done here. The bill, in the declaration, appears to be for English money, when it is, in fact, for Irish.

This authority goes rather to sustain the declaration, as it shows the pro-

priety, and, indeed, necessity in certain cases, where an instrument is dated at
a particular place, to allege in the declaration in what state or country such
place is situated. This has been held necessary, it seems, in case of specialties. Cowper, 177. Lord Mansfield says, if the declaration states a specialty to
have been made at Westminster, in Middlesex, and, upon producing the deed,
it bears date at Bengal, the action is gone, because it is such a variance between the deed and the declaration as makes it appear to be a different instrument.

In the case of Alder *v.* Griner, 13 John., 449, where the venue was laid in
the margin of the declaration, to wit, "City and county of New York;"
and, at the conclusion of the instrument, it was stated to be "done in Boston,
in the day and year above mentioned," the court held that the variance was
not fatal. They say, had the declaration averred the deed to have been made
at New York, they would, probably, have been bound by authority, whatever
may have been their private opinions as to the wisdom of the rule to set aside
the verdict on the ground of variance.

In the case of Munroe *v.* Cooper, 5 Pick., 412, the note was described in the
declaration as dated at Concord, whereas, on its face, it was dated at Boston.
The judge at the trial admitted the note, though objected to; and the supreme
court say, "as to the supposed variance, it has been usual, certainly, in cases
like the present, to set out the true date of the note, both as to place and time,
and to lay the venue under the form of a *videlicet* and that this was the correct mode of declaring." But the point raised was not decided. To the same
effect is the case in 16 Pick., 381.

In the case of Houriet *et al. v.* Morris, 3 Camp., 303, it was objected that
there was a fatal variance, the declaration having stated that the notes were
made in London, whereas, in fact, they appeared on the face of them to have
been made in Paris. And it was insisted that the constant course is, in declaring on foreign bills, to state that they were drawn at the place where they
bear date, adding the venue under a *videlicet.*

Lord Ellenborough said the contract, evidenced by a promissory note, is
transitory, and the place where it purports to be made is immaterial. And
that he saw no reason why it might not be stated that the note was made in
the parish of St. Mary Le Bow, in the ward of Cheap, though dated at Paris,
in the same manner as if it had been dated at York.

And in the case of Ragan and others *v.* More, 4 Black, 344, it was held
that a promissory note, dated at Union county, state of Indiana, might be declared on in another county, without noticing the words, "state of Indiana."
The court say that this variance is not material.

§ **34.** *Discussion of present state of facts. Instrument to be declared on according to legal effect. Variance.*

Now, the objection in the present case is, not that the declaration does not
state the place at which the note was given, but that it alleges that such place
is in the state of Ohio. Under the strictest rules of pleading, which have, at
any time, been observed, this allegation could only require to be proved. And
this the plaintiff offered to do, as we think, in time for the proof to be received. But the case has been argued without reference to such proof.

There are many cases in which it is material to allege the place of the contract, as where it is materially affected by the local law in regard to interest,
currency, etc. But where this is not the case, and the action is transitory, no
reason is perceived for stating in the declaration the place of the contract.

The contract or note need not be described in its very words, but may be stated in the declaration according to its legal effect. And if the place where the note was made can have no influence on its legal effect, why should it be averred? In such a case the place is not traversable, and, if not traversable, need it be averred or proved.

There are some things which may be omitted, but which, if stated, must be proved. And the rule, in this regard, is laid down by Mr. Chitty to be, "that, if the whole of the statement may be struck out without destroying the plaintiff's right of action, it is not necessary to prove it; but otherwise if the whole cannot be struck out without getting rid of a part essential to the cause of action."

The supreme court, in the case of Ferguson v. Harwood, 7 Cranch, 408, decided that a variance is immaterial when it does not change the nature of the contract, which must receive the same legal construction whether the words be in or out of the declaration.

Now, whether this note was made at Cincinnati, in the state of Ohio, or at Cincinnati, in some other state, is immaterial. It has no effect in the construction of the note or on its legal operation.

By the rules of practice lately adopted in England (4 W. 4), the venue is required to be stated in the margin and not in the body of the declaration. And this would seem to render unnecessary any allegation of the place where the contract was made under a *videlicet*, within "the county from which the jury was to come," even in actions on specialties. If the place, however, where the contract was made, be alleged as matter of description and not as venue, it must, in all cases, be stated truly and according to the fact, under peril of variance, if the matter should be brought into issue. Stephen's Pl., 291. But this issue can be raised only in cases where the law of the place has a material bearing on the contract.

This declaration would have been good if the words, "in the state of Ohio," had been omitted; and if these words were stricken out it would not destroy the plaintiff's right of action. They may then be considered as surplusage and need not be proved. By the late change the rules of pleading in England have been simplified and improved, and we are more disposed to adopt the improvements than to follow antiquated precedents and unmeaning technicalities.

In the case of Covington v. Comstock, 14 Pet., 43, the note purported to be set out in the declaration according to its tenor, and it was stated to have been made payable generally, but on its face it was payable at a particular place; the court held this was a fatal variance and the judgment of the circuit court, on this ground, was reversed. And there can be no doubt that strictness is required where the plaintiff purports to set forth the note in terms. Upon the whole, we think that whether we regard the proof offered, or the words objected to, as surplusage, the objection must be overruled.

FRENCH v. TUNSTALL.

(Superior Court of Arkansas Territory: Hempstead, 204, 205. 1832.)

Opinion of the COURT.

STATEMENT OF FACTS.— The declaration contains two counts. The first is the common count in an action of *assumpsit* for money lent and advanced by the plaintiff to the defendant. The second is also in the form of a count in *assumpsit*, upon a promissory note under seal. The defendant filed a general demurrer to the declaration, which was sustained by the court, and judgment rendered in his favor, from which the plaintiff has appealed to this court.

§ 35. *A count in assumpsit, though bad, is still assumpsit, and may be joined with a good count in the same declaration.*

If the declaration contains one good count a demurrer to the whole declaration will not be sustained, unless there is a misjoinder of actions. The first count is in *assumpsit*, and is clearly a good and valid count. It is equally clear that the second count is also in the form of a count in the action of *assumpsit*. It is true that the cause of action set out in the second count will not support an action of *assumpsit;* debt or covenant being the appropriate action upon a writing obligatory. But because the second count is faulty and defective, and might have been reached by a general demurrer, it does not follow that it is a count in debt, although it states a cause of action for which debt is the appropriate remedy.

We are of opinion, then, that there is no misjoinder of actions, notwithstanding the second count is palpably defective, and sets out no cause of action for which *assumpsit* will lie.

§ 36. *If the declaration contain one good count, a general demurrer will be overruled, unless there be a misjoinder.*

The first count being good, the demurrer to the declaration should have been overruled. The case of Judin *v.* Samuel, 4 Bos. & Pul., 43, is, in principle, analogous to the present case. The declaration contained three counts. The first was in trover for bills of exchange, and the second and third counts, after stating the delivery of the bills to the defendant, in order that he might get them discounted for a certain commission, and his having got them discounted, stated that he converted and disposed of the money to his own use.

The defendant demurred, generally, on the ground of a misjoinder of tort and contract, the subject of the two last counts being matter of contract; but the court held that, on a general demurrer, as all the counts were in the form of tort, judgment must be for the plaintiff if any one count was good. We think the principle decided in the above case is decisive of the case now before the court.   *Judgment reversed.*

DAVIS *v.* ABBOTT.

(Circuit Court for Michigan: 2 McLean, 29, 30. 1839.)

Opinion of the COURT.

STATEMENT OF FACTS.—This action is founded upon a promissory note. The declaration states that on the 22d October, 1838, the defendants, by the name and description of Abbott and Layton, made and signed their promissory note for the payment of $669.32, etc. The defendants demurred to this count in the declaration, and for cause of demurrer stated, that in the count it is averred the defendants made the note in the name and description of Abbott and Layton, without stating a partnership, etc.

§ 37. *The averment of a partnership unnecessary where the instrument sued on shows a joint liability.*

The averment of a partnership, where the instrument on which the action is founded shows a joint liability, is unnecessary. The defendants assumed the name of Abbott and Layton; and the declaration avers that the note was thus executed by them; and if the proof shall sustain this averment it will show a right of recovery in the plaintiff.

The suit is not brought against Abbott and Layton without any further designation, but the christian names of the defendants are stated, and the averment is that these persons so named gave the instrument in the name and description of Abbott and Layton. This averment, we think, is sufficient. It may not be very technical, but it leads to no uncertainty, and is substantially good. Why need a partnership be alleged when the instrument shows it, and the declaration also states the names of the defendants in full?

Whether a partnership could be proved under this averment, and then that one of the partners signed the name of the firm, does not arise, because the proof offered is that both defendants acknowledged that the signatures to the note were their own proper signatures. The demurrer to the first count is overruled.

SIMMONS v. SPENCER.

(Circuit Court for Colorado: 8 McCrary, 48–58. 1881.)

Opinion by HALLETT, J.

STATEMENT OF FACTS.— The first and second counts of the complaint set forth, in substance, a sale of certain property, which the plaintiff alleges belonged to him, and conveyances from the plaintiff to McCartney, and from McCartney to the defendant Spencer, which conveyances were deposited with the Merchants' & Mechanics' Bank of Leadville, to be delivered upon payment of a sum of money, amounting to $20,000, for the use of the plaintiff. By instructions given upon the leaving of the deeds with the bank, the money was to be deposited to the credit of the plaintiff in this suit. Plaintiff received $7,000 of this sum, and $13,000, which was afterwards paid by the purchaser, who ever he may be, was not by the bank placed to the credit of the plaintiff, but was, in fact, turned over to the defendant Spencer. And upon this state of facts it is claimed that a liability has arisen upon the part of all the defendants to pay the plaintiff this sum of $13,000. The structure of these two counts is for money due upon a contract; for money had and received by the defendants to the plaintiff's use. Nothing is said about any conversion of the money by the defendants to their own use, and there is nothing in the counts to indicate that they are based upon the theory that a tort was committed by the defendants in receiving this money and appropriating it in the way in which it is alleged they disposed of it.

§ 38. *In an action against several persons jointly for money had and received, it must be alleged that the money was jointly received.*

In order to maintain an action as for money had and received it must appear that the money was *jointly* received by all the defendants, and upon that the law may imply a promise on the part of all to pay it to the rightful owner; and although, upon the facts stated here, there may be a liability in that form of action against Spencer alone, or against the parties constituting the Merchants' & Mechanics' Bank of Leadville alone, there cannot be a joint liability on the part of all these persons in that form of action, because they did not jointly receive this sum of money. The allegation is, in these counts, that the money was received by the Merchants' & Mechanics' Bank of Leadville, and by it wrongfully and fraudulently turned over to the defendant Spencer. That may make a liability as for money had and received on the part of

493

these parties, severally,— that is, upon the part of the persons constituting the bank and upon the part of Spencer, severally; but it cannot be a liability arising by contract on the part of all of them, because they did not jointly and collectively receive this money.

§ 89. *Joining defendants in an action for conversion. Authorities reviewed.*

As to whether the action may be maintained against them jointly as for a tort,— in substance, as an action of trover,— there is some doubt. It is laid down in the case of Orton *v.* Butler, 5 B. & A., 652, that on a money demand merely to allege that the defendant received money and afterwards converted it to his own use, which is the form of declaration in an action of trover, the action cannot be maintained, because, they say, to allow that would be to defeat the defendant's right to set-off; and that the action of trover can only be maintained where the specific thing for which suit is brought can be identified; and that it must be possible in such case, where an action of trover is brought, for the defendant to relieve himself from all liability by tendering the property for which the action is brought to the plaintiff; as, for instance, when it is brought for a horse, he may surrender the horse and relieve himself from liability.

The same view is taken in several cases in Croke's Elizabeth; and there are cases — one in 4 E. D. Smith, N. Y., Donahue *v.* Henry, 162,— which declare that when a sum of money has been received which belongs to the plaintiff in the suit, and concerning which it is the duty of the defendant to turn over the very sum which he received to the plaintiff, *the very money, the same dollars and the same bills,* if he received it in that form, that then, if he makes any other disposition of it, the action of trover may be maintained. Petit *v.* Bonju, 1 Mo., 64, is a case in which the plaintiff brought an action in that form against parties who were conducting a lottery, claiming that he had become entitled to a sum of money as the holder of a ticket in the lottery, and that they had wrongfully refused to pay it over to him, and seeking in trover to recover the amount. The court say, in that instance, that if, in fact, any sum of money had been set apart to the plaintiff —$100, I think, was the amount — if it had been parceled off by itself, by the defendants, as his money, and afterwards they had taken those dollars and converted them to their own use, he might bring an action of trover for the dollars so parceled off; but that he could not, upon the general charge that so much money was due to him and wrongfully detained by the defendants, maintain that action. His action must in that case be in the form of an action on contract, if he would recover at all.

That is the distinction that I think is recognized in all of the cases, and, applying it to the present case, it may be true that the defendants, the Bank of Leadville, as to the very bills, notes or coin, if it was such, which they received for this property, may be liable in an action of trover or an action founded in tort for the conversion of that money, if it be so alleged in the complaint. And if that money — the very same money — was paid over to Spencer he also would be liable, and then and in that case they both might be joined in one action as tort-feasors. To illustrate, I will read a paragraph from Bliss on Code Pleadings: "Under the code, an action for the recovery of personal property will lie against one who has wrongfully parted with the possession of property jointly with one in actual possession." Sec. 83.

And the same principle applies to trover: "Thus, one who has wrongfully pledged plate belonging to the plaintiff is liable to an action of detinue, jointly with the person to whom it had been pledged. So, where one has fraudulently obtained a credit upon a bill of goods and assigned them over for the benefit of his creditors, the vendor having the right to repudiate the sale and pursue the goods may make both the purchaser and his assignee parties to an action for their possession." Id.

For this the case of Nichols v. Michael, 23 N. Y., 264, is cited. The principle declared is that where a party has the right to a specific thing, and he can pursue that particular thing through several hands, he may charge all of these parties consecutively or all who held the property consecutively, in one action for its value. So that here, if it be true that the Smiths, or the persons who constitute the Merchants' & Mechanics' Bank, received this money and turned over the same money to Spencer, they may be jointly charged in proper phraseology as for converting that money, but not otherwise. And it must be the identical money.

These cases, and all the authorities that I have been able to find, go to the point that where an action is founded in tort and maintained upon that principle, it must be for the conversion of the specific thing, and it can only be maintained where the property itself can be traced to the hands of the party to be charged. In that aspect, if the facts are truly stated in the first and second of these counts, no joint action can be maintained against these parties unless the pleader may be able to allege that the same money came to the defendants, the Merchants' & Mechanics' Bank of Leadville, and the defendant Spencer, successively. The plaintiff must allege that it was the same money, and that the defendants converted it to their own use, in order to make it an action for tort.

Upon the other theory there is no difficulty in maintaining an action against either of the defendants separately as for money had and received, and upon that principle, the third count, which states nothing as to the way in which the money came to the hands of the parties, but merely charges that the defendants are liable to the plaintiff for $13,000 received by them for the use of the plaintiff, is not open to any objection.

The ruling upon the demurrer, therefore, must be that it is sustained as to the first and second counts, because there the facts are stated which show that the defendants cannot be jointly liable, and overruled as to the third count, because nothing appears in that count to indicate that they may not be jointly liable.

If I have made myself understood, it will be apparent that the plaintiff must amend so as to make this substantially an action of trover for this sum of money against all these parties, or by dismissing his action against one or the other of the defendants. If the action were dismissed as to Spencer, or as to the defendants who constitute the Merchants' & Mechanics' Bank of Leadville, I would see no difficulty in maintaining it against the other.

PICQUET v. SWAN.

(Circuit Court for Massachusetts: 3 Mason, 469–474. 1824.)

STATEMENT OF FACTS.— *Assumpsit* on several bills of exchange drawn by the defendant in Paris, payable in Boston. On some of these bills the plaintiffs declared as indorsees; on others they declared as having been indorsed to one Jean Claude Picquet, the father of the plaintiffs, in his life-time, and afterwards he died; and the plaintiffs, being his right heirs by the law of France, "*accepted the heirship with the benefit of an inventory*," whereby they became, by the laws of France, "*the beneficiary heirs and administrators* of the estate" of the said J. C. Picquet at his death, "and joint and lawful and only proprietors" of these bills of exchange. The plaintiffs were described in the writ "as aliens and beneficiary heirs of Jean Claude Picquet."

The defendant pleaded in abatement of the suit two pleas: 1. That no probate had ever been made in any probate court of Massachusetts of any last will or testament of Jean Claude Picquet, nor any administration there taken upon his estate; nor were the plaintiffs administrators thereof under any administration taken in any of the United States. 2. That there is a misjoinder of different causes of action in the same suit, viz.: some causes in the plaintiffs' own personal right, and others in their capacity as administrators, executors or heirs of Jean Claude Picquet. The plaintiffs demurred to both pleas, and there was a joinder in demurrer.

Opinion by STORY, J.

It is not necessary to consider how far the pleas in abatement are exact in their form, nor whether both can be pleaded successively to the writ. The substance of the objections raised upon the pleadings is: 1st. That there is a misjoinder of different causes of action, some in a personal and some in a representative character. 2d. As to the causes of action in a representative character, that no administration has been taken out in any court of probate of this state.

§ 40. *Misjoinder of causes and incapacity of plaintiff, how objected to.*

The first objection, though it is pleadable in abatement, is fatal also in every stage of the suit, if well founded. Com. Dig., Abatement, G., 4, Action, G., 1; Chit. Pl., 206, 444. The last is properly pleaded in abatement; for, if the defendant pleads in bar, it is an admission that the plaintiffs are competent to sue in their representative character if they state such character. In the present suit some embarrassment might arise because the representative character is not set forth in the technical language of the common law.

§ 41. *Sufficient allegation of plaintiff's official capacity as administrator.*

Some doctrines are so well settled that they need only to be stated to command assent. Such is the doctrine that in Massachusetts no foreign administrator can maintain any suit without taking out administration in our courts of probate. That principle is obligatory upon this court sitting in the administration of local law. The fact that no such administration has been taken out by the plaintiffs is admitted by the demurrer; and therefore the only inquiry is whether upon the pleadings the first objection is maintained. In other words, are any of the causes of action in point of law brought in a representative character? It appears to me that those in the *third* and *fourth* counts clearly are so, and can be maintained upon no other ground. I lay no stress upon the language of the writ describing the plaintiffs "as aliens and beneficiary heirs of Jean Claude Picquet." That allegation may be gotten over as mere matter of personal description. But the third and fourth counts allege that the bills of exchange therein declared on were indorsed to J. C. Picquet in his life-time, and belonged to him at his decease, and that the plaintiffs are his right heirs and have accepted the heirship with the benefit of an inventory, according to the laws of France, and thereby have by the same laws become "the beneficiary heirs and administrators of the estate of J. C. Picquet," and as such "the joint and sole proprietors" of the same bills. Now, if I am at liberty to examine into the French laws, I cannot but know that this is precisely a description of an administrator in the sense of the common law. The civil law throws the heirship and administration upon the heirs of the deceased, and the acceptance of it with the benefit of an inventory is the same as accepting it with a liability only for the debts of the deceased, co-extensive with the assets coming into the hands of the heir. But the counts plainly state the death of the holder of the bills, and the right asserted is a derivative right under him by operation of law after his decease. It is therefore not a personal right of the plaintiffs upon the transfer *inter vivos*, but a right claimed in virtue of a representation of the deceased under the French laws, which makes the plaintiffs successors to the property in the bills. Under these circumstances the plaintiffs must be deemed to sue here as administrators of the property of the deceased; and therefore the objections are maintained in their fullest extent. There is a misjoinder of counts and the want of a rightful administration under our laws.

§ 42. *Rights arising under foreign laws may be recognized, but remedies depend upon our own laws.*

The French laws may prescribe how rights shall pass to property of the deceased in that country; and we, out of comity, may recognize the like rights as to his property here. But the mode of instituting and pursuing remedies must be decided by our laws. Judgment must be for the defendant on the demurrers.

FAUNTLEROY v. HANNIBAL.

(Circuit Court for Missouri: 1 Dillon, 118. 1871.)

Opinion by DILLON, J.

STATEMENT OF FACTS.— This is an action on certain coupons attached to bonds issued by the city of Hannibal to the Pike County Railroad Company of Illinois, in 1858, to aid in the construction of that railroad. The defendant demurred to the declaration on the ground that the act amending the charter of the city of Hannibal and authorizing it to subscribe to the capital stock of the company was not set forth in the declaration; also that as neither that act nor the charter of the city were declared to be public acts, the courts could not take judicial notice of them.

§ 43. *A declaration depending upon provisions of a municipal charter need not set out the charter.*

The court upon consideration is of opinion that the act is in its nature public, though relating only to the powers of a single municipal or public corporation; and consequently, that it can judicially notice it without a declaration therein that it is a public act. Charters for the government of cities and towns are in this country public in their nature and not special or private acts.

Demurrer overruled.

TREAT and KREKEL, JJ., concur.

BANK OF THE METROPOLIS v. GUTTSCHLICK.

(14 Peters, 19-32. 1840.)

ERROR to the Circuit Court of the District of Columbia.

Opinion by MR. JUSTICE BARBOUR.

STATEMENT OF FACTS.— This was an action of *assumpsit*, brought by the defendant in error against the plaintiff in error, in the circuit court of the United States, in the county of Washington and District of Columbia.

The declaration contains three special counts, and a count for money had and received. The three special counts are all founded upon an agreement in writing, which, after reciting that the plaintiff in the court below had bought of the defendant in the court below lot No. 5, in square No. 489, in the city of Washington, for which he had paid a part of the purchase money, and executed his note for the residue, contains the following stipulation: "The Bank of the Metropolis, through the president and cashier, is hereby pledged, when the above sum (that is, the amount of the note) is paid, to convey the said lot, namely, lot No. 5, in square 489, in fee-simple, to the said Ernest Guttschlick, his heirs or assigns forever." Each of these counts avers the payment, at the time agreed, of the amount of the note, and the failure of the bank, on demand, to convey the lot. At the trial several bills of exception were taken, and a verdict was found and judgment rendered in favor of the plaintiff. To reverse that judgment this writ of error is brought.

In the argument at the bar various objections have been urged to the sufficiency of the declaration, which we will briefly notice in the order in which they were made.

§ 44. *Want of formal conclusion to special count in assumpsit cannot be taken advantage of on error.*

The first objection is that the special counts have no conclusion. There is certainly no formal conclusion to either of these counts; each of them, after alleging the breach, terminating with the words, "Whereby, etc." Whether counts thus concluding would have been sufficient, upon a special demurrer in the court below, it is not necessary to decide; because we are clearly of opinion that the thirty-second (1 Stats. at Large, 91) section of the judiciary act would cure the defect, if it were admitted to have been one.

§ 44a. *Allegation that a bank made an agreement "through the president and cashier," without alleging their authority, is sufficient.*

The second objection which was taken applies to the first count, viz.: That the agreement sued on is averred to have been made by the bank, "through the president and cashier," without averring their authorization by the bank to make it. We consider this objection as wholly untenable. The averment in this count is that the bank, through these officers, agreed to convey the lot. Now, even assuming, for the sake of giving the objection its full force, that the making of this agreement was not within the competency of these officers as such, yet it was unquestionably in the power of the bank to give authority to its own officers to do so. When, then, it is averred that the bank, by them, agreed, this averment, in effect, imports the very thing the supposed want of which constitutes the objection; because, upon the assumption stated, the bank could have made no agreement but by agents having lawful authority.

§ 45. *In pleading facts may be stated according to their legal effect.*

Nay, it would have been sufficient, in our opinion, that the bank agreed without the words "through the president and cashier;" for it is a rule in pleading that facts may be stated according to their legal effect. Now the legal effect of an agreement made by an agent for his principal, whilst the agent is acting within the scope of his authority, is that it is the agreement of the principal. Accordingly, it is settled that the allegation that a party made, accepted, indorsed or delivered a bill of exchange is sufficient, although the defendant did not, in fact, do either of these acts himself, provided he authorized the doing of them. Chitty on Bills, 356, and the authorities there cited. This principle has been applied, too, in actions *ex delicto*, as well as *ex contractu*.

In 6 Term R., 659, it was held that an allegation that the defendant had negligently driven his cart against plaintiff's horse was supported by evidence that defendant's servant drove the cart. In this aspect of the question it was one, not of pleading, but of evidence. If, on the contrary, the act were one in their regular line of duty, then of course the averment was unnecessary. In the case of Fleckner *v.* United States Bank, 8 Wheat., 358 (Banks, §§ 20–27), the court declare the point to be settled, "that a corporation may be bound by contracts not authorized or executed under its corporate seal, and by contracts made in the ordinary discharge of the official duty of its agents and officers."

§ **46.** *Where the breach alleged is a refusal to convey lands, that being the gist of the action, an allegation of eviction will be treated as surplusage.*

The next objection which was raised to the declaration applied to the second count, namely, that the averment that the plaintiff was turned out of possession was insufficient in this, that it is not averred to have been by process of law, or by the entry of one having lawful title. If entry and eviction were the ground of the action, or constituted the *gravamen* of the count, as in covenant on a warranty, or for quiet enjoyment, then, indeed, a declaration or count would be defective which omitted to aver that the plaintiff was evicted by due process of law, or by the entry and eviction of one who, at the time of the covenant, had lawful title to the land, and, having such title, entered and evicted the plaintiff; or which did not contain some averment of equivalent import. But upon examining the count in question it will be found that, although this averment is contained in that count, it is mere surplusage; because the breach alleged is that the defendant refused, on demand, to convey the land. There is nothing, therefore, in the objection, as applied to this count; because it would be good without averring any eviction whatsoever.

§ **47.** *Where the allegation is of an agreement to convey land in fee-simple, free from incumbrance, and that defendant had no fee-simple title, the question of incumbrance need not be decided.*

The next objection to the declaration applies to the third count, and it is this: that the plaintiff, in that count, treats the agreement as importing an undertaking on the part of the bank to convey the lot in fee-simple, by a good and indefeasible title, free from incumbrances. In the view which we have taken of this subject, it is unnecessary for us to decide whether the agreement does or does not import such an undertaking, on the part of the bank, as is ascribed to it in this count of the declaration. This count contains an averment that the bank was not, at the time of the agreement, or at any time after, seized or possessed of the lot in fee-simple. We have seen that the language of the agreement is, that the bank was to convey the lot in fee-simple to the defendant in error, his heirs or assigns forever. Now, it appears from the record that the bank claimed under a deed from Alexander Kerr, who sold the lot as trustee, under a deed of trust from Orr, the former owner, made to secure certain debts therein stated, which deed of trust was executed on the 8th of September, 1819. But Orr had previously, to wit, on the 6th of August, 1818, conveyed the same lot in fee-simple to Joseph Elgar, as trustee, for the purpose of securing certain debts therein stated, and with power to sell in certain events therein mentioned; one of which was, that Samuel Lane, who was indorser of a note of $3,000, secured by this last deed, should be sued, which event occurred as early as the year 1820. Now, from this state of facts, it is apparent that, at the date of the agreement, the bank was not seized of the fee-simple which it contracted to convey. If the deed of trust to Elgar be considered as a mortgage, then, the moment it was executed, the legal estate in fee-simple was in Elgar, subject to be defeated upon the performance of the condition, and so continued in him· from that time down to the year 1835, when, under the trust deed, he sold and conveyed the lot to the Patriotic Bank, which purchased at the sale. The interest of the mortgagor, according to the common law, is not liable to execution as real estate. 8 East, 467; 5 Bos. & Pull., 461. It is treated as equitable assets. 1 Vesey, 436; 4 Kent, 154. In conformity with this doctrine, this court decided (12 Pet., 201) that the wife of a mortgagor was not dowable; and in 13 Pet., 294, that the equity of redemption could not be taken in execution under a *fieri facias*. If this be so in the case of a mortgage, the principle applies more strongly in case of a deed of trust, because the interest of the mortgagor, such as it is, is so far protected by a court of equity that the mortgagee cannot foreclose without a decree in equity; and even in that decree a short time is allowed to the mortgagor within which to redeem by paying the debt; whereas, in the case of the trust, unless in case of some extrinsic matter of equity, a court of equity never interferes; and the only right of the grantor in the deed is the right to whatever surplus may remain after sale of the money for which the property sold. There was, then, a good cause of action, on the ground that the bank had not the fee-simple which it contracted to convey.

We think, then, that the declaration is not liable to any of the objections which have been urged against it.

§ 48. *Where an agreement of a bank is not under its corporate seal, but that of the president and cashier, assumpsit will lie against it.*

Nor have we any doubt but that the action well lies against the bank. For although the agreement is under seal, it is not the seal of the corporation, but that of the president and cashier. It was decided in the case of Randall *v.* Vanvechten, 19 Johns., 60, that covenant would not lie against a corporation on a contract not under their common seal, but that an action of *assumpsit* would lie; and that it makes no difference, in regard to a corporation, whether the agent is appointed under seal or not, or whether he puts his own seal to a contract which he makes in their behalf, the doctrine of merger not applying to such a case. This doctrine we approve, and it is decisive of the objection.

· [The remainder of the opinion is irrelevant to the subject of pleading and is omitted.]   *Affirmed.*

THOMPSON *v.* COOK.

(Circuit Court for Illinois: 2 McLean, 122–126. 1840.)

Opinion of the Court.

STATEMENT OF FACTS.— This action was brought on a promissory note given by the defendants to John W. Taylor & Co., and by them assigned, under the same name, to the plaintiff. The defendants, having filed a special demurrer, take several exceptions to the declaration.

§ 49. *It is sufficient if the citizenship of the plaintiff appear in any part of the pleading.*

The plaintiff, in the declaration, is stated to be a citizen of the state of New York; but it is objected that there is no averment of his being a citizen at the time the suit was commenced. That it does not follow, from his being a citizen of New York at the time the declaration was filed, that he was a citizen at the time the writ was issued. In this respect the declaration is in the usual form, and think it is good. In a late case the supreme court decided that, if the citizenship of the plaintiff appeared in any part of the pleadings, it is sufficient. In that case (Bradstreet *v.* Thomas, 12 Pet. 64; Courts, § 1093) the citizenship of the plaintiff was alleged in the joinder to the demurrer, and, under the circumstances, it was held good.

§ 50. *Jurisdiction over one of joint defendants when the other is beyond the jurisdiction.*

One of the defendants is alleged, in the declaration, to be a citizen of Illinois and the other of Missouri. The writ was served only on the citizen of Illinois. It has often been ruled that, where there are several plaintiffs and defendants, the court must have jurisdiction, as between each of the plaintiffs and defendants. In the case under consideration, the plaintiff being a citizen of New York, the suit being brought in the state of Illinois, the court can take no jurisdiction against the defendant, who is a citizen of Missouri. But as this defendant is not in fact a party to the suit, the process not having been served on him, the act of congress of the 28th of February, 1839, first section, covers the case, and authorizes the suit against one of the parties to the note. And, indeed, without the provisions of this statute, the defendant being liable to pay the note, and the other party not being in any way prejudiced by the proceeding, a judgment might have been entered against the party before the court. But the late law provides for the case and removes all doubt on the subject.

§ 51. *Where title to a note is derived through a firm it is not necessary to state the names.*

It is also objected that the declaration does not show who compose the firm of John W. Taylor & Co., the payees and indorsers of the note. And it is insisted that this is material, in order to give jurisdiction to the court. Where an individual derives his right through an assignment of a firm, as in this case, it is never necessary for him, at common law, to state in his declaration the names composing the firm. In this case the declaration alleges that John W. Taylor & Co. are citizens of the state of New York, and no necessity is perceived for a more specific allegation.

The defendants promise to pay John W. Taylor & Co.; and, by the same name, the note is indorsed to the plaintiff. Why should he be held bound to ascertain and set forth in his declaration the individuals who compose the firm? If the note had been transferred by ten or twenty firms, it would be just as necessary to state the individuals who compose each of them as in the present case. This would not only establish the rule in this court, different from that which exists in other courts, but it would materially affect the negotiable character of bills or notes.

There is nothing in the act of congress referred to, or in the limited jurisdiction of this court, which should change the rule. It is always in the power of the defendant to plead to the jurisdiction of the court, and take advantage of any fact which may exist going to show a want of jurisdiction.

§ 52. *Where note is payable at a certain place, declaration need not state demand was there made.*

In the last place, it is objected that the note, upon its face, is payable at the State Bank of Illinois, and the declaration contains no averment that when due it was presented to the bank for payment. As matter of description, it is proper to state where the note is payable; but the law is now well settled that it is not necessary, where a note is payable at a particular place, to state in the declaration that a demand of payment was made at such place.

There are some conflicting decisions on this point in this country; but the weight of authority is that no demand need be made. And, until lately, in England there was no question which produced more conflicting decisions than this one. The king's bench decided one way and the common pleas another; and this conflict continued until the point was decided in the house of lords, against the king's bench, that a demand of payment at the place where the note was made payable was essential to the right of action on the note.

No one, it is presumed, can read the opinion given in the house of lords and not be struck with the forcible reasoning and superior ability on the side of the minority in the house. Lord Eldon was in favor of the decision given, but eight of the twelve judges were against it and in favor of the decision made by the king's bench. And it does seem that the masterly views presented by the eight judges are conclusive on the subject. The case was Rowe v. Young, 2 Brod. & Bing., 180. This decision of the house of lords does not seem to have been satisfactory, as immediately afterwards an act of parliament (1 & 2 G. 4, ch. 78) was passed which substantially sustained the doctrine of the king's bench.

Where a note is payable at a particular place, as, in the present instance, at a bank, the maker of the note may show a deposit of the money to meet the note, or a readiness to pay had a demand been made. And this seems to be a proper subject-matter for defense. Why should the holder of the paper be required to make a demand of payment at the place designated any more than a demand of the maker at his usual place of residence, where no place is named?

This question, in the case of Wallace v. McConnell, 13 Pet., 144 (BILLS AND NOTES, §§ 1539–43), was fully considered and decided by the supreme court. It is, therefore, no longer an open question before the courts of the United States. The demurrer is overruled; and there being no further defense, judgment is entered for the plaintiff on the note.

METCALF v. ROBINSON.

(Circuit Court for Indiana: 2 McLean, 363–365. 1841.)

Opinion of the COURT.

STATEMENT OF FACTS.— This action was brought on a bill of exchange for $627.33, drawn by the plaintiff on the defendant, accepted by him and protested for non-payment. The first count of the declaration complains, etc., of a plea that the defendant render unto the plaintiff $1,000, which he owes and unjustly detains from him. For that whereas, etc., setting out the bill, its acceptance and protest for non-payment. And that the plaintiff, as drawer, was forced and obliged to pay the holder, etc., of which the defendant had notice, " by means whereof said defendant then and there became liable to pay said plaintiff said sums of money; and being so liable, he, the said defendant, then and there undertook and promised to pay," etc.

The second count states that the defendant was indebted to the plaintiff for so much money, etc., had and received to and for the use of the plaintiff at defendant's request. And, also, in the further sum of $700 for money laid out and expended, etc.; and, being so indebted, he, the said defendant, in consideration thereof, then and there undertook and promised to pay to the said plaintiff said sums of money, when he, the said defendant, should be thereunto requested. Yet the said defendant has refused, etc., to the damage of the said plaintiff $200. To this declaration the defendant demurred, and assigned as cause of demurrer a misjoinder, the first count being in debt and the other *in assumpsit.*

§ 53. *Distinction between assumpsit and debt.*

The forms of a declaration in an action of *indebitatus assumpsit,* and in debt on simple contract, are very similar. There are, however, certain words by which they are distinguished, and which give the one or the other character to the action. The action of debt is founded upon the contract, the action of *assumpsit* upon the promise, and in this consists the principal distinction between the two actions. In the action of debt on simple contract, express or implied, the subject-matter of the debt should be described precisely as in the common counts in *assumpsit.* The consideration for the contract must be stated, as also any inducement necessary to explain the contract or consideration, and it should be stated the party agreed to pay. Stating that he promised to do so would be bad. Emery *v.* Fell, 2 Term R., 28; 2 Bos. & Pul., 78.

In the case of Brill *v.* Neele, 3 Barn. & Ald., 208, the record stated that the plaintiff had brought his bill, etc., in a plea of debt, and the commencement of the declaration was in the common form in debt. The first count then stated that defendant was indebted to the plaintiff for work and labor, etc., and, being indebted, that the defendant undertook and promised to pay upon request, etc. The second count was upon a *quantum meruit,* and in form like the first. The other counts were properly framed in debt. To this declaration there was a demurrer, assigning for cause the misjoinder of debt and *assumpsit.* In support of the demurrer the case of Dalton *v.* Smith, 2 Smith, 618, was cited, where the court held a declaration containing counts precisely similar to be bad; and Lawrence, justice, there said that the counts laid with a promise were counts in *assumpsit* without a breach.

There can be no doubt that in the case under consideration the counts were intended to be in debt. This is plainly seen from the general form and language of the counts. The damages are laid at the conclusion of the declaration, as in debt, in a less amount than the sum demanded. But in both counts it is alleged that the defendant, "in consideration thereof, undertook and promised to pay." This, under the above authority, makes the counts *assumpsit.* They are counts in *assumpsit* without a breach. The breach assigned in the last count, which lays the damages at $200, when the amount demanded is the sum of $1,000, is wholly irregular. Leave given to the plaintiff to amend his declaration.

WILDER v. McCORMICK.

(Circuit Court for New York: 2 Blatchford, 31–37. 1846.)

Opinion by BETTS, J.

Most of the causes of demurrer in this case are of an extremely technical character, touching very slightly the merits of the action. They can be best disposed of by considering them numerically in their order.

§ 54. *Variance between writ and declaration not open on demurrer.*

The first cause is that the declaration is not properly entitled, but the defect or imperfection is not pointed out. It was alleged on the argument that the writ was returnable on the 19th of February, whereas the *placita* was of the 20th. If this objection was intrinsically of ever so great importance, the court most manifestly would not act upon it on a suggestion so made. But if the objection had come up on oyer of the writ, or by setting out the writ *in hæc verba* in the demurrer book, the court would, under the statute, allow an amendment of an error so trivial. Act of September 24, 1789, § 32 (1 U. S. Stat. at Large, 91). Variances between the declaration and the writ cannot, however, be taken advantage of on general demurrer. Duvall *v.* Craig, 2 Wheat., 45. This cause of demurrer is overruled.

§ 55. *Proper allegations in declaring for infringement of patent.*

The second cause assigned is that the declaration does not aver at what time the invention patented was made. Time is not, in this case, a traversable particular, in the sense of special pleading. The patent law nowhere requires the patentee to allege or prove the specific time of his invention. It need only be before his application for a patent, and it is wholly immaterial to the validity of the patent and to the character of the pleading to be interposed by the defendant whether the invention was long antecedent to the application or directly preceded it. The act of July 4, 1836 (5 U. S. Stat. at Large, 119, § 6), entitles the person who invents or discovers a new manufacture, etc., not known or used by others before his discovery, to take out a patent. Should evidence be offered by the defendant tending to defeat the patent because it was taken out before the discovery was made, it would be clearly sufficient for the patentee, in its support, to prove that he made the discovery at any period, however short, previous to his application for the patent. Mellus *v.* Silsbee, 4 Mason, 108; 2 Greenl. Ev., § 492. The averment demanded by this cause of demurrer is not inserted in approved precedents of declarations for infringements of patents. 2 Greenl. Ev., § 487, note 1; Phillips on Pat., 520; 2 Chitty's Pl., 320. The second cause must, therefore, be disallowed.

The third and fourth causes cannot be sustained. The third is that it does not appear that the application for the patent was in writing nor to whom it was made. The fourth is that it does not appear that the commissioner of patents had any rightful authority to grant the patent. These causes are founded upon supposed requisites of the statute, not averred in the declaration to have been complied with, and are also supposed to be supported by general principles governing proceedings in tribunals of inferior jurisdiction. If the matters which it is alleged should be set forth in the declaration would call for the application of those principles in case they were pleaded by way of justification and in defense of acts done, or as a protection to the party pleading them, which would at least be a doubtful proposition (Martin *v.* Mott, 12 Wheat., 19), it would not necessarily follow that the same method of pleading must be pursued in declaring upon a private title or a grant emanating from functionaries acting under statutory authority. Day *v.* Chism, 10 Wheat, 449; Bank of the United States *v.* Smith, 11 Wheat., 171; Carroll *v.* Peake, 1 Pet., 18, 23. The third cause of demurrer rests upon the assumption that the plaintiff must, in his pleading, specify all the acts done by him to obtain a patent, in order that it may appear upon the face of the declaration that the mode of proceeding pointed out by the statute has been pursued. But the case of The Philadelphia & Trenton Railroad Co. *v.* Stimpson, 14 Pet., 448, disposes of this and all the other objections that fall within the same class. The grant of the patent is itself sufficient evidence that all the preliminary steps required by law were properly taken. And as the plaintiff may make his patent the direct and efficient proof, in the first instance, of his right to the grant, so, *a fortiori*, it would seem to be unnecessary for him to plead any of the particulars which conduced to the grant. It is sufficient to set forth the grant in substance. Tryon *v.* White, 1 Pet. C. C., 96.

The fourth cause of demurrer is founded upon a misapplication of a doctrine appertaining to the acts of legal tribunals, where a court of inferior jurisdiction takes cognizance of a case and renders judgment, and he who sets up such judgment in support of his own interests must aver and prove that the tribunal had jurisdiction in the matter. The authority of the commissioner of patents, or of the commissioner of the land office, or of the president (whose former functions in this behalf are now exercised by those officers), to issue grants, is not of the nature of *jurisdiction*, in its common law and technical acceptation. As in regard to patents for land, so in regard to patents for inventions, the proper officer issues the grant when he has evidence satisfactory to his own mind that the claimant is entitled to receive it. But that adjudges nothing as to the real right. That question is unaffected, and remains to be examined and decided between parties contesting it, without prejudice or advantage from the letters patent. We are not aware of any method of pleading by which the courts can be called upon to settle the regularity of the preliminary proceedings in the patent office. Nor does there seem to be any utility in putting in issue the authority of the commissioner, upon the facts before him, to grant a patent, because, if the decision should negative his authority, it could not revoke or supersede the patent. The declaration must tender an issue upon the novelty and utility of the discovery patented, these being essential to the enforcement of any exclusive privilege under the patent. But the question of the regularity of the proceedings in petitioning for and obtaining the patent, and that of the correctness of the judgment of the officer in awarding it, are not material and cannot be inquired into.

§ 56. *Declaring on a writing according to its tenor and effect.*

The fifth and sixth causes of demurrer are founded upon an inaccurate apprehension of the form of the declaration. The fifth cause is that the declaration sets forth the letters patent according to their words and figures, and not according to their legal tenor and effect. The declaration avers the patent and specification to be "in language of the import and to the effect following;" and it cannot be a valid exception that "import" is used instead of "tenor," even if the words are not identical in signification, because the language is that of recital and not of grant.

§ 57. *Sufficient form of profert.*

The sixth cause is that the declaration does not make sufficient profert of the letters patent. The declaration says: "as by the said letters patent and specification, all in due form of law, ready in court to be produced, will fully appear." This is equivalent to profert in the most formal and ample terms. It tenders the entire grant to the inspection of the court and party.

§ 58. *Several torts of one kind may be joined in one count.*

The seventh cause is that the declaration is bad for duplicity, in setting forth three distinct causes of action in the same count, viz.: three distinct infringements of the said letters patent. The patent is for an "improvement in fire-proof chests and safes." The declaration avers, in the same count, that the defendant "made and manufactured and sold five hundred iron safes or chests, in the manner and of the materials described in the said letters patent, and in imitation thereof, in infringement and violation of the said letters

patent, and against the exclusive right so secured by the said letters patent;"
and, also, that he "made and manufactured and sold, and caused to be made
and manufactured and sold," five hundred like iron safes or chests; and, also,
that he "put on sale and offered for sale and sold" five hundred like iron safes
or chests. These various averments, which are supposed to constitute three
separate causes of action, and thus to render the declaration liable to the objection of duplicity, are no more than a specification of the manner in which
the plaintiff's right has been violated. A reiteration of infringements of a
patent, like a repetition of torts of any other kind which are of the same
nature, may be sued for and recompensed in one action. There is no known
doctrine of the law that requires a plaintiff to split up into separate actions
grievances of that character. They are properly united in this case, and the
demurrer cannot be sustained for that cause.

§ **59.** *Conclusion of declaration in case.*

The eighth cause is that the declaration has no proper or formal commencement and conclusion, inasmuch as it commences in the form of an action of
trespass on the case, and concludes in the form of an action of debt. The
conclusion is that the plaintiff has been injured and deprived of profits which
he might otherwise have derived from the improvement, and has sustained
actual damages to the amount of $5,000; and that, by force of the statute,
an action hath accrued to him to recover of the defendant the said actual
damages, and such additional damages, not exceeding, in the whole, three
times the amount of said actual damages, as the court may see fit to order
and adjudge; and that the defendant, though often requested, has never
paid the same nor any part thereof to the plaintiff. If there be any foundation for this cause of demurrer it is of the most technical description, and the
defect would be removable by amendment as of course. But we do not perceive that there is any material incongruity between the commencement and
the close of the declaration. The *gravamen* of the suit is the tortious infringement of the plaintiff's patent, and the conclusion of the declaration is a demand of damages in gross. They are averred to be "actual damages," but
that allegation does not change the nature of the averment. It is still merely
a demand of damages in compensation of the wrong.

The declaration is not formal in its frame. But it embodies all that is
essential to enable the plaintiff to give evidence of his right and of its violation by the defendant, and affords to the defendant the opportunity to interpose every defense allowed him by law. In such a condition of the pleadings
in a cause the court will not encourage objections merely critical and over-
nice, and will seek, even on special demurrer, to sustain pleadings substantially
sufficient, and thus avoid useless delays and expenses.

The demurrer is overruled on all points, but without costs to either party.

§ 60. Proofs must correspond with the allegations of the declaration, but this requirement is fulfilled if the substance of the declaration is proved; and in construing a contract
declared on, the court may use the same light which the parties enjoyed when the contract
was made, placing themselves in the same situation as the parties, so as to view the circumstances as they viewed them. Nash v. Towne, 5 Wall., 689.

§ 61. It is not necessary, it seems, to set forth in the petition points which are merely
matters of proof. Noble v. United States,* Dev., 135.

§ 62. A declaration must contain a statement of facts, which, in law, gives the plaintiff a
right to recover. Stanley v. Whipple, 2 McL., 85.

§ 63. A declaration which alleges a promise by a deceased party to pay, and also a
promise by his administrators, though informal, is not bad on a general demurrer. Curtis v.
Bowrie, 2 McL., 374.

§ 64. **If the plaintiff's title depends upon the performance of certain acts** he must affirm the performance of those acts. Gray v. James, Pet. C. C., 476.

§ 65. **The declaration ought always to show a title** in the plaintiff, and that with sufficient certainty, and set forth all the matters which are of the essence of the action; without these the plaintiff fails to show a right in point of law to ask the court for judgment in his favor. *Ibid.*

§ 66. **A party is bound to abide by his own pleadings,** and cannot be permitted to prove anything in opposition thereto. Therefore, a petition which prays for the confirmation of an indefinite grant, and shows on its face, by express averment, that the same was not surveyed, presents a case in which the claim must be rejected. Winter v. United States, Hemp., 344.

§ 67. **Immaterial statements no ground of demurrer.**— If the facts stated in a complaint constitute a valid cause of action, it is not demurrable though also containing unnecessary, immaterial, redundant statements. The same is true of the answer. The proper method to prune the pleadings in such cases is by motion to strike out. Loomis v. Youle,* 1 Minn., 177.

§ 68. **Joinder of parties.**— Generally speaking, all joint obligors and others bound by covenants, contract or *quasi*-contract ought to be made parties to a suit; and the plaintiff may be compelled to join them all by a plea in abatement for non-joinder; but such objection can only be taken advantage of by a plea in abatement; for if one party only is sued it is not matter in bar of the suit or in arrest of judgment. But the same doctrine does not appear to have been acted upon, to the full extent, in cases of recognizance and judgment, and other matters of record, such as bonds to the crown. In cases of this sort, if it appears by declaration or other pleadings that there is another joint debtor who is not sued, although it is not averred that he is living, the objection need not be pleaded in abatement, but it may be taken advantage of upon demurrer or in arrest of judgment. Gilman v. Rives, 10 Pet., 298.

§ 69. Where a covenant purported to be made between two persons by name of the first part, and the corporate company of the second part, and only one of the persons of the first part signed the instrument, and the covenant ran between the party of the first part and the party of the second part, it was proper for the person who had signed on the first part to sue alone, because the covenant inured to the benefit of those who were parties to it. Philadelphia, Wilmington & Baltimore R. Co. v. Howard, 13 How., 307.

§ 70. In an action on a joint and several bond against several defendants, some of whom are non-residents of the state in which the suit is brought, and there is a return of "no inhabitants" as to them, if the plaintiff declares against all the co-obligors, and those on whom process has been served proceed to trial on the merits, the averment that all the co-obligors are in custody, though irregular, is not fatal, and will not preclude the plaintiff from obtaining a judgment against such of the co-obligors as are really before the court. Pegram v. United States, 1 Marsh., 261.

§ 71. The several obligees in an appeal bond may join in a suit upon it. Arnold v. Frost, 9 Ben., 267.

§ 72. The claimants who have united in this petition are not represented as having any joint interest in the sums demanded, but each as looking after his own. This practice is in violation of all rules of pleading, and the petition is dismissed. Wilson v. United States,* 1 N. & H., 318.

§ 73. The laws of California require that actions shall be prosecuted in the name of the real party in interest, and that all parties having an interest in the subject of the action may be joined. So that this statute is complied with, it is not a fatal objection that the respective interests of parties jointly concerned are not accurately set forth. Lyon v. Bertram, 20 How., 149.

§ 74. In the state of Tennessee the uniform practice has been for tenants in common in ejectment to declare in a joint demise, and to recover a part or the whole of the premises declared for, according to the evidence adduced. Poole v. Lessee of Fleeger, 11 Pet., 185.

§ 75. **Joinder of counts.**— Whenever the same plea may be pleaded to two different counts, and the same judgment given on both, they may be joined in the same declaration. Stockwell v. United States, 3 Cliff., 284.

§ 76. Two actions against the same defendants, for trespass to person and trespass to property, respectively, arising out of the same circumstances, may be joined. In this case they were brought separately, and the court ordered them to be tried together, but did not order them to be joined. Holmes v. Sheridan, 1 Dill., 351.

§ 77. It is proper to consolidate in one action suits of debt brought to recover penalties under the act of congress of 1790, chapter 29, section 1, for shipping a crew without articles, and a single count is sufficient. Wolverton v. Lacey,* 3 Law Rep., N. S., 672.

§ 78. In replevin several counts cannot be joined in the cognizance. Rotchford v. Meade, 3 Cr. C. C., 650.

§ 79. A declaration is bad which joins a count in *assumpsit* for breach of promise of marriage and a count in tort for deceit. Wilkinson *v.* Pomeroy, 10 Blatch., 524.

§ 80. Counts charging the defendants as executors, upon the promise of their testator, and upon their own promise as executors, in consideration of assets, may be joined in the same declaration, and the judgment upon each count will be *de bonis testatoris.* Dixon *v.* Ramsay, 1 Cr. C. C., 472.

§ 81. Action on contract of intestate; plea of limitations; replication that the intestate assumed within three years, and the proof was that the administrator promised within three years. *Held*, that a count upon the intestate's promise, and that of the administrator, may be joined, and the plaintiff was permitted to amend. Wilkings *v.* Murphey,* 2 Hayw. (N. C.), 282.

§ 82. A plaintiff in ejectment may join in one action several trespassers on his single parcel of land. Any defendant taking a defense specifically for a portion of the land disclaims as to the rest, and if he succeeds on trial is entitled to a verdict. Those who plead the general issue are considered as taking a defense for the whole, and if found in possession of any part will be guilty under a general verdict. Greer *v.* Mezes, 24 How., 268.

§ 88. Debt will lie to recover a penalty as provided in the eighty-ninth section of the principal collection act, whether *indebitatus assumpsit* will lie or not. An objection to a joinder of counts to which the same plea may be pleaded, and on which the same judgment may be given, is not valid. Hence counts for recovery of duties and double value may be joined, although duties must be paid in gold and double values in money current. The fact that the importer was the owner does not make the counts inconsistent, because, although he could not import goods and then buy them from himself, he might first import and then conceal them for himself, which would make him liable both for the penalty and duties. Stockwell *v.* United States,* 12 Int. Rev. Rec., 88.

§ 84. In an action of ejectment in California may be included distinct parcels of land, if covered by the same title; also a claim for rents and profits, for damages and waste. Beard *v.* Federy, 8 Wall., 478.

§ 85. It is opposed to the common law system of pleading, which prevails in Illinois, to join actions of covenant and *assumpsit*, and for such joinder a declaration is demurrable. Phillips, etc., Const. Co. *v.* Seymour, 1 Otto, 646.

§ 86. Under the New York code of procedure a count for personal injuries against a railroad corporation cannot be joined with a count to recover a statutory penalty from the corporation for overcharge of fare, provided that both counts are well pleaded. In this case the latter count was ill pleaded, and a demurrer to the declaration for misjoinder was overruled without costs. Sullivan *v.* N. Y., N. H. & H. R. Co.,* 11 Fed. R., 848.

§ 87. Under the New York code a claim for a statutory penalty and a claim for personal injuries cannot be joined in the same complaint. Sullivan *v.* Railroad Co., 19 Blatch., 388.

§ 88. The New York code, making a complaint demurrable which improperly joins two or more causes of action, must be construed to mean good causes of action well pleaded. If two are joined and one is ill pleaded, the complaint is good as to the other. *Ibid.*

§ 89. Allegations of time, quantity, value, etc., need not be proved with precision, though a date, when alleged as description of the instrument declared on, must be accurately given. Under a declaration alleging a contract made on a certain day may be shown a written contract taking effect on a different day. United States *v.* Le Baron, 4 Wall., 642.

§ 90. Whenever time is material, whether in matters of contract or of tort, the plaintiff is strictly bound by the time specified in the declaration. Eastman *v.* Bodfish. 1 Story, 528.

§ 91. The specific date under a *videlicet* is not necessary in a declaration in ejectment, and may be rejected as surplusage, if it sufficiently appears on the face of the declaration that the ouster was after the entry under the several demises. Woodward *v.* Brown, 13 Pet., 1.

§ 92. In an action on the case for failure to perform a parol contract, the time of making it is not material; and hence, where it was alleged to be made on the 19th of September, to take effect in forty days, and the breach of it was assigned to have occurred the next day, it will be presumed, after verdict, that it was proven that the breach occurred after the expiration of forty days. Scull *v.* Higgins, Hemp., 90.

§ 93. An allegation in a declaration that a patent was made on a certain day is supported by proof that several re-issues were granted at a later date on a patent of the date alleged, the re-issues covering the same specification as the original patent. Read *v.* Bowman, 2 Wall., 591.

§ 94. In trespass where a day is laid in the declaration, and from such day to the commencement of the action divers trespasses were committed, one trespass, but not divers, may be proved prior to the day named. But divers may be proved within the time laid. United States *v.* Kennedy, 3 McL., 175.

§ 95. A declaration averring that the note was presented at the bank when due, "to wit, the 28d of July, 1841," the "to-wit" clause was held to be surplusage. Hyslop *v.* Jones, 3 McL., 96.

§ 96. A declaration averring that the bankrupt did on the (blank) day of October, 1869, transfer, assign and convey (the statutory terms) to the defendant, does not limit it to the exact date, but covers any fraudulent transfer during the six months prior to filing the petition in bankruptcy. Andrews, Assignee, v. Graves, 1 Dill., 108.

§ 97. The declaration in ejectment was dated on May 22, 1831, and the judgment was rendered January 14, 1832. The plaintiff in ejectment counted on a demise made by A. B. on the 1st of January, 1828. His title, as shown in the abstract, commenced on the 17th of May, 1828, which is subsequent to the demise on which plaintiff counted. By the Court: Though the demise is a fiction, the plaintiff must count on one which, if real, would support his action. Binney v. Chesapeake & Ohio Canal Co., 8 Pet., 214.

§ 98. Where a patent for the circular saw clapboard machine expired by lapse of time on March 15, 1834, and congress, by act of March 3, 1835, renewed it to A. for the space of seven years from the time when it expired, and the declaration in the writ, which was dated on the 13th of January, 1838, recited the original patent and the subsequent act of congress, and then stated generally a violation of the patent-right for a long time, to wit, for the space of three years and eight months, next preceding the date of the writ, it was held that if the plaintiff intended to claim under the old patent, he should have filed a distinct and independent count; and that he had restricted himself to proof of a violation of the patent-right during the space of the said three years and eight months specified in the declaration. Eastman v. Bodfish, 1 Story, 528.

§ 99. By the custom of the banks in the District of Columbia, payment of a promissory note is to be demanded on the fourth day after the time limited for the payment thereof, in order to charge the indorser, contrary to the law merchant, which requires a demand on the third day. The declaration against the indorser in such a case must lay the demand on the fourth and not on the third day. Renner v. Bank of Columbia, 9 Wheat., 581.

§ 100. Action on judgment — Plaintiff need not describe himself as administrator.— In an action of debt on a judgment recovered by plaintiff as administrator, it is not necessary for plaintiff to describe himself as administrator nor to make profert of his letters of administration; and should he so describe himself the statement may be rejected as surplusage. Biddle v. Wilkins, 1 Pet., 686.

§ 101. Averment of administratorship — Profert of letters.— Where an administrator sues on a bond made to his intestate, he must aver that he is administrator and make profert of his letters. Fugate v. Bronaugh,* 8 Cr. C. C., 65.

§ 102. Allegation of assignment by plaintiff assignee.— A person who sues as assignee is bound to allege an assignment to show title in himself. Earhart v. Campbell, Hemp., 48.

§ 103. Where an inventor sells his invention before he obtains a patent, a declaration filed by the assignee which states the right thus acquired, after the issuing of the patent against the assignor, is not demurrable. Rathbone v. Orr, 5 McL., 131.

§ 104. Husband and wife — Allegations.— The rule is well established that when the right of entry is by ouster of the title of the wife, the demise may be laid in the name of the husband, or in the names of the husband and wife. Woodward v. Brown, 13 Pet., 1.

§ 105. In an action of trover by husband and wife the declaration alleged a conversion before the marriage and concluded to the damage of the husband alone. Verdict for plaintiffs, but the husband had died before. Thereupon the court on motion arrested the judgment and gave surviving plaintiff leave to amend. Semmes v. Sherburne,* 2 Cr. C. C., 534.

§ 106. Trover will not lie against husband and wife for a conversion "to her use" only. Hollenbock v. Miller, 3 Cr. C. C., 176.

§ 107. State statutes need not be pleaded.— The federal courts sitting in a state take judicial notice of the statutes of such state; and where by a general statute authority is given to a corporation to do certain acts, it is not necessary in a declaration to set out such authority, but sufficient if such facts are set out as to bring the case within the operation of the statute. Toppan v. The C., C. & C. R. R. Co., 1 Flip., 74.

§ 108. However it may be in the state courts, it is unnecessary in the federal courts to set out in a declaration or plea statutes of another state, as the court will take judicial notice of them. Jones v. Hays,* 4 McL., 521.

§ 109. The provisions in the act of incorporation in Ohio, that it should be considered a public act, must be regarded in courts, and its enactments noticed, without being specially pleaded, as would be necessary if the act were private. Beaty v. Knowler, 4 Pet., 152.

§ 110. Parol contract made in another state: allegation as to validity of, demurrable.— A declaration is not demurrable, on the ground of not stating a cause of action, which sets out a parol contract and alleges that the contract was made in another state, was valid by the law of that state, and was to be performed there, whether or not the contract actually was valid by the laws of the state in question. So held in an action in New York on a contract made in Connecticut in consideration of past seduction. Liegeois v. McCracken,* 10 Fed. R., 664.

§ 111. **Averments admitted by demurrer.**— In a bill by the assignee of a bankrupt, to get at certain real estate alleged to have been fraudulently and collusively conveyed by the bankrupt to the defendant, the averment of intent to defraud creditors on the part of the bankrupt is an averment of fact, and not a conclusion of law, and is admitted by demurrer. Platt v. Mead. 9 Fed. R., 91.

§ 112. **A declaration charging negligence will not confine the plaintiff to certain acts of negligence alleged;** for, though a plaintiff is bound to state his case, he is not bound to state the evidence by which he intends to prove it. Indianapolis, etc., R. Co. v. Horst, 3 Otto, 291.

§ 113. **Immaterial averments — Surplusage.**— When two breaches of a covenant which are repugnant to each other are assigned in one count, one of them, if immaterial, may be rejected as surplusage. Day v. Chism, 10 Wheat., 449.

§ 114. In a declaration the averment that the assignment of a promissory note was for value received is an immaterial averment and need not be proved. Wilson v. Codman, 3 Cr., 193.

§ 115. **Action by president — Averment of names of persons interested.**— In an action in the name of the president for the benefit of a class of persons, the names of the persons need not be averred. Tyler v. Hand, 7 How., 573.

§ 116. **Interest need not be demanded in the declaration,** nor is its payment negatived in the breach. The uniform practice is to declare for the debt alone, and interest is recoverable as damages. Chinn v. Hamilton, Hemp., 438.

§ 117. **Exchange — Allegations as to rate of.**— The difference of exchange may be recovered on a bill of exchange; but this seems not to be the rule where the action is founded on a promissory note, and there is no count or allegation in the declaration to cover the rate of exchange. Weed v. Miller, 1 McL., 423.

§ 118. **The office of the innuendo in a declaration for slander** is to explain the words spoken and to annex to them their proper meaning. It cannot extend their sense beyond their usual and natural import, unless something is put upon the record by way of introductory matter with which they cannot be connected; then, words which are equivocal or ambiguous, or fall short in their natural sense of importing any libelous charge, may have fixed to them a meaning certain and defamatory, extending beyond their ordinary import. Beardsley v. Tappan, 1 Blatch., 588.

§ 119. **An action of deceit cannot be founded on an allegation of non-performance of a promise** by defendant, but may on an allegation that defendant promised *mala fide* and without intending to perform. Fenwick v. Grimes,* 5 Cr. C. C., 603.

§ 120. **Action on collector's bond, collector's district must be stated.**— In an action by the United States on a tax collector's bond a declaration which does not state the collector's district is bad. United States v. Jackson, 14 Otto, 41.

§ 121. **Deficiency of insurance company's assets; allegation of necessary in action against shareholder.**— In an action at law by a policy-holder of an insurance company against the defendant as a stockholder, to recover from the defendant's unpaid stock an amount claimed to be due on the policy, the declaration must aver that the losses of the company or its liabilities exceed its assets or it is demurrable. Blair v. Gray, 14 Otto, 769.

§ 122. **Allegation of covenant to pay the amount of decree to be rendered sufficient.**— An arrangement was made between A. and B. by which B. paid to A. a certain sum, and covenanted to pay him beside whatever more he should be entitled to in the decree to be rendered in a chancery suit then pending by B. against A. In a suit on this covenant by A. the declaration alleged that a decree had been entered in the supreme court dismissing the bill, and that, by virtue of this decree, plaintiff is entitled to recover a certain sum of defendant. *Held*, on demurrer, that the declaration presented a *prima facie* case, and that how plaintiff became entitled to recover by virtue of the decree need not be stated, as it was a matter of evidence. Hobson v. McArthur,* 3 McL., 241.

§ 123. **Official bond, action on for moneys received subsequent to date of allegation of time.**— If the date of an official bond declared on be later than the beginning of the term of office, the declaration must allege that the moneys received and not accounted for were received subsequent to the execution of the instrument. United States v. Spencer,* 2 McL., 405.

§ 124. **Caption.**— It is sufficient to name the court in the caption of the declaration. Gassett v. Palmer,* 3 McL., 105.

§ 125. A venue "at Boston, in the state of Massachusetts, to wit, at Monroe, in the county of Monroe, and district aforesaid, and within the jurisdiction of this court," is sufficient. *Ibid.*

§ 126. Copy of note in declaration, indorsement omitted — Averment of sufficient.— In an action on a note, wherein the copy of the note was annexed to the declaration, and the indorsement omitted, it was held to be supplied by the averment of indorsement in the declaration. Adams *v.* White,* 2 Pittsb. R., 21.

§ 127. Action by vendor for breach of contract to purchase land — Allegation of title and readiness to convey necessary.— Where, in an agreement to purchase land, the conditions of payment and conveyance are mutual and concurrent, a declaration by the vendor for breach must contain, not merely that he was ready and willing to perform the letter of the contract, but that he had good title and was ready to convey by deed, or it will be bad on demurrer and cannot be cured by the verdict. Washington *v.* Ogden, 1 Black, 450.

§ 128. Contract, when to be set forth specially.— There can be no doubt that, when a special contract remains open, the plaintiff's remedy is on the contract, and he must set it forth specially in his declaration. But if the contract has been put an end to, the action for money had and received lies to recover any payment that has been made under it. The Chesapeake & Ohio Canal Co. *v.* Knapp, 9 Pet., 541.

§ 129. A single bill may be declared upon according to its legal effect. Turner *v.* White, 4 Cr. C. C., 465.

§ 130. In a writ of right on the mise joined on the mere right, under a count for the entire right, a demandant may recover a less quantity than the entirety. Inglis *v.* Trustees of the Sailors' Snug Harbor, 8 Pet., 99.

§ 131. Scire facias under lien law — No declaration necessary.— Where a *scire facias* was issued to enforce a lien upon a house under the lien law of the District of Columbia, there was no necessity to file a declaration. Winder *v.* Caldwell, 14 How., 434.

§ 132. Petition in court of claims — Applications to proper department, averment of.— A petition in the court of claims which does not aver that an application has been made to the proper department to have the claim adjusted will be dismissed unless amended within ten days. Calkins *v.* United States,* 1 N. & H., 382.

§ 133. A petition before the court of claims is defective which does not specify what persons are owners of the claim or interested therein. White & Sherwood *v.* United States,* Dev., 134.

§ 134. Complainants cannot recover in the court of claims on a ground not set forth in the petition as a foundation of recovery. Brown *v.* United States,* 1 N. & H., 377.

§ 135. Eviction, allegation of — Deed bearing scroll for seal.— By the laws of Wisconsin, a scroll, or any device by way of seal, has the same effect as an actual seal. In New York it is otherwise, and an action brought in the latter state upon a deed executed with a scroll in Wisconsin, which contained a covenant of seizin, is properly an action of *assumpsit* and not covenant. Nor is it necessary in the declaration to allege an eviction, because the covenant was broken as soon as made. Le Roy *v.* Beard, 8 How., 451.

§ 136. Seizin — Effect of acts of New York.— The act of New York of 1788, declaring that after the year 1800 no action for the recovery of lands shall be maintained unless on a seizin or possession within twenty-five years next before bringing such action, is valid even if applied to a seizin existing at the time the law was passed, and in such case, where the demandant counted on the seizin of his ancestor within sixty years then last past, it was held that the count was bad. Bockee *v.* Crosby, 2 Paine, 432.

b. Certainty and Sufficiency.

SUMMARY — *Declaration in debt to state amount definitely,* § 137. — *Derivation of title to note sued on,* § 138. — *Allegation of act by agent,* § 139. — *Allegation of damage supplied from ad damnum in writ,* § 140. — *Debt against executor on note,* § 141. — *Averment of consideration "for value received,"* § 142. — *Averment of demand and notice against guarantor,* § 143. — *Breach of contract of guaranty, how assigned,* § 144. — *Declaration on award, averment of publication,* § 145; *same, averment of amount awarded,* § 146; *same, averment of readiness to perform,* § 147. — *Declaration in deceit,* § 148. — *Declaration on judgment, jurisdiction not necessary to be shown,* § 149; *same, contra,* § 150; *same, how set out,* § 151. — *Declaration for account of profits, to aver profits,* § 152; *same, to aver relations of parties,* § 153. — *Declaration rendered uncertain by addition of unnecessary words,* § 154.

§ 137. A declaration in debt on a protested bill which fails to state the amount of charges of protest is bad for uncertainty. Wilson *v.* Lenox, § 155.

§ 138. An executor of the surviving partner of a firm in declaring upon a note due the firm need not allege who had been its members. Childress *v.* Emory, §§ 156–162.

§ 139. An allegation that " A., by his agent B.," made the note in suit is sufficient. *Ibid.*

§ 140. The allegation of damage in an action of debt, if wanting in the declaration, may be supplied by the *ad damnum* in the writ. *Ibid.*

§ 141. The action of debt lies against an executor upon a promissory note. *Ibid.*

§ 142. In declaring on a guaranty it is a sufficient averment of consideration to set out the contract of guaranty containing the words "for value received." Hank *v.* Crittenden, §§ 163-165.

§ 143. A declaration against a guarantor should aver demand and notice to the guarantor, or some excuse, such as insolvency of the principal. *Ibid.*

§ 144. In a declaration against a guarantor, the assignment of the breach should be in the words of the contract of guaranty, or in words co-extensive with the import and effect of it. *Ibid.*

§ 145. When the agreement for an award required notice to the parties, a declaration on the award must aver notice. An allegation that the award was duly made and published is sufficient. Matthews *v.* Matthews, §§ 166-171.

§ 146. A declaration in debt for two sums distinctly awarded, damages and costs, should add the two and ask for the sum. An omission of this, however, will be but a formal defect. *Ibid.*

§ 147. A declaration on an award must aver plaintiff's readiness to perform his part. *Ibid.*

§ 148. In a declaration in deceit the plaintiff must show that the action resulting in his damage was caused and induced by the acts of defendant. Weeks *v.* Ladd, § 172.

§ 149. A declaration upon a foreign judgment, rendered by a court of general jurisdiction, need not show that the court had jurisdiction of the person of defendant, as this is presumed from the allegation of recovery. (See Wilbur *v.* Abbott, *infra.*) Tenney *v.* Townsend, §§ 173, 174.

§ 150. In a declaration upon a foreign judgment it must appear that the defendant resided within the jurisdiction of the foreign court, or else that he was properly served with process, or that he appeared in the suit. (See Tenney *v.* Townsend, *supra.*) Wilbur *v.* Abbott, §§ 175, 176.

§ 151. A declaration upon a foreign judgment rendered by a court of general jurisdiction need not set out particulars of the original cause of action. *Ibid.*

§ 152. Declaration in action of account for account of profits must aver that there were profits. Travers *v.* Dyer, §§ 177-182.

§ 153. Declaration in action of account must aver the relations of the parties whence arises the right to an account. *Ibid.*

§ 154. Declaration against defendant as bailiff to plaintiff of an "undivided moiety" of land, rendered defective by addition of the words "or share," thus making indefinite what had been definite. *Ibid.*

[NOTES.— See §§ 183-321.]

WILSON *v.* LENOX.

(1 Cranch, 194-211. 1803.)

ERROR to the Circuit Court for the District of Columbia.

Opinion by MARSHALL, C. J.

STATEMENT OF FACTS.— In this case there was an objection taken to the plaintiff's declaration, which was in debt on a protested bill of exchange. The declaration claims £300 sterling, with damages, interest and charges of protest, on a protested bill of exchange, without stating in any part of it the amount of those charges. The verdict is for the debt in the declaration mentioned, on which judgment is rendered, to be discharged by a less sum. The objection is that the demand is uncertain, inasmuch as the amount of the charges of protest, which constitute a part of the debt claimed, is not stated.

§ 155. *Declaration in debt on protested bill must state amount of protest charges.*

The clause of the act on which this suit is instituted is in these words: " It shall be lawful for any person or persons," etc., "to prosecute an action of debt for principal, damages, interest and charges of protest against the drawers," etc. The charges of protest constitute an essential part of the debt, and the declaration would not pursue the act if those charges should be omitted. This part, therefore, cannot be considered as surplusage. It is a component part of the debt for which the action is given. Being a necessary part, its amount ought to be stated with as much certainty as the amount of the bill.

As this is a mere technical objection the court would disregard it if it was not a principle, deemed essential in the action of debt, that the delaration should state the demand with certainty. The cases cited by the counsel for the defendant in error do not come up to this case. They relate to different debts; this to a single debt composed of different parts.

Judgment reversed and arrested.

CHILDRESS v. EMORY.

(8 Wheaton, 642–675. 1823.)

Error to U. S. Circuit Court, District of West Tennessee.

Opinion by Mr. Justice Story.

Statement of Facts.— This is an action brought by the executors of John G. Comegys, who was surviving partner of the firm of William Cochran & Comegys, to recover the contents of a promissory note made by Joel Childress, deceased (whose executor the plaintiff in error is), payable to the firm of William Cochran & Comegys. The cause came before the circuit court for the district of West Tennessee upon a special demurrer to the declaration, and the court having overruled the demurrer, it has been brought here by writ of error.

§ 156. *Section 11 of judiciary act of 1789, chapter 20, does not apply to executors.*

The several causes assigned for special demurrer have been argued at the bar; but before we proceed to the consideration of them we may as well dispose of the objection taken to the jurisdiction. The parties executors are, in the writ and declaration, averred to be citizens of different states, but it is not alleged that their testators were citizens of different states and the case has therefore been supposed to be affected by the eleventh section of the judiciary act of 1789, chapter 20. But that section has never been construed to apply to executors and administrators. They are the real parties in interest before the court, and succeed to all the rights of their testators by operation of law, and no other persons are the representatives of the personalty, capable of suing and being sued. They are contradistinguished, therefore, from assignees, who claim by the act of the parties. The point was expressly adjudged in Chappedelaine v. Dechenaux, 4 Cranch, 306, and, indeed, has not been seriously pressed on the present occasion.

§ 157. *An executor deriving title to a partnership note need not allege who were the members.*

The first cause of demurrer is that the declaration states the note to have been made to the firm of William Cochran & Comegys, but does not state who in particular the persons composing that firm were. Upon consideration we do not think this objection ought to prevail. The firm are not parties to the suit; and if Comegys was, as the declaration asserts, the surviving partner of the firm, his executor is the sole party entitled to sue. It is not necessary, in general, in deriving a title through the indorsement of a firm, to allege, in particular, who the persons are composing that firm; for if the indorsement be made in the name of the firm by a person duly authorized, it gives a complete title, whoever may compose the firm. See 3 Chitty's Plead., 2, 39. If this be so in respect to a derivative title from the act of the parties, more particularity and certainty do not seem essential in a derivative title by the act of the law. A more technical averment might, indeed, have been framed upon the rules of good pleading; but the substance is preserved. And there is some convenience in not imposing any unnecessary particularity, since it would add to the proofs; and it is not always easy to ascertain or prove the persons composing firms, whose names are on negotiable instruments, especially where they reside at a distance; and every embarrassment in the proofs would materially diminish the circulation of these valuable facilities of commerce.

§ 158. *Declaration that "A., by his agent B., made" note, good on demurrer.*

Another cause of demurrer is that the declaration does not aver that the note was signed by Joel Childress. To this it is sufficient to answer that the declaration does state that "Joel Childress, by his agent, A. Childress, made" the note; and it is not necessary to state that he signed it: it is sufficient if he made it. The note might have been declared on as the note of the principal, according to its legal operation, without noticing the agency; and though it would have been technically more accurate to have averred that the principal, by his agent in that behalf duly authorized, made the note, yet it is not indispensable; for, if he makes it by his agent, it is a necessary inference of law that the agent is authorized, for otherwise the note would not be made by the principal; and that the demurrer itself admits. See Chitty on Bills, Appx. Sect., p. 528, and notes, id.; Bayley on Bills, 103; 2 Phillips, Evid., ch. 1, sec. 1, pp. 4, 6.

§ 159. *Allegation of damage in action of debt supplied by the writ.*

Another cause of demurrer is that the declaration omits to state any damages; but this, if in any respect material in an action of debt, is cured by the writ, which avers an *ad damnum* of $500.

§ 160. *Court cannot examine where profert is made, but no oyer craved of letters testamentary.*

Another cause of demurrer is that the letters testamentary are not sufficiently set forth to show the right of the plaintiffs to sue. But profert is made of the letters testamentary, in the usual form; and if the defendant would have objected to them as insufficient, he should have craved oyer, so as to have brought them before the court. Unless oyer be craved and granted they cannot be judicially examined. And if the plaintiffs were not executors, that objection should have been taken by way of abatement, and does not arise upon a demurrer in bar. It may be added that, by the laws of Tennessee, executors and administrators, under grants of administration by other states of the Union, are entitled to sue in the courts of Tennessee without such letters granted by the state. Act of Tennessee, 1809, ch. 121, secs. 1, 2.

It was also suggested at the bar, but not assigned as cause of demurrer, that the action ought not to have been in the *detinet* only, but in the *debet et detinet*. This is a mistake. Debt against an executor, in general, should be in the *detinet* only, unless he has made himself especially responsible, as by a *devastavit*. Comyn's Dig., Pleader, 2 D., 2; 1 Chitty's Plead., 292, 344; 2 Chitty's Plead., 141, note *f;* Hope *v.* Bague, 3 East, 6; 1 Saund., 1, note 1; 1 Saund., 112, note 1. And if it had been otherwise, the objection could only have been taken advantage of on special demurrer, for it is but matter of form, and cured by our statute of jeofails. Burland v. Tyler, 2 Lord Raym., 1391; 2 Chitty's Pl., 141, note *f;* Act of 1789, ch. 20, sec. 32.

§ **161.** *Debt on note lies against executors.*

But the most important objection remains to be considered; and that is, that an action of debt does not lie upon a promissory note against executors. It is argued that debt does not lie upon a simple contract generally against executors; and the case of Barry v. Robinson, in 4 Bos. & Pull., 293, has been cited as directly in point. Certainly, if this be the settled rule of the common law, we are not at liberty to disregard it, even though the reason of the rule may appear to be frivolous or may have ceased to be felt as just in its practical operation. But we do not admit that the rule of the common law is as it has been stated at the bar. We understand, on the contrary, that the general rule is that debt does lie against executors upon a simple contract; and that an exception is that it does not lie in the particular case where the testator may wage his law. When, therefore, it is established in any given case that there can be no wager of law by the testator, debt is a proper remedy. Lord Chief Baron Comyns lays down the doctrine that debt lies against executors upon any debt or contract without specialty, where the testator could not have waged his law; and he puts the case of debt for rent upon a parol lease to exemplify it. Com. Dig., Administration, B., 14. See, also, Com. Dig., Pleader, 2 W., 45, tit. 2 D., 2. The same doctrine is laid down by elementary writers. 1 Chitty's Plead., 106; Chitty on Bills, ch. 6, p. 426. Upon this ground the action of debt is admitted to lie against executors in cases of simple contract in courts where the wager of law is not admitted, as in the courts of London, by custom. So, in the court of exchequer, upon a more general principle, the wager of law is not allowed upon a *quo minus.* Com. Dig., Plead., 2 W., 45; Godbolt, 291; 1 Chitty's Plead., 106,· 93; Bohun's Hist. of London, 86. The reason is obvious: the plaintiff shall not, by the form of his action, deprive the executor of any lawful plea that might have been pleaded by his testator; and as the executor can in no case wage his law (Com. Dig., Pleader, 2 W., 45), he shall not be compelled to answer to an action in which his testator might have used that defense. Even the doctrine with these limitations is so purely artificial that the executor may waive the benefit of it; and, therefore, if he omits to demur, and pleads in bar to the action, and a verdict is found against him, he cannot take advantage of the objection, either in arrest of judgment or upon a writ of error. 2 Saund., 74, note 2, by Williams, and the authorities there cited; Norwood v. Read, Plowd., 182; Cro. Eliz., 557. Style, in his Practical Register, lays down the rule with its exact limitations. "No action," says he, "shall ever lie against an executor or administrator, where the testator or intestate might have waged their law; because they have lost the benefit of making that defense, which is a good defense in that action; and, if their intestate or testator had been living, they might have taken advantage of it." Style's Pr. Reg. and Comp. Atty. in Courts of Common Law (1707), p. 666.

In the view, therefore, which we take of this case, we do not think it necessary to · enter into the consideration whether the case in 4 Bos. & Pull., 293, which denies that debt will lie against executors upon a promissory note of the testator, is law. There is, indeed, some reason to question, at least since the statute of Anne, which has put negotiable instruments upon a new and peculiar footing, whether, upon the authorities and general doctrines which regulate that defense, it ought to be applied to such instruments. The cases cited at the bar by the plaintiff's counsel contain reasoning on this point which would deserve very serious consideration. But waiving any discussion of this point, and assuming the case in 4 Bos. & Pull., 293, to have been rightly decided, it does not govern the case now before the court; for that case does not affect to assert or decide that the action of debt will not lie in cases where there can be no wager of law.

§ 162. *Wager of law in United States abolished.*

Now, whatever may be said upon the question whether the wager of law was ever introduced into the common law of our country by the emigration of our ancestors, it is perfectly clear that it cannot, since the establishment of the state of Tennessee, have had a legal existence in its jurisprudence. The constitution of that state has expressly declared that the trial by jury shall remain inviolate; and the constitution of the United States has also declared that in suits at common law, where the value in controversy shall exceed $20, the right of trial by jury shall be preserved. Any attempt to set up the wager of law would be utterly inconsistent with this acknowledged right. So that the wager of law, if it ever had a legal existence in the United States, is now completely abolished. If, then, we apply the rule of the common law to the present case, we shall arrive, necessarily, at the conclusion that the action of debt does lie against the executor, because the testator could never have waged his law in this case.

Upon the whole, the judgment of the circuit court is affirmed, with six per cent. damages, and costs.

HANK v. CRITTENDEN.

(Circuit Court for Ohio: 2 McLean, 557–561. 1841.)

Opinion by LEAVITT, J.

STATEMENT OF FACTS. — The declaration in this case is in *assumpsit*, and sets forth in four special counts the issuing of four several certificates by the Portage Hydraulic Manufacturing and Land Company, dated February 21, 1837, in the following form: "This is to certify that Hank and Niles have ten shares in the capital stock of the Portage Hydraulic Manufacturing and Land Company, on which $1,000 have been paid, transferable on the books of said company by Hank and Niles, or their attorney, on the surrender of this certificate." It is then averred that the defendant on the same day made an indorsement on each of said certificates as follows: "I hereby guaranty unto the holder or holders of the within shares an annual dividend or income of ten per cent. for two years, from the 13th inst., for value received." Then follows an averment that said company, for two years after the said 13th of February, 1837, "neither declared nor paid any dividend or income whatever, of which the defendant had notice," etc.

The defendant has filed a demurrer to the declaration; and the first objection urged is that no sufficient consideration for the promise or guaranty is alleged.

§ 163. *Averment of consideration.*

The principle is well settled that, in declaring on promises or contracts which do not import a consideration, it is necessary to aver a good and sufficient consideration. Specialties and bills of exchange and promissory notes imply a consideration; and in such cases none need be averred.

The promise or guaranty in this case, not being embraced in either of these classes, it is necessary that a consideration should be stated. The only question is whether this is sufficiently set forth in the declaration. It is not averred with the formality and precision usual in such cases; but the promise or guaranty on which the action is founded is copied in the declaration; and from this it appears to have been made "for value received." These words, it may be assumed, were not used without some design; and they clearly amount to an acknowledgment by the guarantor of a benefit received from the other party, as the moving cause of the execution of the guaranty. And in this aspect of the case, we are of the opinion that a sufficient consideration for the promise, stated in the declaration, does appear.

§ **164.** *Averment of demand and notice necessary in declaration against guarantor.*

It is also insisted, by the demurrant, that the declaration is deficient, because it does not aver a demand on the company for the payment of the dividends on the shares transferred to the plaintiff, and a notice to the defendant of such non-payment.

The inquiry which must be decisive of this point is whether the promise on which this action is founded is to be regarded as absolute or collateral. If it can be viewed as an unconditional promise to pay the plaintiff ten per cent. for two years on the stock transferred, it is not necessary to aver a demand upon the company for the dividends, as no such demand can be required to fix the liability of the defendant; but, if it is to be regarded as a promise to pay ten per cent. on the stock transferred to the plaintiff, in the event that the company shall fail to do so, it is clearly one of those collateral undertakings in which it is the right of the promisor, before his liability attaches, that a demand should be made of the party for whom he undertakes, and that notice should be given of the failure of that party to pay. In this latter aspect the promise under consideration must be viewed. And thus considered the principles applicable to it are the same that have been long and uniformly sanctioned by courts, in the numerous cases of commercial guaranties, heretofore decided, both in this country and in England. If an individual guaranty the payment of a note or bill, although the same strictness in regard to the time of making demand and giving notice is not required as in the case of an indorsement of commercial paper, yet the demand and notice are held to be indispensable, unless an excuse, such as the insolvency of the maker or acceptor, be averred. And it is also settled by repeated adjudications, that, to make the writer of a letter of credit responsible for goods sold or advances made upon such letter, he must be duly notified of the acceptance of the letter, and of the amount of sales or advances made; and in default of such notice he is not liable. The position is believed to be sustainable upon principle and authority, that in all collateral undertakings, where the liability of the guarantor depends on the doing of some act by a third person, notice of a demand upon him, or an excuse for not making it, must be alleged.

The averment in the declaration that the company neither declared nor paid any dividend within the two years mentioned in the guaranty does not supersede the necessity of a demand. The undertaking of the defendant in its legal effect is that a profit on the stock transferred, equal to ten per cent. per annum for two years, shall be made; and that if no profit be made the guarantor will be responsible for ten per cent.; or, if a less profit than ten per cent. is made, he will pay the guarantee the difference between that rate and the profit actually made. An averment, therefore, that the company neither declared or paid any dividend or profit is not equivalent to an averment that

no profit was made during the two years; and nothing short of this allegation, or that the company was actually and notoriously insolvent, will excuse
a demand on the company and notice to the guarantor.

§ 165. *In an action on a guaranty the breach must be assigned in the words
of the contract, or in equivalent words.*

In this view of the promise or guaranty on which this action is founded the
assignment of the breach, as stated in the declaration, is defective. The rule
on this subject is that the breach should be assigned in the words of the contract, either negatively or affirmatively, or in words which are co-extensive
with the import and effect of it. And if the breach vary from the sense and
substance of the contract, and be either more limited or larger than the contract, it will be insufficient. In the case before the court the words of the
guaranty, as set forth in the declaration, are: "I hereby guaranty unto the
holder or holders of the within shares an annual income or dividend of ten
per cent. for two years from the 13th February, inst." The breach assigned
is: "That the company, within the two years, neither declared nor paid any
dividend or income whatever." This averment does not negative the contract
or promise, either in its words or according to its legal import. To make the
averment co-extensive with the promise or contract, according to its sense and
substance, it should have alleged not only that the company did not pay or
declare any dividend, but that it made no profit during the two years referred
to. The allegation contained in the declaration may be strictly true, namely,
that the company neither paid nor declared any dividend; and yet, in entire
consistency with that averment, a profit, even exceeding ten per cent., may
have been made by the company. If, instead of declaring and paying a dividend, the officers had deemed it more expedient to set aside the profits as a
surplus or contingent fund; or, if such profits had been added to the capital
stock, it cannot be doubted that this would have been a substantial compliance with the terms of the guaranty, although the company "neither declared
nor paid any dividend whatever." It seems clear to us, therefore, that the
averment of the breach of the guaranty in question is not co-extensive with
the contract; and that on this ground the declaration is defective. The demurrer to the declaration is, therefore, sustained.

MATTHEWS *v.* MATTHEWS.

(Circuit Court for Massachusetts: 2 Curtis, 105–119. 1854.)

Opinion by CURTIS, J.

This is an action of debt upon awards, set out in four counts in the declaration.

§ 166. *A plea to the whole declaration which only answers one count is bad
on general demurrer.*

There are four counts in this declaration purporting to be for four distinct
causes of action, and the second plea is pleaded to all. It begins in bar of the
action. Yet its subject-matter can answer only one count. It avers that "the
instrument referred to by the plaintiff and set forth in his writ as an award
between these parties, and alleged to have been made and published on the
30th day of September last, was not made," etc. There are three such instruments declared on. The plea, if good, can answer but one of them, and there
is no means of knowing which one it is intended to answer. For both these
reasons the plea is bad. First, because it is pleaded to the whole declaration,

when it contains an answer to only one count; second, because it is impossible to decide which of these counts it was intended to answer. This is not the only defect in the plea. As already stated, there are four counts in the declaration. In three of them an award founded on an instrument of submission is declared on. In the other count no instrument of submission is referred to. The plea relies on a revocation of an instrument of submission as a bar to the action. Manifestly it cannot bar the count in which no such instrument is mentioned, and which is in no way dependent on it, and as the plea is to all the counts and fails to answer one of them, it is bad on demurrer.

§ 167. *Plea amounting to general issue.*

The sixth plea denies what the plaintiff would be obliged to prove under the general issue, and consequently is bad for that cause, which has been specially assigned in the demurrer taken to it. 3 Barb. T. C. R., 56; Watson on Arb., 208.

Without making any serious effort to support these pleas, the defendant insists that it will appear that the declaration is also bad.

§ 168. *Notice of an award, when necessary and how averred.*

It was objected to the first count that, though it shows a special agreement in the submission to perform the orders and awards of the referees as the same should from time to time be made known to the parties, it is not averred that notice was given to the defendant of the award therein declared on. Ordinarily, notice by the plaintiff to the defendant, of an award, is not necessary to be averred or proved, because the first lies as much in the knowledge of the defendant as of the plaintiff. 2 Saund., 62, note 4; Child v. Harden, 2 Bulst., 144. But where, as in this case, it is specially provided that notice of the award shall be given to the parties, it is no award until such notice is given. *Ibid.* It should appear in this count, by some sufficient averment, that notice was given to the defendant of the award declared on. The count avers that the award was duly made and published. The word "duly" would not of itself be sufficient to supply the want of a substantive allegation of a fact necessary to the validity of the award. Everard v. Patterson, 2 Marsh. R., 308; S. C., 6 Taunton, 625. But "duly published" is an averment that the kind of publication required by the submission was made. For publication is made by notice from the arbitrator to the parties that his award is in readiness and can be known to them if they choose to know it; this amounts to notice and publication of the award, and such a publication satisfies a requirement in a submission that notice of the award shall be given to the parties. McArthur v. Campbell, 5 B. & A'd., 518; Musselbrook v. Dunkin, 9 Bing., 605.

This objection to the first count is, therefore, not sustained.

§ 169. *Declaration in debt on a divided award.*

It is further objected to the first and fourth counts that the action of debt will not lie for two sums distinctly awarded, the one for damages and the other for costs. This is not tenable. Every action of debt on a judgment is open to the same objection, for judgments are for one sum assessed as damages, or awarded as the debt, and another for costs. There is a technical defect in these counts in the declaration, that they do not add the two amounts together, and go for the sum of both as a sum single; but I do not consider this to be bad on general demurrer. It is also urged that these counts show that the award was of a sum of money "among other things." But it does not appear that any of these "other things" were awarded to the plaintiff, and so it is not a valid objection to an action of debt. The objections which have been made to the first and fourth counts are not sustained.

§ **170.** *Declaration on award must aver plaintiff's readiness to perform his part.*

The second count alleges an award that, upon the payment by the defendant to the plaintiff of a sum of money and the delivery of a release, the plaintiff was to deliver a release to the defendant; and, without an averment that the plaintiff was ready or willing or offered to deliver his release, it goes for the recovery of the money I am of opinion that a readiness by the plaintiff to release, and notice to the defendant of such a readiness, were necessary to be averred.   Taking the statements in the declaration to be true, the acts of the parties were to be concurrent, and an action cannot be sustained by either without averring and proving a readiness on his part to perform and notice thereof, or something sufficient to dispense therewith. 1 Chitty's Pl., 359.   For this cause I hold the second count bad in substance.

Whether an action of debt will lie for a sum of money, where that, to gether with a release, was awarded, I do not determine.   See 1 Saund., 201, a, n. 1; Cro. Car., 137; 12 Mod., 84.   The second count having been held bad for another cause, and that count alone showing an award of releases, it is not necessary to decide that question.

I consider the third count good.   It is very general, but I believe it contains all that is necessary.   It shows certain differences existing between the parties, a submission of them to referees named, and an award, upon those differences, of a sum of money to the plaintiff, pursuant to the submission. This may be a good title; and as it is confessed by the demurrer, it is sufficient.   Having thus held all the counts, except the second, good, it remains to consider the eleventh plea and the replications thereto.

§ **171.** *Moot questions not decided.*

Questions of great nicety have been argued upon the demurrer taken to the replications of this eleventh plea.   But as the first of these replications which are demurred to goes to support the second count only, and as that has already been held to be bad, and as I consider the plea to which this other replication is made as also bad, I shall not express an opinion thereon.   It was suggested at the bar that a decision of these questions might have an important bearing upon questions which are expected to arise on the trial of the issues of fact. But it cannot be now known that those questions will be presented then precisely as they are now, upon these pleadings. .Their aspect may be more or less varied when they shall arise out of the evidence, and I do not think a decision of them can be anticipated without some risk of injustice.   It is far safer to decide them when all the facts on which they depend shall be before the court, rather than to attempt to do so now, upon certain abstract averments in the pleadings.

The eleventh plea is bad for the same cause as the second plea.   It shows, in bar of the whole action, a revocation of one submission only.   Four submissions are shown by the declaration.   The result is that the second count, and the second, sixth and eleventh pleas, are bad.   The other counts are good.

WEEKS v. LADD.

(Circuit Court for Oregon: 2 Sawyer, 520–524. 1874.)

STATEMENT OF FACTS.— Three actions to recover damages suffered by plaintiffs in the sale of their shares in a corporation.

Opinion by DEADY, J.

In Weeks' case the complaint alleges that the plaintiff is a citizen of California, and that the defendants, on August 29, 1867, and prior thereto, and while the plaintiff was the owner of forty-two shares of the stock of the Oregon Steam Navigation Company, were the directors of said corporation, and did by their false and fraudulent acts and representations reduce the market value of said stock sixty-two and a half per centum below its real value; and also that the plaintiff, "being ignorant of the fraudulent acts of defendants, as aforesaid, in diverting the funds of said company, all of which was done secretly by defendants, and in misapplying them, and relying upon the said representations and statements of defendants, and upon their good faith; and believing their said statements and representations so made, as hereinbefore alleged, to be true, was induced to sell, and did actually, on or about August 29, 1877, sell his said forty-two shares of stock in said company for a price greatly below the real value thereof at the time of such sale, and also greatly below what it otherwise would have brought in the market at that time had it not been for the wrongful conduct of the defendants as aforesaid; that your plaintiff, being influenced and induced as aforesaid, by the fraudulent conduct of the said defendants as aforesaid, did, at the date hereinbefore stated, sell, assign, transfer, set over to ——, absolutely, all his forty-two shares of stock in said corporation for the price, and receiving therefor the sum of seventy-two and a half cents, and no more, on the dollar, per value thereof; that the real value of said forty-two shares of stock at that date to the owner and holder thereof was not less than twenty-five per centum premium on the par value thereof to wit, the sum of $625 per share."

The defendants demur to the complaint because: 1. It does not state facts sufficient to constitute a cause of action; and, 2. The action was not commenced within the time limited by law — two years after the cause of action accrued.

In support of the first cause of demurrer the defendant makes the following points: 1. That the acts and representations of the defendants, even conceding them to be fraudulent, and that plaintiff was thereby induced to sell his stock at less than its value, are not sufficient foundation for the action. 2. The complaint does not show that plaintiff was induced by these false acts and representations to part with his stock. 3. That it should be averred that the representations were in writing.

Upon the second of these points the argument stands thus: For the defendants it is maintained that, admitting, as the demurrer does, the defendants did the acts and made the representations complained of, that the plaintiff believed them to be true, and that they had the effect to depreciate the market value of the stock, as alleged, still it does not follow that the plaintiff was thereby induced to sell his stock for less than its real value. There is a failure to connect the alleged cause and effect by proper averment. For aught that appears the plaintiff may have been induced to part with his stock upon considerations altogether different from the apparent depreciation of its value. The alleged loss arose from the sale by the plaintiff of his stock for less than its real value, and unless it appears from the complaint that such sale was induced or caused by the conduct of the defendants, it is insufficient in this respect.

The argument for the plaintiff impliedly admits this proposition, but insists that "it does appear from the complaint that the plaintiff was induced by the fraudulent acts of defendants to sell his stock."

§ 172. *In action of deceit, allegation that plaintiff was induced to act by defendant is necessary.*

In support of this assertion, reference is made to this allegation in the complaint: "That your plaintiff, being influenced and induced as aforesaid by the fraudulent conduct of the said defendants as aforesaid, did, at the date hereinbefore stated, sell, assign, transfer, set over," etc.

But this allegation adds nothing to the complaint in this respect, for to be "influenced and induced as aforesaid" is only to be influenced and induced as before stated. Now, the previous and only allegation to which this "as aforesaid" relates does not state in terms that the plaintiff was induced by the conduct of the defendants to make the sale in question, but only that he "was induced to sell, and did actually . . . sell," etc.

Unless, then, the prior allegation, that the plaintiff believed in and relied on the representations of the defendants, necessarily implies that he was thereby induced to sell, etc., the complaint is insufficient for want of such averment. Without it the alleged wrong and loss are not concatenated as the cause and effect. But the plaintiff does not maintain that there is ground for such implication, and I think it would be unsafe so to conclude.

The immediate inducement to sell may have been the necessity or desire of the plaintiff to convert his stock into money. In all the cases cited on the point there is a direct allegation, in so many words, or to that effect, that the injured party was induced by the conduct of the other to do the act which caused the loss to him.

In Cazeaux v. Mali, 25 Barb., 583, the cause and effect are connected by the averment "that the plaintiff was influenced thereby in making the purchases." In Cross v. Sackett, 2 Bosw., 645, the allegation is: "And so believing, and on the faith and credit of the aforesaid false and fraudulent acts, practices and representations of the said defendants, . . . the said plaintiff did" purchase the stock in question. The court (p. 646) held this allegation equivalent to saying that "by these fraudulent acts they (the defendants) induced the plaintiff to purchase."

In Gerhard v. Bates, 20 Eng. L. & E., 136, the court say: "If the plaintiff had only averred that afterward, having seen the prospectus, he was induced to purchase the shares, objection might have been made that a connection did not sufficiently appear between the act of the defendant and the act of the plaintiff from which the loss arose; but the second count goes on expressly to aver that the defendant, by means of the said . . . representations, wrongfully and fraudulently induced the plaintiff to become the purchaser," etc. Thus the wrong and the loss are clearly concatenated as cause and effect. In Newberry v. Garling, 31 Barb., 131, it is alleged that the "plaintiff was induced by these representations (the representations of the defendant) to purchase."

Upon the argument and authorities cited the point appears to be well taken. The argument for the plaintiff admits that the complaint should show that the plaintiff was induced to make the sale in question by means of the wrongful conduct of the defendants, and rests solely upon the bare assertion, which, in the judgment of the court, is erroneous, that the complaint contains such an allegation.

The cases cited *supra* were cases of the purchase of stock upon false representations, as to its value and condition of the corporation, by the seller. There it was held necessary to aver that the plaintiff was influenced to make the purchase by means of such representations. Without this the loss sustained by the purchaser does not appear to have been caused by the act of the seller.

The case at bar is one of the sale of stock by the plaintiff for a price below its real value, upon false representations as to its value and the condition of the corporation, not by the other party to the sale, but by third persons, who were then directors of the corporation; therefore the allegation as to the influence these representations had upon the plaintiff 'in making the sale should state, not only that he was thereby induced to sell his stock, but also to sell it at a price below its real value, and thus incur a loss which he otherwise would not.

Upon this point the demurrer is sustained, and therefore it is not necessary to consider it further. The complaints in Sanderson and Barker's cases are substantially the same as this, and the demurrers thereto are sustained for the same reason.

TENNEY v. TOWNSEND.

(Circuit Court for New York: 9 Blatchford, 274–277. 1871.)

Opinion by WOODRUFF, J.

STATEMENT OF FACTS.— The action herein is debt on judgment, demanding $539. The declaration avers that the plaintiff is a citizen of the state of Wisconsin; that the defendant Townsend is a citizen of the state of New York; that the superior court of Chicago, within and for the county of Cook, and state of Illinois, was, at the time in the said declaration afterward mentioned, a court of general jurisdiction, duly created by the laws of the said state of Illinois; that, on the 23d of February, 1870, in the said superior court of Chicago, at . . . before the justices thereof, by the consideration and judgment of said court, the said plaintiff recovered against the said defendants the said sum of money above demanded, which, in and by the said court, was then and there adjudicated to the said plaintiff for his damages which he had sustained, as well by reason of the non-performance, by the said defendants, of certain promises and undertakings theretofore made by the said defendants to the said plaintiff, as for his costs and charges, etc., whereof the said defendants were convicted, etc., with the usual averments that the judgment still remains in full force and effect, not reversed, etc., etc., and that the plaintiff hath not obtained execution or satisfaction thereof, etc., whereby, etc., with the usual formal conclusion. To this declaration the defendant Townsend has pleaded their several pleas, to which the plaintiff has demurred, assigning special causes of demurrer. It is not necessary to state the pleas. They are each of them defective, either in form or substance, and that they are so was very properly conceded by the counsel for the defendant on the argument of the demurrer. But, as on demurrer, judgment must be rendered against the party who commits the first fault in substance, the defendant's counsel insists that judgment should be for the defendant because the declaration is insufficient.

§ 173. *Where a judgment of a court of general jurisdiction is declared upon, it is presumed from the fact that plaintiff recovered that the court had jurisdiction of the person of the defendant.*

The sole objection made to the declaration is that it does not aver or in any manner show that the superior court of Chicago had jurisdiction of the person of the defendant Townsend, either by service of process, appearance or otherwise. The declaration is in conformity with the established precedents used in England in declaring upon judgments of the court of king's bench and the court of common pleas, and would have been approved in the state of New York, under the system of pleading in use before the adoption of the Code of Procedure, in declaring on a judgment of the supreme court of that state. The principle governing the subject is, that, when the judgment of a court of general jurisdiction is declared upon, jurisdiction of the person is presumed from the averment of the recovery. This presumption is, however, not conclusive. Want of jurisdiction of the person may be set up as a defense, and may prevail. The presumption, however, suffices to sustain the declaration as a pleading and puts the defendant to plead his defense.

§ 174. *A declaration upon a judgment of a foreign court need not show that the court had jurisdiction.*

By the constitution of the United States (art. 4, sec. 1), full faith and credit are to be given in each state to the judicial proceedings of every other state; and this imports that a judgment shall have, in each state, the same credit, validity and effect as it has in the state in which it was rendered. But, on the other hand, this is qualified in respect to its operation against a defendant in another state by the condition that the court in which it was rendered had jurisdiction of such defendant. In this view it was suggested on the argument that, inasmuch as the defendant was here sued as a citizen of New York, it ought affirmatively to appear, when a judgment of another state was declared upon, that jurisdiction of the person was in fact acquired; and that no presumption arose in the tribunals of this state or district that the court of the state of Illinois, however general its jurisdiction, had any jurisdiction of such a defendant. That the want of such jurisdiction is available as a defense is unquestionable; and it would be no unreasonable rule which required a plaintiff, who wished to rely on such a judgment and assert its conclusiveness under the constitution, to take the affirmative in the very form of his declaration and aver all the facts essential to make the judgment not only valid but conclusive. Under the peculiar relations existing between the states, and this stipulation in the constitution which forbids us to treat the judgment of a sister state as a foreign judgment, such a rule of pleading would harmonize with the construction which is given to the clause in the constitution referred to.

But no case is cited to me which shows that the general rule of pleading has been modified to change the burthen of averment from the defendant to the plaintiff, or which indicates that, upon averring that the court in which the judgment is rendered is a court of general jurisdiction, the plaintiff may not, for the purposes of his pleading, rely upon the same presumption which would avail him if he were declaring thereon in the same state in which it was rendered, and leave the defendant to plead and prove want of jurisdiction if he can. The cases to which I have referred lead to the contrary conclusion; and it may well be suggested that if, in the state in which a judgment is rendered by a court of general jurisdiction, the fact of recovery imports *prima facie* that such court did acquire jurisdiction of the person, and in the absence of counter averment that *prima facie* import would prevail, then like faith and credit which should be here given to such judgment includes the same *prima facie* import, and requires that courts here should accord to the mere averment of recovery in such a court the like presumption of jurisdiction. In support of the declaration in question, and as bearing on the question discussed, see 2 Chitty's Pleading, 225 *et seq.;* 3 id., 228; Wheeler *v.* Raymond, 8 Cowen, 311; Griswold *v.* Sedgwick, 1 Wend., 126; Starbuck *v.* Murray, 5 Wend., 148; Mills *v.* Duryee, 7 Cranch, 481; and that when congress gave the effect of a record to the judgment it gave all the collateral consequences, see Hampton *v.* McConnel, 3 Wheat., 234; Biddle *v.* Wilkins, 1 Pet., 686; D'Arcy *v.* Ketchum, 11 How., 165; Westervelt *v.* Lewis, 2 McLean, 511; Lincoln *v.* Tower, id., 473; Wilson *v.* Graham, 4 Wash. C. C. R., 53; Sumner *v.* Marcy, 3 Woodb. & M., 105. Some conflict of opinion appears to exist on the question whether, if the record of the judgment shows service of process on the defendant or appearance in the action, the fact can be controverted by the defendant. On that question this demurrer calls for no opinion.

Judgment must be given for the plaintiff on the demurrer, but leave is first given to the defendant to amend his pleas on the usual terms.

WILBUR *v.* ABBOT.·

(Circuit Court for New Hampshire: 6 Federal Reporter, 814–816. 1880.)

STATEMENT OF FACTS.— Suit in New Hampshire against E. A. and J. S. Abbot, upon a judgment rendered in a New Orleans city court.

Opinion by CLARK, J.

In this case the defendant demurred to the plaintiff's declaration, and assigned several distinct causes therefor, three of which apply to both counts in the declaration and two to the second count. Those which apply to both counts are: *First,* that it appears that the said Edward A. Abbot, at the time of the rendition of said supposed judgment, was, and ever since has been, a citizen and resident of the state of New Hampshire; *second,* that it is not alleged and it does not appear that the said E. A. Abbot was duly cited to appear and answer to the said supposed suit, nor that any citation or other legal process was issued by or from said fifth district court to the said Joseph S. and Edward A. Abbot, or either of them, to appear and answer to said supposed suit, or that any process was served upon either of them, or that either of them did appear personally or by attorney; and, *third,* that it is not set forth what are the terms, nature or date of the supposed contract upon which the supposed judgment was founded, or the place at which the said supposed contract was entered.

Those which apply to the second count alone are, in substance: *First,* that the second count contains several distinct causes of action; and, *second,* that it is so framed that the defendant is unable to take any single and sufficient issue upon it and in answer thereto. These last two causes of demurrer are substantially the same that were allowed upon a former demurrer in this cause.

§ 175. *In a declaration on a foreign judgment, service of process or appearance of defendant must be alleged if defendant resided without the jurisdiction of the court.*

The declaration has not been since amended in this particular, and as the court has not seen any reason to change its opinion they must be allowed now. The demurrer must be sustained also, for that there is no allegation in the declaration that either Edward A. Abbot or Joseph S. Abbot was served with any proper process, citation or notice of the suit in which the judgment was rendered, or that they appeared or answered thereto. Edward A. Abbot is described as of Concord, in the county of Merrimack, and district of New Hampshire. There is no averment that at the time of the rendition of the judgment, and ever since, he has been, and now is, a citizen and a resident of said state of New Hampshire. Joseph S. Abbot is dead, and there is no distinct allegation of his residence anywhere, but he is described or alleged to be a partner of Edward, and if any presumption arises it is that he resided where Edward did, to wit, at Concord. This being so, and there being no allegation of service upon either of the defendants, or of an appearance by either of them, the presumption is that the judgment is a nullity, because the process of the court cannot run beyond its territorial jurisdiction. ·It is contended that in a court of general jurisdiction, as the court of the fifth district of the city of New Orleans is alleged to be, all things are presumed to be rightfully and legally done, and so if a judgment be rendered against a person it is presumed to be upon a proper notice; and this is so as to all persons within the jurisdiction of the court, when the proceedings are according to the course of the common law. This was expressly decided in Galpin v. Page, 18 Wall., 351. But the same case holds that this presumption is limited to the jurisdiction over persons residing within their territorial limits, and over proceedings which are in accordance with the course of the common law. The Abbots residing in New Hampshire when the judgment was rendered, no presumption can arise that they were duly served with notice of the suit in which the judgment was rendered, or that they appeared and answered thereto, for the reason that the fifth district court of the city of New Orleans is a court of general jurisdiction; nor are the proceedings of said court according to the course of the common law.

§ 176. *Declaration on judgment of a court of general jurisdiction need not set out particulars of cause of action.*

The only remaining cause of demurrer must be overruled. If the fifth district court of the city of New Orleans was a court of general jurisdiction, it would not be necessary to state the term, nature or date of the contract, nor where it was entered into, in order to give the court jurisdiction. Being a personal action it would follow the person.

TRAVERS v. DYER.

(Circuit Court for Vermont: 16 Blatchford, 178–181. 1879.)

Opinion by WHEELER, J.

STATEMENT OF FACTS.— This is an action of account in six counts. The first count is against the defendant as bailiff to the plaintiff of six thousand cords of wood; the second, as receiver of moneys of the plaintiff, to merchandise with for their common profit; the third, as receiver of the moneys of the plaintiff as partner in hotel keeping; the fourth, as bailiff of the plaintiff's moiety of land held by them as tenants in common; the fifth, as bailiff of a moiety of other premises; the sixth, as bailiff of a moiety of other premises. The defendant has demurred generally to each of all the counts but the fourth, and tendered several issues upon that to the country. The cause has now been heard upon the demurrer. As the demurrer is general only, the questions are whether the several counts demurred to are sufficient in substance without regard to form; still sufficient must be alleged, in some form, to constitute a cause of action. A general demurrer supplies nothing toward that.

§ 177. *Action of account.*

The action of account is somewhat peculiar in its proceedings, but the peculiarities will supply no lack of statement of a cause of action, as those in the action of book account in the states of Vermont and Connecticut do, to some extent. The action is for an account by the defendant to the plaintiff for money of the plaintiff received by the defendant by some privity of authority or appointment, or of estate, or of law, and for the recovery of the balance due. There are two judgments in the action — one, that the defendant do account with the plaintiff; the other, after the accounting, for the balance found due. The plaintiff, in his declaration, must set forth enough to entitle him to both judgments. The privity by which he is entitled to an account, and proceedings under or pursuant to it, raising a balance in his favor to be recovered, must both appear. If a plaintiff has not these he is not entitled to maintain the action. If he has them but does not set them forth, he does not show himself entitled to maintain it. These are simple and just rules, by which these counts must be tested.

§ 178. *Declaration for account of profits must aver profits.*

The first count sets forth the relation between the parties clearly enough, by alleging that the defendant, from one day to another named, was bailiff to the plaintiff, and during that time had the care and administration of the wood to be sold and made profit of for the plaintiff; but that is as far as it goes, except that it states that the defendant has not rendered any account, though requested. There is no allegation that any wood has been sold or profit made, nor anything to show there has been anything of the plaintiff's in the hands of the defendant but the wood, and that may all be there yet, ready for the plaintiff. This count seems to be clearly bad.

§ 179. *Declaration for account must show relation of the parties.*

The second count sets forth that the defendant was the receiver of moneys of the plaintiff from a day to a day named, however and by whatever contract accruing for the common use, benefit and profit of both, and during that time received $10,000 to merchandise with and make profits for both, to render a reasonable account thereof, but states no relation or privity under which the plaintiff so became the receiver, nor that he did merchandise with the money received, or did make any profit. In Co. Litt., 172, it is said that "if two joynt merchants occupy their stocke, goods and merchandizes in common, to their common profit, one of them naming himselfe a merchant shall have an account against the other naming him a merchant," etc.; but here that is not done, nor is it alleged that they were in fact joint merchants or partners. This is quite important and material. The defendant has a right to traverse the relation alleged and the extent of the right of the plaintiff claimed, and to have the issues tried and settled before judgment to account, and those matters should be alleged in at least traversable form, that the defendant may avail himself of the right, which is not here done. Wood v. Merrow, 25 Vt., 340. This count is defective in substance.

§ 180. *Declaration defective through clerical error.*

The third count, after alleging the partnership of the plaintiff and defendant, charges that *they* received $10,000 over and above the defendant's just share, but not that the defendant himself had received any more than his share. This may be a mere slip of the pen in alleging that *they* received, intending to allege that he received; but, if so, there is nothing to correct it by. As the count stands there is a plain lack of any allegation that the defendant is in arrear. This count is not good.

§ 181. *Declaration rendered defective by unnecessary addition.*

The fifth count alleges that the defendant was bailiff to the plaintiff of an "undivided moiety or share" of certain lands. It is of importance that the right of the plaintiff should be definitely ascertained by the admissions of the pleadings or by trial. It must be definitely alleged before it can be definitely tried. If this allegation had stopped with "moiety" it would have been clear and exact. But the pleader added "or share," so the allegation stands that the defendant was bailiff of an undivided moiety or an undivided share, without stating of which; and if of the latter, the share may be a moiety or one of any number of parts into which an estate can be divided. This becomes too indefinite. The words *or share* cannot be rejected as surplusage, for they may be the ones on which reliance is placed, and as definite an allegation as could be made. This count is also bad.

§ 182. *Declaration defective through uncertainty of statement.*

In the sixth count it is set up that the plaintiff was seized in fee of an undivided moiety of the premises, with the defendant, which the defendant held, as tenants in common. Perhaps the pleader intended to allege that the plaintiff and defendant were tenants in common, each owning a moiety, but if so he has not done so. As the count stands, they are alleged to be tenants in common of a moiety, which does not at all show what the share of either is. And it does not show who owns the other moiety, whether it is either of them or some other person or persons. If some other person, the action could not be maintained at common law, for it only lies between two and not more. Perhaps, however, the statute of the state would remove that difficulty. Gen. Stat. Vt., 344, § 17. But, however that may be, the defect of not stating the shares of these parties remains, and is not of form merely. This count is, likewise, not good.

The action of account proceeds upon the ground that the defendant rightfully had the money for some purpose. The defendant cannot, therefore, be in default until he has refused or neglected to account and deliver, after being called upon by demand or an equivalent. In each of these counts the allegation in that direction is very faint. It is merely that, although requested, and particularly on a certain day, he refused to account. This may be sufficient, although it hardly seems to be. The counts are judged of upon the other grounds mentioned and not upon this.

The demurrer is sustained, and the first, second, third, fifth and sixth counts are adjudged insufficient.

§ 183. **Definiteness of allegation.**—A declaration for labor and services generally is good, without specifying the labor performed or the services rendered. Edwards v. Nichols,* 3 Day (Conn.), 16.

§ 184. When a note is given payable in foreign coin, the value of each coin in current money must be averred; and, under such averment, evidence of the value may be received. United States v. Hardyman, 13 Pet., 176.

§ 185. When the declaration states that the defendant promised to pay the plaintiff a reasonable commission for certain services, it should allege what a reasonable commission is, or there can be no recovery. Rice v. Montgomery, 4 Biss., 75.

§ 186. A declaration in debt for "$103¼ or 31 pounds Virginia" is bad on special demurrer. It must be for a sum certain. Ashton v. Fitzhugh, 1 Cr. C. C., 218.

§ 187. In an action to recover money alleged to be due on a contract in which the plaintiff promised to furnish sixty-six or more men, for a length of time not exceeding three months, it is not enough for the plaintiff to allege he has duly performed all the conditions of the contract on his part, because these are indefinite; but he must state the number of men actually furnished and how long they worked.   William v. Hallet, 2 Saw., 261.

§ 188. In an action against defendant for breach of contract to build a boat, by the terms of which contract plaintiff was to deliver the plank at one of two specified places, the declaration averred that plaintiff did deliver to defendant the plank necessary, "at the place or places aforesaid mentioned in said contract, according to the tenor and effect thereof." *Held*, that this averment was insufficient, and should have been certain and positive as to where the plank was delivered.   Hart v. Rose,* Hemp., 238.

§ 189. City — Defective streets — Action for damages — Allegation of knowledge of.— In an action against a city for an accident caused to plaintiff by a defect in the street, it is not necessary to allege knowledge of the defect by the defendant in order to make out a *prima facie* case.   Serrot v. Omaha City, 1 Dill., 312.   See § 193.

§ 190. Railway accident — Defective "foreign car" — Allegation as to.— When plaintiff sues for damages for an accident on a railway caused by a defective car, he need not allege that the car on which the accident happened did not belong to the defendant, but was a "foreign car."   O'Neil v. St. Louis, etc., R'y Co., 8 McC., 428.

§ 191. —— certainty required to determine contributory negligence.— In an action for damages for personal injuries on a railroad, the petition set out that the plaintiff was riding "in a hand-car or a push-car." Upon demurrer it was held that the petition was defective for uncertainty, since it would be impossible to determine the question of contributory negligence unless something was known about the character and construction of the car.   Miller v. U. P. R'y Co., 2 McC., 87.

§ 192. Insufficient averment of negligence.— In an action against a stage-coach proprietor for allowing a slave to ride in one of his coaches and thereby escaping, a declaration that defendant "wrongfully and improperly" suffered the slave to ride does not sufficiently aver the negligence or carelessness of defendant, and judgment for the plaintiff will be arrested on motion.   Mandeville v. Cookenderfer,* 3 Cr. C. C., 257.

§ 193. Injury by defective streets — Proper care on part of plaintiff must be alleged.— If neglect to repair a public highway is averred to be on the sides and without the traveled path, and to be injurious in turning out to go by a team with a cart-load of wood, the plaintiff must show that he exercised due care in turning out and passing by, and that the damages arose from the want of proper attention by the town to the sides of the road, and not from himself or some independent accident.   Hull v. The Town of Richmond, 2 Woodb. & M., 337.   See § 189.

§ 194. Sufficiency of allegation as to carrier's legal duty to use care.— A declaration that plaintiff became a passenger in defendant's coach at defendant's request, to be carried for a reward, and that it was defendant's duty to use due care, etc., sufficiently states the defendant's legal duty to use due care.   Stockton v. Bishop,* 4 How., 155.

§ 195. Allegations necessary to charge postmaster for negligence of assistants.— When it is intended to charge a postmaster for the negligence of his assistants, the pleadings must be made up according to the case, and his liability then will only result from his own neglect in not properly superintending the discharge of their duties in his office. In order to make a postmaster liable for negligence, it must appear that the loss or injury sustained by the plaintiff was the consequence of the negligence.   Dunlop v. Monroe, 7 Cr., 242.

§ 196. To support action for deceit false assertions must be averred.— An action upon the case for deceit will not lie unless there was a false affirmation of some fact. A non-performance of promises is not sufficient. The declaration must charge that defendant averred some fact to be true, and that it was false.   Fenwick v. Grimes, 5 Cr. C. C., 439.

§ 197. A scienter need not be averred in an action for a false warranty, whether in contract or tort.   Schuchardt v. Allens, 1 Wall., 359.

§ 198. Fraudulent intent — Sufficiency of allegation of.— An allegation that the defendant wrongfully, fraudulently and falsely certified and represented a certain state of facts as true, whereas none of such facts were true, is a sufficient allegation of fraudulent intent, for to say that the representations were made with intent to deceive would add nothing to the above allegation.   Bank of Montreal v. Thayer, 2 McC., 1.

§ 199. In an action for a libel it is not indispensable to use the word "maliciously" in the declaration. It is sufficient if words of equivalent power or import are used.   White v. Nicholls, 8 How., 266.

§ 200. In an action for libel for charging plaintiff with an attempt to put two ballots in the ballot-box, the declaration must set forth the law so as to show that the act was illegal, etc.   McCleane v. Fowle,* 2 Cr. C. C., 118.

§ 201. If, in an action of libel, the words are actionable *per se*, no innuendo is necessary to connect them with extrinsic facts.   Broad v. Deuster, 8 Biss., 265.

§ 202. The whole of the libel is to be read upon the point whether, in a declaration thereon, the averments are sufficient to make the libel applicable to plaintiff. Cook v. Tribune Association.* 5 Blatch., 352.

§ 203. **Allegation of special damage.**— Where a suit for slander is brought for spoken words not actionable *per se*, special damage must be alleged in the declaration, and an allegation that the plaintiff "has been damaged and injured in her name and fame" is not sufficient to prevent the declaration from being bad in substance. Pollard v. Lyon, 1 Otto, 236.

§ 204. In an action against a carrier, an allegation of a breach, and that the plaintiff was thereby "subjected to great inconvenience and injury," is not a sufficient allegation of special damage. Roberts v. Graham, 6 Wall., 578.

§ 205. In actions of contract or tort, damages which materially and necessarily arise from the breach or *gravamen* need not be stated, as they are covered by the general damages laid in the declaration. Special damages, not necessarily implied, cannot be recovered unless specially stated; and, although the plaintiff has given evidence of special damages by the defendant, yet the defendant may object to their allowance on the trial. Bas v. Steele, 3 Wash., 381.

§ 206. **Certainty of allegation in suits for forfeiture.**— An information to secure the forfeiture of property under the internal revenue laws, though the rules are lax in matters of form, should be as clear and certain, in point of substance, as a declaration at common law. An information describing the property as "all the boilers, stills and other vessels, and all the distilled spirits — being about twelve barrels — now in the distillery, owned by," etc., is defective in not stating the number of vessels, etc., and in not stating definitely the amount of spirits. United States v. Distillery,* 4 Biss., 26.

§ 207. Such an information would be defective if it omitted to state that the distilling charged was done in the use of the property sought to be adjudged forfeited. *Ibid.*

§ 208. In a libel of information under the sixty-seventh section of the collection act of 1796, against goods, on account of their differing in description from the contents of the entry, it is not neccessary that it should allege an intention to defraud the revenue. Two Hundred Chests of Tea, 9 Wheat., 430.

§ 209. An information for a penalty, stating that the defendant refused to permit the collector to examine "paid bank checks," sets out no cause of action under section 3177, Revised Statutes, because it does not allege that the checks were not duly stamped at the time they were made, signed and issued. United States v. Mann, 5 Otto, 580.

§ 210. An averment of performance is always made in the declaration upon contracts containing dependent undertakings, and that averment must be supported by proof. Bank of Columbia v. Hagner, 1 Pet., 455.

§ 211. A plaintiff who sues on a contract in which he was to perform certain things must show that he has done or offered to do what he was required to do. And if no such averment be made the declaration is demurrable. Barbee v. Willard, 4 McL., 356.

§ 212. Declaration, containing general averments of readiness and request have been held sufficient, especially after verdict, unless in very peculiar cases. Carroll v. Peake, 1 Pet., 18.

§ 213. Where J. covenants to sell and convey to S. and B. by a good and sufficient deed, and S. and B. covenant to pay $400, neither is bound to act first; hence the covenants are mutual and concurrent, and if J. brings suit he must aver performance and tender. Snow v. Johnson,* 1 Minn., 48.

§ 214. An averment in a declaration, which might have been framed in more formal and apt terms, of the plaintiff's readiness and willingness to perform a covenant, if coupled with an allegation that the defendant was in default for non-payment for work actually done, is sufficient. Phillips, etc., Const. Co. v. Seymour, 1 Otto, 646.

§ 215. In an action of contract, where certain things must be done by plaintiff to enable defendant to perform his part, plaintiff must allege performance of his conditions. So held in action for breach of contract to build a wall. Plaintiff by the terms was to level the ground, but omitted in the declaration to allege performance. United States v. Beard,* 5 McL., 441.

§ 216. In an action for breach of contract involving mutual conditions, declaration must aver performance or readiness or readiness to perform by plaintiff. Darland v. Greenwood,* 1 McC., 337.

§ 217. **Breach of official bond — Allegation of.**— In a suit on a marshal's bond it is sufficient to allege a breach without averring also that the full amount of the penalty has not hitherto been paid. Sperring v. Taylor,* 2 McL., 362.

§ 218. In debt upon a constable's bond for not conveying to the plaintiff property alleged to have been sold by the defendant under a *fi. fa.*, the breach is defective in not stating that the execution was levied upon the property, and that the lots were the property of the defendant in the execution, and in not describing the property with sufficient certainty; and is bad in averring an alternative breach, namely, in not conveying the property to the plaintiff, or in not permitting him to take possession of it. Hazel v. Waters, 3 Cr. C. C., 420

§ 219. In an action on the bond of a clerk of a United States court the declaration alleged failure to make proper emolument returns and neglect to pay over sums due. A clerk is not required to pay over anything until the attorney-general orders him to do so, upon the coming in of the proper reports showing a surplus. *Held*, the allegation of a failure to pay over may be treated as surplusage, or as an allegation of damage; and the declaration is sufficent in charging a failure to make the proper returns. United States *v.* Ambrose, 2 Fed. R., 552.

§ 220. Where the defendant may replevy the judgment and suspend execution for six months, a declaration against the marshal and his sureties, which avers that he neglected to make the money, is defective. Bispham *v.* Taylor, 2 McL., 355.

§ 221. **Patent causes — Averment of preliminary proceedings.**— The declaration in a patent cause need not state that the stages preliminary to the issuing of a patent were observed. Cutting *v.* Myers, 4 Wash., 220.

§ 222. The declaration in a patent cause must set forth the attestation of the president of the United States, and that the patent was delivered — a want of a statement of either of which is demurrable generally. *Ibid.*

§ 223. It is no cause for demurrer to a declaration in a patent cause that neither the patent nor the declaration states in what the improvement consists. If the defendant wants the specification inserted on the record he must crave oyer of it. *Ibid.*

§ 224. Where the declaration describes the plaintiff's improvement in the words of the patent, it is not necessary that the description of the machine as stated in the specification should be set forth. If the defendant require the specification in his defense, he may have it placed on the record by asking oyer of it. Gray *v.* James, Pet. C. C., 476.

§ 225. To show a violation of a patent the declaration need only aver that the defendant has constructed, used and sold to others the thing patented. Case *v.* Redfield, 4 McL., 526.

§ 226. An averment in a declaration that the defendant has made the thing "in imitation of the patent" is sufficient to sustain the action. Parker *v.* Haworth, 4 McL., 370.

§ 227. In an action for the violation of a patent right on "a new and useful improvement in the cooking stove," the declaration must state, as an essential part of the plaintiff's case, in what the improvement consists, or it is demurrable. Peterson *v.* Wooden, 3 McL., 248.

§ 228. It is no foundation for a nonsuit that the declaration for an invasion of a patent-right does not lay the act complained of to be "against the form of the statute," under which the rights of plaintiff are derived. *Contra formam statuti* is a matter of form, and may be cured by verdict. Tyron *v.* White, Pet. C. C., 96.

§ 229. **Action against defendant for failure to deliver** salt according to contract "at any place along the bank of Red river which may be designated by" plaintiff. The declaration averred failure to deliver at the times and places specified. *Held*, that this was sufficient without any allegation that plaintiff designated places for delivery, as defendant in such case should have delivered at a place of his own selection. Hartfield *v.* Patton,* Hemp., 269.

§ 230. **Agreement to go bail, etc.— What a sufficient allegation of breach of.**— A. was arrested in New York on a promissory note made by him and payable originally to B., of Boston. An agreement was made between the plaintiffs and a third party, C., by which A. was to be discharged from arrest, was to go to Boston and endeavor to arrange the matter with B., and in case of failure to make an arrangement was to surrender himself to any suit begun against him by B., and to accept service therein, and C. was to go bail in such suit if A. should fail to surrender himself. In a suit upon this agreement against C., the declaration was held bad for not averring that a suit had been begun by B. against A., although there was an averment that A. had not gone to Boston according to the agreement. Gill *v.* Stebbins,* 2 Paine, 417.

§ 231. **Abandoned counts** are not in every sense to be considered as stricken from the record. A reference in subsequent counts to the venue as laid in those counts, or to fix the place where an act was done, may be sufficient. Jones *v.* Vanzandt,* 5 McL., 214.

§ 232. A declaration in a common-law action against defendant for secreting plaintiff's slaves need not conclude as against the statute, though at the time a statute exist giving plaintiff an action for a penalty in the same case. *Ibid.*

§ 233. **False imprisonment — Matters of aggravation.**— In an action for false imprisonment matters of aggravation need not be pleaded. Stanton *v.* Seymour, 5 McL., 267.

§ 234. **Action for proceeds of goods sold by consignee — No allegation of collections made by defendants necessary.**— Action for proceeds of goods consigned by plaintiff to defendant for sale. Declaration stated that the goods were sold and the money received by defendant. *Held*, there was no need of allegation that defendant had made collections. Wyman *v.* Fowler,* 3 McL., 467.

§ 235. In the above case it was held that no demand of the proceeds need be alleged, though had the action been for a return of the specific goods, demand would have to be alleged. *Ibid.*

§ 236. Surplusage will not vitiate a count containing sufficient averments. *Ibid.*

§ 237. A venue in the margin is not necessary if it is stated in the body of the declaration. Dwight *v.* Wing,* 2 McL., 580.

§ 238. Survivors of joint obligees must aver non-payment to deceased obligee.— A declaration to recover a sum of money by two survivors out of three who had been jointly interested must allege that the money had not been paid to the deceased party in his life-time. Winter *v.* Simonton,* 3 Cr. C. C., 62.

§ 239. Averment of assets, when necessary in suit against administrator.— *Held,* that "the declaration was bad for the want of averment of assets, inasmuch as the promise was made by the defendant as administrator, and the declaration sought to charge him personally *de bonis propriis.*" Adams *v.* Whiting,* 2 Cr. C. C., 132.

§ 240. Sci. fa. to revive judgment in ejectment — Statement that term is yet unexpired sufficient.— To a *sci. fa.* to revive a judgment in ejectment, where it is stated that the term recovered is yet unexpired, this is sufficient. It is not required that the term as laid in the declaration, and the facts showing its continuance, should be stated. Lessee of Walden *v.* Craig, 14 Pet., 147.

§ 241. An averment of corporate existence need not be positive, but may be by way of recital. Falconer *v.* Campbell, 2 McL., 195.

§ 242. Averment of trusteeship in suit on insurance policy.— A declaration on a policy of marine insurance, which avers that the plaintiffs are trustees, that the insurance was for them, and that they were interested in the vessel at the time of the loss, is sufficient, without setting out the nature and extent of the trust. Henshaw *v.* M. S. Insurance Co., 2 Blatch., 99.

§ 243. Averment of combination to commit fraud.— A declaration against two defendants, charging them with preconcert and combination to defraud plaintiff, is supported by proof of fraud of one of the defendants subsequently participated in by the other. Lincoln *v.* Claflin, 7 Wall., 185.

§ 244. Receivers of public money — Averment of request to pay over, sufficiency of.— Receivers of public money being subject to general orders requiring payments to be made to the government at stated times, a declaration against such receiver averring a request to pay over is sufficient after verdict. Boyden *v.* United States, 13 Wall., 17.

§ 245. A declaration in debt on an arbitration bond must aver that the arbitrators conformed in every material respect to the agreement of arbitration. Gear *v.* Bracken,* 1 Burn, 82.

§ 246. Breach of agreement to buy land — Allegation of title.— If, in a suit seeking damages for breach of an agreement to buy land, the petition does not set forth that the claimant had title, or, except inferentially, that any deed was ever tendered, the petition will be held bad on demurrer, as all pleadings are to be construed most strongly against the person making them. Mer. Ex. Co. *v.* United States,* 1 N. & H., 382.

§ 247. Execution of bonds a condition precedent — Averment of offer to execute insufficient to support action.— Declaration that the defendant had agreed to deliver to the plaintiff $100,000 of its indorsed bonds, if the plaintiff, *before* said delivery, should execute and deliver to the defendant, with sufficient securities, its bond for $100,000; that the plaintiff demanded the indorsed bonds and *offered* to execute its bond in due form, and has always been *ready* to execute it. *Held,* on demurrer, that the plaintiff must allege that it actually executed its bond in due form and tendered it to defendant. Alexandria Railroad Co. *v.* National Junction R. Co., 1 MacArth., 203.

§ 248. Conversion — Only ultimate facts to be proved need be pleaded.— When issue is joined on an averment of conversion in a declaration, it is necessary to show the existence of facts which in law constitute a conversion; but, for the purpose of pleading, the ultimate fact to be proved need only be stated. The circumstances which tend to prove the ultimate fact can be used for the purposes of evidence, but they have no place in the pleadings. McAllister *v.* Kuhn, 6 Otto, 87.

§ 249. Mechanic's lien — Laws of Oregon — Averment as to time when materials were furnished.— As the General Laws of Oregon, page 168, require suit to enforce a mechanic's lien to be brought within one year from the time the materials were furnished, and a later law requires the suit to be brought within one year after the building was completed, it is necessary to show in the complaint the time when materials were furnished. Willamette Falls Transportation and Milling Co. *v.* Smith,* 1 Oreg., 171.

§ 250. Foreign judgment — Foreign court and its jurisdiction must be set out.— If the declaration in an action on a foreign judgment sets out the court in which the judgment was rendered and that it had jurisdiction, that is sufficient without setting out the record and proceedings of such court. Martin *v.* Moore,* 1 Wyom. Ty., 22.

§ 251. Petition for administration of an estate under the Illinois statute.— An allegation in a petition, brought under the Illinois statute for the administration of intestate estates, that a certain person died "leaving" certain real estate, is a sufficient compliance with the direction of the statute that the petition should state what real estate the intestate died "seized of." McNitt v. Turner, 16 Wall., 352.

§ 252. Malicious prosecution — Necessary allegation in suit for damages.— In an action to recover damages for wrongfully bringing a civil action, the petition must allege that the action was brought maliciously and that it has terminated. McCracken v. Covington Bank, 4 Fed. R., 602. See § 268.

§ 253. Tenancy for a term.— In an action of waste an allegation that the defendants held certain portions of the premises as tenants thereof to the plaintiff under a demise for a certain rent sufficiently imports a tenancy for a term. Parrot v. Barney, Deady, 405.

§ 254. Allegation of title by assignee in bankruptcy.— When an assignee in bankruptcy attempts in a declaration to show his title to the bankrupt's goods he must set out an adjudication of bankruptcy, or the declaration will be bad on demurrer. Wright v. Johnson, 8 Blatch., 150.

§ 255. A declaration in trover for "a tool-chest containing divers tools and working utensils," and "a trunk containing clothes," is good for the trunk and chest and tools and clothes. Pall v. Patterson,* 1 Cr. C. C., 607.

§ 256. Letters testamentary — Allegation as to.— It is not necessary to allege in the declaration by whom letters testamentary were granted. Cawood v. Nichols,* 1 Cr. C. C., 180.

§ 257. Seizin; allegation of necessary in ejectment.— To sustain an action of ejectment an averment of seizin is essential, and it must be alleged to have been within the time limited for bringing the action. ˙Bockee v. Crosby, 2 Paine, 432.

§ 258. In assumpsit on a promise to pay a debt due by the promisor, if plaintiff would give time, whenever the promisor should be able, the declaration need not state that the promise was accepted by the plaintiff. It is sufficient to aver that time was given, and that the defendant is able. Lonsdale v. Brown, 4 Wash., 148.

§ 259. A declaration that defendant dug, opened and made an excavation in a sidewalk, by which plaintiff was injured, is a sufficient allegation, though the opening was partly caused by raising the sides by means of a walk. Robbins v. Chicago, 4 Wall., 657.

§ 260. Action on covenant of seizin — Averment of eviction unnecessary.— An action may be supported on a covenant of seizin, although the plaintiff has never been evicted; and the declaration need not aver an eviction. Pollard v. Dwight, 4 Cr., 421.

§ 261. Promise by assignor to refund if property not recovered — Suit by assignee — Allegation.— If a bond of conveyance (then in suit) be assigned, and the assignor agree to refund to the assignee the value thereof if the property should not be recovered on the bond, it is sufficient for the assignee, in a suit against the assignor upon his promise to refund, to aver that the property was not recovered in the suit which was pending when the agreement was made to refund. Ferguson v. Harwood, 7 Cr., 408.

§ 262. Upon a count "for sundry matters properly chargeable in account, as by account annexed, it is not necessary that the account should be such as would be evidence *per se* under the act of Maryland, 1729, chapter 20. McLaughlin v. Turner, 1 Cr. C. C., 476.

§ 263. In a count "for sundry matters properly chargeable in account," if no account be annexed, the words which refer to an account as annexed may be rejected; and money lent may be given in evidence upon that count. Lovejoy v. Wilson, 1 Cr. C. C., 102.

§ 264. Where there has been a special agreement between the parties that has been wholly performed, or if its further execution has been prevented by the act of the defendant, or by the consent of both; or if the contract has been fully performed in respect to any one distinct subject included in it, the plaintiff may recover upon a general *indebitatus assumpsit.* Perkins v. Hart, 11 Wheat., 237.

§ 265. In stating a loss in a declaration on a policy of insurance it is sufficient to show it to have been occasioned by a peril within the policy, without negativing the exceptions of losses from design, invasion, public enemies, riots, etc., which are properly matters of defense. Catlin v. Springfield Fire Ins. Co., 1 Sumn., 434.

§ 266. An averment that John Leonard, "for a certain price," agreed to serve the plaintiff, is supported by evidence that John Leonard, in consideration of eight guineas paid by the plaintiff to a third person, agreed to serve the plaintiff. Milburne v. Byrne, 1 Cr. C. C., 239.

§ 267. Suit against new corporation for debt of old.— A declaration against "the common council of Alexandria" for work and labor done for "the mayor and commonalty" must show how the new corporation is liable for the debts of the old. Lyles v. The Common Council of Alexandria, 1 Cr. C. C., 473.

§ 268. Malicious prosecution.— In an action for maliciously arresting and holding the plaintiff to bail without probable cause, the declaration must aver that the suit in which the plaintiff was so maliciously holden to bail was determined, or it will be bad on general demurrer. Barrell v. Simonton, 2 Cr. C. C., 657. See § 252.

§ 269. In a declaration in an action for maintenance it is necessary to allege the pendency of a suit, in what court pending, together with time, place and circumstances, so as to show the maintenance. Fletcher v. Ellis, Hemp., 300.

§ 270. Garnishment — Citizenship must appear to give court jurisdiction.— A garnishment is a suit or proceeding in which a party has his day in court; and it must, therefore, appear on the face of the pleadings, or by the record, that the judgment creditor and the garnishee are citizens of different states, to give a federal court jurisdiction. Tunstall v. Worthington, Hemp., 663.

§ 271. Suit against administratrix — Laws of Louisiana — Averment of tableau filed.— The laws of Louisiana provide for compelling the executrix to file a tableau of distribution, which is a necessary and preliminary step toward holding the executrix personally responsible, and a petition failing to aver this is defective. McGill v. Armour, 11 How., 142.

§ 272. —— devastavit.— Where a creditor brought an action against an executrix in the United States circuit court for Louisiana, and the petition only averred that the petitioner was shown to be a creditor by the accounts in the state court which had jurisdiction over the estates of deceased persons, and then proceeded to charge the executrix with a *devastavit*, the petition is insufficient. It should have gone on to allege further proceedings in the state court analogous to a judgment at common law, as a foundation of a claim for a judgment against the *executrix de bonis propriis*, suggesting a *devastavit*. *Ibid.*

§ 273. Joint liability — Allegation of partnership.— Where a contract shows a joint liability it is unnecessary to allege or prove a partnership. Kendall v. Freeman, 2 McL., 189.

§ 274. Suit against agent — Allegation of agency.— An action having been brought against a defendant, charging him with an abuse of his powers, as agent of the plaintiff, it is essential that the declaration allege that the defendant acted as agent of the plaintiff. Ætna Ins. Co. v. Sabine, 6 McL., 393.

§ 275. Revenue laws — Variance as to residence, when surplusage.— The act of congress declares that it shall be the duty of every person coming from a foreign territory, adjacent to the United States, into the United States, with merchandise, to deliver the manifest. The declaration averred that the defendant came from a foreign territory, viz., from Montreal, and the evidence was that he came from Caldwell's Manor. *Held*, that after judgment the allegation under the *videlicet* might be rejected as surplusage. Steinham v. United States, 2 Paine, 168.

§ 276. Ejectment — Description of premises.— Formerly it was necessary to describe the premises for which an action of ejectment was brought with great accuracy; but far less certainty is required in modern practice. All the authorities say that the general description is good. The lessor of the plaintiff, on a lease for a specific number of acres, may recover any quantity of less amount. Barclay v. Howell, 6 Pet., 498.

§ 277. Original bill — Allegation of void probate.— An original bill will not be sustained on the allegation that the probate of a will is void. Tarver v. Tarver, 9 Pet., 174.

§ 278. Suit against collector for refusing clearance — Ownership of cargo.— In an action against the collector of customs for refusing a clearance upon a count stating that the plaintiff was the owner of the vessel, laden with a cargo of a certain value, the allegation is sufficient as to ownership of the cargo. Bas v. Steel, 3 Wash., 381.

§ 279. Allegations of citizenship of the parties.— Where the jurisdiction of a federal circuit court depends upon citizenship of the parties in different states, this must appear by proper averment in the record; the omission is fatal at any stage in the cause. Wood v. Mann, 1 Sumn., 578; Hornthall v. The Collector, 9 Wall., 560; Assessors v. Osborne, 9 Wall., 567; Berlin v. Jones, 1 Woods, 639; Godfrey v. Terry, 7 Otto, 171; Teese v. Phelps, McAl., 17; Leavitt v. Cowles, 2 McL., 491; Brown v. Keene, 8 Pet., 112; Turner v. Enrille, 4 Dal., 7; Sullivan v. Fulton Steamboat Co., 6 Wheat., 450; United States v. Alberty, Hemp., 445; Rogers v. Linn, 2 McL., 126; Jackson v. Twentyman, 2 Pet., 186; Dodge v. Perkins, 4 Mason, 435; Cooper v. Dungler, 4 McL., 257.

§ 280. It is not sufficient, to give jurisdiction to the federal courts, to allege that a party is an alien. Wilson v. The City Bank, 3 Sumn., 422; Shedden v. Curtis, 1 Hughes, 246; Michaelson v. Denison,* 3 Day (Conn.), 294; Shedden v. Curtis,* 6 Call (Va.), 241.

§ 281. There must also be an allegation that he is a subject or citizen of some one foreign state. *Ibid.*

§ 282. Where an alien sues in the federal court the defendant must be described as a citizen of some particular state. Stating him to be a citizen of the United States is not sufficient. Piquet v. Swan, 5 Mason, 35; Hodgson v. Bowerbank, 5 Cr., 303.

§ 283. Citizenship of the defendant in a certain state is sufficiently averred in a declaration if it is averred that he is a citizen of the southern district of that state. Delano v. Cargo of Gallatin, 1 Woods, 688; Berlin v. Jones, 1 Woods, 640; Duryea v. Webb,* 16 Conn., 558; Edwards v. Nichols,* 3 Day (Conn.), 16.

§ 284. In a suit brought by a corporation in a federal court, no further allegation of citizenship is required in the declaration than the place where it is located and where its corporate functions are discharged. New York & Erie R. Co. v. Shepard, 5 McL., 455; Covington Drawbridge Co. v. Shepherd, 20 How., 227; Ketchum v. Farmers' Loan & Trust Co., 4 McL., 1; Manufacturers' Nat. Bank v. Baack, 2 Abb., 282; Greeley v. Smith, 3 Story, 76.

§ 285. When the jurisdiction of the federal court depends upon the citizenship of the parties, the jurisdictional facts must appear affirmatively upon the record, and an alleged residence in a state is not equivalent to an allegation of citizenship. Robertson v. Cease,* 18 Alb. L. J., 453.

§ 286. The courts of the United States have not jurisdiction where the record states one party to be a citizen of Pennsylvania and the other to be "of the state of Georgia." Wood v. Wagon, 2 Cr., 9.

§ 287. An averment that "said A. during his life-time was a citizen of the United States and of the state of Pennsylvania," although not very precise, is equivalent to an averment of citizenship in Pennsylvania. Bayerque v. Haley, McAl., 97.

§ 288. The petition filed in the district court of the United States for Louisiana alleged that the defendant had caused himself to be naturalized an American citizen, and that he was, at the time of the filing of the petition, residing in the parish of West Baton Rouge. *Held,* that this was equivalent to an averment that the defendant is a citizen of the state of Louisiana. Gassies v. Ballou, 6 Pet., 761.

§ 289. A plea to the jurisdiction of the federal circuit court must show that the parties were citizens of the same state at the time the action was brought, and not merely at the time of the plea pleaded. The jurisdiction depends upon the state of things at the time of the action brought, and after it is once vested it cannot be ousted by a subsequent change of residence of either of the parties. Mollan v. Torrance, 9 Wheat., 537.

§ 290. The citizenship of persons who may or may not afterward apply to be made parties need not be alleged in the bill. Vallette v. The Whitewater Valley Canal Co., 4 McL., 192.

§ 291. An averment of citizenship in the first count is sufficient to give jurisdiction to the court, although in the other counts there be no such averment. Jones v. Heaton, 1 McL., 317.

§ 292. Where the plaintiffs are averred in the declaration to be citizens of Iowa, and the defendants to be citizens of Ohio, that is sufficient to give the circuit court of the United States for the southern district of Ohio jurisdiction, the return of personal service on the defendants having been made by the marshal of that district, without alleging that defendants were residents or inhabitants of such southern district. Vore v. Fowler, 2 Bond, 294.

§ 293. Where the complainants, citizens of Ohio, brought their bill in the United States court against the Bank of the United States, and certain individuals whose citizenship was not named, that court cannot take jurisdiction. Findlay v. Bank of the United States, 2 McL., 44.

§ 294. That "the plaintiffs are citizens of New York, to wit, of Illinois," where the suit is brought, is a repugnant averment. Leavitt v. Cowles, 2 McL., 491.

§ 295. Where suit was brought against two members of a copartnership composed of three persons, it was not necessary to aver that the third partner was subject to the jurisdiction of the United States courts. Breedlove v. Nicolet, 7 Pet., 418.

§ 296. Where a declaration contained special counts upon promissory notes, and also the common money counts, although the jurisdiction of the court was not apparent upon the special counts, yet the money counts, sustained by evidence, might have been sufficient to sustain it; and the United States supreme court will presume such evidence to have been given if the record is silent upon the subject, and if no objection was made to the jurisdiction in the progress of the trial. Bank of the United States v. Moss, 6 How., 31.

§ 297. A declaration was sufficient which averred that "at a general term of the supreme court of equity for the state of New York," etc. Being thus averred to be a court of general jurisdiction, no averment was necessary that the subject-matter in question was within its jurisdiction. And the United States courts will take notice of the judicial decisions in the several states in the same manner as the courts of those states. Pennington v. Gibson, 16 How., 65.

§ 298. A plea to the jurisdiction that there was no averment of citizenship in the declaration as to one of the defendants who was not served with process was not sustained. Morrison v. Bennett, 1 McL., 330.

§ 299. The declaration, in a suit upon an inland bill of exchange, by the indorsee against the drawer or acceptor, in order to show that the federal courts have jurisdiction, must set out the citizenship of the payee and of the indorsers. Morgan v. Gay, 19 Wall., 81.

§ 300. Where a suit is brought against a remote indorser on a promissory note, and the plaintiff, in his declaration, traces his title through an intermediate indorser, he must show that his intermediate indorser could have sustained his action in the federal circuit court. Mollan v. Torrance, 9 Wheat., 537.

§ 801. Where an action is brought upon a promissory note in a federal court by an indorsee against the maker, not only the parties to the suit, but also the payee, must be stated on the record to be such as to give the court jurisdiction. Turner v. Bank of North America, 4 Dal., 8.

§ 802. The citizenship of a joint promisor, not served with process, must appear in the declaration. If he be a citizen of the same state with the plaintiff the court can take no jurisdiction. Bargh v. Page, 4 McL., 10.

§ 803. The assignee of a promissory note or bill to recover must show by the declaration that his assignor could have sued in the United States courts. Fry v. Rousseau, 3 McL., 106.

§ 804. On a note payable to A. or bearer, suit may be brought in the name of the bearer; he is not an assignee, and need not aver in the declaration the citizenship of A. Sackett v. Davis, 3 McL., 101.

§ 805. Where the assignee of a promissory note sues, the declaration must show that the assignor, by his citizenship, had a right to sue in the federal court, or it is demurrable. Fletcher v. Turner, 5 McL., 468.

§ 806. Though the declaration began with an averment that the drawer and indorser were citizens of the same state, which would oust the jurisdiction of the United States circuit court, yet, as it afterwards averred that the indorser was an alien and citizen of another state, this was sufficient to maintain the jurisdiction. Bailey v. Dozier, 6 How., 23.

§ 807. When a contract is averred under which the court would not have jurisdiction by reason of citizenship, and a subsequent contract under which there would be jurisdiction, and it appears that the former was set out only by way of inducement, the jurisdiction will not be defeated. De Sobry v. Nicholson, 3 Wall., 420.

§ 808. The caption of the bill was in the following terms: "T. J., a citizen of the state of Virginia, W. G. J. and M. C. J., citizens of Virginia, infants, by their father and next friend, the said T. J., v. Rev. W. E. A., a citizen of the state of Pennsylvania, in equity." By the Court: The title or caption of the bill is no part of the bill, and does not remove the objection to the defects in the pleadings. The bill and proceedings should state the citizenship of the parties to give the court jurisdiction of the case. Jackson v. Ashton, 8 Pet., 148.

§ 809. Where the writ had stated both the defendants to be citizens of another state than that of which the plaintiff was a citizen, and one of the defendants has been returned not found by the marshal, under the laws of Alabama it is not necessary, in the declaration, to aver the citizenship of the absent defendant. Smith v. Clapp, 15 Pet., 125.

§ 810. An averment that plaintiffs were a firm of natural persons associated together for the purpose of carrying on the banking business in Omaha, and had been for a period of eighteen months engaged in said business in said place, was held equivalent to an allegation of citizenship. Express Co. v. Kountze Brothers, 8 Wall., 342.

§ 811. An allegation that the defendant is a corporation created by an act of the legislature of New York, located in Aberdeen, Mississippi, and doing business there under the laws of that state, is not a sufficient allegation of citizenship in that state. Insurance Co v. Francis, 11 Wall., 210.

§ 812. An allegation that the defendant corporation is a body politic in the law of and doing business in a certain state is not a sufficient allegation of citizenship in that state. Pennsylvania v. Quicksilver Co., 10 Wall., 553.

§ 813. An averment that complainant was a joint stock association, organized under the laws of New York, having the legal entity and powers therein provided, is not sufficient for jurisdiction purposes, as an allegation that complainant is a corporation. Dinsmore v. Phil. & Reading R. Co.,* 3 Cent. L. J., 157.

§ 814. A declaration in the United States circuit court for the Virginia district stated the plaintiffs to be "merchants and partners, trading under the firm and by the name of D. & Co., of Philadelphia, in Pennsylvania." This was insufficient to give jurisdiction to the court in the action, if the exception had been taken by plea, or by writ of error, within the limitation of such writ. Ross v. Duvall, 13 Pet., 45.

§ 815. A declaration describing plaintiff as "The Third National Bank of Baltimore, a duly incorporated body under the statutes of the United States of America," is defective in omitting an allegation in what state the banking association is established, this being a jurisdictional fact; and is also defective in not alleging that plaintiff is a corporation, a defect which would be cured by verdict. Third National Bank v. Teal,* 5 Fed. R., 503.

§ 816. Where a corporation is sued it is not enough, in order to give jurisdiction, to say that the corporation is a citizen of the state where the suit is brought. But an averment is sufficient, when admitted by a demurrer, that the corporation was created by the laws of the state and has its principal place of business there. Lafayette Ins. Co. v. French, 18 How., 404.

§ 817. The complainants are stated in the bill to be citizens of South Carolina. The defendant, the Bank of Georgia, is a body corporate, but the citizenship of the individual corporators is not stated. The averment in the original bill is that A. B. and C. D. are citizens of Georgia and resident therein; A. B. is afterwards designated in the bill as "president of the mother bank," and C. D. as the "president of the branch bank at Augusta, in the state of Georgia." The United States courts have no jurisdiction of the case. The record does not show that the defendants were citizens of Georgia, nor are there any distinct allegations that the stockholders of the bank were citizens of that state. Breithaupt v. The Bank of Georgia, 1 Pet., 238.

§ 318. Where a suit was brought in which the plaintiff was described as a citizen of France, against the Pennsylvania Railroad Company, without any averment that the defendants were a corporation under the laws of Pennsylvana, or that the place of business of the corporation was there, or that its corporators, managers or directors were citizens of Pennsylvania, the absence of such an averment was fatal to the jurisdiction of the court. Piquignot v. The Pennsylvania R. Co., 16 How., 104.

§ 319. Jurisdictional averments.— To show jurisdiction of federal courts on the ground that the action arises under the laws of the United States there must be shown such facts as show how it arises under such laws, and a mere allegation that it does so arise is insufficient. Dowell v. Griswold, 5 Saw., 39.

§ 320. If a party relies upon a constitutional question being involved to give the federal court jurisdiction, it is not necessary that the special section of the constitution which is supposed to be involved should be stated in the pleadings; but it is enough if the facts set forth necessarily involve a constitutional question. Bridge Proprietors v. Hoboken Co., 1 Wall., 116.

§ 321. The plaintiff in a case brought in the federal court under the act of March 8, 1875, must show by proper and apt averments enough to maintain the federal jurisdiction given under that act. Eaton v. Calhoun, 2 Flip., 593.

c. Written Instruments.

SUMMARY — *Writing sued on, how stated, § 322.— Separate breaches to be separately pleaded, § 323.— Only nominal damages to be recovered unless special damage averred, § 323a.— Papers made part of the instrument declared on, § 324.— Amount demanded in debt, § 325.— Smaller sum may be recovered than amount asked, § 326.— Performance of conditions precedent, § 327.— Breach to be single, § 328.— Damage on appeal bond, how averred, § 329.— Breaches to be assigned on penal bond, 330.— Breaches, when to be assigned, § 331.— Breach, how to be assigned, § 332.— Declaration against joint obligors, § 333.— Breaches to be assigned before judgment by default, § 334.— Averment of ouster on covenant of warranty, § 335.— Omission to show derivation of title, when formal defect only, § 336.— Breach not assigned by averment of non-payment of penalty, § 337.*

§ 322. A writing sued on must be stated according to its legal effect, and not merely annexed as an exhibit. Oh Chow v. Hallett, §§ 338-340.

§ 323. When a contract contains several stipulations, breaches of different ones are separate causes of action and must be separately pleaded. Ibid.

§ 323a. An allegation of a breach of a contract, without averment of special damage, is not uncertain, but only nominal damages can be recovered under it. Ibid.

§ 324. When an insurance policy makes the preliminary proposals, answers, etc., of the insured part of the policy, they must be set out in a declaration on the policy. Bidwell v. Insurance Co., § 341.

§ 325. A declaration in debt by the United States on an embargo bond demanding $20,000, and reciting the statute which allows the United States to demand a sum not exceeding $20,000 and not less than $1,000, is a good declaration. United States v. Colt, §§ 342-347.

§ 326. A declaration in debt must demand a specific sum, but this demand does not preclude the recovery of a smaller sum, where it is diminished by circumstances. Ibid.

§ 327. A declaration on a policy of fire insurance, setting out the terms of the policy, must aver specifically the performance of the various conditions precedent to their recovery. A general allegation of performance will be bad on demurrer. Perry v. Phœnix Assurance Co., §§ 348, 349.

§ 328. In a declaration on an appeal bond the breach assigned must be a single breach, denying each alternative; that is, that the plaintiff in error did not prosecute his writ to effect, nor answer the damages and costs. Tucker v. Lee, §§ 350-358.

§ 329. A declaration on an appeal bond must aver specially the damage. This does not consist of the damages and costs awarded in court, but the loss suffered by the present plaintiff by the failure to pay judgment. Ibid.

§ 880. In an action on a penal bond with collateral conditions, the plaintiff must assign breaches. Burnett v. Wylie, §§ 859, 860.

§ 881. Breaches may be assigned in the declaration or replication, or may be suggested on the record, but a judgment without the assignment of breaches and assessment of damages by a jury will be reversed on error. *Ibid.*

§ 882. A breach of a covenant is properly assigned if it be in words containing the sense and substance of the covenant, and according with its legal effect. Wilcox v. Cohn, §§ 361-363.

§ 883. A declaration against some of joint obligors must aver that all have failed to pay, as the breach laid must be as broad as the obligation. Robins v. Pope, §§ 364-366.

§ 884. The breaches of the bond must be assigned before judgment by default. *Ibid.*

§ 885. In an action on a breach of covenant of warranty of title, an averment that plaintiffs were ousted by due course of law is a sufficient averment of eviction by title paramount. Day v. Chism, §§ 367, 368.

§ 886. An omission by a plaintiff declaring as heir or devisee to show how he derived his title is a defect of form only. *Ibid.*

§ 887. A declaration averring simply non-payment of the penalty does not sufficiently set forth a breach of the condition. Hazel v. Waters, § 869.

[NOTES.— See §§ 370-416.]

OH CHOW v. HALLETT.

(Circuit Court for Oregon: 2 Sawyer, 259, 260. 1872.)

Opinion by DEADY, J.

STATEMENT OF FACTS.— These actions were commenced October 14, 1872, and the motions to strike out were argued and submitted together on November 9. The first named one is brought to recover the balance of $1,982.46, alleged to be due the plaintiff for laborers furnished the defendant to work upon the North Pacific Railway, and the sum of $365.33 damages for a failure on the part of the defendant to furnish transportation to take said laborers and their freight from said railway to the town of Roseburg. The second is brought to recover a balance of $654.26 and the sum of $142 damages, alleged to be due the plaintiffs and incurred in like manner.

In each case the contract sued upon, instead of being pleaded in the complaint according to its tenor or legal effect, is annexed thereto as an exhibit. In each complaint the allegation in regard to the failure to furnish transportation is numbered six, and commences: " And for a further breach of defendant's said contract plaintiffs allege that defendant failed," etc. No facts are stated except the failure aforesaid to show that the plaintiffs sustained damage by reason thereof. The motions to strike out are aimed at these allegations as well as the ones making the contracts exhibits, and the contracts themselves.

§ 338. *A writing sued on must be stated, and not merely annexed as an exhibit.*

As to the allegations concerning the contracts, the motions must be allowed. In pleadings in actions at law there are no such things as exhibits. If a party desires to complain upon or plead a writing he must state it in his complaint or plea according to its tenor or legal effect. Such has always been the ruling and practice in this court.

§ 339. *Where, under a contract, there are several stipulations, breaches of more than one are separate causes of action.*

As to the allegations numbered six, they should have been pleaded, not as "a further breach " of the contract, but as a separate and further cause of action. The practice of assigning more than one breach in the same count or statement of a cause of action, prior to the code, was permitted only in covenant upon a deed, and by statute in debt upon a bond with a condition, or to secure covenants. When an ordinary contract contains various substantive and independent provisions — as, in this case, to pay for labor furnished and to furnish transportation to laborers — if there is a breach or failure to perform more than one of the stipulations there are distinct causes of action, requiring different proofs, and which may admit of different defenses, and therefore should be stated separately. This cause of action, not being pleaded separately, is liable to be stricken out on motion. Or. Code, 163.

§ 340. *Special damage must be alleged.*

But these allegations are not liable to be stricken out upon the ground assigned in the motion, as being "immaterial and irrelevant." True, no special damage could be proven or recovered under them, because no facts showing such damage are stated in them, as that the plaintiffs, by reason of such failure, were compelled to and did furnish such transportation and pay for the same so much. Still the allegations contain an averment of a breach of the respective contracts, for which, if found true, the plaintiffs would be entitled to recover nominal damages. So much of the motions is denied.

BIDWELL v. CONNECTICUT MUTUAL LIFE INSURANCE COMPANY.

(Circuit Court for California: 8 Sawyer, 261, 262. 1874.)

Opinion by SAWYER, J.

STATEMENT OF FACTS.— Action upon a life insurance policy. The complaint contains a copy of the policy, but does not set out, either *in hæc verba* or in substance, the "proposals, answers and declarations" made by the applicant upon which the policy was issued.

§ 341. *Where the "proposals, declarations," etc., are made part of the policy they must be set out in the declaration.*

The policy set out contains the following clause: "And it is also understood and agreed to be the true intent and meaning hereof, that if the proposals, answers and declarations made by the said Alanson C. Bidwell, and bearing date the 15th day of November, 1866, and which are hereby made part and parcel of this policy as fully as if herein recited, and upon the faith of which this agreement is made, shall be found in any respect untrue, then and in such case this policy shall be null and void." The defendant demurs on the ground that the complaint is uncertain and insufficient, it appearing upon its face that the entire contract is not set out. I think this point well taken. It is well settled that, under the provision of the policy cited, the proposals, etc., are not mere representations made as inducement to enter into a contract, but are warranties and a part of the contract itself. Miles v. Conn. M. L. Ins. Co., 3 Gray, 580; 1 Big., 173; Ryan v. World Mut. Life Ins. Co., 4 Ins. Law Jour., 37; Campbell v. N. E. Mut. Ins. Co., 98 Mass., 381; Tibbitts v. Home Mut. Ins. Co., 1 Allen, 305; McLoon v. Conn. Mut. Ins. Co., 100 Mass., 472; Kelsey v. Mon. Life Ins. Co., 35 Conn., 235; Miller v. Mut. Ben. L. Ins. Co., 31 Ia., 227; Lycoming Mut. Ins. Co. v. Sailor, 16 Pa., 108; Rogers v. Charter Oak Life Ins. Co., MSS. Sup. Ct., Conn. The application being a part of the contract, it is necessary to set it out in the complaint, otherwise it does not appear what the contract is. Bobbitt v. The L. & L. & G. Ins. Co., 66 N. C., 70; 8 Am. R., 494; Steph. Pl., 132; Gould's Pl., ch. 4, sec. 28; 1 Ch. Pl., 236.

The demurrer must be sustained, and it is so ordered.

UNITED STATES *v.* COLT.

(Circuit Court for Pennsylvania: Peters, C. C., 145–154. 1815.)

STATEMENT OF FACTS.— This was an action of debt brought upon an embargo bond in the district court in June, 1811, and the declaration demanded $20,000, which the defendant was alleged to owe and detain. It then recited the embargo law, laying the breach by the defendant, "whereby the United States are entitled to demand a sum not exceeding $20,000 and not less than $1,000, viz., $20,000," which it averred to be due to the plaintiffs and detained from them by the defendant. Upon *nil debet* pleaded the jury found a verdict for $4,000. The defendant took out a writ of error, returnable at April sessions, 1812, of the circuit court, and the case now came on for decision.

§ 342. *Object of the action of debt.*

Opinion by WASHINGTON, J.

The question in this case is whether the action is maintainable. The objection to the action of debt, where the penalty is uncertain, is that this action can only be brought to recover a specific sum of money, the amount of which is ascertained. It is said that the very sum demanded must be proved, and on a demand for thirty pounds you can no more recover twenty pounds than you can a horse on a demand for a cow. Blackstone says (3 Blackstone, Com., 154) that debt, in its legal acceptation, is a sum of money due by certain and express agreement, where the quantity is fixed and does not depend on any subsequent valuation to settle it; and, for non-payment, the proper remedy is the action of debt to recover the specific sum due. So, if I verbally agree to pay a certain price for certain goods and fail in the performance, this action lies, for this is a *determinate contract.* But if I agree for no special price debt will not lie, but only a special action on the case; and this action is now generally brought, except in cases of contracts under seal, in preference to the action of debt; because, in this latter action, the plaintiff must prove the whole debt he claims or recover nothing at all. For the debt is one single cause of action, fixed and determined, and which, if the proof varies from the claim, cannot be looked upon as the same contract of which performance is demanded. If I sue for thirty pounds I am not at liberty to prove a debt of twenty pounds and recover a verdict thereon, for I fail in the proof of that contract which my action has alleged to be specific and determinate. But *indebitatus assumpsit* is not brought to compel a specific performance of the contract, but is to recover damages for its non-performance, and, the damages being indeterminate, will adapt themselves to the truth of the case as it may be proved, for if any debt be proved it is sufficient.

The doctrine laid down by this writer appears to be much too general and unqualified, although, to a certain extent, it is unquestionably correct. Debt is certainly a sum of money due by contract, and it most frequently is due by a certain and express agreement, which also fixes the sum, independent of any extrinsic circumstances. But it is not essential that the contract should be express or that it should fix the precise amount of the sum to be paid. Debt may arise on an implied contract, as for the balance of an account stated; to recover back money which a bailiff has paid more than he had received, and in a variety of other cases where the law, by implication, raises a contract to pay. 3 Com. Dig., 365. The sum may not be fixed by the contract, but may depend upon something extrinsic which may be averred; as, a promise to pay so much money as plaintiff shall expend in repairing a ship, may be sued in this form of action, the plaintiff averring that he did expend a certain sum. 2 Bac., 20. So, on promise by defendant to pay his proportion of the expenses of defending a suit in which defendant was interested, with an averment that plaintiff had expended so much, and that defendant's proportion amounted to so much. 3 Levy, 429. So an action of debt may be brought for goods sold to defendant for so much as they were worth. 2 Com. Dig., 365. So debt will lie for use and occupation, where there is only an implied contract, and no precise sum agreed upon. 6 T. Reports, 63.

§ 343. *When debt will lie for an undetermined demand.*

Wooddeson (3d vol., 95) states that debt will lie for an indeterminate demand which may be readily reduced to a certainty. In Emery *v.* Fell, 2 Term R., 28, in which there was a declaration in debt, containing a number of counts for goods sold and delivered, work and labor, money laid out and expended, and money had and received, the court on a special demurrer sustained the action, although it was objected that it did not appear that the demand was certain, and because no contract of sale was stated in the declaration. But the court took no notice of the first objection, and avoided the second by implying a contract of sale from the words which stated a sale. These cases prove that debt may be maintained upon an implied as well as upon an express contract, although no precise sum is agreed upon. But the doctrine stated by Lord Mansfield in the case of Walker *v.* Witter, Doug., 6, is conclusive upon this point. He lays it down that debt may be brought for a sum capable of being ascertained, though not ascertained at the time the action was brought. Ashurst and Buller say that whenever *indebitatus assumpsit* is maintainable, debt is also. In this case two points were also made by the defendant's counsel: first, that on the plea of *nil debet* the plaintiff could not have judgment, because debt could not be maintained on a foreign judgment; and secondly, that on the plea of *nul tiel record* judgment could not be entered for the plaintiff, because the judgment in Jamaica was not on record. The court were in favor of the defendant on the second point and against him in the first, by deciding that debt could be maintained on a foreign judgment, because *indebitatus assumpsit* might; and that the uncertainty of the debt demanded in the declaration was no objection to the bringing of an action of debt. The decision, therefore, given upon that point was upon the very point on which the cause turned. But, independent of the opinion given in this case, is it not true, to use the words of Buller, "that all the old cases show that whenever *indebitatus assumpsit* is maintainable debt also lies."

The subject is very satisfactorily explained by Lord Loughborough, in the case of Rudder *v.* Price, 1 H. Black., 550, which was an action of debt, brought on a promissory note payable by instalments, before the last day of payment was past, in which the court, yielding to the weight of authority, rather than to the reason which governed it, decided that the action could not be supported, because the contract, being entire, would admit of but one action, which could not be brought until the last payment became due, although *indebitatus assumpsit* might have been brought. But his lordship was led to inquire into the ancient forms of action on contracts; and he states that in ancient times debt was the common action for goods sold and for work and labor done. Where *assumpsit* was brought it was not a general *indebitatus assumpsit*, for it was not brought merely on a promise, but a special damage for a non-feasance, by which a special action arose to the plaintiff. The action of *assumpsit* to recover general damages for the non-performance of a contract was first introduced by Slade's Case, which course was afterwards followed. In the case of Walker *v.* Witter, Buller also stated that till Slade's (T. 44 Eliz., 4 Co., 92, b)· Case, a notion prevailed that on a simple contract for a certain sum the action must be debt; but it was held in that case that the plaintiff might bring *assumpsit* or debt at his election.

§ 344. *Debt and indebitatus assumpsit.*

Thus, it appears that in all cases of contract, unless a special damage was stated, the primitive action was debt, and that the action of *indebitatus assumpsit* succeeded principally, I presume, to avoid the wager of law, which, in Slade's Case, was one of the main arguments urged by the defendant's counsel against allowing the introduction of the action of *assumpsit*, as it thereby deprived the defendant of his privilege of wagering his law. Buller seems, therefore, to have been well warranted, in the case of Walker *v.* Witter, in saying that all the old cases show that where *indebitatus assumpsit* will lie debt will lie. The same doctrine is supported by the case of Emery *v.* Fell, 2 Term R., 30, which was an action of debt in which all the counts of *indebitatus assumpsit* are stated, where the objection to the doctrine was made and overruled. So, in the case of Harris *v.* Jameson, 5 Term R., 557, Ashurst refers with approbation to the opinion delivered in the case of Walker *v.* Witter. That debt may be brought for foreign money, the value of which the jury are to find, had been decided before the case of Walker *v.* Witter, as appears by the case of Rands *v.* Peck, Cro. Jac., 618; and in Draper *v.* Rastal the same action was brought, though in different ways, for current money, being the value of the foreign.

Comyns, in his Digest, title Debt, page 366, where he enumerates the cases in which debt will not lie, states no exception to the rule that where *indebitatus assumpsit* will lie debt will lie, but one for the interest of money due upon a loan. But the reason of that is explained by Lord Loughborough in the case of Rudder *v.* Price, who states that until the case of Cook *v.* Whorwood, upon a covenant to pay a stipulated sum by instalments, if the plaintiff brought *assumpsit*, after the first failure, he was entitled to recover the whole sum in damages; because he could not in that form of action, any more than in the action of debt, support two actions on an entire contract. Until that decision the only difference between debt and *assumpsit*, in such a case, was that the former could not be brought until after the last instalment was due; and in the latter, though it might be brought after the first failure, yet the plaintiff might recover the whole, because he could not maintain a second action on the same contract.

§ 345. *Debt is for the recovery of the sum due, not necessarily the sum demanded. Authorities reviewed.*

I proceed with the doctrine of Judge Blackstone before stated. After stating what constitutes debt, he observes "that the remedy is an action of debt to recover the special sum *due.*" It is observable that he does not say that the plaintiff is to recover the sum *demanded* by his declaration, and no person will deny but that he is to recover the special sum due.

After stating what constitutes a debt and prescribing the remedy, Judge Blackstone proceeds to the evidence and recovery, and says, "the plaintiff must prove the whole debt he claims, or he can recover nothing." On this account he adds, "the action of *assumpsit* is most commonly brought, because in that it is sufficient if the plaintiff prove any debt to be due, to enable him to recover the sum so proved in damages." If this writer merely means to say that, where a special contract is laid in the declaration, it must be proved as laid, the doctrine will not be controverted. If debt be brought on a written agreement the contract produced in evidence must correspond, in all respects, with that stated in the declaration, and any variance will be fatal to the plaintiff's recovery. Such, too, is the law in all special actions in the case; but if Judge Blackstone meant to say that, in every case where debt is brought on a simple contract, the plaintiff must prove the whole debt as claimed by the declaration, or that he can recover nothing, he is opposed by every decision, ancient and modern. The old cases before mentioned, in which debt was brought and sustained, are all cases where it is impossible to suppose that the sum stated in the declaration was or could in every instance be proved, any more than it is or can be proved in actions of *indebitatus assumpsit*. They are in fact actions substantially like to actions of *indebitatus assumpsit* in the form of action for debt. The action of debt for foreign money is and can be for no determinate sum, because the value must be found by the jury, either upon the trial of the issue, or upon a writ of inquiry where there is judgment by default. Randall's Peake.

The case of Sanders *v.* Mark is debt for an uncertain sum, in which the debt claimed was for fifteen pounds, eighteen shillings and six pence, and the defendant's proportion of the whole sum was averred to be fifteen pounds, eighteen shillings and eight pence; yet the action was supported. This is plainly a case where the sum due could not be certainly averred, because the yearly value of the defendant's property might not be known to the plaintiff and could only be ascertained with certainty by the jury. In the case of Walker *v.* Witter, Lord Mansfield is express upon this point. He says that debt may be brought for a sum capable of being ascertained though not ascertained at the time of bringing the action; and he adds that it is not necessary that the plaintiff should recover the exact sum demanded. In the case of Rudder *v.* Price, Lord Loughborough, who has shed more light upon this subject than any other judge, says that long before Slade's Case the demand in an action of debt must have been for a thing certain in its nature; yet it was by no means necessary that the amount should be set out so precisely that less could not be recovered."

In short, if, before Slade's Case, debt was the common action for goods sold and work done, it is more obvious that it was not thought necessary to state the amount due with such precision as that less could not be recovered; for in those cases, as the same judge observes, "the sum due was to be ascertained by a jury, and was given in the form of damages." But yet the demand was for a thing certain in its nature; that is, it was capable of being ascertained though not ascertained, or perhaps capable of being so when the action was brought. Whence the opinion arose that, in an action of debt on a *simple contract*, the whole sum must be proved, I cannot ascertain. It certainly was not and could not be the doctrine prior to Slade's Case; and it is clear that it was not countenanced by that case. However, let the opinion have originated how it might, Lord Loughborough in the above case denominates it an erroneous opinion, and says that it has been some time since corrected.

In the case of M'Quillen *v.* Coxe the sum demanded was five thousand pounds, which was fifty more than appeared to be due by the different sums. The objection was made on a special demurrer that the declaration demanded more than appeared by the plaintiff's own showing to be due. The court did not notice the alleged variance between the writ and declaration or the mis-recital of the writ, but overruled the demurrer because the plaintiff might, in an action of debt on a simple contract, prove and recover a less sum than he demanded in the writ.

From this last expression it might be supposed that the court meant to distinguish between the sum demanded by the writ and that demanded by the declaration; but this could not have been the case, because the sum demanded by the writ and that demanded by the declaration was the same, viz., five thousand pounds. There was in fact no variance; for, though the declaration recites the writ, yet the sum demanded, and which the declaration declared to be the sum which the defendant owed and detained, was the same sum as that mentioned in the writ, and the objection stated in the special demurrer was made to the variance between the sum demanded by the declaration and the sum alleged to be due.

The distinction taken in the case of Ingledon v. Cripps, 2 Lord Ray., 815; Salk., 659, runs through all the above cases, and appears to be perfectly rational, viz., that where debt is brought on a *covenant* to pay a certain sum, any variance of the sum in the deed will vitiate. But, where the deed relates to matter of fact extrinsic, there, though the plaintiff demanded more than is due, he may enter a *remitter* for the balance. This shows that debt may be brought for more than is due, and that the jury may give less; or, if they give more than is due, the error may be corrected by a *remitter*.

§ **346.** *Debt will lie for a statutory penalty.*

Thus stands the doctrine in relation to the action of debt on contracts; and if debt will lie on a contract where the sum demanded is uncertain, it would seem to follow that it would lie for a penalty given by statute which is uncertain, and dependent upon the amount to be assessed by a jury. For, when they have assessed it, the sum so fixed becomes the amount of the penalty given. This, however, stands upon stronger ground than mere analogy. The point is expressly decided in the case of Pemberton v. Shelton, Crooke James, 498. That was an action of debt brought upon the first section of the statute (2 Ed. 6, ch. 13), which gives the treble value of the tithes due for not setting them out. The declaration claimed thirty-three pounds as the treble value; and in setting forth the value of the tithes, the whole amount appeared to be more than one-third of the sum demanded; so that the plaintiff claimed less than the penalty given by the statute. Upon *nil debet* pleaded the jury found for the plaintiff twenty pounds, and a motion was made in arrest of judgment, for the reason above mentioned. The court overruled the motion upon the ground afterwards laid down in the case of Ingledon v. Cripps. They held that there was a difference when the action of debt is grounded on a specialty or contract, which is a sum uncertain, or upon a statute which gives a certain sum for the penalty, and where it is grounded on a demand when the sum is uncertain, being such as shall be given by the jury. In the former it was agreed that the plaintiff cannot demand less than the sum agreed to be paid or given by the statute; but in the latter it is said that if the declaration varies from the real sum it is not material, for he shall not recover according to his *demand in the declaration*, but according to the verdict and judgment which may be given for the plaintiff.

§ **347.** *The demand of one sum in a declaration does not preclude the recovery of a smaller sum.*

It cannot be said that this doctrine was laid down in consequence of the court considering this as a statutory action, to which it was necessary to accommodate the recovery by changing general principles of law applicable to other cases; for it will appear, by a reference to the statute, that it prescribes no remedy for enforcing the penalty, and that debt was brought upon the common-law principle that, where a statute gives a penalty, debt may be brought to recover it.   In this case the statute gives the action of debt, and I cannot perceive in what other form than this one which has been adopted the declaration could have been drawn.   Had it claimed the smallest sum, it might have been less than the jury might have thought the United States entitled to recover; and yet judgment could not have been given for more. I know of no precedent for a declaration in debt, claiming no precise sum to be due and detained, nor any principle of law, which would sanction such a form.   On the other hand, I find abundant authority for saying that the demand of one sum does not prevent the recovery of a smaller sum, where it is diminished by extrinsic circumstances.

Rule discharged.

PERRY v. PHŒNIX ASSURANCE COMPANY.

(Circuit Court for Rhode Island: 8 Federal Reporter, 643–646. 1881.)

Opinion by COLT, J.

STATEMENT OF FACTS.— This is an action upon a policy of fire insurance. The question before us arises under a demurrer filed by the defendant to the first count in the plaintiffs' declaration.   The main points raised by the demurrer are whether the count contains sufficient averments — *First*, as to the particular account of loss; and, *second*, as to the magistrate's certificate required to be given by the policy.

The declaration, following out the terms of the policy, alleges, among other things, that the loss was payable "sixty days after notice and proof of the same, upon condition that the plaintiffs, in case of such loss, forthwith gave notice of said loss to the company, and shall, within thirty days, render a particular account of such loss, signed and sworn to by them, stating whether any and what other insurance has been made on the property, what was the value thereof, what was the plaintiff's interest therein, in what general manner said barn was occupied at the time of said fire, also were the occupants the same, and when and how the fire originated, as far as they knew or believed; and should procure a certificate under the hand and seal of a magistrate or notary public most contiguous to the place of the fire and not concerned in the loss as a creditor of the plaintiffs or otherwise, or related to them, stating that he has examined the circumstances attending the loss, knows the character and circumstances of the assured, and does verily believe that they have, by misfortune, and without fraud or evil practice, sustained loss and damage on the property insured to the amount of six hundred and nineteen dollars and seventy-five cents ($619.75)."

The plaintiffs aver the performance of these conditions as follows: "Of which loss the plaintiffs forthwith gave notice to said company, and, as soon as possible after said loss, to wit, within thirty days after said loss, to wit, on the 23d day of October, A. D. 1880, rendered the defendant a particular account of said loss, under their hands and verified by their oaths, and did also declare that no other insurance was made upon said property, and at the same time procured the certificate under the hand and seal of Frederick A. Warner, a magistrate having a seal most contiguous to the place of the fire, not concerned in said loss as a creditor or otherwise, or related to the plaintiffs, and from inquiries made by him into the circumstances and origin of said fire and as to the value of the property destroyed, and he verily believed that the plaintiffs really and by misfortune, and without fraud or evil practice, had sustained by said fire loss and damage to the amount of the sum of six hundred and nineteen dollars and seventy-five cents ($619.75); and the plaintiffs on the same day forwarded to the defendants, at their office at No. 54 William street, New York city, said certificate. And the plaintiffs further aver that thereafterwards, to wit, on the 16th day of November, 1880, and at the request of the said defendants, did procure another certificate of Benjamin M. Bosworth, Jr., a magistrate having a seal and being nearest to the place of the fire, not concerned in the loss as a creditor or otherwise, or related to the plaintiffs, and from inquiries made by him into the circumstances and origin of said fire and as to the value of the property destroyed, and he verily believes that the plaintiffs really and by misfortune, without fraud or evil practice, had sustained, by said fire, loss and damage to the amount named in said certificate,— that is, the sum of six hundred and nineteen dollars and seventy-five cents ($619.75),— which certificate is made a part of this declaration; and the plaintiffs on the same day forwarded to the defendants at their office at No. 54 William street, New York city, said amended and additional certificate as aforesaid."

Then follows the averment that the plaintiffs "have in all things kept, fulfilled and performed all things on their part to be kept, fulfilled and performed under the terms of said contracts, or in any manner connected with their said contract of insurance."

§ 348. *Failure to aver particularly the performance of a condition precedent is fatal on demurrer.*

It will be here observed that while the plaintiffs state that they "rendered the defendant a particular account of said loss, under their hands and verified by their oaths, and did also declare that no other insurance was · made upon said property," they do not aver that this account stated *what was the value of the property, what was the plaintiff's interest therein, in what general manner said barn was occupied at the time of said fire; also, were the occupants the same, and when and how the fire originated, as far as they knew or believed.* And it will further be observed that while the certificate of each of the magistrates conforms in substance to most of the requirements, yet that neither of them state that the magistrate *knows the character and circumstances of the assured,* as required by the policy. By an almost uniform current of decisions in this country and in England, extending back to the first adjudicated cases upon the subject, it has been held that provisions of this character in a policy fire insurance are conditions precedent, the performance of which must be shown to entitle the assured to recover. By this policy of insurance the company agrees to pay the loss only upon conditions that the plaintiffs do certain things which the company deems essential for its own protection. It must appear, therefore, that each and all of these acts, as set out in the contract, have been discharged, or some legal excuse for non-performance given before the plaintiffs have a right of action. Oldman *v.* Bewicke, 2 H. Bl., 577, note; Worsley *v.* Harvey, 20 Eng. Law & Eq., 541; Columbian Ins. Co. *v.* Lawrence, 2 Pet., 25, 50; also 10 Pet., 507; Wellcome *v.* People's Ins. Co., 2 Gray, 480; Campbell *v.* Charter Oak Ins. Co., 10 Allen, 213; Johnson *v.* Phœnix Ins. Co., 112 Mass., 49; Dolbier *v.* Agricultural Ins. Co., 67 Me., 180; Home Ins. Co.

v. Duke, 43 Ind., 418; Doyle *v.* Phœnix Ins. Co., 44 Cal., 265; Dawes *v.* North River Ins. Co., 7 Cow., 462; Rockford Ins. Co. *v.* Nelson, 65 Ill., 415, 418; May, Ins., § 586; Phil. Ins., § 2026. And the failure to aver performance is fatal on demurrer.

Chitty on Pleading, volume 1, page 327, says: "The omission of averment of performance of a condition precedent, or of an excuse for the non-performance, is fatal on demurrer." See, also, Home Ins. Co. *v.* Duke, 43 Ind., 418; Dolbier *v.* Agricultural Ins. Co., 67 Me., 180. The plaintiffs contend, however, that the subsequent general averment that they have performed all things by them to be performed by the terms of the contract is of itself sufficient. But the rule of the common law, as established by the foregoing and other authorities, is clearly the other way. That rule is as Chitty expresses it (p. 985, note *k*): "But if there be anything specific or particular in the thing to be performed, though consisting of a number of acts, performance of each must be particularly stated."

§ **349.** *General averment of performance of conditions precedent insufficient.*

The plaintiffs also argue that it was not necessary for them to aver performance of the various provisions which by the terms of the policy are required to be stated in the particular account, but that their simple allegation that they have rendered the defendant a particular account is sufficient. The policy declares that the particular account must contain statements as to other insurance, value of property, interest of assured, manner the building was occupied at time of fire, who were the occupants, when and how the fire originated. Now it can hardly be said that an averment of performance which simply states that a particular account has been rendered, and only affirming one of the particulars, that relating to other insurance, is enough; because, from all that appears, the account may not have contained anything relating to the other material facts, and consequently upon the face of the declaration a case has not been made out.

It was held in Catlin *v.* Springfield Ins. Co., 1 Sumn., 434, that the words "a particular account of such loss or damage" meant, of themselves, simply a particular account of the articles lost or damaged, and in no way referred to the manner or cause of loss. The legal import, therefore, of these words does not embrace the other important facts called for under this head by this policy, and we are forced, therefore, to the conclusion that the allegation is insufficient. There can be no question but what the magistrate's certificate must be such as the condition requires. Columbian Ins. Co. *v.* Lawrence, 2 Pet., 50; Johnson *v.* Phœnix Ins. Co., 112 Mass., 49.

By the failure in this case to aver knowledge of the character and circumstances of the assured as laid down in the policy, the condition is not complied with. The demurrer is therefore sustained.

TUCKER *v.* LEE.

(Circuit Court for the District of Columbia: 3 Cranch, C. C., 684–692. 1829.)

STATEMENT OF FACTS.— Action against a surety in an appeal bond. Demurrer to declaration because the breach of the condition was not sufficiently assigned.

§ **350.** *How breaches of the condition of a bond must be assigned. Cases cited.*

Opinion by CRANCH, J.

Upon bonds with collateral condition, the plaintiff must, under the statute of 8 & 9 W. 3, chapter 11, section 8, assign the breach or breaches upon which he intends to recover. Hardy v. Bern, 5 T. R., 636; Wilmer v. Harris, 5 Har. & J., 1; 1 Saund., 58, n. 1; 2 Saund., 187a, n. 2. And if he undertakes to set them out in his declaration they must be as precisely averred as in a replication; and if they are all insufficiently set out the declaration must be adjudged bad upon demurrer. T. Jones, 125; Rea v. Burnis, 2 Lev., 124; Anonymous, Ilardres, 320. But if there be one good breach well set out, the demurrer, if to the whole declaration, must be overruled. Gordon v. Kennedy, 2 Binn., 287; 1 Chitty, Pl., 326, n. 1; Adams v. Willoughby, 6 John., 65. Although if some of the breaches assigned be insufficient, and there should be a general verdict for the plaintiff, the judgment would be arrested. Fletcher v. Peck, 6 Cranch, 87.

The counsel for the defendant supposes that the breach assigned in this declaration is insufficient, because it does not set forth specially the damages which the plaintiff has sustained by reason of the judgments not being satisfied and paid after the affirmance in the supreme court.

§ 351. *In an action on an appeal bond the breach assigned must be a single breach, denying each alternative.*

The counsel for the plaintiff contends that there are two breaches assigned in the declaration, namely, that the plaintiff in error "did not prosecute his writ to effect;" "and that he did not answer the damages and costs of the said Henry to the said Henry adjudged by the said supreme court;" and that the first breach is certainly well assigned.

To prosecute his writ to effect is the same thing as to make his plea good. He was not bound to prosecute his writ to effect and also to answer all damages and costs; for he could not prosecute his writ to effect unless he should make his plea good; and if he made his plea good he is not bound to answer the damages and costs.

The condition of the bond, then, is really alternative; so that if the plaintiff in error either prosecuted his writ to effect, or made his plea good, which is the same thing, or answered all damages and costs, the plaintiff has no cause of action.

The breach to be assigned, therefore, must be a single breach, denying each alternative; that is, it must aver that the plaintiff in error did not prosecute his writ to effect, nor make his plea good, nor answer the damages and costs, which damages and costs the plaintiff must set forth specially; for the plaintiff must have sustained damages and costs before the condition can be broken by the non-payment of them.

§ 352. *What are the damages for which the plaintiff in error may be responsible to the defendant in error.*

The condition is not to "answer the damages and costs of the said Henry to the said Henry adjudged in the supreme court," as averred in the declaration. In the case of Catlett v. Brodie, 9 Wheat., 554, the supreme court says: "It has been supposed, at the argument, that the act meant only to provide for such damages and costs as the court should adjudge for the delay; but our opinion is that this is not the true interpretation of the language. The word 'damages' is here used, not as descriptive of the nature of the claim upon which the original judgment is founded, but as descriptive of the indemnity which the defendant is entitled to if the judgment is affirmed. Whatever losses he may sustain by the judgments not being satisfied and paid after the affirmance, these are the damages which he has sustained, and for which the bond ought to give good and sufficient security. Upon any suit brought upon such bond, it follows, of course, that the obligors are at liberty to show that no damages have been sustained, or partial damages only; for which amount only is the obligee entitled to judgment."

It is clear, then, that by the condition of this bond the plaintiff in error is not bound, at all events, to answer the damages adjudged to the defendant in error in the supreme court; and yet the breach assigned is that he has not answered them, and them only. By the decision of the supreme court in Catlett *v.* Brodie he is only to indemnify the defendant in error for whatever losses he may have sustained by the judgment's not being satisfied and paid after the affirmance.

§ 353. *Damages and costs must be made to appear in the allegation of the breach.*

What those losses were is not stated in the declaration, nor can they be judiciously ascertained by any allegation therein. It is not even averred that the plaintiff has sustained any loss for which the defendant is bound to indemnify him. If the breach vary from the sense and substance of the contract, and either be more limited or larger than the covenant, it will be insufficient. 1 Chitty, Pleading, 328. The declaration avers only a single breach, although that breach consists of two negatives; for it was necessary to deny both branches of the alternative condition in order to show a breach. It is bad because it avers that the plaintiff has not done what he was not bound to do; and does not deny that he has done what he was bound to do. Before the defendant can be made liable to the penalty of the bond, for not answering the damages and costs, those damages and costs must be made to appear at least in the allegation of the breach. They are not such as the law implies, and which it is not necessary to state in the declaration, because they are presumptions of law; but they are special damages which must exist before a cause of action can accrue to the plaintiff.

This idea is strongly stated by Mr. Chitty (Civil Pleadings, 385, 386): "General damages," he says, "are such as the law implies to have accrued from the wrong complained of; special damages are such as really took place and are not implied by law. It does not appear necessary to state the former description of damages in the declaration, because presumptions of law are not, in general, to be pleaded. But when the law does not necessarily imply that the plaintiff sustained damage by the act complained of, it is essential to the validity of the declaration that the resulting damage should be shown with particularity."

And again, in page 389, he says, "if the action be not sustainable, independently of special damage, the declaration would be bad on demurrer or in arrest of judgment."

The plaintiff in error is not bound absolutely to prosecute his writ to effect or to make his plea good, and therefore the law does not necessarily imply damages for not doing it. The condition of the bond gives him another alternative, which, as construed by the supreme court, is to indemnify him for whatever losses he may sustain by the judgment's not being satisfied after affirmance. These are losses which must arise before the bond can be forfeited, and must, therefore, be set out in the breach. The only damages which the law would necessarily imply, in this case, would be the damages for not paying the damages actually contracted to be paid. Whenever the amount of these shall be ascertained, the condition of this bond will be equivalent to a condition to pay that sum of money, and, in that case, the only damages which the law would imply would be the damages for the non-payment of that sum.

We are, therefore, of opinion that the breach of the condition of this bond is not well assigned and that the judgment upon the demurrer ought to be for the defendant.

§ 354. *Certainty of allegation.*

There is another objection to the assignment of the breach, and that is that it says "the said Peter did not answer the damages," etc. It might be true that he did not answer the damages and costs on the first day after the affirmance, and yet he might have answered them before the suit brought, so that the plaintiff might not have had a cause of action at the time of bringing the suit. This does not seem to be "certainty to a common intent." However, our opinion is not founded upon this defect.

[After the declaration had, by leave of the court, been amended, the defendant pleaded five pleas, to the first, third and fourth of which demurrers were filed, issue being joined on the second and fifth.]

§ 355. *A plea is bad which purports to be a plea to the whole declaration, but covers only a part.*

Opinion by CRANCH, J.

As to the first plea: The words "after the signing and sealing of the said writing obligatory, in the declaration mentioned and," may be rejected as surplusage, for they are not at all necessary to the validity of the plea. But the plea is bad because it purports to be a plea to the whole declaration and yet covers only a part. The damages alleged in the declaration, the non-payment of which constitutes the breach assigned, consists not only of the $4,616.96, with interest from the 22d of December, 1820, till paid, but of the costs of suit in the circuit court and in the supreme court. The plea does not state the payment of that part of the damages which consists of those costs. It only avers the payment of the whole original debt due by H. Lee, the elder, to Tucker, of which those costs did not constitute a part. It does not aver that the payment made by Jett to Tucker was made for or on account of Beverly; nor that it was made or received in discharge of the judgment of Tucker against Beverly; nor in full of the damages, which plaintiff is entitled to recover under the bond upon which this action is founded. The plea does not expressly aver that any debt was ever due by H. Lee, the elder, to Tucker; nor that Jett and Beverly were bound to Tucker for any debt due to him by the said Lee. It only avers that they were bound to the plaintiff as "securities" for the said Lee, but for what object or purpose does not appear. It does not aver that they were jointly bound, nor bound at the same time, nor that each was bound for the whole; so that it does not appear what right Jett had to pay for Beverly, or what right Beverly had to appropriate to himself the payment made to Jett. Jett may have originally been sole surety for Lee to Tucker, and Beverly may have come in afterward to release Jett. They might have been not simultaneous, but successive sureties. These are possibilities which are left open by the plea, and show that there is not enough stated in the plea to give Beverly a right to avail himself of the payment made by Jett. But if he could, or even if Beverly himself had paid the original debt and interest due by Lee to Tucker, it would be no answer to the present action so long as the judgment against Beverly remained unsatisfied; it would be only matter of argument to show that the plaintiff had sustained no damage covered by the bond upon which this suit is brought.

We are, therefore, of opinion that upon this demurrer the judgment ought to be for the plaintiff.

§ 356. *A plea of non damnificatus is not good if the breach has been specially assigned.*

The third plea is a general *non damnificatus;* that is, "That from the time of making the bond to the day of the commencement of this action the plaintiff was not damnified by reason of anything in the condition of the said writing obligatory mentioned; and this the defendant is ready to verify," etc. The plea does not state that the plaintiff was not damnified by anything in the declaration alleged; nor in manner and form as the plaintiff has averred in his declaration. If he had done so it would have been a direct denial of the gist of the count, and ought to have concluded to the country and not with a verification.

The plea, perhaps, might have been good if the condition of the bond and a special breach of that condition had not been set forth in the declaration. But it is now no answer to the declaration, setting forth such a breach, to say that the plaintiff is not damnified by reason of any thing in the condition mentioned.

The general forms of the plea of *non damnificatus* given in 2 Chitty, 480, 481, are to declarations in which no particular breach nor any particular damages are set forth. So also is the plea in Cutler *v.* Southern, in 1 Saund., 116. This general way of pleading is bad upon special demurrer, even to a declaration for non-payment of the penalty. 1 Saund., 116, note 1. And there is no case where it has been permitted after the assignment of a special breach; for the only design of the general plea of *non damnificatus* is to force the plaintiff to assign a breach of the condition; but when the breach is specially assigned the plea must answer the special assignment. Williams, in his note to 1 Saund., 116, says, "but in all cases of conditions to indemnify and save harmless the proper plea is *non damnificatus;* and if there be any damage the plaintiff must reply it." This shows that the general plea is to precede, not to follow, the special assignment.

§ 357. *Where a condition is in the disjunctive the plea should show which part has been performed.*

But the condition of this bond is, in effect, in the disjunctive. It is to prosecute his writ to effect (that is, to make his plea good), and, if he fail to make his plea good, to answer all damages and costs; and whenever the condition is in the disjunctive, the defendant must, by his plea, show which he has performed. Co. Lit., 303, b.

We are, therefore, of opinion that this third plea is bad, to this declaration; and that the judgment, upon this demurrer also, ought to be for the plaintiff.

§ 358. *Where a plea is not a direct denial of an averment in the declaration it should conclude with a verification.*

The fourth plea is "that another person, to wit, one William S. Jett, hath answered, satisfied and paid to the said plaintiff the said damages, and of this the said defendant puts himself on the country."

To this plea there is a special demurrer. 1st. Because it concludes to the country when it ought to conclude with a verification. 2d. Because, if good, it amounts to the plea of payment, and ought to have been so pleaded.

This plea concludes to the country, as if it were a direct denial of a material allegation in the declaration. The averment to which it purports to be an answer is, "nor did he, nor has he, the said Peter R., or any other person for him, answered, satisfied or paid, though often requested," "the damages and costs sustained by the plaintiff," etc.

The plea does not say that the said Jett paid the damages for the said Beverly, or at his request; nor does it state any facts which show a right in Jett to pay the damages for Beverly, or any right in Beverly to claim the benefit of that payment.

The plea is not a denial of any material fact averred in the declaration, and, therefore, ought not to have concluded to the country. It is therefore bad on general and special demurrer.

The court is of opinion that the judgment upon this demurrer ought also to be for the plaintiff.

BURNETT v. WYLIE.

(Superior Court for the Territory of Arkansas: Hempstead, 197–201. 1832.)

Opinion of the COURT.

STATEMENT OF FACTS.— This is an action of debt, brought by Wylie against Burnett in the Chicot circuit court, upon the following obligation and condition annexed: "Know all men by these presents, that we, John J. Bowie, as principal, and Wm. B. Patton and Moses Burnett, as securities, are held and firmly bound unto Edward Wylie in the sum of $700, lawful money of the United States, to be collected of, as on the following conditions, namely: whereas the said Bowie has this day bargained and sold unto the said Wylie seven hundred acres of Spanish confirmed land claims; now, if the said Bowie should make good and sufficient title to him, the said Wylie, to the aforesaid land, then in that case the above obligation is to be void, otherwise to remain in full force." Which writing is by oyer made part of the record.

The defendant in the court below, having by consent withdrawn his pleas of payment, waived oyer of the writing declared on, and filed a general demurrer to the declaration, which was by the court overruled and judgment rendered against him for $700 and costs, has appealed to this court.

The principal ground of error relied upon by the counsel for the appellant is that the plaintiff in the court below failed to assign breaches of the condition of the writing obligatory on which the action is founded, and that judgment was rendered without a writ of inquiry or the intervention of a jury.

Our legislature, at its last legislature, adopted and re-enacted the statute of William 3, chapter 11, section 8, under the title of "An act concerning suits on penal bonds and other writings under seal." This statute has also been long since re-enacted in the states of New York, Virginia and Kentucky. The adjudications, then, in England and in those states upon this statute will be regarded by this court as high authority.

§ 859. *Assignment of breaches, when necessary.*

In the case of Van Benthuysen v. De Witt, 4 Johns., 213, the supreme court of New York say: "In suits on bonds for the performance of covenants it is compulsory on the part of the plaintiff to assign breaches and have his damages assessed; and when breaches are assigned, the jury at the trial must assess damages for such breaches as the plaintiff shall prove; otherwise the verdict is erroneous, and a *venire facias de novo* will be awarded. 5 Term R.,

636; 2 Caines, 329; 2 Wils. R., 377. It is now settled in England, New York, Virginia and Kentucky that in debt on bonds, with a condition for doing anything else except the payment of a gross sum of money, or the appearance of a defendant in a bail bond, the plaintiff is bound to suggest breaches, either in his declaration, replication or on the roll of record." 1 Saund., 58, n. 1, by Williams, 2; id., 187; Collins v. Collins, 2 Burr., 820; 5 Term R., 538; 8 id., 126; 2 Hen. & Munf. R., 446; 1 Bibb, 242.

The learned editor of Johnson's Reports, in a note to the case before mentioned of Van Benthuysen v. De Witt (2d ed.), lays down the law on this subject, which entirely accords with our own views. He says: "The plaintiff may assign breaches (either one or more) in his declaration, or he may leave the assignment to be made afterwards in consequence of the plea; as, if the defendant pleads performance of the covenant, the plaintiff may set forth his breaches in his replication; or, where the defendant pleads *non est factum*, or judgment be given against him on demurrer, *nil dicit*, or confession, and the plaintiff has not assigned breaches in his declaration, he may, notwithstanding, suggest breaches on the record; and the suggestion may be made as well before as after the entry of the judgment. The judgment to be entered is to recover the penalty of the bond, nominal damages and costs; and if judgment be entered for the damages assessed by the jury it is so far erroneous, and will be reversed as to the damages, and the execution is of course to levy the amount of the judgment, but is indorsed to levy only the damages assessed for the breaches of covenant, together with the costs." In support of these positions numerous authorities are cited.

§ 360. *In an action on a bond with collateral conditions breaches must be assigned and damages assessed by a jury.*

If, then, the present action is founded on a penal bond for the performance of anything else than the payment of a gross sum of money, or the appearance of the defendant in a bail bond (and it is clearly not for either of these), it was incumbent on the plaintiff, after the demurrer to his declaration had been overruled, to assign or suggest a breach or breaches of the covenant contained in the condition of the obligation declared on, and have the damages assessed by a jury upon a writ of inquiry; and for his failure to proceed in this manner we are clearly of opinion that the judgment is erroneous and must be reversed.

It has been argued by the counsel for the plaintiff with great earnestness and zeal that this is not an action brought upon a penalty for non-performance of an agreement or covenant contained in any indenture, deed or writing. By inspecting the writing obligatory, as set out upon oyer, it is manifest that it is a penal bond for the conveyance, by a good, sufficient title, of seven hundred acres of Spanish confirmed land claims. To illustrate this proposition by reasoning would seem to be difficult, since it appears to us to be self-evident. The language used is clear, plain and unambiguous. The obligors bind themselves to pay to the plaintiff $700, conditioned to be void if one of them should make to the plaintiff a good and sufficient title to seven hundred acres of Spanish confirmed land claims which he had that day bargained and sold to the plaintiff, otherwise to remain in force. The plain intention of the parties to this contract is to secure by a penalty, namely, $700, the conveyance, by a good title, of seven hundred acres of Spanish confirmed land claims.

Let us advert to the condition of the bond on which the action was brought in the case of Ramsey v. Matthews, 1 Bibb, 242. It is in these words: "The condition of the above obligation is such, that whereas the above-named Ramsey has hired two negroes of the said Matthews for one year, and for $100 each, to be paid at the end of the year, and to find said negroes in clothing, etc., pay their taxes, and return said negroes at the end of the year to the said Matthews; now, if the said Ramsey does and shall well and truly pay, do and perform, etc., then this obligation to be void." How or in what particular does the condition differ from the condition of the bond before the court? The condition of the present bond is, "Now if the said Bowie should make a good and sufficient title to him, the said Wylie, to the aforesaid land, namely, seven hundred acres of Spanish confirmed land claims, then the above obligation to be void." There is no substantial difference in these two bonds; and Judge Trimble and the whole court held that the obligation in the case of Ramsey v. Matthews was to be regarded as a bond with collateral conditions, in which the law requires breaches to be assigned.

We abstain from further remarks on a question which to us appears so free from doubt. The other objection taken to the declaration we deem untenable.

Judgment reversed.

WILCOX v. COHN.

(Circuit Court for New York: 5 Blatchford, 346–348. 1866.)

Action of covenant. Defendant demurred specially to the declaration on the ground that there was no breach properly stated.

§ 361. *Rules of pleading to be observed in declaring upon a covenant.*

Opinion by SHIPMAN, J.

The rules of pleading by which the issue raised by this demurrer is to be determined are very plain and elementary. In order to avoid prolixity, so much of the covenant as is essential to the cause of action should be set forth and no more. Distinct breaches of separate covenants in the deed may be assigned in the same count. It is sufficient if the breach be assigned in words which contain the sense and substance of the covenant. The breach may be assigned according to the legal effect, or in the words of the deed. When the right of action depends upon a condition precedent, its performance must be averred; but it is never necessary to anticipate and negative matters of defense, such as payment, waiver, discharge, etc.

STATEMENT OF FACTS.—The covenant, for the breach of which this action is brought, is set forth in the declaration as follows: "Nothing in this license contained shall be construed to authorize or permit the said licensee to use the said clasping machine for any other purpose than his own business of manufacturing hoop skirts, to hire the said machine to others, or to suffer any other person to use the said machine gratuitously or for a consideration; and nothing in this license contained shall be construed to authorize, permit or license the said licensee to construct or vend a machine embodying said inventions of the said Maine and said Deforest and said Baird, or either of them, or to have one or more of said machines constructed for him." The next succeeding clause of the deed states the damages agreed upon by the parties for a violation of the foregoing covenant, and it is therein stipulated that the defendant shall pay $500, as liquidated damages, "for each and every machine which the said licensee shall use, or permit another to use, and the same sum for each and every machine which the said licensee shall construct or vend, or procure to be constructed." The machines here referred to are plainly machines other than the machine furnished to the defendant by the plaintiff. These two clauses of the deed are to be construed together, and the latter is somewhat explanatory of the former. Thus construing these clauses, it follows that the defendant would violate the covenant contained in them if he should construct or vend a machine, or cause one or more to be constructed for him, or should use, or permit another to use, a machine constructed by him, or which he had caused to be constructed for himself.

§ 362. *It is sufficient if the breach be assigned in words which contain the sense and substance of the covenant.*

The breach alleged is that the defendant "had and procured three machines, embracing the inventions set forth in said letters patent, to be made and constructed, and did use said three machines, and permit the same to be used." The pleader here states, with certainty to a common intent, which is sufficient in a declaration, and by a fair intendment, that the defendant caused three of these machines to be constructed for himself, and that he used the same. It is explicitly stated that the defendant used the machines, and this alone would constitute a breach of a covenant in the deed. A breach is assigned in words which contain the sense and substance of the covenant, and according to its legal effect.

§ 363. *Matters of defense need not be anticipated.*

It was unnecessary for the pleader to allege that the machines were not procured from the plaintiff by the defendant, or that the defendant had not paid the stipulated damages. These are matters of defense to the action. The demurrer is therefore overruled.

ROBINS v. POPE.

(Superior Court for the Territory of Arkansas: Hempstead, 219-221. 1833.)

Opinion of the Court.

STATEMENT OF FACTS.— This is an action of debt brought in the Phillips circuit court by the governor, for the use of Homer, as administrator *de bonis non* of Wm. H. Smith, deceased, upon the administration bond given by Sylvanus Phillips, the prior administrator of Smith, with Robins and Reece as his securities.

The defendants Robins and Reece, who were alone sued, failed to enter their appearance, and a judgment by default was taken against them at the January term, 1832, of said court, and a writ of inquiry and final judgment at the same term given for the plaintiff for the sum of $663.81. From this judgment a writ of error is prosecuted into this court. Several errors have been assigned as causes for the reversal of the judgment, some of which only will be noticed.

§ 364. *A declaration against some of joint obligors must aver that all have failed to pay.*

The first objection taken is as to the sufficiency of the declaration. Two only of three obligors are sued; the breach is that the defendants have not paid the sum demanded. It is insisted that the breach, as laid, should be as broad as the obligation, and that, as all are bound to pay, it should be averred that all have failed to pay. This objection seems to us to be valid; it may be true that the defendants in this suit may not have discharged the obligation, and that Phillips, who is not sued, may have discharged it or obtained a release from it. The declaration, then, should aver that neither Phillips nor the defendants have paid it. 1 Chitty, 327, 328; Com. Dig., tit. Pleader, 647. The want of such allegation might be cured by a plea of the defendants to the merits, and verdict founded upon a regular issue. But we deem the objection fatal when judgment by default has been rendered.

§ 365. *Writ of inquiry, when to be executed.*

A second objection taken is that the writ of inquiry was improperly executed at the term of the court at which the judgment by default was had. The law contained in Geyer's Digest, page 251, section 7, directs that writs of inquiry should be executed at the next succeeding term after an interlocutory judgment is given. The act of November 21, 1829 (Acts, p. 23), seems to be confined exclusively to cases in which pleadings are made up by the parties. We are of opinion that it does not repeal the provisions of the prior act, and that there is error also in the proceedings of the court below.

§ 366. *Breaches of bond must be assigned before judgment by default.*

A third error assigned is that the breaches of the bond were not assigned till after the judgment by default. This no doubt would be error if the fact were so, and this court has so decided at a former term in the case of Wiley *v.* Burnett. But the record in this case is made out so imperfectly that we cannot say with certainty whether the assignment of breaches was filed before or after the judgment by default. If filed afterwards it will be incumbent on the plaintiff to amend his proceedings in this particular likewise.

For the reasons above stated we think the judgment should be reversed and the cause remanded for further proceedings not inconsistent with the opinion here expressed.   *Judgment reversed.*

DAY v. CHISM.

(10 Wheaton, 449–454. 1825.)

ERROR to U. S. Circuit Court, District of Tennessee.

Opinion by MARSHALL, C. J.

STATEMENT OF FACTS.—This is an action of covenant brought by the heirs and devisees of Nathaniel Day, in the court for the seventh circuit, for the district of Tennessee, on a covenant contained in a deed from the defendant to the said Nathaniel Day, purporting to convey a tract of land therein mentioned. The declaration, which contains six counts, states the covenant in the fourth, in the following words: That the said Obadiah Chism, the defendant, " then and there, by the said indenture, covenanted and agreed with the said Nathaniel Day, his heirs and assigns, to warrant and defend the title to the said premises against the claim of all and every other person whatsoever, as his own proper right in fee-simple." In the fifth count the covenant alleged is, "to warrant and defend the land against all and every person whatever."

In some of the counts the only breach assigned is want of title in the defendant. The fourth and fifth counts charge that " the said Obadiah, the defendant, hath not kept and performed his covenant so made with the said Nathaniel aforesaid, with the said Nathaniel in his life-time, nor with the plaintiffs since his death, but hath broken it in this, that he hath not warranted and defended the title to said premises, described in said covenant, against all and every person whatsoever, to said Nathaniel Day, his heirs and assigns; and also in this, that the said Obadiah had no title to said tract of land, but it was vested in the state of Tennessee; and the said plaintiffs aver that, by reason of said want of title in said Obadiah, the said Nathaniel, in his life-time, and the plaintiffs since his death, were unable to obtain possession thereof, or to derive any benefit therefrom; and also in this, that the said Obadiah had not a good and sufficient title to the said tract of land, and by reason thereof the said plaintiffs were ousted and dispossessed of the said premises by due course of law; and also in this, that the said Obadiah had no title to the said premises, but the same was in the state of North Carolina, by reason whereof the said Nathaniel, in his life-time, and the plaintiffs since his death, were and are unable to obtain possession of the said premises."

The defendant demurred to the declaration, and assigned for cause of demurrer that, 1. "It does not appear in and by the said declaration, any averment or allegation therein, that the said plaintiffs have been evicted by a title paramount to the title of the defendant; and 2. The said declaration is, in other respects, defective, uncertain and informal."

§ 367. *Proper averment of eviction by paramount title.*

The covenant stated in the declaration is, we think, a covenant of warranty, and not a covenant of seizin, or that the vendor has title. In an action on such a covenant it is undoubtedly necessary to allege, substantially, an eviction by title paramount, but we do not think that any formal words are prescribed in which this allegation is to be made. It is not necessary to say in terms that the plaintiff has been evicted by a title paramount to that of the defendants. In this case we think such an eviction is averred substantially. The plaintiffs aver "that the said Obadiah had not a good and sufficient title to the said tract of land; and by reason thereof the said plaintiffs were ousted and dispossessed of the said premises by due course of law." This averment, we think, contains all the facts which constitute an eviction by title paramount. The person who, from want of title, is dispossessed and ousted by due course of law, must, we think, be evicted by title paramount. We think, then, that the special cause assigned for the demurrer will not sustain it.

§ 367a. *When plaintiff declares as heir or devisee, omission to show how he derived his title is a formal defect only.*

There are other defects in the declaration which are supposed by the counsel for the defendants in error to be sufficient to support the judgment. The plaintiffs claim both as heirs and devisees, and do not show in particular how they are heirs, nor do they set out the will.

It is undoubtedly true that their title cannot be in both characters, and that the will, if it passes the estate differently from what it would pass at law, defeats their title as heirs. But a man may devise lands to his heirs, and the statement that they are his heirs, as well as his devisees, though not a strictly artificial mode of declaring, is an error of form and not of substance. Of the same character is, we think, the omission to state how the plaintiffs are heirs, or to set out the will. Although, in the case of Denham v. Stephenson, 1 Salk., 355; 6 Mod., 241, the court says, "that where H. sues as heir he must show his pedigree, and *coment heres*, for it lies in his proper knowledge," the court does not say that the omission to do this would be fatal on a general demurrer, or that it is an error in substance. The plaintiff must show how he is heir on the trial; and the thirty-second section of the judiciary act of 1789, chapter 20, applies, we think, to omissions of this description. The judgment may be given "according to the right of the cause, and matter in law," although the declaration may not show whether the plaintiff is the son or brother of his ancestor, or may not set out the will at large. An averment

that he is the heir or the devisee avers substantially a valid title, which it is
incumbent on him to prove at the trial.

§ 368. *When repugnant breaches are assigned in the same count, one of them,
if immaterial, may be rejected.*

The declaration presents another objection, respecting which the court has
felt considerable difficulty. In the same count breaches are assigned which
are directly repugnant to each other. The plaintiffs allege that, from the defect of title in the vendor, they have not been able to obtain possession of the
premises; and also that they have been dispossessed of those premises by due
course of law. These averments are in opposition to each other. But the
allegation that possession has never been obtained is immaterial, because not
a breach of the covenant, and, the majority of the court is disposed to think,
may be disregarded on a general demurrer.

It is the opinion of the court that the fourth and fifth counts, however informal, have substance enough in them to be maintained against a general
demurrer, and that the judgment must be reversed and the cause remanded
for further proceedings. It will be in the power of the circuit court to allow
the parties to amend their pleadings.

Judgment reversed accordingly.

HAZEL v. WATERS.

(Circuit Court for the District of Columbia: 3 Cranch, C. C., 682–684. 1829.)

Opinion by CRANCH, J.

STATEMENT OF FACTS.— The court has again looked into this case, at the request of the plaintiff's counsel, who has referred us to the case of Minor v. The
Mechanics' Bank of Alexandria, 1 Pet., 67, and supposes that the averment in
the declaration, that by reason of the breach of the condition of the bond, set
forth in the declaration, the plaintiff is entitled to recover the penalty, and
that the defendant has not paid the penalty, is a sufficient setting forth of a
breach of the condition upon demurrer, although the breach of the condition,
as set forth in the declaration, should of itself be insufficient.

§ 369. *The averment of the non-payment of the penalty does not show a
breach of the condition.*

But that case is not applicable to the present. In that case there was a
general plea of performance, and the replication put in issue the whole matter of defense; and the verdict, being general and for the plaintiff, found the
general breach as set forth in the replication. It is true that the court said,
in that case, that the declaration assigned "a good breach, by the non-payment of the penal sum stated in the bond;" but that cannot mean a breach of
the condition of the bond, for it was no part of the condition that the penalty
should be paid. It is evident that by the word "breach" in that sentence
the judge must have meant a cause of action. The declaration in that case did
set forth a good cause of action. It set forth the bond without its condition,
and averred the non-payment of the penalty as the cause of action. In the
present case the condition is set forth in the declaration, which shows that no
cause of action existed, unless there was a breach of that condition; and if,
after setting forth the condition in the declaration, the plaintiff does not, in
the declaration, show a breach of the condition, the mere averment of non-
payment of the penalty does not show a cause of action.

In Minor's Case, the judge, in delivering the opinion of the supreme court, said: "That in a declaration upon a covenant for general performance of duty, if no breach be assigned, or a breach which is bad, as not being in point of law within the scope of the covenant, the defect is fatal, even after verdict."

When the declaration itself sets out the condition of the bond, it is then like a declaration upon a covenant; and the law, as laid down by the judge, is exactly applicable to such a case.

The court, therefore, is still of the opinion that the declaration will not support a judgment for the plaintiff. Judgment arrested.

§ 870. **Allegation of breach of a bond.**—A breach alleged in the terms of the bond is sufficient. Berger v. Williams, 4 McL., 577.

§ 871. Where a breach of the conditions of a penal bond constitutes the basis of the plaintiff's action, it should be assigned with certainty and particularity, so as to show the injury. Campbell v. Strong, Hemp., 265.

§ 872. It is not necessary that a breach of covenant should be assigned in the very words of the covenant. It is sufficient if it show a substantial breach. Fletcher v. Peck, 6 Cr., 87.

§ 873. The declaration on a bond of indemnity must show that the plaintiff has been damnified. Coe v. Rankin, 5 McL., 354.

§ 874. In declaring against principal and sureties on an official bond, which was given after the principal had entered upon his official duties, when the breach alleged is that the principal has failed to account for moneys received by him, it must be alleged that the moneys were in hand at the time the bond was given, or were received by the principal thereafter. United States v. Linn, 1 How., 104.

§ 875. In a declaration on a replevin bond à breach assigned "that the suit was not prosecuted with effect" is sufficient. Gorman v. Lenox,* 15 Pet., 115.

§ 876. Where covenant was brought upon the bond itself, and the breach assigned was the non-performance of a collateral condition inserted therein, it was held bad on demurrer. United States v. Brown, 1 Paine, 422.

§ 877. Upon a submission by one partner of all matters in controversy between the partnership and the person entering into the agreement of reference, an award was made directing the payment of money, and in an action on the bond to abide by the award the breach assigned was that the partner who agreed to the reference did not pay. That is a sufficient assignment of a breach, as he only who agreed to the reference was bound to pay. Karthaus v. Ferrer, 1 Pet., 222.

§ 878. In an action upon an appeal bond to the supreme court of the United States, in setting forth the breach of the condition it must be averred that the plaintiff has sustained damages to a certain amount by the defendant's not making his plea good. Bank of the Metropolis v. Swann, 4 Cr. C. C., 139.

§ 879. The assignment of breaches in an action upon an embargo bond is a very important part of the declaration; and, upon demurrer to the declaration, the plaintiff's attorney will not be permitted to strike out the assignment of breaches, on the ground that the declaration is good without it. Dixon v. United States, 1 Marsh., 177.

§ 880. **When the maker of bonds** sued upon is a county, which has no general power to make such instruments, and can only make them by virtue of special authority, such authority should appear by averment of the act creating it, or by stating the recital of the bond in that respect. Kennard v. Cass County,* 8 Dill., 147.

§ 881. A bona fide holder for value of county bonds, negotiable in their character, is not bound, when suing in the federal courts, to allege in his declaration the election or other facts showing a compliance with the preliminary steps required of the officers before they are authorized to issue and deliver the bonds. Such facts may be pleaded in defense. It is not necessary to attach the bonds to the declaration when the coupons are sued upon. Railroad Co. v. Otoe County, 1 Dill., 338.

§ 882. **Consideration, allegation of—Arrest of judgment.**—Judgment will not be arrested, where no consideration is specially alleged, if the instrument declared on purports a consideration, or shows upon its face that the *assumpsit* was for a valuable consideration. Kemble v. Lull, 3 McL., 272.

§ 883. **Covenant on policy—Abandonment, averment of.**—It is not necessary, in an action of covenant on a policy, that the declaration should aver that the plaintiff had abandoned to the underwriters. Hodgson v. The Marine Ins. Co. of Alexandria, 5 Cr., 100.

§ 884. A separate breach of a contract should be pleaded as a separate cause of action. William v. Hallett,* 2 Saw., 263.

§ 385. Dependent or concurrent covenants — Averment of performance by plaintiff.—
When the covenants in an agreement are dependent or concurrent the plaintiff must aver
and prove performance, or an offer to perform the covenants on his part; and to ascertain
what covenants are of this description, the intention of the parties is to be sought for rather
in the order of time in which the acts are to be done than from the structure of the instrument. Goodwin v. Lynn, 4 Wash., 714.

§ 386. Suit on bonds by indorsee — Performance of terms and conditions, averment of.—
If a township is authorized to issue bonds, and does so, and a person who has purchased them
when circulating as commercial securities brings suit upon them, performance of the terms
and conditions which appear on their face need only be averred in the declaration to make it
good on demurrer. Conditions preliminary to the issue of the bonds need not be set forth, as
these conditions, if of any avail, must be set up by the defendant. Lincoln v. Iron Co., 13
Otto, 412.

§ 387. Breach of agreement to lease by lessor — Allegations by lessee.— In a declaration
upon an agreement by way of lease, by which the lessor stipulated to let a farm from January 1, 1820, to remove the former tenant, and that the lessee should have the tenancy and
occupation of the farm from that day free from all hindrance, the assignment or breaches
was that, although specially requested on said January 1st, the defendant refused and neglected to turn out the former tenant, who was then, or had been, in the possession and occupancy of the land, and to deliver possession thereof to the plaintiff. This assignment is
sufficient. It is sufficient that the averment should state the plaintiff's readiness and offer,
and his request on January 1st, generally, and not at the last convenient hour of that day;
and if an averment of a personal demand is made it need not have been on the land. Carroll
v. Peake, 1 Pet., 18.

§ 388. Mutilation of bond — Averments in declaring thereon.— If a bond be mutilated
by the obligee by mistake or in fraud of the obligor, it may still be declared on as a deed by
making the proper averments in the profert. United States v. Spalding,* 2 Mason, 478.

§ 389. Suit on bond — Matters more properly coming from the other side need not be
pleaded.— It is unnecessary in declaring on a bond to set out in anticipation matters of defeasance, conditions subsequent, and, in general, matters more properly coming from the other
side. So held in suit on a bond to pay plaintiff a certain sum upon plaintiff teaching defendant a new process of making beer. The bond contained a stipulation that defendant might
withdraw from the obligation by abandoning the process before a fixed date. This was held
to be a matter of defeasance and need not be negatived by declaration. Hammer v. Kauf-
man,* 2 Bond, 1.

§ 390. Indebitatus assumpsit for work and labor will lie, although it be objected that
there was a written contract which might have been declared on. Brockett v. Hammond,*
2 Cr. C. C., 56.

§ 391. Declaration on collector's bond which does not identify his district defective.—
An official bond of a collector of taxes, which does not identify the district for which the
officer is appointed, but simply recites that he has been appointed collector of taxes, is void,
and a declaration on such bond is defective and not to be supplemented by evidence. United
States v. Jackson,* 3 Hughes, 231.

§ 392. In Illinois it is necessary to annex to the declaration a copy of any written instrument sued on, and this becomes a part of the pleadings. Nauvoo v. Ritter,* 7 Otto, 389.

§ 393. Averment of demand on a note.— In an action against an indorser upon a note payable at a particular bank the declaration must show that demand was made at that bank.
United States Bank v. Smith,* 11 Wheat., 171.

§ 394. Where, however, the bank in question is the holder of the note, and plaintiff in the
suit, an allegation that the note was presented to the maker and payment refused, under
which competent evidence of a demand was introduced, is sufficient to sustain a verdict.
Ibid.

§ 395. Where a note is payable at a particular bank, the declaration, in an action against
the indorser, must aver demand at that bank. The Bank v. Smith,* 2 Cr. C. C., 319.

§ 396. In an action against the maker of a note it is not necessary to allege that payment
was demanded at the place where the note was made payable; if the defendant was ready at
the time and place, and offered to pay, that is matter of defense to be pleaded and proved.
Kendall v. Badger,* McAl., 523.

§ 397. Where a note is made payable at a particular place, omission to aver this fact in
the declaration is fatal. Sebree v. Dorr, 9 Wheat., 558.

§ 398. An action was instituted in the federal circuit court of Mississippi on a promissory
note dated at and payable in New York. The declaration omitted to state the place at which
the note was payable, and that a demand of payment had been made at that place. The
court held that to maintain an action against the drawer of a promissory note or bill of ex-

change, payable at a particular place, it is not necessary to aver in the declaration that the note when due was presented at the place for payment and was not paid; but the place of payment is a material part in the description of the note, and must be set out in the declaration. Covington v. Comstock, 14 Pet., 43.

§ 399. Notice to indorsee of note — Averment of.— In an action against the indorser of a note, an averment that due notice of non-payment was given indorser is a sufficient averment of notice. Dwight v. Wing,* 2 McL., 580.

§ 400. When a promissory note runs to any one of several payees, a declaration by one of these, describing the note as given to him, is good. Spaulding v. Evans,* 2 McL., 139.

§ 401. Promissory note — Consideration, averment of.— A count upon the indorsement of a promissory note not payable to order, without averring a consideration for the indorsement, is bad in Virginia. Janney v. Geiger, 1 Cr. C. C., 547.

§ 402. Notice to indorser of bill of exchange, averment of.— In an action of debt against the indorser of a bill of exchange, under the statute of Virginia, it is necessary that the declaration should aver notice of protest for non-payment. Slacum v. Pomery, 6 Cr., 221.

§ 403. Foreign bill — Averment of protest.— Where the action is on the protest of a foreign bill for non-payment, an averment of protest for non-acceptance is unnecessary. Brown v. Barry, 3 Dal., 365.

§ 404. Note — Demand on drawer, allegation of, when necessary.— In an action against the assignor or guarantor of a note, demand on the drawer, when it became due, should be alleged in the declaration. January v. Duncan, 3 McL., 19.

§ 405. A declaration on a promissory note in accordance with the New York code is not sufficient in the federal courts in New York; a demand for the amount of the note, with interest, is not a claim for damages, which is necessary in a declaration in assumpsit. Brownson v. Wallace,* 4 Blatch., 465.

§ 406. Consideration — Sufficient allegation of.— A declaration on a bill of exchange alleging that it was drawn in consideration that plaintiff had, at defendant's request, transported goods, etc., is good on demurrer, though not alleging that the goods were the property of defendant. Railroad Co. v. Thompson, 3 Bond, 296.

§ 407. Declaration on note must allege note to be due.— A declaration which states that the plaintiff "has cause of action against the defendant, and expects to recover judgment for a certain sum as per promissory note he holds against him for said sum, dated," etc., is defective because it does not state that the note was due, nor can that fact be implied from the declaration. Williams v. Knighton,* 1 Oreg., 234.

§ 408. Note — Averment of delivery to, and title in, plaintiff.— In a suit upon a note an averment in the declaration that the defendant "made his promissory note in writing, and thereby promised to pay the plaintiff," etc., is sufficient averment of delivery to, and title in, the plaintiff to be good on demurrer. Moss v. Cully,* 1 Oreg., 147.

§ 409. Note payable to agent — Averment of indorsement by such agent.— A declaration upon a note payable to A., and averring that A., "acting by authority, and as agent of said defendant, indorsed the said note for and in behalf of the said defendant by writing thereon the name of him, the said A., as agent of the said defendant," should also aver that the note was made payable to the said A., as the agent, and for and in behalf of the said defendant, otherwise the note will not appear to be indorsed by the said A. in the character in which it was made payable to him, and so no title in the plaintiff. Wilson v. Porter, 2 Cr. C. C., 458.

§ 410. An averment in a declaration that A., by B., made a certain bill is sufficient. Sherman v. Comstock, 3 McL., 19.

§ 411. Notice to drawer of check of non-payment — Averment of.— The holder of a check must give notice to the drawer if payment by the bank be refused, and a declaration on such an instrument is defective if notice be not averred. Ibid.

§ 412. Notice to guarantor of dishonor of note — Averment.— As notice of dishonor is necessary to give a right of action against a guarantor of a promissory note, the declaration must aver that it was given. Lewis v. Brewster, 2 McL., 21.

§ 413. Averment of excuse for not giving notice.— Where there is an excuse for the want of notice of the dishonor of a note it should be stated in the declaration. Ibid.

§ 414. Joint note — Suit against survivors — Averment of non-payment.—An assignee may bring suit against the survivors of one who executed a joint note in his own name, without alleging in the declaration that deceased failed to pay the same. Silver v. Henderson, 3 McL., 165.

§ 415. An averment that the note was assigned on the day or at the time of its execution is sufficient. Ibid.

§ 416. Averment that note is equivalent to sealed instrument, by law of state where made, will not affect recovery thereon in another state where the law is different.— Action of debt brought by the United States Bank upon a promissory note made in the state of

Kentucky, dated June 25, 1822, whereby, sixty days after date, C., V. & Co., as principals, and D. C., S., and D., the defendant, as sureties, promised to pay jointly and severally to the order of the president, directors and company of the United States Bank, $12,877, negotiable and payable at the office of discount and deposit of said bank at Louisville, Kentucky, value received, with interest thereon at the rate of six per cent. per annum thereafter, if not paid at maturity. The declaration contained five counts. The fourth count stated that the principal and sureties "made their other note in writing," etc., and thereby promised, etc. (following the language of the note), and then proceeded to aver "that the said note in writing, so as aforesaid made, at, etc., was and is a writing without seal, stipulating for the payment of money; and that the same, by the law of Kentucky, is placed upon the same footing with sealed writings containing the same stipulations, receiving the same consideration in all courts of justice, and, to all intents and purposes, having the same force and effect as a writing under seal;" and then concluded with the usual assignment of the breach by non-payment of the note. The fifth count differed from the fourth principally in alleging "that the principal and sureties, by their certain writing obligatory, duly executed by them without a seal, bearing date, etc., and here shown to the court, did promise," etc., and containing a like averment with the fourth of the force and effect of such an instrument by the laws of Kentucky. The defendant demurred generally to the fourth and fifth counts, and the district court sustained the demurrer. By the court: We are of opinion that the fourth and fifth counts are, on demurrer, good, and that the judgment of the court below as to them was erroneous. They set out a good and sufficient cause of action in due form of law, and the averment that the contract was made in Kentucky, and that by the laws of that state it has the force and effect of a sealed instrument, does not vitiate the general structure of those counts, founding a right of action on the note set forth thereon. At most they are surplusage, and do not impair the legal liability of the defendants as asserted in the other parts of those counts. Bank of the United States v. Donnally, 8 Pet., 361.

d. Statutes.

SUMMARY — *Conclusion of declaration for penalty,* § 417.— *Declaration under act of January 9, 1808,* § 418.— *Misjoinder, when cured by verdict,* § 419.— *Penalty given to the person suing therefor not to be sued for by more than one person,* § 420.— *Declaration under statute imposing penalty for charging excessive fare,* § 421.— *Declaration under statute enforcing right of citizens to vote,* §§ 422, 423.— *Fraud, when necessary to be alleged, must appear in declaration,* § 424.

§ 417. A declaration to recover a statutory penalty, concluding contrary to the *law* in such case made and provided, is bad on error. The conclusion should have been contrary to the *statute.* Smith v. United States, §§ 425-427.

§ 418. In an action for a penalty under act of January 9, 1808, it is not necessary to allege that neither vessel nor cargo could be seized. *Ibid.*

§ 419. If two good causes of action are shown in the declaration, but only one penalty is sought, the error will be cured by verdict. *Ibid.*

§ 420. Where an act of congress gives a penalty for violation of law to the person who shall sue for the same, an action for this purpose in the name of more than one person is not authorized. Ferrett v. Atwill, §§ 428-431.

§ 421. A claim against a railroad company for a statutory penalty for charging excessive fare must identify the statute relied upon, and must distinctly allege facts enough to show conclusively that the statute has been violated. Sullivan v. Railroad Co., §§ 432-434.

§ 422. A declaration under act of 1870, enforcing the right of citizens to vote, must allege that the plaintiff was a citizen; that he was otherwise qualified to vote; that defendant refused or knowingly omitted to give plaintiff an opportunity to become qualified to vote, and that such refusal or omission was on account of the race, color or previous condition of servitude of plaintiff. McKay v. Campbell, §§ 485-439.

§ 423. A declaration under the act of 1870, to enforce the right of citizens to vote, must show that plaintiff was prevented from voting either by force, bribery, threats, intimidation or similar means. It will not be sufficient to allege that defendant prevented him by unlawfully deciding against his right to vote. Seeley v. Knox, §§ 440-442.

§ 424. Under a statute prohibiting suit against an administrator pending proceedings in the probate court, unless negligence or fraud be alleged, such negligence or fraud must be alleged in the declaration, and it will not be sufficient if it appear in the replication. Walker v. Johnson, §§ 443-446.

[NOTES.— See §§ 447-483.]

SMITH v. UNITED STATES.

(Circuit Court for Massachusetts: 1 Gallison, 260–268. 1812.)

STATEMENT OF FACTS.—This also was an action of debt for the penalty of the double value, under the embargo law, and was in many respects similar to the preceding case. The declaration was as follows:

"Joseph Smith was attached to answer to the United States of America in a plea of debt, for that during the continuance of a certain act of the United States, entitled 'An act laying an embargo on all ships and vessels in the ports and harbors of the United States,' and of the several acts supplementary thereto, to wit, on the 28th day of February now last past, a certain schooner or vessel called the Traveller, whereof the said Joseph was then owner, agent, freighter and factor, did depart from a port of the United States, to wit, the port of Gloucester, in the district aforesaid, without a clearance or permit; and departing as aforesaid, and whilst the said Joseph was owner, agent, freighter and factor as aforesaid, to wit, between the said 28th day of February and the 1st day of March then next following, the said schooner did proceed to some foreign port or place in the West Indies and to Halifax in the province of Nova Scotia, with a cargo of fish, soap and candles and other American produce, *contrary to the law in such case made and provided, and that neither the said vessel nor cargo has been seized;* whereby, and by force of said law, the said Joseph hath forfeited *to the uses therein specified* a sum of money equal to double the value of the said vessel and cargo aforesaid. And the United States do aver that the sum of $2,400 is a sum equal to double the value of the vessel and cargo aforesaid, and that the said Joseph hath forfeited the said sum of $2,400, and an action hath accrued to the United States to have and recover the aforesaid sum accordingly. Of all which the said Joseph hath had due notice; yet, though often requested, he hath not paid said sum nor any part thereof, but detains it."

Upon *nil debet* pleaded and issue joined a verdict was returned for the United States in the following form:

"The jury find that Joseph Smith, Jr., is indebted to the United States in the sum of $400.　　　　　　　　　　　　FITCH HALL, Foreman."

The following errors were assigned:

1st. That the offense supposed in said declaration to have been committed is not therein alleged to have been committed against the form of any statute or statutes, act or acts, not being an offense at common law.

2d. That two distinct offenses, for each of which a penalty is provided by statute, are joined in one count as containing, together, only one offense.

3d. That it is not alleged in said declaration that the said vessel and cargo had not and could not theretofore have been seized for the offense in said declaration supposed to have been committed.

4th. That it is alleged in said declaration that the complainant forfeited, to the uses specified in a law in such cases made and provided, a sum equal to double the value of the vessel and cargo; but it is not, as by law it ought to have been, therein alleged to whom, or to whose use, or to what uses, or by what particular law, said sum was so forfeited.

5th. That it is not expressed in the verdict, as by law it ought to have been, whether the sum which the jury found the said Smith owed to the United States was double the value of the vessel and cargo, or only the single value thereof, by reason of which uncertainty no judgment could legally be rendered thereon by the court.

6th. That the original writ was sued out in the name of the United States of America, but the verdict was returned and judgment rendered for the United States, and not for the United States of America.

§ 425. *A count concluding "contrary to the law in such case made and provided" does not conclude against the form of any statute and is bad on error.*

Opinion by STORY, J.

The first error assigned is, in effect, that a conclusion "contrary to the law in such case made and provided" is not a conclusion against the form of any statute; and if not, then, upon acknowledged principles, the judgment ought to be reversed.

The objection savors a good deal of technical nicety, but as this is a penal action, if it be well founded in law the plaintiff in error ought to have the full benefit of it. At the argument no authority precisely in point was produced, and the objection therefore was endeavored to be supported upon the general rule and upon the meaning of the word "law." It is true that in 12 Mod., 52, Mr. Justice Eyre is made to say that no words will supply the want of *contra formam statuti*, and he cited Cro. Jac., 142. The case in Cro. Jac. was where the conclusion was against the form of a *statute*, when the action depended upon statutes. And in the case before the court, in 12 Mod., 52, the opinion, if it meant to aver that no circumlocution would be sufficient, is at most but an *obiter dictum*, not necessary to the decision of that case. The other authorities cited at the bar prove no more than the general principle that there must in effect be a conclusion against the form of the statute, but do not decide what the form of the allegation should be. 1 Saund., 135, n.; 1 Chitty, Pl., 358; Doct. Pl., 332.

We are left then to consider the interpretation of the expressions used in the declaration. In an enlarged sense, without doubt, the word "law" may include positive as well as common law, but in technical precision the word "law" is usually restrained to the common law, and other words, as "statute or act," are applied to legislative provisions. Now the common law is, without doubt, as much "made and provided" as the statute law, and therefore *proprio vigore* the expression, "law made and provided," does not necessarily imply a public act of the legislature.

I find on examination that this very point was before the supreme court of this state in Comth *v.* Jesse Morse, 2 Mass., 138. The conclusion in that case was, "against the peace of the commonwealth, and the law in such case made and provided," and the court said that the indictment did not conclude against any statute.

It is of great consequence in a public view to preserve the accuracy of pleadings. Every relaxation induces a new irregularity, and brings numerous and embarrassing questions before the court. The opinion of the highly respectable court which I have cited is entitled to great weight; and as I think it stands confirmed by the general current of authority, as to the general principle, and is shaken by no opposing adjudication, I concur on the present occasion.

§ 426. *If two causes of action are declared on, and only one penalty is sought, the error is cured by verdict.*

As to the second error, I do not think it well founded. If two good causes of action are shown in the declaration, and only one penalty is sought, I do not see how it can vitiate the title to a recovery. The party may thereby have imposed upon himself unnecessary proofs, or exposed himself to the suggestion of inartificial pleading; but it is sufficient for the court if a good title anywhere appear on the face of the declaration. This is not denied in the present case.

§ 427. *In an action for a penalty under the act of January 9, 1808, it is not necessary to aver that neither the vessel nor the cargo could be seized.*

As to the third error, the counsel for the plaintiff in error have argued that the declaration ought to have averred " that neither the vessel nor the cargo could have been seized for the offense aforesaid; " for that, upon the true construction of the statute, the United States have not an election to seize the property or to proceed for the penalty, but are limited to a suit against the property, if within their jurisdiction. And I think, upon the authority of The United States v. The Brig Eliza, decided at last February term, this is to be considered as the true construction of the third section of the statute (Act 9th Jan., 1808, ch. 8), on which this prosecution is founded. But it does not follow that the present allegation is not sufficient. It is stated in the terms of the statute, and if the property was within the United States and might have been seized, it was a good matter of defense at the trial under the general issue, and after verdict the inaccuracy, if any, would be cured. It is a general rule, " that wheresoever it may be presumed that anything must of necessity be given in evidence, the want of mentioning it in the record will not vitiate it after a verdict." T. Raym., 487. And this rule extends to actions upon penal statutes. Hab., 78; Carth., 304. It would be but a little defectively set forth, and upon this ground the court proceeded against the first error in Frederick v. Lookup, 4 Burr., 2018, and against the third and fourth errors in Lee v. Clarke, 2 East, 333. But I consider the averment is sufficient, even on special demurrer, and that the fact relied on would be a proper matter to come from the other party by way of defense. 5 T. R., 83; 2 Leon., 5. In general, it is sufficient to remain a suit upon a statute that the case is brought within the terms of it. The case of Spiers v. Parker, 1 T. R., 141, is clearly distinguishable. It was there held that if the enacting clause, which creates an offense, contains exceptions, such exceptions must be negatived by the plaintiff in his declaration for the penalty. In that case the exceptions were not negatived, and the declaration did not therefore contain within its terms sufficient allegations to show that the penalty had accrued.

The fourth and sixth errors have been disposed of in the case of Sears, Jr., v. United States [1 Gall., 257].

The fifth error was overruled in Cross in error v. The United States, at May term, 1812.

On the whole, for the first error I reverse the judgment of the district court.

FERRETT v. ATWILL.

(Circuit Court for New York: 1 Blatchford, 151-158. 1846.)

STATEMENT OF FACTS.—The plaintiffs brought eleven suits against the defendant for violation of the copyright act of February 3, 1831, in a publication with an imprint of a copyright, whereas he had no copyright.

Demurrers were filed by defendant to each suit.

Opinion by BETTS, J.

The decision of the court in this case being limited to two points, we do not consider it proper to discuss the other questions involved in the pleadings, and argued at length by the counsel; and our judgment being peremptory against the action, an attempt now to settle the other points presented by the case will not, as if an amendment were allowed, tend to abridge litigation or to aid the parties in the disposition of the cause.

The declaration contains two counts, each of which demands a distinct penalty of $100. The first count charges that the defendant, on the 1st of July, 1845, at New York, published *a musical composition*, called "*Alethia Waltz*," and falsely inserted therein and impressed upon the face thereof the words: "Entered according to act of congress," etc., without having at the time legally acquired the copyright of the said musical composition. The second count alleges that the defendant, at the time and place aforesaid, published *a volume of music*, called "*Alethia Waltz*," and falsely inserted therein and impressed upon the title thereof the words: "Entered according to act of congress," etc., without having at the time legally acquired the copyright of the said volume of music.

§ 428. *An action for a penalty, imposed by act of congress, and given to the person who shall sue for the same, cannot be brought in the name of more than one person.*

The defendant demurs to the declaration, and, in connection with the general demurrer, assigns various causes of demurrer, only one of which is passed upon by the court, to wit, that the action is brought by two persons jointly, for themselves and the United States of America. Some exceptions were taken to the sufficiency in form of the special demurrer, but we do not regard the question as material, the objection to the declaration being good on general demurrer; because the right of action, if any, is under the statute, and the declaration must show that the party suing is competent to maintain the suit. Almy *v.* Harris, 5 Johns., 175. The decision, accordingly, rests upon this, that the act of congress does not authorize an action in the name of *several persons* and the United States for the recovery of the penalties incurred by its violation.

The provisions governing the question are contained in the eleventh section of the act, which enacts "that, if any person or persons, from and after the passing of this act, shall print or publish any book, map, chart, musical composition, print, cut or engraving, not having legally acquired the copyright thereof, and shall insert or impress that the same hath been entered according to act of congress, or words purporting the same, every person so offending shall forfeit and pay $100; one moiety thereof to the person who shall sue for the same, and the other to the use of the United States, to be recovered by action of debt, in any court of record having cognizance thereof."

In actions directly upon a statute, or on rights derived from a statute, the party prosecuting must allege, and consequently prove, every fact necessary to make out his title to the thing demanded, and his competency to sue for it. Com. Dig., Action on Stat., A., 1, 2, 3, and Pleader, ch. 76. An informer cannot support an action unless there be an express provision in the statute enabling him to sue. Rex *v.* Malland, 2 Stra., 828; Fleming *v.* Bailey, 5 East, 313. And if the statute creating the penalty, and bestowing it upon the informer, does not give the mode of proceeding, he is bound to set forth the special matter upon which the right of action arises, and allege and prove in what way the penalty vests in him. Cole v. Smith, 4 Johns., 193; Bigelow v. Johnson, 13 Johns., 428; Smith v. Merwin, 15 Wend., 184; Fairbanks v. Antrim, 2 N. H., 105; Ellis v. Hall, 2 Aik., 41. The doctrine in effect is applicable to actions founded upon statutes other than for penalties; for, when a statute is made to remedy any mischief or grievance, or to bestow any interest or right upon an individual, the mode of remedy, when one is designated by it, must be exactly followed. Stowell v. Flagg, 11 Mass., 364; Stevens v. The Proprietors of the Middlesex Canal, 12 Mass., 466. And if the form of remedy is not pointed out, and the law supplies one by implication, the plaintiff must aver and prove every fact necessary to show the existence of the right in him under the statute. Bigelow v. The Cambridge and Concord Turnpike Co., 7 Mass., 202; Bigelow v. Johnson, 13 Johns., 428. We think, under these well established rules of law, that the two plaintiffs prosecuting this action do not come within and satisfy the provisions of the statute giving the penalty " to *the person* who shall sue for the same."

§ **429.** *Distinction between penalty given to a common informer and one given to the person aggrieved.*

There is a manifest distinction between giving a penalty to a common informer, and imposing one for the benefit of the person aggrieved by the violation of the statute. In the latter case the term *person* might justly be regarded as comprehending every one affected by the injury; because the design of such enactment must be to give a remedy co-extensive with the mischief or grievance provided against. This consideration has no relation to positive penalties established as sanctions of the law, and not intended to recompense individuals because of their particular injuries.

§ **430.** *Penal laws must be strictly construed.*

The language of the statute is to be particularly adhered to in the construction of penal laws, and, when it has a natural and plain meaning, an artificial or forced one is not to be adopted. 1 Bl. Com., 88; Dwarr. on Stat., 707, 711; Van Valkenburgh v. Torrey, 7 Cow., 252. Courts will not give an equitable construction to a penal law, even for the purpose of embracing cases clearly within the mischief intended to be remedied. United States v. Sheldon, 2 Wheat., 119; Myers v. Foster, 6 Cow., 567; Daggett v. State, 4 Conn., 61. They sedulously limit the action of penal statutes to the precise cases described in them, and reject an interpretation tending to comprehend matters not named by the legislature, although analogous. The authorities cited are explicit to this point, and are in unison with numerous others, English and American. Cone v. Bowles, 1 Salk., 205; Reniger v. Fogossa, 1 Plow., 17; Fleming v. Bailey, 5 East, 313.

The privilege of claiming or enforcing a penalty is one of statutory appointment, and must be construed with like strictness. In an action by husband and wife against executors, to recover a penalty imposed by statute for not proving a will within a fixed period, one-half of the penalty being given to the plaintiff and the other to the legatees, and the wife being a legatee, it was held by the supreme court of Massachusetts that the suit could not be maintained in the name of husband and wife, the action being a popular one, and there being no joint interest in the verdict. Hill v. Davis, 4 Mass., 137. The doctrine was still more fully and explicitly declared in a later case in that court, in which it was held that several persons could not unite in a *qui tam* action as informers, the right to sue in such case resting upon the express provisions of the statute. Vinton v. Welsh, 9 Pick., 87. When the penalty is given to *any person or persons*, a corporation aggregate cannot sue for it. 1 Kyd on Corp., 218; The Weavers' Co. *v.* Forrest, 2 Stra., 1241, *margin.* Hammond, in his Treatise on Parties (48), says: "It seems two cannot join as common informers in a penal action, unless specially allowed by statute."

The plain language and sense of the statute under consideration restrict the right of action to a single person; and we should not be disposed, on general principles, to enlarge its operation, so as to encourage associations of individuals in instituting and conducting penal actions, the nature of those actions in our opinion exacting a rigorous adherence to the terms of the law.

Judgment is accordingly rendered in this case for the demurrant, with costs; and the same judgment is rendered in the ten other suits between the same parties on like pleadings.

[Questions arose as to five items in taxation of costs. The second item was a charge for a rule to declare, and for services in obtaining security for costs. The third item was for perusing demurrer by counsel. The fourth was a charge for a rule to join in demurrer.]

§ 431. *Questions as to allowance of costs.*

Opinion by NELSON, J.

1. The second set of charges for putting in special bail should have been stricken out, because they were incurred by the neglect of the defendant in not causing the bail first put in to justify and for his own benefit. 2. The defendant's attorney is not entitled to a separate charge in each suit for the services embraced in this item. The settled practice is against the allowance. Jackson *v.* Keller, 18 Johns., 310; Schermerhorn *v.* Noble, 1 Denio, 682. 3. This item is taxable in each suit. Rule 27, C. C. U. S. 4. It is urged that this item is distinguishable from the second, because there was a separate rule in each suit. But the principle is the same, and has been so held since the case of Jackson *v.* Clark, 4 Cow., 532. There can be but one charge for the service, as respects attorney's fees. 5. The demurrer books, and brief and points, are taxable in each case, if they were actually made out in each at the time of the argument. The fact must be shown to the taxing officer, if objection be made to the charge. Attorney and counsel fees on argument are taxable in each case.

SULLIVAN *v.* NEW YORK, NEW HAVEN & HARTFORD RAILROAD COMPANY.

(Circuit Court for New York: 19 Blatchford, 388–392. 1881.)

Opinion by BROWN, J.

STATEMENT OF FACTS.— This is a demurrer to the complaint. The action was removed to this court from the supreme court of the state, and the sufficiency of the pleading is, therefore, to be determined according to the provisions of the New York Code of Procedure.

The complaint sets up a claim to $50, as a penalty alleged to have been incurred by the defendant for demanding and receiving from the plaintiff an excessive fare beyond the rate of three cents per mile allowed by law, upon her trip from New Rochelle to Mount Vernon, on May 11, 1880; and also a claim to $5,000 damages for being violently and unlawfully ejected from the defendant's cars, upon her subsequent return trip, on the same day, to her great suffering and injury. The defendant demurs to the complaint because it appears upon the face that two causes of action have been improperly united, viz., one for a statutory penalty, and the other for damages for personal injuries. The New York Code of Procedure (§ 488, subd. 7) allows a demurrer where the complaint contains different causes of action improperly united. Section 484 provides what causes of action may be joined in the same complaint. This section contains nine subdivisions, which are followed by a clause declaring that it must appear "that all the causes of action so united belong to *one of the foregoing subdivisions.*" The second subdivision provides for claims "for personal injuries," and the ninth subdivision provides for "claims arising out of the same transaction, or transactions connected with the same subject of action, and not included within one of the foregoing subdivisions."

§ 432. *Under the New York code a claim for a statutory penalty and one for personal injuries cannot be joined.*

The principal claim, which is for damages for personal injuries, is well pleaded, and manifestly falls within the second subdivision of this section. By force of the concluding clause of this section, above quoted, it follows that no other cause of action can be joined with that except one for personal injuries, since that forms the exclusive subject of subdivision 2. An action for a statutory penalty is not an action for a personal injury, and, therefore, cannot be joined with the other in the same complaint.

The plaintiff claims that, by reason of a duplex or train ticket, so called, for five cents, having been given on the down trip, which was offered as part fare on the return trip, and which, as is claimed, contributed, through misunderstanding by the plaintiff, to her ejection on the latter trip, both claims fall within the ninth subdivision, above stated, as "claims arising out of the same transaction," etc. But that subdivision is further qualified by the amendment adding the words, "and not included within one of the foregoing subdivisions." The claim for personal injuries is included in subdivision 2, and hence cannot fall within subdivision 9, while the latter is the only subdivision under which a claim for a penalty can come, as none of the previous subdivisions would include it.

But aside from this, I think it impossible to consider a claim for a penalty incurred for excessive fare taken on one trip, and an ejection for non-payment of fare on a subsequent trip, to be "claims arising out of the same transaction." The penalty, if incurred, was complete before the latter trip began. I cannot perceive how the duplex ticket given on the first trip, even if refused on the second trip, would tend to make the excessive fare demanded on the first trip and the ejection on the second trip constitute parts of the same transaction. They are perfectly distinct.

§ 433. *Under the New York code a complaint improperly joining two causes of action is bad on demurrer, provided both are well pleaded.*

If there were no other circumstance in the case, therefore, the demurrer would have to be sustained. But, on examination of the complaint, I am satisfied that it does not contain facts constituting a "cause of action" for a penalty. The design of a demurrer, under section 488, is to compel the plaintiff to elect upon which of two causes of action, improperly united, he will proceed. No such election can properly be said to exist where but one good cause of action is set up. For, if the other matter which is insufficient to constitute a cause of action could be supposed to be elected, a demurrer would immediately lie thereto, because it did not constitute a "cause of action," or the complaint could be dismissed therefor at the opening of the trial; and the result would be no action at all. Section 488 should, therefore, be construed to refer to cases of two or more good "causes of action," well pleaded. The words "cause of action" should be held to mean the same thing in subdivision 7 as in subdivision 8 of section 488. So that, if certain facts pleaded do not, under subdivision 8, constitute a "cause of action," then the same facts ought not to be held, under subdivision 7, to constitute a second "cause of action" improperly joined, for which a demurrer will lie. The remedy for such irrelevant matter would be by motion to strike it out.

§ 434. *Claim for a penalty, how declared on.*

The claim for a penalty is not presented as a distinct cause of action and separately numbered, but is presented only as a part of an entire narrative. As a cause of action it is insufficient both in form and substance. It does not set forth, refer to or in any manner identify the statute alleged to have been violated, nor even state whether it refers to a statute of the state of New York, or to a statute of the state of Connecticut, under whose laws it alleges the defendant corporation was chartered. Again, the necessary inference from all the allegations of the complaint on the subject of the excessive fare is, that there was no such "demanding and receiving" of excessive fare as could be held to incur a penalty. The legal rate is alleged to be three cents per mile, the distance traveled three and nine one-hundredths miles, and the customary fare eight cents. The complaint shows that the plaintiff purchased no ticket before entering the cars, and that, when thirteen cents was required of and paid by her, the conductor gave her back a duplex ticket which "he said was good for five cents." The plaintiff took it as such, and it nowhere appears that it was not good for five cents. The complaint goes on to state that the plaintiff being old, and her eyesight poor, she "did not read what was *printed* on the ticket," etc. The necessary inference from this, coupled with the conductor's saying that the ticket was "good for five cents," is that the printed matter upon the ticket showed how and where the five cents was payable. If these conditions were reasonable, and such as the courts have upheld as justifiable regulations to enforce the purchase of tickets before entering the cars, then only eight cents were in effect demanded and received. The complaint does not state what the printed matter was, and it cannot be assumed that the directions for redemption of the ticket were unreasonable, and it does not appear but that the plaintiff either has already received the money for it, or may at any time do so. To incur a penalty there must be an intentional taking and appropriation of excessive fare. If counterfeit coin were given in making change, no action for a penalty would lie; and, in this case, the ticket for five cents given back to the plaintiff shows that no excessive fare was designed to be appropriated by the defendant. Had the ticket not been good for five cents, or had the regulations or printed conditions been unreasonable, the plaintiff was bound to allege these facts.

The complaint contains, therefore, but one cause of action, and that for personal injuries, and the demurrer should, therefore, be overruled with liberty to answer within twenty days, but, under the circumstances, without costs; and the irrelevant matter in reference to the penalty should be stricken from the complaint.

McKAY v. CAMPBELL.

(District Court for Oregon: 2 Abbott, 120–128. 1870.

Opinion by DEADY, J.

STATEMENT OF FACTS.— This action was commenced July 1, 1870, to recover a penalty of $500, under and in pursuance of section 2 of "An act to enforce the rights of citizens of the United States to vote in the several states of this Union, and for other purposes," approved May 31, 1870. Among other things it is alleged in the complaint that on June 6, 1870, as provided by law, a general election was held in the state of Oregon and county of Wasco therein, at which a representative in congress and also state and county officers were voted for and elected, and that on said day and long prior thereto the plaintiff was a citizen of the United States, and a resident of East Dallas, in said county and state, and legally entitled to vote at such election in the precinct aforesaid for all such offices. That on said day defendant was acting as judge of election in said precinct in conjunction with George Corum and Thomas M. Ward, and as such judge was required by law to receive votes from the electors, and perform such other duties as were required by law of such officer; and that on said day the plaintiff appeared at the polls in said precinct and offered his vote for Joseph G. Wilson, as a representative in congress, and for Joel Palmer for governor of Oregon, and others for different state officers, and for John Darrah for sheriff of said county, and for others for the different county offices; and that "the defendant, combining with the other said judges, unlawfully and wrongfully prevented him from voting; that defendant, confederating with said Ward and Corum, unlawfully and wilfully refused his vote; refused to swear him to his qualification as an elector; refused to enter his name on the poll books of said precinct; and refused to enter on record in said book his vote for the different candidates for whom he proffered to vote. All of which duties, though required of him by the laws of Oregon, he, the defendant, wrongfully and wilfully failed and refused to do, though requested to do so by plaintiff; that defendant with said Ward and Corum ordered him away from said polls, and deprived him of his right as a citizen to vote, to his damage. By reason of which unlawful acts of said defendant, so acting and combining with said others, plaintiff has suffered damages; and he, defendant, forfeited and became liable as provided by law to pay said plaintiff therefor the sum of $500, for which sum, with costs and allowances as provided by law, plaintiff now asks judgment of the court."

On July 8 the defendant demurred to the complaint, and for cause of demurrer alleged: I. That it did not state facts sufficient to constitute a cause of action. II. That several causes of action have been improperly united therein.

On August 2 and 3 the demurrer was argued by Mr. Kelly, of counsel for the defendant, and by Messrs. Mitchell and Cartwright, of counsel for the plaintiff.

§ 435. *Duplicity an error of form only.*

Duplicity in pleading, or the statement of more than one sufficient matter as a ground of action or defense thereto in the same count or plea, is forbidden by the common law and the code as tending to useless prolixity and confusion. 1 Chitty, Pl., 259; Gould, Pl., 220; Code, 157, 161, 163. Duplicity in pleading being, however, only an error in form, at common law the objection had to be made by special demurrer. Chitty, Pl., 701; Gould, Pl., 466. The code having practically abolished special demurrers, except in the instances enumerated in title VIII of chapter I, has substituted the motion to strike out for the special demurrer in the case of duplicity in pleading. It provides, section 103:

" When any pleading contains more than one cause of action or defense, if the same be not pleaded separately, such pleading may on motion of the adverse party be stricken out of the case."

For these reasons I conclude that, as to the second ground stated, this demurrer is not well taken, and that the objection should have been made by a motion to strike out the complaint.

§ **436.** *To plead in one count that defendant prevented plaintiff from voting for several officers is duplicity.*

As this demurrer must be sustained upon the ground that the complaint does not state facts sufficient to constitute a cause of action, it may be well enough to briefly consider the question of duplicity in the complaint, so that the plaintiff, if he desires to amend, may frame his amended complaint accordingly.

The complaint contains but one count or statement of a cause of action, and it is alleged therein that the defendant, in conjunction with the other judges of election, unlawfully and wrongfully prevented the plaintiff from voting for representative in congress *and* for governor of the state of Oregon, *and* for sheriff of the county, *and* for other "county offices."

§ **437.** *To plead in one count that defendant in several ways prevented plaintiff from voting is duplicity.*

Now, if it was unlawful to prevent the plaintiff from voting for any one of the candidates for these several offices, that, it appears to me, is a separate and distinct cause of action, and should have been separately stated. But the complaint alleges not only that the defendant prevented the plaintiff from voting for a certain candidate for each of these offices, but that the defendant unlawfully and wilfully *refused* his vote; *refused* to swear him as to his qualifications as an elector; *refused* to enter his name on the poll books; *refused* to enter his vote, etc. Here are four different acts, in addition to the first one stated, alleged to have been committed by the defendant, each of which are assumed by the pleader to be a distinct violation of the act of congress, and consequently a separate cause of action. If so, they should have been stated or pleaded separately, so as to avoid the prolixity and confusion necessarily resulting from jumbling them together in one count or statement.

§ **438.** *What amounts to refusal or wilful omission to give effect to act of 1870, to enforce right of citizens to vote.*

It is a question whether some of these alleged refusals are sufficient to support an action for the penalty given by the act. It does not appear that the penalty given by section 2 of the act, is given for *preventing* a person from voting or for refusing to *receive* or *record* a vote, but for refusing or knowingly omitting to give full effect to such section. Now, this section substantially provides that if the law of the state requires any act to be done as a prerequisite or qualification for voting, and by such law officers are charged with the performance of duties in furnishing to citizens an opportunity to perform such prerequisite or to become qualified to vote, it shall be the duty of such officers to give to all citizens of the United States an *equal* opportunity to perform such prerequisite, and become qualified to vote, *without distinction of race, color or previous condition of servitude.*

What amounts to a refusal or wilful omission to give effect to this section, upon the part of the state officers, depends upon the duties imposed upon these officers in this respect by the law of the state. Upon examination it does not appear that the section commands these officers to admit or permit citizens of the United States " to *vote* without distinction of race, color or previous condition of servitude," but only to give such citizens an equal opportunity to become qualified according to the law of the state, and to perform any act which the law of the state may require as a prerequisite — a condition precedent — to voting. The duty which this section enjoins upon the officers is something or anything which the state law requires the officer to do, so as to enable the citizen to qualify himself to vote, and, from the nature of things, it must precede in point of time and order the *act* of voting, or anything subsequent thereto. If these suggestions be sound, then none of the acts complained of by the complaint are within the purview of the section, except the refusal to swear the plaintiff to his qualifications as an elector.

The law of this state provides (Code, 700):

" Sec. 13. If any person offering to vote shall be challenged as unqualified by any judge or clerk of the election, or by any other person entitled to vote at the same poll, the judges shall declare to the person so challenged the qualifications of an elector; if such person shall then state himself duly qualified, and the challenge shall not be withdrawn, one of the judges shall then tender to him the following oath: You do solemnly swear, etc. (to the effect that the affiant had all the qualifications necessary to authorize him to vote at the poll). And if any person so challenged shall refuse to take such oath so tendered, his vote shall be rejected.

" Sec. 14. If any person so offering such vote shall take such oath, *his vote shall be received*, unless it shall be proven by evidence satisfactory to the majority of the judges that he does not possess the qualifications of an elector, in which·case a majority of such judges are authorized to reject such vote."

It seems to me that whenever a person offering to vote is challenged, that it then becomes necessary that he should take this qualifying oath before he can be said to be qualified to vote. By the interposition of the challenge, it becomes incumbent upon him to perform this prerequisite to entitle himself to vote. But he cannot take this oath and perform this prerequisite without the judge shall furnish him an opportunity so to do. Therefore the law of the state makes it a duty of the judges, or one of them, to tender and administer the oath to him. Then comes the law of congress and makes it the duty of the judges to give all citizens, " without distinction of race, color or previous condition of servitude," the same and equal opportunities to perform this prerequisite — to take this oath — and thereby become qualified to vote. It follows that a refusal or omission to furnish the equal opportunity to any person seeking to vote, on account of either race, color or previous condition of servitude, is a violation of the act.

§ 439. *How to declare under act of 1870, enforcing right of citizens to vote.*
As to the first ground of the demurrer, I think it well taken. The complainant does not state facts sufficient to constitute a cause of action.

The act of congress upon which this action is brought provides for enforcing the amendment to the constitution· which declares:

" Art. 15. Sec. 1. The right of the citizens of the United States to vote shall not be denied or abridged by the United States, or by any state, on account of race, color or previous condition of servitude."

"Sec. 2. Congress shall have power to enforce this article by appropriate legislation."

The act also regulates the elections of representatives in pursuance of section 4 of article 1 of the constitution, which declares:

"The times, places and manner of holding elections for senators and representatives shall be prescribed in each state by the legislature thereof; but the congress may at any time, by law, make or alter such regulations, except as to the place of choosing senators."

Sections 2, 3 and 4 of the act, which relate to the enforcement of the amendment to the constitution, give penalties to be recovered by civil action against persons who violate them, but violations of that portion of the act regulating the election of representatives in congress are only punishable by indictment or information.

In considering the sufficiency of the complaint, therefore, in this action, no special significance can be given to the fact that the plaintiff offered to vote for a candidate for representative in congress.

By the fourteenth amendment to the constitution it is declared that: "Art. XIV. Sec. 1. All persons born or naturalized in the United States, and subject to the jurisdiction thereof, are citizens of the United States, and of the state wherein they reside." . . . This clause of this amendment declares who are citizens of the United States and of the several states, respectively. The fifteenth amendment, above quoted, declares in effect that citizens of the United States and of the several states shall vote in their respective states at all elections by the people, without distinction on account of race, color or previous condition of servitude. But the amendment does not take away the power of the several states to deny the right of citizens of the United States to vote on any other account than those mentioned therein. For instance, notwithstanding the amendment, any state may deny the right of suffrage to citizens of the United States on account of age, sex, place of birth, vocation, want of property or intelligence, neglect of civic duties, crime, etc. The power of congress in the premises is limited to the scope and object of the amendment. It can only legislate to enforce the amendment, that is, to secure the right to citizens of the United States to vote in the several states where they reside, without distinction of race, color or previous condition of servitude. And this appears to be the intention of the act, so far as it relates to the enforcement of the amendment.

Section 1 declares, in effect, that all citizens of the United States, being otherwise qualified by law, shall be allowed to vote at all elections by the people in any state, district, etc., without distinction of race, color or previous condition of servitude.

True, the language of sections 4 and 5, particularly the former, if taken literally, would apply to acts and proceedings intended to prevent citizens of the United States from voting, whether the same were done or carried on on account of the race, color or previous condition of servitude of the citizens in question or not. But they ought to be construed so as to harmonize with the unambiguous sections which precede them, and must, in any view of the matter, be construed so as to have effect only within the limits of the power conferred by the amendment on congress over the subject.

Upon this construction of the act, to maintain this action I think it would be necessary to prove on the trial:

I. That the plaintiff was a citizen of the United States and otherwise qualified to vote at the time and place mentioned in the complaint.

II. That the defendant refused or knowingly omitted to furnish the plaintiff an opportunity to become qualified to vote, as by refusing or knowingly omitting to swear the plaintiff to his qualifications as an elector, when the law of the state made it his duty so to do, and that such refusal or omission was on account of the race, color or previous condition of servitude of the plaintiff.

If it be necessary to prove these facts to maintain this action they ought to be alleged in the complaint. Now the complaint is silent as to the reason of the defendant's refusal or omission to swear the plaintiff as to his qualifications as an elector. It may have been for some other reason than on account of his race, color or previous condition of servitude, and then the plaintiff's remedy, if any, would be found under the state law and in the state tribunals. I know it may be said, with much probability, that disingenuous judges of election who are violently adverse to and prejudiced against the amendment and the act may refuse or omit to allow a citizen to qualify himself to vote, ostensibly for some reason not within the purview of the act, but really and in fact on account of his race, color or previous condition of servitude. But this is a question of fact, and, if the evidence is sufficient, the jury will be bound to disregard the pretenses of the defendant, and find according to what appears to have been the fact. Besides, to prevent a failure of justice on this account, it may be necessary and proper to hold, in this class of cases as in many others, that slight proof on the part of the plaintiff as to the reason of the defendant's refusal or omission is sufficient to throw the burden of proof in this respect upon the latter.

The demurrer must be sustained.

SEELEY v. KOOX.

(Circuit Court for Georgia: 2 Woods, 868–872. 1874.)

Opinion by WOODS, J.

STATEMENT OF FACTS.—Section 4 of the act of congress, approved May 31, 1870, entitled "An act to enforce the right of citizens of the United States to vote in the several states of this Union," and for other purposes (16 Stat., 141), declares:

"That if any person, by force, bribery, threats, intimidation, or other unlawful means, shall hinder, delay, prevent or obstruct any citizen from doing any act required to be done to qualify him to vote, or from voting at any election as aforesaid, such person shall, for every such offense, forfeit and pay the sum of $500 to the person aggrieved thereby, to be recovered by an action on the case, with full costs and such allowance for counsel fees as the court shall deem just; and shall also, for every such offense, be guilty of a misdemeanor; and shall on conviction thereof be fined not less than $500, or be imprisoned not less than one month and not more than one year, or both, at the discretion of the court."

The constitution of the state of Georgia, article II, section 2 (Code of 1873, p. 908), provides that a person to be an elector "shall," among other things, "have resided in this state six months next preceding the election, and shall have resided thirty days in the county in which he offers to vote, and shall have paid all taxes which may have been required of him and which he may have had an opportunity of paying agreeably to law for the year next preceding the election."

Section 1283 of the code of Georgia of 1873 prescribes the following oath to be taken and subscribed by superintendents of elections in the state:

" All and each of us do swear that we will faithfully superintend this day's election; . . . that we will make a just and true return thereof, and not knowingly permit any one to vote unless we believe he is entitled to do so according to the laws of this state, nor knowingly prohibit any one from voting who is so entitled by law," etc.

On the 2d day of October, 1872, the plaintiff, claiming to be an elector under the laws of the state of Georgia, offered to vote at an election held on that day in the city of Savannah for governor and members of the general assembly. The defendant was a superintendent at the poll where plaintiff offered to vote, and refused to receive his ballot.

The plaintiff thereupon brought this suit, the same being an action on the case to recover the forfeit of $500 provided for in section 4 of the act of congress above quoted.

The charge in the declaration is that the defendant " did by unlawful means prevent the plaintiff from voting at said election, the said unlawful means then and there being the holding and deciding that the plaintiff must show that he had paid all legal taxes for the year 1871, the said year not being the year next preceding said election, which the plaintiff admits he had not paid, but avers he had paid all legal taxes for the year 1872 in the manner prescribed by law."

A second count alleges that the defendant did unlawfully hinder and prevent the plaintiff from voting at said election, by refusing his vote, for the reason that the plaintiff had not paid his taxes for the year 1871, when in fact the plaintiff was a legal voter without the payment of any tax whatever.

§ 440. *A statute which prescribes a penalty for certain acts which it also declares a misdemeanor must be construed strictly.*

It will strike the most careless reader of section 4 of the act of congress, above quoted, that the same state of facts that would authorize a recovery in this case would also authorize a conviction of the defendant for a misdemeanor with a penalty of fine or imprisonment, or both, at the discretion of the court. We must therefore construe this section with the same strictness that we would any other penal statute. The question then arises, Would the facts stated in the declaration authorize a conviction in a criminal prosecution under this section? The offense described in the section is the preventing of any qualified elector from voting, " by force, bribery, threats, intimidation, or other unlawful means." It is clear that the words " other unlawful means " refer to something akin to force, bribery, threats or intimidation.

§ 441. *Rule for construing statutes with exceptions and enumerations.*

Lord Bacon observed " that as exception strengthens the force of a law in cases not excepted, so enumeration weakens it in cases not enumerated." Hence, the celebrated rule that " where particular words are followed by general ones, as if, after an enumeration of several classes of persons or things, there is added ' and all others,' the general words are restricted in meaning to objects of the like kind with those specified." 1 Bish. Crim. Law, sec. 275 and cases there cited.

§ 442. *A declaration alleging that plaintiff was prevented from voting by the "decision" of defendant is insufficient under the act of May 31, 1870 (16 Stat., 141).*

The "unlawful means" charged as having been used by the defendant are not of a like kind with those specified, to wit: "Force, bribery, threats or intimidation." The defendant was acting under oath as a public officer in a *quasi*-judicial capacity, and it is charged against him that while so acting he did not construe correctly an obscure clause in the constitution of Georgia. It is not alleged that he decided against the right of plaintiff to vote, knowing that plaintiff had that right, or that his decision was wilfully wrong, malicious or corrupt. Giving the most liberal construction to the averment of the declaration, it only amounts to this, that the defendant fell into error in passing upon the plaintiff's right to vote; that he construed that clause of the constitution which declares that "the elector must have paid all taxes which may have been required of him, etc., for the year next preceding the election," to mean the year which ended on the 31st of December before the election, and not the year current, when the election was held. Can it be possible that congress meant to impose a forfeit of $500, to be recovered in a civil action, and a fine not less than $500, or imprisonment not less than one month nor more than one year, or both, to be inflicted by a criminal prosecution upon an officer, acting under oath, who had made an innocent mistake in judgment? The proposition is too absurd to be entertained.

The declaration then utterly fails to make out a case for recovery. The elector who is prevented from voting cannot recover, unless he shows that he was prevented either by force, bribery, threats, intimidation or other such unlawful means. If it had been averred that the defendant wilfully and maliciously or corruptly decided against the plaintiff's right to vote, well knowing he had such right, and thereby prevented him from voting, it is possible the declaration might be sustained. Without some such averment it presents no cause of action against the defendant. Demurrer sustained, and leave given plaintiff to amend.

ERSKINE, J., concurred.

WALKER *v.* JOHNSON.

(Circuit Court for Indiana: 2 McLean, 92-97. 1840.)

Opinion of the COURT.

STATEMENT OF FACTS.— This action was brought to recover the amount of a promissory note given by Kinnard in his life-time. The defendant pleaded that, the estate being insolvent, he instituted a proceeding before the probate court of the state of the proper county under the statute, and that the plaintiff, having been notified, became a party to those proceedings, which are still pending; and the defendant avers that he has prosecuted the same with diligence, and, without fraud or waste, discharged his trust.

To this plea the plaintiff replied that the defendant had been guilty of negligence in prosecuting the suit in the court of probate, and concluded with a verification. To this replication the defendant demurred specially.

§ 443. *Provisions of Indiana statute as to suits against insolvent estates.*

The twenty-second section of the act to organize probate courts, etc., provides, "if the personal and real estate shall be insufficient to pay the debts the administrator may make application to the court of probate, exhibiting certain inventories, and the court is required to give notice to creditors to file their claims, which are to be duly adjudged and paid, so far as a proportionate distribution shall go.

" And, from the date of filing the complaint, no suit or action shall be brought or sustained against such executor or administrator, unless waste or negligence or fraud in the discharge of the duties of his trust as such be alleged against such executor or administrator; and if any such suit or action be brought after the filing of such complaint, the plaintiff, complainant or claimant alleging such fraud, negligence or waste, and such plaintiff, complainant or claimant shall fail, upon the trial thereof, to establish such fraud, negligence or waste against such executor or administrator, such plaintiff, complainant or claimant shall pay the costs of such suit or action, although he may recover a verdict, decree or judgment against such executor or administrator; for which costs such executor or administrator shall have judgment."

The court of probate, under this statute, has jurisdiction in the mode pointed out when the parties are properly brought before it; and its decision is final and must be so held until reversed. On general principles the pendency of a suit before the court of probate, of which it has jurisdiction, is pleadable in abatement to a subsequent action for the same cause. And there does not appear to be anything in the mode of exercising jurisdiction in this case which should make it an exception to the general rule.

The executor, finding the assets would be insufficient to pay the demands against the estate, instituted before the probate court the proceedings authorized under such circumstances. Notice was given, and the present plaintiff filed his claim and became a party to the proceedings. These proceedings are still pending. And this is the substance of the plea in abatement to the present action, filed by the defendant, with the averment that he has diligently, and without fraud or waste, discharged his duties, and prosecuted the suit in the probate court. To this plea the plaintiff replies that he has been guilty of negligence in the prosecution of the above suit.

§ 444. *Quære, whether two affirmatives may make an issue.*

Regularly, the plaintiff should have negatived the affirmation of diligence in the defendant's plea, and have concluded to the country; or, if he considered the plea defective, he should have demurred to it. It is said that two affirmatives make an issue, when the second is so contrary to the first that it cannot in any degree be true. 1 Chit. Pl., 691; Co. Lit., 126, *a.* It may be said that negligence is opposed to diligence, and that the affirmatives in these pleas come within the rule. If this be admitted, it is still a most awkward and unsatisfactory mode of making up an issue.

§ 445. *A replication tendering issue should conclude to the country.*

But in any view this replication cannot be sustained, as it concludes with a verification instead of an issue to the country.

§ 446. *A declaration under a statute enlarging plaintiff's right to sue under certain conditions should allege the existence of those conditions.*

The demurrer to the replication brings before the court the sufficiency of the pleadings on both sides. It is argued that this proceeding is in the nature of an action against the administrator, suggesting a *devastavit*, and that it must be governed by the same rule. However much in form this may be like an action charging a *devastavit*, in effect it is, in some respects at least, altogether different.

The administrator, by this proceeding, is not, necessarily, made personally responsible for the judgment. If, on the trial, it should be made to appear the defendant had been negligent in the prosecution of the suit in the probate court, that would not make him personally liable as on a *devastavit;* nor would the judgment probably be so entered against him if he were convicted of waste or fraud.

There is another statute which regulates the proceeding against an executor or administrator on suggesting a *devastavit,* and under which a personal liability is established. A procedure under this statute would, undoubtedly, be authorized by the probate act. The statute provides that, after the institution of the suit in the court of probate, "no suit or action shall be brought or sustained against such executor or administrator, unless waste or negligence or fraud, in the discharge of the duties of his trust, as such, be alleged against such executor or administrator."

In the declaration there is no such allegation; and the plea, which sets up the pendency of the suit in the probate court, and avers that such suit has been diligently prosecuted, etc., under the statute, contains matter which, if true, must abate the plaintiff's action. It shows a state of facts which, by the express provision of the statute, prohibits the plaintiff from sustaining his action.

The allegation of fraud, negligence or waste is essential to the maintenance of the plaintiff's action; and this must be found in his declaration. His suit is brought during the pendency of the proceeding before the court of probate; and such suit, the statute declares, shall not be sustained unless the allegation be made. Under this state of facts, the allegation is essential to the plaintiff's right to sue, and, consequently, it must be contained in the declaration.

In pleading upon statutes, where there is an exception in the enacting clause, the plaintiff must show that the defendant is not within the exemption; but if there be an exception in a subsequent clause, that is matter of defense. 1 Chitt. Pl., 264; 1 Term, 144; 6 Term, 559; 1 East, 646; 2 Chitt. Rep., 582. All the circumstances necessary to constitute a legal right of action must appear on the face of the declaration. 1 Chitt. Pl., 276; Co. Lit., 17, *a*, 303; Com. Dig., Pleader, 6, 7.

The statute does not originate the cause of action; but it protects the defendant from an action unless he be charged with fraud, negligence or waste. Now, is this matter of defense to be set up by the defendant, or is it inseparably connected with the plaintiff's right to sue?

An executor or administrator can only be made personally responsible by a suit suggesting a *devastavit,* and this suggestion must always be made in the declaration. Now, in the present case, the defendant is not liable to be sued unless negligence, fraud or waste be charged.

Suppose a statute provided that an executor or administrator should not be liable to be sued until after the expiration of a year from the time his duties commenced, unless he should be charged with fraud, negligence or waste, must not such charge be made in the declaration if the suit be brought before the expiration of the year? And is not the case supposed analogous to the one under consideration?

As before remarked, the court of probate having jurisdiction of the case, no reason is perceived why, on general principles, the pendency of the suit there should not be pleadable in abatement in a subsequent action for the same cause. But the statute authorizes a subsequent action, provided the plaintiff allege fraud, negligence or waste against the executor or administrator. In this view the statute may be considered as enlarging the right of the plaintiff to sue, on certain conditions, and it would seem to be reasonable that he should show in his declaration the defendant is liable to be sued.

The statute provides that if on the trial the plaintiff shall fail to prove the allegation of fraud, negligence or waste, he shall, notwithstanding, recover a judgment for the amount due, but not for costs; but, if he prove fraud, negligence or waste, he may have also a judgment for the costs.

Upon the whole we think, under the statute, it would be the most convenient mode for the plaintiff to make the allegation in his declaration, where he brings the suit under the above circumstances, and that such an allegation would be analogous to the rules of correct pleading.

On this suggestion the plaintiff's counsel asked leave to amend their declaration, and it was granted.

§ 447. State statutes need not be pleaded.— Federal courts will take judicial notice of the statutes of the states in which they sit; and it is sufficient that enough facts be set out to bring a case within the operation of a statute without setting out the statute. Toppan v. Cleveland, etc., R. R. Co.,* 4 West. L. Mo., 67.

§ 448. An authority given by a general statute of a state need not be pleaded, for the courts of the United States take judicial notice of the public acts of the states. Smith v. Tallapoosa Co., 2 Woods, 574.

§ 449. Petition should state act of congress on which founded.— If a claim is founded on an act of congress, such act, it seems, should be stated in the petition. Noble v. United States,* Dev., 185.

§ 450. Assent of voters, required to validate contract sued on, need not be averred.— A plaintiff in suing a city on a contract which required the assent of two-thirds of the legal voters need not aver this sanction. The non-existence of the fact is a matter of defense. Gelpcke v. Dubuque, 1 Wall., 221.

§ 451. Debt will lie for a statutory penalty where the amount of the penalty is fixed only within certain limits, and the particular amount is to be determined by a jury. United States v. Colt, Pet. C. C., 145.

§ 452. Declaration under civil rights act — Citizenship.— A declaration under the civil rights act, which gives a penalty for denying rights, etc., to any citizen, must allege that plaintiff is a citizen. Lewis v. Hitchcock,* 10 Fed. R., 4.

§ 453. A declaration under this act charging that plaintiff was denied privileges at a certain inn, to wit, a restaurant, is sufficient, as the word inn has a definite legal meaning, and is not rendered nugatory by a *videlicet* giving additional circumstances. *Ibid.*

§ 454. The averments of the pleadings and the proof must correspond. The Nevada statute giving damages to the kindred of a person killed by negligence furnishes no exception to this rule; but all facts necessary to bring the case within the statute must be averred in the declaration before proof of them can be introduced. Roach v. Con. Imperial M. Co., 7 Saw., 224.

§ 455. Claim for proceeds of cotton seized and sold by the United States army dismissed on motion because the suit was not brought within two years after suppression of the rebellion, as prescribed by act of congress. Tibbett's Case,* 1 N. & H., 169.

§ 456. The tenth section of act of 3d March, 1863, does not apply to a claim pending at the time of its passage, and cannot be pleaded. The claim was for a bounty for destroying an armed vessel of the enemy in the war of 1812. Parlin v. United States,* 1 N. & H., 174.

§ 457. A charge in the declaration in the alternative, but in the language of the statute, cured after judgment.— An action of debt, founded upon an act of congress, is brought to recover a penalty in which the declaration charges that the defendant "did forcibly rescue, or cause to be rescued, from said collector, or one of them, the said spirits," adopting the phraseology of the act. *Held,* that although the offense might have been stated with more precision, and although the declaration might have been held ill on special demurrer, yet it is a defect of form merely, which, after judgment, is cured by the statute of jeofails. Jacob v. United States, 1 Marsh., 520.

§ 458. Statutory remedy for injury on highway must be strictly followed.— When an action for damages incurred on a public highway, by neglect to keep it in repair, is brought on a statute, the statute must be followed strictly. Hull v. The Town of Richmond, 2 Woodb. & M., 337.

§ 459. **Proceedings under 4 George II.— Allegation of no distress.**— In a proceeding under the statute of 4 George II., it must be alleged and proved that there was no sufficient distress upon the premises on some day or period between the time at which the rent fell due and the day of the demise, and if the time when, according to the proofs, there was not a sufficient distress upon the premises, be subsequent to the day of the demise. Connor v. Bradley, 1 How., 211.

§ 460. **Under the act of August 31, 1851, a petition to the board of land commissioners** must show a claim by virtue of a right or title derived from the Spanish or Mexican government, but the act does not define the character of the right or title, or prescribe the kind of evidence by which it shall be established. It is sufficient if the right is derived from such government, and it may rest only in the general law of the land. Beard v. Federy, 3 Wall., 478.

§ 461. **Conclusion of declaration for statute penalty.**— In debt for a penalty on a statute the declaration must conclude against the form of the statute, or it will be bad. Cross v. United States, 1 Gall., 26; Jones v. Van Zandt, 2 McL., 611; United States v. Babson, 1 Ware, 450.

§ 462. **Conclusion of declaration founded on amendatory act.**— If the declaration is founded on an amendatory act, which refers to and continues the provisions of a former act, it should conclude "against the form of the statute," and not statutes. Falconer v. Campbell, 2 McL., 195.

§ 463. **Action for statutory penalty — Declaration must allege offense to have been committed contrary to the form of the statute.**— A declaration in an action to recover a statutory penalty must allege that the offense charged was contrary to the form of the statute, and it is not a valid substitute to say that "by force of said act" defendant has forfeited. Such a declaration is bad on error. Sears v. United States,[*] 1 Gall., 257; United States v. Batchelder, 9 Int. Rev. Rec., 97.

§ 464. In such an action it is not necessary to refer in the declaration to the statute giving the remedy in addition to that creating the offense. Ibid.

§ 465. —— **brought by an individual.**— In an action for a statutory penalty, brought by an individual, the declaration must state that the act was done or omitted contrary to the form of the statute in such cases made and provided. Briscoe v. Hinman,[*] Deady, 588.

§ 466. The declaration must also allege that, by force of the statute, an action has accrued to the plaintiff to have and demand of the defendant the penalty forfeited. Ibid.

§ 467. A declaration by an individual for a penalty, under act of August 30, 1852, as to transportation of passengers and freight upon steamboats, which alleged that upon certain occasions a boat carried freight or passengers, or which alleged that the defendant, a collector of customs, negligently or intentionally omitted to enforce the law, would be bad for uncertainty. Ibid.

§ 468. **When an offense depends upon several statutes, a conclusion in the declaration** against the form of a single statute would be bad. The converse, however, is not true, and if the offense depends upon one statute only, a conclusion against the form of the statutes is good on error. Kenrich v. United States,[*] 1 Gall., 268.

§ 469. —— **in admiralty**, setting forth the offense clearly enough to bring it within the statute, is sufficient without the contra formam statuti. The Merino, The Constitution and The Louisa, 9 Wheat., 391.

§ 470. **A plea justifying a seizure under the statute of 1794** need not state the particular prince or state by name against whom the ship was intended to cruise. Gelston v. Hoyt, 3 Wheat., 246.

§ 471. A plea justifying a seizure and detention by virtue of the statute of 1794, under the express instructions of the president, must aver that the naval or military force of the United States was employed for that purpose, and that the seizor belonged to the force so employed. Ibid.

§ 472. **Declaration or information for statute penalty must negative exception in enacting clause.**— In a suit to recover a statutory penalty, or an information to secure the forfeiture of property under a statute, if there be an exception in the enacting clause, the declaration or information must negative it; but if the exception is superadded by way of proviso, the party wishing to avail himself of it must set it up in his pleading. United States v. Distillery,[*] 4 Biss., 26.

§ 473. —— **proviso, however, need not be negatived.**— A plea averring that the claimant is an alien, in substantial conformity with the second section of the act of congress, July 27, 1868, but not negativing a provision to the statute allowing aliens the same privilege as citizens in prosecuting claims against the United States, is good on demurrer, as only exceptions to enacting clauses of statutes, not provisos, must be negatived in thus pleading a statute. Muller v. United States,* 4 Ct. Cl., 61.

§ 474. Action to recover taxes paid under protest—Facts showing plaintiff to be within the exception of the statute need not be alleged.— Under section 110 of the revenue act of the United States, as amended on the 13th of July, 1866, providing for a tax upon certain banking institutions, but excepting others from such tax, if the complainant, in a suit to recover the amount of taxes paid by it under protest, denies that it is within the general clause of the act, it need not proceed to allege facts showing that it is within the exception. German Sav. & Loan Co. v. Oulton, 1 Saw., 695.

§ 475. A libel of information does not require all the technical precision of an indictment at common law. If the allegations describe the offense it is all that is necessary; and if founded upon a statute it is sufficient if it pursues the words of the law. The Emily and The Caroline, 9 Wheat., 381.

§ 476. What is mere matter of defense need not be set out in an information, but only enough need be set out to show a violation of the statute under which the information is brought; and it is not necessary to aver that requirements of such statute, which are merely directory to the officers of the government, have been complied with by them, if there has been an actual violation of the statute by the party against whom the information is brought. United States v. 78 Cases of Books, 2 Bond, 271.

§ 477. Action under Revised Statutes, section 4963, for violating copyright law — Complaint must aver it to be within the statute.— In a complaint under Revised Statutes, section 4963, for printing the words "entered according to act of congress," etc., upon a non-copyrighted article, if such article may or may not be within the statute, it must be averred in the complaint that it is within the statute, unless the terms used in describing it necessarily bring it within the statute. Rosenback v. Dreyfuss, 2 Fed. R., 217.

§ 478. An information under the confiscation act of August 6, 1861, should state in distinct articles the causes of forfeiture; should aver that the same are contrary to the form of the statute in such case made and provided; and the allegations must conform strictly to the statute upon which the information is founded, since the proceeding is in the nature of a criminal proceeding. United States v. Huckabee, 16 Wall., 414.

§ 479. Forfeiture of imported merchandise for undervaluation; necessary averments.— An information under section 66 of the act of March 3, 1799, for forfeiture of imported merchandise, because of undervaluation, must aver that the valuation was under cost *at the place of exportation;* but an amendment of an information not so averring will be allowed. United States v. 78 Cases of Books, 2 Bond, 271.

§ 480. Entry upon false invoice — Defective allegation as to.— In an action of debt upon a statute which makes it penal to make an entry *upon* false invoice, an allegation in the declaration that the defendant, upon entry, *left with* the collector a false invoice, is a fatal defect not cured by the verdict. United States v. Batchelder,* 9 Int. Rev. Rec., 97.

§ 481. An information under the slave-trade act of 1794, which describes, in one count, the two distinct acts of "preparing a vessel" and of "causing her to sail," pursuing the words of the law, is sufficient. The Emily and The Caroline, 9 Wheat., 381.

§ 482. Stating a charge in the alternative is good if each alternative constitutes an offense for which a thing is forfeited. *Ibid.*

§ 483. Notice.— In an information on section 3 of the act of January 9, 1809, for not unloading, or giving bonds, the time of receiving the act at the port where the offense was alleged to have been committed, and also of notice to unload, were material and traversable; and it was also held insufficient to allege that notice was given "to discharge the cargo or to give bond, according to the law in such cases provided." The nature of the requisition should have been stated, and to whom notice was given, that the court might judge of its sufficiency. The Schooner Bolina, 1 Gall., 75.

2. Plea.

a. In General.

SUMMARY — *Plea to a part of the declaration not to be treated as a plea to the whole,* § 484.— *Several pleas to different parts of declaration must all be good to obtain final judgment,* § 485.— *Several pleas to different parts, all to be determined separately,* §§ 486, 487.— *Pleas must leave no part of declaration unanswered,* § 488.— *Several pleas to different parts, the same as one plea with several verifications,* § 489.— *Traverse to be direct,* § 490.— *Foreign judgments, how to be pleaded,* §§ 491, 492.— *Joint plea must be good as to all,* § 493.— *Plea of alteration of instrument,* § 494.— *General issue without an oath admits instrument,* § 495.— *Duress or fraud in promissory note,* § 496.— *General plea of fraud,* § 497.— *Pleading defense already set up,* § 498.— *Plea to declaration on official bond,* §§ 499, 500.— *Plea to answer declaration, not evidence,* § 501.— *Bad plea by defendant as acceptor,* § 502.— *Double plea,* § 503.— *Set-off,* § 503.— *Failure of consideration,* § 504.— *Fraudulent misrepresentations,* § 505.— *Bad plea in action on penal bond,* § 506.— *Plea that instrument was mere escrow,* § 507.— *Plea varying written contract,* § 508.— *Uncertainty,* § 509.*

§ 484. When a plea professes to answer only part of the actionable matter in the declaration the plaintiff, by treating it as a plea to the whole, discontinues. Kerr *v.* Force, §§ 510–518.

§ 485. When several independent pleas are filed to different parts of a count they are not double, and plaintiff may demur or reply to each, taking *nil dicit* judgment as to all matters not covered by the plea in each case. Final judgment, however, is upon the whole record, and if all the pleas are good it will be for defendant. *Ibid.*

§ 486. When several pleas are filed, each to the whole count, final judgment will be for defendant if one of them be good. *Ibid.*

§ 487. When several pleas are filed to different parts of a count, and issues taken thereon, damages will be assessed on those found for plaintiff, and defendant will have judgment on those found for him. *Ibid.*

§ 488. When any actionable part of declaration is left unanswered by a sufficient plea plaintiff may have *nil dicit* judgment for so much. *Ibid.*

§ 489. Pleading several pleas to different parts of a count is the same as pleading one plea with several verifications. *Ibid.*

§ 490. A plea should traverse a fact in the declaration directly, not argumentatively. Mower *v.* Burdick, § 519.

§ 491. Foreign judgments are not records, and should not be pleaded as such. Burnham *v.* Webster, §§ 520–525.

§ 492. A plea setting up a foreign judgment must allege that the court rendering it had jurisdiction. *Ibid.*

§ 493. A joint plea by several defendants, if bad as to one is bad as to all. United States *v.* Linn, §§ 526–528.

§ 494. A plea by defendant, alleging alteration of the instrument sued on after signature, without charging the alteration on the plaintiff, is bad in substance. *Ibid.*

§ 495. When statute requires the denial of an instrument declared on to be sworn to, the general issue without an oath may be pleaded, which, though admitting the instrument, allows other defenses to be proved. McClintick *v.* Johnston, §§ 529–537.

§ 496. The plea of duress or of fraud by the maker of a bill in a suit by the assignee is bad without an averment of notice. *Ibid.*

§ 497. A general plea of fraud to a declaration on a bill is not demurrable. *Ibid.*

§ 498. A plea by one defendant, setting up a defense already pleaded by all the defendants jointly, is useless, and a motion to strike out or a demurrer will be sustained. *Ibid.*

§ 499. To a declaration in debt on an official bond a plea is bad which sets up a subsequent bond as received in satisfaction and discharge of the first. United States *v.* Gerault, §§ 538–513.

§ 500. To such a declaration a plea is bad in which sureties set up a fraud of their principal as a defense. *Ibid.*

§ 501. A plea must answer the declaration, and not the evidence, which it is assumed will be given to support the declaration. *Ibid.*

§ 502. Where the declaration is against defendant, as acceptor, in his individual capacity, of a bill of exchange drawn in payment for the transportation of a particular lot of goods, for a firm of which defendant is a member, a plea is bad in substance which seeks to avoid liability by setting up that, in various shipments for the firm, the plaintiff had failed to perform his agreements and had greatly damaged the firm. Railroad Co. *v.* Thompson, §§ 544–547.

§ 503. A plea is double when, after averring non-performance in bar of the action, it sets up a counter-claim against plaintiff. Such a claim should be made in a separate plea of set-off, or by notice of special matter. *Ibid.*

§ 504. A plea of failure of consideration should state precisely what was the consideration; also to what extent and in what respect consideration has failed. Grunninger *v.* Philpot, §§ 548–531.

§ 505. A plea of fraudulent misrepresentations should state what they were, with necessary incidents; also that defendant entered into the contract relying upon them, and should allege the consideration. *Ibid.*

§ 506. In an action on a penal bond, a plea that the breach is less in extent than that charged in the declaration is bad. United States *v.* Dair, §§ 552, 553.

§ 507. A special plea of *non est factum*, on the ground that the instrument declared on was only an escrow and not the deed of defendant, must aver that the instrument was delivered to a third person, to be delivered to the obligee only on performance of a certain condition. *Ibid.*

§ 508. A plea is bad which sets up that the written contract as set out in the declaration is not the contract as made between the parties, this being an attempt to vary a written contract by parol testimony. McDonald *v.* Orvis, §§ 554–556.

§ 509. This plea is bad also for uncertainty, in not stating wherein the contract as set out differs from the contract as made. *Ibid.*

[NOTES.— See §§ 557–648.]

KERR *v.* FORCE.

(Circuit Court for the District of Columbia: 3 Cranch, C. C., 8–46. 1826.)

STATEMENT OF FACTS.— This was a suit charging the defendant with having published a libel against the plaintiff, in stating that the plaintiff had altered a note made by a Mrs. Moulton and indorsed by John Q. Adams, making the instrument materially different from what it was when the parties respectively signed and indorsed it.

The plea was apparently intended to be in justification, and was to the effect that the defendant did publish the matters and things in said (alleged) libel contained, as he might lawfully do. The court having adjudged the plea defective, upon leave given the defendant filed fourteen additional separate pleas, of which the court refused to receive six. Plaintiff moved for judgment by *nil dicit* as to so much as the pleas did not cover.

§ 510. *Discussion of authorities as to pleas answering only part of the actionable matter in declaration.*

Opinion by CRANCH, J.

The case of Patcher *v.* Sprague, 2 Johns., 462, is cited by the plaintiff to show that "whatever is traversable in pleading, and which is not traversed, is admitted." This is certainly true. 1 Chitty, 591. But in that case the replication, which was supposed to admit the fact not traversed, was a replication which purported to be an answer to the whole plea. That case, therefore, only shows that the doctrine applies to such pleas as purport to answer the whole count, or, at least, such traversable matter as is within that part of the count which the plea purports to answer when the plea purports to answer only a part of the count.

In the case of Currie & Witney *v.* Henry, 2 Johns., 437, Spencer, J., in delivering the opinion of the court, said: "Pleas pleaded under the leave of the court must contain in each of them sufficient matter in law to bar the plaintiff's action, and they cannot be made to depend on facts stated in other pleas." This doctrine is stated as the reason for adjudging the defendant's third and fifth pleas in that case to be bad on special demurrer. Each of those pleas purported to answer the whole count. The doctrine, therefore, so far as that case goes, is only applicable to pleas which profess to answer the whole count.

"When the body of a replication contains an answer to a part of a plea the commencement should recite or specify that part intended to be answered; for should the commencement assume to answer the whole plea, but the body contain an answer only to part, the whole replication will be insufficient, and so *vice versa.*" "In this case," says Mr. Chitty, "the form may run thus: 'And the said A. B., as to so much of the said plea of the said C. D. by him secondly above pleaded as relates to the said supposed recognizance in the said plea mentioned, says that he ought not to be barred from having or maintaining his aforesaid action thereof against him, because he says,' etc., and the other part of the plea may commence as follows: 'And the said A. B., as to the residue of the said plea, saith, *"precludi non,"* etc., "because,"' etc.

"On the other hand, when the matter to be replied is equally an answer to several pleas, it is proper, in order to avoid expense, to answer all the pleas in one replication." "In these cases the commencement should apply to and profess to answer all the pleas. So where to a plea of judgment outstanding the plaintiff replied that each is fraudulent, he may conclude with one verification. 1 Chitty, 573.

"It is said that matter which is the ground of the suit, or upon which issue might be taken, cannot be protested, and that a protestation which is repugnant to or inconsistent with the plea is inartificial and improper. In these cases the replication should either admit the part of the plea which is not disputed, by saying 'true it is that,' etc., or should at once deny the matter intended to be tried, though the latter mode, as being the most concise, appears preferable, for whatever is not traversed is, in effect, admitted." 1 Chitty, 590.

"The qualities of a replication in a great measure resemble those of a plea, which are, that it answers so much of the plea as it professes to answer; and that if bad in part it is bad for the whole, and that it must be single. If it do not answer so much of the plea as it professes to answer it will be a discontinuance." 1 Chitty, 617; Marsteller v. McLean, 7 Cranch, 156; Com. Dig., Pleader, F. 4, W. 2; Hancock v. Prowd, 1 Saund., 338. See, also, 1 Chitty, 511, 512, 540, 592, 618; Co. Lit., 304, a; Coombe v. Talbot, Salk., 218; Curtis v. Bateman, 1 Sid.. 39; Wilson v. Law, Carth., 334; S. C., Skin., 554; Middleton v. Cheeseman, Yelv., 65; Bray v. Fisher, 2 Roll., 390; 1 Roll. Ab., 487, b, 43; 7 H. 6, 27; Johnson v. Turner, Yelv., 5; S. C., 1 Brownlow, 192; Penton v. Robert, 2 East, 88; 4 Co., 62; Herlakenden's Case, Gilb. Hist. C. L., 155, 185; Woodward v. Robinson, 1 Str., 302; Wilson v. Dodd, 1 Roll., 176; Wats v. King, Cro. Jac., 353.

§ **511.** *The rule where the plea professes to answer only a part of the actionable matter in declaration.*

From all the cases which I have found the rule seems to be, that where the plea professes to answer only a part of the actionable matter charged in the count; if the plaintiff, by his replication or demurrer, treats it as a plea to the whole matter, it is a discontinuance. But if the plaintiff, by his replication or demurrer, treat it as a plea to that part only which it purports to answer, it is no discontinuance; provided that at the time of replying or demurring he take judgment, by *nil dicit,* for that part of the count which is unanswered by the plea.

§ 512. *The rule where several distinct and independent pleas are pleaded to different and separate parts of a count.*

Where several distinct and independent pleas are pleaded to different and separate parts of a count the pleas are not double, and do not require the aid of the statute; and if the plaintiff may reply or demur to each plea and take judgment by default, or *nil dicit* (which is the same thing), as to all the matter not covered by each plea, in succession, so as ultimately to get judgment for all the matter contained in his declaration, yet by the same process the defendant, if his pleas are all good, and the issues or demurrers be decided in his favor, will have made out a complete bar to the whole of the same matter; and, as the final judgment of the court must be upon the whole record, that judgment must be for the defendant. Tippet *v.* May, 1 B. & P., 411; 8 Co., 120, b; Bonham's Case, 3 Co., 52, b; Ridgeway's Case, 8 Co., 133, b; Turner's Case, Hobart, 199, S. P.

§ 513. *The rule where several pleas are pleaded to the same count.*

Where several distinct and valid pleas in bar are by the leave of the court, under the statute, pleaded to the same count and issues taken thereon, if one of the issues be found for the defendant and the residue for the plaintiff, yet the judgment must be for the defendant. Coke *v.* Sayer, 2 Wils., 85. So if several distinct and valid pleas in bar be, by the leave of the court, pleaded to one and the same part of the count and issue be taken thereon, and one of the issues be found for the defendant, the judgment, as to so much of the count as is answered by the plea, must be for the defendant, although the other issues be found for the plaintiff.

§ 514. *The rule when separate pleas are pleaded to different parts of the same count.*

Where there are separate and distinct pleas to different parts of the count and issues taken thereon, and some of the issues be found for the plaintiff and some for the defendant, several damages should be assessed, and judgment will be entered for the plaintiff as to the issues found for him, and for the defendant as to the issues found for him. And if, instead of taking issue, the plaintiff should demur to those pleas (as he may safely do without fear of a discontinuance if he confine his prayer for judgment on the demurrers to so much of his count as the plea professes to answer, and pray judgment by *nil dicit* for the residue), and some of the demurrers should be decided in favor of the plaintiff and some in favor of the defendant, the plaintiff would have judgment and a writ of inquiry of damages as to those decided in his favor, and the defendant would have judgment upon the others.

§ 515. *The rule in case any part of plaintiff's declaration remains unanswered.*

If it appear upon the whole record that any actionable part of the plaintiff's declaration remain unanswered by a sufficient plea, the plaintiff must have judgment for so much if he shall have prayed judgment at the proper time, so as to avoid a discontinuance. But if it appear from the whole record that every actionable part of the declaration has been fully answered by a valid plea in bar, the truth of which has either been admitted in the pleadings or found by the jury, the judgment must be for the defendant.

§ 516. *Pleading several pleas to different parts of a count is practically the same as pleading one plea with several verifications.*

The form of pleading offered by the defendant in the present case seems to be fair, and more likely to result in a just judgment than if he had pleaded all the matters in one plea, unless in that plea he had tendered as many verifications as there are now pleas. And if he had done that I see no substantial difference between that and the present manner of pleading. In that mode of pleading the defendant would come and say that the plaintiff his action aforesaid thereof against him ought not to have or maintain, because he says that as to so much, etc., he says, etc., and this he is ready to verify; and as to so much, etc., he says, etc., and this he is ready to verify; and so on as to each particular set of words, and then conclude with a general prayer for judgment as to the whole count, instead of inserting after every verification a special prayer for judgment as to the particular part of the count to which the matter thus offered to be verified applies. The difference seems to be only a difference of form; for in the mode of pleading which the plaintiff's counsel supposes to be right, each separate matter of defense pleaded to the distinct and different parts of the count would, in effect, be a distinct and separate plea. It could derive no aid from the other matters of defense pleaded to a different part of the count. If it be not a good justification of the matter which it professes, in its introductory part, to justify, it must be the subject of a separate demurrer on the part of the plaintiff. Douglass *v.* Satterbee, 11 John., 16. If some of the several matters pleaded be good justifications of what they profess to justify, and others be not, the plaintiff must demur to the latter, and plead over to the others. If he were to demur to the whole as one plea, and one of the several matters pleaded should be a good justification of what it purports to justify, the demurrer must be overruled in the same manner as a demurrer to a whole declaration would be overruled if any one of the counts should be good. Com. Dig., Pleader, 2, 3; 1 Chitty, 643; Powdick *v.* Lyon, 11 East, 565; Seddon *v.* Senate, 13 East, 76, 77.

If none of the several matters pleaded to the respective parts of the count should be a good justification of what it purports to justify, perhaps one demurrer to the whole might be good, if it purported to be a demurrer to the separate matters pleaded; but then it would be good only *reddendo singula singulis;* and because it would, in effect, be equivalent to a separate demurrer to each matter of offense pleaded. The two modes of pleading differ only in form; and I can see no disadvantage to the plaintiff from the mode adopted by the defendant; nor any benefit which the plaintiff could derive from that which he seems to suppose to be the most correct.

§ 517. *When a count is wholly answered by several pleas to various parts, plaintiff cannot have nil dicit judgment as to any part.*

If the difference be only in form, then if, by pleading in the form which the plaintiff contends for, he could not take judgment by *nil dicit,* so here where all the pleas are pleaded *uno flatu,* although they have not one common commencement and conclusion, I should think the plaintiff could not have judgment by default on any part of his count. If in replying to each plea he should take judgment, by default, as to all the matter in the count not covered by the plea, it would be only matter of form, to save a technical or formal discontinuance. It is said that one plea cannot be aided by another. This is true, whether each plea be entire, or whether it purport to answer only a part. If an entire plea do not answer the whole count, or if a plea to a part of a count do not answer the whole part which it professes to answer, it is bad upon demurrer, and cannot derive aid from any other plea. But when a plea to a part of a count is an answer to such part, it needs no aid from any other plea; it is sufficient for all that it professes to answer. So when the defend-ant, in what the plaintiff's counsel supposes to be one plea, pleads several dis-tinct matters to several distinct parts of the count, each distinct matter pleaded must be sufficient in itself to answer what it professes to answer, and can de-rive no aid from another distinct matter pleaded to another distinct part of the count; so that the rule applies equally to both forms of pleading.

§ 518. *Necessity of properly answering a good plea of justification.*

If a plea be a good justification of what it purports to justify the plaintiff cannot treat it as a nullity, and take judgment by *nil dicit* for the whole mat-ter contained in his declaration. He must demur or reply to the plea, and take judgment, by default, for what remains unanswered. If the plaintiff de-mur and pray judgment for the whole matter in his declaration, he admits that the defendant has answered to the whole matter, but answered badly (Tay-lor *v.* Cole, 1 H. Bl., 562); and as the plea professes to answer only a part of that matter, the plaintiff, by such demurrer, impliedly abandons all that part which the plea does not profess to answer, and therefore, and thereby, discon-tinues his suit for so much; and a discontinuance as to part (as before observed) is a discontinuance as to the whole. Every demurrer concludes with its ap-propriate prayer for judgment, and if it be to a particular count, or breach, it is qualified accordingly. 1 Chitty on Pleading, 644. If it be to a plea in abatement, and conclude as if it were a plea in bar, it will be a discontinuance. In Hughes *v.* Phillips, Yelv., 38, the court said: "It is not all one *nihil dicere ac insufficienter dicere;* for then upon every insufficient bar judgment should be upon *nil dicit,* which is not so." See, also, Story's Pleadings, 311, the form of a demurrer to a particular breach of covenant and joinder; and in pages 303 and 322, a demurrer to several pleas. See, also, in 1 Harris' Entries, 90, the form of a judgment against the defendant who had neglected to plead as to part of a particular count, and where the plaintiff takes judgment by *nil dicit* as to that, in order to prevent a discontinuance. See, also, in 1 Har. Ent., 212, the form of a verdict in slander, part for the plaintiff and part for the defendant.

For these reasons the court refused to give judgment by *nil dicit,* either as to the respective parts uncovered by each plea when taken separately; or to consider the several pleas as nullities, and to give judgment by default for the whole matter in the plaintiff's declaration.

MOWER v. BURDICK.

(Circuit Court for Michigan: 4 McLean, 7, 8. 1845.)

Opinion of the Court.

STATEMENT OF FACTS.— This action is brought upon a sealed instrument, dated the 9th of June, 1839, in which the defendant agreed to indemnify the plaintiffs and save them harmless against the payment of a promissory note, made and signed by the plaintiffs jointly and severally, with one Samuel Mower, then of Michigan city, Indiana, for the sum of $1,700, payable in one year, for the benefit and use of the said Samuel Mower. And the plaintiffs aver that on the 12th day of July, 1842, they paid the said note. The second count in the declaration was substantially the same on another note.

§ 519. *Argumentative plea is demurrable. The traverse must be direct.*

The defendant pleaded that the said Samuel Mower did himself take up and pay each of the said several promissory notes when they became due, without this, that the said plaintiffs paid the sums due upon the said promissory notes when they became due, or any part of all or either of them in manner and form, etc., which the said defendant is ready to verify. To this plea the plaintiffs demurred.

This plea is bad. The plaintiffs aver that they paid the notes after they became due; the plea alleges that Mower paid them when they became due, which is not a direct answer to the averment in the declaration. This may be a good argument to show that the plaintiffs could not have paid the notes as they allege, but it is an argumentative denial of the fact stated in the declaration, which should be traversed. Stephen, Pl., 385, 175-7, 181. [Case discontinued.]

BURNHAM v. WEBSTER.

(District Court for Maine: Daveis, 236-242. 1845.)

STATEMENT OF FACTS.— *Assumpsit* on a note for $1,000. Defendant pleaded the general issue, and secondly, a foreign judgment rendered by a New Brunswick court. To this latter plea plaintiff replied that the New Brunswick court was a foreign court, had no jurisdiction of the subject-matter when it rendered judgment, and that the note was withdrawn by consent and with the leave of the court before verdict and judgment. Defendant demurred because the replication was double and argumentative.

Opinion by WARE, J.

By the rules of pleading there can be but one replication to one plea. The defendant may indeed put into the cause several pleas, but each plea is distinct and must be single; it must contain but one matter of defense, that is, it must not contain two or more facts or points, each of which would be an answer or defense to the action.

§ 520. *A replication which contains two answers to a plea is bad for duplicity.*

The replication in like manner must be single, and confined to a single answer, and if it contains more than one, each of which would be a full answer to the plea, it will be held on demurrer bad for duplicity, for it must tender a single issue.

Tried by this test can this replication stand? It alleges in the first place that the court had no jurisdiction of the subject-matter of this suit. This alone is a complete answer to the plea, on which the defendant might take issue, and if found for the plaintiff that the court had not jurisdiction, there is an end of the defense set up by the plea. For, if the court had no jurisdiction, the judgment would be considered as a nullity, and not in any way affecting the rights of the parties.

In the second place, the replication alleges that the note now declared on was, by consent of parties and leave of court, withdrawn from the case before the verdict and judgment. This allegation admits the jurisdiction of the court over the parties and the subject-matter at the time when the action was commenced, and then shows that it was withdrawn from the jurisdiction by the leave of the court and consent of the parties, so that no adjudication was in fact had on the note. This is also by itself, and independent of any other matter, a complete answer to the plea, on which the defendant in a rejoinder might take issue. If the defendant had rejoined instead of demurring, the rejoinder must, to answer the replication, have been double and presented two distinct and independent issues.

591

It is contended in favor of the replication that it is not double, because it presents but a single point, and that is that the judgment is not conclusive. But it is obvious that a judgment may not be conclusive on the parties for more reasons than one. But in replying to a plea the plaintiff is not allowed to put in several replications to a single plea, as a defendant may put in several pleas to a declaration. When a foreign judgment is declared on, the defendant may in different pleas allege several distinct and different reasons why it should not be conclusive on his right, as the want of jurisdiction in the court, or fraud in obtaining the judgment, or that it is invoked to affect the rights of third persons by collusion between the parties. But when it is pleaded in defense to an action, though the plaintiff may believe that the judgment is not legally binding for several reasons, he is by the rules of pleading precluded from availing himself of more than one. He must select from his various means of defense the one on which he chooses to rely. The plaintiff having in this case included in his replication two distinct matters, either of which is a complete answer to the plea, the replication must be adjudged bad.

But then it is contended that if the replication is bad, so also is the plea, and that a bad replication is good enough for a bad plea, the general rule being that where there are successive faults in pleading we must go back to the first fault. The plea, it is contended, is bad for two causes. 1. It is pleaded without a profert. 2. Because the plea does not allege that the court had jurisdiction of the parties and of the subject-matter.

§ 521. *A former judgment should not be pleaded with a profert.*

The first objection cannot prevail. In causes where a profert is necessary, the omission can only be taken advantage of by special demurrer, and the objection is waived by pleading over. Chitty on Pleading, 350, 512. And when a judgment is relied on in a declaration as a ground of action, or in a plea as a defense, it is never declared on or pleaded with a profert. See precedents in American Precedents, page 347, and 2 Chitty's Pleading, 232, and 3 Chitty, 227, for Declaration; 2 Chitty, 536 and 673, plea *nul tiel record*, and replication. The profert is made in reply to the plea of *nul tiel record*, and the party then has time to produce the record. 3 Black. Com., 331.

§ 522. *Foreign judgments not records.*

And further, foreign judgments are not considered by the common law as records and cannot be declared on and pleaded technically as such. In the case of Walker *v.* Witter, 1 Doug., the plaintiff declared in debt on a judgment recovered in the colonial court of St. Jago de la Vega, "as by the record and proceedings thereof remaining in said court will more fully appear," and the defendant replied *nul tiel record*. The court said the *prout patet per recordum* was absurd because the foreign judgment, in the view of the common law, was no record, but that it might be rejected as surplusage; but that the plea of *nul tiel record* was a nullity, and gave judgment for the plaintiff.

§ 523. *Effect of foreign judgments.*

The second objection involves a question of more difficulty. The plea is in the common form of a plea of domestic judgment. Whatever difference of opinion there may be as to the binding force of foreign judgments, all agree that they are not entitled to the same authority as the judgments of domestic courts of general jurisdiction. They are but evidence of what they purport to decide, and liable to be controlled by counter evidence, and do not, like domestic judgments, import absolute verity and remain incontrovertible and conclusive until reversed; and the question of the jurisdiction of the court over the matter which it acts upon is always an open question. As to the authority and effect of such judgments, they are rather assimilated to the judgments of domestic courts of limited and special jurisdiction. Now, with respect to the judgments of these courts when they are relied upon, it must always appear that the court rightfully exercised jurisdiction. There is no presumption in favor of their authority, as in the proceedings of courts of general jurisdiction, but that must appear on the face of their proceedings, or their judgments will be held not merely voidable but absolutely void and nullities. Walker *v.* Turner, 9 Wheat., 947–9; Elliot *v.* Piersol, 1 Pet., 340–1.

§ 524. *In pleading a foreign judgment it must appear that the foreign court had jurisdiction.*

Formerly it was held, in pleading the judgment of an inferior court, whether of record or not of record, that the whole proceedings must be set out at large. Nothing was presumed in favor either of their jurisdiction or of the regularity of their proceedings. It was therefore not sufficient to allege *taliter processum fuit,* but the whole must be spread upon the record by the party relying on the judgment, that it might be seen that the court had jurisdiction and that the proceedings were regular. Comyn's Digest, Pleader, E., 18. But the rigor of the old rule has been relaxed in modern times, and it is now held not to be necessary to set out the cause of action and the whole proceedings at large, but that it is sufficient to allege that the suit was for a cause of action arising within the jurisdiction of the court. 1 Saunders' Rep., 92, note 2; Story's Pleading, 134. And the regularity of the proceedings will be presumed unless excepted to by the other party. But still it must appear that the court had jurisdiction, either by a suitable allegation of the party relying on the judgment, or by spreading on the record so much of the proceedings that the court may see that the inferior tribunal could rightfully take cognizance of the cause. For the court will not presume the jurisdiction unless it is distinctly alleged or is apparent on the record.

It is indeed said by Lord Mansfield, in the case of Rowland *v.* Veale, Cowp., 18, that the same liberality holds in pleading the judgment of an inferior court with regard to the jurisdiction as does with regard to the regularity of its proceedings; that is, that it will be presumed to be rightful unless the contrary is shown; and therefore that it is unnecessary to allege that the party "became indebted within the jurisdiction." For if the cause of action did not arise within the jurisdiction, it should have been shown to the court below; or, if it was not alleged in the court below, it would be bad on error or in a writ of false judgment. This, however, was but an *obiter dictum,* for in the case before the court it was alleged in the plea that the cause of action came within the jurisdiction. But with the exception of this *dictum* the precedents and the authorities are the other way.

Foreign judgments are held to have no greater sanctity or authority than domestic judgments of inferior courts. It must appear by the proceedings or be alleged in the plea that the court had jurisdiction of the cause, for the court will not presume, nor can it be contended that it is a presumption of law, that a foreign court has jurisdiction over parties who are inhabitants and residents of this country. Now it is not alleged in the plea, nor is there anything spread on the record which shows, that the foreign court had jurisdiction over the parties or the cause in this case. It appears to me, therefore, that the plea is bad, not in form merely, which might be cured by pleading over, but in substance,

§ 525. *A foreign judgment is no more binding on the party suing than on the party sued.*

The only question of doubt, as it appears to me, that can arise, is whether it lies in the mouth of the plaintiff to say that a court to which he had himself voluntarily appealed, and whose authority he had invoked, had no jurisdiction to determine the matter, and that its proceedings might be treated as a nullity. If the question stood entirely clear of authority, it is one on which I should feel inclined to pause.

It seems to me to be repugnant to the first principles of social order and civil justice, that a party should be allowed to deny the competence of a tribunal of his own choosing, and to whose authority he had compelled the other party to submit. If he may, I do not see but that he may harass the adverse party with a new suit in every new jurisdiction where he may be found, without prejudice from prior judgments which may have been rendered against him by other courts. But the language of the authorities does not appear to indicate any distinction of the kind, or that a foreign judgment is binding any further on the party bringing the suit than on the party defendant.

UNITED STATES *v.* LINN.

(1 Howard, 104–118. 1843.)

Opinion by Mr. Justice Thompson.

Statement of Facts.— This case comes up on a writ of error from the circuit court of the United States for the district of Illinois. The writ or summons issued in the cause purports to be in a plea of debt for $100,000. And the declaration contains three counts upon the following instrument, which, upon oyer craved by the defendants, is set out upon the record:

"Know all men by these presents that we, William Linn, David B. Waterman, Lemuel Lee, James M. Duncan, John Hall, William Walters, Asahel Lee, William L. D. Ewing, Alexander P. Field and Joseph Duncan, are held and firmly bound unto the United States of America in the full and just sum of $100,000, money of the United States, to which payment, well and truly to be made, we bind ourselves jointly and severally, our joint and several heirs, executors and administrators, firmly by these presents, sealed with our seals and dated this 1st day of August, in the year 1836." They also crave oyer of the condition of the said supposed writing obligatory, and it is read to them in these words: "The condition of the foregoing obligation is such, that whereas the president of the United States hath, pursuant to law, appointed the said William Linn receiver of public moneys for the district of lands subject to sale at Vandalia, in the state of Illinois, for the term of four years from the 12th day of January, 1835, by commission bearing   12th February, 1835: Now, therefore, if the said William Linn shall faithfully execute and discharge the duties of his office, then the above obligation to be void and of none effect; otherwise it shall abide and remain in full force and virtue.

"Sealed and delivered in the presence of Presley G. Pollock, as to Wm. Linn, D. B. Waterman, Lemuel Lee, J. M. Duncan, John Hall, Wm. Walters,

Asahel Lee, Wm. L. D. Ewing and A. P. Field; A. Caldwell as to Joseph Duncan.

" WILLIAM LINN, [L. S.]	D. B. WATERMAN, [L. S.]
" LEMUEL LEE, [L. S.]	J. M. DUNCAN, [L. S.]
" JOHN HALL, [L. S.]	WM. WALTERS, [L. S.]
" ASAHEL LEE, [L. S.]	WM. L. D. EWING, [L. S.]
" A. P. FIELD, [L. S.]	JOSEPH DUNCAN. [L. S.]

" GENERAL LAND OFFICE.

"*Approved August 30, 1836.* ETHAN A. BROWN."

To the first count, which purports to be debt on the bond, the defendants plead jointly *non est factum*, and several other pleas not necessary here to be noticed. To the second and third counts, which are upon the same instrument, not described, however, as a bond, but as a certain instrument in writing. To these counts the defendant Joseph Duncan put in the following plea:

" And the said Joseph Duncan, impleaded as aforesaid, by Logan & Brown, his attorneys, comes and defends the wrong and injury, when, etc. And, as to the said second and third counts in the said plaintiffs' declaration contained, says that the said plaintiffs their said action on the said second and third count sought not to have or maintain against him, this defendant, because, he says, that protesting that he executed the supposed written instrument declared upon in the said second and third counts of the plaintiffs' amended declaration, he says that after he had signed said instrument and delivered it to his co-defendant Linn to be transmitted to the plaintiffs, and after the securities to the said written instrument had been affixed (approved) by the Hon. Nathaniel Pope, judge of the district court of the United States for the state of Illinois, it was, without the consent, direction or authority of said Joseph Duncan, materially altered in this: that scrawls, by way of seals, were affixed to the signature of said Joseph Duncan to said written instrument, and to the signatures of the other parties to said written instrument, whereby the character and effect of the said written instrument declared in the second and third counts aforesaid was materially changed and said instrument declared on vitiated.

" And so said Duncan says that the said supposed written instrument declared on in the second and third counts of plaintiffs' amended declaration is not his act and instrument; and of this he puts himself upon the country."

To which plea there is interposed a special demurrer, and the court gave judgment for the defendant Joseph Duncan upon the demurrer, thereby adjudging that the plea was sufficient in law to bar the plaintiffs from maintaining their action against him. And issues being joined upon the pleas to the first count the cause came on to be tried by a jury, and under the instructions of the court a verdict was found for the defendants upon the issues of fact. Exceptions were taken to the instructions of the court to the jury. And the correctness of such instructions is the first question presented on this writ of error.

Upon the trial, after reading the bond to the jury, the defendants called a witness who testified in substance that he saw the bond, after it had been signed by the obligors, in the hands of William Linn, the obligor first named therein, after it had been returned from the district judge with his certificate indorsed of the sufficiency of the sureties; that the district judge, in a note in writing, accompanying the bond, had pointed out the omission of seals to the names of the signers of the instrument; and said Linn, saying he would obviate that difficulty, took a pen, and, in the presence of the witness, added scrawls, by way of seals, to each name subscribed as makers of the instrument. · Other testimony was given, under the issues of fact, which it is not material to notice.

§ 526. *Upon a joint plea of non est factum by several defendants, if the plea is proved bad as to one it is bad as to all.*

Upon this evidence the court gave the following instruction to the jury: "If they shall find from the evidence that, after the instrument upon which the action is brought was signed by the defendants, it was altered by William Linn, one of the defendants, without the knowledge or assent of the other defendants, by adding to the names of the defendants the scrawl seals which now appear upon the face of the instrument, and such defendants have not at any time since the alteration sanctioned it, the instrument is not the deed of such defendants, and the jury will find a verdict in their favor." And the question is whether this instruction was in point of law correct, under the pleadings and evidence in the cause. All the defendants united in a joint plea of *non est factum,* and the proof was that the scrawls were added by Linn to his own name and to the names of the other defendants. The adding the scrawl by Linn to his own name did not vitiate the instrument as to him; he had a right to add the seal, or at least he can have no right to set up his own act in this respect to avoid his own deed. It was therefore his deed, and the plea of *non est factum* as to him is false. And the question is whether it is not false as to all who joined him in the plea of *non est factum.* It is laid down by Chitty, in his Treatise on Pleading, that a plea which is bad in part is bad *in toto.* If, therefore, two defendants join in a plea, which is sufficient for one but not for the other, the plea is bad as to both. For the court cannot sever it, and say that one is guilty and that the other is not, when they put themselves on the same terms. Chitty, 598. A plaintiff may, in an action in form *ex delicto* against several defendants, enter a *nolle prosequi* as to one of them. But in actions in form *ex contractu,* unless the defense be merely in the personal discharge of one of the defendants, a *nolle prosequi* cannot be entered as to one defendant without discharging the other, for the cause of action is entire and indivisible. Chitty, 599. The rule laid down by Chitty is fully sustained by the English and American decisions. In Smith *v.* Bouchin, 2 Str., 993, the action was trespass and false imprisonment; plea not guilty by all, and a justification as to eight days' imprisonment. And the court held that although the officer and jailer might have been excused if they had pleaded severally, but having joined in a plea with others who could not justify, they had forfeited their justification. In Moors *v.* Parker, 3 Mass., 310, the action was trespass *de bonis asportatis* against several, and all join in the plea of not guilty, and also in a plea of justification. The court held that the bar set up was no justification for one of the defendants, and if several defendants join in pleading in bar, if the plea is bad as to one defendant it is bad as to all.

So in the case of Schermerhorne *v.* Tripp, 2 Caines, 108, which was in error from a court of common pleas. The action was trespass against a justice of the peace, the constable and the plaintiff, and all joined in a plea of not guilty. The court said, the constable having joined with the others in the plea of the general issue, they are all equally trespassers. If he had pleaded separately he would probably have been excused; but he has now involved himself with others, and we cannot separate their fates.

It is unnecessary to multiply authorities on this point; the books are full of them, and it is a well settled and established rule in pleading. The reason is, because, the plea being entire, cannot be good in part and bad in part, an entire plea not being divisible; and consequently if the matter jointly pleaded be insufficient as to one of the parties it is so *in toto.* 1 Saund., 28, n. 2, and cases there cited.

It has been suggested that this objection is waived by the following entry in the bill of exceptions: "A judgment having been obtained against Linn for the full amount of his defalcation, a judgment on this bond was not asked against him or any of the defendants, unless the jury shall find against all the defendants." It is not perceived how this can be considered a waiver of any error. No judgment could have been given against Linn separately, the plea of *non est factum* being joint. But the plaintiffs, according to the express terms of this memorandum, did ask a verdict and judgment against all the defendants; and if from the pleadings and evidence they were entitled to judgment against all, as we think they were, there was no waiver that will justify the instructions given to the jury.

§ 527. *Conclusion of a plea. A plea by one who has signed an instrument, that it was altered after signature, without charging the plaintiff with the alteration, is bad on demurrer.*

The next question arises upon the special demurrer to the plea of Joseph Duncan to the second and third counts of the declaration. This plea sets up new matter to avoid the instrument upon which the action is founded, and concludes to the country. And it may well be questioned whether, upon the best and soundest rules of pleading, it ought not to have concluded with a verification. Chitty, in his Treatise on Pleading (1 Chitty, 590), says it is an established rule in pleading that, whatever new matter is introduced on either side, the pleading must conclude with a verification, in order that the other party may have an opportunity of answering it. And this rule has the sanction of many adjudged cases. In the case of Service *v.* Heermance, 1 Johns., 92, the court say there is no rule in pleading better or more universally established than that, whenever new matter is introduced, the pleading must conclude with an averment. And the reason, say the court, is obvious, because the plaintiff might otherwise be precluded from setting forth matter which would maintain his action, although the matter pleaded by the defendant might be true. And in Henderson *v.* Wittry, 2 Durn. & East, 576, Buller, justice, in giving the judgment of the court, said: By the rules of pleading, whenever new matter is introduced the other party must have an opportunity of answering it. So that the replication setting up new matter concluded properly with an averment. Numerous authorities, both in England and the United States, might be cited in support of this rule. But there is certainly no little confusion and diversity of opinion appearing in the books with respect to the question when the pleadings ought to conclude to the country, and when with a verification. Many of these discrepancies may grow out of rules said by Mr. Chitty to have been recently established in the English courts, relating to pleadings, which have not fallen under our notice.

We will, however, pass by the demurrer for that cause in the present case, and proceed to an examination of the special matter set up in the plea in bar of the action. If this mode of pleading be adopted, the special matter set up must, as in a special plea, be such that, if true in point of fact, it will bar the action and defeat the plaintiffs' right to recover. The matter set up in this plea, when stripped of some circumlocution, is that, after he, Joseph Duncan, and the other parties to the instruments had signed the same, it was without his consent, direction or authority, altered by affixing seals to their signatures. The plea does not indicate in any manner by whom the alteration was made. It does not allege that it was done with the knowledge or by the authority or direction of the plaintiffs, nor does it even deny that it was done with the knowledge of the defendant, Joseph Duncan. The plea does not contain any allegation inconsistent with the conclusion that it was altered by a stranger, without the knowledge or consent of the plaintiffs; and, if so, it would not have affected the validity of the instrument. It is said that the demurrer admits the truth of the matter set up in the plea. The demurrer admits whatever is well pleaded. But it does not admit any more, and certainly does not admit what is not pleaded at all. The demurrer then admits nothing more than that the seals were affixed after the instrument had been signed by the parties and delivered to Linn to be transmitted to the plaintiffs, and that this was done without the consent, direction or authority of him, the said Joseph Duncan. Is this enough to avoid the instrument and bar the recovery? It certainly is not, for the seals might have been affixed by a stranger without the knowledge or authority of the plaintiffs, and would not have affected the validity of the. instrument. The plea not alleging by whom the seals were affixed, it is open to two intendments. Either that this was made by the plaintiffs, which would make the instrument void, or that it was done by a stranger, which would not invalidate it. And what is the rule of construction of such a plea? It is, that it is to be construed most strongly against the defendant. This is the rule laid down by Chitty (1 Chitty, 578), and in which he is supported by numerous authorities. And the reason assigned for this rule of construction is that it is a natural presumption that the party pleading will state his case as favorably as he can for himself. And if he do not state it with all its legal circumstances the case is not in fact favorable to him; and the rule of construction in such case is that, if a plea has on the face of it two intendments, it shall be taken most strongly against the defendant; that is, says he, the most unfavorable meaning shall be put upon the plea; a rule which obtains also in other pleadings, and a number of cases are put illustrating this rule. The present plea falls directly within it. The plea not alleging by whom the seals were affixed, it is left open to intendment that it was done either by plaintiffs or by a stranger. In the first case it would make the deed void; in the last it would not vitiate it. And under the rule that has been stated, the most unfavorable meaning must be put upon the plea; that is, that which will operate most against the party pleading it. And the alteration must be presumed to have been made so as not to vitiate the instrument if the plea will admit of such construction. Suppose the plea had concluded with a verification, and the plaintiffs had replied that the affixing the seal was done without their knowledge, consent or authority, and this state of the case had been sustained by the proof, it would not have avoided the instrument.

But it is said the law imposes upon the party who claims under the instrument the burden of explaining the alteration. This is the rule, undoubtedly, where the alteration appears on the face of the instrument, as an erasure, interlineation, and the like. In such case the party having the possession of the instrument and claiming under it ought to be called upon to explain it. It is presumed to have been done while in his possession. But where no such *prima facie* evidence exists there can be no good reason why this should devolve upon a party simply because he claims under the instrument. The plea avers the alteration, and the defendant, therefore, holds the affirmative; and the general rule is that he who holds the affirmative must prove it. And this, under the present plea, can impose no hardship on the defendant, for his affirming the fact of alteration affords a reasonable presumption that he knew by whom the alteration was made. And, in addition to this, it is a circumstance deserving considerable weight that the defendant, in his plea, does not deny his having such knowledge. He avers that the seal was affixed without his consent, direction or authority; but he does not say it was done without his knowledge. And it is not an unreasonable inference that if he had, in his plea, disclosed by whom it was done, it would appear to have been done in a way that did not affect the validity of the instrument. There is not upon the face of this instrument anything indicating an alteration, or casting a suspicion upon its validity, that should put the plaintiffs upon inquiry. The instrument upon its face admits it was sealed with the seals of the defendants, and purports to have been sealed and delivered in the common conclusion of a sealed bond. So that, when the instrument came into the possession of the plaintiffs, there was nothing on the face of it to raise a suspicion against its validity. The case of Henman v. Dickinson, 5 Bing., 183, has been relied upon to show that the *onus* of accounting for the alteration is thrown upon the plaintiffs. All that this case decides is that the party who sues on an instrument which, on the face of it, appears to have been altered, it is for him to show that the alteration has not been improperly made. The circumstance of the alteration appearing on the face of the instrument is emphatically relied upon by the court to show that the party claiming under the instrument must account for the alteration. This was a question of evidence upon the trial, and did arise upon the pleadings, and the report of the case does not furnish us with the pleadings. Many other cases might be cited to the same effect.

In the case of Taylor v. Mosely, 6 Car. & P., 273, the bill upon which the suit was brought appeared on its face to have been altered, and there was no evidence on either side when or by whom the alteration was made; and the question was submitted to the jury by Lord Lyndhurst with the remark that it lay on the plaintiff to account for the suspicious form and obvious alteration of the note, and they must judge from the inspection of the instrument, and if they thought the alteration was made after the completion of the bill the verdict must be for the defendant. In the case now before the court the inspection of the instrument furnishes no ground of suspicion, and from the facts stated in the plea there must have been a considerable distance of time after the instrument was signed by Duncan before it came into the possession of the plaintiffs. The plea alleges that it was delivered to Linn, one of the defendants, to be transmitted to the plaintiffs. But the plea does not allege that the alteration was made after the instrument came into the possession of the plaintiffs; and under the state of facts alleged in the plea, the *onus* of proving when and by whom altered is more properly cast upon the defendant. We are accordingly of opinion that the plea is bad. But it is a settled rule that when the demurrer is to the plea, the court, having the whole record before them, will go back to the first error; and when the demurrer is by the plaintiff his own pleadings must be scrutinized, and the court will notice all exceptions to the declaration that might have been taken on general demur-

rer. We are accordingly thrown back on the record to examine the sufficiency of the declaration in the second and third counts.

§ 528. *The liability of a security who incurred the obligation after his principal took office. How such liability should be declared upon.*

The second count sets out the instrument as of the date of the 1st of April,
1836. That Linn's commission bears date the 12th of February, 1835, and
that he was appointed receiver for four years from the 12th of January, 1835.
And the count then alleges that after the making and delivering the said instrument in writing, and after the appointment of the said Linn, he entered
upon the duties of his office, and that within four years from the said 12th
day of January, and while he was receiver of public moneys, there came into
his hands, as receiver, the sum of $4,000,000, which it was his duty to pay
over to the plaintiffs when requested, yet the said William Linn hath not, nor
would he, although often requested so to do, to wit, on the 2d day of April,
in the year 1838, account for and pay over to the said plaintiffs the said sums
of money or any part thereof, but hath wholly neglected and refused so to do.
It is said this count is bad because from the time stated in the count he might
have received the money after the 12th day of January, 1835, the commencement of his office, and before the 1st day of April, 1836, when the instrument
signed by the sureties bears date, and that the sureties cannot be responsible
for any moneys received before they became sureties. The count alleges a
demand of the money and a refusal to pay it on the 2d day of April, in the
year 1838, long after the defendant became surety. In the case of Farrar and
Brown *v.* The United States, 5 Pet., 373 (which was an action upon a bond
given for the faithful discharge of the duties of a surveyor of the public lands),
the breach assigned was that at the time of the execution of the bond "there
were in the hands of the surveyor large sums of money to be disbursed for the
use of the United States, which he had neglected to do." And one of the
questions which arose was whether the sureties could be made liable for any
moneys paid to the surveyor prior to the execution of the bond; and the court
said there is but one ground on which the sureties can be made answerable,
and that was on the assumption that the money was still remaining in his
hands when the bond was given. And in the case of The United States *v.*
Boyd, 15 Pet., 208, the court said it matters not at what time the moneys had
been received, if after the appointment of the officer they were held by him
in trust for the United States, and so continued to be held at and after the
date of the bond. In these cases there was a direct allegation that the money
was in the hands of the officer at the date of the bond. In the case now before the court there is no such direct allegation, and this count is therefore
bad on this ground. The third count is also bad for the same reason.

The judgment of the circuit court must accordingly be reversed and the
cause sent back for further proceedings.

Mr. Justice McLean dissented.

McCLINTICK v. JOHNSTON.

(Circuit Court .for Indiana: 1 McLean, 414–428. 1839.)

Opinion of the COURT.

STATEMENT OF FACTS.— This action is brought on the following promissory note:

"$715.08.   MADISON, INDIANA, Aug. 28, 1837.

"Nine months after date, we jointly and severally promise to pay at the Branch of the State Bank of Indiana, at Madison, to Riley & Van Amaringe, merchants of Philadelphia, or to their order, seven hundred and fifteen dollars and eight cents, without defalcation, for value received.

"I. D. JOHNSTON.
"DAVID CUMMINS."

Indorsed:

"For value received, pay the within to John McClintick.

"RILEY & VAN AMARINGE."

The defendant filed the following pleas:

1. *Non assumpsit.*

2. "That at the time of making the said supposed note, etc., the said Imley D. Johnston was unlawfully imprisoned by said Riley & Van Amaringe, and others in collusion with them, and then and there detained in prison until the force and duress of imprisonment of him, said Johnston, and to obtain the liberation of him, said Johnston, from such imprisonment, he, said Johnston, together with said David Cummins, as his surety, made said note," etc.

3. That said supposed note was made and delivered to said Riley & Van Amaringe without any consideration whatsoever for so doing; and the same was indorsed over by said Riley & Van Amaringe to said plaintiff without any consideration whatsoever, and with full notice to said plaintiff that the same had been made by said defendants without consideration.

4. That said note was obtained from them by fraud, covin and misrepresentation.

5. That said defendant Johnston, who is impleaded with the said David Cummins, says he did not undertake and promise in manner and form as said plaintiff has alleged.

To the first, second, fourth and fifth pleas the plaintiff has filed demurrers, and assigned the following causes of demurrer to the fourth plea:

1. The said fourth plea is double, containing two substantive bars to said action, if the matters pleaded are pleadable in bar; that is to say, 1. Fraud, covin and false representation; and 2. That the said note declared on was made without any consideration whatever.

2. Fraud, covin and false representation cannot be pleaded without setting out the particular facts that constitute the fraud, covin and false representation, so far as relates to the consideration, but only to the making of the instrument declared on.

And in answer to the third plea, the plaintiff filed the following replication: That the defendant ought not, etc., because he saith that said note was not made and delivered to said Riley & Van Amaringe without any consideration whatever, and that the same was not indorsed over by said Riley & Van Amaringe to said plaintiffs without any consideration whatever, and that said plaintiff had not any notice that said note had been made by said defendants without any consideration.

To this replication the defendant filed a demurrer, and for cause of demurrer states that said replication is double, etc.   And a joinder to the demurrers to the first, second, fourth and fifth pleas is filed.

The first question raised by these pleadings is whether the plea of *non assumpsit* can be filed in this action.   It is contended by the plaintiff's counsel that it cannot be pleaded, 1, to a bill of exchange; and 2, that it cannot be pleaded against an indorsee.

§ 529.   *The general issue without an oath may be pleaded to declaration on a bill, though denial of the execution of the instrument be required to be under oath.*

Upon general principles there can exist no doubt that the drawer or acceptor of a bill may put in this plea.   It denies the execution of the instrument, and requires the plaintiff to prove it.   But it is insisted that under the twenty-first section of the "act to regulate the practice in suits of law" in this state, the plea unless sworn to, cannot have this effect, and that in this case it can be pleaded for no other purpose.   The act provides that "no plea in abatement, plea of *non est factum*, non-assignment, nor any other plea, replication or other pleadings, denying or requiring proof of the execution or assignment of any bond, bill, release, or instrument of writing, etc., shall be received, unless supported by oath or affirmation."

This statute having been passed subsequent to the enactment of the process act of 1828, by congress, can have no force to regulate the practice of this court, unless the court adopt it as a rule of practice.

If not sworn to the plea does not put the plaintiff to the proof of the instrument; but no reason is perceived why the plea should not be held good for every other legitimate purpose, though filed without affidavit.   Under it the defendant may give payment in evidence, accord and satisfaction, etc., and to let in these defenses the plea is not required to be sworn to.   And if it may be used for this purpose without affidavit, the demurrer cannot be sustained.   We think the plea admits the execution of the note and the assignment, on which the action is brought, not being sworn to, but that it is good for other purposes, and that the demurrer must be overruled.

§ 530.   *The plea of duress by the maker of a note in a suit brought by an assignee is bad, unless notice be averred.*

The demurrer to the second plea raises the question whether the duress of Johnston can be jointly pleaded with his co-defendants.   However this may be, there is a conclusive objection to this plea.   This suit is brought by the indorsee of the note, and the plea does in no way, by notice or otherwise, connect him with the duress so as to affect the validity of the note in his hands.   We are clear, therefore, that the plea is bad and the demurrer to it is sustained.

§ 531.   *A plea of fraud in obtaining a note, although expressed in general terms, is good.*

The fourth plea, to which there is a demurrer, alleges that the note was obtained by fraud, covin and misrepresentation.   The additional allegation in this plea, that the note was given without consideration, has been struck out, and this removes one of the causes of demurrer specially assigned to this plea.   And the only objection to the plea, as it now stands, is that fraud, covin and misrepresentation cannot be pleaded on these general grounds.   From the remarks of the counsel, this plea was principally objected to as presenting two distinct grounds of defense: fraud and want of consideration.   But the plea having been amended, it is unnecessary to consider this objection.

Fraud may be given in evidence in this case under the general issue, but the plea is not demurrable on that ground. The defense it sets up is not a matter of fact which amounts to a denial of the allegation which the plaintiff is bound to prove in support of his declaration. It would seem to follow, if fraud may be given in evidence in this case under the general issue, that the plea is not objectionable on account of its generality. 1 Chitty, Pl. (ed. 1839), 570; 9 Co., 110; 2 Maul. & Selw., 378.

§ 532. *A plea of fraud in the payee must aver notice to the holder.*

But it contains no averment that the indorsee participated in the fraud or had any knowledge of it. In this respect the plea is fatally defective. In the case of Bramah *v.* Roberts, 27 Com. L. Rep., the chief justice says, "the third plea in this case, which is pleaded to an action brought by the indorsees against the acceptors of a bill of exchange, is in effect no more than this, that the defendants were defrauded of the bill of exchange, and that the acceptance was given by them without consideration. Now, inasmuch as the indorsee of a bill of exchange is, by law, *prima facie* assumed to hold it for consideration, inasmuch as we are not to presume a notice which would make him a fraudulent agent in taking a bill of exchange, and inasmuch as this plea is silent upon the subject of want of consideration on the part of the indorsees, or of notice of fraud, we are to ask ourselves whether, upon the transfer of a bill of exchange, the circumstance of the acceptor having been defrauded at the time when he gave the acceptance is an answer against an innocent indorsee for a valuable consideration without notice. It seems to me that it is not a sufficient answer." The demurrer to this plea must be sustained.

§ 533. *A plea which is a repetition of a former plea is useless and demurrable.*

In the fifth plea Johnston pleads *non assumpsit,* having previously filed the same plea in connection with his co-defendant. This is clearly irregular, and this plea would have been struck out on motion. A defendant cannot incumber the record by a repetition of the same pleas, which can in no respect change the nature of his defense.

§ 534. *The indorsement of a bill imports a consideration.*

We come now to consider the demurrer to the replication to the third plea. This plea averred a want of consideration in the note, and that the indorsee had full notice of it, and that it was assigned without consideration. To this the plaintiff replies that the note was not given without consideration, that it was not assigned without consideration, and that he had no notice. The defendant demurs to this replication. He alleges it is double and therefore bad.

The pleading is in accordance with the rules lately adopted in England. The plea of *non assumpsit* on bills and notes, and in the action of *assumpsit* generally, is abolished, and all matters in evidence are required to be specially pleaded by these rules. If this shall produce some perplexity in pleading and no little awkwardness in requiring a party to plead negatively, yet it will give greater point and certainty to the controversy in actions of *assumpsit.*

Until very recently it is believed not to have been doubted that the indorsement of a negotiable instrument was *prima facie* evidence of a consideration. This is the doctrine laid down by Mr. Chitty and other writers on bills of exchange and promissory notes. And the doctrine is abundantly sustained by numerous adjudications. Chitt. on Bills (ed. 1839), 79; Philips *v.* Pluckwell, 2 M. & S., 395; 1 Black. Rep., 445; 1 Salk. 25; 2 Ld. Raym., 760; 2 Bl. Com., 446; Selw. N. P. (4th ed.), 340.

But in a late case in the exchequer, where the plea alleged that the defendant accepted without consideration, and that the plaintiff (the indorsee) was a holder without consideration, the latter allegation being denied by the replication, which admitted the former, Lord Abinger is represented to have questioned the principle that the indorsement imported a consideration. And he seems to have expressed surprise that doubts were entertained on the subject. The view of his lordship seems to have been very much influenced by the practice of the London bankers, who receive indorsed bills for collection. If an indorsement on a bill should be held not to import a consideration, it must shake the credit of commercial paper and produce injurious consequences on commercial transactions. And we think the principle has been too long and too beneficially settled to be now questioned.

If it be made to appear that the assignment was without consideration, then the drawer or acceptor of the bill may set up any defense to the bill which he might have done before it was negotiated. For, in the language of Mr. Chitty, in such a case the indorser is in privity with the first holder, and will be affected by everything which would affect him. The title of the plaintiff not being founded on a consideration, he shall not be permitted to enforce it against good faith and conscience. Pearson *v.* Pearson, 7 John., 26; Store *v.* Wadley, 3 John., 124; Ten Eyck *v.* Vanderpool, 8 John., 120; Denniston *v.* Bacon, 10 John., 198, 231; Bayler *v.* Haber, 6 Mass., 451; Slade *v.* Halsted, 7 Cowen, 322; Lawrence *v.* Stonington Bank, 6 Conn., 521; Hill *v.* Buckminister, 5 Pick., 301.

§ 535. *To a plea that the note was given and the assignment made without consideration, issue should be taken on one and not on both the allegations.*

In this case the defendant avers a want of consideration both in the making and assignment of the note. And the plaintiff answers that the note and the assignment were not made without consideration. To this the defendant demurs, and alleges that the replication is multifarious in traversing the want of consideration of the note and of the assignment; that the issue should be joined on one of these allegations, which would admit the truth of the other.

The same principle would seem to apply to this case as to pleas of accord and satisfaction and of arbitrament and award. Mr. Chitty says that the replication to a plea of accord and satisfaction may either deny the delivery of the chattel in satisfaction, or, protesting against the fact, may deny the acceptance. And he observes, if an award be pleaded the plaintiff may either deny the submission or the award; but it appears he may not deny both the submission and the award. And yet it is essential to the defense that the allegations of the plea should extend to both these facts; and a denial of the award admits the submission. The precedents are in conformity with this rule.

Now in the present case the averment of want of consideration in making the note and also the assignment was essential to the defense set up; and yet it would seem that the plaintiff must take issue on the one allegation or the other, and that he cannot traverse both.

This narrows the plaintiff's right to one of the grounds taken in the defense, both of which were essential to the sufficiency of the plea. But the same thing may be said of the replication to a plea of arbitrament and award. To make that plea good, both the submission and the award must be alleged; but the plaintiff must limit his answer to the denial of one or the other.

In the case of Bramah *v.* Roberts, 27 Com. L. Rep., 460, the second plea alleged that the defendants, the acceptors, had been defrauded of the acceptance; that notice of the fraud was given to the plaintiffs, and that they received the bill by indorsement, without a full and valuable consideration. The replication took issue on the consideration of the assignment. And in the case in the exchequer above referred to the issue was made up in the same way.

§ 536. *An issue must be single although embracing several facts.*

An issue consists of a single, certain and material point. But this point may embrace several facts if they be dependent and connected, and go to establish the main point of the plea. Now, the facts alleged in the plea, in this case, are distinct and independent of each other. The facts which go to show a want of consideration in the note are in no way connected with the consideration of the assignment. No two facts could be more disconnected than the making of the note and the assignment of it, and the consideration on which these acts were done.

In the case of Webb *v.* Weatherby, 27 Com. L. Rep., 474, the defendant pleaded that he paid and the plaintiff received a full satisfaction of the said promise, etc., a certain sum. The plaintiff replied that the defendant did not pay the said sum in full satisfaction and discharge of the promise, nor was the said sum accepted in full discharge, etc.

It was contended that in an action for damages it may well be stated that the defendant has paid something, and yet the plaintiff has not accepted it in satisfaction of his entire demand, or *vice versa.* It is necessary, therefore, in such an action, for the defendant to aver acceptance in satisfaction as well as payment. 1 Stra., 573; 3 East, 256. And both the payment and acceptance being material allegations, the plaintiff ought to elect on which of them he will tender an issue. But Tindal, C. J., said this is not a plea of accord and satisfaction, but of a payment received in satisfaction of the plaintiff's demand; the receipt in satisfaction virtually implies that the payment was made in satisfaction; and I cannot see how the defendant is injured by the plaintiff's taking issue on the entire allegation.

In that case the replication was held to be good, on the ground that the receipt of the money in satisfaction virtually included the payment of it in satisfaction. The payment and the receipt in satisfaction were connected, and might be included in the same allegation. The plea would have been good, however, had it alleged only the receipt of the money in satisfaction. But there is no such connection and dependence in the distinct grounds alleged in the plea under consideration.

§ 537. *An issue should consist of an affirmative and a negative.*

There is another objection to this replication which it may be well to suggest, although the special causes of demurrer do not embrace it, and our opinion is formed on the ground above stated. The replication states in answer to the plea that the note and the assignment were not made without consideration. This answer is negative, and it seems to us it should be in the positive. Mr. Chitty says (1 Chitt. Pl., 629) that an issue should in general be upon an affirmative and a negative, and not upon two affirmatives, etc., nor should the issue be on two negatives, thus: "if the defendant plead that he requested the plaintiff to deliver an abstract of his title, but that the plaintiff did not, when so requested, deliver such abstract, but neglected and refused so to do, the plaintiff cannot reply that he did not neglect and refuse to deliver such abstract; but should reply either denying the request, or affirmatively that he did deliver the abstract."

The pleas in the cases above referred to were all drawn affirmatively, that the note was given and the assignment made for a good and valuable consideration. This averment will not throw the proof of the consideration on the plaintiff beyond that which the execution of the note and of the assignment import. He may introduce evidence to rebut that given by the defendant, going to show a want of consideration. Upon the whole, we think the demurrer of the defendant must be sustained to the replication to the third plea; and that the demurrer of the plaintiff to the second, fourth and fifth pleas must be sustained, and the one to the first plea overruled.

UNITED STATES v. GIRAULT.

(11 Howard, 22–33. 1850.)

Opinion by MR. JUSTICE NELSON.

STATEMENT OF FACTS.— This is a writ of error to the district court held in and for the northern district of Mississippi. The action was brought on the official bond of Girault, a receiver of the public money, against him and his sureties. The bond is dated the 8th of July, 1838, and conditioned that he shall faithfully execute and discharge the duties of the office of receiver. The breach assigned is, that on the 2d of June, 1840, the said Girault had received a large amount of the public moneys, to wit, the sum of $8,952.37, which he had neglected and refused to pay over to the government.

All the defendants were personally served with process. The sureties appeared and pleaded:

1. That after the making of the bond in the declaration mentioned, and before the commencement of the suit, to wit, on the 25th of September, 1840, a certain other official bond was given by Girault and others to the plaintiffs, describing it, which they accepted in full discharge and satisfaction of the first one.

2. That on the 2d of June, 1840, and on divers days before that day, the said Girault gave receipts as receiver for moneys paid on the entry of certain lands therein specified, and returned the same to the treasury department, to the amount of $10,000, and of which the amount in the declaration mentioned was part and parcel. And that neither the $10,000, nor any part thereof, was paid to or received by him, the said Girault.

3. The same as the second, except that the receipts given were for several parcels of land entered by Girault for his own use.

4. That no public moneys of the United States came to the hands of Girault, as receiver, after the execution of the bond, nor were there any received by him, for which the defendants were accountable by virtue of said bond, prior to the execution of the same, remaining in his hands as such receiver at the time of the execution, or at any time afterwards, which had not been paid over and accounted for according to law before the commencement of the suit.

To these several pleas the plaintiffs put in a general demurrer, to which there was a joinder. The court gave judgment for the plaintiffs on the first plea; and for the defendants on the second, third and fourth. Upon which the plaintiffs bring error.

§ 538. *A plea to declaration on an official bond is bad which sets up a subsequent bond as a discharge.*

The first plea is not before us, as judgment was rendered for the plaintiffs. It is undoubtedly bad, as the new bond could be no satisfaction for the damages that had accrued for the breach of the condition of the old one. Lovelace v. Crocket, Hob., 68; Bac. Abr., tit. Pleas, 2, 289.

§ 539. *A plea must answer the declaration, not the evidence expected to be given under it.*

The second and third pleas are also bad, and the court below erred in giving judgment for the defendants upon them. They are pleas, not to the declaration or breach charged, but to the evidence upon which it is assumed the plaintiffs will rely at the trial to maintain the action. The breach is general, that the defendant Girault has in his possession $8,952.37 of the public moneys which he neglects and refuses to pay over.

The defendants answer that the evidence which the receiver has furnished the plaintiffs of this indebtedness is false and fabricated; and that no part of the sum in question was ever collected or received by him; thereby placing the defense upon the assumption of a fact or facts which may or may not be material in the case, and upon which the plaintiffs may or may not rely in making out the indebtedness. A defendant has no right to anticipate or undertake to control by his pleadings the nature or character of the proof upon which his adversary may think proper to rely in support of his cause of action, nor to ground his defense upon any such proofs. He must deal with the facts as they are set forth in the declaration; and not with the supposed or presumed evidence of them.

If the defendants are right in the principle sought to be maintained in their second and third pleas, a denial of any public moneys being in the hands of the receiver for which they were liable within the condition of their bond would have answered all their purposes. For if the plaintiffs possess no other evidence of their liability than that of the fabricated receipts, and the sureties are not responsible for the moneys thus acknowledged, nor estopped from controverting them, a plea to the effect above stated would have enabled them to present that defense.

§ 540. *Sureties for a public officer are estopped from setting up his fraud as operating their release from the penalty of the bond.*

The principle, however, upon which these pleas are founded, is as indefensible as the rule of pleading adopted for the purpose of setting it up. The condition of the bond is that Girault shall faithfully execute and discharge the duties of his office as a receiver of the public moneys. The defendants have bound themselves for the fulfillment of these duties, and are, of course, responsible for the very fraud committed upon the government by that officer, which is sought to be set up here in bar of the action on the bond.

As Girault would not be allowed to set up his own fraud for the purpose of disproving the evidence of his indebtedness, we do not see but that, upon the same principle, they should be estopped from setting it up as committed by one for whose fidelity they have become responsible. This is not like the case of The United States v. Boyd, 5 How., 29. There the receipts which had been returned to the treasury department, upon which the indebtedness was founded, and which had been given on entries of the public lands without exacting the money, in fraud of the government, were all given before the execution of the official bond upon which the suit was brought.

The sureties were not, therefore, responsible for the fraud; and it was these transactions on the part of the receiver, which had transpired anterior to the time when the sureties became answerable for the faithful execution of his duties, in respect to which it was held that they could not be estopped by his returns to the government. No part of them fell within the time covered by the official bond.

The fourth plea affords a full and complete answer to the breach assigned in the declaration, and should not have been demurred to. As it takes issue upon the breach it should have concluded to the country; but this defect is available only by a special demurrer.

§ 541. *Upon a general demurrer to several pleas if any one is good the demurrer is bad.*

As the demurrer put in is general to the four several pleas, if any one of them constituted a good bar to the action the demurrer is bad. On this ground the judgment was properly given against the plaintiffs in the court below. They should have asked leave to withdraw the demurrer as to the fourth plea, and have taken issue upon it, instead of allowing the judgment to stand and bringing it to this court on error.

Indeed, when these pleas were put in, the plaintiffs, in order that the case might be disembarrassed of any technical objections or difficulties on account of the pleadings, should have amended their declaration by assigning additional breaches covering the malfeasance in office set up in the second and third pleas. This would have met the grounds of the defense raised by them, and have presented the issues appropriately upon the condition of the bond, whether or not the receiver had faithfully executed the duties of his office.

§ 542. *No final judgment may be entered until the case has been disposed of as to all the defendants.*

The defendant Girault, it appears, was personally served with process, but did not appear. The plaintiffs have not proceeded to judgment, nor discontinued their proceedings as to him. As the case stands, therefore, there is a joint suit against four defendants on the bond, a judgment in favor of three, and the suit as to the fourth undisposed of.

According to the practice in Mississippi, founded upon a statute of the state, in the case of a joint action on a bond or note, separate judgments may be taken against the several defendants, whether by default or on verdict; and the plaintiff may take judgment against some of the defendants, and discontinue as to others. But it is there deemed error, for which the judgment will be reversed, if final judgment is entered up by the plaintiff before the case is finally disposed of in respect to all the parties on the record. 2 How. (Miss.), 870; 4 id., 377; 6 id., 517; 7 id., 304.

In the case in 6 Howard, above cited, the plaintiffs brought a suit against two defendants on a sealed note. The writ was returned served as to one of them, and *non est* as to the other. The declaration was filed against both, and the one personally served appeared and defended; and a verdict was found against him on which judgment was entered, the case remaining undisposed of as to the other defendant. On appeal the court reversed the judgment, remarking that the case should have been disposed of as to all the parties; there is no judgment of discontinuance or dismissal as to one of the defendants.

The same point was ruled in the case in 2 Howard, above referred to; and also in that in 7 Howard. In the last case it is said that it is irregular to enter a final judgment against part of the defendants without disposing of the cause against the others; that it was regular to take judgment by default against those who did not plead; but the judgment in the case should not have been finally entered until the cause was ready for final disposition as to all.

§ 543. *Where the judgment of the court below is not final, a writ of error will be dismissed.*

The practice in this court, in case the judgment or decree is not final, is to dismiss the writ of error or appeal for want of jurisdiction, and remand it to the court below to be further proceeded in. 4 Dall., 22; 3 Wheat., 433; 4 id., 75; 6 How., 201, 206. This is also the rule of the king's bench in England. Metcalfe's Case, 11 Co., 38. It is there laid down in the second resolution, that by the words in the writ, *si judicium inde redditum sit*, etc., are intended, not only a judgment in the chief matters in controversy, but also in the whole of them, so that the suit may be at an end. The reason given is, that, if the record should be removed before the whole matter is determined in the court below, there would be a failure of justice, as the king's bench cannot proceed upon the matters not determined, and upon which no judgment is given, and the whole record must be in the common pleas or king's bench. It is entire, and cannot be in both courts at the same time.

The writ is conditional, and does not authorize the court below to send up the case unless all the matters between all the parties to the record have been finally disposed of. The case is not to be sent up in fragments by a succession of writs of error. Peet *v.* McGraw, 21 Wend., 667.

It is supposed that, inasmuch as judgment is allowed to be entered separately against two or more defendants sued jointly upon a bond or note, according to the statute of Mississippi, the severance of the cause of action is complete; and that any one defendant against whom judgment may be thus entered can bring error, although the case has not been disposed of as to the other defendants. And for a like reason, when a judgment is rendered in favor of one defendant against the plaintiff, the latter may bring error before the suit has been disposed of in respect to the others.

But we have seen that the practice is otherwise under this statute, and that final judgment cannot be properly entered against any of the parties until the whole case is disposed of; and that any neglect in the observance of the rule exposes the judgment to a reversal on error in the appellate court. According to the practice of this court, the judgment cannot be reversed on account of the error, but the case must be dismissed for want of jurisdiction, and remanded to the court below, to be proceeded in and finally disposed of.

As the case must come before that court for further proceedings, it may, in its discretion, on a proper application, relieve the plaintiffs from the embarrassments in which the justice of it seems to have been involved, on account of the unskilfulness of the pleader, by opening the judgment on the demurrer and permitting them to amend the pleadings. It is apparent that judgment has been rendered against them without at all involving the merits of the case. The writ of error is dismissed and the cause remanded to the court below.

CENTRAL OHIO RAILROAD *v.* THOMPSON.

(Circuit Court for Ohio: 2 Bond, 296–304. 1869.)

Opinion of the COURT.

STATEMENT OF FACTS.—The questions now before the court arise on a special demurrer to the third plea of the defendant.

The declaration, in four separate counts, sets forth the grounds on which the plaintiffs seek a recovery. The first and second counts aver that the plaintiffs are the holders and owners of the drafts or bills described in said counts, alleged to have been drawn by the defendant through his agent on himself, payable at one day's sight at the Bank of the Metropolis, in the District of Columbia, with exchange on New York. These drafts, it is averred, were drawn on a sufficient consideration, and were duly accepted by the defendant, and, not being paid, were protested, whereby the defendant became liable to pay to the plaintiffs the amount of said several drafts. The third count is on another draft or bill, drawn in the same manner as those described in the first and second counts, and for a like consideration; but not accepted or paid by the defendant. The fourth is a general count, averring an indebtedness to the plaintiffs for the transportation of horses and mules for the defendant, and at his request, with the usual averment of a promise to pay.

§ 544. *A declaration on bills of exchange stating that they were drawn in consideration of transportation of goods, etc., is good on demurrer although it does not state that the goods were the property of defendant.*

As introductory to the plaintiffs' right of action on the bills or drafts described in the first, second and third counts of the declaration, and explanatory of their ownership of and legal right thereto, the declaration avers, in substance, that on October 1, 1861, in consideration that the plaintiffs, before that time, at the instance and request of the defendant, had transported a large number of mules from and to the places named in the declaration, the defendant was indebted to the plaintiffs in the several sums stated in the several counts, agreed and undertook to pay the same by drafts, to be drawn by his agent or himself, to be accepted by him as already stated. There is no averment, however, that the mules transported were the property of the defendant; and the basis of the plaintiffs' right to a recovery in this action is the promise and undertaking of the defendant to accept and pay the bills or drafts drawn on him by his agent, and his neglect or refusal to do so.

As the demurrer to the defendant's third plea, by a familiar rule of pleading, reaches to the declaration, it will be proper here to inquire preliminarily whether the plaintiffs, in the case made by them, have shown a right to maintain an action to recover the sums stated in the first, second and third counts, on the several bills or drafts described, upon the averment that they are the holders and owners of the same, without indorsement to them. This cannot be a question on this demurrer, for the reason that the supreme court of the United States, in the case in chancery between these parties appealed from this court, adjudged that the remedy of the plaintiffs was not in equity, but by action at law, and therefore remanded the case to this court to be tried in an action at law. 6 Wall., S. C., 134.

And there seems to be no room for a doubt that the averments of the declaration show a promise and undertaking by the defendant, creating a legal liability for which an action may be sustained. There is set forth a promise, upon an alleged consideration, to do an act which the defendant has failed to perform, by reason of which a right of action has accrued to the plaintiffs.

FURTHER STATEMENT OF FACTS.— The only inquiry for the court on this demurrer is, therefore, whether the third plea of the defendant sets forth legal and sufficient grounds to defeat the plaintiffs' right to a recovery in this action.

Without reciting in detail the defendant's third plea, which is of great length, and seemingly obnoxious to the charge of prolixity, it will be sufficient to state its substance. It begins with an averment that the several causes of action stated in the declaration are all parts of one and the same transaction, growing out of the same contract, in which the promises of the defendant were conditional and dependent on obligations to be performed by the plaintiffs, which they did not and would not perform. The plea then avers that on August 30, 1861, and prior and subsequent to that date, the plaintiffs were two railroad companies, each constituting a part of a through line for the transportation of live stock and other property from Cincinnati to Pittsburg, Harrisburg, Baltimore, and other places; that the joint agent of the two companies at Cincinnati, on the said August 30, 1861, submitted a proposition in writing, by which the railroads offered to transport all the horses and mules that Thompson & Groom, and such other persons as they might be interested with, might wish to transport within the next forty days from Cincinnati, by way of Columbus, Steubenville or Bellair, to Pittsburg and Harrisburg, or Baltimore, at certain rates for each car-load, as named in the proposition. And after other stipulations, not material to notice, the written offer of the agent proposed that, for the transportation of horses and mules, William Stuart, as agent of the plaintiffs at Pittsburg, should be authorized to draw on the defendant at the Bank of the Metropolis, in Washington, D. C., at one day's sight for each shipment separately as forwarded from Pittsburg, the drafts to be paid promptly in exchange on New York.

The plea then avers that on the same day, and as a part of the same transaction, the defendant accepted in writing the said offer of the plaintiffs' agent, signing the name of Thompson & Groom. The plea then sets forth that, at the same time, the defendant, in his individual name, signed a written stipulation to the effect that, in pursuance of the foregoing agreement, he authorized William Stuart, as his agent at Pittsburg, to draw on him at one day's sight at the Bank of the Metropolis, Washington City, payable in exchange on New York, for each shipment by Thompson & Groom, as the same should be forwarded from Pittsburg.

The plea then avers that pursuant to this arrangement large numbers of horses and mules were offered to the plaintiffs for transportation, and were received by them; and that, although some were transported under said agreement, in relation to other portions of the animals the plaintiffs were guilty of sundry wrongful acts of commission and omission whereby the animals were greatly injured, and the owners suffered damage to an amount exceeding $24,000, and largely in excess of the sum claimed in this action as due to the plaintiffs. These alleged tortious acts on the part of the plaintiffs are set forth at great length and with great particularity in the plea; but, for the purposes of the question on this demurrer, it is unnecessary to notice them in detail.

§ 545. *A plea in avoidance defective in not responding to allegations of declaration.*

This statement presents, in brief, the grounds of defense set up in the third plea. It purports to be, in its main features, a plea in bar. It is certainly somewhat peculiar in its structure, and has not been drawn with a very strict reference to the rules of special pleading still in force in this court. It is not proposed to notice the numerous points made by the counsel for the plaintiffs in his very elaborate argument in support of the demurrer. There are two objections to the plea which seem to be decisive, and these will be noticed very briefly. The first is that the plea, without denying the material allegations of the declaration on which the plaintiffs base their right to recover, avers, in avoidance of the defendant's liability, the failure of the plaintiffs to perform another agreement between other parties, the performance of which is alleged to be a condition precedent to any liability by the defendant on his promise or undertaking as set out in the declaration. As before stated, the contract obligation of the defendant, as averred, is, in substance, that in consideration that the plaintiffs had agreed to transport horses and mules at the rates stated, for Thompson & Groom and the persons with whom they might be associated, from and to the places named, the defendant authorized Stuart, as his agent, to draw on him for each shipment made from Pittsburg; the bills so drawn to be in exchange in New York. The declaration avers that shipments were made from Pittsburg, in consideration of which the defendant's agent drew the several bills in payment described in the declaration, two of which were accepted by the defendant but not paid — the third not accepted or paid. Then follows the averment of the defendant's liability to pay these bills, in virtue of his agreement to accept and pay them.

There would seem to be no ground for a doubt that the facts averred in the declaration show a good cause of action against the defendant. His promise to accept and pay the bills to be drawn by his agent is clearly a valid promise, and his failure to do so imports a liability to the plaintiffs as the owners and holders of the bills. The only question, therefore, arising on the demurrer is whether the matters set forth in the plea are a legal and valid ground of objection to the plaintiffs' claim. And it seems clear that the plea does not respond to the cause of action asserted by the plaintiffs. It does not deny that shipments of animals were made pursuant to the agreement between the parties, for which the bills were severally drawn; but avers that, under the agreement to transport horses and mules for Thompson & Groom and their associates, the plaintiffs failed to perform their agreement and were guilty of sundry torts, whereby they sustained great injuries. But there is no averment in the plea of any non-performance or tort in reference to the shipments for the freight of which the bills were drawn. In a word, there is no averment in the plea of any facts in avoidance of the defendant's liability on his separate, individual promise that the bills should be drawn, accepted and paid by him; that in making this promise the defendant incurred an individual responsibility distinct from any liability by him as a member of the firm of Thompson & Groom is a legal inference from the facts set out in the declaration. In the written acceptance of the offer, by the plaintiffs, to transport stock for Thompson & Groom and the persons with whom they might be interested, he had signed the name of that firm, of which he was a member. But as no mode of payment for freight was provided for in the plaintiffs' proposition or the written acceptance of the firm, the defendant, in his own name, took upon himself the responsibility of agreeing to accept and pay bills to be drawn on him for each shipment from Pittsburg.

It seems to the court, therefore, that the plea is defective in not responding to the allegations of the declaration, which assert the cause-of action against the defendant.

§ 546. *A plea is double when, being a plea in bar, it sets up a counter-claim.*
There is, also, as it seems to the court, another still more obvious objection to the plea. While it sets forth, as a bar to the action, substantially the non-performance of a condition precedent, it avers, by way of set-off, counter-claim or recoupment of damages, a claim for a large sum, based on the alleged tor-. tious acts of commission or omission by the plaintiffs in the transportation of the animals, and claims judgment for a large sum against the plaintiffs on that ground. The amount thus claimed, as before noticed, largely exceeds the sum claimed by the plaintiffs in this action. There is no rule of pleading

known to the court by which such a claim can be set up in a plea in bar of the action. If there is a basis for such a claim it must be set forth in a separate plea of set-off, or by notice of special matter. Its insertion in this plea clearly subjects it to the charge of duplicity; and upon this ground, if upon no other, the demurrer must be sustained.

§ 547. *Unliquidated damages accruing to third persons cannot be set off upon a contract made by defendant, although he may be the factor or bailee of the parties injured.*

But the court cannot perceive that in any way the matter set forth in the plea can be available to the defendant as a matter of set-off, counter-claim or recoupment. The alleged tortious acts of the plaintiffs affect, not the property of the defendant, but the property of Thompson & Groom, and the unknown persons with whom they were associated. If, on the theory assumed by the court, the plaintiffs have set out a good cause of action against the defendant, it is clearly not competent for the defendant, in avoidance of his liability, to assert a claim against the plaintiffs for tortious acts affecting the property, not of himself, but of Thompson & Groom and other persons. It needs no citation of authority in support of this proposition. It is not necessary to decide whether, as a claim for unliquidated damages arising from alleged torts, it can, under any circumstances, be set up as a set-off to a claim founded on contract. If Thompson & Groom, or other parties interested in the property injured by the torts of the plaintiffs, have a ground of action against the plaintiffs, their redress is open to them in a suit for that purpose. But, clearly, the defendant cannot set off in this suit a claim for damages accruing to property of other persons. And this objection, as it seems to the court, is not obviated by the averment of the plea that the defendant was the bailee or factor of the owners of the animals alleged to have been injured, and as such had a qualified interest in them, and a right to maintain an action in his own name for the tortious acts of the plaintiffs. It is argued that if he had such a right to sue he may defend in this suit by setting up the injuries sustained by the owners on account of his interest in the property as bailee or factor. If such a plea were sustainable, it is not perceived how it could be available to the defendant, as asserted in this third plea. It would seem to be incongruous with other allegations and grounds of defense set up in the plea, and therefore subjecting it to the charge of duplicity. But if separately pleaded it is liable to objection. In the first place the defendant, as the partner of the firm of Thompson & Groom, had a proprietary interest in the property, and I do not perceive that in any legal sense he can be held to be a bailee or factor. And again, his liability to plaintiffs, as set forth in the declaration, is based on his individual contract, liability or promise, in answer to which he cannot assert, by way of set-off or otherwise, that he was bailee or factor for the owners, and that the property was injured by the wrongful acts of the plaintiff in its transportation.

These are all the points which it is deemed material to notice. In passing on this demurrer I have not supposed it necessary to enter on a more elaborate consideration of the points adverted to, for the reason that the more important of them were brought to the notice of the court and decided when this case was before it, as a suit in chancery, prior to its removal to the supreme court. In that case the court expressed the opinion that if the allegations of misfeasance and malfeasance against the railroads, in the transportation of the animals in question, could be sustained by evidence, the owners had a plain remedy by suit for the injuries alleged, but that a recovery for these injuries is not available to the defendant as a defense to his liability on the special contract or promise set up by the plaintiffs. The demurrer is sustained.

GRUNNINGER *v.* PHILPOT.

(Circuit Court for Illinois: 5 Bissell, 82–85. 1869.)

Action upon a note. Several pleas were filed, to which plaintiff demurred. Opinion by DRUMMOND, J.

I think that these pleas should be amended. The history of the case, as stated in the pleas, seems to be that several persons agreed to form a joint stock company, the capital of which was to consist of various oil wells which they were to run; that the deceased, whom the present executrix represents, agreed to be a party to this arrangement and transfer certain portions of his interest which he had in the oil wells and oil lands, etc., to this company; and that as a part of the consideration of his entering into this agreement the note, which is the subject-matter of this suit, was given by these defendants. The allegations set forth in the pleas are that the consideration has failed in whole or in part; also that there were some misrepresentations made by Mr. Grunninger.

§ **548.** *Plea of failure of consideration,— distinctness and precision required.*

The question is whether the account is presented with that distinctness and precision which the rules of pleading require in order to constitute a defense; and in looking over the pleas to which the demurrer has been interposed, viz., the third, fourth, fifth, sixth and seventh pleas, it has struck me that they are wanting in that precision of language and distinctness of averment that are necessary. I will state, in the first place, what I understand to be the rule in such cases. When the defense is the failure of consideration to an action on a promissory note, either in whole or in part, the plea should allege distinctly and with precision what was the consideration for which the note was given, and that there was no other consideration. Where the plea alleges a total failure of consideration it should also state that the consideration has failed, and should set forth in what respect, and where the plea alleges a partial failure of consideration it should set forth to what extent there has been a partial failure and wherein; not that as to the amount it is absolutely necessary that the proof should correspond with the plea in that respect, but the court should see from the averment in the plea to what extent there has been a failure of the consideration where a partial failure of consideration is relied upon. Where fraudulent representations are relied upon it must appear what they were, with all the necessary incidents of time and circumstance, and also that the party, relying upon the representations that were made, entered into the contract and gave the note, also of course alleging, as in the other case, what was the consideration, and the only consideration, of the note.

§ **549.** *Distinction between motive of giving a note and consideration therefor.*

The third plea does not distinctly set forth what was the only consideration of the note, and it also sets forth that there was some fraud and deceit practiced by Mr. Grunninger; "that if they would purchase from him a certain interest which he pretended to have in certain oil lands situated in the county of Venago, Pa., for a certain price, he would become a party to the enterprise which is referred to in the second plea, upon the terms proposed in a writing obligatory," — which writing obligatory, by the way, is not very distinctly set forth. "And thereupon the said defendants executed to the said Lawrence Grunninger the said promissory note in the said first and second counts in said plaintiff's declaration mentioned." There is no statement here as to what was the only consideration upon which that note was given. What was the consideration? Why the note was executed is one thing. There may have been a great many motives for the execution of the note; what is the consideration of the note is another thing, and it must be distinctly and substantially set forth. As has been suggested, there may be a *bona fide* debt due from one party to another which may be an open book account or in any other form, and from various motives the debtor may give a note. Now why he gave the note may be because the man asked him under particular circumstances, or at a particular time; but the consideration of the note would be an entirely different thing; it might be goods sold and delivered, or for land sold, or for any other good consideration.

§ 550. *How and to what extent consideration failed should be alleged.*

The remaining pleas are all, I think, liable to the criticism of want of precision, in this respect: that they allege that Grunninger would pay into and contribute toward the assets of the company which was to be formed certain property; that Grunninger executed a certain writing, and that to secure the payment of the sum of $3,000, so agreed to be paid by the defendants, the promissory note was given. And they allege that although the company was duly and within a reasonable time formed and incorporated as proposed in the agreement, "yet that said Lawrence Grunninger did not nor would not contribute toward the assets nor pay into the property of said company the property in said writing obligatory mentioned, but wholly refused so to do." It does not distinctly appear to what extent or in what respect there was a failure to comply with the obligation on the part of Grunninger as entered into by him, nor is the consideration for which the note was given set forth with that distinctness that I think is necessary. I think the same objection exists to all the pleas.

§ 551. *Profert.*

Where profert is made of an instrument in writing, and a question is made on that writing, it ought to be presented to the court so that the court can see it. Demurrer sustained to the third, fourth, fifth, sixth and seventh pleas, with leave to amend.

UNITED STATES *v.* DAIR.

(District Court for Indiana: 4 Bissell, 280–283. 1869.)

Opinion by McDONALD, J.

STATEMENT OF FACTS.— Debt on a penal bond against the principal and his sureties. The condition of the bond is that Jonathan M. Dair, the principal, a distiller, should, in all respects, comply with the requirements of the law in relation to distilled spirits. The breach laid is that Dair unlawfully removed from his distillery eight thousand two hundred and fifty gallons of distilled spirits otherwise than into a bonded warehouse. Dair and his sureties, William F. Davison and Abraham Briggs, all plead separately. And the government demurs to all the pleas except two pleas of general *non est factum* filed by the sureties.

§ 552. *A plea that the breach is less than that charged in the declaration is bad.*

Dair files but one plea. It seems to be intended as a traverse of the breach of the condition of the bond charged in the declaration. It is substantially as follows: That it is untrue that he removed eight thousand two hundred and fifty gallons of distilled spirits from his distillery otherwise than into a bonded warehouse; that it is untrue, as is alleged in the declaration, that there is due to the plaintiff $16,500 for taxes unpaid upon spirits distilled by Dair; but that, on the contrary, the number of gallons of distilled spirits unlawfully removed by him is less than is stated in the declaration, and the amount of taxes unpaid on spirits unlawfully removed by him is less than that stated in the declaration.

This plea is so obviously and outrageously bad that it deserves no consideration by the court. It looks very much like a sham plea. The demurrer to it is sustained; and an interlocutory judgment on it against Dair will be rendered.

§ 553. *A plea of non est factum, on the ground that the instrument is an escrow, must aver that the instrument was delivered to some third person, to be delivered to the obligee only on performance of a condition.*

Davison, one of the sureties, has filed three pleas — a general plea of *non est factum* and two special pleas of *non est factum.* To the two last there are demurrers. The first of these special pleas of *non est factum* avers that Davison signed the bond when it was in blank as to the names of the other obligors; that he signed it at the request of one William F. Sanks, on his assurance that it should be executed by one James Dair before it should be delivered to the obligee; that said James Dair never executed it; and that Davison never would have signed it but on condition that said James Dair should also sign it.

This plea is an attempt to show that, as to Davison, the instrument is a mere escrow. But this it fails to do. To make the instrument such the plea ought to have averred that the supposed bond was delivered to some third person to be delivered to the obligee only on the performance of the condition pleaded. For want of such averment the plea is bad and the demurrer to it is sustained.

The second special plea of *non est factum* filed by Davison is like the first, except that it adds that "said supposed writing," after he signed it, "was left with William F. Sanks as an escrow, to be delivered by him to the plaintiff's agent in case the same was so afterwards executed by James Dair, and not otherwise."

This is a good plea to show that, as to Davison, the supposed bond is a mere escrow and not his deed. It shows a signing and delivery to a stranger, to be delivered to the obligee only on the performance of a condition precedent, which it avers was never performed. If the facts thus pleaded are true, it is certain that the instrument sued on is not the deed of the defendant Davison. Demurrer overruled.

The defendant Briggs has filed four pleas, to the second, third and fourth of which there are demurrers. The second of these pleas is substantially the same as the plea of the principal obligor, Jonathan M. Dair, which we have already considered. And for the same reason on which that plea is held bad the demurrer to this is sustained. The third and fourth pleas of Briggs are copies of the second and third pleas of Davison, already discussed, and the ruling on them must be the same. The demurrer to the third plea of Briggs is therefore sustained, and the demurrer to his fourth plea is overruled.

McDONALD v. ORVIS.

(Circuit Court for Illinois: 5 Bissell, 183-185. 1870.)

STATEMENT OF FACTS.— Action upon a contract. Defendant in his plea avers that the contract set forth in the declaration does not set forth the contract as made between the parties, but that the same is drawn up by plaintiff, and is a fraud upon defendant's rights. To which plea plaintiff demurs.

§ 554. *A plea is bad if it seeks to change a written contract by parol evidence.* Opinion by BLODGETT, J.

This plea amounts to an averment that the written contract, or the modification of the original contract, which is set up in plaintiff's declaration, is not the true contract made between the parties, but that it is a fraud upon the defendant.

I cannot conceive that an averment of that kind would allow the introduction of any testimony such as would sustain the averment on a trial of the cause at law. It is, in substance, an attempt to modify or change a written contract by parol testimony. The preceding plea avers that the contract was different from what is set up in the declaration, and concludes with this proposition to offer parol evidence to show wherein it differs. I think the demurrer to the plea is well taken, not only for this cause, but for the cause of want of certainty in the plea itself in not stating wherein it is different. I do not think there is enough certainty in the plea, even if it did not seek to change a written contract by parol evidence.

§ 555. *When the declaration contains one good count a general demurrer thereto will be overruled.*

But it is answered on the part of the defendant that a bad plea is a good and sufficient answer to a bad declaration, which I understand, of course, to refer to a well-known rule of pleading, that a demurrer, when taken to a plea, may be made to reach back to the declaration or pleading where the first defect originated; and under many circumstances that rule is applied; but in this case the declaration contains two counts — a special count on a special promise, and the common counts. The plea purports to answer the entire declaration, and of course, if a general demurrer had been introduced to the whole declaration, the demurrer would have to be overruled, because there is one good count in the declaration — the common count for goods sold and delivered, money lent, etc.

§ 556. *A demurrer does not cut back to the declaration if the general issue has been pleaded.*

There is also an exception to the rule contended for by the defendant's counsel which is well recognized, viz.: That a demurrer cannot be carried back to the declaration if the general issue has been pleaded; because if it should it would enable a party, after having tendered an issue of fact on the declaration, to raise an issue of law by putting in a bad plea. If a party wishes to demur to the declaration he must do it before he tenders an issue of fact. The proposition is undoubtedly sound where there is not an issue of fact made, but here, inasmuch as the demurrer is general, if carried back, the declaration, as a whole, would be sustained, because it has one good count, and because the defendant has already made an issue of fact on the declaration. The demurrer must be sustained.

§ 557. **A plea must be single** and rest the defense on a single point. Stanton v. Seymour, 5 McL., 267.

§ 558. A plea in bar must show that the plaintiff has no right to recover. Smith v. Ely, 5 McL., 76.

§ 559. Opposed to record.— A plea cannot contradict the record. Hall v. Singer, 3 McL., 17.

§ 560. Hypothetical pleas, which neither admit nor deny the matter charged, are bad upon general demurrer. Dunlop v. Monroe, 1 Cr. C. C., 536.

§ 561. Certainty to a common intent is sufficient in a plea in bar. Martin r. Bartow Iron Works,* 35 Ga., 320.

§ 562. Each plea must stand on its own merits, and cannot be aided or explained by reference to others. Ibid.

§ 563. The allegations of a plea which are immaterial may be regarded as surplusage, and, if the other matters set forth in the plea are well pleaded and constitute a sufficient answer to the declaration, the immaterial allegations do not vitiate the plea even on special demurrer. Derby v. Jacques. 1 Cliff., 425.

§ 564. An answer should be, what its name purports, a counter-statement of facts, a confutation of what is alleged by the other party, and should be neither evasive nor argumentative. Pollock v. Laurence Co.,* 2 Pittsb. R., 187.

§ 565. Sham, redundant and frivolous defenses, what constitutes.— A sham defense is one that is palpably false. A redundant defense is one that has prolixity of statement or unnecessary repetition. A frivolous defense is one that contains nothing which affects the plaintiff's case, and sets up no defense thereto. So, in an action to recover possession of land, a plea that the defendant has right of possession as assignee of an unsatisfied mortgage is frivolous, as not showing that the defendant entered with the consent of the mortgagor; but such plea is neither sham nor redundant. Witherell v. Wiberg, 4 Saw., 232.

§ 566. The defendant is required to set forth his matter of defense specifically, and with the same precision and accuracy which are required of a plaintiff. Meeker v. Wren,* 1 Wash. T'y, 87; Roeder v. Bonn,* 1 Wash. T'y, 130.

§ 567. Equitable defenses under section 914, Revised Statutes.— Section 914, United States Revised Statutes. conforming pleadings in federal courts to those of the local courts, does not authorize setting up merely equitable defenses in answer to a suit on a judgment. Montejo v. Owen, 14 Blatch., 324.

§ 568. A plea on the merits waives antecedent irregularities set up in pleas in abatement or demurrers. Bell v. Railroad Co., 4 Wall., 598.

§ 569. A plea that answers only part of a count in the declaration is demurrable. Culbertson v. The Wabash Navigation Co., 4 McL., 544.

§ 570. A plea which begins by assuming to answer the whole declaration and concludes by admitting a part thereof is demurrable; for a plea in bar must either deny that the plaintiff ever had the cause of action complained of, or admit he once had but insist that it no longer subsists; and the measure of damages, whether involving questions of law or fact, is not properly the subject-matter of a plea. King v. American, etc.. Co.. 1 Flip., 1.

§ 571. A plea in discharge or avoidance of a bond must state the matter in discharge plainly.— No rule in pleading is better settled, nor upon sounder principles, than that every plea in discharge or avoidance of a bond should state positively and in direct terms the matter in discharge or avoidance. It is not to be inferred arguendo, or upon conjectures. United States v. Bradley, 10 Pet., 343.

§ 572. Statute of limitations, second pleading of.— If the statute of limitations is pleaded and the plea overruled, it cannot be again put in by the same parties or their privies. Fisher v. Rutherford, Bald., 188.

§ 573. Effect of Illinois statute prohibiting defendant to deny his signature.— The provision of the Illinois statute prohibiting defendants sued on written instruments from denying their signatures, except by sworn plea, has no application where the fact of signature is admitted by demurrer, and the only question is as to its legal effect. Hitchcock v. Buchanan,* 15 Otto, 416.

§ 574. A plea purporting to answer the whole declaration, but which really answers but one count, is bad on general demurrer; a fortiori if it cannot be determined for which count it is intended. Matthews v. Matthews, 2 Curt., 105.

§ 575. A plea purporting to cover the whole declaration, but really covering only a part, is bad. Tucker v. Lee, 3 Cr. C. C., 684.

§ 576. A plea of non damnificatus is bad if the breach has been specifically assigned. Ibid.

§ 577. A plea not directly denying some averment of the declaration should conclude with a verification. Ibid.

§ 578. The titling is no part of a plea, but an indication to the clerk in what cause to enter the plea. (Bank of Columbia v. Jones, 2 Cr. C. C., 516, overruled.) Bank of Columbia v. Ott,* 2 Cr. C. C., 529.

§ 579. A plea of payment referring to the instrument as the "supposed writing obligatory" is not bad for inconsistency with itself. The description of the writing may be rejected as surplusage. Murphy v. Byrd,* Hemp., 221.

§ 580. A general plea of fraud is inadmissible. *Ibid.*

§ 581. A plea is bad which only traverses matter of inducement, or which, admitting its allegations as true, does not constitute a bar. White v. How,* 3 McL., 291.

§ 582. A plea of bankruptcy setting up the certificate and discharge required by section 4 of the bankrupt law is good. *Ibid.*

§ 583. Denying written contract must be under oath.— A plea denying the execution of a written contract by joint defendants must be under oath. Frazer v. Wolcott,* 4 McL., 365.

§ 584. Plea cannot contradict record as to appearance of a party.— Where from the record it appears that the defendant appeared in the action, that fact cannot be denied by plea or otherwise. Thompson v. Emmert, 4 McL., 96.

§ 585. The sixty-fifth section of the duty collection act of 1799 interdicted imparlance and sham pleas for delay, but not a good defense founded upon real and substantial merits. *Ex parte* Davenport, 6 Pet., 661.

§ 586. Pleas in bar not subject to technical construction.— Pleas in bar are not to receive a narrow and merely technical construction, but are to be construed according to their entire subject-matter. Withers v. Green, 9 How., 213.

§ 587. Plea in bar answering only in part bad.— A plea professing to be in bar of the whole demand, but answering it only in part, is bad on special demurrer. Postmaster-General v. Reeder, 4 Wash., 678.

§ 588. Attorney's answer not accepted for that of defendant.— The answer of the attorney of a defendant in a suit at law will not be accepted in lieu of the answer of the defendant himself. Read v. Consequa, 4 Wash., 174.

§ 589. Plea cannot set up matters occurring after commencement of suit.— A plea is bad on demurrer which sets up matters which occurred after the commencement of the suit. Lockington v. Smith, Pet. C. C., 466.

§ 590. Plea admits everything in declaration not denied.— A plea which sets up new matter and does not traverse the statements of the declaration admits those statements to be true. Greathouse v. Dunlap, 3 McL., 303.

§ 591. Pleas in avoidance should give color.— A plea is bad which sets up matters in defense, and neither denies nor admits, and avoids the plaintiff's allegations. It should give color to the plaintiff's right. Halsted v. Lyon, 2 McL., 226.

§ 592. Two or more defenses.— A plea is bad if it set up two distinct matters of defense, either of which is sufficient to defeat the plaintiff's action. *Ibid.*

§ 593. Traverse in the negative.— A traverse to an averment, in an information on the acts of 1814, March 1, 1809, and March 2, 1811, that the goods were imported in a vessel not neutral, merely in the negative, is bad. United States v. Hayward, 2 Gall., 497.

§ 594. Plea to certain counts — Plaintiff may reply to part and demur to part.— When a plea is pleaded to certain enumerated counts, the plaintiff may reply to it specially as it applies to some counts, and demur to it as it applies to other counts. Dunlop v. Monroe, 1 Cr. C. C., 536.

§ 595. Conclusions of law cannot be traversed.— A traverse must not be taken on a mere matter or conclusion of law; but if the conclusion is a mixed one of law and fact then it is traversable. So a denial of fraudulent intent in paying one creditor in bankruptcy, if the payment is not denied, is not a sufficient defense. Silverman's Case, 2 Abb., 243.

§ 596. Although a traverse cannot be taken to mere matter of law, still a traverse may be taken to mixed questions of law and fact; for only in this way can the facts be settled on which the law depends. Toppan v. The C., C. & C. R. R. Co., 1 Flip., 74.

§ 597. Evidence should not be pleaded.— So, in an action of trespass upon land, an answer which merely sets up facts from which it might be inferred that the defendant had cause to think he had a right to enter upon the land is irrelevant pleading. Neff v. Pennoyer, 3 Saw., 495.

§ 598. If a plea merely states evidence it is irrelevant; and if the evidence so stated shows no defense it is also frivolous. Wythe v. Myers, 3 Saw., 595.

§ 599. In Texas a party pleading fraud must point out, at least in general terms, the act upon which he relies. Hitchcock v. Galveston, 3 Woods, 287.

§ 600. New matter in answer — California statute.— By California statute, adopted as a rule of pleading by the United States circuit court for California, new matter in the answer is deemed to be controverted by the adverse party. Cheang Kee v. United States, 3 Wall., 320.

§ 601. —— Louisiana practice.— By the practice of the Louisiana courts, adopted in the circuit court of the United States sitting in that state, new facts alleged by the defendant in his answer are considered as denied by the plaintiff without any replication. Levy *v.* Stewart, 11 Wall., 244.

§ 602. **Plea when amounting to a conclusion of law.**— In an action for causing the overflow of land by building a dam the defendant set up a statute allowing him to build a dam of a certain kind, and averred that the dam built was of the kind authorized. *Held*, such plea was bad as stating a conclusion of law instead of stating the facts on which the court could construe the law. Pumpelly *v.* Green Bay Co., 13 Wall., 166.

§ 603. **Setting forth facts as matter of denial — Oregon practice.**— When a defendant cannot deny under oath the *words* of a contract set forth in a declaration, he may adopt, in Oregon, the prudent course of setting forth facts as matter of denial; but after stating that the facts were thus and thus, he should add "and not otherwise," if it is possible that the agreement may be as the defendant says, and as much more as the plaintiff claims, or a demurrer to the plea will be sustained. Naylor *v.* Beeks,* 1 Or., 215.

§ 604. **Conclusion and verification.**— A plea not concluding to the country or with a verification is no plea at all. Wilkinson *v.* Pomeroy,* 9 Blatch., 513.

§ 605. A plea not certified in accordance with the rules of court may be treated as a nullity. *Ibid.*

§ 606. A plea not verified in accordance with the statute would not, as a general principle, be demurrable: but, where it is so held by the state courts, the federal courts will follow the practice. Bell *v.* Vicksburg,* 23 How., 443.

§ 607. An irrelevant and impertinent plea is scandalous and may be stricken out. *Ibid.*

§ 608. The refusal of an inferior court to receive an additional plea, or an amendment to one already filed, can never be assigned as error. This depends on the discretion of the court below, which is regulated more by the circumstances of the case than by any precise rule of law. Insurance Co. *v.* Hodgson,* 6 Cr., 206.

§ 609. **Special matters of defense to be specially pleaded.**— In an action of covenant on a sealed policy of insurance, evidence tending to vacate the policy cannot be introduced under the general issue, as the rule is inflexible that special matters of defense must be specially pleaded. *Ibid.*

§ 610. **Nil debet and non est factum are not inconsistent pleas.** Where, however, the second of these is stricken out on the ground of inconsistency with the first, and it is apparent that defendant was in no way prejudiced thereby, the ruling will not be a ground of reversal, especially as the right to plead more than one plea rests in the discretion of the court. Grand Chute *v.* Winegar,* 15 Wall., 355.

§ 611. **Plea in bar covering same matter as plea in abatement.**— When a plea in abatement is found by a jury against defendant, a plea in bar setting up the same defense may be stricken out. *Ibid.*

§ 612. **May be struck out, when.**— When two pleas are filed to an action, the first denying the cause of action, and the second practically admitting it, the first cannot be stricken out on the ground that it is shown by the second to be false. A plea must stand or fall by itself, and is not sham unless palpably false upon its face. Bachman *v.* Everding,* 1 Saw., 70.

§ 613. When a plea confesses the cause of action and does not avoid it, plaintiff should not move to strike out the plea as frivolous, but should ask for judgment on the pleadings. *Ibid.*

§ 614. —— **special plea after plea of guilty.**— When defendants have pleaded jointly in an action, a special plea by one of them will be inadmissible, and if filed will be stricken out. Varnum *v.* Campbell,* 1 McL., 313.

§ 615. —— **joint plea followed by single plea setting up same defense.**— When defendants jointly plead one defense, and one of them files a single plea setting up the same defense, the latter will be stricken out on motion as unnecessary. Hacker *v.* Stevens,* 4 McL., 540.

§ 616. **Several pleas.**— On demurrer to several pleas, if any one of them going to the whole merits of the case is well pleaded and contains a full and sufficient answer, it will entitle the defendant to judgment. State of Vermont *v.* The Society for the Propagation of Gospel, etc., 2 Paine, 545.

§ 617. The allowance of double pleas and defenses is discretionary with the court, and *mandamus* will not lie for refusal to allow them. *Ex parte* Davenport, 6 Pet., 661.

§ 618. Under section 167 of the code of Oregon several inconsistent defenses may be set up, but each must stand or fall by itself. Hall *v.* Austin, Deady, 104.

§ 619. The law of Louisiana allows general and special pleas to be pleaded together if not inconsistent; and in an action under the code of that state to rescind a sale of slaves on account of their being diseased, alleging knowledge of that fact by the defendant, a special plea that the purchaser was requested to examine them, and refused to do so, is not inconsistent with a general denial. Andrews *v.* Hensler, 6 Wall., 254.

§ 620. **Admission of plea after office judgment — Virginia practice.**— The courts of Virginia have been very liberal in admitting any plea at the next term after an office judgment, which was necessary to bring forward the substantial merits of the case; but at a subsequent term it is a matter of discretion with the court whether they will allow any plea at all. A writ of error will not lie in a case where this discretion has been exercised. Resler v. Shehee, 1 Cr., 110.

§ 621. Plea denying allegation of cross-bill filed.— To a declaration averring that a bill filed by plaintiff was in the nature of a cross-bill, a plea that it was not a cross-bill is bad. Sagory v. Wissman,* 2 Ben., 240.

§ 622. Debt on bond secured by mortgage — Plea of possession taken by mortgagee.— To a declaration in debt on a bond secured by power of sale in a mortgage, a plea is bad which states that plaintiff, who was mortgagee, had entered on the lands to sell and dispose of them, but that instead of doing so he had continued in possession, claiming to be owner; and that the lands were of greater value than the debt. Ibid.

§ 623. Action on distiller's bond — Traverse in the words of the charge.— To a declaration on a distiller's bond, that defendant, having manufactured spirits, had sold and removed for sale the same without first paying the required taxes, a plea traversing this breach in the same words is good on general demurrer. United States v. Hammond,* 4 Biss., 283.

§ 624. A plea is good which craves oyer of the conditions of the bond in suit and alleges generally compliance with all of them. If one of these conditions be performance with certain articles of association, the plea will be sufficient without setting out the articles. Jackson v. Rundlet, 1 Woodb. & M., 381.

§ 625. Covenant — Plea of performance without oyer.— To a declaration on a bond which does not set out the condition of the bond, a plea of performance which does not crave oyer is fatally defective. United States v. Arthur,* 5 Cr., 257.

§ 626. Jurisdiction — Plea as to.— Objection to the jurisdiction of the court by reason of the citizenship of the parties must be specially pleaded. A plea to the merits admits jurisdiction in this respect. Blachley v. Davis,* 1 McL., 412.

§ 627. A plea that the cause of action did not arise within the jurisdiction of the court is a plea in bar, and is good even after office judgment. Smith v. M'Cleod,* 1 Cr. C. C., 43.

§ 628. Manner of giving notice may be given.— A plea may show in what manner, whether by personal service or by attachment, notice is given, as this does not contradict the record, but limits its operation. Lincoln v. Tower, 2 McL., 473.

§ 629. A plea that property was attached and lost is defective in not showing how the loss occurred. Starr v. Moore, 3 McL., 354.

§ 630. Unliquidated damages — Set-off.— Unliquidated damages cannot be pleaded as a set-off. Homas v. McConnell, 3 McL., 381.

§ 631. Payment by note and mortgage — Receipt of proceeds to be averred.— Where a plea alleges that the payee of a note received another note and mortgage, to be applied to the note, it is to be construed that the proceeds of the note and mortgage are to be applied when received; and to make such a plea good it is necessary to aver the receipt of proceeds. Ibid.

§ 632. Plea of foreign judgment — Averment of jurisdiction. — The court being presumed to know the laws of the various states, it is not necessary in a plea setting up a judgment of a state court other than that in which the action is brought to aver that it had jurisdiction. Woodworth v. Spaffords, 2 McL., 168.

§ 633. No authority to sell assigned as breach — Averment of authority not good plea in bar.— If the breach of covenant assigned be that the state had no authority to sell the land, it is not a good plea in bar to say that the governor was legally empowered to sell, although the facts stated in the plea as inducement are sufficient to justify a direct negation of the breach assigned. Fletcher v. Peck, 6 Cr., 87.

§ 634. Denial of part of the allegation as made.— Action on a bond, in the penalty of £20,000, conditioned for payment of £10,000, with an averment that the £20,000 equaled $140,000. Plea, that the £20,000 did not equal $140,000, and that the defendant did not owe that amount. Held, that the pleas were bad; that judgment must be rendered for plaintiff on demurrer; and, the sum being uncertain, either party might demand a jury. Gurney v. Hoge,* 6 Blatch., 499.

§ 635. Action on replevin bond, various pleas to.— In action on a replevin bond, pleas of general performance and non damnificatus are bad; also, no such record, where no record is averred; also, that the plaintiff had no property, where no property is averred; also, a plea to the whole declaration, when it answers only one of the breaches assigned. Wood v. Franklin,* 3 Cr. C. C., 115.

§ 636. Nul tiel record.— Where the record set forth in the declaration is not the foundation of the action, but only matter of inducement, the plea of nul tiel record is not good. United States v. Little,* 3 Cr. C. C., 253.

§ 637. Record, denial of operation of.— Where the record is "showed forth" in the declaration the defendant may deny its operation. Ibid.

§ 638. Performance — When facts constituting should be stated.— In an action on a contract, where the condition precedent is not definitely limited and settled, it is not sufficient to aver that plaintiff has performed all the conditions on his part; the facts showing performance should be stated. William v. Hallett.* 2 Saw., 262.

§ 639. As, for example, where plaintiff agreed to furnish sixty-six or more men for a period not less than three months. *Ibid.*

§ 640. A plea of estoppel must show that defendant was ignorant as to the truth of the matter, and that the defendant could not have conveniently ascertained the same; and it must appear that defendant has acted upon the matter claimed as an estoppel, and has incurred liability and expense. Wythe v. City of Salem,* 4 Saw., 88.

§ 641. Hypothetical plea — Plea of agency.— A demurrer will lie to a plea which is hypothetical, and seeks to avoid a cause of action without admitting it; and a demurrer will lie if a plea sets up that the defendant acted as an agent, and does not give the name of the person for whom he claims to have acted. Morse v. Davis, 5 Blatch., 40.

§ 642. Postmaster's bond — Counter-claim for extra allowance under act of congress, how pleaded.— Where the defendant, a postmaster, sued on his bond, sets up a counter-claim for extra services allowed to certain postoffices under an act of congress, the answer must allege that the postoffice of the defendant was one within the provisions of the act. United States v. Davis, Deady, 294.

§ 643. Private statute, how pleaded — Kansas statute.— The statute of Kansas providing that a private statute is sufficiently pleaded if referred to by its title, and day of its approval, only gives an example, and does not make a reference to the day of its approval absolutely necessary; but if such date is lost the statute may be referred to and fixed in some other way. The Territory of Kansas v. Reyburn, McCahon, 134.

§ 644. Defense in counter-claim.— In an action for treble damages for trespass upon land a defense should not be inserted in a counter-claim, but should be pleaded separately. Neff v. Pennoyer, 3 Saw., 495.

§ 645. Plea of general issue and of confession and evidence — Demurrer to latter.— Where the defendant pleads the general issue, and also a plea of confession and avoidance going to the whole cause of action, and to the latter plea the plaintiff demurs, not replying to the first plea, but, upon the overruling of the demurrer, allowing judgment to be entered on the second plea, judgment on the whole case may be entered for the defendant. United States v. Ballard, 14 Wall., 457.

§ 646. Action against sureties on bond — Plea charging fraud must set out facts constituting the fraud.— A plea by sureties on a bond, who were sued for malfeasance of an agent, that the plaintiff required an agreement by the agent that all his commissions thereafter earned should be applied to his past indebtedness to the plaintiff; that they were so applied ; that the defendant sureties were ignorant of the indebtedness and of this agreement; that if they had been informed of them they would not have executed the bond; and that the agreement as to the commissions and its execution were a fraud on them, was a bad plea, because it does not set forth any of the circumstances attending the execution and delivery of the bond. It does not aver that there was any misrepresentation, anything fraudulently kept back, or any opportunity to make disclosures on the part of the plaintiff, or any inquiry by the sureties before the bond was delivered. Nor does it aver that the sureties were ignorant of the facts complained of. Magee v. Manhattan Life Ins. Co., 2 Otto, 93.

§ 647. Illegal attachment — Plea of officer.— An officer sued for an illegal attachment of plaintiff's goods should in his plea deny that the goods were the property of the plaintiff, or else aver that they were subject to be taken under the writ. Buck v. Colbath, 3 Wall., 334.

§ 648. Verification of plea by municipal corporation — Texas practice.— In Texas a plea requiring an affidavit, if made by a municipal corporation, in an action where the acts of the mayor are questioned, is properly sworn to by a member of the common council; and an affidavit to the best of knowledge and belief is sufficient. Hitchcock v. Galveston, 3 Woods, 287.

b. General Issue.

SUMMARY — *General issue not sworn to admits what*, § 649.— *Plea amounting to general issue*, § 650.— *Nil debet a bad plea to an action on a foreign judgment*, § 651.— *Some defenses proper to general issue or special plea*, § 652.— *Color*, § 653.— *Plea to state facts only*, § 654.

§ 649. When a rule of court requires a plea denying the execution of an instrument sued on to be sworn to, a plea of the general issue not sworn to, though it may be good for some purposes, admits the execution as alleged in the declaration. Thomas v. Clark, § 655.

§ 650. To a declaration on a marine policy, a special plea that the action was not brought within one year, or that the vessel when lost was doing something which vitiated the policy, amounts to the general issue, and will be overruled on special demurrer. Van Avery v. Insurance Co., § 656.

§ 651. *Nil debet* is not a good plea in an action founded on a judgment of another state. *Nul tiel record* should be pleaded as the general issue. Mills v. Duryee, §§ 657-659.

§ 652. Some defenses competent under the general issue may be specially pleaded. Dibble v. Duncan, §§ 660-664.

§ 653. A special plea amounting to the general issue is bad. A special plea, therefore, should give color to the plaintiff's rights. *Ibid.*

§ 654. A plea should state facts only, not law. A matter of law so stated may be regarded as surplusage. *Ibid.*

[NOTES.— See §§ 665-732.]

THOMAS v. CLARK.

(Circuit Court for Michigan: 2 McLean, 194, 195. 1840.)

Opinion of the COURT.

STATEMENT OF FACTS.— This action is brought against the defendants, who are partners, as indorsers of a bill of exchange to the plaintiff. A rule of court requires a plea of the general issue, denying the execution of an instrument, or of an indorsement on which the action is brought, to be sworn to. The general issue in this case being filed without oath, a question is made whether the ground of the action is admitted. The defendants' counsel contends that the signatures of Clark and Cole, as they appear to be indorsed on the note, only are admitted, and not the partnership, and that it is necessary for the plaintiff to prove the partnership.

§ 655. *A plea denying the execution of an instrument, not sworn to as required by rule, admits the execution as alleged in the declaration.*

The rule was designed to prevent delays by filing issues which are not true in fact. A plea of the general issue under the rule may be good for some purposes, but it admits the instrument on which the action is brought. In this case the indorsement by the defendants is admitted. Smith v. McManus, 7 Yerg., 477. But to what extent does this admission go? Most clearly the admission is that the defendants indorsed the note, as they are alleged to have done in the declaration. In the declaration they are stated to be partners, and as such indorsed the note in the partnership name.

This construction of the rule imposes no hardship on the defendants. If the note were not indorsed by them as partners, they might have sworn to the plea, which would have thrown on the plaintiff the necessity of proving their signatures, as alleged in the declaration.

·*Judgment.*

VAN AVERY v. PHŒNIX INSURANCE COMPANY.

(Circuit Court for Illinois: 5 Bissell, 193, 194. 1870.)

Opinion by BLODGETT, J.

STATEMENT OF FACTS.— In this case a demurrer is interposed to the special pleas of the defendant. The first plea is in substance that the suit has not been brought within one year from the time the loss occurred, upon the policy of insurance. The second plea is in substance that the loss occurred while the steamer was engaged in saving a stranded vessel off a reef, whereby it is claimed that she vitiated her policy and that the insurers are not liable. The pleader who drew the declaration has averred the specific manner in which the loss occurred, that she was relieving a stranded vessel, and that it was in pursuance of an immemorial custom among persons engaged in the navigation of these waters that such relief should be rendered.

§ **656.** *Special plea amounting to the general issue is bad.*

I am inclined to think that both these pleas, in view of the averments of the declaration, are nothing more than what can be given in evidence under the general issue. I do not think that the second plea, the last plea in reference to showing the manner in which the loss occurred, is anything more than a reiteration of the matter in the declaration. The question as to whether it does present a defense is one to be decided when the evidence is taken as to whether such a custom exists. I think that the defense under the first plea can be given under the general issue. It is a mere question of fact to be determined on the trial. Demurrer to special pleas sustained.

MILLS *v.* DURYEE.

(7 Cranch, 481–487. 1813.) •

ERROR to the Circuit Court for the District of Columbia.

Opinion by MR. JUSTICE STORY.

STATEMENT OF FACTS.— The question in this case is whether *nil debet* is a good plea to an action of debt brought in the courts of this District on a judgment rendered in a court of record of the state of New York, one of the United States.

§ **657.** *Nil debet is not a good plea to a declaration on a judgment of another state.*

The decision of this question depends altogether upon the construction of the constitution and laws of the United States. By the constitution it is declared that "full faith and credit shall be given in each state to the public acts, records and judicial proceedings of every other state; and the congress may, by general laws, prescribe the manner in which such acts, records and proceedings shall be proved, and the effect thereof."

By the act of May 26, 1790 (1 Stats. at Large, 122), chapter 11, congress provided for the mode of authenticating the records and judicial proceedings of the state courts, and then further declared that "the records and judicial proceeding, authenticated as aforesaid, shall have such faith and credit given to them in every court within the United States as they have by law or usage in the courts of the state from whence the said records are or shall be taken."

It is argued that this act provides only for the admission of such records as evidence, but does not declare the effect of such evidence when admitted. This argument cannot be supported. The act declares that the record duly authenticated shall have such faith and credit as it has in the state court from whence it is taken. If in such court it has the faith and credit of evidence of the highest nature, namely, record evidence, it must have the same faith and credit in every other court. Congress have therefore declared the effect of the record by declaring what faith and credit shall be given to it.

It remains only then to inquire in every case what is the effect of a judgment in the state where it is rendered. In the present case the defendant had full notice of the suit, for he was arrested and gave bail, and it is beyond all doubt that the judgment of the supreme court of New York was conclusive upon the parties in that state. It must, therefore, be conclusive here also.

§ 658. *Nul tiel record may be pleaded though the record cannot be inspected by certiorari.*

But it is said that, admitting that the judgment is conclusive, still *nil debet* was a good plea; and *nul tiel record* could not be pleaded, because the record was of another state, and could not be inspected or transmitted by *certiorari.* Whatever may be the validity of the plea of *nil debet* after verdict, it cannot be sustained in this case. The pleadings in an action are governed by the dignity of the instrument on which it is founded. If it be a record, conclusive between the parties, it cannot be denied but by the plea of *nul tiel record;* and when congress gave the effect of a record to the judgment it gave all the collateral consequences. There is no difficulty in the proof. It may be proved in the manner prescribed by the act, and such proof is of as high a nature as an inspection by the court of its own record, or as an exemplification would be in any other court of the same state. Had this judgment been sued in any other court of New York, there is no doubt that *nil debet* would have been an inadmissible plea. Yet the same objection might be urged that the record could not be inspected. The law, however, is undoubted that an exemplification would in such case be decisive. The original need not be produced.

§ 659. *Objections answered.*

Another objection is that the act cannot have the effect contended for, because it does not enable the courts of another state to issue executions directly on the original judgment. This objection, if it were valid, would equally apply to every other court of the same state where the judgment was rendered. But it has no foundation. The right of a court to issue execution depends upon its own powers and organization. Its judgments may be complete and perfect and have full effect, independent of the right to issue execution.

The last objection is that the act does not apply to courts of this District. The words of the act afford a decisive answer, for they extend to "every court within the United States." Were the construction contended for by the plaintiff in error to prevail, that judgments of the state courts ought to be considered *prima facie* evidence only, this clause in the constitution would be utterly unimportant and illusory. The common law would give such judgments precisely the same effect. It is manifest, however, that the constitution contemplated a power in congress to give a conclusive effect to such judgments. And we can perceive no rational interpretation of the act of congress, unless it declares a judgment conclusive when a court of the particular state where it is rendered would pronounce the same decision.

On the whole the opinion of a majority of the court is that the judgment be affirmed, with costs.

MR. JUSTICE JOHNSON dissented.

<hr/>

DIBBLE *v.* DUNCAN.

(Circuit Court for Ohio: 2 McLean, 553–557. 1841.)

Opinion of the COURT.

STATEMENT OF FACTS.—This is an action of *assumpsit*. The declaration contained a count on a promissory note, one for goods sold and delivered, another for money had and received, etc. Two pleas were filed: First, the general issue; and secondly, Duncan pleaded that he was not a joint maker with the said Converse and Birkey of said promissory note, nor was he in anywise interested in the subject-matter of said contract, but that his name was placed upon said promissory note as an indorser merely and guarantor of the payment of the same.

The plaintiffs demurred to this plea, and assigned three causes of demurrer as follows: First. That the plea amounts to the general issue. Second. It states a conclusion of law. Third. If the facts alleged be true they constitute no bar.

§ 660. *Some defenses competent under the general issue may be specially pleaded.*

It may be admitted that the matters set up in the plea might be proved under the general issue, but it does not follow that the special plea is therefore improper. In the action of *assumpsit* there are many defenses which may be pleaded specially or given in evidence under the general issue. Of this character are all such matters as go to discharge the action, such as infancy, a release, want of consideration, accord and satisfaction, foreign attachment, or that a higher security had been given, payment, etc.

§ 661. *Nature of a special plea. Color.*

A special plea which amounts to the general issue is bad, and, therefore, a special plea must give express or implied color to the plaintiffs' right, and not deny it, as is done by the general issue. By the Reg. Gen. Hil. T., 4 W. 4, all matters in defense in England, except a denial of the promise, are now required to be pleaded specially, and this is justly considered a great improvement in the rules of pleading.

The plea in this case admits the signature of the defendant on the note, but alleges that it was placed there as a security and not as principal. And this is admitted by the demurrer. Now if the defendant Duncan undertook, as a guarantor, to pay the note, and not as principal, he can only be made liable in the character he assumed. As guarantor he was entitled to notice, and it is incumbent on the plaintiffs to show that they have used legal diligence.

The plea gives color to the plaintiffs' right, and it therefore does not amount to the general issue. As regards the present action, the effect of the plea, if true, may be the same as the general issue; but the form is substantially different. In many cases it is advisable to plead specially rather than to give the facts in evidence under the general issue, as it may narrow the grounds of defense. The plaintiffs are called upon either to admit or deny the special matter pleaded.

§ 662. *A plea should state facts only, not law.*

In pleading, facts only are to be stated, and not arguments or inferences, or matter of law. Should a matter of law be stated it may be regarded as surplusage. It is not perceived, however, that the above plea is liable to this objection. 1 Chitt. Pl., 245 (ed. 1837). In the case of Bright *v.* Carpenter, 9 Ohio, 39, it was held "that, where a stranger to a promissory note indorse it in blank at the time of making it, the payee of that note may sue him with the maker as a joint maker of the note, and he is entitled to the privileges of a surety."

"That such blank indorsement may be filled at any time in form to oblige the indorser as principal, or the court may regard it as so filled up. And that proof was admissible to show the intention of the parties as to the extent of the indorsee's liability."

And in Dean *v.* Halt, 17 Wend., 214, "where a note was made by A., payable to B., or bearer, C. indorsed it, and an action was brought by a third person claiming, by transfer from B., charging C. as the maker of the note, it was held on demurrer that the declaration was bad."

"It seems that where an indorser to such a note is privy to the consideration he may be charged directly as maker or as indorser, and that a *bona fide* holder may, in all cases, write a bill of exchange over the name of the indorser, or fill up the blank in any form consistent with the intent of the parties."

§ 663. *Plea that defendant was only guarantor.*

It is objected to the plea that it does not allege the defendant signed the note as guarantor after its execution. The plea states that the defendant was not in anywise interested in the subject-matter of the contract, but that he signed it as guarantor. This, we think, is sufficient. It shows that the undertaking of the defendant was collateral, and that he cannot be sued as principal.

§ 664. *Semble, that the intent with which a name is indorsed may be shown by parol.*

It may be doubted whether, on general principles, evidence is admissible to show that the defendant is surety when by the terms of the note he appears to be a principal. In Laxton *v.* Peat, 2 Campb. N. P., 185, it was held that an acceptor of a bill of exchange might show that he was merely an accommodation acceptor. And under this authority the case of Collett *v.* Haigh, 3 Campb., 281, was decided; but these cases were overruled in the case of Fentum *v.* Pocock, 5 Taunt., 192. In Rees *v.* Berrington, 2 Ves. Jun., 540, Lord Loughborough says, where two are bound jointly and severally, the surety cannot aver by pleading that he is bound as surety; and to this effect is the case of Garrett *v.* Jull, Selwyn, N. P., 393.

It is not important on what part of the note a guarantor shall sign his name. It may be placed on the back or face of the note; and the intent with which the name was indorsed, it would seem, might be shown by parol. There could be no doubt of this if the effect of the indorsement was in itself doubtful, and the note was in the hands of the payees. This would be in explanation of the indorsement, and not against its terms or legal effect.

As appears from the plea, the defendant Duncan was not privy to the consideration, and the case in Wendell, above cited, sustains the plea.

The decision from the Ohio reports, in the admission of parol evidence, may have been influenced by a statute which requires an execution to be levied first on the property of the principal.

Upon the whole, we think that the demurrer to the plea must be overruled.

§ 665. **Issue, what constitutes.**— An issue is a single, certain and material point, arising out of the allegations or pleadings of the parties; and generally should be made up by an affirmative and negative. Simonton *v.* Winter, 5 Pet., 140.

§ 666. **Assumpsit — Defendant may show no cause of action when suit brought.**— Under the general issue in *assumpsit* it may be shown not only that the cause of action never existed, but that it did not exist when the suit was brought; so held where the note in suit had been merged in a prior judgment which would bar this action, and which therefore was allowed to be shown under this plea. Mason *v.* Eldred, 6 Wall., 231.

§ 667. **Execution of instrument, denial of must be sworn to — Indiana practice.**— The general issue, which denies the execution of the instrument, must be sworn to, under the statute of Indiana, which is adopted as a rule of practice in the federal court of the seventh circuit. McClintick *v.* Cummins, 2 McL., 98.

§ 668. **Joint plea of non est factum.**— When several defendants sued on a bond plead jointly *non est factum*, they must sustain that plea as to all or they fail as to all. United States *v.* Halsted, 6 Ben., 205.

§ 669. **A plea of non est factum must conclude with a verification.** Contee *v.* Garner, 2 Cr. C. C., 162.

§ 670. **At common law non assumpsit put the plaintiff to the proof of all the material averments** in the declaration, and where he relied on an indorsement it was necessary for him to prove it. Stroud *v.* Harrington, Hemp., 116.

§ 671. **An answer which denies each and every material allegation** of the declaration "in manner and form as therein set forth" is bad, the denial referring only to the manner and form in which the plaintiff has stated his cause of action. Dole *v.* Burleigh,* 1 Dak. T'y, 227. An answer which denies each and every material allegation is not sufficient. Kimball *v.* County of Stanton,* 4 Fed. R., 325.

§ 672. **General denial of each allegation — Affirmative matters of defense — Missouri statute.**— Under the Missouri act of 1875, as to pleadings, a general denial may be put in as to each allegation on which plaintiff's right of recovery depends, instead of, as formerly, denying such allegations *seriatim*. But affirmative matters of defense must be specially pleaded according to the rules pertaining thereto. Mack *v.* Insurance Co.,* 1 McC., 20.

§ 673. **Nil debet in debt on specialty.**— *Nil debet* is an improper plea to an action of debt on a specialty which is the foundation of the action. Sneed *v.* Wister,* 8 Wheat., 690.

§ 674. *Nil debet* is not a good plea in debt on a bond. United States *v.* Spencer,* 2 McL., 405.

§ 675. **Non assumpsit in tort.**— *Non assumpsit* is not a good plea in an action of tort. Garland *v.* Davis, 4 How., 131.

§ 676. **Redundant plea to be stricken out.**— In an action of debt on a bond two pleas of payment were filed covering the defalcations, which were the breaches assigned, and also another plea alleging payment of the full penalty of the bond. *Held*, that this latter plea was useless and must be stricken out as an incumbrance to the record. *Ibid.*

§ 677. **Nil debet in action on foreign judgment.**— *Nil debet* is a bad plea in an action on a judgment obtained in another state. Reed *v.* Ross,* 1 Bald., 36; Maxwell *v.* Stewart, 22 Wall., 77; Short *v.* Wilkinson, 2 Cr. C. C., 22; Westervelt *v.* Lewis, 2 McL., 511; Jacquette *v.* Hugunon, 2 McL., 129; Bergen *v.* Williams, 4 McL., 125; Bastable *v.* Wilson, 1 Cr. C. C., 124.

§ 678. **Suit on judgment — Nul tiel record proper plea.**— Where, in suing on a judgment, it appears from the record that process was served or that there was an appearance, the fact cannot be controverted; *nul tiel record* is the only proper plea. Westervelt *v.* Lewis, 2 McL., 511.

§ 679. Upon an action on a judgment record the plea of *nul tiel record* is the only available and proper plea; for if such a judgment has been rendered it is conclusive upon the merits and cannot be impeached in a court of co-ordinate jurisdiction or in a collateral proceeding. Amory *v.* Amory, 3 Biss., 266.

§ 680. **Payment on a judgment cannot be proved under nul tiel record,** and if a party would avail himself of it he must plead it. Tunstall *v.* Robinson, Hemp., 229.

§ 681. **Suit on foreign judgment — Nul tiel record bad.**— A foreign judgment is not considered as a record, and a plea to such judgment of *nul tiel record* is bad. The opposite party may treat the plea as a nullity and take judgment. Burnham *v.* Webster, Dav., 236.

§ 682. **What is denied under the general issue.**— A plea of the general issue admits the capacity of an alleged corporation to sue. Existence as a corporation should be directly traversed. United States *v.* Insurance Companies, 22 Wall., 99; Pullman *v.* Upton, 6 Otto, 328.

§ 683. In an action of ejectment to recover a lot of land, the plaintiffs are described in the writ as "The Society for the Propagation of the Gospel in Foreign Parts, a corporation duly established in England within the dominions of the king of the United Kingdom of Great Britain and Ireland, the members of which society are aliens, and subjects of said king." The defendants pleaded the general issue of not guilty. The general issue admits the competency of the plaintiffs to sue in the corporate capacity in which they have sued. Society for the Propagation of the Gospel *v.* Town of Pawlet, 4 Pet., 480.

§ 684. The averment of the citizenship of the parties, to give jurisdiction to a United States circuit court, is a necessary averment, and must be proved under the general issue. Catlett *v.* Pacific Ins. Co., 1 Paine, 594.

§ 685. The plea of the general issue in actions of trespass or case does not necessarily put the title in issue. Richardson *v.* City of Boston, 19 How., 263.

§ 686. *Non cepit* in replevin puts in issue the question of general property only, and not of special property; at least in a suit between the principal and his agent. On *non cepit* the issue must be for the defendant if there was no wrongful taking of the goods from the possession of another. Meany *v.* Head, 1 Mason, 319.

§ 687. In an action of *assumpsit* on certain county bonds defendant pleaded that a step required by the act authorizing the bonds had not been taken, and that plaintiff is not a *bona fide* holder without notice. Plea overruled and parties went to trial on general issue, verdict being rendered for plaintiff. *Held*, on error, that although the special plea was good and should have been sustained, yet the general issue placed in issue all questions raised by the plea, and judgment should be sustained. Chambers County *v.* Clews,* 21 Wall., 317.

§ 688. The plea of *nul tiel record* brings before the court the validity of a judgment on which an action is brought, and the description of it as set forth in the declaration. Jacquette *v.* Hugunon, 2 McL., 129.

§ 689. *Nul tiel record* can only put in issue the fact of the judgment. Bergen *v.* Williams, 4 McL., 125.

§ 690. Plea of *non assumpsit*, sworn to, to a note puts in issue its execution, and the burden is upon plaintiff of proving execution. Gray *v.* Tunstall, Hemp., 558.

§ 691. A general denial puts in issue all the material allegations of a petition brought under the thirty-fifth section of the bankrupt act; and devolves upon the plaintiff the necessity of proving the case stated in his petition, and of recovering upon such case alone. Craigin *v.* Carmichael, 2 Dill., 520.

§ 692. Under the code of Missouri, a general denial puts in issue only the substantive allegations of the declaration; and if a defendant wishes to set up an affirmative defense in the nature of an avoidance he must plead it specially. Walker *v.* Flint, 3 McC., 507.

§ 693. **What may be shown under the general issue.**—A record of a former judgment between the same parties, upon the same cause of action, may be given in evidence on *non assumpsit*. Ridgway *v.* Ghequier, 1 Cr. C. C., 87; Stone *v.* Stone, 2 Cr. C. C., 119; Young *v.* Black, 7 Cr., 565.

§ 694. Upon the plea of *non cepit* to an action of replevin, the plaintiff must prove that the defendant took the property from the possession of the plaintiff. Calvert *v.* Stewart, 4 Cr. C. C., 728.

§ 695. No question involving the capacity of the parties in the cause to litigate in the circuit court can be raised by a plea of the general issue. Philadelphia, etc., R. R. Co. *v.* Quigley, 21 How., 202.

§ 696. In trespass to real property, a freehold or mere possessory right in the defendant may be given in evidence under the general issue. Cooley *v.* O'Connor, 12 Wall., 391.

§ 697. In an action of *assumpsit* brought on a note, under the plea of *non assumpsit*, any evidence tending to show no title in the plaintiff is admissible, and therefore evidence that the ownership is in a third party is admissible. Hartshorn *v.* Green.* 1 Minn., 93.

§ 698. The defense against a bill brought by a corporation, that it was not legally organized under the laws of a state, must be pleaded in abatement and not in bar, nor may it be given in evidence under the general issue; for the general issue, under the rules of the supreme court, is an admission of the corporate existence of the complainants. Dental Vulcanite Co. *v.* Wetherbee, 2 Cliff., 555.

§ 699. In an action of libel, truth of the publication must be specially pleaded, and cannot be availed of under the general issue; and such plea must show specific instances of the misconduct imputed to the plaintiff, if the charge has been general in its nature. Barrows *v.* Carpenter, 1 Cliff., 204.

§ 700. In an action on a fire insurance policy the defendant, under a denial of the allegations of the declaration, cannot set up the breach of any condition in the policy except such as the plaintiff is bound to show affirmatively. Bennett *v.* Maryland Fire Ins. Co., 14 Blatch., 425.

§ 701. Under the general issue, in an action to enforce a forfeiture under the internal revenue laws, the defendant may plead the limitations provided for in those laws. United States *v.* Six Fermenting Tubs, 1 Abb., 268.

§ 702. In ejectment upon the general issue the death of the lessor of the plaintiff cannot be taken advantage of. Worthington *v.* Etcheson, 5 Cr. C. C., 302.

§ 703. In trespass the defendant cannot justify under the general issue. Goddard *v.* Davis, 1 Cr. C. C., 33.

§ 704. A defendant cannot avail himself of the statute of limitations upon the general issue. Neale *v.* Walker, 1 Cr. C. C., 57.

§ 705. The act of limitations cannot be given in evidence upon the plea of *nil debet*. Gardner *v.* Lindo, 1 Cr. C. C., 78; McIver *v.* Moore, 1 Cr. C. C., 90.

§ 706. Upon the plea of "not guilty," in trespass *quare clausum fregit*,* and notice of "defense on warrant," the defendant may give his title in evidence as a justification, without pleading it specially. Pancoast *v.* Barry, 1 Cr. C. C., 176.

§ 707. If all the members of a partnership are not named as plaintiffs the defendant may avail himself of the objection upon *non assumpsit*. Carne *v.* McLane, 1 Cr. C. C., 351.

§ 708. Infancy cannot be given in evidence upon the plea of *nil debet* to an action of debt on a promissory note in Virginia. The promissory note of an infant is voidable but not void. Young v. Bell, 1 Cr. C. C., 842.

§ 709. A former-recovery may be given in evidence upon *nil debet.* Welsh v. Lindo, 1 Cr. C. C., 508.

§ 710. Unless notice of a set-off be given before the suit is called for trial, it cannot be given in evidence upon *non assumpsit.* Deneale v. Young, 2 Cr. C. C., 418.

§ 711. Under a plea of *non assumpsit* testimony cannot be received relating to the residence of a party and bearing upon the jurisdiction of the court. Sims v. Hundley, 6 How., 1.

§ 712. **Pleas amounting to general issue.**—A special plea which amounts to the general issue is demurrable. Curtis v. The Central R'y, 6 McL., 401; Halstead v. Lyon, 2 McL., 226.

§ 713. A plea which amounts to the general issue, or does not answer the whole charge or count, is bad. Parker v. Lewis, Hemp., 72.

§ 714. Where a plea expressly admits the execution of a note, but sets up matter in avoidance, it is not bad on demurrer as amounting to the general issue. Thomas v. Page, 8 McL., 167.

§ 715. To an action on a coupon bond payable to bearer the defendant pleaded that the plaintiff was not the bearer. *Held,* such plea is argumentative and amounts to the general issue. This defect can be taken advantage of only upon special demurrer; upon general demurrer the court will not overrule the plea, but will proceed to consider the merits of the question as a material allegation if the declaration has been traversed. Pendleton Co. v. Amy, 13 Wall., 297.

§ 716. An action was brought against two partners trading under the name of one of them, on a promissory note signed with that name, and claimed in the declaration to be a firm note. The partner whose name did not appear pleaded that plaintiff had accepted the note in full payment, as the individual note of the other partner. On special demurrer this was held bad as amounting to the general issue. Van Ness v. Forrest,* 8 Cr., 30.

§ 717. To a declaration on a note the general issue was pleaded, and a special plea that no consideration passed from plaintiff to defendant. This latter was rejected as amounting to the general issue. Vowell v. Lyles,* 1 Cr. C. C., 329.

§ 718. In a writ of right brought under the statute of Kentucky, where the demandant described his land by metes and bounds, and counted against the tenants jointly, it was held that this was matter pleadable in abatement only, and that by pleading in bar the tenants admitted their joint seizin, and lost the opportunity of pleading a several tenancy. The tenants could not, in this case, severally plead, in addition to the mise or general issue, that neither the plaintiff nor his ancestor, nor any other under or from whom he derived his title to the demanded premises, was ever actually seized or possessed thereof, or of any part thereof; because it amounted to the general issue, and was an application to the mere discretion of the court, which is not examinable upon a mere writ of error. Liter v. Green, 2 Wheat., 306.

§ 719. **Infringement of patent — Defendant not limited to general issue.**—*Semble,* that a defendant in an action for the infringement of a patent is not limited to pleading the general issue, though his defense might be shown under that plea. Day v. New Eng. Car Spring Co., 3 Blatch., 179.

§ 720. **Assumpsit for breach of promise to marry —{Proper plea.**—The general issue in an action of *assumpsit* for breach of promise of marriage is *non assumpsit,* and a plea of not guilty will be stricken out on demurrer. Wilkinson v. Pomeroy, 10 Blatch., 524.

§ 721. **Exception in statute, when must be set out.**—When plaintiff claims a title to land by prescription under a statute, and the defendant relies on coming within an exception to the general rule as to the length of time required to gain such title, if the plaintiff does not set out the statute, or the nature of the title, under which he claims in his declaration, the defendant need not plead the exception specially, but may set it up in evidence. Palmer v. Low, 2 Saw., 248.

§ 722. **Nul tiel record — Misdescription of the record.—Effect of.**—As the plea of *nul tiel record* puts in question the identity of the record, if circumstances descriptive of the record be untruly stated, though it was not necessary they should be stated at all, it will be fatal. Whitaker v. Bramson, 2 Paine, 209.

§ 723. **Plea of former recovery — Record.**—Although a party under a plea of former recovery be precluded from giving the record in evidence, on account of variance, yet he may avail himself of it under the general issue. *Quære,* whether such proof can be received without notice of the special matter? *Ibid.*

§ 724. **Usury — Special plea — General issue — Admission of evidence.**—If usury be specially pleaded, and the court reject the evidence offered upon such special plea, it may be admitted upon the general issue, notwithstanding it has been refused upon the special plea. Levy v. Gadsby, 3 Cr., 180.

§ 725. **Action by administrator — General issue — Production of testamentary letters.—** Letters testamentary issued under the authority of one state are not available in another. But if, to an action brought by an executor, on a cause of action arising in the life-time of the testator, the defendant plead the general issue, the plaintiff cannot be required on the trial to produce any letters testamentary. Champlin v. Tilley,* 8 Day (Conn.), 303.

§ 726. **Sealed instrument — Non est factum, when proper, when special plea.—** Whenever a contract or obligation under seal is void ab initio the general plea of non est factum is proper. Where it is merely voidable, a special plea, setting forth the special circumstances, is necessary. Bottomly v. United States, 1 Story, 135.

§ 727. **Waiver by plea of non assumpsit.—** If one of the counts be "for matters properly chargeable in account, according to an account herewith filed," according to the Maryland practice, and there be no account filed, and non assumpsit be pleaded to all the counts, the plaintiff may give evidence upon that count; the defendant by his plea having waived the objection to the same. Semmes v. Lee, 3 Cr. C. C., 439.

§ 728. **In replevin,** upon the plea of property in the defendant, the burden of proof is on the plaintiff. Williamson v. Ringgold, 4 Cr. C. C., 39.

§ 729. **In assault and battery** the plaintiff, being a mulatto, cannot, at the trial upon the general issue, be compelled to prove his freedom. Murray v. Dulany, 3 Cr. C. C., 343.

§ 730. **A notice of special matter** to be given in evidence, filed with a plea of the general issue, must contain all the substantial matter of a special plea. Its form must depend in some degree upon the circumstances. It is not a part of the record, and cannot be disposed of on demurrer. Fowler v. Colton,* 1 Burn. (Wis.), 175.

§ 731. **Trespass to try title — Not guilty — Special plea — Texas practice.—** In Texas a defendant in an action of trespass to try title may plead not guilty, and also set up the invalidity of the plaintiff's title, provided the defendant pleads a special title in himself under the statute of limitations. Sheirburn v. Hunter, 3 Woods, 261.

§ 732. **An act of limitations must be pleaded.—** The act of Virginia of December 19, 1792, section 5, limiting the time of issuing writs of scire facias, in certain cases, is an act of limitations and must be pleaded. The defendant cannot avail himself of it by plea of nul tiel record, nor by motion to quash the scire facias, nor by motion in arrest of judgment. Offutt v. Henderson, 2 Cr. C. C., 553.

c. Special Pleas in Bar.

SUMMARY — *Plea of impossibility of performance, § 783. — Plea need not anticipate, § 784. — Good plea on record will always bar judgment, § 785. — Plea of justification to show authority, §§ 786, 787. — Uncore prest, § 788. — Readiness to perform, §§ 789, 740. — Non tenure, §§ 741, 742. — Ne unques administrator, § 743. — Argumentativeness, § 744. — Plea to a record showing a judgment, § 745.*

§ 783. In an action for breach of warranty, a plea that performance was rendered impossible by an act done with plaintiff's consent is a good plea. Clearwater v. Meredith, §§ 746–58.

§ 784. The plea need not negative any part of plaintiff's case until averred by the latter. *Ibid.*

§ 785. A good plea in bar of the action on record will always prevent judgment for the plaintiff whatever other pleas may appear on file undisposed of, as judgment for defendant on such a plea would make the others immaterial. *Ibid.*

§ 786. When one justifies in a special plea an act which at common law constitutes a wrong, upon the order or authority of another, he must set out substantially, and not merely in its legal effect, the order or authority relied upon. Bean v. Beckwith, §§ 754, 755.

§ 787. This rule is not changed by the statutes of 3d March, 1863, and 2d March, 1867, to protect persons from liability for acts done under authority of the president during war. *Ibid.*

§ 788. In an action for non-delivery of goods sold, or wherever the condition of the bond is not part of the obligation, the averment of uncore prest is unnecessary in a plea of readiness to perform. Savary v. Goe, §§ 756–760.

§ 739. In an action for the non-delivery of goods, when the goods were to have been delivered at any time during a certain month, a plea of readiness to perform must aver that defendant was ready to perform the last convenient hour of the last day of the month; also that he was present at the place agreed upon for the delivery. *Ibid.*

§ 740. *Quære,* whether such plea should aver an offer to perform, though plaintiff or his agent was not present. *Ibid.*

§ 741. *Non tenure* is to be pleaded in abatement, though in some states it has been allowed as a plea in bar. Fiedler v. Carpenter, §§ 761–763.

§ 742. *Non tenure* is no defense to an action for the foreclosure of a mortgage, when the cause of action appears in the declaration. *Ibid.*

§ 743. In an action of debt on a judgment recovered by plaintiff as administrator, a plea of *ne unques administrator*, or its equivalent, is bad. Biddle v. Wilkins, §§ 764–766.

§ 744. In an action by plaintiff as administrator, a plea that defendant at a certain time and by a certain court was appointed administrator, and that he undertook the office and had continued to act as administrator, is bad on special demurrer for argumentativeness, and is also defective in not stating the date of plaintiff's appointment. *Ibid.*

§ 745. In an action of debt on a judgment a plea cannot attack the validity of the record, though it may attack its operation by showing want of jurisdiction, or that the judgment is void. *Ibid.*

[NOTES.— See §§ 767–878.]

CLEARWATER v. MEREDITH.

(1 Wallace, 25–43. 1863.)

STATEMENT OF FACTS.— Plaintiff brought suit on a guaranty made by defendant Meredith, that the stock of the Cincinnati, Cambridge & Chicago Short Line Railway Company, two hundred shares of which had been transferred by the defendant to the plaintiff in payment of a farm, should be worth par, $50 per share, in Cincinnati, on October 1, 1855. The plaintiff alleged that the shares were, at that date, worthless. The defendant pleaded, among other things, that the said railroad company had consolidated with another company, under the laws of Indiana, whereby said stock had become of no value, and that said consolidation was with plaintiff's acquiescence and consent.

§ 746. *Demurrer reaches back to first defective pleading.*

Opinion by MR. JUSTICE DAVIS.

In order to arrive at a correct solution of this question, it is important to consider whether the *plea* is a good one, for a demurrer, whenever interposed, reaches back through the whole record, and "seizes hold of the first defective pleading." The plea in controversy confesses the original cause of action, but sets up matter which has arisen subsequent to it to avoid the obligation to perform it. It acknowledges that the guaranty was given as claimed, but insists that the consolidation of the interests and stock of the three railroad companies necessarily destroyed and rendered worthless and of no value the guarantied stock, and that Clearwater, having consented to the transfer, is in no position to claim redress from Meredith and his co-defendants.

§ 747. *Contract, non-performance of excused when caused by act or fault of opposite party.*

If Clearwater was a consenting party to a proceeding which, of itself, put it out of the power of the defendants to perform their contract, he cannot recover, for "promisors will be discharged from all liability when the non-performance of their obligation is caused by the act or the fault of the other contracting party." 2 Parsons on Contracts, 188.

§ 748. *Character and purposes of a corporation not to be changed without consent of stockholder.*

The Cincinnati, Cambridge & Chicago Short Line Railway Company, whose stock was guarantied, was, as stated in the pleadings, organized under a general act of the state of Indiana, providing for the incorporation of railroad companies. This act was passed May 11, 1852, and contained no provision permitting railroad corporations to consolidate their stock. It can readily be seen that the interests of the public, as well as the perfection of the railway system, called for the exercise of a power by which different lines of road could be united. Accordingly, on the 23d February, 1853, the general assembly of Indiana passed an act allowing any railway company that had been organized to intersect and unite their road with any other road constructed or in progress of construction, and to merge and consolidate their stock, and on the 4th of March, 1853, the privileges of the act were extended to railroad companies that should afterwards be organized.

The power of the legislature to confer such authority cannot be questioned, and without the authority railroad corporations organized separately could not merge and consolidate their interests. But in conferring the authority the legislature never intended to compel a dissenting stockholder to transfer his interest because a majority of the stockholders consented to the consolidation. Even if the legislature had manifested an obvious purpose to do so, the act would have been illegal, for it would have impaired the obligation of a contract. There was no reservation of power in the act under which the Cincinnati, Cambridge & Chicago Short Line Railway was organized which gave authority to make material changes in the purposes for which the corporation was created, and without such a reservation in no event could a dissenting stockholder be bound.

When any person takes stock in a railroad corporation he has entered into a contract with the company that his interests shall be subject to the direction and control of the proper authorities of the corporation to accomplish the object for which the company was organized. He does not agree that the improvement to which he subscribed should be changed in its purposes and character at the will and pleasure of a majority of the stockholders, so that new responsibilities, and it may be new hazards, are added to the original undertaking. He may be very willing to embark in one enterprise and unwilling to engage in another; to assist in building a short-line railway and averse to risking his money in one having a longer line of transit.

§ 749. *The consolidation of railroad companies dissolves the old corporation and creates a new one.*

But it is not every unimportant change which would work a dissolution of the contract. It must be such a change that a new and different business is superadded to the original undertaking. The Hartford, etc., R. Co. v. Croswell, 5 Hill, 383; Banet v. The Alton, etc., R. R., 13 Ill., 510. The act of the legislature of Indiana allowing railroad corporations to merge and consolidate their stock was an enabling act — was permissive, not mandatory. It simply gave the consent of the legislature to whatever could lawfully be done, and which without that consent could not be done at all. By virtue of this act the consolidations in the plea stated were made. Clearwater, *before* the consolidation, was a stockholder in one corporation, created for a given purpose; after it he was a stockholder in another and different corporation, with other privileges, powers, franchises and stockholders. The effect of the consolidation "was a dissolution of the three corporations, and at the same instant the creation of a new corporation, with property, liabilities and stockholders derived from those passing out of existence." McMahan v. Morrison, 16 Ind., 172. And the act of consolidation was not void because the state assented to it, but a non-consenting stockholder was discharged. McCray v. Junction R. Co., 9 id., 358. Clearwater could have prevented this consolidation had he chosen to do so; instead of that he gave his assent to it and merged his own stock in the new adventure. If a majority of the stockholders of the corporation of which he was a member had undertaken to transfer his interest against his wish, they would have been enjoined. Lauman *v.* Lebanon Valley Railroad, 30 Penn. St., 46. There was no power to force him to join the new corporation and to receive stock in it on the surrender of his stock in the old company. By his own act he has destroyed the stock to which the guaranty attached and made it impossible for the defendants to perform their agreement. After the act of consolidation the stock could not have any distinct market value. There was in fact no longer any stock of the Cincinnati, Cambridge & Chicago Short Line Railway.

Meredith and his co-defendants undertook that the stock should be at par in Cincinnati if it maintained the same separate and independent existence that it had when they gave their guaranty. Their undertaking did not extend to another stock created afterwards, with which they had no concern, and which might be better or worse than the one guarantied. It is not material whether the new stock was worth more or less than the old. It is sufficient that it is another stock and represented other interests.

§ 750. *Plaintiff's case to be pleaded affirmatively.*

But it is said that the plea is defective because it does not aver that the consolidation was an act done without the consent of the defendants. The pleadings do not aver that the defendants were stockholders in any of the roads whose interests were merged, and, if they were not, it is not easy to see what right they had to interpose objections to consolidation, nor how their consent was necessary to carry out the object contemplated. If the plaintiff consented because they did, and it is meant to be argued on that account they would still be liable on their contract, the answer is that this is not a matter to be negatived by the defendants, but the plaintiff should reply the fact. 1 Chitt. Pl., 222.

It follows that the fifth plea presented a complete defense in bar of the action.

§ 751. *Replication tendering issue of law held bad.*

In this plea there were two points and two only which the plaintiff had the right to traverse. He could deny either the act of consolidation or that he gave his consent to it. He could not deny both, for that would make his replication double. And if either fact was untrue, the defense was destroyed. The truth of both was essential to perfect the defense. But traverse can only be taken on matter of fact, and it is always inadmissible to tender an issue on mere matter of law. 1 Chitt. Pl., 645.

The last replication *does* traverse a conclusion of law. Whether the stock of the Cincinnati, Cambridge & Chicago Short Line Railway Company was destroyed and rendered worthless and of no value was not a question for a jury to try. If the roads were consolidated with the consent of the plaintiff, then it followed as a conclusion of law that the stock was destroyed and of no value. The stock passed out of existence the very instant the new corporation was created. The issue, therefore, tendered by the plaintiff in his last replication was an immaterial one, and the court did not err in sustaining a demurrer to it.

§ 752. *Filing new replication waives demurrer to former one.*

But the plaintiff claims the right to have the decision of the court below on the sufficiency of his previous replications reviewed here. This he cannot do. Each replication in this cause is complete in itself; does not refer to, and is not a part of, what precedes it, and is new pleading. When the plaintiff replied *de novo* after a demurrer was sustained to his original replication, he waived any right he might have had to question the correctness of the decision of the court on the demurrer. In like manner he abandoned his second replication when he availed himself of the leave of the court and filed a third and last one.

§ **753.** *A good plea in bar of the action will prevent judgment for plaintiff, whatever other pleas may be on file not disposed of.*

But the plaintiff insists that even if his replication was bad, that still upon the whole record he was entitled to judgment, because the first and fourth pleas were undisposed of. If an issue in fact had been joined on the fifth plea, and found for the defendants, judgment was inevitably for them, because the plea was *in bar* of the action, and the other pleas would then have presented immaterial issues. If the plea was true, being a complete defense, it would have been useless to have tried other issues, for, no matter how they might terminate, judgment must still be for the defendants. The state of pleading leaves the fifth plea precisely as if traverse had been taken on a matter of fact in it, and determined against the plaintiff. "On demurrer to any of the pleadings which go to the action, the judgment for either party is the same as it would have been on an issue in fact, joined upon the same pleading and found in favor of the same party." Gould's Pleading, ch. 9, § 42. "And when the defendant's plea goes to bar the action, if the plaintiff. demur to it and the demurrer is determined in favor of the plea, judgment of *nil capiat* should be entered, notwithstanding there may be also one or more issues in fact; because, upon the whole, it appears that the plaintiff had no cause of action." Tidd's Practice, 4th Am. ed., 741-2. There is no error in the record. Judgment affirmed, with costs.

BEAN v. BECKWITH.

(18 Wallace, 510-516. 1873.)

CERTIFICATE OF DIVISION from U. S. Circuit Court, District of Vermont.

STATEMENT OF FACTS.— Bean sued Beckwith and Henry for assault and battery and false imprisonment, alleging that they kept him in prison for over seven months. They pleaded generally that being military officers, acting in the course of their duty as such, they had arrested Bean, who was charged with having been guilty of disloyal practices in enticing soldiers to desert from the army of the United States. The plea further alleged that the defendants, in so arresting plaintiff, acted under the authority and by order of the president of the United States, whose orders as commander-in-chief, etc., they were bound to obey. Plaintiff demurred to both the pleas, there being two of them to the above effect, and the circuit court, being divided in opinion as to their sufficiency, certified that fact to this court according to law.

§ **754.** *Where one justifies for an alleged trespass he must so set forth his cause of justification, with essential details, that the plaintiff may be apprised of its nature, and may take issue upon it.*

Opinion by MR. JUSTICE FIELD.

There is no averment in the pleas that at the time the plaintiff was arrested any rebellion existed in the state of Vermont against the laws or government of the United States; or that any military operations were being carried on within its limits; or that the courts of justice were not open there, and in the full and undisturbed exercise of their regular jurisdiction; or that the plaintiff was in the military service of the United States, or in any way connected with that service.

Nor is there any averment in the pleas as to the manner in which, or the parties by whom, the charges of disloyal practices were made. It is not alleged that they were stated in writing or supported by oath.

Nor do the pleas, whilst asserting that the acts which are the subject of complaint were done under the authority and by the order of the president, set forth any order, general or special, of the president directing or approving of the acts in question.

For this last omission all the judges are agreed, without expressing any opinion upon the other omissions, that the pleas are defective and insufficient. It is an old rule of pleading, which, in the modern progress of simplifying pleadings, has not lost its virtue, that whenever one justifies in a special plea an act which in itself constitutes at common law a wrong upon the process, order or authority of another, he must set forth substantially and in a traversable form the process, order or authority relied upon, and that no mere averment of its legal effect, without other statement, will answer. In other words, if a defendant has cause of justification for an alleged trespass and undertakes to plead it, he must set it forth in its essential particulars, so that the plaintiff may be apprised of its nature and take issue upon it if he desires, and so that the court may be able to judge of its sufficiency.

§ 755. *The statutes under which the defendants justify do not change the rules of pleading nor dispense with the proof of the authority under which defendants acted.*

The defendants intended by their pleas to rest the justification of their conduct upon the provisions of the act of March 3, 1863, entitled "An act relating to *habeas corpus*, and regulating judicial proceedings in certain cases" (12 Stat. at Large, 756, § 4), and of the act of March 2, 1867, entitled "An act to declare valid and conclusive certain proclamations of the president, and acts done in pursuance thereof or of his orders, in the suppression of the late rebellion against the United States." 14 id., 432.

These statutes were enacted, among other things, to protect parties from liability to prosecution for acts done in the arrest and imprisonment of persons during the existence of the rebellion, under orders or proclamations of the president, or by his authority or approval, who were charged with participation in the rebellion, or as aiders or abettors, or as being guilty of disloyal practices in aid thereof, or any violation of the usages or the laws of war. Assuming for this case that these statutes are not liable to any constitutional objection, they do not change the rules of pleading, when the defense is set up in a special plea, or dispense with the exhibition of the order or authority upon which a party relies. Nor do they cover all acts done by officers in the military service of the United States simply because they are acting under the general authority of the president as commander-in-chief of the armies of the United States. They only cover acts done under order or proclamations issued by him or under his authority; and there is no difficulty in the defendants setting forth such orders or proclamations, whether general or special, if any were made, which applied to their case.

The views thus expressed render it unnecessary to consider any other objections taken by the plaintiff to the pleas before us. The questions certified must be answered in the negative, and the cause remanded for further proceedings.

SAVARY v. GOE.

(Circuit Court for Pennsylvania: 3 Washington, 140–145. 1812.)

STATEMENT OF FACTS.— This was an action of debt on a bond, in the penalty of $1,920, with condition that the defendant should deliver to the plaintiff or his agent or assigns, at the place of embarkation in Brownsville, the quantity of one thousand nine hundred and twenty gallons of good merchantable proof whisky, in good and tight barrels, in all the month of May, 1809. Upon oyer of the obligation and condition the defendant pleads in bar that in all the month of May, 1809, he was ready, and prepared and willing, to deliver to the plaintiff or to his agent or assigns, at the place of embarkation at Brownsville, the quantity of one thousand nine hundred and twenty gallons of good merchantable proof whisky, in good and tight barrels, according to the tenor and effect of the said condition; but the plaintiff was not then and there ready to accept the same, nor was any agent or assignee of the plaintiff then and there ready to accept the same. There are four other pleas to the declaration, but as they, as well as the one just stated, are all demurred to specially, and the objections made to the first are also directed to the others, they need not be specially set forth.

Opinion by WASHINGTON, J.

It is objected to this and the other pleas — 1. That it does not state that the defendant is still ready to deliver the whisky in the condition mentioned. 2. That it does not allege the readiness and preparation of the defendant *at the last convenient hour of the 31st of May*. It does not state that the defendant was at the place of embarkation, in person or by an agent, ready and prepared to deliver.

§ 756. *Plea of uncore prest unnecessary in action for non-delivery of goods sold.*

The first objection was pressed, not so much upon the authority of adjudged cases as upon the unreasonableness of the doctrine to which it is made, which renders a tender and refusal, or a readiness to perform, and the want of it in the other party, tantamount to performance, so as forever to discharge the obligation. The rule of law was, indeed, admitted to be, and so it undoubtedly is, that if the condition of the bond be not parcel of the obligation, as if it be to deliver certain goods, the obligation being for money, it is not necessary for the defendant to plead *uncore prest;* and if the legal consequence of tender and refusal in such a case be a discharge from the obligation, it belongs not to this tribunal on that account to depart from the established doctrines of law. The objection, therefore, has no validity.

§ 757. *Rule as to the time of tender or of readiness to perform to be alleged in plea.*

The doctrine laid down by the plaintiff's counsel, upon which his second objection is founded, can by no means be questioned. It is clear that if money is to be paid, or any other act to be performed, on a certain day and at a certain place, the legal time of performance is the last convenient hour of the day for transacting the business. This rule is established for the convenience of both parties, that neither may be compelled unnecessarily to attend during the whole of the day. But if the parties meet at the agreed place during any part of the day, a tender and refusal, though not at the last convenient hour, is sufficient; for in this case neither party is put to inconvenience. So, if the place be fixed and the party is to do the act on or before a certain day, or has the whole month to do it in, as in the present case, yet he cannot plead a readiness to perform, and the absence or want of readiness of the other party, at any time prior to the last convenient hour of the last day, and this for the reason before assigned. Whether in this latter case the party bound to perform may appoint an earlier day than the last for doing the act, and in such case may compel the other party, after reasonable notice thereof, to accept or to submit to the consequence of his absence or refusal on the appointed day, need not be decided in this case, as the court will not find it necessary to give an opinion on the second plea, which presents this question. The cases are certainly not clear on this point, and are somewhat at variance with each other. But there is no question as to the doctrine above stated, that the tender or readiness to perform must be stated to be on the last convenient hour of the last day, if an earlier period be not appointed.

§ 758. *Averment of readiness during the whole of May, not sufficient averment of readiness the last hour of the last day.*

In answer to this objection it is insisted by the defendant's counsel that this plea does, in effect, allege a readiness and preparation at the last convenient hour of the 31st of May; because if, in the words of the plea, the defendant was ready *in all the month of May* to deliver, he must have been ready on the last hour of the 31st of May, because that was part of the month during the whole of which it is alleged he was ready. This argument carries with it such strong marks of good sense, and is so entirely logical, that one hardly knows how to raise a sound objection to it; and yet a plea like the present is believed to be without a precedent. It is no vindication, however, of its correctness that the court arrive at the matter and real point of it by argument and logical deduction. The rules of law seem to require that a plea should be direct in stating with sufficient precision the matter of defense, and should not leave it to be found out by inference, however strong and conclusive. It is said that the defendant has assumed upon himself the necessity of proving more even than his contract and the law imposed upon him, to which the plaintiff ought not to object. That he undertakes to prove his own readiness, and the want of it in the plaintiff, not only on the last convenient hour of the 31st of May, but during each and every hour of the whole month of May. To this it may observed that this circumstance constitutes one of the demerits of the plea; because, if the plaintiff had taken issue on the whole plea, it would have been immaterial, since the defendant might have lost the cause in consequence of not being able to prove a readiness during the whole month; and yet it was not material whether he was so or not, provided he was ready at the last convenient hour of the last day of the month. It is true the plaintiff might have selected out of the plea, which runs over the whole month, the last convenient hour of the 31st, and taken issue on the readiness of the defendant, and his own absence or readiness at that time of the day, passing over the rest of the plea with a protestation against its truth. But if, instead of doing this, he chooses to demur, he is certainly at liberty to do so.

In the case of Lancashire v. Killingworth it is laid down in the clearest terms that, if the plaintiff or defendant, as the case may be, plead a tender or a readiness to perform and that the other party was not at the place ready to accept, he must state at what time of the day he was there and how long he continued, that it may appear that he stayed to the last convenient hour of the day. It is true that, in that case, the declaration stated that the plaintiff was at the place *on such* a day, which he might well have been, and yet not be there at the last convenient hour of the day. But yet the court not only condemned the plea on that account, but proceeded to state the proper form of pleading in such a case. This decision as to the form of pleading has never, to the recollection of the court, been overruled or relaxed by any subsequent case; and such undoubtedly has been the usual form of pleading a tender or readiness to perform, in the absence of the other party. In the case of Halsey *v.* Carpenter, Cro. Jac., 359, which was debt on a bond to pay £304 to three persons *tam cito*, as they shall come of age, a plea of payment in the words of the bond was considered bad on a special demurrer, because it did not state the time, place and manner of performance; and yet that plea unquestionably covered every hour of the time after the obligees came of age.

§ 759. *A plea of readiness to perform must show by clear and direct allegations that defendant had done all in his power in order to perform.*

The third objection to the plea stands upon still stronger ground than the one just mentioned; for it is not only uncertain and argumentative, but the conclusion from the premises stated is by no means so inevitable. Because the defendant was, in all the month of May, ready, prepared and willing to deliver the whisky to the plaintiff or his agent, at the place of embarkation; the plea argues that the defendant must have been personally, or by his agent, at the place of embarkation ready to deliver. But the conclusion does not necessarily follow, even if it were proper to get at it in this way. A man may truly say that he is ready and prepared to pay money or deliver an article at a particular place, for instance, at a spot near to and within sight of his own house, and would have done so if the other party had come to receive it; and yet he may not have gone to the spot, in consequence of the non-appearance of the other party. To say the least of such a plea, it is uncertain and ambiguous; whereas, if the party would excuse himself for the want of a strict performance of his contract, he should show, by clear and direct allegations, that he did all on his part that was in his power in order to perform.

§ 760. *Quære, whether an offer to perform must be alleged, though in absence of promises.*

In some cases it is said that though the other party be absent, still the plea must state an offer to perform, which would seem to be rather an idle form. Still this shows that the party must state himself to be present in person, or by an agent, since, if absent, he could not offer, although he might be ready to do so. Indeed, the want of the words "*obtulit solvere*" was deemed fatal on demurrer in the case of Cole *v.* Walton, notwithstanding the plea stated in express terms that the defendant was at the place, and remained till sunset, ready to pay, but that the plaintiff was not there ready to receive. It is unnecessary to decide whether, in such a case, an offer need be made or not; but this and other similar cases are strong to show that the presence of the party bound to perform ought to be distinctly stated, and such appears to be the uniform mode of pleading.

Judgment for plaintiff, and writ of inquiry to be executed before the marshal.

FIEDLER v. CARPENTER.

(Circuit Court for Massachusetts: 2 Woodbury & Minot, 211-216. 1846.)

STATEMENT OF FACTS.— This was a writ of entry for a tract of land situated in Attleborough, counting on the seizin of the demandants within twenty years and a disseizin by the tenants.

The latter pleaded in bar that a portion of the premises belonged to one Joseph Wilkinson and they held it under him as tenants at will only, and as to the residue that he had a mortgage thereof, under which, since this suit was instituted, he had entered and dispossessed them.

The demandants replied that the tenants and one Royal Sibly, long before the date of this suit, conveyed the demanded premises to them in mortgage, to hold the same in fee and mortgage by the defendants, and has since disseized them thereof. To this the tenants demurred.

Opinion by WOODBURY, J.

The first question in this case relates to the propriety of the amendment asked for by the demandants.

§ 761. *A declaration may be amended, though after special plea, replication and demurrer, provided the real cause of action will not be changed thereby.*

There can be no doubt that the suit in point of fact was brought for the purpose of foreclosing a mortgage from the tenants to the demandants, though one is not referred to in the declaration. An amendment is usually permissible when the cause of action is the same and the evidence to be offered is the same. Perly *v.* Brown, 12 N. H., 493. The tenants do not in their plea deny the seizin of the demandant, nor set up any title in themselves to any freehold in the premises. And when the demandants in their replication describe their seizin to be by means of a mortgage from the tenants to them, the demurrer to this replication admits the truth of that allegation.

If an amendment, then, is granted so as to introduce this admitted fact in the declaration, the real cause of action will not be changed thereby, and the recovery will be for less than it might be on the original declaration. That is, it would be then only as in mortgage or conditional, whereas now it would be absolute if at all for the demandants. But as the demandants might now not be entitled to judgment at all against the tenants, if claiming a fee against them not in mortgage, and they pleading *non tenure*, or that they hold less than a freehold estate, the amendment may be very important in respect to costs in this action, and may save the expense of a new suit to foreclose the mortgage.

I shall therefore allow it, but the application for it being so late after plea pleaded in bar, and the change caused by it having so important an influence, it must be on terms. The tenth rule of this court requires special terms if an amendment be not asked till an issue is joined. Those terms would be all the costs to the tenants and none to the demandants till the motion was made, if the tenants had any equities in their defense or could have been at all misled as to the wishes of the demandants originally to do nothing except foreclose their mortgage. As the circumstances stand, however, though not probably misled, yet the tenants have been obliged to plead specially before the leave to amend was asked, and the amendment is an important one. They are, therefore, to have their own costs up to the time of the amendment asked, but nothing since.

§ 762. *Non tenure, whether pleadable in bar or in abatement.* ˑ

The next question is, supposing the amendment made, Can the demandant, after the plea of *non tenure* in bar, have judgment to foreclose his mortgage against the tenants? This question seems fully settled in this state by several adjudged cases, mostly referred to by the counsel for the demandant.

It is well established that after such a plea as this in abatement to such a writ as this was originally, the action cannot proceed, as a fee cannot be demanded of or a seizin restored by a tenant unless claiming at least a freehold estate. Brown *v.* Miltimore, 2 N. H., 442; Stearns, Real Actions, 207. It seems also to have been held in Massachusetts that *non tenure* may, as done here, be pleaded in bar as well as in abatement. Fales *v.* Gibbs, 5 Mason, 465; Jackson on Real Actions, 91, 92; 3 Mass., 312; 10 Mass., 64; 11 Mass., 216.

But the supreme court of the United States have in one case considered the matter properly pleaded in abatement only. 8 Cranch, 229. And the practice accords with that in New Hampshire and England. 2 N. H., 10, 442; Booth on Real Actions, 28; Rastell's Entries, 225. And perhaps the allowance of it in bar is justifiable only in states and courts where pleas in abatement must be filed early in the term. As this court must in the practice in this respect comply with what existed here in 1789 (10 Wheat., 1, 51), and for aught which appears it was the same then as now, this plea would be valid against the original form of the action.

§ 763. *Non tenure no defense to action for foreclosure of mortgage.*

But as it is, after amended, so as to be an action by a mortgagee against the mortgagor to foreclose the mortgage, it seems fully settled in this state that *non tenure*, however pleaded, is no defense to an action appearing in the declaration to be for that purpose. Penniman *v.* Spencer, 13 Mass., 429, 430; Wolcott *v.* Spencer, 14 Mass., 412; 15 Mass., 268. If it was, a mortgage could seldom be foreclosed by a suit, as the mortgagor usually remains in possession, and as a mortgagor he is at law never tenant of the freehold, but commonly a mere tenant at will, and being only such a tenant *quodam modo.* 1 Powell on Mort., 136, 137; 1 N. Hamp. R., 169; Doug., 22, 282; Cholmondeley *v.* Clinton, 2 Jac. & Walk., 183; Waltham Bank *v.* Waltham, 9 Law Rep., 210, 211.

The action to foreclose may, therefore, be against any person in possession. Hunt *v.* Hunt, 17 Pick., 121; Shelton *v.* Atkins, 22 Pick., 74. And it is not brought so much to recover seizin as to collect the debt due, and the demandant is not to be put in possession if the debt is paid within the time allowed by law by any one in possession. In this particular case, where the tenant himself executed the mortgage to demandant, it is argued, also, that the latter is estopped by his deed to deny he is tenant of the freehold to the demandant.

But no precedent is cited to support this view, and, on principle, it strikes me that he would be estopped to deny only that he was once possessed of a freehold when he made the conveyance, rather than that he was when the suit was brought. The deed rather shows that he has parted with a freehold than retains it. It is true that in equity the mortgagor is sometimes considered still to retain an equitable freehold. Pow. on Mort., 157, a; 1 Atk., 603. And that may be one additional reason why in this proceeding, under a statute which, in a suit at law, allows the mortgagor time to redeem, instead of considering the estate as forfeited by non-payment at the day agreed, the mortgagee should recover, though the mortgagor, as tenant, pleads *non tenure.*

A mortgagor is treated in America as having, for most purposes at law, a freehold, till he quits possession, as against all but the mortgagee. 4 Kent,

C., 160; 3 Wheat., 226, note; 6 Johns., 290. Some of the cases seem to hold the same as against the mortgagee, and the latter as possessing only a chattel interest. Clark v. Beach, 6 Conn., 142; 20 Maine, 111; 11 N. Hamp., 55. But this is doubtful, except for certain purposes, as dower, taxation, voting, settlement cases, etc. 2 Greenl. R., 173, 387; 6 N. Hamp., 25; Waltham v. Waltham, 9 Law Rep., 211; 11 N. H., 62, 274; 10 N. Hamp., 504. In these the mortgagor in possession is often to be considered as the owner. 2 Doug., 631; Rigney v. Lovejoy, 13 N. Hamp., 251; 5 N. Hamp., 420, 430.

It may be, also, that when one has disseized or entered on his grantee, he may not be allowed "to qualify his own wrong." Jack. on R. A., 97; Golds., 43. But whichever of these may be the true grounds, or the strongest for the decision of the court, it is in favor of sustaining an action like this in the amended form by the mortgagee against his mortgagor. The demandants must take care to insert in the amendment any averment required by the practice here to justify a judgment of foreclosure, and not a mere judgment for possession to receive the rents and profits.

Let the entry, then, be that the demandants are allowed to amend on paying the tenants their cost till the motion was made, and then that the replication is good, and the demandants entitled to judgment for a foreclosure of the mortgage.

BIDDLE v. WILKINS.

(1 Peters, 686–694. 1828.)

Opinion by MR. JUSTICE THOMPSON.

STATEMENT OF FACTS.—This case comes up from the district court of the United States for the Mississippi district upon a writ of error. The action in the court below was founded upon a judgment obtained in the district court of the United States for the western district of Pennsylvania, in the term of October, in the year 1823, for the sum of $32,957.34. The declaration is in the usual form of an action of debt on a judgment.

The defendant pleads in bar: 1. That the plaintiff is not and never was administrator of John Wilkins, deceased. 2. That at the January term, in the year 1817, of the orphans' court for the county of Adams, and state (then territory) of Mississippi, he, the defendant, was duly appointed sole administrator of John Wilkins, deceased, and entered into bond with security, and took the oath prescribed in such case according to the statute in such case made and provided; and that he took upon himself the duty and office of administrator, and has continued to act as such administrator ever since. 3. That the judgment in the declaration mentioned was obtained by fraud. To the first two pleas a special demurrer was interposed, and issue to the country taken upon the third, and judgment rendered for the defendant upon the demurrer, to reverse which the present writ of error has been brought.

§ 764. *In an action on a judgment recovered by the plaintiff as administrator, a plea of ne unques administrator is bad.*

The first plea of *ne unques administrator* has been abandoned as altogether untenable, and the counsel on the part of the defendant in error have rested their argument entirely on the validity of the second plea, and have treated this as a plea in bar to the jurisdiction of the court in which the judgment was rendered. It is a little difficult to discover what is the true character of this plea. It can, in substance, amount to nothing more than an allegation that the plaintiff was not the lawful administrator of John Wilkins. And in that respect is but a repetition of the same matter set up in the first plea, and that, too, in a more exceptionable form. For the conclusion is drawn argumentatively from the fact set up in the plea that he, the defendant, was duly appointed sole administrator of John Wilkins, in the orphans' court of the county of Adams, in the state of Mississippi, and thence to infer that the plaintiff could not be the lawful administrator in Pennsylvania. Such a plea will not stand the test of a special demurrer. If it was intended by this plea to set up that the defendant was the first and only rightful administrator of John Wilkins, and that the debt due from him thereby became assets in his hands, the plea is defective in not alleging when administration was granted to the plaintiff. The declaration alleges that John Wilkins died a citizen of Pennsylvania, and, from anything that appears to the contrary, administration might have been granted to the plaintiff before it was to the defendant.

§ 765. *A plea in an action on a judgment may attack the operation of the record, but not its validity.*

The simple fact that administration had been granted to the defendant in Mississippi would not raise any question with respect to the jurisdiction of the court, and if it furnished any matter of defense on the merits against the recovery, on the ground that it was taking out of his hands assets, the administion of which belonged to him, it should have been set up in the original action. Nothing appears to invalidate the judgment upon which the present action is founded. The cause of action does not appear, and we cannot say that the subject-matter was not within the jurisdiction of the court when it was rendered, or that there was any disability in the plaintiff to sue in that court, or that the judgment was void for any cause whatever. When the court in which the judgment is rendered has not jurisdiction over the subject-matter of the suit, or when the judgment is absolutely void, this may be pleaded in bar, or may in some cases be given in evidence under the general issue. But the general rule is that there can be no averment in pleading against the validity of a record, though there may be against its operation. And it is upon this ground that no matter of defense can be pleaded in such case which existed anterior to the judgment. Chitty, Plead., 481. Hence it has become a settled practice in declaring, in an action upon a judgment, not (as formerly) to set out in the declaration the whole of the proceedings in the former suit, but only to allege generally that the plaintiff, by the consideration and judgment of that court, recovered the sum mentioned therein. Chitty, 354.

§ 766. *In an action of debt upon a judgment recovered by the plaintiff as administrator, he need not name himself as administrator or make profert of his letters of administration.*

The original cause of action having passed *in rem judicatam*, how far the circumstance that the defendant had taken out letters of administration in Mississippi would have availed as a defense against a recovery of the original judgment cannot now be inquired into. It should have been set up in the former suit. But if the first administrator acquired a right to this debt as assets, and that matter was now open to inquiry, there is nothing appearing on this record to show that the defendant had acquired any such priority. When letters of administration were taken out by the plaintiff does not appear, nor was he bound to show that in his declaration. He was not bound to make profert of the letters of administration. This was so decided in the case of Crawford, Administrator of Hargrove, *v.* Whitall, Doug., 4, note *a.* It was an action of

indebitatus assumpsit, upon a judgment recovered by the plaintiff, as administrator, against the defendant, in the mayor's court at Calcutta. And the
declaration alleged that the defendant was indebted to the plaintiff, as administrator, in the sum therein mentioned, which had been adjudged to him as
administrator, etc. The defendant demurred specially, and showed for cause
that there was no profert of letters of administration. But the court said this
was unnecessary, because in this action (upon the judgment) the plaintiff had
no occasion to describe himself as administrator. If then it was a fact, and of
any importance in deciding the legal rights of the parties in this case, that administration had been first granted to the defendant in Mississippi, that should
have been alleged in the plea, and no objection can be taken to the declaration as containing the first fault in pleading.

That it is not necessary, in cases like the present, for the plaintiff to name
himself as administrator, follows as matter of course from his not being bound
to make profert of his letters of administration, and that when he does so
name himself it may be rejected as surplusage, is well settled by numerous
authorities. In the case of Bonafous *v.* Walker, 2 Term R., 126, it was objected that the action ought to have been brought by the plaintiff as administratrix, because the judgment on which the party had been committed in
execution had been obtained by her as administratrix of her husband. But
the court said that was unnecessary, for the instant the plaintiff recovered the
judgment, it became a debt due her on record, and was assets in her hands,
for which it was not necessary for her to declare as administratrix. See, also,
IIob., 301; L. Ray., 1215. The case of Tallmadge, Adm'r, etc., *v.* Chappell and
others, 16 Mass. R., 71, decided in the supreme judicial court of Massachusetts, is
very full and explicit on this point. The plaintiff declared as administrator, etc.,
in debt upon a judgment recovered by him as administrator in a court of common pleas in the state of New York. The defendant pleaded in bar that the
parties at the time of rendering the judgment were all inhabitants of the state
of New York, and that the plaintiff was appointed administrator in that state,
and had not been so appointed in Massachusetts. To which plea there was a
demurrer and joinder, and the court held the plea bad. That the action, being
on a judgment already recovered by the plaintiff, it might have been brought by
him in his own name, and not as administrator. For the debt was due to him,
he being answerable for it to the estate of the intestate, and it ought to be considered as so brought; his style of administrator being merely descriptive, and
not essential to his right of recovery. That it was important to the purposes
of justice that it should be so; for an administrater appointed in Massachusetts could not maintain an action upon this judgment, not being privy to it;
nor could he maintain an action upon the original contract, for the defendants
might plead in bar the judgment recovered against them in New York. The
debt sued for is, in truth, due to the plaintiff in his personal capacity, and he
may well declare that the debt is due to himself.

If, in the case before us, the judgment is considered a debt due to the plaintiff in his personal capacity, it is totally immaterial whether the defendant was
or was not administrator of John Wilkins in the state of Mississippi. That
could not in any manner affect the rights of the plaintiff. The plea, therefore,
tenders an immaterial issue, and is bad on demurrer. In whatever light,
therefore, we consider this plea, whether as to the matter itself set up, or to the
manner in which it is pleaded, it cannot be sustained as a bar to the present
action.

We are accordingly of opinion that the judgment of the court below must be reversed and the cause sent back with directions to allow the defendant to plead *de novo*, if he shall elect so to do.

§ 767. **Party having affirmative of issue must prove it—Admissions by confession and avoidance.**—The general rule of pleading is that when an issue is properly joined he who asserts the affirmative must prove it; and if a defendant by his plea confesses and avoids the count he admits the facts stated in the count. Simonton *v.* Winter, 5 Pet., 140.

§ 768. **Pleas in bar, tender, etc.—Strict rules applied to.**—The strict doctrines relative to averments in pleading have been applied to special pleas in bar, of tender, and some others of a peculiar character, depending upon their own particular reasons. Carroll *v.* Peake, 1 Pet., 18.

§ 769. **Right to plead specially in bar.**—The option to file the general issue and give notice does not take away the right to set up the special matter in a plea. Phillips *v.* Comstock, 4 McL., 525.

§ 770. **Plea to merits at imparlance term after expiration of rule.**—A defendant was permitted to plead any issuable plea to the merits at the imparlance term, although the rule to plead shall have expired. Darnall *v.* Talbot, 2 Cr. C. C., 249.

§ 771. **Judgment against bad declaration cannot be pleaded in bar against another declaration.**—A judgment that a declaration is bad in substance (which alone, and not matter of form, is the ground of a general demurrer) can never be pleaded as a bar to a good declaration for the same cause of action. Gilman *v.* Rives, 10 Pet., 298.

§ 772. **Statute of limitations.**—Where there is a bar under the statute of limitations it should be pleaded. Johnson *v.* United States, 3 McL., 89.

§ 773. A plea of the statute of limitations is not favored in law. Reed *v.* Clark, 3 McL., 480.

§ 774. The right to plead the statute of limitations, like any other defense, does not depend on the pleasure or discretion of the court. Packet Co. *v.* Sickles, 19 Wall., 611.

§ 775. Where the statute of limitations has run against a judgment it may be pleaded to a *sci. fa.* to revive the judgment. Simpson *v.* Lassalle, 4 McL., 352.

§ 776. A release, the statute of limitations or payment, may be pleaded to an action on a judgment in another state. Jacquette *v.* Hugunon, 2 McL., 129.

§ 777. In an action of ejectment, where the defendant pleads the statute of limitations, he must connect his own possession with the adverse possession and title of another person which is set up as a defense. Otherwise the plea is not good. Doswell *v.* De Le Lanza, 20 How., 29.

§ 778. If there be two counts in a declaration, and the statute of limitations be pleaded to both, it is not necessary that it should be supported as to both; but it may be supported as to both or either. Chew *v.* Baker, 4 Cr. C. C., 696.

§ 779. Upon the plea of the statute of limitations the plaintiff cannot avail himself of the exception in favor of merchants' accounts without stating it in his replication. It is not admissible in evidence upon the general replication to the plea. Clarke *v.* Mayfield, 3 Cr. C. C., 353.

§ 780. Neither the general statute of limitations nor the statute of limitations of Massachusetts can be pleaded in bar of a suit instituted by the United States against an executor or administrator in the federal circuit court. United States *v.* Howe, 2 Mason, 311.

§ 781. The commencement of a suit, to defeat the statute of limitations, must be the same suit to which the plea is pleaded. Delaplaine *v.* Crowninshield, 3 Mason, 329.

§ 782. Where the statute of limitations imposes a bar upon certain species of contracts after three years, and upon others after two years, and the plea did not show that the contract in question was of the latter class, the plea was bad. Lyon *v.* Bertram, 20 How., 149.

§ 783. The statute of limitations may be pleaded on the first day of the term next after office judgment. Mechanics' Bank of Alexandria *v.* Lynn, 2 Cr. C. C., 246.

§ 784. The statute of limitations must be pleaded strictly within the rule day, unless the court, for good cause shown, shall permit it to be pleaded afterward. Union Bank *v.* Eliason, 2 Cr. C. C., 629.

§ 785. Upon re-instatement of a cause after nonsuit, the court will not permit the defendant to plead limitation, unless on affidavit showing it to be necessary for the justice of the case. McIver *v.* Moore, 1 Cr. C. C., 90.

§ 786. The court permitted the statute of limitations to be pleaded to an action of trespass for mesne profits, after the rule day, on payment of all antecedent costs and a continuance of the cause. Marstellar *v.* McClean, 1 Cr. C. C., 550.

§ 787. The court permitted the plea of limitations to be filed after the rule day, upon an affidavit showing it to be a fair defense under the circumstances of the case. Beatty *v.* Van Ness, 3 Cr. C. C., 67.

§ 788. If the statute of limitations be pleaded after the plea day without leave of the court, the plea will, on motion, be ordered to be stricken out. Scott *v.* Lewis, 2 Cr. C. C., 203.

§ 789. Defendant not allowed to plead statute of limitations after expiration of rule to plead. Bank of Columbia *v.* Hyatt,* 4 Cr. C. C., 88.

§ 790. The statute of limitations may be pleaded at the first term after office judgment, it being an issuable plea. Morgan *v.* Evans, 2 Cr. C. C., 70.

§ 791. If the plaintiffs are misnamed in the title of the cause in the margin of a plea of limitations, the plea is bad on special demurrer. Bank of Columbia *v.* Jones, 2 Cr. C. C., 516.

§ 792. **Justification.**—If the facts stated in a special plea do not amount in law to a justification, yet if issue be joined thereon, and if the facts be proved as stated, it is error in the judge to instruct the jury that the facts so proved do not in law maintain the issue on the part of the defendant. Otis *v.* Watkins, 9 Cr., 339.

§ 793. In an action for slander, if it appears from the plaintiff's testimony that at the time of speaking the words the defendant named his author, who was a responsible man, the defendant may avail himself of that testimony, without pleading the matter as a special justification. Hogan *v.* Brown, 1 Cr. C. C., 75.

§ 794. A plea of justification to a declaration for libel is construed most strongly against the pleader. Everything must be precisely alleged, and nothing left to be taken by intendment. By charging the plaintiff in the plea by the use of the words of the original libel defendant does not necessarily justify himself, as in the libel the words are to be taken in the sense in which they were intended by the author to be understood, while in the plea they are to be taken in the strongest sense against the defendant. Kerr *v.* Force, 3 Cr. C. C., 8.

§ 795. A plea of justification to a declaration on a libel must be as broad as the libel itself, and must answer all the material allegations of the declaration. Smith *v.* Tribune Co.,* 4 Biss., 477.

§ 796. When a defendant attempts to justify by several pleas covering different parts of the libel as set out in the declaration, and one material charge in the libel is not answered, the justification is incomplete, and the pleas will be overruled on demurrer. *Ibid.*

§ 797. Every plea of justification to a declaration for libel must contain one, and only one, good defense to all that it professes to answer. It will not avail defendant to make in his plea various charges against the plaintiff, similar in general character to those contained in the libel, but the particular charges in the libel must be justified. Cook *v.* Tribune Association,* 5 Blatch., 352.

§ 798. In a plea of justification by a marshal, for not levying an execution setting forth a remission by the secretary of the treasury of the forfeiture or penalty on which the judgment was obtained, it is not necessary to set forth the statement of facts upon which the remission was founded. United States *v.* Morris, 10 Wheat., 246.

§ 799. A plea, alleging a seizure for a forfeiture as a justification, should not only state the facts relied on to establish the forfeiture, but aver that thereby the property became and was actually forfeited, and was seized as forfeited. Gelston *v.* Hoyt, 3 Wheat., 346.

§ 800. **Former judgment.**—When the record of a former judgment is set up as establishing some collateral fact involved in a subsequent controversy, it must be pleaded as an estoppel; and such a pleading must be framed with great certainty, as it cannot be aided by any intendment. When, however, a former judgment is set up in bar of an action, or as having determined the entire merits of the controversy, it is not required to be pleaded with greater strictness than any other plea in bar. Aurora *v.* West,* 7 Wall., 82.

§ 801. A plea of a foreign judgment must contain an allegation that the court had jurisdiction, or so much of the proceedings must be spread on the record as will show affirmatively that the court had jurisdiction. Burnham *v.* Webster, Dav., 236.

§ 802. In pleading a former judgment at law it is sufficient to say that the cause of action was the same or identical with that set forth in the complaint in the new action; the facts need not be stated.' Wythe *v.* City of Salem,* 4 Saw., 91.

§ 803. Where a plea of a prior suit in a state court is entered in a suit begun in a federal court, such plea must show jurisdiction of the former suit, if pending in a court not under the same sovereignty. White *v.* Whitman, 1 Curt., 494.

§ 804. Where a suit is founded on the record of a judgment, in which the court has jurisdiction, no errors in the pleadings can be considered; nor, in such a case, can *nil debet* be pleaded. French *v.* Lafayette Ins. Co., 5 McL., 461.

§ 805. In pleading the judgment or decree of a court having plenary jurisdiction of the subject, it is not necessary to set forth the proceedings preliminary to such judgment or decree; they are presumed. Lathrop *v.* Stuart, 5 McL., 167.

§ 806. **In patent suits.**—In an action at law for the infringement of a patent, a special plea setting up a license under the patentee, and not denying the validity of the patent, nor the use by him of the invention, is a good plea. Day *v.* New Eng. Car Spring Co., 3 Blatch., 179.

§ 807. Where the defendant in a patent suit pleaded the general issue and special pleas, and also gave a notice of special matter under section 15 of the patent act of July 4, 1836 (5 U. S. Stat. at Large, 123), and the matters set forth in the special pleas were those of which notice might have been given under said section 15, the court, on plaintiff's motion, struck out the special pleas, with costs. Wilder v. Gayler, 1 Blatch., 597.

§ 808. Notice must be given of the several matters specified in section 15 of the patent act of July 4, 1836 (5 U. S. Stat. at Large, 123), if they are relied on as a defense. They cannot be pleaded specially. There may be grounds of defense not specified in section 15 which might be set up in bar of the action by special plea. Ibid.

§ 809. To an action for an infringement of a patent-right a plea that the thing claimed to have been invented was in use and for sale before the application for the patent is demurrable unless the plea aver an abandonment or that such sale or use was more than two years before the application. Root v. Ball, 4 McL., 177.

§ 810. The defendant in a patent case may plead a special plea or file the general issue with notice. Ibid.

§ 811. " Not guilty within three years " is a good plea in trover. Barnard v. Tayloe, 5 Cr. C. C., 403.

§ 812. Non assumpsit within five years is not a good plea to an action of assumpsit upon a promise to collect money and account for it. Gardner v. Peyton, 5 Cr. C. C., 561.

§ 813. Time as bar to suit on note, manner of pleading.— A plea of non assumpsit infra tres annos is not a good plea to a count upon a promissory note payable thirty days after date. Ferris v. Williams, 1 Cr. C. C., 475.

§ 814. In an action against the indorser of a promissory note payable sixty days after date, non assumpsit infra tres annos is a bad plea upon a general demurrer; it ought to be actio non accrevit. Bank of Columbia v. Ott, 2 Cr. C. C., 575.

§ 815. Upon the plea of " no rent arrear " the tenant may give evidence of work done and goods sold and delivered to the landlord without notice of set-off. Fendall v. Billy, 1 Cr. C. C., 87.

§ 816. Upon the issue of " no rent arrear " the plaintiff in replevin will not be permitted to show that the defendant " had nothing in the tenements." White v. Cross, 2 Cr. C. C., 17.

§ 817. On plea of no rent arrear in replevin the whole burden of proof is on the party pleading it. Hungerford v. Burr, 4 Cr. C. C., 349.

§ 818. A plea of no rent arrear admits the demise as laid in the avowry. Greer v. Nourse, 4 Cr. C. C., 527.

§ 819. Fraud consists in intention, and that intention is a fact that must be averred in a plea of fraud. Moss v. Riddle, 5 Cr., 351.

§ 820. A plea of fraud generally is not sufficient to admit of evidence in a bankrupt case, where the bankrupt had been engaged in an extensive commercial business; the latter is entitled to notice of the acts which are alleged to be fraudulent. Lathrop v. Stewart, 6 McL., 630.

§ 821. In replevin, upon the issue of non cepit, proof that the defendant took the goods as marshal is sufficient proof of the taking. D'Wolf v. Harris, 4 Mason, 515.

§ 822. In an action of replevin a plea that the goods were not the property of the plaintiff is good in substance. Dermott v. Wallach, 1 Black, 96.

§ 823. Plea of former recovery — Nonsuit as bar.— A plea is not valid as a plea of former recovery which merely sets up that a former suit was brought which was " dismissed agreed " or disposed of in any way which would be equivalent to a nonsuit. If there was any agreement of parties at the time which would bar a future suit, this should be set up in the plea. Haldeman v. United States, 1 Otto, 584.

§ 824. Assumpsit — Plea of attachment holding debt, held bad.— In an action of assumpsit, a plea that before this action the present defendant had sued the present plaintiff in the state court, and in that suit had attached under the state law the debt now sued for, that that suit had been removed into this court, where it was now pending, and that the attachment held the debt, is a bad plea upon demurrer. New Eng. Screw Co. v. Bliven, 3 Blatch., 240.

§ 825. Court of claims — Right of United States to plead statute of limitations in.— It has generally been supposed that, when a petition is presented to the court of claims, the United States occupy the position of an ordinary defendant in a suit at law: but there is no reason to suppose that all the laws, decisions and principles which regulate dealings between man and man were to be applied to the United States; that they might, for instance, plead the statute of limitations, without express authority. Todd v. United States.* Dev., 175.

§ 826. Plea to representative character of plaintiff may be pleaded with another plea in bar.— A plea to the representative character of the plaintiff, in a suit brought by an alleged administrator, may be a plea in bar as well as in abatement, and, therefore, may be pleaded along with another plea in bar to the merits, although the two may be inconsistent. If there
647

were only one plea, and that was to the merits, the representative character of the plaintiff would be admitted. The remedy of the plaintiff when such pleas are put in is not by demurrer, but by motion to strike out one of the pleas, or for the defendent to elect which he will abide by. Noonan v. Bradley, 9 Wall., 394.

§ 827. Paymaster's bond, action on for not accounting — Plea that part of money was stolen, bad.— In an action on the official bond of a paymaster for not accounting to the government for the moneys received by him, a plea that a part of the money to be accounted for was stolen, without a tender of the balance, is bad, and is not cured by going to issue on the question of the theft. United States v. Dashiel, 4 Wall., 182.

§ 828. Usury must be specially pleaded to be available as a defense. Cleveland Ins. Co. v. Reed, 1 Biss., 180.

§ 829. Property in the defendant must be specially pleaded, and cannot be given in evidence under *non cepit.* Dickson v. Mathers, Hemp., 65.

§ 830. The party pleading a record with a prout patet proffers that issue, and it is incumbent on him to maintain it literally, and this as well where the averment has reference to particulars which need not be specifically stated upon the record as to those which must be stated. Whitaker v. Bramson, 2 Paine, 209.

§ 831. Plea setting up forfeiture.— The statute of 1794, prohibiting the fitting out any ship for the service of any foreign prince or state, to cruise against the subjects of any other foreign prince or state, does not apply to any new government, unless it has been acknowledged by the United States or by the government of the country to which such new state belonged. And a plea which sets up a forfeiture under that act, in fitting out a ship to cruise against such new state, must aver such recognition or it is bad. Gelston v. Hoyt, 3 Wheat., 246.

§ 832. Conversion — Justification — New assignment.— To trespass for taking and detaining and converting property, it is sufficient to plead a justification of the taking and detention, and if the plaintiff relies on the conversion he should reply it by way of new assignment. *Ibid.*

§ 833. Plea of never executrix.— An office judgment may be set aside on the plea of "never executrix." Alexander v. West, 1 Cr. C. C., 88.

§ 834. Covenant for rent — Plea ground-rent unpaid.— To an action of covenant for rent the defendant cannot plead that his lessor had not paid the ground-rent according to his covenant. Gill v. Patton, 1 Cr. C. C., 143.

§ 835. To avoid circuity of action a covenant may be pleaded as a release; but it must be a covenant between those parties only; and if it contains no words of release, it will not be construed such, unless it gives the covenantee a right of action which will precisely countervail that to which he is liable; and unless, too, it was the intention of the parties that the last instrument should defeat the first. Garnett v. Macon, 2 Marsh., 185.

§ 836. A general plea of plene administravit may be good, where all the property of the intestate has been exhausted in a regular course of administration. But if exhausted in paying debts, without notice of a debt having a legal priority, that fact should be specially pleaded. United States v. Hoar, 2 Mason, 311.

§ 837. Justification by collector for detention of vessel.— If a collector justify the detention of a vessel, under the eleventh section of the embargo law of the 15.h of April, 1808, he need not show that his opinion was correct, nor that he used reasonable care and diligence in ascertaining the facts upon which his opinion was formed. It is sufficient that he honestly entertained the opinion upon which he acted. Otis v. Watkins, 9 Cr., 339.

§ 838. Suit for seaman's wages, defense, misconduct — Facts constituting must be pleaded.— In a suit for wages, or for a share in a whaling voyage, if the defense sets up misconduct there must be a special allegation of the facts, with due certainty of time, place and other circumstances: otherwise the court will reject it. Loose allegations of general misconduct are insufficient. Macomber v. Thompson, 1 Sumn., 384.

§ 839. Outstanding judgments cannot be given in evidence on plene administravit, but must be specially pleaded. Hines v. Craig, 1 Cr. C. C., 340.

§ 840. Insolvency, answer to averment of.— A plea that the maker of a note had, at the date of the writ, goods and chattels to a greater amount than the plaintiff's claim, is no answer to an averment of insolvency. Janney v. Geiger, 1 Cr. C. C., 547.

§ 841. A plea of the statute of gaming to a promissory note is substantially defective in not stating what debt or judgment the note was given to secure; by what court the judgment was rendered, and the names of the persons who won and lost the money. Welford v. Gilham, 3 Cr. C. C., 556.

§ 842. Justification for distress made.— When a party who has made a distress comes to answer for it he may justify in different rights, by several avowries, and thus bring each right distinctly before the court. Ross v. Holtzman, 3 Cr. C. C., 391.

§ 843. Upon a plea of "payment" to a declaration on a single bill it is not necessary to produce in evidence the single bill. The plea admits its execution and that it is truly stated in the declaration. Turner v. White, 4 Cr. C. C., 465.

§ 844. Plea of "no assets" by administrator in suit instituted against his intestate.— If, after verdict and before judgment, the defendant die, and his administrator become a party to the suit and judgment pass against him, and execution issue thereon and be returned unsatisfied, on *scire facias* against the administrator he may well plead no assets or insolvency, for he had no time to plead such plea in the original suit. Hatch v. Eustis, 1 Gall., 160.

§ 845. Burden of proof.— A plea of another action pending is an affirmative plea, and casts the *onus probandi* on the party pleading it, and the proof to sustain it must be record evidence. Fowler v. Byrd, Hemp., 213.

§ 846. Justification under warrant must be specially pleaded.— In trespass any matter done by virtue of a warrant must be specially pleaded. Martin v. Clark, Hemp., 259.

§ 847. Peremptory exceptions.— Under the practice of Louisiana peremptory exceptions must be considered as specially pleaded when they are set forth in writing, in a specific or detailed form, and judgment prayed on them. Phillips v. Preston, 5 How., 278.

§ 848. Surrender of goods by clerk of court without taking bond — Justification.— Where a clerk of court was sued upon his official bond, and the breach alleged was that he had surrendered certain goods without taking a bond with good and sufficient securities, and the plea was that the bond which had been taken was assigned to the plaintiffs, who had brought suit, and received large sums of money in discharge of the bond, this plea was sufficient, and a demurrer to it was properly overruled. Bevins v. Ramsey, 15 How., 179.

§ 849. A plea that a note had been assigned should be supported by some proof that the right was in the assignee. Conant v. Wills, 1 McL., 427.

§ 850. Note for land — No title in vendor may be pleaded in suit on.— Where the defendants gave their note for a tract of land which belonged to the United States, and to which the plaintiff could have no title, the defendants may plead the fact to an action on the note. Scudder v. Andrews, 2 McL., 464.

§ 851. Plea of another suit pending.— To make the plea of the pendency of another suit effectual it must show that the court where the suit is pending has jurisdiction. *Ex parte* Balch, 3 McL., 221.

§ 852. Bankruptcy — Jurisdictional facts must be pleaded.— Certain things are required to give jurisdiction to a proceeding in bankruptcy, and all these must appear in the plea. *Ibid.*

§ 853. Bankruptcy should be pleaded at law and in equity. Fellows v. Hall, 3 McL., 281.

§ 854. Assumpsit — Former recovery.— In an action of *assumpsit* or on the case the defendant is not bound to plead a former recovery, and may give it in evidence. Lonsdale v. Brown, 4 Wash., 86.

§ 855. Tort action against consul — Justification insufficient.— In an action of tort to recover the value of certain chattels, a plea that defendant was United States consul in Egypt, and that in the exercise of his functions in accordance with the laws of nations and the statutes of the United States he had attached the goods sued for at suit of another, is bad on general demurrer for not setting up the laws or usages on which his jurisdiction depended. Duinese v. Hale, 1 Otto, 13.

§ 856. A plea of general performance, to an assignment of a special breach, tenders no issue and is bad. So held in an action upon a charter-party by the terms of which plaintiff was to be paid certain specified sums at particular times. Declaration averred that defendant had chartered the ship, that the ship was lost during the voyage, and that a large sum of money was at that time due the plaintiff for its hire. Plea craved oyer of the charter-party, and averred that defendant had paid plaintiff all sums due and payable by the terms thereof. Simonton v. Winter,* 5 Pet., 141.

§ 857. Such a plea, when held by the court to be bad, is a nullity and cannot be considered as an admission of the cause of action. *Ibid.*

§ 858. Declaration on bond alleged specific breaches — Plea alleged performance of all conditions, etc.— To a declaration in debt upon a replevin bond, setting forth the condition and the breaches, by not prosecuting the writ of replevin to effect, and by not returning the property, and by not paying the damages and costs, a plea that the defendant hath performed, etc., all and singular the matters and things in the said condition mentioned, which he according to the force, form and effect of the same condition ought to have observed, performed, etc., is bad upon general demurrer. Lenox v. Gorman, 5 Cr. C. C., 531.

§ 859. Matters in avoidance of a deed must be pleaded. Greathouse v. Dunlap, 3 McL., 303.

§ 860. Every plea in discharge or avoidance of a bond should state particularly the matters of discharge or avoidance. *Ibid.*

§ 861. **Suit by assignee of " single bill "— Obligee's fraud pleaded by obligor — Alabama practice.**— In Alabama, where the obligor of a "single bill " — a sealed instrument — was sued by an assignee, and pleaded that such bill was given for the purchase of horses, which were not as sound nor of as high a pedigree as had been represented by the seller, such plea was admissible. Withers *v.* Green, 9 How., 213.

§ 862. **Action on embargo bond — Plea laden with a negative pregnant.**— In an action by the United States on an embargo bond, in which the condition was that defendant's vessel should not touch at any port in Great Britain or France, and that he should prove within six months that the cargo had been discharged elsewhere, a plea that the vessel had not touched at a prohibited port "during said voyage " is a negative pregnant and is bad in substance. United States *v.* Sawyer,* 1 Gall., 86.

§ 863. A plea in the above case that defendant had furnished a certificate of the discharge of the cargo at a permitted port. but that it had been objected and refused by the collector as informal, is bad as a plea of performance. *Ibid.*

§ 864. **Action on appeal bond — Plea of appeal to United States supreme court.**— In an action on a bond given on an appeal from the district to the supreme court of a territory, it is not sufficient to plead that defendant had carried up the case on error from the latter court to the supreme court of the United States, and had filed his bond, which operated as a *supersedeas* of the judgment of the territorial court, that no mandate or *remittitur* had been issued by the United States court, and that the judgment was still stayed by the bond and *supersedeas.* It is necessary for defendant to aver distinctly not only that the appeal had been taken, but that it had been perfected and is still pending. Gillette *v.* Bullard,* 20 Wall., 571.

§ 865. **Plea of payment of note to assignor before notice of assignment.**— In an action on a promissory note, brought by the assignee, a plea is defective which alleges that defendant paid the note to the assignor before notice of the assignment, without an allegation that the note was paid before it was due or before it was assigned. Patterson *v.* Atherton,* 3 McL., 147.

§ 866. In the above action a plea is defective which alleges that defendant before notice of the assignment paid a certain sum to the assignor, and, before suit, the remainder to the plaintiff, without an allegation that plaintiff accepted the sum in discharge of the note. *Ibid.*

§ 867. **Plea of insolvency by administrator.**— To a declaration in debt against an administrator, a plea that the estate is insolvent does not set up a defense to the action. Peyatte *v.* English,* Hemp., 24.

§ 868. **Replevin against sheriff — Pleas by plaintiff repelling justification, held bad.**— A sheriff, sued in replevin, avowed and justified under two writs of attachment covering the same property in question, one of the writs being against the plaintiff in replevin and the other against a third party. To this avowry the plaintiff pleaded the following pleas, all of which were held bad as not repelling the justification: 1. Payment to the plaintiff in attachment without allegation of notice to the sheriff, or a discontinuance. 2. Accord with plaintiff in attachment without discontinuance or notice. 3. Discontinuance after institution of the replevin suit. 4. That when the goods were attached as property of plaintiff they were in possession of the sheriff under an attachment against a third person. 5. That the goods were the property of plaintiff and not of the third person, without showing that plaintiff had disembarrassed his own case of the attachment against himself. Livingstone *v.* Smith,* 5 Pet., 90.

§ 869. **Action on note given for goods — Plea, goods of no value.**— A plea to an action on a note given for the consideration, which avers that the goods purchased are of no value to defendant, is not good. Christy *v.* Cummins, 3 McL., 886.

§ 870. **Seizin of the vendor.**— In a plea of a purchase for a valuable consideration without notice of the plaintiff's title, it is necessary to aver that the person who conveyed was seized, or pretended to be seized, at the time when he executed the purchase deeds. Flagg *v.* Mann, 2 Sumn., 486.

§ 871. **Want of consideration, on general principles, cannot be pleaded to a bond; nor fraud,** except to the execution of the instrument. But under the statute of Ohio, both of these defenses to a sealed instrument may be made. Greathouse *v.* Dunlap, 3 McL., 303.

§ 872. **To take advantage of the statute of frauds the defendant must plead it, and if he** does not the statute will be presumed to have been complied with. Lamb *v.* Starr, Deady, 350.

§ 873. **Plea of ownership bad if statement shows no title.**— While a simple allegation of ownership in the defendant may be a good plea to an action to recover possession of land, it becomes bad if it is coupled with a statement of his title, showing that the alleged ownership does not exist. Wythe *v.* Myers, 3 Saw., 595.

§ 874. **Plea in detinue must deny special property in plaintiff.**— A plea in detinue which merely sets up a general property in the defendant and does not exclude or deny a special property in the plaintiff, with right of possession, is bad. Elgee *v.* Lovell, 1 Woolw., 102.

§ 875. **Allegation of seizin—Insufficient plea denying plaintiff's title—Statute of limitations—Texas practice.**— In Texas the technical forms of pleading, fixed by the common law, are dispensed with, but the principles which regulate the merits of a trial by ejectment and the substance of a plea of title to such an action are preserved. Christy v. Scott, 14 How., 282.

§ 876. Therefore, where the plaintiff filed a petition that he was seized in his demesne as of fee of land from which the defendant had ejected him, and defendant pleaded that if the plaintiff had any paper title it was under a certain grant which was not valid, this plea was bad. So also was a plea denying the right of the plaintiff to receive his title because he was not then a citizen of Texas. So also where, under a plea of the statute of limitations, the defendant claimed certain land by metes and bounds, and disclaimed all not included within them; there was nothing to show that the land so included was part of the land claimed by the plaintiff. And lastly, where the plea was in substance that the plaintiff had no good title against Texas, no title in the defendant being shown. For the action may have been maintainable although the true title was not in the plaintiff. *Ibid.*

§ 877. **Plea of payment.**— B., in Philadelphia, agreed to pay A.'s agent one hundred and seventy thousand guilders, in Amsterdam, on March 1st; and if he should fail so to do, then to repay to A. the value of the said guilders at the rate of exchange current in Philadelphia at the time demand of payment is made, together with the damages at twenty per cent. in the same manner as if bills of exchange had been drawn for the said sum, and they had been returned protested for non-payment, and lawful interest for any delay of payment which may take place after the demand. B. paid the one hundred and seventy thousand guilders, in Amsterdam, to the agent of A. on the 18th of May instead of the 1st of March. A. is not entitled to the twenty per cent. damages, but may, in a suit on the bond given to perform the contract, recover interest on the one hundred and seventy thousand guilders from March 1st to May 18th. It is not a good plea for the defendants to say that they paid the one hundred and seventy thousand guilders to A.'s agent, for the use of A., at Amsterdam, on May 18th, without averring it to be the whole sum then due. United States v. Gurney, 4 Cr., 333.

§ 878. **Special breach assigned — Plea of general performance bad.**— Action of covenant on a charter-party, by which the owners of the brig James Monroe let and hired her to the plaintiff in error for a certain time, the money payable for the hire of the vessel to be paid at certain periods, and under circumstances stated in the charter-party. After some time, and after the vessel had earned a sum of money, while in the employment of the charterer, she was lost by the perils of the sea. The declaration set out the covenants and averred performance on the part of the plaintiffs, and that the sum of $2,784.17 was due and unpaid upon the charter-party. The defendant pleaded that he had paid to the plaintiffs all and every such sums of money as were become due and payable from him, according to the true intent and meaning of the articles of agreement. On the trial of the issue upon this plea, the court, at the request of the plaintiffs, instructed the jury that the plea did not impose any obligation on the plaintiffs to prove any averment in the declaration, but that the whole *onus probandi*, under the plea, was upon the defendant to prove the payment stated in the same, as the plea admitted the demand as stated in the declaration. *Held*, that there was no issue properly joined. The breach assigned in the declaration is special — non-payment of a certain sum of money for particular and specified services alleged to have been rendered. The plea alleges generally that the defendant had paid all that was ever due and payable, according to the tenor of the agreement, and not all of the specified sum. This does not meet the allegations in the declaration, or amount to an admission that the vessel had earned the sum demanded; and there was error in the court in instructing the jury that the plaintiffs were not bound to prove the allegations in the declaration. Simonton v. Winter, 5 Pet., 140.

d. Puis Darrein Continuance.

SUMMARY — *Admits cause of action,* § 879.— *Filed as of right, and waives prior issues,* § 880.

§ 879. Plea *puis darrein continuance* admits the plaintiff's cause of action, and everything else except the matter contested by the plea. Wisdom v. Williams, § 881.

§ 880. A plea *puis darrein continuance,* properly pleaded and verified, must be received by the court, and waives all prior issues. Spafford v. Woodruff, § 882.

[NOTES.— See §§ 883-890.]

WISDOM v. WILLIAMS.

(Circuit Court for Arkansas: Hempstead, 460. 1846.)

§ 881. *Effect of plea puis darrein continuance.*

Opinion of the COURT.

A plea *puis darrein continuance* admits the plaintiff's cause of action, and even if the plea is established still the plaintiff is entitled to costs. It has the effect of displacing all other pleas and previous defenses, and the party is obliged to stand on that alone. 10 Wend., 679; 1 Chitty, Pl., 441; 2 Pet., 548; Stephen, Pl., 81, 83; 13 Pet., 152; Story, Pl., 53, 54. By operation of law the previous pleas are considered as stricken from the record, and everything is confessed except the matter contested by the plea *puis darrein continuance.*

SPAFFORD v. WOODRUFF.

(Circuit Court for Michigan: 2 McLean, 191, 192. 1840.)

Opinion of the COURT.

STATEMENT OF FACTS.— This is an action of *assumpsit* brought against the defendant as the indorser of a note. The general issue was pleaded, and, since the last continuance, a plea *puis darrein continuance,* which alleged that this action is brought against the defendant as indorser of a note, on which the plaintiffs, who are the holders, since the last continuance of this cause, obtained a judgment against the maker and the first indorser, and that they gave time to the defendant, which operates as a release to the defendant in this action. This plea is sworn to, as the rule of the court requires. And a motion is now made to set aside this plea by plaintiffs' attorney on the ground that it is irregular and a nullity.

§ 882. *Requisites and effect of plea puis darrein continuance.*

Great certainty is required in pleas of this description. The plea may be in abatement, or in bar of the action, and the matter of defense must be specifically stated, and the time it arose. In these respects the present plea is not defective, and it is verified by affidavit. Under such circumstances it is said the court cannot set the plea aside on motion, but are bound to receive it. Bro. Abr., Continuance, Pl., 5, 41; Jenk., 160; Prince v. Nicholson, 5 Taunt., 383; Lovell v. Eastaff, 3 Term R., 554.

The interposition of this plea waives all prior issues; nor can the plaintiff, afterwards, proceed thereon. 1 Chitty, Pl. (ed. 1837), 697; 1 Salk., 168; 2 Strange, 1105; 5 Taunt., 333. The matter set up in this plea, so far from appearing to be fraudulent or evasive, presents a serious question; and the facts should either be traversed by a replication, or admitted by a demurrer. The motion is therefore overruled.

§ 883. **Matters of defense arising after commencement of suit — Before or after issue joined.**— The rule is that, when matter of defense has arisen after the commencement of a suit, it cannot be pleaded in bar of the action generally; but must, when it has arisen before the plea or continuance, be pleaded as to the further maintenance of the suit, and when it has arisen after issue joined, *puis darrein continuance.* Yeaton v. Lynn, 5 Pet., 224.

§ 884. **Disability of plaintiff occurring during pendency of suit.**— A distinction is made between an action brought by a person who has no right to sue, and an action brought by a person capable of suing at the time, but who becomes incapable while it is depending. In the first case the plaintiff may be nonsuited at the trial; in the last the disability must be pleaded. *Ibid.*

§ 885. How far a waiver of preceding plea.— At common law any matter of defense arising after a plea was pleaded as a matter arising *puis darrein continuance*, and might be either in abatement or bar of the action; but in either case such plea was a waiver of any plea or defense which preceded it, at least when the former was inconsistent with the latter. Elliott *v.* Teal, 5 Saw., 188.

§ 886. It seems that a plea of *puis darrein continuance* is considered as a waiver of all previous pleas; and the cause of action is admitted to the same extent as if no other defense had been urged than that contained in the plea. Wallace *v.* McConnell, 13 Pet., 136.

§ 887. Judgment on.— If matter in abatement is pleaded *puis darrein continuance*, the judgment, if against the defendant, is peremptory. Renner *v.* Marshall, 1 Wheat., 215.

§ 888. Accord and satisfaction — Waiver.— After the commencement of a suit and issue formed, a party, to avail himself of accord and satisfaction occurring afterwards, must specially plead *puis darrein continuance*, and establish it by evidence if disputed, and pleading *puis darrein continuance* waives all previous defenses. Good *v.* Davis,* Hemp., 16.

§ 889. Mandamus — Resignation — Plea puis darrein.— To a *mandamus* to compel a township clerk to fulfill an official duty, resignation before service of process was averred in the answer, and the appointment of a successor was offered in evidence, but was held inadmissible unless set up by a plea *puis darrein continuance*, or its equivalent. Thompson *v.* United States, 13 Otto, 480.

§ 890. Foreign attachment commenced in state court after commencement of suit cannot be pleaded puis darrein.— An action was instituted on a promissory note against the drawer, by which the drawer promised to pay at the office of discount and deposit of the Bank of the United States at Nashville, three years after date, $4,080. In the declaration, which set out the note according to its terms, and alleged the promise to pay according to the tenor of the note, there was no averment that the note was presented at the bank, or demand of payment made there. The defendant pleaded payment and satisfaction of the note, and issue was thereon joined. At the succeeding term the defendant interposed a plea of *puis darrein continuance*, stating that $4,204, part of the amount of the note, had been attached by B. and W. in a state court of Alabama, under the attachment laws of the state, and a judgment had been obtained against him for $4,204 and costs, with a stay of proceedings until the further proceedings in the case, which remains undetermined. A demurrer to this plea was sustained, and judgment given for the plaintiff for $679, the residue of the note beyond the amount attached, and a final judgment for the whole amount of the note. *Held*, that there was no error in the judgment of the federal court. Wallace *v.* McConnell, 13 Pet., 136.

e. Dilatory Pleas.

SUMMARY — *Want of jurisdiction not apparent on the record to be taken by plea in abatement,* §§ 891, 892.— *Demurrer for want of jurisdiction not a waiver of right to plead in abatement to declaration after amendment,* § 893.

§ 891. An objection for a want of jurisdiction not apparent on the record must be taken by plea in abatement, and this plea is waived if a plea in bar be filed at the same time. Evans *v.* Davenport, §§ 894, 895.

§ 892. A plea in abatement on account of the citizenship of defendant must aver his citizenship and not merely his residence. *Ibid.*

§ 893. By filing a demurrer for want of jurisdiction defendant does not waive his right to plead in abatement to an amended declaration subsequently filed in the same case. Donaldson *v.* Hazen, §§ 896, 897.

[NOTES.— See §§ 898–945.]

EVANS *v.* DAVENPORT.

(Circuit Court for Michigan: 4 McLean, 574–576. 1849.)

Opinion of the COURT.

STATEMENT OF FACTS.— This is a declaration in ejectment, under the forms provided by a statute of the state. The defendant first pleads the general issue. 2d. To the jurisdiction of the court, alleging the defendant to be a resident of New York, instead of Michigan. And the plaintiff demurs for irregularity in the order of pleading. The declaration alleges the plaintiff to be a citizen of New York and the defendant to be a citizen of the state of Michigan.

It is contended that the facts stated in the plea are conclusive against the jurisdiction of the court. The plea denies a material averment in the declaration, which can only be traversed by special plea. And it can make no difference that another plea taking issue generally is on record first. The pleas are filed simultaneously; both are good, it is contended, as pleas in bar. And it is further urged that a want of jurisdiction in a court of special and limited jurisdiction may be shown at any stage of the cause. A plea in abatement should give the plaintiff a better writ. But in this case, if the facts be true as stated, they show that this court can exercise no jurisdiction in the case.

§ 894. *Want of jurisdiction, not apparent on the record, must be objected to by plea in abatement, and this is waived if filed with another plea.*

This court follows the rules of the common law, which requires that the jurisdiction of the court shall first be pleaded. And it is well established (1 Chitt. Pleadings, 440), to file any other plea is a waiver of the want of jurisdiction of the court. From the face of the declaration it appears that there is jurisdiction on the ground of the parties being citizens of different states, the plaintiff being stated to be a citizen of New York and the defendant a citizen of Michigan.

It was laid down by Mr. Justice Washington, in his reports, that a want of jurisdiction may be taken advantage of at any time in the progress of the cause; and it was held at one time that as the averment of citizenship, in the declaration, was a material one, it was denied by the general issue, and the plaintiff was bound to prove it on the trial. But these decisions have long since been overruled, and the settled practice now is to require a plea to the jurisdiction where there is no want of jurisdiction apparent upon the face of the declaration. Where this averment of citizenship is omitted in the declaration, advantage may be taken of it in a motion to arrest the judgment or by a writ of error.

The circuit courts of the United States, though exercising a limited jurisdiction, yet are not inferior courts, which must show in their proceedings jurisdiction, or their judgments will be nullities. This is not the case with the judgments of the circuit court, although the citizenship does not appear in the proceedings. Their judgments are valid until reversed. The order of pleading by the common law is founded in good sense and practical convenience. If the plea to the jurisdiction be sustained, there is an end to the cause on the state of the pleadings, and this necessarily arrests the further progress of the case. And this plea should always be the first pleaded, for this and other considerations.

§ 895. *A person may reside in one state and yet be a citizen of another.*

But there is an objection to this plea which has not been noted in the argument. It avers that the defendant is a resident of New York. Now the plea may be true and yet the court have jurisdiction of the case. A citizen of Michigan may reside in New York for any length of time, and still maintain his citizenship in Michigan. A change of citizenship from one state to another is shown by the acts of the party. If he refrains from exercising the rights of a citizen in the state where he resides, and claims to be a citizen of the state he left, he does not lose his citizenship in such state. We suppose that the attention of the pleader was not particularly drawn to the difference between a citizen and resident. Leave will be given to the defendant to amend his plea, both as to the order of pleading and the averment of the plea.

DONALDSON v. HAZEN.

(Circuit Court for Arkansas: Hempstead, 423–425. 1840.)

Opinion of the COURT.

STATEMENT OF FACTS.— This action of debt was brought by the plaintiff against the defendant upon three promissory notes alleged to have been executed by the defendant to Laughlan Donaldson and by him assigned to the plaintiff. In his declaration the plaintiff failed to aver the citizenship of the assignor of the notes, and at the last term of this court the defendant filed a general demurrer to the declaration, which was sustained by the court, on the ground that the plaintiff had failed to state a case of which the court could take cognizance. The plaintiff then, with the leave of the court, amended his declaration by averring L. Donaldson to be a citizen of the state of Kentucky. On the 28th of October, 1839, the defendant filed a plea to the jurisdiction of this court, averring both the plaintiff and defendant to be aliens. The plaintiff now moves the court to strike out this plea, and whether the motion should be sustained is the only question now to be considered.

§ 896. *Demurrer for want of jurisdiction does not admit jurisdiction.*

The plaintiff contends that the defendant, by a general demurrer to his declaration, has waived the question of jurisdiction and is no longer at liberty to raise it by plea. It may be conceded for argument that if the demurrer to the original declaration did not reach the question of jurisdiction, but went only to the merits of the case, that even to the amended declaration the defendant would not be permitted to file a plea to the jurisdiction of the court. But this would not help the case, because the demurrer was sustained on the sole ground that the plaintiff had failed to state a case in his declaration of which the court could take cognizance. That this judgment of the court upon the demurrer was in accordance with the well-settled principles of law can hardly admit of a doubt.

It is settled by uniform and repeated decisions of the supreme court that the facts or circumstances upon which the jurisdiction over the case depends must be set forth in the declaration. Thus, in a suit between an alien and a citizen, the alienage of the one and the citizenship of the other must be stated. Hodgson v. Bowerbank, 5 Cranch, 303; Jackson v. Tentyman, 2 Pet., 136. When the suit is between citizens of different states, the citizenship of the parties, to show not only that they are citizens of different states; but also that one of them is a citizen of the state where the suit is brought, must be stated. 3 Dall., 382; 1 Cranch, 343; 2 id., 9, 126; 3 id., 515; 5 id., 57; 6 Wheat., 450; 1 Peters, 238.

And in a suit to recover the contents of a promissory note, or other chose in action, except foreign bills of exchange and debentures, brought by an assignee of such note, it is necessary to aver that the original promisee, through whom the plaintiff claims to recover, is an alien or citizen of another state, as the case may be, so as to show that he also might have maintained the action in the court to recover such contents. Montalet v. Murray, 4 Cranch, 46.

And when the want of jurisdiction is apparent upon the face of the declaration by reason of the omission of a statement of the facts requisite to bring the case within the cognizance of the court, it is well settled that the defendant may take advantage of such omission, either by motion, at any time before judgment, to dismiss the suit, or after verdict he may move in arrest of judgment, or after judgment he may bring a writ of error and have thé judgment reversed. 4 Wash., 624; 9 Wheat., 537; Pet. C. C., 431; 5 Cranch, 57; 1 id., 343; 2 Pet., 136.

If, then, the omission is a good ground to arrest the judgment, or to reverse it on a writ of error, it can admit of no doubt that it is a good ground of demurrer; for no principle is better established than that a demurrer will reach every defect in the pleadings which would be fatal on a motion in arrest of judgment, or on a writ of error to reverse the judgment. The defendant, then, by demurring to the original declaration, did not admit the jurisdiction of the court; for indeed the decision upon the demurrer was given upon the express ground of want of jurisdiction.

§ 897. *Demurrer for want of jurisdiction does not waive defendant's right to plead in abatement to an amended declaration.*

The plaintiff then amended his declaration, and for the first time stated a case within the jurisdiction of the court, and which became, as it were, a new case. The defendant could then only call in question the jurisdiction of the court by an appropriate plea, traversing the facts alleged by the plaintiff. Shall the defendant be precluded from filing a plea denying the facts upon which the jurisdiction of the court rests, because he demurred to the original declaration on the ground that it failed to state a case within the cognizance of the court? I think not. Such a rule would be unjust. The motion to strike out the defendant's plea to the jurisdiction of the court is overruled.

§ 898. **Pleas in abatement, not being received with favor, require the greatest accuracy and precision in their form, and must be certain to every intent, and are not amendable; they must not be double.** Anonymous, Hemp., 215.

§ 899. **How waived.**— A plea in bar waives all pleas and the right to plead in abatement. Railroad Co. v. Harris, 12 Wall., 65.

§ 900. The right to plead in abatement is lost by pleading to the merits. Cook v. Burnley, 11 Wall., 659.

§ 901. It is a stringent and unbending rule of law in regard to dilatory pleas that they must be pleaded in a preliminary stage of the suit; and if a plea in bar has been filed and the cause is down for trial, such plea in bar cannot be withdrawn to allow a plea in abatement to be pleaded. Yeatman v. Henderson,[*] 1 Pittsb., 20.

§ 902. A plea in abatement must be pleaded before a plea in bar; for if they are pleaded together the plea in abatement will be held to be waived. Dowell v. Cardwell, 4 Saw., 217.

§ 903. A plea in abatement, filed in connection with pleas in bar, is irregular. Spencer v. Lapsley, 20 How., 264.

§ 904. By common law a plea in abatement is overruled by a plea in bar, and no rule of court is required to confirm this practice. Fenwick v. Grimes,[*] 5 Cr. C. C., 603.

§ 905. A plea in abatement not on oath may be treated as a nullity and set aside. *Ibid.*

§ 906. A plea in abatement that there are other defendants not taken will not be received by the court unless it first be put in upon oath. Edmondson v. Barrell, 2 Cr. C. C., 228.

§ 907. **If a plea in abatement be bad the plaintiff need not demur, but may treat it as a nullity and sign judgment.** Anonymous, Hemp., 215.

§ 908. **A plea in abatement is not a waiver of process.** The plea may be abandoned, and a motion to quash the writ for defective service may be substituted. Halsey v. Hurd, 6 McL., 14.

§ 909. **Not allowable after general issue pleaded.**— The court will not suffer the general issue to be struck out to give the defendant leave to plead in abatement. Bank of Columbia v. Scott, 1 Cr. C. C., 184.

§ 910. **Plea in abatement to jurisdiction — Burden of proof.**— A defendant who would question the jurisdiction of a federal court for causes outside of the record should allege the causes in a plea in abatement, and the burden of proof is upon him to sustain them. Sheppard v. Graves,[*] 14 How., 505.

§ 911. **Waived by plea to merits.**—A plea in abatement is waived if a plea to the merits be filed at the same time or subsequently. Sheppard v. Graves,* 14 How., 505; 14 How., 512.

§ 912. **Withdrawal of plea to merits by plea to jurisdiction.**—Filing a plea to the jurisdiction under special leave of the court is in effect to withdraw a former plea to the merits, and if a demurrer to the special plea is sustained the defendant must plead over or allow judgment to be pronounced. Kern v. Huidekoper, 13 Otto, 485.

§ 913. **Plea to jurisdiction, when too late.**—A plea to the jurisdiction comes too late after a mandate has gone down from the United States supreme court to the court below. Whyte v. Gibbs, 20 How., 541.

§ 914. **Citizenship may be the subject of plea in abatement.**—Formerly it was held in some of the federal circuit courts that the averment of citizenship in a different state from the one in which the suit was brought, and which it is necessary to make in order to give jurisdiction to the federal courts, must be proved on the general issue. But the rule now is that if the defendant disputes the allegation of citizenship which is made in the declaration he must plead so in abatement. Jones v. League, 18 How., 76.

§ 915. **Jurisdictional plea—Colorable assignment to evade insolvent law.**—A plea to the jurisdiction, on the ground that a demand has been colorably assigned in order to evade a discharge under the insolvent law, is not to be treated as dilatory and captious, like some pleas in abatement. Wallace v. Clark, 3 Woodb. & M., 359.

§ 916. **Formal plea to jurisdiction, when unnecessary.**—When the nature of an action is such that the court is incompetent to try it, no formal plea to the jurisdiction is necessary; but the question can be raised by demurrer. Stewart v. Potomac Ferry Co., 12 Fed. R., 296.

§ 917. **A plea to the jurisdiction concludes to the cognizance of the court** by praying judgment, if the court will take cognizance of the suit; it should be most precisely stated; it should be signed by the defendant in person, and the affidavit thereto should be positive. A plea in bar waives a plea in abatement. Adams v. White,* 2 Pittsb. R., 21.

§ 918. **Objection to jurisdiction, how made.**—When want of jurisdiction appears on the face of the pleadings the objection should be taken by demurrer; when not, then by plea. Varner v. West, 1 Woods, 493.

§ 919. **The question of citizenship** of a party can only be raised by a plea in abatement in an earlier stage of the cause than a trial on the merits. D'Wolf v. Rabaud, 1 Pet., 476.

§ 920. **Plea to jurisdiction, form of.**—A plea to the jurisdiction ought to begin with the allegation that the court ought not, on account of the facts stated in the plea, to take cognizance of the action, and ought to conclude with the prayer whether the court will take cognizance of the action. Leonard v. Grant, 6 Saw., 603.

§ 921. **Pendency of probate suit subject of.**—As a general rule, the pendency of a suit before a probate court having jurisdiction is pleadable in abatement to a subsequent action for the same cause. Walker v. Johnson, 2 McL., 92.

§ 922. **Variance** between writ and declaration may be noticed only by a plea in abatement. McKenna v. Fisk, 1 How., 241.

§ 923. **Objection to right of executor or administrator to sue.**—The objection that plaintiff has no right to sue as executor may be taken only by plea in abatement. Childress v. Emory, 8 Wheat., 642.

§ 924. In a suit by an administrator, the objection that the plaintiff is not qualified to sue as administrator may be taken only by plea in abatement. Picquet v. Swan, 3 Mason, 469.

§ 925. **A plea in abatement for misnomer** will lie in ejectment, but the plea does not abate the suit, and the defendant having disclosed his true name must plead in chief by that name. Dixon v. Cavanaugh,* 1 Overt. (Tenn.), 366.

§ 926. **Appointment of assignee pleaded to suit by bankrupt.**—To a suit in the name of a bankrupt a defendant may plead the bankruptcy and the appointment of an assignee in abatement. Cook v. Lansing, 3 McL., 571.

§ 927. **Rulings as to, how far subject to appeal**—Under the twenty-second section of the judiciary act of 1789 the United States supreme court cannot reverse the judgment of the court below for error in ruling any plea in abatement other than a plea to the jurisdiction of the court. Piquignot v. The Pennsylvania R. Co., 16 How., 104.

§ 928. **Jurisdiction—Citizenship—Assignment of mortgage.**—The question of jurisdiction arising in a case where a mortgagor and mortgagee were citizens of the same state, and the mortgagee had assigned the mortgage to a citizen of another state, should have been raised by a plea in statement. Upon the trial of the merits it was too late. Smith v. Kernochen, 7 How., 198.

§ 929. **The pendency of a prior suit in a state court** is not a good plea in abatement to a suit in personam in the federal circuit court. White v. Whitman, 1 Curt., 494.

§ 930. The pendency of a suit between the same parties and respecting the same subject-matter in another state may be pleaded in abatement in the United States courts. *Ex parte* Balch, 3 McL., 221.

§ 981. A plea of pendency of a former suit in another court must offer to produce the record of such suit. Riddle *v.* Potter, 1 Cr. C. C., 288.

§ 982. Non-joinder of parties.— To support a plea in abatement for not naming all the joint promisors, it is not necessary for the defendant to prove that the plaintiff knew he was dealing with a copartnership, 1 Cr. C. C., 327.

§ 983. Jurisdiction — Citizenship.— The exception to the jurisdiction of a federal court, by denial of the fact of citizenship, is of a preliminary nature, and must be taken by plea in abatement, and not by any general answer. Wood *v.* Mann, 1 Sumn., 578.

§ 984. Non-joinder of bankrupt's assignee.— Where, in the answer to a bill in equity, it was set forth that as the plaintiff was a bankrupt, and his assignee was not made a party to the bill, the plaintiff was not entitled to relief, it was held that the objection of bankruptcy should have been taken *in limine* by way of plea, and could not be insisted on to avoid exceptions taken by the plaintiff to the answer. Kittredge *v.* The Claremont Bank, 3 Story, 590.

§ 985. Non-joinder of copartner.— If a contract was with the defendant and another as joint partners, the defendant cannot take advantage of it but by plea in abatement. Clementson *v.* Beatty, 1 Cr. C. C., 178.

§ 986. The defendant may take advantage of a partnership upon a plea of *non assumpsit.* But where the partnership is on the part of the defendant he must plead it in abatement. Coffee *v.* Eastland,* 1 Cooke (Tenn.), 159.

§ 987. Suit commenced in another state after continuance.— The commencement of another suit for the same cause of action in the court of another state since the last continuance cannot be pleaded in abatement of the original suit. Renner *v.* Marshall, 1 Wheat., 215.

§ 988. Want of capacity in corporation to sue.— Where a defendant desires to insist on a want of corporate capacity in a plaintiff corporation to sue, he should insist upon it by a special plea in abatement or bar. Pleading to the merits has been held by the United States supreme court to be an admission of the capacity of a plaintiff to sue. The general issue admits not only the competency of the plaintiff to sue, but to sue in the particular action which he brings. Society for the Propagation of the Gospel *v.* Town of Pawlet, 4 Pet., 480.

§ 989. Illegal tax — Suit brought before appeal required by statute.— Section 19 of the act of July 13, 1866, provides that no suit shall be maintained for the recovery of a tax alleged to have been erroneously or illegally assessed or collected until an appeal has been taken to the commissioner of internal revenue. Failure to take such appeal must be pleaded in abatement, or the right to set it up will be lost. Hendy *v.* Soule, Deady, 400.

§ 940. A plea to an action on a note that the plaintiff is not the owner of the note, but that the name of the plaintiff was used by the owner to acquire standing in the federal court, is a plea in bar as well as in abatement to the jurisdiction; an issuable defense is made; and a verdict for the plaintiff is on the merits and will not be set aside. Lanning *v.* Lockett, 11 Fed. R., 814.

§ 941. In a plea of alien enemy an averment that the plaintiff possessed that character at the time of the commencement of the suit is necessary. Elgee *v.* Lovell, 1 Woolw., 102.

§ 942. Time of bringing suit under insurance company's charter, not subject of.— The charter of a mutual fire insurance company required that action should be brought only in the term of the court held next after loss, but this clause cannot be brought in under a plea in abatement to the jurisdiction. Smith *v.* Atlantic Mutual Fire Insurance Co.,* 2 Law Rep. (N. S.), 408.

§ 943. Ejectment — Colorable title.— In a suit of ejectment an objection that the plaintiff's title is merely colorable may be pleaded in abatement, but cannot be availed of after joinder upon the merits. Boyreau *v.* Campbell, McAl., 119.

§ 944. Plea in abatement after plea in bar.— It is within the discretion of a federal court to allow a plea in bar to be withdrawn, and a plea in abatement denying jurisdiction on account of citizenship to be filed. Eberly *v.* Moore, 24 How., 147.

§ 945. Objections to, when not ground of demurrer.— An action was brought in the federal circuit court of Mississippi against the Commercial and Railroad Bank of Vicksburg, Miss., by parties who were citizens of Louisiana. The defendants pleaded in abatement, by attorney, that they were a corporation aggregate, and that two of the stockholders resided in the state of Mississippi. The affidavit to the plea was sworn to by the cashier of the bank before the "deputy clerk." It was not entitled as of any term of the court. The plaintiffs demurred to the plea. *Held*, that the appearance of the defendants in the circuit court by attorney was proper; and that if any exceptions existed to this form of the plea they should have been urged to the receiving of it when it was offered, and are not causes of demurrer. *Held*, also, that the circuit court of Mississippi had no jurisdiction. The Commercial and Railroad Bank of Vicksburg *v.* Slocomb, 14 Pet., 60.

3. Demurrer.

SUMMARY — *Not inconsistent with general issue,* § 946.— *Demurrer in abatement,* § 947.— *Frivolous demurrer,* § 948.— *General and special,* § 949.— *Demurrer cannot question authority or consideration,* § 950.— *Abatement,* § 950a.— *Variance between writ and declaration,* § 951.— *Misjoinder,* § 952.— *Statute of limitations,* § 953.— *Demurrer to several pleas,* § 954.— *Duplicity, how reached,* § 955.— *General and special,* § 956.— *Duplicity defined,* § 956a.— *Demurrer generally, though not always, reaches back,* § 957.

§ 946. A demurrer admitting all the facts well pleaded, and the general issue denying all the facts, are not necessarily inconsistent, and, if they were, such inconsistency might be allowable by statute. Furniss *v.* Ellis, §§ 958-961.

§ 947. A demurrer is necessarily in bar of an action, and although it only assign matter of abatement, yet it must be treated as a general demurrer. If it be heard, final judgment will be rendered for the plaintiff; and if, on the other hand, the latter fail to join, there will be a discontinuance. *Ibid.*

§ 948. The English practice of giving judgment against a party demurring merely on the ground that it is frivolous does not prevail in this country. *Ibid.*

§ 949. Questions of substance only may be raised by general demurrer, and questions of form only by special demurrer. Tyler *v.* Hand, §§ 962-965.

§ 950. Want of authority in the plaintiff to receive the bonds sued on, and want of consideration for the bonds, cannot be called in question by demurrer. *Ibid.*

§ 950a. A demurrer in abatement entitles plaintiff to final judgment. *Ibid.*

§ 951. Variance between writ and declaration cannot be reached by a demurrer. Wilkinson *v.* Pomeroy, §§ 966-970.

§ 952. Misjoinder of counts in the declaration is a radical defect and will be reached by demurrer. *Ibid.*

§ 953. When the date mentioned in the declaration is not material, a demurrer cannot raise the objection that the action is barred by the statute of limitations. *Ibid.*

§ 954. A demurrer to "the several pleas" will be overruled if one good plea be on record. Brown *v.* Duchesne, §§ 971, 972.

§ 955. An objection on the ground of duplicity may be taken only by special demurrer. Jackson *v.* Rundlet, §§ 973-979.

§ 956. A special demurrer assigns specific causes, while a general demurrer does not. This is a modern distinction, not belonging to early common law. *Ibid.*

§ 956a. Duplicity which would render a pleading bad on demurrer consists of joining distinct causes of action, defenses or breaches, not of alleging several facts which make up one cause of action, etc. *Ibid.*

§ 957. A demurrer ordinarily reaches back to the first fault in pleading, though there are exceptions, as where the fault has been cured or would be reached only by special demurrer. *Ibid.*

[NOTES.— See §§ 980-1059.]

FURNISS *v.* ELLIS.

(Circuit Court for Virginia: 2 Marshall, 14-19. 1822.)

STATEMENT OF FACTS.— Action of *assumpsit.* The clerk, in filling out the writ and the declaration, by mistake wrote the name of one of the plaintiffs *Staney* instead of *Stacey,* as in the memorandum given him by counsel. Defendants pleaded the general issue, in which plaintiffs joined, and also filed a demurrer on the ground that the plaintiffs were not the persons named in the writ and declaration. Plaintiffs refused to join in this, and judgment upon it was entered for defendants. Plaintiffs now move to strike out the demurrer, and for leave to amend on the ground of clerical misprision.

§ 958. *Clerk's discretion in receiving pleadings.*

Opinion by MARSHALL, C. J.

This motion is sustained by the allegation that the demurrer ought not to have been received by the clerk, and consequently admits of no inquiry into its sufficiency farther than is necessary to determine on the right to offer it.

It was offered at a time when the right to plead was complete, and under a law which authorizes the defendant to plead as many several matters, both of law and fact, as he may think necessary for his defense.

From the comprehensive letter of this law there would be some difficulty in excluding any plea which the defendant might offer at a time when he had a right to offer it. The sufficiency of the plea is not submitted to the clerk. He cannot judge of it; consequently it would seem he must receive it if it be tendered in proper time.

§ 959. *Inconsistency in defenses, how far allowed.*

But the plaintiffs contend that there is, in the nature and fitness of things, an objection to the allowance of inconsistent matter to be pleaded in the same cause which must enter into the construction of the act of assembly, and control, or at least influence, the meaning of its words. There is, they say, this inconsistency in a demurrer to the whole declaration and a plea to the whole. The demurrer confesses all the facts, and the plea denies them all.

But a demurrer confesses those facts only which are sufficiently pleaded; and the plea, as the plea of *non assumpsit*, though it admits nothing, is not false, though many of the facts alleged in the declaration are true. It amounts to pleading double, but not to a positive inconsistency. I cannot, however, admit that it is beyond the power of the legislature to pass an act allowing inconsistent pleas, or that a court can disregard such an act.

The plaintiffs' counsel supports his argument by reference to several English authorities, to all of which it may be observed that the law which governs the practice in England is different from that which governs the practice in Virginia. The statute of 4 and 5 Anne, chapter 16, allows the defendant to plead several matters only with the leave of the court. The English statute gives to the court a controlling power over the admission of the plea; the statute of Virginia gives the court no such power. In the exercise of this controlling power the courts of England have prescribed rules by which they will be governed in granting or refusing an application to plead different matters, but the courts of Virginia can prescribe no such rules. The law declares that the defendant may plead as many several matters of law and fact as he pleases without making any application to the court necessary. The defendant in England is, when he first pleads, in the same situation as to a double plea that the defendant in Virginia is after his right to plead depends on the favor of the court.

§ 960. *When a demurrer in abatement is filed, and plaintiff joins, final judgment will be rendered for plaintiff. If the latter does not join it will be a discontinuance.*

But the cases quoted to show that the demurrer is not good do not show that, even in England, it ought not to be received if tendered in proper time. In 5 Bac. Abr., 459, it is said, "if a defendant demur in abatement the court will, notwithstanding, give a final judgment, because there cannot be a demurrer in abatement." This does not prove that the demurrer itself shall be rejected, but that it shall be received and that the judgment upon it shall be final. A judgment on a plea in abatement, or on a demurrer to a plea in abatement, is not final, but on a demurrer which contains matter in abatement it shall be final, because a demurrer cannot partake of the character of a plea in abatement. Salkeld, 220, is quoted by Bacon and is to the same purport, indeed in the same words. These cases show that a demurrer being in its own nature a plea to the action, and being even in form a plea to the action, shall not be considered as a plea in abatement, though the special causes alleged for demurring be matter of abatement. The court will disregard those special causes, and, considering the demurrer independently of them, will decide upon it as if they had not been inserted in it.

These cases go far to show that the court would overrule this demurrer, and decide the cause against the party demurring, not that it should be expunged from the pleadings.

[1 Tidd, 475.] "If the defendant plead in abatement," etc. These cases show that if a plea in abatement be tendered when it is not receivable, the plaintiff may proceed as if no plea had been offered, or he may move the court to strike it out. It is obvious that they do not apply directly to the case at bar. This demurrer was receivable when it was tendered.

But the counsel brings this case within their reasoning by considering the demurrer as a plea in abatement. Now this it cannot be. The cases cited from Bacon and Salkeld show that a demurrer cannot be in abatement. The court, therefore, can consider this only as a general demurrer, and, of course, it was offered in proper time.

Tidd (484, 485) shows that where a defendant is under a judge's order to plead issuably, and he pleads a plea which is not issuable, or puts in a sham demurrer, the plaintiff may consider it as a mere nullity.

But these defendants were not under a judge's order to plead. They were not acting under the guidance of the court, but acting by authority of the law of the land, according to their own judgment. Had they permitted a writ of inquiry to be entered against them, and the term at which it might be set aside to pass away, or had they been in a situation in which they could not plead but under the direction of the court, this doctrine would certainly be applicable to the case. At present I think it is not.

Tidd (482) (1) shows that the court will set aside irregular proceedings. But this is not an irregular proceeding. It is perfectly regular. The demurrer was offered in proper time, and though it may not be sustainable it must be considered. Any plea in bar may be unsustainable; but it is not on that account to be discarded without being considered. The cases cited from the Term Reports only confirm the doctrines of Tidd.

§ 960a. *Frivolous demurrers.*

In another book of practice which has been cited it is said: "But if the demurrer be frivolous, only to put off the trial or for delay of the proceedings, they will not allow of such a demurrer, nor cause the other party to join, but will give judgment against the party upon his frivolous demurrer."

It would require a person more conversant with the English practice than I am to understand precisely the bearing of this *dictum.* The court must examine the declaration to determine whether a demurrer be frivolous. Although the special causes assigned for demurring may be frivolous, the demurrer itself may be substantial. But be this as it may the rule is inapplicable to this case, and perhaps to the practice of this country. The demurrer, according to our practice, can produce no delay, cannot put off the trial of the cause. Had the plaintiffs joined in demurrer, and it had appeared to be frivolous, a writ of inquiry would have been awarded and executed immediately, or the issue would have been tried without allowing a continuance. A frivolous demurrer, therefore, in this case, could not put off the cause, or have occasioned any delay. I do not know what delays, according to the practice in England, a frivolous demurrer may occasion. But this doctrine is founded on the controlling power of the courts of England over pleading, a power which the courts of this country do not possess.

If the demurrer in this case was receivable, and I think it was, the refusal to join in it was a discontinuance which is provided for in the act of assembly. The plaintiffs must be nonsuited. This proceeding, however, is now under the direction of the court, and the cause may certainly be reinstated.

§ **961.** *Amendments; clerical misprision.*

I come now to consider the application to amend. I have no doubt of the power of the court to allow amendments in all cases of clerical misprision, where there is anything to amend by, but I had doubted whether the memorandum of counsel was a document by which an amendment would be made. The cases cited by Mr. Call have in a great measure removed that doubt, and I am inclined to permit an amendment of the writ. An amendment of the declaration will be allowed also, but not on the ground of clerical misprision. To copy a declaration in order to file it is no part of the duty of the clerk. He acted as the agent of the plaintiff's attorney. It is to be considered as a declaration drawn and filed by the attorney himself. In every such case the amendment will be allowed; but it is a new declaration, and the defendants are permitted to plead *de novo*.

This motion involves no question about the recognizance of the bail. I do not at present perceive how that recognizance can avail the party, but I do not understand that the motion extends to it.

TYLER *v.* HAND.

(7 Howard, 573–586. 1848.)

ERROR to U. S. Circuit Court, Northern District of Mississippi.

Opinion by MR. JUSTICE WAYNE.

STATEMENT OF FACTS.— This suit is brought upon ten bonds payable to Martin Van Buren, president of the United States, and his successors in office, for the use of the orphan children provided for in the nineteenth article of the treaty with the Choctaw Indians of September, 1830. 7 Stats at Large, 336. The principal and interest due upon the bonds are demanded, and the plaintiff in the action, John Tyler, sues as successor of Martin Van Buren, and trustee for the orphan children.

The defendants have demurred to the plaintiff's declaration, pursuing the usual form of a general demurrer, and have added thereto several special causes of demurrer. There is a joinder in demurrer. Upon these pleadings the court below sustained the demurrer of the defendants. It is that judgment which is now before this court by writ of error.

In our opinion there is error in the judgment. We shall reverse it with an order to the court below to enter up a final judgment for the plaintiff. The cause is not before us on the grounds upon which it was placed in argument by the counsel of the defendants, except as to the insufficiency of the facts averred in the plaintiff's declaration to entitle him to recover, or to enable the defendants to sustain their demurrer.

§ **962.** *Demurrers, general and special; their functions.*

A demurrer is an objection made by one party to his opponent's pleading, alleging that he ought not to answer it, for some defect in law in the pleading. It admits the facts, and refers the law arising thereon to the court. Co. Lit., 71*b*; 5 Mod., 132. The opposite party may demur when his opponent's pleading is defective in substance or form, but there can be no demurrer for a defect not apparent in the pleadings. This being so, the question now is, whether or not, notwithstanding the objections in substance and form which the defendants have made to the plaintiff's declaration, sufficient matter appear in the pleadings, upon which the court may give judgment according to the very right of the case. Five special causes of demurrer are assigned; they were of course meant to be objections for defects in form, as none other can be assigned in a special demurrer. A general demurrer lies only for defects in substance, and excepts to the sufficiency of the pleading in general terms, without showing specially the nature of the objection. A special demurrer is only for defects in form, and adds to the terms of a general demurrer a specification of the particular ground of exception.

Our first remark, then, is that neither of the special causes of demurrer alleged in this case is for a matter of form. They are as follows:

" 1. That there is no sufficient averment in the proceedings or record showing the citizenship or place of abode of the plaintiff, or that he is, by reason of the nature of his place of abode and citizenship, entitled by law to maintain said suit.

" 2. That the plaintiff shows no title to the bonds or obligations sued on, nor such an interest in the suit as will authorize him to maintain the same.

" 3. That the parties for whose use the suit is brought (who, by the laws of Mississippi, are the real plaintiffs, and responsible for costs) are not named in the record.

" 4. The said bonds sued on were taken without authority of law, the said Martin Van Buren, president of the United States, having no such delegated power, and having no right to make the same payable to himself and his successors in office, or to assume to himself or his successors in office a legal perpetuity and succession unknown to the said office, and not given by law.

" 5. That said bonds in the declaration mentioned appear, from the face of the pleadings, to have been given without any actual consideration, and by virtue of an assumption of authority on the part of said Martin Van Buren to dispose of said orphan Indian lands at public sale, without any legal right to sell the same. And because the said declaration is in other respects informal and insufficient."

§ 962a. *Want of authority in plaintiff to receive the bonds sued on, and want of consideration, cannot be called in question by demurrer.*

The case, then, is before the court upon a general demurrer, in which must be considered the whole record, and judgment should be given for the party who on the whole appears to be entitled to it. Le Bret *v.* Papillon, 4 East, 502. It cannot be better shown in this case for whom the judgment should be, than by showing that the special causes of objection assigned, supposing them to have been made as matters of substance, are not sufficient in law to prevent a recovery by the plaintiff. We will first speak of the fourth and fifth, because they are the chief reliance of the defendants to show that no judgment can be rendered against them.

The fourth is that the bonds given by the defendants were taken without authority of law. The fifth is that it appears from the face of the pleadings they were given without any actual consideration. Neither of these points can be raised in this case by a demurrer. As to the first of the two, it was not necessary to aver in the declaration that the bonds were taken with the authority of law, nor is it so averred. The bonds are made to the president of the United States and his successors in office, for the use of the orphan children provided for in the nineteenth article of the treaty with the Choctaw Indians of September, 1830. They are so recited in the declaration, and are admitted by the defendants to have been given by them. In point of law, then, they are valid instruments, though voluntarily given, and not prescribed by law. United States v. Tingey, 5 Pet., 115. It is not the case of a bond given contrary to law, or in violation of law, but that of bonds given voluntarily for a consideration expressed in them to a public officer, but not happening to be prescribed by law. Nor does it matter that they are made to the president of the United States and his successors in office, if the political official character of the president is recognized in them, and is so averred in the declaration. This cause of demurrer, whether well taken or not, admits the fact that the bonds were given, and estops the defendants from denying it as a matter of form, or from contesting by a demurrer the right of the obligee and his successors in office to sue the obligors at law. As to the alleged want of consideration for these bonds, as stated in the fifth special cause of demurrer, that affords no ground for a demurrer, as a bond cannot be avoided at law either for a want or failure of consideration, and anything illegal in the consideration can only be pleaded in bar to the action. Fallowes v. Taylor, 7 T. R., 475.

But it is said that these bonds were given without any actual consideration, the president, as it is alleged, having no authority to dispose of the land. What of that? The declaration does not state of whom the purchase was made, or by what authority the sale took place. The defendants admit that a sale did take place, that they were purchasers of the lands, and that they gave the bonds voluntarily, according to the terms of sale. Neither of these questions, then, can be raised under the demurrer of the defendants, and could not have been the foundation of the judgment given in their favor.

§ 963. *A demurrer in abatement of the action entitles plaintiff to final judgment.*

Having disposed of the fourth and fifth special causes of demurrer, we will now inquire, in their order, whether or not the judgment which was given can be sustained upon either of the other alleged grounds.

The first is, "that there is no sufficient averment in the proceedings showing the citizenship or place of abode of the plaintiff, or that he is, by reason of the nature of his place of abode and citizenship, entitled by law to maintain this suit." This cannot justify the judgment, because it is demurring in abatement. In such a case the plaintiff is entitled to final judgment. If the matter of abatement be extrinsic the defendant must plead it. If intrinsic, the court will act upon it, upon motion, or notice it of themselves. Dockminique v. Davenant, Salk., 220. But it does not follow, because a demurrer in abatement cannot be available for the defendant, that it is to be rejected altogether from the pleading, if tendered in proper time. It will be received, but being erroneously put in, it entitles the plaintiff to final judgment, so that for this reason the judgment of the court below would have to be reversed.

Perhaps the best exposition of this point of pleading anywhere to be found is that given in Furniss et al. v. Ellis and Allen, in 2 Brockenbrough's Reports, 17, by Chief Justice Marshall. He says: "The cases quoted to show that the demurrer is not good do not show that even in England it ought not to be received, if tendered in proper time. In 5 Bac. Abr., 459, it is said if a defendant demur in abatement the court will, notwithstanding, give a final judgment, because there cannot be a demurrer in abatement. This does not prove that the demurrer shall be rejected. but that it shall be received, and that the judgment upon it shall be final. A judgment on a plea in abatement, or on a demurrer to a plea in abatement, is not final, but on a demurrer which contains matter in abatement it shall be final, because a demurrer cannot partake of the character of a plea in abatement. Salk., 220, is quoted by Bacon, and is to the same purport; indeed, in the same words. These cases show that a demurrer, being in its own nature a plea to the action, and being even in form a plea to the action, shall not be considered as a plea in abatement, though the special cause alleged for demurring be matter of abatement. This court will disregard these special causes, and, considering the demurrer independently of them, will decide upon it as if they had not been inserted in it." And then the chief justice adds, in respect to the particular case then in hand, that "these cases go far to show that the court would overrule the demurrer, and decide the cause against the party demurring, not that it should be expunged from the pleadings."

§ 964. *Questions of form only may be raised by special demurrer.*

The second ground of special demurrer is that the plaintiff shows no title to the bonds or obligations sued on, nor such an interest in the suit as will authorize him to maintain an action on the same. Neither fact stated is a matter of form, and cannot, therefore, be a cause for a special demurrer. But taking them as matters of substance, the insertion of them in the plaintiff's declaration is not necessary to show his right to sue and recover upon these bonds, or material for the defendants in their plea. This objection will not avail to sustain the judgment.

§ 965. *In a suit in the name of the president, for the benefit of a class of persons, the names of the persons need not be averred.*

The remaining objection to be considered is the third in order stated, and may be as briefly and as satisfactorily disposed of as some of the rest have been. It is that the parties for whose use the suit is brought are not named, who, by the laws of Mississippi, are the real plaintiffs and responsible for costs. We remark that for whose use the bonds were taken is not recited as personal to any of the Choctaw orphans, but as an aggregate for all such as were entitled to lands under the nineteenth article of the treaty. The demurrer admits that the bonds were so made by the defendants, and that the recital in the declaration is as the fact is expressed in the bonds. The inquiries, then, into who are individually the orphan children residing in the Choctaw nation, or who by name are entitled to a quarter-section of land, or any such averments in the plaintiff's declaration, were not necessary to entitle him to recover, and could not be shown either as a cause of special demurrer or be urged under a general demurrer to prevent a recovery in this case.

All of us are of the opinion that there is nothing in the causes of demurrer which were shown in argument, or in the special causes assigned, to sustain the demurrer; and thinking, as we all do, that nothing has been shown to lessen the obligation of the defendants to pay these bonds or their liability to be sued for them at law, we shall direct the judgment of the court below to be reversed with costs, and shall order the cause to be remanded to the district court with directions to that court to enter judgment in this case (principal and interest) for the plaintiff in that court.

WILKINSON v. POMEROY.

(Circuit Court for New York: 10 Blatchford, 524–530. 1878.)

Action for breach of promise of marriage. The defendant pleaded not guilty, and the plaintiff demurred.

Opinion by SHIPMAN, J.

The questions presented for consideration in the present stage of this case, and now to be disposed of, arise on the special demurrer interposed by the plaintiff to the first plea of the defendant. The demurrer is, in substance, that the plea should have been " *non assumpsit* " instead of " not guilty." It appears from the record that the defendant had been ordered by the court to file the general issue, and that under such order he filed the plea of " not guilty " to the first count in the declaration.

§ 966. *The general issue in an action of assumpsit for breach of marriage promise is non assumpsit, not not guilty.*

(1) The plaintiff claims that the first count in the declaration is a count in *assumpsit*, and that the general issue proper to be pleaded to such a count is *non assumpsit*. This claim is undoubtedly correct. The first count sets forth a promise of marriage made by the defendant to the plaintiff, May 30, 1866, the breach of such promise by the defendant, his subsequent marriage to another woman, and a claim for damages of $25,000. This count is based upon a breach of contract, and is properly a count in *assumpsit*. The general issue appropriate to such a count is *non assumpsit*. The plea of not guilty to this count is therefore bad, and must be stricken out. Chitty's Pl., vol. 3, p. 908, note.

§ 967. *A writ is not incongruous which requires defendant to answer in tres-pass ac etiam for damages for deceit and breach of marriage promise.*

(2) The defendant, on the other hand, claims that the demurrer reaches back through the whole record, and attaches to the first substantial defect, and that there are defects of this character both in the writ and in the declaration; that one count in the declaration is in tort, and the other is in contract, while the writ is an action in trespass and for deceit and breach of promise of marriage; and that the whole is incongruous. These objections certainly deserve consideration.

The first question is whether any incongruity in the writ, or any variance between the writ and the declaration, is reached by a demurrer. The writ requires the defendant to answer unto the plaintiff " in a plea of trespass, and also to a certain bill of the said plaintiff against the defendant for damages in the sum of $25,000, for deceit and breach of promise of marriage." Does this language describe a valid cause of action; and, if so, is that cause of action variant from the first count in the declaration? It is to be observed that the writ in this case was served upon the defendant as a separate process from the declaration, which was filed afterwards. This practice has come to us from English parentage. We should therefore look for light upon these questions at the common-law practice as it existed when our American colonies became separated from the mother country.

Under the old English practice the whole original writ was repeated in the declaration, and, if a material variance appeared between the writ and the declaration, the defendant might take advantage of it, either by motion in arrest of judgment, writ of error, plea in abatement or demurrer. But this was altered by rule of court in 1654, ordering that declarations in actions upon the case and general statutes, other than debt, should not repeat the original writ, but only the nature of the action. After this rule was made the only way in which the defendant could take advantage of a bad original, or of a variance between the original and the declaration, was by praying oyer of the writ, or, in case of a bad original, by writ of error. But the practice of praying oyer of the original having been much used for delay, the courts came to a resolution not to grant oyer of the original writ, so that no advantage whatever could be had of a defective original or of a variance between it and the declaration. 1 Saund., 318, note 3. The effect of this rule was to abolish all pleas in abatement for any variance between the writ and the count, and it extended to all pleas in abatement which could not be proved without an examination of the original writ. Gould's Pl., ch. V, § 64, note 9, and §§ 82, 101. By statute of 13 Car. II. (Stat. 2, ch. 2), it was provided that "the certainty and true cause of action" should be "expressed particularly" in writs, bills and process issuing out of the courts of king's bench and common pleas, and in all bailable actions where the penalty exceeded the sum of forty pounds. If this provision was not complied with, the defendant was to be bailed upon his own bond for appearance. Blackstone says: "This statute (without any such intention in the makers) had like to have ousted the king's bench of all its jurisdiction over civil injuries without force; for, as the bill of Middlesex was framed only for actions of trespass, a defendant could not be arrested and held to bail thereupon for breaches of civil contract. But, to remedy this inconvenience, the officers of the king's bench devised a method of adding what is called a clause of *ac etiam* to the usual complaint of trespass, the bill of Middlesex commanding the defendant to be brought to answer the plaintiff of a plea of trespass, and also to a bill of debt, the complaint of trespass giving cognizance to the court, and that of debt authorizing the arrest. 3 Black. Comm., 288. The same practice was afterwards extended to the court of common pleas.

A question very similar to the one now under consideration was decided in 1769 in the case of Callaghan v. Harris, 2 Wilson, 392. The sheriff was commanded to attach the defendants to answer the plaintiff "in a plea of trespass, and also that the defendants answer the plaintiff, according to the custom of the said court, in a certain plea of trover, and for converting of the goods and chattels of the said plaintiff," etc. The defendants having been arrested upon this writ and held to special bail, a motion was made for a rule to show cause why a common appearance should not be accepted for the defendants, alleging that the *ac etiam* in the writ did not particularly express the cause of action, as the statute of 13 Car. II., statute 2, chapter 2, directs, for that there is no such cause of action as a plea of trover, but it ought to have been in a certain plea of trespass upon the case for converting the goods and chattels of the plaintiff, etc. But it was resolved by the court that the cause of action was fully and clearly expressed, and that although the *ac etiam* was not exactly clerical, yet nobody who read it could doubt of the cause of action. So in the case under consideration, although the cause of action expressed in the *ac etiam* clause is " for deceit and breach of promise of marriage," which is not exactly clerical, yet actions for deceit belong to a class of actions well known as actions on the case, and the words, " breach of promise of marriage," may be regarded as explanatory of the subject-matter to which the deceit was applied, or they may be rejected as surplusage. Gould's Pl., ch. III, sec. 170. The writ then may be regarded as disclosing a cause of action in trespass on the case.

§ 968. *A variance between the writ and the declaration cannot be reached by demurrer.*

Upon the question of variance between the writ and the first count, the authorities already cited show that a defect of this character cannot be reached by a demurrer. In Thompson *v.* Dicas, 2 Dowl. Pr. Cases, 93, the writ was trespass on the case, and the declaration was trespass. On a rule for setting aside the declaration for variance, the court held that under the uniformity act the declaration must be conformable to the writ, and the declaration was set aside, with leave to the plaintiff to declare properly under the writ if he could do so. But the court held, by Bayley, B., that the variance could not be taken advantage of on demurrer because it was a "mere irregularity." Chitty lays down the rule in such cases as follows: "Before the uniformity of process act (4 W. IV., ch. 39), upon common process, the plaintiff might declare in any cause of action whatever. But in bailable actions the declaration must have corresponded with the cause and form of action in the affidavit, and the *ac etiam* part of the *latitat* or other process; for otherwise the defendant would be discharged on filing common bail, and the court would not allow the declaration to be amended in that respect; but that was the only consequence, for the court would not in such case set aside the proceedings for irregularity." Chitty's Pl., vol. 1, p. 253. "If the body of the declaration state a cause of action that is not nor could be properly declared for in the form of action stated in the writ, then the deviation would constitute an irregularity and ground for setting aside the declaration, but not a ground for demurrer." Id., p. 254. In our own courts it has been decided that a variance between the writ and declaration must be pleaded in abatement. Wilder *v.* McCormick, 2 Blatch., 31; Duval *v.* Craig, 2 Wheat., 45. But in this case the defendant has pleaded to the merits, and therefore it is now too late for him to plead in abatement. Prosser *v.* Chapman, 29 Conn., 515.

§ 969. *A count in assumpsit for breach of promise of marriage and a count in tort for deceit cannot be joined, and the defect may be reached by demurrer.*

(3) It remains now to consider the objections raised by the defendant to the declaration. Some of these objections are merely formal, and, not having been pointed out in the special demurrer, are not reached by it. Only defects of substance in the declaration can be taken advantage of under a special demurrer to a plea. Gould's Pl., ch. IX, part 1, sec. 20.

It is claimed that there is a misjoinder of counts in the declaration, one count being in contract and the other in tort. If such misjoinder exists it is a radical fault, and is reached by the demurrer. Gould's Pl., ch. IV, sec. 98.

As has already been remarked, the first count is in *assumpsit.* The second count sets forth the deceit of the defendant, in representing that he was a single man, when, in fact, he was married, and, under that misrepresentation, entering into a promise of marriage with the plaintiff, and thereby preventing her from receiving the attentions of other men and making a suitable marriage, and keeping her a single woman for the last six years, and injuring her good name, and hurting her feelings, etc. This is a count in trespass on the case (1 Ch. Pl., 137), or, as it is generally denominated, an action on the case. It sounds in tort. So that there is a count in *assumpsit,* and a count in case, joined in the same declaration. These counts cannot be so joined at common law. Gould's Pl., ch. IV, secs. 87, 88, 91. If the writ be regarded as substantially for trespass on the case, and the second count for the same cause of action, then the first count, being in *assumpsit*, is manifestly out of place. The first count, therefore, should be stricken out. Gould's Pl., ch. IV, sec. 101.

As both parties have been greatly in fault in pleading, and as a portion of the pleadings of both parties is to be stricken out, this may be done by both parties without costs.

§ **970.** *Demurrer on ground of statute of limitations.*

A further objection is raised to the declaration, that it shows, upon its face, that the cause of action arose more than six years before suit brought, and is, therefore, barred by the statute of limitations of New York. But the date mentioned in the declaration is not material, and, as the plaintiff can prove any date within the statutory period, such objection cannot be raised on demurrer.

BROWN *v.* DUCHESNE.

(Circuit Court for Massachusetts: 2 Curtis, 97. 1854.)

§ **971.** *A demurrer to all the pleas must be overruled if one is good.*

Opinion by CURTIS, J.

This is an action on the case for the violation of a patent-right. The defendant pleaded the general issue and two special pleas. The plaintiff demurred as follows: "And the said plaintiff says that the several pleas by the said Duchesne, in manner and form aforesaid pleaded, and the matters therein contained, are insufficient to bar the plaintiff," etc., in the usual form of a demurrer. And he assigns several causes of demurrer specially. Without regard to the defects of form specially pointed out, if this demurrer is taken to all the pleas, and any one is found good, the demurrer is overruled. There is certainly one good plea, for the general issue, in the usual form, is upon the record. And it is clear the demurrer covers all the pleas. It applies in terms to the several pleas, which means all the several pleas.

§ **972.** *Form of replying separately to one or more pleas.*

There is a settled form of replying to one or more pleas to the exclusion of others, which is "as to the said pleas by the said defendant secondly, or secondly and, thirdly, above pleaded," etc. When not thus restricted, the legal intendment is that all are included in the answer made to them.

The demurrer must be overruled.

JACKSON *v.* RUNDLET.

(Circuit Court for New Hampshire: 1 Woodbury & Minot, 381-388. 1846.)

STATEMENT OF FACTS.— Action of debt on a bond. After oyer the defendant pleaded *non est factum* and a second plea of general performance. There was an issue on the first plea, and a replication to the second that defendant had received money that he did not use or account for according to his duty. To this there was a demurrer for duplicity.

§ **973.** *Duplicity to be objected to only by special demurrer.*

Opinion by WOODBURY, J.

It is well settled that an objection founded on duplicity in pleading can be taken advantage of only by a special demurrer. Otis *v.* Blake, 6 Mass., 336. Because the defect is in form rather than substance, tending to prolixity, unnecessary expense in recording and copying, and confusion with courts and juries by multifarious and mixed issues. 1 Chit. Pl., 513. The duplicity must also be specially pointed out. 1 Saund., 337, *b;* 10 East, 73; Currie *v.* Henry, 2 John., 433. In this case the designation of the duplicity is imperfect, but the demurrer may be regarded as special, rather than general, since the breaches are alleged to be two in number, and independent of each other.

§ 974. *Distinction between general and special demurrers.*

It runs, however, very near the brink; and hence the plaintiff objects that the demurrer is in form a general rather than special one. The distinctions between these demurrers are modern, there being none at common law, and now the only established difference is that just alluded to, in respect to the pointing out of the duplicity, viz.: That a special demurrer assigns some specific cause, and a general demurrer does not, and either refers to no causes whatever, or only to general ones. 1 Inst., 72; 4 Bl. C., 132; 1 Chit. Pl., 646. Since the 27th Elizabeth all matters of form can be reached only by special demurrer. 1 Saund., 337, *b;* Tidd, 648; Com. Dig., Pleader, 27. A special one, therefore, is always safest. And this must be considered such a demurrer, as one cause is assigned specifically to a certain extent, though the rest are like a general demurrer. 1 Mass., 500, *arguendo.*

§ 975. *Demurrer reaches back to the first fault. Exceptions to the rule.*

But it is contended by the plaintiff that whether his replication be double or not is immaterial, and need not be examined even on a special demurrer, as the plea is bad, and the judgment must be on the first fault in the record. Such is doubtless the general doctrine on this subject when a plea is bad in substance. 1 Chit. Pl., 647; 5 Cranch, 257; 1 Gall., 91; 2 John., 465; 3 id., 366; 11 id., 482.

But there are several exceptions to this rule. In courts of error the judgment will not always be against him committing the first fault, because it may be cured by a verdict, and because the decision below may have been made on other grounds entirely; and the party may wish, and it may be proper, to allow him to amend. So the judgment may be reversed to enable the court to have the matter presented suitably, and then the whole case is left open to amendment and another trial, without rendering judgment for either the plaintiff or the defendant. See Davis *v.* Garland, 4 How., 431.

Nor can the court where the suit is brought go back in a case like this to the first fault, unless it be one bad on general demurrer. For objection should have been taken to it specially, by the opposite party, before pleading over.

§ 976. *Particularity required in a plea in action on a bond.*

In this case the defendant is a surety in a bond, and the objection to his plea is that it is bad for not setting out the articles of association, and denying a breach of them, as well as of the condition to perform them. But the idea that he should go into this greater particularity is, in my opinion, not well founded.

The defendant is not supposed to have those articles in his possession like the plaintiff or the deceased principal in the bond. When, therefore, he gets oyer of the conditions of the bond, all of which are affirmative, and among them one to fulfill these articles, and then proceeds to allege a performance generally, or in the language of the condition, he does all that is at first necessary. 1 Chit. Pl., 514; 8 D. & E., 459; 2 Saund., 413; Hughes *v.* Smith, 5 John., 168; 2 id., 413.

Some cases seem to have required sums and dates to be given, such as

Doug., 214, and 2 N. H., 130. But if that is the true construction of them, it is apparent that they cannot be sustained as sound law. Sneed v. Wister, 8 Wheat., 690, is cited against this conclusion. But the court merely ruled in that case that the defendant could not crave oyer of a deed named in the condition of the bond; and, if he wishes to use it, must produce it himself or show an excuse. But here no oyer of the articles is craved, nor any use made of them by the defendants.

§ 977. *What constitutes duplicity. Authorities reviewed.*

Let us then proceed to examine the replication, to see whether the charge of duplicity against it is well sustained. What constitutes duplicity in such a case? Not more than one fact being alleged, not a connected proposition made, embracing several facts, but distinct defenses, in case of pleas, or separate and independent breaches in replication, or different causes of action set out in writs. 1 Chitty, Pl., 261; 2 Wm. Bl., 1022; 1 Burr., 316; 2 John., 433–462; 3 id., 315; 3 Caines, R., 160. See various other cases showing that any number of facts are not double if they go to establish a single point as a breach or a single justification. Stephen on Pl., 274; Gould on Pl., 421–427; 7 Bacon's Abr., Pl.; 9 Wend., 143; 6 Mass., 338; 6 Brown's P. C., 27; 5 Pick., 221; Story, Pl., 283–287.

Examples, however, throw more light on questions like this than any general definition. Thus, a defense that the plaintiff had married and her husband released the cause of action is good as a plea, because, though two facts are alleged, they both unite to constitute but one defense. While a plea justifying a trespass, as moderate correction, and averring also a release, is double; the two facts being disconnected and constituting two independent defenses.

So a justification by an assistant to a deputy-sheriff, that the warrant was regularly issued and delivered to the deputy-sheriff, that he seized the property by virtue of its being the property of the judgment debtor, but in possession fraudulently of the plaintiff, and that the defendant acted in aid and by command of the deputy-sheriff, are dependent facts, making but one defense. Patcher v. Sprague, 2 John., 462.

As to the English precedents since William III., it is to be noticed that they are not always applicable, being made under a statute in that reign, by which double breaches are allowed to be assigned in replications in actions on bonds to secure the performance of covenants. 1 Chitty, Pl., 688. And this act is in analogy to the common-law rule in actions in covenants, where a double breach is not considered as duplicity. But that statute is not in force in New Hampshire, and is a departure from the common law generally as well as the practice in this state. Mooney v. Demerrit, 1 N. H., 187.

Here a forfeiture is settled by the trial of one breach, and damages are then assessed for all that can be proved in a hearing afterwards in chancery (Parker v. Colcord, 2 id., 38, 39); while there, no damages were assessed but on the breaches assigned and tried. 1 id., 188. The cases in England, where the assignment of a breach must still be single, are numerous, and some of them are much like the present, where the assignment has been considered not double. In a part of them the objections there are made for other reasons, such as want of sufficient particularity. Yet, if open to objections for duplicity, they would probably have been taken or made.

Thus in Shum v. Farrington, 1 Bos. & Pull., 640, the case was debt on bond and the plea craving oyer. It appeared by the condition that the defendants became bound for the faithful conduct of R. S., as agent to the plaintiff, to receive and pay money, and account truly, etc. The plea then alleges general performance. Replication, that the agent received £2,000 belonging to the business, and hath not paid to the plaintiffs and given a fair account thereof. Special demurrer, that the names of the persons from whom he received the money and the time are not set out. No objection was made that the replication was double.

In Cornwallis v. Savery, 2 Burr., 772, the breach was the receipt of a sum and not accounting for it. This was held to be single, as both must unite, the receipt and not accounting, in order to constitute a breach of the condition of a bond. Barton v. Webb, 8 D. & E., 459. If the breach was averred to be receipts of money from different persons, A. and B. and C., then it would be double. 1 Str., 227; case cited, 2 Burr., 773.

In Adams v. Mack, 3 N. H., 493, a similar view was taken, and the court held that a plea justifying the sale as well as the taking of the goods sued for, was not double, both being necessary to constitute a full defense to the charge of converting them. See, also, Galusha v. Cobleigh, 13 id., 79.

The conclusions of the court, then, may be summed up as follows: The demurrer is to be considered as a special one; and if duplicity existed in the replication, it could thus be taken advantage of, and judgment be rendered against the plaintiff for it, unless there was such previous fault in the plea as is bad in general demurrer. See some exceptions. Stephen's Pl., 163, 164; 5 Barn. & Ald., 507; Garland v. Davis, 4 How., 131. But the plea, I think, contains no such fault.

§ 978. *A plea is good which craves oyer of the conditions of the bond, and alleges generally a compliance with them.*

The plea avers a general performance of all the previous duties named in the condition of the bond, and, as before suggested, seems sufficient, especially as the articles of the association were not in the possession of the sureties. After craving oyer of the bond and condition in which they are named, but are not produced with it, it is enough to allege generally a compliance with them all. One of them was to keep fair and honest books and accounts of all his doings with the association; another was, faithfully to keep their secrets; another, to conform to articles and by-laws; and another, to obey all written instructions from the association.

§ 979. *A replication is good which assigns a single breach though consisting of many facts.*

The replication evidently does not intend to assign any breach of the first, second or fourth heads of duty, except as some of them may be included in the third, to conform to the articles and by-laws. But after averring what the articles and by-laws were in respect to his making purchases as agent for the association, and also to contract to pay for labor required in waiving, etc., and once in three months or oftener, if requested, account for money received for them, and likewise give statements of what was received and services rendered, the replication alleges that J. S. Rundlet became agent, and while so received $35,566.66 for said association on account of it, and his duty to use it, and that he was directed to use and pay it in the business of said association; yet he hath not so used it nor accounted for it, nor paid the same to or for the association.

Though inartificial in some degree, this breach is much like those assigned in Shum v. Farrington, and Cornwallis v. Savery. And though no question was raised as to duplicity in the first case, it was in the last, and it was held to' be single (not needing to be cured by the statutè of William III.).

Here the duty was to use the money in behalf of the association; there, to account for it. Here, then, the breach is that he did not so use the money, and the other allegations which follow are merely connected with that averment, to make this single breach complete and full by adding, not new breaches and independent ones, but facts showing him liable for not so using the money, because he had not, instead of that, paid it over or in any way accounted for it. But these last allegations do not seem meant, nor are they fairly to be construed, as separate and independent breaches. They are rather component parts or elements tending to show the first breach existing unatoned for, and not in any way satisfied or commuted.

Strange as it may seem, also, it is not averred. that any duty to pay over the balance existed, and hence of necessity on that account, also, an averment of not paying them over cannot be considered as an averment of a second distinct breach of what there is not stated to have been any duty to be broken or fulfilled. For reasons like these the replication is adjudged good.

§ 980. Formal objections.— Where objections merely formal are stated as causes of demurrer the party taking them is entitled to the benefit of them if they are well founded. Lockington v. Smith, Pet. C. C., 466.

§ 981. Speaking demurrers.— When a demurrer states a fact which does not appear on the face of the pleading demurred to, it is a speaking demurrer and is bad. Lamb v. Starr, Deady, 350.

§ 982. A demurrer when overruled is waived by a replication subsequently filed and ceases to be a part of the record. Young v. Martin, 8 Wall., 354.

§ 983. Withdrawal of plea to admit demurrer.— The court will not permit a plea to the merits to be withdrawn to enable the defendant to demur specially. Alricks v. Slater, 1 Cr. C. C., 72.

§ 984. A defendant will be permitted to withdraw the general issue and file a general demurrer. Deakins v. Lee, 1 Cr. C. C., 442.

§ 985. Waiver of by pleading over.— Pleading over to a declaration adjudged good on demurrer, without any reservation, is a waiver of the demurrer. Watkins v. United States, 9 Wall., 759; Campbell v. Wilcox, 10 Wall., 421.

§ 986. Leave to reply after demurrer overruled.— After a demurrer to a plea of set-off overruled, plaintiff should have leave to reply. Rochell v. Phillips, Hemp., 23.

§ 987. Withdrawal of demurrer to plead de novo.— After judgment for the plaintiff on the defendant's demurrer, and writ of inquiry awarded, the court will not permit the defendant to plead de novo unless he will withdraw his demurrer. Woodrow v. Coleman, 1 Cr. C. C., 192.

§ 988. Demurrer to issue overruled — Same issue cannot be again tendered.— The court, in the present case, would not permit the defendant to tender an issue which he had refused to join, and to which he had demurred when tendered by the plaintiff, there having been judgment rendered against him by the United States supreme court on the demurrer. Hodgson v. Marine Ins. Co., 1 Cr. C. C., 569.

§ 989. A demurrer in a case proceeded on under the civil law does not prevent the party who demurred controverting the facts confessed in the demurrer and compelling the opposite party to prove them. Crawford v. The William Penn, 3 Wash., 484.

§ 990. The legal effect of a demurrer to a scire facias is the same as that of a demurrer to a declaration. Vermont v. The Society for Propagating the Gospel, 1 Paine, 652.

§ 991. How far a demurrer cuts back.— On demurrer the court will give judgment upon the whole record. Hart v. Rose,* Hemp., 238.

§ 992. On a demurrer to any pleading the court may go back to the first fault. Greathouse v. Dunlap, 3 McL., 303; Sprigg v. Bank of Mount Pleasant, 10 Pet., 257; Blossberg, etc., R. Co. v. Tioga R. Co., 5 Blatch., 387; Wright v. Johnson, 8 Blatch.. 150.

§ 993. Defects in a declaration may be waived by pleading to it. But if the plaintiff demurs to the plea the court will look to the first defect in pleading. Bank of Illinois v. Brady, 3 McL., 268.

§ 994. The rule that a demurrer goes back to the first substantial fault in the pleadings applies, although a former demurrer to the faulty pleading has been overruled and waived by pleading over. Aurora *v.* West,* 7 Wall., 82.

§ 995. On demurrer to any pleadings which are in bar of the action the judgment for either party is final, just as it would have been on an issue of fact joined on the same pleading, and found for such person, and such judgment may be pleaded in bar of another suit. *Ibid.*

§ 996. Demurrer reaches back to first defective pleading. Clearwater *v.* Meredith, 1 Wall., 25.

§ 997. When a demurrer to a replication has been sustained, the filing of a replication *de novo* waives the plaintiff's right to question the correctness of the decision. *Ibid.*

§ 998. A demurrer to a special plea ordinarily cuts back to the declaration, but not when the general issue has been pleaded. McDonald *v.* Orvis, 5 Biss., 183.

§ 999. A demurrer ordinarily goes back to the first fault in pleading, but does not go beyond the general issue. Townsend *v.* Jemison. 7 How., 706.

§ 1000. The rule that a demurrer opens the record, and allows judgment to be given against the party who committed the first fault in pleading, does not apply when that fault is one of form merely and not of substance. Railroad Co. *v.* Harris, 12 Wall., 65.

§ 1001. It is an ancient rule in pleading that upon demurrer the whole record is presented, and judgment goes against the party who commits the first substantial fault. The same rule is applicable under the code of New York. United States *v.* Central Nat. Bank, 10 Fed. R., 612.

§ 1002. Upon demurrer to a plea in abatement the court will look back to the first fault in pleading, and if the declaration is bad the judgment will be against plaintiff. Bockee *v.* Crosby, 2 Paine, 432.

§ 1003. A demurrer in *scire facias* proceedings does not reach back to the original suit, nor to any proceedings before those pending. Dickson *v.* Wilkinson,* 3 How., 57.

§ 1004. Upon a general demurrer judgment must be against the party who commits the first substantial fault in pleading. McCue *v.* Corporation of Washington,* 3 Cr. C. C., 639.

§ 1005. General and special.— A special demurrer operates as a general demurrer as to all the pleadings of the party demurring. *Ibid.*

§ 1006. A general demurrer to a declaration will be overruled if the latter contain one good count. *Ibid.*

§ 1007. A special demurrer brings into question the substantial validity of the pleading of the demurring party. Vowell *v.* Lyles, 1 Cr. C. Cr., 428.

§ 1008. If a complaint is defective there should be a special demurrer to the defective part. Lafleur *v.* Douglass,* 1 Wash. T'y, 215.

§ 1009. A special demurrer will not be admitted to set aside an office judgment. Whetcroft *v.* Dunlop, 1 Cr. C. C., 5.

§ 1010. A special demurrer may be filed in all actions in the federal courts. Cage *v.* Jeffries, Hemp., 409.

§ 1011. What is admitted by a demurrer.— A demurrer only admits facts which are well pleaded. Commercial Bank of Manchester *v.* Buckner, 20 How., 108; Greathouse *v.* Dunlap, 3 McL., 303.

§ 1012. A demurrer admits no conclusions of law, but only facts well pleaded; therefore, upon demurrer, questions as to certain legal conclusions, or as to the admissibility of certain evidence, are open to the defendants. Dillon *v.* Barnard, 1 Holmes, 386.

§ 1013. A demurrer in one cause between the same parties, whereby a particular fact is considered in law as admitted, is not evidence of that fact in another cause between the same parties. Auld *v.* Hepburn, 1 Cr. C. C., 122.

§ 1014. Facts well pleaded are admitted by demurrer, but not matters of inference or argument, nor the alleged construction of an instrument when the instrument itself is set forth, and the construction assumed is repugnant to its language, nor any mere legal conclusions. A demurrer cannot be held to work an admission that parol evidence is admissible to enlarge or contradict a sealed instrument which has become a matter of record. United States *v.* Ames, 9 Otto, 35.

§ 1015. In an action by the United States to recover a penal sum under the revenue laws, the plaintiff alleged fraud upon the government by the omission of certain acts prescribed by law. The answer denied the allegation, and averred whatever fraud was committed was effected through other means. To this the plaintiff demurred, and it was held, as the demurrer admitted the truth of the answer, the plaintiff had admitted away its cause of action. United States *v.* Chouteau, 12 Otto, 603.

§ 1016. A defendant, being sued on certain bonds, made defense that plaintiff bought the bonds with notice of a certain defect that would render the instruments invalid. Plaintiff replied, denying the notice, and defendant demurred. *Held,* that this demurrer admitted the facts of the plea to be untrue, and that plaintiff was a *bona fide* holder without notice. City of Lexington *v.* Butler, 14 Wall., 282.

§ 1017. A demurrer for want of jurisdiction does not admit the jurisdiction of the court. Donaldson *v.* Hazen, Hemp., 423.

§ 1018. Defendants made a bill of exchange as officers of the corporation, and were sued upon it as individuals. The bill was determined to be a corporation bill, and it was held that the allegation in the declaration that the defendants made "their" bill was inconsistent with the terms of the writing sued upon, and was not admitted by demurrer. Hitchcock *v.* Buchanan,* 15 Otto, 416.

§ 1019. Action by the postmaster-general against a deputy-postmaster and his sureties on a bond executed by them. The sureties pleaded that the plaintiff did not, as he was bound by law to do, call upon the deputy to settle his accounts, or cause suits to be commenced against him for not so settling them, and paying the balance due by him; nor did he notify the sureties of the defaults of the deputy, but fraudulently, and in violation of his duty to the United States and to the sureties, neglected to bring such suits and to give notice. The plaintiff demurred generally. The demurrer to the plea admitting the fraud stated in it, the plaintiff cannot recover. Postmaster-General *v.* Ustick, 4 Wash., 347.

§ 1020. Demurrer to several pleadings.— If a demurrer be filed to a declaration which sets forth several breaches, and one breach is well averred, the demurrer must be overruled. Gill *v.* Stebbins,* 2 Paine, 417.

§ 1021. When a demurrer is taken "to the complaint," which consists of several counts, if either count is good the demurrer will be overruled. Parrott *v.* Barney, Deady, 405.

§ 1022. In the theory of pleading different counts are supposed to represent different claims or offenses; and upon demurrer it will not be taken for granted that each of two counts is for the same cause of action. So held when the counts were for false imprisonment and malicious prosecution respectively. Castro *v.* De Uriarte, 12 Fed. R., 250.

§ 1023. When an answer to a declaration sets up several inconsistent defenses, under a system allowing such pleading, a demurer will be overruled if any one of the defenses set up be good. Dallas County *v.* Mackenzie,* 4 Otto, 660.

§ 1024. When an answer in a suit on county bonds, among other defenses, denies that the bonds were issued by the county, plaintiff should not demur, as by admitting that the bonds were not issued he destroys his cause of action. *Ibid.*

§ 1025. In covenant where several breaches are assigned, some of which are sufficient and others not, the defendant should only demur to such as are bad; and if he demur to the whole declaration, judgment must be given against him. Gill *v.* Stebbins, 2 Paine, 417.

§ 1026. Want of proper averments in the declaration cannot be made the ground of a nonsuit. Bas *v.* Steel, Pet. C. C., 406.

§ 1027. Statute of limitations as subject of.— When it is apparent on the face of a petition the statute of limitations may be set up under a demurrer. Bonnifield *v.* Price,* 1 Wyom. T'y, 172.

§ 1028. Demurrer overruled on appeal, with permission to plead.— A case came before the United States supreme court on a judgment in a federal circuit court for the defendant, the avowant in replevin, he having demurred to the pleas of the plaintiff in an action of replevin. The court, having reversed the judgment in the circuit court, remanded the cause, with instructions to the circuit court to overrule the demurrer and permit the defendant, the avowant, to plead. Lloyd *v.* Scott, 4 Pet., 206.

§ 1029. Citizenship as ground of.— A defective allegation of citizenship is a good ground of demurrer. Ketchum *v.* Driggs, 6 McL., 13.

§ 1030. A defect of jurisdiction on account of citizenship apparent on the declaration may be relied upon by a demurrer, and a plea in abatement is not necessary. Coal Co. *v.* Blatchford, 11 Wall., 172.

§ 1031. Joinder of counts.— A count alleging the loan of a mare, and an injury of the mare through negligence, may be joined with a count alleging a loan and an agreement to return the mare safe; if such joinder is not strictly proper the remedy is by special demurrer. Dobbin *v.* Foyles,* 2 Cr. C. C., 65.

§ 1032. Limit to number of demurrers that may be taken.— After defendants had three times demurred to and answered the petition or complaint, the case went to the supreme court, which sustained the petition. Defendant then filed other demurrers, and plaintiff moved to strike them out. Held in the discretion of the court that they should be struck out, as there should be some limit to raising legal objection, and apparently every material defense could be presented on the points already raised. Hitchcock *v.* Galveston,* 3 Woods, 270.

§ 1033. General and special demurrer.— A general demurrer enables the party to assail every substantial imperfection in the pleadings of the opposite party without particularizing any of them in the demurrer; a special demurrer goes to the structure merely and not to the substance, and it must distinctly and particularly specify wherein the defect lies. Martin v. Bartow Iron Works,* 35 Ga., 320.

§ 1034. If a pleading is double it is bad on special demurrer, but the demurrer must point out wherein the duplicity consists. Ibid.

§ 1035. The ancient rule, that failure of consideration could not be pleaded to a specialty, has been much relaxed. Ibid.

§ 1036. Patents — Mixed questions of law and fact not subject to demurrer.—Whether a given improvement is a patentable invention is a mixed question of law and fact, and should not, in ordinary cases, be disposed of on demurrer and without the intervention of a jury. Teese v. Phelps, McAl., 19.

§ 1037. Duplicity — Defective allegation of time and place.— Objections to a replication for not alleging time and place, and for duplicity, can be taken by special demurrer only. Blossberg & Corning R. Co. v. Tioga R. Co., 5 Blatch., 387.

§ 1038. No questions not raised by the complaint can be considered on demurrer thereto. Pettit v. Town of Hope, 18 Blatch., 180.

§ 1039. Waste — Demurrer, prayer of complaint not noticed on.— The prayer of the complaint in an action of waste, asking for treble damages, will not be noticed by the court in passing upon a demurrer. The relief in such an action depends upon the facts stated and not upon the prayer. Parrot v. Barney, Deady, 405.

§ 1040. Demurrer to "so much of answer as," etc., bad.— When an answer sets up a special contract in addition to other matter, a demurrer "to so much of the answer as sets up the special contract" is bad, since the clerk would not know, nor would any one, what is meant by sustaining the demurrer "to so much of the answer as sets up the special contract." Ormsby v. U. P. R'y Co., 4 Fed. R., 170.

§ 1041. Service of process.— A defendant cannot raise, by demurrer, the question whether he has been properly served with process. Robinson v. Nat. Stock Yard Co., 12 Fed. R., 361.

§ 1042. Want of jurisdiction, when ground of.— The defendant can raise the question of jurisdiction by demurrer only when the want of jurisdiction appears on the face of the pleadings; and if such want does not so appear, and is not taken advantage of by plea to the jurisdiction, it is waived. Bliss v. Burnes, McCahon, 91.

§ 1043. Declaration charged "unlawful building," etc.— Legality of the building not to be decided on demurrer.— In an action to recover damages for injuries to real estate the declaration averred that the defendant, a city of another state, built a dike unlawfully on the Mississippi river, which caused the plaintiff's land to be washed away. Held, upon demurrer, the defendant could not raise the question as to its right to build the dike, but the court must be informed by answer, on trial, whether the dike interfered with the navigability of the river, and transcended the power of the state in the premises. Rutz v. City of St. Louis, 2 McC., 344.

§ 1044. Allegations of fraud — Objections to form must be taken by special demurrer.— Under a general demurrer it cannot be objected that a plea which sets up fraud does not give the particular acts constituting the fraud; but such an objection being to the form and not to the substance of the plea, a special demurrer is necessary. Christmas v. Russell, 5 Wall., 290.

§ 1045. Want of stamp on note as required by law, not subject of.— The want of a stamp, as required by act of congress, upon a promissory note cannot be taken advantage of upon demurrer, such a note being invalidated for want of a stamp only when the omission is with fraudulent intent, and it being necessary that such fraudulent intent be specially set up or urged at the trial. Moreover, if the declaration avers the making and delivery of a note it implies that the note was properly made, and the existence of a stamp is matter of evidence and not of pleading. Campbell v. Wilcox, 10 Wall., 421.

§ 1046. Action on judgment — Attachment, levy as ground of.— In an action on a judgment, in which the record shows that a levy upon an attachment has been made, and personal property of the defendant taken into the possession of the sheriff, a defense of payment through such levy cannot be made by demurrer, at any rate unless the record shows that the value of the property taken was equal to the amount of the judgment. Such defense should be pleaded; and it should be affirmatively shown that the property levied on was applied to and extinguished the judgment. Maxwell v. Stewart, 22 Wall., 77.

§ 1047. Marginal memorandum annexed to.— A demurrer, to which is annexed a marginal memorandum stating matters of proof as relied upon to sustain the demurrer, will be set aside. Such matters should be asserted by way of replication. Alexander v. Willet,* 1 MacArth., 564.

§ 1048. Demurrers raising questions of fact.— Claim for increase in salary as a "laborer" under a joint resolution of congress. Special demurrer that the claimant was employed in a certain menial service, which placed his compensation under a certain act of congress. The menial service, specified is a fact, and cannot be considered under a demurrer. Demurrer overruled. Graham v. United States,* 1 N. & H., 188.

§ 1049. Written contracts set out in declaration, when validity of may be decided on demurrer.— When a declaration brought up on demurrer sets out the written contracts on which the action rests the court may examine the contracts and decide as upon their validity and construction. This rule applies, however, only when the contracts are set out *in hæc verba*. If a partial statement only is made, and defendant wishes to bring up the question, he should crave oyer and then demur. Hobson v. McArthur,* 8 McL., 241.

§ 1050. Informal plea to merits — Demurrer, not motion to strike out, proper.— When a plea, though informal, goes to the substance of an action, as *nil debet* to debt on a bond, the proper practice is to demur, and a motion to strike out the plea will be overruled. United States v. Spencer,* 2 McL., 405.

§ 1051. When may be struck out by party demurring.— A defendant who had demurred to a declaration, and within due time pleaded the statute of limitations, moved to strike out his own demurrer and leave the plea. The motion was granted against the opposition of plaintiff, who contended that the whole pleading was inconsistent and should be treated as a nullity. Suckley v. Slade,* 5 Cr. C. C., 123.

§ 1052. Variance between writ and declaration cannot be called in question by demurrer. Wilder v. McCormick, 2 Blatch., 31.

§ 1053. On a demurrer to the evidence everything is admitted which the jury could reasonably infer from the evidence. United States Bank v. Smith,* 11 Wheat., 171.

§ 1054. Venue, special demurrer to.— A declaration containing a defective venue, or none at all, should be specially demurred to. The defect is cured by verdict or judgment. Crittenden v. Davis,* Hemp., 96.

§ 1055. No cause of action — Iowa code.— Under the Iowa code a demurrer is properly overruled when the declaration, by a fair and natural construction, shows a substantial cause of action. McFaul v. Ramsey, 20 How., 523.

§ 1056. Statute of limitations as subject of — Wisconsin practice.— Under the Revised Statutes of Wisconsin, and the decisions of the state courts thereon, the statute of limitations may be brought up by demurrer if the bar appears upon the face of the declaration. Chemung Canal Bank v. Lowery, 3 Otto, 72.

§ 1057. Plea and demurrer in same case — Virginia act.— The act of Virginia, passed in 1792, authorizes a defendant to plead and demur in the same case. Fowle v. Common Council of Alexandria, 3 Pet., 898.

§ 1058. Under the law of Virginia the defendant may demur and plead to issue to the whole declaration. Fowle v. Alexandria, 3 Cr. C. C., 70.

§ 1059. Special demurrers abolished in Arkansas.— In the territory of Arkansas, defects in pleading, only reachable at common law by special demurrer, must be disregarded, special demurrers having been abolished by statute. Chandler v. Byrd, Hemp., 222.

4. *Replication and Subsequent Pleadings. Issue.*

SUMMARY — *Replication to plea of authority*, § 1060. — *Replication de injuria*, § 1061. — *Verdict on two issues*, § 1062. — *Replication insufficient in substance*, § 1063. — *Rejoinder, requirements of*, § 1064. — *Nil debet a bad rejoinder in action on a bond*, § 1065.

§ 1060. When defendant in an action of trespass justifies on the ground that the act complained of was done by him in the course of his duty as collector of taxes, a replication that the assessment was not chargeable against plaintiff, and that his taxes had all been paid, is bad, as the collector is a ministerial officer, and cannot examine the justice of an assessment. Erskine v. Hohnbach, §§ 1066-70.

§ 1061. A replication *de injuria* puts in issue all the material averments of the plea, and may be used when defendant justifies under an authority not from a court of record. *Ibid.*

§ 1062. A verdict rendered on two issues, one material and the other immaterial, will stand unless the court exercises its discretion to award a repleader. *Ibid.*

§ 1063. Where a marshal, sued on his official bond for taking insufficient security, pleaded that he had levied on goods and lands of sufficient value, a replication showing that the lands levied upon had been previously attached and would not satisfy the debt was held insufficient, as not fully answering the plea, which mentioned goods as well as lands. Sedam v. Taylor, § 1071.

§ 1064. A rejoinder must fully answer the breach alleged in the replication, and must tender issue on a single point. United States v. Cumpton, §§ 1072, 1073.

§ 1065. *Nil debet* is a bad rejoinder in an action on a bond. *Ibid.*

[NOTES.— See §§ 1074-1101.]

ERSKINE v. HOHNBACH.

(14 Wallace, 613–620. 1871.) *

ERROR to U. S. Circuit Court, Eastern District of Wisconsin.

STATEMENT OF FACTS.— Trespass was brought by Hohnbach against Erskine for a seizure and sale by the latter of his property. Pleas, general issue, and two special pleas, setting up substantially the same defense, to wit, that the acts complained of were done by defendant as collector of internal revenue, under an assessment regularly made by the assessor in the exercise of the latter's jurisdiction. *De injuria* was set up to the first special plea, and to the second plaintiff replied that the said tax was never chargeable to him, because he, during the time mentioned in the assessment, did not manufacture, remove or vend the property described, and that he had paid his taxes. Rejoinder, that plaintiff had not paid the assessment as stated in the plea. Issue was joined. Jury found for plaintiff. Motion in arrest of judgment was made because the replication failed to answer the plea, and did not state that the plaintiff had taken an appeal from the assessment to the commissioners of internal revenue, according to section 19 of act of July 13, 1866. Motion overruled, and judgment for plaintiff.

§ **1066.** *An appeal to the commissioner of internal revenue from an assessment is only a condition precedent to an action for the recovery of taxes paid.*

Opinion by MR. JUSTICE FIELD.

We do not think that the omission, in the replication, to allege that the plaintiff had taken an appeal from the assessment to the commissioner of internal revenue affected the character of the replication, or that the insertion of the allegation would have aided it. The defect of the replication consisted in the fact that it raised an immaterial issue. An appeal to the commissioner of internal revenue from an assessment is only a condition precedent to an action for the recovery of taxes paid. It is not a condition precedent to any other action where such action is permissible.

The collector could not revise nor refuse to enforce the assessment regularly made by the assessor in the exercise of the latter's jurisdiction. The duties of the collector in the enforcement of the tax assessed were purely ministerial. The assessment, duly certified to him, was his authority to proceed, and, like an execution to a sheriff, regular on its face, issued by a tribunal having jurisdiction of the subject-matter, constituted his protection.

§ **1066a.** *Order of competent tribunal as protection to a ministerial officer acting thereunder.*

Whatever may have been the conflict at one time, in the adjudged cases, as to the extent of protection afforded to ministerial officers acting in obedience to process or orders issued to them by tribunals or officers invested by law with authority to pass upon and determine particular facts, and render judgment thereon, it is well settled now that if the officer or tribunal possess jurisdiction over the subject-matter upon which judgment is passed, with power to issue an order or process for the enforcement of such judgment, and the order or process issued thereon to the ministerial officer is regular on its face, showing no departure from the law, or defect of jurisdiction over the person or property affected, then, and in such cases, the order or process will give full and entire protection to the ministerial officer in its regular enforcement against any prosecution which the party aggrieved thereby may institute against him, although serious errors may have been committed by the officer or tribunal in reaching the conclusion or judgment upon which the order or process is issued. Savacool v. Boughton, 5 Wend., 171; Earl v. Camp, 16 id., 563; Chegaray v. Jenkins, 5 N. Y., 376; Sprague v. Birchard, 1 Wis., 457.

§ 1067. *Replication to plea of collector who justifies under regular assessment.*

Now the replication to the second special plea did not deny the jurisdiction of the assessor to make an assessment under the circumstances alleged in the plea; nor that the assessment made by him was duly certified to the defendant as collector of the district, with an order to proceed to enforce it, nor that the property assessed was subject to taxation; but only averred that the assessment made was not chargeable against the plaintiff, because he had not manufactured and sold or removed the property assessed within the period mentioned, and had paid all the taxes chargeable against him upon such property — an averment which, if true, would only have shown that the assessor had erred in his judgment in making the assessment, and could not have controlled the action of the collector, nor have justified him in suspending the enforcement of the tax. A judgment debtor might as well complain of the enforcement of an execution by a sheriff on the ground that the court erred in finding that he was indebted to the plaintiff and so giving judgment against him.

§ 1068. *Practice when two issues are formed, one material, the other immaterial.*

An immaterial issue having been thus tendered, the proper course for the defendant to pursue was to demur to the replication, and thus force the plaintiff to join issue on the merits of the defense pleaded, or to allow judgment to pass against. Had the issue here made been the only one in the case tendered to the defense pleaded by the second special plea, the defendant, not being able to set up that defense under the general issue, would have been entitled after verdict to an arrest of judgment and an award of repleader. Gould on Pleading, ch. X, § 29. But such was not the fact here. The first special plea set up the same defense as the second. In both of the special pleas the defendant justified the seizure and conversion of the property, described in the declaration, as collector of internal revenue, under an assessment against the plaintiff duly made by the assessor of the district and certified to him. The difference in the language used in the two pleas, and in the particularity with which the assessment of the tax and the distraint and sale of the property were set forth, did not change the substantial identity of the defense made.

Now the replication of *de injuria*, which was interposed to the first special plea, put in issue the material averments of that plea. It threw upon the defendant the burden of proving so much of the plea as constituted a defense to the action. As no error in the ruling of the court on the trial is presented, we are forced to presume that the defendant was afforded every opportunity allowed by law to establish the facts averred by him. To arrest judgment upon the verdict rendered on this issue because an immaterial issue was formed upon a replication to another plea setting up the same defense, and award a repleader, would be in effect to allow the same matter to be twice tried. Such being the case, the granting or refusing the motion rested in the discretion of the court below, with which this court will not interfere.

§ 1069. *Replication de injuria, when to be used.*

We are aware of numerous decisions in this country to the effect that the replication *de injuria* is only a good replication where the plea sets up matter of excuse, and is not good where the plea sets up matter of justification, though the justification be under process from a court not of record, or rest upon some authority of law other than a judgment of a court. Such are the decisions of the supreme court of New York (Griswold *v.* Sedgwick, 1 Wend., 131; Coburn *v.* Hopkins, 4 id., 577), and they proceed upon the supposed doctrine of the resolutions in Crogate's Case, 8 Coke, 132. But an examination of that case will show that the doctrine is not supported to the extent laid down in the New York decisions. The third resolution in Crogate's Case does not state that a replication *de injuria* is bad where the justification is under authority of law, but, as observed by Mr. Justice Patteson in Selby *v.* Bardons, 3 Barn. & Ad., 2, this, if taken to the full extent of the terms used, is inconsistent with that part of the first resolution which states that where the plea justifies under proceedings of a court not of record the replevin may be used. In that case the declaration was in replevin for goods and chattels. The avowry of the defendant stated that the plaintiff was an inhabitant and occupier of a tenement in a certain parish; that a rate for the relief of the poor of the parish was duly made and published, in which the plaintiff was rated at seven pounds; that he had notice of the rate, and was required by the defendant, as collector, to pay the same, which he refused; that he was then summoned before two justices to show cause why he refused; that he appeared, but showing no cause, the justices issued a warrant to the defendant to distrain the plaintiff's goods and chattels, under which he, and the other defendant as his bailiff, took the goods and chattels mentioned in the declaration. To this avowry the plaintiff filed the plea of *de injuria*, to which a special demurrer was interposed, assigning for cause that the plea offered to put in issue several distinct matters, and was pleaded as if the avowry consisted wholly in excuse of the taking and detaining and not as a justification and claim of right. The court considered at length both causes, and held that the plea was good. On error to the court of exchequer chamber this ruling was affirmed (3 Tyrw., 430), and the decision, it is believed, has never been departed from in the English courts. The plea *de injuria* in this case to the avowry stands like the replication *de injuria* to a plea setting up similar matter in an action of trespass. There is no distinction in the effect of the plea, in one case and the ;replication in the other. This was held by the king's bench in the case cited, and by the court of exchequer chamber on error.

This case is authority for the sufficiency of the replication to the first special plea. Other cases might be cited to the same purport. The decisions in England on this point will be found collected in a learned note to Crogate's Case by Mr. Smith in his Leading Cases, and the decisions in this country will be found collected in an equally learned note by the American editors of that work.

§ 1070. *The replication de injuria, where specially demurrable, cannot be objected to after verdict.*

But aside from the considerations mentioned, however the replication might be regarded in some courts on special demurrer, its defective character, if at all defective, was cured by the verdict. The objection to its sufficiency to put the averments of the plea in issue cannot be raised after verdict. See Lytle *v.* Lee, 5 John., 112, and the cases there cited.

Judgment affirmed.

SEDAM v. TAYLOR.

(Circuit Court for Indiana: 3 McLean, 547, 548. 1845.)

Opinion of the COURT.

STATEMENT OF FACTS.— This action is brought on the official bond given by the defendant Taylor, as marshal, for taking insufficient security on a replevin bond. The defendants pleaded that, after the taking and return of the replevin bond, a *fi. fa.* was issued and placed in the hands of the marshal, who, before the bringing of this suit, did levy on divers goods and chattels, lands and tenements of the said sureties in the replevin bond, to the full value of the judgment, interest and costs, which levy remains undisposed of, etc.

To this the plaintiff replies.that the lands and tenements levied upon by the *fi. fa.* were subject to a prior lien of a judgment against the said sureties for the sum of $2,760.38, on which execution was issued, and the above land sold, the proceeds of which sale were insufficient to pay that judgment, etc. To this replication the defendants demurred.

§ 1071. *Replication must fully answer plea.*

The replication is bad as it does not answer the plea. In the plea the levy is alleged to have been on divers goods and chattels, lands and tenements. The plea does not answer to the goods and chattels, but to the lands and tenements only. The replication may be true and the plea of the defendant may, notwithstanding, be a bar to the plaintiff's action.

The sureties of the marshal were bound collaterally for the performance of his duty. The plaintiff, in this action, seeks to make them liable where the plea avers there was a levy on goods, etc., to the full value of the judgments. This is clearly a bar to the action. Such a levy is a bar to an action on an injunction or appeal bond. Cass v. Adams, 3 Ohio, 223; M'Intosh v. Chew, 1 Black, 289.

UNITED STATES v. CUMPTON.

(Circuit Court for Indiana: 3 McLean, 163–165. 1843.)

Opinion of the COURT.

STATEMENT OF FACTS.— Cumpton, the defendant, having been postmaster, and failing to account, etc., the above action was brought on his official bond. He pleaded that he had in all things performed his duties faithfully, and accounted for moneys received, etc. The plaintiffs replied that he did not at all times after the making of the said writing obligatory and the said condition thereof well and truly observe, perform, fulfill or keep all and singular the conditions, etc., in the said writing, as in said plea is alleged, but that he broke the same. 1. That he did not make returns every three months. 2. Rendered no account since the 2d April, 1840; and that between the 1st April and 30th of the same month, divers sums came to his hands as postmaster. 3. That on the 13th April, 1840, there was in his hands the sum of $68.

To this the defendants rejoined, 1st. That the said Cumpton did heretofore, and before the commencement of this suit, to wit, the 5th July, 1841, at said district, render accounts of his receipts and expenditures as postmaster to the general postoffice, which were then and there received. 2d. That said Cumpton, as postmaster, did not, at divers times between the 1st April, 1840, and the 10th of the same month, receive divers sums amounting to $68, and that he does not owe. 3. That he owes nothing, etc.

To this rejoinder the plaintiffs demurred.

§ 1072. *Rejoinder must fully answer the breach alleged in replication.*

The demurrer must be sustained. The rejoinder does not answer the breach, to which it was intended to apply. The breach assigned is, that the said Cumpton did not once in three months faithfully render accounts of his receipts, etc., as postmaster. The rejoinder is that Cumpton, on the 5th July, 1841, rendered accounts, etc., which were received, etc. The law requires quarterly accounts to be rendered. Cumpton was postmaster from 6th November, 1838, to 13th April, 1841. The rejoinder is, therefore, defective in this, that it does not show or aver that accounts were rendered once in three months. The postoffice law imposes a penalty on postmasters who neglect to make their quarterly returns. They are liable to pay double the amount of postages, ordinarily received, in each quarter, if the quarterly return be not made.

§ 1073. *Rejoinder must tender issue on a single point.*

The second part of the rejoinder is double, and is, therefore, demurrable. It denies certain allegations of the replication, and also avers that Cumpton owes nothing. The issue must be tendered on a single point, though it may include several facts. Here, however, two distinct issues are tendered.

Nil debet is a bad rejoinder in an action on a bond. The third part of the rejoinder, which is *nil debet*, is also demurrable. This plea can never be pleaded when a specialty is the foundation of the action. It is proper in a case where the deed is mere inducement to the action. 1 Chitty, Pl., 423; 1 Saund, Pl. and Ev., 406. The demurrer is sustained, and judgment.

§ 1074. Issue tendered on matter of law.—A replication which tenders issue only on matter of law is bad. Clearwater *v.* Meredith, 1 Wall., 25.

§ 1075. Conclusion of, when tendering issue.—A replication tendering issue and concluding with a verification is bad on special demurrer. Walker *v.* Johnson, 2 McL., 92.

§ 1076. Single breach supported by many facts.—A replication is good which assigns a single breach, though many facts are averred as constituting the breach. Jackson *v.* Rundlet, 1 Woodb. & M., 381.

§ 1077. When double.—A replication which alleges two distinct and independent facts, either of which is a complete answer to the plea, is double, and is bad on special demurrer. Burnham *v.* Webster, Dav., 236.

§ 1078. Defects in declaration, when cured by.—An insufficient declaration may be cured by additional averments in the replication, which are admitted by demurrer to be true. Railroad Co. *v.* Harris, 12 Wall., 65.

§ 1079. When a plea sets up a defense consisting of two affirmative facts, the replication should take issue on one of these only. McClintick *v.* Johnston, 1 McL., 414.

§ 1080. But one replication may be filed to a plea, and that must contain but one defense. Where the plea set up a foreign judgment, a replication was held bad which set up that the court had no jurisdiction, and that the note in suit had been withdrawn by consent before verdict and judgment. Burnham *v.* Webster, Dav., 236.

§ 1081. Replication to evidence improperly set out in declaration, bad.—In an ejectment suit a replication which replies to evidence of defendant's title, which defendant has improperly set out in his plea, is bad, the proper reply being a motion to strike out for redundancy such parts of the plea as set out evidence. Fitch *v.* Cornell, 1 Saw., 156.

§ 1082. Plea of statute of limitations—Reply, disability.—The defendant having pleaded the statute of limitations, if the plaintiff wishes to set up a disability, caused by the taking of an appeal, he should set forth when the appeal was taken, in order to show the duration of the disability; and an averment that it was "duly" taken, being a conclusion of law and not of fact, has only the effect to aver that the statute was suspended for a time. Braun *v.* Sauerwein, 10 Wall., 218.

§ 1083. A replication to a plea in bar of a former recovery, that the evidence was wholly insufficient to establish the claim, or that no evidence was offered or received by the court, will not avoid the bar. Ramsey *v.* Herndon, 1 McL., 450.

§ 1084. Plea, judgment, no assets ultra — Nul tiel record, assets ultra fraudom.—If an administrator defendant plead judgment and no assets *ultra*, replication thereto may be either *nul tiel record* or assets *ultra fraudom*, or any other fact properly triable by a jury. Teasdale v. Branton,* 2 Hayw., 877.

§ 1085. Administrator's plea, statute of limitations — But one replication allowed. — Where an administrator was defendant, the federal circuit court sitting at Alexandria, D. C., permitted him to plead the statute of limitations at the trial term, to which plea the plaintiff could not make more than one replication. Offut v. Hall, 2 Cr. C. C., 363. *

§ 1086. Statute of limitations — Discontinuance of suit within six years. — To a plea of the statute of limitations it is not a good replication that a suit for the same demand was commenced in a court in another state and discontinued within six years. Delaplaine v. Crowninshield, 3 Mason, 329.

§ 1087. —— leave of court to file several replications, no adjudication of their sufficiency — Defenses held bad. — To a plea of limitations in an action of *assumpsit*, the court under special order allowed the plaintiff to file the following four replications, to which the defendant demurred: (1) A promise for a consideration not to plead limitations. It was held doubtful whether this was matter for replication, as an application to a court of equity to restrain the defendant from the plea would be the proper remedy, but as the defendant made no objection it was allowed. (2) A new promise to pay. This held good. (3) Defendant absent from the state eleven months. This was held to be bad and frivolous, because, if true, it would not follow that six years had not elapsed since the defendant resided out of the state. (4) That an act of congress discharged the defendant from personal liability and substituted the secretary of the treasury in his place, should judgment be declared against the defendant in his official capacity, and that the secretary had promised not to plead limitations and had made a new promise. This was called extraordinary pleading. It was double, and contained no substantial matter of avoidance. The leave of the court to file the several replications was held no adjudication of their sufficiency, which was to be determined afterwards, as shown above. Andreae v. Redfield,* 15 Int. Rev. Rec., 105.

§ 1088. Suit in name of one for benefit of another — Bar to plaintiff not bar to interest of third person. — If a suit is rightly brought in the name of the plaintiff for the benefit of a third person, and the defendant's plea shows a sufficient bar against the plaintiff, it is competent for the plaintiff. in his replication, to show that a third person had an equitable interest which ought not to be affected. Brown v. Hartford Fire Ins. Co.,* 21 Law Rep., 726.

§ 1089. Plea, pendency of another suit — Replication, suit dismissed. — When, in a suit on a promissory note, the pendency of another suit in the state court was pleaded in bar, a replication, that since the filing of the plea the suit had been dismissed, was held to be a good replication in Illinois. Chamberlain v. Eckert, 2 Biss., 124.

§ 1090. Where the defendant pleads a record of the same court, the replication denying it concludes with a verification, and a day is given to the parties to hear judgment. If the record be of another court the replication *nul tiel record* may either conclude by giving the defendant a day to bring in the record, or with an averment and prayer of the debt and damages. In the former case the issue is complete on the replication; in the latter there must be a rejoinder, re-asserting the existence of the record, on which account the former is to be preferred. Bobyshall v. Oppenheimer,* 4 Wash., 888.

§ 1091. Replication must traverse — Statement of facts inconsistent with plea, insufficient. — In an action by the United States on a claim assigned to it by a third party, defendant pleaded that the transaction was a private one between him and the assignor and set up the statute of limitations. Plaintiff, without traversing the allegation that the transaction was private, replied that the money belonged to the United States and was advanced by the assignor as an officer of the United States to defendant as an officer. *Held*, that although these facts were inconsistent with the facts stated in the plea, yet no issue was raised, and judgment must be for defendant. United States v. Buford,* 3 Pet., 12.

§ 1092. Statute of limitations — A replication must answer the plea. — When the plea sets up the statute of limitations a replication that plaintiff lived out of the state is not good, unless this is one of the exceptions provided for in the statute. Jones v. Hays, 4 McL., 521.

§ 1093. To a plea of the statute of limitations it is a good replication that plaintiff has been hitherto beyond sea. Chomqua v. Mason,* 1 Gall., 341.

§ 1094. Action on sheriff's bond — Whether facts have already been tried by law of state question of law, not subject of replication. — By the laws of Alabama, where property is taken in execution, if the sheriff does not make the money, the plaintiff is allowed to suggest to the court that the money might have been made with due diligence, and thereupon the court is directed to frame an issue in order to try the fact. In a suit upon a sheriff's bond, where the plea was that this proceeding had been resorted to by the plaintiff and a verdict found for the sheriff, a replication to this plea, alleging that the property in question in that trial was not the same property mentioned in the breach assigned in the declaration, was a bad replication, and demurrable. Chapman v. Smith, 16 How., 114.

§ 1095. **Rejoinder, excuse for non-performance after plea of performance.**— After a plea of general performance, a rejoinder stating an excuse for not performing is bad. McGowan v. Caldwell, 1 Cr. C. C., 481.

§ 1096. **Rejoinder — Issuable plea.**— Debt on auctioneer's bond; plea, general performance; replication, that the auctioneer did not pay over money to A. and B.; rejoinder, that it had not been established, by a judgment, that money was due to them by the auctioneer, is an issuable plea to set aside an office judgment. Alexandria v. Moore, 1 Cr. C. C., 440.

§ 1097. **Inducement in rejoinder containing new and substantive matter, bad.**— To an action in Michigan on a judgment rendered in New York, defendant pleaded the statute of limitations. Plaintiff replied that he had lived continuously in New York from the time judgment was rendered until within a year. Defendant rejoined that both plaintiff and defendant had lived in New York for eight years after the recovery, and traversed the replication. *Held*, that the inducement in this rejoinder was new and substantive matter not denying the plaintiff's action, being an attempt in Michigan to rely on the New York statute, and the rejoinder was bad. Egberts v. Dibble,* 3 McL., 86.

§ 1098. **An issue is made by an affirmative** and a negative, and consists of a single point, though this may embrace several facts. McClintick v. Johnston, 1 McL., 414.

§ 1099. **Two affirmatives.**— *Quære*, whether two affirmatives may make an issue. Walker v. Johnson, 2 McL., 92.

§ 1100. **Plea in abatement — Affirmative with defendant.**— When, upon an issue on a plea in abatement, the affirmative rests with the defendant, and the only evidence introduced is wholly in favor of the plaintiff, it is not error for the judge to direct a verdict for plaintiff. Grand Chute v. Winegar,* 15 Wall., 355.

§ 1101. **Issue in form one of fact, but in substance one of law.**— An issue raised by the pleadings, which is in form an issue of fact, but in substance an issue of law, cannot be heard by the court without overturning all the established principles of pleading. United States v. Sawyer,* 1 Gall., 86.

5. *Profert and Oyer.*

SUMMARY — *Profert unnecessarily made*, § 1102.

§ 1102. Profert of a writing being made, though unnecessarily, the writing is presumed to be in court, and oyer may be demanded. Hammer v. Klein, § 1103.

[NOTES.— See §§ 1104–1132.]

HAMMER v. KLEIN.

(Circuit Court for Ohio: 1 Bond, 590–592. 1865).

Opinion of the COURT.

STATEMENT OF FACTS.— This case is before the court on a motion by the counsel of the defendants for an order on the plaintiff for oyer of the bond and agreement set forth in the declaration.

For the purposes of this motion it is not necessary to state in detail the particulars of the plaintiff's claim as set out in the declaration. The plaintiff's cause of action is based on a bond executed by one of the defendants in the penalty of $30,000, in connection with a collateral agreement signed by the parties, by which the plaintiff bound himself to do certain acts therein specified before the defendants should incur the penalty named in the bond. These acts, the declaration avers, have been performed by the plaintiff, whereby the defendants have become liable to pay the penalty of the bond. The declaration makes profert both of the bond and the collateral agreement.

The counsel for the plaintiff insists that in this state of the case the defendants are not entitled to oyer as prayed for, either by the rules of pleading in this court, or by the common law.

§ 1103. *When in a declaration profert is made of any paper, even unnecessarily, oyer may be demanded of it.*

There can be no question that, under the common-law system of pleading, oyer of any instrument of writing of which profert is made in the declaration, may be demanded, and will be granted of course. As to the instruments of writing collateral to the bond, it is clear, if profert is made of them, oyer may be craved, although the profert may have been made without any necessity for it. Profert being made the writing is presumed to be in court, and oyer may be required. 1 Chitty's Pleadings, 363 (Ad. edition); Stephen on Pleading, 447. In this case it seems profert of the agreement was properly made, as it was essential to give the plaintiff a right of action on the bond. It is, in fact, the sole basis of his claim to recovery on the bond, and oyer may be claimed both of the bond and the collateral agreement.

It seems to be supposed by plaintiff's counsel that the right of a party in a case in this court to demand oyer is abrogated by the operation of the seventh rule of this court, adopting certain provisions of the Ohio code as rules of this court. But this rule clearly applies only to such papers or instruments of writing which are to be used incidentally as evidence, and not to such as are in the possession of the plaintiff, and which constitute the basis of the action. Neither the rule referred to, nor any other rule of this court, has abolished the common-law system of special pleading. Though the system has been greatly modified it still exists, and has existed and been recognized from the first organization of the federal courts in this district. And the right to demand oyer in proper cases being a part of this system of pleading, the court has no hesitation in making the order prayed for in this case. Oyer is accordingly ordered.

§ 1104. Profert necessary for oyer.— Where profert is not made oyer cannot be demanded. Campbell v. Strong, Hemp., 265.

§ 1105. Profert of original, copy as oyer.— A copy will not be received as *oyer* when a *profert* has been made of the original; and if a copy is offered the defendant may demur. Wellford v. Miller, 1 Cr. C. C., 514.

§ 1106. Subject of oyer part of record.— Where oyer of any instrument is prayed, or there is a demurrer to any part of the pleadings, such instruments or pleadings become a part of the record. Suydam v. Williamson, 20 How., 427.

§ 1107. Oyer of a deed set forth in the first count does not make that deed a part of the record so as to apply it to the other counts in the declaration. Hughes v. Moore, 7 Cr., 176.

§ 1108. Profert is sufficiently made in the declaration in these terms: "As by the said letters patent and specification, all in due form of law, ready in court to be produced, will fully appear." Wilder v. McCormick, 2 Blatch., 31.

§ 1109. Claim of oyer, when too late.— After plea, replication, rejoinder and demurrer, it is too late for defendant to crave oyer of plaintiff's letters of administration. Graham v. Cooke,* 1 Cr. C. C., 116.

§ 1110. Letters of administration, profert of, when necessary.— An administrator suing on a judgment obtained by him in such capacity need not make profert of his letters of administration. Biddle v. Wilkins, 1 Pet., 686.

§ 1111. Instrument to be presented to court.— Where profert is made of an instrument, and question is made on that instrument, it ought to be presented to the court. Grunninger v. Philpot, 5 Biss., 82.

§ 1112. Where profert of letters testamentary is made and oyer is not craved the question of plaintiff's right to sue as executor is not open on demurrer. Childress v. Emory, 8 Wheat., 642.

§ 1113. Oyer craved of the condition of a bond does not entitle the party to oyer of the bond. United States v. Sawyer,* 1 Gall., 86.

§ 1114. Upon oyer of the condition of a bond demanded in a plea the condition becomes a part of the declaration and not of the plea. *Ibid.*

§ 1115. A former judgment is never pleaded with a profert, but this is made in reply to a plea (or replication) of *nul tiel record.* Burnham v. Webster, Dav., 236.

§ 1116. The plaintiff is not bound to give oyer of a bond on which the action does not rest, of which profert is not made, and which is on file in the clerk's office, equally accessible to both parties. Rockhill v. Hanna,* 4 McL., 200.

§ 1117. **Profert of bond, whole instrument before court.**— When profert is made of a bond the whole instrument is before the court, and it is not necessary to make separate profert of the condition. United States *v.* Spalding.* 2 Mason, 478.

§ 1118. **Oyer of one part of bond not oyer of whole bond.**— If defendant wishes oyer of the whole instrument he must pray it. Oyer of the obligatory part is not oyer of the condition, and each must be prayed for if each is wanted. *Ibid.*

§ 1119. **Profert of bond from which seal is lost.**— If the seal is torn off a bond with the assent of the obligee, by mistake or by fraud upon the obligor, the instrument may still be declared on as a deed by making the proper averment of the facts upon the profert. *Ibid.*

§ 1120. **Oyer is not demandable of a record,** and when defendant, in an action on an appeal bond, craved oyer of the records referred to in the declaration, a special demurrer to his plea was sustained on this ground. Sneed *v.* Wister,* 8 Wheat., 690.

§ 1121. **Oyer of deed in action on bond for performance of deed.**— In an action on a bond for the performance of the covenants in another deed, oyer of such deed cannot be craved, but defendant must show it, with a profert of it, or an excuse for the omission. *Ibid.*

§ 1122. **If oyer be improperly demanded** the defect will be open on special demurrer, but will be cured by general demurrer. *Ibid.*

§ 1123. **Oyer — Letters patent.**— Oyer is not demandable of letters patent. Smith *v.* Ely, 5 McL., 76.

§ 1124. **Oyer of note.**— A note sued on is not part of the record unless produced on oyer. Cook *v.* Gray, Hemp., 84.

§ 1125. **Variance — Oyer necessary to sustain demurrer.**— A defendant cannot take advantage of a variance between the writ and declaration by demurrer without praying oyer of the writ. Triplet *v.* Warfield, 2 Cr. C. C., 237.

§ 1126. **Letters of administration — Profert necessary for oyer.**— Although the plaintiffs name themselves administrators, yet, if they have not made profert of their letters of administration, they are not bound to give oyer of them. Mason *v.* Lawrason, 1 Cr. C. C., 190.

§ 1127. **Letters patent, profert of.**— A motion having been made in arrest of judgment, on the ground that no description of the patent was set forth in the declaration in a suit instituted for an infringement of such patent, it was held that the profert of letters patent made them, when produced, a part of the declaration, and gave the invention all the requisite certainty. Pitts *v.* Whitman, 2 Story, 609.

§ 1128. **A former judgment is not pleaded with a profert,** but a profert is tendered in reply to the plea or replication of *nul tiel record.* Burnham *v.* Webster, Dav., 236.

§ 1129. **Oyer cannot be twice demanded.**— After oyer prayed and demurrer by the defendant the plaintiff is not bound to give oyer at a subsequent term. The defendant should have spread the oyer upon the record. Offut *v.* Beatty, 1 Cr. C. C., 213.

§ 1130. **Oyer on plea-day, right to plead after.**— If the defendant on the plea-day demand oyer, which is not given until the subsequent term, the court will give the defendant time to plead after oyer. Calvert *v.* Slater, 1 Cr. C. C., 44.

§ 1131. **Expiration of rule to plead.**— Oyer of the record of a judgment of another state will not be given if not prayed before the expiration of the rule to plead. Cull *v.* Allen, 1 Cr. C. C., 45.

§ 1132. **Oyer of letters testamentary.**— Where plaintiff dies, and the appearance of the administrator is entered, he must give oyer of his letters whenever demanded before the expiration of the rule to plead. North *v.* Clark,* 8 Cr. C. C., 93.

II. Pleading in Equity.

1. *Bill. Cross-bill.*

SUMMARY — *Bill to state whole case,* § 1133.— *Must allege facts necessary to the construction of the language involved,* §§ 1134-85.— *General certainty in bill ordinarily sufficient,* § 1136.— *Consideration, how stated in bill for fraud,* §§ 1187, 1138.— *Bill charging shareholders of insolvent corporation,* § 1189.— *Bill to show how each defendant is concerned as party,* § 1140.— *Parties to suit to enjoin judgment,* § 1141.— *Allegation of payment of note,* § 1142.— *Averments of citizenship in removed cause,* § 1143.— *Bill to dissolve partnership treated as bill for partition,* § 1144.— *Multifariousness,* §§ 1145-48.— *Laches under statute of limitations,* §§ 1149-51.— *Multifariousness,* §§ 1152-57.— *Discovery,* §§ 1158-59.— *Infringement of copyright,* § 1160.

§ 1133. **A bill in equity must contain** enough matter in itself to sustain the case and enable the court to make a decree therein, without being supplemented by the answer or the evidence. Harrison *v.* Nixon, §§ 1161-63.

§ 1134. When a decision depends upon the meaning as used in a will of a technical expression having different meanings in different localities, it is absolutely necessary for the bill to allege the testator's domicile, as the language must be construed as used in that locality, and the court must know by what law to construe the expression. *Ibid.*

§ 1135. If such a bill comes to the supreme court after final judgment in the circuit court, the case will be remanded, that the bill may be amended and proceedings had de novo. *Ibid.*

§ 1136. In most cases general certainty is sufficient in pleadings in equity, and it is only necessary to distinctly apprise defendant of the precise case he will be obliged to meet. A *prima facie* case thus made out should be answered and not demurred to. St. Louis *v.* Knapp Co., § 1163.

§ 1137. A bill to set aside a conveyance as fraudulent may allege either that the conveyance was without consideration, or that plaintiff has offered to return the consideration, or that plaintiff is ignorant whether or not there was a consideration, and that this fact was known to defendant; but the allegations must be harmonious, and must not charge lack of consideration and inadequacy at the same time. Railroad Co. *v.* Alley, §§ 1164-65.

§ 1138. Such a bill, if resting on the ground of inadequacy, should state the value of the property specifically and not doubtfully. *Ibid.*

§ 1139. A bill to charge shareholders in an insolvent corporation must show by averments all the facts necessary to make them liable under the law. United States *v.* Globe Works, §§ 1166-68.

§ 1140. A bill is demurrable which joins a party as defendant without showing how he is liable or is interested as a party. *Ibid.*

§ 1141. A bill in equity against the holder of a bill to enjoin a judgment obtained thereon, and alleging that the holder had already been paid by the drawer, need not make the latter a party to the suit. Atkins *v.* Dick, §§ 1169-72.

§ 1142. An allegation that the note was fully paid is sufficient, without giving the details of the method of payment. *Ibid.*

§ 1143. When a case is removed by defendant from a state to a federal court and an amended complaint is then filed, the jurisdiction of the court is not lost by the omission of the amended complaint to aver the citizenship of the parties. Briges *v.* Sperry, §§ 1173-75.

§ 1144. When a bill is filed for the dissolution of a partnership and the sale of the partnership property, and a decree for that purpose is rendered, the decree may be sustained on appeal by treating the bill as if it were a bill for partition, provided sufficient allegations for that purpose are contained therein. *Ibid.*

§ 1145. The rule as to multifariousness is founded on convenience to defendants, and forbids the joining of distinct matters in one bill, whether against one or many defendants. In each case it is a question of fact and the test is whether one defense may be made to the whole bill. Gamewell Fire Alarm Telegraph Co. *v.* Chillicothe, §§ 1176-78.

§ 1146. A bill is not multifarious which is based on several letters patent, when all the inventions therein secured are set out as constituting one machine, the use of which makes the cause of action. *Ibid.*

§ 1147. No universal rule as to multifariousness can be given, each case necessarily depending on its own circumstances. Sheldon *v.* Keokuk Northern Line Packet Co., §§ 1179-84.

§ 1148. A bill is not multifarious in which separate judgment creditors unite in assailing transactions of their common debtor, by which he has concealed all of his property from them. *Ibid.*

§ 1149. If the question of laches can ever be raised in a suit where the statute of limitation applies, a demurrer insisting upon the lapse of time short of the statutory period should not be sustained unless the bill itself makes out a clear case of unreasonable delay. *Ibid.*

§ 1150. If consistent with the bill that the fraud charged was not discovered until some time after it was committed, the court will not assume unreasonable delay, after discovery, from the fact that suit was not brought until several years after the fraud. *Ibid.*

§ 1151. It will not be assumed on demurrer that the fraud charged was discovered more than six years previous to bringing suit merely because the bill does not allege the contrary. *Ibid.*

§ 1152. Multifariousness is the improperly joining in one bill distinct and independent matters and thereby confounding them. There is no inflexible rule as to what constitutes multifariousness and permits the joinder of questions to a certain extent distinct, when it can be done without inconvenience. Stafford National Bank *v.* Sprague, §§ 1185-86.

§ 1153. A bill is not necessarily multifarious which is brought to foreclose a judgment lien on certain land, and also to set aside a prior deed of the same land. *Ibid.*

§ 1154. It is not true, as a general proposition, that where there is a joinder of distinct claims between the same parties, the bill is necessarily demurrable for that cause alone; but a bill for infringement, brought against a defendant on several patents which are distinct, and are not alleged to have been connected with each other or used at the same time in an infringing machine, is multifarious, and a demurrer on that ground will be sustained. Hayes v. Dayton, §§ 1187–89.

§ 1155. A bill against three defendants cannot be objected to as multifarious by one defendant on the ground that it exacts answers from his codefendants in regard to matters which do not concern them. Atwill v. Ferrett, §§ 1190–95.

§ 1156. This is especially true when it appears that neither of the co-defendants is within the jurisdiction of the court. Ibid.

§ 1157. It would probably be a sufficient answer to this objection that the bill was brought against the three defendants as copartners for acts done in the copartnership character. Ibid.

§ 1158. A bill to enforce penalties cannot enforce discoveries in aid thereto. Ibid.

§ 1159. A discovery will not be decreed in aid of an action at law when it appears that the wrong action is brought, and plaintiff will therefore be unable to avail himself of the discovery. Ibid.

§ 1160. A bill for infringement of a copyright of an opera does not sufficiently show title in plaintiff by alleging that the work was arranged, adapted, printed and published by or for him; but sufficient title will be shown if it be also alleged that plaintiff made many additions and alterations to the music; that he added new matters of his own; that he indicated the pieces so altered and composed and took out a copyright therefor in proper form. Ibid.

[NOTES.— See §§ 1198–1344.]

HARRISON v. NIXON.

(9 Peters, 483–540. 1835.)

Opinion by MR. JUSTICE STORY.

STATEMENT OF FACTS.— This is the case of an appeal from a decree of the circuit court of the district of Pennsylvania in a suit in equity. The bill was filed by Samuel Packer, and asserts that one Matthias Aspden, a citizen of Pennsylvania, made his will, dated in Philadelphia on the 6th of December, 1791; and thereby bequeathed all his estate, real and personal, to his heir at law, and afterwards died in August, 1824; and his will was proved and letters testamentary were taken out in Pennsylvania by the appellee, under which he has received large sums of money; and the bill then asks for a decree in favor of Packer, who asserts himself to be the true and only heir at law of Matthias Aspden, and that he is solely entitled under the bequest. The answer of the executor states, from information and belief, that the testator was born in Philadelphia, which was the residence of his parents, about 1756; that he continued to reside there, doing business as a merchant with some success, before he was twenty-one years of age; that before the breaking out of the war between Great Britain and America in 1776, being still a minor, he went to England, with what view the executor is not, from his own knowledge, able to say, but he believes that he went with an impression that the power of Great Britain must soon prevail in putting down resistance in America; that the testator subsequently came several times to the United States, and invested large sums in government stocks and other securities; but whether after so returning to the United States the testator went back to England as his home, or only for the purpose of superintending his property, and whether the testator did in fact change his domicile, the executor (save and except as appears from the facts) doth not know, and is unable to answer; but he believes that the testator, when in England, considered himself as an alien, etc.; and he died in King street, Holborn, London. The answer also states that the executor proved the will and took out letters testamentary in England; and states certain proceedings had upon a bill in chancery in England by one John Aspden there, claiming to be the heir at law of the testator; and annexes to his answer a copy of the bill. He also alleges that several other persons have made claims to the same property as next of kin of the testator, of whose names, etc., he annexes a schedule.

Various proceedings were had in the circuit court of Pennsylvania, and a reference was made to a master to examine and state who were all the heirs and next of kin of the testator. The master made a report, which was afterwards confirmed, and thereupon a final decree was made by the court in favor of John Aspden, of Lancashire, in England, one of the persons who made claim before the master, as entitled, as heir at law to the personal estate in the hands of the executor, and the claims of the other persons claiming as heirs at law were dismissed; and the present appeal has been taken by several of these claimants. The cause having come before this court for argument upon the merits, a question occurred whether the frame of the bill, taken by itself, or taken in connection with the answer, contained sufficient matter upon which the court could proceed to dispose of the merits of the cause and make a final decision.

§ 1161. *A bill in equity must contain enough matter in itself to sustain the case, without being supplemented by answer or evidence.*

The bill contains no averment of the actual domicile of the testator at the time of the making of his will, or at the time of his death, or at any intermediate period. Nor does the answer contain any averments of domicile which supply these defects in the bill, even if it could so do, as we are of opinion, in point of law, it could not. Every bill must contain in itself sufficient matters of fact, *per se*, to maintain the case of the plaintiff, so that the same may be put in issue by the answer and established by the proofs. The proofs must be according to the allegations of the parties, and if the proofs go to matters not within the allegations the court cannot judicially act upon them as a ground for its decision, for the pleadings do not put them in contestation. The *allegata* and the *probata* must reciprocally meet and conform to each other. The case cited at the bar of Matthew v. Hanbury, 2 Vern., 187, does not in any manner contradict this doctrine. The proofs there offered were founded upon allegations in the bill, and went directly to overthrow the consideration of the bonds set up in the answer, in opposition to the allegations of the bill, the latter having asserted that the bonds were obtained by threats and undue means, and not for any real debt or other good consideration. Is, then, any averment of the actual domicile of the testator, under the circumstances of the present case, proper and necessary to be made in the bill, in order to enable the court to come to a final decision upon the merits? We think that it is, for the reasons which will be presently stated.

The point was never brought before the circuit court for consideration, and, consequently, was not acted on by that court. It did not attract attention (at least, as far as we know), on either side, in the argument there made, and it was probably passed over (as we all know matters of a similar nature are everywhere else) from the mutual understanding that the merits were to be tried, and without any minute inquiry whether the merits were fully spread upon the record. It is undoubtedly an inconvenience that the mistake has occurred; but we do not see how the court can on this account dispense with what in their judgment the law will otherwise require.

§ **1162.** *When the interpretation of a will turns upon the meaning of a technical expression differently used in different localities, it is absolutely necessary that the bill allege testator's domicile, that the court may know from what standpoint to view the expression.*

The present is the case of a will, and, so far at least as the matter of the bill is concerned, is exclusively confined to personalty bequeathed by that will. And the court are called upon to give a construction to the terms of a will, and in an especial manner to ascertain who is meant by the words "heir at law" in the leading bequest in the will. The language of wills is not of universal interpretation, having the same precise import in all countries and under all circumstances. They are supposed to speak the sense of the testator according to the received laws or usages of the country where he is domiciled, by a sort of tacit reference, unless there is something in the language which repels or controls such a conclusion. In regard to personalty in an especial manner, the law of the place of the testator's domicile governs in the distribution thereof, and will govern in the interpretation of wills thereof, unless it is manifest that the testator had the laws of some other country in his own view.

No one can doubt if a testator, born and domiciled in England during his whole life, should by his will give his personal estate to his heir at law, that the *descriptio personæ* would have reference to and be governed by the import of the terms in the sense of the laws of England. The import of them might be very different if the testator were born and domiciled in France, in Louisiana, in Pennsylvania or in Massachusetts. In short, a will of personalty speaks according to the laws of the testator's domicile, where there are no other circumstances to control their application; and to raise the question what the testator means, we must first ascertain what was his domicile, and whether he had reference to the laws of that place or to the laws of any foreign country. Now the very gist of the present controversy turns upon the point who were the person or persons intended to be designated by the testator under the appellation of "heir at law." If, at the time of making his will and at his death, he was domiciled in England and had a reference to its laws, the designation might indicate a very different person or persons from what might be the case (we do not say what is the case) if, at the time of making his will and of his death, he was domiciled in Pennsylvania. In order to raise the question of the true interpretation and designation, it seems to us indispensable that the country by whose laws his will is to be interpreted should be first ascertained, and then the inquiry is naturally presented what the provisions of those laws are.

If this be the true posture of the present case, then the bill should allege all the material facts upon which the plaintiff's title depends; and the final judgment of the court must be given so as to put them in contestation in a proper and regular manner. And we do not perceive how the court can dispose of this cause without ascertaining where the testator's domicile was at the time of his making his will and at the time of his death; and if so, then there ought to be suitable averments in the bill to put these matters in issue.

In order to avoid any misconception, it is proper to state that we do not mean in this stage of the cause to express any opinion what would be the effect upon the interpretation of the will if the domicile of the testator was in one country at the time of his making his will, and in another country at the time of his death. This point may well be left open for future consideration. But being of opinion that an averment of the testator's domicile is indispensable in the bill, we think the case ought to be remanded to the circuit court for the purpose of having suitable amendments made in this particular; and that it will be proper to aver the domicile at the time of making the will and at the time of the death of the testator, and during the intermediate period (if there be any change), so that the elements of a full decision may be finally brought before the court. The petitions of the claimants should contain similar averments.

It appears from the motions which have been made to this court, as well as from certain proceedings in the court below, which have been laid before us in support thereof, that there are certain claimants of this bequest, asserting themselves to be heirs at law, whose claims have not been adjudicated upon in the court below on account of their having been presented at too late a period. As the cause is to go back again for further proceedings and must be again opened there for new allegations and proofs, these claimants will have a full opportunity of presenting and proving their claims in the cause; and we are of opinion they ought to be let into the cause for this purpose. In drawing up the decree remanding the cause, leave will be given to them accordingly. The decree of the circuit court is therefore reversed, and the cause is remanded to the circuit court for further proceedings in conformity to this opinion.

MR. JUSTICE BALDWIN dissented.

ST. LOUIS v. KNAPP COMPANY.

(14 Otto, 658–661. 1881.)

APPEAL from U. S. Circuit Court, Eastern District of Missouri.

STATEMENT OF FACTS.— Bill in equity to abate a nuisance caused by the erection of a run-way and piling by the defendants within the corporate limits of the city of St. Louis, by which it was alleged the navigation of the Mississippi river within those limits would be impaired. A demurrer was filed by defendant, which was sustained by the court. The bill was dismissed, and the city appealed.

Opinion by MR. JUSTICE HARLAN.

Upon the hearing of the demurrer two questions were considered by the court: *First*, whether the bill, upon its face, shows that the construction of the run-way will intrude upon the city's rights and cause special damage; *second*, whether, upon its allegations and in advance of the construction of the work, a decree to prevent its completion should be rendered in favor of the city. The court, in disposing of the demurrer, waived a final decision of the first question, expressing, however, some doubt whether the case was within the general rule that a suit in equity to enjoin or abate a public nuisance must be brought by one who has sustained, or is in danger of sustaining, individual special damages, apart from those suffered by the community at large.

Touching the second question, the court below remarked it was very clear that a public navigable stream must remain free and unobstructed; that no private individual has a right to place permanent structures within the navigable channel; and that if the proposed run-way, when completed, proved to be a material obstruction to the free navigation of the river, or a special injury to the rights of others, it might be condemned and removed as a nuisance. It was, however, of opinion that the case presented was one of a threatened nuisance only, and that the reasons assigned for interference by injunction, in advance of the construction of the run-way, were not sufficient.

§ **1168.** *A bill alleging that a structure, when completed, will be a public nuisance, obstructing the navigation of a river' should be answered, not dismissed on demurrer.*

We are of opinion that the demurrer should have been overruled, and the defendant required to answer. The bill makes a *prima facie* case, not only of the right of the city to bring the suit, but for granting the relief asked. It distinctly avers what the defendant proposes to do, and that averment is accompanied by the general charge or statement that the driving of the piles in the bed of the river, and the construction of the run-way, will not only cause a diversion of the river from its natural course, but will throw it east of its natural location, from along the river bank north and south of the proposed run-way and piling, creating in front of the city's improved wharf a deposit of mud and sediment, and rendering it impossible for boats and vessels engaged in the navigation of the Mississippi river to approach or land at the improved wharf north and south of defendant's premises. This is not, as ruled by the circuit court, merely the expression of an opinion or apprehension upon the part of the city, but a sufficiently certain, though general, statement of the essential ultimate facts upon which the complainant rests its claim for relief. It was not necessary, in such a case, to aver all the minute circumstances which may be proven in support of the general statement or charge in the bill. While the allegations might have been more extended, without departing from correct rules of pleading, they distinctly apprise the defense of the precise case it is required to meet. There are some cases in which the same decisive and categorical certainty is required in a bill in equity as in a declaration at common law. Cooper, Eq. Pl., 5. But in most cases general certainty is sufficient in pleadings in equity. Story, Eq. Pl., secs. 252, 253. Let the case go back for preparation and hearing upon the merits. If it should be again brought here, we may find it necessary to discuss the numerous authorities cited by counsel. In its present condition we do not deem it wise to say more than we have in this opinion.

The decree will be reversed with directions to overrule the demurrer, and for further proceedings according to law; and it is so ordered.

DES MOINES & MINNEAPOLIS RAILROAD COMPANY *v.* ALLEY.

(Circuit Court for Iowa: 3 McCrary, 589–591. 1882.)

Opinion by McCRARY, J.

STATEMENT OF FACTS.— This is a suit brought to set aside a deed executed by the complainant to the respondent, John B. Alley, on the 23d of May, 1879, conveying two thousand three hundred and sixty-two acres of land. The amended bill charges that, at the time of said conveyance, the respondent, John B. Alley, was the owner of the majority of the stock of the corporation, and by reason of that ownership exercised a controlling influence over the officers and directors of the complainant corporation, whereby he induced the board of directors and the president of the corporation to consent to the said conveyance, and to execute a deed good and sufficient in form. It is further alleged that the said respondent, John B. Alley, fraudulently procured and caused said conveyance to be executed. With respect to the consideration paid by the said Alley for said conveyance, there are two allegations in the amended bill as follows: It is first alleged "That, in truth and in fact, the said defendant did not pay anything whatever for said lands; that the books of said company were then under his charge and control; and that he caused to be charged to himself, on account of said lands and said conveyance, the sum of $4,600, and over against said charge on said book he caused to be credited certain fraudulent entries."

§ 1164. *A bill should not aver lack of consideration and inadequacy of consideration at the same time.*

If the allegation stopped here, it would amount to a charge that the conveyance was without any consideration whatever, and would be entirely sufficient. But the bill further avers as follows: "That if, in truth and fact, it shall be made to appear that any portion or all of said $4,600 was in any manner paid by the said Alley, by just and proper credits, then the said sum or price of said lands was, and is, grossly inadequate to its true value; and the said defendant, by reason of his relationship to the said company plaintiff, and such inadequacy of price, is bound to surrender said lands to the plaintiff. That said lands were then worth, as plaintiff is informed and believes, $10,000 and more, and have been since then steadily increasing in value; and defendant well knew that said lands were worth much more than the sum of $4,600, and that they would greatly increase in value from that time forward."

It is necessary that the several allegations of the amended bill should be harmonious and consistent with each other. The amended bill would be sufficient if it distinctly alleged either of three things, to wit: 1. That the conveyance was wholly without consideration; or 2. That it was fraudulent, and there was a consideration, which the complainant has offered to return to the respondent John B. Alley; or 3. That complainant is not informed, and has no means of ascertaining, whether there was a consideration, or what the value of the consideration was, if there was any, and that these facts are peculiarly within the knowledge of the defendant John B. Alley.

If the case is placed upon the latter ground, then the amended bill should pray a discovery of the facts, and should offer to return any consideration actually paid, to the respondent John B. Alley, as soon as the same is ascertained and determined by the court. It will be seen that it is necessary to amend the bill in order to conform to these suggestions.

§ 1165. *In alleging inadequacy of consideration the value should be stated specifically, not doubtfully.*

The allegation concerning the value of the land should also be made specific. It is not sufficient to state that the complainant believes the land to be worth $10,000. In these respects, and to this extent, the demurrer is sustained, and the complainant has leave to amend by the February rules, and will serve a copy of his amendment upon the counsel for respondent.

UNITED STATES v. THE GLOBE WORKS.

(Circuit Court for Massachusetts: 7 Federal Reporter, 590–593. 1881.)

Opinion by LOWELL, J.

STATEMENT OF FACTS.—This is a demurrer to a bill filed by the United States against the Globe Works and John Souther, George Souther, Daniel

N. Pickering and Aristides Talbot. The bill alleges that the Globe Works, formerly called the Globe Locomotive Works, were incorporated by the legislature of Massachusetts in 1854, with a capital stock of not more than $300,000; that June 30, 1868, they were indebted to the United States in $8,725.20, for taxes on certain steam-engines manufactured by them, and in the further sum of $436.26, penalty for non-payment; that in April, 1867, the defendants John Souther and George Souther, being a majority in number and interest of the stockholders of said company, filed a bill in the supreme judicial court of Massachusetts against Daniel N. Pickering, the only other stockholder, and against one Cate, a creditor, asking for a dissolution of the corporation, and for a receiver; that such an order was passed, and the defendant Talbot was appointed such receiver April 22, 1867, with very full powers, which are set out in the bill; that Talbot entered upon his duties, but never filed an account, and never paid the plaintiffs said sums so due them; that in June, 1876, all the parties to that suit made the following agreement, which was filed in and made part of the records of said court:

"John Souther v. The Globe Works and others. It is agreed between all the parties in the above-named case, which has been settled between them, that the receiver shall settle no account therein, and that the bill shall be dismissed without costs, and that the receiver shall deliver up all property, assets and effects in his hands or possession to said John Souther, the same to be held by him as his own property."

That in pursuance of this agreement, all the capital, property and assets of the corporation were delivered up, in fraud of the creditors of the company, by the defendant Talbot, to the defendant John Souther, who has ever since held the same, and the proceeds of the same, as his own property, and has never paid the plaintiffs. That by such surrender the company was made, and has ever since remained, insolvent and unable to pay said sums, and were deprived of all property from which a judgment at law for the same could be satisfied. That they owe the above-mentioned sums to the plaintiffs, with interest.

The prayer is that the defendants John Souther, George Souther, Daniel N. Pickering, and Aristides Talbot may answer the premises, but not on oath; and may be ordered to apply to the payment of said sums and interest, such property and effects belonging to said corporation, and the proceeds of the same, as may be in their possession or control; and, if these are insufficient, may be ordered to pay said sums and interest out of their individual property and effects. The demurrer to this bill must be sustained.

§ 1166. *Allegations necessary to charge shareholder with the debts of a corporation.*

1. There are no allegations or charges by which it is possible to ascertain whether the shareholders of the company, or either of them, are accountable for the assets, or any of them. It appears that in 1876 all the remaining assets were made over to one stockholder, but whether he paid money down for them, or took them for a debt to himself, or for debts of the company which he had paid, or under what other circumstances, I cannot tell. It is settled in this country that the capital is a sort of trust fund for creditors; and if it is taken back by its owners and divided among them before the debts are paid a bill will lie to subject the assets so divided in the hands of the shareholders to an equitable lien for the debts; and if the creditor is one against whom the statute of limitations does not avail no doubt the bill will lie even

at a remote time. Whether such a division has been made of these assets the bill does not inform me.

§ **1167.** *The bill must show how a party defendant is interested in the suit.*

2. There is nothing in the bill to show why Aristides Talbot, the receiver, is made a party. If the assets were bought of him and paid for he might be called to account for the purchase money in the state court; and, under some possible circumstances, might be sued in this court. Whether the facts would bring this case within that rule in either court the bill does not disclose. It is nowhere charged that Talbot was ever notified of the existence of this debt. If not, he is under no personal liability in respect to it.

§ **1167a.** *What is necessary in Massachusetts to charge shareholders in a manufacturing corporation.*

3. No reason is given for subjecting the stockholders personally to the payment of this debt if the assets fail. In a manufacturing corporation, organized under the laws of Massachusetts, the shareholders are liable for debts if the capital has not been fully paid up, or if certain annual notices have not been given; but nothing of the sort is alleged here.

§ **1168.** *Priority of payment to the United States.*

There are no averments which make the case one in which the United States are entitled to priority of payment. That depends upon whether the corporation was insolvent when it was being wound up and the receiver was notified of the debt. As the bill now stands the order must be: demurrer sustained.

ATKINS *v.* DICK.

(14 Peters, 114-121. 1840.)

Opinion by MR. JUSTICE BARBOUR.

STATEMENT OF FACTS.—This is an appeal from a decree of the circuit court of the United States for the southern district of Mississippi.

The appellant was the payee of a bill of exchange drawn by Cain & Lusk, which he indorsed to Parham N. Booker, who indorsed it to N. & J. Dick & Company. The bill having been dishonored, Dick & Company brought suit thereon and recovered a judgment against Atkins, the first indorser. Upon this judgment an execution was issued, a forthcoming bond was taken and forfeited, by reason whereof the bond, according to a statute of Mississippi, had the force of a judgment, on which execution was issued. Atkins thereupon filed his bill in equity, in which he alleged that he had ascertained and verily believed that Dick & Company had been paid the amount of the bill of exchange before the institution of their suit against him, but that he had no knowledge of it at the time of the giving and forfeiture of the forthcoming bond. That he was advised and verily believed that the bill of exchange was paid to Dick & Company by Parham N. Booker before the suit was brought, and that it was paid, because of effects placed in the hands of said Booker by Lusk, one of the drawers of the bill of exchange. That he was advised and believed that he would have had a good defense against Booker on account of said effects received by him from Lusk with which to pay the bill, in case said Booker had sued in his own name thereon. That the names of Dick & Company were used with the intent to defeat him of that defense, in case he became advised that said effects had been placed in the hands of Booker by Lusk, with which to pay and satisfy the bill. The bill charged that in these proceedings the appellant had been most palpably defrauded, and that, in order to consummate the fraud, Dick & Company had caused execution to issue on the judgment created by the forfeited forthcoming bond, which was then in the hands of the marshal; and it prayed an injunction, a perpetuation thereof, and for general relief. An injunction was granted. The defendants demurred to the bill, assigning three causes of demurrer, to wit: 1. That Booker was not made a party. 2. That neither the amount, nor the value, nor the nature of the effects, charged in the bill to have been paid to the second indorser, was specified; and that it was not stated what part or portion was discharged, nor whether any of such effects proved to be productive. 3. That the bill contained no matter or grounds on which the court could grant the relief prayed for. The court sustained the demurrer, and gave the plaintiff leave to amend his bill; and he declining to make any amendment, they dissolved the injunction and dismissed the bill for want of proper parties.

From that decree this appeal was taken. The defendants having demurred to the bill, in the consideration of the case we are to take all its allegations to be true.

§ **1169.** *A bill in equity to enjoin a judgment, which alleges that the debt has been paid before judgment, and charges fraud in attempting to collect it again, will be sustained though the language be not artificial.*

The bill is somewhat inartificially drawn, but it substantially alleges that, before the institution of the suit at law against the plaintiff, the amount of the bill of exchange in question had been paid to Dick & Company, by means of effects furnished by one of the drawers. The particular language of the allegation is that it was paid to them because of effects placed in the hands of Parham N. Booker by Lusk, one of the drawers. Now we understand the import of this to be, that these effects constituted the means by which the payment was effected; whether Booker sold the effects and paid the bill out of the proceeds of the sale, or detained them himself, and in their stead advanced their value in money, is an inquiry of no moment; because, in either aspect of the case, the effect would be that the bill was paid by means furnished by one of the drawers. And upon this state of facts, it is clear that the same operation which satisfied the claim of Dick & Company at the same time extinguished all the rights as well as liabilities growing out of the bill of exchange; because they, being the last indorsers, were the persons entitled to receive the amount of the bill; and the drawers being liable to every other party, and the funds by which the payment was effected being furnished by them, there was no longer any person who could have a claim against any other, founded upon a bill thus paid.

Upon this view of the subject, the question is whether a party who has received payment of his debt shall be permitted by a court of equity to avail himself of a judgment at law to enforce a second payment, and that, too, against a party who did not know of that payment until after the judgment was obtained. To state such a proposition is to answer it.

The bill further charges the defendants with fraud, and this, too, is admitted by the demurrer. If there be any one ground upon which a court of equity affords relief with more unvarying uniformity than on any other, it is an allegation of fraud, whether proven or admitted. Whilst, therefore, a case stands before us upon such a bill and demurrer, we cannot hesitate to say it must be considered as entitling the party to the aid of a court of equity.

§ 1170. *A bill in equity against the holder of a bill to enjoin a judgment obtained thereon, and alleging that the holder had already been paid by the drawer, need not join the latter as a party to the suit.*

It is contended that Booker ought to have been made a party. And the ground taken is (and this is the first cause of demurrer assigned) that every person ought to be made a party who has an interest in the subject of controversy; and it is said that Booker is in that situation. We think that he has no interest in the object of this suit; in other words, that he is not interested in the question between these parties. The ground of equity is that Dick & Company, the plaintiffs in the judgment at law, received payment of the amount recovered by them before they brought their suit. Now, if he were made a party at all, it must be as defendant. But the plaintiff neither sought, nor could he obtain, any decree against him. He only asked a perpetual injunction against Dick & Company, on the ground of an equity attaching upon them personally. If the plaintiff should prevail against them, it would be upon the ground that the amount of the bill had been paid to them by the drawers; supposing that to be the case, then Booker would not be liable to them as indorser. If, on the contrary, the plaintiff should fail, Booker's rights would in nowise be concluded or affected; but if, as indorser, he should be made liable to Dick & Company, then, as indorser, he could recover against the plaintiff Atkins as indorsee to him. But again: Booker's right and liability upon the bill are at law. We cannot, therefore, perceive any ground upon which, in a contest between two parties to a bill, founded upon an allegation of equity attaching personally to one of them, a third party can be brought into a court of equity to mingle in that litigation, when the attitude in which he stands is purely legal. If the equity attached to him, then he ought to be made a party; but as it does not, a court of equity is not the forum in which to discuss or to decide either his right or liability. A very familiar case will illustrate this principle. Suppose an obligee to assign a bond, on which the assignee recovers a judgment, where, by statute, he may sue in his own name; and that the obligor thereupon files his bill in equity, praying for a perpetual injunction, on the ground of some equity attaching upon the obligee before the assignment. In such a case the assignor must be made a party because he is directly interested in discussing the equity alleged to exist against him. But if, on the contrary, the bill were filed upon the ground of some equity not existing against the assignor, but arising between the obligor and assignee after the assignment, then there would be no pretense for saying that the assignor ought to be a party; plainly, because in that particular question he has no interest whatsoever. Whichever way that question may be decided, the relation between the assignor and assignee, and the liability of the former to the latter, growing out of the assignment, are purely questions of law, wholly unaffected by the decision of the case in equity.

§ 1171. —— *an allegation that the bill was fully paid is sufficient without giving all the details.*

The second ground of demurrer is that neither the amount, nor value, nor nature of the effects charged to have been paid, is specified; nor is it stated what portion of the debt was discharged, nor whether any of such effects proved to be productive. This cause of demurrer we consider altogether untenable. The allegation in the bill is that the money mentioned in the bill of exchange was paid to Dick & Company. This allegation covers the whole equity of the case, because it asserts that there was a payment, and that a payment of the money mentioned in the bill; that is, the whole amount of the bill.

§ 1172. *The bill shows ground for relief in equity.*

The third cause of demurrer, that there is no ground laid in the bill for relief, has been already discussed; and we have shown that bill does contain sufficient allegations to entitle the complainant to the aid of a court of equity.

We are of opinion that the circuit court, instead of sustaining the demurrer, ought to have overruled it and ordered the defendants to answer.

The decree is therefore reversed and the cause remanded to the circuit court, to be proceeded in in conformity with this opinion and as to equity and justice shall pertain.

BRIGES v. SPERRY.

(5 Otto, 401–407. 1877.)

APPEAL from U. S. Circuit Court, District of California.

STATEMENT OF FACTS.— Sperry filed a bill in a state court of California, against Briges and others, who, being citizens of France, removed the case into the federal court. Sperry filed in that court an amended bill, in which he stated that he and the defendants were partners in the hotel business at the "Calaveras Big Trees," and tenants in common of two tracts of land upon which stood the mammoth trees, that as a natural curiosity rendered the hotel a popular resort. The bill made sundry charges against the defendants, and prayed the appointment of a receiver, the dissolution of the partnership and a sale of the property. The answer denied the charges of misconduct and resisted the proposed sale of the property because it was not divisible, etc. The decree was according to the prayer of the bill, and defendants appealed.

Opinion by MR. JUSTICE MILLER.

The appellee, Sperry, brought suit in the state court for the county of San Joaquin against the appellants, who duly appeared and caused the suit to be removed into the circuit court of the United States for the district of California. In that court Sperry filed an amended or new complaint.

§ 1173. *The jurisdiction of the circuit court of a case removed from a state court is not lost for want of an averment of citizenship.*

One of the errors alleged as grounds for reversing the decree in favor of Sperry is that this amended bill shows no jurisdiction in the circuit court. If nothing else be looked at but the bill there is no jurisdiction shown. But the proceedings in the state court, which are properly here as part of the record of the case, show that it was removed from the state court to the federal court on account of the citizenship of the parties; and this of itself must have given jurisdiction to the United States court before the amended bill was filed. That jurisdiction is not lost because the facts on which it arose are not set out in the old or the new complaint. Railway Company v. Ramsey, 22 Wall., 322.

§ 1174. *A bill for the dissolution of a partnership may, after decree, be treated as a bill for partition of property, and the decree sustained on that ground, if the bill contain sufficient allegations.*

The appellants treat the bill as one for a dissolution of a partnership, a settlement of the partnership affairs, a sale of the partnership property, and a distribution of its proceeds. They therefore insist that the decree of the court ordering a sale of real estate of the estimated value of $40,000, which the parties held as tenants in common, and which they insist was not partnership property, was erroneous, and should be reversed. On the other side it is said that the real estate was partnership property, and by the rules of chancery practice ought to be sold on a decree for the dissolution of the partnership, and the proceeds divided as in case of personalty; and it is argued further that, if they are mistaken in this view of the matter, the complaint may be treated as a bill for partition; and that as a partition *in specie* could not be made without loss or injury to the value of the property it was rightfully decreed to be sold and the money divided.

As we are clearly of opinion that the decree of the circuit court can be sustained on this latter view, we need not inquire whether, under all circumstances, the real estate was subject to the rules which in equity govern that kind of property when it is bought and used for partnership purposes.

Supposing a bill to wind up a partnership, and a bill to partition real estate to be so distinct in character that a court must hold it to be one or the other, we think the complaint before us has all the necessary elements of the latter, and is as much entitled to be called a suit for partition as for the dissolution and winding up of a partnership.

It begins by describing the real estate, and declaring that plaintiff and defendants are now, and have been, tenants in common of the land since the month of July, 1874. It then alleges the plaintiff to be the owner of an undivided half, the defendant, the Marquis de Briges, of three-eights, and the Marquise de Briges, the other defendant, who, it seems, is his mother of one-eighth. It shows that the land consists of two separate parcels, which, by the congressional subdivisions, of which they consist, must be five or six miles apart, and that one of them is a large tract used as a summer resort for visitors, and that the whole property is of the value of about $40,000. It is also alleged that by reason of the connection of the hotel with the lands,— the latter constituting the Big Tree Groves of Calaveras,— a partition cannot be had without seriously impairing the value of the property. Amongst other relief prayed for is a sale of this property, and a distribution of the proceeds amongst the owners. Here seems to be everything requisite for a suit in partition.

There is, however, in addition to this, an allegation that the parties had been engaged in keeping this hotel in partnership, and that a difference had arisen by the fault of the defendants, which made a dissolution of that partnership necessary, and this dissolution is prayed for, and a settlement of the accounts; and another prayer of the bill is for a sale of the partnership property and proper distribution. The bill is inartificially drawn as a bill in chancery, but is after the model of the code of procedure of California, which justifies such a complaint in the courts of that state. The stating part of it is accordingly divided into seven paragraphs, and they are so numbered. If we are at liberty to disregard the fifth and sixth paragraphs, which alone set out the partnership and the grounds of dissolution, we have no difficulty in finding a bill for partition, with prayer for a sale as a mode of partition, because it would be an injury to the interest of the owners to divide it up.

§ 1175. *An objection to a bill for multifariousness should be taken by demurrer, and is not open on appeal.*

As there was no demurrer to the bill, as the answer sets up no objection to the jurisdiction, but denies that there is anything in the condition of the land to forbid actual partition, we see no reason why the bill may not be treated as sufficient for a partition suit.   If there is anything in the allegations which concern the partnership, which introduces another matter, the objection should have been taken by demurrer for multifariousness.   It is not fatal to the bill on appeal.

[The remainder of the opinion, being merely a discussion of the evidence, is omitted.]

Affirmed.

GAMEWELL FIRE-ALARM TEL. CO. v. CITY OF CHILLICOTHE.

(Circuit Court for Ohio: 7 Federal Reporter, 851–855. . 1881.)

§ 1176. *Multifariousness defined and explained.*

Opinion by SWING, J.

The rule of pleading as to multifariousness is founded on convenience — convenience to the defendant.   McLean, Assignee, v. Bank of Lafayette, 4 McLean, 418; Fellows v. Fellows, 4 Cow., 682.

This rule forbids the joining of distinct and independent matters in one bill, and thereby confounding them; as, for example, the uniting in one bill of several matters perfectly distinct and unconnected against one defendant, or the demand of several matters of different natures against several defendants in the same bill.   Story's Eq. Pl., 271; Mitford's Eq. Pl., 181.

Whether this rule applies to any particular bill or not is a question of fact — of fact, as to the nature and extent of interest of the complainant, or some of the complainants, in the causes of action; or of the defendant, or some of the defendants, as to the nature of the causes of action, whether they are distinct in character as well as independent in form, as to the scope of the relief prayed.   Story's Eq. Pl., 280, 538, 540.   To lay down any rule applicable to all cases cannot well be done.   Id., 539.

The cases upon the subject are various, and the courts, in deciding them, seem to have considered what was convenient under particular circumstances, rather than to have laid down any absolute rule.   Campbell v. Mackay, 1 Mylne & C., 603.   But it may be drawn from the cases, and is in accordance with the reason of the rule, that the test of multifariousness is: What is the burden imposed on the defendant? to what defense is he forced? can he make one defense to the whole bill?   Attorney-General v. St. John's College, 7 Sim., 241; Story's Eq. Pl., 530, 540; Daniell's Ch. Pr., 834–346, notes 1 and 2.   The facts in this case present no complication.

§ 1177. *A bill is not multifarious which is based on several letters patent, when all the inventions are set out as constituting one machine, the use of which makes the cause of action.*

The bill shows that re-issues Nos. 8,891 and 8,896 are for improvements in fire alarms, and that the complainant has the right, under re-issue 4,588, of constructing apparatus for fire alarms and the transmission of municipal intelligence, and alleges that the defendant uses each of these inventions in one machine — uses them all in the same machine.   It is plain that the use of all these inventions together, to cohstitute a machine, is the cause of action set out in the bill; the construction of a fire alarm, such as defendant now uses, being the injury complained of and against which an injunction is prayed. Discovery is asked, not of how many machines containing separately the inventions in the several patents mentioned, but how many machines containing all of these inventions used together to construct the machine, have been made.

A single defense — we do not make such a machine — meets the whole bill in its allegations and prayer founded on the allegations. The mere setting out of more than one letters patent in a bill does not of itself render the bill multifarious. Case v. Redfield, 4 McLean, 526; Nourse v. Allen, 4 Blatch., 876.

And it may be said generally that a demurrer for multifariousness will not lie to a bill founded on several letters patent, where all the inventions are set out as constituting one cause of action, and the prayer relates singly, as to discovery and remedy, to a machine constructed according to and containing all said inventions.

§ 1178. *How to escape multifariousness in praying discovery as to infringement of several letters patent.*

Where the discovery is prayed for under special interrogatories as to each letter patent in a manner so particular as to each invention that it is evident on the face of the bill that the relief sought is for infringement of each and every invention, and not for an injury arising from the making and using one machine constructed according to such letters patent, the bill is demurrable. To escape the objection of multifariousness such a bill should aver that said inventions are capable of conjoint as well as separate use, and are in fact so used by defendant. Nellis v. Lanahan, 6 Fisher, 286. In the bill under consideration the letters patent are properly joined, and, in fact, constitute one and the same cause of action.

The demurrer is therefore overruled.

BAXTER, J., concurred.

SHELDON v. KEOKUK NORTHERN LINE PACKET COMPANY.

(Circuit Court for Wisconsin: 8 Federal Reporter, 763–777. 1881.)

Opinion by HARLAN, J.

STATEMENT OF FACTS.— The defendants demur upon these grounds: "*First*, that the bill is multifarious, in that it seeks to enforce independent judgments in which the complainants have no joint interest, and also because it unites with the cause of action against the Keokuk Northern Line Packet Company, in which the defendant Davidson has no interest, a cause of action against Davidson in which his co-defendant has no interest; *second*, that if complainants ever had any cause of action against the defendants or either of them, the delay which occurred without suit was so unreasonable as to deprive them of any right to relief in equity; *third*, that the suit is barred by the statute of limitations of Wisconsin."

The objection of multifariousness will be first considered. Passing by many details of the transactions set out in the bill, it is sufficient now to say that the suit proceeds upon these general grounds:

" That the complainants are judgment creditors (with returns of no property found) of the Northwestern Union Packet Company, an insolvent corporation, organized for the purpose of engaging in the business of transporting persons and property; that the property of the common debtor was all withdrawn from their reach through transfer thereof made to the defendants, the Keokuk Northern Line Packet Company and Peyton S. Davidson, in pursuance of a plan or scheme to which they and the debtor were parties, though in different degrees, and, in some respects, by different acts; and that such plan or scheme was devised or carried out, by the parties thereto, with the intent to hinder, delay and defraud the complainants and other creditors of the Northern Union Packet Company."

The relief sought is a decree adjudging such transfer to have been fraudulent and void as to the complainants, and other then existing creditors of the Northern Union Packet Company, and subjecting, so far as it may be necessary to the demands of complainants and other creditors who may come into this suit, such of the property, so transferred, as may still be in the possession of defendants; and also requiring the Keokuk Northern Line Packet Company to account for the earnings received from that portion transferred, or which has been lost, destroyed or used up since the transfers were made.

§ 1179. *Principles upon which the question rests whether a bill is multifarious or not.*

It has been held by the supreme court of the United States to be impracticable to lay down any fixed, unbending rule as to what constitutes multifariousness or misjoinder of causes of action. Oliver *v.* Piatt, 3 How., 411; Gaines *v.* Chew, 2 How., 619; Barney *v.* Latham, October term, 1880–1. The court must necessarily exercise a large, though of course a sound, discretion in allowing the union in the same suit of matters which do not alike or equally affect all the parties. Each case' must depend upon its special circumstances, and the necessities which may arise out of the due administration of justice in that case. As a general rule, the court will not compel parties to incur the expense, vexation and delay of several suits, where the transactions constituting the subject of the litigation, or out of which the litigation arises, are so connected by their circumstances as to render it proper and convenient that they should be examined in the same suit, and full relief given by one comprehensive decree. A different rule would often prove to be both oppressive and mischievous, and could result in no possible benefit to any litigant, whose object was not simply to harass his adversary, but to ascertain what were his just legal rights. As to the general propositions there can be no doubt under the authorities.

§ 1180. *Bill in which separate judgment creditors join in attacking one transaction of their common debtor is not multifarious. Authorities reviewed.*

Is the bill objectionable because two separate judgment creditors unite in assailing transactions which have resulted, according to the allegation made, in sweeping away all tangible property of their common debtor from their reach? I think not. Nothing is more common than for several judgment creditors, having exhausted their legal remedies, and having equal right to resort to the property of the same debtor for the satisfaction of their claims, to unite in assailing a fraudulent conveyance or transfer of the debtor's property. "For they all have a common interest in the suit; and, if they succeed, the decree will be equally beneficial to all in proportion to their respective interests." Story, Eq. Pl. (9th ed. by Gould), §§ 537a, 533, 286; Brinkerhoff *v.* Brown, 6 Johns. Ch., 139; Hamlin *v.* Wright, 23 Wis., 494. It is equally clear, I think, that the bill is not multifarious, and that there is no misjoinder of causes of action, because Davidson and the Keokuk Northern Line Packet Company are united as defendants.

Taking (as we must upon demurrer) all the material allegations of the bill to be true, it appears that the transfers complained of were all made in execution of a plan or scheme to strip the Northern Union Packet Company of all its tangible property, so that its creditors, some of whom were then pressing their claims by suit, could not reach any of it by the ordinary process of law. Those two defendants are, in effect, charged to have been confederates with the managers of the Northern Union Packet Company in carrying out the fraud to the injury of the creditors of the insolvent corporation. They conspired (one, perhaps, by more distinct and numerous acts than the other) with the corporation to hinder, delay and defraud its creditors. They are charged with being in the possession of the fruits of a fraudulent scheme of which they were cognizant, and in the execution of which, it is alleged, they were active participants. They are, consequently, upon the theory of the suit, interested in defeating the complainants upon the issue, sharply defined, that the property demanded by complainants was disposed of to the defendants in pursuance of a fraudulent scheme, in the execution of which they give their aid. The relations which, according to the bill, the defendant Davidson held to all the property transferred, as well as to the various corporations which at different times controlled its use, being of such a character as to preclude the possibility (the allegations of the bill being sustained) of upholding the conveyance to him, the transfers to the Keokuk Northern Line Packet Company are adjudged to have been fraudulent and void. It cannot be that the established rules of equity practice would, under these circumstances, compel complainants to institute separate suits against the present defendants.

A leading authority upon this point of the case is Brinkerhoff v. Brown, 6 Johns. Ch., 139. That suit was by several complainants holding distinct judgments against an insolvent corporation. There were several defendants, all of whom were sought to be held liable, in different proportions and in different characters, upon the general ground that the property of the corporation had been withdrawn from the reach of complainants by the fraudulent acts of the several defendants. After analyzing the bill Chancellor Kent said:

"It thus appears from the bill that all the defendants were not jointly concerned in every injurious act charged. There was a series of acts on the part of the persons concerned in the company, all produced by the same fraudulent intent, and terminating in the deception and injury of the plaintiffs. The defendants performed different parts in the same drama, but it was still one piece, the entire performance marked by different scenes; and the question now occurs whether the several matters charged are so distinct and unconnected as to render the joining of them in one bill a ground of demurrer."

After reviewing the authorities he remarks: "That the principle to be deduced from them is that a bill against several persons must relate to matters of the same nature, and having a connection with each other, and in which all the defendants are more or less concerned, though their rights in respect to the general subject of the case may be distinct."

Again he remarked: "When we consider that the plaintiffs are judgment creditors, having claims against the Genesee Company perfectly established, and not the subject of litigation in this suit, and that the general right claimed by the bill is a due application of the capital of that company to the payment of their judgment; that the subject of the bill and of the relief, and the only matter in litigation, is the fraud charged in the creation, management and disposition of the capital, and in which charge all the defendants are implicated, though in different degrees and proportions,—I think we may safely conclude that this case falls within the reach of the principle, and that the demurrer cannot be sustained."

The case is cited with approval in Story, Eq. Pl., section 286, note, where it is said that "The same principle has been supposed properly to justify the joining of several judgment creditors in one bill against their common debtor, and his grantees, to remove impediments to their remedy created by the fraud of their debtor in conveying his property to several grantees, although they take by separate conveyances, and no joint fraud in any one transaction is charged against them all."

To the same effect speaks the supreme court of Wisconsin in Hamlin *v.* Wright, 23 Wis., 494, where it is said that "the fact that all the grantees have become accessory to the fraudulent attempt of the debtor to place his property beyond his creditor's reach gives them such a common connection with the subject-matter of the suit that they may be joined, although the purchase of each was distinct from the others and each is charged with participating in the fraud in respect to his own purchase. . . . There was, therefore, no misjoinder of causes of action in uniting the different fraudulent defendants, although they purchased at different times and each is charged only with fraud in his own purchase." See, also; Story, Eq. Pl. (9th ed.), §§ 271–280, 530–540; Adams, Eq. (6th Am. ed. by Sharswood), 617, note 2; Blake *v.* Van Tilborg, 21 Wis., 680; Bassett *v.* Warner, 23 Wis., 673.

§ 1181. *Doctrine of laches under a statute of limitations.*

As to the second point raised by the demurrer, that complainants, independent of any statute of limitations, have lost their right to relief by delay in suing, I do not think it well taken. The authorities cited under this head by counsel for defendants apply to suits not strictly within any statute of limitations. The legislature here has declared that actions for relief on the ground of fraud, in cases heretofore solely cognizable by the court of chancery, "may be commenced within six years after the discovery of the facts constituting the fraud." Administering the law in this suit, I do not think relief should be denied even if it appeared that the complainants might have applied for relief at an earlier date, when the frauds complained of were first discovered. The court should not assume or infer unreasonable delay, after such discovery, from the isolated fact that the fraud charged was committed several years before the commencement of the suit. It is consistent with the bill that the fraud, and the facts constituting the fraud, were not discovered until some time after they were committed. If the doctrine of laches or lapse of time can ever be asked in a suit as to which there is a statute of limitations prescribing the period within which such suit may be commenced, a demurrer, insisting upon lapse of time short of the statutory period, should not be sustained, unless the bill upon its face, without resorting to inferences, makes a clear case of unreasonable delay upon the part of the complainants after the discovery of the fraud charged.

§ 1182. *Application of the Wisconsin statute of limitations.*

This brings me to the question of the statute of limitations. In considering this question I have carefully examined the several revisions of the statute of Wisconsin, as well as those of New York, to which counsel refers. I have also read the decisions of the New York court to which complainants refer. My best judgment — and perhaps as much may be inferred from what I have already said upon the question of laches and lapse of time — is that the ten-year limitation has no application to this case, for the reason that suits are "provided for" in the previous section, prescribing a limitation of six years where relief is sought on the ground of fraud in a case therefor "solely cognizable by the court of chancery." The contrary view is maintained by counsel upon the authority mainly of Corning v. Stebbins, 1 Barb. Ch., 589; Lawrence v. Trustees, 2 Denio, 577, and Spoor v. Wells, 3 Barb. Ch., 199. The first of those cases was a suit by a receiver appointed upon a creditor's bill after the return of an execution unsatisfied. The object of the suit was to reach the equitable interests and things in action of the defendant. The chancellor said: "And I know of no limitation of that right short of the ten years which the statute has fixed, within which suits purely of equitable cognizance must be brought in this court." When (1846) that case was decided the limitation prescribed by the statutes of New York and Wisconsin were, as to suits in equity, the same. It was true, in 1846, of the Wisconsin statutes, that there was no provision expressly fixing a period for the commencement of suits " purely of equitable cognizance," and therefore such cases were then held in the New York courts to be embraced by the ten-year limitation, which was the period prescribed for "all other cases not (1) herein provided for." But the ten-year limitation did not, after the Wisconsin revision of 1858, apply to suits "purely of equitable cognizance," because such suits wherever relief is sought on the ground of fraud, were provided for in a previous section, subjecting them to the six-year limitation. The Wisconsin revision of 1849 provided that the limitation applicable in suits at law should govern in cases of which equity courts had concurrent jurisdiction with the courts of law, and should not apply in suits of which a court of equity had "peculiar and exclusive jurisdiction;" also that "bills for relief on the ground of fraud shall be filed within six years after the discovery, by the aggrieved party, of the facts constituting such fraud, and not after that time." The revision of 1858, as it seems to me, either for the purpose of providing a uniform limitation in all actions "for relief on the ground of fraud," or to reduce the limitations in suits purely of equitable cognizance, expressly declares that the six-year limitation shall apply to actions for relief on the ground of fraud " in cases which were heretofore solely cognizable by the court of chancery" — the cause of action to be deemed as accruing upon the discovery of the fraud. In respect to such suits there is, it seems to me, a manifest difference between the revision of 1858 and the law previous to that date. What I have said about the case of Corning v. Stebbins seems to be applicable to cases in 2 Denio and 3 Barb. Ch., *supra.*

§ 1183. *The statute of limitations may be set up by demurrer.*

Assuming, then, that the present suit must have been commenced within six years after the discovery of the facts constituting the fraud charged, the important inquiry is whether it appears, from the face of the bill, to be barren. Many courts have held that such a defense could not be made by demurrer. But the doctrine is now settled otherwise. Story, Eq. Pl. (9th ed. by Gould), § 484, note 1, and § 503. That this objection may be made by demurrer is the doctrine of the Wisconsin supreme court, notwithstanding its statutes (1858) declare that "the objection that the action was not commenced within the time limited can only be taken by answer." Howell v. Howell, 15 Wis., 59; Hyde v. Supervisors, 43 Wis., 135.

The present action was commenced June 3, 1879, and counsel for defendant contends that the cause of action must be deemed to have accrued April 1, 1873, "on or about" which time, the bill states, not only the amount agreed to be contributed by the Northwestern Union Company to the Keokuk Northern Line Packet Company was delivered into the custody of the latter corporation, but the pretended sale of real estate to Davidson occurred. But the bill also shows that the agreement with the packet company contemplated an appraisement of the property to be transferred to it, and that it should be paid for in the stock of the new company upon the basis of such appraisement. The bill further shows that the appraisement did not, in fact, take place until July, 1873; that the several bills of sale, from the Northwestern Union Packet Company to the Keokuk Northern Packet Line Company, were executed on divers days between March 31 and October 31, 1873. How many of such bills of sale were executed before, and how many after, June 3, 1873, is not stated. The bill also shows that the stock was not delivered to the vendor corporation until some time in the year 1874. It is also alleged that the conveyance of real estate to the defendant P. S. Davidson was not executed until August 19, 1873. Certainly, the transaction by which defendant Davidson secured the title to the real estate in La Crosse was not consummated until that conveyance was made. And it does not distinctly appear that the sales to the Keokuk Northern Packet Line Company became irrevocable or were consummated prior to June 3, 1873. An instructive case upon this point is Muir v. The Trustees, etc., 3 Barb. Ch., 481, where Chancellor Walworth said: "It may be proper to say, however, that although it is alleged in the bill that the executors of Leake obtained possession of his property, etc., in or about the year 1830, it does not distinctly appear that it was more than ten years before the filing of the complainant's bill. And to enable a defendant to take advantage of the statute of limitations upon demurrer, it must distinctly appear, by the bill itself, that the complainant's remedy is barred by the lapse of time."

§ 1184. *It will not be assumed on demurrer that the fraud was discovered more than six years previous to the commencement of the suit, because the bill does not allege that it was not.*

Aside, however, from this view, I am of opinion that it does not, in the sense of the authorities, appear upon the face of the bill that the suit is barred by the limitation of six years, unless it be true (which cannot be conceded) that the failure of complainants to allege that the frauds complained of were discovered within six years before suit is as false to their suit as if they had admitted, on the face of the bill, in terms, that the frauds were discovered more than six years before the commencement of the suit. This position rests, I suppose, upon the general statement in some of the books that demurrer will lie where the bill shows, upon its face, that the suit is barred. The cases cited in the books, in support of the general rule, show that defendants' counsel misinterpreted the rule. For instance, in Hoare v. Peck, 6 Sim., 51, it appeared on the face of the bill not only when the fraud occurred, but when it was discovered by complainants. So in Hovenden v. Lord Annesley, 2 Scho. & Lef., 636, it appeared, upon the face of the bill, that the fraud was discovered nearly sixty years before suit. So in Foster v. Hodgson, 19 Ves., 182, it appeared on the bill that the fraud charged had occurred twelve years after the complainant might have discovered it, with very slight diligence.

Since the statute declares that the cause of action shall not be deemed to have accrued until the discovery of the facts constituting the fraud charged, and since the utmost which defendants can claim is that the bill shows the fraud to have been committed more than six years before the commencement of the suit, it cannot be said to be apparent from the bill that six years passed after the fraud was discovered — that is, after the right of action accrued —

before suit. A demurrer, therefore, does not meet the objection here urged. And such is the construction of a somewhat similar statutory provision by the courts of New York. In Radcliff v. Rowley, 2 Barb. Ch., 31–2, the court gave a construction to the provision which declares that "bills for relief, on the ground of fraud, shall be filed within six years after the discovery, by the aggrieved party, of the facts constituting such fraud, and not after that time." Chancellor Walworth said:

"But it does not appear on the face of the bill when W. Radcliff discovered the alleged fraud, or that he ever did discover the fact, now stated by his heirs — that the judgment had been paid by Rowley, as the agent of the judgment debtor, with funds in his hands belonging to the latter, before the sheriff's sale. . . . And I think, upon a proper construction of the statute, it is not necessary that the complainant should allege in his bill that he has discovered the fraud complained of within six years. A demurrer, therefore, will not lie to a bill for relief on the ground of fraud, although it appears that the fraud occurred more than six years before the commencement of the suit, unless it also appears positively, or by necessary intendment, that the fraud was discovered by the party aggrieved more than six years before he filed his bill for relief. Where that does not appear the defendant must be left to make his defense by plea or answer, so as to prevent an affirmative issue upon the question of the discovery of the fraud." The position thus taken by the New York court I regard as sound.

What has been said necessarily leads to the conclusion that the court will not, in support of a demurrer setting up the statute of limitations, infer from the fact that the alleged fraud occurred more than six years prior to the commencement of the suit, that the complainants discovered the facts constituting the frauds before that period of six years.

For the reasons given an order will be entered overruling the demurrer, and giving the defendants thirty days within which to plead or answer.

STAFFORD NATIONAL BANK v. SPRAGUE.

(Circuit Court for Connecticut: 19 Blatchford, 529–533. 1881.)

Opinion by SHIPMAN, J.

STATEMENT OF FACTS.— This is a demurrer to the plaintiff's bill upon the ground of multifariousness. The plaintiff originally brought its petition in equity to the state court, alleging, in substance, that it was a judgment creditor of Amasa Sprague and William Sprague, and that to secure its unsatisfied judgment it had duly, on June 10, 1880, filed its judgment lien upon a large amount of real estate in this state, described in the petition, and situate in the towns of Sterling, Canterbury, Scotland, Windham and Franklin, alleged to belong to the said Spragues or one of them, which land had been attached in the suit upon which said judgment was obtained; that in September, 1873, Zachariah Chaffee caused to be recorded in the land records of the towns of Windham, Sterling and Scotland, a trust deed, dated November 1, 1873, by which deed said Amasa and William Sprague pretended to convey to said Chaffee all the lands described in said certificate of lien; and that said deed is fraudulent and void as to the plaintiff for sundry alleged reasons, one being that at the time of its execution and delivery the grantors were hopelessly insolvent, and executed and delivered the deed without consideration, for the purpose of placing the property beyond the reach of their creditors, and to delay and hinder them in the collection of their claims. It is further alleged that said deed provided that after the payment of certain extension notes, to be accepted by the Sprague creditors in discharge of their original claims, the residue of the property should be returned to the grantors; that the plaintiff was not a party to the deed and never assented thereto; and that on April 6, 1874, new assignments were made to said Chaffee by A. & W. Sprague, as a firm and individually, of said property covered by said certificate of lien, which assignments were also fraudulent and void as to the plaintiff, for divers alleged reasons, one of which was that the object of said assignments was to postpone and delay the creditors of the said Spragues. The petition further alleged that Amasa Sprague, William Sprague and said Chaffee are in possession of said real estate, and prayed for a foreclosure of said judgment lien; for possession of said premises; that the trust deed and assignments be declared to be void and of no effect; that the title of Chaffee may be postponed to that of the plaintiff, and for damages. The joinder of causes of action at law and in equity is permitted by the recent practice act of this state. The action was removed to this court, and the defendants demurred upon the ground that the complaint joins in one proceeding a cause of action at law for damages and a cause of action in equity, and that said complaint contains distinct matters, in which the defendants are not both interested, viz., the foreclosure of a judgment lien and the setting aside a trust deed to Chaffee.

§ **1185.** *An amendment of a petition permitted in order to make it conform to the equity rules of United States courts.*

As to the first cause of demurrer the plaintiff admits that, by the equity rules and practice of the United States courts, legal and equitable grounds of relief cannot be joined in a bill in equity, and moves for leave to amend by erasing the prayer for damages, which motion is granted, without costs.

§ **1186.** *Multifariousness. A bill not necessarily multifarious which is brought to foreclose a judgment lien on certain land, and also to set aside a prior deed of the same land.*

The second cause of demurrer presents the question which is in dispute. Judge Story (Eq. Pl., sec. 271) defines multifariousness to be "the improperly joining in one bill distinct and independent matters, and thereby confounding them; as, for example, the uniting in one bill of several matters perfectly distinct and unconnected, against one defendant, or the demand of several matters of a distinct and independent nature against several defendants, in the same bill." It is said by the defendants that, in this bill, there are two subjects, which are distinct and independent — 1st, the foreclosure of a judgment lien upon the interest of the Spragues in the land; and 2d, the setting aside of a prior deed to Chaffee.

While this twofold prayer may come within the letter of the definition of multifariousness, I do not think that it comes within the evil which the rule was intended to prevent, viz., the uniting in one suit questions which it was impracticable to deal with at the same time, by reason of their independent character, or which could not be so dealt with without burdening the parties with expense and inconvenience. In fact, because the circumstances of each case differ, there is no arbitrary and inflexible rule as to what constitutes fatal multifariousness, and courts of equity are wont to permit joinder of questions which are to a certain extent distinct, when it can be done without inconvenience. Story's Eq. Pl., sec. 539; Gaines *v.* Chew, 2 How., 619; Hoggart *v.* Cutts, 1 Craig & Phill., 204. "And in new cases it is to be presumed that the court will be governed by those analogies which seem best founded in general convenience, and will best promote the due administration of justice, without multiplying unnecessary litigation on one hand, or drawing suitors into needless and oppressive expenses on the other."

An examination of the allegations of this bill will, I think, satisfy the mind that the joinder of these two matters would prevent needless multiplicity of suits, and would not be inconvenient to any of the defendants. In 1873 the Messrs. Sprague became insolvent, and executed a deed of trust of their lands in Connecticut to Mr. Chaffee, upon certain trusts. The plaintiff says that this deed and the subsequent assignments are fraudulent and void as to those creditors who did not assent to their provisions, and that it, being a non-assenting creditor, attached these lands, or a part of them, obtained judgment, and filed its certificate of lien. The object of the plaintiff is to perfect its title to the lands by a decree of foreclosure, and by a removal of a cloud upon the title which was created by a void deed of the judgment debtor. In some cases the cloud has been so placed, perhaps by third persons, or has so arisen, as in Banks v. Walker, 2 Sandf. Ch., 344, as to make the examination of both questions in one suit impracticable, or very inconvenient to the parties and to the court. In this case there is no difficulty in investigating the two questions at the same time. The cloud was placed by the Messrs. Sprague, both they and Chaffee have either a title or an interest in the lands, and both are in possession. All the defendants are desirous to defend the validity of the trust deed, and to protect the property from the attack of non-assenting creditors. It is a question in which they are all interested.

Again, the practical and substantial question in this case is in regard to the validity of the trust deeds. Apart from that question the foreclosure would be a mere formal proceeding. The bill for foreclosure is a means by which the plaintiffs place themselves in proper position to attack the deed. It would be an unnecessary delay to compel the plaintiff to obtain a decree of foreclosure and then to commence the suit which is to determine the only seriously mooted question in the litigation. The law's necessary delay frequently causes inconvenience and injuries to suitors. Courts should be careful not to create delay and multiply expenses by unnecessary technicalities. If the questions are severed, the severance will unnecessarily postpone the adjudication of the substantial and vital question in dispute, while the union of the questions will subject the defendants to no inconvenience and to no additional expense.

The second cause of demurrer is overruled.

HAYES v. DAYTON.

(Circuit Court for New York: 18 Blatchford, 420–426. 1880.)

Opinion by BLATCHFORD, J.

STATEMENT OF FACTS.— The bill in this case states that the plaintiff invented certain "improvements in ventilators, skylights, skylight turrets, conservatories and other glazed structures and ventilating louvres," described in "several letters patent and re-issues thereof." It then avers that he obtained six several patents, Nos. 94,203 and 100,143, and 106,157, and 112,594, and 143,149, and 143,153; that he obtained re-issues of all of them, the re-issues being six in number, one of each (though it does not appear of which original any particular re-issue is the re-issue), the re-issues being numbered 8,597 and 8,674, and

8,675, and 8,676, and 8,688, and 8,689; and that, since the re-issues, the defendant has, without authority, infringed said several re-issues, and made, used and sold said inventions. The bill interrogates the defendant as to whether he has made and sold "ventilators, skylights, skylight turrets, conservatories and other glazed structures and ventilating louvres, and embraced within any or either" of the said "several letters patent and re-issued letters patent;" also, in four several questions, as to whether he has made, sold or used what is claimed in each one of four claims in re-issue No. 8,597, quoting it; and the like as to each one of fifteen claims, in re-issue No. 8,674, and of seven claims in re-issue No. 8,675, and of two claims in re-issue No. 8,676, and of seven claims in re-issue No. 8,688, and of three claims in re-issue No. 8,689, there being thirty-eight several claims thus inquired about. The bill prays for a recovery of the profits and damages from the said unlawful making, using and selling, by the defendants, of the said "improvements in ventilators, skylights, skylight turrets, conservatories and other glazed structures and ventilating louvres."

The defendant demurs to the whole bill, and in the demurrer shows, for cause of demurrer, "that it appears by the said bill that it is exhibited against this defendant for several and distinct matters and causes, in many whereof, as appears by said bill, the defendant is not in any manner interested or concerned, and which said several matters and causes are distinct and separate one from the other, and are not alleged in said bill to be conjointly infringed by said defendant. . . . By reason of the distinct matters therein contained, the complainant's bill is drawn out to considerable length, and the defendant is compelled to take a copy of the whole thereof, and, by joining distinct matters together, which do not depend on each other, in the said bill, the pleadings, orders and proceedings will, in the progress of the said suit, be intricate and prolix, and the defendant be put to unnecessary charges in taking copies of the same." The defendant, "not waiving his said demurrer, but relying thereon," has put in, simultaneously, an answer to the whole bill.

§ 1187. *Form of demurrer for misjoinder of causes of action.*

This demurrer does not use the word "multifarious." A bill is multifarious when it improperly unites in one bill, against one defendant, several matters perfectly distinct and unconnected, or when it demands several matters of a distinct and independent nature against several defendants in the same bill. The reason of the first case is that the defendant would be compelled to unite, in his answer and defense, different matters, wholly unconnected with each other, and thus the proofs applicable to each would be apt to be confounded with each other, and delays would be occasioned by waiting for the proofs respecting one of the matters, when the others might be fully ripe for hearing. The reason of the second case is, that each defendant would have an unnecessary burden of costs by the statement in the pleadings of the several claims of the other defendants, with which he has no connection. Story's Eq. Pl., § 271. The demurrer in this case is intended to be a demurrer for misjoining causes of suit against one defendant. Yet much of it is inapplicable to such a case, and is taken from a form which applies only to the case of a demurrer by one of two or more defendants who has no concern with causes of action stated against the other defendants, such a demurrer being really a demurrer for a misjoinder of parties. Story's Eq. Pl., § 530, and note 3, where is to be found the form improperly used in this case. Yet there seems to be enough left, after rejecting as surplusage the improper and unnecessary part, to raise the point intended. The demurrer, in regard to misjoining causes of suit against the defendant, substantially avers that the bill is brought for several matters and causes which are separate and distinct one from the other, and are not alleged to be conjointly infringed by the defendant. This means that the patents sued on are distinct one from the other, and that they are not alleged to be conjointly infringed in any one article which the defendant has made or used or sold. This averment of the demurrer is true.

§ 1188. *A bill in equity for infringement, brought against a defendant on several patents, distinct, and not alleged to be conjointly infringed, is demurrable. Authorities reviewed.*

Where there is a joinder of distinct claims between the same parties, it has never been held, as a general proposition, that they cannot be united, and that the bill is, of course, demurrable for that cause alone. Nor is there any positive, inflexible rule as to what, in the sense of courts of equity, constitutes a fatal multifariousness on demurrer. A sound discretion is always exercised in determining whether the subject-matters of the suit are properly joined or not. It is not very easy, *a priori*, to say exactly what is or what ought to be the true line regulating the course of pleading on this point. All that can be done in each particular case as it arises is to consider whether it comes nearer to the class of decisions where the objection is held to be fatal, or to the other class where it is held not to be fatal. In new cases the court is governed by those analogies which seem best founded in general convenience, and will best promote the due administration of justice, without multiplying unnecessary litigation on the one hand, or drawing suitors into needless and oppressive expenses on the other. Story's Eq. Pl., §§ 531, 539; Horman Patent Mfg. Co. *v.* Brooklyn City R. R. Co., 15 Blatch., 444.

We are not without cases on this subject, in suits on patents in this country. In Nourse *v.* Allen, 4 Blatch., 376, in 1859, before Mr. Justice Nelson, a bill on four patents was held good on demurrer, where it alleged that the machine used contained all the improvements in all the patents. The court thought that the convenience of both parties as well as a saving of expense in the litigation seemed to be consulted in embracing all the patents in one suit in such a case; and that, although the defenses as respected the several improvements might be different and unconnected, yet the patents were connected with each other in each infringing machine.

In Nellis *v.* McLanahan, 6 Fish. Pat. Cas., 286, in 1873, before Judge McKennan, it was held that where a suit in equity is brought for the infringement of several patents for different improvements, not necessarily embodied in the construction and operation of any one machine, the bill must contain an explicit averment that the infringing machines contain all the improvements embraced in the several patents, or it will be held bad for multifariousness on demurrer.

In Gillespie *v.* Cummings, 3 Saw., 259, in 1874, before Judge Sawyer, the bill was founded on two patents for the manufacture of brooms. There was a demurrer on the ground of the joinder of two separate and distinct causes of action. It appearing by the bill that the defendant's broom, in infringing, must be an infringement of both of the patents, and that there was, therefore, a common point to be litigated, and much of the testimony must, from the nature of things, be applicable to both of the patents, the bill was held good.

In Horman Patent Mfg. Co. *v.* Brooklyn City R. R. Co., 15 Blatch., 444, in 1879, before Judge Benedict, a bill in equity on two patents alleged that the defendant was using machines containing in one and the same apparatus the inventions secured by each of the two patents. It was demurred to on the ground that it did not allege that the devices were used conjointly or connected together in any one apparatus, but the demurrer was overruled. The court held that, as the bill did not show the controversy to be of such a character that prejudice to the defendant would result from the joinder in one action of the causes of action joined, the bill must be sustained. The court was of opinion that, in the absence of any other fact, the circumstance that the two transactions complained of were the use, in a single machine, of two patented devices connected with the mechanism of the machine, warranted the inference that no prejudice would result to the defendant from the joinder of the two transactions.

The decisions above cited all tend in one direction. The decision in *Case v. Redfield*, 4 McLean, 526, if limited, as it apparently ought to be, to the case of an original patent, and of another patent granted in terms as an improvement on the original patent, is not like the present case as shown by the bill. It is a case difficult to understand, and if it were like the present case in its facts, whatever there is in the decision of it tending to sustain the bill in this case is opposed to all the other cases on the subject.

The present case appears to be a suit on thirty-eight claims in six different patents. There is nothing to show that any two or more of the patents are in fact, or are capable of being, used in making a single structure, much less that the defendant has so used them. So far as the bill shows, the causes of action are as distinct as the patents. The patents are not shown to be connected with each other in any infringing machine, or to be used at the same time in any infringing machine. The controversy in this suit appears, from the bill, to be of such a character that prejudice will result to the defendant from being called on to defend in one suit against thirty-eight claims in six different patents, no two of which claims, so far as the bill shows to the contrary, are employed in any one machine. On this ground the bill must be held bad.

§ **1189.** *A demurrer to the whole bill is waived by an answer to the whole, but plaintiff, by going to argument on the demurrer, waives the objection.*

The plaintiff contends that the putting in of an answer to the whole bill is a waiver of the demurrer. Rule 32 in equity permits a demurrer to a part of a bill, a plea to a part, and an answer as to the residue. If, impliedly, that rule forbids a demurrer to the whole bill, and at the same time an answer to the whole bill, the plaintiff's remedy is by moving to strike out either the answer or the demurrer, or to compel the defendant to elect which he will abide by. By going to argument on the demurrer the plaintiff waives the benefit of the objection now taken, if otherwise he would have it. Moreover, rule 37 in equity provides that " no demurrer or plea shall be held bad and overruled upon argument, only because the answer of the defendant may extend to some part of the same matter as may be covered by such demurrer or plea." This rule was first made in March, 1842, to take effect August 1, 1842. 17 Pet., lxvii. There was no such rule in the prior rules of March, 1822 (7 Wheat., v), although rule 18 in such prior rules was the same as the above present rule 32. Under the rules of 1822, not only had it been held (Ferguson *v.* O'Harra, Pet. C. C., 493) that, where there was a plea going to the whole bill and also an answer to the whole bill, the court would, on the plaintiff's motion, disallow the plea, on the ground of its being overruled by the answer, but Judge Story had held in 1840, in Stearns *v.* Page, 1 Story, 204, that where a plea stated a ground why the defendant should not go into a full defense, and yet the defendant answered putting in a full defense, it would be held, on the argument of the plea, that the answer overruled the plea. Then rule 37 was made. It applies to the present case. The demurrer is allowed, with costs.

ATWILL v. FERRETT.

(Circuit Court for New York: 2 Blatchford, 39-49. 1846.)

STATEMENT OF FACTS.—"The Bohemian Girl," an opera, was reproduced in New York by Atwill, who added much matter to it, interspersed throughout the work. He made many alterations, changing duetts to solos, trios to duetts, and published and caused to be produced in New York; in December, 1844, the opera thus altered, and, as he alleges, improved, and duly copyrighted the same. His bill charges that Ferrett & Co., a firm composed of Ferrett and Arthur, of Philadelphia, and Galusha, of New York, infringed his copyright, and he brought an action at law in New York against Galusha, the only one of the firm residing in New York, and files this bill for a discovery from him and his partners, which discovery he alleges he is entitled to, and without which he cannot safely try the cause.

Opinion by BETTS, J.

Three separate demurrers are filed to the bill in this case by the defendant Galusha. The other two defendants have not entered their appearance, and it does not appear that they have been served with the subpœna.

§ 1190. *A special demurrer is insufficient if it fails to point out distinctly the matter demurred to.*

The defendant attempts to call in question distinct parts of the bill by severing his demurrers, and also takes objection to the whole by general demurrer. The special causes of demurrer are excepted to by the plaintiff as informal and insufficient, in not pointing out precisely the parts of the bill intended to be embraced by them. They adopt the general formulary, "that, as to so much of the bill as seeks," etc., without specifying by paragraph, page or folio, or other method of reference, where the objectionable matter is to be found. We think this mode of demurring to the statements of a long and involved bill is too obscure and indefinite to be admissible. Mitford's Pl., 214; Robinson v. Thompson, 2 Ves. & B., 118; Weatherhead v. Blackburn, id., 121. The business of a special demurrer is to point out, by the clearest indications, the features alleged to be defective in the pleading, and to relieve the court from the labor and delay incurred by repeated searches for the parts to which the demurrer may apply. Story's Eq. Pl., §§ 457-459; Devonsher v. Newenham, 2 Schoales & Lefroy, 199. In the present case the court have abridged the bill paragraph by paragraph, and in that way have been enabled to select various statements which were undoubtedly intended to be embraced by the special demurrers; but we are not inclined to sanction so loose a mode of pleading. We therefore hold the special demurrers to be informal and insufficient, except in respect to the multifariousness of the bill, and to its demand of discoveries involving penalties and forfeitures against the defendant. In those particulars we think that the causes of demurrer assigned designate, with sufficient explicitness, the parts of the bill to which they are intended to apply.

§ 1191. *Multifariousness.*

(1) The bill is objected to as multifarious by the defendant Galusha, on

the ground that it makes charges against and exacts answers from his co-defendants in regard to matters involved in the suit at law commenced against him, which do not concern them, they not being parties to the suit at law. But the matters referred to concern him, and he cannot make the objection of irrelevancy in respect to his co-defendants, more especially as it appears on the face of the bill that they reside out of the jurisdiction of the court. Story's Eq. Pl., § 544, note 3. Another feature of the bill might also probably rescue it from this objection, inasmuch as it charges the acts complained of to have been committed by the three defendants as partners and in their copartnership character, provided they are all connected by other proper allegations with the object and purpose of the discovery prayed for. Mitford's Pl., 182, 183. The demurrer for multifariousness is overruled.

§ 1192. *A bill to enforce penalties cannot compel discovery in aid thereto.*

(2) It is an incontrovertible principle of equity law that a defendant cannot be compelled to make discoveries in answer to a bill which seeks to enforce penalties and forfeitures against him by means of such discoveries. Story's Eq. Pl., § 521, note 3, and §§ 522, 575, 598; Mitford's Pl., 194–197. In this case the bill claims a forfeiture under section 7 of the act of February 3, 1831 (4 U. S. Stat. at Large, 438), of the plates and pieces of music on hand. Had the forfeiture been waived by the plaintiff, the defendants might be compelled to disclose the number of their publications, the quantity on hand and the amount realized from sales, in aid of the recovery of damages in a suit at law. So, probably, on such discovery equity might compel the defendants to deliver up to the plaintiffs the forfeited copies. But the bill is clearly faulty in directly requiring the defendants to convict themselves of the act which carries with it the forfeiture sued for.

§ 1193. *A bill for infringement of copyright does not show title in plaintiff by alleging that the matter was arranged and adapted by or for him.*

The decision of these two points leaves untouched, however, the principal features of the bill which are supposed to be brought in question by the demurrers, and to the discussion of which the argument was mainly directed; and it therefore remains to be considered whether advantage can be taken of those matters by general demurrer.

The objections which may be taken on general demurrer are: 1. That the plaintiff sets forth no title in himself to the subject-matter of his alleged copyright; and 2. That the bill lays no legal foundation for the discovery sought.

1. The insufficiency of the plaintiff's title on the face of the bill is claimed to be this: that he alleges the musical composition, or considerable portions of it, to have been arranged, adapted, printed and published *by or for* him, instead of averring that it was composed *by* himself. The plaintiff, on the other hand, contends that, even admitting this to be so, his title is complete upon the legal adage, *qui facit per alium facit per se*, and that he can appropriate as his own the alterations and improvements of the music made by others at his procurement and for him.

The act of congress (4 U. S. Stat. at Large, 436, § 1) secures by copyright to any person who is *the author of any musical composition* the exclusive property in his composition for a terms of years. The statute contains a more detailed description of the subjects of copyright than is given in the English acts of 8 Anne and 54 George 3 (Godson on Pat., App., 384 and 422); but the construction given to those acts by the English courts makes them include, under the name of *books*, pieces of music, etc. So that our system has no broader operation in this respect than the English, and no doubt a just construction of both statutes will render their provisions concurrent. The counsel for the plaintiff insists that the doctrine of the English law enables a man to secure to himself as his own composition whatever he has had prepared for him by the labors of others. We think, however, that the cases of Tonson *v.* Walker, 3 Swanst., 672, 680; Nicoll *v.* Stockdale, id., 687; Cary *v.* Longman, 3 Esp., 273, 274, and Mawmann *v.* Tegg, 2 Russ., 385, rest upon wholly different principles. They recognize the right of authorship, although the *materials* of the composition were procured by another, and also an equitable title in one person to the labors of another when the relations of the parties are such that the former is entitled to an assignment of the production. But, to constitute one an author, he must, by his own intellectual labor applied to the materials of his composition, produce an arrangement or compilation new in itself. Gray *v.* Russell, 1 Story, 11. And the rules of the common law and of equity are the same upon this subject. Cary *v.* Longman, 1 East, 358; Sayre *v.* Moore, id., 361, note; Jeremy's Eq., 322. The title to road-books, maps, etc., rests upon this principle (2 Story's Eq. Jur., § 940); and the cases cited by the plaintiff's counsel have relation to new productions arranged or compiled from materials before known or obtained by others for the author, and not to the appropriation by copyright of those materials in the same state in which they are furnished.

§ 1194. *What amounts to an allegation of plaintiff's title.*

If, therefore, the plaintiff's title rested only upon the allegation referred to, we should hold the bill to be defective on general demurrer. But we find repeated averments in the bill to the effect that "he made many alterations of and additions to the said music"—that "he added new matters of his own, not in the original opera"—that he affixed a copy of the record on the title-page "of each piece of music composed, arranged and adapted by him for publication"—and that a copyright was taken out for such pieces "as arranged, adapted and published by the plaintiff, with the new titles and original matter introduced therein by him," whereby he became entitled to vend the music "as arranged and adapted by him, and to the original matter introduced by him therein;" and the bill charges the defendants with having sold such music "printed from and in exact imitation of the music so arranged and adapted and published by the plaintiff, with the original matter introduced therein by him, and with his titles to some of such pieces of music." These allegations amount to an assertion of authorship in terms sufficiently explicit and full to constitute a perfect title at law, and, the facts being admitted by the demurrer, we must hold the right of the plaintiff established upon these averments, notwithstanding their defectiveness and their inconsistency with others contained in the bill. Mitford's Pl., 212. Such imperfect pleading is matter of form and can be taken advantage of only by special demurrer. The general demurrer in this behalf must, therefore, be overruled. Verplank *v.* Caines, 1 Johns. Ch., 57; Higinbotham *v.* Burnet, 5 id., 184; Kuypers *v.* The Reformed Dutch Church, 6 Paige, 570.

§ 1195. *An action of trespass will not lie for a violation of copyright. Case is the proper remedy.*

2. The discovery prayed for is to aid the plaintiff in his suit at law prosecuted against the defendant Galusha, and the averment in the bill is that he has commenced an action of *trespass* against that defendant for the violation of his copyright. The demurrer raises the question whether the bill alleges such a suit at law as will afford foundation for the discovery sought, no relief

consequent on the discovery being prayed for. It is clear that the plaintiff has adopted a form of action at law which cannot be supported. . The English statute of 54 George 3, section 2, gives specifically an action on the case as the remedy for the violation of a copyright. Our act (4 U. S. Stat. at Large, 438) only indicates the form of action when a manuscript is published without the consent of the author (§ 9), or when a suit is brought to recover the pecuniary penalty given by the sixth section. On general principles of law, however, it is clear that *trespass* cannot be brought for an injury merely consequential in its character, unaccompanied by force as against the person or property, or by wrongful intermeddling with the possession of property. 1 Chitty's Pl., 126, 127. The act of 8 Anne, chapter 19, did not designate the form of action, yet no doubt was ever expressed that *case* was the appropriate one. Beckford *v.* Hood, 7 T. R., 616; Cary *v.* Longman, 1 East, 358; Roworth *v.* Wilkes, 1 Campb., 94.

§ 1196. *What must be shown to authorize a discovery in aid of an action at law.*

To obtain a discovery in aid of a suit at law, the bill must show it to be necessary for the plaintiff, and that, when made, it can be used to his advantage. Jeremy's Eq., 161; Story's Eq. Pl., §§ 319, 321. It necessarily follows, from these principles, that a discovery will not be decreed in aid of an action at law, where it is manifest that the plaintiff cannot avail himself of it in the suit he is attempting to prosecute. It is, perhaps, also to be regarded as a substantive defect in the bill that it seeks a discovery from three defendants to aid a suit instituted against one alone. In so far, then, as the maintenance of the bill depends upon the plaintiff's right to a discovery, we think it defective in substance, and bad on general demurrer.

§ 1197. *A general demurrer will not avail if any part of the bill be sufficient, and a protestation will not avoid the force of this rule.*

This bill, however, prays for an injunction, and, making title on its face in the plaintiff to the copyright set forth, and showing a wrongful and wilful violation of the copyright by the defendants, and serious injuries inflicted by and apprehended from such violation, it is sufficient in substance and form to entitle the plaintiff to an injunction. This relief is not dependent upon the discovery prayed, but rests on the equities set forth in the bill, and may be refused or granted irrespective of the discovery. A general demurrer to the whole bill takes exception, therefore, to this branch of it, and the principle of equity pleading is universal that a general demurrer to the whole bill must be overruled if any independent part of the bill is sufficient. Higinbotham *v.* Burnet, 5 Johns. Ch. R., 184; Kuypers *v.* The Reformed Dutch Church, 6 Paige, 570; Story's Eq. Pl., § 443. The formal protestation accompanying the demurrer is of no avail to protect it against this defect, as it cannot serve the purpose of a plea or answer, or form an excuse for not putting in the one or the other. · Story's Eq. Pl., §§ 452, 457, 458. We think, therefore, that the general demurrer must be overruled on both points.   •

As faults in pleading have occurred on both sides, each party may amend without paying costs to the other.

§ 1198. Certainty of averments.—Some degree of strictness is required in the averments of a bill in equity, but in general certainty to a common intent is sufficient. The general statement of a fact is usually enough, and the circumstances which go to establish it need not be minutely charged. These are more properly matters of evidence than of allegation. Dunham *v.* Railroad Co.,* 1 Bond, 492.

§ 1199. **What matters of fact bill must contain.**— Every bill in equity must contain in itself sufficient matter of fact to maintain the cause of the complainant. Gale v. Cutler,* 1 Burn. (Wis.), 92.

§ 1200. **In pleading in equity facts must be specifically stated**, and conclusions upon inference or argument are not tolerated. The rule of evidence that a state of facts once shown to exist is presumed to continue does not obtain in construing pleadings. Wilkinson v. Dobbie, 12 Blatch., 298.

§ 1201. **Sufficient equity to warrant relief must appear on face of bill — Allegations.**— There must be a sufficient equity apparent on the face of the bill to warrant the court in granting the relief prayed, and the material facts on which the plaintiff relies must be so distinctly alleged as to put them in issue. Harding v. Handy, 11 Wheat., 103.

§ 1202. **Matter of law, etc., need not be averred.**— Matters of law and public statutes, of which the court takes judicial notice, need never be averred in a bill in equity. Young v. Montgomery, etc., R. Co., 2 Woods, 606.

§ 1203. **Bill must state essential facts.**— Facts essential to maintain a suit in equity must be stated in the bill; and no facts are properly in issue unless charged in the bill, nor proofs admissible to establish what is not alleged. The *allegata* and the *probata* must concur in supporting the same charge or ground of relief. Bradley v. Converse, 4 Cliff., 366.

§ 1204. **Allegations must show title or interest.**— A complainant in equity has no standing in court if his allegations do not show that he has some title or interest in the subject-matter. Selz v. Unna, 6 Wall., 327.

§ 1205. **Plaintiff's argument cannot controvert allegations of bill.**— If the bill alleges a particular fact, the plaintiff cannot, in argument, urge that the fact is otherwise. He is bound by his admission, unless, before hearing, he obtains leave to amend. Prevost v. Gratz, 3 Wash., 484.

§ 1206. **Inferential or argumentative pleading is not admissible.**— A fact can only be put in issue by a direct allegation in such a way that the party can take issue directly upon it. So a complainant in a bill in equity, if he wishes to allege ownership of a certain amount of land, should not allege that land was conveyed to him "described as follows" in the deed, since this is merely an allegation of what the deed contains, and not of the amount of land actually owned by him. Kinney v. Con. Virginia M. Co., 4 Saw., 388.

§ 1207. **Names and surnames in bill.**— The full christian names and surnames of all persons referred to in the bill must be inserted therein, but a defect in this particular may be amended. Barth v. Makeever, 4 Biss., 206.

§ 1208. **There is no rule in equity pleading requiring the filing of exhibits** or copies of papers mentioned in the bill. Putnam v. New Albany, 4 Biss., 365.

§ 1209. **Allegations in bill passed over in answer admitted.**— Material allegations well pleaded in the bill, and omitted and passed over in the answer, are conclusively admitted. Cahoon v. Ring, 1 Cliff., 592.

§ 1210. **If the answer neither admits nor denies the allegations of the bill** they must be proved on final hearing; but upon a question of dissolution of an injunction they are to be taken to be true. Young v. Grundy, 6 Cr., 51.

§ 1211. **Signing of bill — Indorsement by counsel.**— A bill not signed is demurrable therefor, but an indorsement by counsel is a sufficient signature within the rule. Dwight v. Humphreys,* 3 McL., 104.

§ 1212. A bill in equity, filed without being signed by the plaintiff or his counsel, will be ordered to be taken off the files, because it cannot be received under the sixteenth rule of the federal courts. Roach v. Hulings, 5 Cr. C. C., 637.

§ 1213. **Bill for injunction — Oath of agent to — Texas practice.**— Held, in Texas, that an oath by an agent of plaintiff to a bill for injunction would satisfy the statute. *In re* Fendley,* 3 Am. L. Rec., 105.

§ 1214. **Motion for leave to file bill before supreme court.**— A motion for leave to file a bill before the supreme court is usually heard *ex parte* except in peculiar circumstances, as when a bill was brought against the president. Georgia v. Grant, 6 Wall., 241.

§ 1215. **Bill to enjoin judgment not an original bill.**— A bill to enjoin a judgment in a United States circuit court is not considered as an original bill between the same parties, as at law, but as growing out of, and as auxiliary to, the suit at law. But if other parties are introduced and different interests involved, it is to that extent an original bill, and the jurisdiction of the federal court must then depend on the citizenship of the parties; and one of the parties must be a citizen of the state where the suit was brought. Williams v. Byrne, Hemp., 472.

§ 1216. **Citizenship of the parties.**— A bill in equity brought in the federal court on the ground of citizenship of the parties must contain clear and positive averments of citizenship, as this is a jurisdictional fact. An averment of residence is insufficient. Hilliard v. Brevoort,* 4 McL., 24; Meserole v. Union Paper Collar Co., 6 Blatch., 356; Conwell v. White Water Valley Canal Co., 4 Biss., 195.

§ 1217. Where the jurisdiction of the federal court depends upon the citizenship of the parties, such citizenship must be clearly and positively set out in a bill in equity, and no appearance, demurrer or answer to the bill will waive such an omission in it. Speigle v. Meredith, 4 Biss., 120.

§ 1218. An allegation of citizenship is sufficiently explicit to sustain the jurisdiction of the federal courts if the citizenship disclosed by the allegation does not displace that jurisdiction. The bill must show of what states the respective parties are citizens. Jones v. Andrews, 10 Wall., 327.

§ 1219. If an averment necessary to give the court jurisdiction, having been omitted in the declaration, appears in the joinder in demurrer, no objection having been made by defendant to the omission, the averment as made, though irregular, is sufficient. Bradstreet v. Thomas, 12 Pet., 59.

§ 1220. The grantor is a necessary party in a suit to set aside an alleged fraudulent conveyance, and his citizenship must be alleged when jurisdiction depends upon this ground. Gaylords v. Kelshaw, 1 Wall., 81.

§ 1221. Where a bill in equity alleged the plaintiffs to be citizens of the United States, and this is not denied in the answer, it must be considered as admitted, although no other evidence of citizenship is offered. Webb v. Powers, 2 Woodb. & M., 497.

§ 1222. An averment in a bill that the defendant is a corporation and a citizen of a state named is a sufficient averment of citizenship to give the federal courts jurisdiction. Covington Drawbridge Co. v. Shepherd, 21 How., 112.

§ 1223. Where in a bill in equity the complainants and part of the respondents are described as of one state, and those of the respondents, on whom service is made, and who appear, as of the state where the suit is brought, a demurrer to the bill for want of jurisdiction cannot be sustained. Heriot v. Davis, 2 Woodb. & M., 229.

§ 1224. If a suit is brought in a federal court against a corporation it must be made to appear that the corporation was brought into existence by the law of some state other than that of which the adverse party is a citizen. Such an averment is usually made in the introduction or stating part of the bill. It is always made there if the bill is formally drafted. But if made anywhere in the pleadings it is sufficient. Muller v. Dows, 4 Otto, 444.

§ 1225. Authority of corporations to contract — Allegations as to. — An allegation in a bill that the plaintiff, a corporation, had authority to enter into a certain contract must be assumed to mean that the corporation had such authority by virtue of the law of its being; and such allegation makes necessary an examination of the statutes under which the corporation was organized and by which its powers were defined and limited. W. U. Tel. Co. v. U. P. R'y Co., 1 McC., 418.

§ 1226. Bills of discovery. — An allegation in a bill of discovery that it is material for plaintiffs to have the discovery is not necessary. Heath v. Erie R. Co., 9 Blatch., 316.

§ 1227. A bill which charges a fraud, the particulars of which are unknown to plaintiff, and that defendants are in a conspiracy to perpetrate the fraud, which gives all the particulars known to plaintiff, and which upon the general knowledge, which is all that plaintiff has been able to discover, calls upon the defendants to answer and disclose the particular facts as to a certain transaction alleged to be part of the fraud, includes all the requirements for a bill of discovery; and the complainant will not be required to set out the particulars of a fraud in a bill which, as to these particulars, is a bill for discovery. Forbes v. Overby,* 4 Hughes, 441.

§ 1228. A bill seeking discovery as to defendant's property must point out what property is inquired about, and cannot compel a detailed answer by a general charge that defendant has or has had property. Buerk v. Imhaueser, 10 Fed. R., 608.

§ 1229. The statute of Virginia against usury provides that "any borrower of money or goods may exhibit a bill in chancery against the lenders and compel them to discover, on oath, the money they really lent, and all bargains, contracts or shifts which shall have passed between them relative to such loan or the repayment thereof, and the interest and consideration of the same; and if thereupon it shall appear that more than lawful interest was reserved, the lender shall be obliged to accept his principal money without interest or consideration, and pay costs, but shall be discharged of all the other penalties of this act." The complainants in the circuit court of Alexandria county, District of Columbia, filed a bill to obtain relief under the statute against an alleged usurious loan, and made a contingent and prospective offer to pay the principal when the affairs of the intestate (the borrower) "would admit it;" and there was no averment that the complainants were unable to prove the facts sought from the conscience of the defendant by other testimony. Held, that the bill was deficient in material averments, essential to all such bills of discovery. Brown v. Swann, 10 Pet., 497.

§ 1230. **Fraud.**— If a bill charge fraud as the ground of relief it must be proved; and the proof of other facts, though included in the charge, and sufficient, under some circumstances, to constitute a claim to relief under another head of equity, will not prevent the bill from being dismissed. Fisher *v.* Boody, 1 Curt., 206.

§ 1231. A bill charging falsehood and fraud in a sale, as to the exaggerated quantity of timber on lands, may contain enough to justify setting the sale aside for a gross mistake in the quantity, without setting up the latter as a specific and separate cause; but it is better to have such cause stated independently, in order to give clearer notice to the respondents of what may be contested. Smith *v.* Babcock, 2 Woodb. & M., 246.

§ 1232. In a bill in equity accusations of fraud as to probate accounts, formally settled thirty years before, must be specific and point out the items alleged to be false. Badger *v.* Badger, 2 Cliff., 187.

§ 1233. If a patent of certain lands is sought to be invalidated on the ground of fraud it is not enough to allege that the patent was "fraudulently" obtained by means of "false proof," but the bill should set forth the substance, at least, of the acts constituting the fraud, or should state wherein the proof was false. United States *v.* Tichenor, 12 Fed. R., 415.

§ 1234. A bill to set aside a decree on the ground of fraud is bad upon demurrer if it does not allege that the complainant was ignorant of the facts constituting the fraud pending the original suit; that he could not by due diligence have made them known to the court at that time; and that he could not, by the use of due diligence, have pleaded them to the original suit. Pacific R. R. *v.* Mo. Pacific R'y Co., 2 McC., 227.

§ 1235. In a bill to set aside a decree on the ground of fraud it is not enough to set forth in general terms that a particular transaction was fraudulent, but the facts constituting the fraud must be so stated that the court, and not the pleader, may determine whether, if true, they constitute fraud; and an intent to deceive must be charged either by express averment or by such words as necessarily imply such intent. Moreover, allegations of fraud must never be in the alternative. Brooks *v.* O'Hara, 2 McC., 644.

§ 1236. A general allegation of fraud is not demurrable if the bill sets out that the defendants have concealed the details of the fraudulent transactions, because, when discovered, such details may be set out by way of amendment, and until then the general allegation may stand, if for no other purpose, as a foundation for such amendment. Northern Pacific R. Co. *v.* Kindred, 3 McC., 627.

§ 1237. Where a bill sets forth such leading facts as do not when analyzed show a case of fraud or mistake, allegations or averments in the bill that there was fraud or mistake, and the expressions "fraudulently," "deceitfully," "by mistake," etc., interspersed throughout it, will not bring the case within equitable jurisdiction, even on a demurrer to the bill. Magniac *v.* Thompson, 2 Wall. Jr., 209.

§ 1238. In a bill against a fraudulent grantee of a deceased person it is not necessary to aver a deficiency of the personal estate of the deceased; it is sufficient to aver the fraud and the waste of the personal assets by such grantee, who was also a personal representative. McLaughlin *v.* The Bank of Potomac, 7 How., 220.

§ 1239. In order that a court of equity will open and review accounts which are barred by the statute of limitations, the bill must state distinctly the particular act of fraud, misrepresentation and concealment; must specify how, when and in what manner it was perpetrated; the charges must be definite and reasonably certain; if a mistake is alleged it must be stated with precision and made apparent, so that the court may rectify it with a feeling of certainty that they are not committing another and perhaps greater mistake; and especially must there be distinct averments as to the time when the fraud, mistake and concealment or misrepresentation was discovered, and what the discovery is, so that the court may clearly see whether, by the exercise of ordinary diligence, the discovery might not have been made before. Stearns *v.* Page, 7 How., 819.

§ 1240. **Patent suits.**— The fact that the subject-matter of a contract sought to be enforced is a patent-right does not *per se* give the courts of the United States jurisdiction, and a bill filed for the specific performance of such a contract must contain averments to show that the court has jurisdiction. Burr *v.* Gregory, 2 Paine. 426. See PATENTS.

§ 1241. The general allegation in a bill that the defendant has infringed the plaintiff's letters patent, without setting forth a description of the patented invention and the infringing machine, is sufficient to put the defendant upon his answer. Turrell *v.* Cummerrer,* 3 Fish. Pat. Cas., 462.

§ 1242. A bill in equity purporting to be brought by the United States at the relation of certain persons, but signed not by the district attorney, but by counsel for the plaintiffs, and praying that certain letters patent should be canceled, is bad on demurrer for want of equity. United States *v.* West, 7 Blatch., 424.

§ 1243. A plaintiff in a bill for infringement, claiming title under an unrecorded assignment, need not aver the recording, but may leave defendant to show himself a *bona fide* purchaser without notice. Perry *v.* Corning, 7 Blatch., 195.

§ 1244. A bill for an injunction against the infringement of a patent is not defective because it fails to aver that plaintiff marked the articles sold under the patent, as required by statute. Goodyear *v.* Allen, 6 Blatch., 83.

§ 1245. A bill in equity upon a patent is sufficient if it aver title to the patent to be in the plaintiff, though the deduction of title is not given. Nourse *v.* Allen, 4 Blatch., 376.

§ 1246. A licensee of a patent, who is immediately injured by infringement, is properly joined as plaintiff with the owner of the legal title in an equity suit for the infringement; and he, not the legal owner, is the proper party to verify the bill. Goodyear *v.* Allyn,* 3 Fish. Pat. Cas., 374.

§ 1247. An allegation that the plaintiff marked, as required by statute, the articles sold under the patent sued, is not necessary when an injunction is sought and not damages. It is questionable whether the statute applies to equity suits at all. *Ibid.*

§ 1248. Where a bill in equity alleged that one of the several defendants contracted to transfer a patent (not then obtained) for a machine, and that, after it was obtained, he refused to do so; and that the other defendants, knowing these facts, bought machines of him, it was held that, as the suit could be maintained against him alone, the fact that some of the other defendants were citizens of the same state with the plaintiffs was not fatal to the jurisdiction. Nesmith *v.* Calvert, 1 Woodb. & M., 84.

§ 1249. On an application for an injunction to restrain the infringement of a patent-right, it should be stated in the bill, or by affidavit, that the complainant is the inventor; and the bill must be sworn to; it is not sufficient that he swore to this fact when he obtained his patent. Sullivan *v.* Redfield, 1 Paine, 441.

§ 1250. Where a bill is filed to enjoin the defendant from running a machine, in violation of the right of the assignee of the patent, and the defendant sets up a license which the complainant alleges has been abandoned, but no such statement is made in the bill, proof of abandonment cannot be received. Wilson *v.* Stolley, 4 McL., 275.

§ 1251. Notice of an asserted fraud must be charged directly.— A bill charged notice of an asserted fraud against one of the defendants in general terms, to wit: "that the defendant then and there well knowing all and singular the premises," etc. *Held,* that the bill should be amended so as to charge notice more directly. Wood *v.* Mann, 1 Sumn., 506.

§ 1252. Codicils must be set out in bill as well as the will, or they cannot be given in evidence.— A bill in equity by executors, to recover certain property wrongfully withheld by defendant, set up a will without codicils. The proofs offered, as well as the title of the plaintiffs as executors, rested chiefly upon certain codicils which were offered in evidence. *Held,* the court could not proceed with the case, as the proofs offered were inadmissible, not being in support of or in contradiction to any allegations of the pleadings. The codicils should have been fully set out in the bill; and one which had been revoked and so not probated, either must be set out in the bill, if it were to be used, or its existence must be alleged and defendant called on to produce it. Langdon *v.* Goddard,* 2 Story, 267.

§ 1253. A bill in equity to foreclose a mortgage of an insolvent corporation need not allege a demand of payment of the bonds at the designated place of payment. Shaw *v.* Bill, 5 Otto, 10.

§ 1254. Bill to reform instrument — Mistake of law.— It is not sufficient, in a bill to reform a written agreement, for plaintiff to allege that he had believed the legal effect of a certain clause in the agreement to be what he alleges the agreement really was, the mistake so alleged being one of law and not of fact. Hoover *v.* Reilly, 2 Abb., 471.

§ 1255. Bill to set aside deed for want of consideration — Fatal allegation.— An averment in a bill to set aside a deed for want of consideration, that the deed was thus made to protect the complainant from the result of a then pending suit (to wit, slander), is fatal to it, and the complainant will be left to the consequences of his own act. Fletcher *v.* Fletcher,* 2 MacArth., 38.

§ 1256. An injunction to restrain the prosecution of a suit at law may be granted although no discovery is asked in the bill, and if granted it need not be upon terms that the defendants at law submit to a judgment with costs, although the rule may be such in England. Lawrence *v.* Bowman, McAl., 419.

§ 1257. Former suit as estoppel — Bill must aver judgment.— If complainants wish to bring up a former suit between the same parties as matter of estoppel the bill must aver the judgment, as every material fact upon either side must be set up in the pleadings; allegations being as necessary as proofs. Blandy *v.* Griffith,* 3 Fish. Pat. Cas., 609.

§ 1258. Matter of defense need not be averred in bill.— A deed of trust providing for foreclosure upon default in Little Rock water bonds, "provided the default is not caused by the city of Little Rock," does not necessitate an averment in a bill to foreclose that the failure to pay was not by fault of Little Rock, as that is matter of defense. Water Works Co. v. Barret, 13 Otto. 516.

§ 1259. **Bill to set aside decree of court — Particular allegations of fraud necessary.—** A bill in equity to set aside a decree of a court of competent jurisdiction must not be confined to general allegations of fraud, but full particulars of fraudulent acts and parties must be given. A bill to set aside a decree of a federal district court confirming a land patent seventeen years before, dismissed on demurrer for failure to comply with this rule. United States v. Atherton, 12 Otto, 372.

§ 1260. **Bill by assignee in bankruptcy, when treated as bill in equity.—** Where the pleading filed by an assignee in bankruptcy is appropriate in form for a petition in the bankrupt suit, but is equally good in substance as a bill in equity, and all irregularities are waived, the case may be treated as a suit in equity and may be brought to the supreme court by appeal. Milner v. Meek, 5 Otto, 252.

§ 1261. **The statute of limitations cannot be avoided by general averments of fraud** and concealment in a bill. The particular acts of fraud or concealment as well as the time when discovered must be set forth in distinct averments, to enable the court to see whether the discovery might not have been before made by the exercise of due diligence. Beaubien v. Beaubien, 23 How., 190.

§ 1262. **When a bill seeks to enforce a merely legal title, for which there is adequate remedy at law** by action of ejectment, the bill will be dismissed by the court *sua sponte*, if the defect is not brought up by demurrer, plea or answer, nor is suggested by counsel. Lewis v. Cocks, 23 Wall., 466.

§ 1263. **If a bill avers** that the defendant collected certain judgments and holds the money for the use of the complainant, there is a complete remedy at law. It cannot be called a bill for discovery, and the aid of a court of equity is not needed. French v. Hay, 22 Wall., 231.

§ 1264. **Misjoinder of plaintiffs — Dismissed without prejudice.—** A bill demurred to on three grounds, and held to be defective on one ground, to wit, misjoinder of plaintiffs, cannot be dismissed generally, as the decree would not show upon which ground it was dismissed, and it might, therefore, be pleaded in bar to a new suit brought by one of the misjoined parties. The dismissal should be without prejudice, or the decree should state that the dismissal was for misjoinder. House v. Muller, 22 Wall., 42.

§ 1265. **Deed signed by feme covert under compulsion — Bill for relief — Statute of limitations.—** A bill asking relief on the ground that the complainant signed a deed for land under compulsion cannot be demurred to as showing a bar by limitations, if the bill avers that the complainant was a *feme covert* from the time she parted with possession until within three years of filing the bill. *Ibid.*

§ 1266. **No relief can be claimed unless supported by allegations.—** A complainant in equity can make no claim for relief upon the argument unless such claim is supported by allegations in the bill, for recovery must be had upon the case made by the pleadings or not at all. Grosholz v. Newman, 21 Wall., 481.

§ 1267. **Facts, not law, to be stated.—** A bill to set aside conveyances made by a bankrupt before his bankruptcy ought not to set out the sections of the bankrupt law under which the plaintiff claims relief, for a bill should state facts and not law. Pratt v. Curtis, 2 Low., 87.

§ 1268. **Waiver of penalties.—** In a bill to restrain infringement of a copyright the fact that the bill does not waive the forfeitures and penalties provided by statute for such infringement is not ground for demurrer. Farmer v. Calvert, etc., Co., 1 Flip., 228.

§ 1269. **Title of executor — Allegation of capacity, when mere matter of inducement.—** A bill in equity alleged that the plaintiff held certain property as executor, and it appeared upon proof that he held as surviving partner. It was not material to the case how the property came into plaintiff's hands. *Held*, the allegation of plaintiff's capacity was mere inducement, and a disproof of it would not therefore cause the bill to fail. McCay v. Lamar, 12 Fed. R., 367.

§ 1270. **Sequestration of property, sufficiency of allegation as to amount of.—** In a bill against a corporation by a judgment creditor for a sequestration of its property, it is a sufficient allegation of the value of the defendant's property to allege that it is more than sufficient to pay plaintiff's debt. Winans v. McKean R. R. & N. Co., 6 Blatch., 215.

§ 1271. **Illegal subscription subsequently ratified — Ratification should be set out — Effect of issue tendered thereon by answer.—** Where a subscription of a city to railroad stock is illegal, but is subsequently ratified by act of legislature, an averment of such ratification should be set out in a bill to enforce payment of the subscription; but if such ratification is not set out and there is no demurrer to the bill, but the answer sets out the ratification, and issue is taken on it in the replication, that will supply the defect in the bill. Putnam v. New Albany, 4 Biss., 365.

§ 1272. Lex loci contractus to be averred in bill.— In a suit brought on a debt contracted in a foreign country, the *lex loci contractus* governing the case should be averred in the bill. Vose *v.* Philbrook, 8 Story, 835.

§ 1278. Bill dismissed where pleadings show that plaintiff has no standing in court.— If the complainant by his bill, or respondent by his plea, set forth facts from which it appears that the complainant, by the statutes of the state, has no standing in court, and for the sake of repose and the common good of society is not permitted to sue his adversary, it is the rule of the court to dismiss the bill. Harpending *v.* The Dutch Church, 16 Pet., 455.

§ 1274. A bill asking relief from usury will not be entertained if it does not aver readiness to pay principal and interest. Stanley *v.* Gadsby, 10 Pet., 521.

§ 1275. A bill in equity to enjoin a judgment at law is not to be considered as an original bill, and therefore it is not necessary in a court of limited jurisdiction to make other parties, if the introduction of those parties should create a doubt as to the jurisdiction of the court. Simms *v.* Guthrie, 9 Cr., 19.

§ 1276. Confessions of defendant need not be charged in bill.— The confessions, conversations and admissions of the defendant need not be expressly charged in a bill in equity in order to entitle the plaintiff to use them in proof of facts charged, and in issue therein. Smith *v.* Burnham, 2 Sumn., 612.

§ 1277. Insolvency — A bill to charge the executors of a deceased partner with a partnership debt, where the other partner survives, must express an insolvency of the survivor. Reimsdyk *v.* Kane, 1 Gall., 371.

§ 1278. In a bill of discovery to aid a prosecution at law, the bill should aver the materiality of the facts and that they can only be proved by the oath of the defendant. Bell *v.* Pomeroy, 4 McL., 57.

§ 1279. Injunction, general allegation of injury to property insufficient to obtain.— Where the complainant in an injunction bill, to restrain the erection of certain dams in a river, alleged generally that he would be injured in his property by the construction of said dams, and on this ground prayed an injunction, but failed to show how he would be injured, he was held not to be entitled to the process of injunction. Spooner *v.* McConnell, 1 McL., 837.

§ 1280. Bill to enjoin judgment at law dismissed for lack of necessary allegations.— Where a bill in chancery was filed for the purpose of enjoining a judgment at law obtained upon a promissory note, and the bill did not allege that adequate relief could not be had at law, and did not contain any charges of fraud; neither did it aver that it was owing to the contrivance or unfairness of the defendant that an adequate remedy could not be had at law, nor did it show the necessity of interference by a court of equity to obtain a discovery, the bill must be dismissed. Hungerford *v.* Sigerson, 20 How., 156.

§ 1281. Assignment of judgment — Allegation of release improperly recorded.— Where a judgment, which had been recorded under the laws of Louisiana, and thus made equivalent to a mortgage at law upon the property of the debtor, was assigned, it was not necessary for the assignee, who was defending himself in chancery by claiming under the assignment, to notice in his pleading an allegation in the bill that a release of the judgment was improperly entered upon the record. His assignment was not charged as fraudulent. Stockton *v.* Ford, 11 How., 232.

§ 1282. Bill to restrain collection of purchase money — Charge of fraud, when necessary — Insolvency.— A bill in chancery, filed by the purchaser of land against his vendor to restrain the collection of the purchase money upon the two grounds of want of title in the vendor and his subsequent insolvency, without charging fraud or misrepresentation, cannot be sustained. Patton *v.* Taylor, 7 How., 132.

§ 1283. Objection to misjoinder or non-joinder cannot be taken for first time at hearing.— When a complainant omits to bring before the court persons who are necessary parties, but the objection does not appear on the face of the bill, the proper mode to take advantage of it is by plea and answer. The objection of misjoinder of complainants should be taken either by demurrer or on the answer of the defendants. It is too late to urge a formal objection of the kind for the first time at the hearing. Story *v.* Livingston, 13 Pet., 359.

§ 1284. Loss of instrument as ground for relief — Affidavit of loss must be annexed to bill.— If, in a case where the loss of a deed or other instrument is made the ground for coming into a court of equity for discovery and relief, an affidavit of its loss must be made and annexed to the bill, and the absence of such affidavit is good cause for demurrer to the bill, yet, if the party charged by the bill failed to demur for that cause, but answered over to the bill, or permitted it to be taken for confessed by default against him, it seems that the absence of the affidavit is not a sufficient cause for the reversal of the decree. Findlay *v.* Hinde, 1 Pet., 241.

§ 1285. Prayer.— Under the general prayer in a bill in chancery, other relief than that particularly prayed for may be granted, if agreeable to the case made by the bill, but not otherwise. English v. Foxhall, 2 Pet., 595.

§ 1286. Under a prayer for general relief in a bill in chancery, the court will grant such relief only as the case stated in the bill and the proof justify. Hobson v. M'Arthur, 16 Pet., 182.

§ 1287. No relief can be granted under a general prayer except such as is agreeable to the case made by the bill; but if the objects of the bill can be seen, relief will be granted under such prayer in spite of a want of absolute directness and distinctness in the allegations and interrogatories. Texas v. Hardenberg, 10 Wall., 68.

§ 1288. A prayer for general relief is a prayer for any relief the court can give, except injunction, upon the facts averred in the bill. Railroad Co. v. Macomb, 2 Fed. R., 18.

§ 1289. If the plaintiff mistakes the relief to which he is entitled in his special prayer, the court may yet afford him the relief to which he has a right under the prayer of general relief, provided it is such relief as is agreeable to the case made by the bill. Moore v. Mitchell, 2 Woods, 483.

§ 1290. Where the bill seeks to correct a mistake and reform an instrument the allegations must be most particular, and the bill must conclude with a prayer for a correction of the mistake and a decree according to the reformed instrument. United States v. Munroe, 5 Mason, 572.

§ 1291. An account of profits may be decreed to the owner of a copyright as incidental to the relief by injunction, but it must be prayed for in the bill. Stevens v. Cady, 2 Curt., 200.

§ 1292. A court of equity cannot act on a case which is not fairly made out by the bill and answer. But it is not necessary that these should point out in detail the means which the court shall adopt in giving relief. Under the general prayer for relief the court will often extend relief beyond the specific prayer, and not exactly in accordance with it. Walden v. Bodley, 14 Pet., 156.

§ 1293. Interrogatories.— Under the fortieth rule of the federal practice the defendant is not bound to answer unless special interrogatories be put in the bill. Such a bill is clearly demurrable. Treadwell v. Cleaveland, 3 McL., 283.

§ 1294. A bill requiring an answer must, under the rules of the United States supreme court, contain interrogatories. Wilson v. Stolley, 4 McL., 272.

§ 1295. Where discovery is the object, or the principal object, distinct interrogatories should be affixed to the bill. Parsons v. Cumming,* 1 Woods, 463.

§ 1296. Under the ninety-third equity rule, rendering it unnecessary to interrogate a defendant specially to obtain a discovery, a bill may be a bill for a discovery without an allegation that a discovery is necessary, or special interrogatories, and complainant may have an answer under oath under his prayer. Perry v. Corning, 6 Blatch., 134.

§ 1297. Interrogatories by plaintiff are not framed upon the theory that everything appearing in the bill is true, strictly and in detail. The possibility of plaintiff's misinformation may be taken into account. Interrogatories are proper if they touch with sufficient directness the subject-matter of the suit. Railroad Co. v. Macomb, 2 Fed. R., 18.

§ 1298. Where the question of notice is material, and the bill charges the defendant with notice, he is bound to answer without a special interrogatory. He is not bound to answer irrelevant interrogatories. Mechanics' Bank of Alexandria v. Lynn, 1 Pet., 376.

§ 1299. Laches.— A complainant seeking to enforce a stale claim in equity should set forth in his bill what were the impediments to an earlier prosecution of his claim; how he came to be so long ignorant of his rights, and the means used by the respondent to fraudulently keep him in ignorance; and how and when he first came to a knowledge of the matters alleged in his bill. Badger v. Badger, 2 Wall., 87. See LIMITATIONS.

§ 1300. A bill for an account, after a great lapse of time, should state the reason why it was not brought sooner, so as to repel the presumption of laches. If the case turns upon fraud, mistake or concealment, it should be stated what this was, and how brought about. The charges must be reasonable, definite and certain as to time and occasion and subject-matter. Especially must there be distinct averments as to when and how the fraud, etc., was discovered; for if by ordinary diligence the discovery might have been before made, the bill has no standing on account of laches. Stearns v. Page,* 1 Story, 204.

§ 1301. The question whether or not a bill is bad for laches depends upon the circumstances of the case. A bill is not defective in this respect which charges a fraud committed ten years previously, but only discovered by plaintiff within a year. Forbes v. Overby,* 4 Hughes, 441.

§ 1302. A delay of five years in bringing a bill to vacate a decree in a former suit on account of fraud must be satisfactorily explained, and the time when knowledge of the fraud was discovered set forth. Harwood v. Railroad Co., 17 Wall., 78.

§ 1303. If a bill to rescind a deed is filed after a considerable lapse of time, and the exercise by the plaintiff of the powers of an owner over the property, so as to change its character or value materially, the bill must state sufficient reasons for the delay, and those reasons must be made out in the proof. Fisher v. Boody, 1 Curt., 206.

§ 1804. Though lapse of time be not pleaded as a bar, the judgment of the court will be influenced by delay, not accounted for, when the bill seeks to rescind a sale. Ibid.

§ 1805. Multifariousness.— A bill cannot be sustained in equity which is multifarious and embraces distinct matters, affecting distinct parties, who have no common interest in the distinct matters. West v. Randall, 2 Mason, 181.

§ 1806. By multifariousness is meant improperly joining in one bill independent matters and thereby confounding them, as by uniting distinct and unconnected matters against one defendant, or by demanding several such matters against several defendants in the same bill. A prayer for alternative relief, however, never makes a bill multifarious. Kilgour v. New Orleans Gas Light Co., 2 Woods, 144; Haines v. Carpenter, 1 Woods, 262.

§ 1807. A bill is not multifarious where it does not unite titles which have no analogy to each other, whereby the defendant's litigation and costs are increased. Turner v. The American Baptist Missionary Union, 5 McL., 344.

§ 1808. Two inconsistent causes for relief must not be united in a single bill, although a bill may be framed with a double aspect and alternative relief be demanded, if neither relief is inconsistent with a state of facts conceded by the bill. Wilkinson v. Dobbie, 12 Blatch., 298.

§ 1809. Equity permits the joinder of several causes of action in one bill, provided such joinder does not embarrass the defendant or introduce unnecessary confusion into the cause. Herman Patent Mfg. Co. v. Brooklyn City R. R. Co., 15 Blatch., 444.

§ 1810. There is no absolute rule on the subject of multifariousness of a bill in equity. The decisions are contradictory, and each case depends chiefly on its own facts. M'Lean v. Lafayette Bank, 3 McL., 415.

§ 1811. Courts of equity do not allow a multifarious bill as a remedy for a multiplicity of suits, and a bill which unites a controversy as to the validity of certain bequests in a will with a claim of the heirs of the husband of the testatrix to the property as not passing by the will, and with a suit of a creditor of the succession to recover judgment against the estate, and with a demand for an executor's account, is multifarious. Haines v. Carpenter, 1 Woods, 262.

§ 1812. A bill which by the accepted canons of equity pleading would be bad on demurrer for multifariousness, both as to subjects and parties, cannot be objected to on that account, if these defects arise from conformity with an act of congress directing such a bill to be filed in a federal court. United States v. Union Pacific R. Co., 8 Otto, 569.

§ 1813. Several defendants who have no connection with each other in interest, in estate or in contract, and against whom, jointly, the plaintiffs have no cause of suit, either at law or in equity, cannot be joined in one bill. United States v. Alexander, 4 Cr. C. C., 311.

§ 1814. A bill which seeks to have the purchase by which the defendant became possessed of an estate per autre vie set aside, and also to have him charged with certain taxes on the estate, is not multifarious, but alternative, and is an ordinary form of pleading necessary for economy in litigation. Elliot v. Lamon,* 1 MacArth., 647.

§ 1815. Bill in equity by several distributees against administrator to enforce foreign decree for their several shares is not multifarious. Shields v. Thomas, 18 How., 253.

§ 1816. A bill filed against the executors of an estate and all those who purchased from them is not, upon that ground alone, multifarious. Gaines v. Chew, 2 How., 619.

§ 1817. A bill in equity to adjudge the plaintiff to have the equitable title to certain land, and also that a certain person in possession of the land be made party defendant to the bill, be compelled to disclose the nature of his claim to such land, and to account for the rents and profits thereof, is multifarious. Coper v. Flesher, 1 Bond, 440.

§ 1818. A bill by a railroad, joining the various counties through which the road runs as parties defendant, to restrain them from selling, for non-payment of taxes, certain land claimed by the complainant, is not multifarious if the question on which the case turns is common to all, and the counties are in fact the agencies of the state as to that part of the taxes which they must pay into the state treasury. Union Pac. R. Co. v. McShane, 3 Dill., 303.

§ 1819. Where a suit in equity was brought against a company which was alleged to be the fraudulent transferee of another company, on the property of which the plaintiff claimed a lien, joining such transferring company and asking for a decree to establish such lien, for an injunction against further sale, and for a moneyed judgment, it was held that the president of the transferring company was not a proper party, and that the bill as against the two companies was not multifarious. Hibernia Ins. Co. v. St. Louis, etc., Co., 10 Fed. R., 596.

§ 1820. When a bill sets out one general conspiracy to defraud the complainant it is not multifarious because it charges numerous distinct transactions, if each of these is embraced in the general scope of the conspiracy. Northern Pacific R. R. Co. v. Kindred, 3 McC., 627.

§ 1821. Where certain land is held by numerous defendants, claiming distinct and separate parcels by a similar title, and threatening distinct actions for injuries to their respective parcels, a bill brought against such numerous defendants to quiet title, being in the nature of a bill of peace, is not multifarious on account of the joinder of such defendants. Central Pacific R. R. Co. v. Dyer, 1 Saw., 641.

§ 1822. A bill to restrain infringement of a patent is not bad for multifariousness because the article made by the defendants infringes two patents of the plaintiffs, if both are used in the manufacture of one thing, nor because the plaintiff is assignee of both patents, and one patent is assigned for the Pacific coast and the other for the state of California only. Gillespie v. Cummings, 3 Saw., 259.

§ 1823. A bill against an administrator charging fraud, and seeking among other things to open settlements with the probate court, and also to cancel a receipt given by the complainant to the defendant, is not multifarious, if the only object of the bill is to determine the condition of an estate and compel an account by the administrator. Payne v. Hook, 7 Wall., 425.

§ 1824. A bill to collect assessments, charged upon land by the front foot and against the same defendant, is not multifarious because brought to enforce the lien against several lots. Fitch v. Creighton, 24 How., 159.

§ 1825. A bill may be demurred to for multifariousness, both for misjoinder of parties and causes, when one complainant has no standing in court, and the causes are antagonistic because in one, one set of parties are interested, in another, another set. Walker v. Powers, 14 Otto, 245.

§ 1826. A bill founded upon several patents for improvement in reaping machines, intended for use in all such machines, and not necessarily connected, is not multifarious when the machine upon which the suit is brought contains all the improvements. Nourse v. Allen, 4 Blatch., 376.

§ 1827. A bill in equity was held not to be multifarious, which was brought to set aside conveyances of land, against several different defendants, holding different tracts under different purchases, on the ground that the main defense, the validity of a certain will, was common to all the defendants, and though details of the various purchases might be different, yet they might be ascertained without inconvenience to co-defendants. The bill avoided multiplicity of suits, without subjecting defendants to unreasonable expense or inconvenience. It was not important that a separate bill might have been brought against each defendant. Gaines v. Mausseaux,* 1 Woods, 118.

§ 1828. A bill to set aside an insurance policy is not rendered multifarious by joining a prayer to restrain one of the defendants from further prosecuting a suit at law to recover premiums paid. Equitable Life Ass. Soc. v. Patterson, 1 Fed. R., 126.

§ 1829. A count upon a promise to pay in consideration that the plaintiff, who had arrested the other partner upon a ca. sa., would, at the present defendant's request, forbear to prosecute that other partner upon the ca. sa., and would not trouble him, but let him go out of custody of the marshal, and in further consideration that the debt was a partnership debt for which the present defendant was equally liable with the other partner, and which he had promised that other partner to pay, is not double or multifarious, and is even good upon special demurrer. Rice v. Barry, 2 Cr. C. C., 447.

§ 1830. The objection of multifariousness in a bill must be made before answer; it cannot be made after; and can be tested only by the structure of the bill itself. Nelson v. Hill, 5 How., 127.

§ 1831. The objection of multifariousness can be taken by a party to the bill only by demurrer, or plea, or answer, and cannot be taken at the hearing of the cause. But the court itself may take the objection at any time — at the hearing or otherwise. The objection cannot be taken by a party in the appellate court. Oliver v. Piatt, 3 How., 333.

§ 1832. Certain timber land was purchased by A. of X. and Z., A. agreeing to pay therefor at the rate of $1 per thousand feet for all the good pine timber, to be ascertained by certain persons appointed by all parties, who were accordingly appointed and made estimate. A. subsequently conveyed a portion to D., D. agreeing with X. and Z. to pay therefor one-fourth in money and the remainder in notes, and they giving a bond to convey him the land on full payment of the notes. D. died insolvent and A. became his administrator, and agreed with X. and Z. in his behalf to surrender the bonds for the notes, which was done. The present bill was afterwards brought by A., as administrator of D., and charged that there was a gross error in the original appraisement, unknown to him, A., by which D. had been induced to make the said bargain, and prayed that the bargain should be set aside, and the purchase money paid by D. should be refunded. But A. made no personal claim for relief. Held, (1) that the bill was objectionable for multifariousness in mixing up the independent claims which A. had personally and which he had as administrator; (2) that it set forth no case for canceling the original agreement; (3) that even if it had, it was too defective and loose to support such a claim, in not bringing the proper parties before the court, and in alleging a mere mistake without fraud as a ground of relief, which, under the circumstances, was not sufficient.   Carter *v.* Treadwell, 8 Story, 25.

§ 1883. Cross-bill. — A cross-bill is a mere auxiliary suit, and may be brought by a defendant against the plaintiff or against other defendants, or against both, but it must be touching the matters in question in the bill, and must not introduce a new controversy not necessary to be decided in order to have a final decree on the original bill.   Cross *v.* De Valle, 1 Wall., 5.

§ 1884. A bill which brings up new matter not touched by the original parties is no proper cross-bill.   Hence, when the original bill asked nothing about future rights in an estate devised, nor sought to avoid anything as tending to a perpetuity, these matters could not be brought up by cross-bill.   *Ibid.*

§ 1885. In a cross-bill brought for relief as well as defense, necessary parties may be joined who were not parties to the original bill.   Brandon Manuf. Co. *v.* Prime, 14 Blatch., 371.

§ 1886. A cross-bill goes no further than to give the party filing it the reciprocal right enjoyed by the complainant in the original bill, in respect to their mutual title or interest in the subject-matter of the suit; and if, in a patent suit, the cross-bill is one of discovery, it must rest on a title in the party filing it either in common with or hostile to the patentee.   Young *v.* Colt, 2 Blatch., 373.

§ 1887. A defendant cannot file a cross-bill until the original bill is answered.   Allen *v.* Allen, Hemp., 58.

§ 1888. If a controversy between co-defendants does not affect the rights of the complainant, or qualify the decree in his favor, it is not properly the subject of a cross-bill.   To allow a cross-bill to lie, the settlement of the controversy embraced by it must be necessary for a complete decree upon the subject-matter of the original bill.   Weaver *v.* Alter, 3 Woods, 152.

§ 1889. Any affirmative relief sought by a defendant in equity must be by cross-bill, and can never be granted upon the facts stated in the answer.   Chapin *v.* Walker, 6 Fed. R., 794.

§ 1840. When a lien on a bond is set up in answer to a bill brought to remove the defendant from trusteeship under a deed to secure payment of the bond to the complainant, and to compel the defendant to deliver up the bond, a cross-bill should be filed to enforce the lien, but if none is filed, still the court will take the lien, if deemed valid, into consideration in making its decree, although no affirmative remedy to enforce it can be given.   McPherson *v.* Cox, 6 Otto, 404.

§ 1841. A cross-bill cannot be filed after leave to file it has been asked of the court and refused.   Bronson *v.* La Crosse R. Co., 2 Wall., 288.

§ 1842. Where several plaintiffs have brought a bill and obtained a decree against defendants for the infringement of a patent, the latter cannot maintain, as a cross-bill, a bill to compel the former plaintiffs to disclose in what proportions they claimed payment of the amount of the judgment, so that the present plaintiffs might set off a judgment obtained by them against one of the former plaintiffs.   Rubber Co. *v.* Goodyear, 9 Wall., 807.

§ 1843. Unless there has been fraud or mistake a party is bound by a cross-bill filed by his solicitor; and the fact that he never saw the cross-bill or read it will not allow him to repudiate it.   Putnam *v.* Day, 22 Wall., 60.

§ 1844. The equity practice of the United States courts recognizes no such pleading, as an "answer in the nature of a cross-bill" authorized by the code of Georgia.   Hicks *v.* Jennings, 4 Fed. R., 855.

·2. *Demurrer.*

SUMMARY — *Demurrer to part, certainty,* § 1845. — *Demurrer not to rely upon answer,* § 1846. — *Demurrer to interrogatories,* § 1847. — *Demurrer waived by answer,* § 1848. — Laches, § 1849. — *Demurrer to cross-bill,* § 1850. — *Demurrer to whole bill,* § 1851. — *Demurrer for unnecessary parties,* § 1852. — *Demurrer to cross-bill,* § 1853. — *Demurrer ore tenus,* § 1854.

§ 1845. A demurrer to a part of a bill must point out with certainty the part demurred to. Though this be done properly, the addition of the words "or elsewhere" will be sufficient to vitiate the demurrer by rendering it uncertain.   Railroad Co. *v.* Macomb, §§ 1855-60.

§ 1846. A demurrer to the bill must depend solely upon what appears in the bill and not at all upon the answer.   *Ibid.*

§ 1847. It is no function of a demurrer to interrogatories to raise the question whether the party demurring has sufficiently answered the interrogatories.   *Ibid.*

§ 1848. By putting in an answer to the whole bill a defendant waives a previous demurrer to the whole bill.   If, however, he be allowed to elect between them and elect to rely on his demurrer, he will probably be held to waive thereby his right to answer.   Adams *v.* Howard, § 1861.

§ 1849. A defense grounded upon laches or staleness of the claim presented may be raised by demurrer. Landsdale v. Smith, §§ 1362-63.

§ 1850. A demurrer to a cross-bill, on the ground that another court has prior jurisdiction, cannot be sustained. Brandon Manuf. Co. v. Prime, §§ 1364-67.

§ 1851. A demurrer to the whole bill will be overruled if any part be good. Ibid.

§ 1852. Defendants properly joined cannot demur on the ground that others are improperly joined. Ibid.

§ 1853. A cross-bill, for relief as well as for defense, is not subject to demurrer on the ground that it adds parties not joined in the original bill, provided these parties are necessary to the cross-bill. Ibid.

§ 1854. A demurrer ore tenus should be co-extensive with the demurrer on record. Equitable Life Ass. Soc. v. Patterson, §§ 1368-71.

[Notes.— See §§ 1372-1420.]

CHICAGO, ST. LOUIS & NEW ORLEANS RAILROAD COMPANY v. MACOMB.

(Circuit Court for New York: 2 Federal Reporter, 18-23. 1880.)

Opinion by Choate, J.

Statement of Facts.— The complainant, claiming to have succeeded to the rights of purchasers under a foreclosure sale in a certain railroad, has brought this bill for discovery and relief, in respect to certain bonds issued or alleged to have been issued under two earlier mortgages on parts of the road, praying, among other things, that certain of said earlier mortgage bonds, in the possession of the defendants, be delivered up to be canceled. The bill also contains a prayer for general relief.

The defendant Macomb has filed an answer, in which he has answered part of the bill. He has also filed thirty-two demurrers to different parts of the bill, and the demurrers have been argued.

The first demurrer is to "so much and such part of said bill as in the fourth, fifth, sixteenth, eighteenth, twenty-first, twenty-third, twenty-fourth, twenty fifth, twenty-sixth, twenty-seventh and twenty-eighth interrogatories, or elsewhere, seeks that this defendant may answer and set forth the matters as to which he is thereby interrogated of and concerning said first mortgage bonds, etc., not therein and thereby referred to as having been issued without the consent of the trustees in said mortgage, or without the certificate of such trustees." And the special cause of demurrer alleged is that the plaintiff has not stated such a case as entitles it to such discovery.

An objection is taken to this demurrer that, even without the addition of the words "or elsewhere," the demurrer would be sufficiently certain, yet those words make the demurrer bad because it does not point out with certainty the parts of the bills demurred to.

§ 1355. *Demurrer to part of a bill must point out with certainty what part.*

The rule undoubtedly is that a special demurrer to part of a bill must point out with certainty the part demurred to. This is not only necessary for reasons of convenience, but, unless the demurrer has this precision, there must be great uncertainty in the judgment, if a judgment is entered, sustaining the demurrer. Atwill v. Ferrett, 2 Blatch., 39. The defendant's counsel relies, however, on the case of Claridge v. Hoar, 14 Ves. Jr., 65, as an authority for rejecting the words "or elsewhere" as surplusage. That was not a case of a demurrer, but of a plea, and I think it has no relevancy to this question.

It would seem that if the demurrer is sustained it must be sustained as a whole. And if that is so the judgment would evidently be uncertain as to what parts of the bill under the judgment on the demurrer the defendant would be excused from answering. But as both parties have also fully argued this demurrer on the merits, as if it were a demurrer to the discovery sought in the enumerated interrogatories only, I have examined it as if the words "or elsewhere" had been omitted or could be rejected.

§ **1356.** *Interrogatories are not framed on the theory that everything in the bill is strictly true in detail.*

The bill alleges that the first mortgage bonds to which these interrogatories relate are void in the hands of the defendant, on several grounds, and among other things alleged in respect to all of that class of bonds held by this defendant it is stated in the bill that they had not the certificate of the trustees to their genuineness, as required by the mortgage. This defect is alleged as one of the grounds for holding them void in the hands of the defendant, who is also alleged to hold them with notice of their invalidity, and without having parted with value for them.

The objection to these interrogatories is, as stated in defendant's brief, that "inasmuch as the bill only charges Macomb with holding *uncertificated* bonds, can the plaintiff have a discovery as to any other bonds?" It is also objected that the plaintiff is not entitled to any discovery as to any bonds not held by the defendant Macomb. The interrogatories referred to are undoubtedly broad enough to call for answers as to first mortgage bonds held by Macomb, other than uncertified bonds, and also as to bonds other than those held by Macomb, certified or uncertified. But I think the plaintiff is entitled to the discovery sought for in both particulars. It is true it is alleged in the bill that the bonds held by this defendant are uncertified, but on this point the plaintiff may be misinformed; and, in fact, the defendant's bonds may be in part certified, and interrogatories are not to be framed and limited upon the theory that everything stated in the bill is precisely and in every detail true.

§ **1357.** *Office of prayer for general relief.*

And, as to the other point, the bill shows such grounds of relief against this defendant and his associates, for alleged fraud in the disposition of these bonds generally, the rights of the complainant not being limited to those held by this defendant, that the interrogatories are proper for the purpose of discovering what disposition has been made of any of that issue of bonds. The point is also made that the prayer for relief is limited to the bonds held by the defendant. But the bill states a case larger than that, and the prayer for general relief is a prayer for any relief the court can give, except by injunction, upon the facts averred in the bill. Story, Eq. Pl., 404!.

The second, third, fourth, sixth, seventh, eighth, ninth, tenth, eleventh, twelfth, fifteenth, sixteenth, seventeenth, nineteenth and twentieth demurrers are clearly bad because they do not point out with certainty the parts of the bill demurred to.

§ **1358.** *A demurrer must depend solely upon what appears in the bill, and not at all upon the answer.*

The fifth demurrer is to "so much and such part of said bill as in the fifth, seventh, nineteenth, twenty-first, twenty-third, twenty-fourth, twenty-fifth, twenty-sixth, twenty-seventh and twenty-eighth interrogatories, or elsewhere, seeks that this defendant may answer and set forth the matters, etc., concerning the payment or redemption of any second mortgage bonds, etc., not alleged in the bill, or appearing by this defendant's answer to have been at the time of the commencement of this suit or now to be in the hands and possession of this defendant. The ground alleged is that no such case is stated in the bill as entitles the plaintiff to the discovery.

This demurrer is open to the same objection in matter of form as the first demurrer, and to this further objection, that it is not based upon what appears in the bill, but refers to averments in the answer for the purpose of defining the part of the bill demurred to. This is objected to as a fatal defect in the demurrer, and I think the objection is well taken. It violates the rule that a demurrer "relies merely upon matter apparent on the face of the bill." Mitf. Eq. Pl., 249. It also leaves the parts demurred to uncertain. But upon the merits I think the plaintiff is entitled to the discovery sought, and that the objection made to the bill, that the fraud alleged is not averred with sufficient certainty, is not well taken.

§ **1359.** *Interrogatories proper which touch directly the subject-matter of suit.*
The thirteenth demurrer is to the discovery sought by the eleventh interrogatory as to the books and accounts of the "Mississippi Central Railroad Company." The grounds of demurrer are that that company has no interest in the cause; that the discovery is not material to the relief prayed for; and that the plaintiff has not stated such a case as entitles it to such discovery. The fourteenth demurrer is to the twelfth interrogatory, which seeks similar discovery as to the books and accounts of the "Southern Railroad Association." The same grounds of demurrer are alleged. The bill alleges, on information and belief, that the books of both said corporations are in the possession and under the control of the defendant Macomb, who is also alleged to be an officer of the first-named company, and the president of the second. It is alleged in the bill that these books and accounts were kept under the direction of the defendant, and contain very material evidence of the dealing of said companies with each other, and with this defendant and his associates, touching the redemption of the mortgage bonds, the subject-matter of the suit, and I can see no reason why the interrogatories should not be answered.

The eighteenth demurrer is to the seventh interrogatory, which seeks discovery as to whether the defendant holds or owns the bonds held by him in his own right, or holds them for other parties or jointly with others, and if for or with others, for and with whom. The ground of this demurrer is that as to any bonds not held by the defendant he is a mere witness. But the interrogatory does not call for any discovery as to any bonds not held by the defendant, and as to those held by him it is averred that he has received them, with notice and without consideration, from parties having no right to them, and he is asked to disclose what interest he has.

§ **1360.** *It is no function of a demurrer to raise the question whether the party demurring has sufficiently answered the interrogatories.*
The remaining demurrers, which are to the discovery sought by particular interrogatories, seem not to be well taken. To many of these interrogatories the defendant has answered, and the object of the demurrers appears to be to obtain the opinion of the court whether he should answer further. If the interrogatories are too broad, and he has answered so far as the plaintiff has shown himself entitled by his bill to a discovery, a demurrer to the interrogatory is unnecessary and improper. If the plaintiff is satisfied with the answer, then, so far as that part of the bill is concerned, the answer is complete. If the plaintiff is not satisfied, it is the special office of an exception, and not of a demurrer, to raise the question whether the answer is sufficient.

The demurrers are overruled.

ADAMS v. HOWARD.

(Circuit Court for New York: 9 Federal Reporter, 347. 1881.)

Opinion by BLATCHFORD, J.

STATEMENT OF FACTS.— The defendant Morse has demurred to the whole bill and has put in an answer to the whole bill. The suit is one for the infringement of a patent. The grounds of demurrer set forth in the demurrer are all of them also set forth in the answer. They relate solely to the title set forth in the bill to the patent and to the allegations in the bill respecting infringement. A replication to the answer has been filed. The plaintiffs now move for an order, either that the defendant elect between his demurrer and his answer, or that the demurrer be set down for argument.

§ 1361. *An answer to a whole bill is a waiver of a previous demurrer to the whole bill.*

By rule 32 in equity a defendant may demur to the whole bill and may demur to a part of the bill and answer as to the residue. But there is nothing that allows him to demur to the whole bill and at the same time to answer to the whole bill, especially where the answer sets up everything that is in the demurrer. Putting in such an answer is a waiver of such a demurrer. The defendant must elect between his demurrer and his answer; and, to guard against misunderstanding, if he should elect his demurrer and it should be overruled on argument, he would be held probably to have waived what ordinarily and otherwise would be under rule 34 his right to answer.

The defendant moves to dismiss the bill. The ground of the motion is not specified in the notice of motion. From the affidavit made in support of the motion, one ground would seem to be that the plaintiffs did not under rule 38 set down the demurrer for argument within the time required, and that they did not take any testimony within three months after the replication was filed. I think the plaintiffs sufficiently excuse the omissions. The demurrer ought to be disposed of before any testimony is taken. The motion is denied.

LANDSDALE v. SMITH.

(16 Otto, 391-395. 1882.)

APPEAL from the Supreme Court of the District of Columbia.

STATEMENT OF FACTS.— In July, 1818, Van Ness conveyed to Stinchcomb certain lands, to be held for a term of ninety-nine years, renewable forever, at a certain fixed annual rent. In 1833 Van Ness repossessed himself of the land on account of non-payment of rent. In 1841 Stinchcomb died, and this bill is filed forty years thereafter, by his administratrix, offering to pay arrears of rent, interest, etc., and proposing to redeem the land. The bill was dismissed on demurrer, and complainant appealed.

§ 1362. *A defense grounded on the staleness of the claim and the laches of the claimant may be set up by demurrer.*

Opinion by MR. JUSTICE HARLAN.

It has been a recognized doctrine of courts in equity from the very beginning of their jurisdiction to withhold relief from those who have delayed for an unreasonable length of time in asserting their claims. Elmendorf v. Taylor, 10 Wheat., 152; Piatt v. Vattier, 9 Pet., 405; Maxwell v. Kennedy, 8 How., 210; Badger v. Badger, 2 Wall., 87; Cholmondeley v. Clinton, 2 Jac. & W., 1;

2 Story, Eq. Jur., sec. 1520. In Wagner v. Baird, 7 How., 234, it was said that long acquiescence and laches by parties out of possession are productive of much hardship and injustice to others, and cannot be excused except by showing some actual hindrance or impediment caused by the fraud or concealment of the party in possession, which will appeal to the conscience of the chancellor.

And, contrary to the view pressed in argument, a defense grounded upon the staleness of the claim asserted, or upon the gross laches of the party asserting it, may be made by demurrer, not necessarily by plea or answer. A different rule has been announced by some authors and in some adjudged cases; generally, however, upon the authority of the case of The Earl of Deloraine v. Browne, 3 Bro. C. C., 633. Lord Thurlow, who decided that case, is reported to have declared, when overruling a demurrer to a bill charging fraudulent representations as to the value of an estate, and praying an account of rents, profits, etc., that his action was based upon the ground that length of time, *proprio jure*, was no reason for a demurrer; that it was only a conclusion from facts, showing acquiescence, and was not matter of law; and that he could not allow a party to avail himself of an inference from facts on a demurrer. But in Hovenden v. Lord Annesley, 2 Sch. & Lef., 607, decided in 1806, Lord Redesdale expressed his disapproval of the decision of Lord Thurlow, as reported by Brown, and said that it was rendered in a hurry, when the latter was about to surrender the seals, and when much injury might have been done to parties had judgments not been given before the latter retired from office. The rule, as announced in Hovenden v. Lord Annesley, was "that when a party does not by his bill bring himself within the rule of the court, the other party may by demurrer demand judgment whether he ought to be compelled to answer. If the case of the plaintiff, as stated in the bill, will not entitle him to a decree, the judgment of the court may be required by demurrer, whether the defendant ought to be compelled to answer the bill." That, the court said, was matter of the law of a court of equity, to be determined according to its rules and principles.

Such is, undoubtedly, the established doctrine of this court as announced in many cases. In Maxwell v. Kennedy, *supra*, the court, speaking by Mr. Chief Justice Taney, approved the rule as announced by Lord Redesdale. After referring to Piatt v. Vattier, *supra*, and to McKnight v. Taylor, 1 How., 161, and Bowman v. Wathen, id., 189, it was said that "the proper rule of pleading would seem to be that, when the case stated by the bill appears to be one in which a court of equity will refuse its aid, the defendant should be permitted to resist it by demurrer. And as the laches of the complainant in asserting his claim is a bar in equity, if that objection is apparent on the bill itself, there can be no good reason for requiring a plea or answer to bring it to the notice of the court." In the more recent case of Badger v. Badger, *supra*, the court, speaking by Mr. Justice Grier, said that a party, who makes an appeal to the conscience of the chancellor, "should set forth in his bill specifically what were the impediments to an earlier prosecution of his claim; how he came to be so long ignorant of his rights, and the means used by the respondent to fraudulently keep him in ignorance; and how and when he first came to a knowledge of the matters alleged in his bill; otherwise the chancellor may justly refuse to consider his case, on his own showing, without inquiry whether there is a demurrer or formal plea of the statute of limitations contained in the answer." Page 95.

§ **1363.** *Instance of laches in neglecting rights for forty years.*

These principles are decisive of the case before us. It is plainly one of gross laches on the part of Stinchcomb and those claiming under him. His right under the deed of 1818, to repossess himself of the premises by paying rents and charges in arrear, accrued the moment Van Ness re-entered. But the assertion of it could not be safely neglected for an unreasonable length of time. The bill discloses no plausible, much less sufficient, explanation of the long delay ensuing, after 1833, without an attempt by Stinchcomb, his representatives or his heirs, to recover the property by discharging the rents and charges in arrear, and re-entering, as might have been done, in pursuance of the provisions of that deed. On the contrary, the facts set out in the bill justify the conclusion either that he elected in his life-time to abandon his claim, or that it was, in some way, satisfactorily arranged or discharged. The complainant and those whom she represents have slept too long upon their rights. The peace of society and the security of property demand that the presumption of right, arising from a great lapse of time, without the assertion of an adverse claim, should not be disturbed. In such cases sound discretion requires that the court should withhold relief.

Some reference has been made to the decisions of the supreme court of Maryland, the laws of which state, as they existed on the 27th of February, 1801, except as since modified or repealed by congress, continue in force in this District. It is only necessary to say that the principles to which we have referred have been steadily upheld by that court, not upon the ground of any changes in the law of the state since 1801, but in deference to the established doctrines governing courts of equity in giving relief to those who seek the enforcement of antiquated demands. Hepburn's Case, 3 Bland (Md.), 95; Hawkins *v.* Chapman, 36 Md., 83; Nelson *v.* Hagerstown Bank, 27 id., 51; Syester *v.* Brewer, id., 288; Frazier *v.* Gelston, 35 id., 298.

For the reasons given we are of opinion that the court below properly sustained the demurrer, and dismissed the bill for want of equity.

Decree affirmed.

BRANDON MANUFACTURING COMPANY *v.* PRIME.

(Circuit Court for New York: 14 Blatchford, 871–875. 1878.)

Opinion by WHEELER, J.

STATEMENT OF FACTS.— This cause has been heard on the several demurrer of defendant Strong, and joint demurrer of defendants Prime, Meacham and Luce, to the cross-bill. The causes of demurrer assigned are the same in each. They are, in substance, that this court has not jurisdiction, because the court of chancery of the state had acquired prior jurisdiction on a bill brought by the orator in the cross-bill, there, for the same relief; that some of the relief prayed is not cognizable in equity; that some of the subjects of the cross-bill are not the same as those of the original bill; and that Strong and another, made parties to the cross-bill, were not parties to the original bill. Both are demurrers to the whole bill.

§ **1364.** *A plea of jurisdiction in another court is not a good plea to a cross-bill.*

The orators in the original bill commenced the litigation involved in this court, and compelled the orator in the cross-bill to come here and join in it. Having brought it here they have no right to say that the whole or any part of its belongs anywhere else. If the cross-bill is appropriate to the original, it must relate to the subjects of it and embrace a part, at least, of the litigation introduced by it, so that by filing the cross-bill the orator in that has merely met those in the original where called upon by them to meet them. For this reason a plea of jurisdiction in another court is not a good plea to a cross-bill. 2 Dan. Ch. Pr. (4th Am. ed.), 636; Welford's Eq. Pl., 229; Ld. Newburg v. Wren, 1 Vern., 220. And for the same reason it is not necessary to show, in a proper cross-bill, that the relief sought by it is cognizable in equity. Story's Eq. Pl., § 399.

§ 1365. *A demurrer to the whole bill will be overruled if any part be good.*

It has not been claimed in argument, and could not successfully be claimed, but that this cross-bill relates to the subject of the original in some respects, nor but that some of the relief prayed in the cross-bill is properly prayed. And it follows that some of it is proper to be answered, in some form, by some of the parties; and that some of it may not be is no good reason for not answering what should be answered. As the demurrers are to the whole, and a part clearly should be answered, and the demurrers must be overruled or sustained as a whole, as to the causes relating to jurisdiction and relief, they must be overruled.

§ 1366. *Proper defendants cannot demur on the ground that others are improperly joined.*

So far as the defendants Prime, Meacham and Luce are concerned, it would be sufficient to say, as to the other causes of demurrer, that, because other parties are improperly called upon to answer the cross-bill in this form, it is no good reason why they, who are properly called upon to answer it, should not do so. But if the others are properly called upon to answer it, *a fortiori* they are and should answer it.

§ 1367. *When a cross-bill is brought for relief as well as defense, and shows that persons not parties to the original are necessary parties, they may be added.*

The question hereupon is merely whether the cross-bill should be answered at all or not by these other parties. That depends, of course, upon whether the subjects of it are so presented here by it that they are properly called upon to answer it in the form in which they are presented. The original bill sets forth, in substance, that the orators in that have a patent that the orator in the cross-bill is infringing, and prays appropriate relief. The cross-bill sets forth that the defendant Strong had the record title to the patent, and the orator the equitable title to it, and that the orators in the original bill acquired Strong's title with notice of the outstanding equity, and were endeavoring to assert it against the equitable title, and prays restraint and a conveyance. It is unquestionably the proper office of a cross-bill to afford relief in such a case, if the case is made out. Story, Eq. Pl., § 391; Calverley v. Williams, 1 Ves. Jr., 210. A cross-bill is like an original bill, except that it must rest on what is necessary to the defense of an original bill. In an original bill, brought by the orator in the cross-bill for the same relief, there could be no fair question but that these new parties, of whom Strong is one, would be proper parties. In this original bill, as it is framed, these do not appear to be necessary parties, but when the facts set up in the cross-bill appear they become so. Following the ordinary rule, when the orator in the cross-bill resorts to it for defense and relief, and makes it appear that they are not only proper but necessary parties to the litigation, that orator not only might, but ought, to make them parties. If there were no authorities and was no practice on the subject, on principle that would seem to be the proper course. That the practice in this state, which professes to follow the English chancery practice, the same that is followed in this court, would warrant making him a party, is well known and appears in the state reports. Blodgett v. Hobart, 18 Vt., 414. It does not appear expressly from such English reports or text-books as have been examined what the actual practice in such cases there has been. In this country, in Curd v. Lewis, 1 Dana, 351, a decree was reversed for the reason that an assignor of the subject of litigation in an original and cross-bill was not a party to either, and should have been made a party to the cross-bill, and that he might be made such a party. Wickliffe v. Clay, id., 585, was heard by consent only, without making a party, that by the cross-bill appeared necessary, a new party by the cross-bill. In Sharp v. Pike, 5 B. Mon., 155, a new party was added by cross-bill against his own express objection. In Walker v. Brungard, 13 S. & M., 723, new parties were added and new matters brought in by cross-bill, and heard without objection. In disposing of the case, the chancellor, delivering the opinion of the court, said that, if they had been objected to, the new matters would all have been kept out, without saying that the new parties would have been. In Costers v. Bank of Georgia, 24 Ala., 37, it was expressly held that new parties should be added by cross-bill, when so interested in the litigation involved by it as to be proper parties to it.

Opposed to all this, there is the remark of Mr. Justice Curtis in Shields v. Barrow, 17 How., 130, and the reasons given by him in support of it, to the effect that new parties cannot in any case properly be added by cross-bill, without citing any authority for it, and books and cases that have followed that remark without citing any other authority. That precise question was not involved in that case, but the mere *dictum* of such a judge of such a court would ordinarily be followed, especially by lower courts. An examination of his reasoning shows that he made the suggestion without much examination, probably, and his reasoning does not cover the whole ground as to all classes of cases. The modes of procedure he suggests would probably be ample in all cases of cross-bills brought for discovery in aid of a defense merely to the original bill, but not in cases of those brought for relief as well as defense, where new parties would be necessary to the relief sought. As in this case, the methods he states as the proper ones, if successfully followed, would enable the defendant in the original bill to defeat the orator therein, but not to reach the affirmative relief prayed in the cross-bill, if entitled to it. Weighty as that remark is, it is not thought to be sufficient to control the reasons and authorities to the contrary of it. The result of what is thought to be the soundest reasoning and the best considered authorities is that, where a cross-bill shows that there is a party to the subjects of the litigation as presented by it, who has not been before made a party nor appeared to be a necessary one, and then does appear to be such, that party should be brought in by the cross-bill.

The result is that this cross-bill should be answered by all those made defendants to it. The demurrers are overruled, and it is thereupon ordered that the defendants to the cross-bill answer over.

EQUITABLE LIFE ASSURANCE SOCIETY *v.* PATTERSON.

(Circuit Court for Massachusetts: 1 Federal Reporter, 126, 127. 1880.)

Opinion by NELSON, J.

STATEMENT OF FACTS.— The infant defendants, Kate Kirby Patterson and Edwin Croswell Patterson, by their guardian *ad litem,* demur to the plaintiff's bill and assign as causes of demurrer: *First,* that they have no interest in the matters complained of in the bill; and *second,* multifariousness. The plaintiff is a New York corporation, and the policy of insurance was issued and is payable there.

§ 1868. *Necessary parties.*

The insurance money, by the terms of the policy, is payable to the children at the decease of Charles G. Patterson, the father, if Fannie E. Patterson, the mother, is not then living. This clearly gives the children a contingent interest in the policy, and they are, therefore, proper and necessary parties to a bill in equity to set aside the policy for any cause. Eadie *v.* Slimmon, 26 N. Y., 9; Barry *v.* Equit. L. Ass. Soc., 59 N. Y., 587; Knickerbocker Ins. Co. *v.* Weitz, 99 Mass., 157.

§ 1869. *Multifariousness.*

The joining in the bill a prayer for an injunction to restrain Charles G. Patterson, one of the defendants, from further prosecuting a suit at law in this court to recover back the premiums already paid, is not such a distinct and independent matter as to render the bill multifarious.

§ 1870. *Demurrer ore tenus.*

The guardian *ad litem* assigns another cause of demurrer *ore tenus,* that the bill prays for an answer, under oath, by the infant defendants. There are two reasons why this demurrer cannot prevail. The first is that a demurrer *ore tenus* must be co-extensive with the demurrer upon the record. 1 Dan. Ch. Prac., 589; Story's Eq. Plead., § 464. The demurrer on the record here is to the whole bill, while the demurrer *ore tenus* is to the prayer only.

§ 1871. *Oath to an infant's answer.*

The second reason is that an infant's answer is by his guardian, and should be upon the oath of the guardian, though he is required to swear only to his belief in the truth of the infant's defense. 1 Dan. Ch. Prac., 753; Story's Eq. Plead., § 871. Demurrer overruled.

§ 1872. **Definition.**— A demurrer is an answer in law to a bill, though not, in a technical sense, an answer according to the common language of practice. New Jersey *v.* New York, 6 Pet., 323.

§ 1873. **The office of a demurrer to a bill in equity** is to bring before the court the right to maintain the bill, admitting all the allegations to be true, and the court will not look *aliunde* to search out or conjecture what other facts might or might not exist to defeat the bill, that being the office of the plea or answer. Ocean Ins. Co. *v.* Fields, 2 Story, 59.

§ 1874. **A demurrer to a whole bill** will be overruled if any part of the bill is maintainable. Perry *v.* Littlefield, 17 Blatch., 272; Livingston *v.* Story, 9 Pet., 632.

§ 1875. **Defendant may answer proper and demur to improper matter in bill.**— It is a universal rule of pleading in chancery that a defendant may meet a complainant's bill by several modes of defense. He may demur, answer and plead to different parts of the bill, so that if a bill for discovery contain proper matter for the one and not for the other, the defendant should answer the proper and demur to the improper matter; and if he demurs to the whole bill the demurrer must be overruled. Livingston *v.* Story, 9 Pet., 632.

§ 1876. **Objections to equity of bill to be taken by demurrer.**— An objection to the equity of the bill which might have been made by demurrer is not favorably received at the hearing of the cause after answer. United States *v.* Sturges, 1 Paine, 525.

§ 1877. Answering in part does not withdraw demurrer in part.—A demurrer in part to a bill, followed by an answer as to the rest, is not overruled or withdrawn by the rules of the United States courts, though it might be in England. Pierpont v. Fowle, 2 Woodb. & M., 23.

§ 1878. Waiver of defect by demurrer.— When a plea is filed to a bill in equity, the omission of a certificate of counsel or affidavit of the party, as required by the thirty-first equity rule, is waived by a demurrer. Goodyear v. Toby, 6 Blatch., 130.

§ 1379. —— by plea of co-defendant.— The demurrer of one defendant cannot be held to be overruled by the plea of another defendant. Dakin v. Union Pac. R'y Co., 5 Fed. R., 665.

§ 1380. Demurrer not to be sustained in part and overruled in part — Irregularity, how waived.— A bill to enforce forfeiture and also to obtain compensation was demurred to, and the demurrer sustained as to part and overruled as to part. If, after this, the plaintiff files an amended bill and the defendant answers thereto, the objection that a single demurrer cannot be divided, but must be wholly overruled or wholly sustained, is waived. Marshall v. Vicksburg, 15 Wall., 146.

§ 1381. Demurrer must be certified by counsel.— A demurrer not certified by counsel, in accordance with the rules of court, is no demurrer, and plaintiff may on motion have a decree pro confesso. Secor v. Singleton,* 3 McC., 230.

§ 1382. A demurrer to a plea in equity raises the question as to the sufficiency of the bill. Beard v. Bowler,* 2 Bond, 13.

§ 1383. A special demurrer to a bill in equity points out particular defects in the pleading; a general demurrer shows no particular defect, but calls in question the equity of the bill; the former is indispensable when the objection is to the defects of the bill in point of form. In either case the objection or defects must be apparent on the face of the bill. A demurrer admits matters of fact well pleaded; but does not admit conclusions of law drawn therefrom, although said conclusions are alleged in the bill. Gindrat v. Dane, 4 Cliff., 260.

§ 1384. Objections to form and manner of bill not good on general demurrer. Chouteau v. Rice,* 1 Minn., 106.

§ 1385. Although a bill of review wrongfully sets out the evidence in the original cause, yet a general demurrer to it will be overruled if any error is apparent in the proceedings. A special demurrer assigning this as a cause would be sustained. Buffington, v. Harvey, 5 Otto, 99.

§ 1386. A special demurrer will be overruled on exception, if it fail to point out distinctly the part demurred to. Atwill v. Ferritt, 2 Blatch., 39.

§ 1387. When a bill prays for a discovery and also for an injunction, and makes out a case for one of these, though not for the other, a general demurrer to the bill will be overruled. Ibid.

§ 1388. A demurrer to a bill sufficient in substance will be overruled. An allegation under a demurrer that there is no equity in a bill is unknown to equity pleading, and is merely equivalent to a general demurrer. If defendants wish to contest the right of complainant to sue in the character assumed, they must make the objection by plea denying the right, and a cause to that effect set forth in a demurrer is not proper. A special demurrer to the jurisdiction of the court is insufficient. Nicholas v. Murray,* 18 N. B. R., 469.

§ 1389. What is admitted by a demurrer.— A demurrer to a bill admits all the material allegations contained in it. McLean v. Lafayette Bank, 3 McL., 415; Burnley v. Jeffersonville,* 3 McL., 336; Pagan v. Sparks, 2 Wash., 325; Bayerque v. Cohen, McAl., 113; Woodworth v. Edwards, 3 Woodb. & M., 120; Foote v. Linck, 5 McL., 616.

§ 1390. A demurrer to a bill admits the averments therein so far as they are well pleaded; but not the conclusions drawn by the pleader from the facts stated. Pullman Co. v. Mo. Pacific R'y Co., 3 McC., 645.

§ 1391. A demurrer to a bill in equity admits all relevant facts that are well pleaded; but does not admit conclusions of law drawn from such facts, although such conclusions are also alleged in the bill. The allegations of the existence of a trust are allegations of fact and not conclusions of law. Hosmer v. Jewett, 6 Ben., 208.

§ 1392. A demurrer to a bill in equity does not admit conclusions of law. Boucicault v. Hart, 13 Blatch., 47.

§ 1393. Reasonable presumptions are admitted by demurrer as well as the matters expressly alleged. Amory v. Lawrence, 3 Cliff., 523.

§ 1394. A demurrer does not admit the accuracy of an alleged construction of an instrument, when the instrument is set forth in a bill in equity, or a copy annexed, against a construction required by its terms; nor does it admit any legal inference or conclusion of law, but only matters of fact well pleaded. Dillon v. Barnard, 21 Wall., 430.

§ 1395. When the averments of an original bill are incorporated with and make part of a supplemental bill they form one pleading, and, so far as they conflict, destroy each other;

nor are conflicting and repugnant matters admitted by demurrer, only such matters as are well pleaded being admitted. Chouteau v. Rice,* 1 Minn., 106.

§ 1896. A demurrer admits only such facts as are properly pleaded. Questions of fact are not open for re-examination on a bill of review for errors in law appearing on the record, which consists of the pleadings, proceedings and decree. The truth, therefore, of any fact averred in that kind of a bill of review, inconsistent with the decree or any other part of the record, is not admitted by a demurrer, because no error is assigned on such a fact, and it is, therefore, not properly pleaded. Shelton v. Van Kleeck, 16 Otto, 552.

§ 1897. Want of equity.— As a general rule, a demurrer for want of equity cannot be sustained unless the court is satisfied that no discovery or proof called for or founded upon the allegations of the bill can make the subject-matter of the suit a proper case for equitable interference. Hosmer v. Jewett, 6 Ben., 208.

§ 1898. A motion to dismiss a bill for want of equity cannot be entertained before the final hearing of a suit. Before final hearing want of equity can only be taken advantage of by demurrer. La Vega v. Lapsley, 1 Woods, 428.

§ 1899. If the bill states a substantial case, showing gross and palpable fraud, demurrer to it on the ground that no case entitling complainant to relief is shown will not lie, because of a special and technical defect, such as lapse of time or a mistake in the form. A demurrer on the ground that the bill does not state facts sufficient to constitute a cause of suit is equivalent to a demurrer for want of equity. Nicholas v. Murray, 5 Saw., 320.

§ 1400. A bill alleging facts which go to show that the defendant city is about to do injury to plaintiff's land, without authority of law, is not demurrable for want of equity. Griffing v. Gibb,* 2 Black, 519.

§ 1401. A demurrer in equity for want of parties should name the parties omitted. Dwight v. Central Vermont R. Co.,* 9 Fed. R., 785.

§ 1402. Defect of parties.— The addition of a party plaintiff, in a bill in equity, who has no interest in the suit, and who is not a necessary or proper party upon the record, can be taken advantage of by a general demurrer for want of equity. Hodge v. North Mo. Railroad, 1 Dill., 104.

§ 1403. A defect of misjoinder apparent on face of the bill will be waived unless objected to by demurrer or answer; and the court will hesitate to dismiss a bill for such defect if justice can be done to all parties otherwise. Bunce v. Gallagher, 5 Blatch., 481.

§ 1404. A bill is demurrable for joining an unnecessary party defendant, if it be apparent on the face that such party has no interest in the suit. In such case an amendment will be granted. Dwight v. Humphreys,* 3 McL., 104.

§ 1405. Parties who are proper defendants cannot demur to a bill for a misjoinder of defendants; only those misjoined can demur. An assignee in bankruptcy may join in a bill to collect money fraudulently paid over, and to set aside conveyances, if made by fraud, without multifariousness, all matters that might have been included by creditors in a creditor's bill. Spaulding v. McGovern,* 10 N. B. R., 188.

§ 1406. Causes for demurrer.— If a bill of complaint shows on its face that the plaintiff has a remedy at law demurrer to the bill will lie. Ivinson v. Hutten,* 1 Wyom. T'y, 178.

§ 1407. Where fraud is alleged in a bill and relief prayed against a judgment and a judicial sale of property, a demurrer to the bill, that relief can be had at law, is not sustainable. Shelton v. Tiffin, 6 How., 163.

§ 1408. Where, upon the case stated in the bill, the complainant is not entitled to relief by reason of lapse of time and laches on his part, the defendant may demur. Maxwell v. Kennedy, 8 How., 210.

§ 1409. The rule appears now to be well settled, and with reason, that whenever a bill is so framed as to present the objection of the lapse of time, a demurrer for that cause will lie. Hall v. Russell, 3 Saw., 506.

§ 1410. The objection of the statute of limitations may be taken by demurrer. Sheldon v. Keokuk Northern Line Packet Co., 8 Fed. R., 763.

§ 1411. Where a bill in equity states a case to which the act of limitation applies, without bringing it within some one of the savings, the defendant may take advantage of the bar by demurrer. Wisner v. Barnet, 4 Wash., 631.

§ 1412. When it appears on the face of a bill that the case which it makes is barred by the statute of limitations, and that the excuse of concealment of "the cause of action" by the defendants is not so alleged as to avail the complainant, this defect can be taken advantage of by demurrer. National Bank v. Carpenter, 11 Otto, 567.

§ 1413. A statute of limitations to a bill by a patentee against an infringer should be pleaded rather than relied on by way of demurrer; and a demurrer, so far as it rests on such ground, will be overruled. In this case permission was given to set up same defense by plea or answer. Steven v. Kansas Pac. R'y, 5 Dill., 486.

§ 1414. Bill laying a foundation for some relief not demurrable.— A bill is not as a whole demurrable if it lay a foundation for some of the discovery and relief asked for. Buerk v. Imhaeuser,* 8 Fed. R., 457.

§ 1415. A demurrer for multifariousness cannot be filed by one who is not affected by the fault. Ibid.

§ 1416. Lapse of time, etc., cannot be considered on demurrer.— No circumstance such as lapse of time, statute of limitations. or any other defense, can be taken into consideration on demurrer. Burnley v. Jeffersonville, 3 McL., 336. (Overruled.)

§ 1417. A defense depending upon a state statute should be set up by plea or answer, and not by demurrer. Griffing v. Gibb,* 2 Black, 519.

§ 1418. Capacity of assignee in bankruptcy cannot be questioned by demurrer.— The defendant cannot raise by demurrer to the plaintiff's bill the question whether the plaintiff is the lawful assignee of a bankrupt, the plaintiff having brought the bill in that capacity; but such defense must be set up in a plea. Nicholas v. Murray, 5 Saw., 320.

§ 1419. Demurrer to allegation in bill of discovery, an answer to which would subject defendant to penalty.— If an answer to an allegation in a bill for discovery may subject the defendant to a penalty or forfeiture under United States statutes concerning copyrights, the defendant may demur to such allegation; and such demurrer will be sustained. Chapman v. Ferry, 12 Fed. R., 693.

§ 1420. Evidence cannot be forced into pleadings for the sake of demurring to it.— Bill for injunction against a bankrupt to prevent him from collecting and applying to his own use the debts. The bankrupt prays oyer of the petition in bankruptcy, recites it at large, and demurs to it. This is an endeavor to force evidence into the pleadings and demur to it, which is not allowable. The demurrer will therefore be taken to apply to the bill only, and the recital of the bankruptcy petition will be rejected as surplusage. Blackburn v. Stannard,* 5 L. R., 250.

3. Plea.

SUMMARY — *Requisites of a good plea, § 1421.— Plea to jurisdiction, when heard, §§ 1442-23.— Dilatory plea not different from any other, § 1424.— Plea to jurisdiction, when without oath, § 1425.— What facts are to be sworn to, §§ 1426-27.— Unsupported plea must answer whole bill, § 1428.— Plea of good faith and valuable consideration must state considera- tion, § 1429.— Substance of plea not to be questioned by motion to strike out, § 1430.*

§ 1421. A plea is a special answer to the bill, relying upon one point sufficient to bar, delay or dismiss the suit. It need not admit or deny all allegations of the bill, and, when it pro- fesses to go to the whole bill, does not require to be supported by an answer covering the allegations irrelevant to the point relied upon. If it go only to a part of the bill the remain- der must be answered. Sims v. Lyle, § 1431.

§ 1422. The pendency of a plea to the jurisdiction precludes all action of the court till it is decided. Ewing v. Blight, §§ 1432-33.

§ 1423. An immediate hearing of a dilatory plea will be ordered if necessary in aid of justice. Ibid.

§ 1424. A plea to the jurisdiction need not be filed within four days, as in actions at law, there being no distinction in equity between dilatory and other pleas. Ewing v. Blight, §§ 1434-37.

§ 1425. A plea to the jurisdiction or in bar of any matter of record may be put in without oath, provided the truth of the plea appear by some record. Ibid.

§ 1426. When the facts averred in the plea are of defendant's own knowledge they must be sworn to positively; if they are not necessarily within his knowledge, they need not be sworn to positively, but an affidavit of belief will be sufficient. Ibid.

§ 1427. Domicile of plaintiff is not a fact to which defendant must necessarily swear posi- tively. Ibid.

§ 1428. When a bill charges fraudulent misrepresentations, and avers also an agreement on part of defendant to execute a mortgage of real estate, and a failure to perform this agree- ment, it is not sufficient for defendant merely to plead the statute of frauds, but he must also answer the charges and allegations of the bill. Bailey v. Wright, § 1438.

§ 1429. To a bill by one claiming to be owner of a patent-right against one who is alleged to have obtained the title thereto fraudulently, a plea that defendant is a *bona fide* purchaser for a good and valuable consideration must state the consideration and the amount thereof. Secombe v. Campbell, § 1439.

§ 1430. If a plea be regular in form its sufficiency cannot be inquired into upon motion to strike out. Tyler v. Hyde, § 1440.

[NOTES.— See §§ 1441-1496.]

SIMS *v.* LYLE.

(Circuit Court for Pennsylvania: 4 Washington, 301-304. 1822.)

STATEMENT OF FACTS.—A plea being filed which professed to go to the whole bill, a motion was made to overrule the plea upon grounds appearing in the opinion.

Opinion by WASHINGTON, J.

The ground of the present motion is that the plea does not admit or deny all the allegations stated in the bill, and therefore an answer to that extent is so indispensable that the court must overrule the plea, whether the matter pleaded amount to a bar or not.

§ 1431. *What is a good plea in bar in equity.*

The court can by no means accede to this proposition. The practice of the courts of equity is quite otherwise. A plea, being nothing more than a special answer to the bill, setting forth and relying upon some one fact, or a number of facts, tending to one point, sufficient to bar, delay or dismiss the suit, it would be a vice in the plea to cover any other parts of the bill than such as concern the particular subject of the bar, its office being to reduce the cause, or some part of it, to a single point, and thus to prevent the expense and trouble of an examination at large. It is true that all facts essential to render the plea a complete defense to the bill, so far as the plea extends, must be averred in it or it will be no defense at all. If the plea be to the whole of the bill it must cover the whole; that is, it must cover the whole subject to which the plea applies and which it professes to cover, or it will be bad. As if the bill respect a house and so many acres of land, and the plea, professing to cover that charge, pleads only in bar as to the house; but if it cover the whole subject, and contains a full defense in relation to it, there is no necessity, nor would it be proper, to notice other parts of the bill not involved in the subject to which the plea applies. If the plea be only to a part of the bill the rest of the bill ought to be answered, or else the court would consider the parts not embraced by the plea, or answered, as true.

But there is no instance where the plea contains in itself a full defense to the bill that an answer is necessary, unless it is rendered so in order to negative some equitable ground stated in the bill for avoiding the effect of the anticipated bar; as where fraud, combination, facts intended to avow the force of the statute of frauds, or to bring the plaintiff within some of the exceptions to the act of limitations, as the one or the other of these defenses may be expected; and in those and similar cases the defendant is bound not only to deny those charges in his plea, but to support his plea by an answer also denying them fully and clearly. If every plea required an answer to accompany it there would be no use for the twentieth rule lately established by the supreme court (which is conformable to the English practice), which declares that, if the plea be overruled, the defendant shall proceed to answer the bill, since the argument supposes that the bill has already been answered.

In this case the plea professes to go to the whole bill and does not, in fact, cover the whole subject to which the plea applies, and if the matter of it be a full defense to the suit it is unnecessary to answer other parts of the bill not involved in the subject which forms the ground of the defense.

The plaintiff's counsel will be at liberty to argue the plea on its merits, or to reply to it, as he may think proper.

EWING v. BLIGHT.

(Circuit Court for Pennsylvania: 8 Wallace, Jr., 139, 140. 1855.)

STATEMENT OF FACTS.— During the pendency of a plea to the jurisdiction an application was made for an injunction and a receiver.

§ 1432. *The court will not grant an injunction or appoint a receiver while its jurisdiction is in question.*

Opinion by GRIER, J.

The pendency of a plea to the jurisdiction of the court necessarily precludes all further action of the court till it is decided. This rule of practice is founded on reason as well as fortified by authority. 13 Ves., 164.

While the jurisdiction of the court or the equity of the bill is in doubt by the pendency of a plea or demurrer, it would be highly improper for the court to interfere by the exercise of such high powers over men's property.

§ 1433. *An immediate trial of the dilatory plea will be ordered if necessary.*

The court have it always in their power to guard against the abuse of dilatory pleas. If any irremediable mischief should impend, which it is absolutely necessary to meet with promptness, or if there be any just suspicion that the plea or demurrer is merely intended for delay, the court will order an immediate hearing or trial of the plea.

If an issue be desired to try the plea of jurisdiction in this case it will be ordered, or any other rule which complainant may desire, for the purpose of expediting the final hearing in case the jurisdiction should be found to exist.

EWING v. BLIGHT.

(Circuit Court for Pennsylvania: 8 Wallace, Jr., 134-138. 1855.)

STATEMENT OF FACTS.— Plea to the jurisdiction was filed twenty-five days after the bill was filed. The plea denied that complainant was a resident of another state as alleged in the bill.

§ 1434. *Rules at law in the matter of dilatory pleas.*

Opinion by GRIER, J.

The rules in courts of law, with regard to dilatory pleas, are very stringent, and require them to be put in within four days after the term to which the declaration is filed, counting both days inclusive. They require also that the affidavit to the truth of the plea be positive and not according to the belief of the deponent. In the practice of those courts, also, a dilatory plea, not filed in time or subsequently authenticated, may be treated as a nullity, and the party making it defaulted for want of a plea.

§ 1435. *Equity practice as to dilatory pleas.*

But such is not the course of practice in courts of equity. By the rules of this court the defendant may enter his plea, demurrer or answer to the bill at any time before or on the next rule day succeeding that of his appearance. There is no distinction made between pleas to the jurisdiction, or that called dilatory pleas and any other pleadings. Nor can the complainant treat the plea filed as a nullity and enter an order taking the bill *pro confesso*, where the plea is not sufficiently verified. The proper mode of taking advantage of a formal defect of this description is by an application for an order setting aside the pleading, or to take it off the files for irregularity. Wall *v.* Stubbs, 2 Ves. & B., 385; Heart *v.* Corning, 3 Paige, 570.

Entry in clerk's office rescinded.

Upon motion to set aside the plea because it was not adequately verified the following opinion was delivered:

§ **1436.** *Rule for verification of pleas to the jurisdiction — and exception to that rule.*

Opinion by GRIER, J.

It has been said by Lord Redesdale "that pleas to the jurisdiction of the court, or in disability of the person of the plaintiff, as well as pleas in bar of any matter of record, may be put in without oath." But this is true only where the truth of the plea appears by some record. For it is now well settled that wherever the plea puts in issue matter *in pais*, or which may be established on the hearing by the testimony of witnesses, it should be verified by oath.

The principle upon which the court acts in requiring pleas to be put in upon oath is that it will not permit a defendant to delay or evade the discovery sought unless he will first pledge his oath to the truth (or at *least to his belief of the truth*) of the facts upon which he relies in all cases where the facts are those of which the court does not take official notice.

Where the facts averred in the plea are of the defendant's own knowledge, or acts done by himself, they must be sworn to positively. If they are acts done by others, not necessarily within his knowledge, they need not be sworn to positively. It is sufficient if he swears to his belief of their truth, and this more especially where the plea is negative and denies some fact alleged affirmatively in the bill; as where the bill alleges that the complainant is heir, executor, or partner. Drew *v.* Drew, 2 Ves. & B., 169; Heart *v.* Corning, 3 Paige, 570. There is no distinction in equity between pleas to the jurisdiction or other pleas.

§ **1437.** *Domicile of opposing party need not be sworn to as of knowledge.*

The bill in this case avers that the complainant is a citizen of New Jersey, and of course *not* a citizen of Pennsylvania. This averment is necessary to give the court jurisdiction. The plea denies the fact as averred, and affirms the negative inference assumed from it. Although in strictness it may be said to deny the allegation of the bill by affirming a positive fact, inconsistent with such averment, it may, nevertheless, be considered a negative plea taking issue on an averment of the bill necessarily within the personal knowledge of defendant. Domicile or citizenship depends not only on the acts, but the secret or declared intentions, of the party of whom it is averred. It is the predicate often of very nice legal distinctions, as well as facts and intentions of which another may not be cognizant. It is generally an opinion of belief founded partly on facts known, and partly on information from others. In many cases one man may have such a thorough knowledge of the birthplace and residence of another, and the acts of his whole life, that he may conscientiously swear to his citizenship or domicle absolutely and positively. But in many cases a defendant cannot have such knowledge, and can only swear to his belief.

Where an answer sets forth a detail of numerous facts, some on the knowledge of the defendant and others on information, the oath usually makes such distinction. But a plea denying the citizenship of the complainant, being to a single fact, never sets forth the particular facts or reasons which enter into the result. Hence the form of the oath to an answer is not usually found attached to a plea denying a single fact.

If the fact denied be not within the personal knowledge of the deponent he can but swear to his belief, and the rules of pleading in chancery require no more. It is not necessary to set forth the reasons of such belief, or to distinguish between how much of it is founded on information, how much on personal knowledge, and how much on legal investigation or instruction of counsel. Few persons are capable of such an analysis of their own faith. The law should not compel a party to swear rashly, under penalty of losing his rights. The motion to strike out the plea for want of a sufficient verification is therefore refused.

BAILEY v. WRIGHT.

(Circuit Court for Ohio: 2 Bond, 181-188. 1868.)

Opinion of the COURT.

STATEMENT OF FACTS.—The bill in this case alleges, in substance, that upon certain false and fraudulent representations by the defendants the complainant was induced to make an advance to them of $20,000, to be invested in the purchase of cotton for the benefit of all the parties. It is averred, also, that as an inducement for making said advance, and an indemnity therefor, the defendant Wright represented himself as the owner of valuable real estate in Cincinnati, which he promised to mortgage to the complainant to secure him against loss for said advance in money. The bill contains direct allegations of fraud on the part of defendants, prays for an account, and for a decree requiring the defendant Wright to execute a mortgage on the real estate in Cincinnati, according to his promise.

The defendant Wright has filed a plea to the bill, denying all the allegations of fraud, and averring, as to the averment of the bill that he promised to execute a mortgage of real estate, that if any such promise was made it was verbal, and therefore void under the statute of frauds.

§ 1438. *When a bill shows facts which tend to take a parol contract out of the statute of frauds the defendant cannot merely plead the statute, but must answer the charges of the bill.*

The pending motion in the case is for an order to withdraw the plea from the files, and to require an answer to the merits. The only question intended to be presented on this motion is whether, under the allegations of the bill, the defendant Wright can rely on his averment that the promise to execute the mortgage was void under the statute of frauds, without an answer in response to the charges of fraud in obtaining the advances of money by the complainant.

The defendant has an undoubted right to set up that the agreement to mortgage was by parol, and therefore void. But the law seems now to be well settled, that where facts are asserted in a bill, the effect of which may be to take a verbal agreement out of the operation of the statute of frauds, it is incumbent on the respondent to respond by answer to such facts. This would seem to be the fair construction of the thirty-second rule of the rules of practice in chancery, adopted by the supreme court for the guidance of the courts of the United States. And such seems to be the law applicable to the question as laid down by Judge Story. Story's Eq. Plead., 591.

It is clear that a plea merely setting up the invalidity of an agreement under the statute of frauds, where other facts are averred in the bill in support of the complainant's equity, and which may be of a character to require a court to ignore the plea of the statute, the defendant should be required to file his answer to such facts. Such, it seems to the court, is in accordance with the spirit and design of the thirty-second rule before referred to. And without deeming it necessary, in deciding the present motion, to refer to the frauds alleged in the bill, and without intimating any opinion upon the question whether, if the frauds charged were proved, the legal effect would be to supersede the plea of the statute of frauds, and present the entire transaction for inquiry on the broad principles of equity, an order will be entered requiring the defendants to file their answer to the bill. There can be no hardship in such an order. The defendants should gladly avail themselves of the opportunity of denying the frauds charged. I trust they will be able to acquit themselves of all imputations impugning their integrity in the transactions set out in the bill.

SECOMBE v. CAMPBELL.

(Circuit Court for New York: 18 Blatchford, 108, 109. 1880.)

Opinion by WHEELER, J.

STATEMENT OF FACTS.— This bill is brought upon re-issued letters patent, division A, No. 4,143, to Helen M. Ingalls, assignee of Marcus P. Norton, dated October 4, 1870, for an improvement in postoffice post-marking and postage canceling stamps, and alleges that she assigned this, with other patents, to the plaintiff's intestate and others to the Secombe Manufacturing Company, of which he was president; that the Secombe Manufacturing Company and he, president, joined in a re-assignment to her, which by the contract was not to, and by what the plaintiff claims to be its true construction does not, include this one; but that if by any construction this one is included, the assignment was drawn to include it by the fraud of her agent; that she has assigned it to the defendant Campbell, who has obtained a decree against the defendant James for an account of profits and damages for infringement; and prays that if the instrument of re-assignment is held to include this patent, it may be reformed so as not to include it, and that the profits and damages be decreed to the plaintiff.

The defendant Campbell has pleaded to so much of the bill as alleges fraud in making the instrument of re-assignment that he is a *bona fide* purchaser of these letters patent from Helen M. Ingalls, for a "good and valuable consideration, to wit, a certain sum of money then advanced and paid by him to her," without notice of the fraud. This plea was set down for argument by the plaintiff and the argument has been heard.

§ 1439. *A plea that the defendant is a bona fide purchaser for a good and valuable consideration must set forth the amount of such consideration.*

There is no fair question but that the fact that the defendant was such a purchaser for a valuable consideration without notice would be a sufficient reason for his not answering that part of the bill, and be a good plea to it. Story's Eq. Pl., § 805. The titles to patents are required by law to be recorded, and a purchaser has the right to rely upon the apparent record title so long as he acts in good faith, the same as the purchaser of real estate has where the title is required to be shown. In either case the purchaser must have parted with a consideration large enough to make it inequitable for him to be required to give up the property to one who has not the apparent legal title. Boone v. Chiles, 10 Pet., 177. In this plea there is no allegation of the consideration paid other than the one recited. The words "good and valuable" may refer to what would be good and valuable between the parties, which might be very slight, and "a certain sum of money" might be a very small sum, and wholly inadequate to make his equity superior to Secombe's if the fraud did in fact exist. The rules of pleading as to this are the same as at law, and the consideration ought to be set forth in amount in traversable form, so that the plaintiff can traverse it if he chooses, or the court see that it is adequately valuable if not traversed.

Although this plea is apparently good in other respects it is wanting in this, and must be overruled.

TYLER v. HYDE.

(Circuit Court for New York: 2 Blatchford, 399, 400. 1852.)

STATEMENT OF FACTS.— A demurrer to a plea pleaded *puis darrein continuance* having been sustained, defendant, by leave, pleaded a special plea, which plaintiffs moved to strike out on the ground that it was a repetition of the former plea.

§ 1440. *A plea regular in form cannot be displaced by motion.*

Opinion by BETTS, J.

The court will not, on this motion, enter into a consideration of the sufficiency of the plea in point of substance, or inquire whether it is founded upon the rightful decree of the circuit court in Louisiana. It may, possibly, become necessary for this court to determine, when the proofs are presented, which decree of that court is the valid one governing the case, should two be certified from it which are in conflict in particulars affecting the merits.

The privilege accorded to the defendants to plead over was subject to no restrictions, and they are entitled under it to interpose any plea which would have been good if put in independently of that leave. The defendants plead at their peril, and their plea, being regular in form, cannot be displaced by motion. The plaintiffs must demur to it or take issue on the facts it sets up. Motion denied.

§ 1441. **Definition — Office of the plea.**— A plea in equity is a special answer showing why the suit should be dismissed, delayed or barred, made for the purpose of enabling the defendant to avoid the inconvenience and expense of an answer filed in detail. Two matters of defense cannot be stated in one plea, nor should a plea contain various facts unless they are all conducive to a single point which constitutes a single defense. Two pleas in a suit are never allowed, even in bar, except in a particular case, by leave of the court first obtained, where great inconvenience might otherwise be sustained. Newby v. Oregon Central R. Co., 1 Saw., 68.

§ 1442. **Respondent may put his defense in plea.**— A respondent is not bound to put his defense upon the answer, and reserve it for a final hearing, but may, if it be a fit subject for a plea, put it into that shape, in order to save the expense of going into a general examination. Wilson v. Graham, 4 Wash., 53.

§ 1443. **The plea must set up a bar to every equitable allegation in the bill or it will be set aside.** Piatt v. Oliver, 1 McL., 295.

§ 1444. **A plea in bar to a bill must be full and complete to every part of the bill,** and fraud charged must be denied by an answer filed in support of the plea. *Ibid.*

§ 1445. **A plea is always in avoidance of a bill, and stands for nothing as evidence.** Gernon v. Boscaline, 2 Wash., 199.

§ 1446. **A plea to a bill in equity may be good in part, and not so in the whole; and a** court will allow it as to so much of the bill as it is properly applicable to, unless it has the vice of duplicity in it. Kirkpatrick v. White, 4 Wash., 595; Wythe v. Palmer, 8 Saw., 412.

§ 1447. **A plea in equity must contain but one matter or point, and only one plea may be** filed to the whole bill or to any specific part thereof. A plea mingling matters of abatement, of demurrer, and in bar, will be overruled. Gaines v. Mausseaux,* 1 Woods, 118.

§ 1448. **A defendant has a right to file one plea, but only one, and the court will in its** discretion allow double pleas only when great inconvenience might otherwise result, and then upon payment of costs by defendant. Noyes v. Willard,* 1 Woods, 187.

§ 1449. A defendant filing several pleas without leave should be put to his election upon which to rely. *Ibid.*

§ 1450. In equity a defendant is not allowed to plead more than one plea to the bill without special leave of the court first obtained, and such leave will only be given in particular cases when the necessity therefor is obvious. Lamb *v.* Starr, Deady, 350.

§ 1451. Defenses apparent on face of bill.— A plea that the court is without jurisdiction on the ground of citizenship, or that plaintiff has mistaken his remedy, will be overruled, as defenses apparent on the face of the bill should be set up by demurrer. *Ibid.*

§ 1452. Plea sets up fact outside bill showing that no answer is needed.— A proper plea in equity sets up some fact outside of the bill, which shows that the bill should not be answered at all, and need not be supported by answer. Anomalous pleas denying some single part of the case may be allowed for convenience to save trying the whole case, when the failure of that part would be fatal, and also for safety against enforced discovery in a suit by those not entitled to the discovery. But as to that part denied the defendant cannot avoid fully answering it by merely pleading to it. He must answer that part, although his plea and answer show that the rest of the bill should not be answered. If his unsupported plea should be allowed the plaintiff would be deprived of the discovery on oath to which he is entitled as to that part of the case as evidence upon the traverse to the plea, should he wish to traverse it. Dwight *v.* Central Vermont R. Co.,* 9 Fed. R., 785.

§ 1453. Defendant's right to demur, plead and answer the bill.— Under the thirty-second equity rule a defendant may demur to a part of the bill, plead to a part and answer to a part; and no demurrer or plea is bad simply because the answer may extend to *some* part of the matter covered by the plea or demurrer. But no rule allows a defendant to plead, answer and demur, each to the whole bill, at the same time. Crescent City Co. *v.* Butchers' Co., 12 Fed. R., 225.

§ 1454. Plea must be verified.— The absence of an affidavit verifying the matters of fact alleged in a plea is fatal. White *v.* Whitman, 1 Curt., 494.

§ 1455. —— irregularly filed.— Pleas which are irregularly filed and defective under the thirty-first equity rule for the federal courts, for lack of affidavit that they were not interposed for delay, and of certificate of counsel that in his opinion they were well founded in point of law, need not be traversed or set down for argument, but may be disregarded; so too if they merely allege matters of law and not of fact. National Bank *v.* Insurance Co., 14 Otto, 54.

§ 1456. Plea made to stand for answer.— Where one defense is made by plea, and another by answer, the plea will be ordered to stand for an answer. Lewis *v.* Baird, 3 McL., 56.

§ 1457. Plea heard without reply, facts admitted.— When a plea in equity is set down for hearing without being replied to by the complainant, all the facts therein alleged which are well pleaded are considered as admitted for the purpose of determining the question whether the plea constitutes a sufficient answer to the suit. Mellus *v.* Thompson, 1 Cliff., 125.

§ 1458. Plea undenied taken as true.— A plea not denied by a replication, but set down for argument, is taken as true. Gallagher *v.* Roberts,* 1 Wash., 320.

§ 1459. Plea must deny equitable ground for relief.— When the bill lays an equitable ground for relief, a plea setting up a former judgment, but not denying the ground laid, will not bar the suit. *Ibid.*

§ 1460. Several pleas filed without leave.— When more pleas than one are filed without special leave therefor, they may all be overruled. Wheeler *v.* McCormick,* 8 Blatch., 267.

§ 1460a. The act of congress of April 3, 1818, limiting the jurisdiction of the circuit court for southern New York, intended only to prohibit jurisdiction over causes arising in northern New York, and a plea in that court that the cause of action arose out of the jurisdiction of that court, to wit, in Illinois, is bad. *Ibid.*

§ 1461. Plea overruled by answer touching same matter.— As a rule, if defendant answer to the same matter which is covered by his plea the latter is thereby overruled. The only exception to this is the case where an answer is necessary to support a plea, as where the bill charges circumstances calculated to avoid the anticipated bar of the defendant. There the plea must contain all averments to meet those circumstances, and the answer also must deny the same circumstances in order that plaintiff may have an opportunity for exception. Ferguson *v.* O'Harra,* Pet. C. C., 498.

§ 1462. If a plea go only to a part of the bill the remainder must be covered by answer or demurrer. *Ibid.*

§ 1463. Disposition of plea in discretion of court.— In many cases, when a plea is not overruled, the court in its discretion will refuse to allow it the full effect of a plea, and will sometimes save to defendant the benefit of it at a hearing, and at other times order it to stand for an answer, as in their judgment will best secure the ends of justice. Rhode Island *v.* Massachusetts,* 14 Pet., 210.

§ 1464. **Plea not allowed to prejudice merits of the case in suits to determine boundary of state.**— A suit between two states upon a question of boundary will not be decided upon a plea by which any of the merits of complainant's case will be shut out of consideration. *Ibid.*

§ 1465. Although suits between states upon a question of boundary are conducted according to the rules of the court of chancery, yet, from the dignity and importance of the contest, the court will see that technical rules do not operate to prevent either party from presenting its case in the best possible light, nor oppose an obstacle to the accomplishment of final justice. *Ibid.*

§ 1466. **Duplicity.**— A plea setting up the separate defenses of accord and compromise, and title by prescription, will be overruled for duplicity. *Ibid.*

§ 1467. **Bill charging matters avoiding statute of limitations, plea must negative such matters.**— When the bill charges fraud or other matters which would avoid the bar of the statute of limitations, a plea simply setting up the statute, without negativing the other matters, will be insufficient. The plea itself must offer a complete bar, and it will not be sufficient if an answer in support of the plea contain denials of the allegations in the bill. Stearns v. Page,* 1 Story, 204.

§ 1468. **Plea overruled by answer.**— When the answer in support of the plea contains more than is necessary for this purpose, it overrules the plea. A plea states ground why defendant should not go into a full defense, but an answer by going into a full defense necessarily overrules it. *Ibid.*

§ 1469. If a plea contains a positive denial of the equity of the plaintiff's bill, a decree cannot be rendered for plaintiff on the testimony of a single witness without corroborating circumstances. Hughes v. Blake,* 6 Wheat., 453.

§ 1470. **Issue on plea is one of fact.**— If an issue be formed on a plea the question before the court is of fact only and not of the sufficiency of the plea. Hughes v. Blake,* 1 Mason, 515.

§ 1471. **Plea supported by answer, how overcome.**— If a plea be supported by an answer the latter is good evidence, and will prevail unless overcome by two witnesses or equivalent evidence. *Ibid.*

§ 1472. **Statute of limitations.**— That a demand is stale, or barred by the statute of limitations, must be pleaded. The Steamboat Swallow, Olc., 334.

§ 1473. —— **without answer.**— The defendant to an attachment in chancery in Virginia may plead the statute of limitations without answer. Wilson v. Koontz, 7 Cr., 202.

§ 1474. —— **where defendant has removed from county.**— A defendant who removes from one county in Virginia to another is not thereby prevented from pleading the statute of limitations, unless the plaintiff has been, by such removal, actually defeated or obstructed in bringing or maintaining his action. *Ibid.*

§ 1475. —— **in pleading the statute of limitations** to a bill in chancery it is not necessary that there shall be an express reference to the statute of the state in which the proceeding is instituted. The court is judicially bound to take notice of the statutes of limitations when the facts are stated and relied on as a bar to further proceedings, if they are found sufficient. Harpending v. The Dutch Church, 16 Pet., 455.

§ 1476. **Fraud must be denied in a plea** as well as in an answer. Lewis v. Baird, 3 McL., 56.

§ 1477. **A plaintiff's authority to sue in equity as executor** should be questioned, if at all, by plea or answer. Rubber Co. v. Goodyear, 9 Wall., 788.

§ 1478. **Plea denying particular allegations held bad.**— A bill filed against one alleged to be a legatee, to recover a debt due from the testate, alleged that the executors of the testate had either refused to accept the trust or had died leaving no property, or had disappeared to parts unknown, and that defendant was possessed of property belonging to the testate's estate. A plea setting up where some of the executors might be found, and that some of them had died leaving property, and that defendant was ignorant about plaintiff's claim, was held a bad plea. Milligan v. Milledge,* 3 Cr., 220.

§ 1479. **Bill for infringement of patent by railroad — Plea as to ownership of road.**— A bill for infringement of a patent-right alleged that the invention had been used upon a certain railroad in June, 1861, and that defendant as the owner of the railroad had infringed the patent. Defendant pleaded that since January 1, 1861, the railroad had been owned by a joint stock company, and admitted that he, defendant, was one of the directors therein. *Held,* on demurrer, that this plea was good, as the ownership of the railroad was a material allegation and was denied by the plea. Beard v. Bowler,* 2 Bond, 13.

§ 1480. **A plea to a part only of a bill** need not respond to the other allegations of the bill. *Ibid.*

§ 1481. **Plea of non-joinder.**— A plea to a bill brought by certain stockholders of a railroad, that there were other stockholders who should have been joined as parties, whose names were known to the plaintiffs, but not to defendants, is not a good plea. If there were such stockholders, whose existence would defeat the suit unless they were joined, defendants should state who they were, as plaintiffs are entitled to an opportunity to traverse the fact. A traverse of the plea as filed would only put in issue the knowledge on part of the plaintiffs of persons unknown to defendants. Dwight v. Central Vermont R. Co.,* 9 Fed. R., 785.

§ 1482. Plea of another suit pending.— A plea stating the pendency of another suit on the same ground of action in another court is a good plea; but when the plea sets out the bill in the other suit, making it a part of the plea, the court will compare the bill as set out with the bill in the present case, and, if the cases be found to be not identical in their causes of action, will overrule the plea. Wheeler v. McCormick,* 8 Blatch., 267.

§ 1483. Plea merely denying averment of bill bad, if plaintiff might recover, although plea be true.— Plaintiff in his bill averred that defendant had made soda-water fountains, each of which contained inventions claimed by plaintiff under each of five patents. The defendant in his plea merely denied such averment. Such plea is bad in substance because the plaintiff may recover, although the plea is true, if an infringement of any one of the patents is shown. Matthews v. Lalance, etc., Manuf'g Co., 18 Blatch., 84.

§ 1484. Plea that administrator suing had not taken out his letters, good.— Where a bill was brought by the plaintiff as administrator, and the defendant pleaded that he was not administrator, inasmuch as he had not taken out administration in New Hampshire before filing his bill, held, that the plea was sufficient on general principles, and also that the statute of New Hampshire in relation to actions commenced by persons acting as administrators did not govern the rule of the United States court in equity, but was confined to suits at law, and was addressed only to the state courts. Carter v. Treadwell, 3 Story, 25.

§ 1485. Bill to set aside conveyance on ground of fraud — Insufficient plea by bona fide purchaser.— Where a bill in equity was brought to set aside a conveyance asserted to have been procured by fraud, and one of the defendants pleaded that he was a bona fide purchaser under the grantee of parcel of the premises, without notice of the asserted fraud, and that he had paid a part of the consideration money, and that the residue was secured by mortgage, held, that this plea furnished no bar to the bill; that it should have averred that the whole consideration of the purchase had been paid before notice of the plaintiff's title. Wood v. Mann, 1 Sumn., 506.

§ 1486. Dilatory pleas.— Pleas in bar, which seek to avoid the equity of the case, are not to be favored; but great strictness in their form and substance is required. Piatt v. Oliver, 1 McL., 295.

§ 1487. A plea to the jurisdiction is not a submission to the jurisdiction. Van Antwerp v. Hulburd, 7 Blatch., 426.

§ 1488. A plea to a bill that the court has no jurisdiction, because the parties have not the requisite citizenship, need not be verified by oath; and the complainant cannot move to have the bill taken pro confesso, because the plea is not so verified. Ewing v. Blight,* 1 Phil., 576.

§ 1489. Matter in abatement of a suit in equity, as that plaintiff is not a citizen of another state, or that there is no such person as the plaintiff, must be alleged by plea and not by answer. Chapman v. School District,* Deady, 108.

§ 1490. If citizenship be properly averred in a bill in equity, filed in the United States courts, and the defendant means to deny the fact of citizenship, he must take the exception by way of plea, and cannot do it by general answer, for it is a preliminary inquiry. Dodge v. Perkins, 4 Mason, 435.

§ 1491. If no defect to the jurisdiction of the court appears on the record the proper mode to avail of it is by plea, and if the suit is a bill for an injunction, and the court believes the mischief alleged would be irreparable, a temporary injunction may be issued until the plea is disposed of. Fremont v. The Merced Mining Co., McAl., 267.

§ 1492. Where a bill shows apparent jurisdiction, and defendant desires to contest the allegation or introduce new allegations in avoidance of the jurisdiction, this should be done by plea to the jurisdiction, and not by a collateral proceeding, such as a motion to dismiss, with affidavits. Pond v. Vermont Valley R. Co., 12 Blatch., 280.

§ 1493. A plea for want of parties is not matter for abatement. It is a plea in bar. If this defect is apparent on the face of the bill the bill may be demurred to. If not apparent, it may be propounded by way of plea or be relied upon in a general answer. If apparent and vital, as in the case at bar, where the cancellation of title deeds shown to belong to persons interested but not made parties is asked, the defect may be insisted upon at the hearing. Tobin v. Walkinshaw, McAl., 26.

§ 1494. Where a bill in chancery in the United States circuit court avers that the defendant is a citizen of another state, this averment can only be impugned in a special plea to the jurisdiction of the court. The answer is not the proper place for it under the thirty-third rule of equity practice established by the United States supreme court. Wickliffe v. Owings, 17 How., 47.

§ 1495. A plea in abatement to a suit brought in a circuit court of the United States by a citizen of Massachusetts, that all the defendants are not citizens of California or of the United States, but several, naming them, are each and all aliens and citizens of China, excepting one, "who is an alien," is bad on demurrer — first, for uncertainty; secondly, because the court has jurisdiction over suits between citizens of the United States and aliens; thirdly, because the words "who is an alien" do not disclose the party's citizenship. Hinckley v. Byrne, Deady, 224.

§ 1496. The twenty-third rule of the United States supreme court for the regulation of equity practice in the federal circuit courts is understood to apply to matters applicable to the merits, and not to mere pleas to the jurisdiction; and, especially, to those founded on any personal disability or personal character of the party suing, or to any pleas merely in abatement. The rule does not allow a defendant, instead of filing a formal demurrer or a plea, to insist on any special matter in his answer, and have also the benefit thereof, as if he had pleaded the same matter or had demurred to the bill. In this respect the rule is merely affirmative of the general rule of chancery practice, in which matters in abatement and to the jurisdiction, being preliminary in their nature, must be taken advantage of by plea, and cannot be taken advantage of in a general answer, which necessarily admits the right and capacity of the party to sue. Livingston v. Story, 11 Pet., 351.

4. Answer.

[See EQUITY.]

SUMMARY — Information and belief, §§ 1497-99, 1501, 1502.— Insufficient answer, § 1500.— Answer under thirty-ninth equity rule, §§ 1503-1506.— Answer, joint and several, § 1507.— Signature, § 1508.— Answer to interrogatories by corporation, §§ 1509-10.— Answer when no note is appended, § 1511.— Exceptions to part, § 1512.— Whether part of answer may be heard separately, § 1513.— Impertinence, §§ 1514-15.— Answer to interrogatory, when necessary, § 1516.— Answer as evidence, § 1517.

§ 1497. When defendant is required to answer as to his knowledge, remembrance, information and belief, it will not be sufficient for him to answer as to his knowledge only. Brooks v. Byam, §§ 1518-22.

§ 1498. If the answer state that defendant believes an allegation of the bill to be true it will be taken as true. If the statement be that defendant has no knowledge of the fact there will be no such admission, but the answer will be insufficient. Ibid.

§ 1499. No universal rule can be given as to answers upon information and belief, as there may be many shades of doubt and uncertainty in defendant's mind. In every case he must answer conscientiously as to his state of mind, and as fully as circumstances permit. Ibid.

§ 1500. A plaintiff is not obliged to accept a doubtful or insufficient answer, though it would be interpreted favorably to him. Ibid.

§ 1501. When defendants are required to answer an interrogatory it is not sufficient for them to state that they are ignorant; they must give their information and belief. Kittredge v. Claremont Bank, §§ 1523-24.

§ 1502. Officers of a bank, when required to answer upon their information and belief, must ascertain, as nearly as may be, the truth of the matters, by consulting records, asking their predecessors, etc. Ibid.

§ 1503. Under the thirty-ninth equity rule of the supreme court a defendant need not answer further than he would be obliged to answer upon filing a plea, and an answer supporting it, provided he sets out in his answer the matter of such plea in bar to the merits of the bill. Gaines v. Agnelly, §§ 1525-31.

§ 1504. If the bar set up be sufficient it is immaterial whether or not the defendant answer the allegations of the bill. If he does notice allegations outside of the strict line of his defense he is not held thereby to have waived his bar, and to be obliged to answer fully, as under the former practice, in case of an answer supporting a plea. Ibid.

§ 1505. Under the thirty-ninth rule, if defendant sets up a bar in his answer plaintiff must prove his bill, and has not the benefit of a full answer from defendant, but he has a right to call defendant as a witness. Ibid.

§ 1506. If the bar set up in the answer be insufficient, plaintiff may either except, when defendant would require leave of court before amending, or he may go to proofs, in which case he must prove his bill; or he may set the cause down for hearing on bill and answer, when the answer would be taken as true, the bar as proved, and the bill would be dismissed unless the answer admitted those allegations on which the prayer for relief was grounded. *Ibid.*

§ 1507. A joint answer of defendants need not be made several also, though such is the general practice. Davis *v.* Davidson, §§ 1582–83.

§ 1508. An answer in equity must be signed by counsel, unless the answer is taken by commissioners. *Ibid.*

§ 1509. In an equity suit against a corporation, where the note appended to the interrogatories only requires the officers of the corporation to answer, the corporation need not answer, nor the officers, unless they are parties defendant. French *v.* First National Bank, §§ 1534–36.

§ 1510. A corporation required to answer interrogatories may answer them under seal and without oath, the answer being stated to be according to the knowledge, information and belief of its officers. *Ibid.*

§ 1511. Where, under the equity rules, a defendant is obliged to answer only such interrogatories as by note he is required to answer, and no note is appended, a general answer to the stating part of the bill is all that is necessary from him. Buerk *v.* Imhaueser, § 1587. *

§ 1512. When the answer contains, among other things, a single substantive defense, not responsive to the bill, plaintiff cannot except to this part alone of the answer. Adams *v.* Bridgewater Iron Co., §§ 1588–89.

§ 1513. *Quære,* whether a defense set up in a part of the answer may be heard separately, without going into the whole case. *Ibid.*

§ 1514. An allegation in an answer impeaching the due execution of a codicil already probated by the proper court is impertinent. Langdon *v.* Goddard, §§ 1540–42.

§ 1515. An allegation in an answer setting up an attempted settlement by defendant, which was never accepted by plaintiff, is impertinent. *Ibid.*

§ 1516. Though an interrogatory be not as full as it might have been made, yet, in so far as it states the plain import and object of the question, the defendant will be required to give a full and direct answer. *Ibid.*

§ 1517. An answer in equity will prevail in favor of defendant, unless overcome by the testimony of two witnesses, or of one witness and corroborating circumstances. Hayward *v.* Eliot National Bank, § 1548. See EQUITY.

. [NOTES.—See §§ 1544–1665.]

BROOKS *v.* BYAM.

(Circuit Court for Massachusetts: 1 Story, 296–307. 1840.)

STATEMENT OF FACTS.— Bill in equity for an injunction against the further prosecution of a suit at law brought by present defendants against present plaintiff. Plaintiff excepts to the answer of one of the defendants.

§ 1518. *Proper method of excepting for insufficiency of answer.*

Opinion by STORY, J.

The question arising in this case is upon the exception taken by the plaintiff in equity to the answer of Prentiss Whitney, one of the defendants, "because, in stating in his answer what he has been informed of by Byam (another defendant), he does not say whether he actually believes the same to be true." Certainly this exception is taken in a form and manner entirely too general to be upheld by the court. The exception should have stated the charges in the bill, and the interrogatory applicable thereto to which the answer is addressed, and then have stated the terms of the answer *verbatim*, so that the court without searching the bill and answer throughout, might at once have perceived the ground of the exception and ascertained its sufficiency. It is very properly observed by the vice-chancellor, Sir John Leach, in Hodgson *v.* Butterfield, 2 Sim. & Stu., 236, that, "if the plaintiff complains that a particular interrogatory of the bill is not answered, he must state the interrogatory in the very terms of it, and cannot impose upon the court the trouble of first determining whether the varied expressions of the interrogatory and the exception are to be reconciled." See, also, Gresley on Evid., 21. To which it may be added, that the same rule applies in respect to the necessity of stating the charge or fact in the bill on which the interrogatory is founded; for, if the interrogatory be irrelevant to the matters charged in the bill, the defendant need not answer the interrogatory at all. Mitford, Eq. Pl. by Jeremy, 45; Cooper, Eq. Pl., 12; Gilb. For. Roman, 91, 218; Story on Equity Plead., § 36; Gresley on Evid., 17 to 20, Am. edit. 1837; Story on Equity Plead., § 853; Harrison, Ch. Pract. by Newland, ch. 31, p. 181. The court ought, therefore, without searching through the whole bill, from the form of the exception, to have the materials fully before it by which to ascertain at once its competency and propriety. In this respect the exception is in itself insufficient and exceptionable. The objection, however, has not been insisted upon at the bar.

§ **1519.** *When defendant is required to answer as to his knowledge, remembrance, information and belief, it is not sufficient for him to answer as to his knowledge alone.*

Nothing is more clear in principle than the rule that, in the case of an interrogatory pertinent to a charge in the bill, requiring the defendant to answer it " as to his knowledge, remembrance, information and belief " (which is the usual formulary), it is not sufficient for the defendant to answer as to his knowledge; but he must answer also as to his information and belief. The plain reason is that the admission may be of use to the plaintiff as proof if the defendant should answer as to his belief in the affirmative without qualification. Thus, although a defendant should state that he has no knowledge of the fact charged, if he should also state that he has been informed and believes it to be true, or simply that he believes it to be true, without adding any qualification thereto, such as that he does not know it of his own knowledge to be so, and therefore he does not admit the same, it would be taken by the court as a fact admitted or proved; for the rule in equity generally (although not universally) is that what the defendant believes the court will believe. 2 Daniell, Chan. Prac., 257; id., 402; Gresley on Evid., 19, 20; Potter *v.* Potter, 1 Ves., 274; Carth *v.* Jackson, 6 Ves., 37, 38; Story on Eq. Plead., § 854. The rule might, perhaps, be more exactly stated as to its real foundation by saying that whatever allegation of fact the defendant does not choose directly to deny, but states his belief thereof, amounts to an admission on his part of its truth, or that he does not mean to put it in issue as a matter of controversy in the cause. But a mere statement by the defendant, in his answer, that he has no knowledge that the fact is as stated, without any answer as to his belief concerning it, will not be such an admission as can be received as evidence of the fact. 2 Daniell, Ch. Pr., 257; id., 402; Coop. Eq. Pl., 314; Harris, Ch. Pract. by Newl., ch. 31, p. 181. Such an answer is insufficient; and, therefore, the defect properly constitutes a matter of exception thereto, since it deprives the plaintiff of the benefit of an admission to which he is justly entitled. *Ibid.* However, courts of equity do not, in this respect, act with rigid and technical exactness as to the manner in which the defendant states his belief or disbelief, if it can be fairly gathered from the whole of that part of the answer what is, according to the intention of the defendant, the fair result of its allegations. 2 Daniell, Ch. Pr., 257; Amhurst *v.* King, 2 Sim. & Stu., 183.

§ **1520.** *No universal rule as to answers upon information and belief. How in general they should be framed.*

It is obvious that, in answers as to the information and belief of the defendant, there may be, and, indeed, ordinarily will be, partial admissions and partial denials of every shade and character, some of which may be delivered in terms of great ambiguity and uncertainty, and some mixed up with various qualifications and attendant circumstances. Gresley on Evid., 2d edit., 1837. No general rule, therefore, can be laid down which will govern all the different classes of cases which may thus arise as to the sufficiency or insufficiency of an answer in this respect. A man may have an undoubting belief of a fact, or he may disbelieve its existence, or he may believe it highly probable, or merely probable, or the contrary, or he may have no belief whatsoever, as to it. In each of these cases he is bound to answer conscientiously as to the state of his mind in the matter of his belief; and if he does, that is all which a court of equity will require of him. If a man truly states that he cannot form any belief at all respecting the truth of the fact or information, that is sufficient, and it puts the plaintiff upon proof of it. If, on the other hand, the defendant should state (as in the present case the defendant does in effect state) that he "has no knowledge, information or belief that the fact or information inquired about is not true," or if he states (as in the present case) that he has been informed by a party, and verily believes, that such party did not possess any knowledge, information or belief of the fact which the interrogatory points out,— in each of these cases it seems to me that the answer, if expressive of the true state of mind of the defendant, might at least, for some purposes, be held sufficient. But then, if such language were unaccompanied by any other qualifications or explanations, I should understand that the defendant did mean to assert his belief of the truth of the information or statement of fact, because, if he had no knowledge, information or belief that it is not true, he must be presumed to give credit to it; and if he did not intend so to be understood, it would be his duty to say in express terms that he had no belief about the matter; and he ought not to be allowed to shelter himself behind equivocal or evasive or doubtful terms, and thereby to mislead the plaintiff to his injury.

§ 1521. *Plaintiff is not bound to accept a doubtful answer, though it would be interpreted favorably to him.*

And this leads me to remark, and it is the real and only point of difficulty which I have felt upon the exception, whether, although the plaintiff may agree to take and accept such an admission, interpreting it as affirmative of the defendant's belief, if in that sense it would be beneficial to himself, he is positively bound to receive it, when it is clearly susceptible of a different, or even of an opposite, interpretation, which may affect the nature and extent of his proofs at the hearing of the cause. Upon full reflection, I think that he is not positively bound to receive it, although certainly I should interpret it as an affirmative, if it would be favorable for the plaintiff; but he has a right to require that the defendant should state in direct terms, or, at least, in unequivocal terms, either that he does believe, or that he does not believe, the matter inquired of, or that he cannot form any belief, or has not any belief concerning the matter; and according as the answer shall be the one way or the other, that he calls upon the plaintiff for proof thereof, or he admits it, or he waives any controversy about it.

Upon this ground my opinion is that the exception is well founded, at least, as to some of the allegations in the answer. It may, perhaps, be sufficient for the court merely in this general manner to intimate its present opinion upon the case; and it will be easy for the counsel to make its application to the various parts of the answer complained of. But to make myself more clearly understood, I wish to give an illustration of the principle, drawn from the present bill and answer, especially as the nature of the objection may thereby be seen in a more strong and exact light.

§ 1522. *Illustration drawn from the present state of facts.*

The object of the bill is to obtain, among other things, a perpetual injunction to a suit now pending on the law side of this court, brought by the defendants in the bill (Byam and others) against the plaintiff (Brooks), for a violation of a patent, which they claim title to as assignees of the patentee; and, among other charges, the bill for this purpose alleges that the original patentee (Alonzo D. Phillips) had before his assignment to these parties assigned a limited right therein to one John Brown, under whom the defendant claims a still more limited title, as a sub-purchaser, *pro tanto*, and insisted that his acts done in supposed violation of the patent are rightfully done under this sub-title. The patent is alleged to bear date on the 24th of October, 1837; the assignment to Brown on the 2d of January, 1837; the assignment to Brooks on the 18th of September, 1837; but it was not recorded until the 15th of July, 1839; and the assignment to Byam on the 28th day of July, 1838, under whom the other defendants (Whitney and others) derive title, which only was recorded within the time prescribed by law, whereas the assignment to Brown was not. Under these circumstances the bill charges that Byam, at the time of the assignment to him, and the other defendants (and among them Whitney), at the time of the assignment to them by Byam, had knowledge and information and good cause of belief of the prior assignment to Brown. And in the interrogatory part of the bill the defendants are required "full, true, direct, particular and perfect answer and discovery to make, and that not only according to the best of their knowledge, but to the best of their respective information, hearsay and belief, to all and singular the matters and allegations and charges aforesaid."

Now, the answer of the defendant Whitney (which is excepted to) states that he (the defendant) does not of his own knowledge know whether, at the time of the assignment to Byam, he (Byam) had any information or knowledge, or had any cause to believe, that Phillips had previously made any conveyance to Brown, or Brown to the plaintiff (Brooks), as alleged in the bill; but this defendant has been informed by said Byam that, at the time when the said Phillips conveyed and assigned to him all his right and interest in and to the patent-right, the said Byam had no knowledge, information or cause to believe that the said Phillips had made any conveyance to the said Brown, or that the said Brown had made any conveyance to the complainant; *and this defendant has no knowledge, information or belief that the information so derived from the said Byam is not true.*" Now, it is to the matter and form of this last clause (and a like allegation is to be found in other parts of the answer) that the objection is taken by the exception. The argument is that the clause is ambiguous; that it does not assert, in direct terms, that the defendant believed or disbelieved the statement of Byam; or that the defendant had no belief, or was unable to form any belief, about the matter, and, therefore, required the plaintiff to prove the knowledge, information or belief of Byam at the time of the assignment to him. So that, in fact, the defendant, by the form of his allegation, does not positively put the asserted fact in controversy, as to the knowledge, information or belief of Byam, by affirming his own belief of Byam's statement; neither does he dispense with the proof thereof by denying his own belief thereof; neither does he assert that he is unable to

form any belief upon the subject, and therefore calls for proof of the allegation of the bill on this point; but he leaves the matter in a state of ambiguity
and open to different interpretations as to the true intent and meaning of the
answer.

It appears to me that in this view the exception is well founded. When
the defendant says that he " has no knowledge, information or belief that the
information so derived from the said Byam is not true," he merely pronounces
a negative, which may, indeed, in some sort, amount to a negative pregnant,
arguendo, that, as he has no information or belief that it is not true, therefore
he believes it to be true, which would certainly be a natural, although not an
irresistible, presumption. But it seems to me that the plaintiff has a right to
more than this; to know whether the defendant himself has placed confidence
in the statement or not, or whether his mind hangs *in dubio*, and he is unable
to form any belief either way. In the latter case, certainly, less evidence
would be necessary to infer presumptively the knowledge, information or
belief of Byam himself, than if the defendant himself believed Byam's statement, and acted upon that belief; for a court is not bound, in favor of a defendant, to have a more confident belief in a party than the defendant himself
professes to have. But what I rely on is that the defendant, by such a form
of answer, leaves it entirely equivocal whether he believes or is unable to form
any belief; and the plaintiff has a right to know positively which of the two
is his real predicament.

The exception, therefore, on this point, ought to be allowed.

KITTREDGE v. THE CLAREMONT BANK.

(Circuit Court for Maine: 1 Woodbury & Minot, 244-247. 1846.)

STATEMENT OF FACTS.— The answer of defendant to the bill in this case was
held insufficient and an additional answer was filed which was also excepted to.

§ 1523. *A respondent in his answer to pertinent interrogatories in a bill in
chancery must answer not only as to his knowledge, but his information and
belief.*

Opinion by WOODBURY, J.

One of the exceptions in this case is that the last answer by the bank does
not state whether the original notes of $400 and $850 were for loans made for
the benefit of Bingham. It states that the present officers have no knowledge on this point, but does not add what is their information or their belief
concerning it. The first answer by the bank stated that both Bingham and
the plaintiff appeared as principals on the books, but professed ignorance for
whose benefit the loan was made. And though the court then decided that
the answer should be fuller in this matter, it still omits to set out what is the
information or belief of the present officers on that point.

But both of these should be given when required. Woods v. Morrell, 1
John. Ch., 103. And much more should they have been given in this instance
after a special direction to make the answers in this respect fuller. On this
point the new or amended answers of Briggs and Stevens are nearly in the
same condition; not stating their information and belief as to the matters
urged in the interrogatories, but only their knowledge as set out in the original answer. It is the duty of a respondent, when requested, to state not only
his own knowledge on the matter, but what he has been informed by others,
and the belief which all of his knowledge and information have produced.

§ **1524.** *The officers of a corporation, to answer a bill properly, must make inquiries of their predecessors, etc., if necessary.*

The officers of the bank, if they are not the same persons who were in office at the time of a transaction inquired about, ought to go not only to the records, books and files for information, but to the former officers, if living, and ascertain as near as may be the truth of the matters about which they are interrogated.

These answers are also defective for not denying all which is not admitted on these points, so that a proper issue can be presented and tried. The last exceptions are, therefore, in these respects sustained; and I feel constrained to add, that should another set of answers come in, either evasive or failing .again to comply with the order of the court, some different mode must be taken than merely awarding costs to insure what is proper. Let all the costs of this term be paid by the respondents for leave to amend the present answers and file fuller ones, and let these be filed in thirty days.

Exceptions allowed.

GAINES v. AGNELLY.

(Circuit Court for Louisiana: 1 Woods, 238–245. 1873.)

Opinion by BRADLEY, J.

STATEMENT OF FACTS.— The complainant excepts to the answer of the defendants in this case for insufficiency. She complains that they have not, to the best of their knowledge, information, remembrance and belief, answered and set forth the matters required to be answered by the bill, especially those which were called for by the special interrogatories annexed to the bill.

The complainant claims certain lands, mostly in the city of New Orleans, which she alleges were the property of Daniel Clark at the time of his decease in 1813, were by him devised to her by a will dated July 13, 1813, and have since been taken possession of by the defendants. The bill describes the lands, sets out the will and the probate thereof granted in 1855, and calls upon the defendants severally to show the particular portions of property claimed by them. The bill also states several pretenses which it is supposed will be set up by the defendants: as, first, title derived under a sale of the land by Richard Relf and Beverly Chew, executors of Daniel Clark under a prior will made in 1811, which was revoked by the will of 1813, and as attorneys of Mary Clark, the mother of Daniel Clark, who was devisee under the will of 1811; and secondly, prescription; but the bill charges that the sale by Relf and Chew was unauthorized and void, and would appear to be so on the face of the proceedings; all which must necessarily have been known to the defendants when they purchased. The defendants are called upon, according to the best of their knowledge, information, remembrance and belief to answer: First. Whether the property described was not a part of the estate of Daniel Clark, of which he died seized? Second. Whether the defendants severally claim to be owners of any portion of it? and if so, what portion and by what right? setting forth metes, bounds and titles. Third. How long the defendants have severally been in possession, and what revenue the property has yielded? Fourth. Whether they have sold any part; if so, what, and for what consideration?

These are in substance the interrogatories annexed to the bill, and all the defendants are required to answer them. The bill prays for a discovery of all.

the matters alleged, that the defendants may be decreed to hold the property as trustees for the complainant, may account for the rents and profits, and for general relief. The answers on the point of Daniel Clark's ownership and seizin of the property described in the bill simply say in each case that the defendant has no knowledge whether said Daniel Clark did or did not hold the legal title thereto, and that therefore he cannot admit, but denies, that Clark was seized or lawfully possessed of the same.

The answers then severally set forth and describe by metes and bounds the lands claimed by the defendants, with a statement of the immediate title of the defendants, making the answer and such antecedent acts of title from which the same was derived as are sufficient to carry back the defendants' title far enough to set up prescription under the laws of Louisiana, with averments on information and belief that the successive owners purchased in good faith, believing their vendors to be lawful owners of the property; and had continuous, uninterrupted and peaceable possession for the time requisite for the prescription pleaded.

The answers further state that proceedings have been instituted in one of the state courts for a revocation of the probate of the will of 1813, under which Mrs. Gaines claims the property; that a decree of revocation has already been made in the court of first instance; and that an appeal from that decree to the supreme court has been taken and argued, and the case is now under the final consideration of that court; and the defendants claim that if the decree of revocation shall be affirmed, it will have the effect to deprive the complainant of all foundation of any right to the land claimed. And they pray that they may have the benefit of such decree if it shall be affirmed. They submit that they are not bound in law to make any other or further answer to any matter or thing contained in the bill.

The answers fail to state, except as it may impliedly appear from the descriptions given by streets and by metes and bounds, whether the lands claimed by the defendants were or were not portions of the land described in the complainant's bill, or whether the defendants have any information or belief on the subject; or whether they have any information or belief on the question whether the lands claimed by them belonged to Daniel Clark's estate, or to the lands of which he died seized, as set forth in the bill. The defendants were required to answer fully on these points, not merely upon personal knowledge (which at this day they could not be expected to have), but upon their information and belief as well.

§ 1525. *Under the thirty-ninth rule in equity a defendant is no longer compellable to answer fully as to matters of discovery in cases where he might by plea protect himself, provided that in his answer he sets out the matter of such plea in bar to the merits.*

The defendants, however, to obviate the force of this objection, refer to the thirty-ninth rule in equity, established by the supreme court of the United States, by which the well-known rule of chancery pleading, that if a defendant submits to answer he shall answer fully to all matters of the bill, is abrogated in cases where the defendant might by plea protect himself from such answer and discovery, and in his answer sets forth the matter of such plea as a bar to the merits of the bill. The thirty-ninth rule declares that in such answer the defendant shall not be compellable to answer any other matters than he would be compellable to answer and discover upon filing a plea in bar and an answer in support of such plea, touching the matters set forth in the bill, to avoid or repel the bar or defense.

The defendants claim that prescription is such a bar, and that having set that up in their answer they are excused from answering further.

§ **1526.** *Former practice as to answers and pleas.*

Under the old practice, if a plea were filed and issue taken upon it, and that issue were decided in the complainant's favor, he was entitled to a decree without proving the allegations of his bill. If the same matter were set up in an answer he was obliged to prove his bill, but in aid of such proof he was entitled to the defendant's answer to the whole bill.

§ **1527.** *Under the new rule plaintiff must prove his bill, but may summon defendant as a witness.*

The new rule, which allows a defendant to set up a bar in his answer and excuses him from answering further, still leaves the complainant under the burden of proving his bill, and takes from him the benefit of the defendant's answer. But this disadvantage is compensated for, in some degree, by the liability of the defendant to be called as a witness in the cause. Still, the general effect of the new rule being such as I have stated, it seems to be no longer a ground of exception where the answer sets up a bar to the whole bill and claims the benefit of it, as of a plea in a bar, that it does not fully answer the allegations of the bill.

§ **1528.** *The courses that complainant may pursue if the bar set up in the answer be insufficient.*

If the bar set up and claimed as such be insufficient, or if it be unsupported by proper averments or by a proper answer, to rebut allegations of the bill repugnant to the bar, the complainant may except for insufficiency, set the cause down on bill and answer only, or file a replication and proceed to proofs, according to the exigency of the case. If the bar set up should be insufficient as such, I think the complainant would be entitled to except, as for want of a full answer, and, to avoid answering the exceptions, the defendant, in such case, would require leave of the court before he could amend the bar set up in the answer. If, instead of excepting, the complainant should go to proofs, the burden would be on him to prove his bill and on the defendant to prove his bar, each being entitled to examine the other as a witness. If, on the other hand, he should set the cause down for hearing on bill and answer only, the answer would have to be taken as true, and the bar therein as proved; and though insufficient as a defense, the complaint could not have a decree unless the answer admitted those allegations of the bill on which the prayer for relief was founded.

These are the general rules which seem to me to govern the pleadings in equity, as affected by the introduction of this new rule.

§ **1529.** *If the bar set up be sufficient, it is immaterial whether defendant answer or not.*

From this view of the subject it is manifest that, if the bar set up in the answer is a sufficient defense to the whole relief sought by the bill, it is immaterial whether the defendant answer the allegations of the bill or not. He is not bound to answer them, and the rule no longer applies that if the defendant does answer at all, even on matters outside of the bar, he must answer fully. If that rule did apply it would have the effect of converting the answer, in such a case, into a strict plea in bar. Any divergence of statement, any notice of the allegations of the bill outside of the strict line of the defense, would be held a waiver of the bar, and would subject the defendant to the old burden of a full answer. I do not think that this would be a sound construction of the rule. If there are any authorities favoring this view I should have been glad to have had a reference to them. As counsel has not produced any, I feel the greater confidence in the conclusions to which I have come.

§ **1530.** *What is requisite for a good plea in bar of prescription under the laws of Louisiana.*

The question then is whether the bar set up is, by the laws of Louisiana, a sufficient defense, and whether it is sufficiently averred. And I do not understand the counsel of the complaint to contend that it is not. It seems to me that the bar is very fully and carefully drawn. It sets out all those circumstances which the laws of Louisiana require to exist as the basis of a prescription. Just title, good faith, the requisite period of possession, and that possession continued peaceably and without interruption. All these circumstances are fully alleged. And the defendant has also traversed the effect of the interruption of prescription resulting from the litigation referred to in the bill. How far the proofs, when taken, will sustain the defense, is another matter with which the court has at present no concern. Whether, if the complainant shows that the title of the defendants really originated in a void sale and conveyance by the executors of Daniel Clark, it will effect the defense, on the point of good faith, is a question I do not decide. In the case of Gaines *v.* Hennen and Gaines *v.* New Orleans (24 Howard, and 6 Wallace), the answers admitted that the defendants obtained their title through the sales made by Relf and Chew; and the supreme court held that the illegality of the proceeding was apparent, and constituted a vice in the title, which took from the vendees all pretense of being purchasers or possessors in good faith; and that the interruptions in the prescription prevented its becoming a bar on any other ground. But in this case the defendants do not set up any claim of title under the executors of Daniel Clark. They rely on certain titles which they exhibit as just titles, and which they allege to have been obtained with good faith, and under the honest belief that the author was the real owner. This is, at least, *prima facie* sufficient to lay the foundation of the prescription claimed. Any knowledge, information or belief, obtained since the possession commenced, to the effect that the property once belonged to Daniel Clark, would not, as I understand the law of Louisiana, impair the efficacy of such possession as a ground of prescription. The code expressly says: "It is sufficient if the possession has commenced in good faith; and if the possession should afterward be held in bad faith, that shall not prevent the prescription." Art. 3448. Therefore, the allegations in the bill that the property once belonged to Daniel Clark, and that he died seized thereof, are not inconsistent with or repugnant to the plea of prescription. Hence, any present knowledge or belief of the defendants on those points is perfectly immaterial. Their claim by prescription is independent of those facts, and perfectly consistent with them. These allegations, therefore, do not belong to that class of allegations which it is necessary for a defendant to meet and deny in order to support and maintain his plea in bar.

Had the bill charged that the defendants claimed title to the lands in their possession under Relf and Chew, acting as executors of Daniel Clark, it might perhaps have been incumbent on the defendants to have cleared their possession of the imputation thus cast upon it. But no such charge is made in the bill. On the contrary, the bill expressly states that the complainant is ignorant of the title and claim of title by which the defendants severally hold, and calls upon the defendants to show their title. The defendants do show title sufficient to lay the foundation of a prescription, and on that defense they take their stand.

It seems to me that they are not called upon to answer further. The bar set up is *prima facie* a good defense, and the exceptions must be overruled. As to the answers which the defendants have brought into court and now ask leave to file, I shall allow them to be filed as of the 6th of May instant, without prejudice to the complainant as to proceeding with proofs in the cause, and bringing it on for hearing. ·

§ 1531. *Order as to defendants in default.*

As to those defendants who are in default and· now apply for further time to answer, I shall grant a decree *pro confesso* against them, subject to this qualification and these terms, to wit: that during the taking of proofs in the cause they shall be at liberty, severally, to file· with the master or examiner and serve on the solicitor of the complainant a description of the property which they claim, with the chain of title thereto extending back to the period at which the complainant claims it belonged to the estate of Daniel Clark; and to prove, if they can, a legal prescription for the same; subject also to this further qualification, that if, before the proofs are closed, the decree of the second district court of the parish of Orleans, in the case of Joseph Fuentes *et al. v.* Myra Clark Gaines, revoking the will of Daniel Clark of 1813, be affirmed by the supreme court of Louisiana, the said defendants may have the benefit of said decree for what it may be worth, as if they had pleaded the same. Provided, however, that any further answers of said defendants which may be filed before the 1st day of June next may be filed as of the 6th day of May instant, as are mentioned in reference to answers above allowed to be filed as of said day.

DAVIS v. DAVIDSON.

(Circuit Court for Michigan: 4 McLean, 186–188. 1846.)

Opinion of the COURT. .

STATEMENT OF FACTS.— A motion is made to set aside the answer to a bill in chancery on two grounds.

§ 1532. *A joint answer of defendants need not be several also.* .

1. Because it is the answer of three· individuals and is sworn to by three. In the caption it purports to be the joint answer of the three, but not their several as well as joint answer. This is erroneous, it is contended, for two reasons: 1st. Because all established precedents require them to be several as well as joint. And 2d. Because, in case one of the defendants should swear falsely in the answer, he could not be indicted separately for such false swearing upon a joint answer without joining all the joint respondents.

The precedents are, generally, as stated by the counsel. They are drawn jointly and severally. But we are not prepared to say that this form is indispensable. We see no satisfactory reason why a joint answer, responsive to the bill, would not be sufficient. The reason assigned, that one of the defendants could not be indicted for false swearing without including the others, is not satisfactory. Each individual who answers jointly is responsible for the facts sworn to, the same as if his answer had been separate. And it is not perceived why he might not be indicted without uniting the other defendants.

§ 1533. *Answers should be signed by counsel.*

The answer is not signed by counsel, which is undoubtedly a defect. Except in certain specified cases the answer must be signed by counsel. Under peculiar circumstances, the signature of the defendant may be dispensed with; but the signature of the counsel is required, unless the answer is taken by commissioners. The signature is necessary, that the person signing may be responsible to the court for the contents of the answer. Story's Eq. Pl., sec. 876; Mit. Eq. Pl. by Jeremy, 315. Leave is given to amend the answer.

FRENCH v. FIRST NATIONAL BANK OF THE CITY OF NEW YORK.

(District Court for New York: 7 Benedict, 488-490. 1874.)

Opinion by BLATCHFORD, J.

STATEMENT OF FACTS.— The defendant is a corporation, and is the sole defendant. The bill pleads for relief, and avers facts which lay a foundation for a discovery, and prays a discovery. A corporation must answer a bill under its common seal, and not on oath. This is well settled. Bronson *v.* La Crosse Railroad Co., 2 Wall., 283, 302. The bill in this case prays that the corporation " may, upon the several and respective corporal oaths of its proper officers, agents and servants, according to the best and utmost of their several and respective knowledge, remembrance, information and belief," answer "such of the several interrogatories hereinafter mentioned and set forth as by the note hereinunder written they are respectively required to answer." The note appended to the bill does not require the defendant to answer any of the interrogatories, but says: " The president and cashier of the defendant and its agent, surnamed Brown, are severally required to answer the interrogatories." The corporation has answered under its corporate seal. In its answer it states that it declines to answer the interrogatories. The plaintiff now excepts to the answer, " for that the said defendant hath not, to the best of its knowledge, and to the best of the knowlege, remembrance, information and belief of its officers and agents, answered and set forth, whether," etc.

§ 1534. *A defendant corporation is not obliged to answer interrogatories when the note only requires the officers to answer.*

Under the rules of equity practice established by the supreme court, a defendant is not bound to answer any interrogatories except such as, by the note at the foot of the bill, he is required to answer. In the present case the note does not require the defendant to answer any of the interrogatories, but only requires its president and cashier, and its agent, Brown, to answer them. But the bill could be amended so as to require the defendant to answer them. Yet this would probably be of no use, for, as corporations answer under seal, and without oath, a discovery on oath could not be compelled from the corporation, except through the medium of such a discovery from its agents and officers, and by making such agents and officers parties defendant. Fulton Bank *v.* N. Y. & Sharon Canal Co., 1 Paige, 311; Brumly *v.* Westchester Co. Mfg. Society, 1 Johns. Ch., 366.

§ 1535. *Officers of a defendant corporation are not obliged to answer unless they are parties defendant.*

Under this bill the officers and agents of the defendant cannot be compelled to answer the interrogatories under oath, because they are not defendants. The equity rules (41 to 44) clearly import that no one but a defendant can be compelled to answer the interrogatories in a bill. Officers of a corporation may be made parties defendant to a bill against the corporation, in order to obtain a discovery from such officers. Angell & Ames on Corporations, §§ 674, 675; Story's Eq. Pl., § 235; 2 Story's Eq. Juris., § 1501.

§ 1536. *A defendant corporation may be required to answer under its seal, but not under oath.*

There is nothing in Kittredge v. The Claremont Bank, 3 Story, 590, and 1 Woodb. & M., 244, which conflicts with these views. The plaintiff can, if he desires, so amend his bill as to require the defendant corporation to answer the interrogatories. It may answer them under its seal and without oath. But its answer must be stated therein to be made according to the knowledge and information and belief of its officers, ascertained from all proper sources of information.

The exceptions are overruled, with costs, with leave to the plaintiff to apply on notice for permission to amend the bill by adding new parties and otherwise.

BUERK v. IMHAEUSER.

(Circuit Court for New York: 10 Federal Reporter, 608. 1882.)

Opinion by WHEELER, J.

STATEMENT OF FACTS.— This cause has now been heard on exceptions to the answer for insufficiency. The bill states the recovery of judgments by decree against the defendants for the payment of money; that execution cannot be satisfied for want of property to be found; that the defendants have or have had property, without specifying any in particular; and prays a discovery of their property in hand or held in trust for them. The interrogatories make more specific inquiries. The answer denies generally that the defendant answering has any property in his hands, or that any is held in trust for him, or that he has conveyed away any since the decree, at all, or before, in view of it, to defeat it.

§ 1537. *What interrogatories defendants are required to answer.*

The rules in equity require defendants to answer only such interrogatories as they are specifically required by note to answer. This bill, accordingly, required the defendants to answer such interrogatories as by the note thereunder written they should be required to answer. There is no note thereunder written; therefore there were no interrogatories to be specifically answered. They were only required to answer the stating part of the bill. This the defendant answering has done as specifically as he is by the bill charged. No ground is known for making a defendant give a particular account of all the property he has ever had, or deny specifically having had particular property, upon such general charge as to having had property before which cannot be found now to satisfy judgments. At least, the particular property sought to be reached should be pointed out before anything more than a general answer should be compelled. Exceptions overruled.

ADAMS v. BRIDGEWATER IRON COMPANY.

(Circuit Court for Massachusetts: 6 Federal Reporter, 179, 180. 1881.)

Opinion by LOWELL, J.

STATEMENT OF FACTS.— The defendant corporation, by its answer to the bill, makes all the defenses usual in a patent suit, and adds that it has received from the plaintiff Adams a release, under seal, of all actions for infringement, if it has committed any. A copy of the release is set out, and the defendants pray to have the same benefit of these facts as if they had been pleaded in bar. The plaintiffs except to the answer on the ground that this release, if given precisely as it is averred to have been given, is insufficient in law to bar the plaintiffs' suit.

§ **1538.** *A part of the answer containing a single defense, not responsive to the bill, is not subject to exception.*

A substantive defense, not responsive to the plaintiffs' inquiry in his bill, is not the subject of exception. That form of objection applies only to an insufficient discovery, or to scandal and impertinence.

The plaintiffs intended by their exceptions to procure a hearing upon the validity of this defense as if it were a plea and they had set it down. But it is not a plea. It is part of the answer, and is merely one of several defenses. By the thirty-ninth rule in equity a defendant may make a plea part of his answer, and, if he does so, he shall not be compellable to answer more, or otherwise, than if he had filed a regular plea. The defendants have taken no advantage of this rule; they have answered the whole bill fully; and their request to have the same advantage as if they had pleaded the release has no meaning. As it stands it is, as I have said, one substantive defense not used by way of plea at all, but by way of alternative answer. It stands precisely like the defense of the statute of limitations, which they also rely on in another part of their answer, and which they might have used by way of plea or demurrer.

§ **1539.** *Quære, whether there may be a hearing on part of the answer without going into the whole case.*

Whether the court may not have power to hear such a defense before requiring the whole case to be gone into is not now the question. There is no regular authorized mode of pleading, like a demurrer, to test the legal validity of part of an answer; but possibly, on motion, some order might be taken to dispose of part of a case in the first instance, if it should be found that great delay and expense might thereby be avoided. I do not decide that point. Exceptions overruled.

LANGDON *v.* GODDARD.

(Circuit Court for New Hampshire: 3 Story, 13–25. 1843.)

STATEMENT OF FACTS.—This cause was heard upon exceptions to the answer of defendant Goddard to complainants' bill. The first exception was that a certain allegation on the ninth page of the answer was impertinent, and should be stricken out. The allegation in question was to the effect that the testatrix, Elizabeth Sewall, executed a codicil to her will on August 21, 1838, being moved thereto by the importunities of complainants, and charging the complainants with, in effect, dictating the codicil. The will and codicil in question had, prior to the filing of the answer, been duly admitted to probate by the proper court. The second exception was to a statement that he, defendant, had sought to procure Mr. Emerson to effect a settlement of the disputes between him and complainants, and that he and Emerson had agreed upon terms, to which, however, complainants would not afterwards adhere. This statement, it was insisted, was impertinent.

The third exception was that defendant had not, to the best of his knowledge and belief, answered a certain interrogatory of plaintiffs.

§ 1540. *A statement in an answer impeaching the due execution of a codicil, which has been already probated, is impertinent.*

Opinion by STORY, J.

I am of opinion that all the exceptions to the answer are well taken, and ought to be allowed. The first exception turns upon the allegations in the answer therein referred to, by which an attempt is made by a side wind to impeach the *bona fides* and due execution of the codicil to the will of Mrs. Sewall, and by implication to insinuate that it was procured by fraud and imposition. Now, it is well known that the courts of probate have a full and exclusive jurisdiction, as well in New Hampshire as in Maine, over the probate of wills, and that their decree, affirming the validity of a will or codicil, and allowing the same, is conclusive upon the subject-matter, and is not re-examinable elsewhere. The present codicil has been duly admitted and allowed by the probate courts of both states. The allegation of the answer here excepted to is, therefore, at once impertinent and immaterial, and endeavors to cast a shade upon the transaction, which is not justifiable or excusable. It is not a matter which can be filed in controversy in the present suit, or admitted to proof.

§ 1541. *To set up in an answer an attempted settlement by the defendant, which was never accepted by the plaintiff, is impertinent.*

The second exception is to the allegation in the answer setting up an attempted settlement and arrangement, of the nature and terms of which no account is given, by the defendant with the plaintiffs, through the means of a professional friend, which was not accepted or adhered to by the plaintiffs, and therefore failed of its purpose. What is this but to stuff the answer with immaterial and impertinent suggestions for the purpose of giving a false gloss and coloring to the controversy? Besides, as the nature and terms of the proffered settlement and arrangement are nowhere stated, it is impossible for the court to see what possible bearing it could properly have upon the cause.

§ 1542. *Although an interrogatory may not be as full as it should be, yet if it be sufficiently explicit to show its plain import, a full disclosure in reply to it will be required of the defendant.*

The third exception is the insufficiency of the answer to the eighth interrogatory propounded by the bill, and states the very words of that interrogatory. That interrogatory undoubtedly was intended to refer to the following allegation in the bill, viz.: "Your orators further say that thereafterwards the said Elizabeth frequently called upon the said Goddard to refund to her the amount of the said notes so sold by her to him, or return the same, and that the said Goddard repeatedly promised so to do. That on the 20th day of August, 1838, the said William Goddard prepared with his own hand an instrument purporting to be a codicil to the will of said Elizabeth, and procured the said Elizabeth to sign the same, therein and thereby bequeathing to him the aforesaid notes of Floyd and Harris, and also all sums of money due from him to the said Elizabeth, which codicil was so signed by the said Elizabeth by inducement of the said Goddard, and by reason of the confidence subsisting between the said Elizabeth and the said Goddard, and was thereafterward revoked by the said Elizabeth, which codicil was, after its execution, carried away by the said William, and is now in his possession." It is certainly not as pointed, full and precise as it ought to be to meet all the stress of the allegations of the bill. It does not interrogate as to the present possession by the defendant of that codicil, or as to what has become of it, and when he last saw it, and what were the exact purport and words thereof; nor does it call upon the defendant to produce it. Still, however, it is sufficient to call upon the defendant for a fair and full answer to the plain import and objects thereof. I cannot but consider the answer put in to this point as inexplicit and evasive, if it does not deserve the stronger imputation of being disingenuous. I shall therefore direct that the defendant put in a more full and direct answer to the interrogatory and allegation in the bill, applicable thereto, so that the justice of the case may on this point be fully presented to the court. I shall also give leave to the plaintiff to put additional interrogatories to the defendant applicable to this same allegation, so as to compel a direct and positive disclosure of the facts appertaining thereto. The defendant is to pay the costs of the hearing upon and allowance of these exceptions, which I shall direct to be taxed at $10.

HAYWARD v. ELIOT NATIONAL BANK.

(Circuit Court for Massachusetts: 4 Clifford, 294-300. 1874.)

STATEMENT OF FACTS.—Bill in equity for account, and that complainant might redeem shares of mining stock pledged by him to the respondent as collateral security for a loan.

§ 1543. *Effect of answer as evidence for defendant.*

Opinion by CLIFFORD, J.

Controversies like the present cannot be satisfactorily determined without some reference to the pleadings which immediately respect the material matters in issue; as where the answer is responsive to the bill, and positively denies the matter charged, and the denial has respect to a transaction within the knowledge of the party making it, the answer is evidence in his favor, and unless the answer is overcome by the testimony of two opposing witnesses, or of one witness corroborated by facts and circumstances which give the opposing evidence greater weight than the answer, the rule in equity is that the answer is conclusive, so that the court will neither make a decree in favor of the complainant, nor send the case to trial, but will simply dismiss the bill of complaint. Badger v. Badger, 2 Cliff., 146. Repeated decisions of the supreme court have established the rule that an answer responsive to the allegations of the bill, if it have respect to matters within the knowledge of the pleader and be duly sworn to, must be taken to be true, unless disproved by two witnesses, or by one witness and corroborative circumstances which give the opposing testimony greater weight than the answer. Clark v. Van Reims-dyk, 9 Cranch, 160; Hughes v. Blake, 6 Wheat., 453; Same Case, 1 Mason, 518.; Union Bank v. Geary, 5 Pet., 111. Unsworn answers do not have that effect, but if the answer be duly sworn to, even though the suit be against a corporation, and the oath be by one of its principal officers, the answer will have that effect if it be responsive to the bill, and be clear and positive in its terms. Carpenter v. Ins. Co., 4 How., 219; Salmon v. Clagett, 3 Bland, 165; Parker v. Phettyplace, 1 Wall., 689; Tobey v. Leonards, 2 Wall., 430; 2 Story, Eq. Jur., 1528. Apply that rule to the case, and it is clear that the complainant cannot recover unless the proofs introduced by him are sufficient to overcome the allegations of the answer, giving to the answer the probative force which that rule prescribes, as the bill distinctly charges that no valid sale of the shares was made; that if the respondents pretend that they did any act tending to transfer the title to the shares, or that they have procured or permitted certificates of the shares to issue to any other parties, it has been done without notice to the complainant, without right, and in fraud of his just rights. Nothing further can be required to show that the issue of notice is distinctly tendered by the complainant; and the record shows that the answer is directly responsive to the bill, and alleges that the vote of the directors to instruct the president of the bank to sell the shares, if the pledgor failed to make the required payments, was communicated to the complainant; and that he declined to make the payments, and stated that he would not pay anything, and would not do anything about it, and that the sale was made with the full concurrence of, and with the prior assent and subsequent approval of, the complainant. Beyond all doubt the complainant is bound to disprove the material averments of the answer, or he is not entitled to a decree for relief, as the rule is that the answer shall otherwise prevail.

[The remainder of the case, being merely a discussion of facts, is omitted.]

Dismissed with costs.

§ 1544. **If no answers be filed** to a bill in equity plaintiff may have a decree *pro confesso.* Secor *v.* Singleton,* 5 McC., 230.

§ 1545. **An answer consisting of a general denial** of the allegations of the bill in the form of the general issue is wholly unknown in equity, though, if it be filed, plaintiff possibly should file a *pro forma* replication. *Ibid.*

§ 1546. **Where an answer neither admits nor denies the allegations of the bill** such allegations must be proved upon the final hearing. Rogers *v.* Marshall, 8 McC., 76.

§ 1547. **An admission made in an answer** will be of no use to the plaintiff unless it is put in issue by some charge in the bill. Battle *v.* Insurance Co., 10 Blatch., 417.

§ 1548. **Requisites of answer in absence of interrogatories.**— If a bill does not contain specific interrogatories the complainant must be satisfied with such answer to his allegations as would fairly occur to the professional mind as meeting them in a substantial manner. Parsons *v.* Cumming,* 1 Woods, 461.

§ 1549. **A general answer** is sufficient for a general allegation. *Ibid.*

§ 1550. **If an answer is insufficient** parties may be called to the stand and examined on oath. *Ibid.*

§ 1551. **When second answer will be required.**— If it is apparent that defendant has omitted to answer any material allegation, or has evaded giving an answer, or has answered disingenuously, the court will compel him to file another answer. *Ibid.*

§ 1552. **Plea, demurrer or answer may be put in any time before bill is taken as confessed.**— In a suit in equity the defendant may, at any time before the bill is taken for confessed, plead, demur or answer; and the plaintiff is to pursue the same course as if the plea, demurrer or answer had been filed before the expiration of the three months limited for answer by the rules of the court. Oliver *v.* Decatur, 4 Cr., 458.

§ 1553. **A bill and answer** should be construed together. Cahoon *v.* Ring, 1 Cliff., 592.

§ 1554. **Answer may be put in after plea overruled.**— Under equity rule 34 of the supreme court, a defendant, upon the overruling of his plea, has a right to answer, and leave so to do must be given him. Wooster *v.* Blake,* 7 Fed. R., 816.

§ 1555. **Admissions in answer, effect of.**— No admissions in an answer to a bill in chancery can, under any circumstances, lay the foundation for relief under any specific head of equity, unless it be substantially set forth in the bill. Jackson *v.* Ashton, 11 Pet., 229.

§ 1556. **Allegations in answer and proof must agree.**— The general rule is that the allegations in the answer or plea in an action and the proof must agree. Where there were no averments in a plea to authorize the proof offered by a defendant, it was properly rejected by the court. Wilcox *v.* Hunt, 13 Pet., 378.

§ 1557. **What matter may be insisted upon in answer.**— The twenty-third rule of the supreme court in equity, declaring "that the defendant, instead of a formal demurrer or plea, may insist upon any matter in his answer, and have the same benefit thereof as if he had pleaded the same matter or demurred to the bill," is simply in affirmance of the common practice of courts of equity, and applies to matters to the merits, and not to such objections as are in abatement merely. Wood *v.* Mann, 1 Sumn., 578.

§ 1558. **Defects in title not apparent in pleading will not be noticed.**— When a paper title is set out in the pleadings in equity, the court will notice any defect apparent therein;

but if the defect depend upon extraneous facts, it must be averred or the court will not take it into account, even though practically all the proof has been directed to that point. So held when the bill was brought to recover a certain tract of land, and the question depended upon the validity of a certificate of settlement. The certificate was sufficient on its face and was not attacked in the pleadings, but upon trial a decree was rendered adverse to the certificate, upon testimony showing that the location was too vague. This decree was overruled by the supreme court as not conforming to the pleadings. Crocket v. Lee,* 7 Wheat., 522.

§ 1559. **Sufficiency of verification of answer.**— An answer in chancery is not sufficiently authenticated unless the authority of the justice of the peace before whom it was sworn be sufficiently shown. Addison v. Duckett, 1 Cr. C. C., 349.

§ 1560. —— **in foreign country.**— Under an agreement that an answer should be sworn to before some officer qualified by the law of France to administer oaths, an oath before the American consul is not sufficient. Herman v. Herman,* 4 Wash., 555.

§ 1561. An answer in equity executed in a foreign country should be sworn to before a commissioner authorized under a *dedimus potestatem* from the court having jurisdiction of the case. Reed v. Consequa,* 4 Wash., 335.

§ 1562. —— **by infant.**— An infant's answer in equity, if required to be under oath, should be sworn to by the guardian *ad litem* as to his belief in the truth of the defense. Equitable Life Ass. Soc. v. Patterson, 1 Fed. R., 126.

§ 1563. —— **by corporation.**— A corporation must answer a bill under its common seal and not on oath. Hence, if the bill prays a discovery that various officers of the corporation answer on oath, the corporation is not required to answer, nor are the officers if not made parties. French v. The First Nat. Bk. of N. Y.,* 11 N. B. R., 189.

§ 1564. **Specific denial in answer — Montana statute.**— Under a Montana statute of 1872, providing that the answer of the defendant shall contain a specific denial to allegation intended to be controverted, denial upon information and belief is not permissible. That the verification provided by the code speaks of "matters stated on information and belief" does not alter this ruling, and if the denials are thus made the complainant can take judgment without motion to strike out the answer. Sands v. Maclay,* 2 Mont. T'y, 35.

§ 1565. **Time for filing — Controversy between states.**— The rules which govern courts of equity as to the allowance of time for filing an answer and other proceedings in suits between individuals will not be applied by the United States supreme court to controversies between states of the Union. The parties in such cases must, in the nature of things, be incapable of acting with the promptness of an individual. Rhode Island v. Massachusetts, 13 Pet., 23.

§ 1566. **When plea overruled by.**— An answer being broader than a plea overrules it. Lewis v. Baird, 3 McL., 56; Taylor v. Luther, 2 Sumn., 228.

§ 1567. **Demurrer overruled by.**— Double pleading in a court of equity is not allowable; and therefore if there is a general answer and a demurrer, the answer overrules the demurrer, and the case stands on the bill and answer. United States v. Parrott, McAl. 271.

§ 1568. **Denial accompanied by allegations equivalent to admission.**— A denial by a defendant in the answer that he took a certain action alleged in the bill is of no avail when in the same answer he admits other facts which are legally equivalent to the act denied. Adams v. Adams, 21 Wall., 185.

§ 1569. **Amendatory answer repeating former defense stricken out.**— If an amendatory answer repeat what was said in the answer filed before, without varying the defense, it may be considered as impertinent, and will be referred to a master and stricken out. Gier v. Gregg, 4 McL., 202.

§ 1570. **If the material allegations of a bill are admitted and the immaterial denied in the answer,** the complainant may move to strike out the answer, and for judgment, because the whole answer is bad, but this could not be done were there any merit in the answer. Freman v. Curran,* 1 Minn., 169.

§ 1571. **New matter in nature of cross-bill in.**— A defendant cannot introduce new matter in the nature of a cross-bill in his answer, and require the plaintiff to answer it. Federal courts follow the English practice and require a cross-bill. Morgan v. Tipton, 3 McL., 339.

§ 1572. **English practice.**— It is not the English practice to set up a matter in the answer which shall have the effect of a cross-bill. And the practice in the United States courts is derived from that of the high court of chancery in England. Hubbard v. Turner, 2 McL., 519.

§ 1573. **A departure from the defense alleged in the answer** is not permitted in courts of chancery, where the complainant is entitled to call upon the defendant to answer under oath. Such answer must be held to be the true and only answer the defendants have. Russell & Erwin Manuf. Co. v. Mallory,* 5 Fish. Pat. Cas., 632.

§ 1574. **An averment in an answer not responsive to any allegation in the bill throws the burden** of establishing it affirmatively upon the defendant. Gaines v. Hennen, 24 How., 553.

§ 1575. Averments in the answer not responsive to anything in the bill must be supported by proof in order to be of any avail as defenses. Roach v. Summers, 20 Wall., 165.

§ 1576. Answer by way of confession and avoidance — Burden of proof.— The rule in chancery is, if the answer of the defendant admits a fact, but insists on matter by way of avoidance, the complainant need not prove the fact admitted, but the defendant must prove the matter in avoidance. Clarke v. White, 12 Pet., 178.

§ 1577. Charge of fraud — Plea and answer.— There must be an answer denying the fraud charged in the bill in support of the plea. Lewis v. Baird, 3 McL., 56.

§ 1578. Defendant need not answer immaterial interrogatories.— When an answer in equity set up an agreement that upon the settlement of a claim by the Brazilian government defendant was to pay over a certain sum to one Wells, and the remainder to "certain parties in Brazil," and alleged that defendant had acted in accordance with this agreement, and that plaintiff had ratified and approved of his action, but did not allege that the names of the parties in Brazil had been communicated to plaintiff, and it did not appear that the names were relevant to the case or important to the cause of action or defense, held, that plaintiff's interrogatory as to the names was immaterial, and that defendant need not answer it. United States v. Webb,* 8 Ben., 844.

§ 1579. Adequate remedy at law as defense in answer.— Objection to a bill in equity that the complainant has an adequate remedy at law, when the jurisdiction in chancery and at law are concurrent, may sometimes be taken under the answer and at the hearing as well as by demurrer. Pierpont v. Fowle, 2 Woodb. & M., 23.

§ 1580. Information and belief.— Where the respondent has no personal knowledge of the matter set forth in any particular allegation of the bill of complaint, a denial by the respondent upon information and belief is sufficient to make it necessary for the complainant to prove the allegation. Robinson v. Mandell, 3 Cliff., 169.

§ 1581. A defendant is not permitted to deny an allegation in plaintiff's bill upon information and belief, when, from the nature of the charge, his knowledge, if any, must be direct and personal. Burpee v. First National Bank,* 5 Biss., 405.

§ 1582. Such a denial does not raise an issue, and the allegation referred to will be taken as true in deciding the case. Ibid.

§ 1583. It is good cause of exception to an answer, that, to a denial that a defendant has no knowledge of the facts charged, it is not added "that he had no information or belief of them." Bradford v. Geiss, 4 Wash., 513.

§ 1584. Where exceptions were taken to the answer, by the plaintiff, on the ground that the statements of the defendants therein contained were not "to the best of their knowledge, remembrance, information and belief," as required by the bill, and were imperfect and insufficient, and the exceptions were allowed by the court, it was held that the defendants were bound to answer as to their information, and remembrance, and belief, as well as to their knowledge. Kittredge v. The Claremont Bank, 3 Story, 590.

§ 1585. Where the plaintiff in his bill in chancery directly charged upon the defendant that he had made and entered into a certain agreement, a simple denial by the defendant in his answer, "according to his recollection and belief," is insufficient, and must be treated as a mere evasion. Taylor v. Luther, 2 Sumn., 228.

§ 1586. Exceptions.— Matter in an answer which is in response to the bill cannot be excepted to for impertinence. Lownsdale v. Portland, Deady, 1.

§ 1587. Exceptions for impertinence are only allowed when it is apparent that the matter excepted to is not material or relevant, or is stated with needless prolixity. If the matter may be material an exception will not be allowed. Chapman v. School District,* Deady, 108.

§ 1588. An allegation in an answer will be allowed to stand if it is proper as matter of inducement, though it would be impertinent if standing alone. Ibid.

§ 1589. An allegation of the answer may be evasive and insufficient and yet not subject to exception for impertinence. A portion of an answer setting up a defense which rests on an assumption of law manifestly wrong is impertinent. Ibid.

§ 1590. A portion of an answer seeking affirmative relief for defendant is impertinent. Ibid.

§ 1591. An exception for impertinence must be allowed as a whole or not at all. Ibid.

§ 1592. An exception for insufficiency of an answer to an interrogatory should state the charges of the bill, the interrogatory applicable thereto, and the terms of the answer verbatim, so that the court may at once perceive the ground of exception without searching through the pleadings. Brooks v. Byam, 1 Story, 296.

§ 1593. Upon exceptions to an answer for impertinence and scandal the court will give the answer a liberal construction, and will take into account the nature of the case presented in the bill. Griswold v. Hill, 1 Paine, 390.

§ 1594. When a bill was brought to revive a partnership, alleging that an agreement had been made, and subsequently given up by desire of defendant upon the failure to obtain certain privileges from the government of Chili, an answer that a stronger reason in defendant's mind was that he had become convinced that any connection in business with plaintiff would be, in a high degree, inexpedient and unsafe, is not open to exception as impertinent and scandalous; also an allegation in the answer that plaintiff had required, as a condition precedent to giving up the agreement, that defendant should give him a certificate in favor of his character; also an allegation in the answer insinuating that plaintiff's pecuniary condition had become doubtful, yet showing that it had been restored; also an allegation in the answer as to a certain letter written by plaintiff to defendant, asking a renewal of the partnership agreement, that defendant did not believe plaintiff wrote the letter with any intent or view of forming or renewing a business connection, plaintiff having neither sufficient funds nor credit to enable him so to do. *Ibid.*

§ 1595. An omission of the answer to admit or deny a wholly immaterial charge of the bill is no ground for exception. So held where a bill was brought for an injunction against a judgment at law obtained against present plaintiff as surety on a bond. The bill alleged that the principal on the bond was dead and his estate insolvent, and the answer neither admitted nor denied the fact. An exception to the answer on this ground was overruled. Hardeman *v.* Harris,* 7 How., 726.

§ 1596. When a bill alleged that the decision in a certain suit was made after full consideration, an answer denying that it was made after full consideration, but alleging that on the contrary it was made under circumstances which would go to show the opposite, is not in so far impertinent or scandalous, and an exception on that ground will be overruled. Miller *v.* Buchanan,* 5 Fed. R., 866.

§ 1597. Plaintiff's exceptions to defendant's answer were filed two months after the answer, but before defendant had left with the clerk a rule to reply. *Held*, that the exceptions were filed in time. Brent *v.* Venable,* 3 Cr. C. C., 227.

§ 1598. Where an exception to the jurisdiction was taken in the answer it was properly struck out, on reference to a master, for impertinence. Wood *v.* Mann, 1 Sumn., 578.

§ 1599. Joint and several answer of three sworn to by two only.— An answer in the name of three defendants as their joint and several answer, signed and sworn to, however, by two only, is irregular, though plaintiff may, if he choose, waive the irregularity by replying. If he does not this, but moves to strike the answer from the files and for judgment *pro confesso*, an order will be given to strike out the answer, with leave to the two defendants to erase the name of the third, and to file the answer as their own only. Bailey Washing Machine Co. *v.* Young, 12 Blatch., 199.

§ 1600. An order giving leave to answer without oath or signature will be granted, if circumstances render it proper. *Ibid.*

§ 1601. Answer may admit contract but plead statute of frauds.— In a suit for a specific performance of a parol agreement to convey lands, although the defendant answer and admit the agreement, he may, nevertheless, protect himself against a performance of it by pleading the statute of frauds. Thompson *v.* Tod, Pet. C. C., 380.

§ 1602. Purchase under judicial sale — Fraud, when to be set up by cross-bill instead of answer.— A purchaser under a judicial sale having filed a bill and obtained an injunction upon a creditor of the estate — who had obtained a judgment and levied an execution upon the purchased property — to stay the execution, it was an irregular mode of raising the question of fraud in the sale for the creditor to file an answer setting it forth, and alleging the sale to be void upon that ground; he should have filed a cross-bill. Ford *v.* Douglas, 5 How., 143.

§ 1603. Bill of discovery — Answer that A. can prove the facts, insufficient.— It is no sufficient answer to a bill of discovery brought against a defendant in a suit at law — where the facts are material and can only be proved by the oath of the defendant — to say that A. B. can prove the facts, where the person so referred to is interested. Bell *v.* Pomeroy, 4 McL., 57.

§ 1604. Rescission by deed.— Lying by, and acquiescence, may be sufficient to induce the court to refuse to rescind a deed, though not pleaded as a bar. Fisher *v.* Boody, 1 Curt., 206.

§ 1605. Upon a motion to vacate an order pro confesso, and for leave to answer, the respondent must satisfactorily account for his laches, and exhibit by answer or affidavit a meritorious defense. Scott *v.* The Propeller Young America, Newb., 107.

§ 1606. Charge of notice of fraud — Argumentative denial.— The following denial was entered to the notice of fraud asserted in the bill, to wit: "That this defendant had no notice whatever of any title, claim or demand of the complainant, or of any other person, to or in the lands so purchased by this defendant, as aforesaid, which would affect the same, or any of them, or any part thereof." *Held*, that this is argumentative and insufficient. It should expressly and in terms deny, by proper averment, notice of the fraud charged in the bill. Wood v. Mann, 1 Sumn., 506.

§ 1607. Answer setting up dismission of former bill.— An answer in chancery setting up as a defense the dismission of a former bill filed by the same complainant is not sufficient unless the record be exhibited.   United States Bank v. Beverly, 1 How., 134.

§ 1608. Answer to injunction bill, how treated.— An answer to an injunction bill, though filed without a rule, will be treated as an answer on a motion to grant or continue an injunction.\ Brooks v. Bicknell, 8 McL., 250.

§ 1609. Answer admitting acceptance of proposal but denying contract.— If an answer in chancery admits that a proposal for insurance was made and accepted, but adds that no contract was made, the court will not intend that this denial includes any new matter of fact, but will treat it only as containing respondent's view of the legal consequences of the facts admitted.   Union Mutual Ins. Co. v. Commercial Mutual Marine Ins. Co., 2 Curt., 524.

§ 1610. Answer not responsive to bill.— Where a bill alleged than an agreement of compromise was made, and the answer goes into a history of the dispute compromised, it is not responsive to the bill.   Sargent v. Larned, 2 Curt., 340.

§ 1611. Want of jurisdiction, parties or equity — Objection for, how taken.— An objection to jurisdiction for want of parties, of equity in the bill, or of there being a remedy at law, need not be made by demurrer, plea, or in the answer; it may be made at the hearing or on appeal. Baker v. Biddle, 1 Bald., 394.

§ 1612. The staleness of a demand may be relied on at the hearing, though there is no plea or demurrer, or the answer does not insist on it.   Ibid.

§ 1613. Infringement of patent — Requisites of answer.— Where a bill alleges an infringement of a patent the respondent must answer it distinctly and unevasively.   Jordan v. Wallace,* 1 Leg. Gaz. R., 354.

§ 1614. —— issue of fraud, how raised.— The issue of fraud, in a patent case, can be raised only by distinct and special allegations in the plea or answer.   Blake v. Stafford, 6 Blatch., 195.

§ 1615. —— pleadings must be single.— Pleadings in equity, as well as at law, should be single, clear and free of evasion: and in a patent case the respondent cannot set up as a defense that if the complainant's patent be so construed as to cover the machine made and sold by him, then the invention embraced in said patent was known and used prior to the invention thereof by the patentee.   More than one defense, however, may be presented in the answer, provided each is separately and clearly alleged, without any conditions or undefined qualifications.   Graham v. Mason, 4 Cliff., 88.

§ 1616. —— denial must be unequivocal.— In a suit to restrain infringement of a patent, if the defendant wishes to deny the infringement, he must do so distinctly and unequivocally.   Jordan v. Wallace,* 8 Phil., 165.

§ 1617. If the defense of the statute of limitations, set up in an answer to certain parts of a bill, is well taken, no further answer need be made to such parts of the bill.   Samples v. The Bank, 1 Woods, 523.

§ 1318. Bill to set aside conveyance for duress — Insufficient answer.— A bill in equity to set aside a conveyance on the ground of duress, brought against the grantee and a judgment creditor of the grantee claiming a lien on the land, set up title in the complainant, and alleged that the conveyance to the respondent was made under duress.   The answer of the judgment creditor set up that the title was in the grantee without further particulars; did not deny the duress; alleged that the respondent was informed and believed that the complainant was in possession of the land as tenant only; but set up no other title.   Held, the allegation in the answer of title in the grantee must be taken to refer to the title derived through the deed sought to be set aside, since no other title was set up; the answer is evasive and insufficient, and, the grantee having put in no answer, the conclusion is inevitable that the title was in the complainant and that he parted with it under duress.   Brown v. Pierce, 7 Wall., 205.

§ 1619. Bill filed by agreement, but void for champerty — Objection to, how taken.— An objection that the bill was filed under an agreement made between the plaintiffs and certain other parties, which is void for champerty, ought to be raised formally by answer, and not by motion to take the bill from the files.   Sperry v. Erie R'y Co., 6 Blatch., 425.

§ 1620. Patent suit — Extent of admission as to infringement.— Where in a patent suit the answer admitted that defendants had manufactured locks as described in the plaintiff's patent, this admission need go no further than its terms necessarily imply, and the court may assume that the smallest number of locks were made, consistent with the use of that word in the plural.   Jones v. Morehead, 1 Wall., 155.

§ 1621. —— averments unnecessary to let in evidence.— In a patent case in equity the answer need not make averments as to the state of the act in question in order to let in evidence of it.   Brown v. Piper, 1 Otto, 87.

§ 1622. —— Insufficient answer.— An averment in an answer to a suit on a patent for infringement, that. after rejection of the application for want of novelty in the invention, the plaintiffs "abandoned said application for over two years, well knowing that a certain company were making and using this pretended invention, and that the patent afterwards granted was obtained upon false and fraudulent representations by the plaintiffs, or some of them, made to the commissioner of patents, and is wholly void in law," is frivolous and void, because abandonment to the *public* is not set up, and the averment of false representations is too general to raise a triable issue. Clark v. Scott,* 5 Fish. Pat. Cas., 245.

§ 1623. The statute of limitations, if relied on in equity as a defense, must be set up in the plea or answer. Sullivan v. Railroad Co., 4 Otto, 806.

§ 1624. Allegation in answer of fraud in sale wrongfully stricken out.— An action was brought in the United States circuit court of Louisiana against the sheriff of New Orleans, to recover the value of a steamboat sold by him under an execution as the property of A., one of the defendants in the execution, B., the plaintiff, alleging the boat was his property. The defendant in his answer alleged that the sale of the steamboat by A. to B. was fraudulent, and that it was made to defraud the creditors of A. Before the jury was sworn, the court, on motion of counsel for the plaintiff, struck out all that part of the defendant's answer which alleged fraud in the sale from A. to B. *Held*, that there was error in this order of the court. Hozey v. Buchanan, 16 Pet., 215.

§ 1625. Verification of answer, waiver of, by bill.— The waiver by the bill of the oath of the respondent to his answer does not amount to anything unless accepted by the respondent. Amory v. Lawrence, 3 Cliff., 528.

§ 1626. Defendants have a right to answer a bill upon oath, although the plaintiff has waived such an answer; the waiver amounts to nothing unless the defendants accept it; and the tender of the waiver is no ground of demurrer to the bill. Heath v. Erie R'y Co., 8 Blatch., 347.

§ 1627. Complainant cannot deprive a defendant in a bill in equity of his right to answer under oath by waiving such oath; and if, after a waiver, the defendant nevertheless answers under oath, he is entitled to the benefit of such an answer. Clements v. Moore, 6 Wall., 299.

§ 1628. Answer as evidence.— An answer responsive to the bill is evidence in favor of the defendant. Russell v. Clark, 7 Cr., 69; Hough v. Richardson, 3 Story, 659; Morgan v. Tipton, 3 McL., 339; Lenox v. Notrebe, Hemp., 251. See EQUITY.

§ 1629. The answer of a defendant is evidence against the plaintiff, although it be doubtful whether a decree can be made against such defendant. Field v. Holland, 6 Cr., 8.

§ 1630. The answer of a defendant in chancery is not evidence of new matter set up by way of defense, and not responsive to any allegation in the bill. Robinson v. Cathcart, 3 Cr. C. C., 877.

§ 1631. An allegation in an answer which is not responsive to the bill is not evidence; and the *onus probandi* is on the defendant to establish it. Flagg v. Mann, 2 Sumn., 486.

§ 1632. An answer of the defendant, in order to be evidence in his favor, must be an answer to a fact averred in the bill, and not an answer to a mere inference of law. Robinson v. Cathcart, 2 Cr. C. C., 590.

§ 1633. The answer of a defendant in chancery, who has no personal knowledge of the facts he states, and whose conscience cannot be affected thereby, is not evidence in the cause, although responsive to the allegations in the bill. The only effect of such an answer is to present an issue and to put the plaintiff to the proof of his allegations. Dutilh's Adm'r v. Coursault, 5 Cr. C. C., 349.

§ 1634. If a matter charged in a bill in equity is one within the defendant's own knowledge he must answer positively; and it is not sufficient for him to answer that he has no recollection of doing a certain thing with which he is charged, and that he does not believe he did it. Upon such an answer the testimony of a single witness is sufficient to establish the fact alleged in the bill. Slater v. Maxwell, 6 Wall., 268.

§ 1635. The sworn answer of a defendant in equity, when responsive to material allegations in the bill, must be taken as true, unless overcome by the testimony of two witnesses, or of one witness and corroborative circumstances equivalent to another witness. Lenox v. Prout, 3 Wheat., 520; Union Bank of Georgetown v. Geary, 5 Pet., 99; Tobey v. Leonards, 2 Wall., 423; Voorhees v. Bonesteel, 16 Wall., 16; Vigil v. Hopt,* 14 Otto, 441; Delano v. Winsor, 1 Cliff., 50; Clark v. Hackett, 1 Cliff., 269; Tobey v. Leonard, 2 Cliff., 40; Parker v. Phetteplace, 2 Cliff., 70; Badger v. Badger, 2 Cliff., 137; Gilman v. Libbey, 4 Cliff., 447; Daniel v. Mitchell, 1 Story, 173; Langdon v. Goddard, 2 Story, 267; Gould v. Gould, 3 Story, 515; Cushing v. Smith, 3 Story, 556; Higbee v. Hopkins, 1 Wash., 230; Gernon v. Boecaline, 3 Wash., 199; Harper v. Dougherty, 2 Cr. C. C., 284; Pomeroy v. Manin, 2 Paine, 476; Jones v. Brittan, 1 Woods, 667; Towne v. Smith, 1 Woodb. & M., 115; Walker v. Derby, 5 Biss., 134.

§ 1636. When the complainant in a bill offers to receive an answer without oath, and the defendant accordingly files the answer without oath, denying the allegations of the bill, the complainant is not put to the necessity, according to the general rule, of contradicting the answer by the evidence of two witnesses, or of one witness and corroborating circumstances. The answer being without oath is not evidence, and the usual rule does not apply. Patterson v. Gaines, 6 How., 550.

§ 1637. An answer of a defendant in equity cannot be used as evidence against his co-defendant. Clark v. Van Reimsdyk,* 9 Cr., 153.

§ 1638. It is a general rule that an answer in equity will prevail unless contradicted by two witnesses, or by one witness and corroborating circumstances. This must be taken with qualifications, however. The reason of the rule is that plaintiff, by calling upon defendant to answer, admits his answer as evidence. As the burden of proof is upon plaintiff, it will require more than one witness to turn the balance. But circumstantial evidence is sometimes strong enough to outweigh the testimony of any single witness, especially as in this case, where the answer of defendant, though positive in its terms, asserted a fact which could not in the nature of things be within the actual knowledge of defendant. Ibid.

§ 1639. The rule that when a defendant, by his answer under oath, expressly negatived the allegations of the bill, and the testimony of one witness only has affirmed what has been negatived, the court will not decree in favor of the complainant, does not extend to averments not directly responsive to the allegations of the bill. Seitz v. Mitchell, 4 Otto, 580.

§ 1640. Where a defendant in equity discredits his own answer by contradictory and unreasonable statements, or by positive denials of matters as to which he could have no personal knowledge, the testimony of one disinterested witness will be sufficient to sustain the bill against the answer. Parish v. Gear,* 1 Burn. (Wis.), 99.

§ 1641. An answer in equity supported by positive testimony of one witness will outweigh an allegation in the bill supported only by circumstantial and argumentative evidence. Parker v. Phetteplace, 1 Wall., 684.

§ 1642. If there is an absolute denial contained in the answer to a bill in equity, the complainant should not have a decree upon the uncorroborated testimony of one witness, certainly not where such witness has bias, prejudice or interest adverse to the respondent. Andrews v. Hyde, 8 Cliff., 516.

§ 1643. Where a bill alleged a sale to be in fraud of creditors, and joined vendor and vendee as defendants, and both the latter denied the fraud, alleging payment of consideration, the circumstances of the case, together with the fact that the details were peculiarly within their knowledge, and were not shown in evidence, were allowed to rebut the truth of the answer. Callan v. Statham, 23 How., 477.

§ 1644. A positive denial in the answer to a bill in equity must be overcome by the plaintiff's proofs; and in this case, it seems, the circumstances which it was claimed tended to establish the allegations of the bill did not overcome such answer. Roots v. Shields, Woolw., 340.

§ 1645. The answer of one defendant in equity is not evidence in behalf of another defendant. Morris v. Nixon, 1 How., 118; Texas v. Chiles, 10 Wall., 127; Dexter v. Arnold, 3 Sumn., 152; Robinson v. Cathcart, 2 Cr. C. C., 590; Lenox v. Notrebe, Hemp., 251.

§ 1646. The separate answer of one defendant in equity is not evidence to sustain the complainant's case against a co-defendant except when the defendants stand in such a relation to each other that the admission of each, if not under oath, would be evidence against the others; as, for instance, in the case of copartners. Dick v. Hamilton, Deady, 322.

§ 1647. The answer of one defendant in equity cannot be used as evidence against his co-defendant, nor the answer of an agent as evidence against his principal. Leeds v. Marine Insurance Co.,* 2 Wheat., 380.

§ 1648. Where a case is set for hearing upon bill, answer and exhibits, the answer must be taken as true. Ibid.

§ 1649. The plaintiffs cannot avail themselves of the answer of a defendant who is substantially a plaintiff; and it is not evidence against a co-defendant. Field v. Holland, 6 Cr., 8.

§ 1650. The answer of one defendant is evidence against other defendants claiming through him. Ibid.

§ 1651. In general the answer of one defendant in equity cannot be read in evidence against another. But where one defendant succeeds to another, so that the right of the one devolves upon the other, and they become privies in estate, the rule does not apply. Osborne v. United States Bank, 9 Wheat., 738.

§ 1652. In general, in a bill in equity, the answer of one defendant is not evidence against another; but this rule does not apply to the case where the defendants are all partners in the same transaction, for in such case the answer or confession of either is evidence against the others. Van Reimsdyk v. Kane, 1 Gall., 630.

§ 1653. In equity, where an answer which is put in issue admits a fact and insists upon another fact by way of avoidance, the former fact is established, but the latter fact must be proved. Clements *v.* Moore, 6 Wall., 299.

§ 1654. If an answer sets up matter in avoidance of the complaint such answer is not evidence, but its allegations must be proved, and the burden is upon the respondent. Howe *v.* Williams, 2 Cliff., 245.

§ 1655. If new facts are set forth in an answer to a bill in equity, and are relied on to effect a discharge or avoidance or as a defense, which are not responsive to the bill, they must be established by independent proof. The answer is not evidence to support them. Randall *v.* Phillips, 3 Mason, 378.

§ 1656. New matter set up in the answer to a bill strictly and purely of revivor is impertinent, and no formal replication is necessary to avoid its effect as evidence. Gunnell *v.* Bird, 10 Wall., 304.

§ 1657. When a cause is set down for hearing on bill and answer the answer is taken as true. If, therefore, the bill rely on a fraudulent conveyance, and the answer deny fraud and aver good faith, the bill will be dismissed. United States *v.* Scott,* 3 Woods, 334.

§ 1658. A court cannot render a decree for plaintiff on a bill which is denied by the answer, when no replication has been filed and there is no evidence on the record contradicting the answer. Gettings *v.* Burch,* 9 Cr., 372.

§ 1659. The answer of a corporation under its seal, denying the material allegations of the bill, and sworn to by its president according to the best of his knowledge and belief, imposes an obligation on the complainant to prove the facts alleged by something more than the testimony of one witness. Carpenter *v.* Providence Washington Ins. Co., 4 How., 185.

§ 1660. If notice is alleged by a bill in chancery and is denied by the answer, it must be proved by two witnesses, or one witness and strong circumstances. Smith *v.* Shane, 1 McL., 22; Piatt *v.* Vattier, 1 McL., 146.

§ 1661. The rule of equity pleading, that allegations in the bill which are neither admitted nor denied must be sustained by proof, does not prevail when the statements in the answer can be construed into an admission of or acquiescence in the allegations of material facts. Surget *v.* Byers, Hemp., 715.

§ 1662. After the answer to a bill for an injunction is put in issue new matter set up by way of avoidance must be proved by the defendant; but on a motion for, or to dissolve, an injunction it is deemed evidence in favor of the defendant, as his affidavit or sworn statement. Tobin *v.* Walkinshaw, McAl., 26.

§ 1663. A general allegation in a bill against an executor, that he retains the money of the estate in virtue of a pretended claim from the testator by a pretended contract, which the bill denies, and the prayer of the bill is generally for an answer to the matters charged therein, does not make the answer of the executor evidence to support such debt, when he admits there is money of the estate in his hands for which he must account if he does not establish the debt. Tilghman *v.* Tilghman, 1 Bald., 464.

§ 1664. An answer denying the right of the complainant is evidence in favor of the defendant. But if he admits the right and sets up new matter in bar; if he admits the charge, and avers a discharge at a different time by a distinct transaction, or sets up an affirmative claim in his own right to the subject-matter claimed by the complainant, it is not evidence in his favor; the defendant must make out his case as a complainant ought to do. *Ibid.*

§ 1665. In the state courts of Connecticut an answer in chancery stands on the same footing as a plea, and is not evidence unless the complainant seeks a disclosure by an appeal to the conscience of the defendant. Pomeroy *v.* Manin, 2 Paine, 476.

5. *Replication.*

§ 1666. The purpose of the general replication is to put in issue any new matter set forth in the answer; and it does not nullify the effect of an admission in the answer of an allegation of the bill. Cavender *v.* Cavender, 8 Fed. R., 642.

§ 1667. Admissions by.— By replying to a plea in equity the plaintiff admits its sufficiency if the facts it sets up are established. Myers *v.* Dorr, 13 Blatch., 22.

§ 1668. A replication in equity admits the legal sufficiency of the plea, and if the latter is proved the bill will be dismissed. Hughes *v.* Blake,* 6 Wheat., 453.

§ 1669. If a replication be inadvertently filed the court would have no difficulty in permitting it to be withdrawn. *Ibid.*

§ 1670. Special replications setting up new matter have quite gone out of use, and if plaintiff wishes to do more than deny the allegations of the answer he should move to amend his bill, and introduce his new matter in that way. If, however, such a replication contain the essential qualities of a general replication, denying such parts of the bill as are not intended to be admitted, and the parties go to a hearing, the new matter will be considered as surplusage, and the plaintiff will lose the benefit of it, though supported by proof. Duponte v. Mussy,* 4 Wash., 128.

§ 1671. By a general replication every allegation not responsive to a bill is denied, and must be proved before it can be taken as true. Hence good matter in bar first appearing in the answer was held not to prevent a bill from being dismissed under a decree based upon the pleadings alone. Humes v. Scruggs, 4 Otto, 22.

§ 1672. Replication omitted.— When a case had been set down for hearing upon bill and answer through mistake of counsel, in a state where equity practice was unfamiliar, the court allowed plaintiff to file a replication. Pierce v. West,* Pet. C. C., 351.

§ 1673. When the plaintiff files no general replication in a suit in equity, but the parties proceed to take testimony as if such replication had been filed, and no motion is made to dismiss for want of a replication, it may be considered as filed and the case considered on its merits, or a replication may be filed instanter. Jones v. Brittan, 1 Woods, 667.

§ 1674. Effect of on new matter in answer.— If a general replication is filed, new matter in avoidance, set up in the answer to a bill in equity, must be proved. Seymour v. Osborne. 11 Wall., 516.

§ 1675. Where a replication denies all the matter of a plea the latter must be supported by evidence. Gernon v. Boecaline,* 2 Wash., 199.

§ 1676. Replication merely to deny answer, unnecessary.— According to the practice in this district the formality of a replication merely denying the truth of the answer is not necessary. Taber v. Jenny, 1 Spr., 315; 9 Law Rep., N. S., 27.

§ 1677. Failure to file replication in time.— Under the sixty-sixth United States equity rule a failure to file a replication within the proper time entitles the defendant to an order to have the bill dismissed, and such order may be entered by the clerk without action of the judge. Robinson v. Satterlee, 3 Saw., 134.

§ 1678. The court may, under rules 66 and 69 in equity, allow a replication filed late to stand as if filed in time. Fischer v. Hayes, 19 Blatch., 26.

§ 1679. Supreme court rules as to.— Under rule 66 of the rules in equity prescribed by the supreme court, the answer of every defendant, when sufficient, must be replied to without reference to the state of the cause or of the pleadings in regard to any other defendant. The replication must be a general one. Rule 45 abolishes special replications. Any defendant whose answer is sufficient has a right to have the cause, as to him, put at issue, so that he may, under rules 67, 68 and 69, proceed to take his testimony if he wishes to. But where the cause is not at issue as to all the defendants, and where it is not proper to compel the plaintiff to go to proofs until it is at issue as to all of them, the court will, on a proper application, enlarge the time, under rule 69, for the plaintiff to take proofs in respect of the defendants as to whom the cause is at issue. Coleman v. Martin,* 6 Blatch., 291.

§ 1680. Statute of limitations, replication to plea of.— Where the statute of limitations is pleaded at law or in equity, and the plaintiff desires to bring himself within its savings, it would be proper for him in his replication, or by an amendment of his bill, to set forth the facts specifically. Miller v. McIntyre, 6 Pet., 61.

§ 1681. Replication cannot ask for relief other than that claimed in bill.— A plaintiff who has set forth a claim in his bill, and prayed for the conveyance to him by the defendant of a certain tract of land, cannot, in his replication, ask for the conveyance of a part of the tract upon a different claim than that in the bill, in case the court should not make a decree in his favor in accordance with the prayer of the bill. Warren v. Van Brunt, 19 Wall., 646.

§ 1682. An objection that there is no replication in the record of an equity court cannot be made in the supreme court. A replication need not be filed to an answer setting up new defenses to a bill of revivor intended to make a deceased defendant's executor and sole legatee a party defendant, as such new defenses are not pertinent. Fretz v. Stover, 22 Wall., 198.

§ 1683. The want of a replication cannot be assigned for error on appeal when leave to file one was granted by the court and the cause was heard on bill, answer and proofs, although the transcript does not show that a replication was filed. National Bank v. Insurance Co., 14 Otto, 54.

6. Supplemental Pleadings.

SUMMARY — *Special replication not allowed,* § 1684.— *Supplemental bill, for what used,* §§ 1685-86.— *Motion to dismiss for laches in prosecution,* § 1687.

§ 1684. Special replications setting up new matter are no longer allowed. *Mason v. Railroad Co.*, §§ 1688-91.

§ 1685. New matter arising since the commencement of the suit must be set up, if at all, in a supplemental bill, not in an amendment to the original bill. *Ibid.*

§ 1686. A supplemental bill cannot be used to show plaintiff's right to sue, acquired since the commencement of the suit, when in the original bill he had no right at all. *Ibid.*

§ 1687. A motion to dismiss plaintiff's bill for laches in prosecution will be denied if plaintiff has used reasonable diligence. *Ibid.*

[NOTES.— See §§ 1692-1709.]

MASON v. HARTFORD, PROVIDENCE & FISHKILL RAILROAD COMPANY

(Circuit Court for Massachusetts: 10 Federal Reporter, 334-338. 1882.)

Opinion by COLT, J.

STATEMENT OF FACTS.— In this cause a bill of revivor was filed August 14, 1880, by the alleged administrators and trustees of Earl P. Mason, the original complainant. To this bill one of the defendants, William T. Hart, put in a plea setting up that it did not appear by said bill of revivor that the plaintiffs named therein had ever been appointed administrators of said estate by any court of competent jurisdiction in the state of Massachusetts, and that therefore the plaintiffs had no right to file said bill, that the court had no jurisdiction thereof, and praying that the bill might be dismissed. The New York & New England Railroad Company, another defendant, demurred to the bill upon this as well as other grounds. To this plea and demurrer the complainants in the bill of revivor filed separate replications, setting out, among other things, that since the filing of the plea and demurrer they had been apppointed administrators of the estate of said Earl P. Mason in the state of Massachusetts.

The defendant William T. Hart now moves, *first*, that the replication to his plea be stricken from the files because it is special, and sets up new matter and matter accruing after the filing of the bill of revivor; and *second*, that the bill of revivor be dismissed, because the complainants have not taken issue on the plea nor set the same down to be argued, though the same has been filed more than a year.

§ 1688. *Special replications setting up new matter are no longer allowed.*

The New York & New England Railroad Company also move that the replication to the demurrer be stricken from the files, and that the bill of revivor be dismissed, because the complainants have not set the demurrer down for argument, though filed over one year before.

It is apparent that the replications here filed are special, setting up new matter and matter accruing since the filing of the bill of revivor; therefore they are irregular. By equity rule 45 of the United States court, "no special replication to any answer shall be filed."

In Vattier v. Hinde, 7 Pet., 252, 274, the supreme court declare that no special replication can be filed except by leave of the court; holding it to be contrary to the rules of a court of chancery for the plaintiff to set up new matter necessary to his case by way of replication; that omissions in a bill cannot be supplied by averments in the replication; and that a plaintiff cannot be allowed to make out a new case in his replication. This is equally true whether it is an answer or plea that is replied to. See Daniell, Ch. Pl. & Pr. (4th ed.), 828, n. 1. "Matters in avoidance of a plea, which have arisen since the suit began, are properly set up by a supplemental bill, not by a special replication," citing Chouteau v. Rice, 1 Minn., 106. In Mitford & Tyler, Pl. & Pr. in Eq., 412, 413, we find, "special replications, with all their consequences, are now out of use, and the plaintiff is to be relieved according to the form of the bill, whatever new matters have been introduced by the defendant's *plea* or *answer*." The replications to the plea and demurrer cannot be sustained.

§ 1689. *Motion to dismiss plaintiff's bill for want of prosecution denied under the circumstances.*

The second motion of the defendants, that the bill of revivor be dismissed, is based upon equity rule 38, which provides that if the plaintiff shall not reply to any plea, or set down any plea or demurrer for argument, on the rule day when the same is filed, or on the next succeeding rule day, he shall be deemed to admit the truth and sufficiency thereof, and his bill shall be dismissed as of course, unless a judge of the court shall allow him further time for the purpose.

It appears in this case that the bill of revivor was filed August 14, 1880; the plea and demurrer September 6, 1880; the replications July 30, 1881; and that soon after (August 4) the plaintiffs' counsel asked the court to fix a day for the argument. It further appears that after the filing of the plea and demurrer, September 6, 1880, a stipulation was entered into by counsel upon both sides extending the time for hearing to the November rule day, 1880, meantime the complainants to be allowed to file proper pleadings in reply to said plea and demurrer. By further written agreements between counsel the postponement provided for by this stipulation was extended monthly until February, 1881. Then we find a further stipulation as follows:

"It is hereby agreed that no movement on either side shall be made in this cause until May, 1881, without prejudice to complainants' right to file evidence of appointment as administrators in Boston."

By the affidavit of Mr. Payne, one of complainants' counsel, it appears that in October or November, 1880, Mr. Lothrop, one of defendants' counsel, stated in effect that, while he would sign the stipulation, the complainants' counsel might take their own time about bringing the case to a hearing.

In the light of all these circumstances it is fair to presume that complainants' counsel understood that any rigid enforcement of the rule now invoked had been waived, impliedly by acts and conduct, if not in express terms; and we are of this opinion.

Considering the repeated postponements which had taken place for the mutual accommodation of both sides, so far as appears, the language used by defendants' counsel as to time of hearing; and bearing also in mind that the replications were filed within three months after May, 1881; and that within a week thereafter the plaintiffs moved the court to set a time for hearing,— it would, we think, be inequitable to allow the defendants' motion to dismiss to prevail. Indirectly, as bearing on this question of laches, reference is made to the fact that the original bill in this case was brought in 1871, the answer filed in 1873, the replication not put in until 1875; also that the original complainant died in 1876, and that the bill of revivor was not brought until 1880. In answer to this charge the complainants say that the delay has been owing to the pendency of another suit in the state court of Rhode Island, the determination of which might affect the prosecution of this suit, and that consequently the delay was acquiesced in by both sides. They further state that within a short time after the final decision by the Rhode Island state court the bill of revivor was filed, and that they are now anxious to speed the cause. Under these circumstances, and in the absence of any motion on the part of the defendants to speed the cause, we do not see how the charge of laches can be seriously pressed; at least so far as the present motion is concerned.

§ 1690. *New matter arising since the commencement of the suit must be set up in a supplemental bill.*

The complainants, in the event of their replications being held to be bad, ask leave to withdraw them and to amend their bill of revivor by inserting, among other things, the fact that they were, on the 25th day of July, 1881, by the court of probate for the district of Suffolk, in the state of Massachusetts, duly appointed administrators of the estate of Earl P. Mason. The defendants object upon the ground that this is new matter, accruing since the filing of the bill, which cannot be set up by amendment, but only by supplemental bill. It is true that events which have happened since the filing of a bill cannot be introduced by way of amendment, and that as a general rule they may be set out by supplemental bill. Equity Rule 57, U. S. Court.

In Daniell, Ch. Pl. & Pr. (4th ed.), 1515, note 1, we find "an original bill cannot be amended by incorporating anything therein which arose subsequently to the commencement of the suit. This should be stated in a supplemental bill." And again, on page 828, note 1 (already cited), it is laid down that matters in avoidance of a plea, which have arisen since the suit began, are properly set out by a supplemental bill. Mitford & Tyler, Pl. & Pr. in Eq., 159; Story, Eq. Pl., § 880.

§ 1691. *A supplemental bill cannot be used to show plaintiff's right to sue, acquired since the commencement of the suit.*

But in this case it is difficult to see how a supplemental bill can be brought. The bill of revivor has not become defective from any event happening after it was filed. But originally, when it was brought, it was wholly defective; for the fact that the plaintiffs were appointed administrators by the proper court in Massachusetts was necessary to its maintenance. Mellus v. Thompson, 1 Clif., 125. And yet this event happened, as the record discloses, nearly a year after it was brought. If the bill is wholly defective, and there is no ground for proceeding upon it, it cannot be sustained by filing a supplemental bill founded upon matters which have subsequently taken place. Candler v. Pettit, 1 Paige, Ch., 168.

In Pinch v. Anthony, 10 Allen, 471, 477, the court observe: " We have found no authority that goes so far as to authorize a party who has no cause of action at the time of filing his original bill to file a supplemental bill in order to maintain his suit upon a cause of action that accrued after the original bill was filed, even though it arose out of the same transaction that was the subject of the original bill." Daniell, Ch. Pl. & Pr. (4th ed.), 1515, note.

We are of the opinion that this new matter cannot be incorporated in the bill of revivor by amendment, nor introduced in a supplemental bill, and that the proper course for the complainants to pursue is to bring a new bill of revivor.

(1) The defendants' motion to strike from the files complainants' replica-

tions to plea and demurrer is granted.   (2) The defendants' motion to dismiss bill of revivor is denied.   (3) The complainants' motion to amend bill of revivor is denied.

§ 1692. Office and scope of.— A supplemental bill containing matters having no necessary connection with the original bill will be dismissed.   Minnesota Co. v. St. Paul Co., 6 Wall., 742.

§ 1693. A party cannot introduce a material fact which has occurred since the filing of his original bill in an amended bill; but must file a supplemental bill.   Copen v. Flesher, 1 Bond, 440.

§ 1694. Discovery as to matters not stated in original bill.— A supplemental bill which seeks discovery from the defendant as to particulars not stated in the original bill will be admitted though it contains new matters which should properly be introduced by way of amendment to the original bill.   Parkhurst v. Kinsman, 2 Blatch., 72.

§ 1695. Ancillary bill not necessarily supplemental.— A bill in equity ancillary to another suit in the federal court is not necessarily a supplemental bill in a sense to bring it under the rules of pleading applicable to supplemental bills.   Minnesota Co. v. St. Paul Co., 2 Wall., 609.

§ 1696. Sufficiency of petition for.— Under rule 57 in equity, a petition for leave to file a supplemental bill is sufficient if it inform the court and the defendant of the ground on which relief is sought.   It may state matters upon information and belief, and need not contain all the averments intended to be set up.   Parkhurst v. Kinsman. 2 Blatch., 72.

§ 1697. Matters proper for supplemental bill and for amendment.— It is a general rule in equity pleading that matters existing at the time the bill was filed, but omitted in the original bill, are to be introduced by amendment; and that matters pertinent to the case occurring after the bill is filed are to be introduced by supplemental bill.   Sometimes, however, as in the case of a suit brought by an administrator appointed in one state, and suing in another before letters of administration have been taken out in such other, a right acquired subsequently to the bringing of the suit may be brought in by amendment to the original bill. Swatzel v. Arnold, 1 Woolw., 383.

§ 1698. Suit on re-issued patent surrendered pending litigation brought by.— If a patent is surrendered and re-issued pending litigation, suit on the re-issued patent cannot be brought by supplemental bill, because surrender extinguishes the old patent.   New suit must be brought.   But if remedy is sought by supplemental bill, and no objection is made by respondent, but the suit is regularly tried and decree entered in the court below, the irregularity will be held as waived.   Reedy v. Scott, 23 Wall., 352.

§ 1699. —— agreement to arbitrate as plea to.— To a suit on a re-issued patent, irregularly brought by supplemental bill instead of by a new bill, an agreement to arbitrate, made during the pendency of the original bill and before the supplemental, may properly be pleaded to the supplemental as it might have been to the original, provided the identity of the invention covered by the surrendered patent and the re-issued is plain.   Ibid.

§ 1700. Bill for dissolution on ground of fraud — Supplemental bill to plea of settlement.— Bill for dissolution of copartnership on ground of fraud, etc., settlement pleaded and allowed; a supplemental bill then filed, impeaching the settlement for fraud, etc.; demurrer. Held, proper to set up the matter of avoidance by supplemental bill, as special replications are now disused, and amendment may not be used to bring in matters which have arisen subsequent to the bill.   Chouteau v. Rice,* 1 Minn., 106.

§ 1701. Assignee of pending action cannot continue by.— When plaintiff, suing in his own right. assigns his whole interest to another, the assignee cannot continue the proceedings by a supplemental bill, but must bring an original bill in the nature of a supplemental bill.   Tappan v. Smith, 5 Biss., 73.

§ 1702. Release brought in collaterally by agreed statement of facts cannot be considered — Supplemental bill necessary.— A bill in equity alleged that plaintiff bought certain property of defendants at auction, and that the price was greatly enhanced by by-bidders.   Upon the argument an agreed statement of facts was used, from which it appeared that plaintiff had given the auctioneer a release from all liability in the matter, which release, by the agreement, might be referred to and used in the case, and the whole agreement was to be made a part of the case and to be filed therein.   Argument of counsel was directed to the question whether this release to the auctioneer released also the defendant, his principal. But it was held that, as the release was not set up in the pleading, it could not be considered as in issue, although thus brought before the court in argument.   In order that the question might be brought properly before the court, it would be necessary for plaintiff to file a supplemental bill, setting up the release with suitable averments, so that defendants may fully answer. Veazie v. Williams,* 8 Story, 54.

§ 1703. **To compel discovery of assets by defendant after appointment of receiver.**— When a receiver appointed under a bill in equity has reduced to possession the assets of defendant, a supplemental bill could not be used to compel a discovery by defendant of his assets. Dunham v. Railroad Co., 1 Bond, 492.

§ 1704. But if it does not appear that the receiver so appointed has taken any steps to that purpose, nor that he has accepted the trust, a supplemental bill may be used for such discovery. *Ibid.*

§ 1705. **Bill for specific performance against firm creditor in suit to wind up partnership.**— When plaintiff, after bringing a bill to wind up a copartnership, brings a second bill against a creditor of the copartnership to enforce specific performance of a contract with the copartnership, such second bill is an original and not a supplemental bill. Myers v. Dorr, 13 Blatch., 22.

§ 1706. **New matter discovered after answer filed.**— A supplemental answer is the proper course when a new matter of defense is discovered after filing the answer, but which existed before. The motion to file is addressed to the discretion of the court, and if the additional matter was known before the answer was filed the motion will be refused, especially if the addition is calculated to embarrass the proceedings, and is not necessary to the defense. Suydam v. Truesdale,* 6 McL., 459.

§ 1707. When a motion was made to file a supplemental answer, and was accompanied by an affidavit that the new matter had been discovered since the answer was filed, but it appeared in a cross-bill already filed by defendant that the matter was known at the time the answer was filed, the motion was refused, especially as this did not materially interfere with the presentation of the defense. *Ibid.*

§ 1708. **A supplemental answer is in the nature of a plea puis darrein continuance** under the old practice, and therefore must be filed at the first opportunity and before the next continuance. It can be filed later only by leave of court upon showing satisfactory excuse. French v. Edwards, 4 Saw., 125.

§ 1709. **Supplemental answer setting up former judgment.**— If, after a refusal by a judge of a federal court to allow a supplemental answer to be filed setting up a former judgment on the ground that an appeal from such judgment is still pending, the appeal is decided, it is matter of discretion for another judge of the same federal court to allow the supplemental answer to be filed. Robinson v. Satterlee, 3 Saw., 134.

III. Pleading in Admiralty.

1. *In General.*

§ 1710. **The rules of pleading in admiralty are not as rigid as at common law;** there are no technical rules of variance or departure; and the court is not precluded from granting the relief appropriate to the case appearing on the record, and prayed for in the libel, because the entire case is not distinctly stated in the libel. West v. Steamer Uncle Sam, McAL., 505.

§ 1711. The rules of pleading in admiralty do not require all the technical precision which is required at common law, but they require that the cause of action should be clearly set forth, so that a plain and direct issue may be made upon the charge, and the evidence must be confined to the matter put in issue. Jenks v. Lewis, 1 Ware, 51.

§ 1712. —— **unity of causes of action.**— The strict rules of the common law as to unity of causes of action or community of interest or responsibility of parties to actions are not observed in the maritime courts. The Sloop Merchant, Abb. Adm., 21.

§ 1713. —— **variance or departure.**— There are no technical rules of variance or departure in pleading in admiralty. Dupont de Nemours v. Vance, 19 How., 162.

§ 1714. **In admiralty the proofs and allegations must coincide.**— Proofs to facts not put in contestation by the pleadings, and allegations of facts not established by proofs, will both be rejected. The Brig Sarah Ann, 2 Sumn., 206.

§ 1715. —— **proof alone insufficient.**— It is a cardinal rule in equity proceedings that no decree can be rendered upon proofs alone if the subject-matter of those proofs is not alleged in the pleadings. Davis v. Leslie, Abb. Adm., 123.

§ 1716. **Evidence confined to point in issue.**— Under admiralty rule 23 the evidence must be confined strictly to points put in issue by the allegations of the libel and denial of the answer. The Rocket, 1 Biss., 354.

§ 1717. **Collision — Variance.**— In a collision case the libel did not aver (1) that the steamer changed her course, but averred (2) that the schooner kept hers — and thus brought on the collision. The answer not denying (2) sets up (1). The court found both allegations true, but that the steamer's change was justifiable, and that, therefore, the libel need not be dismissed under rules of pleading for variance between allegations and proof, or for surprise. The Iris, 1 Low., 520.

§ 1718. If questions are not raised by the pleadings they are not before the court; but this objection not having been taken in this case the points made in the argument were considered in their order. The Camanche, 8 Wall., 448.

§ 1719. Collision — Defense by way of answer or plea.— The rules of the supreme court in regard to the limited liability of ship-owners in cases of collision were intended, not to restrict parties claiming the benefit of the law, but to aid them by formulating a proceeding that would give them full protection in such cases. The rules, therefore, do not prevent defense by way of answer to a libel, or plea to an action, if the ship-owners deem such a mode of pleading adequate to their protection. The "Scotland," 15 Otto, 24.

§ 1720. Answer once replied to, not to be treated as nullity.— When an answer in admiralty has been filed and replied to by the libelant, the latter cannot subsequently, upon discovering an irregularity in the answer, treat it as a nullity, and enter a default, though this in turn would be an irregularity which might be waived. Gaines v. Travis, Abb. Adm., 297.

§ 1721. Exceptions in admiralty have the effect of a demurrer and also that of a motion to make more definite and certain. The Steamboat Transport,* 1 Ben., 86.

§ 1722. —— when well taken.— An exception to a libel that it does not state facts sufficient to constitute a cause of action or forfeiture is not well taken, unless it states in what the insufficiency consists. The Active, Deady, 165.

2. Libel. Cross-libel. Information.

SUMMARY — *Information, conclusion, §§ 1723–24.— Information to be exact in describing statutory offense. § 1725.— Innocent articles, § 1726.— Conclusion, § 1727.— Defect in substance not remedied by evidence, § 1728.— Pleading under act of 1845 as to navigable lakes, § 1729.— Description of vessel, § 1730.— Averment of subsisting seizure necessary, § 1731.— Averment of negligence, § 1732.*

§ 1723. An information for an offense created by statute must conclude against the form of the statute, or refer to some statute upon which the prosecution may rest. The Nancy, §§ 1733–34.

§ 1724. A conclusion against the statute is inadequate to supply the deficiency of material allegations to show that the act was unlawful. *Ibid.*

§ 1725. An information not describing exactly the offense created by the statute is defective. The Hoppet v. United States, §§ 1735–39.

§ 1726. To secure the forfeiture of innocent articles in the cargo the information must charge that they belong to the owner of the prohibited articles. *Ibid.*

§ 1727. A condemnation will not be justified by a conclusion against the statute unless a case is fully made out independently of such allegation. *Ibid.*

§ 1728. A defect of substance in the information cannot be cured by evidence. . *Ibid.*

§ 1729. The act of 1845, extending the admiralty jurisdiction over navigable lakes and rivers, was inoperative to change the methods of pleading, since the jurisdiction already covered them. The Illinois, §§ 1740–41.

§ 1730. In describing a vessel in the libel it is sufficient to say the ship, bark, sloop, schooner, steamboat, steamer, barge, or as the case may be, and giving the name, without further specification or qualification. The maritime character of the vessel follows from the meaning of the terms. *Ibid.*

§ 1731. The failure to aver a good subsisting seizure at the time of filing the libel is a defect fatal at any stage of the cause. The Washington, § 1742.

§ 1732. It is not sufficient for a libel to assert of the colliding vessel that she was negligently and carelessly handled, but the facts should be given so that the court may see judicially that negligence contributed to the result. The H. P. Baldwin, § 1743.

[NOTES.— See §§ 1744–1838.]

THE SLOOP NANCY.

(Circuit Court for Massachusetts: 1 Gallison, 66–68. 1812.)

Opinion by STORY, J.

STATEMENT OF FACTS.— The sloop Nancy was libeled in the district court for exporting from the port of Boston divers goods and merchandise of domestic growth and manufacture, during the existence of the embargo, contrary to the prohibition of a certain act of the United States; and 2, for trading with, and putting on board of another ship or vessel, a quantity of goods and merchandise of domestic growth and manufacture, contrary to a certain other act of the United States.

The facts appear to be these: That the sloop Nancy is a lighter, whose employment has been confined to the port and bay of Boston, and as such, at the time of the seizure, she was under bonds at the custom-house, pursuant to the provisions of the act of January 9, 1808, chapter 8. On the 15th of July, 1808, she departed from Boston, stood off into the bay, and at the distance of about four or five leagues met with another vessel, and immediately came along-side, and hoisted out into said vessel all the cargo which she had on board (which seems to have been flour), but the quantity does not appear. She remained along-side about an hour, and then quitted the other vessel. There seems no reason to doubt that during this time a considerable quantity of flour was discharged.

§ 1733. *An information for a forfeiture must conclude against the form of the statute.*

These facts present a clear case of a violation of the embargo acts, and if the libel contains sufficient allegations to enable the court to pronounce a sentence of forfeiture, it is their duty so to do. The first count seems to be founded upon the fourth section of the act of March 12, 1808, chapter 33; but it concludes against an act whose title, as stated in the libel, is not known among our statutes. As this count stands, therefore, it does not warrant the court to proceed to condemnation. For it is a general rule, that where an offense is created by statute it must, on the face of the information or libel, conclude against the form of the statute, or at least refer to a subsisting statute authorizing the offense; and we have so held the doctrine in other cases at this term.

§ 1734. *A conclusion against the form of the statute will not supply the place of essential averments.*

The second count contains a very dry allegation, that the sloop on the high seas, in or near the harbor of Boston, on the 14th of July, 1808, did trade with, or put on board, another certain ship or vessel, then being on the high seas, in or near the harbor of Boston, a quantity of goods, wares and merchandise of domestic growth and manufacture, to wit, flour, contrary to the act of January 9, 1808, chapter 8.

Now it is material to observe that it is not every trading with or putting on board of another vessel of such goods, wares and merchandise that subjects the property to forfeiture. The act declares that it must be a trading with, or putting on board, contrary to that act or the act of 22d December, 1807. But a trading with, or putting on board, in the port where the goods are first laden, is not prohibited; and so it has been held by the supreme court of the United States. Nor is a trading or putting on board by foreign vessels on the high seas within the purview of the act. Sufficient matter, therefore, ought to have been alleged to have shown that this trading or putting on board was clearly against the acts above stated. A mere conclusion against a statute has been uniformly held inadequate to supply the deficiency of material averments to bring the case within the statute. Hardr., 4; Bunb., 78, 119, 177. It ought at least to have been averred that the vessel was a vessel owned by citizens of the United States, and proceeded from some port of the United States, with her cargo, during the continuance of the embargo. As this libel now stands, without amendment, I do not feel at liberty to affirm the decree of the court below, and I shall therefore suspend a decree until the question of amendment has been argued and considered. (After amendment allowed, the decree was affirmed.)

SCHOONER HOPPET AND CARGO *v.* UNITED STATES.

(7 Cranch, 389–395. 1813.)

Opinion by Marshall, C. J.

STATEMENT OF FACTS.— This is an appeal from a sentence of the court for the district of Orleans, condemning the schooner Hoppet and her cargo as forfeited to the United States for violating the non-intercourse law. In the district court two informations were filed by the attorney for the United States, one claiming the ship as being forfeited, and the other claiming the cargo. Objections have been made to each of these informations, which will be separately considered.

The information against the vessel charges that while the act entitled " An act to interdict commercial intercourse," etc., was in force, certain goods of the growth, produce or manufacture of France were imported into the United States, to wit, into the port of New Orleans, in the said vessel from some foreign port or place, to wit, from St. Bartholomews, contrary to and in violation of the fourth, fifth and sixth sections of the act. By reason of which, and by virtue of the act of congress entitled " An act," etc., the said vessel, her tackle, apparel and furniture have become forfeited to the United States.

The charge contained in this information, and the only charge it contains, is an importation into the United States of certain prohibited articles while the prohibitory act was in force. How far does this crime affect the vessel?

§ 1735. *The information must keep closely to the offense created by the statute.* The question must be answered by the law. The sixth section of the act enacts, in substance, that if any article, the importation of which is prohibited, shall be put on board of any ship, etc., with intention to import the same into the United States or the territories thereof, contrary to the true intent and meaning of this act, and with the knowledge of the owner or master of such ship, etc., such ship, etc.; shall be forfeited.

This is the only section of the act which imposes a forfeiture on the vessel. It will be perceived that the crime consists in the prohibited articles being laden on board a ship with intent to be imported into the United States, and with the knowledge of the owner or master of the vessel. A union of a lading with the intention to import, and with the knowledge of the owner or master, is necessary to constitute the crime. Without these essential ingredients, the particular offense which alone incurs a forfeiture cannot be committed.

In the information under consideration neither of these offenses is charged. It is neither alleged that the prohibited goods were put on board the ship with intention to be imported into the United States, nor with the knowledge of the owner or master.

§ 1736. *Innocent articles are not liable to forfeiture unless the information alleges that they belong to the owner of the prohibited articles.*

The information against the cargo charges, in substance, that certain prohibited articles, and certain other articles not stated to be prohibited, were brought into the United States, to wit, into the port of New Orleans, while the act entitled "An act to interdict commercial intercourse," etc., was in force, from some foreign port or place, by reason of which, and by virtue of the act, the whole cargo of the Hoppet has become forfeited.

The fifth section of the act, under which this prosecution was sustained, inflicts forfeiture on the prohibited articles imported contrary to law, and also on "all other articles on board the same ship or vessel, boat, raft or carriage belonging to the owner of such prohibited articles."

The innocent articles are liable to forfeiture only where they belong to the owner of the prohibited articles. It is this association, and this alone, which constitutes their crime. Their being in the same vessel exposes them to no forfeiture unless they belong to the same person. In the case under consideration the information does not allege that the innocent and the prohibited articles did belong to the same person.

§ 1737. *A condemnation will not be justified by a conclusion against a statute, unless a case is fully made out independently of this allegation.*

The first question made for the consideration of the court is this: Will this information support a sentence of condemnation pronounced against the vessel and the innocent part of the cargo? That the information states a case by which no forfeiture of the ship or the innocent part of the cargo has been incurred, unless its defectiveness be cured by the allegation that the act was done contrary to and in violation of the provisions of the statute, has been already fully shown.

It is not controverted that in all proceedings in courts of common law, either against the person or the thing for penalties or forfeitures, the allegation that the act charged was committed in violation of law, or of the provisions of a particular statute, will not justify condemnation, unless, independent of this allegation, a case be stated which shows that the law has been violated. The reference to the statute may direct the attention of the court, and of the accused, to the particular statute by which the prosecution is to be sustained, but forms no part of the description of the offense. The importance of this principle to a fair administration of justice, to that certainty introduced and demanded by the free genius of our institutions in all prosecutions for offenses against the laws, is too apparent to require elucidation, and the principle itself is too familiar not to suggest itself to every gentleman of the profession.

Does this rule apply to informations in a court of admiralty?

It is not contended that all those technical niceties which are unimportant in themselves, and standing only on precedents of which the reason cannot be discerned, should be transplanted from the courts of common law into the courts of admiralty. But a rule so essential to justice and fair proceeding as that which requires a substantial statement of the offense upon which the prosecution is founded must be the rule of every court where justice is the object; and cannot be satisfied by a general reference to the provisions of a statute. It would require a series of clear and unequivocal precedents to show that this rule is dispensed with in courts of admiralty, sitting for the trial of offenses against municipal law.

It is, upon these and other reasons, the opinion of the court that the information is not made good by the allegation that the offense was committed against the provisions of certain sections of the act of congress.

It is cured by any evidence showing that in point of fact the vessel and cargo are liable to forfeiture?

§ 1738. *A defect of substance in the information cannot be cured by the evidence.*

The rule that a man shall not be charged with one crime and convicted of another may sometimes cover real guilt, but its observance is essential to the preservation of innocence. It is only a modification of this rule that the accusation on which the prosecution is founded should state the crime which is to be proved, and state such a crime as will justify the judgment to be pronounced.

The reasons for this rule are, 1st. That the party accused may know against what charge to direct his defense. 2d. That the court may see, with judicial eyes, that the fact alleged to have been committed is an offense against the laws, and may also discern the punishment annexed by law to the specific offense. These reasons apply to prosecutions in courts of admiralty with as much force as to prosecutions in other courts. It is, therefore, a maxim of the civil law that a decree must be *secundum allegata* as well as *secundum probata.* It would seem to be a maxim essential to the due administration of justice in all courts.

It is the opinion of the court that this information will not justify a sentence condemning the schooner Hoppet, and that part of her cargo which is not alleged to be of the growth, produce or manufacture of either France or Great Britain, or the dependencies of either of these powers, whatever the fact may be.

§ 1739. *French wines imported into the United States before the non-intercourse act, re-exported to a Danish island, and thence imported to New Orleans during the operation of that act, are liable to forfeiture.*

There are certain wines imported in this vessel alleged to be of the growth, produce or manufacture of France. These wines were exported from the United States to St. Bartholomew's, where they were purchased by the consignee and shipped to New Orleans. It is contended that, having been imported into the United States previous to the passage of the non-intercourse law, their exportation and re-importation does not subject them to the penalties of that law. But the court is unanimously of opinion that they come completely within the provisions of the act of congress.

It is the opinion of the court that there is no error in that part of the sentence in the district court of Orleans which condemns the wines in the information mentioned as forfeited to the United States, but that there is error in that part of the sentence which condemns the schooner Hoppet and the residue of her cargo.

This court doth therefore adjudge and order that so much of the sentence of the district court as condemns the schooner Hoppet, and the thirty-five hogsheads of molasses, five barrels of molasses, twelve dozen of cocoa-nuts, and twelve pounds of starch, part of the cargo of the said schooner, be and the same is hereby reversed and annulled; and the said sentence, as to the residue of the cargo, is in all things affirmed.

THE ILLINOIS.

(District Court for Michigan: 1 Brown, 497, 498. 1874.)

§ 1740. *Form of libel not affected by the act of 1845, as to jurisdiction over lakes, etc.*

Opinion by LONGYEAR, J.

The libel is in the usual form of libels *in personam* under the general maritime law. 2 Conk. Adm., 478 *et. seq.*, 482, 488; Ben. Adm., 484, No. 83. The allegations, the absence of which constitute the first three grounds of demurrer, were necessary in order to confer jurisdiction under the act of congress of February 26; 1845 (5 Stat. at Large), 726, entitled "An act extending the jurisdiction of the district courts to certain cases upon the lakes and navigable waters connecting the same." 2 Conk. Adm., 491 and note *a*. But the supreme court in the case of The Eagle, 8 Wall., 15, adopting the only logical conclusion from their earlier decision in the case of The Genesee Chief, 12 How., 443, authoritatively decides that general admiralty jurisdiction was not limited in this country to tide-waters, but extended to the lakes and the navigable waters connecting them, and hence that the act of 1845 was inoperative and ineffectual, with the exception of the clause which gives either party the right of trial by jury when requested. Since that decision the limitations as to jurisdiction imposed by the act of 1845 have had no existence, and the necessity of inserting in the libel the allegations in question has ceased; and consequently a libel which is sufficient under the general maritime law is now sufficient in cases upon the lakes and their connecting waters. See The General Cass, 1 Brown, 334. The first, second and third grounds of demurrer are therefore not well taken.

§ 1741. *Description of the vessel in a libel.*

As to the fourth ground of demurrer I find no adjudications or opinions of text-writers upon the point; but judging from the forms adopted and universally used from an early period in admiralty jurisprudence down to the present time, it seems to have always been considered sufficient to describe a vessel in a libel, whether *in rem* or *in personam*, as the ship, bark, sloop, schooner, steamboat, steamer, barge, or as the case may be, giving her name, without further specification or qualification. See Conk. Adm., 490, note *a*. These terms seem always to have been considered sufficient to denote the maritime character of the subject. In their ordinary meaning they signify maritime things, and, independently of the consideration of long usage, the use of those terms alone is no doubt sufficient to confer jurisdiction without further description or qualification. The rest follows by necessary implication. If the fact be different it must be taken advantage of by way of special allegation and cannot be by way of demurrer. The fourth ground of demurrer is, therefore, also not well taken.

The demurrer must be overruled, with costs of the demurrer to libelant, with leave to respondent to answer the libel on condition of payment of the costs of the demurrer, including a counsel fee of $10.

Demurrer overruled.

THE WASHINGTON.

(Circuit Court for New York: 4 Blatchford, 101–108. 1857.)

STATEMENT OF FACTS.— Vessel libeled for alleged violation of revenue laws and her forfeiture demanded. The claimant excepted to the libel that it contained no averment of seizure of the vessel within the district. The case came up on appeal from the district court.

Opinion by NELSON, J.

The libel contains no averment whatever of the seizure of the vessel for a violation of the revenue laws, the proctor for the libelants relying altogether upon the seizure by the marshal upon the warrant.

§ 1742. *A subsisting seizure of a vessel is necessary to give the court jurisdiction for purposes of forfeiture, and a failure to aver such seizure in the libel is fatal at any stage of the cause.*

In the case of The Ann, 9 Cranch, 289, it was held that if a seizure by a collector under the revenue laws be abandoned, and the property be restored before the libel or information is filed and allowed, the district court has no jurisdiction of the cause. The court say that the jurisdiction is given to the court of the district, not where the offense was committed, but where the seizure was made; and further, that it follows from this, that, before judicial cognizance can attach upon a forfeiture *in rem* under the statute, there must be a seizure; for, until the seizure, it is impossible to ascertain what is the competent form to hear and determine the cause, and that it must be a good subsisting seizure at the time when the libel or information is filed. See, also, The Abby, 9 Mason, 360; The Merino, 9 Wheat., 391; Benedict's Admiralty, p. 171, sec. 303, and cases there cited; rule 22, in admiralty, of supreme court.

The seizure being a jurisdictional fact necessary to give to the court below cognizance of the cause, and no such fact having been averred, it is well settled that advantage may be taken of the defect at any stage of the proceedings. The district court was therefore right in dismissing the libel for this reason.

Decree affirmed.

THE H. P. BALDWIN.

(District Court for Michigan: 2 Abbott, 257–260. 1870.)

Opinion by LONGYEAR, J.

STATEMENT OF FACTS.— The libelant's vessel, the schooner Marquette, was bound on a voyage from Oswego to Chicago, and when in the straits of Mackinaw was collided with by the bark H. P. Baldwin. The manner and cause of the collision are stated in the third article of the libel, in the following language: "Third. That when the said schooner had so far proceeded on her said voyage as to have reached the straits of Mackinaw, and were off and a little above "Old Mackinaw," so called, and while running on the wind upon the port tack, with her proper watch, officers and crew properly placed and vigilantly attentive to the care and safe navigation of their said schooner, with the proper signal lights properly placed and brightly burning, the bark H. P. Baldwin, in passing up by the starboard side, was so carelessly, negligently, unskilfully and recklessly navigated by those in charge of her that she was made to run into, upon, and collide with the said schooner, the said bark striking the said schooner on the starboard side," etc. There are no other allegations in the libel as to the manner and cause of the collision. Articles

4 and 6 were alluded to on the argument as throwing further light upon this subject. But article 4 is confined to a statement of what efforts were made by the master and crew of the schooner to avoid the collision, and states, by way of fixing the period in the occurrences which resulted in the collision when such efforts were made, that they were made "as soon as the said bark headed towards and for the said schooner." And article 6 is the usual general allegation that the bark was solely in fault.

Is the allegation above quoted, then, that the bark "was so carelessly, negligently, unskilfully and recklessly navigated," as the cause of collision, a sufficient allegation?

§ 1743. *In a libel for a collision it is not sufficient to allege that the colliding vessel was careless or negligent; the facts should be stated.*

There does not seem to be any well defined rule laid down in the books as to the degree of certainty requisite in stating the cause of collision. Mr. Parsons says: "How these things should be stated we can better indicate by the forms we give in the appendix than in any other way; saying now only that the demand of the libelant should be so clearly stated that the respondent may know, without any doubt, what claims he must repel. The facts should be stated, also, that they may be understood by all interested in knowing them, and the judge be able to see judicially that they bring the case within his jurisdiction and within the law of his court." 2 Pars. Shipp. & Adm., 380. On an examination of the precedents to which we are referred by Mr. Parsons, and also of those laid down by other authors, we find that in every instance of a libel for collision resulting from carelessness, etc., it is stated wherein the carelessness, negligence, unskilfulness or recklessness consisted. I believe this to be the only correct, practical and safe rule. To state that the navigation of the colliding vessel was careless, negligent, unskilful or reckless, without stating wherein the carelessness, etc., consisted, is stating a mere conclusion. The facts should be stated, so that the court may be able to see judicially that carelessness, etc., existed, and contributed to or was the cause of the collision. I cannot see, in the application of this rule, any of the hardships contemplated by counsel for libelant in this case. It is true the libelant cannot be presumed always to know and be able to state in his libel just what orders were given on the colliding vessel, or all that was done upon it that resulted in the manœuvers which brought about the collision, but he can state what those manœuvers were, for, if he has the necessary lookout, they can be and are always seen and known on board his own vessel. If the manœuvers of the colliding vessel were such as to bring about the result when it was within the power, or it was the duty, of the colliding vessel to avoid the other, then it is sufficient to state what such manœuvers were, accompanying such statements, of course, with a statement of the position, course, etc., of the respective vessels at the time such manœuvers occurred, by which the court may be able to see what was the necessary result of such manœuvers. I say such statement would be sufficient, because, if such manœuvers were in violation of the duty of the colliding vessel under the circumstances of the case, then they necessarily constitute, in and of themselves, careless, negligent, unskilful and reckless navigation. For instance, in this case, if the colliding vessel, when in dangerous proximity to the libelant's vessel, suddenly changed her course, and the collision was thereby brought about, it would be sufficient to state that fact; or, if the two vessels were crossing, and so were within article 12 of the collision act (13 Stat. at Large, 60), or, if the colliding vessel was overtaking the other, and so was within article 17 of said act; and if in either of these cases the colliding vessel failed to observe the requirements of those articles, it would be sufficient to state these facts, for then the carelessness, etc., complained of would clearly appear from the facts stated.

I think the libel in this case falls far short of the necessary requisites as above indicated, in its statement of the cause of the collision. We might infer several things from the statements which are contained in the libel; but this is not sufficient in a matter of pleading. The facts must be clearly and positively stated, and not be left to inference, nor alleged by way of reference or recital merely. The exceptions are sustained, and the libelant will be granted leave to amend his libel.

§ 1744. Particularity in pleading.— Libels in admiralty should state the subject-matter in articles with certainty and precision, and with averments admitting of distinct answers. The Schooner Boston, 1 Sumn., 328.

§ 1745. In admiralty particularity in pleading is not considered a fault, but the reverse. The rule is the pleader must state all the essential particulars of the alleged tort or misconduct, with the circumstances of time and place. Holmes v. Oregon, etc., Co., 6 Saw., 262.

§ 1746. No form prescribed — Notice, waiver of.— No form of libel is prescribed by law. Intelligibility is the only requirement. The object of the monition or citation is to give notice, and if the respondents voluntarily appear and answer notice is waived. The Brig Joseph Gorham,* 7 Law Rep., 135.

§ 1747. Undisguised omission of material facts.— In admiralty an omission to state some facts which prove to be material, but which cannot have occasioned any surprise to the opposite party, will not be allowed to work any injury to the libelant, if the court can see there was no design on his part in omitting to state them. The Quickstep, 9 Wall., 665; The Steamer Syracuse, 12 Wall., 167.

§ 1748. Unnecessary allegations in libel — Evidence.— In a libel it is not necessary to state any fact which constitutes the defense of the claimant. Brig Aurora v. United States, 7 Cr., 382.

§ 1749. It is unnecessary to spread out the evidence upon which the allegations of a libel rest. The particulars and accounts which make up the claim are matters for reference, or for investigation on trial, if the claimants come into court upon answer. Whittock v. Barque Thales,* 20 How. Pr., 447.

§ 1750. Libel should show jurisdiction.— The libel should always show the jurisdiction of the court. Boon v. The Hornet, Crabbe, 426.

§ 1751. —— tort — Averments as to place.— Every libel for a tort must contain on its face sufficient averments as to place to show that it is within the admiralty jurisdiction, otherwise it must be dismissed. Thomas v. Lane, 2 Sumn., 1.

§ 1752. Allegations in libel not denied by answer.— All allegations in a libel not denied in the answer are not to be taken as true; but where the answer is silent or evasive in relation to a fact alleged in the libel supposed to be peculiarly within the knowledge of the respondent, it is within the court's discretion to take the fact pro confesso. Whether the libelants were designated in the crew list as prescribed by law must have been known to the master. Campbell v. Steamer Uncle Sam, McAl., 77.

§ 1753. Jurisdiction destroyed by proof.— Although district courts are courts both of admiralty and of common law, these jurisdictions are wholly distinct. Therefore when a libel in admiralty charged that certain wines were seized upon navigable waters, and it appeared that the seizure was made upon land, the jurisdiction ceased and the libel should have been dismissed or amended. The impaneling of a jury at the instance of claimants cannot be treated as a consent that the libel stand amended, and a sentence of condemnation by the district court after verdict was reversed by the supreme court, and the case remanded with directions to permit the libel to be amended. The Sarah,* 8 Wheat., 391.

§ 1754. Libel must be particular and certain.— A libel not particular and certain in all material averments will not sustain a sentence of condemnation. The Caroline v. United States,* 7 Cr., 496.

§ 1755. Decree reversed for lack of averments in libel.— A decree will be reversed if founded on a libel wanting in substantial averments. The Anne v. United States,* 7 Cr., 570.

§ 1756. Name of respondent in prayer.— Where a respondent is proceeded against by name in the body of the libel he need not be named in the prayer for relief. Nevitt v. Clarke, Olc., 316.

§ 1757. **The authority of an attorney in fact to attest a libel** may be proved when called in question, and need not appear in the libel; but a mere general employment as attorney at law or proctor gives no such authority, and a defendant could not be held to bail on a libel so attested. Martin v. Walker, Abb. Adm., 579.

§ 1758. **In admiralty a sworn libel is required** as a foundation of any process of arrest or attachment. *Ibid.*

§ 1759. **No oath required to libels in rem in civil causes.—** Libels *in rem* in civil causes within the admiralty jurisdiction of the federal courts need not be sworn to, and need not state the occupation and residence of the libelant. The Hoyle, 4 Biss., 234.

§ 1760. **The oath of calumny is not now in use;** in admiralty practice, a general verification by affidavit is all that is required. Pratt v. Thomas, 1 Ware, 427.

§ 1761. **Cause of action should be verified.—** The debt or cause of action on which a libel is filed in admiralty should be verified by affidavit as a good and subsisting cause of action. In like manner the respondent is required to verify his answer by oath. Hutson v. Jordan, 1 Ware, 386.

§ 1762. **Joinder of actions.—** A joint tort against two or more cannot in admiralty be united in one action with a tort against one separately. Roberts v. Skolfield,* 8 Am. L. Reg., 156.

§ 1763. Although in an action at law on a charter-party it would be a fatal variance to include among the plaintiffs a person not proved to be a party in interest, it is only an irregularity in pleading to include such a person among the libelants in admiralty, and will not work defeat. Talbot v. Wakeman,* 19 How. Pr., 36.

§ 1764. Whether proceedings *in rem* and *in personam* can be joined in the same libel is doubtful. Bondies v. Sherwood, 22 How., 214.

§ 1765. A proceeding *in rem* cannot be joined with a proceeding *in personam* except in the cases specially provided for by the admiralty rules of the supreme court. The Alida, 12 Fed. R., 843.

§ 1766. Under the nineteenth admiralty rule, a joinder of actions *in rem* and *in personam* in the same libel for salvage of the same goods is not permitted. Actions *in rem* against both vessel and cargo may be joined, or *in personam* against both the owner of the vessel and the owner of the cargo; but if the actions are joined they must be pursued in the same manner, either both *in rem* or both *in personam*. Nott v. The Sabine,* 2 Woods, 211.

§ 1767. Where a cause of action in admiralty arises out of a contract, which, if the respondents are liable, binds also the property, and the respondents claim the property, it is no objection to the libel that it joins an action *in rem* with one *in personam*. Vaughan v. 630 Casks of Sherry Wine, 7 Ben., 506.

§ 1768. Where a libel is filed against a vessel and its master for a cause of action in which both may be unitedly liable, the libelant will not be compelled to elect between his remedy *in rem* and *in personam*. The Zenobia, Abb. Adm., 48.

§ 1769. An exception to a libel because it improperly joined a suit *in rem* against a vessel with a suit *in personam* against her owner allowed. An exception because all the owners of the vessel not joined as libelants also allowed. Woolman v. The Richard Doane,* 7 Int. Rev. Rec., 77.

§ 1770. Proceedings *in rem* against two vessels jointly and *in personam* against the owner of a third cannot be joined in the same libel. The Young America, 1 Brown, 462.

§ 1771. When there are several sets of salvors claiming to have performed separate and distinct services, and especially where the interests of the various salvors are somewhat antagonistic, as is often the case, it is not only proper but sometimes necessary that several libels be filed. The Steamship Merrimac, 1 Ben., 68.

§ 1772. Separate and distinct trespasses cannot be joined in the same libel against defendants who are not jointly liable. Thomas v. Lane, 2 Sumn., 1.

§ 1772a. A claim for the bounty and for an account of the fish taken in a voyage may be united in the same libel, as they relate to the same subject-matter, and if bounty is additional compensation are both of admiralty jurisdiction. The Lucy Anne,* 13 Law Rep. (N. S.), 545.

§ 1773. A claim for damages to the person cannot be joined in the same libel with a claim for the fine imposed by the act of 1840, chapter 48, section 19. Knowlton v. Boss, 1 Spr., 163.

§ 1774. A libel *in rem* against a vessel may properly be joined with a libel *in personam* against her owner under the fifteenth admiralty rule; and when a libel was brought against the vessel, the master, who was also part owner, and the pilot, it was held that it should be amended by dismissing it as to the pilot. Newell v. Norton, 3 Wall., 257.

§ 1775. An article in a libel against two jointly for a tort committed by them cannot be joined with an article against one of these for another tort. Roberts v. Skolfield, 3 Ware, 184.

§ 1776. A claim for wages and for money advanced for the use of a ship may be joined in one action *in rem;* and to such an action a party claiming wages only may be a party. But such a joint action will not lie *in personam.* The Sloop Merchant, Abb. Adm., 12.

§ 1777. An action against the master for assault and battery cannot be joined in the same libel with an action for wages if it be excepted to. Pratt *v.* Thomas, 1 Ware, 437.

§ 1778. Parties may join in one libel causes of action arising *ex contractu* and those arising *ex delicto,* where the causes of action are so united that the same evidence will apply to all; *e. g.,* a claim for wages, and a claim for damages for an assault and battery committed on the same voyage. Borden *v.* Hiom, Bl. & How., 293.

§ 1779. A libelant may unite in one libel an allegation founded on the hypothecation implied by law for money advanced for repairs, with an allegation on a bottomry bond given for the same consideration. The Brig Hunter, 1 Ware. 249.

§ 1780. **Collision cases.**— The true mode of declaring in collision cases in admiralty is for each party to allege what happened on his own vessel; and he may undoubtedly add whatever he believes to have been done by the other; but he ought not to be held to prove too strictly the latter part of his allegations. The Cambridge, 2 Low., 21.

§ 1781. The libel and answer should clearly and explicitly set forth the facts relied on by both parties. This is especially important in collision cases; and the court has power at any stage to require the parties to supply any defects in the pleadings, though counsel can appeal to the court for this purpose only by exceptions filed at the proper time. The Bark Havre, 1 Ben.. 295.

§ 1782. A libel is not required to state with precise accuracy the location where a collision occurred, unless the description be material to the main question. The Suffolk County, 9 Wall., 651.

§ 1783. Cross-actions brought at the same time upon double pleadings. The Mazeppa fails to aver the course she was steering. The Washington sets forth distinctly in the pleading her course by compass, and as the court has a right to an unreserved and explicit statement on the pleadings of every material fact known to the parties, a neglect to supply this will always be taken against the vessel omitting it, but as no exception was taken to the defect the court proceeded to consider the proof. Post *v.* The Schooner Washington Sturges,* 9 N. Y. Leg. Obs., 321.

§ 1784. A libelant is not excused from setting out a full statement of the facts of the case, where his vessel was injured in a collision between two steamboats, one of which was towing her, she thus being a passive object. All the circumstances known to the libelant, or seen by the persons in charge of his vessel, should be fully set out for the information of the court. The Steamboat Transport,* 1 Ben., 86.

§ 1785. **The twenty-second rule** in admiralty, prescribing the mode of procedure in petitory and possessory suits, requires a joint proceeding *in rem* and *in personam;* and to allow a libel, in such a case, to be amended so as to proceed for damages *in personam,* would be inconsistent with the established rules of admiralty practice. Kynoch *v.* The Propeller S. C. Ives, Newb., 205.

§ 1786. A libel **in personam,** resting upon a common cause of action. may be filed for the libelants, and for all others interested. whenever the whole subject-matter can be disposed of in one suit. American Ins. Co. *v.* Johnson, Bl. & How., 9.

§ 1787. Where it appears on the face of the libel that the court has not jurisdiction, or that the libelant has not capacity to sue, the respondent may demur; but if the incapacity does not appear, though true in point of fact, the respondent must take advantage of it by pleading in bar. Knight *v.* The Brig Attila, Crabbe, 326.

§ 1788. A libel brought before the right of action is perfected must be dismissed, if duly excepted to on that ground, though such right becomes perfected during the progress of the suit. The Martha, Bl. & How., 151.

§ 1789. **Seaman's libel for wages** — Notice required to render his statements proof of contents of shipping articles.— If a seaman ships under articles at Boston, in December, 1842, and at New Orleans in March. 1843, and leaves the ship at Bordeaux in June. 1843, and in his libel filed against the vessel in the United States circuit court for wages on those voyages he "prays "the shipping articles may be produced by the master or owner," that is not such notice or requirement as will render his statement proof of their contents. The Brig Osceola, Olc., 450.

§ 1790. **Libel for damage to cargo** — Libelant cannot claim ground of complaint not set up in libel.— In case of damage to a cargo, where the libel alleges the fault of the master to be, first, that he falsely represented his vessel to be tight, staunch and seaworthy; and second, that the danger resulted from the master's carelessness, negligence and improper conduct, the libelant cannot claim another specific ground of complaint not set up in the libel, as that the danger was caused by the fault of the master in not putting into some other port to repair his vessel and take measures to preserve his cargo. Soule *v.* Rodocanachi, Newb., 504,

§ 1791. Libel for non-delivery of cargo — Jettison — General average.— Where a libel alleged a shipment of cargo under a bill of lading and its non-delivery, and prayed process against the vessel, and the answer set up a jettison, rendered necessary by a peril of the sea, and this defensive allegation was sustained by the court, it was held that the libelant was entitled to a decree for the contributory share of general average due from the vessel. Dupont de Nemours v. Vance, 19 How., 162.

§ 1792. Libel for salvage — Parties.— In a libel for salvage all the parties should be inserted and brought before the court. The Schooner Boston, 1 Sumn., 328.

§ 1793. Lien — Allegation showing foreign character of vessel.— Where a libel is filed to enforce a lien under the general maritime law, such facts must be set forth in the libel which, if proven, would satisfy the court that the vessel was a foreign vessel at the time the lien attached. The Propeller Charles Mears, Newb., 197.

§ 1794. —— before employment of vessel, necessary allegations.— Where a libel is filed to enforce a lien against a vessel before she is actually employed in navigation, the libel must show that the vessel is of the size and build fitted for maritime employment, and that her business was to be maritime navigation upon the lakes or high seas. *Ibid.*

§ 1795. —— domestic vessels.— Law giving lien to be set forth.— Where a libel is filed to enforce a lien upon a domestic vessel, it must be distinctly set forth in the libel by what municipal regulation or state law such lien is conferred. *Ibid.*

§ 1796. In a libel for wages the allegations of the hiring, voyage, etc., should be drawn accurately and with reasonable certainty, otherwise it may be excepted to. The most correct course is to state the facts, etc., in distinct articles, which is the usual course in admiralty proceedings. Orne v. Townsend, 4 Mason, 541.

§ 1797. In debt for the double value under section 3 of the embargo act, January 9, 1808, chapter 8, it is not necessary to allege the particular articles which compose the cargo, nor that the owner was knowingly concerned in the illegal voyage. Cross v. United States, 1 Gall., 26.

§ 1798. Marine tort — Each separate wrong to be alleged.— In a libel for a marine tort the libelant must set forth in a distinct allegation each separate wrong on which he intends to rely and for which he claims damages; and if he intends to rely on general ill-treatment and oppression on the part of the master in aggravation of damages, it must be propounded in a distinct allegation to enable the master to take issue upon it in his answer. Pettingill v. Dinsmore, Dav., 208.

§ 1799. Neglect to aver ownership, waiver of.— Where a libel was filed for non-delivery of certain goods without averring that the libelant was the owner, and the answer did not contain an averment that he was, nor did it except to the libel for so not averring, the point that the libelant was not the owner must be taken as having been waived. Steamship Ville de Paris, 8 Ben., 276.

§ 1800. A petition in admiralty to set aside a sale on the ground of fraud must set forth the facts which constitute the fraud. The Kaloolah, 1 Brown, 55.

§ 1801. To charge carrier with loss of goods — In personam — In rem.— A libel *in personam* for the loss of goods shipped in a certain vessel must charge the vessel as a common carrier; but a libel *in rem* for the same cause of action need not so charge; but, in the latter case, it must be shown in evidence that the vessel was employed as a common carrier. The Pacific, Deady, 17.

§ 1802. Tort action — Averment of contract by way of inducement.— In a libel for the destruction of a boat the reciting of a contract of towage by way of inducement does not transform the action from one of tort to one upon the contract of towage. The Quickstep, 9 Wall., 665.

• § 1803. Salvage — Contract averred.— A clause in a libel alleging it to be "a cause of contract, maritime and civil, and of extra services rendered," will not prevent a claim for salvage if the general scope of the several allegations shows that the services rendered were such as to constitute a legal foundation for such a claim. Adams v. Bark Island City and Cargo, 1 Cliff., 210.

§ 1804. After answer and replication libelant cannot except to claimant's right to contest.— After an answer has been received and a replication filed to it, and the cause been brought to a hearing on the merits, a libelant cannot be allowed to interpose an exception that the claimant had no legal right to contest the case. A proper allegation should have been filed, putting that fact in issue preliminarily, or else the irregularity will be regarded as waived. Thomas v. The Steamboat Kosciusko,* 11 N. Y. Leg. Obs., 38.

§ 1805. Libel in prize — Necessary allegations.— A libel in prize must allege generally the fact of capture as prize of war and need not state why it has become prize. The Andromeda, 2 Wall., 481.

§ 1806. **Libel for wages — Statement of account unnecessary.**— It is not necessary to annex to a libel for wages an account stating the rate of wages and the precise balance due. It is sufficient if the contract is stated and the service alleged in proper form. Pratt *v.* Thomas, 1 Ware, 427.

§ 1807. **Libel for loan to be paid out of earnings — Allegations.**— Plaintiff made a written agreement with the owner of the brig Cadmus to sail her as master, and also loaned him $300, a stipulation being included that this sum should be paid out of the first earnings of the vessel, and that the vessel stood accountable to plaintiff for this sum until paid. A libel against the vessel, to enforce payment of this sum, stated the facts and alleged generally that the whole of said sum was still due and unpaid, but did not allege that there were no earnings out of which the sum might have been paid. For want of this allegation the district court dismissed the libel. Held by the circuit court on appeal that the general allegation was sufficient, reversing the decree of the district court. Brown *v.* The Cadmus,* 2 Paine, 564.

§ 1808. **Strictness of admiralty rules of pleading.**— The same strictness is not required in admiralty pleading as in common-law pleadings. *Ibid.*

§ 1809. **Informations.**— A libel in admiralty in the nature of an information need not be expressed with the technical nicety of an indictment at common law. The Samuel, 1 Wheat., 9.

§ 1810. An information on a seizure under the internal revenue laws is subject to the same general rules, as to its structure and amendment, as an ordinary libel. It may contain different causes of forfeiture, and the government cannot be compelled to elect on which to rely. If it be ambiguous or wanting in plain allegations of fact the court will, on motion, order it to be reformed. 18,000 Gallons Distilled Spirits,* 5 Ben., 4.

§ 1811. A libel is sufficient if it follows the language of the statute which inflicts the forfeiture. Exceptions or provisos in the statute are matters of defense. Two Hundred Chests of Tea, 9 Wheat., 430.

§ 1812. When a libel is filed, claiming a forfeiture of the vessel libeled, and the facts of the case do not authorize the forfeiture alleged in the libel, but show an offense against other provisions of the same law under which the forfeiture is asserted to have arisen, the court will dismiss the libel. United States *v.* The Hunter, Pet. C. C., 10.

§ 1813. An information for a forfeiture of a vessel need not be more technical in its language than an indictment, and in general will be sufficient if it sets forth the offense in the words of the statute creating it, with sufficient certainty as to the time and place of its commission. The Neurea,* 19 How., 92.

§ 1814. A libel, under the passenger act of 1847, averring that the master took on board, to carry to the United States, a certain number of passengers; that this number was greater than in proportion to the space occupied by them, viz., on the lower deck or platform one passenger for every fourteen clear superficial feet; that he brought them to the United States, and that the passengers exceeded the number which could be lawfully brought to the number of twenty in the whole, etc., is a sufficient libel, though it does not state that the excess of passengers was carried in the lower deck or the orlop deck. *Ibid.*

§ 1815. In a count in a libel upon the fiftieth section of the collection law of March 2, 1799, for unloading goods without a permit, it is not necessary to state the time and place of the importation nor the vessel in which it was made, but it is sufficient to allege that they were unknown to the attorney. Locke *v.* United States, 7 Cr., 339.

§ 1816. In a libel against a ship for failure to enter goods on the manifest as provided in the statutes of the United States of March 2, 1799, and July 18, 1866, it is not necessary to aver a seizure of the ship within the district, the word "seized," as used in such statutes, referring not to a revenue seizure, but to the seizure under process of court, which forms part of every proceeding *in rem* in admiralty. The Steamer Missouri, 3 Ben., 508.

§ 1817. In a libel of information to recover a penalty of a steam tug for not having been inspected under the act of February 23, 1871, a seizure of the vessel must be alleged in order to give the court jurisdiction. The Tug Oconto, 5 Biss., 460.

§ 1818. A libel for seizure of a vessel under the thirty-second section of the act of February 18, 1793, need not state the particular trade in which the vessel was engaged at the time of the seizure. It is sufficient, in a libel of this kind, if the case is brought within the words of the act; and technical rules of pleading are not so much regarded in libels of this description as in indictments and informations at common law. United States *v.* Schooner Paryntha Davis, 1 Cliff., 532.

§ 1819. If an information to secure the forfeiture of a vessel sets forth a proper cause of forfeiture within the main part of a statute, the fact that it does not allege that the case is not within the proviso will not prevent the operation of the statute. This is a matter of defense to be set up by the claimant, if he relies upon it as exempting him from the operation of the main cause of forfeiture in the statute. The Mary Merritt,* 2 Biss., 381.

§ 1820. A libel under act of March 8, 1799, which prohibits the unloading of a vessel under certain conditions within four leagues of the coast, should conform to the words of the statute, and not charge the offense as committed within four leagues of a collection district, as the expressions would not always be synonymous. However, a decree of the district court will not be reversed in the circuit court for this inaccuracy, but an amendment will be allowed. The Betsy,* 1 Mason, 354.

§ 1821. When an act of congress requires that every captain of a vessel in a certain trade shall deliver to the collector of the port from which he sailed a manifest, a libel charging that the captain sailed from two ports, and did not deliver manifests to the collectors of those ports, is fatally defective, as it requires more than the law requires. The Mary Ann,* 8 Wheat., 380.

§ 1822. A charge that the manifest required by law was not delivered before the vessel sailed is good on demurrer, and the question does not arise by this means whether the charge would be disproved by producing a libel not strictly conformable to law. Ibid.

§ 1823. The ninth section of the act of congress of March 2, 1807, as to vessels carrying negroes, comprehends only vessels of forty tons' burden or more, and a libel for forfeiture of a vessel under this section must allege that the vessel was of forty tons or more. Ibid.

§ 1824. By the fifteenth section of the act of 1799 a ship is not forfeited for unlading goods without a permit unless they are of the value of $400, and counts of a libel alleging goods unladen to be of a less value must be adjudged insufficient. The Washington,* 7 Law Rep., 497.

§ 1825. A libel for forfeiture for violation of United States laws should set out a seizure before the filing of such libel. United States v. Steamboat Corn,* 1 Dak. T'y, 1.

§ 1826. Before there can be a libel in rem for forfeiture there must be a seizure; and a plea of no seizure is like a plea of not guilty to an indictment, and puts in issue all the material allegations of the libel. If, therefore, upon trial, a seizure previous to filing the libel does not appear, the libel is not sustained. The Schooner Silver Spring, 1 Spr., 551.

§ 1827. A libel under the navigation laws does not lie unless there has previously been a seizure of the property, and therefore an allegation of such seizure in the libel is necessary to give the court jurisdiction. Fideliter v. United States, 1 Saw., 153.

§ 1828. Under section 50 of the collection act of March 2, 1799, a suit to enforce forfeiture need not allege that the goods unladen were of foreign growth or manufacture if it is alleged that they were brought from a foreign port; it is sufficient to allege that they were unladen in the collection district of Oregon without alleging that they were unladen in the United States, since the court will take judicial notice that such district is in the United States; and it is not necessary to allege that the goods were unladen at a port; for it is sufficient if they were unladen at any place or district within the United States. The Active, Deady, 165.

§ 1829. A libel against a vessel for violating the embargo laws must contain a substantial statement of the offense, and it must be made with reasonable precision. But, inasmuch as the embargo act of December, 1807, prohibits all vessels, whether foreign or domestic, registered or coasting vessels, from sailing to any foreign port or place, and the supplemental act of January, 1808, annexes the penalty of forfeiture to any vessel which violates either act, it is not necessary that the libel should set forth the particular character of the vessel. United States v. The Schooner Little Charles, 1 Marsh., 347.

§ 1830. An act of congress declares that "no person shall build, fit, equip, load, or otherwise prepare, any ship or vessel, etc., within any port of the United States, nor shall cause any ship or vessel to sail from any port of the United States, for the purpose of carrying on any trade or traffic in slaves, to any foreign country;" and it declares that "if any ship or vessel shall be so fitted out as aforesaid, or shall be caused to sail as aforesaid, such ship or vessel shall be forfeited to the United States." Held, that an information against a vessel which charges "that she was built, fitted, equipped, loaded or otherwise prepared, etc., or caused to sail," is bad for uncertainty as to which of the several offenses is charged. The Case of the Brig Caroline, 1 Marsh., 384.

§ 1831. Cross-libels.— If a claimant of a vessel libeled for collision wishes to recover damages for his injury he should file a cross-libel. The Dove.* 1 Otto, 381.

§ 1832. A libel and cross-libel are usually tried together though separate decrees are entered. If one of these be appealed from and the other not, the question in the latter is finally settled, but the rights of the parties in the former are not at all affected; nor is either of them estopped from setting up anything warranted by the pleadings, by the decree not appealed from. Ibid.

§ 1833. New and distinct matters not included in the original libel cannot be included in the cross-libel, which may include only matters auxiliary to the cause of action set forth in the original suit. Ibid.

§ 1834. A cross-libel may not be necessary in every case where the libeled vessel was injured and claims damages, but it may be questioned whether such injury should not appear in the answer. At any rate the claim cannot be made for the first time on appeal. The Sapphire, 18 Wall., 51.

§ 1835. Respondents in admiralty who wish to file a cross-libel should do so in regular form, and not file an answer under an agreement that this should operate as a cross-libel. Ward v. Chamberlain, 21 How., 572.

§ 1836. To a libel against a common carrier for failure to deliver goods, a claim for freight cannot be set up as a defense; such a claim can only be used against the libelant by setting it up in a cross-libel. Maxwell v. The Powell, 1 Woods, 99.

§ 1837. If a respondent sets up a deviation from the contract by the libelant as a mere defense to a libel on a charter-party, and not by way of set-off or recoupment, he may afterwards file a cross-libel claiming damages for misconduct of the libelant in making such deviation. Nichols v. Tremlett, 1 Spr., 361.

§ 1838. No general doctrine of set-off is recognized in admiralty. The respondent may set off damages by way of recoupment, but if the damage be greater than the whole freight, there can be no decree against the libelant for the excess. To recover damage more than the amount of the freight the respondent must bring a cross-libel; but he cannot do this if he has set up the damage by way of recoupment. He must elect between recoupment and cross-libel. Snow v. Carruth, 1 Spr., 324.

3. Plea.

§ 1839. A plea to the jurisdiction must be interposed by the defendant in person and on oath, and not by any agent or attorney. Teasdale v. The Rambler,* Bee, 9.

§ 1840. Suit prematurely brought — Plea in abatement proper.— A claimant or respondent in admiralty, to obtain judgment on the ground that the action was prematurely brought, must raise the point by plea in abatement. Otherwise the action will not be dismissed for this reason, if the right is perfected before final hearing. The Isaac Newton, Abb. Adm., 11.

§ 1841. Pendency of another suit.— An objection grounded on the pendency of another suit for the same cause of action is preliminary in its character, and should be taken in admiralty by a special plea in the nature of a plea in abatement, known as a dilatory or declinatory exception. Certain Logs of Mahogany, 2 Sumn., 589.

§ 1842. A plea to a libel that it shows no cause of action, or, if it does, that the remedy is in a court of common law, amounts to a demurrer, and will be overruled. The Sea Gull, Chase's Dec., 145.

§ 1843. Salvage — Replevin suit pending — Plea in abatement.— It cannot be pleaded in abatement to a libel in rem for salvage that a replevin suit is pending in a court of law brought by the owner of the salved property against the salvor to recover possession, in which replevin suit the validity of the salvor's lien may be determined. A Raft of Spars, Abb. Adm., 291.

§ 1844. The non-joinder of proper respondents in an action in personam can be taken advantage of only by plea in abatement. Reed v. Hussey, Bl. & How., 525.

§ 1845. Plea to jurisdiction.— Where no want of jurisdiction appears on the libel, but a plea to the jurisdiction is put in, and the case heard on that question alone, the plea will be overruled. Knight v. The Brig Attila, Crabbe, 326.

4. Answer.

SUMMARY — *Plea, clearness but not excessive formality required,* § 1846.— *Plea of former adjudication,* § 1847.

§ 1846. Pleas or exceptions in admiralty must set out the matter of defense clearly, but excessive formality is not required. The Navarro, §§ 1848–49.

§ 1847. A plea setting up a former adjudication is good, though the former suit was in personam and the pending suit in rem. Ibid.

[NOTES.— See §§ 1850–1906.]

THE SCHOONER NAVARRO.

(District Court for New York: Olcott, 127-129. 1845.)

Opinion by BETTS, J.

STATEMENT OF FACTS.— This is a cross-action, *in rem*, on a charter-party, on which the claimants heretofore brought suit against the libelant and had a decree in their favor in this court. The vessel was chartered to the libelant on a vovage from La Guyana to a plantation about twenty miles to the windward, from thence to La Guyana and Puerto Cabello, with the privilege of going to Maracaibo for a cargo.

The libel charges that the vessel proceeded only to the port of Maracaibo, at the head of the lake, and no sufficient cargo being found for her there, the master was requested to proceed up Lake Maracaibo to other ports, where cargo would be found, which he refused to do; and it avers that the usage in that trade is for vessels chartered to Maracaibo to go up the lake for cargo when required, without mention of such obligation in the charter.

Damages are demanded against the vessel because of the non-performance of such implied contract by the master. The claimants, by way of exception, set up the former action and the decree of the court therein in bar of this suit, and aver that the same matters sought to be drawn in controversy in this cause have been adjudicated and decreed by this court between the libelant and the claimants herein, and pray that the libel be dismissed.

§ **1848.** *Pleas or exceptions in admiralty must set forth the matter of defense clearly, but excessive formality is not required.*

The libelant by an exceptive allegation takes issue in law upon the sufficiency of the bar. The alleged insufficiencies of the bar might, most of them, be grounds of special demurrer at law; such as that the averments are not positive, but are merely by way of recital; the want of certainty as to the identity of the subject-matter of the two suits; the want of proper form and verification of the plea, etc.

Others are inappropriate to this court, as that the parties are not *nominatively* the same in the proceedings in both cases, this being *in rem*, the former *in personam;* that the issue tendered by the plea is partly *in pais* and in part to this court (Betts' Adm. Pr., 48), and that the particulars of the former action are not alleged in the plea. The general principle governing pleas or exceptions in admiralty practice is that they must set forth the matter of defense in perspicuous and definite terms, and it is in no way necessary they should embody the formalities which obtain in common-law pleas, or even those used in chancery. 2 Browne's Civ. & Ad., 110; Dunlap, 196, 197; Betts' Admiralty Practice, 48.

The gist of the plea is that the present claimants brought their action on this charter-party against the libelant, averring full performance of its engagements on their part; that the libelant contested the action, and the court on the pleadings and proofs decreed in favor of the claimants, and that the libelant now seeks to bring the same matters in controversy in this suit.

§ **1849.** *A plea setting up a former adjudication is good, though the former suit was in personam and the pending suit in rem.*

The defense is sufficient in its material point — the identity of the cause of action in this and the former suit. The substitution in this of the vessel for the owners does not constitute a distinct cause of action. The vessel being chargeable in admiralty with the responsibilities of her owners takes also all their legal privileges and exemptions in respect to the charter-party, and it is substantially sufficient in its frame, it not being necessary to the validity of the bar that more of the former pleadings be rehearsed than is here set forth. To do so would load the files to no useful end, and the rules of court inhibit all useless prolixities in referring to antecedent pleadings in a cause, with a view to bring a point under the consideration of the court which may be material in a new proceeding.   Rule 7.

The exception to the plea is accordingly overruled, with costs, with leave to the libelant to reply to the plea within ten days.

Ordered and adjudged that the exception filed by the libelant to the plea of the respondents of a former trial and decree upon the subject-matter of the suit be overruled, with costs to be taxed, the libel of the libelant be decreed barred and be dismissed, with costs to be taxed, unless the libelant shall elect to reply to said plea, and in that case that he have leave to file a replication thereto within ten days, on payment of the costs created by such exception to be taxed.

§ 1850. General requirements of.— An answer in admiralty must fully and explicitly answer the several articles of the libel, either denying them or confessing and avoiding. United States v. Propeller Sun,* 10 Am. L. Reg., 277.

§ 1851. The authorities are unanimous that an answer in admiralty should be full, explicit and distinct to each separate article and allegation of the libel; and if the answer sets up that the vessel of the libelants lay in an improper place and in an improper manner, the answer should show the facts leading to such conclusions. Commander-in-Chief, 1 Wall., 43.

§ 1852. In admiralty the answer must either deny the articles of the libel, or confess and avoid them by a proper allegation of facts. The Propeller Sun, 1 Biss., 373.

§ 1853. An answer to a libel in admiralty should meet each material allegation of the libel with an admission, a denial or defense. The Schooner Boston, 1 Sumn., 328.

§ 1854. Proof must correspond with allegation.— In admiralty the facts as proved must correspond with the facts as alleged in the answer in order to give the party setting them up the benefit of them. The Washington Irving, Abb. Adm., 336.

§ 1855. —— surprise.— The libelants must recover on the allegations in their libel, and the respondents rely exclusively on the grounds they have selected in their answer, in order to prevent surprise. Campbell v. Steamer Uncle Sam, McAl., 77.

§ 1856. An answer which neither admits nor denies a material averment in the libel is insufficient, and may be excepted to on that ground. The Elizabeth Frith, Bl. & How., 195.

§ 1857. Impertinent and irrelevant allegations in an answer will be stricken out on motion. The Gustavia. Bl. & How., 189.

§ 1858. Particular matters of defense.— When the respondent wishes to avail himself of any particular matter of defense he must present it with proper averments in his answer, or by plea. The William Harris, 1 Ware, 367.

§ 1859. Only issue raised can be considered.— The issue raised by the libel and answer in admiralty is the only point which can be considered by the court. McKinlay v. Morrish, 21 How., 343.

§ 1860. Verification.— An answer to a libel in admiralty should be sworn to by the respondent, but the libel need not be. Coffin v. Jenkins, 3 Story, 108.

§ 1861. Neglect to file answer.— In admiralty a deliberate omission to file an answer must be taken as an absolute waiver of the right to do so. Ferryboats Roslyn and Midland, 9 Ben., 119.

§ 1862. Pendency of motion as excuse for failure to answer.— In admiralty the pendency of a motion to test the validity of a levy by the marshal does not excuse failure to answer to the merits. Ibid.

§ 1863. Agreement to arbitrate dispenses with answer.— An agreement to refer to arbitrators takes away the necessity for an answer, and not until the rule to refer is set aside is an answer necessary or proper. The Nineveh, 1 Low., 400.

§ 1864. One part of answer inconsistent with another.— Where an answer is not excepted to, and one part is inconsistent with another, the court must accept as true the allegation most adverse to the claimant. The Bark Olbers, 8 Ben., 148.

§ 1865. Amended answer inconsistent with original answer.— In admiralty where an amended answer, inconsistent with the original answer, and susceptible of easy proof, but not satisfactorily proved, was set up, the court held that the defense was not established. The Mabey and Cooper, 14 Wall., 204.

§ 1866. **Matter of abatement in answer.**— The practice of courts of admiralty admits matter of abatement to be set up in the answer, but the answer must in such case demand the same judgment, and be subject to the same rules, as if a formal dilatory plea had been employed. Reed v. Hussey, Bl. & How., 525.

§ 1867. **Answer not filed until bail is perfected.**— When a respondent has been arrested in a suit *in personam* in admiralty, the answer is not filed, within the meaning of the eighteenth rule, until bail is perfected. Thomas v. Gray, Bl. & How., 493.

§ 1868. **Verification — Special interrogatories.**— In causes on the instance side of the admiralty court, the answer of the claimant should be verified by oath; and in a suit for wages the libelant may compel the adverse party to answer special interrogatories. Gammell v. Skinner, 2 Gall., 45.

§ 1869. **Claim to property.**— The first step in a defense in a proceeding in rem in instance causes, in courts exercising admiralty jurisdiction, is to interpose a claim to the property libeled. This claim should be made by the owner or by his agent, or by the agent of a foreign government whose subjects are interested in the property in question; should state the facts showing the right of the party to the property in a direct and issuable form, alleging a true and *bona fide* interest, and that no other person is the owner thereof; and should be verified by the oath of the party or his agent or consignee; and if verified by the oath of agent or consignee, there must be an oath that such agent or consignee is authorized by the owner to verify; or if the property be, at the time of the arrest, in the possession of the master of a ship, that he is a lawful bailee thereof for the owner. Steamer Spark v. Lee Choi Chum, 1 Saw., 713.

§ 1870. **Libel cannot be met by general issue.**— A libel or information, or libel of information, cannot be met by the general issue, but the defendant should answer each articulation of the libel; the technical conclusion should be a mere prayer for restitution. When an allegation in the libel must be met by sworn matter, the form should be, not that the claimant "denies" or "believes," but that "it is or is not true;" and, if he has no direct knowledge, he may state in his oath that they are true according to his information and belief. The United States v. Twenty-five Barrels of Alcohol,[*] 10 Int. Rev. Rec., 17.

§ 1871. **Foreign attachment — Garnishee's right to answer.**— The process of foreign attachment is governed primarily by the rules of the supreme court. It is not borrowed from the custom of London or the local laws of the states. Its rules give the garnishee a right to answer. If he fails to answer, the libelant may proceed to execution if he can prove his libel. If a disclosure is indispensable to give the libelant evidence, he may compel answer. After execution the garnishee has no right to answer the libel. Possibly he might be allowed to appear upon terms and show matter in discharge. After default the court may, in its discretion, allow answer upon terms. Shorey v. Rennell & Kimball, Garnishes, 1 Spr., 418.

§ 1872. **Where an answer admits that a bill of lading was signed for the ship** the authority of the agents who signed it is admitted also. The Steamer Saragossa, 3 Ben., 544.

§ 1873. **Joint tort — Separate answers liberally construed.**— Where, in an action against two parties for a joint tort, the respondents put in separate answers, each respondent must rely for his defense upon his own answer and the proofs, without reference to the answer of the other respondent; but, unless the answers are excepted to by the libelant, for insufficiency or uncertainty, they will be liberally construed. Gardner v. Bibbins, Bl. & How., 356.

§ 1874. **Technical exactness not required.**— While technical exactness is not required in admiralty pleading, the libelant must set forth in distinct allegations each substantive wrong, such as separate and independent assaults, upon which he relies. If a master wishes to justify punishment by proof of libelant's habitual sloth, or show it in mitigation, it must be set out in a distinct allegation in the answer. Pettingill v. Dinsmore,[*] 6 Law Rep., 255.

§ 1875. **Statute of limitations must be pleaded.**— A respondent in admiralty cannot avail himself of the statute of limitations unless he pleads it. Brown v. Jones, 2 Gall., 476.

§ 1876. —— **staleness.**— If a respondent to a libel intends to rely on staleness it should be regularly pleaded, for in admiralty a defense that does not meet the merits cannot be used unless notice thereof is given by a plea or distinct allegation in the answer. The Platina,[*] 21 Law Rep., 397.

§ 1877. **Misconduct, particular facts must be pleaded.**— If misconduct is intended to be pleaded as a cause of forfeiture or diminution of wages, the particulars of the alleged neglect and mismanagement should be stated, with circumstances of time and place. The Pioneer, Deady, 58.

§ 1878. **Justification of charge in libel.**— An answer in admiralty should be positive in its terms. If it seek to justify the charge in the libel the charge should be admitted, and not stated hypothetically. Treadwell v. Joseph,[*] 1 Sumn., 390.

§ 1879. A charge in the libel that respondent compelled libelant, a seaman, to scrape the masts for an excessive length of time, in rough weather, is not justified by an answer that scraping the mast was a part of the ship's duty, which libelant was bound to perform, as it does not show that such length of time is proper or necessary. If this were intended to be justified as a punishment the fact should be expressly so stated, and also the cause for which it was inflicted. *Ibid.*

§ 1880. **Payment in full and release — Date of release need not be averred.**— An answer to a libel for wages, setting up payment in full and a release under seal executed by libelant, is sufficient, without any averment as to the date of release, time of making or consideration, the payment being a bar to the suit, and the release being merely evidence thereof. The Western Metropolis,* 2 Ben., 212.

§ 1881. **Admission of receipt as admission of agreement.**— Where a libel averred that by agreement between libelant and respondent the vessel, for $100 additional compensation, was to go to a port not stipulated in the charter-party and take in cargo; that the vessel took the extra voyage, and that the $100 was paid by the agent of libelant to the agent of the respondent, and a receipt therefor given, an admission in the answer of the receipt and the payment of the money would be a sufficient, though informal, admission of the whole agreement, and an exception for insufficiency on that ground would be overruled. The Brig Aldebaran,* Olc., 130.

§ 1882. **The answer need not respond to mere narrative statements** not made the ground of a demand for relief. *Ibid.*

§ 1883. **Admitting agreement and performance thereof.**— An answer admitting an agreement as charged in the bill, and performance thereof. need not go further and state specifically that the performance was in pursuance of the agreement. *Ibid.*

§ 1884. **Libel for wages — Answer setting up misconduct.**— When a libel for wages showed that libelant had been hired by the month, and was suing for several months' wages, a statement in the answer that he was discharged because he, by mismanagement and neglect, had caused great damage to the machinery of the boat, is impertinent, and an exception on that ground will be allowed. The Pioneer,* Deady, 58.

§ 1885. —— **mutinous conduct, incompetence.**— An averment in the answer that the wages were forfeited by reason of mutinous conduct, incompetence and malicious mischief, causing damage, is wholly insufficient; first, because it is too vague and indefinite; and also because the hiring, being by the month, the misconduct of one month is overlooked or waived by retention in the employment after an opportunity for discharge, and wages earned one month are not forfeited by misconduct another. *Ibid.*

§ 1886. —— **answer setting up garnishment by claimant.**— An averment in an answer to a libel for wages, that part of the amount due has been garnished by the present claimant and owner of the vessel in the hands of the last owner in a suit against libelant, is insufficient without an averment that libelant has been served with process in that suit. *Ibid.*

§ 1887. **In rem for wages — Answer may bar the action.**— Although, in an action *in rem* for wages, a warrant is issued under a certificate of sufficient cause of complaint for admiralty process, conformably to the statute (Act of July 20, 1790; 1 U. S. Stat. at Large, 133), yet the owner of the vessel may intervene by answer, and bar the action by proving that the libelant had no right to sue. The Warrington, Bl. & How., 335.

§ 1888. **Suit for physician's bill — Answer that vessel was supplied with medicine chest.** An answer averring in general terms that a vessel was supplied with a medicine chest according to law is not of itself sufficient evidence to discharge a master from his liability for a physician's bill for attendance upon a sick seaman. Freeman *v.* Baker, Bl. & How., 872.

§ 1889. **Libel by bottomry holder — Answers by owner and mortgagee claiming proceeds.**— When the owner and mortgagee of a ship both appear and file answers to the libel of a bottomry holder, it is competent for each to claim in his answer or by separate petition that the proceeds of the vessel, after satisfaction of the bottomry security, be paid to him. The Ship Panama, Olc., 343.

§ 1890. **Forfeiture for misconduct.**— There can be no specific forfeiture or deduction for misconduct which is not specially charged in the answer. Hart *v.* The Otis, Crabbe, 52.

§ 1891. **Libel by material-man — Answer need not deny that articles were necessaries.**— Whether supplies furnished to a vessel are necessary is a conclusion of law, and the claimant in answer to a libel by a material-man is not required to either admit or deny that the articles furnished were necessaries. The Gustavia, Bl. & How., 189.

§ 1892. **An averment in a libel by a seaman for wages** who has signed articles for a voyage from New York to Pernambuco, thence to a port in Europe and back to the United States, is sufficiently supported, in case the master or owner does not produce the articles on trial, by proof that the agreement was that the first terminus was some port in South America not designated. Piehl *v.* Balchen, Olc., 24.

§ 1893. **Justification by master for punishing seamen.**—When a master is prosecuted in admiralty for punishing a seaman, he may be permitted, in justification or in mitigation of damages, to show that the seaman was habitually careless, disobedient or negligent. But in order to be admitted to this defense, he must set forth such habitual misconduct in a defensive allegation in his answer, in order that the libelant may be enabled to meet the charge by counter-evidence. Pettingill *v.* Dinsmore, Dav., 208.

§ 1894. **Claim of extra wages for short allowance of provisions**—Where a libel claims extra wages in satisfaction of a short allowance of provisions, under the ninth section of the act of July 20, 1790 (1 U. S. Stats. at Large, 135), the answer must set forth precisely whether the vessel shipped the quantity and quality of provisions required by the statute, or an exception will lie for insufficiency. The Elizabeth Frith, Bl. & How., 195.

§ 1895. **Defense for discharging seaman in foreign port.**—A discharge of a seaman in a foreign port can be ordered by the consul only with the seaman's consent, and to prove such discharge as a defense the consent of the seaman must be shown by the party relying upon the discharge. The Atlantic, Abb. Adm., 451.

§ 1896. **In a prize case the defense should set out** specifically the owner of the vessel, the place of her outfit and the course of her trade or employment. The Hannah M. Johnson, Bl. Pr. Cas., 2.

§ 1897. All the answer that is required in a prize case is a brief assertion that the property seized is not liable to condemnation and forfeiture. The Lynchburg. Bl. Pr. Cas., 3.

§ 1898. **Answer to suit by carrier for freight.**—If a suit is brought by a carrier for freight the respondent may set up in answer damage to the goods, and if the damage is proved to be by fault of the carrier and to exceed the amount of the freight the libel will be dismissed. Bearse *v.* Ropes, 1 Spr., 331.

§ 1899. **"Contrary to shipping articles," meaning of in answer setting up desertion of seaman.**—An allegation in an answer to a libel for wages, that the libelant left "contrary to the shipping articles," will be taken to mean contrary to the usual articles, and under it proof of leaving contrary to special and peculiar articles cannot be set up, but if relied upon should be specifically averred in the answer. Heard *v.* Rogers, 1 Spr., 536.

§ 1900. **In order to bar a claim for salvage** a distinct agreement must be alleged and proved between the parties for a given sum, and such a contract will not be implied from the fact that the relief was undertaken at the request of the vessel's owners. Adams *v.* Bark Island City and Cargo, 1 Cliff., 210.

§ 1901. **Set-off no defense to tort action.**—A set-off, being a right or title founded on contract, is no defense to a libel founded on a tort, although when loss of service of a minor is the gist of the tort advances to him may be taken into consideration. The Platina,* 21 Law Rep., 397.

§ 1902. **Answer as evidence.**—The answer of the respondent upon oath in reply to interrogatories does not, in the admiralty, constitute positive evidence in his own favor. Its true effect is, either to furnish evidence for the other party, or, in a case doubtful in point of proof, to turn the scale in favor of the respondent. Cushman *v.* Ryan, 1 Story, 91.

§ 1903. The rule of courts of equity as to overcoming the denial in the answer by two witnesses, etc., does not apply in courts of admiralty. Sherwood *v.* Hall, 3 Sumn., 127; Steamboat H. D. Bacon, Newb., 274.

§ 1904. In an action *in rem* for a collision, the answer of the owners of the colliding vessel, admitting facts to their prejudice, will prevail in favor of the libelants against the testimony of the pilot of the vessel to the contrary. The Santa Claus, Olc., 428.

§ 1905. **Insufficiency.**—In admiralty, if the libelant wishes to object to the answer as insufficient, he must do so before the taking of testimony. The Rocket, 1 Biss., 354.

§ 1906. In admiralty, as in equity, if the answer of the respondent is not full, explicit and distinct as to each separate allegation of the libel, exceptions to the answer for insufficiency will be allowed; and the respondent must make a further and better answer. An answer in admiralty may be excepted to as impertinent if a defensive allegation, not responsive to any allegation of the libel, is blended with a response to an allegation of the libel. Such a defensive allegation should be separately stated in an article framed after the manner of an article in a libel. When an answer is responsive to the allegations of the bill, but is not sufficient to constitute a defense, exceptions to it should be for impertinence and not for insufficiency. The California, 1 Saw., 463.

5. *Replication and Supplemental Pleadings.*

§ 1907. **Replication necessary to put in issue truth of answer.**—A replication is necessary in admiralty pleadings, as in equity, to put in issue the truth of the answer, and if a cause be set down for hearing without such replication, the answer will be taken as true. The Mary Jane,* Bl. & How., 390.

§ 1908. **A special replication by the libelant under oath** is not admissible, unless it be demanded by the respondent or ordered by the court, and then it is in the nature of a cross-bill or *reconventio* of the civil law. Coffin *v.* Jenkins, 3 Story, 108.

§ 1909. **An answer need not be under oath unless required by a sworn libel;** and if an answer is not under oath no replication, or notice in place of a replication, that testimony to contradict the answer will be taken, is required. The Infanta, Abb. Adm., 265.

§ 1910. **Where a replication is not filed within the time required** by the rules of the court of admiralty, the libelant will be held to have waived the benefit of the rules in that respect, unless he takes advantage of the point when evidence is offered at the hearing. Thomas *v.* Gray, Bl. & How., 493.

§ 1911. **Proof allowed under pleadings.**— Libel for destroying spirits by carelessness of storing. Answer, that the spirits were well stored, and any damage was owing to defects in barrels. Replication joined. Under this state of the pleading, proof of destruction by a natural cause was not allowed, on the ground that it would be departure from the answer. Turner *v.* The Ship Black Warrior, McAl., 181.

§ 1912. **Replication, when not necessary.**— When a libelant intends merely to deny the truth of the allegations in the answer a replication is not necessary; but when the allegations of the answer are admitted, and intended to be avoided by new facts, the matter in avoidance should be put upon the record; and this is usually done by a supplemental libel though sometimes by replication. Gladding *v.* Constant, 1 Spr., 73; Taber *v.* Jenny, 1 Spr., 315.

§ 1913. **Effect of general replication.**— A general replication has only the effect to put both parties to the proof of the allegations in their respective pleadings not admitted to be true; or of permitting the cause, when the answer operates as a plea in bar, to be set down for hearing upon the libel and answer; and if the libelant wishes to impugn a certain stipulation set up in the answer as a bar to a libel for wages, by introducing facts outside such stipulation, he should do so by amending his libel or filing a special replication. He may, under a general replication, however, contend that the stipulation was void as a matter of law, such general replication operating as a demurrer or exception to the answer. The Atlantic, Abb. Adm., 451.

§ 1914. **Denial of validity of award pleaded in answer.**— If an answer sets up an award of referees as a bar to the libel, and the libelant not denying that such an award was made, but insisting, for certain reasons, that it was not binding, this is new matter in avoidance, which should be put on the record. This is sometimes done by replication, but the more regular mode is by supplemental libel, to which the respondents should answer. Upon engagement to file supplemental libel and answer the court heard the cause. Taber *v.* Jenny,* 9 Law Rep., N. S., 27.

§ 1915. **Where a supplemental libel is filed before the process is returnable** it becomes part of the pleadings without further notice to the respondent, and he is bound to answer it. Thomas *v.* Gray, Bl. & How., 493.

§ 1916. **Supplemental bill for extra compensation.**— When the libelants are pilots and they cannot recover on a salvage claim, but have a valid claim for extra compensation as pilots, they will be allowed to file a supplemental bill for such extra compensation. Dexter *v.* Bark Richmond,* 4 Law Rep., 20.

IV. ADMISSIONS IN PLEADING.

§ 1917. **Allegations as admissions.**— Allegations in pleading are admissions by the pleader, and need no proof unless denied and put in issue; and, as against the pleader, will be taken as matter conceded. Ward *v.* The Brig Fashion, Newb., 8; Fashion *v.* Wards, 6 McL., 152.

§ 1918. **Averments not denied.**— It is a rule of pleading in the courts of common law that every material averment which is not denied will be regarded as admitted; and that rule would seem to apply *a fortiori* in equity, where formal exceptions are discouraged. Surget *v.* Byers, Hemp., 715.

§ 1919. **Where an averment is not traversed it is held to be admitted,** but the rule does not apply to a negative averment not essential to the effect of the pleading. Toland *v.* Sprague, 12 Pet., 300.

§ 1920. Failure to answer matter not well pleaded.— If matter be not well pleaded, and there is no answer to the breach assigned in the declaration, it cannot be considered as an admission of the cause of action stated in the declaration. Simonton *v.* Winter, 5 Pet., 140.

§ 1921. Patents — Effect of neglect to answer.— When no answer is made to an alleged infringement of a patent the charge is admitted. Parker *v.* Bamker, 6 McL., 681.

§ 1922. Plea in bar admits ability of plaintiff to sue.— The rule is general that a plea in bar admits the ability of the plaintiff to sue; and if the parties go to trial on that issue the presumption is reasonable that this admission continues. Yeaton *v.* Lynn, 5 Pet., 223.

§ 1923. Administrator's ability to sue, how admitted.— When a suit is brought by an administrator during the minority of the executor, his powers as administrator are determined when the executor has attained his majority; and the fact that he has not attained his full age must be averred in the declaration. But if this averment be omitted, and the defendant pleads in bar, he admits the ability of the plaintiff to sue, and the judgment is not void. *Ibid.*

§ 1924. Failure to deny averment of citizenship.— An averment that plaintiffs are aliens, uncontradicted, is admitted. Breedlove *v.* Nicolet, 7 Pet., 413.

§ 1925. Pleading to the merits admits plaintiff's capacity to sue. Couard *v.* The Atlantic Insurance Co., 1 Pet., 386.

§ 1926. Infants unprejudiced by omissions of guardians.— Infants cannot be prejudiced by misstatements or omissions of their guardian in his answer. Lenox *v.* Notrebe, Hemp., 251.

§ 1927. A plea of payment admits all the allegations in the plaintiff's declaration essential to support the action, and it is unnecessary for the plaintiff to prove them. Archer *v.* Morehouse, Hemp., 184.

§ 1928. The plea of no rent arrear admits the demise as laid in the avowry. Alexander *v.* Harris, 4 Cr., 299.

§ 1929. Allegations not denied — Iowa code.— By the code of Iowa every material allegation of a declaration must be specifically denied, or it will be held to be admitted. Per Clifford, J., dissenting, in Smith *v.* Sac. Co., 11 Wall., 139.

V. Errors and Defects in Pleading. Waiver. Aider by Verdict.

Summary — *Defects of form and substance, how reached,* §§ 1930-31.— *Motions to strike out apply only to entire pleadings,* § 1932.— *Variance between record and recital thereof,* § 1933.— *Variance between writ and declaration not ground for arrest of judgment,* § 1934.— *Variance between writ and declaration, how objected to,* § 1935.— *Immaterial issue,* § 1936.— *Repleader not awarded by court of error,* § 1937.— *Repleader rarely in favor of party making first fault,* § 1938.— *Immaterial matter, when to be rejected,* § 1939.— *Informality in plea, when cured by verdict,* § 1940.— *Demurrer, though not disposed of, may sometimes be considered as waived,* §§ 1941-42.— *Clerical misprision,* § 1943.— *Law favors curing of defects in pleadings,* § 1944.— *Extension of time for pleading waives no rights,* § 1945.— *Exceptions and motions to strike out in equity,* § 1946.— *Motion to dismiss,* § 1947.— *Motion to substitute one answer for another,* § 1948.

§ 1930. When a pleading has not issuable facts sufficient to constitute a cause of action or a defense, the opposite party should demur. Gause *v.* Knapp, §§ 1949-50.

§ 1931. When a pleading is confused by the intermingling of material and immaterial, issuable and non-issuable allegations, the opposite party should move to make the pleading more definite and certain. *Ibid.*

§ 1932. Motions to strike out must be directed not to special sentences, but to entire pleadings or counts. *Ibid.*

§ 1933. A material variance between the record of a recognizance of special bail and the recital of it in *scire facias* is fatal. Barnes *v.* Lee, §§ 1951-53.

§ 1934. A variance between the writ and declaration is no ground for arrest of judgment. Wilson *v.* Berry, §§ 1934-55.

§ 1935. Variance between writ and declaration should be objected to by plea in abatement or special demurrer. How *v.* McKinney, § 1956.

§ 1936. When the charge is that goods were unladen at Boston without permission from the collector, and the plea that the goods were not unladen without a permit from the collector of the port where they were first entered, to wit, Memphremagog, an issue formed on this plea is immaterial, as the plea does not deny nor confess and avoid the matter of the information. United States *v.* Burnham, §§ 1957-62.

§ 1937. When a verdict for defendant is rendered on bad plea and replication, a court of error can only award final judgment for plaintiff, as it cannot award a repleader. *Ibid.*

§ 1938. Repleader is not ordinarily awarded in favor of the party making the first fault, but it may be done if required by substantial justice. *Ibid.*

§ 1939. That immaterial matter may be rejected as surplusage is not always true. If it constitute a part of a material averment, so that the whole cannot be stricken out without destroying the cause of action or defense, the immaterial matter cannot be rejected as surplusage, but may be traversed, and must be proved as laid. *Ibid.*

§ 1940. Informality in a good plea will be cured by verdict. A bad plea also will be cured, provided it contain enough of substance to put in issue the material parts of the declaration. Garland *v.* Davis, §§ 1968-70.

§ 1941. A demurrer appearing on the record not disposed of may be deemed from circumstances to have been waived. Townsend *v.* Jemison, §§ 1971-80.

§ 1942. A demurrer may be deemed to have been waived by defendant from his proceeding in the case without securing a hearing or decision thereon. *Ibid.*

§ 1943. Clerical misprision is not a ground for reversing the judgment if substance enough appear on the record. *Ibid.*

§ 1944. It is the policy of the law that defects, as far as possible, be cured by verdict. *Ibid.*

§ 1945. A defendant, by allowing an extension of time for filing the declaration, estops himself from taking advantage of the plaintiff's laches in the matter, but waives no other rights. Ricard *v.* New Providence, §§ 1981-83.

§ 1946. *Semble,* that filing of exceptions is not the only method of testing the sufficiency or regularity of an answer, but that in some cases a motion to strike from the files may be entertained. Allis *v.* Stowell, § 1984.

§ 1947. A motion to dismiss a suit for want of a replication will not be granted pending a motion to strike the answer from the files for irregularity. *Ibid.*

§ 1948. A motion to take one answer from the files and substitute another, though not as favorably received as a motion for amendment, yet may be granted in a clear case. Coster *v.* Wood, §§ 1985-86.

[NOTES.— See §§ 1987-2082.]

GAUSE *v.* KNAPP.

(Circuit Court for Missouri: 1 McCrary, 75-78. 1880.)

Opinion by McCRARY, J.

STATEMENT OF FACTS.— This is a motion to strike out a special defense. This cause was before the court at a previous term, Judge Dillon presiding, at which time it was suggested that the questions designed to be raised could be presented in a better form under a special answer. Since then an amended petition and an answer thereto have been filed.

It is of importance, not for this cause alone but for the general practice of the court, that the modes of proceeding should be clearly understood, and I therefore take this occasion to restate some well settled rules which prevail in this court.

§ 1949. *Rules of pleading.*

Mr. Justice Miller, at an early day, with the concurrence of Judges Dillon and Treat, held:

First. That in pleading the parties respectively must aver the issuable facts and nothing more.

If irrelevant and redundant matter is inserted in the petition or answer the court will not entertain a motion to eliminate the same, but will receive a motion to make said pleading more certain and definite. The reason for this ruling is based not only on the essential requisites of good pleading, but on the duty of attorneys to so plead as not to drive the opposing attorney, with the aid of the court, to do the pleading for the party. The function of the court is to pass upon the papers filed, and not to become the pleader for the parties. Let the plaintiff and defendant respectively come to an issue, not on matters of evidence, relevant or irrelevant, but on the ultimate facts determining their respective rights. There is nothing in the Missouri practice act which abrogates these essential rules of pleading. The very object of pleading is to bring the parties face to face with the issuable facts on which their rights depend.

Second. If a pleading has not issuable facts sufficient to constitute a cause of action or a defense, or is mixed with statements as to evidence to support the same, the opposite party may demur, so that the court, disregarding the irrelevant matter, may determine whether the alleged cause of action or special defense has any foundation in law.

Third. If the vicious pleading is so vague and confused that the material and immaterial allegations are intermixed, or a mass of statements are contained therein, some issuable and others non-issuable, the proper practice is a motion to make the pleading more definite and certain.

Fourth. Motions to strike out special clauses or sentences in a pleading this court will not entertain, for it cannot determine in advance of the trial to what issuable facts they may pertain; nor will the court, through such motions, be driven to the necessity, after repeated experiments, of doing practically the pleading for the party in default. This court recognizes, therefore, demurrers and motions to make pleadings more definite and specific. A motion to strike out, if admissible at all, must be directed to an entire pleading or a whole count or division. Matter appearing to be scandalous would form an exception to the rule.

There is a very important consideration in this ruling, which every good pleader will recognize, viz.: that while a demurrer cuts back to the first bad pleading it is by no means sure that a motion to strike out will effect the same end; nor is it sure that the decision on such a motion could be considered a final judgment, entitling the party to a writ of error or appeal.

These general propositions are now reduced to form, not because this case requires the statement of them, but that it may be understood that the rulings of Mr. Justice Miller, and Judges Dillon and Treat, heretofore made on the points stated, are to be adhered to.

As to the motion now before the court it must suffice to say that the question intended to be presented would have been more properly raised on demurrer to the answer, instead of a motion to strike out. But, waiving that technical question, we find that the answer as to the special defense is somewhat vague; yet, if true, it makes it appear that the alleged agreement set up in the petition, if made, was fraudulent and void. The defendants ought to have put themselves distinctly on record by positive averments, yet they have, by liberal construction, done so, and if a demurrer instead of a motion had been interposed, the objection made would have cut back to the petition.

§ 1950. *A contract to give one creditor a preference over others, for consenting to a composition, is void.*

The cause of action as set out discloses imperfectly a contract on the part of plaintiffs to receive a sum of money beyond what other creditors were to receive, for assenting to a *quasi* composition; and such a contract, if the assent of all was required, the law pronounces void.

We regard the answer, liberally construed, as charging in substance that the contract sued on, if made, was one under which the plaintiffs were to receive a secret preference over other creditors of the same debtor, and this, if true, is a perfect defense.

The motion to strike out is overruled. If plaintiff desires a more specific statement of the points of defense he may move therefor, or he may demur to the answer and thus secure a more concise and clear statement. But the present motion, for reasons stated, cannot prevail.

BARNES v. LEE.

(Circuit Court for the District of Columbia: 1 Cranch, C. O., 430–432. 1807.)

Scire facias against special bail.

§ 1951. *Material variance between the record and its recital in the scire facias is fatal.*

Opinion by CRANCH, J.

To this *scire facias* Mr. Lee has pleaded *nul tiel record*, upon which an issue is joined which must be decided by the court upon inspection of the record. If there be such a record as that set forth in the *scire facias* the judgment must be for the plaintiff. But if there be a material variance between the record and the recital of it in the *scire facias* the judgment must be for the defendant.

The first question is, What is the record? The record as made up at large in the record-book is in these words: "Whereupon Edmund J. Lee came into court and undertook, for the said defendant, to satisfy and pay the condemnation of the court, if he should be cast at the trial of this suit, or render his body to prison in execution for the same."

The *scire facias* states, "Edmund J. Lee heretofore," "to wit, on," etc., "came before the court and became pledge and bail for the said David Easton, that if it should happen that the said David Easton should be convicted at the suit of the said John Barnes, in the action aforesaid, then the same bail granted that as well the said damages as all such costs and charges as should be adjudged to the said John Barnes in that behalf should be made of the goods and chattels of the said Edmund J. Lee, and to be levied to the use of the said John Barnes, if it should happen that the said David Easton should not pay the said damages and costs aforesaid, or should not on that account render himself to the prison of our said county."

It is contended by the defendant that the undertaking, as stated in the record, is materially variant from that set forth in the *scire facias*, because the former does not show that the defendant "granted that the damages and costs should be made of his goods and chattels" in case Easton did not pay them or render himself to prison on that account. The undertaking of the defendant, as stated in the record, is only that Easton should pay or render himself to prison; it does not include the usual alternative, "or that the bail will pay it for him," which is the very substance and essence of the undertaking upon which the *scire facias* is grounded.

But it is answered on the part of the plaintiff: 1st. That the obligation of special bail is well known and settled by law and cannot be altered, and when the record states that he came into court and acknowledged himself to be special bail, it states in substance that he acknowledged himself to be bound by all the legal obligations of bail; and that when the record states that he undertook for Easton to pay or render himself to prison, in execution, it implies that if he did not the bail would do it for him; so that the record states the substance of the whole legal obligation of special bail, and the *scire facias* has stated nothing more. 2d. It is also contended that the entry on the minute-book of the day, in these words, "Edmund J. Lee, special bail," au-

· thorized the clerk to make up the records of the recognizance of bail in the legal form, and in no 'other. That the true records of the court are the minutes extended into form, according to their legal import. That if the clerk has erroneously extended the minutes in this case, it is as if he had done nothing; and that the record may now be made up in due form, when it will exactly correspond with the *scire facias*. There is much ingenuity and seems to be some weight in this argument, and it brings us back to the question, what is the record in this case?

§ 1951a. *What is the record of a cause and how made up.*

The daily minutes, taken by the clerk and sanctioned by the court, are only memoranda to assist the memory of the clerk in making up the records of the court. The record is the history of the proceedings in an action made out at full length and in technical language. When the clerk has once made out this history and written it in the record-book his power over it ceases. It has become a public document, and cannot be altered unless by order of the court under certain circumstances. The record, therefore, to which the court is referred by the issue in this case, I take to be that which is entered at length in the record-book, and although the court may perhaps order a clerical error to be corrected, yet such correction now made could not affect the issue in this case, which must be decided according to the record as it stood at the time of the plea pleaded. This principle seems to be settled by the cases of Coy *v.* Hymas, 2 Str., 1171; King's Case, 2 Ld. Raym, 1014, and Salk., 329; Hillier *v.* Frost, 1 Str., 401, and Gray *v.* Jefferson, 2 Str., 1165.

§ 1952. *Liability of special bail not to be enlarged by intendment.*

If, then, the record in the record-book is that which we are to compare with the *scire facias*, the question remains whether there be a substantial variance between them. That there is apparently such variance seems to be admitted; but it is said that when a man undertakes that another shall do a thing, if this other fails to do it, there is an implied obligation on the part of the former that he will do it for him. This may perhaps be true in some cases of contract, and such implied obligation may perhaps support an action; but it does not therefore follow that such implied obligation can arise upon a recognizance, nor that it will authorize an execution to issue without a previous judgment. A recognizance is a solemn acknowledgment upon record, and contains all the terms of the obligation which the party takes upon himself. In the present case the court deems the omission of the usual alternative (" or that he will do it for him ") to be fatal.

§ 1953. *Quære, as to power of amendment over record.*

I have a doubt whether, if the plaintiff chooses to quash his *scire facias* and then apply to have the record amended, I should not think it ought to be amended; and that he might then bring a new *scire facias* upon the amended record. But upon this last point the court has not made up an opinion.

WILSON v. BERRY.

(Circuit Court for the District of Columbia: 2 Cranch, C. C., 707-716. 1826.)

STATEMENT OF FACTS.— In this case the *capias* was in trespass on the case, and the declaration in covenant on a sealed instrument. Verdict for plaintiff, and motion in arrest of judgment.

§ 1954. *A variance between the capias ad respondendum and the declaration will not warrant an arrest of judgment. Authorities reviewed.*

Opinion by CRANCH, J.

This is a motion in arrest of judgment for variance between the writ of *capias ad respondendum* and the declaration; the writ being in trespass on the case, and the declaration being in covenant.

"Arrests of judgment arise from intrinsic causes appearing on the face of the record; of this kind are, 1. Where the declaration varies totally from the original writ; as where the writ is in debt, and the plaintiff declares in an action upon the case for an *assumpsit;* for the original writ out of chancery being the foundation and warrant of the whole proceedings in the common pleas, if the declaration does not pursue the nature of the writ the court's authority totally fails." 3 Bl. Comm., 393.

In England, pleas in abatement to the count could only be pleaded in actions by original writ. After declaration, formerly, the defendant might demand *oyer* of the writ, and then, the same being set forth on the roll, if there were any variance between the count and the writ, and a record or specialty, etc., mentioned in the count, the defendant might plead such variance in abatement or demur, move in arrest of judgment or sustain error. 1 Chitty's Pleadings, 438; Hole *v.* Finch, 2 Wils., 394; Com. Dig., Abatement, G., 8; 3 Instr. Cl., 62; Reg. Pl., 277, 278. But as the variance between the writ and count could in no case be pleaded without craving *oyer* of the writ (Hole *v.* Finch, 2 Wils., 394, 395), and the defendant cannot now have such *oyer*, such variance or defect is no longer pleadable in abatement, and if it be pleaded in abatement the plaintiff may sign judgment or move the court to set the plea aside. 1 Chitty, 438; Murray *v.* Hubbart, 1 B. & P., 646, 647; Gray *et al. v.* Sidneff, 3 B. & P., 395; Deshons *v.* Head, 7 East, 383; Boats *v.* Edwards, Doug., 227; Spalding *v.* Mure, 6 T. R., 364. Nor will the court set aside the proceeding in respect of the variance, as *oyer* of the writ cannot now be craved. Hole *v.* Finch, 2 Wils., 393; Oakley *qui tam v.* Giles, 3 East, 167; 1 Chitty, 247, 249; Boats *v.* Edwards, Doug., 227.

It is one of the general requisites of a declaration that it corresponds with the process (Com. Dig., Pleader, C., 13), and in bailable actions with the *ac etiam* and affidavit to hold the bail. 1 Chitty, 248.

Regularly the declaration should correspond with the process; but as, according to the present practice of the courts, *oyer* of the writ cannot be craved, and a variance between the writ and declaration cannot in any case be pleaded in abatement (1 Saund., 318, n. 3; Gray *v.* Sidneff, 3 B. & P., 295; Spalding *v.* Mure, 6 T. R., 364), and as there are several instances in which the court will not set aside the proceedings on account of a variance between the writ and declaration, many of the older decisions are no longer applicable in practice. In the king's bench, when the proceedings are by special original, the venue must be laid in the county into which the original was issued, or in bailable cases the bail will be discharged; but in the common pleas the bail would not be discharged by such variance. Smithson *v.* White, Welles, 461; Smithson *v.* Smith, Barnes, 94; Stroud *v.* Lady Gerard, Salk., 8; Doo *v.* Butcher, 3 T. R., 611; Hole *v.* Finch, 2 Wils., 393; Bac. Ab., tit. Pleas, I, 11; Tidd, 582, n. i; Benson *v.* Derby, 1 Ld. Raym., 240, cont.

Chitty (vol. i, p. 254) says, "Upon common process by bill in the king's bench, or upon a *capias*, or original *quare clausum fregit* in the common pleas, the plaintiff may declare in any cause of action whatever although the writ in each case is in trespass. Foster v. Bonner, Cowp., 455. But in bailable actions the declaration must correspond with the cause and the form of action in the affidavit and the *ac etiam* part of the *latitat* or other process, for otherwise the defendant will be discharged out of custody upon filing common bail; but this will be the only consequence, for the court will not in such a case set aside the proceedings for irregularity." And even, " When the proceeding has been by special original, if thère be a variance between it and the declaration the defendant will be discharged on entering a common appearance; but the proceedings will not be set aside merely on account of a variance in the cause of action; and therefore the only consequence of the mistake is that the plaintiff loses the security of the bail."

In Hole v. Finch, and Jackson v. Doleman, 2 Wils., 395, the court said, " One reason why the court should not interpose is that after the defendant hath appeared and is in court there is an end of the *mesne process;* and if the defendant craves *oyer*, it must be of the original writ; he cannot have it of the *mesne process;* and if application was to be made to the master of the rolls, he certainly would not refuse to order right originals to be made out in both these cases."

In the case of Murray v. Hubbart, 1 B. & P., 647, Eyre, C. J., said: " The arrest, however, is not the operation of the writ, but of the *mesne process*, which is out of the question, after appearance."

"The objection to the *mesne process* being cured by appearance in the true name, the writ, whenever it is properly called for, will be found to be a writ against the party by his true name." " The case, therefore, comes to this: that so long as it is the practice of the court to issue the *mesne process* first and to allow an original to be sued out afterwards, if necessary to substantiate the proceedings, no advantage can be taken after appearance of a misnomer in *mesne process*."

In Gray et al. v. Sidneff, 3 B. & P., 348, Lord Alvanley, C. J., in delivering the opinion of the court, said, " It has been long the practice not to grant *oyer* of original writs; and though, perhaps, such refusal may be considered in the first instance to have been a strong measure, yet it was the necessary consequence of assuming jurisdiction without original." " When courts adopt a fiction they must necessarily support it. The court of king's bench would not allow a party to say that he was not in the custody of the marshal; nor the court of exchequer that he was not the king's debtor. By this doctrine no right is taken away from the subject, nor is he proceeded against in any way injurious to himself. If such a plea were to be allowed, the master of the rolls would issue a new writ agreeable to the declaration. If the court thinks itself at liberty to proceed without an original, it will never permit a mode of proceeding to be adopted which will have the effect of compelling the plaintiff to sue out that original which the court feels itself justified in acting without." See, also, Dèshons v. Head, 7 East, 383; 1 Saund., 318, n. 3.

In England, neither the original writ nor the *mesne process* is entered on the roll, so as to form any part of the record, either in the king's bench or common pleas.

A record in the king's bench commences in this form: " London, *ss*. Memorandum that on Monday next, after three weeks of St. Michael, in that term, before our lord the king at Westminster, came R. B. by D. S., his attorney, and brought here into the court of our said lord the king, then and there, his certain bill against C. D. in the custody of the marshal, etc., of a plea of trespass on the case; and there are pledges of prosecution, to wit, John Doe and Richard Roe, which said bill follows in these words, to wit: London, *ss.* R. B. complains of C. D. in the custody of the marshal of the marshalsea of our lord the king, before the king himself being, for this, to wit," etc. See 1 Modus Intrandi, 1; Barker *v.* Thorald, 1 Saund., 40.

A record in the court of common pleas commences in this form: "Essex, *ss.* Elizabeth Savil, late of, etc., in the county aforesaid, administratrix, etc., was summoned to answer to Thomas Wallford of a plea that she render to him £300, which she detains from him; whereupon the said Thomas, by John Reynolds, his attorney, says," etc.

A record in the king's bench, when sent up by writ of error, is headed thus: "Pleas before our lord the king at Westminster, of the term of the Holy Trinity, in the second year of the reign of our lord James the Second, now king of England," etc. Rot., 139; Gray *v.* Briggs, 1 Lutwyche, 889. A record from the common pleas is headed thus: "Pleas at Westminster, before George Treby, knight, and his associate justices of our lord the king of the bench, *ss.* In the term of St. Hilary in the tenth and eleventh years of the reign of our lord William the Third," etc. Rot., 1337.

It appears by the case of Longville *v.* Hundred of Thistlewood, 6 Mod., 27, that judgment cannot be arrested for variance between the original writ and declaration, unless the writ be made part of the record by oyer. There is no case in the books where judgment has been arrested for variance between the declaration and the process.

In the case of Bragg *v.* Digby, 2 Salk., 658, "the defendant, without praying oyer of the original writ, pleaded variance between the writ and count, showing particularly wherein; and the plaintiff demurred; and it was adjudged that the defendant should answer over, for he ought to have demanded oyer of the writ before he could take advantage of the variance; because, although the writ is in court, yet not being upon the same roll with the count, the defendant cannot plead to it without demanding oyer."

And in Ellery *v.* Hicks and Wife, 4 Mod., 246, upon a motion in arrest of judgment on the ground of a variance between the original writ and declaration, "the exception was disallowed, because the defendant cannot take advantage of an ill original without demanding oyer of it, which had not been done." See, also, Stephens *v.* White, 2 Wash., 212, Mr. Justice Lyon's opinion. In Lindo *v.* Gardner, 1 Cranch, 344, there is a note of the reporter, intimating that in Maryland the *capias ad respondendum* is considered as part of the record; but this is the mere *dictum* of the reporter, unsupported by any authority.

In the case of Lowry *v.* Lawrence, 1 N. Y. T. R., 71, the court said "that the declaration must be captioned (entitled) of the term when the writ is returned served;" and the court must (from the recital at the head of the declaration, that "heretofore, to wit, on the third Tuesday of July, in July term, 1801, came William Lowry and brought into the said court then and there his bill," etc.) "necessarily intend the fact that the writ was returned in July term, 1801, and of course the action, both in fact and technically speaking, commenced previously to that time."

This reasoning shows that the writ itself was not considered as part of the record; because, if the writ itself had been officially before the court, the judges would not have resorted to inference for proof of the time of its issuing or of its return, but would have looked at the writ itself.

Finch, in his "Common Law" (folio 54 b, French edition, p. 172 of the English edition of 1759, lib. 3, ch. 1) says, "such is the commencement of the suit" (that is, the original writ). "The proceeding until judgment consists of two parts, the parol and the process, and this is proved by the form of the writ of error; because in the record and process and the giving judgment of the plaint, etc. Reg. Bre., 116; 8 Co., 157 b. The parol which is called the plaint is that which depends in plea, namely, all the time until judgment; for after judgment the suit is not said depending. And all this is entered of record in a roll, which is called the plea-roll; but the entry of the original writ in the roll is but superfluous, forasmuch as the writ always remains of record and is sufficient by itself; but it shall not have any roll, although the contrary is used. Variance in any part of the original writ shall be amended at any time." "Stat. 14 E. 3, c. 6; 9 H. 5, c. 4; 4 H. 6, c. 3; 8 H. 6, c. 12, 15; 5 G. 1, c. 13;" 8 Co., 156 b.

And, again, in p. 177 (folio 56 a) he says: "After the count, the defendant, for his aid to plead better, shall have oyer, if he demand it, of everything which is not parcel of the record, as of the writ and return thereof; of an obligation and the condition, and the like."

In Arthur Blackmore's Case, 8 Co., 156 b, 157 a, Lord Coke says: "So, at the common law, the judges might amend as well their judgment as any other part of the record, etc., in the same term (Co. Lit., 260 a; 5 Co., 74 b); for during the same term the record is in the breast of the judges and not in the roll. But at the common law the misprision of clerks, in another term, in the process, was not amendable by the court; for in another term the roll is the record, and therefore, by 14 E. 3, ch. 6, it is enacted, etc., that no process shall be annulled," etc. "But this statute doth not extend to an original writ, nor to a writ which is in the nature of an original, for that is not included in this word process." "Recordum" (in the writ of error) contains "the plea-roll;" "Processus, all the proceedings out of it till judgment." 8 Co., 157 b. "And the first part of the record is the count." 8 Co., 161 a.

Blackstone (3 Bl. Com., 272, 273) says the original writ, issued out of chancery, "is the foundation of the jurisdiction of the court; being the king's warrant to proceed to the determination of the cause. For it was a maxim, introduced by the Normans, that there should be no proceedings in the common pleas before the king's justices without his original writ, because they held it unfit that those justices, being only substitutes for the crown, should take cognizance of anything but what was thus expressly referred to their judgment." Flet., b. 2, c. 34; Gilb., Com. Pleas, Introduction, X; Gilb., Com. Pl., 2; Flet., 58. See, also, Finch, 198, as to the definition of process, mesne process, and judicial process. Finch, 168, says, "Until the original writ be returned the suit is not said depending;" "nor can the courts hold plea but upon an original returned before them."

Gilbert, in his History of the Practice of the Common Pleas, page 26, says: "The appearance of the plaintiff and defendant in propria persona, at the return of the writ, is recorded by the philazer" (the officer who issues process), "because he was to continue the process of the court till the prothonotary took it upon the declaration; this prothonotary sets forth the authority by which the court proceeded, that the court might appear to have cognizance of the cause, and that they pursued their warrant; and therefore in all actions where the first process is by summons, though he did not appear at the return of the summons, and they had issued several mesne writs, yet they only took notice of the summons, and said *summonitus fuit ad respondendum*, and so in trespass, *attachiatus fuit ad respondendum*." See, also, pages 96, 97. And in page 42 Gilbert says further, "But where there is a variance between the original and the count, or the bond, and oyer prayed, there the variance may be pleaded, because it was usual for the pleaders to show it to the court and have the writ abated; these, taken down by the prothonotary, were the original of those pleas in abatement; but when the recital of the writ and the count itself were entered on record, if there were any material variance, the defendant might take advantage of it, not only by way of plea, but by motion in arrest of judgment after the verdict, or by a writ of error; because the writ being the foundation and warrant of the whole proceedings, if the plaintiff did not pursue it by his count there was no authority to the court to proceed in such cases."

A mistake in the recital of the writ is immaterial after verdict; and if there be a variance between the recital of the writ and the count, the court, unless the contrary appears, will, after verdict, intend that there was a good original, and that the plaintiff's clerk had made a mistake in the recital of it. Redmond *v.* Edlon, 1 Saund., 317, 318.

Again, in chapter 10, page 86, Gilbert says, " that matter amendable, and matter of form, as the law now stands, will not arrest judgment." And in page 87 he says, "That part of the count which recites the writ was amendable at common law;" and in page 95, "The writ" (meaning the original writ) "is amendable if there be false Latin, if it be only in the form of the writ; but if it be in the substance it shall not be amendable; for the statute gives the court leave, where they have sufficient authority to proceed, to amend the form, but not to make an authority for themselves by altering the substance of the writ." See, also, Tidd's Pr., 124, and Davis *v.* Owen, 1 B. & P., 343, that the *capias* is no part of the record and may be amended.

§ **1955.** *Result of authorities. Distinction between the office of the writ in England and in the United States.*

The result of my reflections is this: In England, the reason why a variance between the original writ and count was fatal was because the original writ was the foundation of the authority of the court to take cognizance of the cause and the warrant to the judges to proceed to judgment. It was necessary that they should pursue their authority strictly. Their acts, if not warranted by the writ, were void. But as these writs have, for a long time, been grantable of common right (*ex debito justitiæ*), and as the jurisdiction of the courts has been so long established and precisely ascertained, it became apparent to the whole nation that a particular warrant to the judges, in every case, was wholly unnecessary and had become a mere matter of form. The judges themselves, finding that justice was often defeated or delayed by exceptions taken to the accidental variance between the count and the writ, even after the parties had pleaded and gone to trial upon the merits, decided that the defendant should not take advantage of such variance without oyer of the writ; and finally that oyer should not be granted when that was the object, and that if a variance appeared between the recital of the writ and the count, they would, after verdict, intend that there was a good ·original, which had been misrecited by the misprision of the clerk, so that, at this time, no advantage can, in England, be taken of any such variance.

In that country the judicial power is not separated from the executive. The king is the source of all judicial authority. In theory, he himself is supposed to exercise judicial power. The judges are his delegates or substitutes, and can hear no cause unless it be referred to them by the king, or be brought before them by his order. Hence the necessity, at first, of original writs.

But in this country the judicial power is a separate branch of the national sovereignty. It does not emanate from the executive; and after being organized by the legislature it is independent of both. It exercises its functions *suo jure*, although the jurisdiction of each particular tribunal is described and defined by the legislature at the time of its erection. It is not necessary that each particular case should be referred to the court by a higher authority. It requires no original writ to warrant its proceedings. Every person has access to it, as of common right. It is bound to hear and determine every case brought judicially before it, of which it has jurisdiction. The writ which is issued to compel the appearance of the defendant is what, in England, is called process, issued from the court itself, and not an original writ issuing from another tribunal. Although it may be called the original writ because it is the first writ which issues in the cause, yet it has not the qualities of the English original writ; and no variance between it and the count can abate it, because it is not the foundation of the authority of the court; and, if it could be thus abated, the abatement of the process, issuing from the court itself, could not deprive the court of that cognizance of the cause which it must have had before it issued the process.

There is no instance in the English books of a plea in abatement, or of an arrest of judgment for variance between the count and the process. Such variance is seldom noticed, unless it affect the interest of third parties, as in bailable cases, or unless it be very material. The mode of taking advantage of such variance is not by plea, but by motion either to discharge the bail or to set aside the proceedings for irregularity. It is a motion to the discretion of the court, not as a matter of strict right; and the court varies the remedy according to the justice of the case. 1 Chitty, Pleadings, 248, 254.

When we find that the English courts have deemed it necessary for the purposes of justice to throw obstacles in the way of taking advantage of a variance between the original writ and the count, and that no advantage, by way of plea, or motion in arrest of judgment, can there be taken of a variance between the process and the count, it would seem strange that we, who have no original writ sent to us as the foundation of our jurisdiction, should decide that the process is abated by its variance from the declaration, or that judgment should be arrested for that cause. The English doctrine respecting the original writ is wholly inapplicable to our courts, and a doctrine which for its injustice and inconvenience has been reprobated there ought not to be gratuitously assumed here. The reason why, in England, judgment was arrested for variance between the original writ and count was that the court had no jurisdiction of the cause actually prosecuted; and it is never too late, before judgment, to show that the court has no authority to give the judgment which is asked. But in this country an error in the process does not affect the jurisdiction or authority of the court, especially when the defendant has appeared upon that process and pleaded to the action. The process is only the means of bringing the defendant into court. If he appear and do not object to the process, nor move to be discharged on account of its irregularity, but submit himself to the jurisdiction of the court, it is immaterial by what sort of process he is brought in.

But it may be asked, shall a man arrested for trespass be obliged to answer to the plaintiff in an action of debt? In answer it may be asked, why not here as well as in England? No inconvenience is felt there in this course of proceeding. The only objection would be on behalf of the bail, and he might be relieved on motion.

I think it quite immaterial whether the *capias ad respondendum* be or be not part of the record; for if it be, a variance between it and the count is not fatal, for the reasons before stated; and if it be not a part of the record the variance does not judicially appear, and cannot be noticed by the court. The motion in arrest of judgment is overruled.

HOW v. McKINNEY.

(Circuit Court for Indiana: 1 McLean, 319, 320. 1838.)

Opinion of the COURT.

STATEMENT OF FACTS.— In this case a motion was made by Mr. Pettit, who appears for the defendants, to quash the writ on the following grounds: 1. Because the declaration varies from the writ. 2. Because the writ is in case, and the indorsement on it is special, on a promissory note, and bail required. 3. The writ is too general, being simply trespass on the case.

§ 1956. *In case of variance between writ and declaration a plea in abatement or special demurrer is the proper remedy.*

The second and third objections to the writ are not sustainable. The writ is in the usual form and is good. And, as to the objection of variance between the writ and the declaration, that should be taken advantage of by plea in abatement or a special demurrer. A practice, it is said, has been adopted in one of the judicial circuits of this state to take advantage of any variance between the writ and declaration by a motion in this form. And it is insisted that this is in conformity with the English practice.

It is true that a plea in abatement or demurrer for this variance is not now filed, as formerly, in England; and the reason is because, under a rule of court, oyer of the writ is refused; and without craving oyer this matter cannot be pleaded. 2 Wils., 394–5; 1 Bos. & Pull., 646–7; 3 Bos. & Pull., 395; 7 East, 383. Nor will the court set aside the proceeding in respect of the variance. 2 Wils., 393; 3 East, 167. But this practice has not been adopted by the courts of the United States, nor does it appear that any decision of the supreme court of this state has sanctioned the practice of the circuit referred to.

In the case of Duval v. Craig *et al.*, 2 Wheat., 45, the supreme court held that variances between the writ and the declaration are matters pleadable in abatement only, and cannot be taken advantage of upon general demurrer to the declaration. And also in the case of Chirac *et al.* v. Reinecker, 11 Wheat., 280, the court say variances between the writ and declaration are, in general, matters proper for pleas in abatement, and if in any case such variances can be taken advantage of by defendant, it is an established rule that it can only be done upon oyer of the writ, granted in some proper stage of the cause. The motion to quash is overruled.

UNITED STATES v. BURNHAM.

(Circuit Court for Massachusetts: 1 Mason, 57–70. 1816.)

STATEMENT OF FACTS.— This was a writ of error from a district court, rendered upon an information *in rem* against certain goods and merchandise seized on land by the collector of the district of Boston and Charlestown.

Opinion by STORY, J.

Rarely has any record come before the court, attended with more embarrassing circumstances, where the merits of the cause lay in so narrow a compass. The information in substance charges that the goods and merchandise being of foreign growth and manufacture, and liable to the payment of duties, were imported and brought into the United States from some foreign port or place unknown, and, being so imported, were afterwards unladen and delivered from the said vessel within the United States, to wit, at the port of Boston, in the district of Boston and Charlestown, without a special permit or license from the collector, naval officer, or other competent officer of the said port, for such unlading and delivery, contrary to the statute in such case made and provided; and it further avers that the duties to which said goods and merchandise were liable had not been paid or secured to be paid according to law; by reason of all which, and by force of the said statute, they became forfeited. It is obvious from this summary statement that the information rests on the fiftieth section of the collection act of 2d March, 1799, chapter 128; and to bring the case within that section, it was neither material nor proper to allege that the goods were of foreign growth or manufacture, or liable to the payment of duties, or that the duties due thereon had not been paid or secured to be paid according to law; for no such qualifications are incorporated into the language of the section, or are implied by intendment of law. It was the policy of the legislature, in order to suppress smuggling, to prohibit any goods brought in any vessel from any foreign port, whether of foreign or domestic growth or manufacture, or whether liable to duties or free, from being unladen without a permit from the proper officer at the port of unlivery. It is generally unnecessary and often perilous, in informations upon revenue laws, to make the allegations more broad or more narrow than the terms in which the prohibition is expressed in the statutes themselves; and the present case is an example of the inconvenience of any deviation from the strictness of pleading.

The plea of the claimant alleges that the duties to which the goods and merchandise were liable have been paid or secured to be paid according to law; and that they were not unladen or delivered within the United States without a special license or permit from the collector of the United States at the port or district where said goods and merchandise were first entered, viz., the district of Memphremagog; and that the goods have not become forfeited as alleged in the information. The replication alleges that the duties to which the goods were liable had not been paid or secured to be paid according to law, and that the same were unladen and delivered within the United States without a special license or permit from the collector of the customs at the port where the goods were entered; and that the same have become forfeited, as in the information alleged; and concludes with an issue to the country, which is joined by the claimant.

§ 1957. *Immaterial issues formed by the plea and replication.*

Independent of the objections to these pleadings on account of their inartificial structure and duplicity, the fact put in issue, as to the payment or security of the duties, is upon this information wholly immaterial. If the goods were unladen without a permit they would be clearly forfeited under the statute, although the duties had been paid or secured; and on the other hand, although the duties might have been paid or secured to be paid, yet, if there had not been an unlading without a permit, the goods would be safe from the penalty of the statute. A verdict, therefore, finding the payment or non-payment of the duties would be in every view of the information without any legal efficacy.

The other allegation of fact in the plea, upon which issue was taken in the republication, was doubtless intended as a traverse of that averment in the information, which constituted the very *gist* of the action, but in the terms in which it is expressed it does not meet the point.

The information charges "that the said goods and merchandise, being imported and brought as aforesaid, were afterwards, to wit, on the same day of January, unladen and delivered from the said vessel within the United States, to wit, at the port of Boston, in the district aforesaid, without a special license or permit from the collector, naval officer, or any other competent officer of the said port, for such unlading and delivery;" the traverse on the plea is "that they were not unladen or delivered within the United States without a special license ȯr permit from the collector of the customs of the United States at the port or district where said goods were first entered, viz., the district of Memphremagog." The substance of the charge in the information is that the goods were unladen at Boston without a permit from the collector, etc., of that port; the substance of the plea is that the goods were not unladen without a permit from the collector of the port or district where they were first entered, to wit, the district of Memphremagog. The plea, therefore, contains neither a denial, nor a confession and avoidance, of the matter in the information; but alleges matter totally distinct (and even that by way of negative allegation), which, whether true or false, has nothing to do with the controversy between the parties; and the plea might be strictly true in point of fact, and yet the forfeiture charged in the information might have been incurred, for the goods might have been unladen from a vessel at Boston without a permit from the collector of that port, notwithstanding they might have been first entered and the duties secured, and a permit granted, in the district of Memphremagog. The issue joined on this allegation in the plea is therefore immaterial, and it has this additional vice, that as it neither traverses nor denies the material averments of the information, it must be deemed in law to admit them. Nicholson *v.* Simpson, 1 Str., 297; Blake *v.* West, 1 Ld. Raym., 504.

§ 1958. *When plea and replication are so bad that a verdict on them cannot stand, final judgment goes for plaintiff, if the complaint contains matter enough to warrant it.*

It follows that, as the plea and replication are in this view bad, the verdict founded on them cannot avail the defendant, even supposing that the point of law raised in the bill of exceptions should be decided in his favor, for the court must pronounce upon the whole record, and if the plea and replication are bad and immaterial, and the information contains sufficient matter to warrant a judgment (as this certainly does), there must be a final judgment for the United States.

§ 1959. *Repleader never awarded by a court of error.*

If this had been a case originally depending in this court, a repleader might perhaps have been proper to be awarded, for although, in general, a repleader is not grantable in favor of the person who made the first fault in pleading, nor where the court can give judgment upon the whole record, yet if it appear that substantial justice will not otherwise be done the court might award it. But this court sits in this cause as a court of error, and although the practice was anciently otherwise, a repleader is now never awarded by a court of error. Holbage v. Bennet, 2 Keble, 739, 769, 825; Bennet v. Holbeck, 2 Saund., 317; Crosse v. Bilson, 6 Mod., 102.

§ 1960. *Immaterial allegations, when to be rejected and when to be proved.*

To avoid the effect of these principles, and to save the defendant from the perils of mispleadings, it is argued that in the allegation of the information that the goods "were unladen and delivered from the said vessel within the United States, to wit, at the port of Boston, in said district aforesaid," the words under the *videlicet* may be rejected as surplusage, so as not to tie up the proof to an unlading at Boston; and in like manner the words under the *videlicet* in the plea ("viz., the district of Memphremagog") may be rejected as surplusage so as not to tie up the proof to the district of Memphremagog, and then the issue, though informal, will yet meet the point of the information. This argument proceeds upon the supposition that the matters stated under the *videlicet* are immaterial, and that whatever is immaterial may be rejected as surplusage. But it is by no means generally true that whatever is immaterial may be rejected as surplusage. If the immaterial matter constitute a part of a material averment, so that the whole cannot be struck out without destroying the right of action or defense of the party, there the immaterial matter cannot be rejected as surplusage, but may be traversed in pleading, and must be proved as laid, though the averment be more particular than it need have been. 2 Saund., 206, note 27; Williamson v. Allison, 2 East, 446; Bristow v. Wright, Doug., 665; Savage v. Smith, 2 W. Black., 1101. The doctrine has, in some cases, been pressed somewhat further, and a distinction taken between immaterial and impertinent averments, that the latter need not be proved, though the former must, because relative to the point in question. Doug., 665; 2 W. Black., 1101; 2 East, 446. The true rule seems to be, that whenever the whole allegation may be struck out without affecting the legal right set up by the party, it is impertinent and may be rejected as surplusage. But if the immaterial matter be sensible in the place where it occurs, and constitute a part of a material allegation, then it cannot be rejected, but may be traversed, and must be proved if put in issue. Nor is it true, as urged in the argument, that matter stated under a *videlicet* is mere surplusage. It is sometimes used to explain what goes before it, and if the explanation be consistent with the preceding matter it is traversable; so it is sometimes used to restrain the generality of the former words, where they are not express and special, and then it is traversable. And whenever a *videlicet* contains matter which is material and necessary to be alleged, it is considered as a direct and positive averment, and, as such, traversable in the same manner as if no *videlicet* had been inserted. Skinner v. Andrews, 1 Saund., 170; Stukely v. Butler, Hob., 175; Hayman v. Rogers, 1 Str., 232; Bissex v. Bissex, 3 Burr., 1729; Knight v. Preston, 2 Wils., 332; Grimwood v. Barrit, 6 Term R., 460; Dakin's Case, 2 Saund., 291, and note 1; King v. Stevens, 5 East, 254. If the matter alleged under the *videlicet* in the information or plea be tried by these rules, it will not be easy to reject it as surplusage. It is evidently explanatory of the generality of the preceding words, and consistent and sensible in the place where it occurs, and, therefore, just as much a part of the preceding allegation as if it had been stated without a *videlicet*. The matter, also, under the *videlicet* in the information was material, and pertinent to be alleged.

The fiftieth section of the collection act, on which this information is founded, manifestly contemplates that the goods are unladen within some port or place of a district of the United States, without a permit from the collector of the particular port or district where they are unladen. If the unlading be within the maritime limits of the United States, before an arrival at any port, the case seems properly to fall within the twenty-seventh section, and not within the fiftieth section of the act. 1 Gall., 115. To bring the case within the purview of the fiftieth section it is therefore necessary to allege in the information that the goods were unladen within some port, or other place within a collection district, without a permit from the collector of such district. I do not say that it is necessary to specify the particular port or district by its legal name, for it would be sufficient to state it to be unknown to the attorney of the United States; but it must judicially appear in the information to be an unlading within some port or district, and if the United States should choose to specify the particular port or district, they are bound by the specification. In the present information the matter under the *videlicet* would, independent of this ground, have been material, because it is referred to in the subsequent part of the allegation. The unlading is alleged to be without a permit from the collector of the same port, and if the words under the *videlicet* were struck out there would be a material defect in the information; for even supposing that the words " the said port" could then be referred to the introductory part, so as to mean the port of Boston, still, as a collector has no authority to grant a permit, nor is there any necessity of obtaining one from him, except for an unlading within his district, there would be nothing remaining in the information to show that the unlading was within the district of Boston and Charlestown, so as to render a permit from him necessary, or to make its non-existence a cause of forfeiture.

The matter also alleged under the *videlicet* in the plea (even supposing that the plea, as containing a negative allegation of new matter, could be sustained) is open to many of the observations which have been already made, and upon other distinct grounds must be held material. It is, however, unnecessary to review these grounds, because, for the reasons already stated, the plea has a fatal defect.

§ 1961. *Bill of exceptions, how to be drawn up.*

The insufficiencies of the pleadings render it unnecessary to consider the point of law intended to be raised by the bill of exceptions. I say intended to be raised, for the bill of exceptions is so inartificially drawn that it is very doubtful if it presents any distinct question of law. The bill contains a very unnecessary and prolix recital of all the evidence given on the trial in the very language of the depositions and witnesses, the greater part of which evidence is totally impertinent to the point of law. And the district attorney then prays the court to instruct the jury, among other things, that a forfeiture of the merchandise must, therefore, " under all the circumstances of the case," be considered as resulting of course. What those circumstances were was matter of fact for the consideration of the jury, and did not properly fall within the province of the court to ascertain or decide. It is very clear, therefore, that the court was not bound to give the instruction in the manner in which it was asked. Smith *v.* Carrington, 4 Cr., 62. The proper course would have been, if the facts on which the point of law arose were not in dispute, to have stated them shortly and succinctly, as facts in proof, and prayed the court to instruct the jury on the law arising out of them; and if the facts were in dispute, to have prayed the court to instruct the jury as to the law, if they should find the facts as the party alleged them.

§ 1962. *Disadvantage of irregularity in pleading.*

I regret extremely that I have been compelled by a sense of duty to take notice of the irregularities in the pleadings and exceptions in this case, which I am quite sure were simply owing to the unavoidable haste in which they were prepared by the learned counsel. Nothing could have been a more unwelcome and irksome task to me. Irregularity in pleading tends greatly to increase the embarrassments as well as the labors of the court. It also very frequently commits the substantial interests of the parties, and defeats the purposes of justice. It is a melancholy reflection that much of the time of courts of justice is employed in ingenious devices and laborious technical study to disentangle the merits of causes from the difficulties in which they are involved by the parties.

I recommend to the counsel in this case to enter into an agreement to set aside the judgment and all the pleadings, and to plead anew, so that the real merits of the cause may be tried at the bar of this court. If such an agreement be not entered into, for the reasons which have already been mentioned, I shall feel myself compelled to pronounce a reversal of the judgment of the district court, and to award a final judgment in favor of the United States.

. GARLAND *v.* DAVIS.

(4 Howard, 131-155. 1845.)

ERROR to the Circuit Court for the District of Columbia.

Opinion by MR. JUSTICE WOODBURY.

In the examination of this case a defect has been discovered in the pleadings and verdict which was not noticed in the court below nor suggested by the counsel here. And the first question is whether, under these circumstances, it can be considered by us; and, if it can be, and is a material defect, not cured or otherwise capable of being overcome, whether it ought to be made a ground for reversing the judgment and sending the case back for amendment and further proceedings.

§ 1963. *Where the whole record is brought before this court notice will be taken of defects apparent thereon.*

There can be no doubt that exceptions to the opinions given by courts below must all be taken at the time the opinions are pronounced. But it is equally clear that when the whole record is before the court above, as in this case, any exception appearing on it can be taken by counsel which could have been taken below. Roach *v.* Hulings, 16 Pet., 319. So it is the duty of the court to give judgment on the whole record and not merely on the points stated by counsel. Slacum *v.* Pomeroy, 6 Cranch, 221; Baird & Co. *v.* Mattox, 1 Call, 257; 16 Pet., 319.

In United States *v.* Burnham, 1 Mason, 62, the court alone took notice of the defect which was the sole ground of its opinion. In Patterson *v.* United States, 2 Wheat., 222, it is stated that "the points made were not considered by the court, and judgment was pronounced on other grounds;" and Justice Washington says (p. 224): "The court considers it to be unnecessary to decide the questions which were argued at the bar, as the verdict is so defective that no judgment can be rendered upon it;" and on that account the proceedings below were reversed. See, also, Harrison *v.* Nixon, 9 Pet., 483, 535.

STATEMENT OF FACTS.—I proceed, then, to consider the nature and character of the difficulty in this case appearing on the record. Since discovering it, an opportunity has been given to the counsel for the original plaintiff, which has been improved, to attempt to remove it by argument and authorities. But it still remains and consists in this.

The declaration is an action on the case, sounding in tort. It sets out no contract except one by way of inducement, made by Mr. Franklin, the predecessor in office of the defendant, and it then proceeds to make the gist of its complaint a wrongful and injurious neglect and refusal by the defendant to furnish a copy of certain laws to the plaintiff, as had been agreed by Franklin. We are required to take this view of the declaration, not only by the averments in it, but by both the present and past positions of the counsel for the plaintiff, that it was intended to be founded on a misfeasance. The plea, however, instead of being "not guilty," as was proper in such case (Com. Dig., Pleader), is *non assumpsit*, and the plaintiff below, not demurring thereto, nor moving for judgment notwithstanding such a plea, joined issue upon it, and the verdict of the jury conforms to the plea and issue, and merely finds "that the defendant did assume upon himself in manner and form," etc., and assesses damages, "sustained by reason of the non-performance of the promise and assumption aforesaid."

§ 1964. *Non assumpsit is a bad plea to an action of tort.*

Beside the general reasoning in the books, that pleas amounting to the general issue should traverse the material averments in the declaration, and, where the action is one on the case for a tort, should deny the tort by pleading "not guilty," it is laid down in most elementary treatises that "not guilty" is the proper general issue in such cases. See Com. Dig., Pleader. Beyond this, it has been actually adjudged in an action on the case, after full hearing, that *non assumpsit* was a bad plea. Noble *v.* Lancaster, Barnes' Notes, 125. That action was trover, but being still an action on the case, the same principle applied. Nor is the difference merely formal or technical between actions founded in tort and in contract. 1 Chit. Plead, 229, 418. Because, when in tort or *ex delicto*, a set-off is not admissible, nor can infancy be pleaded as to one *ex contractu*, nor can a plea in abatement be sustained, that all concerned in the wrong are not joined, as it may be in counts on contracts, and a writ of inquiry must issue to ascertain the damages, which is often unnecessary in suits on contracts. A declaration is bad which unites a count in tort with one in contract. 2 Chit., 229, 230; 1 Chitty, 625, note; 4 D. & E., 794; 8 D. & E., 33.

Various other cases analogous to this might be cited, which tend to show that the present plea is improper, but it is not deemed necessary, in this stage of the inquiry, to enlarge on that point; and I proceed to the next and more difficult question, whether such a plea, though bad on demurrer, should not be considered as good after verdict, and cured by the statute of jeofails.

§ 1965. *Bad pleas, how far cured by verdict.*

As a general rule, all informality in a good plea is held to be cured by a verdict, and ought to be, in order not to delay, through a defect of mere form, what may seem to be just. 1 Levinz, 32; 6 Mod., 1; Com. Dig., Pleader, 18; 6 Johns., 1.

Here, however, there appears to be no informality in a good plea; on the contrary it looks more like formality in a bad one. And if it be asked whether there are no cases of bad pleas which are cured by a verdict, we answer that several exist, but that they are cases where the pleas, though bad on demurrer, because wrong in form, yet still contain enough of substance to put in issue the material parts of the declaration. That is the test.

In the opinion of a majority of the court the plea under consideration does not contain enough for that purpose; and my apology for examining this point somewhat more in detail must be found in the circumstance that the court are divided upon it.

The provision by congress in relation to amendments is to be found in the thirty-second section of the judiciary act of September 24, 1789 (1 Stats. at Large, 91), and is similar to that in the 32 Henry VIII., but certainly not broader. See the former, in 1 Little & Brown's ed., 91, and the latter in 1 Bac. Abr., Amendment and Jeofail, B.

Under both of these statutes it has frequently been adjudged that defects in substance are not cured by a verdict; "for this," says Bacon (Abr., before quoted, E.), "would have ruined all proceedings in the courts of justice;" and a defect in substance, in a plea or verdict, is conceded, in all the books, to exist when they do not cover "whatever is essential to the gist of the action."

The present plea, if tried by this test, seems not to be remedied by the verdict; because, so far from traversing all that is essential, nothing is denied, unless it be the inducement. Thus it traverses a promise simply; but the only promise set out in the declaration is one introductory to those material averments, which, as before stated, are the wrongful and injurious acts of the defendant. So far from denying those acts, the plea entirely passes them by, and they are neither put in issue, nor a verdict returned upon them one way or the other. It is true that, in some actions for a tort, a promise may be referred to in the declaration, which sometimes will constitute one material fact among several others. But it is only one, and not the whole, nor is it the most material fact; that being, in such cases, the misfeasance of the defendant. Nor does the verdict here find this one fact or promise such as averred in the inducement. There it is stated to be made by Mr. Franklin; but, on the contrary, the verdict finds a promise made by the defendant.

§ **1966.** *Authorities reviewed.*

On recurring to precedents several are found which confirm these conclusions. In respect to pleas they show that, when so imperfect and immaterial as this, they are not cured by verdict. And the reason generally assigned, and which pervades the whole, is that before mentioned, namely, that they do not cover or traverse all the *gravamen* of the declaration. Staple v. Heydon, 6 Mod., 10; Willes, 532; Tidd's Prac., 827; Gilb. C. P., 146.

Hence it has been decided that a plea of *non assumpsit* to an action of debt is not thus cured (Brennan v. Egan, 4 Taunt., 164; Penfold v. Hawkins, 2 Maule & Selw., 606), because it covers too little or is irrelevant. While in pursuance of the same rule it has been held that *nil debet* to *assumpsit* (1 Hen. Bl., 664), and "not guilty" either to *assumpsit* (Cro. El., 470, and 8 Serg. & R., 441), or to covenant (1 Hen. & Munf., 153), or to debt for a penalty (Coppin v. Carter, 1 D. & E., 462, note), are cured by a verdict because they contain enough to put in issue all which is important in the declaration.

In the present case the issue manifestly reaches only a part of the case and is therefore incurable (Hardres, 331); and it comes expressly within the definition of an immaterial issue, which is also incurable. Carth., 371; Bac. Abr., Verdict, K.; 2 Levinz, 12; 2 Saund., 319; 2 Mod., 137; Gould's Pl., 506, 509.

This is undoubted from Williams' definition in Bennet *v.* Holbeck, 2 Saunders, 319, *a.* He says: "An immaterial issue is where a material allegation in the pleadings is not answered, but an issue is taken on some point which will not determine the merits of the case, and the court is often at a loss for which of the parties to give judgment."

So in Benden *v.* Manning, 2 N. H., 291, it is laid down on circumstances like the present, that "if, instead of *assumpsit*, a special action on the case had been brought for misfeasance, it is very clear that no consideration need have been alleged or proved. The gist of such an action would have been the misfeasance, and it would have been wholly immaterial whether the contract was a valid one or not." 5 D. & E., 143; 2 Wils., 359; 1 Saund., 312, note 2.

If we should next compare this plea and issue in their substance with a few others less general that have been solemnly adjudged to be bad, and not cured by verdict, though found for the plaintiff, the result will be the same.

It may be seen in Tryon *v.* Carter, 2 Str., 994, that, in debt on bond payable on or before the 5th of December, the defendant pleaded payment on the 5th of December, an issue being joined and found against him, the court still awarded a repleader, as it could not be inferred from these pleadings that payment may not have been made before the 5th.

See another in Enys *v.* Mohun, 2 Str., 847, where, to covenant on a lease to C., averred to come by assignment to the defendant, the plea was that C. did not assign to him, and verdict was for plaintiff. But the court awarded a repleader, as the issue found does not cover all the important points of the declaration, namely, that the lease may have come to the defendant, not from C. direct, but by mesne assignments. Same case in 1 Barnardiston, 182, 220. See also other cases. Yelv., 154; Beck *v.* Hill, 2 Mod., 137; Read *v.* Dawson, id., 139; Stafford *v.* Mayor of Albany, 6 Johns., 1; Com. Dig., Pleader, 1 and 2, V., 5; Chit. Pl., 625, 695; 6 D. & E., 462; 1 Saund., 319, n.

In Patterson *v.* United States, 2 Wheat., 225, Judge Washington lays down the whole law precisely as we view it in respect to a verdict varying materially from the issue, and which principle applies equally well to a plea varying from the substance of the declaration. He says: "Whether the jury find a general or a special verdict, it is their duty to decide the very point in issue, and although the court in which it is tried may give form to a general finding so as to make it harmonize with the issue, yet if it appear to that court or to the appellate court that the finding is different from the issue, or is confined only to a part of the matter in issue, no judgment can be rendered on the verdict." And on error the proceedings below were reversed.

After all this it is hardly necessary to state further, by way of precedent, that in Noble *v.* Lancaster, Barnes' Notes, 125, before cited, this very point was decided. *Non assumpsit* was pleaded to an action on the case (e. g., trover), and was held not to be cured by a verdict, but was bad in arrest of judgment.

Looking, then, to many precedents as well as correct principles in pleading, the issue presented and tried here is not only an improper one for the case, but not containing enough to cover all that is material in the declaration, and being thus imperfect in substance, it "does not determine the right between the parties," and is not cured by the verdict or the statute of jeofails.

§ 1967. *Defective verdict.*

A moment as to the defects in the verdict. It is difficult to see how an immaterial and bad plea can be cured by a verdict, which, as in this case, is quite as immaterial as the plea. Indeed, in some respects the verdict here compared with the declaration is more defective and irremediable than the plea. It is laid down in Comyn's Dig., Pleader, S., 24, that a verdict is even void if it be "variant from the declaration;" and he gives as one illustration from 2 Roll., 703, l. 35, "in *assumpsit*, if he finds a different promise."

In the present case the promise is found not only different from that laid in the declaration as inducement, but the verdict varies in other essential respects from the declaration, finding nothing of any of the misfeasance charged in it on the defendant. The defect here, then, is in the verdict as well as plea, and though a mere informality in the former is cured by the act of congress as to amendments (16 Pet., 319), yet the defect here is similar in both, and, as just shown, being on principle in both a defect in substance no less than form, is uncured. Stearns *v.* Barrett, 1 Mason, 170, and 2 Mason, 31.

§ **1968.** *Whether or not justice is done though the forms are incorrect. Authorities.*

But several arguments have been offered against a reversal of the judgment and further proceedings, and in favor of rendering judgment for the plaintiff, on this record, though the plea, issue and verdict are all defective in substance, and do not show which party is entitled to recover on the real merits in dispute, or that they have been legally tried.

These arguments it is our duty to examine. One is that the whole merits, according to the evidence reported, may have actually been considered and passed upon in the court below under this plea and issue. But it is a sufficient answer to this, that if so done it was illegally done, no evidence being competent under that issue except the promise described in it, and no opinion of the jury or court being regular or proper under it, except as to that promise alone. Harrison *v.* Nixon, 9 Pet., 483.

There are many cases showing that the evidence must be limited to the plea. Mar. Ins. Company *v.* Hodgson, 6 Cranch, 206; 4 Wheat., 64, in case of The Divina Pastora. The court says you must "not admit the introduction of evidence varying from the facts alleged." 9 Pet., 484. The *probata* should conform to the *allegata.* Boone *v.* Chiles, 10 Pet., 177.

In Barnes *v.* Williams, 11 Wheat., 416, it is said: "Upon inspecting the record, it had been discovered that the special verdict found in the case was too imperfect to enable the court to render judgment upon it." A certain fact was important to the recovery. "Although in the opinion of the court there was sufficient evidence in the special verdict from which the jury might have found the fact, yet they have not found it, and the court could not upon a special verdict intend it."

These illustrations and cases tend to show the difficulties in forming an opinion on anything not found or apparent on the record, and the impropriety of conjecturing and pronouncing on the real merits when both the issue and verdict are defective in substance in relation to them. But, in this case, if the promise averred to have been made by Franklin was treated at the trial as one made by Garland, so far as regarded its operation and his duty, which has been the argument of the original plaintiff's counsel before us, and which may, for aught we now decide, be correct, then we should be called upon to render judgment against Garland merely on such promise and a breach of it.

That is everything which the verdict finds or the issue presents in the most favorable view. But that being a promise confessedly on the whole evidence made by the original defendant or his predecessor, as a public agent, if now rendering final judgment, we should probably, in that view of the record (no tort having been put in issue or found by the verdict), be obliged to decide against the original plaintiff on the merits, because public agents are not usually liable on mere contracts or promises made in behalf of their principals. See on this, Hodgson v. Dexter, 1 Cranch, 345; Macbeath v. Haldimand, 1 D. & E., 172; Fox v. Drake, 8 Cowen, 191; 2 Dall., 444; Osborne v. Kerr, 12 Wend., 179; Story on Agency, §§ 302–308; Lord Palmerston's Case, 3 Brod. & Bing., 275; Freeman v. Otis, 9 Mass., 272, *quære* in part.

On the contrary, however, if the action is to be considered as brought, not on any promise except as inducement, but on a wrongful act or misfeasance, as the plaintiff sets out his case in his declaration, and still contends to be the truth, then it seems manifest that — nothing on that misfeasance, the essential point of the action, having been either traversed in the plea or found by the verdict — there is nothing upon which judgment can legally be rendered for either party on the merits. It will be seen that we come to this conclusion, not because cases are wanting which hold that officers not judicial, nor having any discretion to exercise on the subject (Wheeler v. Patterson, 1 New Hamp. R., 88; Kendall v. Stokes, 3 How., 98; 11 Johns., 114; 2 Lord Raym., 938), are liable in tort for misfeasances whenever they are violations of public laws or official duties (Shepherd v. Lincoln, 17 Wend., 250; 5 Burr., 2709; 6 D. & E., 445; Gidley, Ex'r of Holland, v. Lord Palmerston, 7 J. B. Moore, 91; 15 East, 384; 9 Clark & Fin., 251; 1 Bos. & Pul., 229; Little v. Barreme, 2 Cranch, 470; 13 Johns., 141; Tracy v. Swartwout, 10 Pet., 95), though others consist of unsuccessful attempts to charge persons in tort for matters which originated and existed in fact only as contracts (Bristow v. Eastman, 1 Esp. N. P., 172; Jennings v. Rundall, 8 D. & E., 335); or which were mere nonfeasances (20 Johns., 379; 12 Mod., 488; 1 Ld. Raym., 466; 4 Maule & Selw., 27; Story on Agency, § 308); but because the issue and verdict present nothing in relation to any such misfeasance, and our opinion is intended to be confined to the questions on the pleadings, without any decision upon the merits. Indeed, it would be difficult to express one on them, where we have been unable to agree on one, and where a majority of the court think the pleadings are not in a proper state to enable us to give one satisfactorily.

§ 1969. *When final judgment may be awarded on defective pleadings, and when opportunity for correction given.*

In this state of things the most obvious course to assist us to "reach the law and justice of the case" would be to reverse the judgment below and award a repleader. This would not deprive either party of any merits they may have and may be able hereafter to show on proper pleadings, and costs would indemnify the party who has been delayed by any bad pleading, so far as he ought to be indemnified, considering his own fault, in this case, in joining and trying an issue immaterial or radically insufficient to settle the cause of action, rather than demurring to the plea seasonably. But such a course is objected to on certain grounds not yet considered, and which it is our duty to notice. One of them is that, when a plea or verdict is radically defective, judgment ought to be rendered, notwithstanding the verdict, for the party whose pleadings are right; and another, a branch of this, is that a court ought in no case to permit the party who commits the first error to have the judgment reversed and be allowed a repleader, unless, perhaps, when the verdict is in his favor.

Though several of the text-books lay down rules like these in broad terms, it is first to be noticed that some state them with a *quære* or doubt. 1 Chit. Pl., note, 522, 633, and Com. Dig., Pleader. In others, the cited authorities do not support them, as Gilbert, quoted in Tidd, 828. In others, the counsel, rather than the court, recognize them. Kempe *v.* Crews, 1 Ld. Raym., 170; Taylor *v.* Whitehead, Doug., 749. In others, the court refer to them, but do not appear to have founded their decision on them, as Webster *v.* Bannister, Doug., 396, where the issue-covered the merits, 3 Hen. & Munf., 388; and in others matters still different existed, which justified the judgment given, independent of these rules.

Thus, if a plea be bad, but still confesses the cause of action without setting out a sufficient avoidance, judgment can with propriety be rendered for the plaintiff on such confession, if the declaration be good. Rex *v.* Philips, 1 Str., 397; Jones *v.* Bodingham, 1 Salk., 173; Gould on Pl., 509; Simonton *v.* Winter *et al.,* 5 Pet., 141; Kirtley *v.* Deck, 3 Hen. & Munf., 388; 6 Mod., 10; Tidd, 827.

So, if the plea be a mere nullity, putting nothing material in issue, judgment is at times allowed to be signed as for want of a plea, as if *nil dicit*, provided the declaration be good. 4 Taunt., 164; 2 Maule & Selw., 606.

So, if the plea be evidently a sham plea or fictitious, a like course is warranted. 10 East, 237; Tidd, 831.

Or if the plea, though neither of these, still be defective, but sets out such facts as demonstrate that the party has no merits, and that no amendment could be made which would avail him anything, or, in other words, nothing is left in the case that can be mended. Gould on Pl., 514, § 39; Tidd, 831; Henderson *v.* Foote, 3 Call,'248.

It is incidental circumstances like these, affecting the merits, and not adverted to always in decisions or elementary treatises, which have governed most of the opposing cases, rather than a mere technical and in some degree arbitrary rule, without reference to the merits, and which would bar a party claiming to possess them from having them tried on a repleader or amendment on complying with equitable terms.

In the case now under consideration the plea comes under neither of these categories, neither confessing a cause of action, nor appearing to be a sham or fictitious plea, nor disclosing enough to show the defendant to be without any good defense. On the contrary, a defense appears which the original defendant seems always to have urged with great confidence as being good. Under these circumstances, then, repleading or something equivalent would seem proper to do justice between the parties, and to carry out the principle of the statutes of jeofails, so as not to prevent a judgment on the merits, because some "slip," as Lord Mansfield calls it, has happened on the part of the defendant in his plea. Rex *v.* Philips, 1 Burr., 295; Tidd, 828; Gould on Pl., 508, §§ 31, 40. If the right be not put in issue, and may be, a ruling to permit it seems reasonable. Staple *v.* Heyden, 6 Mod., 2.

The true meaning of these technical rules can be made rational and consistent if they are held to apply to cases where good grounds are apparent for rendering final judgment. Then it may well be rendered against him who committed the first material fault in the pleadings, and which fault has not afterwards in any way been cured.

But if no such grounds appear, in consequence of the imperfections of the pleas and verdict, final judgment cannot properly be rendered and the rules are inapplicable; and the judgment below should be reversed, so as to furnish an opportunity to remove those imperfections and reach the justice of the case by amendments or repleaders. And so far from the party not being permitted to enjoy this indulgence who committed the first fault, he is the only one who needs it, and in whose behalf, under the liberal spirit of modern times, all statutes of jeofails are passed. Nor can the opposite party suffer by this course in respect to the merits, as they are left open. Or in respect to cost and delay, as he should be indemnified for them, in the manner before mentioned, by equitable terms for allowing any amendments.

In this view of the subject it is of no consequence for which party the defective verdict was found, except at times the fact in it may be an indication of merits in that party who has the *postea*, so far as that fact can affect the merits. But in this case the fact found was immaterial in relation to the merits, as already shown, and the object now is to prevent such immaterialities from making a final disposal of the case, to prevent substance from being sacrificed to form, and, where merits may exist, to adopt such a course as will present them to the court intelligibly for a final adjudication of the real justice of the case.

To all this, in an advanced era of jurisprudence, it will hardly do to repeat from some of the old books, that a party is forever to be barred either for the badness or the falsity of his plea, if it happens to be imperfect and is found against him, though he has not confessed the declaration, nor stated any facts in his plea inconsistent with the merits.

Much more, too, is it proper, if not indispensable, in a case like this, so defective on the record as not to justify any decision about the merits, to adopt a course which shall not bar the due consideration of them in the end, and which shall be for the benefit and guide of the court even more than a party, so as to prevent a leap in the dark, and which for these and other reasons shall let the cause be re-opened, and prepared and tried in a manner to bring the whole of the merits legally before both the court and the jury. Cro. Eliz., 245; 3 Hen. & Munf., 393; Baird & Co. v. Mattox, 1 Call, 257.

Considering the character and position of this tribunal, as one of the last resort in administering justice, and considering the increased disposition of the age in which we live to eviscerate the truth, and decide ultimately only on the real merits in controversy between parties, or, in the words of Justice Story (1 Story, 152, in Bottomley v. United States) as to "technical niceties," considering "the days for such subtilties in a great measure passed away," it seems a duty of our own motion to give all reasonable facility to get the record in an intelligible and proper shape before we render final judgment.

As proof that such a course is sometimes deemed proper to aid a court as well as a party, notwithstanding the technical rules before mentioned, it is stated in Gould on Pl., 507, § 28, that judgment may be arrested after verdict "if the issue is immaterial, so that the court cannot discover from the finding upon it for which party judgment ought to be given." §§ 22 and 23.

So, though Gould lays down these rules before named, he says [page 514, § 40] if a special plea show there may be a good justification, though it has been badly pleaded, judgment must be arrested and a repleader awarded, as it appears a good issue might be formed, and when this is the case "the ends of justice require that an opportunity for forming such an issue should be afforded." And in respect to objections in such cases to indulgence to a party whose plea is bad, Gould, 508, says in a note: "The true answer to this inquiry appears to be, that the awarding a repleader in such case was originally rather an act of indulgence to a party who tendered an improper issue than a matter of strict right; an indulgence grounded on the presumption that the issue was misjoined through the inadvertence and oversight of the pleaders, and that a further opportunity to plead would probably result in a material issue decisive of the merits of the cause," etc.

There are also some very high precedents against the application of these technical rules in cases and circumstances like those now under consideration. Such was the case of Rex v. Philips, 1 Burr., 302. The reasoning of Lord Mansfield on this whole subject is directly in point, as well as the case itself, and contains that beautiful correction by him of a much abused maxim, in which he says it is the duty of a good judge to amplify justice rather than his jurisdiction, *boni judicis est ampliare justitiam,* not *jurisdictionem.* There, after verdict for the plaintiff, he allowed an amendment of the plea on payment of costs, being satisfied that "the ends of justice require that an opportunity for forming a proper issue be allowed."

There are many other cases, some ancient and some modern, which fully support the same conclusion. See Enys v. Mohun, 2 Strange, 847, and S. C., Barnardiston, 182, 220; Tryon v. Carter, 2 Strange, 994; Love v. Wotton, Cro. Eliz., 245.

In Serjeant v. Fairfax, 1 Levinz, 32, the plea was defective as not taking issue on enough, though it denied part of what was material in the declaration. Verdict was found for the plaintiff. This is in substance the very case now under consideration. Counsel contended: "When the issue is found against the pleader, judgment shall be for the plaintiff, but if for him (the pleader), not. But Justice Twysden said that if an improper issue is taken, and verdict given thereon, judgment shall be given thereupon, be it for the plaintiff or defendant. 2 Cro., 575. But an immaterial issue is where, upon the verdict, the court cannot know for whom to give judgment, whether for the plaintiff or for the defendant, as in Hob., 175; and with him the chief justice and Wyndham wholly agreed, and awarded a repleader."

In Simonton v. Winter, 5 Pet., 141, the verdict was for the plaintiff, and yet, the plea being bad, the court reversed the judgment, as the cause of action was not confessed in the plea, and remanded the case with an order for a *venire de novo.* See, also, in point, Green v. Baily, 5 Munford, 246, and Baird & Co. v. Mattox, 1 Call, 257.

And in 9 Wheat., 729, the pleadings are not given, but Justice Story said there was great irregularity and laxity in them, and "it is impossible, without breaking down the best settled principles of law, not to perceive that the very errors in the pleadings are of themselves sufficient to justify a reversal of the judgment and an award of a repleader," and without "appropriate pleas," "it would be difficult to ascertain what was to be tried or not tried." See, also, Harrison v. Nixon, 9 Pet., 483.

§ 1970. *Repleader having gone into disuse, judgment should be reversed and the cause remanded for further proceedings.*

All that remains is to consider the best form of carrying these conclusions into effect. In some of the cases before cited the court have not only reversed the judgment but ordered a repleader. But in others it is said that this cannot be done after a writ of error. 6 Mod., 102; 2 Keb., 769; Com. Dig., Pleader and Verdict. Such, probably, has always been the practice in relation to not ordering it by the court below, after a writ of error is sued out, till the case is again re-opened; but it was once not the practice in the higher courts of error in England. See 2 Saund., 319; Holbech *v.* Bennett, 2 Levinz, 12. Nor is it the practice now in some of the higher courts in this country. In Green *v.* Baily, 5 Munford, 251, judgment was reversed on the writ of error, the pleadings set aside after the plea, and a repleader awarded.

The thirty-second section of the judiciary act, before referred to, expressly empowers "any court of the United States," "at any time, to permit either of the parties to amend any defect in the process or pleadings." Little & Brown's ed., 91. All know that a repleader is little more in substance than permitting an amendment. But most of the precedents in this court allowing amendments after a writ of error are in maritime or admiralty proceedings, and I have found none of those in the form of repleaders. In 4 Wheat., 64 (though one in admiralty, where less strictness prevails in pleading than at common law), Chief Justice Marshall said: "The pleadings in this case are too informal and defective to pronounce a final decree on the merits;" and the judgment was therefore reversed and the cause remanded, with directions to permit the pleadings to be amended. See, also, a like order in The Divina Pastora, 4 Wheat., 63, and in case of The Edward, 1 Wheat., 264, and case of The Samuel, 1 Wheat., 13; Harrison *et al. v.* Nixon, 9 Pet., 483.

In cases at common law the form is usually somewhat different. In 5 Pet., 141, the form was suited to the case, and judgment not only reversed, but a *venire de novo* ordered; and in United States *v.* Hawkins, 10 Pet., 125, Justice Wayne says: "A *venire de novo* is frequently awarded in a court of error, upon a bill of exceptions, to enable parties to amend," and "amendment may, in the sound discretion of the court, upon a new trial, be permitted." See, further, 2 Wheat., 226; Barnes *v.* Williams, 11 Wheat., 416; Bellows *v.* Hallowell & Augusta Bank, 2 Mason, 31; Peterson *v.* United States, 2 Wash. C. C., 36. See the form in England. Parker *v.* Wells, 1 D. & E., 783, and Grant *v.* Astle, Doug., 722. In Pollard *v.* Dwight, 4 Cranch, 433, the court said let judgment "be reversed and the cause remanded for a new trial." Mr. Lee prayed "with leave for the defendants below to amend their pleadings." The court said "that the court below had the power to grant leave to amend, and this court could not doubt but it would do what was right in that respect." Similar to this was the course in Day *v.* Chism, 10 Wheat., 449.

And in United States *v.* Kirkpatrick, 9 Wheat., 738, the court not only reversed the judgment and awarded a *venire de novo*, but gave "directions also to allow the parties liberty to amend their pleadings." So 9 Wheat., 540. See on this, further, Mar. Ins. Co. *v.* Hodgson, 6 Cranch, 218; 7 id., 47, 497; 9 id., 244; 1 id., 261, 13; 10 id., 449; 4 id., 52; 16 Pet., 319; Moody *v.* Keener, 9 Porter, 252.

In conclusion, then, as by several cases in England the allowance of a repleader in courts of error seems to have gone into disuse in modern times, and as the practice in common-law cases in this tribunal, though otherwise in some of the states, has usually been not to direct either amendments or repleaders in cases like these, but to reverse the judgment and remand the cause to the court below for further proceedings there, we shall conform to that practice in the present instance.

Let the judgment below be reversed, and the case remanded for further proceedings.

TOWNSEND *v.* JEMISON.

(7 Howard, 706–726. 1848.)

ERROR to U. S. District Court, Northern District of Mississippi.

Opinion by MR. JUSTICE WOODBURY.

STATEMENT OF FACTS.— The original action in this case was *assumpsit*. Though the declaration contained several counts, some on a special promise and some for money paid and received, it was indorsed on the original summons that the action was " brought to recover the sum of $4,000 and interest at ten per cent., paid for defendant, from 27th of January, 1840, to Mississippi Union Bank," etc., etc.

There was a demurrer and other pleadings as to this declaration, which it is not necessary to repeat, as leave was given to amend throughout, and, on the 6th of December, 1842, a new declaration was filed, consisting of three special counts and the usual money counts, all of which must, of course, be for the original cause of action.

On the 9th of December, 1842, the defendant pleaded the general issue of *non assumpsit* to the whole declaration; and, for further plea to the three special counts, averred that the suit was brought to charge him for the debt of John B. Jones, and for no other purpose; and that, there being no evidence of his promise in writing, the suit was barred by the statute of frauds and perjuries. To this the plaintiff replied that the suit was not so brought, but on original promises made by the defendant. The latter filed a general demurrer to this replication.

On the 12th of December the general issue joined as to the whole declaration appears to have been tried, and a verdict returned for $3,451.88, for which sum, at the same time, judgment was rendered and execution issued.

Nothing further took place till June 5, 1845, when this writ of error was brought to reverse the judgment, assigning as the ground for it that the demurrer to the replication should first have been disposed of, and that the statute of frauds pleaded in the preceding plea was a full defense to the matters alleged by the original plaintiff.

§ 1971. *When there is an issue of law and fact before the court in the same action the practice in this country is to decide the question of law first.*

This case presents some questions of practice and of pleading which possess no little difficulty. They must be settled chiefly by the reasons which may be applicable to them; and when precedents in this court are not found for a guide in aid of those reasons, they may be strengthened by analogies established in the state courts or in England, where the systems of pleading and practice are somewhat similar. It seems proper, and is conceded, that in a cause where several pleas are filed, as here, and some terminate in a demurrer and others in an issue to the jury, they should all, as a general rule, unless waived or withdrawn, be in some way disposed of by the court. The leading inquiry then is, if enough appears in all the proceedings here to render it probable that the issue, in law no less than in fact, was in some way disposed of, though this is not, *eo nomine*, mentioned in the record. Assuredly it is usual in this country, as a matter of practice, when there is an issue of fact and another of law in the same action, to have the question of law heard and decided first. Green *v.* Dulany, 2 Munf., 518; Muldrow *v.* M'Cleland, 1 Litt., 4; Co. Litt., 72, *a;* Com. Dig., Pleader, Demurrer. 22. The twenty-eighth rule for the circuit courts accords with this by directing that, in such cases, "the demurrer shall, unless the court shall otherwise, for good cause, direct, be first argued and determined;" because a decision on that, if one way, that is, if in favor of the demurrer, will frequently dispose of the whole cause, and supersede the expense and necessity of a jury trial of the other issue, as well as give an opportunity to move for an amendment. 5 Bac. Abr., Pleas and Pleading, No. 1; Tidd's Pract., 476; Duberley v. Page, 2 D. & E., 394.

§ 1972. *A demurrer appearing on the record not disposed of may be deemed from the circumstances to have been waived.*

Yet this course, being a matter of sound discretion in the court rather than of fixed or inflexible right, it cannot always be absolutely presumed to have been pursued. See twenty-eighth rule, *ante*, and cases before cited; 2 D. & E., 394; 1 Saunders, 80, note 1. But as it is usual, and the defendant in this case did not file any exception, as if there had been a refusal by the court to decide first on the demurrer, the presumption does not seem so strong that there had been a refusal or neglect to do it, as that the demurrer had been waived by the defendant, or, if not waived, had been decided, and the particular minute of this on the record omitted by a mistake of the clerk. Several other circumstances exist which, in connection with these, contribute to strengthen this last presumption, and to justify us on legal grounds in inferring that one of the above events, either a waiver or decision of the demurrer, actually took place here. First, as to those in favor of the position that the demurrer was waived. Only one cause of action existed here, though set out in several counts. This is stated not only, as before mentioned, in the summons by the original plaintiff, but by the defendant in his special plea and in the argument of his counsel. The general issue, which was joined and tried, went to the whole declaration, and under that, at the trial, any parol evidence offered in its support could have been objected to as within the statute of frauds, which seems to have been the whole defense, as well as under the special plea setting up this statute against the special counts. This is clear from the books of practice. 1 Chit. Pl., 515; 2 Leigh's N. P., 1066; 1 Tidd's Pract., 646. Though, to be sure, it could be pleaded specially also, and this may now be necessary under the new rules of court in England. 1 Bingh. N. C., 781; 2 Cromp., Mees. & Rosc., 627. Hence, from abundant caution lest this objection might not be admissible under the general issue, the special plea here was probably at first filed. But before the trial came on, which was three days after, it is likely that the defendant had become convinced that it was admissible under the general issue, and therefore went to trial without having the demurrer first argued and decided, or even joined, but waived it. If, on the contrary, he concluded to try the issue to the jury first, and then, if not allowed there to make his objection as to the statute, to argue the demurrer afterwards, the inference would be equally strong that he was allowed to urge the objection at the trial, and had a decision on it there, and therefore waived his special plea and demurrer, and a separate and unnecessary decision on them afterwards. Such was the presumption in the case of Bond v. Hill, 3 Stew. (Ala.), 283, more fully explained hereafter. It was held likewise in Morrison v. Morrison, 3 Stew., 444, that if a demurrer and an issue of fact were to the same matter, and the latter was tried first, it must be presumed that the other had been waived.

In Dufau v. Couprey's Heirs, 6 Pet., 170, a writ of error was brought for the same general cause as here, that one of the pleas intended for the court did not appear by the record to have been decided. But the court sustained the judgment below; the other plea, on examination, as will soon be shown to be the case here, being found immaterial after the finding of the jury. Where one material issue is decided, going to the whole declaration, it is of no consequence how an immaterial issue going only to a part of it is found, if no injury be done by it to either party. 6 Mo., 544. And by parity of reasoning it would be of no consequence whether it was decided at all or not, if enough else is decided to dispose properly of the whole case.

What fortifies these views is the fact that the defendant never procured a joinder to his demurrer by the plaintiff. As he interposed this defense in a special plea and filed the demurrer to the replication, it would be material for him, if wanting a decision on them, to get the pleadings finished. He should have moved for a joinder or got a rule for one (1 Chit. Pl., 628), and should likewise have moved for a decision on them, if desired, before a final judgment was rendered on the verdict. It is true that some books appear to consider it the duty of the plaintiff to join a demurrer soon after it has been tendered by the defendant. But this, it is believed, generally depends upon a positive rule of court, which may exist, to require it. 33d Rule of Practice for Courts of Equity, 1 How., 51; Williams' Case, Skinner, 217. And without such rule, as in this case, he may need and take time to decide on making a motion to amend before joining; and the harshest penalty proper for delay in the joinder would seem to be that the demurrer may be considered, when requested by the party making it, though no formal joinder has taken place. 3 Levinz, 222; Skinner, 217. The omission of the defendant, then, to obtain a joinder to which he was by law entitled (1 Chit., 647; Barnes, 163), the omission to add one himself, which is sometimes permissible (5 Taunt., 164, and 1 Pike, Ark., 180), and the omission to request a decision without any joinder, as he may after much delay (Skinner, 217), all appear on the record, and look not only like a waiver of a decision on the demurrer by the defendant, but a neglect of his own duties on the subject. A waiver of a demurrer often takes place, and is, by law, permissible. 1 Tidd's Pr., 710; 1 East, 135; 2 Bibb, 12; 1 Burrow, 321; 2 Strange, 1181. *Quilibet renuntiare potest jure pro se introducto.* The want of a decision would, in this aspect of the subject, seem to be by his own consent, and *consensus tollit errorem.* The course of the defendant appears to have been, practically and substantially, if not formally, an abandonment of a wish for any separate decision on the demurrer. See cases of this kind. Wright *v.* Hollingsworth, 1 Pet., 165; Bac. Abr., Error, K., 5; Vaiden *v.* Bell, 3 Randolph, 448; Patrick *v.* Conrad, 3 Marsh., 613; 2 Marsh., 227; Casky *v.* January, Hard., 539. As a plea of the general issue, while a demurrer is pending undisposed of, is considered a waiver of it. Cobb *v.* Ingalls, Breese, 180.

§ 1973. *A demurrer may be deemed to have been waived by defendant from his neglect to secure a decision thereon.*

In another view of the subject, looking to the defendant's own neglect as the cause, a party cannot be allowed to take advantage of his own wrong or inattention. Thus, it has been decided that a writ of error will not lie for one's own neglect or irregularity. 1 McCord, 205; 1 Pike (Ark.), 99; Kincaid *v.* Higgins, 1 Bibb, 396; 2 Blackf., 71; 3 McCord, 302, 477; Kyle *v.* Hoyle, 6 Mo., 544. It strengthens these conclusions that the original defendant seems to have long acquiesced in what he now excepts to,— that he does not appear to have asked for a decision on the demurrer, to have made any complaint at the time of the demurrer not being decided to have filed any motion about it, offered any bill of exceptions, or even brought any writ of error till after the lapse of nearly three years. So much as to the waiver of the demurrer. But if the demurrer was not, in truth, waived or withdrawn by the defendant, or cannot be now so considered, from all which appears on the record, the presumption from all is evident that the demurrer and special plea were actually decided on by the court, and the omission to enter it on the record may be cured by the statute of jeofails. Such a decision would have been its ordinary and proper course of proceeding.

This court has held in a state of things much like this, as will soon be more fully explained, that it was bound to presume that "justice was administered in the ordinary form." 4 How., 167. And hence, in 3 Stew. (Ala), 447, 448, where a decree was averred in the record, but not its form, it was presumed to have been in the ordinary form. The court could not properly have decided and given judgment for the plaintiff in this case as it did, and, as must be presumed, properly, in the first instance, if the demurrer had not been waived or settled in favor of the plaintiff. Nor was the defendant likely to have acquiesced in the judgment without putting an exception on the record, unless one of these circumstances had occurred. This question has arisen in several of the states, and been decided in conformity with these views. In the case of Cochran's Executors v. Davis, 5 Litt., 119, the court very properly adopt a like principle, saying: "To this plea there was a demurrer, and although there is no order of record expressly disposing of the demurrer, yet, as the court gave judgment for the plaintiff on the whole record, it must be taken that the demurrer was sustained and the plea overruled." So in substance it was held in McCollom v. Hogan, 1 Alabama, 515; and in Bond v. Hill, 3 Stewart, 283, where, as in this case, there was a plea amounting to the general issue, or containing what was admissible under it, and it did not appear distinctly to have been disposed of, but the general issue was tried, it was held to be presumed that the defendant had the full benefit of the objection on the trial, and error will not lie. It is true that where one issue in a cause is found one way, and another. on a matter entirely distinct is not disposed of, it may not be proper always to consider it as decided. Pratt v. Rogers, 5 Mo., 51. But here the questions involved in both issues were the same; both related to the same cause of action, and both to the same defense. The cases on this subject are so much more numerous in the states than in England or in this court, that we oftener find it necessary to resort to them for analogies in support of our reasoning as to what should, under all the facts, be presumed. But in this court, at this very term, we have a strong illustration of the correctness of truth of such a presumption. in the case of Harris v. Wall; where, on similar findings by a jury on some pleas and a demurrer to others, and a judgment for the defendant without any entry made specifically that the demurrer was disposed of. it happens, in point of fact, that it was decided, and the judge on that circuit. now present, has with him his written opinion which he delivered when deciding it. So in Stockton v. Bishop, 4 How., 167, in a writ of error where a verdict appeared and a judgment, but not for any particular sum, with several other important omissions, this court, by Catron, justice, remarked: "Still, we are bound to presume, in favor of proceedings in a court having jurisdiction of the parties and subject-matter, that justice was administered in the ordinary form, when so much appears as is found in this imperfect record."

§ 1974. *Some things not appearing on the record may be assumed on writ of error.*

Again, on a writ of error, many things will always be presumed or intended, in law as well as fact, to have happened which are not *ipsissimis verbis*, or substantively so set out on the record, but are plainly to be inferred to have happened from what is set out. Cro. Eliz., 467; 4 How., 166. Thus in this case numerous circumstances stated on the record, and already referred to, indicate that the demurrer and special plea, if not withdrawn or waived, were actually disposed of. Among them, raising a strong presumption that way, is the fact that three days elapsed after the pleas and demurrer were filed before the trial of the other issue; that within this period the court had time to hear the question of law argued; that it is the usual practice to hear such a question before going to a trial of the facts; and hence, unless the demurrer was waived, that the court, before the trial, did probably hear and decide the demurrer against the defendant. Again, the court would have been still less likely to have proceeded to final judgment without first disposing of the question of law, unless waived or settled either before, at or after the trial. Such, too, being the duty of the court, they are to be presumed, till the contrary appears, to have done their duty. Wilkes *v.* Dinsman, 7 How., 89. Nor is such a presumption here, as some have suggested, against the record, because the record says nothing on the subject. But it is consistent with everything that is there said, and with what is fairly to be inferred from the whole record, carrying with us the probable idea, in that event, of some omission or misprision by the clerk in noting all which happened.

§ 1975. *Clerical misprision.*

The omission of the clerk to enter on the record the judgment upon the demurrer, or to state its waiver if it was abandoned, would be merely a clerical mistake; and it is well settled at common law that a misprision by a clerk, if the case be clearly that alone, though it consist of the omission of an important word or expression, is not a good ground to reverse a judgment, where substance enough appears to show that all which was proper and required was properly done. Willoughby *v.* Gray, Cro. Eliz., 467; Weston's Case, 11 Mass., 417.

§ 1976. *Policy of the law that defects be cured as far as possible by verdict.*

The statutes of jeofails usually go still further in remedying defects after verdicts and judgments. Considering this, under those statutes, as a case of defect or want of form in the entry by the clerk, and not of error in the real doings of the court, the statute of jeofails of the United States, curing all defects or want of form in judgments, is explicit against our reversing this for such a cause. Sec. 32 of Judiciary Act of 1789 (1 Stats. at Large, 91). If the state laws are to govern, the words of the statute of jeofails are equally explicit and more minute in Mississippi in curing such defects, resembling more the English statutes. Hutchinson's Code for Mississippi, 841. It is not a little singular that the unwillingness in England to have judgments disturbed by writs of error for defects in them or in the prior pleadings, where a verdict of a jury has been rendered for a plaintiff, is such that something like five or six acts of parliament were passed before our ancestors emigrated hither, and several more since, to prevent writs of error from being maintained for defects in form as well as to empower amendments in such cases. See those in 1 Bac. Abr., Amendment and Jeofails; O'Driscoll *v.* McBurney, 2 Nott & McCord, 58. Some of the defects cured seem to be very near as strong as the present

case. 11 Coke, 6, *b;* Act of 32 Hen. VIII., ch. 30. The difficulty is in deciding "what is substance and what is form," and that is governed by no fixed
text, but it is laid down that it "must be determined in every action according
to its nature." 1 Bac. Abr., Amendment and Jeofails, E, 1; 1 Saund., 81,
note 1.

At common law defects in collateral pleadings, or other matters not preceding the verdict, and not to be proved in order to get a verdict, were not cured
by it. Yet those were cured which related to matters necessary to be shown
to get a verdict, and hence, after it, are presumed to have been shown. Renner *v.* Bank of Columbia, 9 Wheat., 581; Com. Dig., Pleader, Count, ch. 87;
Carson *v.* Hood, 4 Dall., 108; 1 Sumn., 314; 1 Gall., 261; 1 Wils., 222; Burr.,
17, 25; Cotterel *v.* Cummins, 6 Serg. & R., 348; 1 Sumn., 319; 16 Conn., 586;
11 Wend., 375; 7 Greenl., 63. But these defects in collateral matters, as here,
when they relate to form, are as fully cured by the statutes of jeofails as those
connected with the verdict are by intendment at common law. Stennel *v.*
Hogg, 1 Saund., 228, note 1; Dale *v.* Dean, 16 Conn., 579. Any omission like
this would certainly be amendable below, and some cases have gone so far as
to hold, in error, that any defect amendable below will be considered as actually amended. Cummings *v.* Lebo, 2 Rawle, 23.

In conclusion on this point, this court, by Catron, J., in the writ of error
before named, of Stockton *v.* Bishop, 4 How., 164, stated that "it must be admitted that congress acted wisely in declaring that no litigant party shall lose
his right in law for want of form; and in going one step further, as congress
unquestionably has done, by declaring that, to save the parties' rights, the
substance should be infringed on to some extent when contrasted with modes
of proceeding in the English courts, and with their ideas of what is substance."

After this it would seem hypercritical, and contrary to the whole spirit of
the statutes of jeofails, both of the United States and of Mississippi, to allow
an exception so contrary to legal presumption as this to be sustained. Nor
does it promote the ends of justice to let parties lie by and not take exceptions, and afterwards reverse judgments for omissions, which, if noticed at
the time, would have been corrected. McCready *v.* James, 6 Whart., 547.
And this court, where the issues were three, and the verdict and judgment not
separate on each, but general on all, and the objection was taken on the writ
of error, in Roach *v.* Hulings, 16 Pet., 321, said, by Daniel, J.: "Objections of
this character that are neither taken at the usual stage of the proceedings, nor
prominently presented on the face of the record, but which may be sprung
upon a party after an apparent waiver of them by an adversary, and still more
after a trial upon the merits, can have no claim to the favor of the court, but
should be entertained only in obedience to the strictest requirements of law;"
and they were in that case accordingly overruled or considered as cured.

§ **1977.** *In Mississippi one good count will sustain a verdict.*

Another ground for affirming the judgment, which the plaintiff in error
cannot easily overcome, is that, if the three counts to which the special plea
is filed cannot be sustained, the defendant in error has obtained a verdict on
all the counts; thus showing, at least, that there was no valid defense to the
others. And if those three were conceded to be bad, the others are good, and,
notwithstanding a verdict and judgment on all, the latter must not in such
case be reversed on error. By an express statute in Mississippi, passed June
28, 1842, one good count, though others are bad, will sustain a judgment.
Hutch. Code for Miss., ch. 5, art. 1. This is not a peculiarity confined to

Mississippi, but a like rule prevails in several other states. 2 Bibb, 62; 2 Litt., 100; 2 Bay, 204; 2 Hill, 648; 1 Blackf., 12; 1 Stewart, 384; 2 Conn., 324. And though in some it is otherwise (1 Caines, 347; 11 Johns., 98; 9 Mass., 198), and is otherwise in England (Grant v. Astle, Doug., 722), yet it has been regretted by some of her eminent jurists as "inconvenient and ill-judged."

If this provision, then, in Mississippi should be regarded as a rule of practice, it existed there when the last process act of May, 1828 (4 Stats. at Large, 278), passed, and hence, by acts of congress and the rules of our circuit court, binds them; but if it be a right conferred by her statute, it equally must govern us, by the judiciary law of 1789 (1 id., 73), in all cases tried like this in that state. 16 Pet., 89, 303.

§ 1978. *On a demurrer judgment goes against party committing the first fault.*

But besides these reasonings and views, to some of which a portion of the court except, there exists another ground for affirming the judgment below, which appears to us fully established both on principle and adjudged cases. The first fault in the pleadings connected with the demurrer seems to have been committed by the defendant himself, and no reason appears on the whole record why the original judgment should not have been rendered against him on that ground. His only defense set up was the statute of frauds and perjuries. This statute was pleaded specially; but on the facts and the law it does not seem to have been applicable to the case. The case was a transaction of money paid by the plaintiff on account of the defendant, and must have been considered by the court and jury as done under an original undertaking to repay it in a particular way, which the defendant had not fulfilled, and which was not within the provisions of the statute. The defendant was misled, by the mode of payment being special and to a third person, into an impression that the original promise was to a third person. The suit is not brought by the third person to whom the original plaintiff owed a debt, nor was the promise made to a third person; but it is brought by the person who advanced money on account of the defendant on a consideration moving from him alone, and on the promise made to him alone for its payment in a particular manner. See, on this, Read v. Nash, 1 Wils., 305; 2 Leigh's N. P., 1031; King v. Despard, 5 Wend., 277; Towne v. Grover, 9 Pick., 306; Hodgson v. Anderson, 3 Barn. & Cres., 842.

This was virtually, therefore, an undertaking by the defendant to pay his own debt, but simply specifying a particular manner of doing it; and unless it was found at the trial that the statute of frauds did not apply, it is to be presumed that a recovery would not have been had before the jury, where it was competent to make this an objection.

The matter of the plea, then, having been clearly bad, it appears to be well settled that, when a demurrer is filed to a replication, if the plea is bad, judgment ought to be given for the plaintiff. Anon., 2 Wils., 150; *semble,* Moor, 692; Com. Dig., Pleader, Proceedings in Error, 3, B., 16; 1 Levinz, 181. The whole record connected with the demurrer is open on the writ of error, and judgment goes against the earliest fault. Breese, 207; Morgan v. Morgan, 4 Gill & John., 395.

In regard to the suggestion that the demurrer might have applied to some other objection than the statute of frauds, either in the plea, or, going back to the declaration, some defect there (as the first defect bad on general demurrer is the fatal one, 1 Chit. Pl., 647), it is enough to say that no other appears then or now to have been pointed out, and none is intimated in the argument for the plaintiff in error.

§ 1979. *A demurrer does not reach back beyond the general issue.*

It is very doubtful, also, if in this particular case a defect in the declaration would be considered at all on this demurrer, as the general issue is pleaded to all of the declaration covering these three special counts. And an issue in fact and a demurrer cannot both be allowed to reach the same count. Bac. Abr., Pleas and Pleading, n. 1; 2 Blackf., 34; 5 Wend., 104. If there be an exception to this rule, it must be by some local law or practice not existing here. 1 Litt., 4; 4 Munford, 104.

From the whole record, therefore, it appears that the judgment below in favor of the plaintiff was probably correct, even if the demurrer had not been waived, and in this event it is clear that the judgment should not, on this writ of error, be reversed. Hobart, 56; Com. Dig., Pleader, Demurrer, Q., 2; Saunders v. Johnson, 1 Bibb, 322; 6 Monroe, 295, 606; Phelps v. Taylor, 4 id., 170; *semble*, 3 Bibb, 225; McWaters v. Draper, 5 Monroe. 496; Hard., 164. In Foster v. Jackson, Hob., 56, the opinion says: "It is the office of the court to judge the law upon the whole record." The other cases cited show that in writs of error, as well as demurrer, the same rule prevails.

§ 1980. *A reversal of judgment would not benefit the defendant.*

The propriety of our conclusions in this case becomes more manifest when we consider that a reversal of the judgment would be of no use to the original defendant; because, if reversed, the order here could not be to render judgment for the defendant, but to have a record made of the waiver or decision of the demurrer. if either occurred, and if not, then a joinder in demurrer and an opinion below on the question presented by it, and which opinion, as already shown, must probably be for the plaintiff, and then the same judgment be entered again on the verdict which exists now. McGriffin v. Helm, 5 Litt., 48; 2 Strange, 972; Jackson v. Rundlet, 1 Woodb. & M., 381.

Finally, so far as any presumptions or doubts on any of these considerations should operate against either party in forming our conclusions, we are unable to see anything in the acquiescent conduct of the original defendant before the judgment, or in the merits of his original defense, or in his writ of error, brought after such an uninterrupted silence and assent for years, which entitle him to any peculiar favor.

The plaintiff in error, likewise, must always make out his case clearly and satisfactorily, as every reasonable intendment should be in favor of a judgment already rendered. Ventris v. Smith, 10 Pet., 161; Lander v. Reynolds, 3 Litt., 16; Lou. Code of Pract., 909, note, and cases there cited; 3 Martin (N. S.), 29; 15 Louis., 480, etc. This not having been done in the present case, we think that the judgment below must be affirmed.

Opinion by TANEY, C. J., CATRON, J., concurring.

I think the judgment of the district court may be supported on the ground that the decision on the demurrer had become immaterial after the verdict on the general issue. The special plea out of which the demurrer arose applied only to three counts. There was a fourth count, to which no defense was made except by the plea of the general issue; and according to the law and practice of Mississippi one good count is sufficient to support the judgment when there are several counts in a declaration and the others bad. And after the verdict on the general issue the decision of the demurrer was immaterial, and the judgment must still have been for the plaintiff, even if the demurrer was decided for defendant. The omission to dispose of an immaterial issue is not a ground for reversing a judgment, as the decision of such issue could not influence the judgment of the district court. But I do not concur in the other portions of the opinion, and think that many of the positions taken in it cannot be supported.

Dissenting opinion by MR. JUSTICE DANIEL.

Regarding the opinion just delivered as in direct opposition to the very canons of pleading at law, I feel constrained to declare my dissent from it. I cannot subscribe to, and can hardly comprehend, a doctrine of presumptions which, in proceedings at law and on questions of pleading, infers that the parties or the court have acted in direct contravention of the facts apparent upon and standing prominently out upon the record, operating by such presumption a false feature of the record itself. In this case the defendant has tendered an issue in law to the replication to the third plea; the record discloses the fact that this issue has never been tried; it is, therefore, undeniable that there is a chasm in the proceedings, and that the court has not passed upon the whole case. If presumption can be admitted to warrant the conclusion that this demurrer was withdrawn, where shall such presumption end? Would it not be equally regular to presume that any other plea or issue on the record had been withdrawn? Then, if any other source than the record itself can be resorted to in order to ascertain what was in truth involved in the trial, conjecture or evidence *aliunde* must be introduced to determine; and that which, by legal intendment, is the only evidence or proof of the proceedings — the record — becomes the weakest of all proof, or, rather, becomes no proof at all. I think the judgment should be reversed, and the cause remanded for a trial on all the issues of law and of fact.

RICARD v. NEW PROVIDENCE.

(Circuit Court for New Jersey: 5 Federal Reporter, 433-435. 1881.)

Opinion by NIXON, J.

STATEMENT OF FACTS.— This is a motion to open and set aside a judgment as improvidently entered. The summons in the case was returnable on the 23d of March, 1880. Before the time expired for filing the declaration, to wit, on the 21st of April, the attorneys for the defendant corporation signed a consent in writing, as follows: " We hereby consent and agree that the time within which plaintiff's declaration in the above cause may be filed be extended thirty days from date, to wit, until the 22d day of May next."

On the 18th day of May, before the expiration of the extended time, the plaintiff filed his declaration and gave written notice thereof to the attorneys of the defendant, and, at their request, furnished to them a copy of the declaration as filed. No further steps seem to have been taken in the cause until the 22d day of November following, when the plaintiff entered a rule for judgment by default, and had his damages assessed by the clerk of the court.

§ 1981. *Pleadings to conform to state practice.*

Is such a judgment regular? By section 914 of the Revised Statutes of the United States the practice, pleadings and forms and modes of proceeding in civil causes, other than equity and admiralty causes, in the circuit and district courts, shall conform, as near as may be, to the practice, pleadings and forms and modes of proceeding existing at the time in like causes in the courts of record of the state within which such circuit and district courts are held, any rule of court to the contrary notwithstanding. It hence becomes necessary to turn to the statutes and the rules of the law courts of the state to ascertain the forms and modes of proceeding in such a case.

§ 1982. *Practice act of New Jersey.*

Under the practice act of New Jersey (§§ 103–4), the plaintiff is required to file his declaration against the defendant within' thirty days after being returned "summoned," and the defendant his plea within thirty days after the expiration of the time limited or granted for filing the declaration. By section 110 of the same act, if any party shall not file his pleading in the cause within the time required by law, and shall file the same after the expiration of such time, he shall give the adverse party notice in writing of the time of filing such pleading, and the adverse party shall not be required to plead in reply thereto until ruled so to do.

§ 1983. *Defendant's consent to extend time of pleading estops him from taking advantage of plaintiff's laches in the matter, but waives no other rights.*

It is admitted that the declaration was not filed within the time required by law, but within the time in which the defendant consented that it might be filed. What was the legal operation of such consent? It estopped the defendant from taking advantage of the laches of the plaintiff in regard to the time of filing the declaration, but it had no other effect. It cannot properly be construed, as the counsel for plaintiff insists, into a waiver of any right which resulted to the defendant by extending the time, and the last clause of section 110, *supra*, absolved the defendant from the duty of putting in any plea, when the declaration is not filed within the time required by law, until ruled so to do by the plaintiff. As no rule was taken, the judgment is irregular.

This view renders it unnecessary to consider the other ground of irregularity taken by the defendant under section 113 of the practice act, viz., that the plaintiff ought to have moved for his judgment at the opening of the next term of the court after the default, and that, having failed so to do, he was not authorized to enter a judgment during the continuance of the term without an order of the court. The judgment is set aside. The plaintiff has leave to enter a rule that the defendant plead within twenty days after service of the rule, or that judgment be entered for want of a plea.

ALLIS *v.* STOWELL.

(Circuit Court for Wisconsin: 5 Federal Reporter, 203–206. 1880.)

Opinion by Dyer, J.

Statement of Facts.—This is a bill to restrain the infringement of two patents for saw-mill dogs, known as the Selden and Beckwith patents. On a previous hearing upon bill, answer and proofs, a decree was entered in favor of complainants, sustaining the validity of both patents. Subsequently the defendant moved that the cause be opened for a rehearing on the ground of newly-discovered evidence. The court granted a rehearing as to the Selden patent, but denied it as to the Beckwith patent, and it was ordered that the defendant have leave to amend his answer as prayed in said petition for a rehearing. By this order it was intended and understood that the controversy between the parties should be re-opened, but only to let in the newly-discovered matter, and to the extent only that the Selden patent might be thereby affected. The defendant filed an amended answer, which set up the new matter relied on to defeat the Selden patent, and also embraced all the original defenses to both patents. The complainant then filed a motion to strike the answer from the files for the reason that it was not limited in form and substance to the new matter, and therefore was not, as it is claimed, such an answer as the order for a rehearing authorized. The defendant then moved to dismiss the suit, under the sixty-sixth rule in equity, for the reason that no replication had been filed to the amended answer, and this is the motion now to be decided.

§ 1984. *A motion to dismiss for want of a replication to an amended answer will not be entertained while a motion to strike such answer from the files is pending.*

It is claimed by counsel for defendant that if the complainant desired to raise any question as to the regularity or sufficiency of the amended answer, he should have excepted to it; that a motion to strike from the files is irregular and cannot be entertained; and that as the answer was not excepted to, and a replication was not filed, he is entitled to have the suit dismissed, as of course, under the rule.

It is not intended now to pass upon the merits of the motion to strike the amended answer from the files. The only question to be presently determined is, Is the defendant entitled, in the face of that motion, to have the suit dismissed for want of a replication? In other words, is the complainant in such default as to entitle the defendant to such action by the court as he invokes? It must be presumed that the motion to strike the amended answer from the files was made in good faith, and an inspection of the answer shows that it contains all the defenses which appeared in the original answer, in addition to those embraced in the new matter, on account of which a rehearing was granted. Whether this form of pleading, in the present attitude of the case, be regular or not, I do not, as before remarked, now decide. But it seems very clear that the court cannot treat the motion to strike the amended answer from the files as such an act of non-conformity to correct practice as leaves the complainant in default, and as entitles the defendant to a dismissal of the suit for want of a replication. Rule 66 provides that "whenever the answer of the defendant shall not be excepted to, *or shall be adjudged or deemed sufficient*, the plaintiff shall file the general replication thereto on or before the next succeeding rule day thereafter. . . . If the plaintiff shall omit or refuse to file such replication within the prescribed period, the defendant shall be entitled to an order, as of course, for a dismissal of the suit."

So it appears that if the answer shall be excepted to, or shall be adjudged *or deemed insufficient*, a replication is not to be filed. And I do not think that the only method that may be pursued to test the sufficiency or regularity of an answer is that of filing exceptions. Where a question is presented like that here involved, I am of opinion that it may be raised by motion to strike the answer from the files, and the rule does not necessarily exclude such a course of procedure.

Whether or not, in a given case, exceptions should be filed, or a motion should be made to strike the pleading from the files, may depend upon the character of the objections which are made to the pleading. Authority upon the correct course of practice is meager, but in Strange v. Collins, 2 Ves. & B., 162, it was held by Lord Eldon that where a supplemental answer contained not only the new matter which the party had obtained leave to allege, but also other matter which was contained in a former answer, the supplemental answer could be ordered off the file, on motion. In the case at bar the pleading involved is an amended and not a supplemental answer, but that ought not to make any difference in the application of a rule of practice.

It is understood to be true, as claimed by counsel for defendant, that exceptions to this answer could not, in the present aspect of the case, be filed without leave. Barnes *v.* Tweddle, 10 Sim., 481. But I hardly think that leave of the court was a necessary prerequisite to a motion to strike the pleading from the files. On the whole, I am of opinion that whether that motion can be ultimately sustained on its merits or not, the complainant cannot be regarded as in such default for want of a replication as to entitle defendant to a dismissal of the suit.

The motion to dismiss will be denied; and, as it deems desirable that proper issue in the cause shall be joined without unnecessary delay, the motion to strike the answer from the files may be brought to a hearing on ten days' notice by either party.

CASTER *v.* WOOD.

(Circuit Court for Pennsylvania: 1 Baldwin, 289-291. 1831.)

Statement of Facts.— This was an application to file an additional answer, upon affidavit that the respondent had since the former answer acquired further information.

§ 1985. *Answers are not amendable as of course.*

Opinion of the Court.

Applications to amend an answer are not grantable of course, but depend on the discretion of the court; they are viewed more favorably when made to reform an answer than when made to take it off the file and substitute a different one; the former is allowed in many cases, the latter only in special cases, where the conscience of the court is satisfied that the purposes of justice require it. 4 Madd., 28; 4 J. C., 375, 376.

§ 1986. *In a clear case the court may allow an answer to be taken off the file and a new one substituted.*

As a general rule, the plaintiff is entitled to the benefit of all the admissions of the defendant on oath, and it must be a clear case where the answer will be permitted to be taken from the file. But the present motion is merely to amend and explain matter not fully stated in the answer, on account of the partial information then possessed by the defendant, and the introduction of new matter since come to his knowledge, deemed material to the case. We think it comes within the established rules of courts of equity, and therefore allow the amendments, imposing on the defendant the condition of furnishing the opposite party with the names of the witnesses whose depositions he intends to take.

§ 1987. Striking out pleadings.— Where a plea, by way of traverse, includes other matter not responsive to any allegations, it is not error to strike out such matter on motion of plaintiff. Hart *v.* United States, 5 Otto, 816. After issue joined the defendant will be allowed to traverse the allegation, necessary in the declaration to give the court of claims jurisdiction, that the claimant was loyal. The court of claims will be controlled by substance in pleadings rather than by the exact rules of special pleading. A motion to strike out a plea which would merely cumber the record allowed. Pierce *v.* United States,* 1 Ct. Cl., 195.

§ 1988. The mode of disposing of pleas, which seems to be growing in favor in the territorial courts, by striking them out on motion, is an unscientific and unprofessional mode of raising and deciding a pure question of law. It should be confined to pleas filed irregularly, those not sworn to if that is required, or those wanting signature of counsel, or showing any defect of that character; but if a real and important issue of law is to be made, that issue should be raised by demurrer. Bates v. Clark, 5 Otto, 201.

§ 1989. Where a declaration contained two counts, one of which set out an injunction bond with the condition thereto annexed, and averred a breach, and the second count was merely for the debt in the penalty; and the pleas were all applicable to the first count, which was upon trial stricken out by the plaintiff, and the court gave judgment upon the second count for the want of a plea, this judgment was proper and must be affirmed. Hogan v. Ross, 13 How., 173.

§ 1990. A motion to make the pleadings more definite and certain is the proper practice where the pleadings are confused by the intermingling of material and immaterial, issuable and non-issuable, allegations. Gause v. Knapp, 1 McC., 75.

§ 1991. Motions to strike out are to be directed not to special sentences, but to entire pleadings or counts. Ibid.

§ 1992. While a demurrer cuts back to the first bad pleading, it is by no means sure that a motion to strike out will have this effect, nor that on such a motion final judgment may be given. Ibid.

§ 1993. When a defect of jurisdiction appears on the pleadings, advantage may be taken of it by motion in arrest of judgment, or by writ of error. Blachley v. Davis,* 1 McL., 412.

§ 1994. Incorrect title of officer used in pleadings.— An allegation in a petition that services were rendered by order of the general postmaster equivalent to an allegation that they were rendered by order of the postmaster-general. White & Sherwood v. United States,* Dev., 135.

§ 1995. Defective pleadings.— In a case where, after replication, an amended bill was filed without leave, and without terms, where a hearing was had upon answers to which no replications had been filed, where a cross-bill had been put in which joined nobody as defendant, thus being a nullity, and where a decree had been given on this cross-bill, it was held that although none of these errors had been noticed in the court below, yet the court on appeal cannot overlook a combination of errors of so grave a character. Washington Railroad v. Bradleys, 10 Wall., 299.

§ 1996. If the plea is defective in omitting facts which give jurisdiction to the secretary of the treasury, the replication admitting that jurisdiction cures the defect. United States v. Morris, 10 Wheat., 246.

§ 1997. In a declaration in ejectment various demises were laid, and the verdict of the jury and judgment of the United States circuit court were entered on one of the demises only; and it was contended that the court ought not to have entered a judgment on the issue found for the plaintiff, but should have awarded a venire facias de novo, and that this irregularity might be taken advantage of on a writ of error. Held, that if this objection had been made in the circuit court on a motion in arrest of judgment, the plaintiff would have been permitted to strike out all the demises in the declaration but that on which the verdict was given. That omission was only an omission of form, and the act of congress of 1789 expressly provides that no judgment shall be reversed for any defect or want of form, but that the federal courts shall proceed to give judgment, according as the right of the cause and matter in law shall appear to them, without regarding any imperfections, defects or want of form in the judgment except that specially demurred to. Van Ness v. Bank of the United States, 13 Pet., 17.

§ 1998. A judgment against some out of several defendants, and the case against the rest not being disposed of, all having been served with process, is irregular and not final, and a writ of error based thereon will be dismissed. United States v. Gerault, 11 How., 22.

§ 1999. A motion for a venire de novo is a motion for a new trial upon matter appearing upon the record, and is addressed to the discretion of the court. It will be granted when a general verdict for plaintiff has been rendered upon several counts, one of which proves bad, provided that evidence has been offered upon the bad count among others. Mandeville v. Cookenderfer,* 3 Cr. C. C., 257.

§ 2000. Where a verdict has been rendered as if the pleadings had been complete, a failure to answer one of the pleas filed in the case will not be ground for reversing judgment. Nauvoo v. Ritter,* 7 Otto, 389.

§ 2001. If a defendant has had the benefit of a defense under one of his pleas, on which issue was taken, a verdict will not be set aside because a demurrer to another plea setting up the same defense was wrongly sustained. Railroad Co. v. Bank of Ashland, 12 Wall., 226.

§ 2002. When the pleadings are so defective that the verdict rendered thereon is immaterial, the court, on error, will endeavor to accomplish justice by giving all reasonable facility to get the record in proper and intelligible shape before rendering final judgment. Garland v. Davis, 4 How., 181.

§ 2003. In such case judgment will be reversed and the case remanded for further proceedings, the practice of awarding a repleader having gone into disuse. *Ibid.*

§ 2004. A repleader is never awarded in favor of him who commits the first fault in pleading, nor where one issue raised is material. Hartfield v. Patton,* Hemp., 269.

§ 2005. A court of error cannot award a repleader. United States v. Sawyer,* 1 Gall., 86.

§ 2006. Non obstante veredicto.—If the defendant plead in bar a matter which is no defense at all, and it be found for him, still he cannot have judgment, but the court will give judgment for the plaintiff, *non obstante veredicto;* provided the defect in the plea is not in the form but in the matter of it. If it be in the form, or can be made better by other pleadings, a repleader will be awarded. The rule is the same if the facts stated in a demurrer to evidence maintain such a plea. Postmaster-General v. Reeder, 4 Wash., 678.

§ 2007. A judgment *non obstante veredicto* may be rendered in favor of the plaintiff when the cause of action shown by the declaration is confessed by the plea and no bar pleaded. But a defendant cannot have such judgment, and a motion therefor will be treated as a motion in arrest. He can only move in arrest if the bar shown by the plea be sufficient, and the matter found by the verdict does not answer it. Brown v. Hartford Fire Ins. Co.,* 21 Law Rep., 726.

§ 2008. Departure.—If the defendant to an action on a note plead the bankruptcy of the indorser in bar, a replication stating that the note was given to the indorser in trust for the plaintiff is not a departure from the declaration, which alleges the note to have been given by the defendant for value received. Wilson v. Codman, 3 Cr., 193.

§ 2009. A judgment had been recovered by the United States for a penalty which was afterwards remitted. The marshal, to whom an execution was issued, had made a levy, but, on being served with the warrant of remission, redelivered the goods to the debtors. An action was thereupon brought against him in the name of the United States for the moiety of the penalty allowed to the officers, but the declaration alleged no interest in them but only in the United States. The defendant pleaded the remission. The plaintiffs replied the interest of the officers. On special demurrer, held to be a departure. United States v. Morris, 1 Paine, 231.

§ 2010. Duplicity consists of joining distinct causes of action, defenses or breaches in one pleading, but not of alleging several facts which make up one cause of action, etc. Jackson v. Rundlet, 1 Woodb. & M., 381.

§ 2011. Duplicity is an error of form only. McKay v. Campbell, 2 Abb., 120.

§ 2011a. A replication to a plea setting up the statute of limitations, that the debt sued for arose upon an account between merchant and merchant, and that the plaintiff was beyond seas when the cause of action arose, is double. Craig v. Brown,* Pet. C. C., 443.

§ 2012. A replication of non-payment on the day and non-acceptance in satisfaction is bad for duplicity. United States v. Gurney,* 1 Wash., 446.

§ 2013. To plead in one count that defendant prevented plaintiff from voting for several officers, or that defendant in several ways prevented plaintiff from voting, is double. McKay v. Campbell, 2 Abb., 120.

§ 2014. The statement of more than one sufficient matter as a ground of action or defense in the same count or plea is forbidden by the common law and by the code of Oregon. But by the code objection to duplicity is to be taken by motion to strike out, instead of by special demurrer as at common law. McKay v. Campbell, 1 Saw., 374.

§ 2015. Waiver.—An answer is an appearance and waives a plea to the jurisdiction, and therefore no such plea can be set up in an answer. Vose v. Reed, 1 Woods, 647.

§ 2016. Pleading over to a declaration adjudged good on demurrer is waiver of the demurrer. Stanton v. Embrey, 3 Otto, 548.

§ 2017. A refusal or omission by the defendant to join in a demurrer to a plea is a waiver of the plea. Morsell v. Hall, 13 How., 212.

§ 2018. If a misjoinder of parties is not taken advantage of by a plea in abatement it is waived by pleading to the merits. Minor v. Mechanics' Bank of Alexandria, 1 Pet., 46.

§ 2019. When the record does not disclose what disposition was made of a demurrer, but an answer was subsequently filed on which the parties went to a hearing, the presumption is that it has been abandoned. Basey v. Gallagher, 20 Wall., 670.

§ 2020. Allegations and pleadings to the merits are a waiver of the preliminary inquiry as to the proprietary interests, and an admission that the party is rightly in court and capable of contesting the merits. United States v. 422 Casks of Wine, 1 Pet., 547.

§ 2021. When one count in a declaration was left unanswered, so that plaintiff might have had judgment upon *nil dicit*, yet as he did not move for this, and both parties proceeded throughout the trial as if that count did not exist, it was held, when the case came up upon exceptions, that in the light of the proceedings the count must be understood to be waived. Aurora v. West,* 7 Wall., 82.

§ 2022. A plaintiff, having failed to file his replication within the time required by law, asked leave to file it, and defendant objected. No decision was given, but plaintiff filed his replication with the clerk, and the parties proceeded to trial as if it were properly in. Plaintiff obtained judgment, which the court on motion reversed. *Held*, on error, that defendant had waived his objection and his right to move for judgment, and a mandate was issued to enforce judgment for the plaintiff. Osgood v. Haverty,* McCahon, 182.

§ 2023. Misjoinder of actions should be taken advantage of by demurrer, motion to strike out, or perhaps by motion to compel plaintiff to elect; and the right to object for misjoinder is waived by taking issue upon the plaintiff's petition. Fraley v. Bentley,* 1 Dak. T'y, 25.

§ 2024. A party who means to except to the jurisdiction of the court in a case of seizure must plead to that jurisdiction. If he files a claim and plea to the merits, on which the parties are at issue, it is a waiver of any exception to the jurisdiction. On such claim and plea no question as to the place of seizure is before the court. The Abby, 1 Mason, 360.

§ 2025. If a plea to the jurisdiction and a plea of *non assumpsit* be put in, and the issue be made up on the latter plea only, no notice being taken of the former, and upon this state of the pleadings the cause goes on to trial, the plea to the jurisdiction is considered as waived. Bailey v. Dozier, 6 How., 23.

§ 2026. Where a *scire facias* was issued against special bail, who pleaded two pleas, to the first of which the plaintiff took issue, and demurred to the second; and the cause went to trial upon that state of the pleadings without a joinder in demurrer, and the court gave a general judgment for the plaintiff, this was not error. Morsell v. Hall, 13 How., 212.

§ 2027. If a foreign consul, being sued in a state court, omits to plead his privilege of exemption from the suit, and afterwards, on removing the judgment of the inferior court to a higher court by writ of error, claims the privilege, such an omission is not a waiver of the privilege. Davis v. Packard, 7 Pet., 276.

§ 2028. A plea since the last continuance waives the issue previously joined, and puts the case on that plea. Yeaton v. Lynn, 5 Pet., 223.

§ 2029. If plaintiff demurs to the defendant's plea to a chancery attachment, he thereby waives his right to move to strike out the plea on the ground that it was pleaded without giving special bail. Irwin v. Henderson, 3 Cr. C. C., 167.

§ 2080. L., as executor of W., instituted an action of *assumpsit* on April 6, 1826. The declaration stated L. to be executor of W., and claiming as executor for money paid by him as such. The defendant pleaded *non assumpsit*, and a verdict and judgment were given for the plaintiff. After the institution of the suit and before the trial the letters testamentary of L. were revoked by the orphans' court of the county of Alexandria, D. C., he having, after being required, failed to give bond with counter security, as directed by the court. As the plaintiff was incontestably executor when suit was brought and issue joined, and could then rightfully maintain the action, and the revocation of the letters testamentary was not brought before the court by a plea since the last continuance, as it might have been, the defendant must be considered as having waived his defense and resting his cause on the general issue. Yeaton v. Lynn, 5 Pet., 223.

§ 2081. Under the Missouri code of pleading every defense must be taken by demurrer or by answer; and all defenses except want of jurisdiction, and that the facts stated in the petition, which is the first pleading, do not show a cause of action, unless taken by demurrer or special answer, are waived. Tyler v. Magwire, 17 Wall., 253.

§ 2082. **Variance.**—A party is not allowed to state one case in a bill or answer, and make out a different one by proof; the *allegata* and *probata* must agree, and the latter must support the former. Boone v. Chiles, 10 Pet., 177.

§ 2083. A variance is immaterial which does not change the nature of the contract. Ferguson v. Harwood, 7 Cr., 408.

§ 2084. Variance must be objected to when the evidence is introduced. Roberts v. Graham, 6 Wall., 578.

§ 2085. All the particulars set forth in pleading, descriptive of a record or instrument on which the party relies, must be established by proof, or the variance will be fatal. Whitaker v. Bramson, 2 Paine, 209.

§ 2086. Variances between the writ and declaration are pleadable in abatement only; they cannot be taken advantage of by general demurrer. Duvall v. Craig, 2 Wheat., 45.

§ 2087. Any misdescription of a record in pleading is fatal. Hence, in an action of debt on a judgment, misdescriptions in the declaration of the amount and the parties were both fatal variances. Lawrence v. Willoughby,* 1 Minn., 87.

§ 2088. In declaring upon a decree for a certain sum of money with interest, the omission to state the clause of the decree giving interest will constitute a variance. Thompson v. Jameson,* 1 Cr., 283.

§ 2039. A declaration which misstates the date of a bond sued on is bad for variance on general demurrer. Cooke v. Graham,* 3 Cr., 229.

§ 2040. Upon an allegation of negligence of defendant and his servant, it is not a variance to prove negligence of the servant. Dobbin v. Foyles,* 2 Cr. C. C., 65.

§ 2041. In an action of debt against Daniel Carroll and William Brent, survivors of Charles Carroll and Eli Williams, upon articles of agreement, and averring the articles to be "sealed with the seals of the said Williams and Carrolls, and the said William Brent," if on profert and oyer the articles appear to be signed and sealed thus: "Williams & Carrolls (seal)," "Wm. Brent (seal)," "Thomas Tingey (seal)," the variance is fatal on general demurrer. Tingey v. Carroll, 3 Cr. C. C., 693.

§ 2042. An averment that the plaintiffs have an entire interest in themselves in the subject insured cannot be supported by evidence of a joint interest with others; nor can an averment of a joint interest with others be supported by proof of a sole interest. Catlett v. Pacific Ins. Co., 1 Paine, 594.

§ 2043. In pleading a record it is not indispensable that the precise words of the record shall be observed. Surplusage or immaterial omissions in matters of substance, in pleading records, are attended with no other consequences than in other cases. But as to matters of description it is otherwise, and there the record produced must conform strictly to the plea. Whitaker v. Bramson, 2 Paine, 209.

§ 2044. An allegation of a combination between the master and mate to ill-treat and oppress a seaman is not supported by proof that each of them separately assaulted and ill-treated him, without some presumptive evidence of concert between them. Jenks v. Lewis, 1 Ware, 51.

§ 2045. An action for a certain sum, stated in the declaration to be the amount of a decree obtained by the plaintiff, cannot be supported by evidence of a decree for the same sum, with interest from a certain day to the day of passing the decree. Thompson v. Jameson, 1 Cr., 282.

§ 2046. The interest of a copartnership cannot be given in evidence on an averment of individual interest, nor an averment of the interest of a company be supported by a special contract relating to the interest of an individual. Graves v. Boston Marine Ins. Co., 2 Cr., 419.

§ 2047. Where the declaration alleged an undertaking in consideration of a contract entered into by the plaintiff to build a ship, and the evidence was of a contract to finish a ship partly built, it was held that the variance was fatal. Smith v. Barker,* 3 Day (Conn.), 303.

§ 2048. A by-law, approved on the 27th of March, will not support an averment of a by-law passed on the 26th. Common Council of Alexandria v. Brockett, 1 Cr. C. C., 505.

§ 2049. In slander, evidence of words spoken in the second person will not support an averment of words spoken in the third person. Birch v. Simms, 1 Cr. C. C., 550.

§ 2050. An averment of a demise from year to year for three years, at $120 a year, is not supported by evidence of a demise from year to year for two years, at $120 a year, and for one year at $100. Dorsey v. Chenault, 2 Cr. C. C., 316.

§ 2051. An award, signed by A. and B., as an award made in pursuance of a reference to them, will not support an averment of an award or umpirage made by the said B. as umpire, upon the failure of the two original arbitrators, A. and C., to deliver their award within the time limited by the bond. Goldsborough v. McWilliams, 2 Cr. C. C., 401.

§ 2052. A note payable in sixty days, "with interest from date," will not support a declaration upon a note payable in sixty days without interest. Coyle v. Gozzler, 2 Cr. C. C., 625.

§ 2053. In an action of ejectment, if the plaintiff count upon a lease to himself from a person whom the evidence shows to have been dead at the time, it is bad. Connor v. Bradley, 1 How., 211.

§ 2054. A declaration averring that a due-bill was made dum sola precluded the admission as evidence of a due-bill made to the wife during the coverture, and for a consideration accruing during the coverture. Smith v. Clarke, 4 Cr. C. C., 293.

§ 2055. The declaration in an action against one partner only never gives notice of the claim being on a partnership transaction. The proceeding is always as if the party sued was the sole contracting party; and if the declaration were to show a partnership contract, the judgment against the single party could not be sustained. Barry v. Foyles, 1 Pet., 311.

§ 2056. When the declaration professes to set forth the specification in a patent as part of the grant, the slightest variance is fatal, and the defendant is entitled to claim a nonsuit. In general it is sufficient to state the grant in substance in the declaration. Tyron v. White, Pet. C. C., 96.

§ 2057. A nonsuit was entered by direction of the court where the evidence varied from the case stated in the declaration; the latter stating the goods as belonging to the plaintiff, of which the defendant, as bailiff, was to make profit for him, and charging the defendant as receiver by the hands of A., B. and C., being the money of the plaintiff; and the evidence proved that the money received was that of himself and his partners and was received on joint account. Jordan v. Wilkins, 2 Wash., 483.

§ 2058. A variance in pleading which would be fatal at common law may not be so in courts which proceed according to the civil law; as the rules which govern the former courts are seldom applicable to proceedings in the latter. Crawford v. The William Penn, 3 Wash., 484.

§ 2059. A court proceeding under the civil law will not allow a party to be surprised by evidence materially variant from the case stated in the pleadings, but will allow an amendment. *Ibid.*

§ 2060. When an information for violating a by-law of a town stated that the penalty accrued to the state, and by charter it appeared that the penalty accrued to the town, judgment was arrested. Virginia v. Hoof,* 1 Cr. C. C., 31.

§ 2061. Where the writ is brought by the United States of America a verdict for the United States is sufficient. Sears v. United States,* 1 Gall., 257.

§ 2062. A variance between a petition under the Louisiana code and the facts found by the court, when the latter were warranted by the proofs, and the judgment conforms with law and justice, will not be a fatal defect on error. Railroad Co. v. Lindsay, 4 Wall., 650.

§ 2063. The declaration contained two counts. The first, setting out the cause of action, stated, "for that whereas the said defendants and copartners, trading under the firm name of J., T. & Co., in the life-time of said W. T., on the 1st of March, 1821, were indebted to the plaintiffs, and being so indebted," etc.; the second count was upon an *insimul computassent*, and began, "and also whereas the said defendants, afterwards, to wit, on the day and year aforesaid, accounted with the said plaintiffs of and concerning divers other sums of money, due and owing from said defendants," etc. The defendants, to maintain the issue on their parts gave in evidence to the jury that W. T., the person mentioned in the declaration, died on January 6, 1819, that he was formerly a partner with J. and P. T., the defendants, under the firm of J., T. & Co., but that the partnership was dissolved in October, 1817, and that the defendants formed a copartnership in 1820. The defendants prayed the court to instruct the jury that there was a variance between the contract declared on and that given in evidence, W. T. being dead. By the court: The only allegation in the second count in the declaration from which it is argued that the contract declared upon was one including W. T. with J. and P. is "that the said defendants accounted with the plaintiffs." But this does not warrant the conclusion drawn from it. The defendants were J. and P. T.; W. T. was not a defendant, and the terms, "the said defendants," could not include him. There was no variance between the contract declared upon in the second count and the contract proved upon the trial with respect to the parties thereto. Schimmelpennick v. Turner, 6 Pet., 1.

§ 2064. **Aider by verdict.**— A good cause of action defectively stated in the declaration will be aided by verdict; but if it appear that the cause of action was defective a verdict will not aid it. McDonald v. Hobson,* 7 How., 745.

§ 2065. Where a fact must necessarily have been proved at the trial to justify the verdict, and the declaration omits to state it, the defect is cured by the verdict, if the general terms of the declaration are otherwise sufficient to comprehend the proof. Dobson v. Campbell, 1 Summ., 319.

§ 2066. Want of averment of citizenship in a declaration filed in the United States court is a defect of substance and not cured by verdict; so also of the averment of value of property in dispute when necessary to give jurisdiction. Smith v. Jackson, 1 Paine, 486.

§ 2067. A plea purporting to answer all the breaches in the declaration, which answers only some of them, is good after verdict. Such defect can only be taken advantage of by special demurrer. United States v. Willard, 1 Paine, 539.

§ 2068. Where an action is for foreign money, and its value is not averred, a verdict cures the defect. Brown v. Barry, 3 Dal., 368.

§ 2069. If a proper case is laid in the declaration or libel, but not described with precision, the court after verdict will presume that the want of precision was supplied by evidence; *aliter*, if no ground is laid at all. United States v. The Virgin, Pet. C. C., 7.

§ 2070. Surplusage in pleading does not in any case vitiate after verdict. Carroll v. Peake, 1 Pet., 18.

§ 2071. A verdict does not cure a variance between the covenant alleged in the declaration and that produced on oyer. Ingle v. Collard, 1 Cr. C. C., 152.

§ 2072. Non-joinder of a party plaintiff is a defect which is cured by verdict. Greenleaf v. Schell, 6 Blatch., 225.

§ 2073. Where three pleas were filed and a replication was put in to only-one of them, the other two, which should have concluded to the country being improperly concluded with a verification, but the trial proceeded as if the pleadings were complete, the defect will be cured by verdict; and this though the jury accidentally found the "issue" for plaintiff instead of "issues." Laber v. Cooper, 7 Wall., 565.

§ 2074. Where there is an informal plea to an action of trespass, which is not demurred to, but on which issue is taken and a trial had, such informality cannot be considered upon a writ of error. Deitsch v. Wiggins, 15 Wall., 539.

§ 2075. In an action for the infringement of a patent, an omission to aver that the assignment was properly recorded is cured by verdict. Dobson v. Campbell,* 1 Sumn., 326.

§ 2076. Where a matter is so essentially necessary to be proved, to establish the plaintiff's right to recover, that the jury could not be presumed to have found a verdict for him unless it had been proved at the trial, the omission to state that matter in express terms in the declaration is cured by verdict if the general terms of the declaration are otherwise sufficient to comprehend it. Ibid.

§ 2077. Where it was omitted to allege in the declaration on a note a demand of payment on the person of the maker, but it averred a demand at the bank "where the note was negotiable," such averment in the declaration could not be true, unless there was an agreement between the parties that the demand should be made there. Brent v. Bank of the Metropolis, 1 Pet., 89.

§ 2078. And the averment must have been proved at the trial or the plaintiff could not have obtained a verdict and judgment; and after a verdict judgment will be sustained. Ibid.

§ 2079. The omission of the declaration to allege a material date is a defect cured by verdict. Stockton v. Bishop,* 4 How., 155.

§ 2080. Though the record does not state who the jurors were nor that they were sworn, yet a court of error will presume that justice was administered in the ordinary form. Ibid.

§ 2081. When the record is brought before the court on error, defects of form are to be disregarded. Ibid.

§ 2082. Where a statute (of Illinois) provides that an assignee of a note may sue an assignor if suit against the maker would be unavailing, a general averment in the declaration that suit would be unavailing is bad on demurrer; but as such an averment will permit proof of the facts thus imperfectly stated, it will be presumed after verdict that they were proved, and the defect will be cured. Wills v. Claflin, 2 Otto, 135.

VI. AMENDMENTS.

SUMMARY — *Allowance of amendments not open to revision in court of error, § 2083.— Rights after substantial amendment to declaration, § 2084.— Amendment to answer allowed as of course to supply inadvertent admission, § 2085.— New cause of action not to be introduced at trial, § 2086.— Libel in rem not to be changed into libel in personam, § 2087.*

§ 2083. The act of the circuit court in allowing the amendment of the declaration by the addition of a count is not subject to revision in the supreme court, though the amendment amount to the addition of a new cause of action. Wright v. Hollingsworth, §§ 2088-90.

§ 2084. When the declaration is amended by the addition of a count, defendant has a right to plead de novo, but will waive the right by going to trial without objection. Ibid.

§ 2085. When the answer in a libel suit omitted to deny plaintiff's allegations as to the amount of damage sustained, and this was evidently the result of inadvertence, held, that an amendment would be allowed, and plaintiff's counsel should have anticipated that such a motion would be made and granted. Goodyear Dental Vulcanite Co. v. White, § 2091.

§ 2086. An amendment introducing a new cause of action cannot be made at the trial. Postmaster-General v. Ridgway, § 2092.

§ 2087. A libel in rem cannot be changed by amendment into a libel in personam. The Young America, §§ 2093-94.

NOTES.— See §§ 2095-2130.]

WRIGHT v. LESSEE OF HOLLINGSWORTH.

(1 Peters, 165-169. 1828.)

Opinion by MR. JUSTICE TRIMBLE.

STATEMENT OF FACTS.— This action of ejectment was commenced in the circuit court held in East Tennessee by suing out a writ of *capias ad respondan-*

dum, accompanied with the declaration, and the tenants in possession held to bail to answer to the action in the manner provided for by a statute of the state. The original declaration contained two counts, the first on the demise of Hollingsworth and Kaighn, citizens of Pennsylvania; the second on the demise of Joseph Blake and Daniel Green, citizens of Massachusetts.

The tenants appeared and pleaded not guilty, upon which issue was joined. A trial was had, and a nonsuit suffered by the plaintiff, which was set aside on the payment of costs. After these proceedings, the court, on the motion of the plaintiff, permitted the declaration to be amended by adding a count on the demise of Benjamin Spencer, a citizen of Missouri. The parties went to trial without any other pleadings, and a verdict having been found for the plaintiff, upon the third or new count, judgment was thereon rendered in his favor, to reverse which the defendants have prosecuted this writ of error.

They allege the judgment is erroneous and should be reversed: 1. Because the count on which judgment was rendered against them does not show that Missouri is one of the United States. 2. Because the court permitted the declaration to be amended by adding a new count on the demise of Benjamin Spencer, and especially as the amendment was permitted without payment of costs. 3. Because no plea was filed to the new count, nor any issue made up thereon.

§ 2088. *Courts take judicial notice of the admission of states into the Union.*
The first objection was very properly not pressed in argument. The count alleges Benjamin Spencer to be a citizen of the state of Missouri. This count was filed after Missouri was admitted as a state into the Union; and there can be no question but that this and every other court in the nation are bound to take notice of the admission of a state as one of the United States, without any express averment of the fact.

§ 2089. *The action of courts of original jurisdiction in allowing and refusing amendments in pleading, and in granting or refusing new trials, will not be reviewed in the supreme court.*
In support of the second objection it is urged that the admission of the new count, on the demise of a new lessor, made a material alteration in the suit; that, the suit having been originally commenced under the state practice, by writ of *capias ad respondendum*, to which the former lessors only were parties, the amendment was, in substance and effect, the institution of a new suit, or at least grafting a new one upon the old, and produced an incongruity upon the record; the first and second counts, and the proceedings on them, being proceedings under the statute, and the third or new count a proceeding at common law, and that, according to established principles of practice, it should have been allowed, if at all, only on payment of costs.

This argument would be entitled to great and perhaps decisive influence, if addressed to a court having any discretion or power over the subject of amendments.

But the allowance and refusal of amendments in the pleadings, the granting or refusing new trials, and indeed, most other incidental orders made in the progress of a cause before trial, are matters so peculiarly addressed to the sound discretion of the courts of original jurisdiction as to be fit for their decision only, under their own rules and modes of practice. This, it is true, may occasionally lead to particular hardships; but, on the other hand, the general inconvenience of this court attempting to revise and correct all the intermediate proceedings in suits between their commencement and final judgment would be intolerable. This court has always declined interfering in such cases; accordingly it was held by the court in Wood *v.* Young, 4 Cranch, 237, that the refusal of the court below to continue a cause after it is at issue is not a matter upon which error can be assigned; that the refusal of the court below to grant a new trial is not matter for which a writ of error lies (5 Cranch, 11, 187, and 4 Wheat., 220); and that the refusal of the court below to allow a plea to be amended, or a new plea to be filed, or to grant a new trial, or to continue a cause, cannot be assigned as a cause of reversal or a writ of error. We can perceive no distinction in principle between these cases and the one before the court. We must take the declaration, including the amendment, as we find it on the record. Nor can we interfere because the court below did not, as it ought, require the costs formerly accrued to be paid as a condition of the amendment.

§ 2090. *Where the declaration is amended by adding a new count, the defendant has a right to plead de novo, but may waive the right.*

The authorities cited by the learned counsel do not, we think, support his last position, that the judgment is erroneous because a plea was not filed to the new count. They prove, unquestionably, that, upon the amendment being made to the declaration by adding a count, the defendants had a right to plead *de novo;* they prove nothing more. They do not show that the defendant in such cases must necessarily plead *de novo,* or that judgment may be entered by default for want of a plea to the new count, if, before the amendment, he has pleaded the general issue. We think the practice is well settled to the contrary. The defendant has a right, if he will, to withdraw his former plea and plead anew either the general issue or any further or other pleas which his case may require; but he may, if he will, abide by his plea already pleaded and waive his right of pleading *de novo.* His failure to plead and going to trial without objection are held to be a waiver of his right to plead, and an election to abide by his plea; and if it in terms purports to go to the whole action, as is the case in this instance, it is deemed sufficient to cover the whole declaration, and puts the plaintiff to the proof of his case on the new as well as on the old counts.

This is the general doctrine in other forms of action, such as trespass and *assumpsit;* and we see no reason to distinguish the action of ejectment or take it out of the general rule.

Judgment affirmed, with costs.

GOODYEAR DENTAL VULCANITE COMPANY *v.* WHITE.

(Circuit Court for New York: 17 Blatchford, 5–9. 1879.)

Opinion by WALLACE, J.

STATEMENT OF FACTS.— The defendant moves for leave to amend his answer so far as to deny certain allegations of the complaint, which, not being denied in the answer, stand as admitted. The action was commenced in May, 1875, and the complaint alleges that the defendant published certain libelous matter concerning a patent of the plaintiff. "knowing that the plaintiff was then offering for sale, and was about offering for sale, licenses or office rights to use said invention under said letters patent, and maliciously contriving to cause it to be believed that the plaintiff was not the lawful owner of the exclusive rights secured by said letters patent, and could not lawfully sell licenses to use said invention, and could not lawfully compel the payment of royalties for the use of the invention, and to prevent the plaintiff from effecting sales of licenses as aforesaid to dentists." The complaint further alleges, "that by reason of said several false and defamatory publications, great numbers of the dentists, and particularly the persons mentioned in Schedule A, hereto annexed, were dissuaded from purchasing said licenses, and refused, and still refuse, to purchase the same in consequence thereof," and that the plaintiff has sustained damages in the sum of $75,000. Schedule A sets forth the names and residences of over fourteen hundred dentists residing in all parts of the United States. To this complaint the defendant interposed a pleading which combined demurrers to each count in the complaint with pleas of the statute of limitations, and matter in defense which could only be urged in mitigation of damages. The demurrers were noticed for argument from time to time, but the hearing upon the demurrers was delayed, and the decision was not had until October, 1878, at which time the demurrers were overruled and the pleading permitted to stand as an answer upon the payment of the costs of the demurrers. The defendant then moved to amend the answer, and the motion was granted, but upon the hearing of that motion it was first discovered that the answer, as amended, did not contain a denial of the allegation in the complaint which states that, by reason of the publications of the defendant, the dentists in Schedule A were dissuaded from purchasing licenses of the plaintiffs, or of the allegation that the plaintiff has sustained damages in the sum of $75,000; and thereupon leave was obtained to move for the further amendment now asked for.

§ 2091. *Where, in an answer, defendant omits to deny the statements in the complaint of the manner and amount of damages suffered, an amendment will be permitted if it appears that the omission was the result of mistake or inadvertence.*

It is palpable that the defendant did not intend to admit the truth of these averments, and that, upon the issue as it now stands, the defendant will be precluded from disputing his liability for very heavy damages. It is urged, in opposition to the motion, that the plaintiff has relied upon the implied admission in the answer, and, resting upon this from 1875 until this motion was made, it has not issued commissions and taken testimony *de bene esse* as it otherwise would have done, and, in consequence, by the death, or removal, or forgetfulness of many of the dentists mentioned in Schedule A, it will be unable to produce proof, as to a large number of these dentists, that they were influenced by the defendant's publications and were thereby dissuaded from taking licenses from the plaintiff; and it is further stated in the plaintiff's affidavit that the additional expense of obtaining its testimony at the present time, owing to peculiar circumstances, will be very onerous.

It would be a great hardship upon the defendant to preclude him from controverting so important an issue in the case, in consequence of a slip of his counsel in framing the answer, and the court will struggle against the result, and, in furtherance of justice, give him an opportunity to present the truth of the matter, unless constrained to the contrary because of the countervailing hardship which such action would impose upon the plaintiff.

Was the plaintiff justified in relying upon the implied admission in the answer? Had he a right to suppose that the issue, which would eventually be tried, was that which was tendered by the answer? Here was a pleading containing demurrers which went to the whole complaint, and also matter by way of defense. By the demurrers the defendant admitted all the facts in the complaint, while, by another part of the pleading, he sought to deny the plaintiff's right to recover. What was the legal effect of such a pleading? A defendant may demur to part of a complaint and answer as to the residue, when the complaint joins several causes of action, but he cannot demur and answer to the same cause of action. He must either demur or answer. Old Code of Procedure, §§ 143–148, 151. There can be no doubt that the plaintiff could have stricken out either the matter in defense or the demurrers, upon a motion for that purpose. Instead of adopting this course, he preferred to notice the demurrers for hearing. By doing this he elected to treat the demurrers as the regular pleading on the part of the defendant. Upon the decision overruling the demurrers, unless leave had been given to the defendant to answer, there would have been no answer in the case. This motion, then, is to be considered as though there had never been an answer in the case until leave was given, upon the decision of the demurrers, by which the defendant's pleading was allowed to stand as an answer, and the position of the plaintiff is the same as though the defendant had then, for the first time, served the answer which he now moves to amend. It is true, the error in the pleading was the fault of the defendant, but the plaintiff has no just cause to complain that he has been prejudiced by relying upon an admission in an answer, when he should have known that, as matter of law, there was no answer in the case.

But I prefer to place the decision of this motion upon broader grounds and consider it as though the answer sought to be amended had been the only pleading served, when issue was originally joined in the action. I think the plaintiff's counsel were not justified in the belief that the defendant intended to admit such an important allegation of the complaint, and should have regarded it as inadvertent and a slip in pleading. Defendants who contest the plaintiff's right to recover in an action for a wrong are not accustomed to accept the plaintiff's own statement of his damages; and to concede, as was apparently done here, that the plaintiff sustained $75,000 damages by reason of a libel, would be such a startling departure from the line of action usually adopted by a defendant, as to suggest, almost necessarily, mistake or ignorance. If there had been an express admission in the answer to this effect it would have excited surprise and incredulity.

Aside from the extraordinary character of the admission, the rest of the answer indicated that the defendant intended to contest the amount of the plaintiff's damages, because the last defense pleaded in the answer, while inartificially pleaded, was in substance a defense by way of mitigation of damages. Under the circumstances, the plaintiff's counsel should have anticipated that a motion to amend the answer would be made at the trial, if not before, and should also have assumed that the motion would appeal so strongly to the equitable consideration of the court that it could hardly be refused. The motion to amend is granted.

POSTMASTER-GENERAL *v.* RIDGWAY.

(District Court for Pennsylvania: Gilpin, 135–189. 1829.)

Action to enforce liability on a bond.

§ 2092. *An amendment introducing a new cause of action cannot be made at the trial.*

Opinion by HOPKINSON, J.

This suit was brought eighteen years after the bond was executed, and fourteen years after the surety's liability by reason of the default of the principal. It is a suit on a sealed instrument, which is described by the plaintiff in his declaration, and which the defendant in his plea has alleged not be his deed. A bond is now offered in evidence which is not the bond so described, nor that which the defendant has denied to be his; it is a joint bond given by himself and another person, while the former is expressly stated in the declaration to be a joint and several bond of the defendant, and it is not alleged that any other person is joined with him. It is no doubt true that amendments may be made, not only in form but even in substance. But surely the court is not to be put to sea; nor is this privilege to be so construed as to introduce suddenly, and on the trial, new parties and a new cause of action. My difficulty is that the proposed amendment would introduce an entirely new cause of action. The bond, as set forth in the new count now offered as an amendment, differs in the most essential particulars from that originally declared on, as it is described in the declaration. It is impossible for us to decide that they are the same instruments, merely from similarity in certain particulars. The same parties may, on the same day and in the same penalty, have given a joint and several bond as well as a joint bond. What are pleadings? They are the manner and form in which a party is required to present his case to the court, and if he has made a mistake in this form, which is peculiarly under the direction of the court, he may be allowed to amend it. But here there is no error in the manner and form of stating the plaintiff's case, but in the case itself. He has mistaken his cause of action. He has brought the defendant here to answer his complaint; he has formally stated and declared what that complaint is; the defendant has put in his answer to it; and the parties appear, each to maintain his allegation. But now the plaintiff informs the court that he has no such complaint as he has averred, although he has another which he prays may be substituted for that which he cannot maintain.

On the whole, I am of opinion that the amendment ought not to be now made, and on the ground that it introduces a new cause of action.

THE YOUNG AMERICA.

(District Court for Michigan: 1 Brown, 462–469. 1874.)

Opinion by LONGYEAR, J.

STATEMENT OF FACTS.— The question presented involves two considerations: 1. As a libel against the scow alone, could the court allow it to be changed by amendment from a libel *in rem* against the vessel to a libel *in personam* against the owner? 2. In case of a joint liability of two or more vessels for a collision, can a joint action be maintained *in rem* against one or more of the vessels, and *in personam* against the owners of the others?

§ 2093. *A libel in rem cannot be changed by amendment into a libel in personam. Authorities reviewed.*

First. Touching the first question the counsel on either side have not referred the court to any reported or unreported decision in point, and after a pretty thorough investigation I am satisfied that none exists. This would seem to indicate that the matter is so well understood at the bar that the question has never been raised, or, if it has, that it has not been considered by the courts of sufficient importance to demand the promulgation of an opinion.

But upon which side of the question does this seeming acquiescence of court and bar bear? This question must be answered, if at all, by ascertaining what the courts have decided in cases involving principles lying at the foundation of the question under consideration.

In several instances in England and in this country the question has arisen in collision cases as to the right to ingraft upon or blend with an action *in rem* a proceeding *in personam* for the recovery of a deficiency against the owner, where the proceeds of the vessel were not sufficient to meet the damages pronounced for; and also whether an action *in rem* against the vessel, and an action *in personam* against the owner, could be joined in the same libel. In the United States, however, the latter question was settled by a rule of the supreme court in 1845 (Admiralty Rule 15). Since that time the decisions in this country have all turned upon the construction of the rule, and therefore throw but little light upon the question, and will not be noticed

The first case in England which has come to the notice of the court was The Triune, in 1834 (3 Hagg., 114). In this case Sir J. Nicholl granted a monition to the owner, who had intervened and bonded the vessel, to pay a deficiency, failing to do which he was imprisoned upon an attachment. When the motion was made Sir J. Nicholl put this pertinent interrogatory to counsel: "Is there an instance of a warrant of arrest under circumstances such as are in this case against the master and part owner?" The interrogatory does not appear to have been answered, but at a subsequent date he allowed the process to issue. The matter does not appear to have been discussed or very much considered, and altogether the report of the case is quite unsatisfactory.

The question next arose in England in 1840, in the case of The Hope, 1 W. Rob., 155. In this case Dr. Lushington decided directly the contrary to Sir J. Nicholl in The Triune, and held that it was not competent for the court to ingraft upon a proceeding *in rem* a personal action against the owner to make good the excess of damage beyond the proceeds of the ship. His attention had not at that time been called to the decision of Sir J. Nicholl in The Triune. Subsequently, however, in the case of The Volant, in 1842 (1 W. Rob., 383), where the same question was again presented, his attention was called to Sir J. Nicholl's decision. Dr. Lushington then went over the subject quite fully, and finally disagreed entirely with Sir J. Nicholl, and fully adhered to his former opinion in the case of The Hope; and such appears to have been the settled doctrine in England ever since.

In Citizens' Bank *v.* Nantucket Steamboat Company, in 1841 (2 Story, 16, 57, 58), Judge Story held that in collision cases it was not competent to proceed in the same suit *in rem* against the vessel and *in personam* against the owner. And this appears to be the only reported case in which any question of this kind arose in the courts of the United States before the promulgation of rule 15.

But we are not concerned here so much with the particular points decided in those cases as we are with the reasons upon which the decisions were founded. In the case of The Hope, 1 W. Rob., 155, Dr. Lushington held substantially, that, looking to the general principles upon which the proceedings in admiralty are conducted, it was wholly incompetent to ingraft a proceeding *in personam* against the owner upon a proceeding *in rem* against the vessel for the recovery of a deficiency.

Applying that declaration to the present question, it may be remarked that if, in view of those general principles, it is wholly incompetent for the recovery of a part of the damages only, that is, the excess of damages over value of vessel, for a still stronger reason it is incompetent to change the whole proceeding from one *in rem* to one *in personam*, in which the owner may be made liable for the whole damages without regard to the value of the vessel against which the libel was filed.

In the case of The Volant, 1 W. Rob., 383, Dr. Lushington says: "The jurisdiction of this court does not depend upon the existence of the ship, but upon the origin of the question to be decided and the locality. Looking to a proceeding by the arrest of the vessel, it is clear that, if no appearance is given to the warrant arresting the ship, there can be no proceedings against the owners, for the court cannot know who the owners are; the court cannot exercise any power over persons not before the court and never personally cited to appear." That is to say, in a proceeding *in rem* for a collision, in which the owners are never personally cited to appear, there is no process or proceeding by which the court can obtain jurisdiction of the owners, or know who they are, even in cases where the vessel has been arrested, other than by their voluntary appearance. This doctrine commends itself to my judgment, and, applied to the present case, it seems to me unanswerable.

How can it be said that, in a case like the present, where the vessel has not been arrested even, and there has been no appearance, the court can change the proceeding *in rem* against the vessel to a proceeding *in personam* against the owner, of whom the court has acquired and can acquire no jurisdiction, and whom the court does not and cannot know, by virtue of any process or proceeding incident to the proceedings *in rem?* The allowance of the amendment making the change, on the petition of the libelant, necessarily involved a determination by the court of the fact as to who was the owner, thus giving judgment beforehand, in an *ex parte* proceeding, and in a proceeding *in rem*, as to an essential and traversable fact in actions *in personam* in like cases — a thing no court ever does wittingly, and which, having done, through inadvertence or for want of due consideration, will be at once undone on attention being called to it.

In Citizens' Bank *v.* Nantucket Steamboat Company, 2 Story, 53, Judge Story says: "In cases of collision the injured party may proceed *in rem*, or *in personam*, or successively in each way, until he has full satisfaction. But," he says, "I do not understand how the proceedings can be blended in the libel." And in another place, in the same opinion, he says: "In the course of the argument it was intimated that in libels of this sort the proceedings might be properly instituted both *in rem* against the steamboat and *in personam* against the owners and master thereof. I ventured at the time to say that I knew of no principle or authority, in the general jurisprudence of courts of admiralty, which would justify such a joinder of proceedings, so very different in their nature and character and decretal effect. On the contrary, in this court, every practice of this sort has been constantly discountenanced as irregular and improper."

It will be observed that the ground upon which the objection to joining the two proceedings in one libel was sustained by Judge Story was that the two are so very different in their nature and character and decretal effect. The same objection, as it seems to the court, applies with increased force to changing the one proceeding into the other by way of amendment. And besides that, there is what seems to the court the further unanswerable objection, that such change involves an entire change of the party proceeded against. It is, in fact, the institution of a new suit by way of amendment, a proceeding never tolerated, I believe, in this or any court.

§ 2094. *Proceedings in rem and in personam cannot be blended in one libel.*
Second. The foregoing considerations, I think, are equally conclusive against joining in one suit proceedings *in rem* against the two vessels and *in personam* against the owner of the other.

The original libel was brought against the three vessels, upon the theory, of course, that they were guilty of a joint tort. The action was joint as to the three. With the amendment the action remains joint as to the two vessels which were arrested, but has necessarily become several as to the owner of the third, because, as an action *in personam*, it involves other and additional proof and a different decree. The amendment has, therefore, wrought a palpable misjoinder of actions.

But in the view taken as to the first point, it is unnecessary to elaborate this one further for present purposes. It results that the amendment was irregular, and therefore that the order allowing the same must be vacated, the amended libel taken from the files, and the citation be dismissed, with costs of the motion against the libelant.

Motion granted.

§ 2095. **After demurrer.**— Whether or not, after a demurrer, the pleadings can be amended is a question entirely within the discretion of the court. Bonnifield v. Price,* 1 Wyom. T'y, 172.

§ 2096. **To show citizenship and jurisdiction.**— An amendment to the declaration to show the jurisdiction of the court on the ground of citizenship of the parties is not a new suit, and may be allowed, though if the suit were dismissed a new suit would be barred by the statute of limitations. Robertson v. Cease,* 18 Alb. L. J., 453.

§ 2097. **After plea, replication and demurrer.**— An amendment may be allowed to a declaration though after plea, replication and demurrer, provided the cause of action be not changed thereby. Fiedler v. Carpenter, 2 Woodb. & M., 211.

§ 2098. **Refusing or granting no ground for writ of error.**— The refusing or granting by the court below of amendments or motions for new trial affords no ground for writ of error, and cannot be examined in the supreme court, though the decision was based on an erroneous construction of a written contract. United States v. Buford,* 3 Pet., 12.

§ 2099. **Mistake in pleading made by clerk.**— Where the clerk at request of counsel makes out a declaration, and makes a mistake therein, an amendment, if allowed, will not be on the ground of clerical misprision, as the clerk was acting merely as agent of counsel. Furniss v. Ellis, 2 Marsh., 14.

§ 2100. **Power of court to amend record on scire facias.**— Quære, whether, on motion of plaintiff in *scire facias*, the court has power to amend the record as brought up, on which, as amended, plaintiff might bring a new *scire facias*. Barnes v. Lee, 1 Cr. C. C., 430.

§ 2101. **Amendment of record after having been taken to the supreme court.**— The circuit court, on a motion to amend the statement of facts in the record of a cause which had gone up to the supreme court on error, refused to make the amendment, on the ground that it was put out of their power so to do by the writ of error. (CRANCH, J., dissenting.) United States v. Hooe,* 1 Cr. C. C., 116.

§ 2102. **Amendment of declaration dissolves attachment, when.**— The allowance of an amendment to the declaration will dissolve the attachment in those states where the federal courts have adopted the state practice of allowing attachments, and where the highest state court has decided such to be the effect of an amendment. Third National Bank *v.* Teal,* 5 Fed. R., 503.

§ 2103. **The power of a court over amendments,** under the thirty-second section of the judiciary act, is at least as great as that given by any British statutes. Walden *v.* Craig,* 9 Wheat., 576.

§ 2104. The power over amendments should be exercised liberally in ejectment suits, and a motion by plaintiff for an enlargement of the term of a judgment obtained in such a suit ought to be granted, especially when the time has lapsed through excessive delays practiced by defendant. Writ of error does not lie to any decisions of the court upon motions for amendments. *Ibid.*

§ 2105. **Admission of affidavit to deny execution of instrument.—** When the execution of an instrument is to be denied by plea under oath, the court will not grant a motion of defendant upon trial to add an affidavit denying his signature to the instrument, as this would be a surprise to the plaintiff. Benedict *v.* Maynard,* 6 McL., 21.

§ 2106. **Time allowed for reply to.—** When a substantial amendment is made in a declaration the defendant should be allowed until the next succeeding term to plead. Wyatt *v.* Harden, Hemp., 17.

§ 2107. **New plea after issue joined.—** After the issue joined upon *nul tiel record,* and the cause is called for trial on that issue, the court will not permit the defendant to plead that the plaintiff was never administrator. Duvall *v.* Wright, 4 Cr. C. C., 169.

§ 2108. **Parties, right of amendment as to.—** When some of the defendants have been taken, and others not arrested, the plaintiff may amend his declaration at the trial term in that respect as a matter of right, and such amendments will not authorize the defendants to plead the statute of limitations. Bell *v.* Davis, 3 Cr. C. C., 4.

§ 2109. A party will be allowed to amend his writ and declaration before trial by striking out the name of one of the defendants. Tobey *v.* Claflin, 3 Sumn., 379.

§ 2110. **Non est factum after issue joined.—** After a cause has been at issue eighteen months, leave will not be given to a defendant to plead *non est factum* without affidavit denying the execution of the bond. Bullock *v.* Van Pelt, Bald., 463.

§ 2111. **The averment of citizenship** of a party may be added at any stage of the cause, if the amendment is moved for in a reasonable time after the defect is suggested. Fisher *v.* Rutherford, Bald., 188.

§ 2112. **Statute of limitations — Right to withdraw demurrer and rejoin.—** After judgment for the plaintiff upon demurrer to the replication to the plea of limitations, the defendant will not be permitted to withdraw the demurrer and rejoin specially, unless he can show by affidavit that it is necessary to the justice of the case. Wilson *v.* Mandeville, 1 Cr. C. C., 452.

§ 2113. **Manner of stating citizenship in.—** In an amended declaration it is proper to state citizenship of the parties in the present tense, and it is not necessary that such citizenship should be stated as existing at commencement of suit. Birdsall *v.* Perego, 5 Blatch., 251.

§ 2114. **Action brought within statute time — Amended petition filed after.—** When a statutory action, brought within the proper time, alleged that the plaintiff's intestate was injured by the falling of a bridge, and set out the cause of the fall, and on disproof of this cause of the fall an amended petition was brought giving another explanation of the fall, which petition was brought after the time allowed by statute for bringing such actions had expired, the court considered the falling of the bridge the gravamen of the suit, and entertained the amended petition as being simply explanatory of what had occurred, and not barred. Yager *v.* The Receivers, 4 Hughes, 192.

§ 2115. **Petition in name of three — Amended petition, naming two only, dismissed.—** Where a petition on a contract is brought in the name of three persons, as parties to a contract, and an amended petition is then filed in the name of the same three upon the same contract, but naming only two as parties to the contract, the record precludes inadvertence in the omission, or that the amended petition was intended as a substitute, but fatal misjoinder of parties and interests is established and the petition must be dismissed. Parish *v.* United States,* 1 N. & H., 345.

§ 2116. **Removal from state to federal court — Amendment to make action conform to practice of latter.—** When an action joining a legal and an equitable cause of action is begun in a state court which permits that practice, and is then removed into a federal court, an amendment to the action, making it conform to the equity rules of the United States courts, will be allowed without costs. Stafford National Bank *v.* Sprague, 19 Blatch., 529.

§ 2117. **Amendment of bill relates to time of filing.—** An amendment of a bill generally relates to the time of filing the bill; but where a new title is introduced by the amendment, affecting the interests of new parties, no relation can withdraw such title from the statute of limitations. Miller v. McIntire, 1 McL., 85.

§ 2118. To make bill conform to proofs.—An amendment to a bill in equity to make it conform to the proofs submitted may be allowed by the court, even after the cause has been heard, if justice demands it. Neale v. Neales, 9 Wall., 1.

§ 2119. Introduction of new parties by.—The rule as to parties in equity is not inflexible, and the court will not readily grant an amendment introducing new parties, when the effect would be to cause the bill to be dismissed for want of jurisdiction, and when justice could be done without the new parties; nor would the interests of the present parties be in any way prejudiced. Suydam v. Truesdale,* 6 McL., 459.

§ 2120. When a bill is amended by the joining of a new defendant, under the twenty-ninth equity rule, which allows a plaintiff at any time before replication filed, upon motion, without notice, to obtain from any judge of the court an order for an amendment, it is not possible for the defendant so joined to get rid of the amendment by a motion to have the order set aside. The amendment under the rule was a matter of right to the plaintiff. Lichtenauer v. Cheney,* 3 McC., 119.

§ 2121. Bill to wind up corporation — Breaches of trust.—To a bill by a stockholder asking that the corporation be wound up because of mismanagement and breaches of trust on the part of the directors, a plea that, by the laws of the state, a corporation can be wound up under certain specified circumstances only, and that these circumstances were not in this case present, is good; but the plaintiff, upon amendment of his prayer, may have relief for the breaches of trust set forth in the bill. Hardon v. Newton, 14 Blatch., 376.

§ 2122. An amendment to an answer in equity setting up a new defense will not be allowed when this defense might by reasonable diligence have been introduced into the answer at an earlier stage. India Rubber Comb Co. v. Phelps, 8 Blatch., 85.

§ 2123. Patent suit—Admissions in answer struck out by.—In a suit for infringing a patent the defendants were allowed, under special circumstances, and there being no laches, to strike out an admission in their answer that they had made certain articles, their making of which the complainant was seeking by the bill to enjoin. Morehead v. Jones, 3 Wall. Jr., 306.

§ 2124. Admiralty practice — New facts by.— In admiralty pleadings the better practice is to present new facts, when necessary, by an amendment to the libel and answer, as in chancery, and not by way of replication and rejoinder. The Brig Sarah Ann, 2 Sumn., 206.

§ 2125. —— striking out unnecessary allegations.—A libel may be amended on motion by striking out unnecessary and impertinent allegations. American Ins. Co. v. Johnson, Bl. & How., 9.

§ 2126. —— allowable any time before final decree.—A court of admiralty has the power to allow amendment of the pleadings at any stage of the case before final decree, but in its discretion. Not allowed to the libelant in this case because the fault was his, because it would cause delay, increase expense, and its necessity to attain substantial justice not clear. Pettingill v. Dinsmore,* 6 Law Rep., 255,

§ 2127. —— allowable of course until concluded by judgment.—Under the twenty-fourth admiralty rule of the supreme court the libelant is entitled of course to have amendment of his pleadings until he shall be concluded by judgment upon exceptions taken to the libel. The claimants having taken no steps to enforce their exception, a motion to amend the libel in particulars of form, pointed out to claimants' proctors by notice, is therefore allowed. Town v. Steamship Western Metropolis,* 23 How. Pr., 288.

§ 2128. The twenty-fourth rule of the supreme court, allowing amendments in matters of substance to be made in admiralty on motion at any time before the final decree, in the court's discretion, applies to the circuit as well as the district courts. Some of the unwritten rules followed by the court in the exercise of this discretion given in full. Lamb v. Parkman,* 11 Law Rep. (N. S.), 589.

§ 2129. —— after opportunity to ascertain facts.—An answer to a libel cannot be amended if it was put in after the respondents had the fullest opportunity to ascertain a material fact in regard to a collision, especially when the amendment is not based on mistake, erroneous information or misunderstanding, and the court is besides satisfied of the substantial truth of the statements desired to be expunged. The Brig Iola,* 11 N. Y. Leg. Obs., 268.

§ 2130. —— defense omitted in answer.— In admiralty the fact that when an answer was originally filed a certain defense was not set up can be taken into consideration at the hearing, if there is a conflict of testimony, although the answer was subsequently amended and such defense inserted. Steamboat Empire State, 1 Ben., 57.

VII. In General.

SUMMARY — *Object of written pleadings,* § 2131. — *Less technicality than formerly necessary,* § 2132. — *Pleadings in federal courts conformable to those in state courts,* § 2133. — *Law and equity not to be blended,* § 2134.

§ 2131. Written pleadings terminating in one or more integral propositions of law or fact are necessary in order that the whole case may appear on record for revision by a court exclusively concerned in questions of law. McFaul v. Ramsey, §§ 2135–39.

§ 2132. Modern times have greatly modified the excessive accuracy and technicality required by early common law, but the attempt to abolish all system by legislation, only destroys certainty and simplicity and introduces great and needless confusion. *Ibid.*

§ 2133. Pleadings and practice in the federal courts are to conform as nearly as may be to the pleadings and practice in the state courts at the same time. Lewis v. Gould, § 2140.

§ 2134. In the federal courts legal and equitable causes of action are not to be blended in one suit. Hurt v. Hollingsworth, §§ 2141–43.

[NOTES. — See §§ 2144–2165.]

McFAUL v. RAMSEY.

(20 Howard, 523–527. 1857.)

Opinion by MR. JUSTICE GRIER.

STATEMENT OF FACTS. — Ramsey, the plaintiff below, instituted this suit in the district court of the United States for the district of Iowa. The parties have been permitted by that court to frame their pleadings, not according to the simple and established forms of action in courts of common law, but according to a system of pleadings and practice enacted by that state to regulate proceedings in its own courts. This code commences by abolishing "all technical forms of actions," prescribing the following curt rules for all cases, whether of law or equity:

"Any pleading which possesses the following requisites shall be deemed sufficient: 1. When to the common understanding it conveys a reasonable certainty of meaning. 2. When, by a fair and natural construction, it shows a substantial cause of action or defense. If defective in the first of the above particulars the court, on motion, will direct a more specific statement; if in the latter it is ground of demurrer."

§ 2135. *Necessity and object of pleadings.*

If the right of deciding absolutely and finally all matters in controversy between suitors were committed to a single tribunal it might be left to collect the nature of the wrong complained of, and the remedy sought, from the allegations of the party *ore tenus,* or in any other manner it might choose to adopt. But the common law, which wisely commits the decision of questions of law to a court supposed to be learned in the law, and the decision of the facts to a jury, necessarily requires that the controversy, before it is submitted to the tribunal having jurisdiction of it, should be reduced to one or more integral propositions of law or fact; hence it is necessary that the parties should frame the allegations which they respectively make in support of their demand or defense into certain writings called pleadings. These should clearly, distinctly and succinctly state the nature of the wrong complained of, the remedy sought and the defense set up. The end proposed is to bring the matter of litigation to one or more points, simple and unambiguous.

§ 2136. *Early and modern pleading compared.*

At one time the excessive accuracy required, the subtlety of distinctions introduced by astute logicians, the introduction of cumbrous forms, fictions and contrivances which seemed only to perplex the investigation of truth, had brought the system of special pleading into deserved disrepute, notwithstanding the assertion of Sir William Jones that " it was the best logic in the world except mathematics." This system is said to have come to its perfection in the reign of Edward III. But in more modern times it has been so modified by the courts, and trimmed of its excrescences, the pleadings in every form of common-law action have been so completely reduced to simple, clear and unambiguous forms, that the merits of a cause are now never submerged under folios of special demurrers, alleging errors in pleading which, when discovered, are immediately permitted to be amended. This system, matured by the wisdom of ages, founded on principles of truth and sound reason, has been ruthlessly abolished in many of our states, who have rashly substituted in its place the suggestions of sciolists, who invent new codes and systems of pleading to order. But this attempt to abolish all species and establish a single genus is found to be beyond the power of legislative omnipotence. They cannot compel the human mind not to distinguish between things that differ. The distinction between the different forms of actions for different wrongs, requiring different remedies, lies in the nature of things; it is absolutely inseparable from the correct administration of justice in common-law courts.

§ 2137. *Danger of abolishing slowly matured system in pleading.*

The result of these experiments, so far as they have come to our knowledge, has been to destroy the certainty and simplicity of all pleadings and introduce on the record an endless wrangle in writing, perplexing to the court, delaying and impeding the administration of justice. In the case of Randon *v.* Toby, 11 How., 517, we had occasion to notice the operation and result of a code similar to that of Iowa. In a simple action on a promissory note, the pleadings of which, according to common-law forms, would not have occupied a page, they were extended to over twenty pages, requiring two years of wrangle, with exceptions and special demurrers, before an issue could be formed between the parties. In order to arrive at the justice of the case, this court was compelled to disregard the chaos of pleadings and eliminate the merits of the case from a confused mass of *fifty* special demurrers or exceptions, and decide the cause without regard to these contrivances to delay and impede a decision of the real controversy between the parties. In the case of Bennett *v.* Butterworth, 11 How., 667, originating under the same code, the court were unable to discover from the pleading the nature of action or of the remedy sought. It might with equal probability be called an action of debt, or detinue, or replevin, or trover, or trespass, or a bill in chancery. The jury and the court below seem to have labored under the same perplexity, as the verdict was for $1,200, and the judgment for four negroes. In both these cases this court have endeavored to impress the minds of the judges of the district and circuit courts of the United States with the impropriety of permitting these experimental codes of pleading and practice to be inflicted upon them. In the last mentioned case, the chief justice, in delivering the opinion of the court, says: "The constitution of the United States has recognized the distinction between law and equity, and it *must* be observed in the federal courts.

In Louisiana, where the civil law prevails, we have necessarily to adopt the forms of action inseparable from the system. But in those states where the courts of the United States administer the common law, they *cannot* adopt these novel inventions which propose to amalgamate law and equity by enacting a hybrid system of pleadings unsuited to the administration of either.

We have made these few introductory remarks before proceeding to notice the merits of the controversy as developed by the record, in order that the bar and courts of the United States may make their records conform to these views, and not call upon us to construe new codes and hear special demurrers or pleadings, which are not required to conform to any system founded on reason and experience. To test such pleadings by the logical reasoning of the common law, after requiring the party to disregard all forms of action known to the law under which he seeks a remedy, would be unwarrantable and unjust.

The plaintiff's petition sets forth his grievances in plain, intelligible form, if not with technical brevity and simplicity.

1st. He alleges a contract with defendant to deliver to him eight hundred hogs on or before a certain day; in consideration whereof, the defendant agreed to pay plaintiff $5.50 per hundred pounds net. He avers that he did deliver according to contract, at the time and place, the number of eight hundred hogs; that defendant refused to receive over five hundred and fifty of them, or pay for the remainder.

2d. He complains that defendant refused to receive and butcher the hogs in accordance with the agreement, and, thus caused by his delay, that the plaintiff was put to expense in feeding the hogs, and exposed to a great loss in the *net weight.*

3d. That defendant did not make a true return of the net weight, but defrauded plaintiff on that behalf.

4th. That he slaughtered twenty-four more hogs than he accounted for, and improperly cut off parts of others to reduce their weight.

5th. The plaintiff alleges, in what might be called a second count, another contract to deliver fourteen hundred hogs to defendant, at $5.60 per hundred net.

He avers delivery according to contract, and charges defendant with delay in slaughtering them; causing great loss in the weight, and expense to plaintiff in feeding them in the meanwhile.

6th. He charges defendant with taking one hundred other hogs of plaintiff, for which he refused to account.

7th. That in consequence of delay in receiving, many of the hogs died, to the great loss of plaintiff.

8th. That defendant returned false weights of these fourteen hundred, and cut off parts before weighing.

9th. The plaintiff also sets up a third contract for five hundred hogs, which were delivered, and avers the same delay and consequent injury to plaintiff; and the same frauds in weighing, etc.

To this catalogue of grievances the defendant, in his answer, pleads thirty-three distinct denials of the averments in the petition. A jury was called to try these thirty-three issues, and found a verdict for plaintiff, and assessed his damages. No exception was taken on the trial to the admission or rejection of evidence; no error is alleged in the charge of the court, and a regular judgment was entered on the verdict.

§ 2138. *Decision of motion for continuance or change of venue is not subject to review in supreme court.*

The only bills of exception were to the refusal of the court to grant a continuance and change the venue, both of which were matters of discretion in the court below, and not the subject of review here.

§ 2139. *Under the Iowa code a demurrer is properly overruled when the petition states a substantial cause of action.*

The cavils to the sufficiency of the plaintiff's statement, under the name of a special demurrer, were overruled by the court below, and justly, because.the code permits a demurrer only when the petition "by a fair and natural construction does not show a substantial cause of action." As we have already shown, it contains a dozen. The judgment of the court below is affirmed, with.costs.

LEWIS *v.* GOULD.

(Circuit Court for New York: 13 Blatchford, 216–218. 1875.)

·Opinion by JOHNSON, J.

STATEMENT OF FACTS.— The defendants move to set aside the replication upon the ground that the pleading is not authorized by law. It is entirely clear that, if this suit were in the supreme court of the state of New York, the pleading in question would be unauthorized, and might be set aside. The question is whether that is also the law of the United States courts in this district.

§ 2140. *Pleadings and practice in the federal courts are to conform as nearly as may be to the pleadings and practice in the state courts at the same time.*

The answer to this question is given by section 914 of the United States Revised Statutes, which enacts that "the practice, pleadings and forms and modes of proceeding in civil causes, other than equity and admiralty causes, in the circuit and district courts, shall conform, as near as may be, to the practice, pleadings and forms and modes of proceeding existing at the time, in like causes, in the courts of record of the state within which such circuit or district courts are held, any rule of court to the contrary notwithstanding." No language can be more direct or plainer than this to convey the will of the congress that the pleadings in the circuit and district courts shall be conformed to those employed in the state practice, ·" as near as may be." The qualification contained in this last phrase is not to be construed to subvert the command of the statute. "As near as may be" allows only necessary variations from the state methods, growing out of the different organization of the courts, and other similar matters.

No one can doubt that, if the code of procedure of New York had existed as the law of the state in 1789 and 1792, the practice, pleadings and modes of procedure which it contains would, by force of the process acts of those years, have been adopted into and become the law of the circuit and district courts of the United States within this state. Nor is there any more doubt that such was the intent and is the effect of the section in question. The common-law forms of pleading are no longer necessary in the United States courts within the state of New York, nor are they admissible, except as they may be deemed to be substantially a compliance with the requirements of the code of civil procedure of the state as to pleadings. The same view of this statute was taken in Butler *v.* Young, by Sherman, J., in the circuit court for the northern district of Ohio (7 West. Jur., 59), and the same principles of interpretation were applied to the former process acts. Fenn *v.* Holme, 21 How., 481; United States *v.* Keokuk, 6 Wall., 514. The motion to set aside the replication must be granted.

HURT v. HOLLINGSWORTH.

(10 Otto, 100–104. 1879.)

ERROR to U. S. Circuit Court, Eastern District of Texas.

Opinion by MR. JUSTICE FIELD.

STATEMENT OF FACTS.— This suit was brought by the plaintiff, in a district court of Texas, to quiet his title to certain real property situated in Galveston in that state. On application of the defendant it was removed to the circuit court of the United States.

The petition, which is the first pleading in a suit according to the practice which obtains in Texas, sets forth that the plaintiff is the owner of the premises; that he purchased them of one Molsberger and wife in June, 1874; that those parties acquired them in December, 1865, and had subsequently, until the sale to the plaintiff, claimed and held them as a homestead; that in April, 1867, certain parties, designated as Marsh, Denman & Co., recovered judgment against Molsberger, in the county court of Galveston, on a debt contracted in 1866, while the premises constituted the homestead of himself and family; and in October, 1873, under an execution issued thereon, the premises were sold by the sheriff of the county, for the sum of $30, to the defendant Hollingsworth, one of the members of that firm, and to him the sheriff executed a deed of the premises, which has been recorded in the county.

The petition avers that this deed is a cloud upon the title of the plaintiff, and prays that the cloud may be removed and his title quieted. The defendant filed in the circuit court an answer to this petition, in which he admits that the plaintiff was in possession of the premises and had obtained a deed of them from Molsberger and wife, who had purchased them in 1865, but denies that they constituted a homestead of Molsberger and family continuously from that time until the alleged sale to the plaintiff, or that they were such homestead when the sale was made by the sheriff to him.

The answer then avers that the defendant became the owner of the premises by his purchase; that the plaintiff wrongfully withholds the possession from him, and the rents and profits, which are of the value of $75 a month. He therefore prays that the title may be declared to be in him, and that he may have judgment for the possession of the premises and the value of the rents.

These pleadings were subsequently amended so as to show the value of the property and the amount of its rents, and in some other particulars not material to the question now presented.

The case was considered by counsel and treated by the court as an action at law, and by stipulation made at the December term of 1875 the parties waived a jury trial and submitted "the matters therein, as well of facts as of law, to the court." The evidence was then heard; and at a subsequent term the court gave judgment that the plaintiff take nothing by his action, and that the defendant recover the title and possession of the property, and also the sum of $420, as damages for its use and occupation, and have a writ of possession.

This judgment was subsequently vacated and a rehearing granted, when a motion was made by the plaintiff to transfer the cause, it being one seeking equitable relief, from the law docket of the court, upon the ground that it had been improvidently placed there by the defendant, to the chancery docket, to be there proceeded with according to the rules and practice of the circuit court sitting in chancery; and also a motion to take from the files of the court so much of the answer as purported to be "a cross-suit, reconvention suit, or cross-bill," because the court, sitting as a law court, had no jurisdiction to grant in that suit the relief prayed by the defendant. These motions were accompanied with a petition for leave to amend the bill of complaint. But the court, considering that the case was on its law docket and had been submitted for its judgment, refused to sustain the motions. In disposing of them it observed that it was a court both of law and equity and had cognizance of both kinds of cases; that though the cause was an equity cause the court had cognizance of it, and the question presented was, therefore, simply one of regularity of pleadings and proceedings; that the parties had waived all matters of mere form by going to final hearing on the merits and submitting the case to the court, and that their substantial rights had not been violated by this mode of proceeding. The court thereupon heard the evidence presented by the parties; which related principally to the point whether the premises had been abandoned as a homestead at the time of the sheriff's sale mentioned 'in the pleadings, and rendered a similar judgment to that previously entered. The case is brought · here both on writ of error and on appeal, the plaintiff adopting both modes to obviate a possible objection, which otherwise might have been taken to our jurisdiction.

· § 2141. *In the federal courts legal and equitable causes of action are not to be blended in one suit.*

There would be great force in the observations of the court below if the different causes of action presented by the parties could, by the usual forms of proceeding, either at law or in equity, be disposed of in one suit. It might then very well be said that as by stipulation the case had been submitted to the court for determination, it was too late to object to the form of the proceedings. If it was an equity case, then it was properly before the court; if it was a case at law, a jury having been waived, it was also properly there. In either view, the relief warranted by the facts would be administered. But here no such disposition could be made of the case presented by the petition and the one presented by the answer. The first is strictly a suit in equity seeking special relief, which only a court of chancery can grant. The second is an action at law for the recovery of real property with the rents and profits. The two cases are entirely different in their nature, and can be determined, where the distinctions between legal and equitable proceedings are maintained, only in separate suits. In the one case, if the allegations of the plaintiff be sustained, the judgment must be declaratory and prohibitory, adjudging that the deed of the sheriff to the defendant constitutes a cloud upon his title, and enjoining the defendant from asserting any claim to the premises under it. In the other case, if the defendant establishes his averments the judgment must be for the possession of the premises and the rent and profits.

In the federal courts such a blending of equitable and legal causes of action in one suit is not permissible under the process act of 1792, substantially re-enacted in the Revised Statutes, which declares that in suits in equity in the circuit and district courts of the United States the forms and modes of proceeding shall be according to the principles, rules and usages which belong to courts of equity. 1 Stat., 276, sec. 2; R. S., sec. 913. This requirement has always been held obligatory upon parties and the court whenever the question has been raised. Thompson *v.* Railroad Companies, 6 Wall., 134. A party who claims a legal title must, therefore, proceed at law; and a party whose title or claim is an equitable one must follow the forms and rules of equity proceedings as prescribed by this court under the authority of the act of August

23, 1842. 5 Stat., 518, sec. 6. The case of Hornbuckle v. Toombs, reported in the 18th of Wallace, does not conflict with this view; it only decides that the process act of 1792 does not extend to proceedings in the courts of the several territories, which may be regulated by their respective legislatures.

In this case there is nothing in the answer of the defendant which would render it good as a cross-bill, even had it been drawn in due form and filed as such bill by leave of the court, for it seeks legal and not equitable relief. Story, Eq. Pl., sec. 398.

§ 2142. *Parties may insist upon following provisions of process act, though variant from state practice.*

We are of opinion, therefore, that the court below should have granted the motions of the plaintiff. So long as the process act, respecting the modes and forms of procedure in equity cases, remains in force, parties have a right to insist that its provisions, however variant from the practice of the state courts, or open to objection, shall be followed, and should be permitted to recede from a stipulation waiving them, improvidently made, as the one in this case evidently was, at any time before final hearing and judgment.

§ 2143. *Abandonment of homestead.*

There is an additional reason for sending the case back — that the evidence as to the abandonment of the homestead of the plaintiff is very unsatisfactory and leaves great doubt on our minds whether the conclusion reached by the court below on this point was correct. We do not think that a homestead can be considered as abandoned because occupied by tenants and the owner is temporarily residing elsewhere. According to the decisions of the supreme court of Texas it would appear that, in order to work a forfeiture of the right to the homestead, the owner's cessation of occupancy must be with an intention of total relinquishment, shown by clear and decisive circumstances. The trifling sum at which the premises were suffered to be struck off would seem to indicate that at the sale little confidence was felt in the validity of the title which would be acquired. On the rehearing this matter will receive a more full and careful consideration.

The judgment will be reversed and the cause remanded with directions to the court below to allow the plaintiff to amend his petition or bill of complaint, as he now designates it, and to strike out of the answer of the defendant his prayer for the possession of the premises and the value of the rents and profits; and it is so ordered.

§ 2144. **Wager of law,** if it ever existed in the United States, was abolished by the constitution. Childress *v.* Emory, 8 Wheat., 642.

§ 2145. **Construction of pleadings.**— An uncertain pleading is taken most strongly against the pleader. Lamb *v.* Starr, Deady, 350; Foreman *v.* Bigelow, 4 Cliff., 508.

§ 2146. —— **Montana practice.**— The provision in the Montana practice act, that in the construction of pleadings the allegations shall be liberally construed with a view to substantial justice, is a modification of the common-law rule requiring pleadings to be construed most strongly against the pleader. Gillette *v.* Bullard,* 20 Wall., 571.

§ 2147. **Exceptions to form in equity.**— Pleadings are viewed with very little regard to form in courts of equity, and exceptions are never allowed if they are made under circumstances calculated to effect a surprise on either party, and might have been made at a different stage of the cause, and consistent with fairness to all. Surget *v.* Byers, Hemp., 715.

§ 2148. —— **In court of claims.**— The forms of pleading in the court of claims are not of so strict a character as to preclude a claimant from recovering what is justly due to him upon the facts stated in his petition, although due in a different aspect from that in which his demand is conceived. Clark *v.* United States, 5 Otto, 539.

§ 2149. The court of claims in deciding upon the rights of claimants is not bound by any special rules of pleading. United States *v.* Burns, 12 Wall., 246.

§ 2150. **Territorial courts.**—The practice, pleadings, and forms and modes of proceeding of the territorial courts, subject to a few express or implied conditions in the act itself, were intended to be left to the legislative action of the territorial assemblies, and to the regulations which might be adopted by the courts themselves. Accordingly, where, by the territorial law, legal and equitable remedies are allowed to be blended in one action, this cannot be assigned as error in the supreme court. Hornbuckle v. Toombs, 18 Wall., 648; Hershfield v. Griffith, 18 Wall., 657; Davis v. Bilsland, 18 Wall., 659.

§ 2151. **Equity practice not to be varied by agreement of parties.**— Practice in a court of equity is regulated by law or rule, and cannot be varied by the agreement of parties. Hence a federal court will not hear an equity case upon an agreed statement of facts and without pleadings. Nickerson v. A., T. & S. F. R. R. Co., 1 McC., 383.

§ 2152. **Negotiable paper — Questions which cannot arise by agreement of parties.**— Upon a common declaration to recover the amount of an accepted bill from the acceptor, the question cannot arise, even by agreement, whether plaintiff, who was the original payee, has a right to recover from defendant the costs and damages which had been recovered against plaintiff in a suit by the indorsee of the bill. King v. Phillips,* Pet. C. C., 350.

§ 2153. **Joinder of legal and equitable causes of action — Removal.**— A party cannot unite legal and equitable causes of action in the same case in the federal court; but he must replead if he has removed to the federal court a case uniting such causes from a state court where such joinder is allowed. La Mothe Manuf'g Co. v. Nat. Tube Works, 15 Blatch., 432.

§ 2154. **State practice adopted by federal courts.**— The modes of proceeding in force in a state furnish the rule by which the pleadings in the United States courts in that state should be controlled. United States v. Boyd, 15 Pet., 187.

§ 2155. Under 17 Stat., 196, the forms of pleading and procedure in United States, circuit and district courts, except in admiralty and equity, are conformed, as near as may be, to the pleading and procedure in the courts of the state where such United States courts are held; and the federal courts will follow the decisions of the supreme court of the state upon such matters. Taylor v. Brigham, 3 Woods, 377.

§ 2156. **There is no such thing as an exhibit in pleadings** in an action at law. A record or instrument must be stated in a pleading according to its legal effect or according to the tenor thereof, and its legal operations referred to the court. Fitch v. Cornell, 1 Saw., 156.

§ 2157. —— **ejectment.**— In ejectment plats are part of the pleadings; in trespass they are evidence only. Pancoast v. Barry, 1 Cr. C. C., 176.

§ 2158. **Written instruments, contradiction of.**— No averment is admissible to contradict the terms of a written instrument. United States v. Thompson, 1 Gall., 388.

§ 2159. **Decree not founded on facts put in issue.**— A decree must be sustained by the allegations of the parties as well as by the proofs in the cause, and cannot be founded upon a fact not put in issue by the pleadings. Carneal v. Banks, 10 Wheat., 181.

§ 2160. **Trespass — Breach of promise of marriage — Surplusage.**— A writ requiring the defendant to answer to an action of trespass, and also for damages for deceit and breach of promise of marriage, sets forth an action of trespass on the case, and the breach of promise clause may be regarded as explanatory, or rejected as surplusage. The writ, therefore, is not incongruous. Wilkinson v. Pomeroy, 10 Blatch., 524.

§ 2161. **Statute of limitations — Proofs not founded on facts put in issue.**—A bill was filed in the United States circuit court of Ohio for a conveyance of the legal title to certain real estate in Cincinnati, and the statute of limitations of Ohio was relied on by the defendants. The complainant claimed the benefit of an exception in the statute of non-residence and absence from the state; and evidence was given tending to show that the person under whom he made his claim in equity was within the exception. The non-residence and absence were not charged in the bill, and of course were not denied or put in issue in the answer. *Held,* that the court can take no notice of the proofs; for the proofs, to be admissible, must be founded upon some allegations in the bill and answer. Piatt v. Vattier, 9 Pet., 405.

§ 2162. **Informal pleadings — Tennessee code.**— Under the Tennessee code any declaration which states a cause of action, however informally, or any plea which states a defense either by general denial equivalent to the general issue, or special plea showing the facts, will be good, whether good at common law or not. Brown v. M. I. C. R. Co., 4 Fed. R., 37.

§ 2163. —— **Kansas code.**— The code of Kansas of 1858 does not make good any pleading bad in substance at common law. Bliss v. Burnes, McCahon, 91.

§ 2164. —— **New York.**— Under the system of pleading in New York, judgment should be rendered in accordance with the facts pleaded and proved, without regard to the form of the pleadings or the theory upon which they were pressed. Whalen v. Sheridan, 17 Blatch., 9.

§ 2165. **Ejectment — Title acquired after issue joined.**— Under California pleadings in an ejectment suit a title acquired subsequent to issue joined must be set up by a supplemental answer in the nature of a plea *puis darrein continuance.* Hardy v. Johnson, 1 Wall., 371.

TABLE OF CASES.

BOATS AND VESSELS.

E.

F.

H.

Spring Co. v. Knowlton, 18 Otto, 49. Pay't, § 244.
Stanley v. Gadsby, 10 Pet., 521. Pl., § 1274.
Stanley v. Whipple, 2 McL., 35. Pl., § 62.
Stanton v. Embrey, 3 Otto, 548. Pl., § 2016.
Stanton v. Seymour, 5 McL., 267. Pl., §§ 233, 557.
Starr v. Moore, 3 McL., 854. Off., § 45; Pay't, § 83; Pl., § 629.
Starr v. Taylor, 3 McL., 542. Off., §§ 188, 189; Pay't, § 84.
State of Indiana v. Baldwin, 6 Fed. R., 80. Off., § 198.
State of New York v. Dibble, 21 How., 366. Police Powers, § 10.
State of Vermont v. Society for Propagating the Gospel, 1 Paine, 652. Pl., § 990.
State of Vermont v. Society for the Propagation of Gospel, etc., 2 Paine, 545. Pl., § 616.
Steam Engine Co. v. Hubbard, 11 Otto, 188. Penalties, § 57.
Steamship Co. v. United States,* 13 Otto, 721. P. O., §§ 155, 156, 158.
Stearns v. Page, 7 How., 819. Pl., § 1239.
Stearns v. Page,* 1 Story, 204. Pl., §§ 1300, 1467, 1468.
Stearns v. United States, 2 Paine, 300. Penalties, §§ 100, 101, 104.
Steinham v. United States, 2 Paine, 168. Pl., § 275.
Stevelie v. Read, 2 Wash., 274. Name, § 24.
Stevens v. Cady, 2 Curt., 200. Pl., § 1291.
Stevens v. Kansas Pac. R'y, 5 Dill., 486. Pl., § 1413.
Stevens v. The Railroads, 4 Fed. R., 97. Notice, § 49.
Stewart v. Hamilton, 4 McL., 534. Off., §§ 124, 314.
Stewart v. Potomac Ferry Co., 12 Fed. R., 296. Pl., § 916.
Stimpson v. Pond, 2 Curt., 502. Penalties, §§ 55, 77.
Stockton v. Bishop,* 4 How., 155. Pl., §§ 194, 2079–2081.
Stockton v. Ford, 11 How., 232. Pl., § 1281.
Stockwell v. United States, 3 Cliff., 284. Partn., § 219; Pl., § 75.
Stockwell v. United States,* 12 Int. Rev. Rec., 88. Pl., § 83.
Stockwell v. United States, 13 Wall., 531; S. C., 12 Int. Rev. Rec., 88. Partn., § 548.
Stone v. Mason, 2 Cr. C. C., 481. Off., § 146.
Stone v. Mississippi, 11 Otto, 814. Police Powers, § 26.
Stone v. Stone, 2 Cr. C. C., 119. Pl., § 693.
Stoppage of Letters,* 7 Op. Att'y Gen'l, 76. P. O., §§ 46, 47.
Story v. Livingston, 13 Pet., 359. Pay't, § 209; Pl., § 1283.
Stoughton v. Dimick, 3 Blatch., 356; 8 L. Rep., 557; 29 Vt., 535. Off., § 411.
Strain v. Gourdin, 2 Woods, 380. Pay't, § 71.
Strauss, In re,* 2 N. B. R., 18. Notary, § 23.
Strong v. United States, 6 Wall., 788. Off., §§ 400–402.
Stroud v. Harrington, Hemp., 116. Pl., § 670.
Sturges v. Colby, 2 Flip., 108. Pay't, § 84.
Suckley v. Slade,* 5 Cr. C. C., 123. Pl., § 1051.
Sullivan v. Fulton Steamboat Co., 6 Wheat., 450. Pl., § 279.
Sullivan v. Railroad Co., 4 Otto, 806. Pl., § 1623.
Sullivan v. Redfield, 1 Paine, 441. Pl., § 1249.
Sullivan v. N. Y., N. H. & H. R. Co., 19 Blatch., 383–392. Pl., §§ 432–434, 87, 88.

Sullivan v. N. Y., N. H. & H. R. Co.,* 11 Fed. R., 848. Pl., § 86.
Supervisors v. United States, 4 Wall., 435. Off., § 139.
Surget v. Byers, Hemp., 715. Pl., §§ 1661, 1918, 2147.
Sutton v. Mandeville, 1 Cr. C. C., 2. Partn., § 428.
Suydam v. Truesdale,* 6 McL., 459. Pl., §§ 1706, 1707, 2119.
Suydam v. Williamson, 20 How., 427. Pl., § 1106.
Swatzel v. Arnold, 1 Woolw., 383. Pl., § 1697.
Swift v. Hathaway, 1 Gall., 417. Pay't, § 86.
Swift v. United States,* 14 Ct. Cl., 208. Pay't, § 312.

T.

Tabb v. Gist, 6 Call (Va.), 279; 1 Marsh., 38. Partn., §§ 154, 155.
Taber v. Jenny,* 1 Spr., 315; 9 Law Rep., N. S., 27. Pl., §§ 1676, 1912, 1914.
Talbot v. Wakeman,* 19 How. Pr., 36. Pl., § 1763.
Talcott v. Delaware Ins. Co., 2 Wash., 449. Notary, § 2.
Tappan v. Smith, 5 Biss., 73. Pl., § 1701.
Tarver v. Tarver, 9 Pet., 174. Pl., § 277.
Tayloe v. Merchants', etc., Ins. Co., 9 How., 390. Pay't, § 74.
Tayloe v. Sandiford, 7 Wheat., 13. Partn., § 177.
Taylor v. Bemis, 4 Biss., 406. Partn., §§ 69, 70.
Taylor v. Benham, 5 How., 233. Powers, §§ 26, 27, 35.
Taylor v. Brigham, 3 Woods, 377. Pl., § 2155.
Taylor v. Luther, 2 Sumn., 228. Pl., §§ 1566, 1585.
Taylor v. Rasch, 1 Cent. L. J., 555; 11 N. B. R., 91. Partn., §§ 510, 513.
Taylor v. Rasch, 1 Flip., 385–388. Partn., §§ 506, 507.
Taylor v. Rasch,* 5 N. B. R., 399. Partn., § 193.
Taylor v. Smith,* 8 Cr. C. C., 241. Partn., § 427.
Teal v. Felton, 12 How., 284–293. P. O., §§ 89–93, 43.
Teasdale v. Branton,* 2 Hayw., 377. Pl., § 1084.
Teasdale v. The Rambler,* Bee, 9. Pl., § 1839.
Teese v. Phelps, McAl., 17. Pl., §§ 279, 1036.
Teller v. Patten, 20 How., 125. Partn., § 53.
Tenney v. Townsend, 9 Blatch., 274–277. Pl., §§ 173, 174.
Territory of Kansas v. Reyburn, McCahon, 134. Pl., § 643.
Terry, In re, 5 Biss., 110. Partn., § 268.
Texas v. Chiles, 10 Wall., 127. Pl., § 1645.
Texas v. Hardenberg, 10 Wall., 68. Pl., § 1287.
Thacher's Distilled Spirits, 13 Otto, 679. Penalties, § 3.
Thatcher v. United States,* 12 Law Rep. (N. S.), 82. Pensions, §§ 23, 24, 28.
Thistle v. United States,* Dev., 131. Penalties, § 71.
Thomas v. Clark, 2 McL., 194, 195. Pl., § 655.
Thomas v. Gray, Bl. & How., 493. Pl., §§ 1867, 1910, 1915.
Thomas, In re, 6 Cent. L. J., 151; 8 Biss., 139. Partn., § 540.

United States v. Bixby, 9 Fed. R., 78. Off., § 185; Notary, § 1.
—— v. Blaisdell, 3 Ben., 132; 9 Int. Rev. Rec., 82. Off., § 43).
—— v. Bloomgart, 2 Ben., 356. Off., § 33.
—— v. Bogart,* 3 Ben., 257. Off., §§ 32, 68.
—— v. Bougher, 6 McL., 277–282. Penalties, §§ 90–92, 108, 116, 143.
—— v. Bowen.* 10 Otto, 508. Pensions, § 17.
—— v. Boyd, 15 Pet., 187. Pl., § 2154.
—— v. Bradbury, Dav., 146–154. Pay't, §§ 154–158.
—— v. Bradley, 10 Pet., 343. Pl., § 571.
—— v. Brodhead,* 3 Law Rep., 95. Off., § 121.
—— v. Bromley,* 12 How., 88. P. O., §§ 18, 39.
—— v. Brown,* 9 How., 487. P. O., §§ 56, 74.
—— v. Brown, 1 Paine, 422. Pl., § 376.
—— v. Buford,* 3 Pet., 12. Pl., §§ 1091, 2098.
—— v. Burnham, 1 Mason, 57–70. Pl., §§ 1957–1962.
—— v. Burns, 12 Wall., 246. Pl., § 2149.
—— v. Cambuston, 7 Saw., 575. Off., § 61.
—— v. Central Nat. Bank, 10 Fed. R., 612. Pl., § 1001.
—— v. Chaloner,* 1 Ware, 214. P. O., § 25.
—— v. Child, 12 Wall., 232. Pay't, § 315.
—— v. Chouteau, 12 Otto, 603. Pl., § 1015.
—— v. City Bank, 6 McL., 130. Off., § 142.
—— v. Clarke,* Hemp., 315. Pay't, § 278.
—— v. Clyde, 13 Wall., 35. Pay't, § 303.
—— v. Cochran, 2 Marsh., 274. Pay't, § 178.
—— v. Collier, 3 Blatch., 325. Off., §§ 118, 397, 398.
—— v. Collins, 4 Blatch., 142. P. O., §§ 68, 69.
—— v. Collins, 1 Woods, 499. Off., § 64.
—— v. Colt, Pet. C. C., 145–154. Pl., §§ 342–347, 451.
—— v. Corrie,* 23 Law Rep., 145. Off., § 428.
—— v. County Court of Knox County, 1 McC., 603. Off., § 130.
—— v. Crusell, 14 Wall., 1. Off., § 59.
—— v. Cumpton, 3 McL., 163–165. Pl., §§ 1072, 1073.
—— v. Custis, 1 Cr. C. C., 417. Off., § 346.
—— v. Cutter, 2 Curt., 617. Pensions. § 32.
—— v. Dair, 4 Biss., 280–283. Pl., §§ 552, 558.
—— v. Daniel, 6 How., 11. Off., § 277.
—— v. Dashiel, 4 Wall., 182. Pl., § 827.
—— v. Davis, Deady, 294. P. O., § 79; Pl., § 642.
—— v. Davis, 3 McL., 483. P. O., § 129.
—— v. Deming, 4 McL., 3. Oaths, § 8.
—— v. De Mott, 3 Fed. R., 478. P. O., § 37.
—— v. Denvir, 16 Otto, 536. Off., § 405.
—— v. Dewitt, 9 Wall., 41. Police Powers, § 9.
—— v. Distillery,* 4 Biss., 26. Pl., §§ 206, 207, 472.
—— v. Dobbins,* 1 Penn. L. J., 9. Privilege, § 25.
—— v. Dodge, Deady, 186. Name, § 11.
—— v. Doughty, 7 Blatch.. 424. Off., § 423.
—— v. Duncan, 4 McL., 607. Partn., §§ 391, 392.
—— v. Durling, 4 Biss., 509. Off., § 425.
—— v. Duval,* Gilp., 356. Off., §§ 372, 373, 384, 385, 391, 396.
—— v. Eckford, 1 How., 250. Pay't, §§ 203, 212.
—— v. Eighteen Barrels of High Wines, 8 Blatch., 475. Penalties, § 168.
—— v. Ellis, 1 Cr. C. C., 125. Penalties, § 117.
—— v. Ellsworth, 11 Otto, 170. Pay't, § 241.

United States v. Fairchilds, 1 Abb., 74; 1 Am. L. T., 58. Pensions. §§ 1, 2.
—— v. Faw, 1 Cr. C. C., 457. Off., § 106.
—— v. Fifty-six Barrels of Whisky, 6 Am. L. Reg. (N. S.), 32; 1 Abb., 93. Penalties, §§ 16, 17.
—— v. Fillebrown,* 7 Pet., 28. Off., § 392.
—— v. Four Hundred and Twenty-two Casks of Wine, 1 Pet., 547. Pl., § 2020.
—— v. Fourteen Packages of Pins, Gilp., 235. Penalties, §§ 40, 158.
—— v. Gadsby, 1 Cr. C. C., 55. Penalties, § 118.
—— v. Gaussen, 19 Wall., 198. Off., §§ 394, 395.
—— v. George, 6 Blatch., 37–47. Penalties, §§ 179–181.
—— v. Germaine, 9 Otto, 508. Off., § 31; Pensions, § 18.
—— v. Giles, 9 Cr., 212. Pay't, § 130.
—— v. Girault, 11 How., 22–33. Pl., §§ 538–543, 1998.
—— v. Goggin, 1 Fed. R., 49; 9 Biss., 269. Pensions, § 4.
—— v. Griswold, 5 Saw., 25–31. Penalties, §§ 93–96.
—— v. Gurney, 4 Cr., 333. Pl., § 877.
—— v. Gurney,* 1 Wash., 446. Pl., § 2012.
—— v. Hack, 8 Pet., 271. Partn., §§ 395, 401.
—— v. all,* 9 Am. L. Reg., 232. P. O., § 29H
—— v. Hall, 6 Cr., 171. Penalties, § 63.
—— v. Hall, 8 Otto, 343. Pensions, § 3.
—— v. Hall, 2 Wash., 366. Penalties. § 76.
—— v. Halsted, 6 Ben., 205. Pl., § 668.
—— v. Hammond.* 4 Biss., 283. Pl., § 623.
—— v. Harden, 10 Fed. R., 802; 4 Hughes, 455. Off., §§ 299, 300, 332, 368, 429.
—— v. Hardyman, 13 Pet., 176. Pl., § 184.
—— v. Harris, 1* Abb., 110–119. Penalties, §§ 204, 205.
—— v. Hartwell,* 12 Int. Rev. Rec., 50. Off., §§ 83, 431.
—— v. Hartwell, 6 Wall., 385. Off., §§ 27–29
—— v. Haynes, 9 Ben., 22. Pensions, § 29.
—— v. Hayward, 2 Gall., 497. Pl., § 593.
—— v. Hoar, 2 Mason, 311. Pl., §§ 780, 836.
—— v. Hodge, 13 How.. 478. P. O., § 114.
—— v. Hoffman,* 4 N. Y. Leg. Obs., 8. Penalties, § 49.
—— v. Hooe,* 1 Cr. C. C., 116. Pl., § 2101.
—— v. Howard, 1 Saw., 507. Name, § 27.
—— v. Huckabee, 16 Wall., 414. Pl., § 478.
—— v. Hudson, 3 McL., 156. Off., § 44.
—— v. Humason, 5 Saw., 537. Off., § 54.
—— v. Ingersoll, Crabbe, 135. Off., § 435.
—— v. Insurance Cos., 22 Wall., 99. Pl., § 682.
—— v. Jackson,* 3 Hughes, 231. Pl., § 391.
—— v. Jackson, 14 Otto, 41. Pl., § 120.
—— v. Jailer of Fayette County, 2 Abb., 265. Off., §§ 88, 104, 103, 274.
—— v. James, 13 Blatch., 207. P. O., § 16
—— v. January, 7 Cr., 572. Pay't, § 216.
—— v. Jones, 1 Marsh., 285. Penalties, § 189.
—— v. Justices of Lauderdale County, 10 Fed. R., 460. Off.. § 213.
—— v. Keehler, 9 Wall., 83. Off., §§ 77, 78, 399; P. O., § 109.
—— v. Kellum, 19 Blatch., 372. Penalties, § 141.
—— v. Kelly,* 15 Wall., 34. Pensions, § 15.
—— v. Kendall, 5 Cr. C. C., 163. Off., § 84; P. O., §§ 63, 83.
—— v. Kennedy, 3 McL., 175. Pl., § 94.
—— v. Kershner, 1 Bond, 432. P. O., § 135.

TABLE OF CASES CITED.

891

Camp v. Grant, 21 Conn., 41. Partn., § 255.
Campbell v. Charter Oak Ins. Co., 10 Allen, 213. Pl., § 348.
Campbell v. Mackay, 1 Myl. & C., 603. Pl., § 1176.
Campbell v. N. E. Mut. Ins. Co., 98 Mass., 381. Pl., § 341.
Candler v. Pettit, 1 Paige, Ch., 168. Pl., § 1691.
Carlisle v. United States, 16 Wall., 147. Pay't, p. 358.
Carpenter v. Ins. Co., 4 How., 219. Pl., § 1543.
Carpenter v. Pennsylvania, 17 How., 463. Penalties, § 204.
Carroll v. Peake, 1 Pet., 18. Pl., § 55.
Carson v. Hood. 4 Dall., 108. Pl., § 1976.
Carter v. Ken, 2 Bay, 112. Off., § 261.
Carth v. Jackson, 6 Ves.* 37. Pl., § 1519.
Cartwright v. Rowley, 2 Esp., 723. Pay't, § 235.
Carver v. Waugh, 2 H. Bl., 235. Partn., § 9.
Carvick v. Vickery, Doug., 653, n. Partn., § 123.
Cary v. Longman, 1 East, 358. Pl., §§ 1193, 1195.
Cary v. Longman, 3 Esp., 273. Pl., § 1193.
Case v. Beauregard, 99 U. S., 119. Partn., § 367.
Case v. Beauregard, 101 U. S., 688. Partn., § 367.
Case v. Redfield, 4 McL., 526. Pl., §§ 1177, 1188.
Case v. Rorabacher, 15 Mich., 537. Privilege, § 14.
Caskhuff v. Anderson, 3 Binn., 9. Partn., § 66.
Casky v. January. Hard., 539. Pl., § 1972.
Cass v. Adams, 3 Ohio, 223. Pl., § 1071.
Cassaday v. Cavenor, 37 Ia., 300. P. O., § 14.
Cassidy v. Stewart, 4 Scott, N. R., 432. Privilege, § 14.
Catlett v. Brodie, 9 Wheat., 554. Pl., § 352.
Catlin v. Springfield Ins. Co., 1 Sumn., 434. Pl., § 349.
Cazeaux v. Mali, 25 Barb., 583. Pl., § 172.
Chaffee v. Jones, 19 Pick., 261. Privilege, § 14.
Champion v. Bostwick, 18 Wend., 184. Partn., § 7.
Chapman v. Koops, 3 Boss. & Pull., 289. Partn., § 354a.
Chappedelaine v. Dechenaux, 4 Cr., 306. Pl., § 156.
Chardon v. Calder & Co., 2 Const. (S. C.), 685. Partn., § 148.
Chase v. Dwinal, 7 Greenl., 134. Pay't, § 235.
Chase v. Taylor, 4 Harr. & Johns., 54. Pay't, § 235.
Cheap v. Cramond, 4 Barn. & Ald., 663. Partn., §§ 9, 11.
Chegaray v. Jenkins, 5 N. Y., 376. Pl., § 1066a.
Chesterfield v. Jansen, 2 Ves., 155. Partn., § 365.
Child v. Harden, 2 Bulst., 144. Pl., § 168.
Chirac Reinecker, 11 Wheat., 280. Pl., § 1956.
Cholmondeley v. Clinton, 2 Jac. & W., 1. Pl., § 1363.
Cholmondeley v. Clinton, 2 Jac. & Walk., 183. Pl., § 763.
Chouteau v. Rice, 1 Minn., 106. Pl., § 1688.
Claridge v. Hoar, 14 Ves. Jr., 65. Pl., § 1355.
Clark v. Beach, 6 Conn., 142. Pl., § 763.
Clark v. Mundall, 1 Salk., 124. Pay't, § 7.
Clark v. Van Reimsdyk, 9 Cr., 160. Pl., § 1543.
Clarke v. Dutcher, 9 Cow., 681. Pay't, § 284.
Clarke v. Shee, Cowp., 200. Partn., § 140.

Clayton's Case, 1 Mer., 572. Partn., § 138; Pay't, §§ 156, 163.
Clementson v. Williams, 8 Cr., 72. Partn., § 148.
Clones, Ex parte, 2 Bro. C. C., 595. Partn., § 141.
Clute v. Goodell, 2 McL., 193. Off., § 266.
Cobb v. Dows, 10 N. Y., 335. Partn., § 139.
Cobb v. Ingalls, Breese. 180. Pl., § 1972.
Cobb v. Smith, 16 Wis., 661. P. O., § 14.
Coburn v. Hopkins, 4 Wend., 577. Pl., § 1069.
Cochran v. Davis, 5 Litt., 119. Pl., § 1973.
Coke v. Sayer, 2 Wils., 85. Pl., § 513.
Cole v. Hawkins, Andrews, 275. Privilege, § 10.
Cole v. Smith, 4 Johns., 193. Pl., § 428.
Coles v. Trecothick, 9 Ves., 284. Partn., § 208.
Collett v. Haigh, 3 Campb., 281. Pl., § 664.
Collins v. Blantern, 2 Wils., 341. Off., § 17.
Collins v. Collins, 2 Burr., 820. Pl., § 359.
Comth v. Morse, 2 Mass., 138. Pl., § 425.
Cone v. Bowles, 1 Salk., 205. Pl., § 430.
Cook v. City of Boston, 9 Allen, 393. Pay't, § 282.
Cookson v. Cookson, 8 Sim., 529. Partn., § 68.
Coombe v. Talbot, Salk., 218. Pl., § 510.
Coombes' Case, 9 Co., 766. Powers, § 6.
Coover's Appeal, 29 Pa. St., 9. Partn., § 359.
Coppin v. Carter. 1 D. & E., 462. Pl., § 1966.
Corning v. Stebbins, 1 Barb. Ch., 589. Pl., § 1182.
Cornwallis v. Savery, 2 Burr., 772. Pl. § 977.
Costers v. Bank of Georgia, 24 Ala., 37. Pl., § 1367.
Cotterel v. Cummins, 6 Serg. & R., 343. Pl., § 1976.
Covington v. Comstock, 14 Pet., 43. Pl., § 34.
Coy v. Hymas, 1 Str., 401. Pl., § 1951a.
Crawford v. Whitall, Doug., 4, n. a. Pl., § 766.
Crew v. Vernon, Cro. Car., 97. Off., § 267.
Cropper v. Coburn, 2 Curt., 465. Partn., § 353a.
Cross v. Sackett, 2 Bosw., 645. Pl., § 172.
Crosse v. Bilson, 6 Mod., 102. Pl., § 1959.
Cummings v. Lebo, 2 Rawle, 23. Pl., § 1976.
Cunningham v. Boston, 16 Gray, 468. Pay't, § 282.
Cunningham v. Monroe, 15 Gray, 471. Pay't, § 282.
Curd v. Lewis, 1 Dana. 351. Pl., § 1367.
Currie v. Henry, 2 John., 433. Pl., §§ 510, 973.
Curtis v. Bateman, 1 Sid., 39. Pl., § 510.
Cutler v. Southern, 1 Saund., 116. Pl., § 856.

D.

Daggett v. State, 4 Conn., 61. Pl., § 430.
Dale v. Dean. 16 Conn., 579. Pl., § 1976.
Dalton v. Smith, 2 Smith, 618. Pl., § 53.
Daniel v. Cross, 3 Ves., 277. Partn., § 239.
D'Arcy v. Ketchum, 11 How., 165. Partn., § 150; Pl., § 174.
Davis v. Garland, 4 How., 431. Pl., § 973.
Davis v. Owen, 1 B. & P., 343. Pl., § 1934.
Davis v. Rendlesham, 7 Taunt., 679. Privilege, § 13.
Dawes v. North River Ins. Co., 7 Cow., 462. Pl., § 348.
Day v. Chism, 10 Wheat., 449. Pl., §§ 55, 1970.

I.

J.

K.

L.

M.

V.

W.

Y.

INDEX.*

ANSWER IN EQUITY. See *Plea; Supplemental Pleadings.*
 information and belief. Pl., §§ 1497–1499, 1501, 1502, 1519, 1520, 1522, 1523, 1580–1585.
 insufficient. Pl., §§ 1500, 1518, 1528, 1632.
 under thirty-ninth equity rule. Pl., §§ 1503–1506, 1525–1531.
 joint and several. Pl., §§ 1507, 1532, 1599.
 signature. Pl., §§ 1508, 1533.
 to interrogatories. Pl., §§ 1509, 1510, 1511, 1516, 1528, 1524, 1534–1537, 1542.
 verification. Pl., §§ 1559–1563, 1599, 1625–1627.
 infringement of patent. Pl., §§ 1613–1616, 1620–1623.
 when no note is appended. Pl., §§ 1511, 1537.
 exceptions to. Pl., §§ 1518, 1521, 1586–1598.
 exceptions to part. Pl., §§ 1512, 1538.
 whether part may be heard separately. Pl., §§ 1513, 1539.   .
 impertinence. Pl., §§ 1514, 1515, 1540, 1541.
 as evidence. Pl., §§ 1517, 1543, 1628–1665.
 insufficient bar in. Pl., § 1528.
 sufficient bar in. Pl., § 1529.
 order as to defendants in default. Pl., § 1531.
 illustrative cases. Pl., §§ 1544–1558, 1564–1579, 1599–1612, 1617–1624.

APPEARANCE.
 to suit by partner. Part., §§ 110, 150, 151.

APPELLATE PRACTICE. See *Amendments; Practice.*

APPLICATION OF PAYMENTS. See *Payment and Settlement.*

APPOINTMENT. See *Officers.*
 power to make. Pow., §§ 38–42.

ARREST. See *Officers; Privilege.*

ASSIGNEE. See *Bankruptcy.*

ASSIGNMENTS. See *Partnership.*
 right of insolvent debtor to prefer creditors in Mississippi. Part., § 869.
 for creditors by partner. Part., §§ 98, 99, 127–130, 188–192.
 of debts by partner. Part., §§ 102, 181.

ASSISTANTS. See *Officers.*

ASSUMPSIT. See *Answer; Declaration; Plea; Pleading.*

ATTACHMENT.
 right of private creditors to attach partnership property. Part., §§ 253, 253a, 255, 334.
 proof of allegation to defraud creditors. Part., § 366.
 mail of debtor not subject to. Post., § 52.
 to bring party before court; practice. Off., § 260.   .
 United States courts may compel observance of rules by. Off., § 262.

ATTORNEY-GENERAL. See *Officers.*

ATTORNEY, POWER OF. See *Powers.*

AUTHORITIES REVIEWED.
 as to variance between writ and declaration. Pl., §§ 1954, 1955.
 as to how far bad plea cured by verdict. Pl., § 1906.
 as to whether or not justice is done though the forms are incorrect. Pl., § 1968.
 as to multifariousness of bill in equity. Pl., § 1180.
 as to demurrability of bill for infringement of patent. Pl., § 1188.
 as to statement of venue of instrument declared on. Pl., § 83.
 as to joining defendants in action for conversion. Pl., § 89.
 as to what constitutes duplicity. Pl., § 977.
 as to recovery in action for debt. Pl., § 845.
 as to right to change by amendment a libel *in rem* to libel *in personam.* Pl., § 2093.
 as to illegal partnership, particular case. Part., § 206.
 as to existence of partnership by participation in profits. Part., § 7.
 as to equitable rights of surviving partner in realty. Part., § 68.
 as to distinction between dormant and open partners. Part., § 118.
 as to equity of innocent partner where trust money is misappropriated. Part., § 141.
 as to notice in dissolution of partnership. Part., § 250.
 as to right of partnership creditors. Part., § 255.
 as to resignation of officers. Off., § 208.
 as to effect of appointment upon incumbent of office. Off., § 289.

AWARD.   .
 action on original demand cannot be maintained after. Off., § 18.

B.

BAIL.
 special, liability of, not to be enlarged by intendment. Pl., § **1952.**

BAILIFFS.
 to United States marshal. Offi., §§ 274, 275.

BANKRUPTCY.
 notarial acts in. N. P., §§ 19–26.
 rule in, for distributing assets of partnership and separate assets of partners. Part., § 124.
 effect upon dissolution of partnership. Part., § 275.
 receiver of property in sheriff's possession, right of assignee in. Part., § **375.**

BELIEF. See *Answer in Equity.*

BILL IN EQUITY. See *Pleading.*
 to state whole case. Pl., §§ 1133, 1161.
 must allege necessary facts to construe language involved. Pl., §§ 1134, 1135, **1162.**
 general certainty in, ordinarily sufficient. Pl., §§ 1136, **1163.**
 consideration, statement of, in bill for fraud. Pl., §§ 1137, 1138, **1164, 1165.**
 bill charging shareholders of insolvent company. Pl., §§ 1139, 1166, 1167a.
 to show how each defendant is concerned as party. Pl., §§ 1140, **1167.**
 parties to suit to enjoin judgment. Pl., §§ 1141, 1169, 1170, **1172.**
 allegation of payment of note. Pl., §§ 1142, 1171, 1172.
 averment of citizenship in removed cause. Pl., §§ 1143, 1173.
 to dissolve partnership, treated as bill for partition. Pl., §§ 1144, 1174.
 multifariousness. Pl., §§ 1145–1148, 1152–1157, 1175–1180, 1186, 1191, 1305–1332, 1369.
 laches under statute of limitations. Pl., §§ 1149–1151, 1181–1184, 1261.
 discovery. Pl., §§ 1158, 1159, 1192, 1196, 1226–1229.
 infringement of copyright. Pl., §§ 1160, **1193, 1195.**
  of patent. Pl., § 1188.
 allegation as to title. Pl., §§ 1194, 1204.
 certainty of averments. Pl., § 1198.
 statement of facts. Pl., §§ 1199–1203.
 citizenship of parties. Pl., §§ 1216–1225.
 fraud. Pl., §§ 1230–1239.
 patent suits. Pl., §§ 1240–1251.
 supplemental pleadings, special replication not allowed. Pl., §§ 1684, **1688.**
  bill, for what used. Pl., §§ 1685, 1686, 1690, 1691.
   illustrative cases. Pl., §§ 1692–1709.
   motion to dismiss for laches in prosecution. Pl., §§ 1687, **1689.**
  illustrative cases. Pl., §§ 1205–1215, 1252–1284.
 prayer. Pl., §§ 1285–1292, **1357.**
 interrogatories. Pl., §§ 1293–1298.
 laches. Pl., §§ 1290–1304.
 cross-bill. Pl., §§ 1333–1344.

BILL OF EXCEPTIONS.
 how to be drawn. Pl., § **1961.**

BILL OF EXCHANGE.
 when debt of drawer to acceptor is one. Paym., § 167.

BONA FIDE PURCHASER. See *Notice.*

BONDS. See *Declaration; Official Bonds; Plea; Pleading; Postmaster; Principal and Surety.*
 delivery by United States marshal. Offi., § 272.
 replevy by United States marshal. Offi., § 282.
 made to United States marshal, he is to collect. Offi., § **288.**

BOUNTIES. See *Pensions and Bounties.*

BURDEN OF PROOF. See *Evidence.*

C.

CARRYING MAIL. See *Mail.*

CHANGE OF NAME. See *Name.*

CITIZENSHIP. See *Answer in Equity; Bill in Equity; Declaration; Demurrer; Plea; Pleading.*
 in one state, and residence in another. Pl., § **895.**

COSTS.
 question as to allowance of. Pl., § 431.
 quo warranto, plaintiff may recover when defendant surrenders office. Off., § 246.

COUNT. See *Declaration*.

COUNTER-CLAIM. See *Plea; Set-off*.

COUNTY OFFICERS. See *Officers*.

COURTS. See *Jurisdiction; Supreme Court*.
 powers, etc., as to attachment of persons, etc. Off., §§ 260-264.

CREDITORS. See *Compromise; Partnership*.

CROSS-BILL.
 nature of, etc. Pl., §§ 1333-1844.

CROSS-LIBEL. See *Pleadings in Admiralty*.

CUSTOM. See *Usage and Custom*.

D.

DAMAGES.
 measure of, in actions against officers. Off., §§ 101-103.

DEATH. See *Abatement; Partnership; Powers*.
 simple power, irrevocable during life of donor, extinguished by his death. Pow., § 6.

DEBT. See *Declaration*.
 object of action of. Pl., § 842.
 will lie for undetermined demand. Pl., § 343.
 and *indebitatus assumpsit*. Pl., § 844.
 is for recovery of sum due, not sum demanded. Pl., § 345.
 will lie for statutory penalty. Pl., §§ 846, 451.

DECLARATION. See *Evidence; Pleading; Pleadings in Admiralty; Profert and Oyer*.
  1. IN GENERAL.
  2. CERTAINTY AND SUFFICIENCY OF.
  8. ON WRITTEN INSTRUMENTS.
  4. UNDER STATUTES.

 1. IN GENERAL.
 variance between writ and declaration. Pl., §§ 1, 26, 54.
 venue for trial sufficient. Pl., §§ 2, 27.
 venue necessary for every material fact. Pl., §§ 8, 28.
 venue in margin sufficient. Pl., §§ 4, 30, 31.
 illustration of good venue. Pl., §§ 5, 33, 34, 125.
 count in wrong form of action. Pl., §§ 6, 35, 36.
 proper joinder of count improperly framed. Pl., §§ 7, 86.
 averment of fact of partnership not always necessary. Pl., §§ 8, 37.
 money had and received against joint defendants. Pl., §§ 9, 88, 89.
 trover against joint defendants. Pl., §§ 10, 39.
 joinder of causes by plaintiff in two capacities. Pl., §§ 11, 12, 40-42.
 facts within judicial notice not averred. Pl., §§ 13, 43.
 want of formal conclusion. Pl., §§ 14, 44.
 averment of act by agent. Pl., §§ 15, 44a.
 allegations of time, quantity, value, etc. Pl., §§ 89-99.
 action on judgment; plaintiff as administrator. Pl., § 100.
 averment of administratorship; profert of letters. Pl., § 101.
 allegation of assignment. Pl., §§ 102, 103.
   husband and wife. Pl., §§ 104-106.
 state statutes need not be pleaded. Pl., §§ 107-109.
 averment of title to note in suit. Pl., §§ 19, 51.
 suit on note; allegation of demand at place of payment not necessary. Pl., §§ 20, 52.
 distinction between, in debt and *assumpsit*. Pl., §§ 21, 58.
 for infringement of patent. Pl., §§ 22, 55.
 setting out instrument declared on. Pl., §§ 23, 56, 57.
 sufficient form of profert. Pl., § 57.
 surplusage. Pl., §§ 16, 46, 113, 114.
 assumpsit on an agreement improperly sealed. Pl., §§ 17, 48.
 averment of citizenship at time of filing. Pl., §§ 18, 49.
 joinder of torts in one count. Pl., §§ 24, 58.
 informality in conclusion for damages. Pl., §§ 25, 59.
 sufficient allegation of plaintiff's official capacity as administrator. Pl., § 41.
 depending upon municipal charter, need not set out. Pl., §§ 18, 48.

DECLARATION, On Written Instruments — continued.
　breaches, when to be assigned.　Pl., §§ 331, 359, 360.
　　how to be assigned.　Pl., §§ 332, 350, 351, 361–363.
　against joint obligors.　Pl., §§ 333, 364.
　assignment of breaches before judgment by default.　Pl., §§ 334, 366.
　averment of ouster on covenant of warranty.　Pl., §§ 335, 367.
　derivation of title, when formal defect.　Pl., §§ 335, 367a.
　immaterial repugnant assignment of breach rejected.　Pl., § 368.
　breach not assigned by averment of non-payment of penalty.　Pl., §§ 337, 369.
　allegation of breach of bond.　Pl., §§ 370–381.
　illustrative cases.　Pl., §§ 382–393.
　in actions on notes and bills.　Pl., §§ 393–416.

4. Under Statutes.
　conclusion of declaration for penalty.　Pl., §§ 417, 425.
　under act of January 9, 1808.　Pl., §§ 418, 427.
　misjoinder, when cured by verdict.　Pl., §§ 419, 426.
　fraud, when to be alleged.　Pl., §§ 424, 443–446.
　under statute enlarging right to sue.　Pl., § 446.
　suits against insolvent estates in Indiana.　Pl., §§ 443–446.
　claim for penalty and personal injury cannot be joined in New York.　Pl., § 432.
　　bad on demurrer, when.　Pl., § 433.
　claim for penalty; how declared on.　Pl., § 434.
　penalty to person suing therefor.　Pl., §§ 420, 428, 429.
　under statutory penalty for imposing excessive fare.　Pl., §§ 421, 432–434.
　under statute enforcing right of citizen to vote.　Pl., §§ 422, 423, 435–442.
　state statutes need not be pleaded.　Pl., §§ 107–109, 447, 448.
　should state act of congress on which founded.　Pl., § 449.
　assent of voters to validate contract sued on.　Pl., § 450.
　debt will lie for statutory penalty.　Pl., § 451.
　under civil rights act; citizenship.　Pl., §§ 452, 453.
　illustrative cases.　Pl., §§ 454–483.

DEED OF TRUST.　See *Notice.*

DEFECTS IN PLEADINGS.　See *Pleading.*

DELIVERY BOND.
　by United States marshal.　Offi., § 273.

DEMURRER.　See *Amendments; Practice.*
　　　　　1. In General.
　　　　　2. At Law.
　　　　　3. In Equity.

1. In General.
　undisposed of; when considered waived.　Pl., §§ 1941, 1942, 1972, 1973.
　judgment goes against party committing first fault on.　Pl., § 1978.
　does not reach back beyond general issue.　Pl., § 1979.

2. At Law.
　not inconsistent with general issue.　Pl., §§ 946, 959.
　in abatement.　Pl., §§ 947, 959a, 960, 963.
　frivolous.　Pl., §§ 948, 960a.
　general and special.　Pl., §§ 949, 956, 962, 964, 974, 1005–1010, 1068, 1069.
　cannot question authority or consideration.　Pl., §§ 950, 962a.
　variance between writ and declaration.　Pl., §§ 951, 968.
　misjoinder.　Pl., §§ 952, 969.
　statute of limitations.　Pl., §§ 953, 970, 1027, 1056.
　reaches back to first defective pleading.　Pl., § 746.
　　though not always.　Pl., §§ 957, 975.
　how far it cuts back.　Pl., §§ 901–1004.
　what is admitted by.　Pl., §§ 1011–1019.
　to several pleas.　Pl., §§ 954, 971, 972, 1020–1025.
　duplicity, how reached.　Pl., §§ 955, 973.
　　defined.　Pl., §§ 956a, 977, 1037.
　properly overruled, in Iowa, where petition states a substantial cause of action.　Pl., § 2139.
　for want of jurisdiction, does not admit it.　Pl., § 896.
　to several pleas, if any one is good, demurrer is bad.　Pl., § 541.
　special may be filed in all actions in federal courts.　Pl., § 32.
　illustrative cases.　Pl., §§ 980–990, 1026, 1028, 1031, 1034–1036, 1038–59.
　citizenship as ground of.　Pl., §§ 1029, 1030.
　limit as to number.　Pl., § 1032.

3. In Equity.
　definition; office.　Pl., §§ 1372, 1373.
　illustrative cases.　Pl., §§ 1374–1382, 1414–1420.
　what is admitted by.　Pl., §§ 1389–1396.

DEMURRER, In Equity — continued.
    want of equity. Pl., §§ 1397–1401.
    defect of parties. Pl., §§ 1402–1405.
    causes for. Pl., §§ 1406–1413.
    to part, certainty. Pl., §§ 1345, **1355**.
    not to rely upon answer. Pl., §§ 1346, **1358**.
    to interrogatories. Pl., §§ 1347, **1356, 1359, 1360**.
    to whole bill. Pl., §§ 1351, **1365**, 1374.
    for unnecessary parties. Pl., §§ 1352, **1366, 1367**.
    ore tenus. Pl., §§ 1354, **1368–1371**.
    waived by answer. Pl., §§ 1189, 1348, **1361**.
    laches. Pl., §§ 1849, **1362, 1363**.
    to cross-bill. Pl., §§ 1350, 1353, **1364–1367**.
    special, must point out distinctly matter demurred to. Pl., §§ 1190, **1383–1388**.
    form of, for misjoinder of causes of action. Pl., § **1187**.
    general, not proper if part of bill is sufficient. Pl., § **1197**.
    statute of limitations may be set up by. Pl., § **1188**.
    assumption as to discovery of fraud under. Pl., § **1184**.

DEPARTMENTS. See *Officers*.

DEPUTIES. See *Officers; United States Marshal*.

DILATORY PLEAS. See *Plea*.

DISCOVERY. See *Bill in Equity*.

DISSOLUTION. See *Partnership*.

DISTRIBUTION. See *Penalties and Forfeitures*.

DISTRICT ATTORNEY. See *Officers*.

DISTRICT OF COLUMBIA.
    United States marshal of. Off., §§ 289–293.

DOMICILE.
    of opposing party, need not be sworn to as of knowledge. Pl., § **1487**.

DORMANT PARTNER. See *Partnership*.

DUPLICITY. See *Answer in Equity; Declaration; Demurrer; Plea; Pleading; Pleadings in Admiralty; Replication*.

DURESS. See *Plea*.
    recovery of money paid under. Paym., §§ 225, 228, 231, **234, 235**, 239–243.
    in settlement. Paym., § 303.
    in compromise. Paym., § 315.

E.

ELECTION.
    party not compelled to elect between suit at law and bill in equity, touching same matter. Part., § **185**.

EQUITY. See *Amendments; Answer in Equity; Bill in Equity; Demurrer; Injunction; Plea; Pleading; Replication; Supplemental Pleadings*.
    rights of surviving partner in, as to partnership realty. Part., § **68**.
    rule of, for distributing assets of partnership and separate assets of partners. Part., § 124.
    right of retiring partner of notice of acceptance of new firm as debtor. Part., § **260**.
    government bound by same rules of, as other plaintiffs. Paym., § **229**.
    will give relief when effect of instrument is misunderstood. Pow., § 8.
    powers, relief in. Pow., §§ 8, 45–48.

EQUITY RULES. See *Answer in Equity*.

ERRORS AND DEFECTS IN PLEADINGS. See *Pleading*.

ERROR, WRIT OF. See *Writ of Error*.

ESTOPPEL.
    rule of. Part., § **370**.
    when sureties estopped from setting up fraud. Pl., § **540**.

EVIDENCE.
    in partnership suits. Part., §§ 428, 485–490.
    of acceptance of new firm as debtor. Part., §§ **256–259**.

EVIDENCE — continued.
 of notice of dissolution of partnership. Part., § 253.
 statements and declarations in proving partnership. Part., §§ 5, 6, 14, 15.
 as to participation in profits of partnership. Part., § 8.
 proof of partnership. Part., §§ 53-62, 120.
 admissions by partner after dissolution. Part., §§ 109, 145-148.
 answer in equity as. Pl., §§ 1517, 1543, 1628-1666.
 judicial notice taken of admission of states into the Union. Pl., § 2088.
 intent with which a name is indorsed may be shown by parol. Pl., § 664.
 proof of allegation in attachment of disposition of property to defraud creditors. Part.,
  § 360.
 declaration of public agent as to power to act, etc. Offi., § 126.
 presumption in favor of acts of officers. Offi., §§ 51-66.
 extrinsic, admissible to prove identity of grantee of patent. Name, § 10.
 name may be proved by reputation or hearsay. Name, § 11.
 notarial acts as. N. P., §§ 16-26.
 what admissible to support plea of payment. Paym., §§ 14-18.
 burden of proof in actions for penalties and forfeitures. Pen., §§ 146-155.

EXCEPTIONS. See *Pleading.*
 to insufficient answer in equity. Pl., §§ 1518, 1521, 1586-1598.
 bill of, how to be drawn. Pl., § 1961.

EXCHANGE.
 membership in, as property. Prop., § 10.

EXEMPTIONS.
 notice of. Notice, § 84.

EXTRA COMPENSATION. See *Mail.*

F.

FEES.
 of officers. Offi., §§ 376-399.

FEDERAL COURTS. See *Courts; Jurisdiction; Supreme Court.*

FOREIGN JUDGMENTS. See *Declaration; Plea; Pleading.*
 not records. Pl., § 522.
 effect of. Pl., §§ 523, 525.

FOREIGN LAWS.
 rights arising under may be recognized, but remedies depend upon our laws. Pl., § 42.

FORFEITURES. See *Declaration; Penalties and Forfeitures; Pleadings in Admiralty.*
 wines subject to, under non-intercourse act. Pl., § 1739.

FORMER JUDGMENTS. See *Plea.*

FRAUD. See *Bill in Equity; Declaration; Plea.*

FRAUDULENT CONVEYANCES.
 notice of. Notice, § 80.

G.

GARNISHMENT.
 of firm debtor on suit against partner. Part., §§ 254, 255, 335.

GOOD WILL.
 as property. Prop., §§ 15, 16.

GOVERNMENT.
 right of, to make contract. Offi., § 14.
 contract by; essential elements of. Offi., § 15.
 is bound by same rules of equity that affect other plaintiffs. Paym., § 229.
 how far bound by act of officers. Offi., §§ 141-179.
 as partnership creditor. Part., §§ 391-395.

GUARDIAN.
 appointment of, notice. Notice, § 81.

H.

HEADS OF DEPARTMENTS. See *Officers.*

HEARSAY. See *Evidence.*

HOMESTEAD. See *Partnership.*
    abandonment of. Pl., § 2148.

I.

IDENTITY. See *Evidence; Name; Notary Public.*

ILLINOIS.
    resignation of town officers in. Offi., §§ 201, 202, 204.

IMPEACHMENT. See *Officers.*

IMPERTINENCE. See *Answer in Equity.*

INFANT. See *Minor.*
    oath of, to answer in equity. Pl., §§ 1371, 1562.

INFORMATION. See *Answer in Equity; Bill in Equity; Penalties and Forfeitures; Pleadings in Admiralty.*

INJUNCTION.
    between partners. Part., §§ 444–446.
    will not be granted when jurisdiction is in question. Pl., § 1432.

INNOCENT PURCHASER. See *Notice.*

INQUIRY.
    writ of, when to be executed. Pl., § 865.

INSOLVENCY.
    notice of. Notice, § 86.

INTENT.
    with which a name is indorsed, may be shown by parol. Pl., § 664.

INTEREST. See *Declaration.*

INTERPRETATION. See *Construction; Words and Phrases.*

INTERROGATORIES. See *Answer in Equity; Bill in Equity; Demurrer.*

INVENTION. See *Patents.*
    developed by partnership. Part., §§ 195, 196, 201–204.

ISSUE. See *Plea; Pleading.*
    made by affirmative and negative, and single point. Pl., § 1098.
    quære, whether two affirmatives may make. Pl., § 1099.
    in form one of fact, but in substance one of law, cannot be heard. Pl., § 1101.
    must be single, although embracing several facts. Pl., § 536.
    should consist of an affirmative and negative. Pl., § 537.
    immaterial. Pl., §§ 1936, 1957, 1958.

J.

JOINDER. See *Declaration.*

JUDGES.
    privilege of, from arrest, etc. Priv., §§ 1–3, 8 et seq., 20.

JUDGMENT LIEN.
    partnership property is subject to. Part., § 66.

JUDGMENTS. See *Declaration; Plea; Pleading.*
    final, cannot be entered to case disposed of as to all defendants. Pl., § 542.
    when not final, writ of error will be dismissed. Pl., § 543.

JUDICIAL NOTICE. See *Declaration; Evidence.*
    courts take, of admissions of states into the Union. Pl., § 2088.

MANDAMUS.
    nature of writ of.   Offi., § 235.
    issue of *mandamus* is exercise of original jurisdiction.   Offi., § 237.
    may compel performance of ministerial duties by postoffice department.   Post., §§ 82, 83.
    bars action for damages on same cause.   Offi., §§ 20, 21.
    is inconsistent with action for damages.   Offi., § 21.

MARSHAL.   See *United States Marshal.*

MAXIMS.
    cujus est donare ejus est disponere.   Pen., § 205.
    every wrong has its appropriate remedy.   Offi., § 234.
    damnum absque injuria.   Offi., § 234.
    in re præsenti, hoc est statim, at que solutum est.   Paym., § 154.
    quod verisimile videretur diligentum debitorem admonitu iia suum negotium gesturium
        fuisse.   Paym., § 157.
    quilibet renuntiare postest jure pro se introducto.   Pl., § 1978.
    qui facit per alium facit per se.   Pl., § 1193.
    qui tam pro domino Rege quam pro se ipso in hac parte sequitur.   Pen., § 93.
    si nihil eorum interveniat vetustior contractus ante solvitur.   Paym., § 157.
    solvitur in modum solventis.   Paym., § 164.
    satius est petere fontes, quam secreturi rivulos.   Part., § 116.

MEASURE OF DAMAGES.   See *Damages.*

MICHIGAN.
    resignation of officers in.   Offi., §§ 203, 206–208.

MIDDLE NAME.   See *Name.*

MILITARY OFFICERS.   See *Officers.*

MINOR.   See *Infant.*
    may be notary public at common law.   N. P., § 1.
    may hold ministerial office.   Offi., § 135.

MISJOINDER.   See *Demurrer; Plea.*

MISNOMER.   See *Name.*

MISTAKE.
    instrument misunderstood, equity will give relief.   Pow., § 8.
    recovery of money paid under.   Paym., §§ 223, 224, 230, 236–238.

MONEY.
    lawful, of United States, is, for all states.   Pl., § 29.
    title to, passes by delivery.   Part., § 140.

MOOT QUESTIONS.
    not decided.   Pl., § 171.

MORTGAGE.   See *Notice; Partnership; Payment and Settlement.*

MOTION.
    to strike out. substance of plea not to be questioned by.   Pl., §§ 1430, 1440.
    to dismiss bill in equity for laches in prosecution.   Pl., §§ 1687, 1689.
    for continuance, not subject to review.   Pl., § 2188.

MULTIFARIOUSNESS.   See *Bill in Equity; Declaration.*

N.

NAME.
    use of initials.   Name, §§ 12–14.
    presumption as to identity.   Name, §§ 15–19.
    middle name.   Name, §§ 20, 21.
    change of.   Name, § 23.
    amendments in.   Name, § 28.
    two names having same original derivation.   Name, § 1.
    act of attainder against *Henry* Gordon void against *Harry* Gordon, when.   Name, § 2.
    chosen by person, is proper one.   Name, § 3.
    material variance.   Name, §§ 4–6.
    immaterial variance.   Name, §§ 7–9.
    extrinsic evidence admissible to prove identity in grant by patent.   Name, § 10.
    proved by reputation or hearsay.   Name, § 11.
    misnomer in judgment.   Name, §§ 24, 25.
    in pleadings.   Name, § 26.
    misnomer; demurrer.   Name, § 27.

NAVAL OFFICERS. See *Officers.*

NEGLIGENCE. See *Declaration.*
averment of, in libel. Pl., §§ 1732, 1743.

NEGOTIABLE INSTRUMENTS. See *Notary Public; Notice; Partnership.*

NEWSPAPERS. See *Postmaster; Postoffice.*

NON-INTERCOURSE ACT.
wines subject to forfeiture under. Pl., § 1739.

NOTARY PUBLIC. See *Oaths.*
liable for false certificate. Offi., § 335.
identification of official character. N. P., § 7.
clerk of, act by ineffectual. N. P., § 8.
acknowledging deed in which he is interested, good. N. P., § 9.
infant, name by, at common law. N. P., § 1.
use of seal. N. P., §§ 2–6.
powers and liabilities as to commercial paper. N. P., §§ 10, 11.
power to administer oaths. N. P., §§ 12–15.
acts in evidence. N. P., §§ 16–18.
in bankruptcy. N. P., §§ 19–26.

NOTE. See *Declaration.*

NOTES AND BILLS. See *Notary Public; Notice; Partnership.*

NOTICE.
party put on inquiry. Notice, §§ 4, 5.
to be published "once a week." Notice, §§ 6–8.
in writing. Notice, §§ 9, 10.
service on Sunday. Notice, § 11.
printed tariff of charges at dock, not, to master. Notice, § 12.
articles of limited partnership. Part., § 510.
right of retiring partner to, of acceptance of new firm as debtor. Part., § 260.
of dissolution of partnership. Part., §§ 237, 238, 248–252, 322, 326.
by individual, of power of government officials. Offi., § 109.
sale under deed of trust. Notice, § 37.
mortgage. Notice, § 38.
prior deed or mortgage. Notice. §§ 39, 40.
subsequent vendee. Notice, § 41.
lis pendens. Notice, §§ 42–65.
to stockholders of corporation. Notice, §§ 66–70.
transfer of stock. Notice, § 71.
to purchaser of corporation stock. Notice, § 72.
to corporation. Notice, § 74.
commercial paper. Notice. §§ 75–79.
fraudulent conveyances. Notice, § 80.
appointment of guardian. Notice, § 81.
ownership of telegraph. Notice, § 82.
trustee for creditors. Notice, § 83.
exempt property. Notice, § 84.
to counsel. Notice, § 85.
of insolvency. Notice, § 86.
innocent persons. Notice, 87.
by-laws of a town. Notice, § 88.
to deputy-marshal, is notice to marshal. Notice, § 89.
constructive. Notice, §§ 1–3.
how purchaser affected, etc. Notice, §§ 16–33.
in confirmation of land titles. Notice, § 34.
title to personal property. Notice, § 35.
by mail. Notice, § 13.
when to be read. Notice, § 14.
by publication; designation of newspaper. Notice, § 15.
purchase from one executor. Notice, § 36.

NOVATION.
acceptance of new firm as debtor. Part., §§ 241, 243, 256–260.

O.

OATH. See *Notary Public; Plea.*
who may administer. Oaths, §§ 1–11.
acting officer presumed to have taken. Oaths, § 12.
when juror may make affirmation in lieu of oath. Oaths, §§ 13, 14.
to infant's answer. Pl., §§ 1371, 1562.

OBSCENE ARTICLES.
　information; stereoscopic slides. Obscene Articles.

OFFICERS. See *Notary Public; Oaths; United States Marshal.*
　　1. IN GENERAL.
　　2. APPOINTMENT AND REMOVAL.

1. IN GENERAL.
　office and officer defined. Offi., §§ 1, 8–10.
　establishment of offices: agent of fortifications. Offi., §§ 2, 9, 10, 338.
　illegal appointment; liability of appointee. Offi., § 3.
　acts requiring judgment and discretion. Offi., §§ 4, 5, 7, 25, 26.
　liability of sheriff as conservator of the peace. Offi., §§ 6, 22–24.
　liability, etc., of sheriff in general. Offi., §§ 180–200.
　what constitutes a public officer. Offi., §§ 8, 27–33.
　object of act of March 3, 1817. Offi., § 10.
　taking new official bond; sureties on old. Offi., § 11.
　liability of, generally. Offi., §§ 34–47.
　　　acts after expiration of term. Offi., §§ 48–50.
　　　presumptions in favor of acts. Offi., §§ 51–60.
　　　loss of money or property. Offi., §§ 67–85.
　protected by writ. Offi., §§ 86–90.
　individual must take notice of powers of. Offi., § 109.
　taking insufficient security. Offi., § 110.
　power of levee board in making contract. Offi., § 111.
　of county. Offi., § 112.
　permitting escapes. Offi., §§ 113–117.
　deputies and assistants. Offi., §§ 118–124.
　purchasing agents. Offi., § 125.
　declarations as to power to act. Offi., § 126.
　irregular appointment; validity of official bond. Offi., § 18.
　when not liable for official acts. Offi., § 19.
　powers and duties of sheriff are quasi-judicial or ministerial. Offi., § 22.
　　　liability of. Offi., §§ 23, 24.
　sale of perishable or explosive goods. Offi., § 26.
　must act with care and diligence. Offi., §§ 97–100.
　measure of damages. Offi., §§ 101–103.
　arrests by, etc. Offi., §§ 104–108.
　state officers; actions against. Offi., §§ 127–130.
　trial of right to office. Offi., §§ 131, 132.
　captured property. Offi., §§ 133, 134.
　minor may hold ministerial office. Offi., § 135.
　money held by, is *in custodia legis*. Offi., § 136.
　disability; removal; fourteenth amendment. Offi., § 137.
　government, cannot donate or remit taxes. Offi., § 138.
　discretion. Offi., § 139.
　warrant officers. Offi., § 140.
　how far government bound by acts of. Offi., §§ 141–179.
　resignations by. Offi., §§ 210–219.
　　　of town officers in Illinois. Offi., §§ 201, 202, 204.
　　　at common law and in Michigan. Offi., §§ 203, 205–208.
　ministerial, order of competent as protection to, acting thereunder. Pl., § 1066a.
　failure to take oath. Offi., § 334.
　wrongful acts. Offi., § 336.
　liability of collector of port. Offi., § 337.
　commissioners or board of supervisors of county, powers. Offi., § 339.
　presentation of false claim. Offi., § 340.
　levee board in Mississippi. Offi., § 350.
　postmaster-general may discontinue postoffice. Offi., § 351.
　appointment by military governor. Offi., § 352.
　custom-house officers. Offi., § 353.
　road overseer in Virginia. Offi., § 346.
　justice in District of Columbia. Offi., § 347.
　judgment against, not binding on state. Offi., § 348.
　advertisement by Indian superintendent. Offi., § 349.
　commissioner cannot make warrant returnable before another. Offi., § 341.
　pilot commissioners. Offi., § 342.
　tax commissioners. Offi., § 343.
　shipping commissioner. Offi., § 344.
　magistrate. Offi., § 345.
　receiver of public moneys. Offi., § 361.
　quartermaster's department at Key West. Offi., §§ 362, 363.
　pay and expenses. Offi., §§ 364, 365.
　United States commissioner. Offi., §§ 366–368.
　judicial functions. Offi., § 354.
　acts of two of three commissioners. Offi., §§ 355, 356.
　in Utah. Offi., §§ 357, 358.

P.

919

PAYMENT AND SETTLEMENT — continued.

2. APPLICATION OF PAYMENTS.

general rule. Paym., §§ 137, 147, **154–158, 161, 162.**

illustrations. Paym., §§ 168–176.

when the law will apply. Paym., §§ 138, **155.**

by a receipt. Paym., §§ 139, **158.**

running accounts. Paym., §§ 138, 145, 146, 149–153, **154, 156, 163–166,** 199–207.

payment to treasury department. Paym., § 148.

voluntary payments. Paym., §§ 140, 141, **159.**

proceeds of judicial sale. Paym., §§ 142, 143, **159.**

by administrator. Paym., §§ 144, 161, 162.

where debtor owes several sums on various accounts. Paym., §§ **154, 164–166.**

the rule of the Roman law. Paym., § 157.

when payment may be applied to oldest debt. Paym., § **166.**

by the debtor. Paym., §§ 177–179.

by the creditor. Paym., §§ 180–191.

after action commenced. Paym., § 192.

secured and unsecured notes. Paym., §§ 193–198.

interest and principal. Paym., §§ 208, 209.

as between different securities. Paym., §§ 210–222.

PENAL LAWS.

strictly construed. Pl., §§ **430, 440**; Pen., §§ 56, 57.

PENALTY. See *Declaration.*

for violations of the postal laws. Post., §§ 18–29.

PENALTIES AND FORFEITURES.

　　1. IN GENERAL.
　　2. ACTIONS AND PROCEDURE.
　　3. SEIZURE.
　　4. DISTRIBUTION OF PROCEEDS.
　　5. REMISSION AND PARDON.

1. IN GENERAL.

when property forfeited vests in government. Pen., §§ 1–7.

bona fide purchaser. Pen., §§ 8–19.

interest of mortgagee. Pen., § 20.

not attachable by private creditors after commission of act which works forfeiture. Pen., §§ 21, 22.

claims of seamen etc.; preferences. Pen., §§ 23, **24.**

violation of registry act. Pen., § 39.

how affected by fraudulent intent. Pen., §§ 40–45.

forfeitures by piracy. Pen., § **46.**

duties paid on false valuation not protection against. Pen., § 47.

but one penalty for same act. Pen., §§ 48, 49.

by acts of persons other than owner. Pen., §§ 25–31.

how affected by ignorance of law. Pen., §§ 32, 33.

repeal of law while action pending thereunder. Pen., §§ **34–36.**

embargo act; vessel only to be seized. Pen., §§ 37, **38.**

when penalty waived. Pen., §§ 50–52.

limitations. Pen., §§ 53–55.

forfeitures strictly construed. Pen., §§ 56, 57.

relief in equity against forfeiture. Pen., §§ 58–60.

fine for contempt of court. Pen., § 61.

illustrative cases. Pen., §§ 62–82.

2. ACTIONS AND PROCEDURE.

nature of action. Pen., § 104.

when debt will lie. Pen., §§ 105–110.

when *qui tam* action will lie. Pen., §§ 111–113.

by information. Pen., § 114.

by indictment or suit at law. Pen., §§ 115–118.

forfeiture of lands and franchises by legislative action. Pen., § 119.

jurisdiction. Pen., §§ 87, 92, 97–103.

qui tam actions; complaint; signing by district attorney; undertaking for damages. Pen., §§ 88, 89, 93–96.

statute authorizing informer to sue. Pen., § 90.

trial by jury. Pen., § 121.

pleading and practice. Pen., §§ 122–140.

parties. Pen., §§ 141–145.

evidence, burden of proof. Pen., §§ 146–155.

no form of action provided. Pen., §§ 83, 90–92.

debt proper at common law. Pen., §§ 84, 91.

under steamboat act of 1852. Pen., §§ 85, 86.

3. SEIZURE.

validity of; what constitutes. Pen., §§ 156–161.

who may make. Pen., §§ 163–164.

PLEA, GENERAL ISSUE — continued.
    action on bond; which craves oyer of conditions of bond, etc., good. Pl., § 978.
    non assumpsit bad, to action of tort. Pl., § 1964.
    how far cured by verdict. Pl., §§ 1965, 1966.

3. SPECIAL PLEAS IN BAR.
    of impossibility of performance. Pl., §§ 733, 746–753.
    need not anticipate. Pl., §§ 734, 750.
    good plea on record will always bar judgment. Pl., §§ 735, 758.
    of justification to show authority. Pl., §§ 736, 737, 754, 755.
    uncore prest. Pl., §§ 738, 756.
    readiness to perform. Pl., §§ 739, 740, 757–760.
    non tenure. Pl., §§ 741, 742, 761–763.
    ne unques administrator. Pl., §§ 743, 764–766.
    argumentativeness. Pl., § 744.
    to record showing judgment. Pl., §§ 745, 765.
    statute of limitations. Pl., §§ 772–791, 875, 876.
    justification. Pl., §§ 792–799.
    former judgment. Pl., §§ 800–805.
    in patent suits. Pl., §§ 806–810.
    illustrative cases. Pl., §§ 767–771, 811–874.
    allegation of seizin; limitations; Texas. Pl., §§ 875, 876.
    of payment. Pl., § 877.
    special breach; general performance. Pl., § 878.

4. PUIS DARREIN CONTINUANCE.
    requisites and effect of. Pl., §§ 879, 881, 882.
    admits cause of action. Pl., §§ 879, 881.
    filed as of right, and waives prior issues. Pl., §§ 880, 882.
    defenses arising after commencement of suit. Pl., § 883.
    disability of plaintiff occurring during pendency of suit. Pl., § 884.
    how far waiver of preceding pleas. Pl., §§ 885, 886.
    judgment on. Pl., § 887.
    accord and satisfaction; waiver. Pl., § 888.
    mandamus; resignation. Pl., § 889.
    foreign attachment. Pl., § 890.

5. DILATORY PLEAS.
    want of jurisdiction; plea in abatement. Pl., §§ 891, 892, 894.
    demurrer not waiver of right to plead. Pl., §§ 893, 896, 897.
    illustrative cases of. Pl., §§ 898–945.

6. IN EQUITY.
    definition. Pl., § 1441.
    illustrative cases. Pl., §§ 1442–1485.
    duplicity. Pl., § 1466.
    statute of limitations. Pl., §§ 1472–1475.
    requisites of good. Pl., §§ 1421, 1431.
    in bar of prescription in Louisiana. Pl., § 1580.
    to jurisdiction. Pl., §§ 1422, 1423, 1432, 1433.
    without oath. Pl., §§ 1425, 1436, 1437.
    dilatory. Pl., §§ 1424, 1433–1435, 1486–1496.
    regular in form, cannot be displaced by motion. Pl., § 1440.
    what facts are to be sworn to. Pl., §§ 1426, 1427, 1436, 1437.
    unsupported plea must answer whole bill. Pl., §§ 1428, 1438.
    of good faith and valuable consideration. Pl., §§ 1429, 1439.
    substance of, not to be questioned by motion to strike out. Pl., § 1430.
    domicile of opposing party need not be sworn to as of knowledge. Pl., § 1437.
    of jurisdiction of another court, not good, to cross-bill. Pl., § 1864.

PLEADING. See *Amendments; Answer in Equity; Bill in Equity; Declaration; Issue; Penalties and Forfeitures; Plea; Pleadings in Admiralty; Practice; Rejoinder; Replication; Supplemental Pleadings.*
    1. IN GENERAL.
    2. ERRORS AND DEFECTS IN.

1. IN GENERAL.
    resettlement of partnership accounts; defendant need not set forth original account. Part., § 212.
    in actions by and against partners. Part., §§ 474–483.
    plea *puis darrein continuance,* in *quo warranto* to remove from office. Offi., § 246.
    full christian and surname required in; amendment. Name, § 26.
    lis pendens must be pleaded as in *linine litis* in Louisiana. Notice, § 65.
    how accord and satisfaction pleaded. Paym., § 279.
    in actions for penalties and forfeitures. Pen., §§ 122–140.
    object of written pleadings. Pl., §§ 2131, 2135.
    technicality less than formerly. Pl., §§ 2132, 2136, 2137.
    conformable in federal to state courts. Pl., §§ 2133, 2140.
    law and equity not to be blended. Pl., §§ 2134, 2141.

POSTMASTER. See *Mail; Postoffice; Postoffice Department.*
  appointment. Post., § 98.
  duties, etc., in general. Post., §§ 94–97.
  amount of diligence required. Post., §§ 99–101.
  discontinuance of office. Post., §§ 102, 103.
  abandonment of office. Post., § 104.
  default; demand not necessary. Post., § 105.
  right to detain letters addressed to lottery. Post., § 13.
    injunction. Post., § 14.
  deputy's bond; acceptance and approval. Post., §§ 106, 107.
    not vitiated by extension. Post., § 108.
  suit on bond; jurisdiction. Post., § 117.
    defenses. Post., §§ 109. 110.
    evidence. Post., §§ 111–115.
    limitations. Post., §§ 118–121.
    general liability of sureties. Post., §§ 122–125.
    for stamps furnished principal. Post., §§ 126, 127.
    new bond. Post., § 128.
    entitled to benefit of bankrupt law. Post., § 129.
    sureties not relieved by delay in suing. Post., §§ 130, 131.
    rights and liabilities on different bonds. Post., §§ 132, 133.
    notice of defalcation to government. Post., § 134.
    application of payments as affecting sureties. Post., §§ 135–140.
  civil action for money stolen. Post., § 116.
  marks on newspapers; letter postage. Post., §§ 41–43. 66–88, 89–93.
  when suit for conversion will lie against. Post., §§ 92, 93.

POSTMASTER-GENERAL.
  may discontinue postoffice. Offi., § 351.

POSTOFFICE. See *Mail; Postmaster; Postoffice Department.*
  powers of congress; non-mailable matter. Post., §§ 1–8, 9–14, 15, 16.
  right of postmaster to detain letters addressed to lottery. Post., § 13.
    injunction. Post., § 14.
  freedom of the press. Post., § 17.
  penalties for violations of postal laws. Post., § 18.
    for failure to deliver mail. Post., §§ 19–21.
    for unlawfully carrying mail. Post., §§ 22–29.
  private letter carriers. Post., §§ 30–32.
  franking privilege. Post., §§ 33–35.
  postal money orders. Post., § 36.
  obstruction of vehicles carrying mail. Post., § 37.
  adoption of route. Post., § 38.
  what constitutes mailable matter. Post., § 39.
    dutiable articles in mails. Post., § 40.
  illustrative cases. Post., §§ 57–61.
  letter postage; what is a newspaper. Post., §§ 41, 42.
    marks on newspaper subjecting it to. Post., § 43.
  remedy to compel delivery of letters. Post., § 44.
  bonds stolen in mail; replevin. Post., § 45.
  privilege of writer to claim letter *in transitu.* Post., §§ 46, 47.
  suppression of letters calculated to cheat and defraud the public. Post., §§ 48–51.
  mail of debtor not subject to attachment. Post., § 52.
  adverse claimants, rights of to mail. Post., §§ 53–55.

POSTOFFICE DEPARTMENT.
  scope of powers. Post., § 62.
  not subject to control of president. Post., § 63.
  to require bonds from deputies. Post., §§ 64, 66.
  to make mail contracts. Post., §§ 66, 67.
  to fine mail contractors. Post., §§ 68, 69.
  to establish post roads. Post., §§ 70, 71.
  to discontinue postoffices. Post., §§ 72, 73.
  to make loans of public money. Post., § 74.
  to correct mistakes of predecessor. Post., §§ 75, 76.
  to bind successor. Post., § 77.
  to contract for postal cards. Post., § 78.
  to allow extra compensation to deputy. Post., §§ 79, 80.
  re-adjustment of deputy's salary. Post., § 81.
  ministerial duties; *mandamus.* Post., §§ 82. 83.
  discretionary acts not subject to revision. Post., § 84.
  liability of. Post., § 85.
  chief clerk of, not entitled to commissions in addition to salary. Post., § 56.

POWERS. See *Congress; Postmaster; Postoffice; Police Powers.*
  revocation of power of attorney. Pow., §§ 1–3, 5, 6–8.
  coupled with interest, survives. Pow., §§ 4, 7, 56–60.

POWERS — continued.
 execution of. Pow., §§ 9–13.
 how followed and construed. Pow., §§ 14, 15.
 supported by usage. Pow., § 16.
 of disposal by will. Pow., § 17.
 rights of third persons. Pow., § 18.
 of sale. Pow., §§ 19–37.
 of appointment. Pow., §§ 38–42.
 to make partition. Pow., §§ 43, 44.
 relief in equity. Pow., §§ 8, 45–48.
 deed with power of sale. Pow., §§ 49, 50.
 of administrator as to sale. Pow., § 51.
 death; substituted trustee. Pow., § 52.
 death of trustee, power of survivor. Pow., §§ 53–55.
 collateral. Pow., §§ 61, 62.
 irrevocable during life of donor, extinguished by his death. Pow., § 6.

PRACTICE. See *Amendments; Answer in Equity; Bill in Equity; Bill of Exceptions; Demurrer; Exceptions; Issue; Motion; Parties; Penalties and Forfeitures; Pleading; Pleadings in Admiralty; Record; Repleader; Replication; Writ of Error.*
 as to opening partnership settlements. Part., §§ 209–212.
 party not compelled to elect between suit at law and bill in equity, when. Part., § 135.
 rule as to attachment, etc., in Mississippi. Part., § 371.
 in actions by and against partners. Part., §§ 474–483.
 return to *mandamus* estops party from pleading want of notice. Offi., § 209.
 in *quo warranto* party may surrender office by plea *puis darrein continuance.* Offi., § 246.
 attachment to bring party before court, etc. Offi., § 260.
  power of United States courts as to. Offi., § 262.
 amendment of variance in name. Name, § 23.
 as to names in pleading. Name, § 26.
 misnomer in judgment. Name, § 25.
  demurrer. Name, § 27.
 release given in evidence without exception, etc., waived. Paym., § 11.
 in actions for penalties and forfeitures. Pen., §§ 122–140.
 demurrer waived by answer. Pl., § 1189.
 demurrer is properly overruled where petition states substantial cause of action, in Iowa. Pl., § 2139.
 substance of plea not to be questioned by motion to strike out. Pl., §§ 1430, 1440.
 exceptions to insufficient answer in equity. Pl., §§ 1518, 1521, 1586–1598.
 allegation of agreement to convey land in fee-simple, free from incumbrance — question of incumbrance need not be decided. Pl., § 47.
 when two issues are formed — one material and one immaterial. Pl., § 1068.
 replication *de injuria*, cannot be excepted to after verdict, when. Pl., § 1070.
 when verdict for defendant in, to be directed. Pl., § 1100.
 issue in form one of fact, but in substance one of law, cannot be heard. Pl., § 1101.
 writ of error dismissed when judgment not final. Pl., § 543.
 as to profert and oyer. Pl., §§ 1102, 1103, 1104–1132.
 in federal court, when parties may insist upon following process act, though variant from state practice. Pl., § 2142.
 decision of motion for continuance not subject to review. Pl., § 2138.
 moot questions not decided. Pl., § 171.
 on demurrer judgment goes against party committing first fault. Pl., § 1078.
 when things not appearing on record may be assumed on writ of error. Pl., § 1974.
 issue of law and of fact pending, former decided first. Pl., § 1971.
 how bill of exceptions to be drawn. Pl., § 1961.
 as to allowance of costs. Pl., § 431.

PREFERENCES. See *Compromise.*
 contract giving to creditor, void. Pl., § 1950.
 right of insolvent debtor to prefer creditors in Mississippi. Part., § 869.
 creditors of new firm preferred to old, when. Part., § 373.

PRESCRIPTION. See *Limitations.*
 plea of, in bar; Louisiana. Pl., § 1530.

PRESIDENT. See *Officers.*
 power of to remit fine. Pen., §§ 204, 206.
 pardon by, for offense, is bar to civil suit. Pen., § 210.
 effect and extent of pardon by. Pen., §§ 211–215.

PRESS.
 freedom of. Post., § 17.

PRESUMPTIONS. See *Evidence; Payment and Settlement.*

Q.

QUI TAM ACTIONS. See *Penalties and Forfeitures.*

QUO WARRANTO.
to eject party from office; defendant may surrender office at any time. Offi., § 246.

R.

RAILROAD.
consolidation of companies dissolves old and creates new. Pl., § 749.

REAL PROPERTY. See *Partnership.*

RECEIPTS.
prima facie evidence only. Paym., §§ 280-286.
by seaman. Paym., § 287.
of collector. Paym., §. 288, 289.
operation of. Paym., §290.
by attorney, for money paid by himself as attorney to himself as administrator. Paym., § 291.
of payment by note. Paym., §§ 8, 9, 18.

RECEIVER.
court will not appoint, when jurisdiction is in question. Pl., § 1432.
appointment of, of property in sheriff's possession, rights of assignee. Part., § 375.

RECORDS.
right to copies of public. Pub. Rec., §§ 1-3.
what is, of cause, and how made up. Pl., § 1951a.
variance between, and recital in *scire facias*, fatal. Pl., § 1951.
power to amend. Pl., § 1958.
when notice taken of apparent defects of. Pl., § 1963.
what not appearing on, may be assumed on writ of error. Pl., § 1974.

RECOVERY BACK.
payment by mistake. Paym., §§ 223, 224, 230, 236-238.
duress. Paym., §§ 225, 228, 231, 234, 235, 239-243.
under protest. Paym., §§ 226, 232, 233, 250, 251.
legal compulsion. Paym., §§ 227, 234, 235.
tax paid under invalid statute. Paym., § 283.
illegal contract. Paym., §§ 244, 245.
illegal demand. Paym.. §§ 246-249.
taxes. Paym., §§ 252, 253.
illegal attorney fee. Paym., § 254.
money paid on forged indorsement. Paym., § 255.

REJOINDER.
requisites of. Pl., §§ 1064, 1072, 1073.
must fully answer breach alleged in replication. Pl., § 1072.
nil debet bad on action on bond. Pl., §§ 1065, 1073.
must tender issue on single point. Pl., § 1073.
excuse for non-performance after plea of performance. Pl., § 1095.
issuable plea. Pl., § 1096.
inducement, containing new and substantive matter, bad. Pl., § 1097.

RELEASE. See *Settlement and Release.*
mutual, not obligatory upon party not signing. Part., § 201.
given without exception, as evidence, proof of execution waived. Paym., § 11.

REMISSION. See *Penalties and Forfeitures.*

REMOVAL. See *Officers.*

REPLEADER. See *Pleading.*
not awarded by court of error. Pl., §§ 1987, 1959, 2005.
rarely in favor of party making first fault. Pl., §§ 1988, 1959, 2004.
has gone into disuse. Pl., §§ 1970, 2004.

REPLICATION. See *Pleading; Pleadings in Admiralty.*
1. At Law.
2. In Equity.

1. AT LAW.
must fully answer plea. Pl., §§ 1068, 1071.
illustrative cases. Pl., §§ 1075-1084, 1088-1091, 1094.

REPLICATION, At Law — continued.
    statute of limitations. Pl., §§ 1082, 1085–1087, 1092, 1098.
    to plea of authority. Pl., §§ 1060, 1066, 1067.
    de injuria. Pl., §§ 1061, 1069, 1070.
    tendering issue of law, held bad. Pl., §§ 751, 1074.
    filing new waives demurrer to former one. Pl., § 752.
    tendering issue, should conclude to the country. Pl., § 445.
    containing two answers to plea, is bad for duplicity. Pl., § 520.
    action on bond, assigning single breach, good. Pl., § 970.
2. In Equity.
    purpose of. Pl., § 1666.
    admissions by. Pl., §§ 1667, 1668.
    omitted. Pl., §§ 1672, 1678.
    failure to file in time. Pl., §§ 1677, 1678.
    supreme court rules as to. Pl., § 1679.
    statute of limitations. Pl., § 1680.
    illustrative cases. Pl., §§ 1669–1671, 1674–1676, 1681–1683.
    special, not allowed. Pl., §§ 1684, 1688.

REPUTATION.
    name may be proved by. Name, § 11.

RESIGNATION. See *Officers.*

RETIRING PARTNERS. See *Partnership.*

RETURN.
    false, by United States marshal. Off., § 284.
    court will not dictate as to. Off., §§ 308, 309.

REVIVAL. See *Partnership.*

REVOCATION. See *Powers.*

RUNNING ACCOUNTS. See *Payment and Settlement.*

S.

SALE.
    power of. Pow., §§ 19–87.
    deed with power of. Pow., §§ 49, 50.
    under deed of trust; notice. Notice, § 37.
    of perishable or explosive goods by officer. Off., § 26.

SATISFACTION. See *Accord and Satisfaction; Payment and Settlement.*

SEAL.
    use of by notary public. N. P., §§ 2–6.

SECRET PARTIES. See *Partnership.*

SECRETARY OF THE TREASURY.
    remission and pardon by. Pen., §§ 198–201, 206–208, 216–238.

SECRETARY OF WAR.
    possesses no power to appoint agent of fortifications. Off., § 338.

SEIZURE. See *Penalties and Forfeitures.*

SERVICE. See *Notice.*

SET-OFF. See *Plea.*
    unliquidated damages cannot be set off, when. Pl., § 547.

SETTLEMENTS. See *Partnership; Payment and Settlement.*

SETTLEMENT AND RELEASE.
    covenant under seal to come to settlement. Paym., § 293.
    binding effect; subsequent attempt at arbitration. Paym., § 298.
    non-compliance with terms of. Paym., § 294.
    based upon false statements. Paym., § 295.
    in ignorance of right. Paym., § 296.
    by seamen. Paym., §§ 297, 298.
    release, effect of. Paym., §§ 299–301.
        cannot be enlarged. Paym., § 302.
        duress; undue advantage. Paym., § 303.
    agreement to release as a defense. Paym., § 304.
    illustrative cases. Paym., §§ 305, 306.

SHERIFF. See *Officers.*

SIGNATURE.
    of answer in equity. Pl., §§ 1508, 1583.

SLANDER. See *Declaration.*

SOLDIERS. See *Pensions and Bounties.*

STATE.
    acts of, in conflict with powers of congress as to police powers. Pol., §§ 6–31.

STATEMENTS. See *Evidence; Partnership.*

STATE OFFICERS. See *Officers.*

STATUTES. See *Construction; Declaration; Plea.*
    party claiming under, which derogates from general rule of law, must show strict compliance. Part., § 504.

STATUTE OF LIMITATIONS. See *Answer in Equity; Demurrer; Limitations; Plea; Pleading; Pleadings in Admiralty.*

STOCKHOLDERS. See *Notice.*

SUBSTITUTION. See *Powers.*

SUNDAY.
    service of notice on. Notice, § 11.

SUPPLEMENTAL PLEADINGS.
    special replication not allowed. Pl., §§ 1684, 1688.
    in admiralty. Pl., §§ 1907–1916.
    supplemental bill, for what used. Pl., §§ 1685, 1686, 1690, 1691.
    illustrative cases. Pl., §§ 1692–1709.
    motion to dismiss for laches in prosecution. Pl., §§ 1687, 1689.

SUPREME COURT.
    original jurisdiction of, derived from constitution. Off., § 236.
    has jurisdiction on writ of error, when. Post., § 89.

SURETY. See *Official Bonds; Principal and Surety.*

SURVIVING PARTNERS. See *Partnership.*

T.

TAXES.
    illegally paid; recovery back. Paym., §§ 252, 253.

TENDER.
    right of plaintiff on plea of. Paym., § 267.
    what constitutes. Paym., §§ 256, 257.
    must be unconditional. Paym., §§ 258–260.
    must be kept good. Paym., §§ 261, 262.
    when unnecessary; waiver. Paym., §§ 263–266.
    in admiralty. Paym., §§ 268, 269.
    illustrative cases. Paym., §§ 270–272.

TITLE. See *Declaration.*
    to money, passes by delivery. Part., § 140.
    to personal property. Notice, § 35.
    notice in confirmation of land titles. Notice, § 34.

TORT. See *Conversion.*
    by one partner; liability of partnership. Part., §§ 103, 132–135.
    partnership. Part., § 219.

TRADE-MARK.
    partnership. Part., §§ 69, 70.

TRIAL.
    wager of law abolished in United States. Pl., § 162.

TROVER. See *Declaration.*

TRUSTEES. See *Powers.*

U.

UNITED STATES.
　as partnership creditor. Part., §§ 391–393.

UNITED STATES COURTS. See *Courts; Government; Jurisdiction; Supreme Court.*

UNITED STATES MARSHAL. See *Officers.*
　deputy. Offi., §§ 257, **261–264,** 318–331.
　liable for money in hands of deputy. Offi., § 258.
　acts after expiration of term. Offi., §§ 259, **267,** 312–317.
　contracts by. Offi., §§ 268–270.
　executions. Offi., § 271.
　delivery bond. Offi., § 272.
　custody of prisoners. Offi., § 273.
　bailiffs. Offi., §§ 274, 275.
　presentation of false account by deputy. Offi., § 276.
　action against executor of deceased. Offi., § 276.
　taking bail. Offi., §§ 278, 279.
　order to produce prisoner. Offi., § 280.
　failure to sell property. Offi., § 281.
　sureties of replevy bond. Offi., § 282.
　when marshal is to collect bonds. Offi., § 283.
　court will not dictate as to returns by. Offi., §§ 308, 809.
　money in hand. Offi., §§ 310, 311.
　possess powers of sheriff. Offi., §§ 332, 333.
　not removed by appointment of successor until notice. Offi., § **267.**
　false return. Offi., § 284.
　arrears of taxes on property sold. Offi., § 285.
　custody of libeled goods. Offi., § 286.
　act as to alien enemies. Offi., § 287.
　order to bring money into court. Offi., § 288.
　of District of Columbia. Offi., §§ 289–293.
　must pay seized foreign coin into court. Offi., § **265.**
　court may require money paid into court. Offi., § **266.**
　summary remedy against. Offi., §§ 294, 295.
　care of property. Offi., §§ 296–298.
　commitment to jail. Offi., §§ 299, 300.
　in bankruptcy. Offi., §§ 301–303.
　execution of admiralty process *in rem.* Offi., § **304.**
　conflict of authority. Offi., §§ 305–307.

USAGE AND CUSTOM.
　power supported by. Pow., § 16.

V.

VARIANCE. See *Answer in Equity; Bill in Equity; Declaration; Demurrer; Plea; Pleading; Pleadings in Admiralty.*
　in names. Name, §§ 4–9.

VENUE. See *Declaration.*

VERDICT. See *Aider by Verdict.*
　on issue joined as to note and account, good, though informal. Paym., § **10.**
　on two issues, one material and one immaterial, when good. Pl., §§ 1062, **1068.**
　defective. Pl., § **1967.**
　one good count will sustain, in Mississippi. Pl., § **1977.**

W.

WAGER OF LAW.
　abolished in United States. Pl., § **162.**

WAIVER. See *Demurrer; Plea; Pleading; Practice; Replication.*
　release given in evidence, without exception as to proof of execution, is a. Paym., § **11.**
　of tender of payment. Paym., §§ 263–266.
　of penalty. Pen., §§ 50–52.
　of right to share of forfeiture. Pen., § 194.

WAR.
> effect on dissolution of partnership. Part., §§ 271-274.

WHALE.
> killed and in possession is property. Prop., § 11.

WIDOWS. See *Pensions and Bounties.*

WILL.
> power of disposal by. Pow., § 17.
> provisions against dissolution of partnership by death. Part., § 262.
>> general direction to executor to continue business. *Ibid.*

WITNESSES.
> privilege from arrest, etc. Priv., §§ 2, 11, 28-31.

WORDS AND PHRASES. See *Maxims.*
> "once a week," as to publication of notice. Notice, §§ 6-8.
> "the place of publication is nearest the land," in statute as to notice. Notice, § 15.

WRIT. See *Mandamus.*
> variance between, and declaration. Pl., §§ 1954-1956.
> distinction between office of, in England and United States. Pl., § 1955.
> requiring answer in trespass *ac etiam,* and breach of marriage promise, not incongruous. Pl., § 967.

WRIT OF ERROR.
> what not appearing on record may be assumed on. Pl., § 1974.
> when supreme court has jurisdiction on. Post., § 89.

WRIT OF INQUIRY.
> when to be executed. Pl., § 365.

Lightning Source UK Ltd.
Milton Keynes UK
UKHW020110310119

336364UK00006BA/197/P